THE WORLD REACTS
TO THE HOLOCAUST

THE WORLD REACTS TO THE HOLOCAUST

David S. Wyman, Editor

Charles H. Rosenzveig, Project Director

THE JOHNS HOPKINS UNIVERSITY PRESS
Baltimore and London

All rights reserved. Published 1996
Printed in the United States of America on acid-free paper
05 04 03 02 01 00 99 98 97 96   5 4 3 2 1

The Johns Hopkins University Press
2715 North Charles Street
Baltimore, Maryland 21218-4319
The Johns Hopkins Press Ltd., London

Library of Congress Cataloging-in-Publication Data will be found
at the end of this book.
A catalog record for this book is available from the British Library.

ISBN 0-8018-4969-1

WITH NO GRAVE TO VISIT, NO TOMBSTONE UPON WHICH TO lay a wreath, may this work stand instead as one memorial to six million Jews who died *Al Kiddush Hashem,* in the Sanctification of God's Name. The Talmud teaches us that the human psyche must distance itself from the death of loved ones, but we of the generation of the *Shoah* cannot walk free from the shadow their martyrdom casts nor follow with ease the decree of the sage Rashi that the dead shall be forgotten from the heart.

☐

Among those of the Holocaust lost to us are two sisters, Chana Kremnitzer Nivy and Yona Sprechman Nivy, to whom this volume is dedicated.

SOLOMON M. NIVY

CONTENTS

Contents

CONTRIBUTORS

IRVING ABELLA is a professor in the Department of History, Glendon College, York University. He is the co-author of *None Is Too Many: Canada and the Jews of Europe, 1933–1948* and author of *A Coat of Many Colours: Two Centuries of Jewish Life in Canada.*

FRANKLIN BIALYSTOK is in the graduate program in history at York University. His most recent publications on the Holocaust deal with pedagogical issues, collective memory, the impact of the Holocaust on the Canadian Jewish community, and the Americanization of the Holocaust.

RANDOLPH L. BRAHAM is distinguished professor emeritus of political science and director of the Rosenthal Institute for Holocaust Studies of the Graduate School and University Center of the City University of New York. His many publications include *The Politics of Genocide: The Holocaust in Hungary* and *The Hungarian Jewish Catastrophe: A Selected and Annotated Bibliography.*

DAVID CESARANI is Alliance Professor of Judaism in Modern Times in the Department of Religions and Theology at the University of Manchester. He has written *Justice Delayed: How Britain Became a Refuge for Nazi War Criminals* and *The "Jewish Chronicle" and Anglo-Jewry 1841–1991.* He has also edited *The Making of Modern Anglo-Jewry.*

FREDERICK B. CHARY is professor of history at Indiana University Northwest. His published works include *The Bulgarian Jews and the Final Solution, 1940–1944.*

DEBÓRAH DWORK is the Rose Professor of Holocaust History at Clark University. She is the author of *Children with a Star: Jewish Youth in Nazi Europe* and co-author with Robert-Jan van Pelt of *Auschwitz: 1270 to the Present.*

ANDREW EZERGAILIS is a professor of history at Ithaca College. His publications include *1917 Revolution in Latvia* and *The Latvian Impact on the Bolshevik Revolution* and numerous articles.

SEYMOUR MAXWELL FINGER served in the U.S. foreign service for twenty-six years, the last five as an American ambassador at the United Nations. He is now a professor emeritus at the City University of New York. His works include *American Ambassadors at the United Nations* and *Bending With the Winds: Kurt Waldheim and the United Nations* and several edited books.

Contributors

ZVI GITELMAN teaches in the Department of Political Science at the University of Michigan—Ann Arbor. He is the author of several books, including *A Century of Ambivalence: The Jews of Russia and the Soviet Union, 1881 to the Present*.

RADU IOANID is the director of the Registry of Jewish Holocaust Survivors of the U.S. Holocaust Memorial Museum in Washington, D.C., and correspondent for Radio France Internationale. Among his published works are *The Sword of the Archangel: Fascist Ideology in Romania* and numerous articles.

DERMOT KEOGH is a professor with the Institute of Irish Studies at the Queen's University of Belfast. His publications include *Twentieth Century Ireland* and *Ireland and Europe, 1919–1989*.

TETSU KOHNO is professor of English at Hosei University in Tokyo. He has published numerous articles in books and periodicals in both English and Japanese. He also translates English works into Japanese.

DAVID KRANZLER is a retired professor from the City University of New York. His books include *Japanese, Nazis and Jews: The Jewish Refugee Community of Shanghai* and *The Man Who Stopped the Trains to Auschwitz*.

DOV LEVIN is head of the Oral History Division of the Avraham Harman Institute of Contemporary Jewry at Hebrew University in Jerusalem. He is the author of several books in Hebrew and *Fighting Back: The Lithuanian Jewry's Armed Resistance to the Nazis, 1941–1945* and *The Lesser of Two Evils: Eastern European Jewry under Soviet Rule, 1939–1941*.

ROBERT M. LEVINE is a professor of history at the University of Miami, Coral Gables, and is director of Latin American Studies. He has written nearly two dozen books on Latin American history and created the videotape "Hotel Cuba" with Mark D. Szuchman.

ANDREI S. MARKOVITS is professor in and chair of the Board of Studies in Politics at the University of California, Santa Cruz. He is also a senior associate of the Center for European Studies at Harvard University. His publications include *The German Left: Red, Green and Beyond* and *From Bundesrepublik to Deutschland: German Politics after Unification*.

MEIR MICHAELIS is a professor at the Institute of Contemporary Jewry at the Hebrew University of Jerusalem. His published works include *Mussolini and the Jews*.

BETH SIMONE NOVECK is currently completing a J.D. at Yale Law School. She was a Rotary Fellow at Christ Church, Oxford, and a Fulbright Scholar at the University of Innsbruck, where she completed a doctorate in political science.

DALIA OFER is the Max and Rita Haber Professor for Holocaust Studies in the Avraham Harman Institute of Contemporary Jewry and the head of the Vidal Sassoon International Center for the Study of Antisemitism, both at the Hebrew University. She is the author of *Escaping the Holocaust: Illegal Immigration to the Land of Israel, 1939–1944* and *Dead End Journey: The Kladovo Sabac Affair.*

BRUCE F. PAULEY is a professor of history at the University of Central Florida. He is the author of *Hitler and the Forgotten Nazis: A History of Austrian National Socialism* and *From Prejudice to Persecution: A History of Austrian Anti-Semitism.*

JEFFREY M. PECK is a professor of German in the Center for German and European Studies and the German Department, Georgetown University. He has co-written *Sojourners: The Return of German-Jews and the Question of Identity* and co-edited *Culture and Contexture: Explorations in Anthropology and Literary Studies.*

CHARLES H. ROSENZVEIG is the founder and executive vice-president of the Holocaust Memorial Center in West Bloomfield, Michigan. His published works include articles in scholarly journals.

LIVIA ROTHKIRCHEN is a senior researcher in the Holocaust Martyrs' and Heroes' Remembrance Authority of Yad Vashem. For more than fifteen years she served as editor of *Yad Vashem Studies.* She has edited *Hanhagat Yehude Hungaryah be-mivhan ha-sho'ah* (The destruction of Hungarian Jewry) and co-edited with Israel Gutman *Sho'at Yehude Eropah: Reka'—korot—mashma'ut* (The holocaust of European Jewry: background—history—implications).

MILTON SHAIN teaches medieval and modern Jewish history at the University of Cape Town in South Africa. He is the author of *Jewry and Cape Society: The Origins and Activities of the Jewish Board of Deputies for the Cape Colony* and *The Roots of Antisemitism in South Africa.*

MICHAEL C. STEINLAUF is a senior research fellow at the YIVO Institute for Jewish Research in New York. He writes and teaches about Eastern European Jewish history and culture and Polish-Jewish relations.

ROBERT-JAN VAN PELT is a professor of cultural history at the architecture school of the University of Waterloo in Ontario, Canada. His books include *Het Binnenhof, Tempel van de Wereld,* and, with Debórah Dwork, *Auschwitz: 1270 to the Present.*

DAVID WEINBERG is a professor of history at Wayne State University and director of the Cohn-Haddow Center for Judaic Studies. His published works include *A Community on Trial: The Jews of Paris in the 1930s* and numerous articles on modern Jewish history and French Jewry in the Holocaust.

DAVID S. WYMAN is Josiah DuBois Professor of History, Emeritus, from the University of Massachusetts, Amherst. His publications include *Paper Walls: America and the Refugee Crisis, 1938–1941* and *The Abandonment of the Jews: America and the Holocaust, 1941–1945.* He also edited the thirteen-volume document collection *America and the Holocaust.*

FOREWORD

We know so much about the Holocaust. Countless monographs, document collections, memoirs, oral histories, novels, and films have illuminated nearly every aspect of that cataclysm. What happened in the aftermath, after the stunned silence of 1945 gave way to a full realization of the horror, has not been so thoroughly studied. Indeed, there exists no systematic exploration of how the postwar world has dealt with the Holocaust. In 1988 the Holocaust Memorial Center, in West Bloomfield, Michigan, and its editorial board decided to delve into this important but neglected subject. The result is this work, which examines how twenty-two countries and the United Nations have reacted to the Holocaust since 1945.

Unique historical circumstances affected each country's behavior during the war and the Holocaust. These circumstances, coupled with wartime experiences, influenced how each country has reacted to the Holocaust over time. Some have denied the Holocaust, some have denationalized it, some have trivialized it, some have rationalized it, all have universalized it. Some countries have adopted every one of these positions in the period since 1945.

The voices of denationalization emanate mostly from German government officials, and their echoes can be found in Holocaust literature. The proponents of denationalization maintain that the Holocaust was an aberration of German history and culture, that the Third Reich, its Nazi philosophy, and the murder of Jewish people involved an insignificant segment of the German people. They claim that the Germany of today is not the Germany of the Third Reich and thus is not responsible for the crimes of the Third Reich.

The trivialization of the Holocaust advances the position that other nations in the past have also persecuted and murdered Jews, that Germany does not stand alone or apart. Those who endeavor to trivialize the Holocaust in Germany also argue that Germans too were victims of crimes committed by the Western Allies and the Russians during the war. Furthermore, some German scholars claim that the precedents for concentration camps and mass murder were established by the Soviet Union in its struggle against the capitalist class. Some Eastern European countries that were once occupied by or allied with the former Soviet Union equate their treatment by Jewish Communists with the treatment of the Jews by some of their countrymen and the Germans during the Holocaust.

Rationalization is the attempt to transmogrify Holocaust victims into war casualties. Recently this argument was taken one step further with the claim that the Zionists had been allies in the war against Germany. According to this reckoning, the Jews of Europe are viewed as combatants, and those who were murdered, as the simple casualties of war.

Foreword

Universalization, the attempt to dilute the uniqueness of the Holocaust and to deny the particular Jewish tragedy it represents, involves including political and war victims among Holocaust victims or equating other crimes against humanity of the past and present with the Holocaust, or both. Generally, Germany has universalized the crimes of the Holocaust by comparing other historic crimes to the Holocaust. Occupied Europe has universalized the victims. All of occupied Europe became victims of the Holocaust, and all historic persecutions were equated with the Holocaust.

The first official international response to the Holocaust was the Nuremberg trials in 1945–46. At these proceedings the victorious Allies prosecuted major Nazi figures for war crimes, crimes against humanity, and violations of international law. While the trials may have satisfied some in bringing to justice certain war criminals, they fell far short of providing a full, independent, and separate reckoning with the Jewish tragedy. The trials did not distinguish between the crimes committed against prisoners of war, which have precedence in history, and the Holocaust, which has none. The trials represent the first instance of universalizing the Holocaust, though it was probably unintended.

This situation did not change, for the Allies soon began to lose their fervor for prosecuting war criminals. The Cold War struggle for control of Europe preempted other concerns. To open further the wounds of the Holocaust and examine the records of the nations involved in this unique genocide might have alienated the people whose allegiance they thought they needed and thus sought. The West viewed Germany as crucially important to the containment of Communism. The Soviet Union too regarded Germany as essential to the extension of its sphere of influence. Bringing Germany into each of their respective folds was a major consideration in the Allies' decision to deemphasize denazification and war crimes trials after Nuremberg.

Because of serious political and economic concerns, many Europeans were also unwilling to deal with the moral conundrums posed by the Holocaust. Holocaust survivors returned to their communities to find their homes, businesses, and possessions, along with the property of the millions of Jews who perished in the death camps, in the hands of their neighbors. Fearing negative political repercussions, a number of governments discouraged the survivors from claiming their property, much less recovering it. Few countries established laws to restore expropriated property to returning Jews in the immediate postwar period. The vested interest of a significant portion of the population in keeping formerly Jewish property hindered a full and truthful examination of the Holocaust. Internationally, it suited the interests of the countries formally occupied by Germany to downplay the behavior of their citizens toward the Jews during the war. Endeavoring to identify themselves with the Allies and their war effort, they maximized the level of resistance they offered the Germans and minimized the extent of their cooperation and collaboration during the Occupation.

The countries examined in this volume reacted in different ways during and after the Holocaust, but in some respects their reactions were similar. The various chapters reveal that anti-Semitism was present at one time or another in all of these countries before the Holocaust. The characteristics of anti-Semitism in the different countries were remarkably alike. For centuries, Jews in the Diaspora have been accused of deicide by the predominantly Christian societies in which they lived. The prejudice that spawned this accusation gradually grew to include a variety of alleged offenses: Jews used Christian blood in secret rituals; they were infidels who sneered at other religions; they despised manual labor and were economic parasites; they were money-hungry, selfish, and ethically and morally corrupt; they had no national loyalty and did not wish to assimilate into the general society; elitist and cosmopolitan, they controlled the international political and economic levers of power. It rankled many that the Jews, a minority group historically accused by Christian leaders of deicide and of having a variety of vices, did not behave as a despised minority. Economically and educationally the Jews did not inhabit the lowest social strata in the countries in which they lived.

The consequences of anti-Semitism were varied. They ranged from the slaughter of entire Jewish communities during the Crusades to forced conversion, expulsion, isolation, and ghettoization; economic, political, and cultural discrimination; and pogroms. Jewish reactions to these persecutions similarly varied. Some Jews opted for assimilation and/or conversion. Some turned inward in a self-imposed ghettoization and isolation from the larger community. Some found their salvation in emigration. Others turned to nationalism in the form of Zionism. Still others espoused Jewish amalgamation and identification with the international socialist movements. And a small segment of Jews turned to Communism.

The Holocaust and the post-Holocaust reactions have proved that the problem of anti-Semitism cannot be solved by either assimilation or Communist internationalism. Judging by the rhetoric of the intense anti-Semitism that preceded the Holocaust and, in a number of Eastern European countries, even following the Holocaust, it would appear that the small number of Jews who turned to the Left elicited the most virulent form of anti-Semitism.

Jews typically were not active in national politics except when their internal community affairs were involved. With the advent of parliamentary democracy in the nineteenth century, however, Jews, like the rest of the general population, began to become politically active. Consigned to the mostly powerless fringes of society, Jews, when spurred to political activity, tended to align themselves with change. The status quo provided them little advancement or security. In Eastern Europe a small number of Jews became active in the Communist and other revolutionary movements. Some Jews, such as Rosa Luxemburg, Béla Kun, and Leon Trotsky, emerged as leading figures of the Left. In Western Europe Léon Blum was the leader of the French Socialist Party and in 1936 became the prime minister of France, the first socialist and the first Jew to head a French government.

The conspicuous presence of some Jews in the leadership of the Left earned the Jews more pejorative labels: liberals, Communists, revolutionaries. The Right used these labels to combat what they perceived as a divisive and growing force in society. Jews were threatening national unity and the sanctity of Christianity with their foreign, corrupting influence. Although Christian liberals and leftists were also considered disruptive, they were viewed as misguided insiders, whereas the Jews were portrayed as disloyal outsiders.

The Bolshevik revolution in 1917, the realignment of Europe after World War I, the economic upheavals in the 1930s, and the rise of fascism created an unstable environment in which Jews presented a convenient target for the venting of frustrations. The alleged vices of a few Jews became the faults of the entire group. The many prejudices against the Jews that had accumulated through the ages coalesced with the more recent accusations of political radicalism to create a particularly intense form of anti-Semitism. Adolf Hitler summed up this attitude in *Mein Kampf* in 1925: "As I learned to look for the Jew in every field of our cultural and artistic life, I suddenly bumped against him in a place where I had never suspected. The scales dropped from my eyes when I found the Jew as the leader of Social Democracy. This put an end to a long internal struggle" ([New York, 1939], 78).

The intense political anti-Semitism of the 1930s became almost universal, abetted in part by the worldwide economic depression. It even manifested itself in societies with few or no Jews. Before this period such anti-Semitism rarely occurred in one country because of the alleged economic or political vices of Jews in another country. From the 1930s on, however, Jews came to be seen as international economic and political conspirators and manipulators who threatened the livelihood and political stability of nations everywhere. The fear that the Jews would wrest political and economic power from the Christian community proved to be a particularly potent force when combined with religious anti-Semitism. The immediate welfare of peoples and nations lay at stake. Many of Europe's political and economic elite became active, open, and virulent anti-Semites, and the Jews became the scapegoats in a Europe torn by economic depression, political upheaval, and war.

Yet blaming the Jews for the world's ills did not alone create the conditions that led to the Final Solution. After the outbreak of the German-Soviet war in June 1941, Germany became less concerned about world opinion, which had previously acted as a restraint on Hitler. The totalitarian Nazi government and the powerful "leader" cult Hitler fostered were key ingredients. In addition, Germany's cultural orientation toward Realpolitik, in which the pursuit of a nation's interest is unfettered by the restraints of idealism or conscience, served to free perpetrators from moral concerns and permitted the majority of the German people to tolerate the crimes of the Holocaust. Lt. Gen. R. A. Rudenko, the Soviet Union's chief prosecutor at the Nuremberg trials, quoted Hitler in his opening remarks at the trials: "We want to make a selection for a class of new masters who will be deprived of moral pity. . . . I am freeing men from the restraints of an intelligence that has taken charge; from the dirty and degrading self-mortifications of a chimera called conscience" (*Trial of the Major War Criminals before the International Military Tribunal*, vol. 7, *Proceedings, 14 November 1945–1 October 1946* [Nuremberg, 1947], 152–53). Judging from his immense popularity, Hitler's words were favorably received by a significant portion of the German public.

Foreword

One would have thought that the countries represented in this volume, especially those that witnessed the Holocaust, would have reassessed their wartime prejudices and behavior in the post-Holocaust period. Unfortunately, this did not happen in the first twenty-five years following World War II. Most of the countries had reasons not to examine too closely their wartime actions. But the passage of time has made the process less painful, and most have begun to reassess their role. A number of legal scholars and political leaders in several countries have reexamined the Nuremberg trials and questioned their legality, saying that wars of aggression and crimes against prisoners of war and political opponents are not unique in history and therefore did not deserve the unique treatment represented by the international tribunal. The Holocaust, however, is unique. At no other time in history has a nation knowingly and methodically established administrative, military, logistic, and technical facilities to annihilate an entire people, many of them their own citizens.

Throughout history, totalitarian regimes have persecuted both real and imagined political dissidents. Nations have similarly conducted wars of conquest or wars to protect themselves against real or imagined threats to their national security. Tragically, war and its ugly by-products have become accepted as the sometimes necessary results of pursuing and protecting a nation's interests. In times both of war and of peace, persecution of political opponents is one of the destructive consequences of intolerance. The Jewish people, perhaps more than any other, have been victimized by sporadic violence. Unfortunately, history suggests that prejudice, discrimination, persecution, and war are predictable; all we can hope for is to control and modify their emergence.

To compare selective political, racial, or religious persecution or any other historical event to the planned total extermination of a people blunts the revulsion we should feel when we contemplate the Holocaust. One way we can make another Holocaust less likely is to present it as a totally unprecedented and therefore totally reprehensible and unacceptable occurrence. To do otherwise would be to perpetuate a falsehood. The indiscriminate, premeditated murder of Jewish men, women, and children not involved in war or territorial disputes is *not* on a par with the killing of prisoners of war or selective detainees. To fall into this perceptual trap would work to make another Holocaust as acceptable and perhaps as predictable as war and its abuses. No motive, no matter how well intentioned, can justify compromising the uniqueness of the Holocaust. The Holocaust is a singular event, and it is our duty to ensure that it remains so, never to be repeated against any people anywhere.

Fortunately, as many of the authors point out, the end of the Cold War and the passage of time have created a more open environment for coming to terms with the Holocaust. The influence of the World War II generation is fading, and new generations, generations that did not participate in the Holocaust and thus have no particular ideological stance to protect, have begun to explore its moral complexities. As a result, most of the countries studied in this volume are finally grappling with the Holocaust in a more objective manner. One hopes the new willingness to confront unpleasant realities will foster educational, social, and governmental safeguards that will work to prevent the crossing of the line that separates prejudice and Holocaust.

□

I wish to acknowledge my gratitude and give recognition to the editor of this volume, Professor David Wyman. His scholarship, wisdom, and dedication have been indispensable to the success of this project. Dr. Wyman's impressive monographs and document collections have left an indelible imprint on the field of Holocaust studies. His many public lectures based upon his brilliant research have served to awaken the conscience of America regarding its behavior during the Holocaust. This volume is another example of his scholarship and commitment.

CHARLES H. ROSENZVEIG

INTRODUCTION

Except for the perpetrators and the victims, the world gave little attention to the Holocaust while it was happening. Only in the closing weeks of World War II, when the Allied armies came upon the concentration camps, was mankind forced to look intensively at the horrors committed by Nazi Germany. During the early postwar period the Holocaust again intruded into public consciousness, though less dramatically. The Nuremberg trials, while they did not focus sharply on the Holocaust, drew substantial public attention to the genocide of the Jews. For more than three years following the war most of the surviving remnant of European Jewry existed in crowded displaced persons camps, waiting for doors to open in other lands. These people were a constant reminder to the world of the hell that they had endured and of the fact that for each Jew who had survived, many had not. During the same years the Holocaust continually hovered over the international deliberations concerning Palestine. It was also a powerful stimulus for the Jewish drive to establish a state there.

By the early 1950s the war crimes trials, the displaced persons problem, and the issue of Jewish statehood had been essentially resolved. But the most difficult and sensitive questions about the Holocaust had barely been raised. These issues included, but were certainly not restricted to, questions about the guilt of the German people, complicity and collaboration in the countries under German occupation, the failure of non-Jews to attempt to save their Jewish neighbors, and the very limited rescue efforts on the part of the outside world. Nor were these issues confronted during the 1950s; instead, in that decade the Holocaust all but disappeared from public consciousness in most of the world. The near silence was broken in 1961 by the Eichmann trial and the months of publicity that it generated. Structured by the Israeli government for maximum educational impact, the trial was closely watched throughout the world, and it made some inroads into the widespread ignorance about the Holocaust. But outside Israel the most sensitive questions still were not confronted in any depth; nor were they confronted during the decade that followed, when the world's interest in Holocaust issues was again nearly quiescent.

In many countries the early 1970s saw an increase in attention to and discussion of the Holocaust. Then in the late seventies and into the mid-eighties, especially in several nations outside the Iron Curtain, the level of interest rose noticeably. In those years world consciousness of the Holocaust was spurred by—among other developments—the remarkable international impact of the American television miniseries *Holocaust* and the fortieth anniversaries of several significant Holocaust events. The impact of the Holocaust became increasingly apparent in literature, scholarship, film, and, to a lesser extent, educational systems. More and more governments recognized the importance of Holocaust-related issues and responded to them. And the deeper

Introduction

questions about the destruction of the European Jews began to be more widely raised.

In 1988 a group of scholars who were interested in the world's changing reactions to the Holocaust met at the Holocaust Memorial Center in the Detroit suburb of West Bloomfield. At that gathering the center's founder, Rabbi Charles H. Rosenzveig, proposed that a book be prepared and published that would deal with the responses of several of the world's nations to the Holocaust in the years *since* the Holocaust. Those at the meeting were enthusiastic about the rabbi's suggestion and offered to serve on an editorial board that was soon expanded to include additional scholars. The Holocaust Memorial Center agreed to sponsor the project.

The plan for the book called for a separate chapter for each nation. Each chapter was assigned to a highly qualified scholar who possessed the specialized knowledge required for analyzing the particular country under consideration. Many of the authors selected are leading experts in their fields, and all have published important works on the Holocaust and Jewish history. Originally each essay was to cover developments up to 1990, but the momentous events of the late 1980s and early 1990s on the world scene, especially those in Eastern and Central Europe, persuaded us to extend our original time frame to the mid-1990s. This change was made possible by the patient cooperation of the authors, who reworked and updated their chapters. The outcome was the inclusion in the book of much recent and very significant material. Of special importance were the dramatic changes in the responses to the Holocaust that occurred in most of the formerly Communist nations in conjunction with or shortly after the remarkable political changes.

I do not intend in this introduction to undertake a systematic analysis of the information presented in this book. Instead, I shall briefly preview a very few of the findings that are of particular interest.

The post–World War II responses of the Netherlands and France to the Holocaust reveal interesting similarities as well as intriguing differences. Both nations came out of the war committed to mythologies about their supposedly strong and extensive resistance to the German Occupation. The Dutch further believed that they had gallantly, if not successfully, tried to protect the Dutch Jews, incurring great risk and sacrifice in doing so. By 1970, however, developments in the Netherlands had demolished the myths. The Dutch people had come to recognize that accommodation and collaboration had been the norm and that few Dutch citizens had resisted the Nazis and few had helped Jews. In the process of reconsideration, the tragic fate of the Dutch Jews moved into a central place in the Dutch perception of World War II. In France the mythology about widespread resistance, though challenged and weakened over the decades, has persisted. Meanwhile, the French, despite several near encounters with the fact of France's complicity with the Nazis in carrying out the Holocaust, have begun only in the 1990s to move toward direct confrontation with that reality.

Britain and the United States, nations with a shared heritage and numerous commonalities, were similar also in their reluctance to aid the Jews during the Holocaust. Britain made virtually no attempts at rescue, while the United States launched a very limited rescue program in 1944. Yet these nations have responded very differently to the Holocaust in the years since World War II. In the United States questions arising out of the Holocaust began to be fairly widely discussed in the 1970s. One important factor in this development was an earlier initiative, a meaningful Christian-Jewish dialogue that dated back to the first postwar years. Those involved had not hesitated to face such difficult issues as the connection between the Holocaust and the anti-Semitism that the Christian churches had harbored for centuries. Since the 1970s the Holocaust and many of the questions connected with it have received extensive attention in the United States. In Britain reaction to the Holocaust was very limited until the 1990s. Even the attention given it by British Jews was not widespread until the 1980s. Whether the higher level of public consciousness of the Holocaust that accompanied the recent World War II anniversaries will be sustained cannot be predicted. And whether the British will eventually confront their nation's policies regarding the Jews during the Holocaust remains to be seen.

This book offers a large amount of new information on the formerly Communist nations of Europe. Until the late 1980s these countries all followed the Soviet Union's approach to the Holocaust: they universalized it and forced it into a Communist ideological mold. The destruction of the Jews was seen as merely a small part of racist fascism's murder of millions of Eastern European civilians. Since fascism was considered the ultimate form of capitalism, capitalism had been at the root of the massive killing. According to this perception, nothing was different or special about what had happened to the Jews. Thus, in the Communist countries the Holocaust was virtually ignored by the governments, the historians, and the people. It was omitted from textbooks about World War II. It very infrequently appeared in literature. Because the Holocaust was not addressed, there was no need to face sensitive issues such as collaboration with the Germans in the killing of the Jews, widespread though it had been in several of these countries.

With the fall of Communism and the end of Soviet hegemony, new perspectives on the Holocaust began to take form in the Eastern European nations. Free discussion of the Holocaust started to occur in the press, markers and monuments were placed at deportation and mass killing sites, memorial services were initiated, and serious scholarly inquiry was undertaken. In Poland and Hungary, where Soviet controls loosened earlier, the first steps toward facing the Holocaust occurred before the 1970s ended. Elsewhere, the changes began only with the demise of the Communist governments at the end of the 1980s and the start of the 1990s. In some nations (Lithuania, Latvia, Slovakia, East Germany) the new leaderships expressed official regret for the participation of some of their people in the killing of the Jews, thereby opening up the difficult and painful issue of complicity in the Holocaust. But in all of the formerly Communist countries the early 1990s brought only the beginnings of serious efforts to confront the reality and the implications of the Holocaust. At the same time, resistance to those realities and implications became evident in several quarters, especially in Lithuania and Hungary. And in Romania after the fall of the Ceausescu regime, the longtime denial of any Romanian involvement in the Holocaust only solidified in an atmosphere of anti-Semitism that was sufficient to bring about the rehabilitation of the executed war criminal Ion Antonescu.

Introduction

Communist ideology considered the territory held by the East German state to have been under "occupation" by the Nazis in World War II. According to this theory, the East Germans were victims of the Nazis, bore no responsibility for the treatment of the Jews, and had no need to confront the Holocaust. Even before the termination of the East German state, however, its leaders, seeking to improve relations with the United States, dropped this absurd thesis and began to acknowledge the Holocaust, particularly through numerous events related to the fiftieth anniversary of Kristallnacht during 1988. Early in 1990 the new (and soon to dissolve) East German government entirely reversed the old position. It recognized the responsibility of all Germans for the Nazi regime and asked the Jews of the world to forgive them for the persecution and for East Germany's years of anti-Israel policies.

Through the decades, many West German political leaders, intellectuals, and members of the general public have turned their attention to the Holocaust and have attempted steps to deal with it. Yet West Germany has still not really confronted this part of its past. A key reason is that in the immediate postwar period the German response to the Holocaust was to repress it and forget it rather than to face it honestly. Then the failure of denazification meant that when the West German Federal Republic emerged four years after the war there was no clear break between it and the Nazi regime. The political leadership of the new state did not come to terms with the Nazi atrocities, and it allowed the German people to continue to avoid any real confrontation with them. Even though German writers and historians have probed extensively into the Nazi era over the years, no adequate confrontation with the Holocaust has occurred on that front either, because little of their examination has gone specifically and deeply into the actual destruction of the Jews. The airing of the television miniseries *Holocaust* in 1979 did ignite a long-delayed, frank discussion of German guilt, a discussion that still has a considerable distance to go.

The foregoing paragraphs represent a small sampling of the materials presented in this work. I have confined myself to only a few of the many important issues discussed by our authors, and I have drawn on only half of the essays in this volume. Limited though my scope is, I hope I have given some impression of the richness of the findings offered in this book.

Throughout *The World Reacts to the Holocaust,* the authors have endeavored to follow the same general format in presenting their research. The essays begin with a concise history of the Jews in the country under consideration prior to the Holocaust. The topics addressed include the characteristics of the Jewish settlements, the presence of anti-Semitism and any related violence, the role of Jews in the society, and the nature of the relationship between Jews and non-Jews. A brief narrative of the Holocaust in the country follows. Among the issues examined are the extent of the human destruction, the degree of collaboration, Jewish reactions, and efforts to save the Jews.

The major part of each essay concerns the post–World War II era, and here the authors investigate the reactions of each country to the destruction of the European Jews. They consider official and unofficial governmental responses to the Holocaust;

reactions of religious communities, other voluntary associations, and the general public; the treatment of the Holocaust by the media and in the educational system; and the role of the Holocaust in scholarship, literature, and film and in the country's culture in general.

We believe that the information and insights in this book will be useful to people of various degrees of historical knowledge and diverse areas of interest. Though it is a scholarly work, it is aimed at the serious general reader as well as at a scholarly audience.

I wish to express my deep appreciation to the Holocaust Memorial Center and to its founder and executive vice president, Rabbi Charles H. Rosenzveig. The Holocaust Memorial Center, the first freestanding Holocaust museum in the United States, was dedicated in October 1984. It is an independent institution, not politically indebted to any government or other body. The museum's exhibits portray and document the destruction of European Jewry and the events that led up to it. Also highlighted are the two-thousand-year history of the European Jews and the rich culture that was destroyed with them. Essential to the center's mission is its Morris and Emma Schaver Library-Archive. A research facility whose holdings document the history and impact of the Holocaust, European Jewish history, and the Judeo-Christian relationship, the library-archive offers an extensive collection of books, documents, correspondence, photographs, maps, and documentary films. In addition, it houses the John J. Mames Oral History Department, which records and collects the testimonies of survivors, liberators, rescuers, and eyewitnesses. The Holocaust Memorial Center also sponsors scholarly conferences, teachers' seminars, and public lectures. Rabbi Rosenzveig, who originated the concept that led to *The World Reacts to the Holocaust,* grew up in Poland. Only he and one other member of his family were not lost in the Holocaust. After the war he studied in France for one year and then came to the United States, where he attended Yeshiva University. He became an ordained rabbi in 1949. Without the steadfast support of the Holocaust Memorial Center and the insights and the many hours of dedicated work provided by Rabbi Rosenzveig, this book could not have become a reality.

I would like also to extend my sincere gratitude to our distinguished editorial board and especially to Dr. Guy Stern for his wise and practical guidance; to Dr. Melvin Small, whose advice and editorial assistance have been indispensable; and to Dr. Bernard Goldman, who has always responded helpfully to our requests for guidance and scholarly advice. Anne Adamus, who assisted in the editing of this volume, deserves special recognition. She has managed the day-to-day work of this project with professionalism, creativity, and exceptional skill.

Finally, a very great debt of gratitude belongs to Solomon and Aliza Nivy, whose generous grant to the Holocaust Memorial Center made this book possible. Their support remains unstinting and unqualified. It is only fitting that Solomon Nivy have the honor of dedicating this volume.

DAVID S. WYMAN

WESTERN EUROPE

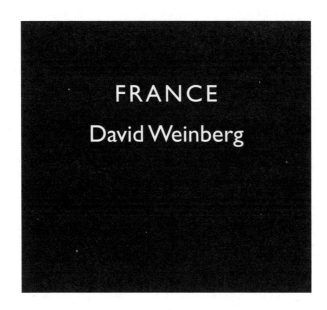

FRANCE
David Weinberg

The phantoms are always there; like living dead that cannot be buried, embedded in our consciences, they periodically return from afar to pull us out of our torpor.

Bernard-Henri Lévy, *L'Idéologie française*

BEFORE THE HOLOCAUST

The history and consciousness of the Holocaust in France are marked by profound contradictions and ironies that reflect both the tortured path of France's political development and the ambiguous nature of its collective memory. In 1791 France became the first country to emancipate Jewry. Throughout much of the nineteenth and early twentieth centuries it prided itself in being the most ardent defender of religious freedom and civil liberties. Yet one hundred and fifty years after the French Revolution the popularly supported Vichy regime initiated brutal discriminatory policies against its Jewish inhabitants and later openly assisted the Third Reich in the implementation of the Final Solution.

For more than three decades after Liberation, French society denied its painful wartime past and ignored the fate of its Jewish inhabitants under Vichy. Yet the memories of collaboration and deportation could not be repressed. Despite the collapse of the collaborationist government of Philippe Pétain and the return to democracy, antirepublicanism and anti-Semitism continued to plague postwar French society. It took a series of events in the 1970s and 1980s to suddenly catapult the Holocaust into the center of French public debate as part of a general reevaluation of the comfortable myths concerning resistance to Nazism that formed the ideological basis of postwar national revival and reconstruction. The result is that no other country in the contemporary era, with the possible exception of Germany, has become as obsessed with the deportation and destruction of its Jewish community during World War II. Indeed, Vichy would replace the Dreyfus Affair in the postwar era as the central symbol in twentieth-century French political life. The fact that the events and the perpetrators of the Holocaust under Vichy continue to make front-page headlines in French newspapers in the 1990s, fifty years after the deportations, suggests that France continues to have difficulty coming to terms with its past.[1]

While Jews and Judaism are a popular topic of discussion and research in contemporary France, for much of the modern era most Frenchmen had little direct awareness of the Jewish community in their midst. In the period before the French Revolution, Jews generally were segregated from the larger society and had few civil rights. Divided between Sephardic descendants of Spanish-Portuguese Jews in the southwest of France and Ashkenazic descendants of German Jews in Alsace, they numbered no more than a few thousand in 1789. Even after their emancipation, French Jews remained small in number and widely dispersed. Unlike their German coreligionists, they played a relatively minor role in the modernization of Jewish thought and society that took place in the first half of the nineteenth century.

It was only after 1848 that French Jewry began to make significant inroads in the social, economic, political, and cultural life of France. As the nation modernized, Jews assumed prominent positions in banking, commerce, and industry as well as in the arts and politics. Gradually concentrating in Paris, they developed a complex communal structure that mirrored the centralized nature of French society as a whole. Increases in the French Jews' standard of living and level of health care enabled them to share in the general increase in population affecting Europe, and Jewry in particular, in the nineteenth century. By the outbreak of World War I, French Jews numbered around 120,000, about 0.3 percent of the total population.

The makeup and attitudes of the community in the period before 1914 generally reflected the ease with which its members integrated into the larger society. For much of the nineteenth and the early twentieth century French Jewry was dominated by so-called native Jews, or *autochtones,* comprising mainly families that had fled Alsace-Lorraine after the defeat of France in 1870. Largely bourgeois and politically centrist, they were committed to the cautious program of economic growth, social stability, and political moderation espoused by leaders of the Third Republic. Beneficiaries of emancipation and largely unscathed by anti-Semitic prejudice, they no longer regarded themselves as *juifs,* or Jews in the classical sense, but as *israélites français,* individuals who could live as equal citizens while retaining their commitment to basic Jewish religious values and beliefs. Even the outbreak of the Dreyfus Affair at the end of the century did not seriously damage the community's commitment to assimilationism.[2]

In actuality, the Jews' status in France was far less favorable than the rosy picture portrayed by community leaders. France had a long history of anti-Jewish sentiment, which took many different forms over the centuries. In the period before the French Revolution, Jews were hated by Christian believers and unbelievers alike—by the former because of the Jews' rejection of religious "truth," by the latter as the forerunners of despised Christianity. Even the granting of full and equal rights during the French Revolution came at a cost. As the proponents of emancipation after 1789 were careful to point out, the decision to allow Jews to participate freely in society was predicated on the assumption that they would willingly give up their communal institutions and identity. In true Jacobin fashion, supporters of rights for Jews were convinced that commitment to *la patrie* necessitated the rejection of all other collective loyalties. As Stanislaus Clermont de la Tonnerre, a deputy to the National Assembly, announced in 1791: "You must refuse everything to Jews as a nation and give Jews everything as individuals . . . they must no longer be a political body or an order in the State."[3]

In general, French Jewry seemed more than happy to acquiesce to society's demands that it dispense with traditional beliefs and practices that hindered its assimilation. Proclaimed by the Sanhedrin (Rabbinic High Court) convened by Napoleon in 1807 and institutionalized in the structure and activities of the community's major religious body, the Consistoire central, modern French Judaism represented a synthesis of the central tenets of classical Jewish religious thought and the liberal values of post-Revolutionary France. Throughout the nineteenth and early twentieth centuries, consistorial rabbis constantly proclaimed the view that loyalty to biblical ideals necessitated active Jewish participation in the development of liberty, equality, and fraternity in France. Beholden to the Republic as the ultimate guarantor of their freedom, French Jews rejected all particularisms that threatened to isolate them from the larger society. As Joseph Reinach, a leading French Jewish writer, noted in response to the rise of Zionism in late-nineteenth-century Europe: "All of our efforts, all of our intellectual activity, all of our love, the last blood in our veins, belong to France, and to her alone."[4]

The close relationship between Jews and the Republic and between French Judaism and the ideals of the Revolution meant that groups and movements that sought to attack the existing political structure after 1848 and especially after 1871 invariably expressed anti-Semitic sentiments. In the nineteenth century, hostility toward Jews could be found on both the Left and the Right. While many leading French socialists denounced the Jew for his association with capitalism, defenders of traditional institutions and values attacked him as a harbinger of modernity, a symbolic manifestation of the evils that had befallen France since the onset of the French Revolution.[5]

The most serious manifestation of anti-Semitism in modern France before the Holocaust could be found in the so-called Dreyfus Affair. The affair had its origins in the court-martial of Alfred Dreyfus, a Jewish captain in the French Army who in 1894 was accused of selling secret military information to the Germans. The case quickly took on the dimensions of a national struggle as supporters of Dreyfus championed the ideals of individual freedom and toleration, while his opponents denounced his rise in the military ranks as a reflection of the decadence and corruption of republican France. Dreyfus was eventually pardoned in 1899, but he was not fully cleared until 1906.

In their attacks upon Dreyfus, anti-Semites often combined contrasting stereotypes of the Jew to create a classical scapegoat for the ills of the nation. In the rhetoric of anti-Dreyfusards such as Charles Drumont and Léon Daudet, traditional imagery of the wandering Jew merged with contemporary caricatures of rootless cosmopolitans, whether capitalists or revolutionaries. Dreyfus thus was the archetypical Jew who allegedly used the freedoms granted him by modern French society to betray his "adopted" nation in the name of ancient tribal loyalties and commitments. Even after the furor over Dreyfus had subsided, anti-Semitism continued to lie just beneath the surface of French public consciousness, rarely articulated yet capable of being aroused in periods of national crisis. Not surprisingly, therefore, many of the anti-Semitic ideas and attitudes first formulated during the Dreyfus Affair would surface again during the period of the Occupation and again in the postwar debate over the involvement of Vichy in the deportations of Jews.[6]

Before World War II native Jews generally chose to dismiss anti-Semitic outbursts as the rantings of an extremist and insignificant minority. Even during the Dreyfus Affair most French Jews either ignored the attacks upon the community or argued for a policy of quiet diplomacy. Unlike their coreligionists in Germany, French Jews remained confident of the support of their government and rarely felt the need to defend their emancipation openly.[7] The result was that championing defense of Jewish interests generally took place beyond the borders of France in areas where they believed Jews had yet to share in the benefits of emancipation. It was not coincidental that the most active organization within the community in the nineteenth century was the Alliance israélite universelle, founded in 1860. As its tripartite name implied, the organization was pledged not only to defend the ideals of a voluntaristic Jewish community and a modern Jewish identity but also to spread the principles of 1789 among coreligionists in areas under French imperialist control.

For many French Jews, the source of modern anti-Semitism in their country could be traced to the arrival at the turn of the century of thousands of immigrants fleeing economic impoverishment and political persecution in czarist Russia. France would experience another influx of Russian and Polish Jews between the wars as a result of continued economic and political unrest in Eastern Europe and the onset of restrictions upon immigration to America in 1924. By 1939 French Jews numbered close to three hundred thousand, almost two-thirds of whom were foreign-born.

Products of a traditional communal structure and distrustful of the larger society, Eastern European Jews' attitudes toward both Judaism and the host community differed markedly from those of their French coreligionists. Clinging to their traditional beliefs and practices, congregating in areas of immigrant settlement, and employed in the "Jewish trades" of clothing and textile production, many Russian and Polish Jews sought to re-create the collective life of the *shtetl* within the more open atmosphere of French society. The immigrant community also contained hundreds of radicals who had been drawn to France by its rich revolutionary heritage and toleration of political refugees. Though immigrant activists were often bitterly critical of Jewish religious values and beliefs, they shared the traditionalists' view of the established Jewish community as assimilationist with little loyalty to Jewish values.

Unlike native-born Jews, newly arrived immigrants from Russia and Poland saw the rise of anti-Semitic mass movements in France as a clear indication of the need for vigilance and an activist response. In the period before World War I, however, they were far too weak and disunited to mount an effective campaign against anti-Jewish attacks. More importantly, with time many of the immigrants' suspicions gradually melted away in the wake of the inexorable power of French cultural assimilationism. The significant participation of thousands of Russian and Polish Jews in the French army during World War I was an important acculturating experience. So too was the gradual embourgeoisement of formerly semiskilled and unskilled immigrant Jewish laborers in the 1920s. Although doubts born of decades of brutal persecution and numbing economic deprivation in the Old Country persisted, the process of assimilation was clearly making inroads in the first decades of the twentieth century among both immigrants and their native-born children.[8]

The 1930s saw an explosion of antiforeignism in the economic, cultural, and political realms and the first significant public manifestations of violence against Jews since the Dreyfus Affair. Such attitudes and behavior would provide the bedrock for Vichy's anti-Jewish propaganda and policies in the following decade. In the period immediately before and after the outbreak of World War I, hostility toward *métèques* (foreigners) had been muted by the grudging recognition of France's need for "fresh blood" to replace a young male population decimated by war and to supply labor for a growing modern economy. The onset of the Depression in the early 1930s, however, led to a clamor for controls on foreigners. Government officials and their advisers, conflating the immigrant labor issue and the problem of refugees, now argued that foreign workers should be expelled from France and insisted that refugees would only be accepted if they promised not to compete for jobs.

The increase in restrictive legislation and policies had a particularly devastating effect upon foreign-born Jews. German Jews who had begun to arrive in France after the accession of the Nazis to power in 1933 were the target of especially bitter criticism, since their high socioeconomic status made them potential competitors with the most articulate and most influential members of the French workforce. In time, Eastern European Jewish merchants and tradesmen, many of whom had lived in France for years, began to face the onslaught of attacks from petit bourgeois groups demanding restrictions on the activities and employment of foreigners in the clothing and textile trades. Even previously sympathetic liberal newspapers now urged French Jews to train their foreign coreligionists to become miners and agricultural laborers so that they would be less visible in society.[9]

Of particular concern was the association of the decline in the prestige and influence of French culture with the influx of foreigners, especially Jews. The outbreak of syphilis and typhoid epidemics in France in the 1920s had been blamed on foreigners concentrated in urban ghettos, that is, Jews, who were accused of weakening the nation's physical and spiritual strength. Polemical tracts distributed in France after World War I associated Jews specifically with such sociobiological "evils" as hermaphroditism, effeminacy, homosexuality, and sexual perversion. Fears of biological infection allegedly spread by new arrivals often merged with concerns over the cultural tainting of the French nation. Respected scholars and government advisers in the interwar period wrote menacingly about the danger of shadowy *clandestins*, who were said to be methodically destroying French society from within.[10]

Such concerns were introduced into public debate in an ominous form in 1934 as a result of the so-called Stavisky Affair. Serge Stavisky was a Russian-born Jew who had been involved in a number of shady financial schemes that bilked hundreds of investors. The fact that he had successfully avoided coming to trial raised suspicions that he was being protected by government officials. Evoking memories of the Dreyfus Affair, right-wing polemicists pointed to Stavisky's corrupt financial activities and political machinations and the suspicious circumstances surrounding his sudden and violent death in January 1934 as proof of the deeply rooted decadence of France's economic and political elite. The sudden resignation of a number of deputies and the formation of a new cabinet led to the bloody demonstrations of February 6, 1934, in which crowds marched on the Chambre des députés demanding an accounting for the "crimes of Stavisky."[11]

As the 1930s progressed, economic retrenchment triggered concerns about France's military capabilities. French military doctrine in the interwar period was predicated on the probability of a prolonged war in which economic and demographic strength would play a determining role. Appeasement was the natural corollary of economic belt-tightening after the onset of the Depression in the early thirties. Economic crisis and a foreign policy that sought to avoid war at all costs easily bred hostility toward Jewish victims of Nazism as warmongers. Hatred of Jews as subversives and fomenters of international conflict was reinforced by the accession of Léon Blum to power in June 1936. Portraying the Popular Front as a Jewish creation to weaken France, extremist elements on the Right denounced Blum as a Polish Jew whose allegiance lay with shadowy forces allied against the nation. Such attitudes climaxed in popular protests against the regime's involvement in the Spanish Civil War that merged anti-Jewish hostility with concerns over the possibility of French military entanglement.[12]

Popular fears of subversion from within and without by Jews and other "aliens" fueled the rise of fascist and extreme nationalist movements in the 1930s. In 1934 alone some 370,000 persons belonged to the four major French movements of the extreme Right—Action française, Jeunesse patriotes, Légion, and Faisceau—more than the total membership of the Nazi Party in 1933 or of the Italian Blackshirts in 1922.[13] Such movements were given respectability by the support of young intellectuals such as Robert Brasillach, Pierre Drieu de la Rochelle, and Louis-Ferdinand Céline, who saw in fascism a program to revitalize the French spirit and transform national values in the wake of economic, political, and cultural decline.[14]

Although not all right-wing groups in the 1930s were anti-Jewish, many of the newer movements regarded previous forms of French anti-Semitism as too passive and tame and called for the adoption of Nazi racial ideology and policy in France. Blending the disparate anti-Jewish sentiments in France during the period into an all-embracing ideology of anti-Semitism, such groups held world Jewry responsible for the international crisis, parliamentary indecision and corruption, the weakening of the national ideal, and the conformism and decadence of bourgeois culture. With little encouragement from the German government, some supporters of French fascism even went so far as to call for mass murder as a solution to the Jewish Problem in France. Even the most successful French fascist movement, the Parti populaire français, which previously had judiciously avoided public expressions of anti-Semitism, took up the battle cry against Jews after the victory of the Popular Front. As its fiery leader, Jean-Jacques Doriot, wrote menacingly in July 1936: "Jews, socialists, and communists for the most part by their tyranny or intolerance will lead to the rapid birth and growth of an anti-Semitism in France that was nonexistent before their accession to power. If terrible things happen to them, they will have brought it upon themselves."[15]

By far the most telling indication of the growth of anti-Semitism in France in the mid- and late thirties was the appropriation of anti-Jewish language and attitudes by "respectable" elements within society. Particularly vocal were professional groups, who in their eagerness to prevent competition from German Jewish doctors and lawyers openly called for the adoption of quotas on their admission into France. Throughout the 1930s all elements of the political spectrum borrowed statements and statistics about Jews and other "foreigners" from extreme right-wing newspapers and made little or no attempt to verify them. Even liberal political factions in the Radical majority of Parliament called for a thorough investigation of problems posed by the continuous influx of foreigners into France.[16] Traditional moral arguments that rested on the image of France as an asylum for political refugees were drowned out by growing hysteria over the impact of "aliens" upon the nation's economy and international standing. By 1939 a lead article in the respected daily *Le Temps* could publicly speak of the need to maintain the "integrity of race," a position that was echoed in articles in many of the French capital's other leading dailies.[17]

The turbulent events of the 1930s only served to reinforce the conflicts between native and immigrant Jews that had been simmering in the interwar period. At the very time when events called for a united stand in the face of oppression and persecution, French Jewry found itself deeply divided over tactics and behavior. In large part, the divisions reflected the differing social and economic conditions of the two groups. As noted earlier, native Jews were largely bourgeois and assimilated into French society. Their view of developments within French society was that of insiders, committed to the national interest and familiar with the individuals and groups that defined and shaped French policy. Immigrants, on the other hand, were generally petit bourgeois and outside the mainstream of French society. Coming from societies where anti-Semitism was often officially inspired and removed from the sources of French political power, they were naturally suspicious of government leaders and policies.[18]

THE HOLOCAUST ERA

In the end, of course, there was little that either group could do to stem the tide of anti-foreigner and anti-Jewish sentiment that arose in the 1930s and reached the level of a torrent with the sudden defeat and occupation of France in June 1940. Not surprisingly, one of the first decisions of the newly created Vichy government was to "punish" immigrants and refugees in the area under its control. Long before any actions were taken by Germany in occupied France, and without any direct orders from the Nazi regime, French officials passed legislation to exclude Jews and other "aliens" from the Unoccupied Southern Zone. Only a month after an armistice was declared, the Vichy government established a commission to review all naturalizations since 1927 with the intention of abrogating the citizenship of all those found to be "undesirable."

There soon followed laws specifically directed against Jews, including procedures for confiscating Jewish property, marking Jewish shops, and prohibiting the sale of books by Jewish authors. Government action against Jews was accompanied by heightened anti-Semitic propaganda triggered by the repeal of the Marchandeau Law, passed in April 1939, which had prohibited racist propaganda, and by the appointment of outspoken anti-Semites to the cabinet.[19] In October 1940 the Vichy regime issued the so-called Statut des Juifs, which defined Jews as a race and excluded them from various public functions. Jews and other refugees were transported to remote villages in the south where they lived under police surveillance or were assigned to forced-labor detachments in France and in North Africa. In an ominous foretelling of future policies, the government authorized prefects to place foreign Jews in "special camps," such as Gurs and Rivesaltes in the Pyrenees, which previously had been used for refugees from Franco Spain. By the end of 1940, forty thousand aliens and refugees, 70 percent of whom were Jews, had been interned in unoccupied France.[20]

In the first two years of the war, the decision by the Vichy government to initiate its own action against Jews in the Unoccupied Zone was met by stupefaction and anger on the part of Nazi officials. Indeed, the goals of the two administrations often seemed to be at cross-purposes as thousands of Jews found themselves caught between attempts by the Vichy government to ship refugees back to Germany and efforts by the invading German forces to expel Jews from areas now under military occupation.[21] For the most part, German treatment of the Jews in the Occupied Northern Zone lagged behind the more enthusiastic efforts of Vichy officials in the south. The one major German ordinance dealing with Jews in this early period, issued in September 1940, merely created a census and required special placards to be displayed in Jewish shops. The differences in the treatment of Jews in the two zones were so marked that many Jews from Paris who had fled southward soon returned to the occupied north to avoid the effects of Vichy's discriminatory legislation.[22]

It was not until the creation of a Commissariat général aux questions juives in February 1941 that any serious effort was made to coordinate Jewish policy in the two zones.[23] On paper, responsibility for Jewish policy throughout France now rested in the hands of Vichy officials. The Commissariat's first minister, Xavier Vallat, espoused a more traditional anti-Semitism and saw his role primarily as expanding upon the policies of previous French governments, which had persecuted hated foreign Jews but generally had spared native-born citizens. In reality, as the balance of power gradually shifted from Vichy to the Third Reich and as German officials began to map out far-reaching plans for dealing with the Jewish Question, Vallat's programs were soon outstripped by more radical policies and actions developed by the occupying authorities. Thus the creation of the Commissariat was accompanied by German calls for the arrest of all Jews in Paris. Throughout 1941 thousands of foreign Jews were methodically rounded up in the French capital, and in December the first *rafles* (roundups) of French-born Jews began. Arrests generally were carried out by French police under the watchful eyes of German authorities. Increasingly, Nazi officials took the lead by initiating anti-Jewish policies in the north, which Vichy officials then rushed to apply in the Southern Zone.[24]

Within a few months of the convening of the Wannsee Conference in January 1942, German authorities began to carry out the program it set forth for the Final Solution in occupied France. In April, in the wake of more stringent measures passed to both define and segregate Jews, German authorities replaced Vallat with Darquier de Pellepoix, a rabid anti-Semite who openly supported the Nazis' radical policies. In June it was decided that France would supply a hundred thousand Jews, to be taken from both zones, for extermination. In a desperate and cynical attempt to retain a modicum of French independence, Premier Pierre Laval promised German officials the complete cooperation of the French police and offered to add to the convoy children of foreign Jews under sixteen in return for sparing French-born Jews. On July 16, after numerous delays, French policemen went from house to house in Paris and rounded up close to thirteen thousand foreign Jews, including six thousand children.[25] *Rafles* continued throughout July and August in the Southern Zone. By the end of the summer close to eleven thousand Jews had been rounded up. Those arrested in the north were immediately sent to so-called transit camps. Some camps, like Pithiviers and Beaune-la-Rolande, which were situated south of Paris, originally had been established by German officials for political prisoners in 1939–40. Others, like Drancy, just north of Paris, were reserved expressly for Jewish deportees beginning in mid-1941. The occupation of the Southern Zone by German troops in November 1942 merely formalized a reality that had become all too apparent in the previous year, namely, the complete domination of France by Nazi Germany. The unification of the two zones also meant that the implementation of the Final Solution could now proceed without interruption and without differentiation between foreign-born and French Jews.[26]

The first deportations of foreign Jews in France to Auschwitz occurred in March 1942. They were soon followed by a convoy of French Jews. Beginning in June 1942 the deportations were accelerated, and they continued almost without interruption throughout 1943. Most Jews were sent to Auschwitz, though a small number were killed in Natzweiler-Struthof, a camp near Strasbourg established largely for political prisoners. Even Jews who had fled to the safety of the Italian Zone, in southeastern France, could not escape the Nazi onslaught. After the overthrow of Benito Mussolini in September 1943, the area was occupied by German troops. Deportations of Jews in Grenoble and Nice quickly followed.[27]

Between March 1942 and August 1944, when the last train left French soil, one hundred convoys, containing between eighty thousand and ninety thousand Jews, were sent to Auschwitz, primarily from Drancy. It is estimated that close to eighty thousand Jews from France, the overwhelming majority of them immigrants and refugees, eventually met their death in extermination camps. About one-third were French citizens, nearly two thousand were under the age of six, and more than six thousand were under thirteen.[28] The fact that three-quarters of the population of the prewar community were not deported can only be attributed to the confused relationship between German and French authorities. It was the desperate effort of French authorities to maintain a fragile independence by bartering foreigners for native-born Jews, rather than a humanitarian concern (as Vichy officials often argued after the war), that limited the tragedy befalling French Jewry.

It is difficult to gauge the response of the average Frenchman to the implementation of the anti-Jewish policies. There is little doubt that in the Unoccupied Zone Vichy's plans for a revitalized France free of foreign elements was greeted enthusiastically by most citizens, who were desperately seeking an explanation for their country's catastrophic defeat and for the resultant confusion attending the Nazi occupation. As tens of thousands of residents of the German-controlled Northern Zone fled southward, newly arrived Jews were singled out and attacked for creating food shortages, engaging in black-market activities, living ostentatiously, and disseminating anti-German propaganda. According to Michael Marrus and Robert Paxton, anti-Semitism was especially strong in villages and towns in rural areas, where Jews were relatively unknown before the war and where food rationing was most acute.[29] Virulent anti-Semitic attitudes could also be found among the *pieds-noirs,* the European residents of France's North African colonies, whose Jewish inhabitants were also subject to Vichy's discriminatory policies. According to the reports of local prefects, many Frenchmen were quick to use the laws passed by the Vichy regime to denounce Jews and to assume control of their property.[30]

It is generally accepted that there was more opposition to anti-Jewish measures in the Occupied Zone, if only because they were imposed by a foreign power. In the first few years of the Occupation, however, Vichy laws still applied in the north, and French Jews were not segregated from the larger society. Until 1942 German officials correctly assumed that as long as anti-Jewish activity was limited to legal measures it would occasion little opposition from the majority of the French public. In the absence of any public statements of concern from their leaders and in the face of their own suffering, most Frenchmen in the north probably paid little attention to the plight of refugees and foreigners.

The indifference and at times open hostility of many Frenchmen toward Jews in their midst clearly owed something to the propaganda of hardened anti-Semites, who found under Vichy an open forum for the expression of their ideas. As noted earlier, Vichy anti-Semitism drew upon anti-Jewish attitudes that had developed over decades and had reached their culmination in the anti-foreigner paranoia of the 1930s. By the interwar period anti-Jewish sentiment had penetrated all segments of French society; it could be found even among those who had never met a Jew and who would have been astonished to be labeled anti-Semitic.[31] It is not surprising, therefore, that elements of the French resistance often were no more sensitive than other Frenchmen to the plight of the Jews. Anti-Jewish prejudices were not unknown among the Free French officials in Charles De Gaulle's inner circle, and many underground groups were hostile to attempts by Jewish members to separate the fate of Jewry from the general struggle against Nazism. Even individuals who spoke out against Vichy policies at an early stage, such as Pastor Marc Boegner of the Reformed Church and Cardinal Gerlier, archbishop of Lyons, often voiced resentment against the immigration and naturalization of foreign-born Jews.[32]

A turning point in French public opinion seems to have come with the roundups of the summer of 1942. It was one thing to persecute foreigners; it was quite another to harm innocent children. For the first time in France there were public outcries against anti-Jewish policies. Particularly vocal were Protestants, who were fearful that discriminatory measures would soon be taken against other religious minorities, and left-wing Catholics, who used the opportunity to condemn the cautiousness of traditional church leadership. The fact that Vichy never officially prohibited emigration even after the occupation of the south meant that there were opportunities for Frenchmen to aid Jews to escape across the Pyrenees and the Swiss border. As the moving story of the Huguenot village of Le Chambon-sur-Lignon suggests, many Frenchmen hid Jews in their homes even at the risk of their own lives.[33] Hundreds of young Jews whose parents were deported were taken in by French families or found refuge in convents and monasteries. The onset of deportations also coincided with the consolidation of the French resistance, and many Jews were able to save themselves by joining either French or Jewish underground movements.[34]

The response of French Jewry itself during the Holocaust tragically replicated the divisions that existed within the community in the interwar period. While natives generally proved willing to trust the Pétain government and to accept its decisions at least at the beginning, immigrants viewed the government with suspicion and demanded a more activist response. The position of the established native-born community was reflected in the activities of the Union générale des juifs de France (UGIF), established by French authorities in March 1941.[35] The Jewish organization was committed to working with Vichy, and its policies rested on a firm belief that the nation's leaders would never betray the basic principles that allegedly underlay French society. Privately, native leaders in the UGIF and the Consistoire central were disturbed by Vichy's early efforts to exclude foreign Jews, but they tended to justify them publicly as extreme responses to economic crisis. Drawing upon the statements of individuals like Xavier Vallat, some native leaders even argued that the expulsion of foreign Jews would end state anti-Semitism and restore the status quo. Within their limited framework, French Jewish organizations, with the help of international agencies such as the Joint Distribution Committee and HICEM, were able to provide assistance to needy Jews through the establishment of orphanages, free kitchens, and vocational training centers. Community leaders also managed to maintain religious activities and institutions in both zones throughout the war.[36]

The tragedy of French Jewry was that its vision of France had little to do with the realities of the German occupation. Not only did the UGIF and the Consistoire seriously misread the intentions of the Vichy government at its inception, but they also failed to anticipate the brutal determination with which the Third Reich would attempt to carry out the Final Solution. With the onset of deportations in 1942, most French Jewish organizations realized the true dimensions of the impending catastrophe and began to supplement their legal action with surreptitious aid to underground movements. Nevertheless, as the tragic histories of many participants in Jewish councils throughout occupied Europe attest, the willingness of many native Jewish leaders in France to cooperate even on a limited basis with French and German authorities forced them into moral dilemmas from which they could not escape. As late as July 1944, less than three weeks before the liberation of Paris, for example, the UGIF refused to intercede with German authorities to prevent the deportation of a convoy of children for fear that it might endanger the organization's continued existence.[37]

Immigrants generally took a more aggressive stand against both Vichy and Nazi measures against Jews. Many of the first acts of resistance against German occupation were carried out by eastern European Jewish political militants, who rejected the French Communist Party's declaration of neutrality after the signing of the Nazi-Soviet Non-Aggression Pact in 1939. Yet as the major targets of discrimination and deportation in an environment that was at best apathetic to their plight, immigrants faced overpowering obstacles in their struggle to survive. Aside from the daily onslaught from both French and German authorities, the Eastern European Jewish community was paralyzed by deep internal divisions over methods of self-defense. While moderate elements grouped around the so-called Amelot Committee (named after the street in Paris's eleventh arrondissement where it secretly met) demanded that Jews pursue their own self-interest in the struggle against Nazism, militant Jews supporting the Solidarity movement argued that Jews must link their activity with the general struggle against Nazism. As Jacques Adler has clearly demonstrated in his work on Paris Jews under Vichy, despite the Amelot Committee's significant aid to Jewish victims and Solidarity's important contribution to sabotaging the Nazi effort, both groups were severely limited in their actions. While the former was weakened by its exclusive dependence upon limited Jewish resources, the latter proved unable to convince the French Communist Party of the distinctive plight of the Jewish community.[38]

Ultimately, one is forced to conclude that there was little that either natives or immigrants could have done in the face of the grim determination of Nazi leaders, with the active support of Vichy, to exterminate all the Jews in France. Even the heroic activity of underground Jewish youth movements such as the Zionist-inspired Armée juive (Jewish Army) and the native-run Eclaireurs (Scouts)—which were later incorporated into the Organisation juive de combat (Jewish Combat Organization)—and of Communist groups in the Union des Juifs pour la résistance et l'entr'aide (Union of Jews for Resistance and Mutual Assistance), or UJRE, could not stem the Nazi juggernaut. Though there is strong evidence that both natives and immigrants moved closer together after the roundups and deportations of July 1942 and as the details of the Final Solution became known—the UGIF increasingly supporting illegal activity to save Jews, and immigrant militants recognizing the primary need to defend Jewish victims—their actions had only a marginal impact on the process of the Final Solution. By January 1944 natives and immigrants of all ideological persuasions were able to come together to form the Conseil représentatif des israélites français (Representative Council of French Jews), or CRIF, an umbrella organization to coordinate relief and resistance efforts. By that time, however, Jews in France no longer were under physical threat and had already begun to look toward the postwar future.[39]

THE POST-HOLOCAUST ERA

As French Jews turned their attention to reconstruction in the days and months after the liberation of France in August 1944, they soon realized that they faced a daunting task.[40] The community had lost nearly one-third of its prewar population, including twenty thousand children, to the ravages of the Final Solution. Of the approximately eighty thousand Jews deported from France during the war, only about thirty-five hundred returned to their homes.[41] The Jewish community of Paris, which before the war had numbered close to two hundred thousand, was weakened seriously by the loss of approximately sixty thousand to seventy thousand members. Throughout France, Jews agonized over the disappearance of hundreds of small communities and the reduction of many large settlements to mere handfuls of Jewish families.[42]

Included among the murdered thousands was the cream of French Jewry's prewar religious and administrative leadership. Of the sixty rabbis who were members of the Consistoire central in 1939, twenty-three were deported to death camps and two were shot. Influential lay leaders, such as Raoul-Raymond Lambert, a former editor of *L'Univers israélite* (the quasi-official newspaper of prewar French Jewry) and a central figure in the UGIF; Jacques Helbronner, president of the Consistoire central; and Léonce Bernheim, a noted prewar Zionist activist, also met their death during the Occupation. Other community leaders had scattered in their flight from Nazism, never to return to France. In addition, many committed young Jews who had served in Jewish resistance groups and who had been expected to assume leadership roles in the community after the war concluded that there was little future for Jews in France and chose to emigrate to Palestine.[43]

And yet in comparison with other European Jewish communities, French Jewry faced a situation after Liberation that was far from hopeless. French Jews were in the unique position of having experienced the Holocaust and yet surviving in large enough numbers to reassert themselves after the war. It is estimated that there were 180,000 Jews in France in 1946—160,000 former residents and 20,000 refugees from Central and Eastern Europe. Of the surviving European Jewish communities outside the Soviet Union, only Romania had a larger population. The continuous influx of Jewish survivors fleeing displaced person (DP) camps and emerging from hiding—more than 35,000 in the first three years after the war—meant that France would soon host the second most populous Jewish community on the European continent.[44]

Of the many pressing problems facing the newly reconstituted community in the early days after the end of the war, three consumed most of its energy and interest: the restoration of spoliated property, the care and feeding of refugees, and the plight of orphaned and "adopted" children. Many Jews who had fled to the south or had been deported during the war found upon their return to cities such as Paris and Strasbourg that their businesses, furniture, and apartments had been expropriated by the Nazis and sold to Frenchmen. Others who had entrusted their shops to French neighbors were now asked to reimburse the latter for having maintained their businesses. To compound their problems, the provisional government seemed more concerned with courting the thousands of bourgeois who had enriched themselves under Vichy than with helping returning Jews. Thus it enacted legislation that required former owners to prove that their property had been forcibly taken from them and that forbade the eviction of any tenant unless he was provided with a new place to live. When Jews protested, they were informed that there was a housing shortage in most major cities and that it was government policy to treat apartments and furniture left by deportees as "abandoned property." In many cases, Jewish efforts to reclaim property were thwarted by corrupt officials who leaked information to comrades, who were then able to lay false claims to lost goods. Police often stood by when organized groups of expropriators of Jewish property such as the Fédération des locataires de bonne foi (Federation of Renters of Good Faith) and the Renaissance du foyer français (Renaissance of the French Household) hurled anti-Semitic slogans and attacked Jews who were attempting to reclaim their goods and apartments. In 1946 the French government passed legislation that restricted restitution of property to dispossessed individuals, thereby effectively establishing a statute of limitations on spoliations. Community organizations tried valiantly to aid Jews to track down stolen property, but they were severely hindered by the lack of resources and personnel. Although there was some discussion in government circles of giving unclaimed property to the Jewish community as reparations, nothing came of the proposal. As late as 1951 only half of the estimated sixty-five thousand Jews in Paris whose homes had been ransacked or sold during the Occupation had been able to reacquire their property. It would take another two decades and the passage by West Germany of a comprehensive indemnification law that applied to all areas under Nazi occupation to finally put the question of French Jews' spoliated property to rest.[45]

In addition to providing for the thousands of dispossessed French Jews without homes and means of support, the community was also burdened with the care and feeding of close to forty thousand displaced persons and refugees who found asylum in France. Although many survivors of the Holocaust viewed France merely as a way station to Palestine or America, a considerable number either chose or were forced to remain in the country as a result of restrictions imposed by the British and American governments. As in the case of dispossessed Jews, the French government proved less than helpful. Though loyal to France's historical role as an asylum for political refugees, the early cabinets of the Fourth Republic did little to facilitate refugee efforts to establish themselves. Ignoring the unprecedented nature of the Jewish refugee problem and blind to the inability or unwillingness of survivors to return to their former homelands, the French government relied upon outdated immigration laws that combined the carrot of limited economic incentive with the stick of enforced expulsion. In Kafkaesque fashion, it gave no means of redress to Jews who were expelled and threw those who were not allowed into neighboring countries into French jails for infractions against the expulsion order.

Despite great difficulties, the French Jewish community, aided by American-sponsored relief agencies such as the Joint Distribution Committee, generally was successful in integrating refugees. Under the guidance of the Comité juif d'action social et de reconstruction (Jewish Committee for Social Action and Reconstruction), or COJASOR, nearly three-quarters of the survivors of the Holocaust who sought refuge in France were housed and fed. Working closely with French officials, the Organization for Rehabilitation through Training (ORT) gained government accreditation and subsidization for its vocational programs, which enabled thousands of previously unskilled and semiskilled refugees to enter French industry.[46] These individuals, who were generally committed to the perpetuation of Jewish communal life, served as important religious and cultural leaven in the reconstruction effort, much as eastern European immigrants in the period after World War I had done.

Yet another urgent need in the immediate postwar period was the rescue and rehabilitation of Jewish youth. It is estimated that between five thousand and fifteen thousand Jewish children in France lost their parents during the war. Many had been placed with Christian families and now had to be searched out. Within days of Liberation, a special office was established in Paris to collect information on abandoned and orphaned children and to defend their legal and property rights. Thanks to the efforts of organizations such as the Oeuvre de protection des enfants juifs (Society for the Protection of Jewish Children), or OPEJ, and the Oeuvre de secours aux enfants (Society to Aid Children), or OSE, nearly one hundred institutions were created to care for orphaned children and to reintegrate them into the community.[47]

While the French Jewish community was able to provide foster parents for orphans, it had little success in recovering Jewish children "adopted" by non-Jews. Many Christian parents baptized Jewish children entrusted to their care during the Occupation. When Jewish relatives tried to regain custody of the orphans, the adoptive parents argued that it would be unfair to tear the children away from a family environment in which they felt comfortable. In some cases they were supported by Jewish leaders who claimed that the return of the children would be a slap in the face to the non-Jews who had risked their lives to save them. Christian families also found support among church leaders who argued sophistically that Jews who had handed their children over to Christians for safekeeping during the war clearly had desired their baptism.[48]

Incidents such as the Finaly Affair in 1953, in which Catholic Church officials conspired to block efforts to allow two young children who were given up by their parents during the war to return to the Jewish community, suggested that in addition to the massive tasks of physical reconstruction and psychological rehabilitation within, French Jews faced a significant challenge from the larger French society.[49] The events of the war had clearly raised questions concerning the alleged symbiosis of *français* and *israélite*. Nor did Liberation signal the end of anti-Semitism. As noted earlier, violent demonstrations and protests often attended efforts by Jews to reacquire stolen property and to rescue children. Anti-Semitism remained strong throughout the late forties and early fifties among segments of the population as many Frenchmen reacted angrily to the arrival of Eastern and Central European Jews fleeing DP camps and occupied zones and to Jewish reintegration into French economic and social life. Graffiti in streets and Metro stations mockingly criticizing Adolf Hitler for "avenging himself by dumping Jews on us," and *plastique* bombings of Jewish-owned stores were vivid reminders of the visceral anti-Jewish sentiments of many Frenchmen.[50]

For much of the early postwar period the tragic events surrounding French involvement in the Final Solution were masked by governmental concerns with reconstruction and reconciliation. Despite his leadership of the Free French, Charles De Gaulle soon realized after his accession to power in 1944 that the troubling issue of collaboration with German authorities during the war could only divide French society and hinder its chances for reconstruction. In addition, the French public showed little interest in undergoing a serious self-examination of its behavior during the Occupation. The result was the gradual emergence of a national myth that viewed the overwhelming majority of Frenchmen during World War II as resisters to Nazism and portrayed the Vichy regime as an aberration whose traitorous deeds resulted from the venality and fanaticism of a crazed few. As in postwar Germany, French government officials and intellectuals spoke of the need to "erase" the wartime regime from French history and to view Liberation as the "year zero."[51]

Nowhere was the masking of Vichy more evident than in the treatment of French collaborators. Thousands of Frenchmen had been summarily tried and in many cases executed by victorious resistance movements in the confused and heated atmosphere of Liberation. With the restoration of governmental control, however, the myth of popular resistance emerged, and brutal purges soon gave way to a concerted effort to punish only the most egregious offenders. A series of show trials in 1945 and 1946 of the most visible leaders of Vichy reflected the government's reinterpretation of recent historical reality. Thus, for example, Pierre Laval, premier from 1942 to 1944, was depicted by the prosecution and in the press as a traitor to French national ideals. Accused of usurping the legally established authority of the Third Republic, he was executed in 1945 with little public protest. Similarly, the courts meted out swift punishment against "antirepublican" ideologues like Charles Maurras, who was said to have demoralized the army and weakened the national defense, and Nazi sympathizers like Joseph Darnand, who was accused of actively participating in the suppression of the resistance. Marshal Pétain proved a more ticklish problem, however, in part because of his military leadership during World War I, in part because of the unwillingness of many Frenchmen to confront the circumstances surrounding the establishment of Vichy in 1940. Portrayed as a well-meaning patriot who nevertheless had to take responsibility for the crimes of those who exercised power under him, he was first condemned to death by zealous judges. Public outcry and political pressure, however, forced the government to commute his sentence to life imprisonment, allegedly because of his advanced age and declining health. Not surprisingly, therefore, Pétain's role during Vichy and his place in modern French history would continue to be a subject of intense controversy long after his death in July 1951.[52]

Despite exhaustive efforts by the prosecution to secure the maximum sentence against the Vichy leadership, no mention was made of the persecution and deportations of Jews. To do so would have compromised the central purpose of the trials, which was to portray Vichy as a betrayal of the shared ideals and values of Frenchmen, by raising disturbing questions concerning the complicity of thousands of citizens in the execution of government-sponsored anti-Jewish measures. In the end, the fate of the Jews during the Occupation could not be easily incorporated into the postwar government's Manichean view, which divided Frenchmen into heroic resisters and cowardly collaborators.

As the years passed, the number of trials decreased and the punishments became less severe. Government action clearly mirrored the changing mood of the French populace, which, according to polls conducted between 1948 and 1949, now seemed willing to forgive and to forget even the most ardent Vichy supporters. Of the 168,287 individuals who had been tried by government courts by the end of 1948, 45 percent had been acquitted; 25 percent had received the punishment of "national degradation," which denied the convicted individual the right to participate in political life; 16 percent had been imprisoned; and 8 percent had been sentenced to forced labor. By 1951, 2,853 individuals had received the death sentence, and 3,910 had been sentenced to death in absentia, but only 767 executions had actually been carried out. The dismantling in the same year of the special courts originally established to try collaborators went almost unnoticed by the general public. Although a law would be passed in 1964 suspending the statute of limitations for so-called crimes against humanity, it was intended for German criminals and made no mention of French collaborators.[53]

Postwar governments were also quick to lift the burden of responsibility from hundreds of thousands of Frenchmen who had aided the Vichy regime as petty bureaucrats and politicians. In 1951 a law was passed that abrogated the penalty of "national degradation" for virtually all those who had received the sentence and provided for the early release of many previously convicted prisoners. Two years later the government passed a law abolishing the penalty completely, while ending electoral ineligibility and restoring the pension rights of many accused collaborators. Of some forty thousand Vichy officials sentenced to imprisonment after the war, only sixty-two remained incarcerated in 1956; by 1958 there were nineteen. By 1964 none remained in jail.[54]

Government amnesties brought many collaborators back to France after years in exile, and in the early fifties there was a noticeable increase in neo-fascist and neo-Nazi activity on the part of the extreme Right. Throughout the 1950s and 1960s the flea markets of Paris conducted a lively business in collaborationist and Nazi memorabilia, while ultranationalist bookstores hawked dozens of publications defending the policies and leaders of Vichy and the Third Reich. Yet collaborators generally remained out of sight, and outright defenses of French and German wartime policies found only a small audience of stalwart loyalists, sensationalists, and curiosity-seekers.

More serious was the anti-Semitism that resurfaced in its classic, anti-Dreyfusard form as a cudgel used by opponents of republicanism to attack the established government. The most significant example of such attitudes could be found in the so-called Poujadist movement, which arose in 1953 and flourished for three years before disappearing in ignominious electoral defeat in 1957. As in the assault upon Léon Blum in the 1930s, antirepublican elements in the 1950s directed their attacks upon a Jewish premier as the source of all the evils befalling France. In an uncertain economic and political climate, the efforts by Pierre Mendès-France to modernize the French economy and to streamline government were denounced by Pierre Poujade and his followers as an assault upon the position of the "little men and women" in French society and as a betrayal of the national interest in the name of big business, corrupt politicians, and radical social reformers. At the same time, the premier and all Jews by implication were blamed for the moral degradation of France. After all, Poujade argued, Mendès-France had even dared to suggest that Frenchmen should drink more milk in place of wine![55]

For the most part, however, such sentiments harked back to a more traditional form of anti-Semitism. Even among rabid anti-Jewish elements there seemed to be little interest in dredging up the experiences of Vichy and of the Final Solution for fear of what they might reveal about collaboration and deportation. Efforts to discuss or remember the tragic events of the war were ridiculed or suppressed. Many Frenchmen undoubtedly shared the view of the French philosopher Emmanuel Mounier that returning deportees were a "nuisance" to most Frenchmen, "whose only wish is to return as quickly as possible to peace and quiet."[56] Memories of Nazi brutalities also clashed with the desire of European leaders to enlist West Germany in the Cold War struggle against Soviet Communism. At national commemorations of the Armistice, officials prohibited deportees from wearing their striped uniforms. It was not until 1954 that the French government instituted a special day of commemoration for deportees.[57]

Most disturbing was the refusal to recognize the distinctive nature of the Jewish genocide. Jewish deportees were not allowed to march as a separate group during commemorations. Although the *Diary of Anne Frank* was a major best seller in France in 1950, its success had more to do with the evocation of Christian ideals of martyrology than with its association with the persecution of a young Jewish girl. Similarly, the first French film on Nazi death camps, Alain Resnais's *Nuit et Brouillard* (Night and Fog), produced in 1956, caused a sensation in France, but it made almost no reference to Jews, despite its discussion of deportations and its graphic depiction of the extermination process.

Nor was there much discussion of the Holocaust within the French Jewish community.[58] Few Eastern European Jews had survived the ordeal; those who had seemed reticent to talk about their experiences. A major exception was a small group of survivors centered around the Centre de documentation juive contemporaine (Center for Contemporary Jewish Documentation), or CDJC. Originally created within the underground movement in Grenoble in 1943, the CDJC was pledged to collect and preserve documents on the Holocaust. After the war, under the leadership of the indefatigable Isaac Schneersohn, the group was able to establish a research library in Paris with more than twelve thousand volumes and to publish a journal and a series of volumes dealing with various issues connected with the Nazi period. In 1951 the CDJC published Léon Poliakov's *Breviaire de la haine* (Harvest of hate), the first scholarly account of the Final Solution to appear in France. Despite considerable opposition from the French Jewish establishment and from Israeli leaders, who argued that the commemoration of the Holocaust was the sole province of Yad Vashem in Jerusalem, in 1956 the CDJC succeeded in constructing a Memorial to the Unknown Jewish Martyr near the historic Jewish area of the "Pletzl" in Paris.[59]

Community opposition to the memorial reflected the fact that despite the revelations of atrocities, many French Jews, like Frenchmen in general, simply could not grasp the immensity of the tragedy. The few survivors who wrote about their ordeal upon returning to France, such as David Rousset, continually stressed the frustrations they felt over the Jewish community's total ignorance of the true nature of the Nazi camp system and its refusal to believe the horrifying reality of the Final Solution.[60] Despite massive publicity on the part of survivor groups, rallies to commemorate the deportation within the Jewish community in the immediate postwar period attracted only a handful of participants.[61] Even those Jews who helped to reintegrate survivors into French society after the war tended to concentrate on the practical problems of housing and employment rather than on the deportees' underlying psychological trauma.

Like the French government itself, the French Jewish community was concerned with reconstruction and did not want to dwell upon the past. In an important sense, survivors forced French Jews to confront their own historical myths concerning the compatibility of French and Jewish values that defined native Jewish identity and behavior before the war. The community's effort to block out the bitter memory of the Holocaust in France was aided by the arrival of hundreds of thousands of Jews fleeing North Africa during the struggles of Algeria, Morocco, and Tunisia for independence in the 1950s and early 1960s. The influx of a dynamic group of Jews from the Maghreb, most of whom were fully familiar with French culture and language, offered hope for the revival of the French Jewish community. With the potential for a bright and vibrant future at hand, it seemed futile and wasteful to dwell upon the past.

The onset of the 1960s seemed to bring a new attitude toward Vichy among the generation of Frenchmen born during or immediately after the war. Of particular significance was the emergence of a new cadre of French historians for whom the myth of the resistance held little personal significance. Supported by the newly established Comité d'histoire de la Deuxième Guerre Mondiale (Committee on the History of World War II), they conducted research that placed emphasis upon the Occupation rather than upon the resistance. French scholars were aided by the works of foreign historians such as Robert Paxton, who attacked the assumption that resistance to Vichy was widespread and that the Pétain regime was unpopular.[62]

Among the general public, the war in Algeria in the early sixties and the student riots of 1968 created a climate of government violence and repression throughout the decade and brought back painful memories of brutalities committed by past regimes. It was not accidental that Daniel Cohn-Bendit, one of the leaders of the 1968 student revolt, attempted to gain sympathy by comparing the students' plight with the fate of German Jews under Nazism.[63]

The 1960s also saw the emergence of a substantial literature on the Holocaust. The publication in 1959 of André Schwarz-Bart's best-selling novel *Le Dernier des justes* (The last of the just), which sought to incorporate the Holocaust into the general history of Jewish martyrdom, introduced hundreds of thousands of Frenchmen to the events of the Final Solution from a Jewish perspective. In 1964 Rolf Hochhuth's play *The Deputy*, which dealt with the Vatican's response to the Nazi persecution of Jews, was staged in Paris amidst bitter debate and violent confrontations between supporters and opponents. The issues of the silence of the world in the face of the Final Solution and the moral complicity of bystanders during the Holocaust troubled sensitive Frenchmen and struck a disturbing chord within the Jewish community. In the same year, readers of the French and Jewish press were introduced to the writings of Elie Wiesel, who quickly emerged as a moral spokesman for survivors of the Holocaust in France. Two years later, the appearance of Jean-François Steiner's controversial work *Treblinka*, which accused Jewish victims of passivity in the face of Nazism, sparked further debate within the general and Jewish communities.[64]

Undoubtedly the most important spur to renewed Jewish interest in the Holocaust in France during this period was the trial of Adolf Eichmann in 1961. Of particular significance was the emphasis that the Israeli prosecutors placed on the specificity of the Jewish tragedy during the war, an issue that often had been ignored in discussions of French victims of Nazism. For the first time the French Jewish press referred to the annihilation of Jews in World War II as a "Holocaust" (or *Khurbn*, as it was translated in Yiddish), indicating a recognition of both its devastating nature and its distinctiveness in the history of Jewish persecutions. In compelling Jews in general to confront what one French Jewish writer called "our solitary death," the trial forced French Jews to recognize their country's role in the implementation of the Final Solution.[65] In chronicling the painful reality of the Holocaust, it enabled a younger generation of French Jews to learn of their parents' tragic past, which all too often had been hidden from them, and to consider appropriate measures to prevent it from happening again.[66]

All of these attitudes were reinforced by the events surrounding the outbreak of the Six-Day War in June 1967. The French government's decision on the eve of the war to place an embargo on the sale of Mirage jets to Israel pointed up the growing gap between French and Jewish interests and reinforced fears that the isolation of the Jewish state in the world community signaled another potential Holocaust. The shocking comments by President De Gaulle at a press conference the following November, in which he described Jews as "an elitist people, sure of itself and domineering," seemed to strengthen such attitudes at the same time that it recalled bitter memories of official anti-Semitism under Vichy.[67]

Similar sentiments were revived in 1973 during the Yom Kippur War, when a number of newspapers, including the prestigious *Le Monde,* raised the issue of the "double loyalty" of French Jewry.[68] Notions that Jews were controlling French politics and endangering the national welfare by supporting Israel gained increasing currency as a result of the threat of an Arab oil embargo of France. Growing tensions led to an outbreak of anti-Semitic incidents in the following year, including the defacement of the Memorial to the Unknown Jewish Martyr. Such incidents seemed to corroborate the findings of the sociologist Edgar Morin, who in a study of an anti-Semitic occurrence in the city of Orléans in 1969 had concluded that anti-Jewish sentiments were deeply rooted in French consciousness and needed only a minor incident to bring them to the surface.[69]

The reawakening of Jewish consciousness of the Holocaust in the 1960s undoubtedly reinforced general French interest in the events of the war in the early 1970s. The unlocking of French collective memory was also facilitated by the death of De Gaulle in 1970, which removed from public discourse the most ardent defender of France's "invented" past of massive resistance to Nazism. Popular fascination with Vichy and the Final Solution in the seventies was also fostered by the release of a number of significant films, including *Le Chagrin et la Pitié* (The Sorrow and the Pity), *Les Violons du Bal* (The Violins of the Ball), and *Monsieur Klein* (Mr. Klein), which challenged the myth of the resistance and boldly confronted the issue of French complicity in the Holocaust.[70]

By far the most traumatic assault upon French collective memory of Vichy in the postwar era, however, occurred in 1978 as the result of three dramatically linked events: an interview with Darquier de Pellepoix, the former head of the Commissariat générale aux questions juives; the screening of the American docudrama *Holocaust* on French television; and the sudden emergence of revisionist tracts that denied that the Final Solution had ever occurred. The confused responses to these events, each of which challenged the nation's distorted perception of its past, suggested that thirty years after the war France had yet to come to grips with Vichy and its role in the implementation of the Final Solution.

Darquier de Pellepoix, hand-picked by the Nazis to assume the post of director of the Commissariat générale aux questions juives in 1942, was one of a number of Vichy activists who had escaped to Franco Spain after the war.[71] Darquier had been condemned to death in absentia in 1947 for consorting with the enemy, but thanks to the statute of limitations, his sentence had lapsed in 1968. In an attempt to boost both magazine sales and popular consciousness of the Holocaust, the French weekly *L'Express* granted him an interview, which appeared in its November 4, 1978, issue. After more than thirty years of self-imposed anonymity and silence, Darquier was unrepentant and unbowed. His brazen comments praising the Vichy regime and his description of the gas chambers and the Holocaust itself as creations of "satanic Jewish propaganda" sent shockwaves through France.

The immediate response of French politicians and journalists centered on the legality of Darquier's extradition from Spain, but it soon became clear that his remarks had reopened a festering wound in the French body politic. Public reactions were sudden and wide-ranging. Within a few months, movements of the extreme Right began to reassert themselves. Anti-Semitic and racist graffiti suddenly reappeared on walls, war memorials, and Metro stations in Paris. Eurodroite, a militantly neo-fascist organization, held a huge mass meeting in Paris at which speakers praised Darquier and attacked Jews and other "foreign elements." Its plans to stage a similar demonstration in Marseilles were foiled at the last moment by municipal authorities, who, fearing street violence, intervened to ban it. Darquier's comments also triggered strong anti-Nazi statements from former resistance members, while the left-wing press warned its readers of the "unworldly beast" of racism and anti-Semitism that lurked within French society.[72] Survivors of the Holocaust also assumed greater visibility. In November Jewish deportees held a meeting to commemorate the fortieth anniversary of Kristallnacht and organized a demonstration against the former *commissaire* in Paris with more than twenty-five hundred protesters in attendance. Faced with the potential polarization of the French public, government leaders responded cautiously, calling for greater responsibility and vigilance on the part of the press and hurriedly canceling plans to inter the ashes of Marshal Pétain at the Douaumont military cemetery.[73]

The publication of the Darquier interview also increased pressure on the French television system, the Organisation de radio et télévision française (ORTF), to broadcast the docudrama *Holocaust*, which had been shown on American television in April 1978. As a state-run facility, the ORTF faithfully adhered to the government's policy of not dredging up memories of Vichy and the Final Solution. In 1971, for example, French television authorities had refused to screen Marcel Ophuls's *Le Chagrin et la Pitié*, which dealt with the response to Vichy during World War II in the town of Clermont-Ferrand, a film they had commissioned. (The film would eventually be shown on French television in 1981, after successful runs in movie theaters in Paris and around the world.) In contrast to previous treatments of the Occupation, which had focused on German occupiers, Vichy officials, and resistance leaders, the young director deliberately chose to study the response of average Frenchmen during the war. His major discovery was that most individuals in the town, one of the centers of the resistance, not only accepted the Pétain regime during the war but actively supported its programs to exclude Jews.[74] It thus was not surprising that seven years later all three French channels turned down the opportunity to broadcast *Holocaust*, despite the fact that France remained the only country in Western Europe that had not screened the American series.

It was the *L'Express* interview and the militant response of veterans' groups that seems to have finally persuaded the ORTF to reconsider its decision. After intensive negotiations between government officials and striking employees, who threatened to sabotage the broadcast, *Holocaust* was finally aired on four separate nights in February and March 1979. The series was accompanied by two roundtable discussions, the first on the origins of anti-Semitism in Germany, the second on the Final Solution. The discussions lasted well into the night, as callers jammed the station lines with questions about the events of the Holocaust. Although no polls were taken, it was generally assumed that the series was the most widely watched program in the history of French television.[75] The varied responses to the docudrama in the French press clearly revealed that, much as in West Germany, *Holocaust* had touched a raw nerve in French society. Many reviewers saw it as an important beginning in the education of a generation that had remained shielded from the horrible truth of the war and for whom television was the sole source of information. Others were convinced that *Holocaust* had served as a much needed emotional catharsis for a French population that had repressed the bitter memory of the events of the Final Solution far too long. So overpowering was the emotional response to the series that even its most bitter critics were torn between openly condemning the docudrama as distorted and melodramatic on the one hand and praising it for triggering thoughtful reflection on the other.[76]

By far the most significant response to the docudrama was to be found among Jewish youth. In particular, the series reinforced a growing malaise among Jewish radicals who had participated in the 1968 student revolt. The failure of Communism both within and outside of France, the need to move beyond their decade-old student perspectives, and growing concerns with the increasingly anti-Semitic nature of left-wing attacks upon Israel had led many young Jewish militants to search for a new direction. As the numerous autobiographies written by French Jewish intellectuals in the 1980s clearly reveal, it was *Holocaust* that influenced them to seek out their Jewish past. The portrayal of Jews as tragic victims of totalitarianism, the depiction of a rich and vibrant prewar Jewish culture, and the emphasis upon militant resistance by youthful Jews all served to reconnect these former radicals, who were largely children of Eastern European immigrants, with their ethnic and religious heritage. The series also seems to have had a certain impact upon children of North African Jews, many of whom had known nothing about the events of the Final Solution, who now found important parallels between the fate of European Jewry during World War II and the plight of the embattled state of Israel.[77]

In the end, however, *Holocaust* had only a minimal impact upon France's understanding of its role in the implementation of the Final Solution. As in the case of the Darquier interview, the discussions about the Holocaust that it brought about engendered confusion and controversy rather than clarification. It did not take long for the disturbing questions of complicity and collaboration raised by the film series to become lost in a cacophony of political and ideological debate. While the Right predictably warned Frenchmen not to forget the Communist menace amidst the anti-Nazi mania allegedly sweeping across the nation, the extreme Left argued that racism and anti-Semitism could only be understood in the context of the class struggle. Some politicians now wondered aloud whether the series had been shown before the elections to the European Parliament in order to create anti-German feelings among Frenchmen and to weaken European unity, while others used the opportunity to raise questions concerning the treatment of Jews and other foreigners in Communist resistance groups during the war. The series was even used by anti-Israel propagandists to equate Zionism with Nazism. The brutalities portrayed in *Holocaust* were hardly unique, a Moroccan writer noted in an article published in *Le Monde*. He claimed that in again demonstrating the "bloody irony" of history, the broadcast had brought back memories of watching a documentary on Nazi atrocities in a Tangiers movie theater in 1948 on the same day that he learned of the massacre of the Arab residents of Deir Yassin by Jewish soldiers! A few weeks after the final installment of *Holocaust* was shown, public interest had waned. Like most television fare, the series and the issues it raised were quickly forgotten by the start of the next broadcast season.[78]

By contributing to public confusion and disbelief over the events of the war, the rhetoric and polemics that attended the Darquier interview and the screening of the *Holocaust* series provided a ready opportunity for so-called revisionists to popularize their ideas denying the Holocaust. The origins of Holocaust revisionism in France are to be found in the late 1940s and early 1950s with the publication of a series of works by Paul Rassinier, a survivor of the concentration camps of Buchenwald and Dora. In his book *Le Mensonge d'Ulysse* (The lie of Ulysses), published in 1950, Rassinier had criticized other survivors for supposed inaccuracies in their eyewitness accounts of camp life. Although admitting that there had been gas chambers in Nazi death camps, he doubted that more than a few hundred thousand Jews had actually been murdered. In any case, there was no proof of a deliberate program to annihilate Jews. Even if German documents eventually became available proving that gas chambers had been used for mass killing, Rassinier concluded, they would clearly reveal that the murders were carried out by a few crazed SS men.[79]

Rassinier's testimony was surprising not only because he had not directly experienced extermination camps but also because he had been a loyal member of the resistance and was a former Communist. At first his main goal in denying the Holocaust seems to have been to attack the evils of capitalism, much as French socialists such as Charles Fourier and Pierre Proudhon had done when they condemned Jewish financiers in the nineteenth century. In a work entitled *Le Drame des juifs européens* (The drama of European Jewry), published in 1964, for example, Rassinier had accused Israel of seeking to gain public sympathy for Jewish victims of Nazism in order to facilitate its effort to establish "a commercial fiefdom that . . . would encircle the entire world."[80] In time Rassinier's attacks upon Jewish finance became intermingled with his growing hostility toward Communists, whom he claimed had used their control of the concentration camps' political apparatus to brutalize other prisoners. It was not coincidental that many of Rassinier's earliest works were republished in the 1970s by La Vielle Taupe (The Old Mole), a press with anarcho-syndicalist leanings whose director, Serge Thion, attacked the Soviet Union and viewed the extermination of the Jews as a plot by German capitalists to save themselves from collapse by sacrificing the Jewish bourgeoisie.[81]

Rassinier's anti-Communism and anti-Semitism soon gained him the attention of leaders of the radical Right as well. In numerous books written in the mid-fifties and published by longtime fascist supporters and anti-Semites such as Henri Coston, he argued that the Nazis were right to consider Jews as foreigners and blamed Jewry for starting World War II. Combining elements of both radical left-wing and right-wing ideology, Rassinier claimed that Jews were in league with American capitalists and Soviet communism in a plot to conquer Europe. In devising the "myth" of the Holocaust and demanding reparations, he claimed, Jewish financiers and revolutionaries were attempting to sow political disunity among European nations, corrupt their societies, and destroy their economies.

For much of the postwar period, Rassinier's ideas languished in the relative obscurity of extremist political circles, and his death in 1967 went almost unnoticed by the general French public. Revisionism gained new visibility in France in January 1979 with the publication of a letter in *Le Monde* by Robert Faurisson, a professor of literature at the Université de Lyons-2.[82] Faurisson prided himself on being an objective scholar and a courageous pursuer of truth. He claimed that his research into the Holocaust had been completely objective, since he had no direct personal or ideological connection with the subject matter. After decades of careful research, Faurisson had become convinced that there was absolutely no proof of the existence of gas chambers in Nazi concentration camps. All previous testimony by German officials concerning the use of gas chambers had been exacted under duress by Allied courts, while survivor accounts were far too emotional and self-serving to be believed. Faurisson was careful not to engage in polemics against Jews or to defend Nazism. Indeed, he was willing to admit that there were two points of view on the subject—"Revisionism" and "Exterminationism"—a position that cleverly served to give intellectual respectability to the denial of the Holocaust. It was Faurisson's guise of objectivity and scholarship that explained not only the willingness of *Le Monde* to publish his letter but also the decision two years later by Noam Chomsky, the noted American linguist, to write a preface to Faurisson's collected writings in which he defended the author's right to express his opinions.[83]

Faurisson's views were bitterly attacked by both Jewish and French historians, and he was eventually indicted for "falsification of history." Yet the basic ideas of Holocaust revisionism soon became common currency in extremist circles in France. The view that gas chambers never existed and that genocide never occurred, the argument that the numbers of Jews killed had been greatly exaggerated and that Jewish "survivors" were actually to be found in America and the Soviet Union, and the notion that the Holocaust was the creation of Zionists to strengthen the state of Israel all became central components of revisionist literature, as did the peculiar methodology of revisionism—the rejection of all Jewish and Nazi testimony that proved the existence of the Holocaust as automatically false; the attempt to demonstrate the technical impossibility of the existence and functioning of gas chambers; and the acceptance of all efforts by Nazi leaders to mask the Final Solution as literally true.[84]

Yet it was the growing respectability of revisionism among elements of the general public in France that most alarmed observers. The failure of French political and intellectual leaders to address the central questions raised by the Darquier interview and the broadcast of the *Holocaust* series opened the way for the acceptance of pseudoscientific analyses and accounts of the events of World War II. For some Frenchmen, the arguments of individuals like Rassinier and Thion only confirmed deeply rooted suspicions and prejudices. The emphasis revisionists placed upon the responsibility of Jewry for the outbreak of the war found a favorable response among those Frenchmen who refused to accept their nation's collapse in 1940 and its responsibility for the deportation of Jews. Their warnings about the threat to Europe posed by alien forces within and without seemed to have contemporary relevance in the 1980s in the face of the influx of hundreds of thousands of foreign workers to France and of renewed interest in Continental unity. Not even intellectuals were immune from revisionist propaganda. Many undoubtedly welcomed the attempt to deny the Holocaust as part of the general onslaught upon the comfortable myths that had developed in France after Liberation. As late as 1986 a university thesis purporting to demonstrate that gas chambers had not existed passed with high marks at Nantes University. It is no wonder that in the early 1980s, at the height of revisionist propaganda, the prominent French historian Pierre Vidal-Nacquet could speak of the revisionist as an "Eichmann de papier" who sought to exterminate through the written word those who had not been destroyed in the Holocaust.[85]

With hindsight, one is forced to conclude that the events of 1978 seem to have done little to clarify France's consciousness of its past. As noted earlier, the Darquier Affair quickly faded into memory, and the showing of *Holocaust* was not followed up by any serious investigation of the French role in the Final Solution. Revisionism continued to attract supporters well into the 1980s, though it no longer generated the intense interest of a decade earlier. Despite the controversy that surrounded the various events, there was little effort to go beyond polemics and symbolic demonstrations to a serious evaluation of their implications for French national identity and collective memory. The fact that the experiences were not seen as directly relevant to the average Frenchman made it easy to downplay their significance. True, Darquier was an important official during the Vichy period, but his extremist views hardly typified French attitudes during the war. And while *Holocaust* raised important questions about World War II, especially for a young generation that had remained completely ignorant of the events, its central concerns were German victimizers and Jewish victims, not Frenchmen. Similarly, revisionism, with its obsession to disprove the existence of gas chambers, focused attention on the experiences of Nazism rather than on Vichy. The few attempts to portray French passive acceptance of the Pétain regime and its policies, such as the 1974 film *Lacombe Lucien,* whose opportunistic peasant hero joins the Gestapo after being turned down by the resistance, came closer to the truth, but by banalizing the history of wartime collaboration they ran the risk of blurring the lines of responsibility.[86] In the face of a complex reality in which heroism and villainy were often intermingled and which could not be explained by the extremes of collaboration or resistance, Frenchmen simply chose to ignore their painful past.

Yet despite efforts to deny the reality of Vichy and its complicity in the Holocaust, the issue refused to go away. An important impetus was the outbreak of anti-Semitic violence in France that began in 1978 and continued throughout the early 1980s. In the most spectacular episode four people were killed and nineteen were injured in an October 1980 explosion outside of a synagogue in the fashionable sixteenth arrondissement of Paris. The situation was exacerbated by a statement issued soon after the incident by Premier Raymond Barre, who noted that the attack on the synagogue had been aimed at Jews but also had struck "innocent Frenchmen" who were crossing the street. More than one observer wondered whether attitudes toward Jews had changed substantially since Vichy, especially when no important cabinet representatives bothered to attend a special ceremony that took place the next day on the street where the explosion had occurred. Despite the fact that both French and Israeli officials ascribed the incident to Arab terrorists, an opinion poll issued soon after the bombing suggested that more than half of the adult French population believed that anti-Semitism was still widespread in their country. Such views were reinforced by scathing if somewhat hyperbolic indictments of the "fascist" and "totalitarian" nature of French political ideology and culture written by two prominent Jewish intellectuals, Bernard-Henri Lévy and Shmuel Trigano.[87]

The events of the Holocaust entered French public debate again in 1982 as part of an anti-Zionist backlash created by the Israeli invasion of Lebanon. From its establishment in 1948 the Jewish state has been a puzzlement to Frenchmen, conjuring up images of both victimized and victimizer during Vichy. On the one hand, the Jewish struggle for independence was enthusiastically supported and even romanticized, representing as it did a historical parallel to the wartime French resistance. Jewish defiance of the mandate authorities also found favor among French government officials who had long resented British involvement in the Middle East. On the other hand, growing concerns about the emerging Third World, fed by the Algerian war against French colonialism, created a strong anti-Zionist response, especially among left-wing intellectuals. From the creation of Israel in 1948, when hundreds of thousands of Palestinian Arabs fled their homes, through the invasion of the Sinai in 1956 and the occupation of the West Bank after the Six-Day War, there were elements of the French Left who equated the Jewish struggle against the Arabs with Nazi treatment of the Jews themselves. Israel was linked with the events of World War II in yet another sense as a result of efforts by elements of the Right and the extreme Right, many of whom who had questionable careers under Vichy, to compare the Jewish state's struggle against Arabs with their own nation's war against the Front de libération nationale algérien (FLN) in Algeria.[88]

The incursion into Lebanon in 1982 brought an intensification of the associations of Israel with Nazism. In bizarre inversions of the history of the Holocaust, the left-wing French press compared the killings at the Sabra and Shatilla refugee camps in September 1982 to the Nazi massacre of French civilians, equated invading Jewish soldiers with storm troopers and *Einsatzgruppen,* and characterized Menachem Begin and his supporters as "a new Hitler and his henchmen."[89] For many observers, the viciousness of such attacks signaled the rise of a new form of anti-Jewish hatred which in using the Holocaust to condemn Zionism sought to deny Jewry both its collective past and future. The politicization and banalization of Nazism and the Holocaust by elements of the French Left also suggested that the tragic events of the Final Solution were rapidly losing their specificity and sanctity for a generation that had not experienced Vichy. The very same elements that in the past had criticized the French government for falsifying the reality of the Occupation and failing to learn the lessons of World War II were themselves distorting the historical past to support their own narrow ideological ends.

The intertwining of the Holocaust and French collective memory surfaced again in 1983 with the capture of Klaus Barbie, a German officer who had been assigned to Lyons as chief of the second largest Gestapo force in France. Given the reluctance of government officials to confront the events of the Final Solution in France, Barbie would probably have lived out his life in relative peace in Bolivia if not for the doggedness of Serge and Beate Klarsfeld. Klarsfeld, whose father had been deported from Nice in 1943, and his wife Beate, a German Christian with a strong personal sense of moral responsibility, had taken it upon themselves to pursue Nazi war criminals and collaborators who had escaped indictment after the war. Among other individuals they had previously tracked down and brought to trial were Jean Leguay, secretary-general of the Paris police under Vichy, who had been responsible for the infamous roundup on July 16, 1942, and René Bousquet, Leguay's superior. Both had avoided serious prosecution while developing successful business careers and busy social lives in France. The Leguay indictment was especially significant, since it marked the first time that the suspension of the statute of limitations had been applied to a French citizen.[90]

Barbie was by far the most important war criminal to be put on trial in France. Thirty-one years earlier the most powerful SS official in occupied France, Karl-Albrecht Oberg, had been tried and convicted by a military tribunal in Paris, but Frenchmen, preoccupied with what one writer called "more timely problems," seem to have paid little attention to the courtroom proceedings.[91] Barbie's case was potentially far more explosive, for aside from his participation in the deportation of Jews, he was also implicated in the torture of Jean Moulin, De Gaulle's representative in France during the war. It was well known that Barbie had depended upon members of the Milice, a paramilitary organization of Nazi supporters in France, to carry out his brutal activity against Jews and the underground, and it had been rumored that Moulin himself had been betrayed by a member of the resistance. As a result, his trial threatened not only to expose French complicity in the Final Solution but also to explode the myth of the collective heroism of the French populace during the Occupation. As Erna Paris, the author of a book on the Barbie Affair noted, the arrival of the war criminal in France raised the fear "that he would point a finger at people who had helped him, people who, having undergone a sudden transformation from collaborator to resistance fighter, from traitor to hero, had been living in relative obscurity for almost half a century."[92]

A peculiar aspect of the affair was the strategy and perspective of Barbie's lawyer, Jacques Vergès. A self-proclaimed revolutionary and a fervent anti-Zionist, Vergès reflected the bizarre synthesis of the approaches of the extreme Left and the extreme Right to Vichy, Nazism, and the Holocaust that were evident in the ideology of French revisionism. In essence, Vergès planned to transform Barbie from a defendant into a prosecutor of Western society and of the Jews. In attacking France and Israel as "Nazi" regimes that oppressed colonial peoples, he hoped to demonstrate that democracies were hypocritical in their denunciation of the Third Reich and that ultimately all governments were totalitarian in their nature. In pointing up the willingness of the UGIF to negotiate with the Vichy regime, he intended both to implicate the Jews in their own destruction and to demonstrate their unscrupulous and corrupt nature.

Ultimately, French fears were assuaged and Vergès's plans were foiled. Even before the trial, bitter quarrels over the demands by former resistance fighters that Barbie's persecution of the French underground be considered as a "crime against humanity" threatened to blur the lines of distinction between French resistance and Jewish victims and to weaken the impact of the case. As we have seen, such a blurring had occurred throughout much of the postwar period, fed in large part by the refusal by government officials to recognize the distinctiveness of the Jewish tragedy. In a tragic turn of events, it now seemed as though Jews and resistance groups were competing for public sympathy as victims of Nazism. Revelations concerning the efforts by the United States Army counterintelligence to shield Barbie from his French pursuers and to help him escape to South America further confused matters.

Barbie himself at first refused to appear at the trial, claiming that the court lacked jurisdiction. In May 1987, however, he finally agreed to cooperate. After a summary trial that lasted less than two months, he was sentenced to life imprisonment. None of Barbie's victims was able to confront him directly. Although pinpointing many of his actions against Jews, French prosecutors judiciously avoided any serious discussion of Barbie's relationship with French collaborators. In doing so, France missed yet another chance to come to grips with its past. As for Barbie, the former Gestapo leader was all but forgotten (except perhaps by relieved government officials) when he died in jail in September 1991.[93]

Not surprisingly, those who are most determined to keep the memory of the Holocaust alive in France today are its seven hundred thousand Jewish citizens. Theirs is a different collective memory from that of the majority of Frenchmen, however. While most French citizens see the war in terms of humiliation and shame, Jews in France associate it with devastation and death. While most Frenchmen wish to repress the painful events of Vichy, for much of the French Jewish community the Holocaust has become an integral part of their collective and personal identity. Efforts by revisionists and anti-Semites to deny or minimize its importance thus represent not only a slur upon the memory of victims but an attack upon the personal raison d'être of many Jews in contemporary France.[94]

In actuality, the events of the Final Solution have had varying influences on the different groups that comprise the present-day French Jewish community. For descendants of Alsatian Jewry still prominent in the community leadership, the growing awareness of the Holocaust has clearly spelled the end of the simplistic association of French with Jewish interests that so dominated the consciousness of their parents' generation. As in the case of French historiography of Vichy, the research of foreign scholars has helped to clarify memory by developing a more nuanced view of the native Jewish response to the Occupation. In particular, Richard I. Cohen and Jacques Adler have demonstrated how the naiveté of community leadership vis-à-vis Vichy in 1939 gave way after 1942 to a growing realization of French complicity in the implementation of the Final Solution.[95]

The new militancy of the French Jewish establishment, especially in regard to the defense of Israel, and its incorporation of immigrants from North Africa into positions of power within the community are important indications of lessons learned from the tragic events of deportation and destruction. Equally significant was the decision by a number of the larger Jewish communities outside Paris, including Lyons, Nice, and Bordeaux, to erect commemorative monuments and plaques to Holocaust victims and to conduct memorial religious services in connection with the observance of Yom Hashoah (Holocaust Remembrance Day). After decades of continued pressure from survivors, community leaders finally also were able to convince the French government to place plaques specifically denoting Jewish victims at various sites in France associated with the Holocaust, such as the Vélodrome d'Hiver in Paris (where Jews were interned after the roundups of July 16, 1942) and the Pithiviers concentration camp.[96]

For North African Jews, who now represent the majority of the community, on the other hand, the Holocaust has little direct relevance to their own past experiences. Although the Jews of France's colonies were subject to Vichy anti-Jewish legislation, they were generally spared the tragedy of the Final Solution.[97] Indeed, many North African Jews in France today view the destruction of much of European Jewry as a demarcation point in the transfer of communal power and cultural hegemony from Ashkenazic to Sephardic Jewry. Thanks in large part to the use of Holocaust symbolism in Israeli political debate, however, the events of the Final Solution have become important components of the collective consciousness of world Jewry. For Jews from Morocco, Tunisia, and Algeria living in France who have strong familial and ideological ties to Israel, the Holocaust thus has become an important object lesson of the vulnerability of Jews living in the Diaspora and tragic proof of the need for a strong and viable Jewish state.

Though the Eastern European Jewish community in France was nearly decimated in World War II, its heritage lives on among the children of survivors, whose Jewish identity was profoundly affected by both the painful reality and memory of the Holocaust. As noted earlier, the *Holocaust* series had a significant effect upon many sons and daughters of Russian and Polish Jews, especially those with radical backgrounds. The search for roots led a number of them to seek out those prewar sources of Eastern European Jewish culture that melded Jewish identity with a commitment to social and economic equality. The result has been a certain revival of secular Jewish culture in France, manifested in the renewed interest in the Yiddish language and Bundism (Eastern European Jewish socialism). Rejecting both assimilationism and Zionism, a small group of young intellectuals have also rediscovered Jewish Autonomism, whose bold affirmation of communal and cultural distinctiveness within prewar Polish society seems to have direct relevance to an increasingly ethnically and linguistically diverse France.[98] In their approach to the Holocaust itself, many of these young Jews have attacked the passivity of the French Jewish establishment during the war and have emphasized the heroic activity of the Jewish resistance. In so doing, they mirror the behavior of their immigrant parents and grandparents, who sought to create a new French Jewish identity that combined loyalty to their community with a commitment to the "progressive" ideals of the French

Left. At the same time, however, their efforts to reduce the complexity of Jewish response during the Holocaust to the activities of a cowardly and corrupt leadership on the one hand and the heroic resistance of the masses on the other directly parallel the French national mythology of the war years.

As the 1990s opened, France was again in the throes of a crisis surrounding the Vichy regime and its role in the Final Solution. The renewed effort to bring aging war criminals to trial, the decade-long tenure of a socialist president who had served in the resistance, the opening up of government archives that had been closed since the end of World War II, and the desire of many educators and communal leaders to set the historical record straight for a new generation that knew nothing of Vichy have all served to again focus French public attention on the wartime regime and especially its role in the deportation of Jews. In some cases the upsurge of interest has signaled a marked break with past attitudes toward Vichy and the Holocaust. In others it seems to have had little impact upon the deeply rooted patterns of denial and mythification that marked collective consciousness of the events of World War II in postwar France. A survey of recent events suggests that the results of the contemporary reevaluation of French collective memory have been mixed.

Many observers have voiced concern that the Front National, led by Jean-Marie Le Pen, is an ominous reflection of the continued vitality of Vichyite and anti-Jewish sentiments among the French public. The party has clearly emerged as an influential force in French national politics. It captured 11 percent of the French vote in the European elections in June 1984, thirty-five seats in the National Assembly in 1986, and nearly 14.5 percent of the vote in the first round of the presidential elections of 1988. French polls and interviews conducted in 1991 and 1992 suggested that nearly a third of the electorate broadly supports Front National policies.[99]

Founded in 1972, the Front National has always catered to anti-Semitic fears. There is reason to believe that works denying the Holocaust were published under its auspices in the 1970s. Le Pen himself received his early political training in 1956 as the youngest Poujadist deputy to the Chambre des députés, where he took part in veiled anti-Semitic attacks upon the French premier, Pierre Mendès-France. Le Pen was one of the few major political figures to express opposition to the trial of Barbie. In interviews conducted in 1989 he dismissed the gas chambers as a mere "detail" that had been exaggerated to serve special interests, spoke of conducting *rafles* in the heavily Jewish Paris suburb Sentier, and denounced Jewish protests against the establishment of a convent at Auschwitz as unacceptable interference in Polish internal affairs. The French right-wing leader has been fined twice for slurring Holocaust victims and was forced to indemnify nine organizations representing former deportees as well as the MRAP, a group that fights racism and anti-Semitism in France.[100]

Although Le Pen rarely misses an opportunity to denounce individual Jews and freely borrows from revisionist propaganda, he has never expressed any particular interest in the Jewish Question per se. Many of his anti-Semitic tirades seem designed to elicit responses from politicians and other public figures, which would be sure to earn him free publicity in the media.[101] Le Pen's primary focus is on immigrants from North Africa, the Middle East, and Asia, whom he accuses of creating unemployment and implicating France in foreign entanglements against her national interest. In this, he reflects the growing visibility of right-wing movements in Europe that have benefited from resurgent nationalism on the Continent. Though he has often opposed the socialist policies of recent governments, Le Pen has judiciously avoided attacking the Republic or openly defending Vichy. His electoral fate seems to ebb and flow with the changing economic climate and the impact of foreign workers.[102]

Indeed, Le Pen's relative lack of interest in the Jewish Question may reflect a general decline in French anxiety about Jews. In 1946 a national poll revealed that 43 percent of the French doubted the national loyalty of Jewish citizens. By 1978 the figure had dropped to 9 percent, with slightly more Frenchmen expressing concerns about the loyalty of Corsicans and only slightly fewer voicing reservations about Alsatians. Surveys conducted between 1966 and 1978 also revealed a noticeable decline in the number of those who would object to a Jewish president, a Jewish son- or daughter-in-law, or a Jewish boss. During the same period the number of Frenchmen who openly declared themselves anti-Semites dropped from 9 percent to 5 percent. The most recent survey, conducted in 1991, revealed that 16 percent of Frenchmen felt "unfriendly" toward Jews, while 69 percent claimed that they had strong pro-Jewish sentiments. Far more hostility was expressed toward gypsies (41 percent) and black Africans (24 percent).[103]

The reasons for the decline in anti-Semitism are not hard to discern. With the modernization of French society many of the traditional sources of anti-Jewish sentiment have disappeared. Dechristianization and widespread education have weakened the religious basis of anti-Jewish hatred, while the growing emphasis upon the rights of ethnic and linguistic minorities in French political life has created greater toleration of cultural difference. Capitalist activity is no longer the bugaboo of the French petit bourgeoisie, and acquisitiveness and money are no longer looked upon as curses by the masses. The relative stability of the recent governments and the absence of a clear external danger have led to a decline in attacks upon the Republic, a major target of anti-Semitic propaganda. On a more practical level, the rapid increase in foreign labor has meant that French xenophobic sentiment has been increasingly diverted from Jews to Africans and Arabs.[104]

Many of those who have maintained that anti-Semitic attitudes were in decline in France were shocked by the desecration of a Jewish grave in the town of Carpentras in May 1990. Despite its profoundly disturbing nature, however, the incident must be seen in perspective. The act itself harked back to more traditional forms of anti-Semitism and appears to have had little to do with the events of Vichy and the deportation of Jews. Equally significant, no group has ever publicly assumed responsibility for the desecration, and the event did not lead to an outbreak of general anti-Jewish violence in France. Most importantly, political leaders of all stripes (with the notable exception of Le Pen) publicly denounced it as an outrage. In response to an appeal for support from the Jewish community, more than two hundred thousand people marched in the streets of Paris on less than forty-eight hours' notice. If the grave desecration suggested that for some Frenchmen the memory of the Holocaust was fading and no longer imposed any restraints upon their actions against Jews, the massive response of French political and religious leaders indicated an unwillingness on the part of a wide spectrum of the populace to allow blatant acts of racial and ethnic hatred to go unanswered.[105]

An important step in confronting Holocaust revisionism was the passage in 1990 of a bill making it a misdemeanor to publicly deny Nazi crimes.[106] At the same time, however, the willingness of even liberal publications such as *Le Monde* to publicize revisionist views would seem to indicate that the denial or at least questioning of the Holocaust has imperceptibly become legitimized in growing circles. Such growing toleration of formerly taboo ideas explains Le Pen's continued ability to employ anti-Semitic statements concerning Jews and the Holocaust in his political campaign without seriously damaging his chances for victory. According to one poll conducted in 1990, one in three Frenchmen doubts that the gas chambers actually existed. Equally disturbing is the manner in which the language of Vichy policy toward Jews has been incorporated into the present debate over foreigners in France. Socialist and Gaullist politicians alike speak openly about "Frenchmen of blood" and the need to "solve" the refugee problem through deportation.[107]

The issue of France's willingness to confront the events of the Holocaust yields similarly mixed results. On the one hand, the events of the Final Solution continue to haunt popular consciousness. Films such as *Shoah* (which was shown on French television during the Barbie trial) and the immensely successful *Au Revoir les Enfants* (Goodbye to the Children) point to a renewed interest in the Holocaust on the part of a new generation of Frenchmen. Similarly, studies of concentration camps and memoirs by survivors continue to be published with regularity.[108] Clearly, the same climate that allows for the unleashing of verbal attacks and anti-Semitic actions that would have been unthinkable forty years ago also enables filmmakers, scholars, and memoirists to treat the subject of the Final Solution in a frank and convincing manner.

While the French populace in the early 1990s showed significant signs of its willingness to confront the events of the Holocaust and the deportations from France, government leaders, including President Mitterrand himself, remained distinctly uncomfortable with its implications for France. Like De Gaulle almost a half-century ago, political leaders were convinced that a frank discussion of Vichy and the Final Solution would only create public unrest in a period of economic and political crisis. In particular, they feared that the wartime regime's acquiescence to the Nazi Final Solution indicated a pattern of French weakness vis-à-vis her powerful neighbor to the east that might have a deleterious impact upon Franco-German relations in the European community. Equally important was the concern that any discussion of racial and ethnic hatred a half-century ago would play into the hands of contemporary racists like Le Pen, whose tirades against immigrants echoed the xenophobic rhetoric of the Pétain regime.[109]

The ostrichlike attitudes of the Mitterrand regime were most clearly evident in its response to efforts to inculcate and to commemorate the events of the deportations. It took nearly forty years for officials in the ministry of education to agree to include discussions of French police complicity in the deportation process in classroom textbooks.[110] Similarly, though some attempts were made to honor the victims of deportations through the construction of monuments and memorials at camp sites such as Drancy and Struthof, French officials continued to be reticent about emphasizing the specificity of the Jewish tragedy. Despite some notable exceptions, most commemorations of deportations in the early 1990s made no differentiation between Frenchmen sent off as forced laborers and Jews marked for extermination. As in the case of national commemorations of the Armistice in the postwar era, memorials linked the tragedy of deportees with the martyrdom of resisters, thereby incorporating the experiences of Jews into the general context of the Nazi occupation of France and perpetuating the myth of popular opposition to Vichy.[111]

Many had hoped that the observance of the fiftieth anniversary of the *rafle* at the Vélodrome d'Hiver in July 1992 would signal a new attitude on the part of the regime. It was certainly significant that prominent government officials participated in ceremonies in Paris, thereby implicitly recognizing the personal tragedy of Jews in wartime France. Nevertheless, the Mitterrand regime rejected the demand of a group of prominent intellectuals that the date be set aside as an annual national day of remembrance and that the government admit the direct involvement of the wartime regime in crimes against Jews. Official France's response was typically evasive. It would be wrong to single out Jews among the millions of Frenchmen who suffered under German occupation, authorities argued. Nor would the regime agree to pass judgment on crimes of past French governments.[112]

At times the response of the Mitterrand government seemed to go beyond denial; at least some officials seemed to be trying deliberately to obscure the nature of anti-Jewish activity during Vichy. In one notorious example, in early 1992, after almost forty years of intensive investigation researchers found comprehensive files of the names of 150,000 Parisian Jews that the French police had compiled and used to conduct *rafles* during World War II. Although government officials adamantly denied knowledge of their whereabouts after the war, the files had actually remained in the hands of the ministry of veterans' affairs, which used them to verify the property and pension claims made by Jewish survivors. In 1973 all references to the lists were deleted from the inventory of government archives. A large number of the files were eventually released for public scrutiny, but the fact that they remained hidden for so long only to be discovered neatly stored in a modern building that was built in 1983 led more than one observer to question whether government officials had deliberately hidden the documents.[113]

Activists like Serge Klarsfeld reacted to these ominous developments in the 1990s by renewing their efforts to try French collaborators for war crimes. Klarsfeld's efforts were fueled by a growing fear that the individuals would die before they were brought to trial. Thanks to the famed Nazi hunter's persistence in the face of considerable foot-dragging by the French judicial system, in 1992 René Bousquet and Maurice Papon, who served as secretary-general of the prefecture of the Gironde during the Occupation,[114] were finally indicted for war crimes. Both men were accused of assisting in the deportation of thousands of Jews from Bordeaux, including children, to Nazi death camps in 1942 and 1943.

In order to reopen both cases, however, Klarsfeld had to fight both government resistance and opposition within the Jewish community. The French lawyer originally brought charges of crimes against humanity against Bousquet in September 1989. A year later the French government indefinitely postponed the decision by assigning the case to the Special High Court of the Liberation, a body that had not convened since the 1940s! At the time, the newspaper *Le Monde* reported that President François Mitterrand had indicated privately that "French public interest" would not be served by a trial of Bousquet.[115] Similarly, the case of Papon had been under study in the courts since 1982. In 1986 an appeals court annulled the first indictment. Court officials initiated a new investigation in 1987, but it was abruptly canceled two years later. It took three years for a third investigation to result in an indictment.[116]

Aside from investigating French war criminals, Klarsfeld has attempted to extradite Alois Brunner, an assistant to Adolf Eichmann who was directly involved in the deportation process in France, from Syria. The Nazi hunter also has been active in countering revisionist propaganda by compiling and publishing a list of all of the victims of the Holocaust who were deported from France.[117] Similarly, Klarsfeld was instrumental in publishing a five-hundred-page study of the technique and operation of the gas chambers at Auschwitz by Jean-Claude Pressac, a pharmacist who began his work doubting that the Holocaust had ever occurred.[118]

By far the most dramatic development in the pursuit of war criminals in recent years was the dismissal of the case against Paul Touvier, head of the Lyons branch and later regional chief of the Milice, in April 1992. In many ways the court's decision was the culmination of a long and tragic process that encapsulates the tortured development of postwar France's treatment of its Vichy past. Tried and sentenced in absentia in Lyons in September 1946 and again in his native Chambéry in March 1947, Touvier managed to escape capture. In March 1967 the death sentence issued against him was canceled as a result of the passage of a statute of limitations on Vichy crimes. Four years later Touvier was pardoned by President Georges Pompidou after Gabriel Marcel, a prominent Catholic philosopher and a converted Jew, intervened on his behalf. Despite massive protests, the French president stood by his decision, arguing that the time had come "to draw a veil over the past."[119] In July 1979 public pressure triggered by the events of 1978 led to Touvier's indictment for crimes against humanity. By the time an arrest warrant was issued, however, Touvier was nowhere to be found. In 1989 he was traced to a Catholic monastery near Nice and arrested. He was later freed pending trial because of ill health.[120]

In its decision to drop legal charges against Touvier the Paris court chose to rest its decision upon a highly questionable analysis of the nature of the Vichy regime's policies toward Jews. While Touvier may have murdered Jews in his role as an agent of the government, it maintained, he could not be convicted of crimes against humanity because of the nature of the Vichy regime. Invoking a judicial decision made during the Barbie trial, the court argued that despite its policies against Jews, Vichy, unlike Nazi Germany, was not engaged in a systematic policy of "ideological hegemony." (In a bizarre mirroring of revisionist arguments concerning Hitler's responsibility for the Final Solution, the court based its decision on the fact that none of Marshal Pétain's public pronouncements contained any anti-Semitic statements.) As a result, Touvier's crime did not fit the commonly accepted definition of crimes against humanity and thus was subject to a statute of limitations. Once again, in the name of civil peace French authority chose to reaffirm the myth of Vichy as an unwilling accomplice of Nazi policy and to deny its central role in the deportation of Jews.[121]

The court's decision in the Touvier case created an unusual outcry among many French citizens. The revelations concerning the efforts by some religious officials to hide Touvier led to a call both within and outside the French Catholic Church for a reassessment of the popularly accepted image of the wartime church as a stalwart opponent of Vichy's anti-Jewish policies. More importantly, many concerned Frenchmen feared that the decision would only benefit those who sought to deny the Holocaust or at least minimize its significance. At least one journalist stated what many thoughtful French citizens were secretly thinking, namely, that the failure to punish a figure who had a major role in implementing Vichy's anti-Jewish policies could only mean that government authorities remained unwilling to confront the true nature of the wartime regime. Almost all political parties, with the exception of Le Pen's Front National, demanded that the ruling be reversed. As a sign of its anger, the French Parliament suspended its session in order to attend a memorial service for Touvier's victims. French officials responded to the public outcry by promising to expedite the prosecution of Bousquet and Papon. In turn, the Supreme Court of Appeals agreed to review the Touvier decision. After numerous delays, in June 1993 it reversed itself and ordered Touvier to stand trial.[122] On April 19, 1994, a French court found Paul Touvier guilty of crimes against humanity during World War II for ordering the execution of seven Jews while he was serving in the Milice.

The impressive response of a wide spectrum of the French populace to the decision has led some observers to argue that with the passing of the generation that directly experienced Vichy, Frenchmen are finally prepared to judge its crimes objectively. According to the historian Henry Rousso, for example, young French citizens have at least partially broken with both the myth and the countermyth of Vichy by recognizing that their countrymen were neither heroes nor villains during World War II.[123] Others, especially those within the Jewish community, are not as certain. What does seem increasingly clear is that there is a growing gap between the populace's and the government's ability and willingness to confront the events of the Holocaust in France. Whether courageous individuals can continue to assert an independent stance in the face of government pressure or apathy is an open question.

In February 1993 the French government made a dramatic announcement making July 16 a national day of remembrance for Jewish and other racial victims of Vichy policies. The decree also called for monuments to be built at the Vélodrome d'Hiver and other sites throughout France where victims were concentrated or held before deportation. In addition, commemorative plaques were to be erected in every department in France. A special committee headed by the secretary of state for veterans and including representatives of the Jewish community, in consultation with local authorities, was to decide on the text that would appear on each plaque.[124]

It is too early to assess the implications of the government's action. On the one hand, the unprecedented decision marks an important departure from the tendency of postwar French governments to ignore the role of their country in the implementation of the Holocaust. The fact that the decree was announced in a period in which there had been a disturbing increase in the incidences of anti-Semitism and xenophobia in Europe makes it even more significant. Yet one must not forget that the French government's willingness to confront the crimes of Vichy came only in response to massive protests by Jewish and resistance groups. In addition, little has been said so far about the need to teach the lessons of the Holocaust to the next generation through the incorporation of its history in school curricula. Most disturbingly, the statement in October 1994 by a terminally ill François Mitterand concerning his involvement in the Vichy regime and his lack of concern at the time with its anti-Semitic laws, as well as his expressions of longstanding friendship with René Bousquet, one of the officials responsible for the infamous roundup of July 16, 1942, cast doubts on the sincerity of the government's commitment to honestly confront France's wartime activity, while again highlighting the gap that continues to exist between French and Jewish perceptions of World War II.[125]

The postwar history of France suggests that its citizens have often fallen into what the philosopher Bernard Henri-Lévy has called an "amnésiaque somnolence" concerning Vichy. One can only hope that Serge Klarsfeld is correct in describing France's decisions to commemorate the victims of the Holocaust and to prosecute Touvier as "an important stage in the fight to recover our memory."[126] The pronouncement on July 16, 1995, by the newly elected president, Jacques Chirac, that France must take full responsibility for the deportation of its Jews during World War II is yet another hopeful sign that French society has finally decided not to obfuscate its past.[127] For it is only by choosing to remember the tragic events of Vichy that France will once again find its national identity and purpose in the contemporary world.

NOTES

1. An indispensable source for understanding the development of French collective memory of the Vichy regime in the postwar era is Henry Rousso, *The Vichy Syndrome: History and Memory in France since 1944* (Cambridge, 1991). Two other useful overviews are the chapter on France in Judith Miller, *One, by One, by One: Facing the Holocaust* (New York, 1990), 112–57; and the essay "Une Mémoire conquise: La Choa au miroir du judaïsme français, 1945–1990," *L'Arche*, no. 402 (January 1991), 122–25.

2. For general studies of the history of Jews in France in the nineteenth century, see Bernhard Blumenkranz, ed., *Histoire des juifs en France* (Tou-louse, 1972), 265–361; and David Feuerwerker, *L'Emancipation des juifs en France de l'ancien régime à la fin du second empire* (Paris, 1976).

3. Stanislaus Clermont de la Tonnerre, cited in Pierre Birnbaum, *Un Mythe politique: "La République juive": De Léon Blum à Pierre Mendès France* (Paris, 1988), 44–45. All translations are by the author. For an examination of the nature of Jewish emancipation during the French Revolution, see Feuerwerker, *L'Emancipation,* 3–445; and Arthur Hertzberg, *The French Enlightenment and the Jews* (New York, 1968), 314–68.

4. Joseph Reinach, cited in Birnbaum, *Un Mythe politique,* 47. For studies of French Jewish

attitudes in the nineteenth century as reflected in the thought and behavior of the community lay and religious leaders, see Phyllis Albert, *The Modernization of French Jewry: Consistory and Community in the Nineteenth Century* (Hanover, N.H., 1977); and Jay R. Berkovitz, *The Shaping of Jewish Identity in Nineteenth-Century France* (Detroit, 1989). For a general study of French Jewish ideology in the nineteenth century, see Michael Graetz, *Les Juifs en France au XIXe siècle: De la Revolution française à l'Alliance israélite universelle* (Paris, 1989).

5. A useful general survey of French anti-Semitism in the nineteenth century is Robert Byrnes, *Antisemitism in Modern France: The Prologue to the Dreyfus Affair,* vol. 1 (New Brunswick, N.J., 1961). For information on French socialist anti-Semitism in the nineteenth century, see Edmund Silberner, *Ha-sotsializm ha-maaravi u-she'elat ha-yehudim* (Western socialism and the Jewish Question) (Jerusalem, 1955), 13–130.

6. It is a testament to the persistence of such sentiments in twentieth-century French consciousness that in 1945 the lifelong anti-Semite Charles Maurras would greet his sentencing to prison for collaboration during Vichy with the cry: "This is Dreyfus's revenge" (Rousso, *The Vichy Syndrome,* 81). For discussions of anti-Semitism during the Dreyfus Affair, see Michel Winock, *Edouard Drumont et Cie: Antisémitisme et fascisme en France* (Paris, 1982); Stephen Wilson, *Ideology and Experience: Antisemitism in France at the Time of the Dreyfus Affair* (Rutherford, N.J., 1982); and Michael R. Marrus, "Popular Anti-Semitism," *The Dreyfus Affair: Art, Truth, and Justice* (Berkeley, 1987), 50–61.

7. For the attitudes and behavior of native Jewry during the Dreyfus Affair, see Michael R. Marrus, *The Politics of Assimilation: A Study of the French Jewish Community at the Time of the Dreyfus Affair* (Oxford, 1971).

8. For a study of the attitudes and behavior of Eastern European Jews in France before World War I, see David Weinberg, "'Heureux comme Dieu en France': East European Jewish Immigrants in Paris, 1881–1914," *Studies in Contemporary Jewry* 1 (1984), 26–54; and Nancy L. Green, *The Pletzl of Paris: Jewish Immigrant Workers in the Belle Epoque* (New York, 1986). The impact of assimilation upon the French Jewish community in the period between the Dreyfus Affair and World War II is discussed in Paula Hyman, *From Dreyfus to Vichy: The Remaking of French Jewry, 1906–1939* (New York, 1979). For an examination of the attitudes, socioeconomic makeup, and institutions of the Paris Jewish community in the 1930s, see David Weinberg, *A Community on Trial: The Jews of Paris in the 1930s* (Chicago, 1977), 1–71.

9. Michael R. Marrus, *The Unwanted: European Refugees in the Twentieth Century* (Oxford, 1985), 145–49.

10. See, e.g., Georges Mauco, *Les Etrangers en France* (Paris, 1932); and Raymond Millet, *Trois millions d'étrangers en France* (Paris, 1938).

11. For a study of the events surrounding the Stavisky Affair, see Maurice Chavardès, *Le 6 février 1934: La République en danger* (Paris, 1966).

12. Marrus, *The Unwanted,* 148; Weinberg, *A Community on Trial,* 178–88.

13. Robert Soucy, *French Fascism: The First Wave, 1924–1933* (New Haven, 1986), xi–xii.

14. For a general discussion of the role of intellectuals in the French fascist movement in the 1930s and during Vichy, see Pierre-Marie Dioudonnat, *Je Suis Partout, 1930–1944: Les Maurrassiens devant la tentation fasciste* (Paris, 1973).

15. Jean-Jacques Doriot, cited in J. Plumyène and R. Lasierra, *Les Fascismes français, 1923–1963* (Paris, 1963), 129–30.

16. Jean Charles Bonnet, *Les Pouvoirs publics français et l'immigration dans l'entre deux guerres* (Lyon, 1976), 217–22, 214.

17. *Le Temps,* April 15, 1939, cited in *Les Juifs en France,* special issue of *Histoire* 3 (November 1979), 88.

18. For an examination of the response of the Jews of Paris to the rise of anti-Semitism in the 1930s, see Weinberg, *A Community on Trial,* 72–211.

19. The most thorough discussion of Vichy policy toward Jews is to be found in Michael R. Marrus and Robert Paxton, *Vichy France and the Jews* (New York, 1981). Serge Klarsfeld's *Vichy-Auschwitz: Le Rôle de Vichy dans la solution finale de la question juive en France—1942* (Paris, 1983) contains a valuable collection of Vichy documents that deal with the deportations of Jews.

20. Marrus and Paxton, *Vichy France,* 67. For information on life in one internment camp, see Hanna Schramm and Barbara Vormeier, *Vivre à Gurs: Un Camp de concentration français, 1940–1944* (Paris, 1979).

21. Marrus and Paxton, *Vichy France,* 9–10, 70.

22. Ibid., 3–21.

23. For a comprehensive study of the activities of the Commissariat général, see Joseph Billig, *Le Commissariat général aux questions juives (1941–1944),* 3 vols. (Paris, 1955–60).

24. Klarsfeld, *Vichy-Auschwitz,* 11–37.

25. For a history of the *rafle,* see Claude Lévy

and Paul Tillard, *La Grande Rafle du Vel d'Hiv (16 juillet 1942)* (Paris, 1967).

26. For a general discussion of the *rafles* of 1942 in both the North and the South, see Klarsfeld, *Vichy-Auschwitz,* 89–162.

27. For a study of the fate of Jews in the Italian Zone, see Léon Poliakov, *Jews under the Italian Occupation* (New York, 1983).

28. Jacob Lestschinsky, "Bilan d'extermination," *Le Monde juif,* March 1947, 19–20; *La Terre retrouvée,* October 15, 1947; Marrus and Paxton, *Vichy France,* 343.

29. Marrus and Paxton, *Vichy France,* 186.

30. Michel Abitbol, *Les Juifs d'Afrique du Nord sous Vichy* (Paris, 1983), 17–32.

31. Marrus and Paxton, *Vichy France,* 32.

32. Ibid., 197–203, 271–74; Klarsfeld, *Vichy-Auschwitz,* 163–74.

33. The story of Le Chambon is movingly recounted in Phillip Hallie's *Lest Innocent Blood Be Shed* (New York, 1980).

34. Blumenkranz, *Histoire des juifs en France,* 415–17.

35. For a discussion of the establishment and activity of the UGIF, see Richard I. Cohen, *The Burden of Conscience: French Jewry's Response to the Holocaust* (Bloomington, Ind., 1987).

36. Jacques Adler, *The Jews of Paris and the Final Solution: Communal Response and Internal Conflicts, 1940–1944* (New York, 1987), 143–45.

37. Ibid., 154–55, 167–68, 220–21; Cohen, *Burden of Conscience,* 94–104, 137–47.

38. Adler, *Jews of Paris,* 227–28.

39. Ibid., 230–31; Cohen, *Burden of Conscience,* 183–84. For a contemporaneous view of CRIF, see *La Terre retrouvée,* December 1944, 4–5.

40. The discussion of French Jewry in the immediate postwar period is taken from David Weinberg, "The Reconstruction of the French Jewish Community after World War II," in *Shearit Ha-Pletah, 1944–1948: Proceedings of the Sixth Yad Vashem International Historical Conference* (Jerusalem, 1990), 168–86. The article was also published in the Hebrew volume of the proceedings, *Sh'erit ha-pleta, 1944–1948: Hartzaot vi-diyunim bi-kinus ha-benleumi ha-shishi shel hokre ha-shoah* (Jerusalem, 1990), 149–66.

41. For information on the repatriation of deportees, see Olga Wormser-Migot, "Le Rapatriement des déportés," in *La Libération de la France: Actes du Colloque international tenu à Paris du 28 au 31 octobre 1974* (Paris, 1976), 721–38.

42. For discussions of the plight of various Jewish communities after Liberation, see *Bulletin de nos communautés,* January 25, 1945; *Unzer Vort,*

January 10, 1945, January 18, August 15, 1946, February 9, 1947; *Bulletin du Grand Rabbinat du Nord,* July–August 1946, 1; *La Terre retrouvée,* September 15, 1947, October 15, 1948, September 15, 1949; and *Droit et liberté,* March 1, 1948.

43. For a typical example of the attitudes of young Jews who emigrated to Palestine after the war, see Isaac Pougatch, *Un Bâtisseur: Robert Gamzon* (Paris, 1971), 143–53.

44. The figures are taken from the *Bulletin du Centre israélite d'information* 3 (May 1–15, 1946). According to one observer, by 1948 there were as many Polish Jews in Paris as in all of Poland (*Unzer Vort,* June 10, 1948).

45. For contemporaneous discussions of the problem of the restoration of spoliated property, see *Droit et liberté,* April 27, May 31, 1945; *Quand Même,* December 1944, 2; and CRIF, *Bulletin intérieur d'information,* January 15, 1951.

46. F. Schrager, *Un Militant Juif* (Paris, 1979), 197–98.

47. *Le Monde juif,* June 1949, 20; *La Terre retrouvée,* October 15, 1947. For the testimony of deportee children, see Denise Baumann, *La Mémoire des oubliés: Grandir après Auschwitz* (Paris, 1988).

48. See, e.g., the article by Fr. Robert Braun in *La Terre retrouvée,* January 15–February 1, 1946.

49. For more information on the Finaly case, see Wladimir Rabi, *L'Affaire Finaly* (Marseilles, 1953). Another incident that caused great concern to the Jewish community was the so-called Hochberg Affair. In 1957 a French court ruled that a child of a French father and a Polish Jewish mother should remain with the father. In its brief, the court noted that it would reverse its finding if the child were to go to live in Poland or Israel. The decision was eventually struck down in 1964.

50. For an example of French hostility toward the arrival of Jewish refugees in France, see the remarkable article by J. J. Bernard, a deportee, in *Le Figaro,* April 14, 1945. In the article, Bernard claimed that refugees were attempting to impose themselves on France. The article concluded with the ringing affirmation that refugees would be opposed as strongly as France opposed Hitler. For information on the French anti-Semitic press during the late forties and early fifties, see *Le Monde juif,* February 1949, 27–28; and CRIF, *Bulletin intérieur,* November 16, 1953.

51. For a discussion of the creation of the myth of the resistance, see Rousso, *The Vichy Syndrome,* 15–60.

52. For a discussion of contemporary attitudes towards Pétain, see ibid., 283–95.

53. Peter Novick, *The Resistance versus Vichy: The*

Purge of Collaborators in Liberated France (London, 1968), 187–88.

54. Ibid., 188.

55. Gordon Wright, *France in Modern Times* (Chicago, 1964), 541–42; Birnbaum, *Un Mythe politique,* 272; Pierre Birnbaum, "Anti-Semitism and Anticapitalism in Modern France," in *The Jews in Modern France,* ed. Frances Malino and Bernard Wasserstein (Hanover, N.H., 1985), 218. For a contemporaneous analysis of Poujadism, see "Le Mouvement Poujade," *Evidences* 7, no. 54 (1956), 5–12. For Jewish reactions to Poujade, see *La Terre retrouvée* 7 (January 1, 1956), 8 (January 15, 1956), and 9 (February 1, 1956).

56. Emmanuel Mounier, cited in Rousso, *The Vichy Syndrome,* 26.

57. For a discussion of the ambiguities surrounding the commemoration of the Armistice, see ibid., 219–26.

58. In 1956 an article reviewing French Jewish literature after the war bemoaned the fact that it was unlikely that anything would ever be written about the experiences of French Jews under Vichy (*La Revue du FSJU* 5, no. 18 [1956], 46).

59. For information on the activity of Schneersohn and the construction of the memorial, see Annette Wieworka, "Un Lieu de mémoire et d'histoire: Le Mémorial du martyr juif inconnu," *Revue de l'Université de Bruxelles* 1–2 (1987), 107–32. For examples of community opposition to the memorial, see *La Terre retrouvée* 2 (October 1, 1956), 3 (October 15, 1956), and 6 (November 15, 1956).

60. David Rousset, *A World Apart* (London, 1951), 107. See also Jacqueline Mesnil-Amar, *Ceux qui ne dormaient pas* (Paris, 1957), 119; and Suzanne Birnbaum, *Une Française juive est revenue* (Paris, 1946), 193–96.

61. See, e.g., the article on a rally held in August 1945 in *L'Unité,* August 3, 1945.

62. Robert Paxton, *Vichy France: Old Guard and New Order, 1940–1944* (New York, 1975).

63. Adrien Dansette, *Mai 1968* (Paris, 1974), 230.

64. For contemporaneous discussions of Holocaust literature in France, see the articles in *L'Arche,* nos. 60 (January 1962), 22–25, 63, and 84 (January 1964), 15–17. For a general examination of the treatment of deportations and the Holocaust in French literature, see Cynthia Haft, *The Theme of Nazi Concentration Camps in French Literature* (The Hague and Paris, 1973). For an extremely critical analysis, see Roger Errera, "La Déportation comme best-seller," *Esprit* 18 (December 1969), 918–21.

65. Jacques Mosel in *L'Arche,* no. 52 (May 1961), 19.

66. For an examination of the treatment of the capture of Adolf Eichmann in the Franco-Jewish press, see ibid., no. 43 (June 1960), 21–30.

67. For a general discussion of the impact and significance of De Gaulle's statement, see Raymond Aron, *De Gaulle, Israél et les juifs* (Paris, 1968).

68. See, e.g., Claude Bordet, "Les 'Amis' d'Israél," *Le Monde,* November 14, 1973. The issue of "double loyalty" was also brought up after American Jewish activists harassed President Georges Pompidou during his visit to the United States in March 1970. See esp. "M. Pompidou et les juifs," ibid., March 4, 1970.

69. Edgar Morin, *Rumour in Orléans* (New York, 1971). See also idem, "L'Antisémitisme ordinaire," *Histoire* 3 (November 1979), 127, 132.

70. Annette Insdorf, *Indelible Shadows: Film and the Holocaust* (New York, 1983), 98–101, 149–53, 195–201.

71. For a discussion of Darquier's activity during the war, see Blumenkranz, *Histoire des juifs en France,* 392.

72. See, e.g., the article by René-Victor Pilhes in *Le Monde,* November 4, 1978.

73. For a general analysis of the response to Darquier's statements, see Bernard Chaouat, "L'Affaire Darquier de Pellepoix et la classe politique française," *Combat pour le Diaspora* 1 (February 1980), 65–78.

74. For the text of the film, see Marcel Ophuls, *Le Chagrin et la Pitié* (Paris, 1980). For information on the circumstances surrounding the ORTF's rejection of the film, see Rousso, *The Vichy Syndrome,* 100–114.

75. *Le Monde,* February 11–12, 15, 1979.

76. For representative responses see ibid., February 11–12, 27, 1979; and *Esprit* 28 (April 1979), 116–24.

77. For representative examples of the reactions of children of Eastern European immigrants to *Holocaust,* see Luc Rosenzweig, *La Jeune France juive: Conversations avec des juifs d'aujourd'hui* (Paris, 1980), 21; and André Harris and Alain de Sédouy, *Juifs & Français* (Paris, 1979), 9–10. The attitude of North African Jews is reflected in Shmuel Trigano, "From Individual to Collectivity: The Rebirth of the 'Jewish Nation,'" in Malino and Wasserstein, *The Jews in Modern France,* 245–81.

78. For a synopsis of the responses of the Left and the Right to *Holocaust,* see *Le Monde,* February 21, 1979; for a discussion of the impact of the

series on elections to the European Parliament, see ibid., February 15, 1979; for the article by the Moroccan writer, see ibid., February 18, 1979.

79. For a discussion of Rassinier's views, see N. Fresco, "Les Redresseurs de morts," *Les Temps modernes* 37, no. 407 (1980), 2164–67, 2204–10.

80. Paul Rassinier, *Le Drame des juifs européens* (Paris, 1964), 8, cited in ibid., 2205.

81. Fresco, "Les Redresseurs de morts," 2167–68; Pierre Vidal-Nacquet, "Un Eichmann de papier," in *Les Juifs, la mémoire et le présent,* ed. Pierre Vidal-Nacquet (Paris, 1981), 204–10.

82. *Le Monde,* January 16, 1979.

83. Noam Chomsky, preface to Robert Faurisson, *Mémoire en défense: Contre ceux qui m'accusent de falsifier l'histoire: la question des chambre à gaz* (Paris, 1980).

84. Vidal-Nacquet, *Les Juifs,* 218–20, 222–26.

85. Ibid., 226, 270.

86. Insdorf, *Indelible Shadows,* 101–3.

87. For a discussion of the incident, see Michael R. Marrus, "Are the French Antisemitic? Evidence in the 1980s," in Malino and Wasserstein, *The Jews in Modern France,* 224–25. For Lévy's comments on the nature of French political ideology, see Bernard-Henri Lévy, *L'Idéologie française* (Paris, 1981), 224; for Trigano's, see Shmuel Trigano, *La République et les juifs après Copernic* (Paris, 1982), 202.

88. For a general discussion of the French public attitudes toward Israel in the years immediately after the establishment of the Jewish state, see David Lazar, *L'Opinion française et la naissance de l'Etat d'Israël: 1945–1949* (Paris, 1972).

89. *Le Monde,* September 21–25, 1982; *Les Temps modernes* 39, no. 435 (1982), 639–55. For the response of a left-wing Jewish intellectual, see Claude Lanzmann, "Un Criminel de guerre vous parle: Brève réponse à Elisabeth de Fontenay," ibid., 39, no. 436 (1982), 39–46. See also Marrus, "Are the French Antisemitic?" 228.

90. For further information on how the Klarsfelds tracked down Barbie and the circumstances surrounding his discovery in and extradition from Bolivia, see Erna Paris, *Unhealed Wounds: France and the Barbie Affair* (New York, 1985), 116–29; and Miller, *One, by One, by One,* 115. The activities of Bousquet and Leguay are covered extensively in Klarsfeld, *Vichy-Auschwitz.*

91. See Paris, *Unhealed Wounds,* 14.

92. Ibid., 15.

93. For a general discussion of "L'Affaire Barbie" written in the wake of Barbie's death, see *Le Monde,* September 29, 1991.

94. For discussions of contemporary French Jewish attitudes toward Vichy, see *Penser Auschwitz,* special issue of *Pardes* 9–10 (1989).

95. Cohen, *Burden of Conscience;* Adler, *Jews of Paris.*

96. On the memorial at the Vélodrome d'Hiver, see *Le Monde,* July 18, 1990; on Pithiviers, see ibid., May 8, 1990.

97. For a discussion of the fate of North African Jews under Vichy, see Abitbol, *Les Juifs d'Afrique du Nord,* 49–110.

98. The most extensive exposition of this point of view is to be found in Richard Marienstras, *Etre un peuple en diaspora* (Paris, 1975). See also the editorial in the first issue of the journal *Combat pour le Diaspora* (February 1980), 5–6.

99. For a study of Le Pen's supporters, see Orfal Birgitta, *L'Adhésion au Front National: De la minorité active au mouvement social* (Paris, 1990).

100. For information on the history of the Front National and the role of Le Pen, see Jean Chatain, *Les Affaires de M. Le Pen* (Paris, 1986); and Edwy Plenel and Alain Rollat, comps., *L'Effet Le Pen* (Paris, 1984). For other examples of Le Pen's anti-Semitism, see Chatain, *Les Affaires,* 26.

101. See, e.g., the response to Le Pen's attack upon the "Jewish International," which he claimed was responsible for the "anti-national spirit" in France, as noted in *Le Monde,* August 12, 14, 1991; and his attack on "left-wing Jewish intellectuals," who he alleged controlled the French press, cited in ibid., August 26, 1991.

102. For an insight into Le Pen's views on immigrants and immigration, see Jean-Marie Le Pen, *La France est de retour* (Paris, 1985), 52–54, 156–57, 217–37.

103. The figures are taken from Marrus, "Are the French Antisemitic?" 240–41. See also *Le Monde,* March 22, 1991; and *Jerusalem Report,* April 16, 1992.

104. For a general discussion of the factors leading to a decline in anti-Semitism, see Birnbaum, *Un Mythe politique,* 301.

105. Roger Kaplan, "Incident at Carpentras," *Commentary* 80, no. 2 (1990), 48–51. See also the June 1990 issue of *L'Arche,* which is largely devoted to what the magazine calls "La France de Carpentras."

106. *New York Times,* May 5, 1990.

107. See, e.g., the statements by the Gaullist leader Valéry Giscard d'Estaing cited in *Le Monde,* September 21, 1991, and the various responses by both the Left and the Right cited in ibid., September 24, 25, 28, 30, 1991.

108. See, e.g., Annette Wievorka, *Déportation et génocide* (Paris, 1992).

109. See, e.g., the comments made by Mitterrand in an interview conducted in 1986 as cited in Miller, *One, by One, by One,* 149–53.

110. For an analysis of the teaching of the Holocaust in public-school curricula, see Centre de documentation juive contemporaine, *L'Enseignement de la Choa: Comment les manuels d'histoire présentent-ils l'extermination des juifs au cours de la second guerre mondiale* (Paris, 1982). A more recent discussion can be found in *L'Arche,* no. 415 (February 1992), 30. A text that is used in Jewish schools in France is *Le Temps qu'on n'oublie pas, 1939–1945* (Paris, 1963).

111. For a discussion of the effort to place a memorial plaque at Natzweiler-Struthof, see the Simon Wiesenthal Center's magazine, *Response,* September 1989, 4.

112. *New York Times,* June 22, 1992.

113. *Le Monde,* November 13, December 17, 1991.

114. Papon's activities during the war are discussed throughout Klarsfeld, *Vichy-Auschwitz.*

115. *Le Monde,* September 26, 1990.

116. *New York Times,* October 28, 1990. For a discussion of the controversy over the Bousquet and Papon indictments see Richard Bernstein, "French Collaborators: The New Debate," *New York Review of Books,* June 25, 1992, 37–42. See also Laurent Greilsamer, "Le Réflexe du secret," *Le Monde: Selection Hebdomadaire,* July 7, 1992.

On June 8, 1993, while awaiting trial, Bousquet was assassinated in his Paris home by a publicity seeker who claimed that he had been sent by God to ensure "the victory of good over evil." For further information on the assassination, see *New York Times,* June 9, 1993; and *Le Monde,* June 9, 1993.

117. Serge Klarsfeld, *Memorial to the Jews Deported from France, 1942–1944: Documentation of the Deportation of the Victims of the Final Solution in France* (New York, 1983).

118. *New York Times,* December 18, 1989.

119. Georges Pompidou, cited in Rousso, *The Vichy Syndrome,* 123.

120. For information on the discovery of Touvier, see *Le Monde,* May 26, 1989.

121. Details on the ruling can be found in *New York Times,* April 15, May 10, 1992; and *Le Monde,* April 15, 1992.

122. *New York Times,* May 10, 1992.

123. Rousso, *The Vichy Syndrome,* 305–6.

124. "France Will Remember Jews Sent to Nazi Camps by Vichy," *New York Times,* February 5, 1993, A4.

125. For the Jewish response to the Mitterand statement, see *L'Arche,* November 1994, 25–32.

126. Lévy, *L'Idéologie française,* 70.

127. *Le Monde,* July 18, 1995.

THE NETHERLANDS
Debórah Dwork
Robert-Jan van Pelt

The Jonas Daniel Meijerplein, once the heart of Jewish Amsterdam and later the hub of the ghetto without walls instituted by the Germans during the Occupation, is framed by the Portuguese Synagogue, the four shuls that form the Ashkenazi Synagogue complex, and the statue of the dockworker on strike in February 1941 against the first German-imposed anti-Jewish measures. In a very real sense, the three structures that now make the square famous constitute an architectural exhibition of the history of the Jews in the Netherlands. The Portuguese Synagogue remains as it was in the seventeenth century, untouched by the war in general or the Germans in particular. Gorgeous and empty, it is owned by the Portuguese-Israelite community, but there are few Sephardic Jews in the city to use it. The fate of the Ashkenazi shuls was very different. The complex, dating from the seventeenth and eighteenth centuries, was plundered by the Germans during their five-year rule. The synagogues survived as a deserted hulk. Purchased by Amsterdam's city council in 1955, the Ashkenazi complex ceased to have any connection with the Jewish community. For more than thirty years the building was abandoned; finally, in 1987 it was restored to provide a new home for the city-run Jewish Historical Museum. No longer a living Jewish communal building, it is now a municipal museum to preserve the memory of the Jews in the Netherlands. The dockworker—the quintessential symbol of Dutch resistance—faces the museum, his back to the splendid relic of the Jewish community, the Portuguese Synagogue. It is the victims and not the survivors who command his attention; his loyalty lies with the dead.

The statue of the dockworker was erected in 1952, seven years after the liberation of the Netherlands. Standing in the center of the Dutch capital, it expresses the immediate postwar belief that the Dutch nation as a whole had gallantly, if unsuccessfully, defended its Jewish citizens. By 1970 the self-perception of the Dutch had changed, and another monument was erected far from Amsterdam, in a forest clear-

45

ing near the village of Westerbork. In the 1930s a camp had been built in that bleak and desolate spot. First a compound for German refugees, it then became the transit center on the train route from homeland and haven to destruction and death. More than one hundred thousand Jews were deported to the East from Westerbork.

The creation of the monument in Westerbork marked a watershed in the history of the Dutch response to the Holocaust. Dutch self-satisfaction, expressed in the heroic pose of the dockworker, had given way to a genuinely felt empathy with the victims. This metamorphosis began in 1945 with the conclusion of 350 years of Dutch Jewish history. Starting in the Jonas Daniel Meijerplein in the late sixteenth century, the history of Dutch Jewry was, in a fundamental sense, terminated in Westerbork on September 13, 1944, with a last transport of 279 persons to Bergen-Belsen.

BEFORE THE HOLOCAUST

Arriving in Amsterdam at the end of the sixteenth century, the so-called Portuguese Jews settled in an area adjacent to what is now the Jonas Daniel Meijerplein. They were the first generation of the Jewish community that was to endure until the German Occupation. Expelled from Spain in 1492, these Jews traveled to Portugal, where they made a home for themselves as crypto-Jews. When Spain annexed Portugal a century later, they were driven out of the Iberian Peninsula and fled to the Netherlands. In the Dutch Republic, which was at war with the country that had persecuted them, the Sephardic refugees found a tolerant haven where they were entitled to practice their own religion and participate in economic life. They flourished as a community (with a population of about four hundred in 1610 and three thousand in 1780), they engaged in business and education, and there was always a core of respected scholars and wealthy merchants.[1] The Sephardic community took an active role in the life of the city of Amsterdam and in the affairs of the republic. They were a visible, confident, and accepted minority. It was their privilege to obtain permission to construct a Jewish communal building (the Portuguese Synagogue), which in size competed with and in decoration exceeded major Protestant churches, just inside the most important city gate.[2] It was the site that later became the Jonas Daniel Meijerplein. The community had become an integral and integrated part of the city landscape.

In the 1620s a second group of Jews immigrated to the Netherlands. The new arrivals from Germany formed a semi-autonomous Ashkenazi "nation." The German Jews were joined three decades later by their Polish coreligionists fleeing from pogroms in Ukraine. The two groups together were known as the *Hoogduitse* (High German) nation. With a population of five thousand in 1680 and thirty thousand a century later, theirs was a far larger community than that of their Sephardic cousins. It was also much poorer.

The Christian community was, in general, tolerant of Jewish customs, which were practiced publicly, and of the participation of Jews in Dutch life—in education, publishing, business, trade, colonial enterprises, and so on. In the seventeenth and eighteenth centuries anti-Semitism, such as it was, was directed mainly against the High German nation, perhaps because the Portuguese Jews were seen as an exotic, stable community with a glorious past. The Sephardic Jews' very reason for being in the Netherlands fit the Dutch conception of their own struggle against Spain. They were, in essence, fellow sufferers. All Jews were granted full citizenship in 1796, and the two nations' special legal status of semi-autonomy was revoked. Jews were part of the general community, and the anti-Semitism they experienced was moderate in tone and certainly nonaggressive. It was an anti-Semitism that was not perceived as dangerous, but as a slightly unpleasant element in an otherwise safe, if impoverished, existence.

Dutch Jews on the whole were not well-off financially. Indeed, by the end of the eighteenth century both the Sephardic community and the *Hoogduitse* community were poverty-stricken. In Amsterdam, which was the center of Dutch Jewry, 54 percent of Portuguese Jews and 87 percent of High German Jews were supported in 1799 by richer members of their respective communities. A half-century later, in 1849, the fortunes of the former had declined, while those of the latter had improved; yet the welfare of both was completely out of proportion to that of the general population. Thus, 63 percent of Portuguese Jews and 55 percent of the *Hoogduitse* but only 17 percent of the gentile population of Amsterdam received aid. It was not until the end of the nineteenth century that the situation improved, and even then it was still not very good, with 11.2 percent of the Sephardic and 11.6 percent of the Ashkenazi Jews but only 2 percent of the gentiles requiring assistance.

Unemployment, underemployment, and poorly paid employment were constant. Even those who had work were relatively destitute. The two-fifths of all working Jews who were in trade, most of them peddlers, managed to make a living but were rarely economically comfortable. The diamond industry absorbed two-thirds of all Jews in industrial occupations but was highly fluctuating. Thus, although there was a Jewish bourgeoisie, there was also a real *Lumpenproletariat* that warmly supported socialism and was disaffected from Jewish communal authority. The two main religious bodies, or "churches" *(kerkgenootschappen),* the Portuguese-Israelite and the Dutch-Israelite (successor to the *Hoogduitse* community), were controlled by the rich, which alienated most working-class Jews. The community was divided and fragmented: Ashkenazi and Sephardic, bourgeois and proletariat, economically conservative and socialist.

The economic crisis of the 1930s exacerbated the divisions within the Jewish community, which at the time had 110,000 members, of whom 90,000 lived in Amsterdam. The contrast between rich and poor was sharper than in Dutch society generally. The average income of those Jews who paid taxes was 20 percent higher than that of the general population, while the percentage of Jews whose income was below the line where tax began to apply was at least equal to or greater than the percentage of poor in the Dutch population at large. The poorer and the richer Jews lived in distinct neighborhoods, and they voted differently (the poor voting "red," the rich for one of the liberal parties). Most important, there was no Jewish ideology connecting the two groups. The synagogue had lost its attraction, and the small Zionist movement, which had 3,000 members, was a middle-class affair. It was, in short, a fragmented community without leadership. As one historian put it, seen from a Jewish perspective, Dutch Jewry had already ceased to exist before the Germans arrived.[3]

The disaffection within the Jewish community was not due to, or in reaction to, anti-Semitism. By the 1930s most Jews felt themselves to be very well integrated in Dutch society, even though they had only limited access to the highest government posts and to the officer corps in the armed forces and even though there was not one Jewish mayor and only thirteen of the twenty thousand policemen and gendarmes were Jews. These manifestations of the limitations of acceptance were not experienced as a problem, and in general Jews believed that social advancement was possible. Nevertheless, it was commonly understood that admission came at a price. As the unsentimental, pragmatic Dutch Zionist leader Fritz Bernstein observed wryly in 1935: "The Jew is only admitted to non-Jewish circles when he can bring something with him that compensates for his disadvantage of being a Jew; he must bring a surplus of talent or significance or position or education, or wealth in comparison to the circle in which he desires admittance. . . . *In the best of circumstances the Jew faces a kind-hearted tolerance on the part of truly well-bred gentiles, who consider it their duty not to let it appear to the Jew that his Jewishness makes a difference,* just as a civilized person tries to hide from the invalid that his handicap is noticed."[4]

The essentially mild genre of anti-Semitism that prevailed in the Netherlands must be understood within the unique context of Dutch society. Unlike in other European countries, in Holland there was no clear differentiation between a dominant and relatively homogeneous culture and the "foreign" culture of the Jews. The Dutch nation was itself fragmented into a number of virtually independent societies, none of which could claim a majority. These societies were perceived as columns, or *zuilen,* on which the state rested. In addition to the Catholic *zuil* (which, with 30 percent of the population, was the largest), there were three Protestant *zuilen* and two secular *zuilen,* one social-democratic and the other liberal. Each *zuil* had its own political party, newspaper, trade union, schools, university, sports societies, broadcasting system, and so on. The various *zuilen* considered each other at best with indifference and more usually with suspicion. Thus the Catholic *zuil's* attitude toward the Jews was not very different from their attitude toward members of the other *zuilen.* In only one way did the situation of the Jews differ from that of members of other religious denominations: while the specific character of their group would have justified a Jewish *zuil,* there was none. This was because of both the size and the fragmentation of the Jewish community. Any group that made up at least 10 percent of the population could, if it so wished, form a *zuil,* and at no more than 2 percent the Jews did not qualify. Then too, the Jewish bourgeoisie belonged to the liberal *zuil,* and the Jewish working class to the social-democratic *zuil.*

What united these different societies was the House of Orange, not as the embodiment of the ideology of monarchy, but as the representation of the glorious history of the Netherlands. All groups, including the Jews, shared the history of the Dutch Republic in the late sixteenth and seventeenth centuries. This national-historical consciousness ultimately rested on the notion of what it meant to be a *Nederlander,* a Dutchman. Jews perceived themselves to be, and were recognized by their Christian countrymen to be, *Nederlanders* whose earliest ancestors had lived in Palestine but whose later forebears had participated in writing the most illustrious page in Dutch history, a page of glory and tolerance. Gentile Dutchmen shared the sentiments that Abraham Asscher (owner of a large diamond factory, liberal member of the Provincial Estates of North Holland, chairman of numerous Jewish organizations, and the leader of the Dutch-Israelite community) expressed in 1935 at the official third centennial of the establishment of the *Hoogduitse/Nederlands-Israelitische* community. "As Dutchmen and as people who belong to the Jewish community, we consider it the greatest happiness for our country to have been ruled for centuries by a royal house such as that of Orange, which from generation to generation has maintained the life goal of its brilliant founder, William the Taciturn: the high principles of freedom of conscience and religious tolerance," Asscher declared. "It is well known that Her Majesty our Queen has carried on this tradition for the sake of the happiness of our country. We know that she acts in total accordance with the spirit of the Dutch people."[5]

There were no functional implications or actual manifestations of this concept of the *Nederlander,* however. To be Dutch meant, as the historian Hans Blom has put it, to have "a well-considered contentment about the unique and exemplary nature of Dutch society,"[6] but it did not signify a commitment to an inclusive Dutch nation incorporating all the *zuilen* or all the disparate groups living in the country—Catholics, liberals, Jews, socialists, Protestants, communists, and so on. There was no mutual loyalty among them, only a shared self-satisfaction. In practical terms, the sole unifying element was the extremely efficient bureaucracy of the civil service, which spread its web across the nation. The different *zuilen* of which Dutch society was composed did not drift apart, because each individual was connected to the apparatus of the state through this net. Everyone and everything was registered; everyone and everything had a place and was in place.

The heterogeneous character of the Dutch state had several implications, the most important of which was that each of the participating societies considered itself a minority. The Catholics, for instance, saw themselves as a minority in a generally Protestant country. Thus the Jewish minority had no special function as a scapegoat, and anti-Semitism was of little value as a theme to gain votes. The agenda of the Dutch fascist party, the Nationaal Socialistische Beweging (National Socialist Movement), or NSB, was to transmute the pluralism in which the nation was grounded into unity; their ideal was a single *volk,* or people. Their aim was to destroy the *zuilen* structure of Dutch society and to reconstruct the nation on an ideology of homogeneity. The concept of the *Nederlander* was to be given substance.

Initially, Jews were not excluded from this process. By the mid-thirties, however, the NSB had discovered the political potential of anti-Semitism. According to the Dutch National Socialists, the divisions in Dutch society were not only unnecessary but harmful, and the Jews were to blame for these fissures. Indeed, perhaps it was a ploy of the Jews to divide what was, and ought to have been, one united gentile *Nederlandse* society, thus rendering it powerless. The NSB pointed to the decline of Dutch commercial and cultural preeminence in the second half of the seventeenth century, the adoption of French, and the loss of specifically Dutch characteristics in society, art, and architecture and attributed these trends to the establishment of the *Hoogduitse* Jewish community in the Netherlands. Clearly, the Jews were responsible for the ills of the nation. (The Portuguese Jews, by contrast, were considered with greater benevolence, since their arrival had preceded the period of Dutch glory and thus they were perceived to have participated in it.)

The NSB move toward anti-Semitism was influenced by events in Germany, and the *zuilen* too were susceptible to Nazi ideology and propaganda. They slowly became aware of a Jewish Problem. The Nazi postulate that Europe had suffered a moral degeneration since the beginning of the Industrial Revolution as a direct result of Jewish emancipation began to be accepted in Catholic and Protestant circles. Much of the new philosophy coming out of Germany was interpreted by these elements of Dutch society as staunchly Christian, and they found it attractive. By the end of the 1930s many people believed that a Jewish Problem or a Jewish Question indeed existed and that a solution was needed. Even a relatively mild and not altogether unsympathetic review of the issue, J. van der Ploeg's *Het Joodsche Vraagstuk: Een Maatschappelijk Probleem* (The Jewish Question: A social problem), published shortly before the German occupation, argued that it "is important, both for the Jew and the non-Jew, to come to an arrangement before it is too late. If one allows anti-Semitism and the hatred for Jews to run its course, outbursts will occur in which the Jew will become the victim and the persecutors of Jews will be dishonored. A just and speedy arrangement can prevent this, and is therefore of self-evident interest to both parties."[7] The "arrangement," which van der Ploeg suggested but did not specify, was to be based on the recognition that the Jews were an alien element within Dutch society and should be treated accordingly.

While a more virulent strain of anti-Semitism was articulated in the Netherlands throughout the mid- to late 1930s, the Dutch were rather reserved with regard to Nazism as such, and many rejected it completely. As elsewhere in Europe, however, Nazism was perceived as a preferable alternative to communism, which was greatly feared. This led to a certain relativism vis-à-vis German anti-Semitism. "In Russia the persecution of Christians is worse than the persecution of the Jews in Germany," one paper declared. "We lament what is done east of us against the Jews, but in our own country Christians suffer worse at the hands of revolutionary elements," another proclaimed.[8] In general, however, the Dutch tradition of neutrality prevailed. Christian Holland kept its distance from the events in Germany. The secular liberal and socialist *zuilen* and the Communist Party responded more energetically to anti-Semitism, although there were great differences of opinion concerning how to proceed, and as a result there were no collective actions.

The Dutch Jewish community also kept its distance from the developments in Germany. There were no collective actions against the Nazi government's persecution of the Jews, nor was there an appreciable solidarity between Dutch and German Jews. Dutch Jews considered themselves to be first and foremost *Nederlanders,* while German Jews remained *Duitsers.* The differences between them were more important than the bonds they shared; Judaism, as we have seen, did not greatly signify in prewar Holland. Dutch Jews feared that the arrival of their German coreligionists (whose presence was the result of their Jewishness and who claimed a connection with the Dutch Jews on that basis) would upset the carefully preserved ideology that the Dutch Jew, like the Dutch Catholic or the Dutch Protestant, was an ordinary *Nederlander* like all other *Nederlanders*. And to some extent their fear was rational: it was undoubtedly as a result of the arrival between early 1933 and April 1938 of some twenty-five thousand Jewish refugees, of whom around twelve thousand came to depend on public assistance, that many Dutchmen started to reconsider the position of the Jewish community in relation to other Dutch communities (or Dutch society as a whole, as the NSB claimed).[9]

The Dutch government exploited this tension both to limit immigration and to profit financially. In 1938 the borders effectively were closed to Jewish refugees, and new arrivals were returned to Germany. The sole exception to this policy occurred after Kristallnacht, when the regulations were relaxed for a short time and another seven thousand refugees were allowed into the country. By the time the war began in 1939, there were some thirty thousand Jewish refugees in the Netherlands, as about two thousand of the more than thirty-two thousand who had entered the country had found other havens. The government justified the immigration restrictions by claiming that they would prevent the rise of anti-Semitism at home. Furthermore, The Hague required the Dutch Jewish community to care for the refugees. Thus, Westerbork, the internment camp for German Jewish refugees, was built by the Dutch government, but it was the Dutch Jewish community that paid for its construction and operating costs. It went without saying that "their own community would pay for those of the same race and faith."[10]

The leadership of the Jewish community, insofar as one could speak of a community, allowed this to happen. No one dared to criticize the Dutch government's policy. To the contrary: during a protest meeting against Kristallnacht in November 1938, Asscher thanked the government both

> for the way in which it has demonstrated its recognition of the seriousness of the situation [in Germany] and also for the great amount of work which has been done by a number of its prominent members and civil servants. . . . Indeed we mention with praise the fact that the Dutch government has been the first to express publicly the need to help those unfortunates, the first to try to find other countries to help. We are well aware of the many difficulties the government encounters in its sincere desire to help solve this problem. It is absolutely certain that the Dutch government is not able to realize what really was necessary for the German Jews: safety and hope for the future of all.[11]

In short, the leader of the Dutch Jewish community excused a Dutch government that turned back refugees at the Dutch-German border! The Jewish press agreed. Only a small minority within the Dutch Jewish community expressed disgust with its own leadership and indignation with the government. The Dutch Jewish leadership "did not demand anything," the *Centraal Blad voor Israelieten* (Central Journal for Israelites) wrote in December 1939. "God forbid—not even the application of existing legislation: that could give rise to anti-Semitism. [Our representative] requests in a submissive fashion and trembles at a frown on the forehead of a minister. He fights only when other Jews attempt to normalize the legal situation of the refugees. . . . Then he battles against those Jews. Yes, he thanks the government publicly for the creation of camps, where Jews are imprisoned, instead of simply keeping silent because we must accept these camps."[12] Two years later that same representative, Abraham Asscher, was to head the German-imposed Jewish Council.

The unwillingness of the Dutch Jewish leadership to criticize the refugee policy reveals the extent of their insecurity. The Jewish community had begun to drift into a realm characterized by "instability, uncertainty, anxiety—no concrete fear, but a vague, far echo, as it were, of the persecutions which had victimized their ancestors for centuries."[13]

THE HOLOCAUST ERA

On the eve of World War II the Dutch Jewish community of 140,000 people was vulnerable. This figure included approximately 118,000 people who had been born in the Netherlands or who had acquired Dutch nationality through naturalization, about 14,500 Jews who still carried German passports, and some 7,500 Jews who had obtained passports from other countries, mainly in Latin America. All of them, regardless of their citizenship status or the nationality of their passports, were imperiled. Just how great their jeopardy was became clear six years later, in 1945. Nearly annihilated, with 75 percent of its members murdered, Dutch Jewry suffered even greater losses than did Jews in neighboring Belgium (40 percent) and France (25 percent) or across the North Sea in Norway (40 percent) and Denmark (1.6 percent). A number of factors contributed to this staggeringly high mortality rate.[14] In the Netherlands the SS had a free hand, whereas in Belgium and France there were tensions between the dominant Wehrmacht and the SS and Heydrich's security service, the SD, and in Denmark the government ran the country without direct German interference until the late summer of 1943; after that date the population did not cooperate with the Germans. The Netherlands, moreover, was policed by a greater force (five thousand men) than, for example, was its larger neighbor, France, to which the Germans sent only three thousand men. The specific situation of the Jews within Dutch society was an equally important factor, however. Jews in the Netherlands had never suffered at the behest of the government or the civil service. During their centuries of citizenship they had learned to expect protection from "above," and they were not suspicious of national authority or their own leaders. The system had worked well for nearly three hundred years, and the trust it had engendered blinded the Jews and prevented them from realizing that that very system could be a tool for their destruction. In short, the Jews were like other Dutchmen and reacted to the Germans like other Dutchmen: they were, for the most part, cooperative, administratively efficient, and loyal to the authority, and they assumed that their leaders had the best intentions.

These perceptions and beliefs resulted in a general passivity among the Dutch population in general and among the Jews in particular. For the first three years of the Occupation the general attitude in the Netherlands (shared by gentiles and Jews) was one of accommodation, and the Germans could do as they wished. Deeply divided by the *zuilen* structure of their society, the Dutch did not develop a general spirit of resistance in the sense of Dutchman against German. Indeed, for a time the NSB successfully appropriated the label "true Dutchman" for its own vision of a national regeneration on racial-historical foundations. The various *zuilen* felt no loyalty to each other, and no Jews belonged to the *zuilen* in which the spirit of resistance was strongest, the Christian fundamentalists. Furthermore, the lack of cohesiveness among the Dutch Jews and the ill will between them and the German Jewish refugees crippled the community. Paralyzed by passivity, fragmentation, trust in authority, and suspicion of each other, the Dutch offered little resistance to the German occupation for three years. It was not difficult for the Nazis to achieve most of their goals during that time. Step by step, the move from Holland to Poland was secured on Dutch soil.[15]

The road to Auschwitz was opened with the registration of Jewish enterprises in October 1940. A month later, Jewish public servants, including teachers and professors, were dismissed from their jobs. Registration of Jews followed in January 1941: the official tally was 140,552 Jews, 14,549 half-Jews, and 5,719 quarter-Jews. Within weeks, in early February 1941, the Germans allowed NSB storm troopers to wreak havoc in the Jewish quarter of Amsterdam. To everyone's surprise, however, they were beaten off by the inhabitants of the neighborhood, and one of the storm troopers was mortally wounded. On February 12 the Germans sealed off the Jewish quarter and established a Jewish Council headed by Abraham Asscher and David Cohen, a professor of ancient history at the University of Amsterdam.

Tension and violence mounted quickly. On February 19 a German patrol entered a popular ice cream parlor (the Koco) located outside the Jewish quarter but run by two German Jewish refugees. As it had been a Nazi target, some of the regular clients had installed a primitive self-defense system using ammonia. Sprayed with the fluid as they came through the door, the patrol opened fire and arrested the owners and everyone else on the premises. One of the proprietors, Ernst Cahn, was the first Jew to be killed by the Germans in the Netherlands; he was executed in March. The Germans used the battle in the Jewish quarter and the Koco incident as a pretext to arrest four hundred Jewish men on February 22 and 23; they were sent to Buchenwald and then on to Mauthausen, where they died. The incarceration of these men sparked off a general strike that began on the Amsterdam docks on February 25 and quickly spread to the rest of the city. This act of Dutch gentile solidarity with their Jewish neighbors was ruthlessly suppressed. The Germans immediately informed the Jewish Council that they would continue to arrest, deport, and even shoot large contingents of Jews on a daily basis until the strike ended. Asscher contacted forty industrial leaders and convinced them to bring the strike to an end; by February 27 everyone was back at work.

Throughout 1941 and early 1942 the noose tightened. In July 1941 special identity cards for Jews were issued, and in September the Zentralstelle fuer Juedische Auswanderung (Central Office for Jewish Emigration), headed by Ferdinand aus der Fuenten, began operation. With the start of the new academic year, Jewish children were thrown out of schools; now segregated from their gentile friends, they began to attend schools newly established by the Jewish community. Travel restrictions were imposed that autumn, and by the end of the year the Jews were concentrated in a few designated areas of the country. By that time the Germans had already sequestered most of the Jewish wealth and possessions, allowing Jews to keep only a few personal possessions and no precious metals except a wedding ring, a silver (but not gold) watch, four pieces of table silver per person, and gold and platinum teeth. (These the Germans later retrieved in the undressing rooms of the gas chambers or in little rooms next to them marked "Goldarbeiten.") Finally, in May 1942 the Germans introduced the yellow Jewish star marking.

The first deportations to Poland began two months later. The "resettlements," as they were termed, were announced formally in the newspapers. The evening papers of Monday, June 29, 1942, announced that all Jews were to leave Holland as poor as they had been when they came. Three days earlier the Jewish Council had been informed that the Germans would send "police-controlled labor contingents" of Jewish men and women between sixteen and forty years old to Germany. In a meeting held on June 27, the members of the council had considered resigning in protest, but in the end they decided to cooperate with the Germans in order to save what they could. A week of haggling began in which the Jewish Council tried to obtain exemptions for themselves, their aides, and their families; to improve the transit conditions for those who had to leave; and to reduce the daily quota of deportees.

Aus der Fuenten's Central Office for Jewish Emigration began with the German Jewish refugees. Aus der Fuenten had been notified by Eichmann that the shuttle between Westerbork and Auschwitz was to begin on July 15, and the Central Office for Jewish Emigration marked the fourteenth as the date to load the trains in preparation for the deportation from Westerbork to Auschwitz. Six trains were to take 4,200 Jews from Amsterdam to the transit camp in Drente, whence they were to leave for Poland. Four thousand Jews were called up to register for these transports; most did not respond. A massive dragnet on July 14 caught 500 Jews, who were held as hostages, and the Jewish community was informed that if those who had not responded to the summons for deportation remained obstinate, the 500 would share the fate of the February 1941 hostages. This moral blackmail convinced a number of people: when the first two trains left that night, 962 Jews of the 1,400 who had been called up were on board. The next two trains were not so full: despite the pressure, fewer than half of those summoned presented themselves. Yet registration had risen, and the hostages were released.

During the next twelve months, as transports carried Jews from Amsterdam to Westerbork, and from Westerbork to an "unknown destination" in the East, the Jewish Council concerned itself very little with the fate of those who had left, a bit more with the future of those who, for the moment, remained, and primarily with its own fate. The council's aim was to preserve "the best" for rebuilding the community after the war; it translated into a policy of cooperation. Indeed, the members of the Jewish Council were so convinced of the value to the community of cooperation with the Germans that they beseeched their coreligionists to comply with their directives and enjoined them not to go into hiding. In the end, between twenty thousand and twenty-five thousand Jews hid during the war; of these, fewer than half were caught. Some twenty-one hundred Jews managed to escape to Switzerland despite the extreme difficulties of traversing Belgium and France to get there. And another ten thousand Jews, married to gentiles, survived in Holland.

Between July 1942 and July 1943, when the Jewish community was dismantled, few people resisted the Germans. By the time the spirit of resistance finally spread, it was too late for the Jews. It was not until the end of the summer of 1943 that the resistance movement and the underground press began to expand rapidly. By then 82,000 Jews had been deported, and most of the rest of the 115,000 Jews who were ultimately to be shipped east were already detained in concentration camps such as Vught or the central transit camp at Westerbork.[16]

THE POST-HOLOCAUST ERA

Only 5,450 Jews returned from the camps in 1945; an estimated 2,000 who had survived the war outside the Netherlands were repatriated also. They returned to a country in chaos. Several hundred thousand forced laborers, voluntary workers, prisoners of war, merchant seamen, and other Dutchmen were streaming back into the country. They joined the one million civilians who had been evacuated during the war and were now in search of their homes.[17] Among them were some 10,000 Jews who had survived the war in hiding. With a severe housing shortage, a shattered economy, and serious civil disturbance as tens of thousands of Nazi collaborators were rounded up, the government paid little attention to the Jews. The latter, who numbered approximately 30,000 by 1946 (including those who were partners in mixed marriages and 5,000 surviving German Jews who had arrived as refugees before the war), were not granted special assistance or privileges. To recognize the plight of the Jews as unique was, according to the official position, to continue the German distinction between gentile and Jew. As the minister of interior of the Dutch government-in-exile declared in October 1944, it was the aim of the government to eradicate "as soon as possible, the discriminated position in which the Jews have been put by the occupier."[18]

The problem with this ideology was that it led to another genre of humiliation. The oppression of the Jews by the Germans and their Dutch allies had been different from the abuse others had suffered, and the postwar passion to create parity between gentiles and Jews obscured their special plight. The popular postwar perception of the nation's immediate past was that history had caught up with them; the struggle of their ancestors had been realized in their own time. Holland had faced a supreme test, just as she had three and a half centuries earlier. Many citizens had failed, but the resistance had saved the honor of the Netherlands and had created a new concept of the *Nederlander*. The Jews, however, were found wanting as a group. The common belief was that the Jews had been singled out in the trial but had not resisted. One expression of this view appeared in the 1949 book *De Tyrannie Verdrijven* (Tyranny expelled). The author, Klaas Norel, a resistance fighter and an editor of the underground newspaper *Trouw* (Loyalty), described the deportation of the Jews. "The Jews did not offer resistance against the pogroms," he maintained. "This absence of resistance is no surprise. It was not expected that the Jews, who do not exert themselves when there is no chance of success would fight. . . . The Jews may not be heroes, but they are certainly cunning. . . . Only when the Nazis reached out their claws towards their capital and goods did the Jews awaken. And then very good: with great craftiness they were able to snatch away uncounted millions from the enemy."[19]

The Jews were not part of this new idea of *Nederlanderschap*. They now were perceived as the Other. Their history was now seen as different from the history of "the Dutch people." In the first years after the war there was a real effort to demolish the *zuilen* structure, which had characterized Dutch society. The experience of common suffering and common resistance had brought Catholics and Protestants, liberals and socialists, together. But the Jews did not share this common bond, and they, the outsiders, were accused of having a sense of exclusive community. As one observer complained, "The Jews have a very strong mutual bond—which is laudable, by the way—which brings them to use their energy and influence to help them achieve positions they want; the result of this is the disproportionate representation of the Jewish element." The Jews' behavior, the critic argued, should be countered with a *numerus clausus,* restricting the participation of Jews in the economy and public institutions to their representative percentage in the population. "It is possible that there will be Jews who will consider themselves hurt by this, but such feelings are not justified. It is up to them to prove that we have worried ourselves without any real reason."[20]

In his 1946 book, *Onze Joden en Duitschland's Greep naar de Wereldmacht* (Our Jews and Germany's bid for world power), H. W. J. Sannes described the generally prevalent feeling very well. Most people realized intellectually that the Nazis' racial theories were nonsense and that the Jews were not the great antagonists of the Aryans, as the Germans had claimed. Yet reason was not enough because, as he confessed, "I have my personal experiences with cunning, immodest, impertinent, greedy and fraudulent Jews and this experience cannot be gainsaid. Even if I am not able to describe exactly what I have against them, they are in any case repugnant to me. What happened during the Occupation is revolting, but it is still good that we have got rid of them. This is what one hears in Holland."[21]

Sannes had sympathy for the Jews, and at the end of his book he welcomed them back, emphasizing that he hoped they would be able to rebuild their lives—as Dutchmen. "I feel myself a friend of the Jews. Not because they are Jews, *but because they are Dutchmen* and because they have shown themselves in the past to be good patriots. Their faith is of no interest to me. Their race is as little significant to me as that of an Aryan. Among the good things that I wish for our Jews who have returned, is first: *that they will feel themselves to be Dutch.*"[22]

The only way Jews could participate in the popular postwar conception of Dutch society was to demonstrate their gratitude to the resistance. Blind to the Jews' own resistance to the German murder machinery, gentile Dutchmen demanded grateful acknowledgment from the surviving Jews. In an article that expressed a common sentiment, the resistance newspaper *De Patriot* observed (July 2, 1945) that "all the Jews who were in hiding who emerge again have the noble, principled and consistently Christian feeling of the Dutch population to thank for their lives." Risking everything, Christians had protected Jews on humanitarian grounds. "The emerging Jews may thank God for that help, and must feel themselves to be very small indeed. Perhaps much better people [than they] were killed on their behalf. And those who now come out of hiding should consider also that there is much to repay. Many people encountered difficulties because of the help given to Jews." In conclusion *De Patriot* claimed, "There is no doubt that the Jews, because of the German persecution, enjoyed great sympathy from the Dutch population. Now the Jews must refrain from excessive behavior, they must think constantly how grateful they ought to be, and they must express that gratitude first of all to make good what must be made good to those who have become victims because of the Jews."[23]

Given homecoming messages of this sort, it is not surprising that the first major monument relating to the Holocaust was erected by the survivors to honor those who had helped them. It was the first major war monument erected in Amsterdam. Designed by Job Wertheim, who had survived the war in Theresienstadt, the monument is a wall with five reliefs moving from the Jewish periphery ("Resignation") to a Christian center ("Defense," "Protection," "Resistance") and back to the Jewish periphery ("Mourning"). The texts below the allegorical figures read: "Resigned in God's Will," "United with you in Defense," "Protected by your Love," "Strengthened by your Resistance," and "Mourning with you."[24] The dedication speech of the monument committee chairman, on February 22, 1950, reflected the prevailing ideology. We must not forget, he said, "what non-Jews, at risk to their own lives, have done for us. . . . The remaining 20,000 Jews have that to thank for their salvation. With fervent compassion we remember the more than 100,000 Jews who could find no help. With even more gratitude have we, the survivors, dedicated this monument, to which also the smallest and the poorest have contributed."[25] In his acceptance speech the mayor of Amsterdam proudly expatiated on the activities of the Dutch citizenry on behalf of the Jews. The fact that not everyone had resisted the Germans' orders warranted but a single remark. The monument was not meant to be a reminder of that shame; rather, it was intended to encourage future generations to choose justice over injustice, resistance against suppression. It was, in other words, a command to remain faithful to one's *Nederlanderschap:* to face the oppressor and to act against him. It was a question of choice, and neither the monument committee chairman nor the mayor recognized that Jews also had faced an extreme challenge and that they also had made courageous and righteous choices. The victims had no place in the ideology of the monuments, which invoked Calvinist imagery and depended on Christian phraseology.

As Jews, the survivors had no place at all. It was their task to re-create a material and moral universe in which they could live once again. Among the first of the very practical problems they faced were the administrative struggles and legal battles to regain their possessions. The financial loss to the Dutch Jewish community was 650–700 million guilders, and the survivors attempted to recover their share of this sum. The entire German-imposed structure, which had legitimized every aspect of their material ruin (real estate, stocks and bonds, inheritances, bank account holdings, insurance policies, etc.), had to be dismantled, and the survivors struggled through this web to reclaim what had been theirs. It pitted them against their fellow countrymen; for years they fought with the stock exchange officials, the insurance companies, and the bank presidents. It took a very long time; most of the claims were settled in the early 1950s, but some cases still had not come to closure more than twenty years after the war ended.[26]

The survivors' loss was overwhelming. They had, of course, lost their property, their businesses, their resources, and their security. They had also lost their families. And so there was a succession of legal battles to obtain guardianship of the approximately 1,450 Jewish children who had survived the war in hiding with Christian families and had no relatives left when the war was over.[27]

Finally, the survivors confronted the moral dilemmas posed by the behavior of the Jewish community leaders during the Occupation. It was a complicated issue. Many felt that the destruction of the Dutch Jews was solely the responsibility of the Germans, and they did not want to judge those Jews who, as members or employees of the Jewish Council or as members of the staff at Westerbork, had collaborated with the Germans. Others believed that no one had the moral right to judge, especially as virtually all the survivors had, for a time, accepted the Jewish Council and its policies. Still others feared that an investigation of Jews by Jews would be a gift to anti-Semites. The overwhelming sentiment, however, was the sense of complete desolation and despair: the proceedings would not bring back the dead, and those who survived needed to focus their attention and concentrate their energy on rebuilding their lives.[28]

Despite these deep reservations, a Jewish Council of Honor was established. The first meeting, on December 15, 1946, initiated a very painful period for the Jewish community. The council was to judge only those whom the Nazis had defined as Jews, including half-Jews and quarter-Jews who were born to gentile mothers. It was decided that neither the establishment of the Jewish Council nor membership on it was in itself problematic, so long as one had not participated for personal gain. Similarly, simply to have carried out German orders gave no cause for criticism. But those who had retained their positions after August 15, 1942, when it was obvious that the Jewish Council had become a tool to liquidate the Dutch Jewish community, were to explain their actions. After a year of excruciating hearings, the Council of Honor ruled to exclude Abraham Asscher and David Cohen from any public office in the Jewish community for the rest of their lives. This had no practical significance, as Asscher already had given up his membership in the very community he had tried to serve and Cohen voluntarily had renounced all future positions. As Hans Knoop observed in his study of the Jewish Council, the Council of Honor had not addressed the central weakness of Asscher and Cohen. The tragedy was that they had adapted and adjusted rather than reacted and resisted. They had been philanthropists before the war, and they had carried out their business on the council as if they still had no greater responsibility than to continue to be philanthropists. But philanthropy was not what was needed from the leaders of a community destined for death.

> They issued the deportation notices and urged the Jews in *Het Joodsche Weekblad* [The Jewish Weekly] to obey these summons to the letter. But they found another task to do—or did they consider it to be their primary one?—to ensure that those who left for Auschwitz traveled with at least one extra pair of socks. Cohen declared after the war that "thanks to our efforts no Jew suffered from hunger in occupied Holland." That is the case. But thanks to Asscher and Cohen the deportation of the Jews in the Netherlands achieved a greater measure of perfection and efficiency than anywhere else in occupied Europe.[29]

The attempts of the survivors to reconstruct their individual and communal lives occurred within a radically changed demographic situation. The Portuguese community had been reduced to a few families, who continued to worship in the enormous Portuguese Synagogue in Amsterdam. In Amsterdam there were enough surviving members of the *Nederlandse Israelietische* community to reestablish a shul, although the proud historic center at the Jonas Daniel Meijerplein had to be abandoned, as the Germans had reduced it to a ruin. In a few of the other large cities communities reestablished themselves, albeit on a very modest scale. In the provinces there simply were not enough survivors for viable communities. In many towns only a few Jewish families had returned, and there were neither the financial nor the human resources to maintain a synagogue. The only two groups that increased significantly were the Liberal community, which had been introduced just before the war by Jewish refugees from Germany, and the Zionists. Under the charismatic leadership of Rabbi Jacob Soetendorp, the previously marginal Liberal community grew to equal the Orthodox, building a large new synagogue in Amsterdam and restoring for its own use the gorgeous baroque Portuguese synagogue in The Hague. The Zionists also enjoyed a new popularity. The experience of the war in Europe, the very different War of Independence in Palestine, and the subsequent establishment of the state of Israel and the continued anti-Semitism at home invigorated the movement.

By the end of the 1940s the anti-Semitism of the immediate postwar period had disappeared and the Netherlands had established excellent relations with Israel; in 1948 it was the first country to establish an embassy in Jerusalem. The economic condition of the Jewish community stabilized, and from a financial point of view the relative situation of the average Jewish family improved significantly. Largely proletariat before the war, the Jewish community that emerged in the early 1950s was largely middle and upper middle class. This was due, in part, to reparation settlements, but it was also due to the fact that the survival rate of professional and wealthier Jews had been higher than that of the proletariat. (This had little to do with the Jewish Council's policy to preserve "the best" and much more to do with the ability of those who had not been ruined completely by 1942 to contribute financially to their own salvation.) Surviving Jews began to be increasingly visible in society, but it was clear that they were not part of an energetic or dynamic community.

In fact, the number of Jews had declined from around 30,000 in 1946 to roughly 26,500 a decade later. Emigration to the United States (1,399), Israel (1,209), Canada (440), and Australia (286), and the combined effect of a very low birth rate and a high death rate accounted for this decrease. The population has remained stable since then, and in some of the smaller cities synagogues have begun to function once again, but the Jewish community of the 1990s, much smaller and at least as fragmented as it was before the war, has a limited future.

That the Jews were marginal after the war was manifested in the social life of the nation and in the Dutch self-image, especially with regard to the years under occupation. We have seen how the ideology of the first monument to commemorate the destruction of the Dutch Jews honored the resisters and ignored the victims. It was the former who deserved the monuments, who deserved their place in history. Throughout the 1950s and early 1960s the history of the war was seen as a battle between German suppression and Dutch resistance.[30] This perception of the past was expressed again and again, in print as well as in stone.

The first important scholarship about the war years was a four-volume work published between 1949 and 1954. The title, *Onderdrukking en Verzet* (Suppression and resistance), brackets the popular paradigm and is the central theme of all the articles. In the foreword the editors wrote that the two words "suppression" and "resistance" signified a duality. "Yes, because from the moment that the best of our people were awakened and readied themselves for this task, one could not think of the one without the other. Tyranny and terror were pitted against the imprisoned spirit of Liberty, a magnificent struggle, which in the end brought to the ever-growing legion the 'V' of Victory."[31] Collaborators did not figure in this text. As the editors made clear, those who had placed themselves outside the community had also placed themselves outside the history as understood in *Onderdrukking en Verzet*.

The third volume of the series, published in 1950, included Abel J. Herzberg's "Kroniek der Jodenvervolging, 1940–1945," the first systematic chronicle of the destruction of the Jews. This work, which was to be republished in 1955, 1978, and 1985, applied the dominant perspective to the Holocaust. "The persecution of the Jews in the Netherlands, even if it happened on Dutch soil, is not properly Dutch history," Herzberg maintained. "It did not arise from Dutch circumstances. One can even say with certainty that it could not have arisen from it. The *resistance* against the persecution of the Jews has been a Dutch affair."[32]

The statue of the dockworker (1952) and the official Dutch memorial to the war years, the National Monument (1956), were merely official expressions of this interpretation of the war years. Collaboration had not occurred; the tragedy the Jews had endured was not recognized. For the chairman of the National Monument Committee, Dr. M. L. van Holthe tot Echten, "war dead" meant those of the resistance who had fallen in battle. "All the dead from that time of terror, whose names are engraved in our hearts, considered their lives less than their yearning for freedom," he declared in his dedication speech.[33] "Resistance" signified male combatants, not the women of the underground networks, and certainly not Jewish resistance.[34]

Despite the films and photographs of the slave labor and death camps, the tangible aide-mémoire of returning Jews as well as the intangible reminder of the memory of Jewish life in the Netherlands, the publication of Anne Frank's diary in 1947, and the establishment of the foundation named after her in 1957, the fate of the Dutch Jews remained of marginal interest. Indeed, Anne Frank, who has come to be seen as paradigmatic of the Jews in the Netherlands, was almost forgotten by the early 1950s; she became of interest again only as her fame grew abroad. Her hiding address, 263 Prinsengracht, was of little importance within the historic geography of Amsterdam until the 1960s, after the first monument to honor Jews was erected in 1962. That memorial was constructed in the Hollandsche Schouwburg, a theater in the former Jewish quarter of Amsterdam, which had served as a collection point for the deportation of the Jews between July 1942 and the late summer of 1943. The monument was dedicated in the ruins of the theater's stage, from which the names of those who were to be transported had been called during the war. The auditorium, where the waiting, incarcerated Jews lived in extremely crowded conditions, has been pulled down and replaced by a memorial garden. Yet the facade still stands, symbolic of the fate of the Jewish community after the war. It is a haunted, painful place, a place of doom that, unlike the Anne Frank House, so full of hope and life, never became an important site in Amsterdam. Even its dedication was attended by only a small gathering.[35]

History, however, was closing in on the Netherlands. The received version of the past that had worked so well for a decade and a half began to fall apart. Time, the opportunity for reflection, the advent of prosperity, the well-reported Eichmann trial in Jerusalem, and the debates about what to do with the war criminals imprisoned in the Netherlands led to a reinterpretation of history. In Louis de Jong's television series *Bezetting* (Occupation) the issue of the Jews finally was raised, albeit in a limited context. The twenty-one episodes, aired between 1960 and 1965, became a national event. People who did not have a television went to those who did. The streets were empty.

Like its predecessors, *Bezetting* was a black-and-white vision, with occupiers and resisters, villains and heroes. The great mass of people who accommodated were left out, and everyone could identify with the heroes. But de Jong specifically included the persecution of the Jews. He did not bridge the question of responsibility. According to him, the mass murder of the Jews could not be stopped because no one could imagine it; but for the first time the cataclysm of the Holocaust was addressed. "I feel a great need to speak some words to you as an introduction to what follows," de Jong said in the episode chronicling the early stages of the Shoah in Holland.

As the result of the persecution of the Jews more than 100,000 of our fellow citizens were killed—men, women and children. I do not only want merely to mention these human losses—I want especially to point out that these losses occurred not as the result of a sudden explosion of a bomb, not as the result of death in military battle, but because all these struggling people were caught in the wheels of a merciless machine of destruction that, especially in the years 1942 and 1943, operated right through our own society. Young people who did not live through this period of fathomless horror ask us older people questions, often questions of conscience, which always converge on this one: How could this happen? It is a question with many answers. One of the answers is—and that I want to mention specifically first— that the imagination of most people (Jews and non-Jews) was unable to grasp in time that the National Socialists literally meant what they said when they spoke about the destruction of the Jews.[36]

Nearly twenty years after the end of the war, the murder of the Dutch Jews had become a central event in Dutch history. If Willy Lages, head of the SD in Amsterdam; Ferdinand aus der Fuenten, head of the Central Office for Jewish Emigration and as such responsible for the roundups of Jews; Franz Fischer, nicknamed "Judenfischer" (Jewfisher), who worked for the SD in The Hague and who was responsible for the deportation of thirteen thousand Jews from that city; and Joseph Kotaella, a guard from the concentration camp in Amersfoort, were not released in the early 1960s from prison in the Netherlands, they have de Jong to thank.

De Jong had written the Jews into the history of the Netherlands during the war. In his work these citizens who had been specially identified, segregated, isolated, and murdered were members of Dutch society. The disaster that had befallen them was part of the occupation of the nation. It was the historian Jacob Presser, however, who questioned the paradigm of suppression versus resistance, shaped the problem of responsibility, and, as we shall see, precipitated the recognition of the dull gray of everyday collusion. In 1950 Presser was commissioned by the Rijksinstituut voor Oorlogsdocumentatie (State War Documentation Institute), or RIOD, headed by Louis de Jong, to write the history of the Jews during the Occupation. "We hesitated for a long time before we invited him to write *Ondergang* [Destruction]," de Jong explained later. "I knew what it would unlock. And that happened. He suffered when he wrote the book. But we allowed him to work at his own pace, for ten years. When it was finished [my colleague] Sijes and I had great objections. We objected to the whole work, to the scholarly approach, the method, and the division." One of the main problems was that as Presser began his narrative with the invasion of the Netherlands on May 10, 1940, he failed to include a historical background. Furthermore, Presser did not distinguish between the different phases of the persecution, and he treated the persecutors as a homogeneous group. In short, for him the five-year oppression was a storm that had beaten the Jews senselessly, and the book was written from the victims' perspective alone. According to de Jong, "Long conversations followed. At the end Presser said that he shared our criticism, and that he wanted to think it over again. He took the manuscript with him, but after a week he returned with the statement, 'I'm sorry, you are right, but I have no energy left to change it. This is the way it must be published.'"[37]

Whatever de Jong's criticisms, Presser's *Ondergang* swept the country. His was the voice of lost neighbors, brothers, sisters, parents. "As I became more involved with the subject," Presser explained in the introduction,

> an understanding grew slowly of a special moral obligation, which I prefer to describe, carefully circumventing great words, as the calling to be the voice of those who, fated to an eternal silence, would be heard only here and now, only for this one time. One time more on earth will their lamentation, their accusation, resound.

Nothing was left of their most pitiful possessions in their last hours; their ashes were scattered in the winds. They had no one in the world other than the historian who could hand down their message. I believe that I should not hesitate to call this a holy duty, a duty that I tried to fulfil as far as my powers allowed me to do so.[38]

His story was of their death.

This book concerns the history of a murder. A murder, indeed a mass murder, on a scale never known before, with malice aforethought and committed in cold blood. The murderers were Germans; the murdered, Jews—in the Netherlands roughly a hundred thousand, fewer than 2 percent of the total number of victims the Germans made with their *Endloesung der Judenfrage.* In a process in which they were put outside the law and isolated, the Jews who lived in this country were robbed of all their possessions, deported, and killed in a scientifically systematic, technically almost flawless style. Town dwellers and country folk, the pious and the freethinkers, the healthy and the sick, the old and the young, families and single people, Dutchmen and foreigners: men, women, and children. Without haste, well thought out, registered, and following the proper formalities. Often the murderers were thugs and illiterates, but often, too, educated men and intellectuals with an ineradicable love of literature, the visual arts, and music; many were caring fathers, not without *Gemuet;* almost all of them celebrated Christmas, after which they continued their job: the murder of countless men, women, and children, defenseless people, fellow people.[39]

From the very beginning *Ondergang* was seen as a monument, or testament. "The war is over, the liberation remembered, and there will be much joy, even perhaps at our war memorials. Only one thing is still missing: a memorial for the Jews who succumbed almost defenseless,"[40] the influential *Algemeen Handelsblad* (General Business Journal) observed. The politician Han Lammers urged that the book be subsidized so that anyone could afford to buy it; only thus would it be possible to "make the monument that Presser's book is into a National Monument."[41]

There was no doubt that Presser's work was—and was accepted as—a monument. But was it a monument to the Dutch Jews or to Dutch failure? *Ondergang* was a tremendous achievement, but its great value and its unique genius was that in reaction to it people, ordinary citizens, began to question their own role and perhaps even their own culpability. An editorial in the newspaper *Trouw* began to question the attitude of the Dutch gentiles during the war. It noted that many had felt pity but few had resisted; that all had signed statements that they were not Jews. The civil servants had remained at their posts, and a part of the Dutch police had aided and abetted the Germans at the roundups of Jews; at least one of the Germans responsible for the implementation of the Final Solution in the Netherlands (Lages) had praised the Dutch for the way they had supported him and helped him reach his goal.[42]

So strong was the Dutch identification with *Ondergang* that a debate followed over whether Presser had been the right person to write the book. The argument was that this calamity was part of Dutch history and should not be relegated to the victims alone. A long letter in the authoritative *Nieuwe Rotterdamse Courant* (New Rotterdam Courant) by a certain J. S. Wijne asserted that Presser should not have written the book, since he was emotionally too close to the events he described: someone who had some distance from the subject should have written the history. "This is especially important as it concerns Jewish Dutchmen," the writer continued. "It happens that those who were persecuted and destroyed were not Dutch Jews but Jewish Dutchmen. And this concerns every Dutchman. That is the reason why the task of writing the history of the destruction of the Jewish Dutchmen should not have been given to a Jewish Dutchman. The danger is that many, especially non-Jewish Dutchmen, will consider *Ondergang* a work of Jewish history and will use that as an excuse to feel that it does not concern them."[43] Many people responded to this letter; the vast majority were of the opinion that only a Jew could have written the book. As one woman, B. Buitenrust Hettema, put it, "A person who did not belong to the victims psychologically could never have written this sober and simultaneously deeply touching, complete indictment. An indictment? A judgment? A requisitory? More honest than Professor Presser, more merciful than this talented historian, with more justice?" And she concluded her letter with an insight shared by many in those days in 1965. "We live. Many of those whom we are about to remember would also live today if we had had a little bit more courage, a little bit more sense of responsibility, a little less cowardice, a little less love of ease."[44]

While the general response to *Ondergang* was shame and guilt, there was also a certain sense of self-satisfaction. The book was the result of a government commission, after all. It was the government that had taken the initiative for a description of its own failure and the failure of its people. This was unique indeed. The Jewish community, by contrast, was far less constricted by guilt and considerably less self-satisfied. *Ondergang* was enormously important to the Dutch Jews, but they could afford sharper criticism. The day the book was published the Jewish weekly *Nieuw Israelietisch Weekblad* (New Israelite Weekly) ran a selection of some seven pages, accompanied by a long editorial. In the following weeks the journal traced the responses to the book, quoting long excerpts from various reviews. Avid as interest was, the book's focus on the victims alone raised serious questions for the survivors about their own place in history. In a radio broadcast the Jewish historian Jaap Meijer criticized the title, *Ondergang,* because it implied the total destruction of Dutch Jewry. Where were the survivors? Presser's silence about postwar Jewish history was, Meijer remarked, a symptom of his failure to situate his argument within the context of Dutch Jewish history as a whole.[45]

While the Dutch gentiles were busy with guilt and pride, and the surviving Jews wondered about their historical role, the scholarly community was caught between a concept of professional detachment and a prevailing standard of political correctness. The historian Herman von der Dunk, for example, wrote a fair and sober assessment of Presser's achievement and failure for a prominent Dutch historical journal. Von der Dunk criticized the emotional element in the book, which had so touched the nation. "It is a writing of history that not only emerges from emotion but also cultivates that emotion, and it is not appropriate today. It is as if Presser himself still cannot believe what has happened and assumes that his readers also must share that disbelief." Presser had not tried to write history, but to commemorate. Yet, as von der Dunk concluded, "to commemorate, to commemorate personally, and to write history are two different things."[46] Reasonable as this review was, the editors of the journal rejected it because it lacked the desired reverence for *Ondergang*.

The political consequences of *Ondergang* were immediate and practical as well as long-term and ideological. When war erupted in the Middle East on June 5, 1967, the government and the general population championed the Israelis. The leader of the Social Democratic Party, Joop den Uyl, declared in Parliament that "Holland is party to the conflict, Holland ought to be party and ought to manifest that."[47] As a result, the Dutch state organized a program of financial support of Israel, and it invited all civil servants to donate 0.5 percent of their income to the beleaguered nation for three months. It was the Dutch form of war reparations, or *Wiedergutmachung*.[48]

The Dutch had come to a new understanding of their society and their history.[49] And it was with the realization that Holland had emerged from the war essentially unchanged—that the great revolution had not occurred—that the old order began to crack. In the mid-1960s a generation came of age that had been born during or just after the war. They had been raised with stories of the Occupation in which resistance was considered the norm. But current scholarship showed that very few had been active in the resistance. In the eyes of many young people, the older generation had failed and their structures were obsolete. It was up to them, the younger generation felt, to take up the tradition of resistance, but it now became a resistance against the society they had inherited. They identified government authority with the oppression of the Occupation, and the resistance with the so-called New Left movement or with the more radical, anarchistic "provos" (provocateurs). It was no accident that one of the leaders of the New Left movement was among the first to review Presser's book. Han Lammers summarized its significance: "The fairy tale is finished, the fable of the small Holland that acted so well towards its Jews. . . . To preserve the myth that Holland 'did so well' is in fact to aid a falsification of history."[50]

The role of Presser's book in this political development was explicated by Evert Werkman in the newspaper *Het Parool* (The Password), a former underground publication: "*Ondergang* is a book that no one can finish without getting the feeling that he has lived, and perhaps still lives, in a crazy world, because it is in *this, our society* that this could happen."[51] The essence of this insanity, Werkman argued, was to be found in the small chapter on the Jewish children, the contemporaries of the provo generation. Presser summarized their history in a few sentences. "They wore the star and went into the gas chamber. Many, many thousands of children, in one long night of Herod. A number survived in hiding and a few even came back from elsewhere, where some of them had seen everything, including cannibalism. And as a matter of fact, those children went back to the school benches, just as before. That is, more or less, more or less."[52] The children had been powerless; no one had spoken up for them. They were symbolic of others without power: the poor, the working class.

One of the reasons that Presser's book made such an impact on the reform movement was its explicit thesis that the intellectuals and the rich, who had controlled the Jewish Council, had sacrificed the "little people" in order "to prevent worse." In *Ondergang* Presser reported a joke he had heard during the war. "When Asscher and Cohen [the two co-chairmen of the Jewish Council] were the only Jews left, and the Germans demanded the deportation of one of them, then Cohen would say to his fellow-chairman: 'Go now, Bram, to prevent worse—in the interest of the Jewish community.'" As Presser explained, the principle of the joke guided the Jewish Council until the end. "Even in May 1943, when the Jewish Council was ordered to select 7,000 people for deportation, the cup was not yet full, and the Council tried to preserve 'the best.' The best meant the intelligentsia and the well-to-do, . . . for the salvation of this dwindling group they sacrificed an ever larger group of lesser people and those who were not the best. The orange sellers for the sake of the caste of the rich and the scholars, for the sake of those like the chairmen themselves."[53]

For the New Left, the Jewish Council became a symbol of Dutch society and everything wrong with it. Presser's book also provided a hero, however, who served as an example to the provo movement. Friedrich Weinreb was a shadowy person whose cause the radicals championed in the complicated Weinreb Affair, as it came to be called, which held the public's attention throughout the late 1960s.[54] Weinreb was a Dutch Jew of Galician origin. He was just one of the many victims of Nazism, and he was especially badly treated by the SD. He became famous because of a kind of game he appears to have played with the Germans that allowed him and perhaps a few others to survive the war. At the command of a nonexistent "General von Schumann," Weinreb created a list of Jews who were to be allowed to emigrate. Hundreds of people desperately sought to be registered. In September 1942 the SD heard of the list and arrested Weinreb. Although they knew that the list was non-sense, they believed that it was the product of some Army officers who had duped Weinreb to gain access to Jewish property. The SD released Weinreb as bait and allowed him to continue his work, now under surveillance. In January 1943 the SD realized that there were no German officers behind it, that it had been Weinreb's invention all along, and they arrested him and sent him to Westerbork. All the Jews on the list were deported to the East. The game was over, or so it seemed at the time. In June 1943 Weinreb, who had not yet been deported, was brought back to The Hague. One of the SD officers had decided to revive the list to do precisely what they had suspected the Army officers of doing: to gain access to hidden Jewish property. Weinreb became bait once again, this time to catch not German officers but Jewish property and Jewish people in hiding. A number of Jews in Westerbork profited from this second game because they got a stay of deportation while, unbeknownst to them, the Germans searched for property they were believed to own. When the SD tired of this in February 1944, Weinreb and his family went into hiding. They survived the war.

After the war some Jews believed that they owed their survival to Weinreb, while others believed that they had been duped by him. There were accusations that he had used the money that people paid to get on his list for his own profit and that, to keep his list alive and his game going, he had betrayed people who helped Jews in hiding because he had to satisfy the SD's desire for action. He was tried in 1947 and 1948 and convicted for having committed espionage in prison and for embezzlement of the money entrusted to him by the people on his list. On November 27, 1947, he was sentenced to three and a half years of imprisonment. A year later, on October 25, 1948, a special council increased the sentence to six years, but on December 11 he was freed in an amnesty in honor of the fifty-year jubilee of Queen Wilhelmina's reign.

Herzberg had discussed the Weinreb case in his *Kroniek der Jodenvervolging*. He believed that Weinreb had practiced deceit but that he nevertheless had saved some people. In his analysis of the judgment against Weinreb he remarked, "If I have understood everything well, then the accused Weinreb was reproached not for his poker game and not for his reckless ante and not for the committed deceit but for his flight from the consequences, when it touched his own life, a flight to which he has not admitted. It is as if the judge wants to say: 'He who wants to play poker in history, must bring his own life as his stake. He who does not dare to do that, must remain at home.' A judge can hardly give another judgment. But the unanswered question is, what is more courageous: to play poker or to stay at home? To escape the consequences which may arise in certain situations, or to escape the situations, because one may have to face consequences?"[55]

Presser did not agree with Herzberg's measured judgment. For him Weinreb was an ingenious helper, a savior of many Jews, a kind of counterproof to the accusation that the Jews had allowed themselves to be slaughtered by the Germans without any resistance.[56] As so often happens in history, the Jewish hero had been turned into a villain by the gentiles. According to Presser, Weinreb's conviction had been an attempt by Dutch society (or, better, the Dutch establishment) to elude its own passivity. "The Jew Weinreb has become the scapegoat; he has paid for the failure of countless non-Jews. He must have failed, as they had failed, *because* they had failed. Just as they had not done their duty, neither had he. If there were no Jewish traitors, it was necessary to invent them. The few who came to trial after the war were insignificant. Now here was one of a stature that sufficed."[57] Based on Weinreb's own stories and a rather careless investigation of the trials of 1947 and 1948, Presser's judgment was precipitous, and he did not include his discussion of the Weinreb case in the English edition of *Ondergang*. But that did not matter in 1965. Two prominent journalists linked to the New Left movement, Renate Rubinstein and Aad Nuis, began a campaign to rehabilitate Weinreb. They found him in Switzerland and persuaded him to write his memoirs, which appeared under the title *Collaboratie en Verzet, 1940–1945: Een Poging tot ontmythologisering* (Collaboration and resistance, 1940–1945: An attempt at demystification) in three fat volumes in 1969.[58] Describing himself as a combatant against the establishment who had challenged the bureaucracy and the rules of society, Weinreb depicted himself as the sole precursor of the provo movement. It was a pleasing portrait, and many people were convinced that if everyone had been like Weinreb, no Jews would have been deported. Weinreb, in short, became the patron saint of a new kind of Holland. By the end of the 1960s the old resistance fighters, whose organizations were firmly entrenched in the center right of the political spectrum, were identified with the establishment. An alternative vision of resistance was required, and Weinreb provided it. He came to be seen as a new incarnation of that old Dutch hero Tijl Uilenspiegel, a "point of light of imaginative intelligence . . . in a country of burghers and barbarians."[59]

The whole country began to discuss the case. Champions of both sides wrote articles and pamphlets. There were public meetings and forums to discuss the issue. Weinreb's book was selected to receive the prestigious prose award of the city of Amsterdam in 1970, but the city unprecedentedly rejected the jury's decision and the award was withheld. A television program about Weinreb's theological vision (he had acquired a reputation as a cabalist) was scheduled, withdrawn at the last moment in response to many protests by members of the anti-Weinreb faction, and rescheduled after protests by members of the pro-Weinreb faction. Many people considered it the Dutch Dreyfus case. One of the most prominent Dutch authors, Willem Frederik Hermans, attacked Weinreb and his supporters fiercely in his sarcastic but masterfully written *Van Wittgenstein tot Weinreb* (From Wittgenstein to Weinreb [1970]).[60]

Although Weinreb was at the center of the dispute, the Holocaust was the context of the debate. It was the genocide of the Jews that framed this singularly important attempt by the Dutch to define what a good *Nederlander* ought to be. The answer to which they had come, the new public awareness of the dull gray of everyday collusion, informed the next affair to seize Dutch interest. As the Weinreb case waned, the next episode in the affair of the Four of Breda, the German war criminals in Breda prison in the Netherlands, began to unfold. Willy Lages was released in 1966 because he was said to be dying; he lived comfortably for another five years. This left the Three of Breda, and in 1969 the New Left pressed for their release, which the Right opposed. By 1969, however, the Jews had a voice, and they participated in the public debate. "Soon you will organize a hearing, but 120,000 Dutch Jews cannot be heard anymore," the author Meijer Sluyser reminded the minister of justice. "Invisible, they will be present in the room where you seek counsel and will have to take your decision—witnesses, Jews, like you and me, flesh of our flesh, blood of our blood, mind of our mind."[61] Ironically, the urge to release them was a result of the close reading of *Ondergang*. Presser had forced the Dutch to rethink their behavior during the war, and they were left with the question whether they were so different from the Three of Breda. The left-wing *Vrij Nederland* (which had supported Weinreb) argued for their release. The director of the Catholic Discharged Prisoners' Aid Society neatly framed the dilemma the Dutch faced. "At the same time as we obstinately insist on the imprisonment of the three war criminals in Breda, we repress our own guilt. We also have been guilty of the deportation of the Jews. I myself was a bit involved in the resistance, but I did not actually help Jews. I blame myself for that, that is no secret. The Germans were not the only ones who committed war crimes. Dutchmen helped to find Jews, to transport them; without the help of Dutchmen it would not have been possible."[62] Despite this equation, the three were not released. "Mercy for the victims," as the *Haarlems Dagblad* (Haarlem Daily) called it, prevailed.[63]

The primary victims of the German occupation had become central in the nation's history and memory of the war years. A quarter of a century after Liberation, in the Twenty-Five-Year Jubilee commemorations (1970), the fate of the Jews was the focus of remembrance. It was Presser who had forced the nation to recognize what they formerly had relegated to obscurity, and he was invited to give the keynote speech in the May 5 ceremony in the Lawrence Church in Rotterdam (which had been destroyed in 1940 and only recently rebuilt) in the presence of the Royal House, the government, and other dignitaries. His address was to be aired on national television and radio. A month before the event, however, Presser was hospitalized with stomach cancer. He died on April 30 of complications pursuant to a major operation. His last words were reported to have been "5 May." On the eve of Liberation Day, the national day of commemoration of the war dead (May 4), his body was cremated. A few months later he himself was commemorated in a special session of the Dutch Academy, to which he had been elected as the result of *Ondergang*. De Jong delivered the eulogy. "In *Ondergang*," he said, "[Presser] drowned himself in waves of bewilderment, confronted as he was with a process of massive destruction that he perceived to be completely irrational, absolutely meaningless, and, in essence, beyond comprehension. Whoever dares to speak here about a failure ought to keep in mind that Presser's inability to transcend this most personal grief and his failure to represent that which cannot be represented reveal the sensitive and vulnerable human being Presser was."[64]

Presser's work had fundamentally affected the Dutch memory and remembrance of the war. Shortly after his death the long-overdue monument in Westerbork was unveiled.[65] More than a hundred thousand Jews had been deported to the East from Westerbork, and there had not been a single attempt to blow up the railroad tracks. But gentiles often stood along the crossings and waved to the passing trains. It was a gesture, Louis de Jong wrote, that touched the deportees deeply.

By 1970 Westerbork had become the site of a row of enormous radiotelescopes, for the same reason that it had been a convenient spot for a transit camp: it is the most remote spot in the Netherlands, far away from radio interference and removed from society. The monument is the last bit of track. On one side is the buffer stop, and on the other the ends of the track are turned to the heavens, imitating the gesture of the telescopes. The poet Wim Ramaker visited Westerbork and wrote about the experience.

> Who dares to raise his voice here?
> Departure point of a whole people:
> with known destination left for Auschwitz,
> Sobibor, Theresienstadt, Bergen-Belsen, Kosel . . .
>
> And nobody saved them
> To be sure there was much waving when they passed by
> A gesture that always touched the deported deeply
> but nobody shifted the point to life,
> or changed the track

Scores of trains have left from here,
according to schedule
often Tuesdays,
exactly on time,
because no one was allowed to die too late

Stand for a moment . . .
now the point of departure and arrival have almost caught up with
each other
Here left a whole people:
more than one hundred and two thousand Jewish fellow citizens,
children, mothers, fathers,
fathers, mothers, children
and also babies and those old of days
were gassed, shot, burned alive,
beaten to death, hanged
while we waved

At last the rails are shifted
of sadness twisted
and at the place where they were readied for their journey
stand telescopes
to amplify their silent whispering in the universe
and to wave again
when they wave.[66]

That the war years were a period of exceptional importance to the Dutch and in their history is reflected in their monuments, the context of the numerous public "affairs" that gripped their attention, and their reception first of de Jong's televised series, then of Presser's *Ondergang,* and then, from 1969 through 1988, of de Jong's twelve-part *Het Koninkrijk der Nederlanden in de Tweede Wereldoorlog* (The Kingdom of the Netherlands in the Second World War). Nearly all the parts consist of two six-hundred-page volumes. Printed on special paper reserved for the production of Bibles, it has become something of a bible. There is a scholarly edition with footnotes as well as a popular version without footnotes but otherwise complete.

The enormous size of the work, which is dedicated to a mere five years of Dutch history, and the astonishing sales it commands suggest that this period is of normative significance. It is a caesura in Dutch history, a decisive period that can be neither forgotten nor ignored. The Occupation years were a period of conflict between suppression and resistance, wrong and right, evil and good, and the destruction of the Jews is an important part of that strife.

A fundamental and deeply troubling paradox emerged from this position, however. Although the Occupation years had been an era of struggle between suppression and resistance, wrong and right, evil and good, most people who lived through that time had simply carried on with daily life as usual. Ordinary people followed their ordinary routine as they ordinarily did. Rationing, bombing, and closed borders had inconvenienced them, but the war had not changed them. There was a fundamental continuity between Dutch society before, during, and after the war. It had been a period of normative significance, but few had noticed. The details of this continuity were the focus of a long television production aired on October 15, 1974, that traced the history of the Netherlands between 1938 and 1948, *Vastberaden, maar soepel en met mate* (Resolute, to a Certain Extent, but Flexible). The purpose of this film, inspired by Marcel Ophuls's *Le Chagrin et la Pitié* (The Sorrow and the Pity), which follows the history of Clermont-Ferrand during the Occupation, was to trace, not the highways of Dutch history, but the side streets, that is, the streets where people actually lived.[67] It was not history from above, but the story of those below—of ordinary people.

Vastberaden, maar soepel en met mate differed from *Le Chagrin et la Pitié* in one important aspect. Ophuls's aim had been to demolish the myth that all Frenchmen had been in the resistance. This was no longer necessary in the Netherlands: the idea had been discredited in the mid-1960s. "The myth of the absolutely heroic fatherland that refused to bow under the boot of the tyrant does not live here anymore," one of the filmmakers, H. J. A. Hofland, explained. "This myth is sometimes revived at solemn ceremonies, but on normal days most people are quite able to face the largest part of the truth: that the number of people in the resistance was relatively small, that the Amsterdam streetcar company helped with the deportation of the Jews, that the Dutch train personnel went on strike only in September 1944 and before that had provided many services to the Germans for four long years, that most people did not want to give shelter to the persecuted, that countless people paid for the administrative precision of the state and individual communities with their freedom and their lives, etc." And he concluded, "That people were not so courageous as it appears in our national histories is a fact which crops up again and again automatically. It is more difficult to reveal the continuity within the society."[68]

The prevalent concern to maintain the status quo resulted in daily accommodation and even individual and national collaboration. A striking example revealed in the film was the cooperation of the Dutch authorities with the Germans beginning in September 1944 to ensure that after the German collapse no revolution would occur that would change the structure of society. The most important thing was to maintain order and tranquillity in the period of change. Shown without judgment, "without the interference of a professional moralist, a professional patriot, or a professional historian,"[69] this elucidation of the continuity within Dutch society and of the importance of the ordinary changed Dutch historiography and reeducated the Dutch population.[70]

By the mid-1970s the Dutch had come to an understanding of their individual and national (often silent) collusion and therefore (tacit) collaboration. As a society, they accepted responsibility for their implicit participation in the murder of their fellow Jewish citizens. They understood the Holocaust to be a catastrophe for gentile *Nederlanders* as well as Jewish Dutchmen. In subsequent years the significance of the war, and the lessons Dutch citizens should learn from it and should teach their children, remained part of public discourse. Expressed in films, monuments, books, articles, television productions, and school textbooks, the message that personal behavior was (and is) political action was reiterated again and again.

Jan Wolkers's 1977 monument is an expression of this acceptance of the political significance of private acts. An urn containing ashes of those who had died in Auschwitz had been placed in the Oosterbegraafplaats (East Cemetery) in Amsterdam soon after the war, and it became a custom for mourners to lay flowers there. In January 1977, the thirty-second anniversary of the liberation of Auschwitz, a memorial designed by the Netherlands's most popular author and sculptor was dedicated on that spot. "To make a monument at the site where an urn with the ashes of victims from Auschwitz rests on Dutch soil seems an impossible task," Wolkers explained to the crowd that had gathered for the unveiling. "How can you find a form to commemorate a crime which you feel will not be effaced even when our planet will be dissolved into the universe in two or three thousand centuries? You can beat your brains until they burst to imagine an image which can just begin to represent roughly that shame and that suffering. You look up at the sky and you do not understand how the blue expanse rested over that horror, as untouched and peaceful as over a meadow with flowers. And in a vision of justice you see the blue sky over you crack, as if the horror which happened here on earth below her has violated eternity forever."[71] Wolkers's monument was a two-hundred-square-foot surface of cracked mirrors reflecting the sky. His design—and his address—took the nation one step further: while the annihilation of the Dutch Jews was represented in the Schouwburg monument as a Jewish tragedy and in the Westerbork memorial as a national disaster, in the Oosterbegraafplaats it was seen as a universal cataclysm.

Just how far the popular perception of the war had evolved was clearly seen in the Dutch reaction to the American television series *Holocaust.* Broadcast in Germany in 1978, *Holocaust* had a massive impact. The influential German magazine *Der Spiegel,* which had mocked the series as "gas chambers a la Hollywood" before it was aired, respectfully referred to it as "Holocaust: The Past Returns" a few days later. Learning from the German experience, the Dutch decided to prepare the public, and a whole program was set up to counsel and help people during and after the broadcasts. Schools received information packages, and roundtable discussions by experts and special documentaries to place the series in its historical context were aired. When the series finally was broadcast in 1979, it was an anticlimax, not because the preparation had been so intense (as it transpired, it was unnecessary), but because the questions *Holocaust* engendered had been asked and answered in the Netherlands years earlier.[72]

In Germany the discussion of *Holocaust* centered on the conundrum, How could it have happened? The series marked a moment of revelation. For all the academic study of the "unresolved past" (as the Germans call the Nazi era), it had taken an American television series to affect the public consciousness. It was a very difficult moment for the Germans. The dramatization, which concentrated on the German Jewish family Weiss and the German gentile family Dorf, allowed each German to identify with the Weiss family while simultaneously recognizing themselves in the Dorfs. This paradox gave the series its specific power in the German context. The war, which had been seen in terms of a military-political conflict, was suddenly discovered as a moral issue. The question of culpability, especially that of the responsibility of each individual vis-à-vis his or her neighbors, had not been raised. In the

Netherlands that moment had occurred more than a decade earlier; with Presser's *Ondergang* the paradigm of "suppression and resistance" had been transformed into one of "collective failure." Furthermore, while in Germany the film initiated a debate over the statute of limitations for war crimes, in Holland the affair of the Three of Breda had already raised the problem. The only aspect of the program that excited interest was the one element that had been a secondary Dutch concern throughout their dialogue with the Holocaust since De Jong's *De Bezetting:* Was it in good taste? In an article in the liberal weekly magazine *De Haagse Post* (The Hague Post), the filmmaker H. J. A. Hofland maintained that "it was clear what the answer would be. Anyone who measures with aesthetic norms must consider 'Holocaust' a melodrama with the signature of an American soap opera. In the same way as actors address a hall here as if they actually want to reach a hall beyond, so the Americans have learned to look regularly to a point beyond the horizon, whatever the situation in which they find themselves. That is the hallmark of their tragedy and their pain. You used to see it in Peyton Place . . . and it was also present in *Holocaust.*"[73] Thus the issue at stake was not so much the relationship of the Dutch to their past as it was their relationship to the dominant culture of 1979, that of the United States. The film *Holocaust* was first and foremost American.

Holocaust underscored another lesson, however: it had reinforced and emphasized that the Holocaust becomes meaningful when we can identify with its victims, and with the choices people had to make. The real issue of the 1980s was not the confession of guilt but a genuine attempt to integrate the Holocaust into daily life, as an issue that informs the day-to-day ethics of human life. An obvious example was the application of its lessons to the daily reality of racism. A few days after the last part was broadcast, Rafael Shibboleth, a curator at the Jewish Historical Museum in Amsterdam, remarked that "if people think about what we can do vis-à-vis minorities, then we more or less have reached our goal with the airing of *Holocaust.*" "Each country has its own Jews," Rabbi Sonny Herman added. "Holocaust means that every minority can be persecuted."[74]

This understanding of the Holocaust as an issue that concerns the solidarity of a majority with a persecuted or discriminated-against minority defines the approach to the education about the genocide of the Jews in Dutch schools. The school textbook *Grenzen aan solidariteit* (Limits to solidarity),[75] published in 1990 and adopted for use throughout the Netherlands, pursues the dilemmas of this social ethic. The book is neatly divided into eighteen chapters, half focusing on historical issues and half on ethical questions. In the first part, a short introduction to Judaism, the history of the Jews, and the history of the Jews in the Netherlands are followed by two lessons on anti-Semitism and one on Hitler and the Thousand Year Reich. The last three chapters of the historical section are entitled "From Isolation to Murder," and they delineate the process by which the Jews were segregated and deported to their death. The text then moves to the difficult moral and ethical conundrums raised by the Holocaust. Two chapters focus on the attitude of Dutch gentiles, and two on the attitude of Dutch Jews. Questions about the Jews in the death camps, the perpetrators, whether there are limits to solidarity, whether the Holocaust is unique or one of many genocides, and whether not choosing is also a choice are explored. In *Grenzen aan solidariteit* the issue of the Holocaust begins with the decisions ordinary people make in everyday situations. Treason, suppression, heroism, and resistance are rooted in the problems we must face all the time, even in our own—especially in our own—neighborhoods.

Half a century after the persecution of the Jews began in the Netherlands, how and what the next generation will be taught about the Occupation has emerged as the central issue.[76] No longer looking back with Calvinist, smug self-righteousness or equally Calvinist self-flagellating guilt, the Dutch now identify their responsibility constructively. Their task is to educate. It is this that makes the Dutch response to the Holocaust unique. Like the other European nations, Holland too failed in its responsibility to its Jewish citizens during the Occupation. And after the war was over the Dutch, like other European peoples, reveled in the delusion of a national resistance. What makes the Dutch exceptional is that the same generation that lived through the war caring only about their ordinary concerns came to recognize and accept responsibility for their accommodation, complicity, and collusion.

History and memory frame a commonly accepted social ethic in the increasingly multicultural society of the Netherlands. The primary place of children in this national agenda has led to the juxtaposition of the task the Dutch now face and their treatment of Jewish youngsters fifty years ago. On November 1, 1941, Jewish children were thrown out of all the playgrounds in Amsterdam-Zuid, a neighborhood where some seventeen thousand Jews lived. At the order of the authorities, one of these playgrounds became a Jewish market; the rest were reserved for use by gentile children alone. Just four years later, thirteen thousand of the seventeen thousand Jewish inhabitants had been murdered. In 1986 the people of Amsterdam-Zuid and the local society of market stall owners collected sixty-five thousand guilders to create a monument to that incident. "Remember, so that our children, irrespective of their ancestry, will be able to play together. If we can play with each other as children, we must be able to live together as adults," the text reads.[77] The four-figure statue depicts two gentile children at play and two Jewish children locked out of the playground. It is the counterpart to the dockworker monument. The memorial to those who participated in the February strike against the Germans commemorates a certain form of heroism and resistance. The children's monument, by contrast, illustrates the first step of an oppression that, unstopped, led to mass murder. Acceptance of the German-imposed regulations, accommodation to the Occupation authority, began at home, in the neighborhoods, with children. There is no better place, the Dutch feel, to start anew than with the education of children at home and in the local neighborhood schools.

NOTES

The authors would like to thank Dr. van Galen Last and Dr. Barnouw of the Rijksinstituut voor Oorlogsdocumentatie in Amsterdam for their advice and help. Please note that the authors have used the term "Holocaust" instead of "Judeocide" for consistency of usage in this volume.

1. Statistical information about the situation of the Jews before World War II is largely from Louis

de Jong's monumental standard work on the history of World War II in Holland, *Het Koninkrijk der Nederlanden in de Tweede Wereldoorlog,* 12 vols. ('s-Gravenhage, 1969–88), 5, pt. 1:481ff. See also Joseph Michman, Hartog Beem, and Dan Michman, *Pinkas: Geschiedenis van de Joodsche Gemeenschap in Nederland,* trans. Ruben Verhasselt, ed. Joop Sanders and Edward van Voolen (Amsterdam, 1992).

2. The Calvinist city authorities did not grant a similar privilege to other Protestant denominations or to Roman Catholics. The Lutherans did not obtain permission to build a major church building until twenty years after the completion of the Portuguese Synagogue; the Catholics were obliged to worship in *schuilkerken* (hidden churches) until the end of the eighteenth century.

3. Jaap Meijer, *Hoge Hoeden Lage Standaarden: De Nederlandse Joden Tussen 1933 en 1940* (Baarn, 1969), 35.

4. Fritz Bernstein, *Over Joodsche problematiek* (1935), quoted in Meijer, *Hoge Hoeden Lage Standaarden,* 93–94.

5. Abraham Asscher, quoted in Hans Knoop, *De Joodsche Raad: Het Drama van Abraham Asscher en David Cohen* (Amsterdam, 1983), 22.

6. J. C. H. Blom, *De Muiterij op de Zeven Provincien* (Utrecht, 1975), 27.

7. J. van der Ploeg, *Het Joodsche Vraagstuk: Een Maatschappelijk Probleem* (1940), quoted in Meijer, *Hoge Hoeden Lage Standaarden,* 187.

8. *De Spiegel,* April 8, 1933, quoted in Dienke Hondius, *Terugkeer: Antisemitisme in Nederland rond de bevrijding* (The Hague, 1990), 17.

9. Bob Moore, *Refugees from Nazi Germany in the Netherlands, 1933–1940* (Dordrecht, 1986), 81ff.

10. Dick Houwaart, *Westerbork: Het begon in 1933* (The Hague, 1983), 51.

11. Asscher, quoted in Knoop, *De Joodsche Raad,* 26–27.

12. *Centraal Blad voor Israelieten,* December 28, 1939, quoted in Knoop, *De Joodsche Raad,* 28–29.

13. De Jong, *Het Koninkrijk der Nederlanden,* 5, pt. 1:506.

14. J. C. H. Blom, "De Vervolging van de Joden in Nederland in Internationaal Vergelijkend Perspectief," in *Crisis, Bezetting en Herstel: Tien studies over Nederland, 1930–1950* (The Hague, 1989), 134–50. See also Johannes Houwink ten Cate, "Heydrich's Security Police Forces and Jewish Policy: The Case of Occupied France and Occupied Holland" (paper delivered at RIOD/PONTEG [State War Documentation Institute/National Program in Nineteenth and Twentieth Century History] Congress, "Deportation and Resistance

in [Western] Europe, 1941–1944," Amsterdam, November 23–24, 1992; publication forthcoming).

15. The account of the persecution and deportation of the Dutch Jews is based on de Jong, *Het Koninkrijk der Nederlanden,* and Jacob Presser, *Ondergang: De Vervolging en Verdelging van het Nederlandse Jodendom, 1940–1945,* 2 vols. (The Hague, 1965), published in English as *Ashes in the Wind: The Destruction of Dutch Jewry,* trans. Arnold Pomerans (Detroit, 1988).

16. Guus Meershoek, "The Amsterdam Police and the Deportations," and Peter Romijn, "The Dutch Local Government and the Persecution of the Jews" (papers delivered at RIOD/PONTEG Congress, "Deportation and Resistance in [Western] Europe, 1941–1944," Amsterdam, November 23–24, 1992; publication forthcoming).

17. There were some 430,000 Dutchmen outside the borders who had to be reintegrated in the society, the largest groups among them being 90,000 men pressed into work in Germany in 1944, 250,000 more or less voluntary workers, 10,000 prisoners in concentration camps, 12,000 prisoners of war, 2,000 forced laborers in Norway, and 60,000 men who had served in the Dutch units of the Allied forces or in the Dutch merchant navy or who had been behind Allied lines in Belgium and France. In addition, there were 350,000 Dutchmen who had been in hiding in Holland to escape forced labor in Germany or to escape being picked up by the Gestapo for being known resisters.

18. Quoted in Hondius, *Terugkeer,* 53.

19. Klaas Norel, *De Tyrannie Verdrijven,* quoted in ibid., 92.

20. W. J. Koenig-Soeters, "Ethiek en jodenvraagstuk," *Vrij Nederland,* August 4, 1945, quoted in ibid., 90.

21. H. W. J. Sannes, *Onze Joden en Duitschland's Greep naar de Wereldmacht* (Amsterdam, 1946), 7. Dienke Hondius discusses the problem at length in her study of Dutch anti-Semitism after the war (see *Terugkeer,* 87–104) and confirms earlier discussions of the phenomenon by de Jong (*Het Koninkrijk der Nederlanden,* 12, pt. 1:121ff.) and Presser (*Ondergang,* 2:501, 515f.). Even so cautious a writer as Daniel Schorr, who reported on the postwar situation of the Dutch Jewish community in the *American Jewish Year Book* in 1947, noted that two years after liberation the identity cards carried by Jews were still marked with a *J,* and he acknowledged that Jewish leaders in the Netherlands were troubled by public anti-Semitism ("The Netherlands," *American Jewish Year Book, 1947–1948* [Philadelphia, 1947], 339–40). Indeed, the problem was so public and so acute that a number

of intellectuals in Amsterdam convened a work group to describe and analyze current anti-Semitism. According to Hondius, the group found that the root of the problem was an overblown perception by many Dutchmen of their own role as resisters, while the perceived accommodation of the Jewish Council was considered to be characteristic of Jews (*Terugkeer*, 116–22).

22. Sannes, *Onze Joden*, 299. This message was internalized. For a general discussion of the postwar adaptation of Jewish child survivors, see Debórah Dwork, "My War Began in 1945," *Children With A Star: Jewish Youth in Nazi Europe* (New Haven, Conn., 1991), 253–70.

23. *De Patriot*, July 2, 1945, quoted in Hondius, *Terugkeer*, 96.

24. "Wij spraken met: Joh. Wertheim, beeldhouwer," *Nieuw Israelitisch Weekblad*, February 17, 1950.

25. "Monument van Joodse dankbaarheid te Amsterdam onthuld," *Algemeen Handelsblad*, February 23, 1950.

26. For a comprehensive discussion, see de Jong, *Het Koninkrijk der Nederlanden*, 12, pt. 2:680–708.

27. Elma Verhey, *Om het Joodse Kind* (Amsterdam, 1991); Debórah Dwork, "Custody and Care of Jewish Children after the War: The Case of the Netherlands" (1996, forthcoming). See also Joel Fishman, "The Anneke Beekman Affair and the Dutch News Media," *Jewish Social Studies* 40 (1978), 42–54; idem, "The Ecumenical Challenge of Jewish Survival: Pastor Kalma and Postwar Dutch Society, 1946," *Journal of Ecumenical Studies* 15 (1978), 461–76; idem, "The Jewish Community in Post-War Netherlands, 1944–1975," *Midstream* 22 (1976), 42–54; idem, "Jewish War Orphans in the Netherlands: The Guardianship Issue, 1945–1950," *Wiener Library Bulletin*, n.s. 27, nos. 30–31 (1973–74), 31–36; idem, "The War Orphan Controversy in the Netherlands: Majority-Minority Relations," in *Dutch Jewish History: Proceedings of the Symposium on the History of the Jews in the Netherlands, 1982,* ed. Jozeph Michman (Jerusalem, 1984), 421–32; Jozeph Michman, "The Problem of the Jewish War Orphans in Holland," in *She'erit Hapletah, 1944–1948: Rehabilitation and Political Struggle,* Proceedings of the Fifth Yad Vashem International Conference, 1985 (Jerusalem, 1990), 187–209.

28. See Knoop, *De Joodsche Raad*, 182–220; and de Jong, *Het Koninkrijk der Nederlanden*, 12, pt. 1:469–75.

29. Knoop, *De Joodsche Raad*, 219 f.

30. The changing view of the war in postwar historiography has been the subject of a number of recent works. In 1983 two important studies were published: Jan Bank, *Oorlogsverleden in Nederland* (inaugural lecture, Erasmus University in Rotterdam, October 27, 1983) (Baarn, 1983); and J. C. H. Blom, *In de ban van goed en fout? Wetenschappelijke geschiedschrijving over de bezettingstijd in Nederland* (inaugural lecture, University of Amsterdam, December 12, 1983) (Bergen, 1983). See also Ernst H. Kossmann, "Continuiteit en Discontinuiteit in de Naoorlogse Geschiedenis van Nederland," *Ons Erfdeel* 28 (November–December 1985), 659–68; and the proceedings of a conference on postwar Dutch historiography of the war years, held at the Free University in Amsterdam on May 10–11, 1990 (the fiftieth anniversary of the German invasion in 1940): J. P. B. Jonker, A. E. Kerstens, and G. N. van der Plaat, eds., *Vijftig Jaar na de Inval: Geschiedschrijving en Tweede Wereldoorlog* (The Hague, 1990).

31. J. J. van Bolhuis et al., eds., *Onderdrukking en Verzet: Nederland in oorlogstijd*, 4 vols. (Amsterdam, 1949–54), 1:5.

32. Abel J. Herzberg, *Kroniek der Jodenvervolging, 1940–1945* (Amsterdam, 1985), 9.

33. "Nationaal monument op de Dam door koningin Juliana onthuld," *De Nieuwe Rotterdamse Courant,* May 4, 1956.

34. For a discussion of gendered resistance, see Dwork, *Children With A Star*, chap. 2, esp. 40 f.

35. "Eeuwige Vlam in Schouwburg," *De Volkskrant,* May 5, 1962.

36. L. de Jong, *De Bezetting: Tekst en beeldmateriaal van de uitzendingen van de Nederlandse Televisie-Stichting over het Koninkrijk der Nederlanden in de Tweede Wereldoorlog, 1940–1945* (Amsterdam, 1966), 353.

37. Louis de Jong, quoted in Max Pam, *De Onderzoekers van de Oorlog: Het Rijksinstituut voor Oorlogsdocumentatie en het Werk van Dr. L. de Jong* (The Hague, 1979), 61.

38. Presser, *Ondergang*, 1:viii. We chose to translate directly from the Dutch edition and not to use the English version of the book, *The Destruction of the Dutch Jews,* trans. Arnold Pomerans (New York, 1969), republished in 1988 as *Ashes in the Wind: The Destruction of Dutch Jewry*. Pomerans's translation is imprecise at best, and more often it is simply wrong. It does not pick up the subtle sarcasm and irony of the Dutch original.

39. Presser, *Ondergang*, 1:3.

40. "Monument," *Algemeen Handelsblad*, April 24, 1965.

41. Han Lammers, quoted in *De Groene Amsterdammer*, April 24, 1965.

42. "Zij droegen een ster," *Trouw,* April 24, 1965.

43. J. S. Wijne, "Waarom prof. Presser?" *Nieuwe Rotterdamse Courant,* April 27, 1965.

44. B. Buitenrust Hettema, "Waarom Presser niet?" ibid., May 4, 1965.

45. Jaap Meijer, "Uit de Boekerij," Nederlandse Christelijke Radio Vereniging, May 31, 1965.

46. Herman von der Dunk, "Het boek van Presser," in *Kleio heeft duizend ogen: Over historie en historici* (Assen, 1974), 52.

47. Joop den Uyl, quoted in R. B. Soetendorp, *Pragmatisch of principieel: Het Nederlandse beleid ten aanzien van het Arabisch-Israelisch conflict* (Doctoral diss., Leiden University, 1983), 98.

48. Soetendorp, *Pragmatisch of principieel,* 99.

49. For a concise description of the social context of the Dutch attitude toward World War II in the 1960s, see Kossmann, "In de naoorlogse geschiedenis van Nederland," *Ons Erfdeel* 28 (November–December 1985), 659–68.

50. Han Lammers, quoted in *De Groene Amsterdammer,* April 24, 1965.

51. Evert Werkman, "Ondergang der Joden, boek met aanklacht," *Het Parool,* April 22, 1965.

52. Presser, *Ondergang,* 2:122.

53. Ibid., 1:525.

54. For a succinct description of the Weinreb case, see I. Schoeffer, "Weinreb, een affaire van lange duur," *Tijdschrift voor Geschiedenis* 95 (1982), 196–224.

55. Abel J. Herzberg, quoted in Dick Houwaart, *Weinreb: Een Witboek* (Amsterdam, 1975), 21–22.

56. Schoeffer, "Weinreb," 202.

57. Presser, *Ondergang,* 2:110.

58. Friedrich Weinreb, *Collaboratie en Verzet, 1940–1945: Een poging tot ontmythologisering,* 3 vols. (Amsterdam, 1969).

59. Renate Rubinstein, "Korte Verantwoording," in ibid., 1:vii.

60. Willem Frederik Hermans, *Van Wittgenstein tot Weinreb: Het sadistische universum 2* (Amsterdam, 1970).

61. Meijer Sluyser, "Excellentie Polak op uw hearing kunnen 120,000 joden niet meer worden gehoord," *Nieuw Israelitisch Weekblad,* September 5, 1969.

62. Y. Postma, quoted in J. van den Berg, "Het onmogelijke verhaal van de Drie van Breda," *Vrij Nederland,* September 20, 1969.

63. "Twee soorten barmhartigheid," *Haarlems Dagblad,* October 23, 1969.

64. Louis de Jong, "Jacques Presser" (eulogy delivered before the Literary Section of the Royal Academy of Science, Amsterdam, November 9, 1970; ms., RIOD), 16.

65. Wim Ramaker, *Sta een ogenblik stil . . . : Monumentenboek, 1940/45,* with photos by Ben van Bohemen (Kampen, 1980), 90–91.

66. Ibid., 11.

67. H. J. A. Hofland, Hans Keller, and Hans Verhagen, *Vastberaden, maar soepel en met mate: Herinneringen aan Nederland, 1938–1948* (Amsterdam, 1976), 7 ff.

68. Ibid., 32–33.

69. Ibid., 35.

70. See Bank, *Oorlogsverleden in Nederland;* Blom, *Crisis, Bezetting en Herstel;* Kossmann, "Continuiteit en Discontinuiteit"; Jonker, Kerstens, and van der Plaat, *Vijftig Jaar na de Inval;* and Gerhard Hirschfeld, *Fremdherrschaft und Kollaboration: Die Niederlande unter deutscher Besatzung, 1940–1945* (Stuttgart, 1984).

71. Jan Wolkers, quoted in Ramaker, *Sta een ogenblik stil . . . ,* 128.

72. *Rondom Holocaust: Een onderzoek naar de effecten van een omstreden televisie-serie op jongeren* (Hilversum, 1980), 204–5.

73. H. J. A. Hofland, "Het wonder van Hollywood," *De Haagse Post,* May 12, 1979.

74. Riet Diemer, "Holocaust in Nederland leverde geen 'explosie' op," *Trouw,* May 8, 1979.

75. Paul Vigeveno and Ton van der Meer, *Grenzen aan solidariteit: een lessenserie over de Holocaust* (Malmberg, 1990).

76. For a short discussion on the significance of the jubilee for the remembrance of the Holocaust, see Robert-Jan van Pelt, "After the Walls Have Fallen Down," *Queens Quarterly* 96 (autumn 1989), 641 f.

77. "In Amsterdam herdenkingsbeeld voor Joodse kinderen," *Het Vrije Volk,* September 2, 1986.

EASTERN EUROPE

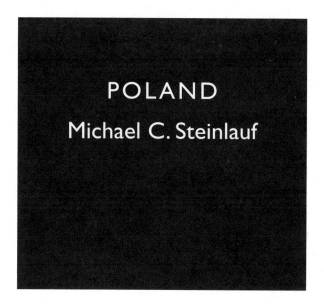

POLAND
Michael C. Steinlauf

Tracing the development of the Polish reaction to the Holocaust in the decades after World War II is both extremely important and extremely difficult. It is important, first and foremost, because of geography. In 1939 Poland was the center of the European Jewish world. It was the site of Europe's largest Jewish population, heir to a highly developed civilization rooted for nearly a thousand years in Polish soil. The destruction of the Jews of Poland accounted for more than half of all the victims of the Holocaust. At the same time, and hardly coincidentally, it was in Poland that most of the ghettos were established and the death camps were built—Chełmno, Treblinka, Sobibor, Majdanek, Bełżec, Auschwitz-Birkenau. It was where the railroad tracks converged, bringing Jews from the farthest corners of Europe to feed the Nazi death machine. At the most fundamental level, therefore, Poland was where the encounter between murderers and victims, Germans and Jews, that we have come to call the Holocaust played itself out. The Holocaust did not involve Poles directly; rather, Poles found themselves witnesses to the Holocaust, from beginning to end. The effects of witnessing murder on such a scale, at such close range, and over such a long time are of course complex. To inquire about the Polish reaction to the Holocaust is to investigate the effects of a mass psychic and moral trauma unprecedented in history.

Superimposed upon this paradigm are the many factors that made Poles more than just witnesses to the Holocaust. They were also victims of the Germans. Indeed, after the Jews and the Gypsies, the Poles were the most relentlessly victimized national group in Hitler's Europe. Publicly at least, Polish memory of the war years has been preoccupied with issues of Polish survival, martyrdom, and resistance. In relation to the Jews, while Poles collectively were powerless to affect their fate, individual Poles could and did help save, or destroy, individual Jews. The majority of Poles did neither, but that too was their own choice.

The World Reacts to the Holocaust

Such moral and psychological complications become even denser when we view the war years within the context of recent Polish history. The development in Poland of modern anti-Semitism, which was particularly influential just prior to the war, played a substantial role in Polish politics and society during and after the war. Anti-Semitism, as not only Poles have pointed out, is hardly identical with mass murder, but when we examine Polish responses to the Holocaust, Polish anti-Semitism, in its numerous historical contexts and functions, is a crucial element. To this must be added the factor that more than any other has crippled the way Poles recall not only the Holocaust but their entire history: Poland's incorporation, for more than four decades, into the Soviet empire. In Poland as elsewhere in Eastern Europe, postwar rulers, whose central legitimation was the alleged historical inevitability of the Communist system, worked especially hard to rewrite history books, redesign school curricula, and reeducate youth to believe that all of history was no more than a prelude to, or the "prehistory" of, the Communist seizure of power. Within this carefully crafted narrative, uses for the Holocaust were also found. The fate of the Jews became an object lesson in the horror of this prehistory and further proof that the only alternative to "progress" was "barbarism." But discussion of the Holocaust, like so much of postwar Polish discourse, evolved in an atmosphere so constricted and politically charged that, as a rule, what counted was not what was said but rather who said it and what forces they represented. Meanwhile, the collective psychic and moral dilemmas that the war had seared into Polish consciousness cried out for an airing as nowhere else in postwar Europe. But they were allowed no public exploration and instead were driven below the surface to fester.

BEFORE THE HOLOCAUST
In the Polish Commonwealth

The Jewish connection to Poland is as old as Polish history: the earliest known reference to Poland is by a Spanish Jew who in the tenth century accompanied an Arab official on a diplomatic mission to Eastern Europe.[1] While the earliest records of Jewish settlement in Poland date from the late twelfth century, the key period of settlement was the fourteenth and fifteenth centuries, when economic, political, and social dislocations combined with persecution to drive thousands of Jews eastward from northeastern France and Germany. This movement of Ashkenazic Jews (*Ashkenaz* being the Hebrew name for Germany) also brought a well-developed culture based in Hebrew texts and Yiddish, a young and particularly flexible vernacular language. During the centuries when the remaining Jewish communities of Western Europe suffered the turmoil that prepared them for the problematic gifts of emancipation, Ashkenazic civilization comparatively peacefully sank deep roots in the East.[2]

In Polish historiography, the years 1500–1650 are known as the golden age. It was a period when Polish kings ruled over a vast Polish-Lithuanian Commonwealth, stretching from the Oder River to the Dnieper, from the Baltic to the Black Sea.[3] At a time when its neighbors to the west were caught up in fratricidal religious strife and those to both the east and the west were experiencing the birth pangs of new absolutist states, the Polish Commonwealth presented a striking contrast: a land of great ethnic and religious diversity, multiple centers of authority, and comparative stability. In addition to Jews, the Commonwealth was home to German Lutherans, Polish Calvinists, Arians, Anabaptists, Armenians, Greeks, Scots, Tatar and Turkish Moslems, and Eastern Orthodox communities, frequently in the throes of schism. The Catholic Church, which saw itself as Rome's last defense against "eastern," that is, Russian, "barbarism," was a relatively youthful institution, still somewhat unsure of itself. Polish religious tolerance was in practice less a question of principle than a necessity for survival: religious uniformity could simply not be enforced.[4] This is the frequently cited historical underpinning of a key ingredient of modern Polish self-perception, namely, the conviction that Poles are at heart a very tolerant people.[5]

Political authority too tended toward comparatively democratic, decentralized forms. Beginning in 1573, Polish kings were elected by a parliament of representatives of the noble estate (szlachta). Membership in the szlachta, which constituted 10 percent of the population (a high proportion by contemporary Western European standards), was of course hereditary but was not entirely closed to those of common birth; non-Poles and even converted Jews were accepted into its ranks. Increasingly, the king's authority was circumscribed by the power of a nobility based in huge landed estates and often encompassing private towns and even private armies. During the golden age, Poland was often called a "noblemen's paradise." It also provided a particularly favorable environment for its numerous ethnic-religious communities not just to practice their way of life in relative tranquility but to enjoy considerable autonomy in the administration of their affairs as well.

All this suggests why Jews found the Polish Commonwealth a hospitable place to live during this period. At first they settled in the western Polish lands, primarily in the crown cities. But beginning in the sixteenth century, Jews increasingly linked their economic fate to the dynamic szlachta, who over the next century and a half acquired huge tracts of land, particularly in the eastern borderlands, the kresy. These ethnically mixed territories on the shifting eastern frontier of the Commonwealth today make up Lithuania, Belarus, a bit of eastern Poland, and most of Ukraine. Jews served the szlachta as lessees and managers of the new properties. They colonized them for the szlachta, founding or expanding towns that often acquired large Jewish majorities. These towns, or shtetlakh, became particularly common in the east but were widespread throughout the Commonwealth. They constituted the typical Jewish settlement in Poland until late in the nineteenth century, when the largest cities again began to attract many Jews.

The shtetl played a fundamental role in the economy of agrarian Poland. While the lord reigned in his nearby manor and peasants toiled in the fields surrounding their tiny villages, the shtetl's marketplace, ringed with stores and workshops, functioned as the sole commercial center for the entire region. Here the Jews had no economic competitors and were relatively free, as long as they paid taxes to the shtetl's lord, to organize their communal life as they saw fit. A community council (kehillah) collected taxes for the landowner and for the shtetl to maintain a cemetery, a synagogue, study houses, a civil court, a ritual slaughterhouse, a bathhouse, a poorhouse, and other similar institutions. Numerous voluntary societies *(khevres)* provided a host of other services. From the cutting of one's fingernails, to the regulation of weights and measures, to the chanting of daily prayers, Jewish life was lived under the sign of Jewish law and custom. While many aspects of this life were common to Jewish communities throughout medieval Europe, in Poland Jews were able to create a particularly coherent culture, one characterized by what Abraham Heschel has called "the highest degree of inwardness."[6] Beginning in the golden age and lasting nearly to the end of the Commonwealth, Polish Jews developed an intercommunal structure unprecedented in the Diaspora: a hierarchy of regional and provincial councils overseen by two supreme deliberative and judicial councils that constituted a kind of "national" Jewish government.[7] In the sixteenth and seventeenth centuries Jews compared communal life in Poland to that in the land of Israel in Second Temple times, while in Polish popular discourse the expression "Poland, paradise of the Jews" joined "noblemen's paradise" as a term with strong ironic connotations.

The golden age came to an end in the second half of the seventeenth century as the Commonwealth was laid waste by invasions of Swedes, Prussians, Tatars, Russians, and Cossacks. The Cossack armies in particular, filled with Ukrainian Orthodox peasants eager for revenge against their Polish Catholic and Jewish colonizers, were responsible for slaughter that imprinted itself for centuries in both Polish and Jewish historical memory. Increasingly, the Commonwealth's virtues of multiplicity and decentralization proved its undoing: royal authority disintegrated; *szlachta* families, often in alliance with foreign powers, plotted and waged war against each other; cities fell into decay; and a once free peasantry found itself bound to the land in serfdom. This process of decomposition led, by the end of the eighteenth century, to the division of the Commonwealth among its three newly powerful neighbors—Prussia, Austria, and Russia—and the disappearance of Poland as a political entity.

The trauma of the Cossack massacres, however, did little to arrest the continuous development of Jewish communities. By the mid-eighteenth century, when there were about 750,000 Jews living in the Commonwealth, one-quarter of all the Jews in the world lived in Polish *shtetlakh*.[8] Jews had become a fixture of the Polish landscape, as familiar an element of the natural order as the peasant village or the landowner's manor. Indeed, one popular *szlachta* conception identified this tripartite division of the social world with the races descended from the sons of Noah: the peasant as Ham, the landowner as Japhet, the Jew as Shem.

While individual relations varied greatly, on the whole relations between Jews and Poles were free of violence. This is hardly to say that Poles and Jews "knew each other." Existing alongside the host of personal contacts between individual Poles and Jews, which may have been characterized by a measure of respect and even affection, was a system of powerfully rooted stereotypes. Peasants attributed to Jews the character traits typical of the preindustrial conception of traders: crafty, deceitful, and miserly. The Jew was also an object of mystery, the possessor of secret lore, an alien being who, as the church never let the peasant forget, had rejected the true faith and was implicated in the murder of Christ. Yet counterbalancing such fears was the Jew's role as an object of laughter: perceived as sober, chaste, nonviolent, and therefore unmanly, the Jew was ridiculous in dress, speech, and customs. The *szlachta* found little that was fearful about the Jew. The landowner's Jewish agent was often a trusted adviser; indeed, every noble was said to "have his Jew." But the land-owner viewed the mass of Jews as contemptible and ludicrous. By the nineteenth century the comic stereotype of the dancing little Jew *(żydek)*, clutching his belly, stroking his beard, and babbling gibberish, had become a fixture of the popular imagination, a kind of Polish Sambo.[9] For his part, the Jew, outwardly subservient, was inwardly contemptuous of both the peasant and the noble, though his attitude toward the latter was colored by awe as well. For the Jew, both peasant and noble, each in his own way, manifested brutality, ignorance, and overall loutishness, characteristics that were antithetical to the Jewish ethos.

Under Three Empires, 1795–1918

For more than one hundred years, while the word "Polish" continued to designate a language and, increasingly, a modern national and cultural identity, Poland itself had ceased to exist. Prussia had taken the western areas, Austria had taken the southern province, called Galicia, while the lion's share, central Poland along with most of the eastern borderlands, had gone to Russia.[10] For the Prussians and the Austrians, their new Polish provinces were agricultural hinterlands. By the end of the nineteenth century, however, Poles in both areas were reaping some of the economic and social benefits of the West, though Bismarck and Franz-Joseph pursued very different nationality policies. In Germany, a campaign was launched to Germanize the Poles (Kulturkampf). In Galicia after 1867 the Poles were left alone. It became a haven for Polish nationalism, and the *szlachta,* still ensconced in their traditional estates, were free to run the province. Russia pursued policies that varied geographically in the huge territories it had annexed. The *kresy,* where a Polish minority of city dwellers and *szlachta* lived in a sea of Lithuanian, Belorussian, and Ukrainian peasant villages and small Jewish towns, were Russified and merged with the Great Russian heartland. Central Poland (also called Congress Poland, after the Congress of Vienna in 1815, which had drawn its boundaries), most of whose population was ethnically Polish, was at first permitted a degree of autonomy.

The *szlachta,* however, were not content with limited autonomy as the western showpiece of the czars. Nurtured by the memory of Tadeusz Kościuszko's last stand against the Russians in 1794, they dreamed of freedom not only at home but throughout Europe as well. Their ethos led them to become a vanguard in the republican struggles that transformed the European political system during the nineteenth century. They fought the old order in Polish legions organized under Napoleon, and a generation later they fought as defenders of the revolutionary cause in Italy, Hungary, and elsewhere in the 1848 "springtime of nations." They also mounted two doomed insurrections against the Russians in 1831 and 1863. "Poland is a symbol," wrote the Danish Jewish critic George Brandes in 1885, "a symbol of all which the best of the human race have loved, and for which they have fought. Everywhere in Europe where there has been any fighting for freedom in this century, the Poles have taken part in it, on all battlefields, on all barricades. . . . Conversely, it may also be said that everywhere [in Europe] where there is any fighting for freedom, there is fighting for Poland."[11] Freedom fighting bore a price. In the aftermath of the second uprising against the czars the name Poland was replaced by the designation Vistulaland, *szlachta* property was expropriated, and, with few exceptions, Polish speech was banned from public use. Polish national consciousness survived above all in the church, which during this period, particularly at the parish level, provided important material aid to the insurrectionists and thereby solidified an intimate alliance with the Polish national cause.

For Polish Jews in the nineteenth century, as for Poles, much depended on who their new masters were.[12] In Prussian Poland, given the sudden opportunity to "Westernize," many Jews moved to the larger German cities, where they were soon indistinguishable from their German coreligionists. In Galicia, Jewish life fell into two different patterns by the end of the nineteenth century. In Cracow, Lvov, and other large cities an educated, emancipated Jewish bourgeoisie had begun to enter Austrian politics; in the countryside, where the *szlachta* still ruled as in the days of the Commonwealth, most Jews continued to live a traditional life in cramped, economically marginal *shtetlakh*.

In Russia the situation was more problematic. For centuries the czars had refused to admit the "enemies of Christ" into their realms; with the partitions, they suddenly found themselves ruling over hundreds of thousands of Jews. Their instinctive response was to isolate them from the Great Russian masses: they created the Pale of Settlement, essentially those areas of conquered Poland where the Jews were settled and to which they were now confined. What to do with the Jews beyond containing them was a question the czars never resolved. Czarist attempts to force reforms of Jewish society were often indistinguishable from punitive decrees. Even an occasional carrot, such as access to universities or permission to reside in Moscow or St. Petersburg, was invariably followed by the stick. After 1881 there were no more carrots: used as scapegoats for everything from peasant drunkenness to the revolutionary movement, Jews were subjected to ever new restrictions, expelled from villages and cities, and murdered in pogroms fomented, beginning early in the twentieth century, by groups with government connections.

Even under siege, traditional Jewish society manifested signs of considerable inner strength and even renewal. Indeed, this tenacity characterized Jewish communities both in the Russian "prison house of nations" and in Galicia under the "enlightened" Habsburg rule. During the ninety years from 1820 to 1910, while the population of the Russian Empire rose from 46 million to 131 million, the number of Jews increased even faster, from 1.6 million to 5.6 million.[13] In Galicia the Jewish growth rate was even higher. A powerful revivalist religious movement also swept Eastern European Jewish communities in the nineteenth century. Hasidism, with its populist spirit, passionate optimism, and crusading combativeness, infused traditional Judaism in Eastern Europe with new life precisely at the time when Western European Jews, unfortified by any comparable revival, were abandoning traditional ways of life for those of the modern citizen. With its network of charismatic leaders *(tsaddikim)* ensconced in "courts" visited by masses of pilgrims and its own houses of worship, schools, printing presses, and sources of income, Hasidism established vigorous new centers of communal authority to withstand the double assault of czarist autocracy and modern Western thought.

Nevertheless, even in the "backward East" secular ideas began to touch the Jews. The Jewish Enlightenment, or Haskalah, moving eastward from Germany in the late eighteenth century, began to gain disciples as a small, Western-oriented Jewish bourgeoisie developed in the larger towns. Eager for knowledge of the world, these Jews turned to non-Jewish languages, first German, then Russian in the *kresy* and Polish in Congress Poland and Galicia. Cultural contacts between Poles and modernizing Jews followed a characteristic pattern: a handful of Jews were attracted to the Polish freedom struggle, while some Poles were sympathetic toward the Jews, but only insofar as they were perceived as allies of the Polish cause.[14] Berek Joselewicz, who formed a Jewish regiment that fought the Russians under Kościuszko and then joined the Polish Legions and fell in battle at Kock defending Napoleon against the Austrians, became a legendary figure for generations of assimilating Jews and their Polish friends. Following in his footsteps, a small number of Jews fought beside their Polish comrades in the insurrections of 1831 and 1863. In 1863, in an act that would symbolize Polish-Jewish cooperation for generations to come, Ber Meisels, the Orthodox chief rabbi of Warsaw, preached support for the Polish uprising.

This was a crucial period in the shaping of a distinctive Polish national identity. Polish Romantic poets, above all the national bard, Adam Mickiewicz, began to see in Polish history a mythic narrative of self-sacrifice at the vanguard of a universal struggle for freedom. Significantly, such conceptions assigned a positive role to Jews. During the period between the two uprisings, Mickiewicz preached a messianic alliance between the Polish "Christ of nations" and his suffering "elder brother." Mickiewicz's epic, *Pan Tadeusz,* verses of which Polish schoolchildren have recited for generations, includes a tavernkeeper named Jankiel, the most well-known Jewish figure in Polish literature. At a gathering of *szlachta,* the bearded Jankiel, a virtuoso dulcimer player, performs a concert of Polish patriotic music that recalls his audience to their sacred national task. "For our freedom, and for yours," the universalistic slogan of the Polish insurrectionists, became the watchword of Jewish solidarity with the Poles against a common oppressor as well.

After the two failed uprisings, however, a new generation of Polish intelligentsia, the Positivists, reacted strongly against the past. Not the noble gesture but the patient, rational development of industry and culture was to be the measure of the nation's progress. In the afterglow of Polish-Jewish insurrectionary solidarity, this period at first seemed also to bode well for Polish-Jewish relations. In contrast to the situation in Western Europe, where an energetic native bourgeoisie anchored in long-established urban centers had vanquished the landed nobility, in late-nineteenth-century Poland Polish industrialists were relatively rare. Neither the *szlachta* nor the peasants, emancipated only during the 1860s, could spearhead the economic transformation of Poland; only the Germans and above all the Jews, Poland's traditional commercial "classes," possessed the economic and psychosocial requirements. From the 1880s until World War I, hundreds of thousands of Jews abandoned the *shtetlakh* for the cities. Warsaw became the commercial hub of the Russian Empire, while the textile mills of Łódź and Białystok produced much of its clothing. For the Positivists, the Jewish banker or industrialist who was prepared to embrace "Polishness" could be seen as an ally of the Polish cause.

Yet in nineteenth-century Europe capitalism was hardly an unmixed blessing. In the eyes of its numerous Polish critics, whose *szlachta* origins were never distant, capitalism seemed particularly ugly and disorienting and inevitably un-Polish. In Poland the turmoil of capitalist development, nowhere in Europe a very pretty thing, became mired not only in class but also in national antagonisms, chief among them hostility to Jews. The rapid overturning of the feudal order was accompanied by a change in the Polish perception of the Jew; amidst the atomization of urban life the familiar stereotypes were swept away, and in their place emerged an unknown and potentially frightening personage who continued, however, to live next door.

This transformation was also fueled by very real changes within the Jewish communities. Beginning in the 1880s the heirs of the Haskalah in the Russian Empire, profoundly discouraged by the prospects for Russian reform and surrounded by the stirrings of Polish and other national movements, embarked on the building of national consciousness among Jews. This effort was to take many competing forms, including various kinds of Zionism, Diaspora nationalism, and Jewish socialism. Whatever their ideology, however, as long as they had to respond to Eastern European realities, all these movements, even Zionism, found it necessary to make demands of the Diaspora, including autonomous political activity in defense of Jewish interests (a struggle for minority as well as civil rights), a modern culture based in Jewish languages, and new relationships to non-Jewish peoples based on mutual respect.

But a Jewish national movement was totally unacceptable to Poles, and it was perceived as the final straw in growing Jewish intractability. By the turn of the century much of the Polish intelligentsia's goodwill toward the Jews had evaporated. Only a relatively small proportion of Jews had decided to assimilate into Polish culture and become "good Poles." Educated Jews in the eastern borderlands had turned to Russian culture, those in Prussian Poland had turned to German culture, and both groups were manipulated by the czar and the kaiser against the Poles. Furthermore, as the Poles saw it, the vast majority of Jews remained outside any European culture: they were desperately poor and clung to outlandish traditional attire and an offensive Germanic jargon. Worse yet, among the new generation of educated Jews, even as the social process of assimilation continued uninterrupted, the ideology of assimilation began to go out of fashion. The notion of an independent Jewish politics profoundly frightened Poles. Combined with the apparent economic power of the small Jewish oligarchy, such fears, cultivated whenever possible by the Russians, raised the specter of a "Judaeo-Polonia," a latter-day "paradise of the Jews" that was supposedly the Zionists' true aim, a Jewish state on Polish soil. In Poland, that staple of European anti-Semitism, the notion of Jews as a "state within a state," rooted itself with particular tenacity. Finally, there was a new personal assertiveness among younger Jews. These were no longer the comical *żydki* or even wise old patriarchs;

in a world increasingly out of joint, here were Jews who did not know their place.[15]

These developments in the Polish perception of the Jews coincided with the emergence of a debate over the nature of Polish national identity that was to leave its mark on subsequent Polish history. It was triggered by a critique of the past, by the need to move out of what was perceived as a historical cul-de-sac. If "Polishness" was the exclusive property of the *szlachta,* then the Polish national struggle, it was perceived, could not hope to advance beyond doomed insurrections. Did Polishness include the peasant, who in 1863 not infrequently had reported his insurrectionist landlord to the Russians? Did it include women? Did it include non–Roman Catholics and those who were not of Polish ethnic stock? Did it, finally, include the Jews? In answer to such questions, two alternatives began to emerge.

The first, which we can term "pluralist," offered a conception of Polishness reminiscent of what had been possible in the old Polish Commonwealth, where a gentleman might describe himself as "a canon of Kraków, a member of the Polish nation, of the Ruthenian [Ukrainian] people, of Jewish origin."[16] This "noble" notion of national identity assumed that Polishness designated a community of cultural and historical values that was inclusive and voluntary. It was a base from which a future campaign to create a "nationalities state" *(państwo narodowościowe)* could be launched. The sustaining ideals would be both Polish and universal, part of the struggle for Polish freedom, whose motto had been "For your freedom, and for ours." By the century's end such tendencies had been integrated into the nondogmatic socialism of the Polish Socialist Party (Polska Partia Socjalistyczna [PPS]), founded in 1897 by Jósef Piłsudski. Here the old *szlachta* beliefs coexisted with modern ideas of social justice. Closely associated with the *kresy,* Piłsudski and his comrades saw the Russians as their chief enemy and entertained notions of tactical alliance with the Austrians. The main goal was an independent Polish state, and in this struggle Jews, insofar as they considered themselves Polish patriots, were welcomed.

In direct opposition to the pluralists were the "exclusivists," who found their political focus in the National Democratic Party (Narodowa Democracja [ND], or Endecja), which was founded by Roman Dmowski and his associates also in the late 1890s. The Endecja advocated what it called "integral nationalism," which narrowly defined Polishness to include only those of ethnic Polish descent and Roman Catholic faith. It dreamt not of a nationalities state but of a nation state *(państwo narodowe).* Strongest in German-occupied western Poland, the Endecja stressed bourgeois over *szlachta* values, Realpolitik over insurrection, compromise with the Russians, and hostility toward the Germans.

Using the popular contemporary language of social Darwinism, Endeks argued that a modern national existence demanded a "national egoism" in the merciless struggle for survival against other peoples. Chief among these struggles was that against the Jews. In the Middle Ages, when a modern Polish nation did not yet exist, Jews had been invited to develop trade in the Polish lands. But now, according to the Endeks, the Polish nation, standing on the threshold of a modern existence, was young and much too trusting in the confrontation with an all too experienced and ruthless opponent. A modern nation cannot exist, they insisted, without a commercial class. But the Jews, they claimed, controlled Poland's commerce, indeed *were* its commercial class. This reasoning led the Endeks to conclude that the Jews had to be driven out of Polish commerce and industry and replaced by ethnic Poles. Endek ideologues were well aware of the progress of modern anti-Semitic movements from France to Russia and learned much from them. But what made Polish anti-Semitism different and gave it a unique logic was its insistence that it was simply the sign of a national conflict, of a struggle between two peoples contending for economic and political dominance in one land. Furthermore, the Endeks saw Poles as the underdogs. The rise of the Jewish national movement was taken as a confirmation of this. Having already subjugated the Poles economically, what could these Jews want, the Endeks argued, but political rule over the Poles as well?

While the conflict between Piłsudski's and Dmowski's followers was a political one, the struggle between the pluralists and exclusivists went beyond the political arena. Theirs involved more than a clash of ideas: they viewed the world in fundamentally different ways. Pluralists, touched with a bit of messianic hope and heirs to a history of exemplary martyrdom, adopted a generous and tolerant stance toward the world. Exclusivists read Polish history as a chronicle of victimization and insisted that Poles learn that they would always stand alone. The weakness of the pluralist stance was the risk of degenerating into empty posturing. The exclusivist stance, under certain circumstances—and the events of this century, as we will see, would provide them in great number—could easily slip into paranoia.

Between the World Wars, 1918–1939

The reconstituted Polish state, like its neighboring successor states, was cast into the twentieth century out of the wreckage of what had been the most destructive war in history. It emerged into an era of nearly continuous economic crisis and was also beset by its own unique problems.[17] After 123 years, Poland was a patchwork of regions with diverse economic, social, and political traditions and needs. Polish industry, which had been based in Congress Poland and oriented to the Russian market, now had to compete in the West; it never regained its prewar vigor. While the great majority of the Polish population continued to live on the land, Polish agriculture was in crisis. Peasant farms, already small, were continually shrinking, subdivided and parceled out from one generation to the next. Meanwhile, in the East powerful *szlachta* families still ruled over giant estates and successfully resisted land reform for the entire interwar period. Among the results was a growing mass of impoverished landless peasants.

Then there was the problem of national minorities. Only two-thirds of the population of interwar Poland was ethnically Polish; the remainder was Ukrainian, Jewish, Belorussian, and German, in that order. In most of the eastern parts of the country, the historical *kresy*, Poles themselves were a minority. Under such circumstances civil harmony would have demanded some sort of pluralist approach to national issues. Despite the fact that the state was dubbed the Second Commonwealth, the exclusivist, ethnically based notion of Polishness proved increasingly influential and led to a rising hostility to non-Poles. This hostility was provoked in part by some of the minorities themselves, who allowed their demands to become the subject of political intrigue by Poland's powerful neighbors. With the Ukrainian and Belorussian Soviet Socialist Republics across the border, Ukrainian and Belorussian activism in Poland, including terrorism, was encouraged by the Soviet Union. In the 1930s the manipulation of ethnic Germans and Ukrainians in Poland became a weapon of Nazi foreign policy. But to view Jews within a comparable context required a rather exaggerated notion of the power of international Jewry, a notion that was a German specialty during this period but hardly unknown in Poland.

These and other problems made the establishment of a stable constitutional government an impossible task. Indeed, for the greater part of its existence the Second Polish Commonwealth was not governed democratically; rather, it was ruled by Józef Piłsudski and his disciples. Piłsudski, who by the 1920s had broken with socialism and the PPS, proved himself a true son of the *szlachta*. A military leader who guided Poland to independence, he then took his army east into the *kresy* and engaged the Soviets, the Ukrainians, and the Lithuanians on the field of battle. In 1922 Piłsudski turned the government over to parliamentary rule, but his charisma was powerful enough for him to seize power from the ineffectual government in 1926 and rule the country until his death nine years later, all the while maintaining great popularity. In an age that produced monstrous despotisms all over Europe, the "Marshal," as he preferred to be called, created a comparatively inoffensive "nonparty" regime under the name Sanacja, implying a moral cleansing of society. He managed to be a dictator without being either a fascist or an anti-Semite, and he held the line against the more aggressive manifestations of Endek nationalism. The clique of military men who succeeded him and led Poland for the remaining four years of its independence was much less successful at this.

Despite enormous changes in the situation of Polish Jews during the twenty years of the Second Commonwealth, their demographic and economic profile remained exceptional.[18] In a country that was nearly three-quarters rural, Jews were increasingly an urban population: although one-third continued to live in the *shtetlakh,* and one-quarter in the countryside, nearly half of all Jews lived in cities with a population of more than twenty thousand. While the Jews constituted 10 percent of the total population, they made up 30 percent of the urban population. Although Jewish population growth in this period was surpassed by that of the Poles, the number of Jews, unlike elsewhere in Central Europe, continued to increase in absolute terms. Jews were vastly overrepresented in commerce and the professions: in 1921 more than 60 percent of those in commerce were Jews, and in 1931 more than half of the doctors in private practice and one-third of the lawyers were Jews. Although foreign investment and state-run enterprises had begun to displace Jewish-owned businesses, on the eve of World War II Jewish firms still employed more than 40 percent of the Polish labor force, and certain industries, textiles and food most notably, were predominantly in Jewish hands. While such statistics were grist for anti-Semitic propagandists, the vast majority of Jews were hardly well-off professionals or captains of industry; typically, Jews were small shopkeepers and artisans making barely enough to survive.[19]

In the Minorities Treaty, which Poland, along with other successor states, had been required to sign at the Paris Peace Conference, Jews were granted both civil and minority rights. Secular Jewish leaders hailed the treaty as the Magna Carta for Jewish national autonomy in Poland. Such optimism proved misplaced, for successive Polish governments, including the Sanacja, in practice consistently rejected claims based on Jewish national rights. Thus, while government-supported Jewish schools were stipulated in the Minorities Treaty, Polish governments refused to finance them and denied them accreditation. Nevertheless, regardless of official attitudes and even as Jews were becoming fully literate in Polish and in certain circles even abandoning Yiddish, they were increasingly using the notion of Jewish nationality to define themselves.[20] On the one hand, this was a reaction to increasing Polish hostility to Jews, even to assimilating Jews. But the new Jewish identity was also shaped by the opportunity to develop Jewish culture and institutions under conditions that were vastly more promising than anything that had been possible under the czars.

One measure of the Jewish world that emerged in interwar Poland was the range of its political life. Jewish voters now cast ballots in three different sorts of elections: for the national Polish Parliament, for their local city or town council, and for the local kehillah. More than a dozen Jewish political parties competed for this Jewish vote. The most successful, particularly in national elections, were the General Zionists. Aspiring both to a Jewish homeland in Palestine and to the leadership of the Jewish community of Poland, the General Zionists waged a militant parliamentary struggle for Jewish national rights and "national dignity." While the Zionist movement included a religious wing, most Orthodox Jews were represented by the anti-Zionist Agudat Israel, the second most popular Jewish party at the national level and the dominant force in kehillah politics. The Agudat maintained a traditional Jewish stance of moderation and pursued a policy of private intercession with the government; after Piłsudski took power it was the only Jewish party that joined the governing coalition. On the left, the anti-Zionist Bund had the overwhelming allegiance of Jewish workers, most of whom were organized in Bundist labor unions. Boycotting the national elections as a bourgeois sham, the Bund contended for influence on the local level and attempted to build bridges to the PPS.

The influence of the Jewish political parties far transcended conventional politics. Indeed, in terms of their ability to effect political change the parties were ultimately impotent.[21] But the Jewish parties and their activists were instrumental in elaborating a dense web of institutions and organizations that affected every aspect of Jewish life. For example, the Zionists supported a school system in which Hebrew was the primary language of instruction, while the Bundists and their allies supported one in which the language of instruction was Yiddish. But the most popular system of Jewish education comprised the network of schools maintained by the Agudah, which included, for the first time, elementary schools for girls as well as a spacious modern rabbinical seminary, the Yeshivat Hakhmei Lublin.[22] Similarly, about a dozen youth groups generally linked to Zionist and socialist parties recruited members throughout Poland. Fixtures of the largest cities and the smallest *shtetlakh* alike were the libraries and clubs where such socially conscious young people gathered to study, debate, and socialize. At the same time, Orthodox Jews continued to fill traditional study and prayer houses maintained by local *khevres* and Hasidic sects.[23] In Warsaw in the 1920s, according to official and doubtless incomplete statistics, there were 442 synagogues and prayer houses for a population of about 350,000 Jews.[24] Cooperatives, credit unions, orphanages, hospitals, newspapers, publishing houses, theater companies, orchestras, choirs, sports clubs, and cultural societies, many sponsored by political parties but many others independent, were the links in a far-flung network that defined what can best be described as the Jewish nationality of interwar Poland.

The result was a community whose influence radiated wherever there were Jews in the world. Even as Polish rabbis fought the flood of secular ideas and lifestyles, Polish yeshivot attracted thousands of American students, while Polish graduates of these yeshivot went on to found new educational centers in Palestine, Western Europe, and the United States. Traditional religious scholarship published in Poland was distributed throughout the world; in particular demand were the volumes produced by the legendary Rom printing house in Vilna.[25] In the realm of secular culture, above all Yiddish literature, a similar situation developed. While Yiddish writers in Poland continually lamented the loss of their readers to Polish literature, nevertheless, in relation to the vicissitudes of Yiddish elsewhere in the world Poland remained the center of the Yiddish printed word. During the interwar period between three and five Yiddish daily newspapers were available at Warsaw kiosks, while more than seventeen hundred different periodicals appeared.[26] Even those Yiddish writers who had permanently settled abroad, usually in New York, would frequently return to Poland and inevitably appear in the clublike quarters of the Yiddish Writers' and Journalists' Union in Warsaw, commonly known by its address, Tłomackie 13. But this address, as well as the Jewish world it represented, was virtually unknown to Poles. Commonly described as an exotic "dark continent," the Jewish world was said to lie behind a mythical "Chinese wall."

The relations between Poles and Polish Jews in the interwar period began badly and ended worse. On the day Polish independence was declared, anti-Jewish violence, hitherto rare in Poland, erupted throughout the country. In the eastern borderlands for the next three years numerous armies, paramilitary units, and bands of outlaws slaughtered each other as well as masses of civilians. Jewish life proved particularly cheap. While Jews fell victim primarily to Ukrainian forces, there were also cases of pogroms staged or abetted by Polish forces, particularly those commanded by General Józef Haller. Typically, each side accused the Jews of aiding the other. Out of this turmoil arose a belief that played a fateful role during World War II and well beyond. Based partly on the anti-Semitic stereotype of the "commie Jew" and partly on the Jewish involvement in the various "revolutionary" and "provisional" committees set up by the advancing Red Army, a conviction arose among Poles that the Jews as a whole were pro-Soviet. Accordingly, in one highly publicized incident during the Polish-Soviet War of 1919–20 a group of Jewish army officers were declared a security risk and interned in a detention camp.[27]

In the meantime, responding to the international outcry over the pogroms, the

Polish government and press heatedly denied the involvement of Polish troops and, launching another accusation that would recur for decades, charged that Polish Jewish activists in collusion with Western Jews had organized an international propaganda campaign to besmirch Poland's honor. This accusation in turn was linked to Polish anger about the role of international Jewish delegations in drafting the Minorities Treaty. The Polish representatives at the Paris Peace Conference, who were primarily Endek activists, denounced the treaty as meddling in Polish internal affairs. For many Poles it may have been difficult to understand why Jews were content with civil rights in the West but demanded additional national minority rights in Poland. The coda to these initial years came in November 1922, when the Polish Parliament selected Gabriel Narutowicz as the first constitutionally elected president of Poland. Narutowicz was chosen with the support of a bloc of Jewish and other minority representatives. Immediately dubbed "President of the Jews" in the Endek press, he was assassinated two days after his inauguration.

During subsequent years, and particularly after Piłsudski's coup, national passions abated somewhat. Yet anti-Semitic propagandists discovered new fields to conquer; much was made, for example, of the alleged Jewish infiltration of Polish culture. By the 1930s Julian Tuwim, the eminent Polish poet of Jewish origin, was regularly being attacked, as Heinrich Heine had been in Germany a century earlier, for polluting the national language. It became increasingly difficult for a Jew to become a "good Pole." Those Jews who were willing to assimilate, indeed even the handful of converts, found themselves isolated, spurned by Poles and ostracized by Jews. Meanwhile, under constant pressure from the Endecja, the Sanacja regime both formally and informally adopted large portions of the Endek program concerning Jews. It became virtually impossible for a Jew to hold a civil-service position; banks made it more difficult for Jewish businesses to qualify for loans; new taxes hurt Jewish shopkeepers and artisans; and a quota system restricted Jewish enrollment at Polish medical schools.

In Poland as elsewhere in Europe, the 1930s brought economic catastrophe and an escalation of social conflict, which in this case worsened the already volatile relations between Poles and Jews. Violence flared particularly in the *shtetlakh* and the universities. Endek agitators went out among the poorest peasants to announce that the time had come not just to boycott Jewish merchants but to expel them from their shops and stalls and take over. The result was bloodshed in numerous towns. Meanwhile, at the universities right-wing nationalists became increasingly aggressive. While Jewish students were forced to sit in the back of lecture halls (the so-called bench ghetto), gangs of "gentlemen" hooligans, armed with canes and razors, assaulted their Jewish classmates on campuses and terrorized Jews in the streets and parks. Despite the traditional Endek aversion to Germany, some youths openly emulated the Nazis; one group, the National Radical Camp (Obóz Narodowo-Radykalny [ONR]), adopted a fascist program and split from the National Democrats. In response to the violence, Jewish unions and youth groups formed self-defense units that collected arms and resisted attacks. But such groups learned that, for a vastly outnumbered minority, violent resistance, while psychologically satisfying, could be counterproductive, for it often provoked even greater violence.[28]

Many in Poland, including the church, were upset by the violence. In 1936 August Cardinal Hlond, the primate of Poland, issued a pastoral letter condemning hatred and violence against Jews. At the same time, however, and this was characteristic of the church's position on the Jewish Question during this period, he gave his clear support to the "moral" struggle against what he termed Jewish atheism, bolshevism, and pornography. He also supported nonviolent boycotts of Jewish businesses.[29] There were some, primarily among the intelligentsia and on the left politically, who opposed the notion of any kind of struggle against the Jews. At its 1937 party congress, the PPS condemned anti-Semitism and fascism and resolved to support national rights for all minorities, including the Jews. The PPS and the Bund, moreover, had developed something of a tradition of cooperation; however, such politics were the exception. By the 1930s, besides the PPS, only the tiny Stronnictwo Demokratyczne (Democratic Party), a left-wing breakaway from Sanacja, and the small Communist Party did not advocate mass Jewish emigration. In the atmosphere that prevailed in Poland in the years just prior to the war, denouncing anti-Semitism was tantamount to declaring oneself "for the Jews" and took considerable political and personal courage.

Following Marshal Piłsudski's death in 1935, his heirs drew politically closer to both the church and the Endecja and diplomatically closer to Nazi Germany. This was a Polish government increasingly preoccupied with the Jewish Question.[30] In December 1938, after Poland had participated in the dismemberment of Czechoslovakia, a government spokesman declared that "the more normal division of the Jews among the countries of the world" was "the pressing matter of the international political scene" and that the Jewish Question was one of "the chief and most difficult problems facing the Polish nation."[31] The solution to this problem was sought in mass Jewish emigration. The most controversial of numerous schemes was the government's negotiations with Vladimir Jabotinsky of the Zionist Revisionists for the "evacuation" of hundreds of thousands of Polish Jews to Palestine, an episode that led to enormous publicity but no results. It is doubtful whether the government seriously expected any of these plans (none of which, it should be noted, involved forced emigration) to succeed. Such schemes emerged out of the same political atmosphere that turned the prohibition of Jewish ritual slaughter into a cause célèbre voluminously debated in the Polish Parliament and press on the eve of World War II.[32] The Polish pluralist tradition was moribund; instead, the Jewish Question hung over Polish public life. Rooted in the most fundamental problems of Polish national development, the Jewish Question made it difficult to see those problems, as well as the truly menacing developments just beyond Poland's borders, with any clarity.

THE HOLOCAUST ERA
Poles and Jews during the Holocaust, 1939–1944

On September 1, 1939, German troops invaded Poland. Polish defenses quickly crumbled before an overwhelming assault that included intensive aerial bombardment of civilian areas. After two weeks Germany controlled the western half of the country with the exception of Warsaw, which, besieged and burning and abandoned by the government and the General Staff, held out for two more weeks. Meanwhile, on September 17 the Soviet Union invaded Poland from the east. For almost two years, according to the treaty signed with Germany just before the war, the Soviets ruled half the territory of prewar Poland, the area east of the Bug River. In June 1941 the Germans turned on the Soviets and forced the Red Army out of Poland. For three years all of prewar Poland was occupied by the Germans. Then in January 1944 the Red Army reentered Polish territory, and by the beginning of 1945 it had pushed the last of the German forces out of Poland.

The German occupation of Poland was the cornerstone of Nazi plans for a Eurasian empire stratified by race in which German masters would rule over "racially inferior," primarily Slavic peoples.[33] The war offered the Nazis the opportunity to begin building this "New Order." Immediately after their conquest of the western half of Poland the Nazis divided it in two. The northwestern regions, including important industrial and mining centers, were directly incorporated into the Reich, and much of the non-German population, primarily Poles and Jews, was expelled into the remaining area, which the Nazis called the Generalgouvernement. Over the next five years the Generalgouvernement, comprising one-third of the territory of prewar Poland, including the cities of Warsaw, Cracow, and Lublin, and nearly half of the population, became the center of the Nazi occupation.[34] As a dumping ground for all the "racial garbage" in occupied Poland, the Generalgouvernement became the focus of Nazi "clean-up" attempts: the organization of slave labor and mass murder.[35] At the same time, it was also where some fifteen million Poles managed to eat, sleep, work, occasionally sit in a café or a theater, and stay alive for the duration of the war.

In the Generalgouvernement the Germans instituted a regime of total exploitation. Their intention was to extract from the Poles the maximum possible labor to support the German war machine, while allowing them as little as possible in return. All Poles fourteen years of age and older were required to work; workers were often bound to their workplace, with work papers used as identification. As a result of frequent, unpredictable roundups, over a million Poles were deported to work in Germany. Other roundups, as well as sentences for a host of major and minor transgressions of Nazi laws, resulted in some two million more being condemned to work in the vast network of Nazi concentration camps, labor camps, and prisons established within Poland.[36] Prices skyrocketed, wages (for those who were paid them) fell, and the official German rationing system barely sustained life.

Nazi policies in Poland were intended not just to control a potentially rebellious population but to begin to shape its future. While the Nazis made use of hundreds of thousands of municipal employees, railroad workers, police, and other local officials, who continued their work under German orders, in Poland, unlike elsewhere in Europe, the Nazis did not seek political collaborators, nor were there many interested in collaborating. Poles were not to be bargained with or cajoled; they were to be broken, reduced to the common denominator of helots for their Nazi lords. In order to do this, the Nazis had to dissolve the structures and values that bound Polish society together. The Nazis began with a campaign to wipe out Polish elites: in 1939 and 1940 thousands of teachers, military officers, landowners, priests, and professors were rounded up and murdered. At the same time, secondary schools and universities were closed, and most cultural activities banned. Education was limited to the fourth grade, entertainment to operettas, cabarets, and pornography. Drinking was strongly encouraged. Above all, random, meaningless violence, unrelated or out of proportion to any crime, was the preferred means of enforcing obedience.[37] The death penalty was the mandated punishment for a slew of transgressions, great and small. Collective punishment—the execution, for an act of real or imagined resistance, of scores or hundreds of innocent people—was common. Nazi terror created an atmosphere conducive to terror of other kinds: banditry and armed attacks by a variety of political and quasi-political groups, including the slaughter in eastern Poland of some one hundred thousand Poles by Ukrainian nationalists.[38]

The Nazi assault on Polish society evoked two different but not necessarily exclusive reactions. Faced with the apparent impossibility of reasoning with the occupier, Poles soon discovered that there was one language the Germans understood well, namely, corruption. Under a system in which Poles had no rights whatsoever, every aspect of life, sometimes life itself, became a privilege to be negotiated with particular officials in return for financial considerations. Money suddenly became the measure of all things, and in this respect corruption complemented the terror by further wrecking traditional values: extortion, blackmail, and informing poisoned human relations. German greed combined with the inadequacy of official rationing to stimulate an alternative economy: the black market provided for some 80 percent of the needs of the Polish population.[39] In cheating the Germans and helping Poles survive the war, corruption played a positive social role as well. In the memoirs of Poles, as in the memoirs of Jews in the ghettos, the smuggler is frequently portrayed as a heroic figure.

But German oppression bred another response as well: the most effective resistance movement in occupied Europe. Amidst widespread demoralization, hundreds of thousands of Poles opted for exaltation and self-sacrifice. The purpose of this underground was less military than social. It aimed less to hurt the Germans than to counteract the atomization of Polish society and restore the social structure the Germans sought to dissolve.[40] The underground organized clandestine secondary and higher education; a variety of cultural events, especially theater; and an underground press, the most extensive in occupied Europe, which issued nearly two thousand separate publications in millions of copies. Most of all, participation bonded conspirators together and endowed them with an exalted sense of mission, a crucial antidote to the depravity fostered by the Nazis. Anti-Nazi resistance could be assimilated into the history of Polish freedom fighting, of martyrdom for the Polish cause. Joining the underground, in other words, meant resisting the Nazis in the most fundamental way: deciding to invest one's life, and probably one's death as well, with meaning.

Ultimate authority over the underground was wielded by the Polish government-in-exile, which was headed by Władysław Sikorski until his death in 1943 and then by Stanisław Mikołajczyk. Headquartered in London, this government ap-pointed a representative to organize in Poland what was known as the Delegate's Bureau (Delegatura), the underground's supreme political authority.[41] The govern-ment-in-exile in certain respects represented a break with the immediate past: it repudiated the prewar Sanacja regime for its political and military blindness as well as for its authoritarianism. Within occupied Poland, every prewar political party went underground and, with the exception of the Communists, was overseen by the Delegate's Bureau. Each party produced its own publications and played a role in underground social and cultural work, as well as in military matters. Similarly, the underground's military arm, the Home Army (Armia Krajowa [AK]), was an um-brella organization of armed groups originally organized under the authority of in-dividual political parties. Of the groups that remained outside the Home Army's authority, the most important were the forces organized by the Communists—the People's Guard (Gwardia Ludowa [GL]) and its successor, the People's Army (Armia Ludowa [AL])—and most of those organized by right-wing nationalists, the Na-tional Armed Forces (Narodowe Siły Zbrojne [NSZ]).

The Home Army, which is estimated to have numbered 350,000 in 1943,[42] di-rected an extensive campaign of sabotage against German factories and railroads and coordinated the work of the partisan groups particularly active in the eastern forests. For most of the war the Home Army undertook only limited direct attacks against German personnel. Vastly superior German firepower and the policy of collective punishment made armed resistance problematic and made mass insurrection seem suicidal.[43] Nevertheless, the underground hid numerous arms in Warsaw and devel-oped plans for a general insurrection that, it was hoped, would finish off the Ger-mans in the final stages of the war. On August 1, 1944, with the Soviets approaching Warsaw, the Home Army launched the long-awaited uprising. On October 2, with some two hundred thousand Warsaw residents dead and the underground de-stroyed, the Poles surrendered to the Germans. The Red Army, unwilling to aid Pol-ish nationalists, had waited outside Warsaw. The Germans marched the surviving population out of the city, and demolition squads dynamited what remained of its monuments. On January 17, 1945, the Red Army occupied the ruins of Warsaw.

The ramified social, cultural, political, and military network that emerged to resist the German occupation of Poland has justifiably been dubbed an "under-ground state" by Polish historians. Its development was facilitated by a number of factors, but above all by the Polish collective memory of resistance against occupiers. In addition, while the underground emerged as a response to oppression, this op-pression, for most of the war and for the great majority of Poles, damaged but did not destroy the fabric of everyday life.[44] The German rationing system might have had terrible consequences for Poles, but because of the black market, hunger rarely led to starvation. Finally, the "underground state" had access to large financial re-sources that were channeled to it from London, beyond German reach.

The situation of the Jews under the German occupation bore little resemblance to that of the Poles. The fundamental difference, of course, was the German inten-tion to murder every Jew. About two million Poles and three million Polish Jews, or, respectively, roughly 10 percent and 90 percent of the prewar Polish and Jewish populations of Poland, died during the German occupation.[45] Nevertheless, nowhere else in Europe would such a comparison be necessary; nowhere else did the murder of Jews unfold amidst such slaughter of the coterritorial people.

Within months of their conquest of Poland the Germans launched the first phase of their "Jewish policy."[46] Throughout Poland, Jews were made to wear the yellow star, uprooted from their homes, and forced into ghettos. The ghettos, walled-off portions of the prewar Jewish neighborhoods, were created in some four hundred cities and towns, primarily in the Generalgouvernement. The Poles living within their boundaries were expelled, and all the Jews in the area, including those from smaller surrounding communities, were crammed into their confines. By the end of 1941, Jews had been despoiled of their possessions and their means of livelihood, and nearly all of the ghettos had been sealed. Traffic in and out was strictly controlled, the regulations enforced with characteristic savagery.

Behind the ghetto walls, the Jews lived under a death sentence, which the Nazis did their best to conceal. Slave labor factories in many ghettos produced apparently important war materiel for the Germans. Jewish councils (*Judenräte*) and Jewish police (*Ordnungsdienst*), though established by German decree and operating under German control, played on the centuries-old tradition of Jewish autonomy: *Judenrat* and kehillah were purposely confounded. Historical memory betrayed Jewish leaders into believing that the survival of at least a portion of the community was possible; entirely helpless, most consented to a degree of cooperation with the oppressor and called for Jewish endurance until the German defeat. Vast amounts of energy were both officially and clandestinely channeled into communal welfare: soup kitchens, hospitals, and schools were established, clothing distributed, housing subsidized, and cultural activities of every kind organized. Clandestine activities, above all smuggling, which typically involved Polish partners, huge profits, and deadly risks, maintained economic breaches in the ghetto walls. Yet all this frenzied activity was insufficient to offset the effects of a German rationing system that in 1941 allowed the Jews of Warsaw only 184 calories per person a day, a little more than one-quarter of the meager Polish ration.[47] In that year in the ghetto, starvation combined with disease and outright murder to produce a death rate of over 10 percent.[48]

With the invasion of the Soviet Union in June 1941, the Nazis began the systematic mass killing of Jews. For Hitler, war in the East heralded the New Order, a world about which much was in doubt but one thing was certain: it would contain no Jews. As the Germans pushed the Red Army through eastern Poland and into Russia, mobile "special operations" units, or *Einsatzgruppen*, operating behind the front lines slaughtered more than one million Jews.[49] In December 1941 at Chełmno, in western Poland, the experimental mass gassing of Jews in vans began. During 1942, camps equipped with gas chambers and crematoriums began to operate throughout the Generalgouvernement. In ghetto after ghetto the same scenario unfolded: the *Judenrat* was told to furnish Jews for "resettlement in the East." Some starving Jews reported voluntarily when promised a loaf of bread and some marmalade or after receiving encouraging postcards from relatives. Many attempted to hide but were rounded up with extraordinary violence. Most were eventually packed into freight cars and dispatched to their death. By the end of 1942 nearly four million Jews had died, including most of the Jews of Poland.[50]

In the ghettos that remained, populated by handfuls of slave laborers and the "illegals" who had managed to avoid deportation, awareness of Nazi intentions was now inescapable. A Jewish underground had existed since the beginning of the German occupation. Composed primarily of youthful Zionist and socialist activists who remained after the flight or murder of the prewar Jewish political leadership, the underground had developed a prolific clandestine press and struggled against divisions in its own ranks and among the masses of starving, isolated ghetto inmates. The survivors of this ghetto underground now offered the surviving Jews their leadership in a fight, not for survival, but for what they called "death with honor." The most effective and symbolically important ghetto revolt occurred in Warsaw several months after the deportation and gassing at Treblinka, from July to September 1942, of more than 250,000 Warsaw Jews. The Warsaw Ghetto Uprising began on April 19, 1943, and pitted about 750 barely armed young people and some 40,000 unarmed Jews dug into underground bunkers against 2,000 superbly armed German troops.[51] This unequal contest lasted for more than a month; the defeat of the uprising required the incineration of nearly every building in the ghetto. Individuals and groups also organized escapes from this and other ghettos. A very few people managed to flee from the death trains and camps. Some of the escapees formed Jewish partisan units or joined existing Russian and Polish groups who fought in the Polish forests. Others attempted to hide among non-Jews, both in cities and in the countryside. During the last two years of the war the Germans expended great effort in tracking down and killing these survivors.[52]

The Polish response to the mass slaughter of the Jews ranged from acts of altruism through indifference to active participation in the killing.[53] The responses of individuals, moreover, were not the same as collective responses, most importantly those of the government-in-exile and the Polish underground. The Polish response to the Holocaust was conditioned by a tangle of political, social, and psychological factors that created immense barriers not just to helping Jews but to wanting to help them.

For a brief period after the German invasion, particularly as Poles and Jews dug trenches side by side in embattled Warsaw, Polish-Jewish relations were transformed. Warsaw Jews, as Emanuel Ringelblum reported, were seized with an enthusiasm reminiscent of the solidarity experienced during the insurrections of the nineteenth century.[54] But the imposition of German rule, specifically intended, among other things, to poison relations between Jews and Poles, marked an irreversible change for the worse. In the first months of the occupation the Nazis orchestrated pogroms by Polish hoodlums in which the Germans were placed in the position of "protecting" the Jews against their neighbors. Although these staged events soon ended, the awareness that street toughs could do what they pleased to Jews accompanied the entire occupation, as did the venomous anti-Semitism of films, posters, and the official Polish-language press.[55]

Moreover, as Poles observed German policy toward the Jews during the first two years of the war, it may not have been entirely clear that Jews had it worse. While it was apparent that the Nazis lavished exceptional sadism on the Jews, prior to the mobilization of the death camps German repression of Jews and Poles may have appeared to differ mainly in intent, being chiefly political in nature, including the murder of elites, against the Poles but primarily economic against the Jews.[56] Ghettos, which the Nazis termed "Jewish residential quarters" to parallel Polish and German "quarters," removed Jews from Polish daily life. Until the ghetto uprisings the Polish underground press stereotyped the Jewish response to the Nazis as passive and contrasted it with the active Polish resistance. When a Jew managed to escape onto an Aryan street from behind ghetto walls plastered with Nazi posters proclaiming, "Jews, Lice, Disease," it required an effort for Poles to remember how recently this Jew had been their neighbor.

To further complicate matters, for many Poles the fate of the Jews proved economically profitable. Beyond the money to be made through smuggling to and from the ghettos as well as blackmailing and informing on Jews hidden on the Aryan side, activities that involved only a small minority of Poles, the German expropriation of the property of 3.5 million Jews amounted to an economic revolution.[57] While the Germans took the lion's share of factories, warehouses, luxury residences, fancy furniture, and clothing, the leftovers went to Poles. Throughout Poland, ownerless stores, merchandise, workshops, raw material, land, and houses quickly found new owners. All of this was strikingly reminiscent of the popular prewar demand of Polish nationalists for eliminating Jews from the Polish economy. Resentment over the alleged Jewish stranglehold on Polish economic life and the conviction that Jewish property rightfully belonged in Polish hands combined with the lure of opportunity to stifle the scruples of the "inheritors" of Jewish property. Indeed, contemporary accounts made it clear that many Poles regarded the new economic situation as a *fait accompli* and would react badly should Jews attempt to return to reclaim their property after the war. Thus, an assessment of the Jewish Question sent to the government-in-exile by an official of the Polish underground in August 1943 included the following:

> In the Homeland as a whole—independently of the general psychological situation at any given moment—the position is such that the return of the Jews to their jobs and workshops is completely out of the question, even if the number of Jews were greatly reduced. The non-Jewish population has filled the places of the Jews in the towns and cities; in a large part of Poland this is a fundamental change, final in character. The return of masses of Jews would be experienced by the population not as restitution but as an invasion against which they would defend themselves, even with physical means.[58]

Such reactions were reinforced by Polish political parties. Most of the parties whose collaboration enabled the "underground state" to function continued to regard the presence of Jews in Poland as a burden. While only the extreme Right condoned killing Jews, the majority of the underground (with the exception of the PPS and several smaller parties) opposed equal rights for Jews in postwar Poland and favored emigration of the one or two million anticipated survivors as the only possible resolution of the Jewish Question.[59] The Poland that would emerge after the war must be a new Poland, free of the debilitating influence of the Jews. In Western Europe, anti-Semites had cordially received the Nazis and often collaborated with them. As a result, after the German defeat anti-Semitism was associated not only with the fate of the Jews but also with treason. It was therefore discredited and banished to the margins of public life. But in Poland, where there was no political collaboration, the most bloodthirsty anti-Semite typically remained a Polish patriot, fought the occupier, and found a place for his views in the underground press. Indeed, part of the Endek heritage was a special antipathy to Germans. Therefore, both during and after the war anti-Semitism remained embedded in Polish society; in many circles, one might easily be a "good Pole" and detest Jews simultaneously. This anti-Semitism, however, was not simply a carryover from the prewar period; it also received a powerful impetus from the Poles' encounter with the Soviet Union, an experience that was to have momentous implications for the future.

From September 1939 to June 1941 the Soviet Union ruled the *kresy*, an area that made up half of the prewar Polish state but in which Poles constituted a minority of the population.[60] The goal of the Soviet occupation was the incorporation of this region into the Soviet system, a transformation of its political, economic, and social structure that, in its own way, paralleled the Nazi effort to make the rest of Poland part of its New Order. The Soviets portrayed themselves as liberators, freeing the region from class and national oppression. This meant appealing to Ukrainian and Belorussian peasants and impoverished Jewish workers. Peasants, for example, were incited to take violent revenge against their Polish landlords. The Soviets established new schools, courts, and other institutions and mounted an assault on religion intended particularly to coopt young people into the new world of "proletarian values."

Finally, the Soviets institutionalized the system of terror that Stalin had perfected in the 1930s. The secret police identified "class enemies" and solicited denunciations of citizens from all corners of society. Poles trembled at the sound of car brakes screeching to a halt in the night before their homes.[61] Immense numbers of people were arrested, imprisoned under barbaric conditions, tortured, executed, or, most commonly, deported to the far reaches of the Soviet Union. In the course of four waves of deportation in 1940 and 1941 over half a million Polish citizens were rounded up without warning and transported to Siberia and Central Asia.[62] As in German-occupied Poland, Polish elites were particular targets of repression.

After the German invasion of the Soviet Union and the rapid retreat of Soviet forces from Polish territory, Stalin initiated relations with the Polish government-in-exile. This uneasy alliance lasted for two years, during which the Soviets released Poles from prisons and labor camps and permitted them to recruit a Polish army in the Soviet Union. But in April 1943, in the Katyń Forest near Smolensk, Germans discovered the bodies of four thousand Polish officers who had been arrested and then murdered by the Soviets at the beginning of the war as part of Stalin's liquidation of Polish elites.[63] The Katyń massacre, which the Soviets denied and then used as a pretext for severing diplomatic relations with the Polish government-in-exile, was to become Communist Poland's greatest historical taboo. It became a symbol of the many atrocities the Soviets had committed against the Poles, which, unlike Nazi crimes, went unpunished and indeed were in danger of being effaced from historical memory.

Having broken with the Polish government-in-exile, Stalin proceeded to plan the country's future independently of it. First he began to build within Poland an underground military and political base devoted exclusively to Moscow. A small group of Polish Communists who had fled to the Soviet Union at the start of the war had been parachuted into the Generalgouvernement in January 1942 to establish a new Communist Party. This was the Polish Workers' Party (Polska Partia Robotnicza [PPR]), the previous Polish Communist Party having been liquidated by Stalin before the war.[64] This cadre then helped set up the People's Guard and later the People's Army, which, even though its membership was small compared with that of the Home Army, proclaimed itself the legitimate Polish underground. Throughout the eastern borderlands, Soviet partisan units fought the Germans and prepared the region for reannexation by the Soviets. Meanwhile, Stalin played his other hand, that of diplomacy. As a result of the three international conferences between 1943 and 1945, at Teheran, Yalta, and Potsdam, he obtained Allied approval for a postwar Poland shorn of the *kresy* and firmly within the Soviet orbit. In October 1944, from positions across the Vistula River, Red Army units, apparently purposely uninvolved, observed the end of an era in Polish history: the defeat of the Warsaw Uprising and the destruction of the Home Army, the last major link to Poland's prewar past.

Even before the Soviet invasion of eastern Poland, the Żydokomuna (Jew Commune) had occupied a prominent place in nationalist diatribes. Here, supposedly, was the modern means to the long-attempted Jewish political conquest of Poland; the Żydokomuna conspirators would finally succeed in establishing a "Judaeo-Polonia." Beginning with the accusation that they sided with the Bolsheviks during the Polish-Soviet War of 1919–20, Jews were accused of masterminding Polish Communism. The interwar Polish Communist Party (Komunistyczna Partia Polski [KPP]) was a small, sectarian organization that Stalin dissolved in 1938 for "Fascist and Trotskyite infiltration";[65] and its leaders were summoned to Moscow, where most of them were murdered. Most Poles saw the KPP as little more than a tool of their eastern enemy; the vast majority of Polish Jews preferred to support Zionist, socialist, or Orthodox parties. Yet while the Jewish representation in the KPP was an insignificant fraction of the Jewish population of Poland, it was far higher than the Jewish share of the general population. During the 1930s, Jews made up about one-quarter of the overall membership of the party; in large cities and in the *kresy* these proportions were considerably higher. Jews comprised over half of the local party leadership, and most of the members of the central committee were of Jewish origin.[66] It should be stressed that most of the Jews in the KPP and certainly those in positions of leadership strongly de-emphasized their Jewish origins. It should not be surprising that an ideology that guaranteed the overcoming of all national antagonisms in an internationalist world of the future would entice Polish Jews more easily than Poles. Soviet practice, moreover, seemed to support the theory: for much of the interwar period, anti-Semitism in the Soviet Union was forbidden and combated, although with diminishing commitment, by state institutions.[67]

The invasion of the eastern borderlands by the Soviet Union signified something quite different for the Jews of the region than it did for the Poles.[68] First and foremost, after years of hearing news reports from Nazi Germany and the stories of refugees from Nazi-occupied Poland, Jews in eastern Poland were convinced that whatever awaited them under the Soviets would be preferable to Nazi rule. Furthermore, in the hundreds of impoverished *shtetlakh* that filled this region, as in Belorussian and Ukrainian peasant villages, there was considerable resentment against Polish rule. In many towns Jews and other minorities greeted the Red Army with flowers and cheers; Jews apparently were particularly conspicuous for kissing Soviet tanks.[69] The Jewish response to the Soviets was also class-related. The middle class, whether tradition-oriented or Polish-assimilating, generally minimized its contact with the occupier. Some of the working-class youth, suddenly offered unprecedented educational and vocational opportunities, enthusiastically embraced a system in which being born Jewish was declared irrelevant; some, indeed, even joined the Soviet security apparatus.

All of this was carefully noted by the beleaguered Poles. After the Germans united all of prewar Poland under their rule in 1941, rumors about what the Soviet occupation of the east had been like inundated the Generalgouvernement. These rumors typically embellished upon the subject of "what *they* [i.e., the Jews] did to us on the other side of the Bug." It was said that Poles had two enemies—the Germans and the Soviets—but the Jews had only one. The irony is that after several months of life under the Soviets, the great majority of Jews, regardless of their initial reactions, were not Soviet devotees.[70] This is best illustrated by the fate of some three hundred thousand Jews from western and central Poland who fled to the Soviet sector during the first months of the war. In the spring of 1940 these refugees were registered by the NKVD and offered two choices: to accept Soviet citizenship or to declare themselves willing to return to their homes in German-occupied Poland. The great majority indicated their readiness to return to the Nazis, whereupon they were accorded the standard treatment for those suspected of disloyalty, namely, deportation to labor camps deep in the Soviet Union. The ultimate irony is that most of these Polish Jews survived the Holocaust, by far the largest group to do so.

Bearing in mind the resentments, hatreds, and misunderstandings that shaped Polish attitudes toward Jews during the war, as well as the severity of Polish suffering, we can return to the question of Polish reactions, both institutional and individual, to the slaughter of the Jews. The Polish underground was involved in a variety of political, social-welfare, and military activities. Despite its democratic structure and its exalted national mission, or perhaps because of them, the "underground state" was essentially for Poles only.[71] In this respect it was a departure from the historical tradition it claimed to represent. Its powerful bond to the community was premised on culture and blood, not formal citizenship; it mirrored popular attitudes, including those about the Jews. In contrast, the government-in-exile had to walk a tightrope. On one hand, contending with Stalin for influence in Washington and London, it was exposed to Western scrutiny, especially that of American and British Jews, who found denouncing Polish anti-Semitism easier than criticizing their own governments' inaction in saving Jews. On the other hand, the government-in-exile was sensitive to reports from Poland stressing the danger of being perceived by Poles as a "government of the Jews." While the government-in-exile had two Jewish representatives on its National Council in London, in Poland Jews were not represented in the Delegate's Bureau.

Beginning in October 1941, the Polish underground relayed accounts of the mass murder of Jews in the eastern territories and then in the gas vans at Chełmno. Several days after the start of deportations from the Warsaw Ghetto to Treblinka, the underground provided a detailed report.[72] Such information was dispatched to the government-in-exile and printed in numerous underground publications. What happened to this information once it arrived in London—how it was treated by the government-in-exile, the BBC, Jewish groups, and Allied governments—is complex. What is undeniable is that, despite occasional vacillation, the Polish government-in-exile was the key channel through which word of the Holocaust reached the West. Crucial in this respect was the work of the Home Army courier Jan Karski. In October 1942 he was smuggled into the Warsaw Ghetto and a concentration camp. He later recounted what he had seen in London and Washington; his visit to the latter city in July 1943 included a personal audience with President Franklin D. Roosevelt.[73]

Both the government-in-exile and the Polish underground accompanied their documentation of the slaughter with expressions of outrage.[74] In October 1942 Prime Minister Sikorski, the main speaker at a protest demonstration at the Albert Hall in London, denounced the Nazi murder of the Jews, warned the Germans that they would pay for their crimes, and promised Jews equal rights in postwar Poland.[75] But with rare exceptions, missing from these statements were appeals to Poles.[76] In the Polish underground press, calls to assist the Jews were no more frequent than condemnations of anti-Semitism; a typical reaction was speculation about whether Poles would be the next to be murdered. For the underground press, the fate of the Jews was a distant second to the fate of the Poles.[77]

While there were sporadic contacts between Polish and Jewish underground groups, chiefly between the PPS and the Bund, from the beginning of the war, it was not until the end of 1942 that the leadership of the Polish underground made attempts to aid Jews. In October of that year, after the deportations from the Warsaw Ghetto, the Warsaw Jewish underground managed to establish contact with the Home Army for the first time. Not long before the start of the ghetto uprising in April 1943 they were given a small quantity of arms and some weapons training. During the uprising, several AK units mounted attacks on the Germans. After the uprising a handful of surviving fighters were led by AK guides through the sewers and out of the burning ghetto. Detachments of the People's Guard also aided the Jewish fighters.[78] The Warsaw Ghetto Uprising marked a high point in the Polish underground's attitude toward the Jews: at last, it was felt, the Jews had responded to the Nazis in a courageous way. Nevertheless, Polish and Jewish interests diverged even here: the Home Army leadership resisted being drawn into a premature insurrection, while the Jews, of course, did not have the luxury of choice. Throughout the war, there were also a few Jews (generally passing as Aryans) who fought in Home Army partisan units, as well as some Jewish units who cooperated with the Home Army. Overall, however, Jews found it easier and safer to work with Soviet and PPR groups, since many right-wing Home Army and NSZ units treated Jews (and Bolsheviks) no differently than they did Germans.[79]

More significant than military aid was the founding in September 1942 of a clandestine Polish organization devoted to helping Jews survive on the Aryan side.[80] Zegota, code name of the Council for Aid to Jews (Rada Pomocy Żydom), was incorporated into the Polish underground and funded until the end of the war by the Polish government-in-exile and Western Jews. Primarily active in Warsaw, the several dozen members of Zegota located housing, produced counterfeit documents, secured regular financial support, and organized medical care for thousands of Jews. The organization developed a special section devoted to hiding children and functioned as an advocate for Jews within the Delegate's Bureau.

The initiative for Zegota's creation was a leaflet written and distributed in Warsaw in August 1942, while Jews were being deported to Treblinka. The author, Zofia Kossak, a Catholic nationalist, reminded Poles of what was taking place behind the ghetto walls, condemned the world's silence, which she equated with complicity with the murderers, and insisted that it was the duty of Catholics and Poles to protest. She then continued: "That is why we, Polish Catholics, are speaking out. Our feelings about the Jews have not changed. We have not ceased to regard them as political, economic, and ideological enemies of Poland. Furthermore, we recognize that they hate us more than the Germans, that they hold us responsible for their misfortunes. Why, for what reason—that remains a secret of the Jewish soul, nonetheless it is a fact that is continually confirmed. Our awareness of these feelings, however, does not free us from *the responsibility of denouncing the crime.*"[81] While Kossak's views were not those of Zegota as a whole, they were hardly unique: there were cases of other anti-Semites who, revolted by the Nazi resolution of the Jewish Question, devoted themselves to saving Jews. But if even a founder of Zegota was an anti-Semite, what could one have expected of the average Pole, lacking, let us assume, Kossak's extraordinary ethical sensibility?

Given the demoralization of much of Polish society under Nazi rule, the fierce anti-Semitism, and the profits to be made from Jews, the prevalence of informing, blackmail, plunder of various kinds, as well as the outright murder of Jews should not surprise us. City streets in the Aryan quarter were the terrain of specialized gangs of blackmailers (the so-called *szmalcownicy,* from *shmalts,* Yiddish for "grease"), who scanned the physiognomy and posture of passersby seeking Jews, whom they turned in to the Germans for a price. In the forests, peasants, with or without German escort, hunted for Jews, whom they killed on the spot or turned over to the Germans. Certainly, not only Jews were betrayed: the first commander of the Home Army,

General Stefan Grot-Rowecki, was denounced to the Nazis by a fellow officer.[82] Hunting Jews was easier, however; all one needed was a knack for "sniffing them out." It was also less dangerous: despite Zegota's efforts, the number of Poles the underground sentenced to death for crimes against Jews was only 1 percent of all the Poles executed by the underground.[83] As Emanuel Ringelblum noted, in Aryan Warsaw the cry "Catch that Jew!" was used by the Nazis to enlist the help of passersby in capturing fleeing members of the Polish underground.[84]

The murder of the Jews evoked a range of responses, from compassion, to the opinion that their fate was "not our business," to the judgment that the Germans had provided an unpleasant but necessary solution to an intractable problem. For the great majority of Poles, however, none of these feelings inspired any action. No different from the majority of other Europeans under Nazi occupation, most Poles were passive witnesses to the fate of the Jews. But for Poles this passivity was reinforced by three factors: the difficulty of daily life under German occupation; the imposition of the death sentence against those accused of aiding Jews; and the widespread perception that Jews were beyond the Polish universe of obligation.[85]

And yet, throughout Poland Jews were helped by thousands of individual Poles, the majority unaffiliated with Zegota. This assistance ranged from the most unpremeditated of gestures, such as offering someone on a death transport a drink of water, to building and maintaining elaborate hideouts where scores of people survived for months and sometimes years. Jews were hidden for the entire war by the Polish families into which they had married, and others were taken off the street and housed and fed for years by total strangers. Some of these Poles were paid for their assistance, but payment could not compensate for the risks involved. There are records of hundreds of Poles who were killed, sometimes along with their families, for sheltering Jews.[86]

Polish aid to Jews was limited not just by fear of the death penalty; it was also limited by Polish popular attitudes about Jews. A person hiding a Jew could be much less certain of his or her neighbor than someone distributing an underground paper. Hiding Jews required a powerful system of personal values independent of social norms. Those who saved Jews came from all classes of society; what many of them had in common was a trait that Nehama Tec has called "marginality," or more positively, "individuality."[87] This rare quality permitted such people to face not only Nazi terror but the indifference and hostility of much of their society. It permitted them to see Jews as humans in need of help. The existence of such individuals is one of the most extraordinary features of Polish-Jewish relations during the Holocaust.

THE POST-HOLOCAUST ERA
1944–1948

The Polish state that emerged from the devastation of World War II differed strikingly from the Second Commonwealth of the interwar years. According to the terms of the agreements worked out by the Allies at Teheran, Yalta, and Potsdam, the boundaries of the new state were shifted greatly to the west. Some seventy thousand square miles of territory, the multiethnic *kresy,* were ceded to the Soviet Union;

in exchange, forty thousand square miles of what had been the German Reich, including East Prussia, Pomerania, and Lower Silesia, became Polish. This geographic transformation, accompanied by the forced expulsion of millions of Germans and Ukrainians from the western and eastern regions, respectively, of the new territory, created a demographic revolution: for the first time in history a Polish state would be populated almost exclusively by ethnic, Roman Catholic Poles. Ironically, this goal of several generations of Polish nationalists, first realized in the experience of the Home Army's "underground state," whose strength had rested in its "Polishness," was attained under Communist rule in the new People's Republic of Poland. The imposition of totalitarian rule transformed everything in Poland, from the structure of its economic development, to the consciousness of its intelligentsia, to the minutiae of everyday life. Politics—the rise, victory, decline, and fall of Communism—is the baseline of postwar Polish history, the ground against which other aspects of that history acquire definition.

The key role of politics is apparent in the immediate postwar period. As Norman Davies points out, it is out of place to speak of a Communist "seizure of power" during the years 1944–48.[88] According to Allied understanding, Poland was to belong to the Soviet sphere of influence; the presence in Poland of the Red Army, accompanied by the inevitable political commissars and secret police, guaranteed this outcome. With the destruction of the Home Army during the Warsaw Uprising of August–October 1944 and the withdrawal of U.S. and British support for the government-in-exile, there remained little significant political opposition to the installation of a Polish government subservient to Moscow. Subsequent events were less a seizure than simply a consolidation of power by the Communists: the succession of provisional governments (beginning with the so-called Lublin Committee, organized in July 1944) consisting of what were termed "all democratic and anti-Nazi elements" that ruled Poland until February 1947; the rigged national referendum of 1946 supporting the government; the elections of 1947 that brought Bolesław Bierut, a Communist who had spent the war years in Moscow, into power as president of the republic; the flight from Poland in late 1947 of Stanisław Mikołajczyk, the last major independent political figure; and the founding the following year (out of the PPR, part of the PPS, and several smaller parties) of the Polish United Workers' Party (Polska Zjednoczona Partia Robotnicza [PZPR]), which was to rule Poland for four decades, with Bierut as its general secretary.

In the immediate postwar years there was a degree of sympathy in Polish society, particularly among workers, peasants, and the intelligentsia, for the program of reconstruction and reform promised by Communist leaders. Yet as Stalin is said to have remarked, imposing Soviet-style Communism on Poland was like trying to saddle a cow. Communism in Poland had had only a limited following, unlike in interwar Czechoslovakia or in Yugoslavia, where the Communists' role in the anti-Nazi resistance legitimated their claim to national leadership after the war. Indeed, in Poland just the opposite was the case: the Home Army and its underground state had been betrayed by the Communists. Communism had no links to either of the national orientations that had developed at the end of the nineteenth century; it traced its origins to a tiny clandestine party that had explicitly renounced the need for Polish independence.[89] In postwar Poland, Communism largely remained an alien system, imposed by the "eastern enemy." The sense of victory at the conclusion of the war was fleeting at best and quickly gave way to the perception that one occupier had simply replaced another and that Poland had been betrayed and abandoned by the West. Such feelings, compounded by the increasing mockery that Communist ideology made of pluralist and universalist discourse, tended to reinforce the exclusivist, almost paranoid tendencies in the Polish popular consciousness. For many Poles the aftermath of the war confirmed their bitter vision of a world filled with enemies and false friends, a world in which the cardinal error was trusting anyone other than oneself.

The consciousness of political defeat played itself out in a general atmosphere of demoralization. Like the years after World War I, but to a much greater extent, the aftermath of the war was marked by widespread lawlessness and violence that approached civil war. Alongside private vendettas, and often indistinguishable from them, paramilitary units linked to three political groups launched attacks against the government and whomever they identified as its sympathizers that claimed thousands of victims. There were the National Armed Forces (NSZ), right-wing nationalists who had remained outside the Home Army during the war; Freedom and Independence (Wolność i Niezawisłość [WiN]), made up of remnants of the disbanded Home Army; and the Ukrainian Insurgent Army (Ukrajinska Powstanska Armija [UPA]), fighting for a Ukrainian state in eastern Poland. At the same time, both responding to the violence and provoking it, the Soviet terror apparatus swung into action: indiscriminate murders, arrests, and deportations swept the country.

This was the atmosphere in which survivors of the Holocaust found themselves when they began to emerge from concentration camps and places of refuge. Determining their number is difficult. There was continuous traffic across the Polish borders, recordkeeping was unreliable, and existing statistics reflect only those Jews who chose to identify themselves as such to local Jewish committees. Statistics from January 1946 reveal 86,000 Jews in Poland, most of whom, we may assume, had hidden on the Aryan side or survived concentration camps, with smaller numbers surviving as combatants in partisan units and in the Polish army and in hiding in forests and bunkers. From February to August 1946, according to the terms of a Polish-Soviet repatriation agreement, more than 100,000 Jews, prewar Polish citizens who had escaped the war deep in the Soviet Union, returned to Poland, swelling the officially registered Jewish population to a postwar peak of 244,000.[90] There is no way to estimate the additional number of Jews who, having passed as Poles on the Aryan side, chose to continue as such.

During these years it briefly seemed as if organized Jewish life in Poland might regain its prewar shape if not its magnitude. Headed by leaders who had returned from the Soviet Union, all the prewar Jewish political parties began to rebuild their activist networks. Alongside them, and involving many of the same leaders, the Central Committee of Polish Jews (Centralny Komitet Żydów Polskich [CKŻP]), established in late 1944 with the cooperation of the pro-Soviet authorities, pursued a program aimed at the economic, social, and cultural revival of the Jewish community in Poland.[91] For psychological reasons and because of security considerations, few Jews attempted to resume their lives in the places where they had lived before the war. With the encouragement of the Polish government and financial support from American Jews, the CKŻP helped settle Jews in the new western areas of Poland, particularly Lower Silesia, where there were industrial jobs. Jewish farming and artisanry were also developed, along with a network of producers' cooperatives. The CKŻP set up Jewish schools to provide primary, secondary, and vocational instruction in Yiddish and Polish, as well as clinics and orphanages (the latter attempting to cope with the unique needs of child survivors). Numerous Jewish periodicals were published, and two Yiddish theaters and a variety of cultural organizations were established. Religious life was organized by local associations modeled on the prewar kehillah; a national union of these congregations was recognized by the government.

At the same time, a handful of surviving Jewish historians founded the Central Jewish Historical Commission (Centralna Żydowska Komisja Historyczna [CŻKH]) under the aegis of the CKŻP and with government support. The commission opened branches in several Polish cities and dedicated itself to gathering documentation on the Holocaust. Its activity paralleled that of Polish historians working in the High Commission to Investigate Nazi War Crimes in Poland (Głowna Komisja Badania Zbrodni Hitlerowskich w Polsce), established by the Polish government in 1945.[92] The primary task of the latter, under the auspices of the ministry of justice, was to gather material for the prosecution of war criminals before the International Military Tribunal at Nuremberg and the Supreme National Tribunal in Poland. The best-known of the Polish trials was that of Rudolf Höss, the commandant of Auschwitz, who was executed at the site of the camp in 1947. Both the High Commission to Investigate Nazi War Crimes and the Central Jewish Historical Commission published considerable material. During the years 1945–48 the Central Jewish Historical Commission issued more than twenty volumes of documents, histories, memoirs, and literary works.[93] In 1947 it moved permanently to Warsaw, changing its name to the Jewish Historical Institute (Żydowski Instytut Historyczny [ŻIH]). There it became the repository of documents relating to Jewish life before and during the Holocaust and of the Ringelblum Archives, which were dug out of the rubble of the Warsaw Ghetto in 1946 and 1950. While most of its founders soon left Poland, the institute nevertheless continued its research and publishing through all the subsequent years of Communist rule, the only Jewish research institution in the Soviet bloc that managed to do so.[94]

The upsurge of Jewish activity in the immediate postwar years was supported by the new Polish government. Until the late 1940s the goodwill of the West and of Western Jews was important both to the Soviet Union and to the new Polish state, especially when such goodwill was accompanied by financial aid. Soviet support for Holocaust survivors in Poland coincided with Soviet politics internationally: in 1947 the Soviet Union voted in the United Nations for the creation of a Jewish state. Nor did the Polish government in the immediate postwar years hinder Jewish emigration to Palestine. Throughout the world these were years that seemed to mark the victory of good over evil. The notion that "peace and progress" had triumphed over "fascist barbarism" was much more than a Communist slogan. Based on these beliefs, official commemorative activity was quickly undertaken. Even before the end of the war the remains of the concentration camps at Majdanek, Stutthof (Sztutowo), and Auschwitz-Birkenau (Oświęcim-Brzezinka) were declared memorial sites by the provisional government.[95] In 1947 the Polish Parliament made these and similar locations the responsibility of the Council for the Protection of Memorials to Struggle and Martyrdom (Rada Ochrony Pomników Walki i Męczeństwa).

The new Polish government legitimized itself by claiming to represent a complete break with everything reactionary in the Polish past, in particular with the heritage of anti-Semitism. This turned out to be only a step along the path to triumphant Stalinism, which would shortly disown the entire Polish past as prehistory. For the time being the government and its supporters constructed an image of the enemy out of the attributes "reactionary," "nationalist," "anti-Semitic," and "criminal."[96] Little distinction was made between the NSZ and the AK: both were attacked as Nazi collaborators who murdered both Jews and partisans. Jewish resistance, and above all the Warsaw Ghetto Uprising, was easily absorbed into this narrative. An extreme but instructive example was provided by the writer Jerzy Andrzejewski, who reported seeing two posters affixed to walls amidst the ruins of Warsaw in April 1945, one reading, "Glory to the Heroic Defenders of the Ghetto," while the one alongside it declared, "Shame to the Fascist Flunkeys of the Home Army."[97] On the fifth anniversary of the Warsaw Ghetto Uprising this distinction was literally graven in stone with the unveiling of Nathan Rapoport's memorial. This celebrated monument and the large public square in front of it quickly became the preeminent site for Polish commemorations of the Holocaust.[98] While official attitudes toward the Home Army softened considerably over subsequent decades, it nevertheless took forty years before a comparable monument was erected to commemorate the Polish uprising. Indeed, at the time the Ghetto monument was raised, the only other war memorial that had been erected in Warsaw was one commemorating fallen Soviet soldiers. Rapoport's monument stood alone in a vast field of rubble, easily read by Poles as a symbol of the new government's decision to honor the Jews, while consigning the Polish national struggle to the dustbin of history.[99] Similarly, Polish secondary school textbooks of the early 1950s devote more attention to the history of anti-Semitism and the Holocaust than any subsequent versions, but the context for this information is a narrative in which the AK is described as hindering Polish resistance.[100]

All this reaffirmed what many Poles already felt they knew, namely, that Jews were the government and the government was Jewish. In the propaganda of the nationalist underground and in the popular consciousness, the enemy became the mirror image of government propaganda: it was assembled out of the attributes "alien," "Communist," "Jewish," and "traitorous." It was an image that long outlived its competitor. The popular and long-lived conviction now arose that the

Żydokomuna had finally conquered Poland. Characteristic is a report written in London in October 1945 by a Polish military courier who had just returned from Poland. He reported that upon the appearance of the new political authorities, Jews "immediately began to falsely accuse those who had concealed them of blackmail and extortion, denounced members of the AK, and permitted themselves to beat and torture Poles in the camps the Jews administered for the Soviets. . . . It is a fact that Jews, along with the Bolsheviks, rule Poland. The ridiculed prewar slogan 'Żydokomuna' has currently been realized. Polish Communists have no power, even in the PPR."[101] Thus the Jews became responsible for the enslavement of Poland.

The kernel of truth in such accusations was related to the vast difference between the situations of Poles and Jews in the new Poland. Because the new government seemed to be the only force capable of defending Jewish rights and safeguarding Jewish life and property in postwar Poland, most Jews in Poland and throughout the world supported it, although not without many reservations. But only a minority of Jews actually served in the government. Except for a handful of Yiddish-speaking Communists who oversaw the officially organized Jewish community in Poland from 1948 to 1968, most Jews who served in the Polish government had assimilated linguistically and culturally to Polish norms or were attempting to do so. The prevalence of such Jews in the postwar Polish government is reminiscent of their prevalence in the KPP, the prewar Polish Communist Party. While they constituted a tiny proportion of all Jews, their representation in the party was considerably higher than their share in the general population.[102]

The Communists who took power in postwar Poland were primarily ex-KPP members who had spent the war in Moscow; their number therefore included a particularly high proportion of individuals of Jewish origin who had thereby survived the Holocaust. For most such lifelong activists the postwar years provided the opportunity to create the kind of Poland they had dreamed of. Other Jews, non-Communists before the war, were attracted by the opportunity to serve in the government, from which Jews had been excluded in the prewar period. Many Jews in the party and the government, partly at the urging of their superiors or the NKVD, adopted more Polish-sounding names in order to arouse less hostility. This practice often backfired and led to widespread speculation about "hidden Jews" for decades to come. It was further believed that Jews controlled the security apparatus, the dreaded UB (Urząd Bezpieczeństwa), and that Jews were thereby responsible for the torture and murder of Polish patriots. The reality was that Jewish representation was greater than the Jewish share of the population but nowhere near the claims of the stereotype.[103]

The development of these notions about the Jews accompanied the worst anti-Jewish violence in the history of Polish-Jewish relations. From 1944 to 1947 between fifteen hundred and two thousand Jews were murdered, the great majority specifically because they were Jews.[104] Most were killed individually or in small groups when they returned to scores of localities in Poland to discover the fate of their families or to reclaim homes and businesses. Jews were pulled from trains to be beaten and murdered, and several Jewish institutions were bombed. Pogroms occurred in about a dozen cities and towns. The worst and the last of these attacks occurred in Kielce in July 1946; forty-two Jews were killed and over one hundred were wounded when a mob attacked a residence for Holocaust survivors.[105] Most of these pogroms, including the one in Kielce, were accompanied by blood libels, accusations originating in the Middle Ages that Jews kidnapped and ritually murdered Christian children.[106] The violence brought international notoriety to postwar Poland and strengthened the government's claim to being the only force that could oppose reactionary backlashes and protect the Jews. Kielce was also a turning point in the attempt to rebuild a Jewish community in Poland. The pogrom convinced most survivors that Poland held no future for them; by 1951, when the government prohibited emigration to Israel, the Jewish population of Poland had shrunk to fewer than eighty thousand.[107] Many of those who stayed had political reasons for doing so; their group profile ever more closely resembled the mythic Żydokomuna.

What caused the waves of anti-Jewish violence that swept Poland after Liberation? Political factors were of great importance. Some of the perpetrators, often still in uniform, were indeed the "fascist bandits" of government propaganda, the "boys from the woods" of the NSZ. Wiping out Jews was as much a part of their political credo as eliminating Bolsheviks; their leaflets ended with the slogan "Kill the Jews and save Poland."[108] The Kielce pogrom has also inspired a good deal of speculation, partly justified, that it was a provocation orchestrated by the NKVD in order to turn world sympathy against the opposition at a time when it was protesting the rigged results of the 1946 referendum.[109] More generally, the Jews found themselves victims of the most explosive conflicts in postwar Poland, and these conflicts were essentially political. As the historian Krystyna Kersten has put it, the core of the problem was "the result of linking the Jewish Question to the system of rule imposed on Poland. Combined in this syndrome in a truly surrealistic manner were the real world and the mythologized world, reason and phobia, political morality and political pragmatism, manipulation and spontaneity, the past and the present, nationalism and Communism."[110] Compared with the prewar period, when hostility to Jews was entangled in economic factors, the postwar situation was a new one. At the same time, there was an abiding continuity in the negative stereotype of the Jew: before, during, and after the war the image of the Jew was that of the spoiler, the avenger, the foe of everything Polish.

But how could this continuity have survived the Holocaust? How could the experience of being the prime witnesses of the Holocaust have left the Poles clinging to their conventional attitudes toward the Jews? It was the Poles, after all, who saw the ghetto walls go up and watched their neighbors imprisoned behind them. Poles observed the ghettos burning, saw Jews herded into sealed trains, watched the transports arrive at their destination, smelled the smoke of the crematoriums, and witnessed the hunting of escapees. It should not have been difficult for Poles to conclude that they were witnessing the attempt to murder every Jew in Poland, perhaps every Jew in Europe.

Is it possible that the Holocaust was not truly or fully witnessed by Poles, that its events were seen but not comprehended? There is testimony that something like this was indeed the case. A student of attitudes toward Jews in Polish literature since 1939 cited the following passage as typical of the Polish reaction to the fate of the Jews: "Collective life and my own life went on beside the life of the ghetto. It occupied me little then; I treated its misery as one of the many astonishing aspects of the war, unnamed in their ghastliness, to which we somehow became accustomed."[111] Krystyna Kersten analyzed references to Jews in memoranda to the government-in-exile written in wartime Poland and pointed out "the nearly total separation of the martyrology of the Jews from the so-called Jewish question. The annihilation of the Jewish people occurring before the eyes of Poles seemed not to have changed in any way the stereotype, encoded in the collective imagination, of the Jew as threat. . . . Between the effect—Poland without Jews—and the cause—a crime without precedent on a scale that does not permit it to be grasped by the imagination of those who were not its witnesses—the link was broken." It was this, according to Kersten, that allowed the Catholic activist Zofia Kossak to demand Polish aid for Jews during the war even as she termed them "enemies of Poland."[112]

The inability to accept, to assimilate, to grasp, that is, truly to witness the events of the Holocaust as they were occurring, was not unique to Poles. It was inherent in the incredulous response of Americans who read the news of death camps printed in the corners of their newspapers because the editors, in turn, had found the information too "unbelievable" to put on the front page; it was true of most of the perpetrators, the bureaucrats who did not want to know and were systematically kept from knowing the truth, carefully cloaked in euphemisms; it was true of Jews in the ghettos, who assumed that making themselves useful to the Germans would guarantee survival, and later, when they entered gas chambers believing they were showers; and it was true of the survivors, who typically questioned whether they could bear witness to themselves, much less to the world, about what they had experienced.[113]

1948–1968

Most of the evidence on Polish reactions to the Holocaust in the period after 1948 concerns the actions and attitudes of the party and the state. With the totalitarian system in place, popular violence, indeed popular expression of any kind, was rare; even when an unplanned outburst occurred, its traces were quickly erased from public record. Certainly, on most issues there was a vast gulf between official pronouncements and the private opinions of "average" Poles. Yet it would be an oversimplification to distinguish absolutely between the rulers and the ruled. The "official" world included several million bureaucrats who had been raised in Poland. Poland under Communism was not simply a creature of Soviet manipulation; it was a product of the interplay between this manipulation and the particular constraints of Polish history. Rulers and ruled in postwar Poland were distinct, but they were all Poles. Nowhere was this more true than in relation to the Jewish Question and the memory of the Holocaust.

As elsewhere in Eastern Europe, Soviet domination was strongest at the start of this period. From 1948 until 1956 Poland was governed by a group of ideologues intimately linked to the Soviet Union under Stalin, who attempted to impose a comprehensive economic, political, and cultural system on the country.[114] But Polish Stalinism, the first and crudest attempt to saddle the Polish cow, never attained the extremes of its counterparts in neighboring Communist countries, and this made a fateful difference in Poland's postwar history. Unlike in other Soviet bloc countries, agriculture remained in private hands. The church, though attacked, was far from crushed. Cardinal Stefan Wyszyński, who had succeeded Cardinal Hlond as primate of Poland, was freed from house arrest in 1956. Over the next quarter of a century he presided over the development of the most powerful church in the Communist bloc. Under a political system in which the state controlled all education and media, the church managed to retain the only exceptions: legalized religious instruction for the young and its own press. At a time when in the Soviet Union Yiddish writers were murdered and Jewish doctors were accused of poisoning Stalin, while elsewhere in the Soviet bloc anti-Semitic show trials were the order of the day, nothing comparable occurred in Poland. The new regime attempted to accustom Poles to austerity through a rhetoric of present sacrifice for future generations. But on the level of daily life the reality was not just scarcity but interminable delays, inefficiency, and growing corruption in the expanding state bureaucracy.

The overthrow of Polish Stalinism in October 1956 and its replacement by a new group of leaders led by Władysław Gomułka was the most significant attempt during the postwar years to reestablish the legitimacy of the ruling system through reform. Gomułka's assumption of power amidst pitched battles between workers and police in the streets of Poznań climaxed a factional struggle within Polish Communism that dated back to the war years. This was a contest between those who, like Bierut, had spent the war in Moscow and those who, like Gomułka, had spent it in Poland. The latter, identified as "fighters" and "patriots," were reputed to be less dogmatic, more practical-minded, and more willing to discover a "Polish road to socialism."

The Polish socialism of Gomułka and his circle, a form of the so-called national Communism that made headway for several decades in the Soviet bloc, was a grab bag of contradictory tendencies advanced by competing factions. There were revisionists, who sought to make the ruling system less repressive politically and culturally. The first years of Gomułka's rule were indeed marked by a new feeling of intellectual freedom, a considerable easing of censorship, and the disappearance of many Stalinist taboos. There were also those who wished to rehabilitate the system by infusing it with "national" values. This direction, supported by a new generation of party functionaries, the "new class," who were primarily of peasant background and who had joined the party after the war, entailed the assimilation of ideas with a direct lineage to the prewar Endecja but with proletarian rhetoric. Here were the beginnings of a peculiar marriage of authoritarian Communist and chauvinist nationalist tendencies that would later be termed "Endo-Communism."[115] Thus, in the process of attempting to develop a greater measure of national legitimacy, Polish Communism began to manifest divisions resembling those characteristic of Polish politics since the end of the nineteenth century.[116]

With Gomułka's rise to power, the Jewish Question began to play an increasingly prominent role in intraparty intrigue. The fall of the Polish Stalinists was hailed by the budding Endo-Communists as the defeat of the Jews who had sat out the war in Moscow and then returned to exploit Polish workers. The revisionists were labeled ex-Stalinists, "cosmopolitans," and "Jews" out of touch with the needs of the Polish masses. In the aftermath of the coup, anti-Semitism flared throughout Poland. While it was not comparable in extent or intensity to that of the immediate postwar years, it did include physical attacks, with abuse directed particularly at Jewish schoolchildren, as well as the expropriation of apartments belonging to Jews.[117] An indication of Polish attitudes during this period was the popularity of a comment attributed, in one of its versions, to a Łódź Jew: "Many of us died, it is true, but there are enough of us remaining to rule over you."[118] While the precise relation between popular anti-Semitism and party agitation is unclear, both were short-lived because the highest party authorities insisted on adhering to ideological orthodoxy and repressing them for the time being. In April 1957 the central committee of the PZPR issued a memorandum to party committees throughout the country denouncing "occurrences of chauvinism, anti-Semitism and racism" as well as "nationalistic, chauvinistic and racist views [propagated by] comrades holding responsible party or state positions."[119] Several years later such concerns prevented *The Merchant of Venice* from opening at the state theater.[120] Until the late 1960s the passions surrounding the Jewish Question would be more or less successfully excluded from the public domain.

The events of the Polish October, combined with the lifting of the ban on Jewish emigration, were nevertheless sufficient to provoke a new wave of Jewish emigration. From 1956 to 1960 more than forty thousand Jews left Poland for Israel. These departures were only partially offset by the repatriation of eighteen thousand Polish Jews from the Soviet Union, some of whom remained in Poland. By the mid-1960s the Jewish community in Poland numbered no more than thirty thousand.[121] This was an aging, fear-ridden group that was supposed to conform to the profile of a Soviet-style "national minority." With no qualified rabbi, nearly no *shokhtim* (ritual slaughterers), and only a handful of functioning synagogues, the community was controlled by a small group of Yiddish-speaking Communists who, with government approval and American Jewish financial assistance, ostentatiously maintained certain vestiges of a secular Yiddish culture: a newspaper (*Folksshtimme* [The People's Voice]), a publishing house (Yidish Bukh), and a theater, directed until 1969 by the celebrated Yiddish actress Ida Kaminska.

The many-sided development, in a host of contexts and mediums, of a narrative of the war years was crucial to the efforts of postwar Polish governments to legitimate themselves in the eyes of their subjects. Such a narrative was also needed for external purposes. At least until the ratification in 1972 of a treaty with West Germany affirming Poland's western borders, memorializing the martyrdom of Poles at the hands of the Germans was a way to demonstrate the historical justice of the new geography. For Communist ideologues the matter was loaded with even more significance. From Marx to Stalin, history had been the foundation of the Communist worldview; everything was done, and justified, in its name. Thus, in the Communist narrative that developed in the postwar years the war was invested with messianic significance, being seen as the product of suicidal class and national hatreds that had climaxed in the destruction of the class system and the establishment of the rule of peace and justice in Poland and throughout the Soviet bloc. Viewed from a suitably dialectical perspective, the war years were about martyrdom and resistance, horror and heroism, all in the interests of a single historically inevitable cause.

The fate of the Auschwitz-Birkenau site is instructive. Here had stood the Nazis' largest and most dreaded slave labor factory, where from 1940 to 1942 tens of thousands of Poles, among them the Polish political and cultural elite, were shipped to be worked to death. Between 1942 and the end of 1944, during which time it was expanded by the addition at Birkenau of four sets of crematoriums and gas chambers, the camp also became the final destination for hundreds of thousands of Jews from Poland and across Europe. According to a recent study, 960,000 Jews, as well as 73,000 Poles, 21,000 Gypsies, 15,000 Soviet prisoners of war, and 10,000 to 15,000 citizens of other nations, died at Auschwitz-Birkenau.[122] Yet according to the mandate of the Council for the Protection of Memorials to Struggle and Martyrdom, ratified by the Polish Parliament in 1947, Auschwitz was one of the sites at which "Poles and citizens of other nationalities fought and died a martyr's death."[123]

Under Communism, Auschwitz became a monument to internationalism that commemorated the "resistance and martyrdom" of "Poles and citizens of other nationalities." In consultation with the International Auschwitz Committee, a group of survivors and relatives of victims dominated by veterans of the largely Communist Auschwitz underground, barracks in the original work camp were turned over to twenty countries for use as "national pavilions." One of these structures became a "Jewish pavilion." In 1967 an International Memorial to the Victims of Fascism, the result of efforts initiated by the International Auschwitz Committee soon after Gomułka's accession to power, was completed at Birkenau near the site of the four crematoriums. One week prior to its unveiling, the monument was changed: a group of three abstract figures of varying sizes that suggested a family was replaced by a polished marble square with a triangle at its center.[124] Thus, the representation suggesting Jewish victims (most of the families murdered were, of course, Jewish) was replaced by one recalling the insignia worn by slave laborers, who had not been gassed immediately and who indeed represented a cross section of nationalities. At the base of the monument were nineteen plaques in as many languages, including Yiddish, all bearing the same inscription: "Four million people suffered and died here at the hands of the Nazi murderers between the years 1940 and 1945." This inflated figure, widely accepted in the Soviet bloc, was based on the unexamined postwar testimony of both Auschwitz survivors and Nazi officials and made it possible to inflate the numbers of Poles, Russian prisoners of war, and other non-Jews murdered at Auschwitz, thus providing further basis both for its "Polonization" and for its "internationalization." Auschwitz could thereby emerge as the central symbol of Polish martyrdom, but within an inclusive internationalist framework. Jews could be relegated to the formulaic "other nationalities" murdered at Auschwitz, a list in which, alphabetically and therefore democratically, "Żydzi" came last.

Nevertheless, until the mid-1960s the fate of the Jews continued to be seen as something exceptional. However, the term "genocide," which was used to designate the fate of the Jews, was incorporated into an ideological narrative. It was seen as the result of passivity in the face of fascism and was counterposed to redeeming acts of resistance. The basis for this interpretation was the decision just after the war to make the Warsaw Ghetto Uprising emblematic of the Holocaust. Rapoport's monument, with its inscription, "To the Jewish people, its fighters and martyrs," was designed to express this idea. On the front of the monument, framed by two large menorahs (lit once a year on the anniversary of the uprising) and dominating the surrounding square, a group of armed ghetto fighters seems to burst out of the stone. On the back of the monument a shallow bas-relief depicts a downcast procession of Jews guarded by German soldiers that includes the monument's only religious figure, a traditionally dressed Jew gazing heavenward and bearing a Torah scroll. This image overlooks a side street.

Narrative accounts of the Warsaw Ghetto Uprising published during most of the Gomułka years are constructed around this duality. Typically, they also stress Polish solidarity with Jewish resistance and parallel Polish and Jewish suffering, thereby tending to blur, though not abolishing, the distinction between the fate of the Poles and that of the Jews. The introduction to a popular volume of photographs of the uprising, for example, mentions both the "inconceivable crime of genocide" and "the invader's plans . . . to be rid of everything that was not Germanic."[125] In a popular pamphlet published by the veterans' association Związek Bojowników o Wolność i Demokrację (ZBoWiD, the Association of Fighters for Freedom and Democracy) on the twentieth anniversary of the uprising, the author Wacław Poterański began with descriptions of the sounds of battle and ended on a note of internationalism, linking the Ghetto Uprising with both the Polish Uprising and the antifascist struggles of "all the freedom- and peace-loving peoples."[126] Poles and Jews are also linked through the intentions of their persecutor: the Nazis, according to Poterański, slated both people for extermination but did not have time to complete the job on the Poles. He noted that "the overwhelming majority of the Polish nation condemned the crimes committed against the Jews and stigmatized those who expressed satisfaction with 'Hitler's solution to the Jewish question' or manifested passivity."[127]

Poterański also drew a parallel between Poles' and Jews' internal struggles concerning armed resistance. In both cases, he explained, "bourgeois and right-wing groups" preached passivity: among Poles, they waited for the Nazis and the Soviets to finish each other off on the eastern front; among Jews, they attended help from the West. Among both Poles and Jews, only the Left, and above all the PPR, consistently organized armed resistance from the beginning. But Poterański considerably moderated the extremity of postwar attacks on non-Communists: only the NSZ was accused of fascism, anti-Semitism, and collaboration. The AK, the government-in-exile, and even the church were assigned roles that were honorable though secondary. The impact of the "Polish road to socialism" on the narrative of the war years is apparent in Poterański's list of those who helped save Jews: "Communists, socialists, populists, democrats, scouts, officers and soldiers of the People's Guard and the AK, Catholics, priests and nuns, professors, doctors, workers, and students."[128]

The great variety of narratives of the war years produced during the Gomułka period included other approaches as well, especially in the earlier years. A large-format volume of photographs entitled *Miasto nieujarzmione* (Unvanquished city) and dedicated to occupied Warsaw was published in the liberal political atmosphere following Gomułka's accession to power. Unabashedly nationalist in tone, it concentrated on the Home Army and the Polish Uprising. The afterword, printed in the national colors, white letters on a red page, refers to the uprising as "yet another insurrectionary impulse" and alludes to the ongoing need for Poles to "uncover the truth about the uprising—raw and grim, yet full of faith in man, his nobility, and courage," and to incorporate it into national memory.[129] Yet, of the 270 pages of photographs in this decidedly unofficial narrative only 2 are devoted to the ghetto, and only 4 to the Ghetto Uprising.

Relatively unmarked by official ideology was much of the Holocaust scholarship produced by the Jewish Historical Institute from the late 1950s to the early 1960s, as well as a short history of wartime Poland whose authors, one of them the director of the High Commission to Investigate Nazi Crimes in Poland, stated that the Nazis had intended to deport, but not to murder, all the Poles.[130] A powerful memorial at Treblinka, where only Jews were killed, was completed in 1964. It consists of thousands of broken stones, some bearing the names of destroyed Jewish communities, set into a huge field of concrete in the middle of a meadow. Overlooking the field is a monument that includes a carved menorah; text panels at the entrance also make reference to Jews. Nevertheless, at the unveiling of this memorial the press spoke of Treblinka's victims as "800,000 citizens of European nations."[131]

How was all this received by its intended audience? Although the evidence needed to answer this question definitively is lacking, it is reasonable to assume that most of it was widely mistrusted, if not dismissed. This doubtless applied to the invocations to internationalism, which were viewed as a cynical reminder of precisely the opposite, namely, the history of Soviet oppression, even under "national Communism." More generally, by the 1960s, as political repression intensified and the economic situation worsened, Gomułka's vaunted "Polish road to socialism" increasingly seemed to be yet another variety of opportunism. The difficulties of daily life undermined the affirmations of public discourse, and the gap between the latter and private belief continued to widen. The following passage from the émigré writer Henryk Grynberg's autobiographical novel, set in Poland in the late 1950s and early 1960s, presents this disjunction, inaccessible through opinion polls, in its extremity:

> Speakers have to pretend that they believe what they say, and listeners that they believe what they hear, and it doesn't bother anyone that everyone knows that no one believes a single word. . . . The press did not believe what it wrote, for it was not so stupid, nor was it embarrassed knowing that its readers could not believe it and perfectly well knew that it knew, and none of this surprised anyone. . . . It was the same

with radio and television, exhibitions, films, books, students and teachers, and pretending no longer tired anyone, for everyone was accustomed to it. . . . One didn't even have to pretend so carefully, knowing that in any case everyone knew. Very little was demanded, just enough for the show to go on.[132]

While the majority of those who lived in Poland may not have perceived the disjunction between public and private discourse in terms that were quite so absolute, what was believed about the war years was doubtless learned behind closed doors, from the personal accounts of family and friends. The prioritizing of private narrative was a cornerstone of popular resistance to Communism, but this narrative, punctuated by the rumors, resentments, and silences inherited from the war years and the years immediately following, was a legacy particularly subject to distortion.[133]

Unlike during the immediate postwar years, however, these beliefs scarcely marked the surface of history. Elsewhere in his novel, Grynberg, who had toured Poland for several years with Ida Kaminska's Yiddish theater troupe, recounted how in one city a group of local residents confronted the actors as they left the theater: "They didn't make any real disturbance, and didn't even throw stones as we departed, but only repeated, over and over, 'Leave us alone!'"[134] In consigning the memory of the Jews to that of the "other nations" victimized by the Nazis or to an official narrative woven around a small number of explicitly "Jewish" sites and symbols, a narrative whose effect was to marginalize, or "ghettoize," its subject, official Polish commemorative activity doubtless reflected a popular need.

1968–1970

As the first postwar generation began to come of age in the mid-1960s, efforts to appropriate the memory of the war years could no longer avoid confronting the memory of the Holocaust. The first of these confrontations, the most extreme and the most destructive, came to a climax in the years 1968–70. In Polish popular awareness and recent Polish historiography, the events of this period have been subsumed under the term "March '68," the month when the government attacked striking Warsaw University students.[135]

The immediate cause of the attack was a conflict about the uses of the past: students had protested the banning of performances of Adam Mickiewicz's national epic *Dziady* (Forefathers' eve), which the government claimed had inspired behavior hostile to Poland's "eastern ally." The government's heavy-handed response quickly escalated events into a full-fledged confrontation between, on one side, students and intelligentsia, the proponents of political and cultural reform, and, on the other side, the most repressive faction within the party, the so-called Partisans led by General Mieczysław Moczar. The Partisans, whose name stressed their self-identification as "fighters" and "patriots" of the anti-Nazi resistance, were strongly represented in the security apparatus. They unleashed against the so-called *bananowcy* (a term implying the students' privileged consumption of delicacies such as bananas) the combined forces of the police, the courts, and the media. Their campaign also included a wave of orchestrated demonstrations of "popular outrage."

In the short run, the Partisans, unimpeded by Gomułka, won notable victories.

The student movement and its allies were crushed, its leaders imprisoned or exiled. In Poland, as throughout the Soviet bloc, revisionism was defeated. And yet the student rebels learned crucial lessons from their defeat, above all that political change was not possible without the active participation of the workers; in 1980 an alliance of workers and intelligentsia would produce the Solidarity movement. From this perspective, March '68 can be seen as a turning point in postwar Polish history, the origin of forces that would overthrow Polish Communism.

But the years 1968–70 also witnessed a state-sponsored campaign of anti-Semitic agitation directed not only at the allegedly "Zionist" student rebels but at Jews in general, both real and imaginary.[136] The campaign was initiated by Gomułka in a speech following the Six-Day War in June 1967 in which he employed the term "fifth column" to refer to Jews in Poland.[137] Beginning in March 1968, at workplaces throughout the country, mass meetings were called to denounce Zionism, and Jewish employees were "unmasked" and dismissed from their positions. While most of those affected were professionals in the big cities—doctors, engineers, academics, journalists, and, above all, government functionaries—the purge extended to smaller cities and to those employed in lower-level positions, even to factory workers. These individuals, who were unable to find work, were permitted to leave Poland under one condition: that they surrender their Polish citizenship in exchange for an exit permit valid only for travel to Israel. In this fashion, over a period of two years some twenty thousand Poles of Jewish descent "proved" their allegiance to Israel through what was actually a forced expulsion. Because they had surrendered their citizenship, no Communist regime would ever readmit them to Poland. Ironically, only a small proportion of these emigrants, most of whom had been indifferent or hostile to Zionism, settled in Israel. Most moved to the Scandinavian countries and to the United States. There was no protest in Poland against the campaign. The church barely reacted, and even the Catholic press, skilled in political commentary designed to skirt the censor's pencil, was silent.[138]

The anti-Zionist campaign has been viewed as the accompaniment to an essentially political struggle. Indeed, Moczar tried but failed to replace Gomułka, who was finally toppled by worker protests in December 1970. The anti-Zionist campaign, which was directed with particular ferocity at party functionaries of Jewish descent, has also been seen as an effort by the new generation of bureaucrats, who joined the party after the war, to advance their careers by making room for themselves in the party hierarchy. Yet these factors hardly explain the significance of the campaign. The reemergence of the myth of the "Jewish menace" at this turning point in Polish history is more than a coincidence.

The second half of the 1960s marked the beginnings of a transformation in the nature of Polish public discourse. Before this period, both the government and the intelligentsia operated within a more or less conventional Marxist worldview; at most the intelligentsia spoke of "socialism with a human face." March '68, as the sociologist Jerzy Szacki put it twenty years later, was "the funeral of Communist ideology."[139] It was gradually replaced by what the historian Marcin Król described as "a patriotic-symbolic-religious language. . . . Traditions that had been reviled and undermined by the authorities, but also by the intelligentsia, returned to public life with their entire ambiguous heritage."[140] These "traditions" were the traditions of Polish nationalism, which had persisted within popular consciousness despite their rejection by the government and the leftist intelligentsia. The events of 1968 represented the first step in discarding a discourse out of touch with the majority of Poles for one that attempted to speak directly to them. Prominent among the traditions uncovered were the competing claims of the exclusivist and pluralist worldviews. The proponents of these two perspectives began to compete in the quest for a usable past, one with an acceptable narrative of the war years. This process could not avoid dealing with the Holocaust.

The first stage of this process was the work of General Moczar and his Partisans, who solidified the alliance between chauvinist nationalism and authoritarian Communism into the formidable political force known as Endo-Communism. Moczar's links to the Soviet Union and the NKVD dated back to the war years. Some of his party associates had roots in the prewar Endecja and its radical offshoots. His influence began to grow after October 1956, when, as a member of the right-wing faction in the PZPR, he helped rebuild the weakened security apparatus and transformed it into his personal power base. Many observers of Moczar and his followers have stressed the Soviet Union's influence on the Polish anti-Zionist campaign. While Soviet manipulation of the Jewish Question certainly played a role in Polish party intrigue, recent research has shown that the Polish anti-Zionist campaign preceded its Soviet counterpart.[141]

Key to Moczar's rise to power was his alliance with the institutions responsible for interpreting the memory of the war years, including the Warsaw office of the International Auschwitz Committee and the High Commission for the Investigation of Nazi War Crimes. Most important was Moczar's leadership of the veterans' association ZBoWiD. This organization, with a membership of three hundred thousand, claimed to speak for all Polish veterans of World War II. For the first time in Poland, tens of thousands of former members of the AK could step proudly into the public arena. Moczar transformed them from outcasts into honorable veterans and thereby assured himself their exclusive allegiance. The support of ZBoWiD in turn gave Moczar and his associates popular legitimation to appropriate the heritage of anti-Nazi resistance. ZBoWiD became Moczar's ideological base, the driving force of both the anti-Jewish campaign and the assault on the students and the intelligentsia. Moczar also made himself a symbol, the incarnation of the Polish anti-Nazi underground. Hundreds of thousands of copies of his war memoirs, *Barwy walki* (The colors of struggle), appeared during the 1960s, making it one of the most widely available books in postwar Poland. Required reading in secondary schools, it was translated into six languages and made into a movie.[142]

Thus situated, Moczar led the campaign in the name of all "fighting Poles" who had sacrificed for the fatherland during the war against a foe that once again sought Poland's humiliation and defeat. Poland was under siege, the Partisans proclaimed, by an international conspiracy that was overseen by American imperialists but implemented by enemies much closer to home, namely, Germans and Jews. The nature of the threat was always somewhat nebulous, but two issues emerged clearly: (1) the supposed West German desire to regain the territories Poland had annexed after the war; and (2) the alleged effort by Jews, both in Poland and abroad, to distort the memory of the war years.

Moczar and his followers cultivated the image of a Poland reeling under a Western propaganda attack directed at Polish attitudes toward Jews during the war. Works such as Leon Uris's *Exodus* and *Mila 18* and Jerzy Kosinski's *Painted Bird* were accused of defaming the honor of the Polish nation. As official news of the "anti-Polish offensive" mounted, history began to be revised: references to Polish informers or indifference to the fate of the Jews during the war were increasingly censored, while accounts of Polish aid to Jews and "exposés" of Jewish collaboration with the Nazis began to proliferate.

All this came to a head during the campaign against the so-called Encyclopedists *(Encyklopedyści)*. At issue was an article on Nazi concentration camps that had appeared in the eighth volume of the prestigious *Wielka Encyklopedia Powszechna* (Great Universal Encyclopedia) published by Państwowe Wydawnictwo Naukowe (the State Academic Publishing House) in 1966.[143] The article differentiated between *obozy koncentracyjne* (concentration camps), where prisoners lived and worked under conditions designed to hasten death, and *obozy zagłady* (annihilation camps), whose only purpose was murder and nearly all of whose victims were Jews. The media joined in the condemnation in August 1967, and shortly afterward "demonstrations" denouncing the Encyclopedists were staged at ceremonies commemorating the beginning of World War II. After much examination, the entire encyclopedia was deemed to have slighted Polish martyrdom and emphasized the suffering of Jews and Germans.[144] Most of the members of the encyclopedia's staff (some of whom, of course, happened to be of Jewish descent) were dismissed, and a "corrected" article was added to the volume. The new article denounced the idea that any distinction existed among Nazi camps and affirmed that they were all intended to exterminate everyone who passed through their gates, be they Poles or Jews.

In the following years a host of other publications developed a greatly changed narrative about Poles and Jews during the war years. Though Moczar's influence waned after 1968, this new official narrative of Polish history persisted well into the 1980s. When Wacław Poterański's pamphlet on the Warsaw Ghetto Uprising was reissued in 1968, on the twenty-fifth anniversary of the uprising, it contained new material on the prewar Jewish community that attributed the political and cultural attainments of the Jews to the Polish environment. It went on to explain that the Jewish community was controlled by "clerical," "bourgeois," and "Zionist elements." The German occupation, introduced as "the most tragic period in the history of the Polish nation," was characterized as follows: "The extermination plans of the Nazi occupier assumed the physical annihilation of the Polish population—Poles as well as national minorities: Jews, Ukrainians, Belorussians, Gypsies."[145] The victims of Nazi concentration and death camps are then discussed within this context. New sections on the *Judenräte* and the Jewish police were added, accusing them of collaboration with the Nazis. Much was also made of Jewish demoralization and passivity. Such material was counterposed to extended discussions about Polish aid to Jews; the Poles who aided Jews included "very many politically unaligned, patriotic Poles—people of good will."[146]

The description of the actual uprising devoted three times as much space to Polish actions of support as to the Jewish fighting. The pamphlet no longer concluded on a note of internationalism; now it quoted warnings by Moczar and Gomułka against West Germans and Zionists. It ended with a protest against "the anti-Polish propaganda of various historical institutes in Israel, as well as Zionist centers in Western Europe and the United States, [which] accuses the Polish nation of anti-Semitism, of participation in the Nazi mass murder of the Jews during the Second World War, while ignoring Polish help to Jews in hiding and in battle and falsifying the truth about the history of the Jews in Poland in order to whitewash and lessen the responsibility of Nazism and its heirs for genocide against Jews and other nations."[147]

The 1973 edition of Poterański's pamphlet did not cite Moczar and Gomułka, but there was a new denial of anti-Semitism in prewar Poland. New material was also added on Jewish Gestapo agents and the AK's efforts against the Polish blackmailers who preyed on Jews in hiding. Less space was devoted to the NSZ, who were described as anti-Semites and anti-Communists but no longer as fascists and Nazi collaborators.[148]

In general accounts of the war years published from the late 1960s until the 1980s the fate of the Jews is nearly indistinguishable from that of "the Polish nation." An excellent example is *Obozy hitlerowskie na ziemiach polskich, 1939–1945: Informator encyklopedyczny* (Nazi camps on Polish soil, 1939–1945: Encyclopedic handbook), jointly produced by the High Commission to Investigate Nazi War Crimes and the Council for the Preservation of Memorials to Struggle and Martyrdom.[149] This seven-hundred-page volume is a source of invaluable information about thousands of concentration, forced-labor, transit, prisoner-of-war, and death camps; prisons; and ghettos established by the Nazis throughout Poland. Czesław Pilichowski, a member of the anti-Semitic prewar ONR who took over as director of the High Commission in 1965 and ran it until his death in 1984, edited the volume and provided the introductory essay.[150] The essay refuted the Encyclopedists by demonstrating that the many types of Nazi camps were all directed toward one end, the "genocide and annihilation of the Polish nation."[151] Accordingly, in every category of camp Jewish victims were subsumed under Polish victims; Jews were specifically discussed only in the context of ghettos. Perusing this volume's otherwise reliable documentation, one can nevertheless arrive at the conclusion that the Holocaust was something that happened to Poles.

Part of this new official narrative received support from an unexpected quarter. Władysław Bartoszewski, a founding member of Żegota, was a Catholic activist who had been imprisoned in Poland during the Stalinist period and was a resolute opponent of the succeeding Communist governments. In 1963, citing as his motive the Western stereotypes of Poles as collaborators in the murder of Jews, Bartoszewski issued a call in the leading Polish Catholic and émigré publications for material documenting Polish aid to Jews during the war.[152] Bartoszewski first published his results in 1966. Primarily a collection of testimonies, *Ten jest z ojczyzny mojej* (He is of my fatherland) was published by the Catholic publisher Znak (Sign), which issued an enlarged edition three years later.[153] But in 1970 the government publishing house Interpress issued an abridged narrative by Bartoszewski, in English, French, and German editions, based on the testimonies.[154] This curious and temporary rapprochement between otherwise implacable enemies is another sign of the degree to which issues connected with the Polish experience of the Holocaust, and indeed only these issues, had the power to transcend the most formidable political differences as the first postwar generation came of age.

Rewriting the history of the war was only one manifestation of the paranoid vision of the world advanced by Moczar and the Partisans. Tadeusz Walichnowski, an official of the ministry of the interior in the 1960s, who was responsible for keeping track of Jews by racial criteria, published *Izrael a NRF* (Israel and West Germany) in 1967. This bestselling book described in detail how West Germans and Jews plotted against Poland. An article with a similar theme is "The Alliance between Victims and Executioners."[155] This title is characteristic of all these publications: in a host of contexts, victims and victimizers, as well as past and present, were conflated. It was written that Germany supported Israel's "genocide" in the Middle East and that the Israelis were Nazis. A government figure declared that one thousand ex-Nazis were advising the Israeli army.[156] Others asserted that Moshe Dayan was actually a disguised Nazi war criminal; that Martin Bormann was hiding in Golda Meir's apartment;[157] and that Dayan's daughter Yael "reminds us" of Ilse Koch, the Buchenwald commandant's wife who reputedly had lampshades made of human skin.[158] Moreover, this alliance between Nazis and Jews supposedly was not a recent occurrence. Zionists, it was alleged, who needed the Holocaust in order to build support for a Jewish state, collaborated with the Nazis, as did Jewish communal leaders in the ghettos. The real victims were clearly the Poles. The conspiracy of Germans and Jews denied the martyrdom of the Polish nation during World War II. Furthermore, it exonerated the Germans of the murder of the Jews and blamed it on the Poles.

The anti-Zionist campaign suggested that the murder of the Jews was an obstacle that stood between Poles and their own past and prevented them from repossessing that past as a narrative of their own exemplary martyrdom. The meaning of the Holocaust had become Polish victimization *by* the Holocaust. The events of the late 1960s may be viewed in several ways: as a struggle for power within the Polish Communist Party; as an attack on independent culture and thinking; as the final gasp of a hopelessly outmoded ideology; and as an attempted exorcism of the worst demons of the Polish national memory. This exorcism initiated the process of recalling a fundamental dynamic of modern Polish history, the struggle between chauvinism and pluralism, the forces Solidarity leader Adam Michnik termed the two faces of Europe.[159] The chauvinist forces' failure to seize political power set the stage for the coming revolution, which would unfold under the signs of optimism, inclusiveness, and multiplicity. Basic to the new era would be an attempt to restructure the values and symbols of the Polish psyche, a quest intimately connected with the effort to integrate the Holocaust into Polish national memory.

1970–1989

Gomułka weathered March '68, but he did not survive the massive worker protests that followed it. Centered in the Baltic shipyards of Gdańsk, Gdynia, and Szczecin in December 1970, the protests were provoked by an increase in food prices. Events escalated to street fighting between workers, on the one hand, and the police and the army, on the other; the burning of party headquarters in Gdańsk; and the death of perhaps as many as several hundred workers. With Gomułka's fall, Polish Communism began to disintegrate. Even the rulers scarcely believed in the legitimacy of the system. The government was staffed by younger apparatchiks, many of them supporters of General Moczar. Like their counterparts elsewhere, this generation was "post-ideological," but in Poland this meant not the transcendence of ideology but its subservience to opportunism. Corruption, which was already widespread, became even more pervasive.

Edward Gierek, an ex-miner from Silesia with a reputation as a strong manager, succeeded Gomułka. Announcing a new era of dynamic growth intended to smother politics with consumer goods, Gierek rolled back the price increases, expanded trade, and secured loans from the West.[160] For several years Gierek projected a liberal image to the West and presided over something of an economic boom. At home, references to patriotism predominated over socialism. The church and other nonparty forces were briefly courted. But Gierek's economic initiatives began to flounder, particularly when Western markets shrank after the oil crisis of 1973. Food prices rose again in 1976, sparking demonstrations, strikes, and riots by workers. Gierek revoked the price hikes, cracked down on political dissidents, and borrowed more money from the West. By 1980, the year of Gierek's ouster, Poland's debt totaled $23 billion.

During these years, changes in thinking began to take place in certain quarters that would greatly influence Poland's political future. Perhaps the most important of these transformations was the gradual realization by elements of the church and the secular intelligentsia that they had a great deal in common. In his influential work *Kościół, lewica, dialog* (The church, the Left, dialogue), first published in Paris in 1977 but widely available in Poland through the growing clandestine press, Adam Michnik cited the poet Antoni Słonimski to account for what it was that had begun to bring together, not without problems, Catholic and progressive secular thinking. It was not a matter of reconciling worldviews, declared Słonimski, but rather the "intensified feeling of responsibility for human dignity threatened today in its very existence."[161] The basis for agreement was the perception that the fundamental evil underlying the Communist system was not ideological but moral. This evil was rooted in the split between private and public realms in Polish society, in the acceptance of lying as a way of life.

This approach bore a clear affinity to the "politics of '68" throughout the world, which typically developed critiques of established political and social systems from moral perspectives that were often antipolitical. It also had roots in Polish history, in the universalism of the insurrectionists and the tradition of independent socialism of the PPS. The secular intelligentsia discovered the church to be a bastion that resisted the split between the public and private worlds, insisting that the essence of Christianity and European civilization was belief in "the autonomous value of truth and human solidarity."[162] Michnik believed that sovietization intended to destroy the basis of European civilization in general and Polish culture in particular. The goal was to transform Poles into "a nation of broken backbones, captive minds, ravaged consciences . . . [for whom] every thought of changing the existing state of things would appear to be an irrational absurdity." The process worked on two levels: first, the destruction of tradition, the consignment to oblivion of huge areas of the Polish past; and second, the replacement of tradition by a counterfeit notion of the past and therefore of the present, a "castrated" history whose only function was to legitimize the existing order.[163]

To counteract the ravages of sovietization, Michnik suggested two sorts of rehumanizing activity. The first was to rediscover the history that had been silenced, to restore the broken connection to tradition. But which tradition? And what was the relation of this tradition to Catholicism? Was Catholicism its primary attribute or, as the church and Endecja had insisted prior to the war, its only attribute? Michnik argued that since the interwar period, when it had allied itself with national chauvinism, the Polish church, tempered by oppression and the ecumenical spirit of Vatican Council II, had greatly changed, that it was prepared to accept a credo comparable to Michnik's "profound conviction that the strength of our culture, what determines its richness and beauty, is pluralism, diversity, multiplicity of hue."[164] Michnik approvingly cited the teaching of Polish bishops in the 1970s that "thanks to the love of our own Fatherland, we are able to love the entire human family. . . . True love of the fatherland is linked to profound respect for everything that constitutes the value of other nations."[165] In this respect, Michnik and his colleagues found a hospitable reception among the Catholic intelligentsia.

The second activity involved reforging social bonds in the present. In 1968 workers had remained aloof from the student protests, and two years later the students and intelligentsia had ignored the workers' appeal for their support. But in 1976, during yet another worker confrontation with the state, this changed. A group of Polish intelligentsia founded the Komitet Obrony Robotników (KOR, Workers' Defense Committee). The members of KOR included Michnik and his colleagues, representatives of the generation of '68, and representatives of an older generation rooted in the PPS and in the Home Army. Their immediate activities centered on providing financial, legal, and medical help to workers and their families who were being persecuted for their protests. Their longer-term strategy was not to confront the state in battles they could only lose but to avoid the state and stimulate the creation of centers of autonomous social activity, organizations built from the ground up. The goal was to begin to restore the human solidarity that the system had gone far toward eradicating. Key to this work were notions linked to a Christian ethos:

social work for the good of others as a transcendent ethical value, nonviolence, and forgiveness of one's enemies. KOR activists also developed an uncensored clandestine press and founded an educational network known as the Uniwersytet Latający (Flying University), which offered independent courses on history and culture. The name, which suggested the need for the classes to keep changing their location to avoid the police, linked this organization to one established under the same name by the Warsaw intelligentsia for similar purposes in czarist times.[166]

Following the anti-Zionist campaign of the late 1960s a profound and nearly universal silence descended on the Jewish Question. The subject of Jews was avoided in public and even in private conversation between intimates.[167] Abroad it was believed that the history of the Jews in Poland had come to an ultimate conclusion; it was common to speak of "the end of a thousand years."[168] The *American Jewish Year Book,* which published news of the tiniest Jewish communities throughout the world, ceased reporting on Poland for most of the 1970s. In Israel the perception was marked by a symbolic transfer of Holocaust memory: in 1975 a smaller version of Rapoport's Warsaw Ghetto monument was installed at Yad Vashem, the Holocaust memorial center in Jerusalem, "where its Jewish national spirit would be preserved."[169] Nevertheless, a tiny, aging, demoralized, and submissive official Jewish community, organized in a handful of secular associations and religious congregations, managed to continue, as did such institutions as the Jewish Historical Institute, the State Yiddish Theater, and the Yiddish newspaper *Folksshtimme.* Nor did the silence about Jewish matters prevent KOR activists from being abused as Jewish "Trotskyists" and "garlic-eaters" in their increasing contacts with the police.[170] More importantly, in the circles of the emerging opposition there were signs of an entirely new approach to the Jewish Question.[171]

The earliest such stirrings occurred within the Catholic intelligentsia. Since the 1940s these circles had gradually evolved into the closest thing possible to forums for independent liberal thought. Their publications, *Tygodnik Powszechny* (Universal Weekly) and the monthly *Znak* in Cracow, the monthly *Więź* (Link) in Warsaw, while subject to censorship, were not organs of the state. Similarly, the Kluby Inteligencji Katolickiej (KIK, Clubs of the Catholic Intelligentsia) undertook the discussion of many taboo issues.[172] In the 1970s the Warsaw club began to organize annual "Weeks of Jewish Culture." Members of the KIK also began regular visits to the huge, devastated Jewish cemetery in Warsaw, where they restored some of the tombstones.

In the summer of 1979 a therapy workshop outside Warsaw with the American psychologist Carl Rogers was organized by some of his Polish disciples. A number of the participants decided to continue meeting together. What most of them had in common was that they had been born after the war, had been raised in entirely assimilated Jewish families, and had experienced the trauma of first confronting their Jewish descent in the anti-Zionist campaign of 1968. Along with some members of the KIK, they organized gatherings for the purpose of exploring Jewish identity and culture. The resulting group, numbering less than one hundred members, became known as the Jewish Flying University.[173]

These young "Jews" and sympathetic non-Jews were above all Poles whose primary identification was with the emerging opposition movement. They knew nothing of Jewish religious practices, languages, or history. They were entirely cut off from the official Jewish community in Poland, whose elderly members might have served as a link to Jewish tradition. However, so long as Communism reigned, they would remain cut off from them, regarding the official community as hopelessly compromised. For this small group of seekers and the many more that would follow in the 1980s, the expulsion of the "last" Jews of Poland was an exorcism that enabled them, as representatives of the postwar generation, to begin to reinvent a Jewish past. This Jewish quest was profoundly Polish, of course, for it was an integral part of the larger movement to regain the Polish past, but it marked the Polish effort in a crucial way by confirming it as inherently pluralist. The Jew would increasingly appear as a legitimate and even honored representative of the new Polish past.

If these developments bore an elitist character, involving only a small number of the intelligentsia, they did not remain that way for long. In October 1978 Karol Wojtyła, the archbishop of Cracow and an important member of the Catholic intelligentsia, became Pope John Paul II. His first encyclical, *Redemptor Hominis,* was about human dignity and the struggle for human rights. In June 1979 he visited Poland. About this visit Jan Józef Lipski, one of the founders of KOR, wrote: "Spiritually, Poland before June 1979 and Poland after June 1979 seemed to be two different countries. Who knows whether the breakthrough that occurred then was not deeper and more essential than the one that took place [with the emergence of Solidarity] in August 1980?"[174] For nine days the pope's presence transformed the nature of social relations. Millions of people, and above all the young, found themselves acting in a manner that the system had heretofore thwarted: they were "kinder to one another, disciplined yet free and relaxed, as they enjoyed these few days of internal, shared freedom."[175] John Paul's message spoke to the very issues addressed by the emerging workers' movement. "Christ will never approve that man be considered, or that man consider himself, *merely instruments of production. . . .* This must be remembered by the worker and the employer and the system of work," he announced in Nowa Huta. He concluded his visit to Cracow before a crowd of one million people. "I ask you to accept . . . the whole of the spiritual legacy which goes with the name 'Poland,'" he asserted. "Do not despair, do not grow weary, do not become disheartened. . . . Never lose *that spiritual freedom* to which He 'calls' humanity."[176]

John Paul II also visited Auschwitz. His words at a mass conducted on that occasion were widely reprinted and hailed in Poland as marking a new era in the Catholic Church's relationship to the memory of the Holocaust. Noting the plaques at the foot of the International Memorial at Birkenau, the pope asked his listeners to

pause . . . for a moment *at the plaque with an inscription in the Hebrew language.* This inscription evokes the memory of the nation whose sons and daughters were intended for complete extermination. This nation originates with Abraham, who is the "father of our faith" (Romans 4:12), as Paul of Tarsus expressed it. This nation, which received from God Jahweh the commandment "Thou shalt not kill," itself experienced killing in special measure. It is not permissible for anyone to pass this plaque with indifference.[177]

The ideas expressed in this statement became the focus for expanding interest in Judaism within the Polish church and among lay Catholics and also inspired dialogue between Poles and Jews, both in Poland and abroad.

The Polish Catholic approach to Jews was hardly unproblematic, however, as the context of John Paul's statement illustrates. His words about the Jews followed remarks dedicated to Maximilian Kolbe, a Franciscan priest imprisoned at Auschwitz who gave his life to save another prisoner. John Paul's praise of Father Kolbe's "victory through faith and love" hinted that the meaning of Auschwitz could be encompassed by a Catholic paradigm. This "exclusivist" vision, along with the discovery that Father Kolbe, whom the pope canonized in 1982, had been the publisher of an anti-Semitic newspaper before the war, fueled growing hostility toward the Catholic Church among Jews throughout the world.

For the moment, however, unity, not division, prevailed.[178] Solidarity emerged when a series of strikes was staged in response to new price increases in the summer of 1980. The climax was a seventeen-day sit-in at the Lenin Shipyards in Gdańsk in August 1980. The strike produced a negotiated settlement and an extraordinary document, the Gdańsk Accords, which included the right of Polish workers to be represented by an independent trade union, the first in the Communist bloc. While both the intelligentsia and the church were indispensable to its formation, Solidarity was above all the achievement of Polish workers, who rejected Marxism-Leninism in favor of the Polish insurrectionary tradition.

Solidarity was immediately much more than a trade union. During the sixteen months of its legal existence it vastly expanded on the transformation the pope's visit had achieved for nine days. The duplicity and corruption of daily life fell away. The public game that Henryk Grynberg had described was no longer played. Instead, "people opened their lips," as one worker recalled, "and sincerely began to say what they had been forbidden to say before."[179] By the end of these months, with ten million members, Solidarity, both as an organization and as a spirit, had penetrated every corner of Polish society, and, indeed, it became that society.

Fundamental to Solidarity's "truth-telling" was an explosion of symbolic activity relating to the past, an attempt to repossess and use what the system had silenced for decades. There was a proliferation of monuments and memorials linking the postwar struggles of Polish workers to the prewar insurrectionary tradition, the anti-Nazi resistance, and Catholic iconography. Solidarity also transformed the Polish calendar, filling it with unofficial commemorations of events of martyrdom and victory in Polish history that typically were celebrated with special masses and solemn gatherings at the appropriate sites. World War II was strongly represented. For example, at the 1980 commemoration at the Warsaw Catholic cemetery of the 1944 uprising, homage was paid to the victims of Katyń.

During this process, "Jews" and the Jewish Question emerged out of the silence and into the public forum. A special supplement of an independent newsletter published shortly after the Gdańsk Accords provided a characteristic expression of this development. The occasion for the publication, entitled "Jews and Poles," was the fortieth anniversary of the closing of the ghettos.[180] The editors' statement began by quoting the pope's words about Jews during his visit to Auschwitz the previous year and then continued, "We have recalled the crime of Katyń and the crime perpetrated [by the Soviets] on the Baltic nations. We should perhaps also have remembered Palmiry [a forest near Warsaw where the Germans murdered many Poles]. WE MUST remember the beginning of the annihilation of the Jews of Europe." This memory must be cultivated as "a turning point in human history. . . . Humanity reached the frontiers of the human and did not hesitate to cross them. This time toward its own shame." The editors continued:

> Let us lay aside the general problem. Let us look at Polish Jews. And not only in order to honor their martyrdom, but because, though Jews themselves are no longer among us, the subject of Jews constitutes a problem for us. The problem is the very language with which we speak of them—that very THEY. But they were a part of US, of our society (regardless of their degree of integration into that society). We say that they lived on our lands. But those lands were also their lands. They lived, quite simply, at home.

With this recognition, rooted in a pluralist conception of Polish history, the editors then listed a series of problems that would prefigure the explorations of the years to come. First was "the problem of our lack of knowledge . . . of the richness of the cultural, religious, social life of Jews in the old lands of the Polish Commonwealth," of their modern history, and of their annihilation. Second was the problem of

> outdated quarrels and (mutual) slanders unexamined for decades. Despite the beautiful stance of many Poles during the occupation years, who came forth to defend the tormented Jews, there is also the problem of our conscience—weighted with the anti-Jewish excesses of the prewar years, the bench ghettos in the universities. And there is the problem of the indifference of part of society during their annihilation.

Finally, there was the problem of the persistence of anti-Semitism in the present, its extent unclear, but with "someone always using it to advance their own interests." The statement concluded: "On the fortieth anniversary of the closing of the ghettos, in the year of the bombing of European synagogues, but also in the year of our moral and social renewal, IT IS NOT PERMISSIBLE TO BE SILENT."[181]

Although the Solidarity era was dedicated to the breaking of a multitude of silences, often the milieu was inappropriate for exploring what was revealed, particularly with respect to the Jewish Question. In December 1980, for example, with press censorship greatly loosened, there appeared in a leading Warsaw weekly a letter signed by, among others, Władysław Bartoszewski, Jan Józef Lipski, and members of the Jewish Flying University.[182] The letter began by stating the need for breaking the silence about "the problem of Polish-Jewish relations." It described "the history of Polish Jews [as] an integral part of the history of Poland" and explained that "the so-called Jewish Question" was above all a Polish problem. The letter then specifically addressed itself to the "anti-Semitic campaign" that erupted in

March 1968, calling for the rehabilitation of its victims and the gathering of accounts by participants and witnesses. It concluded: "It is our hope that in the present times, when truth, though bitter, comes to light, the honest presentation of Polish-Jewish relations, including their most sensitive aspects, will become possible." The editor's response, however, insisted that "the March events should not be reduced to—let us call it—the Jewish aspect." And in March 1981, when, for the first time, the events of the late 1960s were publicly discussed during a series of lectures and colloquiums at the University of Warsaw, the emphasis was on the state's crushing of the student movement, and not on the "sensitive aspects" of Polish-Jewish relations.[183]

For sixteen months, under the apparatchik Stanisław Kania, the state countenanced a breach in its monopoly of power. Much was made of Solidarity's "nonpolitical" goals and its "self-limiting revolution," but the state understood that what Solidarity represented could not be limited and constituted an absolute challenge to its authority. In December 1981 the state finally reacted as many Poles had long feared it would.[184] Assuming the positions of minister of defense, premier, and first secretary of the PZPR and installing a handful of military cronies in other key positions, General Wojciech Jaruzelski proclaimed martial law. Jaruzelski, who considered himself a Polish patriot and claimed that he had acted to avoid a far more sanguinary Soviet "solution," had nothing new to propose beyond smashing Solidarity and "restoring order." Poland slid into an economic crisis; waiting in line for hours for every daily necessity became a way of life. No longer capable of even claiming to deliver the goods, the system's only remaining raison d'être was to stave off the crude threat of Soviet invasion.

While the imposition of martial law was generally bloodless, many thousands of activists were taken into custody and kept in prison without trial for months. A handful managed to elude capture and, aided by many volunteers, established a clandestine organization that soon became the most elaborate underground in the Communist bloc. The struggle against the authorities was waged on a variety of fronts, most of them symbolic. Characteristic of the period of martial law, which ended in July 1983, was the appearance at public sites of giant flower crosses laden with leaflets, communiqués, patriotic symbols, and religious icons of every sort. With stringent censorship reimposed, the underground developed a superbly organized clandestine press. Side by side with the underground press, the legal Catholic press, especially that of the Catholic intelligentsia, greatly expanded its influence.

Martial law did not quell the growing interest in Jews, Judaism, and the Jewish past of Poland. For the postwar generation, which had neither seen a "real Jew" nor witnessed the Holocaust, the Jew became a focus of longing for the Old Poland, a Poland of the multinational Commonwealth, of the *kresy* and the *shtetl.* The image also permitted older Poles a nostalgic return to an idealized prewar youth. Jews became fashionable, evidenced by the popularity of Jewish songs and music, *Fiddler on the Roof,* and even of Jewish food. *Ryba po żydowsku* ("fish Jewish-style," i.e., gefilte fish) became a restaurant staple.

For some the image of the Jew was linked to a moral imperative: the responsibility to uncover and preserve the remaining physical remnants of the Jewish past. Hunting for old Jewish books and discovering ruined synagogues and cemeteries redeemed the past from oblivion and were also acts of resistance. Several of the "new Jews" founded an independent Citizens' Committee for the Protection of Jewish Cemeteries and Cultural Monuments in Poland. Throughout Poland, at sites where there was little or nothing left to restore, monuments were raised commemorating the Jewish communities that once thrived there. In the immediate postwar years Holocaust survivors had done this work before leaving Poland; in this new round of construction the initiative came from local Poles, sometimes with the help of survivors living abroad. These memorials, commonly erected at the site of ruined cemeteries, often consist of fragments of tombstones, an iconography of rupture, discontinuity, and loss.[185] Forty years after the Holocaust it became possible for Poles to begin to mourn for the Jews. Antoni Słonimski's poem "Elegy for the Little Jewish Towns," first published just after the war, was reprinted and recited throughout the 1980s. It begins:

> They are gone, gone from Poland, the little Jewish towns,
> In Hrubieszów, Karczew, Brody, Falenica.
> In vain you would search in windows for lighted candles,
> Or listen for song from a wooden synagogue.[186]

A number of international scholarly initiatives also began to draw Polish historians and intellectuals into contact with their Western Jewish counterparts. The first of a series of international conferences dedicated to Polish-Jewish relations was held in 1983 in New York.[187] In the same year an unofficial delegation of Israeli historians was received at Polish academic institutions. Beginning in 1985 these efforts were coordinated from Oxford, where *Polin: A Journal of Polish-Jewish Studies* began annual publication.[188] New scholarship emerged, as well as a forum where the most controversial historical issues could be aired, especially the issue of Polish-Jewish relations during the Holocaust. Gradually this activity came to the notice of the larger Jewish and Polish communities abroad (the latter now including recently emigrated former Solidarity activists). Even in these communities, where positions were particularly polarized, some dialogue began to occur.

In Poland the 1980s witnessed a wave of publications, dissertations, films, plays, concerts, and exhibitions devoted to Jewish subjects.[189] Some of the publications were products of the clandestine and Catholic presses. Among these was a six-hundred-page double issue of *Znak* dedicated to the Jews in Poland and Catholic-Jewish relations published for the fortieth anniversary of the Warsaw Ghetto Uprising.[190] The great majority of publications, however, were issued by Polish state publishing houses. Alongside popular and scholarly works that continued to blur the difference between the fate of Poles and the fate of Jews during the war, there appeared Holocaust memoirs, local histories of Jewish communities before and during the Holocaust, monographs by young historians on Polish Jewish history and culture, and collections of Jewish jokes and recipes. A great number of literary works were also released, including books by Isaac Bashevis Singer and his Polish counterpart, Julian Stryjkowski. Stryjkowski and several other Jewish authors, such as Adolf Rudnicki and Artur Sandauer, had remained in Poland and continued to write on Jewish themes during the postwar years.[191] Now that they were no longer curiosities, their writings began to reach a large audience, as did the work of the émigré writer Henryk Grynberg, whose cycle of autobiographical novels, beginning with his childhood during the Holocaust, was reprinted by both the official and the underground presses.[192] Polish poetry about the Holocaust also became very popular. Poetry first published just after the war was reprinted, and much new work was written.[193] Indeed, one of Nobel laureate Czesław Miłosz's poems written during the war would become the pretext for an important polemic about Poles and the Holocaust.

Such cultural developments inevitably affected the political arena. Once again the Jewish Question reappeared in Polish political discourse. The party leadership, ever opportunistic, played both sides of the issue. On the one hand, it quietly supported forces that remained nostalgic for the days of General Moczar and Endo-Communism. In March 1981, while the University of Warsaw sponsored its symposium on March '68, members of the new Zjednoczenie Patriotyczne "Grunwald" (Grunwald Patriotic Union), named after the site of a medieval battle in which Poles defeated the Teutonic Knights, demonstrated in front of the building that in Stalinist times had housed the ministry of public security demanding that a plaque be affixed to the building to honor patriots and Communists who had fallen victim to the "Zionist terror."[194] Throughout the 1980s Grunwald issued publications and became a fixture of the government's many-sided attempts to undermine the opposition. It started rumors about the Jewish origins of Solidarity leaders and was the source of anti-German and anti-Semitic disinformation.[195] Other initiatives included a ZBoWiD-sponsored reprint of Poterański's 1968 pamphlet on the Warsaw Ghetto Uprising, in which the statements of Moczar and Gomułka were restored, as well as a book on Polish-Jewish relations that concluded that the Kielce pogrom had been instigated by Zionists.[196]

On the other hand, Jaruzelski and his generals began to flirt publicly with philo-Semitic trends. Hungry for international legitimation and economic aid, the government staged an elaborate commemoration of the fortieth anniversary of the Warsaw Ghetto Uprising. Invitations were issued to Jews and Jewish organizations throughout the world. This affair encountered opposition when Marek Edelman, the last surviving leader of the uprising, published an open letter in the underground press calling for a boycott of the proceedings.

Edelman had been a member of the Jewish socialist Bund before and during the war. He had become a cardiologist after the war and remained out of politics until the Solidarity era, when he was chosen as a delegate to Solidarity's last national conference. He had attracted attention as the subject of a book-length interview by Hanna Krall, *Zdążyć przed Panem Bogiem* (Beating God to the punch), first published in 1977.[197] In the interview Edelman remarked that the meaning of the Holocaust could not be reduced to martyrdom and resistance. Unlike Poles during the war, Edelman pointed out, Jews in the ghettos did not have the option of a "beautiful" or "aesthetic" death, but "died unimpressively: in terror and darkness." And he doubted whether any conventional moral categories and notions of heroism were adequate for coping with the impossible choices faced by Jews in that "other world." In particular, he wondered about the ultimate importance of a handful of "boys and girls" deciding to shoot at Germans. Ironically, in the Poland of the 1980s, Edelman, who his interviewer claimed was "no good at talking because he was unable to yell" and "no good as a hero because he lacked grandiloquence," emerged as a spokesman on the moral significance of the Warsaw Ghetto Uprising.[198] Edelman's open letter, which was reprinted in the West, read, in part:

> Forty years ago we fought not only for life but for a life of dignity and freedom. Commemorating our anniversary here, where today degradation and coercion weigh upon the whole of social life, where words and gestures have been utterly falsified, is to be faithless to our struggle, to participate in something entirely the opposite; it is an act of cynicism and contempt. . . . Far from manipulated commemorations, in the silence of graves and hearts will survive the true memory of victims and heroes, of the eternal human impulse toward freedom and truth.[199]

World Jewish response to Edelman's letter was mixed. Some Jews stayed home, but several thousand attended the official wreath-laying by a military guard of honor in front of the ghetto memorial. Meanwhile, with Edelman's blessing, an "unofficial" ceremony was organized at the same site a few days before the official one. Several hundred people listened to some hurried speeches and watched as a small cross of flowers was laid before the monument. Several of the "new Jews," their heads covered with *kipot,* chanted the *Kaddish* (the Jewish prayer for the dead) before being dispersed by riot police. On another day demonstrators at the site of the notorious Umschlagplatz, the "transfer point" where the Nazis had herded the Jews of Warsaw onto trains for Treblinka, demanded that a memorial mark the location, at which now only a gas station stood.[200]

In the following years, commemoration of the Warsaw Ghetto Uprising and the Holocaust became ever more closely intertwined with the Polish political struggle. In the mid-1980s the underground issued "postage stamps" that were sold clandestinely and sometimes affixed to letters (which, rumor had it, were occasionally delivered by sympathetic mail carriers). The iconography of these stamps included the Solidarity logo, a portrait of Lech Wałęsa, symbols of the 1944 uprising, as well as several images dedicated to Polish Jews, including a ghetto fighter rousted from a bunker during the Warsaw Ghetto Uprising, a terrified little boy with his hands raised over his head (particularly well known in the West), and a wall constructed of broken Jewish tombstones.[201] Competition to appropriate the meaning of the Warsaw Ghetto Uprising climaxed in 1988 with its forty-fifth anniversary. The government used the occasion to dedicate a series of new monuments, developed with input from Israelis, in the streets surrounding the ghetto memorial. These consisted of a Memorial Route of Jewish Martyrdom and Struggle, marked by stones bearing the names of individuals linked with the uprising. The route led from the ghetto memorial to a new monument, the work of architects connected to the opposition, that had finally been erected at the site of the Umschlagplatz. Meanwhile, Solidarity sponsored an unofficial unveiling at the Warsaw Jewish cemetery of a monument in memory of Victor Alter and Henryk Ehrlich, leaders of the Bund who had been murdered in the Soviet Union after they fled Nazi-occupied Poland. Lech Wałęsa wrote a letter to Marek Edelman on that occasion, declaring:

> This land, the Polish land, knows the truth about a struggle against slavery on behalf of freedom, against degradation on behalf of dignity, a struggle on behalf of hope fought without any chance of victory. The struggle of our Jewish brothers, the heroes of the Warsaw Ghetto, was such a struggle. We honor it today in a special manner. For in this land, the land of so many uprisings, the uprising of the Jewish fighters was the most Polish of all Polish uprisings.[202]

A Poland in which an audience could cheer a popular entertainer for donning a *kipa* and performing a Jewish song about a *shtetl*[203] and the Warsaw Ghetto Uprising could be assimilated into the Polish insurrectionary tradition was prepared to confront more problematic aspects of the Holocaust. During the Solidarity era, opposition leaders devoted considerable energy to attacking anti-Semitism, which was seen as an embarrassment and was particularly discredited since it had become a tool of the state. When internal polemics occasionally evoked anti-Semitic slurs (typically directed against the "nonworking" intelligentsia), immediate denunciations followed. In the introduction to the special Jewish issue of *Znak,* the editor, Stefan Wilkanowicz, evoked a "wise patriotism," at home in a pluralist world, that required Poles "to make a national or social accounting of their conscience and to cleanse wounds—in order for time to heal them."[204]

One of the most influential texts in this national accounting was Jan Józef Lipski's essay "Dwie ojczyzny—dwa patriotyzmy (Uwagi o megalomanii narodowej i ksenofobii Polaków)" (Two fatherlands, two patriotisms: Remarks on Polish national megalomania and xenophobia). Lipski defined two traditions in Polish historical thinking. One served "the national megalomania," and the other was the "bitter tradition of reckoning" based on moral judgment. "The struggle for the shape of Polish patriotism," declared Lipski, "will determine the fate of our nation—its moral, cultural, and political fate."[205] The rest of the essay was devoted to a harsh indictment of Polish historical injustices toward Germans, Russians, Lithuanians, Belorussians, Ukrainians, Czechs, and finally, in greatest detail, Jews. He described prewar Polish anti-Semitism, in the face of which, "unfortunately, resistance in society was too weak," and criticized the role of the church. Lipski continued: "In this situation the war and the occupation arrived, as well as the horrendous extermination of the Jews by the occupier. An assessment of the test undergone by Poles in this situation cannot, unfortunately, be straightforward and unambiguous."[206]

Lipski's essay and similar writings circulated clandestinely among the intelligentsia. The issue of Polish-Jewish relations during the Holocaust, however, was thrust into the mainstream again by two disturbing works of art. The first was Claude Lanzmann's film *Shoah,* which premiered in Paris in April 1985. Nine and a half hours long, the film contains no documentary images, but consists entirely of footage of Holocaust witnesses—Jews, Germans, and Poles—interviewed by Lanzmann. The Poles whom Lanzmann presents are nearly all peasants and residents of small towns located near death camps and transport sites. With the exception of Jan Karski, there are no members of the intelligentsia and no heroes among them. They sometimes express sympathy for the Jews, but they also repeat common anti-Semitic stereotypes. In one remarkable scene the only Jewish survivor of a small town, whom Lanzmann brought back to Poland from Israel, stands on the church steps among his well-wishing former neighbors. A procession of white-clad young girls emerges from the church, in which, we have just learned, during the war Jews were locked prior to being gassed. Suddenly one of the people on the steps recounts a story implying that the fate of the Jews was just punishment for their betrayal of God, and the camera focuses on the survivor's face, now bereft of its smile.

Most Poles first heard of the film when a Paris newspaper article about it carried the headline "Poland Accused." The situation was exacerbated by Lanzmann, whose public statements were filled with accusations against Poles, suggesting, for example, that concentration camps had been built in Poland because of Polish anti-Semitism. The Polish press responded by describing the film as "yet another attempt to justify Nazi crimes, and erase from European memory German plans for the biological annihilation also of the Polish nation."[207] Poland officially protested to the French government that the film was an "insulting . . . insinuation of [Polish] complicity in Nazi genocide." Poland also demanded that the film be banned from French television and even threatened to discontinue teaching the French language in Polish schools. By the end of the year, however, the government had calmed down. The parts of *Shoah* dealing with Poland (about one-third of the film) were shown on Polish television and followed by discussions with "experts." The entire film was then released in several theaters. Meanwhile, the government began to reestablish relations with Israel, broken off twenty years earlier, and General Jaruzelski met in New York with Edgar Bronfman, president of the World Jewish Congress.[208]

Shoah provoked impassioned discussion in Poland not only in the official, Catholic, and underground presses but also in "hundreds of thousands of Polish homes."[209] This was doubtless due to the role of television, which gave the entire nation direct access to the disputed images. (As in the West, the complete film had only a limited audience when it was shown in theaters.) The *Shoah* controversy received thorough public exposure in a manner more reminiscent of Western than of Communist societies. That the issue concerned Polish-Jewish relations during the Holocaust was not insignificant. A few people viewed the film with approval and understanding. Solidarity leader Jacek Kuroń wrote that

> Jews were condemned to death because they were Jews. In other words, people were condemned because they were people. And this changed human history in a fundamental way. All of us who lived here in these killing grounds emerged maimed, and this the film *Shoah* shows very well. . . . What was the difference between Poles and Jews during the occupation? It was the following: that on a trolley through the ghetto on my way to a swimming pool I watched people dying on the other side of the wall.[210]

In the great majority of responses, however, the film was denounced as anti-Polish. The differences among the official, Catholic, and underground presses tended to be minimal, although the tone of the official press was more strident.[211] The film was attacked for its choice of witnesses, its supposed manipulation of them, and its omission of testimony from anyone involved in saving Jews. Much energy was devoted to remembering Polish help to Jews during the war; the work of Władysław Bartoszewski was frequently cited. The unique dangers of trying to assist Jews in Poland were stressed, as was the great number of Poles awarded the Righteous Gentile medal by the Israeli government for saving Jews. The attitude of Poles was contrasted to that of Western bystanders, and especially the French, who, it was emphasized, had collaborated politically with the Germans and even participated in deporting Jews to death camps. Despite the negative reactions to *Shoah*, however, in the aftermath of this controversy the notion that there had been no difference between the fates of Jews and Poles during the war slipped out of Polish public discourse.

The controversy over *Shoah* was soon followed by a conflict that revolved around a poem by Czesław Miłosz and a response to it written by Jan Błoński, a professor of literature. Błoński's article was published in *Tygodnik Powszechny* in January 1987.[212] In it he described a conversation that ensued when Poles traveling abroad were asked why Poles were anti-Semites. After detailing the accusations and rebuttals concerning events beginning in the Middle Ages and ending in 1968, Błoński concluded: "And so on, endlessly. The debates of historians resemble this discussion." To escape this cycle he turned to Miłosz's poem "A Poor Christian Looks at the Ghetto," written in 1943 as the poet watched the ghetto burn from the "Aryan" side of Warsaw. Miłosz began by describing a terrible "tearing . . . trampling . . . breaking" followed by fire and the collapse of roofs and walls. Then, underground, he confronted a peculiar apparition: a "guardian mole . . . with a small red lamp fastened to his forehead," who counted burned bodies, "distinguishes human ashes." The poet concluded:

> I am afraid, so afraid of the guardian mole.
> He has swollen eyelids, like a Patriarch
> Who has sat much in the light of candles
> Reading the great book of the species.
>
> What will I tell him, I, a Jew of the New Testament,
> Waiting two thousand years for the second coming of Jesus?
> My broken body will deliver me to his sight
> And he will count me among the helpers of death:
> The uncircumcised.[213]

Błoński interpreted Miłosz's poem as follows:

> This mole burrows underground but also underneath our consciousness. This is the feeling of guilt which we do not want to admit. Buried under the rubble, among the bodies of the Jews, the "uncircumcised" fears that he may be counted among the murderers. . . . [The poem] makes tangible something which is not fully comprehended, something that was, and perhaps still is, in other people's as much as in the poet's own psyche, but in an obscure, blurred, muffled shape. When we read such a

poem, we understand ourselves better, since that which had been evading us until now is made palpable.[214]

Błoński went on to describe the Jews as people who "shared our home, lived on our soil, [whose] blood has remained in the walls, seeped into the soil, [and] has also entered into ourselves, into our memory." But although the Jews "shared our home," they were made to "live in the cellar."[215]

> Eventually, when we lost our home, and when, within that home, the invaders set to murdering Jews, did we show solidarity towards them? How many of us decided that it was none of our business? There were also those (and I leave out of account common criminals) who were secretly pleased that Hitler had solved for us "the Jewish problem." We could not even welcome and honor the survivors, even if they were embittered, disoriented and perhaps sometimes tiresome.[216]

Błoński explained that Poles had blocked the memory of this part of their history because "when we consider the past, we want to derive moral advantages from it . . . we want to be *completely* clean. We want to be also—and only—victims." This desire, however, is "underpinned by fear," accompanied by "the horror," "the mole who burrows in our subconscious." Błoński suggested that the only remedy was to see the past fully, without defensiveness, and then to "acknowledge our own guilt, and ask for forgiveness." Poles must atone for what Błoński termed their "shared responsibility," above all, for the Polish attitude toward Jews *before* the Holocaust.[217]

Błoński's article brought a ferocious response. In the words of Jerzy Turowicz, the editor of *Tygodnik Powszechny,* "When we printed the article, I was, as were my colleagues, aware that it would be an event to which there would certainly be a strong reaction. The reaction was greater than anything known in the course of the 42 years during which I have edited that paper."[218] As with *Shoah,* the reaction was mostly negative. What was rejected above all was the notion that Poles needed forgiveness from Jews. First of all, Błoński was misread as affirming Polish participation in the Holocaust. This view was reinforced when Poles were informed in Western accounts of the controversy that at last they were accepting joint responsibility with the Germans for the murder of the Jews. Most writers rejected the notion that Poles had wronged Jews; many denied the existence of anti-Semitism in Poland altogether. In defending Polish attitudes, many writers drew on the full spectrum of pre-war Endek discourse: Jews had exploited Poles economically, they had been hostile to Polish independence, they had overwhelmed Polish professions and cultural life, and they had constituted a "foreign element" at war with Poland, Poles, and "Polishness." There were also allusions, often veiled, to the Żydokomuna. For Turowicz, the nearly two hundred letters and articles received in response to Błoński's article "disclosed the existence of anti-Semitism still in Poland, today more than forty years after the war." While "one should not exaggerate the size of this phenomenon," his mail convinced him that it was "an attitude which cannot easily be uprooted or overcome, and one that even at times regenerates itself."[219]

Although they were few in number, there were also those who supported Błoński and even refined his ideas. Andrzej Bryk, the young scion of a family rooted in Home

Army traditions, used the occasion to define the dilemma of the Polish experience of the Holocaust as that of "a Polish community raised in a largely anti-semitic culture and subconsciously accepting Jews as aliens suddenly in a situation where its culture offered no moral means to resist an easy acceptance of the fact of the annihilation of the Jews by the Germans." The result, which has molded Polish consciousness since the Holocaust, was what Bryk termed "the hidden complex of the Polish mind," which has prevented Poles from processing the Holocaust according to any "clear-cut dichotomous model" of morality.[220]

Two years after Błoński's article was published, another controversy about Poland and the Holocaust attracted international attention. In 1984 a group of Carmelite nuns had moved into a building abutting the walls of Auschwitz and raised a twenty-foot-high cross in front of it.[221] The convent was part of a nationwide proliferation of sites honoring Polish martyrdom during World War II. At Auschwitz these included the cell where Father Maximilian Kolbe awaited death; the symbolic grave of Edith Stein, a Carmelite nun who had been a convert from Judaism; and the bullet-scarred Wall of Death in the work camp, before which thousands of Polish prisoners were shot. These sites, marked by tablets or crosses and strewn with flowers, attained the status of national shrines and became places of pilgrimage and prayer for millions of Poles.

A Catholic convent at Auschwitz was a particularly emotion-laden issue. Because of the scale of its death machinery and probably also because the majority of death camp survivors and testimonies emerged from it, for Jews and for the West Auschwitz had come to represent the unassimilable absolute evil associated with the word "Holocaust." In the 1980s, as Poland began to emerge from behind the Iron Curtain, Westerners discovered a site containing ruins, restored barracks, watchtowers, barbed wire, a museum, offices, a parking lot, souvenir shops, and a snack bar. It was visited annually by hundreds of thousands of people, most of them Polish tourists and secondary-school students. This place, moreover, scarcely referred to Jews and now included a Catholic convent and a huge cross.

Jewish protests about the inappropriateness of a Catholic place of worship at Auschwitz began in 1985, when a Belgian Catholic organization issued an appeal for support of the convent, "which will become a spiritual fortress and a guarantee of the conversion of strayed brothers from our countries as well as proof of our desire to erase the outrages so often done to the Vicar of Christ."[222] This announcement, which was widely publicized in European Jewish circles and followed soon after the pope's canonization of Father Kolbe, led Edgar Bronfman to raise the issue of the convent with Polish authorities later that year. Direct negotiations between representatives of European Jewry and Polish and Western European Catholics began at Geneva in 1986 and ended in an agreement signed the following year to move the convent to a new Catholic center to be built near Auschwitz within two years' time. When the deadline arrived, however, groundbreaking for the new center had not begun and considerable opposition to the agreement had developed in the Polish church and among lay Catholics.

Jewish protests also continued. In July 1989 a group of Jews wrapped in prayer shawls, led by Rabbi Avi Weiss of New York, climbed over the convent fence and staged a noisy demonstration in front of the convent. They were roughed up and expelled from the grounds by local workers.[223] This event created an international stir. Referring to the failure of the nuns and a local priest to intervene with his attackers, Rabbi Weiss accused them of treating Jews "just like your Church did fifty years ago."[224] In Poland, the intrusion into the Carmelite convent, whose regulations prohibited all contact with the outside world, was called an invasion and was seen as the climax of an international Jewish campaign directed against the church's work at Auschwitz.

In the weeks that followed Rabbi Weiss's protest, readers of the Polish press followed the unfolding affair, which was reported in unaccustomed detail. They read accounts of subsequent, larger Jewish demonstrations and of their confrontation by angry crowds of local Poles, often expressing crudely anti-Semitic views.[225] Sister Teresa, the mother superior of the convent, who was interviewed in the Polish-American press, claimed that since three of the Catholic negotiators at the Geneva Conference had been Jews, "naturally" the outcome of the conference had been "one-sided in favor of World Jewry." She concluded: "You can tell the Americans that we are not moving a single inch. And like the Pauline monks who bravely withstood the Swedish siege of their monastery at Częstochowa in 1655, we are here to stay!"[226]

Meanwhile, Cardinal Franciszek Macharski of Cracow, in whose diocese Auschwitz was located, called for the abrogation of the Geneva accord. He cited "a violent campaign of accusations and insinuations on the part of some Jewish circles in the West . . . insulting aggression expressed not only in words."[227] This was followed by a homily delivered by Cardinal Józef Glemp, the primate of Poland, at the national shrine of the Black Madonna of Częstochowa, in which he spoke of making peace "with those nations towards whom resentment has remained because of the war . . . Germans and Jews." Implying that Rabbi Weiss's group had planned to murder the nuns, and accusing Jews of controlling the world's media, Cardinal Glemp concluded: "If there is no antipolonism, there will be no antisemitism in us."[228] Glemp, who had been appointed by the pope but strongly sympathized with Endek ideologues, outraged many in the opposition and was criticized in the newly legalized Solidarity press. In Israel, Prime Minister Yitzhak Shamir responded to Glemp's remarks by declaring that Poles "suck [anti-Semitism] in with their mother's milk."[229]

The controversy only began to subside with direct pressure from the Vatican. In February 1990 construction began on the Catholic center to which the nuns were expected to move. Three years later the new building was completed, but the nuns were still in their convent. In April 1993, as Jewish groups threatened to boycott the commemorations of the fiftieth anniversary of the Warsaw Ghetto Uprising, the pope sent a letter to the nuns in which he specifically asked them to move.[230]

1989–1993

While the convent controversy raged, Poland was undergoing a political transformation. In May 1988, during another series of strikes, a new generation of workers demanded the relegalization of Solidarity. Roundtable talks in early 1989 between the opposition and the weakening government resulted in the first free elections in Poland in sixty years. The victory of the opposition, of course, marked its obsolescence. Strains began to develop between the church and Solidarity as well as within Solidarity itself. The opposition began to fragment into competing factions, which soon became political parties that followed a traditional configuration ranging from a pluralist Left to a chauvinist Right. In the new Poland, the church championed an agenda of religious education in the public schools and the banning of abortion. The birth of democracy transformed Polish society by allowing a full spectrum of popular opinion to flourish. As elsewhere in Eastern Europe, this development included, especially in the beginning, the expression of resentments and hatreds long suppressed by the system.

The fall of Communism released swarms of petty traders into the streets and public squares of cities and towns. In the bazaarlike atmosphere of the first months of freedom, hoodlums flourished and the police seemed to vanish. Vicious anti-Semitic graffiti proliferated on walls and remained untouched for months. Jewish cemeteries and institutions were vandalized. Amidst stalls, trucks, card tables, and blankets overflowing with cheap goods, anti-Semitic tracts were prominently displayed. In the campaigns of the first free elections candidates representing liberal views were often attacked as Jews. The most notorious example occurred during the presidential elections in 1990, when Lech Wałęsa ran against his erstwhile ally Tadeusz Mazowiecki. Mazowiecki, a member of the Catholic intelligentsia and of *szlachta* descent, drew his base of support from Solidarity's left wing. A significant portion of the electorate believed him to be a Jew. Wałęsa found it politically expedient during the campaign to wonder out loud why some of his opponents "conceal their origins."[231]

As the new political and economic system gained its balance, anti-Semitic graffiti dwindled and the Jewish Question began to disappear from Polish politics. Despite many fears to the contrary, overtly anti-Semitic political parties gained little following. Bolesław Tejkowski, whose entire political program revolved around the struggle against the Jews, became the object of criminal and psychiatric investigations. For the first time in postwar history, anti-Semitism was frequently and publicly discussed, with particular attention devoted to the previously taboo subject of the immediate postwar years. Excerpts from Krystyna Kersten's research on the postwar roots of anti-Jewish stereotypes were published in the daily press, as were articles on issues ranging from the rehabilitation of the fascist NSZ as heroes of the anti-Communist resistance[232] to government attempts to ban the publication of *The Protocols of the Elders of Zion* and *Mein Kampf.*

Surveys of popular attitudes toward non-Poles in the 1990s have indicated antipathy to Jews in a significant minority of respondents, dwarfed, however, by hostility to Gypsies and Arabs.[233] In one poll, when asked who they would prefer to share a seat with in class, secondary-school students ranked Jews as slightly less desirable than Germans and the children of Communists, slightly more desirable than Russians, and much more desirable than those infected with HIV, Gypsies, homosexuals, or the mentally ill.[234] An informal poll conducted somewhat earlier indicated that, regardless of what was in their textbooks, a majority of students were aware that what had happened to the Jews during the war was "unique and incomparable."[235] Unlike Germany and Hungary, Poland has few skinheads. There is little ethnic violence; the most serious case occurred in June 1991 in the eastern town of Mława, where Polish residents destroyed the Gypsy section of the town following a car accident in which a Gypsy driver severely injured several Poles.

Meanwhile, despite the disappearance in post-Communist Poland of its political context, the "Jewish revival" shows no sign of abating; indeed, it continues to grow. Festivals of Jewish culture, modeled after the successful annual spring festival in Kazimierz, the old Jewish quarter of Cracow, are increasingly popular, as are "Jewish" restaurants, cafés, shops, souvenirs, and competing brands of "kosher" vodka. While Jewish travel to Poland has greatly expanded and there are jokes about German tourists paying to see Poles disguised as Jews, much of the interest and the market for Judaica remains Polish.

The early 1990s had witnessed a wave of Jewish publications that dwarfed that of the 1980s. With the Jewish Historical Institute under new leadership and the establishment of new centers of scholarship at other Polish institutions, academic study of Polish Jewish history has blossomed. For example, the first international conference dedicated to the history of Yiddish theater was held in October 1993 in Warsaw; going on at the same time were a festival of Jewish films, Jewish art exhibitions, and Jewish musical and theatrical performances. In the same month, the privately funded Shalom Foundation announced the results of a contest among Polish secondary-school students for the best essays on the subject of Jewish culture in Poland; there had been four thousand entries.

Belying the popular conception that there are no Jews left in Poland, an organized Jewish community has also revived. According to official statistics, in 1993 this community numbered 4,415; those involved in Jewish affairs put the number between 5,000 and 10,000.[236] The leadership of this community is made up mostly of the "new Jews" of the 1980s, who now are much more comfortable with their identity. Alongside the old organizations are new ones, ranging from a Jewish day-care center to a President's Council on Polish-Jewish Relations and a Polish-Israeli Friendship Society, which has been particularly active since Poland's exchange of ambassadors with Israel. Joint Polish-Israeli projects include the revision of school textbooks in Poland and Israel dealing with the history of Polish-Jewish relations.[237] Perhaps most surprising has been the number of people under the age of thirty who have claimed to be Polish Jews. Often the children or grandchildren of hidden Jews who remained in Poland after the war, these young people now study Jewish religion and culture, attend Jewish summer camp, and, among other things, have founded a Maccabi sports club and a periodical called *Jidele* (The Little Jew). Much of their activity is funded by the American philanthropist Ronald Lauder, who also supports Poland's two rabbis.

The work of commemorating the Holocaust initiated in the 1980s also has expanded in the 1990s. At the sites of death camps and ghettos throughout Poland new tablets have been mounted and monuments built, and various gatherings have been held, often with the participation of Holocaust survivors from abroad. That such activity no longer represents political resistance has not diminished the urge to commemorate. Such ceremonies now also celebrate the victory over Communism and the emergence of historical truth. This was the case, for example, at Sobibor, where a tablet referring to 250,000 murdered "Soviet prisoners of war, Jews, Poles and Gypsies" was replaced by one acknowledging "over 250,000 Jews and about 1,000 Poles" murdered there. Similarly, a "march of death" held in 1992 to trace the steps of Jews herded by the Nazis from the town of Rembertów to that of Falenica and then to Treblinka echoed the first such symbolic march, organized clandestinely by a handful of "new Jews" eight years earlier, but this time the local Solidarity committee dedicated a monument at the march's terminus.[238]

Some explorations dug deeper into the past, such as Paweł Łoziński's 1992 documentary film *Miejsce urodzenia* (Birthplace), which follows the writer Henryk Grynberg, a child survivor of the Holocaust who returned to Poland to discover the fate of his father, who had been murdered fifty years earlier. The film documents not only Grynberg's confrontation with a peasant who probably helped murder his father but also Grynberg's discovery of his father's remains. When the film was shown on Polish television, a scene in which a witness identifies the perpetrators of the crime was deleted and replaced by a statement explaining the need to protect the witness. In an interview about the making of the film, Łoziński spoke of meeting a peasant woman who continues to conceal the fact that she hid Jews during the war. "I'm afraid," she told him. "What if someone breaks into my house to look for gold under the floor?"[239]

An elaborate commemoration of the fiftieth anniversary of the Warsaw Ghetto Uprising was organized in April 1993. For a week, Polish television and radio carried programs about Polish Jews and the Holocaust. Photographs of the ghetto wall and of the white-bearded chief rabbi of Poland were on the front page of newspapers and periodicals. One leading weekly published a feature entitled "A Scene I Cannot Forget," which comprised selections from over one hundred responses to an appeal, issued jointly with the Society of Children of the Holocaust, for "unforgettable" Polish memories of the Holocaust.[240] The events included an ecumenical memorial service at the Warsaw synagogue with the unprecedented presence of church officials and climaxed with an official wreath-laying ceremony at the ghetto monument that was attended by President Lech Wałęsa, uprising survivor Marek Edelman, Israeli Prime Minister Yitzhak Rabin, and U.S. Vice President Al Gore. Also participating were thousands of Jews from all over the world, including elderly Holocaust survivors and many young Israelis, who surrounded the monument in a sea of Israeli flags. Most Poles, lacking the special passes required to approach the monument, watched the proceedings from behind distant police barricades.

Prime Minister Rabin's presence at the commemoration was doubtless a result of President Wałęsa's trip to Israel in May 1991. In his speech before the Israeli Parliament, Wałęsa had remarked, apparently spontaneously, "Please forgive us." These words had triggered considerable outrage in Poland. Yet they had come soon after a pastoral letter from Polish bishops, read in all parishes in January 1991, that re-affirmed, on its twenty-fifth anniversary, Vatican II's revocation of the ancient charge of deicide against Jews. The letter also included the following on the Holocaust and Polish-Jewish relations:

> In spite of so many heroic examples of help on the part of Polish Christians, there were also people who remained indifferent to this incomprehensible tragedy. We are especially disheartened by those among Catholics who in some way were the cause of the death of Jews. If only one Christian could have helped and did not stretch out a helping hand to a Jew during the time of danger or caused his death, we must ask for forgiveness of our Jewish brothers and sisters. We are aware that many of our compatriots still remember the injustices and injuries committed by the postwar communist authorities, in which people of Jewish origin also took part. We must acknowledge, however, that the source of inspiration of their activity was clearly neither their origin nor religion, but the communist ideology, from which the Jews themselves, in fact, suffered many injustices. . . . We express our sincere regret for all the incidents of anti-Semitism which were committed at any time or by anyone on Polish soil. . . . In expressing our sorrow for all the injustices and harm done to Jews, we cannot forget that we consider untrue and deeply harmful the use by many of the concept of what is called "Polish anti-Semitism" as an especially threatening form of anti-Semitism; and in addition, frequently connecting the concentration camps not with those who were actually involved with them, but with Poles in a Poland occupied by the Germans.[241]

To agree on the facts of history is considerably easier than to agree on the meaning of history, particularly when the history is that of the Holocaust. Even in this respect, however, recent changes at Auschwitz point to the development of a new kind of official attitude. These changes, after consultations with Jews from Poland and abroad, have included the recaptioning of photographic displays to encompass information about Jewish victims and the translation of captions into Hebrew as well as European languages.[242] In 1990 the new Polish government decided to remove the inscriptions at the International Memorial, which referred to "four million people" murdered at Auschwitz. For two years, while the authorities tried to decide how to revise the text, the monument was surrounded by empty plaques. In 1992 the following statement was finally inscribed on the plaques in nineteen languages:

> Let this place remain for eternity as a cry of despair and a warning to humanity. About one and a half million men, women, children and infants, mainly Jews from different countries of Europe, were murdered here. The world was silent. Auschwitz-Birkenau, 1940–1945.

Nearby, a larger tablet is inscribed with a quotation from the Book of Job:

> O Earth, hide not my blood
> And let my cry never cease.[243]

Half a century after witnessing the Holocaust, Poles are freely confronting the memory of the experience for the first time. It is far too soon, however, to speculate about the meaning of this confrontation. It will gradually assume a coherent form only in the decades to come.

NOTES

Preliminary research for this chapter was funded in part by a grant from IREX. I would like to thank the following people for their invaluable assistance: Monika Adamczyk-Garbowska, Alina Cała, Helena Datner-Śpiewak, Konstanty Gebert, Jerzy Halbersztadt, Jan Jagielski, Jerzy Jedlicki, Ninel Kos, Ewa Koźmińska-Frejlak, Monika Krajewska, Stanisław Krajewski, Hanna Krall, Paweł Śpiewak, Stefan Wilkanowicz, Andrzej Wróblewski (may his memory be a blessing), and Ryszarda Zachariasz.

1. Norman Davies, *God's Playground: A History of Poland*, 2 vols. (New York, 1982), 1:3–4.

2. On Jewish civilization in the Polish Commonwealth, standard works in English are Salo Wittmayer Baron, *A Social and Religious History of the Jews,* vol. 16, *Poland-Lithuania, 1500–1650* (New York, 1976); and Bernard D. Weinryb, *The Jews of Poland: A Social and Economic History of the Jewish Community in Poland from 1100–1800* (Philadelphia, 1972). Important recent studies are M. J. Rosman, *The Lord's Jews: Magnate-Jewish Relations in the Polish-Lithuanian Commonwealth during the Eighteenth Century* (Cambridge, Mass., 1990); and Gershon David Hundert, *The Jews in a Polish Private Town: The Case of Opatów in the Eighteenth Century* (Baltimore, 1992).

3. The best English-language history of the Polish-Lithuanian Commonwealth is in Davies, *God's Playground,* 1:159–469. This otherwise excellent historian is entirely unreliable on matters concerning Polish Jews.

4. Davies, *God's Playground,* 1:199–200. See also Janusz Tazbir, *A State without Stakes: Polish Religious Toleration in the Sixteenth and Seventeenth Centuries* ([Warsaw], 1973).

5. "Być Żydem w Polsce," *Tygodnik Solidarność,* December 14, 1990.

6. Abraham Heschel, *The Earth Is the Lord's: The Inner World of the Jew in East Europe* (New York, 1978), 10.

7. The Council of the Four (Polish) Lands began to meet formally in 1580, the Lithuanian Council in 1623. The system of intercommunal councils was abolished by Polish authorities in 1764.

8. Evyatar Friesel, *Atlas of Modern Jewish History* (Oxford, 1990), 30; Hundert, *The Jews in a Polish Private Town,* xi.

9. On *szlachta* stereotypes of the Jew in Old Poland, see Eugenia Prokopówna, "Śmiech szlachecki w satyrycznych obrazach żydowskiego świata," in *Studenckie zeszyty naukowe Uniwersytetu Jagiellońskiego: Studenckie zeszyty polonisty-* *czne* (Cracow) 7 (1988), 131–51. On Polish stereotypes of the Jew in the nineteenth century, see Aleksander Hertz, *The Jews in Polish Culture* (Evanston, Ill., 1988); and Michael C. Steinlauf, "Mr. Geldhab and Sambo in Peyes: Images of the Jew on the Polish Stage, 1863–1905," *Polin* 4 (1989), 110–18. On the stereotype of the Jew among Polish peasants in the 1970s, see Alina Cała, *Wizerunek Żyda w polskiej kulturze ludowej* (Warsaw, 1987).

10. Two good sources for the history of this period are Davies, *God's Playground,* 2:3–392; and Piotr Wandycz, *The Lands of Partitioned Poland, 1795–1918* (Seattle, 1974).

11. George Brandes, cited in Michael T. Kaufman, *Mad Dreams, Saving Graces: Poland, A Nation in Conspiracy* (New York, 1989), [ix].

12. As yet there exists no comprehensive work on the history of the Jews in the lands of partitioned Poland.

13. Salo Wittmayer Baron, *The Russian Jew under Tsars and Soviets* (New York, 1964), 64. The disparity is even greater than these numbers suggest, since the Jewish figures do not include the two million Jews who migrated westward during the last decades of this period.

14. On this era in Polish-Jewish relations, see Magdalena Opalski and Israel Bartal, *Poles and Jews: A Failed Brotherhood* (Hanover, N.H., 1992).

15. On Polish-Jewish relations at the turn of the century, see Raphael Mahler, "Antisemitism in Poland," in *Essays on Antisemitism,* ed. Koppel S. Pinson (New York, 1946), 156–65; Frank Golczewski, *Polnisch-jüdische Beziehungen, 1881–1922: Eine Studie zur Geschichte des Antisemitismus in Osteuropa* (Wiesbaden, 1981); Alina Cała, *Asymilacja Żydów w Królestwie Polskim (1864–1897)* (Warsaw, 1989); Stephen D. Corrsin, *Warsaw before the First World War: Poles and Jews in the Third City of the Russian Empire, 1888–1914* (Boulder, Colo., 1989); and Opalski and Bartal, *Poles and Jews,* 98–147.

16. Davies, *God's Playground,* 2:12–13.

17. On interwar Poland, see ibid., 2:393–434; and Antony Polonsky, *Politics in Independent Poland, 1921–1939: The Crisis of Constitutional Government* (Oxford, 1972).

18. On the Jews of interwar Poland, an excellent survey is the first chapter of Ezra Mendelsohn, *The Jews of East Central Europe between the World Wars* (Bloomington, Ind., 1983), 11–83. See also Joseph Marcus, *Social and Political History of the Jews in Poland, 1919–1939* (Berlin, 1983); Yisrael Gutman

et al., eds., *The Jews of Poland between Two World Wars* (Hanover, N.H., 1989); and Jerzy Tomaszewski, "Niepodległa rzeczpospolita," in *Najnowsze dzieje Żydów w Polsce w zarysie (do 1950 roku),* ed. Jerzy Tomaszewski (Warsaw, 1993).

19. Szyja Bronsztejn, *Ludność żydowska w Polsce w okresie międzywojennym: Studium statystyczne* (Wrocław, 1963), 126–27; Mendelsohn, *The Jews of East Central Europe,* 24–25, 26–27; Marcus, *Social and Political History of the Jews in Poland,* 113, 116, 120.

20. Mendelsohn, *The Jews of East Central Europe,* 29–32.

21. Thus, Bernard Johnpoll entitled his study of the interwar Bund, which focuses exclusively on such issues, *The Politics of Futility* (Ithaca, N.Y., 1967).

22. In 1936 Tarbut and Yavneh schools, where instruction was primarily in Hebrew, had an enrollment of 60,703 students (33.7 percent of all children in Jewish elementary schools); the Central Yiddish School Organization enrolled 16,486 students (9.2 percent); while the various Orthodox schools had 100,649 students (55.9 percent). To keep these figures in perspective, it should be stressed that over half of all Jewish elementary school students attended Polish public schools, though a substantial portion of these attended additional Jewish classes after school (see Chone Shmeruk, "Hebrew—Yiddish—Polish: A Trilingual Jewish Culture," in Gutman et al., *The Jews of Poland between Two World Wars,* 291–93).

23. Moyshe Kligsberg, "Di yidishe yugnt-bavegung in Poyln tsvishn beyde velt-milkhomes (a sotsyologishe shtudye)," in *Studies on Polish Jewry, 1919–1939,* ed. Joshua A. Fishman (New York, 1974), 137–228.

24. Rafał Żebrowski and Zofia Borzymińska, *Po-lin: Kultura Żydów polskich w XX wieku (Zarys)* (Warsaw, 1993), 84.

25. Ephraim E. Urbach, "The History of Polish Jews after World War I as Reflected in the Traditional Literature," in Gutman et al., *Jews of Poland between Two World Wars,* 223–46; Ben-Zion Gold, "Religious Education in Poland: A Personal Perspective," ibid., 272–82; Żebrowski and Borzymińska, *Po-lin,* 74–90.

26. Michael C. Steinlauf, "The Polish Jewish Daily Press," in *From Shtetl to Socialism: Studies from Polin,* ed. Antony Polonsky (London, 1993), 332–58; Yechiel Szeintuch, *Preliminary Inventory of Yiddish Dailies and Periodicals Published in Poland between the Two World Wars* (Jerusalem, 1986).

27. The camp was at Jabłonna. For sources, see Celia Heller, *On the Edge of Destruction: Jews of*

Poland between the Two World Wars (New York, 1977), 302 n. 5.

28. See Joshua Rothenberg, "The Przytyk Pogrom," *Soviet Jewish Affairs* (London) 16, no. 2 (1986), 29–46.

29. August Cardinal Hlond, *Listy pasterskie* (Poznań, 1936), 192–93, cited in Heller, *On the Edge of Destruction,* 113.

30. See Edward Wynot, "'A Necessary Cruelty': The Emergence of Official Anti-Semitism in Poland, 1936–39," *American Historical Review* 76 (1971), 1035–58.

31. *Gazeta Polska,* December 4, 1938, cited in Heller, *On the Edge of Destruction,* 137. Simultaneously with Hitler's occupation of the Sudetenland, and with his permission, Poland seized Teschen (Zaolzie), a portion of Silesia it had claimed since 1919.

32. Marcus, *Social and Political History of the Jews in Poland,* 358.

33. An enlightening study of the occupation is Jan Tomasz Gross, *Polish Society under German Occupation: The Generalgouvernement, 1939–1944* (Princeton, 1979). See also Richard C. Lukas, *Forgotten Holocaust: The Poles under German Occupation, 1939–1944* (New York, 1986); and Davies, *God's Playground,* 2:435–91.

34. After the German invasion of the Soviet Union, the territory of eastern Galicia, including Lvov, was added to the Generalgouvernement.

35. Treblinka, Sobibór, Majdanek, Auschwitz-Birkenau, and Bełżec were located in the Generalgouvernement. Only Chełmno, the first, "experimental" death camp, was located outside, in the western portion of Poland annexed by the Reich.

36. *Obozy hitlerowskie na ziemiach polskich, 1939–1945: Informator encyklopedyczny* (Warsaw, 1979). This important source must, however, be used with care; see p. 124.

37. On this issue in the concentration camp setting, see the important essay by Primo Levi, "Useless Violence," in *The Drowned and the Saved* (New York, 1988), 105–26.

38. Antoni Szcześniak and Wiesław Szota, *Droga do nikąd: Działalność organizacji ukraińskich nacjonalistów i jej likwidacja w Polsce* (Warsaw, 1973), 166–67, 170, and Ryszard Torzecki, *Kwestia ukraińska w polityce III Rzeszy (1933–1945)* (Warsaw, 1972), 328–30, both cited in Gross, *Polish Society under German Occupation,* 193.

39. Franciszek Skalniak, *Bank emisyjny w Polsce 1939–1945* (Warsaw, 1966), 133, cited in Gross, *Polish Society under German Occupation,* 109. See also the important essay by Kazimierz Wyka, first pub-

lished just after the war, "Gospodarka wyłączona," in *Życie na niby* (Cracow, 1984), 138–75.

40. Gross, *Polish Society under German Occupation*, 256–58, 283–306.

41. Lukas, *Forgotten Holocaust*, 40–60; Davies, *God's Playground*, 2:464–69; Gross, *Polish Society under German Occupation*, 259–83.

42. Gross, *Polish Society under German Occupation*, 281.

43. Ibid., 283–86.

44. Ibid., 160–83.

45. The long-accepted figure of three million Poles killed is no longer tenable. Studies published since the fall of communism, although not definitive, particularly for eastern Poland, have established two million as an upper limit (see Czesław Łuczak, "Szanse i trudności bilansu demograficznego Polski w latach 1939–1945," *Dzieje najnowsze* [Warsaw], no. 2 [1994]: 12–13; and Krystyna Kersten, "Szacunek strat osobowych w Polsce Wschodniej," ibid., 41–50). But the accepted figure of three million Polish Jews killed has been confirmed.

46. On the development of this policy, see Raul Hilberg, *The Destruction of the European Jews*, 3 vols., rev. ed. (New York, 1985). For a summary of the course of the Holocaust in Poland, including Jewish responses, see Lucy Dawidowicz, *The War against the Jews, 1933–1945*, 10th anniv. ed. (New York, 1986), 197–340. See also Yisrael Gutman, *The Jews of Warsaw, 1939–1943: Ghetto, Underground, Revolt* (Bloomington, Ind., 1982). A major work on the Warsaw ghetto, Ruta Sakowska's *Ludzie z dzielnicy zamkniętej*, 2d ed., rev. and exp. (Warsaw, 1993), awaits translation into English.

47. The average Polish ration was 669 calories, the German 2,613 (see Eugeniusz Duraczyński, *Wojna i okupacja: Wrzesień 1939–kwiecień 1943* [Warsaw, 1974], 69, cited in Lukas, *Forgotten Holocaust*, 30). For slightly different figures, see Yisrael Gutman and Shmuel Krakowski, *Unequal Victims: Poles and Jews during World War II* (New York, 1986), 45.

48. Gutman, *The Jews of Warsaw*, 64.

49. Hilberg, *Destruction*, 1:389–90.

50. Ibid., 3:1220.

51. The numbers follow Gutman, *The Jews of Warsaw*; previous estimates have suggested up to two thousand Jewish fighters and a surviving ghetto population of seventy thousand.

52. Gutman and Krakowski, *Unequal Victims*, 172–251.

53. For some studies in English, see Michael Borwicz, "Factors Influencing the Relations between the General Polish Underground and the Jewish Underground," in *Jewish Resistance during the Holocaust: Proceedings of the Conference on Manifestation of Jewish Resistance, Jerusalem, April 7–11, 1968* (Jerusalem, 1971), 343–64; Emmanuel Ringelblum, *Polish-Jewish Relations during the Second World War* (Evanston, Ill., 1992); Shmuel Krakowski, "Holocaust in the Polish Underground Press," *Yad Vashem Studies* 16 (1984), 241–70; Gutman and Krakowski, *Unequal Victims*; David Engel, *In the Shadow of Auschwitz: The Polish Government-in-Exile and the Jews, 1939–1942* (Chapel Hill, N.C., 1987); and idem, *Facing the Holocaust: The Polish Government-in-Exile and the Jews, 1943–1945* (Chapel Hill, N.C., 1993). Krakowski's work suffers from his deliberately provocative tone; see the exchange entitled "Polemic as History" between Krakowski and Stanislaus A. Blejwas in *Polin* 4 (1989), 354–69. A large portion of Richard Lukas's *Forgotten Holocaust* is devoted to a defense of Polish behavior against Jewish "accusations"; see esp. 117–81. In a similar vein, in *God's Playground* Davies devotes three pages to Polish-Jewish relations during the Holocaust (2:263–66), in the course of which he states, "To ask why the Poles did little to help the Jews is rather like asking why the Jews did nothing to assist the Poles" (264).

54. Ringelblum, *Polish-Jewish Relations*, 29.

55. Ibid., 40–53.

56. See, e.g., Gross, *Polish Society under German Occupation*, 185–86.

57. Wyka, "Gospodarka wyłączona," 155–60.

58. Ringelblum, *Polish-Jewish Relations*, 257.

59. A good source is Jan Rzepecki, "Organizacja i działanie Biura Informacji i Propagandy (BIP) Komendy Głównej AK: Zakończenie," *Wojskowy Przegląd Historyczny*, no. 4 (1971), 147–53.

60. See the important study by Jan T. Gross, *Revolution from Abroad: The Soviet Conquest of Poland's Western Ukraine and Western Belorussia* (Princeton, 1988).

61. Ibid., 146.

62. Ibid., 194. The total number of Polish citizens who moved, willingly or unwillingly, into the interior of the Soviet Union during 1939–41 was estimated by the Polish foreign ministry as 1.25 million.

63. Davies, *God's Playground*, 2:452.

64. M. K. Dziewanowski, *The Communist Party of Poland: An Outline of History* (Cambridge, Mass., 1976), 161–63, 146–54.

65. Davies, *God's Playground*, 2:545.

66. Jaff Schatz, *The Generation: The Rise and Fall of the Jewish Communists of Poland* (Berkeley, 1991), 96–98.

67. On Jews and Communism, see also the essay by A. Kainer [Stanisław Krajewski], "Żydzi a komunizm," *Krytyka* (London), no. 15 (1983), 214–47.

68. See Gross, *Revolution from Abroad*, 28–35; Paweł Korzec and Jean-Charles Szurek, "Jews and Poles under Soviet Occupation (1939–1941): Conflicting Interests," *Polin* 4 (1989), 204–25; Dov Levin, "The Response of the Jews of Eastern Poland to the Invasion of the Red Army in September 1939 (As Described by Jewish Witnesses)," *Gal-Ed: On the History of the Jews in Poland* (Tel Aviv) 11 (1989), 87–102; Ben-Cion Pinchuk, *Shtetl Jews under Soviet Rule: Eastern Poland on the Eve of the Holocaust* (London, 1990); and Krystyna Kersten, *Polacy, Żydzi, Komunizm: Anatomia półprawd, 1939–1968* (Warsaw, 1992), 25–33.

69. Gross, *Revolution from Abroad*, 29.

70. See, e.g., Pinchuk, *Shtetl Jews under Soviet Rule*, 100–101, 112–14.

71. Gross, *Polish Society under German Occupation*, 184–85, 297–99.

72. Walter Lacqueur, *The Terrible Secret: Suppression of the Truth about Hitler's Final Solution* (Boston, 1980), 109–10; Engel, *In the Shadow of Auschwitz*, 186–87.

73. See Jan Karski, *The Story of a Secret State* (Boston, 1944).

74. Engel, *In the Shadow of Auschwitz*, 173–202; Gutman and Krakowski, *Unequal Victims*, 65–74.

75. Engel, *In the Shadow of Auschwitz*, 196–97; Gutman and Krakowski, *Unequal Victims*, 88–89. The printed Polish version of his speech omitted the promise of equal rights for Jews.

76. The best-known exception was a radio broadcast by Sikorski one month after the start of the Warsaw Ghetto Uprising. For the relevant text, see Władysław Bartoszewski and Zofia Lewin, eds., *The Samaritans: Heroes of the Holocaust* (New York, 1970), 42.

77. See the important volume of materials from the Polish underground press, Paweł Szapiro, ed., *Wojna żydowsko-niemiecka: Polska prasa konspiracyjna 1943–1944 o powstaniu w getcie Warszawy* (London, 1992).

78. On Polish aid to the Warsaw Ghetto Uprising, see Gutman, *The Jews of Warsaw*, 297–301; and Gutman and Krakowski, *Unequal Victims*, 143–71.

79. Gutman and Krakowski, *Unequal Victims*, 216–20.

80. See Teresa Prekerowa, *Konspiracyjna Rada Pomocy Żydom w Warszawie 1942–1945* (Warsaw, 1982).

81. Ibid., 112 (facing), emphasis in the original, cited in Aleksander Smolar, "Tabu i Niewinność," *Aneks* (London), nos. 41–42 (1986), 93–94. Kossak was a member of the Front Odrodzenia Polski (Front for the Rebirth of Poland).

82. Lukas, *Forgotten Holocaust*, 93.

83. In 1943 and 1944 about twenty out of two thousand (see *Polskie Siły Zbrojne w Drugiej Wojnie Światowej*, 3 vols. [London, 1950], 3:472–73; Prekerowa, *Konspiracyjna Rada Pomocy Żydom*, 294–95; and idem, "The 'Just' and the 'Passive,'" *Yad Vashem Studies* 19 [1988]: 369–77). Żegota also tried unsuccessfully to convince the Delegate's Bureau to publish a fictitious list of death sentences for crimes against Jews.

84. Ringelblum, *Polish-Jewish Relations*, 125–26.

85. The term "universe of obligation" was first employed in this context by Helen Fein (see *Accounting for Genocide: National Responses and Jewish Victimization during the Holocaust* [Chicago, 1979], 33).

86. See Wacław Bielawski, *Zbrodnie na Polakach dokonane przez hitlerowców za pomoc udzielaną Żydom* (Warsaw, 1987).

87. See Nechama Tec, *When Light Pierced the Darkness: Christian Rescue of Jews in Nazi-Occupied Poland* (New York, 1986).

88. Davies, *God's Playground*, 2:575–76. The major work on this period is Krystyna Kersten, *The Establishment of Communist Rule in Poland, 1943–1948* (Berkeley, 1991).

89. Founded by Rosa Luxemburg and others at the turn of the century, the party was named Social Democracy of the Kingdom of Poland and Lithuania (Socjał-demokracja Królestwa Polskiego i Litwy [SDKPiL]).

90. Józef Adelson, "W Polsce zwanej ludowej," in *Najnowsze dzieje Żydów w Polsce, w zarysie (do 1950 roku)*, ed. Jerzy Tomaszewski (Warsaw, 1993), 398; see also 387–91 and 399–400. For other sources, see Lucjan Dobroszycki, "Restoring Jewish Life in Postwar Poland," *Soviet Jewish Affairs* 3, no. 2 (1973), 58–60; and Paul Glikson, "Jewish Population in the Polish People's Republic, 1944–1972," in *Papers on Jewish Demography* (Jerusalem, 1977), 237–39.

91. On the rebuilding of Jewish life in postwar Poland, see the sources in n. 90 as well as Yisrael Gutman, *Ha-yehudim be-Folin aharei milhamat ha-olam ha-shniya* (Jerusalem, 1985); Bernard D. Weinryb, "Poland," in *The Jews in the Soviet Satellites*, by Peter Meyer et al. (Syracuse, 1953), 207–326; and S. L. Shneiderman, *Between Fear and Hope* (New York, 1947).

92. Lucy Dawidowicz, *The Holocaust and the Historians* (Cambridge, Mass., 1981), 98; until the early 1950s the institution was known as the Cen-

tral Commission to Investigate German Crimes in Poland.

93. See Bernard Mark, *Męczeństwo i walka Żydow w latach okupacji: Poradnik bibliograficzny* (Warsaw, 1963).

94. The historical journal *Biuletyn Żydowskiego Instytutu Historycznego* has appeared quarterly since 1951. Other publications, including the Yiddish historical journal *Bleter far geshikhte,* have appeared sporadically. See Abraham Wein, "The Jewish Historical Institute in Warsaw," *Yad Vashem Studies* 8 (1970), 203–13.

95. James E. Young, *The Texture of Memory: Holocaust Memorials and Meaning* (New Haven, 1993), 120.

96. For this approach to the Jewish Problem in postwar Poland, I am indebted to the important work of Kersten in *Polacy, Żydzi, Komunizm.*

97. "Zagadnienie polskiego antysemityzmu," *Odrodzenie,* no. 28 (July 14, 1946), cited in Kersten, *Establishment of Communist Rule in Poland,* 220.

98. On the history of the monument, see Young, *The Texture of Memory,* 175–84.

99. See, e.g., "Problem antysemityzmu," *Kultura* (Paris), nos. 1/111–2/112 (January–February 1957), 60.

100. Anna Radziwiłł, "The Teaching of the History of the Jews in Secondary Schools in the Polish People's Republic, 1949–88," *Polin* 4 (1989), 402–24.

101. Quoted in Kersten, *Polacy, Żydzi, Komunizm,* 108.

102. The figures were considerably more lopsided for the KPP than for the PPR and PZPR.

103. On Jews in the UB, see Kersten, *Polacy, Żydzi, Komunizm,* 83–84; and Schatz, *The Generation,* 222–28. On popular Polish conceptions about Jews in the government, see also the interesting report from Warsaw to the British foreign secretary, September 21, 1948, published in *Soviet Jewish Affairs* 10, no. 1 (1980), 64–68.

104. Dobroszycki, "Restoring Jewish Life," 66; Adelson, "W Polsce zwanej ludowej," 401. The hundreds of Yiddish and Hebrew memorial books (*yizker bikher*) published after the Holocaust by survivors of particular communities provide ample documentation of such attacks.

105. The most comprehensive documentation is in Bożena Szaynok, *Pogrom Żydów w Kielcach 4 VII 1956 r.* (Warsaw, 1991).

106. Aryeh Josef Kochavi, "The Catholic Church and Anti-Semitism in Poland following World War II As Reflected in British Diplomatic Documents," *Gal-Ed: On the History of the Jews in Poland* 11 (1989), 116–28.

107. Adelson, "W Polsce zwanej ludowej," 424.

108. Shneiderman, *Between Fear and Hope,* 181.

109. Kersten (*Polacy, Żydzi, Komunizm,* 113–38) summarizes the current status of this theory.

110. Ibid., 152.

111. S. Łukasiewicz, *Okupacja* (Warsaw, 1978), 246, cited in Józef Wróbel, *Tematy żydowskie w prozie polskiej, 1939–1987* (Cracow, 1991), 117. Written in 1947, Łukasiewicz's book was first published in 1958.

112. Kersten, *Polacy, Żydzi, Komunizm,* 17–18.

113. For some of the diverse material on these subjects, see David S. Wyman, *The Abandonment of the Jews: America and the Holocaust, 1941–1945* (New York, 1984); Deborah E. Lipstadt, *Beyond Belief: The American Press and the Coming of the Holocaust, 1933–1945* (New York, 1986); Hilberg, *Destruction;* Gutman, *The Jews of Warsaw;* and Levi, *The Drowned and the Saved.*

114. For an account of postwar Poland up to the rise of Solidarity, see Davies, *God's Playground,* 2:556–633.

115. See, e.g., Josef Banas, *The Scapegoats: The Exodus of the Remnants of Polish Jewry* (London, 1979).

116. See the important article by K[onstanty] A. Jeleński, "White Eagle Today and Yesterday," *Soviet Survey* (London), no. 35 (January–March 1961), 12–25.

117. For a summary, see *American Jewish Year Book,* vols. 59 (Philadelphia, 1958), 326; and 60 (Philadelphia, 1959), 215.

118. "Problem antysemityzmu," 62. See also the opinion expressed by another respondent from Poland that "today anti-Semitism, in distinction from the prewar period, has been embraced by broad masses of peasants and workers, while the participation of the intelligentsia has diminished" (ibid.).

119. Banas, *The Scapegoats,* 29–30.

120. *American Jewish Year Book,* vol. 62 (Philadelphia, 1961), 292.

121. *American Jewish Year Book,* vols. 60, 216; 61 (Philadelphia, 1960), 265; 64 (Philadelphia, 1963), 360; and 69 (Philadelphia, 1968), 505. Glikson, "Jewish Population in the Polish People's Republic," 243–44.

122. Franciszek Piper, "Estimating the Number of Deportees to and Victims of the Auschwitz-Birkenau Camp," *Yad Vashem Studies* 21 (1991), 49–103.

123. Rada Ochrony Pomników Walki i Męczeństwa, *Miejsca męczeństwa i walki Żydów na*

ziemiach polskich, 1939–1945, with text in Polish, Yiddish, English, French, Russian, and German (Warsaw, 1978), 5.

124. Young, *The Texture of Memory,* 139–40.

125. Council for the Preservation of the Monuments of Struggle and Martyrdom, *Struggle, Death, Memory, 1939–1945: On the Twentieth Anniversary of the Rising in the Warsaw Ghetto, 1943–1963* (Warsaw, 1963), unpaginated.

126. Wacław Poterański, *Walka Warszawskiego Ghetta* (Warsaw, 1963), 52.

127. Ibid., 28.

128. Ibid., 37.

129. *Miasto nieujarzmione* (Warsaw, 1957), unpaginated.

130. Janusz Gumkowski and Kazimierz Leszczyński, *Poland under Nazi Occupation* (Warsaw, 1961), 16–17. For a review of Polish Holocaust historiography published before 1970, see Dawidowicz, *The Holocaust and the Historians,* 88–124. While nearly nothing about the Holocaust was published from 1949 to 1955, more than forty volumes of histories, memoirs and literature appeared from 1956 to 1962 (see Mark, *Męczeństwo i walka Żydow w latach okupacji*).

131. "Musimy pamiętać, będziemy pamiętać," *Prawo i życie,* no. 11 (1964), cited in Young, *The Texture of Memory,* 363–64; on the Treblinka memorial, see Young, *The Texture of Memory,* 186–89.

132. Henryk Grynberg, *Życie osobiste* (Warsaw, 1989), 56; the book was first published in London in 1979.

133. For memories of growing up in a "typical" patriotic Polish family in the 1950s and 1960s, see Marek Turbacz, "1968 and All That," in *Poland: Genesis of a Revolution,* ed. Abraham Brumberg (New York, 1983), 237–39.

134. Grynberg, *Życie osobiste,* 26.

135. A typical example of this approach is the recent book by Jerzy Eisler, *Marzec 1968* (Warsaw, 1991); an important exception is an article by Helena Pobóg, "Spory o marzec," *Krytyka* (Warsaw), nos. 10–11 (1982), 33–52.

136. English sources include *The Anti-Jewish Campaign in Present-Day Poland: Facts, Documents, Press Reports* (London, 1968); Paul Lendvai, *Anti-Semitism without Jews: Communist Eastern Europe* (Garden City, N.Y., 1971); Banas, *The Scapegoats;* and Michael Checinski, *Poland: Communism, Nationalism, Anti-Semitism* (New York, 1982).

137. *The Anti-Jewish Campaign,* 11.

138. When the Polish episcopate finally released a pastoral letter on the subject on May 3, 1968, the letter condemned both Polish anti-Semitism and the "anti-Polish campaign" abroad (see Eisler, *Marzec 1968,* 328).

139. Jerzy Szacki, "8 marca 1968 roku," *Krytyka,* nos. 28–29 (1988), 22.

140. Marcin Król, "O marcu—dziś: Z rozmowy redakcyjnej (fragmenty)," *Res Publica* (Warsaw) 2, no. 3 (1988), 6–7.

141. Those who have strongly argued for the Soviets' influence on the Polish anti-Zionist campaign include M. K. Dziewanowski (see his *Communist Party of Poland,* 299–301). But the Soviet anti-Zionist campaign did not originate, as once assumed, immediately after the Six-Day War, but rather as a response to the subsequent growth of the Jewish national movement in the Soviet Union. The "opening salvo" in this campaign was an article published in *Pravda* on November 30, 1969 (see Jonathan Frankel, "The Soviet Regime and Anti-Zionism: An Analysis," in *Jewish Culture and Identity in the Soviet Union,* ed. Yaacov Ro'i and Avi Beker [New York, 1991], 332).

142. The first edition of Moczar's *Barwy walki* was published in Warsaw in 1961 (see Checinski, *Poland,* 160).

143. *Wielka Encyklopedia Powszechna,* vol. 8 (Warsaw, 1966), 87–89.

144. See Władysław Machejek, "Smutno mi, Boże . . . ," *Życie literackie* (Cracow), August 6, 1967; Tadeusz Kur [Witold Jerzmanowski], "Encyklopedyści," *Prawo i życie,* March 24, 1968; and Adam Bromberg, "Encyklopedyści," *Kultura,* nos. 7–8 (1973): 174–78, 9 (1973): 123–28, 10 (1973): 157–64.

145. Wacław Poterański, *Warszawskie getto: W 25-lecie walki zbrojnej w getcie w 1943 r.* (Warsaw, 1968), 6–7.

146. Ibid., 54.

147. Ibid., 77.

148. Wacław Poterański, *Warszawskie getto: W 30-lecie powstania zbrojnego w getcie w 1943 r.* (Warsaw, 1973), 11, 29, 54.

149. Czesław Pilichowski, ed., *Obozy hitlerowskie na ziemiach polskich, 1939-1945: Informator encyklopedyczny* (Warsaw, 1979).

150. Simon Wiesenthal, "Jew-Baiting in Poland: A Documentation about Prewar Fascists and Nazi Collaborators and Their Unity of Action with Anti-Semites from the Ranks of the Communist Party of Poland" (Vienna, 1969), cited in Lendvai, *Anti-Semitism without Jews,* 136, 357 n. 45.

151. Czesław Pilichowski, "Hitlerowskie obozy i ośrodki przymusowego odosobnienia oraz ich rola w realizacji programu ludobójstwa i zagłady narodu polskiego," in Pilichowski, *Obozy hitlerowskie na ziemiach polskich,* 11. A similar perspective is

adopted by Czesław Madajczyk in his influential history of the war years, *Polityka III Rzeszy w okupowanej Polsce,* 2 vols. (Warsaw, 1970).

152. Władysław Bartoszewski, "Polacy z pomocą Żydom, 1939–1944," *Tygodnik Powszechny* (Cracow), no. 12 (1963), 3, reprinted in *Kultura,* no. 5 (1963), 93–95.

153. Władysław Bartoszewski and Zofia Lewinówna, eds., *Ten jest z ojczyzny mojej: Polacy z pomocą Żydom, 1939–1945* (Cracow, 1966); 2d enl. ed. (Cracow, 1969). There are two English versions, *Righteous among Nations: How the Poles Helped the Jews* (London, 1969), based on the second Polish edition; and *The Samaritans* (see above, n. 76). Polish aid to Jews during the war was also the subject of a monograph published several years earlier by scholars connected to the Jewish Historical Institute in Warsaw: Tatiana Berenstein and Adam Rutkowski, *Pomoc Żydom w Polsce, 1939–1945* (Warsaw, 1963).

154. The English edition is Władysław Bartoszewski, *The Blood Shed Unites Us* (Warsaw, 1970). The following year Interpress published another volume of documents, testimonies, and photographs: Stanisław Wroński and Maria Zwolakowa, eds., *Polacy i Żydzi, 1939–1945* (Warsaw, 1971).

155. Wojciech Zabrzeski, "Sojusz ofiar z katami," *Prawo i Życie,* November 21, 1967.

156. Banas, *The Scapegoats,* 83; the comment is attributed to Kazimierz Rusinek, deputy minister of culture and art, in the period just after the Six-Day War.

157. Piotr Goszczyński, *Głos Robotniczy,* May 12, 1968, cited in Lendvai, *Anti-Semitism without Jews,* 159.

158. Lendvai, *Anti-Semitism without Jews,* 159; the original source is said to be the Polish periodical *Kultura.*

159. Adam Michnik, "The Two Faces of Europe," *New York Review of Books,* July 19, 1990.

160. See Keith John Lepak, *Prelude to Solidarity: Poland and the Politics of the Gierek Regime* (New York, 1988); see also the useful chronology in Lawrence Weschler, *Solidarity: Poland in the Season of Its Passion* (New York, 1982), 137–207.

161. Antoni Słonimski, quoted in Adam Michnik, *Kościół, lewica, dialog* (Paris, 1977), 89, published in English as *The Church and the Left* (Chicago, 1993). Słonimski, to whom the book is dedicated, had been attacked during the interwar period, as Michnik was throughout his career, for his Jewish origins.

162. Michnik, *Kościół, lewica, dialog,* 91.

163. Ibid., 116–19.

164. Ibid., 114.

165. *Listy Pasterskie Episkopatu Polski* (Paris, 1975), 707–8, cited in ibid., 110.

166. See Jan Józef Lipski, *KOR: A History of the Workers' Defense Committee in Poland, 1976–1981* (Berkeley, 1985), 62–78, 208–31.

167. See, e.g., Kersten, *Polacy, Żydzi, Komunizm,* 144–45.

168. This was the title, for example, of a pamphlet published by left-wing Yiddish-speaking Jews: Itche Goldberg and Yuri Suhl, eds., *The End of a Thousand Years: The Recent Exodus of the Jews from Poland* (New York, 1971).

169. Young, *The Texture of Memory,* 182.

170. Lipski, *KOR,* 139–40.

171. On Jews and the memory of the Holocaust in Poland in the 1980s, see Iwona Irwin-Zarecka, *Neutralizing Memory: The Jew in Contemporary Poland* (New Brunswick, N.J., 1989); Andrzej Bryk, "Polish Society Today and the Memory of the Holocaust," *Gal-Ed: On the History of the Jews in Poland* 12 (1991), 107–29; and Young, *The Texture of Memory,* 113–208.

172. *Tygodnik Powszechny,* edited by Jerzy Turowicz, and *Znak,* edited by Stefan Wilkanowicz, were published continuously from the 1940s with the exception of the years 1953–56; *Więź,* edited by Tadeusz Mazowiecki, began publication in the late 1950s.

173. Michel Wieviorka, *Les Juifs, la Pologne et Solidarność* (Paris, 1984), 175–85. For an interview with one of the organizers of the Jewish Flying University, see Małgorzata Niezabitowska, "Finding It (an Interview with Stanisław Krajewski)," *Moment* (Boston), April 1984.

174. Lipski, *KOR,* 331.

175. Ibid., 337–38.

176. "Budowałem razem z wami na fundamencie chrystusowego krzyża," June 9, 1979, and "Bierzmowanie dziejów," June 10, 1979; in *Jan Paweł II na Ziemi Polskiej* (Vatican, 1979), 248, 268, emphasis in the original.

177. "Zwycięstwo przez wiarę i miłość: Homilia Ojca świętego Jana Pawła II," June 7, 1979, in *Jan Paweł II na Ziemi Polskiej,* 207, emphasis in the original.

178. There is a large literature in English on Solidarity. Excellent journalistic accounts of its origins are Neal Ascherson, *The Polish August: The Self-Limiting Revolution* (New York, 1982); Weschler, *Solidarity;* and Timothy Garton Ash, *The Polish Revolution: Solidarity* (New York, 1984). Analyses include Brumberg, *Poland;* David Ost, *Solidarity and the Politics of Anti-Politics: Opposition and Reform in Poland since 1968* (Philadelphia, 1990); and Roman Laba, *The Roots of Solidarity: A Political*

Sociology of Poland's Working-Class Democratization (Princeton, 1991).

179. Józef Przybylski, "Wspomnienia," *Kontakt* (Paris) 1, no. 21 (January 1984), 32, cited in Laba, *Roots of Solidarity,* 131.

180. "Żydzi i Polacy, Dodatek specjalny," *Biuletyn Dolnośląski,* no. 11/18 (November–December 1980); the Hebrew date is also given: "Kislew-Teweth 5741." The Warsaw Ghetto was closed in November 1940; other ghettos were closed during that same year or the following year.

181. Ibid., 1–2, emphasis in the original.

182. "Listy do redakcji: Marzec 1968," *Polityka,* no. 50 (December 12, 1980).

183. See the comments of Stanisław Krajewski in a collection of contemporary documents: Towarzystwo Kursów Naukowych, *Marzec 1968* (Warsaw, 1981), 38–39; another such collection is *Post Factum: Biuletyn specjalny* (Warsaw, 1981).

184. On the final years of Polish communism, see Kaufman, *Mad Dreams, Saving Graces;* Maciej Łopiński, Marcin Moskit, and Mariusz Wilk, eds., *Konspira: Solidarity Underground* (Berkeley, 1990); and Ost, *Solidarity and the Politics of Anti-Politics,* 149–222.

185. James Young uses the term "broken tablets" (see his *Texture of Memory,* 185–208).

186. Antoni Słonimski, "Elegia miasteczek żydowskich," in *Izrael w poezji polskiej: Antologia,* ed. Jan Winczakiewicz (Paris, 1958), 239. The editor gives 1950 as the original date of publication.

187. The conference was appropriately entitled "Poles and Jews: Myth and Reality in the Historical Context." The papers are available from the Institute on East Central Europe, Columbia University. Subsequent conferences have been held in the United States, England, Israel, and Poland.

188. Eight issues of *Polin,* edited by Antony Polonsky, had appeared by 1993.

189. The only comparable period with respect to publications about the Holocaust was 1945–48. But almost two-thirds of the new publications on Jewish topics were not directly about the Holocaust. This wave of publications kept growing; there were 171 "Jewish" books published during 1980–86 and 123 during the subsequent two years (see "Judaica: Bibliografia publikacji polskich za lata 1980–1986" and "Judaica . . . za lata 1987–1988," typescripts available through the Jewish Historical Institute. In English, see also Natan Gross, "Requiem for the Jewish People [Polish Literary Judaica in the Years 1987–1989]," *Polin* 6 [1991]: 295–308).

190. *Znak* 35, nos. 2–3 (1983).

191. On Stryjkowski in English, see Stanisław Eile, "The Tragedy of the Chosen People: Jewish Themes in the Novels of Julian Stryjkowski," *Soviet Jewish Affairs* 13, no. 3 (1983), 27–43; and Laura Quercioli-Mincer, "A Voice from the Diaspora: Julian Stryjkowski," in *From Shtetl to Socialism: Studies from Polin,* ed. Antony Polonsky (London, 1993), 487–501.

192. Grynberg's first novel, *Wojna żydowska,* was first published in Warsaw in 1965, then reprinted by the official press in 1989.

193. See Irena Maciejewska, ed., *Męczeństwo i zagłada Żydów w zapisach literatury polskiej* (Warsaw, 1988), an anthology of poetry and prose based in part on Michał Borwicz's postwar collection *Pieśń ujdzie cało* (Warsaw, 1947). Maciejewska's volume is prefaced by an important essay reviewing Polish literature on the Holocaust. See also the recent study by Natan Gross, *Poeci i Szoa: Obraz Zagłady Żydów w poezji polskiej* (Sosnowiec, 1993).

194. *Literatura,* March 19, 1981.

195. *Grunwald: Biuletyn Informacyjny Zjednoczenia Patriotycznego "Grunwald"* (Warsaw, [1980s]).

196. Wacław Poterański, *Warszawskie getto,* preface by Ryszard Nazarewicz (Warsaw, 1983); Józef Orlicki, *Szkice z dziejów stosunków polsko-żydowskich, 1918–1949* (Szczecin, 1983), 251–63.

197. Hanna Krall, *Zdążyć przed Panem Bogiem* (Cracow, 1977). It was translated as *Shielding the Flame: An Intimate Conversation with Dr. Marek Edelman, the Last Surviving Leader of the Warsaw Ghetto Uprising* (New York, 1986), which has been reprinted under a new title, along with another of Krall's works, in *The Subtenant; and To Outwit God* (Evanston, Ill., 1992).

198. Krall, *Zdążyć przed Panem Bogiem,* 15–16.

199. The full text is reprinted in Władysław Bartoszewski and Marek Edelman, *Żydzi Warszawy* (Lublin, 1993), 178.

200. As a Fulbright scholar in Poland in 1983–84 and on numerous subsequent visits, I was privileged to witness these and similar events.

201. A set of these stamps is in my personal possession.

202. "Letter from Lech Wałęsa to Marek Edelman, April 17, 1988," *Tikkun* 3, no. 5 (1988), 27.

203. For an excellent example, see Kaufman, *Mad Dreams, Saving Graces,* 175–77.

204. "Antysemityzm, Patriotyzm, Chrześcijaństwo," *Znak* 35, nos. 2–3 (1983), 176, 171.

205. Jan Józef Lipski, "Dwie ojczyzny—dwa patriotyzmy (Uwagi o megalomanii narodowej i ksenofobii Polaków)" (Warsaw, 1982), photocopy, 3–4, 6, reprinted in Lipski's *Dwie ojczyzny i inne szkice* (n.p., 1985).

206. Ibid., 25.

207. *Rzeczpospolita* (Warsaw), May 2, 1985.

208. Ibid.; Neal Ascherson, "The *Shoah* Controversy," *Soviet Jewish Affairs* 16, no. 1 (1986), 54–55.

209. Maciej Kozłowski, "Zrozumieć," *Ogniwo* (Wrocław), no. 25 (April 1986), 26.

210. *Tygodnik Mazowsze*, no. 145 (November 7, 1985).

211. See, e.g., Stanisław Kostarski, "Film 'Shoah': Prawda i fałsze Claude Lanzmanna," *Życie Warszawy*, May 11–12, 1985; "Po projekcji 'Shoah': Fałszywy obraz," *Rzeczpospolita*, November 4, 1985; Jerzy Turowicz, "'Shoah' w polskich oczach," *Tygodnik Powszechny*, no. 45 (November 10, 1985); Teresa Pisarek, "'Shoah' i myśl niezależna," *Obecność* (Wrocław), no. 14 (1986), 103–6; and Andrzej Stanisławski, "'Shoah,' czy może 'romantyzm rewolucyjny'?" *Kurs*, no. 18 (1986), 45–50.

212. For translations of Miłosz's poem, Błoński's essay, and selected responses, see Antony Polonsky, ed., *My Brother's Keeper? Recent Polish Debates on the Holocaust* (London, 1990).

213. Miłosz, "A Poor Christian Looks at the Ghetto," in ibid., 51.

214. Błoński, "The Poor Poles Look at the Ghetto," in ibid., 41–42.

215. Ibid., 35, 44.

216. Ibid., 45.

217. Ibid., 43, 45–46, emphasis in the original.

218. Jerzy Turowicz, "Ethical Problems of the Holocaust in Poland: Discussion Held at the International Conference on the History and Culture of Polish Jewry in Jerusalem on Monday, 1 February 1988," in Polonsky, *My Brother's Keeper?* 215.

219. Ibid., 216.

220. Andrzej Bryk, "The Hidden Complex of the Polish Mind: Polish-Jewish Relations during the Holocaust," in Polonsky, *My Brother's Keeper?* 168, 171–72.

221. On the controversy, see Carol Rittner and John K. Roth, eds., *Memory Offended: The Auschwitz Convent Controversy* (New York, 1991); and Władysław Bartoszewski, *The Convent at Auschwitz* (New York, 1991). The latter author is the son of the chronicler of Polish aid to the Jews during the Holocaust.

222. Bartoszewski, *The Convent at Auschwitz*, 7.

223. For a chronology of events relevant to the controversy, see Rittner and Roth, *Memory Offended*, 17–26.

224. Bartoszewski, *The Convent at Auschwitz*, 87.

225. Ibid., 90–93.

226. Francis A. Winiarz, "We're Not Moving a Single Inch," *Polish Daily News*, November 1, 1989, reprinted in Rittner and Roth, *Memory Offended*, 260–61.

227. Translated in Rittner and Roth, *Memory Offended*, 218; the statement was made August 8, 1989.

228. "We Trust in the Capital of Wisdom," homily delivered at Jasna Góra, Częstochowa, August 26, 1989, translated in Rittner and Roth, *Memory Offended*, 220–24.

229. *Jerusalem Post*, September 16, 1989, cited in Rittner and Roth, *Memory Offended*, 24.

230. On Polish sentiment against the nuns' moving, see the interview with Bishop Tadeusz Pieronek published in *Polityka*, no. 16 (April 17, 1993). For the pope's letter to the nuns, see *Gazeta Wyborcza*, no. 88 (April 15, 1993).

231. Dawid Warszawski [Konstanty Gebert], "The Role of Anti-Semitism in the Polish Presidential Elections of 1990," typescript, a copy of which is in my possession. See also Jarosław Kurski, *Lech Wałęsa: Democrat or Dictator?* (Boulder, Colo., 1993), 42–45.

232. See, e.g., the articles and letters to the editor in *Gazeta Wyborcza*, March 6–7, 13–14, 20–21, 25, 26, 27–28, 1993, and September 27, 1993; and the interview with Krystyna Kersten, "Oblicza prawdy," in *Plus-Minus* (weekly supplement to *Rzeczpospolita*), no. 16 (May 8–9, 1993). See also the interesting article by Dariusz Fikus on the term *Żydokomuna* in *Rzeczpospolita*, April 30, 1993.

233. The figures for 1991 were 19 percent expressing antipathy to Jews, 47 percent to Gypsies, 32 percent to Arabs (see Aleksandra Jasińska-Kania, "Zmiany postaw Polaków wobec różnych narodów i państw," in *Bliscy i dalecy*, Studia nad postawami wobec innych narodów, ras i grup etnicznych, vol. 2, ed. Aleksandra Jasińska-Kania [Warsaw, 1992], 224. In English see the pamphlet published by the American Jewish Committee, Renae Cohen and Jennifer L. Golub, *Attitudes toward Jews in Poland, Hungary, and Czechoslovakia: A Comparative Survey* [New York, 1991]). The figures for Poland are based on polls conducted by the Demoskop Research Agency in 1991.

234. "Nie w jednej ławce," *Gazeta Wyborcza*, July 14, 1992.

235. Bryk, "Polish Society Today and the Memory of the Holocaust," 124–27.

236. According to the *Rocznik Statystyczny* (Warsaw, 1994), in 1993 the Związek Religijny Wyznania Mojżeszowego (Union of Congregations of the Mosaic Faith) numbered 1,170 members and the secular Towarzystwo Społeczno-Kulturalne Żydów w Polsce (Social-Cultural Society of the

Jews of Poland) numbered 3,245. There may be some overlap in these figures. A key problem, as usual, is how to define a Jew. Some estimate the number of Poles of Jewish descent at 40,000.

237. Gregorz Polak, "Lekcja prawdy," *Gazeta Wyborcza,* October 26, 1993.

238. Jacek E. Wilczur, "Sobibór—fałsz i prawda," *Życie Warszawy,* December 13, 1991; "Śladami 'marszu śmierci,'" ibid., August 24, 1992.

239. Katarzyna Bielas, "Miejsce dochodzenia," *Gazeta Wyborcza,* October 21, 1993.

240. "Scena, której nie mogę zapomnieć," *Polityka,* no. 16 (April 17, 1993).

241. "Pastoral on Jewish-Catholic Relations," issued November 30, 1990, translated in Ritter and Roth, *Memory Offended,* 265–66.

242. In addition to the organization of a permanent International Auschwitz Advisory Council, there have been two Symposiums of Jewish Intellectuals on the Future of Auschwitz, one in Oxford in 1990 and another in Cracow in 1992. These gatherings have also addressed the problem of the progressive deterioration of the grounds and exhibits at Auschwitz. On this issue, see Timothy W. Ryback, "A Reporter at Large: Evidence of Evil," *New Yorker,* November 15, 1993, 68–81; and Jane Perlez, "Decay of a 20th Century Relic: What's the Future of Auschwitz?" *New York Times,* January 5, 1994, A6.

243. *New York Times,* June 17, 1992, A15. The quotation is from Job 16:18.

CZECHOSLOVAKIA
Livia Rothkirchen

BEFORE THE HOLOCAUST

The fledgling Czechoslovak Republic,[1] which first emerged on the political scene in 1918 after the dissolution of the Austro-Hungarian monarchy, encompassed the Czech crown lands (Bohemia and Moravia-Silesia) as well as Slovakia and Subcarpathian Ruthenia, the former provinces of Hungary.[2] Although it was the richest of the successor states, Czechoslovakia was the least homogeneous. With an area of 54,244 square miles and a population of 13,613,172, the new state constituted an ethnic and cultural amalgam of minorities with a variety of languages and diverse religious traditions. In Bohemia and Moravia-Silesia Roman Catholicism was in decline—many Czechs joined the Independent Czechoslovak Church or the Protestant Church of Czech Brethren or claimed to be unattached. In Slovakia the Roman Catholic Church played an important role in public life, and among the Ruthenes the Uniate (Greek Catholic) and Orthodox Churches were paramount. The most distinctive infirmity of the new state was the Germans and Hungarians settled in the strategic border areas who had been a part of the master nations of the prewar imperial system. Overnight, these nationalities found themselves to have the status of minorities, and they barely acquiesced to the new development. The minority problems were to play a crucial role in both the foreign and internal affairs of the republic.

The Jewish populace, which according to the 1921 census numbered 354,342 in the western and eastern provinces, to all intents and purposes entered the historical map as "Czechoslovak Jews."[3] Although the Jews of each of the above-mentioned provinces had their own particular socioeconomic background and cultural characteristics, the collective term for the Jews gained worldwide currency. (In fact, the term "Czechoslovak Jews" has often been erroneously used in the context of World War II history, 1939–45, during which period the three provinces were separated from one another.)

The Historical Setting

Bohemia ceased to be an independent kingdom in the Middle Ages, when it became affiliated with the Holy Roman Empire. From 1526 it constituted part of the hereditary Habsburg dominion, and after the Battle of the White Mountain in 1620 Bohemia lost its independence; the kingdom was transformed into an administrative province, and its culture and native Czech language were almost destroyed. After three centuries of decline, in the wake of the Czech national revival and the industrialization of the area, the Czechs created a society of well-established and educated bourgeoisie, a politically conscious working class, and a literate peasantry.

In Bohemia and Moravia minute Jewish settlements existed as of the tenth century C.E., first and foremost in Prague, one of the oldest communities in Central Europe, known as "city and mother in Israel" because of its famous Jewish scholars and sages. This enclave later developed into a mainspring of religious and spiritual life that wielded great influence over other Jewish communities.

In the wake of the Edict of Tolerance, issued by Emperor Joseph II (in Bohemia in October 1781 and in Moravia in February 1782), a new era began in every aspect of life. The overall usage of the German language in both everyday and religious life led to the so-called Germanization process that engendered a change in the cultural and political orientation of the Jews. A further development occurred in the wake of the Law of Equality (1848) and the Emancipation Law (1867): assimilation and progress deeply penetrated all strata of life, especially in Prague, where religious practice declined, as did dependence on community life.

By this time the Jews numbered 75,459 (0.72 percent of the total population). Following the Czech national awakening in the mid-1850s, Jews were caught up in the German-Czech conflict for national supremacy, exposed to continuous antagonism and strife between the rival parties.[4] They were blamed by the Czechs for being an instrument of "Germanization." Under the influence of a constant outpouring of virulent anti-Semitic literature—pseudoreligious pamphlets "for the people"—distributed by Catholic preachers, ill feeling mounted. The situation was further aggravated when the steady advancement of the Jews in the economy and in industry and their growing role in the development of the urban centers led Czech nationalists to launch an economic campaign directed mainly against German and Jewish concerns. In due course industrial unrest and mass demonstrations of workers occurred, originally generated by socioeconomic conditions (low wages and mechanization), setting off a chain of rioting in townlets and villages.[5] The anti-Jewish riots peaked during the notorious Hilsner blood libel trial in 1899–1900, which prompted Professor Thomas Garrigue Masaryk to courageously speak out for justice.

In 1876 the nucleus of the "Czech Jewish movement" sprang up within student circles, centered around the Svaz českých akademiků židů (Academic Student's Club), to promote the use of the Czech language in publications and in the synagogue.[6] The students strove for close ties with the oppressed Czech nation, supporting its national aspirations. Initially they were a small but forceful group whose members hailed primarily from the rural areas. In Moravia their number was minute. By the turn of the century the Czech Jewish movement in Bohemia could boast of a cultural elite: journalists, professionals, and several leading authors and thinkers of high caliber, such as Dr. Jindřich Kohn, Dr. Viktor Vohryzek, and Dr. Edvard Lederer. At about the same time, a thin but significant stratum of the Jewish intelligentsia came to be drawn to Zionism under the impact of Theodor Herzl and Ahad Ha'am.[7] Adherents of the two diametrically opposed ideologies, Czech assimilationism and Zionism, gradually became fervent adversaries, challenging each other in perpetual debates.

The last year of the turbulent decade heralded the "national turnabout" of the Jews in Prague. In 1890 about two-thirds of Bohemian Jewry—and three-quarters of the Jews of Prague—declared their language of daily use to be German; ten years later, in 1900, more than 54 percent of both Bohemian and Prague Jews proclaimed Czech to be their daily language.[8] The Jews of Moravia were more conservative and observant in religious practice than their Bohemian brothers. They differed from their coreligionists also in the use of language: in 1900, 77 percent declared German as their mother tongue; 16 percent, Czech; and 7 percent, other languages.

Bohemian Jews had been the moving force behind the "economic wonder" in the development of the Czech provinces, which contained 70–80 percent of the industries and resources of the former Austrian monarchy, the majority of which were located in the border areas, the so-called Sudetenland. As a predominantly urban population, the Jews were associated with the trade and manufacture of glass, textiles, and hosiery and the stone, building, and mining industries.

After the dissolution of the Austro-Hungarian monarchy and the establishment of the Czechoslovak Republic in 1918, Jewish society underwent great changes. Assimilation continued, reflected in the high rate of intermarriage, especially in the highly affluent Prague community, which constituted almost half of the Jewish population (33,425). One of the factors aiding assimilation was the separation of church and state in the newly created republic, the legalization of civil marriage, and the free choice of religious denomination.[9] A large segment of the acculturated generation of Jews viewed "the register of birth as its only link with Judaism," as the writer František Langer put it.[10] Consequently, in Bohemia some of the secularized Jews preferred no affiliation to any religion whatsoever and thus claimed to be "without confession" *(bez vyznání)*. In Moravia, however, Jewish tradition retained a greater hold upon the community, reinforced during World War I by the steady influx of refugees from Galicia and Bukovina, observant Jews for the most part.

According to the 1930 census in the Czech provinces, the Jews numbered 117,551, or 1.01 percent, of the total population. Although 46.4 percent of the Jews in Bohemia and 17.6 percent in Moravia spoke Czech, only a small number were organized within the Czech Jewish movement. The Zionist (national) camp had the support of 20.3 percent of the Jews in Bohemia and 51.7 percent in Moravia. The German-speaking Jews in the two provinces (who claimed German nationality during the 1930 census) constituted around 30 percent of the Jewish population.[11] After 1933 the majority of German-speaking Jews drifted conceptually to the Zionist camp.

Already in the 1920s German Jewish culture in the Czech lands was on the retreat, signaling the end of a historical process. At the same time, the Czech Jewish writers were gaining ascendancy along with a nucleus of the first generation of literati who were imbued with Jewish national aspirations. The deep-seated Jewish commitment to education produced a cultural and intellectual elite that greatly enriched all aspects of life.[12]

Slovakia, known as Upper Hungary (in Hungarian, *Felvidék,* and in Slovak, *Horňáky*) until 1918, was a province of Hungary. Its 3,000,870 residents consisted overwhelmingly of devout Catholic peasants and rural laborers. A thin layer of middle-class village priests and professionals constituted the country's intelligentsia. Although archaeological finds—tombstones with Hebrew inscriptions from the ancient Roman province of Pannonia—indicate early Jewish settlement in this area, historical records point to a Jewish presence in the mid-twelfth century.[13]

The one-time imperial town of Pressburg (renamed Bratislava in 1918), along with some other cities—Trnava, Nitra, and Holíč—having long-established Jewish communities, played an important role in the urbanization process of the country, with many Jewish individuals contributing to the development of commerce and industry. In the eighteenth century the settlements expanded and were spiritually enriched by an influx of Moravian Jews, whose customs and traditions became an integral part of the community life. Following the Chmielnicki pogroms, Jewish emigrants from Poland settled in eastern Slovakia.

The Edict of Tolerance of Joseph II and the opening of the first Jewish schools to have German as the language of instruction introduced new developments in the life of the Jews of this area. In the wake of the Constitutional Compromise *(Ausgleich),* the Austro-Hungarian monarchy came into being (1867). That same year the Emancipation Law was sanctioned, changing considerably the position of a broad stratum of the Jewish population. Many Jewish entrepreneurs became pioneers of industry, manufacturing, and building construction and began to gravitate toward Budapest instead of Vienna, as did a greater part of the local Slovak intelligentsia.

During the 1870s the Hungarians launched their "Magyarization" policy, which mandated that the Hungarian language be used in education and public administration. While to Jews it meant merely substituting Magyar for their German *Umgangsprache,* the nationally conscious Slovaks resented this new language policy. Many years later this policy would provide the basis for accusations of "Magyarizing" voiced by Slovak nationalist circles against the Jews. In reality, however, anti-Jewish sentiments stemmed from religious prejudices and social differences.

As Jews moved gradually into the professions, they tended to become assimilated. The great divide in internal affairs dates back to the Hungarian Jewish Congress that convened under the aegis of the authorities in 1868–69 and altered the former composition by splitting the predominantly Orthodox community into "Orthodox," "Neolog," and "Status Quo Ante" congregations. However, the changes introduced in Slovakia were less radical than in Hungary proper. Communal life as well as social and educational activities continued to center around religious institutions. Intermarriage was virtually unknown.

In the 1870s, following a massive influx of poor and observant Jews from Galicia, who first settled in the neighboring northern provinces, anti-Semitism grew, peaking during the infamous Tiszaeszlár blood libel trial, which rocked all of Hungary. Anti-Jewish riots occurred also in Pressburg in 1882 and 1883. In 1884, the Anti-Semitic Party came into being, fomenting the hatred of Jews on its political platform. In 1896 Father Andreas (Andrej) Hlinka, a Catholic priest, founded the clerical People's Party; antiliberalism became a basic tenet of its platform, and it focused its campaign ostentatiously against the Jews.[14] The clerical movement openly claimed that the influence of the Jews was morally and intellectually harmful and destructive.

The dismemberment of the Austro-Hungarian Empire and the foundation of the Czechoslovak Republic was viewed favorably by the nationally conscious Slovaks. The leadership of the People's Party also saw it as a positive act. Nevertheless, in the 1920s, under the influence of Hungarian irredentism, a number of Slovak activists engaged in hostile activities in an effort to undermine the existence of the new state.

Central Slovakia had a well-established middle-class Jewish population made up mainly of entrepreneurs, professionals, businessmen, and gentrified estate owners whose lifestyle was reminiscent of that of the Hungarian nobility. (It is estimated that during the 1930s around 50 percent of the physicians and 60 percent of the lawyers in Slovakia were Jews.) The Jews of eastern Slovakia, however, were more akin to the neighboring Galician and Subcarpathian Jewry and less willing than their coreligionists in the western area to assimilate or identify with the surrounding Slovak and Hungarian population. The majority were observant Jews to whom religion was the essence of life. Among the strictly Orthodox there were a considerable number of Hasidic congregations. A large proportion of the Jews in eastern Slovakia were engaged in the lumber trade, while others barely eked out a livelihood.

According to the 1930 census, Jews in Slovakia numbered 136,737, or 4.11 percent of the overall population, of which 70.9 percent were Roman Catholic, 6.5 percent were Greek Catholic, and 16.6 percent were Protestants of various denominations.[15] Besides the large Magyar minority (around 700,000), there were medium-sized German Ruthenian and still smaller Czech, Gypsy, and Polish entities.

Subcarpathian Ruthenia (Podkarpatská Rus), with an area of 4,900 square miles, was also a province of Hungary until 1918. When the region was incorporated into Czechoslovakia, the Ruthenians made up more than 50 percent of its overall population (725,568 according to the 1930 census). The Hungarians, who after centuries of domination became a minority, constituted about one-third of the population. The Jews were the third largest ethnic group. Other, less numerous ethnic groups were Germans, Czechs, Poles, and Gypsies.

There is sporadic evidence of a Jewish presence in Subcarpathian Ruthenia as early as the fifteenth century.[16] However, it was only in the eighteenth century that organized communities sprang up, reinforced by a large influx of Jews from neighboring Galicia and Romania as well as from Poland after the Chmielnicki pogrom. The Jews of Subcarpathian Ruthenia were the most vital and the least assimilated element within Czechoslovak Jewry, numbering 102,542 people, or 15.4 percent of the population.[17] (An additional 8,000 Jews were "stateless" individuals.) Almost half of the city of Mukačevo's inhabitants and one-third of those of the capital, Užhorod, were Jewish. Aside from the well-to-do urbanized professionals, the majority of Jews residing in the larger localities engaged mainly in commerce and business; others supported themselves as artisans, craftsmen, and manual laborers.

The great majority of Jews (around 65,000) lived in small rural settlements and villages on close and amicable terms with their Ruthenian neighbors. The percentage of Jews engaged in agriculture was 27.6 percent, a phenomenon rare for European Jewry. Many owned land or rock and salt quarries. Others owned vineyards and tobacco plantations or made their living by breeding livestock and keeping bees. A steady number of the unemployed proletariat, the so-called *luftmenschen,* lived from hand to mouth, with no income whatsoever, relying heavily on handouts and charity. The situation worsened during the Great Depression because of the collapse of the lumber industry and associated businesses. Jewish shopkeepers were particularly hard hit by a new government policy, promoted by certain political parties, that supported workers' union cooperatives and other organized consumers' enterprises.

The Jews of the Verchovina mountain plateaus, in the Maramaros region—the birthplace of the Baal Shem Tov, the founder of Hasidism—were a world apart, akin to the native Ruthenian peasants whose illiteracy, poverty, and rustic backwardness made world headlines in the 1920s. The relief work conducted by the American Joint Distribution Committee and the vocational training provided by the Jewish Colonization Association in basket weaving, pottery, and handicrafts were most useful in turning them into self-supporting, productive people.

The freedom and democratic spirit prevalent in the republic, along with the progress of education, spawned national consciousness among the native Ruthenians. At the same time, Zionism among the Jews was gaining ground; the leftist pioneering youth organization Hehalutz, founded in the late twenties, grew in size each year. Its members attended the *hachsharah* (preparation) training centers and planned to emigrate to Palestine.

One of the dilemmas of the Ruthenian people concerned their national identity: were they a separate nation or part of the Ukrainian or the Russian nation? Was their local Carpatho-Russian language, in certain areas "corrupted" by Magyar and Slovak words, a dialect of Russian or Ukrainian? Since the questions remained unanswered, there was constant chaos in the school system with regard to what textbooks to use as well as what language to teach in. Subsequently the question of language became associated with political issues. The Ruthenians were aggravated by the fact that a great percentage of Jewish children attended Czech schools: of the 20,000 Jewish pupils, 12,479 attended Czech schools; 4,974, Ruthenian schools; 1,084, Hungarian schools; and 751, Hebrew schools. Consequently, Jews were accused of "exploitation," "opportunism," and, mainly, the "Czechization" of the region.

In order to neutralize the Jewish element, the government supported the opening of the Hebrew Reform Real gymnasium in Mukačevo in 1928 and in 1934 another gymnasium in Užhorod, thus reinforcing the existing network of Hebrew elementary schools.[18] This enterprise, though launched with state approval (President Masaryk himself contributed to it from his private funds), was subsidized countrywide by the Zionist organizations, such as the Women's International Zionist Organization (WIZO) and Tarbut, as well as by wealthy donors. It was described as the crowning achievement of the Zionist movement in this area.

The Jewish Minority: Political Affiliation

Under the tutelage of the philosopher-president T. G. Masaryk, Czechoslovakia, although it was surrounded by semifeudal and totalitarian countries, was a bulwark of democracy during the interwar period. Its pioneering efforts were widely acclaimed in the Western world. H. G. Wells viewed the First Republic as "the only positive outcome of World War I."[19] The Czechoslovak Republic was one of the sixteen countries that signed the minorities clause at the Peace Conference at Saint-Germain-en-Laye on September 10, 1919. After prolonged negotiations, the principle was endorsed on February 29, 1920, in the Constitution of the Republic, article 128. According to the preamble, the Jews were recognized as a national minority with political rights. Czechoslovakia thus became the only country in Europe to acknowledge the Jewish entity.[20] One of the objectives of this policy was to reduce the number of Jews who identified themselves as Germans or Magyars, a relic of the Austro-Hungarian past. The political potential of the comparatively large Jewish population of the region, especially in the eastern provinces, caused it to be regarded as a desirable pawn by the competing Ruthenians, Magyars, and Czechs. Within the framework of the republic, fruitful cooperation began between the Jewish populations of the three provinces: Bohemia and Moravia provided the Zionist leadership, Slovakia became the mainstay of the youth movement, and Subcarpathian Ruthenia was the reservoir of the Jewish Party electorate.[21] In 1930 the Jews numbered 356,830, only 2.5 percent of the total population of 14,500,000. Their influence in commerce and industry as well as in the cultural life of the country, however, far exceeded their numerical strength.

One of the weaknesses of Czechoslovakia's constitutional life was its multiethnic composition, which was reflected in a proliferation of political parties. Of the total of twenty-three parties, five Czechoslovak parties of various hues constituted the backbone of coalition governments.[22] The cardinal issue in the multinational setup was the language problem, a decisive matter determining internal policy in the spheres of education, culture, electoral criteria, and religious communal affairs.[23] As far as the use of minority languages was concerned, the law stipulated that they could be used officially in local government agencies within jurisdictions in which at least one-fifth of the population spoke the language in question. Since minority groups were dispersed, it was ultimately this stipulation that became a stumbling block in electing candidates to Parliament.

The Jewish Party suffered several defeats in the initial elections.[24] Although the party entered the political arena in 1919, it was only in the third election, in 1929, following a vote agreement with the Polish minority party, that two representatives of the Jewish Party were elected to the Prague Parliament: Dr. Ludvík Singer, who was succeeded after his death in July 1931 by Dr. Angelo Goldstein, and Dr. Julius

Reisz. During the next elections, in 1935, as a result of an arrangement with the Czech Social Democrats, Goldstein and Dr. Hayyim Kugel were elected. The Jewish Party (which cooperated with other minor Zionist parties, such as the Poalei Zion Workers' Party and the religious Mizrachi Party) competed mainly with the Tradesmen's Party, the German, Hungarian, and Polish ethnic minority parties, and the Communist Party, which also drew Jewish votes.

Throughout the years of the First Republic the most important items on the agenda of the Jewish Party were to improve the economic situation, especially that of the poverty-stricken Jewish population in the eastern provinces; to legalize religious congregations; to attain official recognition of the Hebrew school system in Subcarpathian Ruthenia; and to protest the bureaucratic attitude of the local authorities in their handling of the question of "stateless" persons. In the mid-1930s the Jewish Party representatives were also actively engaged in counteracting the spread of Nazi agitation as well as attacks led by local nationalists and anti-Semites.

The Jewish religious communities of Czechoslovakia were governed by two separate codes: Bohemia and Moravia-Silesia had taken over the old Austrian code of 1890.[25] The main function of the community was to levy taxes and collect fees "to provide for the religious needs and support the institutions needed for the purpose." Slovakia and Subcarpathian Ruthenia carried on according to the legislation enacted by Hungary in 1870. After the establishment of the republic, this arrangement of two separate codes for the religious communities was accorded governmental approval, and no serious attempt was made to change it. In Slovakia the decree of April 14, 1920, which reconstituted the Orthodox Autonomous Congregations, was extended on February 12, 1923, to include the congregations of Subcarpathian Ruthenia. The analogous Federation of the Neolog and Status Quo Ante congregations (as of 1928 known as Jeshurun) was approved by a decree of November 22, 1926. The formation of a new, non-Orthodox federation and the process of democratization, backed by the new generation both in Slovakia and in Subcarpathian Ruthenia, led to bitter controversies and protests against the autocratic Orthodox leadership.

Aside from organizational differences between the two systems, the essential distinction lay in the field of religious instruction. In the eastern provinces the congregations (as "recognized" churches according to the former Hungarian legislation) were permitted to provide and superintend Jewish religious instruction in public schools and other parochial schools, which were subsidized by the government. (The rabbis themselves were entitled to state subsidies, which raised their salaries to the minimum established for conformist clergy.) This, of course, allowed the rabbis to wield considerable influence on the school system. In contrast to the situation in Bohemia and Moravia-Silesia, in Slovakia and Subcarpathian Ruthenia there was hardly a congregation that did not have a *Talmud Torah,* which acted as a preparatory school to yeshivot of higher education, which in turn were the most important sources for the recruitment of rabbis. In the Czech lands it was only in 1926 that a joint Supreme Council of the Federations of Jewish Religious Communities in Bohemia, Moravia, and Silesia (Nejvyšší rada svazu náboženských obcí židovských v Čechách, na Moravě a ve Slezsku) was established.

This situation of separate community organizations prevailed until the late thirties. On January 21, 1937, a "Supplement to the Law of the Organization of the Jewish Religious Community" was finally passed in the Parliament.[26] It was to apply only to the western part of the country. However, because of the political developments that subsequently led to the Munich Crisis, it was never implemented.

Jewish Achievements during the First Republic

Czechoslovakia's concessions to Jewish nationalism were unprecedented. The influence of President Masaryk and of a number of leading intellectuals who openly condemned anti-Semitism and supported Zionism had an enormous impact in forging the identity of the younger generation of Jews.[27] In the first census held in the republic, in 1921, 180,855 persons (53.62 percent of all Jews in Czechoslovakia) claimed Jewish nationality; by 1930, 204,427 (57.20 percent) did so. Although the increase in percentage was slight (in Bohemia altogether 15,463, or 20.26 percent, adhered to Jewish nationality; in Moravia-Silesia, 21,315, or 51.67 percent; and in Slovakia, 72,644, or 53.11 percent), it actually indicated the development of a new political trend. There was a noticeable decline in German orientation in the Czech lands and of Hungarian orientation in the eastern provinces. The most striking change occurred in Slovakia, which registered a substantial rise in the adherence of Jews to Slovak nationality, and in Subcarpathian Ruthenia, where 95,005 (94 percent) declared themselves to be of Jewish nationality. There was concomitantly a remarkable increase in the number of Jewish pupils attending Czech-, Slovak-, and Ruthenian-language state schools, with their numbers in the 1930s estimated at 84 percent of all Jewish students.

The Zionist movement sponsored various publications and prided itself on its excellent press. It could point to the weekly *Selbstwehr* (Self-Defense) and *Židovské zprávy* (Jewish News), as well as papers of all political and ideological hues published in Czech, Slovak, Yiddish, German, and Hungarian, highlighted by the boldly entitled *Medina Ivrit—Judenstaat* (Jewish State), issued by the revisionist movement.[28] The Czech Jewish assimilationist movement was represented by *Rozvoj* (Development), and among its contributors were several leading intellectuals.

Great progress was made in the field of education generally, but especially in the eastern provinces of the republic. For instance, in Slovakia in the last year of the monarchy (1918) there were only 140 public schools; by 1935 there were 3,277. According to Sir Cecil Parrott, the British ambassador to Czechoslovakia during the interwar period, "Schools were better and more democratic than in Britain."[29] The Jewish minority was one of the prime beneficiaries. It has been estimated that 18 percent of all university students were Jews, although their ratio in the overall population was only 2.5 percent. Jewish students from neighboring Poland and Hungary, excluded from educational institutions because of the *numerus clausus* in their countries, flocked to the Czechoslovak high schools and institutions of higher learning. The inculcation of democratic values and the study of Czech history, language, and culture aroused, at the same time, an interest in exploring the history of the Jews both in the Czech lands and in Slovakia and Subcarpathian Ruthenia, where the first

Jewish museums were opened and the study of local Jewish history was begun.

Although a number of Jews held responsible positions, their number in the civil service was negligible. Jewish academics were appointed professors at the Czech and German universities of Prague and other academic institutions. Others made careers as leading journalists and also in political and public life. (Four ministers of Jewish origin served in Czechoslovak governments.)

The Impact of Fascism and the Nazi Ideologies

From the very beginning fascism in Bohemia and Moravia was weak, lacking ideological roots and a raison d'être.[30] The National Fascist Community (Národní fašistická obec), led by General Rudolf Gajda—it was later transformed into a political party—was described as "a grotesque imitation of foreign models."[31] Nevertheless, the rightist daily press, obviously inspired by fascist ideology, carried abusive articles. Anti-Semitic pamphlets and books deriding Jewish traditions and rituals also made their appearance. In the 1920s, following the Italian model, extreme nationalist elements, supported by *völkisch* German students, occasionally staged anti-Semitic demonstrations in Prague.

Autonomist circles in both Slovakia and Ruthenia looked with admiration upon the "dynamic" totalitarian regimes, discontented as they were over the question of autonomy and the friction existing between themselves and the centralist government in Prague. In Slovakia a paramilitary organization, Rodobrana (a home guard militia, a forerunner of the infamous Hlinka Guard shock troops), was formed in 1924. In Ruthenia the Ukrainian-oriented nationalist paramilitary organization Sič was founded in the 1930s on Nazi models. White Russian and Ukrainian teachers, writers, and journalists who had found asylum in the area after World War I also played a predominant role in the dissemination of anti-Semitism. As the economic crisis became aggravated, the Slovak nationalist press launched a campaign against Jewish capital and members of the liberal professions, particularly law, in which the number of Jews was growing. The policy of the autonomist Slovenská ľudová strana (Slovak People's Party), led by Father Andrej Hlinka, was hostile and aggressive: the Jews were stigmatized as the tool of Czechization, the supporters of the ruling power.

The Great Depression of the thirties coincided with the advent of Hitler and the dissemination of Nazi ideology. The vehement propaganda from Berlin exerted considerable influence first and foremost upon the large and truculent German minority (numbering three million, or 23.32 percent of the total population), which for centuries had lived along the interior rim of Bohemia as the dominant national entity.[32] Konrad Henlein's Sudeten Deutsche Party (SDP), striving for territorial autonomy and subsidized by Germany, rose to militancy after the 1935 elections. It polled 1.2 million votes (33 percent of the total German vote), greatly outnumbering the "activists," the moderate German parties that were cooperating with the government. The political activity of the Slovak People's Party increased after the 1935 elections under the influence of the SDP. On February 8, 1938, Hlinka signed an agreement with the Sudeten leaders to coordinate party activities to achieve "common aims."

The aggressive policy of the Sudeten Germans ultimately led to the Munich agreement of September 30, 1938, and the cession of large territories to the Reich.[33] This was soon followed by the Vienna Award of November 2, 1938, according to which parts of Slovakia and Subcarpathian Ruthenia were annexed to Hungary. These agreements maimed Czechoslovakia both economically and strategically. The country lost three-tenths of its territory, one-third of its population, and four-tenths of its national income. On October 5 President Edvard Beneš resigned, and before his departure abroad he appointed a new government headed by General Jan Syrový.

The new Second Czecho-Slovak Republic, encompassing the autonomous provinces of Slovakia and Ruthenia, was short-lived. Abandoned by its Western allies, divided from within, the truncated state was soon drawn into the German sphere of influence. The anti-Jewish campaign launched in the rightist press blamed German-speaking Jews for the loss of Czech territories, generating an overall feeling of disillusionment and frustration. An ever-increasing number of Jews daily inundated the consulate of the United States to apply for emigration visas.[34] The cities Prague, Brno, Moravská Ostrava, and Olomouc, which in 1933 had become havens for thousands of antifascist refugees fleeing from the Nazis, were once again flooded with fugitives in the fall of 1938. Among the fugitives were several hundred democratic-minded Sudeten Germans and about seventeen thousand Jews from the evacuated Sudeten area, which had been ceded to Nazi Germany.

Mid-March 1939 saw the dismemberment of the Second Czecho-Slovak Republic. The Parliament in Bratislava proclaimed Slovakia independent on March 14. On the next day the Wehrmacht occupied what remained of Bohemia and Moravia, and Hungary seized Subcarpathian Ruthenia. From that point on, the three Jewish enclaves became separated; all three suffered persecution, but under different circumstances.

THE HOLOCAUST ERA

Prior to the German onslaught, a total of 136 Jewish religious congregations existed in Bohemia, Moravia, and Silesia. They numbered 118,310 persons defined as Jews according to the criteria of the Nuremberg Laws. The seizure of the Czech lands on March 15, 1939, came as a shock to the Jews. The day after the invasion by the Wehrmacht, Adolf Hitler himself arrived in Prague and proclaimed the Protectorate of Bohemia and Moravia an integral part of the territory of the Reich. Konstantin von Neurath was appointed Reich protector, and all other key positions were filled by Reich officials, who, through the *Landräte* (local German councils), controlled the Czech provincial authorities. Emil Hácha remained president in name; an "autonomous" Czech government functioned, although under complete subordination to the German authorities. When the deportations began, these *Landräte* were instrumental at every stage in clearing the provinces of their Jewish population.[35]

The first anti-Jewish excesses occurred when synagogues in localities such as Vsetín and Jihlava were reduced to ashes. In Pilsen and Brno Jews were dragged out of cafés by members of the local fascist organization, Vlajka (The Flag), and severely harassed and beaten. During a wave of arrests code-named Aktion Gitter (Operation Bars), which took place in the first days following the occupation, the Gestapo arrested Czech public figures and Jews and rounded up émigrés from Germany.

After the outbreak of war in September 1939, around three thousand men from Moravská Ostrava and Frýdek-Místek were forcefully dispatched to "retraining centers" *(Umschulungslager)* in Nisko and in German-occupied Poland. Actually, they built roads and cleared away ruins; many of them were driven eastward at gunpoint to the border between the German and Soviet sectors of Poland, where they were killed by German, Polish, and Ukrainian bandits.

In the wake of the German occupation the Jewish congregations became subjugated to the Zentralstelle für Jüdische Auswanderung (Central Office for Jewish Emigration). The Council of the Jewish Religious Community in Prague (later known as the Council of Jewish Elders), a quasi-autonomous body with jurisdiction over the entire network of congregations in the protectorate, had thirty-seven members. It was headed by Dr. František Weidmann of the Czech Jewish movement. The deputy chairman was Jacob Edelstein, the noted Zionist leader and director of the Palestine Office in Prague, who was assisted by some of his associates, including engineer Otto Zucker, Dr. Franz Kahn, Hanna Steiner, and Dr. František Friedmann.

The desperate situation generated a rapprochement between the various factions of the Jewish leadership and broke down existing barriers and differences. An unwritten truce came about between the two major rivals, the Czech Jews and the Zionists, in an effort to save what they could. Now all efforts were concentrated on emigration. The still vital community organized vocational training in agriculture, various technical areas (handicrafts, industrial arts), and hotel management and maintenance, as well as courses in foreign languages, for prospective emigrants.

The bilingual community weekly *Jüdisches Nachrichtenblatt–Židovské listy* (Jewish Leaves), although censored by the Gestapo, did its utmost to boost morale and campaign for emigration. It is estimated that before October 1941, when emigration was banned, 26,629 Jews managed to leave the country legally. Among these were 2,500 persons who, under the Haavara (Transfer) Agreement, reached Palestine. Others emigrated to Great Britain, the United States, or South America or escaped to neighboring Poland.

After the establishment in 1940 of the Czechoslovak National Council in London, which later became the Czechoslovak Government-in-Exile, under the leadership of Edvard Beneš, Czechoslovak army reservists in Allied and neutral countries were called upon to enlist in the Allied armies.[36] About twelve hundred Czechoslovak Jews who had reached Palestine volunteered to serve in the Czechoslovak army unit. More than seven hundred of these arrived in France, where they formed the nucleus of the troops who fought at Dunkirk. Later they were part of the Allied forces in the Middle East. It is estimated that Jews in the Czechoslovak army units established in the Soviet Union and in the West constituted 30–70 percent of the overall composition of the units at various periods of the war.[37]

The implementation of anti-Jewish laws and the ensuing confiscation of property impoverished the Jewish populace. The "Aryanization" of Jewish enterprises and their transfer to German hands was meant to strengthen the German ethnicity in the protectorate, one of the main stratagems of the Nazi policy in this area. The total value of Jewish assets expropriated by the Germans in the Protectorate of Bohemia and Moravia has been estimated as at least seventeen billion crowns (half a billion dollars). The Jewish community in Prague and in other localities responded by opening up soup kitchens and infirmaries to provide for the needy and to keep the desperate Jewish community above water.

With Reinhard Heydrich's arrival in Prague on September 27, 1941, and the subsequent mass deportations to Lodz, Minsk, and Riga and the establishment of the ghetto Terezín (Theresienstadt), the liquidation of Czech Jewry began.[38] The various departments of the Council of the Jewish Religious Community were gradually turned into the unwilling tools of the German authorities, and their functions were redefined. They were given such tasks as storing and making inventories of sequestrated Jewish assets, assigning Jews to forced labor, and assisting deportees. Any obstruction was regarded as sabotage and was punishable by death.

Between 1941 and 1945, 73,608 Jews were dispatched to the ghetto of Terezín, from which they were transported to various extermination camps in Poland. Most of the Jews ended up at Auschwitz-Birkenau. Others were annihilated in the camps of Belzec, Chelmno, Treblinka, and Lublin (Majdanek). Some were massacred in the Ninth Fort in Kovno.

Only a small number of individuals, mainly those closely associated with local gentile families, were able to find hiding places and eventually join local resistance groups engaging in intelligence and sabotage. Those caught in hiding were brought to trial and sentenced to death by hanging. Czechs found to be sheltering or aiding Jews in some way were also sentenced to death and executed. By 1943 only a minute remnant of the community, consisting mostly of families of mixed marriages living under constant surveillance, remained in Prague and the provinces.

Prior to the liquidation of the communities, upon the initiative of the Jewish leadership in Prague and with the permission of the SS, art treasures and religious objects held over the centuries in synagogues and public institutions were saved from destruction.[39] The Nazis intended to display these collections after the war at a special central museum dedicated to the "Extinct Jewish Race." The Jewish Museum of Prague, inaugurated in the summer of 1945, became the richest depository of Judaica in the world, in silent witness to the terror and destruction inflicted upon this community.

On May 5, 1945, the day of Czechoslovakia's liberation, there were 2,803 officially registered Jews in the Protectorate of Bohemia and Moravia. It is estimated that of the 92,199 Jews living in Bohemia and Moravia before the start of the deportations, 78,154 perished and 14,045 survived the Holocaust.

"Independent" Slovakia

The plight of the local Jewish population began in the autumn of 1938, when Slovakia became an autonomous region. After the Vienna Award, part of southern Slovakia and the town of Košice were ceded to Hungary. This elicited anti-Semitic outbursts in the press: "Magyarizing" Jews were accused of causing the loss of these territories. The Hlinka Guard terrorized and killed several Jewish individuals. In a campaign organized by Adolf Eichmann, groups of "stateless" Jews were expelled to the no-man's-land between the borders of Slovakia and Hungary.[40] The Jewish population shrank to 88,951, or 3.3 percent of the entire population (2,653,654). An estimate of the value of Jewish property in 1938 revealed that Jewish assets amounted to about 4.3 million Slovak crowns, 14 percent in landed property and forest, 30 percent in buildings, 23 percent in enterprises, and 33 percent in capital.

With the declaration of Slovak independence on March 14, 1939, the Jews became subject to constant harassment, and their freedom of movement was restricted. A one-party totalitarian regime, the Hlinkova slovenská ľudová strana (Slovak People's Party of Hlinka), took control under the leadership of the Catholic priest Dr. Jozef Tiso. Henceforth the Catholic clergy played a dominant role in Parliament and in politics. (Of the sixty-three members of Parliament, sixteen were priests.) One of the first acts of the new government was to sign the Treaty of Protection (Schutzvertrag), with the German foreign minister, Joachim von Ribbentrop, proclaiming that the foreign policy of Slovakia would follow the lead provided by the Reich. Shortly afterwards two institutions were created to solve the Jewish Problem in Slovakia: the Central Office for Economy, which was granted total authority to oust Jews from economic and social life and to launch the Aryanization process, and the Jewish Center (Ústredňa Židov), the only body authorized to represent the Jews of Slovakia before the German authorities and to carry out their orders.

The autumn of 1941 brought a number of radical innovations in anti-Jewish legislation. On September 9, 1941, the government promulgated the Jewish Code (Židovský kódex), comprising 270 articles, which contained all previous anti-Jewish restrictions and newly issued orders. The "Aryanization" process was accomplished within one year: 10,025 Jewish businesses were liquidated, and 2,223 others were transferred to "Aryan" owners. The confiscated property was either sold off at bargain prices or distributed to supporters sympathetic to the regime. By special ministerial order, about 10,000 Jews were evicted from Bratislava and resettled in eastern Slovakia.

In the autumn of 1941 Slovak leaders approached Heinrich Himmler about the possibility of ridding themselves of the Jewish population. Shortly after the Wannsee Conference, held in Berlin on January 20, 1942, the Slovak government signed an agreement with the Reich in which it committed itself to paying five hundred Reichsmarks for every deported Jew. Prime Minister Vojtech Tuka, who negotiated the terms on behalf of Slovakia, requested that the Jews not be returned and that the Germans make no claims on their abandoned property. As of March 26 the first trainloads, carrying able-bodied Jews between the ages of sixteen and thirty-five, were dispatched to Auschwitz and the Lublin area. Between May and October 1942 whole families were deported, totaling more than fifty-eight thousand Jews. These deportations were carried out by the Hlinka Guard and the Freiwillige Schutzstaffel, a voluntary paramilitary organization of ethnic Germans.

On May 15, 1942, constitutional law 68/1942, which sanctioned post factum the deportation of the Jews, was passed unanimously. (Only one member of Parliament, the representative of the Hungarian minority, Count Janos Eszterházy, abstained from voting.) Aside from several Slovak bishops and individual priests who spoke out against the persecution of the Jews, the Catholic clergy lent qualified support to the deportation campaign of the government.[41] The sight of the cruelty and terror—the herding of the aged, the sick, and children into cattle cars going to the East—aroused mute horror among the Slovak population, especially among the devout villagers.

The Jews of Slovakia earned a special place on the map of resistance to the Nazi genocide because of the rescue operations undertaken by groups of defiant youngsters and by the united Jewish leadership, the underground Working Group (Pracovná skupina). Led by Gisi Fleischmann and initiated by Rabbi Michael Dov Weissmandel, the Working Group was composed of Zionists, rabbis, and assimilated Jews.[42] In the summer of 1942, when the mass deportations were at their peak, the group initiated a rescue scheme: they bribed the SS chiefs to save the remaining Jews through a "work stratagem" (erection of labor camps in Slovakia) and the so-called Europa Plan, an attempt to save the remnant of European Jewry by paying ransom. Members of the Working Group were the first to unmask the systematic mass murder of European Jewry and to transmit to Jewish organizations abroad detailed accounts written by escapees who in the late summer of 1942 had, miraculously, already made their way back to Slovakia.

A phenomenon that marked the Slovak tragedy was the cessation of the deportations between October 1942 and September 1944, a halt unparalleled in other countries. This could be ascribed partly to the effective campaign led by the clandestine Working Group but mainly to the intervention of the Vatican against the expulsion of Slovak Jews. The Holy See addressed several strongly worded notes to the Slovak government, warning the priest-president Dr. Jozef Tiso of the grave consequences this "inhumane act" might bear on the future of the state.[43]

It was only on March 21, 1943, one year after the intervention of the Vatican, that a pastoral letter signed by the Catholic bishops of Slovakia was read from the pulpits of all Slovak churches. It spoke of "the lamentable fate of thousands of innocent fellow citizens, due to no guilt on their part but purely as a result of their descent or nationality." The Evangelical Church, known for its negative attitude toward the regime, reacted with more sympathy to the Jewish predicament. The Convent of Lutheran Bishops had already issued a pastoral letter (censored by the authorities) on May 20, 1942, condemning the excesses that accompanied the deportation of Jews and stressing "the sanctity of family life and respect for human dignity that should also be observed in the case of the Jews."

In the autumn of 1944, around 1,600 Jewish youngsters, most of them from the demobilized Šiesty prapor (Sixth Flag) labor units or former detainees of the Nováky and Sered labor camps, participated in the Slovak National Uprising at Banská Bystrica. It lasted three months, from the end of August to the end of October 1944, and its suppression by the Nazis sealed the fate of the remaining Jews.

They were deported under the command of the German Security Service, with the aid of special squads of the Hlinka Guard. During the last year of the war individual Slovaks tended to be more forthcoming in helping Jews by hiding them on country farms and in mountain huts. Of the prewar Slovak Jewish population of 136,737, only 25,000 survived.

Subcarpathian Ruthenia under Hungarian Occupation

In concert with the Vienna Award, seventeen hundred square kilometers of Carpathian territory, with a population of 194,000 and including the towns of Mukačevo, Užhorod, and Berehovo, were ceded to Hungary. After the Slovaks proclaimed their autonomy on October 6, 1938, the Subcarpathian Ruthenians followed their example, changing the name of their region to Carpatho-Ukraine (Zakarpatska Ukraïna). However, their autonomy was short-lived. On March 15, 1939, Hungarian troops occupied the area, and Kárpátalja (Subcarpathia) became a separate administrative unit. The autonomy was only nominal: the population had no legal or political rights, and a plebiscite was never held. Administrative and executive powers were placed in the hands of a governor, who was subordinate to the regent. With the annexation of this region the Jews of the area came to share the fate of Hungarian Jewry.[44]

The First and Second "Jewish Laws," passed by the Hungarian Parliament in 1938 and 1939, limited the percentage of Jews who could engage in trade and commerce to 6 percent, with the result that many individuals lost their jobs and became dependent on the support of communal and social institutions. The impoverished Jewish populace, gradually stripped of its property and deprived of its livelihood, was exposed to anti-Semitic agitation and chicanery. Jews who lived in the border areas were frequently subjected to raids by the Kůlföldieket ellenörző országos központi hivatal (KEOKH, or Aliens Control Department, a branch of the ministry of the interior), which rounded up the illegal refugees from neighboring Galicia and Poland who had escaped the massacres in their own countries. The local Jewish communities organized help for these escapees, hiding them temporarily and sharing their scanty rations with them. Special rescue teams made up of members of the Hehalutz Youth Movement, together with the Budapest-based Va'adat haEzra veHazalah (Relief and Rescue Committee), smuggled the fugitives across the border to Budapest on their way to freedom.

Persecution began with a review of citizenship and the registration of about fifteen thousand "stateless" persons of doubtful citizenship (many of whom had lived in the country for many generations), who were subsequently exposed to constant harassment. In the fall of 1939, in the wake of the Ribbentrop-Molotov Agreement, Soviet forces took over the neighboring Galician area, and there was thus a common border between the Soviet Union and Hungary. After the seizure of Galicia by the Wehrmacht in July 1941, the Hungarian authorities expelled around eighteen thousand "stateless" persons (the majority of whom were Jews from the annexed Czechoslovak territories) to Kamenets Podolsk, where they were slaughtered en masse two months later, at the end of August 1941.[45]

Many of the Jewish young people with leftist political inclinations fled to the Soviet Union to escape being drafted into the Hungarian forced-labor battalions. In some cases Jews, members of the Communist Party, fled with their Ruthenian comrades, trying to escape political persecution by the Hungarians. Upon reaching Soviet territory, however, they were treated as "dubious elements" and spies, tried, and sentenced to hard labor for illegally crossing the border. They languished under extremely harsh conditions in Soviet labor camps, where many of them perished. Those who survived were permitted to enlist in 1942 in the Czechoslovak army units under the command of General Ludvík Svoboda.

On June 22, 1941, Hungary entered the war on the side of Germany and sent troops to the eastern front. A considerable number of Jewish males from this area were drafted into forced-labor battalions. They were sent, along with the Hungarian army division, to the Ukrainian front, where they were assigned the tasks of constructing roads and detecting mines. Brutally mistreated, many of them perished or disappeared without a trace. Others succeeded in defecting to the Soviet side, and after much suffering they too joined the Czechoslovak army units.

Back in Subcarpathia, underground cells sprang up in various localities. Composed for the most part of Ruthenian and Jewish members of the Communist Party, they engaged in clandestine activities against the fascist Hungarian regime.

The Wehrmacht occupied Hungary on March 19, 1944, and the Carpathian area was declared a military zone. A month later the Jewish population was concentrated in ghettos established in the district towns. Between mid-May and July 1944 the whole territory was cleared of its Jews (numbering around 112,500), who were loaded onto cattle cars and dispatched to Auschwitz. In spite of the Jews' friendly ties with the indigenous, mainly Ruthenian population, the number who were sheltered by their non-Jewish friends or neighbors was low. Altogether, fewer than 20 percent of the Jews of this area survived the war.[46]

In October 1944 this region was liberated by the Red Army. Under the terms of a treaty between Czechoslovakia and the Soviet Union of June 29, 1945, Transcarpathian Ukraine (Zakarpatskaya Oblast) was incorporated into the Soviet Union. Subcarpathian Jews, primarily veterans of the Czechoslovak army units, were given the option of choosing Czechoslovak citizenship.[47]

THE POST-HOLOCAUST PERIOD

Historians term the immediate postwar years, 1945–48, the period of "pseudo-democracy" to indicate that the reconstructed state was not a continuation of the pre-Munich First Republic. From the outset, in spite of certain similarities and the reinstatement of President Beneš, Czechoslovakia took a different turn, both internally and externally. In the wake of the Teheran and Yalta agreements that determined the "division of spheres of influence," Czechoslovakia was occupied by Russian troops; only Budějovice, Plzeň, and a few other localities in western Bohemia were for a short time under American occupation.

The new government's so-called Košice program of April 4, 1945, delineated domestic policy according to a meticulous draft prepared by leading Czech Communist exiles in Moscow with a view to changing the social order.[48] The latter were to occupy key posts in the cabinet of Klement Gottwald, who became president after Beneš's resignation in June 1948.

As a result of the transfer of the German minority to the Reich and the mass exchange of population with Hungary in 1946, the state's population, which had been multinational before the war, was made up almost entirely of Czechs and Slovaks, constituting more than 94 percent of the population, after the war. In keeping with the newly adopted policy, the status of the Jewish entity was no longer recognized. Henceforth Jews could claim either Czech or Slovak nationality. As a disciple of T. G. Masaryk, Beneš, true to his principles, remained a staunch supporter of Zionism. He was convinced that with the establishment of a new Jewish homeland it would be up to the Jews to decide "whether they are for [emigration to] Palestine or for assimilation (in the national sense) into the nation of the country where they live."[49] Czechoslovakia thus played a unique role in building the Jewish entity prior to the establishment of the state of Israel. The liberated republic became the transit point for thousands of Holocaust survivors from Poland, Romania, and Hungary who desperately sought passage to their coveted destination, Palestine.[50]

The first laws enacted by presidential decree set up special "people's courts" to bring to justice traitors and Nazi collaborators. In order to comprehend the reactions of the Czech and the Slovak establishments—both the people and the media—to the trials and the information that inevitably emerged from them, one needs to understand the different circumstances that prevailed in the Protectorate of Bohemia and Moravia and in "independent" Slovakia. First and foremost, the concepts of "collaboration" with the Nazi enemy and "national treason" were viewed differently in the Czech lands than they were in Slovakia.[51] One should bear in mind that Czechoslovakia was actually the first country that suffered from Hitler's advent to power, in the humiliation of the Munich agreement and the ensuing loss of its sovereignty. Yet the Germans resorted to a certain modus vivendi vis-à-vis the Czechs because of the exigencies of war. Priority was given to the economic exploitation of the protectorate for the war effort. The ultimate goal of the Nazi genocidal policy was to stamp out the elite and patriotic elements, "depriving the Czechs of their nationhood" *(odnárodnění)*.[52]

On November 17, 1939, Czech universities were closed, and for six years students in the protectorate were barred from attending institutions of higher education. Instead, they were recruited for forced labor in Germany; those caught in resistance activities were executed or put into concentration camps. The atrocities, suppression, and suffering of the many, in addition to the destruction of the hamlets of Lidice and Ležáky and the summary execution of Czech patriots (in retaliation for Heydrich's assassination by parachutists), became deeply engraved in the Czech national consciousness. Thus, the trials of the Nazi criminals as well as of a number of Czech collaborators proceeded with the overall approval of the public, which bore a deep animosity toward the German oppressors.

The reaction to retribution and trials was radically different in "independent" Slovakia, a creation of Hitler's. The Catholic, nationalist-minded majority (constituting 74 percent of Slovakia's total population) looked most favorably upon its wartime leadership and priest-president Dr. Tiso.[53] Since it was the Slovak government that had enacted the Jewish Code and later the law on the "evacuation" of Jews (May 15, 1942), the persecution and deportation of Jews as such were viewed as criminality *ex lege*.[54] Only with the subsequent endorsement of standard legal criminal proceedings in liberated Czechoslovakia could the persecution of Jews be dealt with by the special people's courts.

The Bratislava Tribunal, which tried the members of the former government, the leaders of the Hlinka Party, and their accomplices,[55] generated widespread concern among the local population. Attempts were made by nationalist elements to obstruct and sabotage the course of the proceedings.[56] The atmosphere in general became hostile toward Jewish survivors and those who upon returning from the concentration camps demanded the restitution of their property, their homes, and other valuables. Emotions ran wild in eastern Slovakia, where violent riots erupted in several localities. In Snina and Svinná, near Hummenné, fifteen Jews were killed upon their return home.[57] Pogroms also occurred in Velké Topolčany (September 24, 1945), in the capital, Bratislava (August 1946), and in a number of other Slovak localities. These outbursts of hatred coincided with the "spontaneous" anti-Semitic pogroms in the northern industrial cities of neighboring Hungary (e.g., Miskolc and Diósgyör), in which Jews were murdered and their property was plundered.[58]

We can point to five stages in the historiography of World War II in general and the Holocaust in particular: (1) the immediate postwar years; (2) the Moscow-oriented *Gleichschaltung* of the fifties; (3) the liberalization period of the sixties; (4) the so-called normalization (dubbed "abnormalization") following the Prague Spring and the invasion by the troops of the Warsaw Pact; and (5) the *glasnost* of the eighties.

The hallmarks of the newly reconstructed republic became nationalization of industries and land reform, which augured ill for owners of industrial plants, whose property had been Aryanized by the Nazis. A definitive Law of Restitution was promulgated on May 16, 1946.[59] The enforcement of the initial laws concerning indemnity and restitution of property encountered many encroachments by extreme nationalists as well as by fanatical Communists seeking ways of placing the Nazi-expropriated Jewish assets under national administration on the ideological grounds that all means of production belonged to the state.

The repatriation of the Czech and Jewish inmates from the concentration camps liberated by the Allies was widely covered by the national press and radio, arousing compassion and solidarity among the population at large. By the end of 1946 several important publications had appeared, among them a spate of diaries, memoirs, and eyewitness accounts of survivors of the ghetto of Terezín (Anna Auředníčková and Irma Semecká), followed later by a monograph by Mirko Tůma and an analytic treatise by Emil Utitz on the psychology of life in Terezín.[60] Although they were lacking in distance and perspective, these works had the quality of immediacy and authenticity.

In 1946 one of the earliest documentary works on Auschwitz, the now famous

Továrna na smrt (The Death Factory), by Ota Kraus and Erich Kulka, detailing the methods of extermination employed at Auschwitz, appeared in Prague.[61] The first monograph on the fate of the Jews in Bohemia and Moravia, *Židovská tragedie: dějství poslední* (The Jewish tragedy: The final act), written by Rabbi Richard Feder, was published in 1947.[62] *Tragédia slovenských Židov* (The Tragedy of Slovak Jewry), the first documentary and photographic work conveying the horrors of deportation, the labor camps, and the most notorious Nazi concentration camps, was published in Bratislava in 1949 by the Central Union of Jewish Religious Communities.[63]

Nevertheless, in the first three years following the end of the war there was no analytic historical writing to speak of, since documentation was still in the initial stages of being processed and was only partially accessible. Only one topical dissertation on the Holocaust has been discovered from this period. Ota Klein's essay on the impact of the concentration camp on the moral character of Jewish youth was submitted to the Philosophical Faculty of Charles University in Prague in 1948.[64]

The first years after the Communist takeover in February 1948 were marked by a great exodus. Between 1948 and 1950, around nineteen thousand Czechoslovak Jews emigrated to Israel. In October 1950 the Slánský trials came to the fore, masterminded by Moscow.[65] The preparation and staging lasted two years. Even though the political concept of the trial, prepared and approved by the Central Committee of the Czechoslovak Communist Party in February 1951, was directed against Trotskyism and "bourgeois nationalism," the anti-Zionist and anti-Semitic tendency became its main feature. The reason for this was the newly adopted Soviet policy seeking to strengthen the Soviet Union's foothold in the Arab world. Czechoslovakia, once the friendly supporter of Zionism helping along the fledgling Jewish state with arms and a military air base, providing instructors for the Israeli Defense Force, seemed to be eminently suited for this task.

The immense anti-Semitic campaign that accompanied the show trial (with rotated, carefully selected audiences of spectators) was given great play in the press and was relayed over the radio. Thus, after a proliferation of creative writing and recording of the traumatic years of the Holocaust, there followed an embarrassing lull.

Moscow-Oriented Historiography, 1954–1962

Following the Communist coup, Czechoslovak historiography embarked on a course of subservience to the political goals of the Communist Party. In order to grasp the lacunae in Holocaust research up to the mid-1960s and the ambivalent approach to the Holocaust, it is necessary to understand the official stance vis-à-vis the study of history in general and of World War II in particular. Most instructive for tracing the process of this development is the *Československý časopis historický* (Czechoslovak Historical Review), a bimonthly journal published by the Historical Institute of the Czechoslovak Academy of Sciences, which was established in 1953. The first issue, published in 1954, brought into focus the "official" guidelines for historical research. The prime objectives were (1) to neutralize the influence of some periods of history, such as the establishment of the First Czechoslovak Republic in 1918, stressing the direct impact of revolutionary Russia and the impact of Communism on Czechoslovakia in order to prove that "without the Great October Socialist Revolution there would be no independent Czechoslovakia"; (2) to diminish the importance of certain historical periods in the life of the country, such as the years 1945–48, presenting the period as a prelude to the February "socialist revolution"; (3) to reassess certain historical periods from the Marxist perspective, utilizing such concepts as class struggle, social revolution, and peasants' rebellions, in an effort to eliminate the roles played by the intelligentsia and national factions; and (4) to portray the disintegration of the First Republic as a consequence of the reactionary policies of bourgeois parties and financial magnates who were actively aided by Western imperialists. All these criteria constrained those engaged in historical research to resort to distortion and falsification, introducing a plethora of pseudoscientific Marxist terms, such as "sociofascists" for Social Democrats and "imperialist bourgeoisie" or "reactionary circles" for prewar democratic parties.[66]

Leading Soviet historians generously shared their expertise with their Czech colleagues. This is evident from comments made by A. I. Nedorezov at a conference at the Historical Institute on June 21–22, 1955.[67] Discussing the theses of the forthcoming second and third volumes of the *Survey of Czechoslovak History,* which would include the periods of the Second Republic, the Nazi occupation, and the People's Democracy of Czechoslovakia, Nedorezov took issue with the question of periodization. Criticizing the Czech historians' intention to divide the period of Nazi occupation into three phases, he cited the example of Soviet historiography, which viewed this period in two stages, the first from the occupation of the Czech lands by the Nazis to the attack of the Soviet Union, the second from the attack to the liberation of Czechoslovakia by the Red Army in 1945. There is no mention whatsoever of the Holocaust. One should bear in mind that in the Soviet Union the persecution and tragedy of the Jewish population as an ethnic group was not mentioned at all: it was viewed as part of the global antifascist struggle. The Czechs conformed to this line.

A telling illustration of this policy is that the fate of the Jews of Transcarpathian Ukraine, annexed to the Soviet Union after the war, was never separately studied. The number of victims and the number of participants in the local resistance groups were anonymously tallied in the figures of total losses.[68] The same principle applied to monuments erected in several localities to commemorate heroes and the sites of massacres: the victims' Jewish origin is not mentioned.

Historical research on the post-Munich developments and the fate of the Jews in the Czech lands was neither encouraged by teachers nor pursued by students at academic institutions. General works on the history of the First Czechoslovak Republic and World War II made only marginal reference to the Jews.[69] There were, however, select subjects, such as life in the ghetto of Terezín, which fell in line with the Marxist conception of class struggle. A small number of Terezín survivors pursued research on the history of the ghetto, and their papers were featured occasionally in magazines and academic journals.

Reminiscences, poetry, belles-lettres, and docu-fiction were treated differently. For one thing, they were not censored as stringently as historical accounts. In a category of their own are the many Jewish writers in postwar Czechoslovakia, most of them survivors of concentration camps, such as Norbert Frýd, Josef Bor, Ludvík Aškenázy, Arnošt Lustig, František Kafka, and Jiří Weil, the quality of whose work and whose achievements stand out as unique.[70] Their work was exceedingly popular; many of their books appeared in new editions, and their works were also published in Polish, German, Russian, Hungarian, and English. Two of their counterparts in Slovakia, Ladislav Grossman and Emil Knieža, wrote extensively on the topic of the Holocaust.[71]

By 1959 indications of impending change could be observed. The most palpable was the unveiling of the memorial erected to the Jewish martyrs of Bohemia and Moravia, 77,297 names engraved on the walls of the Pinkas Synagogue.[72] Changes were evident in literature as well. The book *Die aussähen unter Tränen mit Jubel werden sie ernten* (They that sow in tears shall reap in joy), on the fate of the postwar Jewish communities in Bohemia and Moravia, and the mimeographed booklet *Cedry Libanonu* (The cedars of Lebanon), on the postwar Jewish communities in Slovakia, put out by the Central Publishing House of Churches, appeared in 1959 and 1960–61, respectively. Books on the Holocaust by leading non-Jewish Czech authors, such as Josef Škvorecký, Jan Otčenášek, Hana Bělohradská, Ladislav Fuks, and Jindřiška Smetanová,[73] published in the late 1950s and 1960s reveal great empathy toward Jewish suffering. Some of these novels had been scripted as radio plays, adapted for the screen, or, in the case of Otčenášek's, produced as an opera.

The fate of the Jewish population had been given more attention in Slovakia than in the Czech lands, mainly because of the involvement and complicity of the clero-fascist Slovak regime, headed by the Catholic priest-president Dr. Jozef Tiso. The role played by the Catholic clergy in Slovakia during World War II conformed with the antireligious propaganda of the Communist Party.

The initial attempt to review the birth of the Slovak state was made by the prewar minister of justice, Ivan Dérer, in his *Slovenský vývoj a ľudácká zrada, fakta, vzpomínky a úvahy* (The Slovak state and the treachery of the Ľudaks: Facts, memories, and thoughts).[74] The first writer to set a novel against the background of the years of Slovak independence was Dominik Tatarka in his *Farská republika* (The parish republic).[75] Tatarka depicted the misguided policy and the corrupt leadership that ultimately led to the wholesale deportation and destruction of the Jewish population. Other authors, such as Hela Volanská and Katerína Lazarová, portrayed the heroic stance of Jewish participants in the Slovak National Uprising.[76] *The History of Modern Slovakia,* the first in-depth study to disclose the policy of the Nazi puppet regime and to describe at great length the persecution of Slovak Jewry, was published in New York in 1955 by Dr. Jozef Lettrich, a chairman of the Slovak National Council who had fled after the Communist coup.[77] The role of the Hlinka Guard and the Jewish plight were analyzed by Imrich Staněk, himself a survivor, in the 1958 *Zrada a pád: hlinkovští separatisté a tak zvaný Slovenský stát* (Treachery and downfall: The Hlinka separatists and the so-called Slovak state), written from a strictly Marxist-Leninist viewpoint.[78]

The capture of Adolf Eichmann in May 1960 by the Mossad and his subsequent trial in Jerusalem were widely covered in the national press and media. Eichmann, notorious for engineering the deportation of both Czech and Slovak Jewry, was of major interest to the local population. (He had commuted between Berlin and Prague, where he resided in the elegant, confiscated Rosenthal villa, in the Střešovice district.) The Czech and Slovak press sent special reporters to cover the proceedings of the trial. One of these reporters, the writer Ladislav Mňačko, later published a book portraying Eichmann's satanic role in the Holocaust.[79] The testimonies given at the trial by survivors appeared frequently in the press and in *Věstník ŽNO,* the weekly bulletin of the Jewish Religious Communities in Prague. Many of these related to the wholesale deportation of Slovak Jewry orchestrated by the Tiso regime. During one of the sessions of the trial Eichmann's claim that "the Slovaks gave away their Jews as one spills sour beer," from *Life* magazine's interview with him, was quoted.[80] Widely repeated in the international press, this assertion provoked reactions among leading Slovak figures in exile. The Munich-based Fraňo Tiso, in an effort to whitewash the Slovak wartime leadership, published an article in which he stressed the endeavors of the "moderate parish regime" to save Jews from deportation.[81] In response, Edo Friš took up the topic in the article "In the Background was Heydrich," published in the Bratislava weekly *Kultúrny život.* The controversy focused on the visit of SS Obergruppenführer Reinhard Heydrich to Bratislava on April 10, 1942. Friš challenged Tiso's claim that the reason for Heydrich's visit was to pressure the Slovak government to continue implementing the Final Solution.[82] Citing documents referred to in *The Destruction of Slovak Jewry,* published some months earlier,[83] Friš stressed the initiative and involvement of the Slovak leaders in the mass deportation of Jews; the aim of Heydrich's visit, Friš added, was to assist the Slovak government in formulating a fallacious reply to the Vatican's March 14, 1942, protest against the deportations of Jews.[84] This was the first discussion of this sensitive issue in more than a decade.

The Period of Liberalization, 1962–1968

Vladimir V. Kusin observed that the impetus to change the approach to historiography originated in the late 1950s.[85] According to Kusin, the process was triggered by the Communist Party's endeavors to rectify some wrongs committed in the recent past. Following the 1962 twelfth Party congress, a committee of investigation was created in Prague to scrutinize certain aspects of the Slánský trials. A special commission of economists, jurists, and historians, headed by Drahomír Kolder, was to examine secret documentary material relating to charges leveled against several defendants (Frejka, Fischl, Loebl, Outrata, etc.) who had been sentenced to death or long-term prison terms for economic "crimes," direct sabotage, and subversion of economy and finance. The material put at the disposal of the researchers in the former Barnabitky Nunnery at the Prague Castle acted as a boomerang.[86] The perusal of the documentation enabled the team to gain insight into the entire political system. It soon realized that monstrous crimes and injustice had been committed by the state during the show trials.

The ensuing breakthrough described in historiography as the "de-Stalinization period" coincided with liberalization in several spheres of public life,[87] resulting in the rehabilitation of several Slovak "bourgeois nationalists" as well as Jewish Communists sentenced to long-term imprisonment during the Slánský trials.[88] This liberalization was also apparent in the official attitude toward the various churches and religious denominations as well as toward the Jewish community. The new atmosphere spurred intensified cultural activities, reflected in open meetings and discussions held for young people eager to learn about Jewish history and the Holocaust.

On the whole, it could be asserted that the discoveries of the above-mentioned special commission actually generated the reform movement, which culminated in the revolution in January 1968, dubbed the Prague Spring. The thrust of the reform movement was expressed in Alexander Dubček's famous slogan "Communism with a Human Face." After the quelling of this revolution and the invasion by the troops of the Warsaw Pact in August 1968, a new period began in Czechoslovakia, marked by political oppression and cultural stagnation.[89]

Among the books of general interest from this hopeful period, Josef Škvorecký's *Sedmiramenný svícen* (The seven-branched candelabrum) stands out for its novel approach to questioning society's responses to the Jewish issue. His heroine, a survivor, encounters upon her return cool indifference on the part of former neighbors, who are reluctant to return valuables entrusted to them for safekeeping before the deportations. Also noteworthy is *Město za mřížemi* (City behind bars), by Karel Lágus and Josef Polák, and the anthology *Terezín, 1941–1945*, the first and only officially sponsored publication produced by the Council of the Jewish Religious Communities in the Czech lands.[90]

A cursory perusal of titles of doctoral dissertations dealing with the history of World War II submitted to Prague and Bratislava universities reveals that up to the sixties most of them examined the decisive role of the Soviet Union in defeating Nazi Germany and the Communist-led underground resistance.[91] Even if Slovak historians have pursued research of modern history at a rate surpassing their Czech colleagues (Czech students have preferred to delve into medieval history, the Hussite period, and other chapters of their past), they too have been selective in their choice of subjects, avoiding topics such as the birth of the independent Slovak state and the fate of the Jewish population during World War II and preferring the Slovak National Uprising, on which a plethora of books and papers have appeared.

Three dissertations dealing with the Jewish plight can be ascribed to the liberalized atmosphere: Jan Džugas, "Ľudácké riešenia 'židovskej otázky' za tzá. Slovenského štátu" (The Populist solution of the Jewish Question in the so-called Slovak state), submitted to the Philosophical Faculty of the Komenský University, Bratislava (1965); Ivan Kamenec, "Židovská otázka v politike ľudáckej vlády na Slovensku v rokoch 1938–1945" (The Jewish Question in the policy of the Populist government in Slovakia in the years 1938–1945), submitted to the Historical Institute of the Slovak Academy of Sciences in Bratislava (1971);[92] and Ján Čarnogurský, "Rasové zákonodárstvo Slovenského štátu" (Racial legislation of the Slovak state), submitted to the Law Faculty of the Komenský University, Bratislava (1971).[93] Of special note is the fact that Čarnogurský, a Catholic dissident in the 1980s who was among the twenty-four signatories of the "Proclamation Concerning the Deportation of the Jews from Slovakia" (October 1987), after the November 1989 revolution became prime minister of the Slovak Federal Republic.

None of the theses submitted to the Philosophical Faculty of Charles University of Prague dealt comprehensively with the fate of Jewry during the protectorate. The four dissertations touching on the topic were Zdeněk Jirotka, "Židovské listy v letech 1939–1944" (The Jewish Community Bulletin in the years 1939–1944 [1967]); Eva Šormová, "Divadlo v Terezíně 1941–1945" (Theater in Terezín, 1941–1945 [1966]); Jiří Kocur, "Viktor Ullmann" (1966); and Blanka Müllerová, "Hans Krása" (1966), all of which assessed the role of culture in the ghetto of Terezín.[94]

No comprehensive work has yet been written on the home resistance or the situation of the Czech population during the Nazi occupation. A most perceptive recent study by Jan Křen, *Blank Spots in Our History?* raises some thought-provoking ideas on this topic.[95]

It is not without interest that Aleš Veselý's *Kaddish* (Prayer for the dead), a multidimensional sculpture in memory of the martyrs created of actual human bones for the memorial at Terezín, originated between August 1967 and May 1968.[96]

The festivities planned by the community to celebrate the millennium of Jewish settlement in the Czech lands, scheduled for 1966, were twice postponed by the authorities for political reasons. The main reason was the growing Arab-Israeli crisis and the anti-Jewish campaign launched in the press first and foremost in Poland and throughout Eastern Europe.[97] The atmosphere was further aggravated when Charles Jordan, one of the heads of the American Joint Distribution Committee, was murdered in August 1967 by a group of Palestinian students of the "University of 17 November" in the Egyptian Embassy in Prague.[98]

Despite the pro-Arab policy of the Czechoslovak government, prior to the Six-Day War "public opinion almost unanimously sided with Israel." The Union of Czech Writers issued a proclamation in support of Israel. The writer Pavel Kohout compared the crucial position of the state of Israel, threatened by Arab "genocide," to that of Czechoslovakia during the Munich crisis in 1938.[99] At the same time, however, within anti-Semitic circles resentment spread, directed mainly against Jewish intellectuals who participated in the reform movement. The most telling example was the case of Professor Eduard Goldstücker, the chairman of the Union of Czech Writers, against whom was waged a smear campaign, accompanied by a massive outpouring of articles slandering the Jews of Czechoslovakia in a manner and a vocabulary reminiscent of the Nazis.[100]

Apparently this campaign against the Jews prompted the writer Ludvík Vaculík to publish his now famous statement "2,000 Words to Workers, Farmers, Scientists, Artists, and Everyone." Vaculík scathingly criticized the Communist bureaucracy and the prevailing state of affairs, advocating spontaneous initiatives to force out remaining conservatives who had misused their power.[101]

The Czech reform movement grew stronger, and in 1968 the process of democratization gained new impetus. Spurred by the spirit of freedom, the Jewish community leadership rose to the occasion and on May 6 issued a statement in support of Israel, demanding rights previously denied to the community and voicing their grievances.[102] The declaration criticized the authorities for their disdain and lack of respect toward the victims of the Holocaust. It referred to the misconduct of the ministry for national defense in barring access to the site on the bank of the River Ohře where the ashes of some twenty thousand victims of Terezín had been dumped. It also criticized the security services for their hostile attitude toward the Jewish community as a whole and for insulting the memory of the murdered victims by charging them with collaboration.

The reform movement generated a historiographic renaissance in the late sixties. In an attempt to clarify some of the controversial issues in Czech history, scholars demonstrated a more balanced approach, "achieving a remarkable level of quality." In the crucial year 1968 alone the bibliography of Czech history registered two thousand titles;[103] however, there were only sporadic articles dealing with Jewish topics. Noteworthy is Eduard Vavruška's perceptive study *Terezínská předkapitola* (The pre-Terezín chapter), published in 1967.[104]

The Period of Normalization, 1968–1985

In August 1968 Warsaw Pact troops invaded Czechoslovakia. Alexander Dubček was replaced as party leader by Gustav Husák, who reverted to a particularly vindictive form of Stalinism. (Dubček from then until 1989 lived as a virtual recluse in Bratislava, working as a clerk in the Slovak forestry commission.) The period of "normalization"—known in Czechoslovakia as Absurdistan—had begun.

Nevertheless, the momentum generated during the Prague Spring did not expire overnight; it carried over after the invasion and even in the years 1969–71. Publications spurred by the spirit of freedom continued to appear in small numbers until 1974. By that time the Communist Party had managed to weed out its more liberal elements, and a solid number of writers, artists, actors, and musicians were prohibited from publishing their work or continuing their activities. Thousands of Czechoslovak intellectuals and professionals were forced to leave their jobs, and many others left the country.

Persecution came to a head in the late seventies. Actions like the mass arrest of young people for the crime of making music, the arrest of Czech rock groups, and unwarranted police interrogations stirred some courageous intellectuals to act. On January 6, 1977, an informal citizens' initiative, Charter 77, was created in response to the Helsinki International Agreement on Human Rights, signed in 1976.[105] Among the first signatories were the playwright Václav Havel, the philosopher Jan Patočka, Dubček's foreign minister Jiří Hájek, and dissidents Petr Uhl and Pavel Kohout. They asserted their intentions to take the Husák regime, which was a co-signatory of the Helsinki Treaty, at its word: to speak up against every kind of abuse of power, defend the accused, and, in the words of Václav Havel, "live in truth."

Major Institutions: Publications and Activities

The State Jewish Museum in Prague, which resumed its activities in liberated Czechoslovakia in May 1945, could be described as a kaleidoscope of the constantly changing political climate. Its main task was to disseminate knowledge about the history of the Jewish communities in Bohemia and Moravia through publications and exhibits of its unique collection of memorabilia (amounting to two hundred thousand items) amassed from the uprooted communities during the deportations in 1942 and 1943.[106] In April 1950 the museum was nationalized and put under state administration. Dr. Hana Volavková, a well-known art historian and a survivor of the wartime museum staff—the other members had been sent to their death in Auschwitz in October 1944—was appointed its first director. The museum underwent several radical changes, and in 1955, in line with the overall Communist *Gleichschaltung*, it was charged with conducting its research from the Marxist-Leninist point of view. This policy was reflected in the management and staff of the museum, whose directors were gradually replaced by state-appointed officials. (In 1961 Dr. Volavková was forced to retire for political reasons, as was her successor, Vilém Benda, in 1969.) The director who held this position at the time of the November 1989 revolution was a party functionary with no qualifications or knowledge of Judaism whatsoever.

In its early years of operation the Jewish Museum could list publications and cultural activities on a wide range of subjects, including exhibitions of works by leading Terezín artists, such as Bedřich Fritta, Otto Ungar, Karel Fleischmann, Leo Haas, František Nágl, and Malvina Schalková. The climax of the exhibition was the show "Drawings and Poems of the Children of Terezín" (1955). This unique collection of children's art was first published as *Dětské kresby na zastávce smrti. Terezín 1942–1944* (Children's drawings on a stop before death) in 1956 and later translated into English as *I Never Saw Another Butterfly*. It appeared in many other languages as well.[107]

Judaica Bohemiae, the official publication of the museum, was launched in 1965 and dealt mainly with the documentation concerning the centuries-long history of the Jewish communities and Hebrew manuscripts and literature. It occasionally featured articles on Terezín and reviews of books on the Holocaust. Destined solely for readers abroad, the publication included articles printed in German, French, English, or Russian, which, however, were never made available in a Czech version.[108]

Věstník ŽNO was the only Jewish newspaper to appear during the Communist era. Although it lacked the vitality of the buoyant, free, prewar Jewish press, it played a more important and very special role in the crucial years of the Communist regime. Aside from publishing each week an excerpt of the Torah that stressed the universal values of Judaism in conformity with the official "peace-seeking" policy, the newspaper primarily featured articles dealing with the traumatic issues of the Holocaust, announcements of commemorative wreath-laying ceremonies, and information such as the dates of liberation of concentration camps by the Red Army. (Camps set free by the Western allies, such as Bergen-Belsen and Dachau, were not mentioned.) Also featured regularly were reports of events and memorial rallies held in the communities in Hungary, Poland, Yugoslavia, Romania, and East Germany. The bulletin carried reviews of new books, vignettes on literary talents who perished in the camps, and sketches of Czechs who saved Jews during the war. Beginning in 1972 *Věstník* appeared as a monthly and was distributed strictly on a subscription basis. Preoccupied with the trauma of the Holocaust, it was the only outlet through which the Jews could express themselves freely and without restraint or fear of official reaction.

Věstník also carried excerpts of stories from the daily press, especially from *Hlas revoluce* (The Voice of Revolution, the organ of the Union of Anti-Fascist Fighters) and its Slovak counterpart, *Tribúna,* highlighting the heroism of members of the army units, the resistance movement, and partisan groups. (It should be noted that these newspapers avoided reference to the Jewish origin of these heroes, referring to them rather as "antifascists.")

In 1972 an anti-Zionist campaign was launched in the Czech and Slovak press, obviously influenced by a two-part article that appeared in the Moscow *Pravda* on February 18–19, 1971, on the occasion of the anniversary of the Babi Yar massacre. The article described the Zionists as "accomplices and followers of the Nazis."[109] From this point on, the wartime Jewish leadership in Prague and the ghetto of Terezín was consistently charged with collaborating with the Nazi chieftains "in order to save their own skin." The Jewish community representatives did not remain silent at this attack. At the commemorative rally marking the thirtieth anniversary of the dissolution of the Prague community by the Nazis (September 1943), František Fuchs, head of the Council of Jewish Communities in Czechoslovakia, courageously defended the leadership, asserting that it "did its utmost to halt the deportations to the death camps."[110] For making this statement, Fuchs was suspended from his post.

As a rule, *Věstník* conspicuously ignored news about cultural or scientific events in Israel. Government declarations condemning Israeli policies were, however, duly reproduced. (The Jewish community leadership was to print, *inter alia,* an appeal to President Reagan to prevent the production of a neutron bomb.)[111] However, considering the extremely hostile tone of the vicious anti-Israel tirades in the national press and media, one could on the whole detect a certain restraint in the wording of the community bulletin.

In the late 1970s the community issued the quarterly German-language *Informationsbulletin* (mimeographed) for distribution abroad. It contained select items from *Věstník* with English-language summaries. Some items reflected upon the mutual cooperation between the various Christian churches and the Jewish community. In fact, the newsletters issued by the Christian communities frequently featured articles on Jewish topics, especially the Holocaust. The collection of writings of Dr. Gustav Sicher, Chief Rabbi of Prague, who was highly regarded both by the Jewish and the non-Jewish public, which appeared under the title *Volte život* (Choose life!),[112] was reviewed in *Katolické noviny* (Catholic News), and the review was reproduced in the *Informationsbulletin.* The review noted his erudition in both Judaism and Christianity and stressed the unprecedented suffering of his people during World War II.[113]

Židovská ročenka (The Jewish annual), first published by the Council of Jewish Communities in 1953, presented a wide range of historical and literary essays by Jewish as well as non-Jewish authors. It also included items from well-known Jewish writers abroad and featured poetry, excerpts from diaries, recollections of survivors, and vignettes highlighting the bravery of Jewish soldiers and partisans.

The Terezín Memorial (Památník Terezín) was established upon the wave of the reform movement in 1968 on the site of the former ghetto and concentration camp as a long overdue tribute to the Jewish martyrs. Its research institute was to address a wide scope of hitherto neglected activities. The first issue of *Terezínské listy* (Terezín Leaves), the official annual publication of the memorial, published in 1970, included an article by Miroslav Kryl, "A New Source for the History of the Ghetto of Terezín," describing the diary of Egon Redlich ("Gonda"), a Zionist youth leader and a member of the Jewish Council in Terezín, written secretly in the ghetto during the war.[114] (Redlich's diary, discovered in 1967, was later exploited to attack the Zionist leadership.) In 1973 *Terezínské listy* printed Ludvík Václavek's article "The Literary Work of Petr Kien," in which he paid tribute to the young painter's unique artistic and literary talents. In the same issue, Oliva Pechová wrote another assessment, "The Artistic Legacy of Petr Kien."[115]

By 1974 the Terezín Memorial had come to serve as an educational tool to inculcate class awareness. It was used by government officials in their anti-Zionist and anti-Israeli propaganda campaign. The inmates of Terezín were presented as a society engulfed in a class struggle between Zionists and Czech assimilationists. Wartime Jewish leaders were accused of collaborating with the Nazis in order to save their lives and those of privileged persons. Most instructive is the opening article of the 1974 issue of *Terezínské listy*, entitled "State Care for the Terezín Memorial."[116] It outlines the memorial's role as an educational center that will focus its exhibitions on five major themes: (1) the Communist resistance to the Nazis; (2) the suffering of Czechoslovakia; (3) the suffering of the inmates of all nationalities in Terezín; (4) the military and historical documentation of the various phases of both the Little Fortress, the prison where Czech political prisoners were incarcerated, and the ghetto; and (5) the parallels between the fate that befell the Jews during the Nazi period and the conduct of the Zionists. In the late 1970s the last theme became part of an indoctrination effort that bordered on vulgarity. As they conducted groups of schoolchildren and visitors from abroad through the memorial, the official guides would add political asides condemning imperialism and Zionist crimes perpetrated against the Palestinians. These "enlightening" ideas, also included in lectures and in the official guidebooks of the museum, can occasionally be found in readers' letters addressed to the various local papers and magazines.[117]

This extreme thinking cannot be discerned, however, in academic publications or topical journals of a more serious nature. In the mid-seventies a number of well-documented studies and articles on the history of the Terezín concentration camp began to appear in *Judaica Bohemiae*.[118] The authors of these studies, Anita Franková, Anna Hyndráková, and Miroslav Kárný, were survivors of Terezín. Kárný was, in fact, the only author of Jewish origin whose articles dealing with anti-Jewish policy in the protectorate appeared in Czech magazines and periodicals. Written from the Marxist point of view, his topical papers utilized documents held in Czechoslovak archives. Kárný's first article, "Terezínský koncentrační tábor v plánech nacistů"

(The concentration camp in Terezín in the plans of the Nazis), was published in *Československý časopis historický* (Czechoslovak Historical Review) in 1974.[119]

Film, Television, and Radio

Czech cinematography can be credited with major achievements as far as the portrayal of the Holocaust is concerned.[120] It can boast of several documentary films, such as *Nezapomeneme* (Lest We Forget [1945]), a protest film portraying the horror of the concentration camps, made after the liberation; *Motýly Tady Nežijí* (There Are No Butterflies Here [1960]), based on the children's drawings from Theresienstadt; and *77,297* (1963), directed by František Bližek, whose title is the number of Jewish victims whose names were listed on the walls of the Pinkas Synagogue. One of the most outstanding films is Alfred Radok's *Daleká cesta* (Distant Journey), produced in 1948, portraying the story of Nazi persecution through the dramatic love story of Tony, a gentile, and Hannah, a Jewish doctor, who marry in wartime Prague. The second part of the film describes the horrors of life in Terezín, the "model ghetto." Radok's film, labeled "existential" and "formalistic" by the political commissars, was withdrawn after a brief and successful run and kept locked away in the censor's vault at the Barandov Film Studio for almost two decades. Another film that won wide acclaim was *Sweet Light in a Dark Room*, based on the novel *Romeo, Julie a tma* (Romeo, Juliet, and darkness) by Jan Otčenášek (1959) and directed by Jiří Weiss. It is the love story of a Jewish woman and a non-Jew set in the time of the Nazi occupation in the protectorate.

Five of Arnošt Lustig's books were produced as films. One of the first movies that actually heralded the Czech "New Wave" was Zbyněk Brynych's *Transport z Ráje* (Transport from Paradise [1962]), based on Lustig's *Noc a naděje* (Night and hope), a collection of autobiographical stories on life and death in Terezín highlighting preparations for the visit of the International Committee of the Red Cross and the massive deportation the day after. Another of Lustig's books, *Darkness Casts No Shadow*, was adapted and directed by Jan Němec as *Démanty Noci* (Diamonds of the Night [1964]). It relates the plight of two youngsters who escape from a deportation train and struggle to reach their home in Prague. Hana Bělohradská's best-selling novella *Bez krásy a bez limce* (Without beauty, without a collar), produced by Brynych under the title *The Fifth Horseman Is Fear* (1965), concentrates on the terror perpetrated by the Nazis against the victims and on the bystanders. The main plot concerns Braun, a Jewish doctor in Prague, who treats a wounded resistance fighter and pays with his life for his heroic deed. The most successful film, earning an Oscar, was Jan Kadar and Elmar Klos's *Obchod na Korse* (released in English as *The Shop on Main Street* [1965]), based on the book by Ladislav Grossman. It relates the story of a simple carpenter in a small Slovakian town who becomes an Aryanizer of a neglected button shop owned by a deaf, aged Jewish woman.

In 1968, with the quelling of the Prague reform movement, the flourishing Czech cinema was abruptly brought to an end. It was only eleven years later that the topic of the Holocaust was again revived on the screen. *Zlatí Úhoři* (The Golden Eels

[1979]), based on a novel of the same name by Ota Pavel, won first prize in an Italian television competition.[121] In this story set against the background of Nazi occupation, Pavel's love for his father is symbolized by an eel and his deep affection for his mother is represented by the river. Another film made from a novel by Pavel, *Smrt Krásných Srnců* (Death of the Beautiful Roebucks), was directed by Karel Kachyňa in 1987. It presents a portrait of a Czech Jewish family torn apart by the Holocaust. All of these films were adapted for television and became very popular with the Czech public.

Theater

The stage, it would seem, was a medium less conducive to conveying the trauma of the Holocaust. No Czech play has been written about the Jewish plight. One may surmise that because of censorship, the dialogues on stage were more difficult to handle. The opera *The Emperor of Atlantis,* on the eternal motif of dictatorship, written in Terezín by Petr Kien (libretto) and Victor Ullmann (music), was produced on many European stages in the late 1970s and widely acclaimed. Its production was barred in Czechoslovakia, however, even though both authors were from that country and perished in Auschwitz.[122] Throughout the years, Czech theaters did produce a number of plays from the European repertoire, such as *The Diary of Anne Frank, The Deputy,* by Rolf Hochhuth, and *The Investigation,* by Peter Weiss.

Propaganda and the Cynical Abuse of the Holocaust

The events of World War II provided the most important fodder for Communist propagandists. As a rule, their two main objectives were to depict the failure of Western capitalism and its disastrous consequences and to present the Soviet Union as a major force in liberating Eastern Europe from fascist tyranny. Highlighting the feats of the Red Army and the activities of the Communist-led resistance during the Nazi persecution, the regime most effectively disseminated its political ideas.

In the mid-1950s the Czech Secret Security Police harassed former Jewish community leaders in the protectorate and in "independent" Slovakia, investigating their activities during the war. Dr. Tibor Kováč of the Bratislava-based Working Group, which engaged in rescue acts during the war, apparently was one of these victims. Unable to cope with the harassment, he committed suicide. Erich Kraus, deputy of the last elder of the Jewish Council in Prague, was also investigated in 1955 and was ordered to prepare an outline of the activities of the Jewish community leadership between 1939 and 1945.[123]

It appears that in addition to ideological and political objectives, some of the propaganda campaigns had financial aims as well. Concealment, trickery, and mischief were employed. One plot framed by the disinformation section of Czechoslovak Intelligence involved the discovery of "new" documents, which bona fide news agencies, publishing houses, and representatives of the Jewish community were to help publicize. (The story posited that a selection of World War II documents taken from Soviet and Czechoslovak archives had been dumped by intelligence agents into Black Lake, on the Czechoslovak–West German border, only to be retrieved as "secret Nazi archives" and made available for dissemination in various countries.) This scheme, undertaken in May 1964 and given the code name Operation Neptune,[124] had several objectives, one of which was to resuscitate ill feelings toward Germany in the Western Hemisphere, since the statute of limitations for war crimes in West Germany would be reached in May 1965. The sensational "discovery" of documents relating to the brutal treatment of Allied prisoners of war and the massacre of Jews coincided with the trials being held in Frankfurt of a number of notorious SS guards from Auschwitz, which were attracting worldwide attention. The Czechoslovak ministry of foreign affairs and the Czechoslovak Press Agency acted as agents for the distribution of the discovered documents. The Council of the Jewish Religious Communities in the Czech lands and the Central Union of the Jewish Communities in Slovakia jointly issued a volume of the Gestapo documents dealing with the fate of the Jews of Moravská Ostrava ("retrieved from the Black Sea"), published by the Central Publishing House of the Churches, under the title *Nazi Dokumente sprechen* (Nazi documents speak).[125] For both financial and political reasons, two state-run publishing houses, the military Naše Vojsko and the House of the Union of Fighters against Fascism, prepared special editions of the finds entitled *Na dně byla smrt* (On the bottom was death [1964]) and *Tajemství Černého jezera* (The mystery of Black Lake [1965]).[126] Czechoslovak radio and television stations featured programs on the new books. A wide range of articles in the press described the documents. *Hlas revoluce* and *Věstník ŽNO* were instructed to publicize the books to Jewish groups and organizations abroad. After serving the immediate political purposes, however, the furor was allowed to die down, and the affair had little lasting impact.

In concert with the "peace-loving" policy, the content of radio programs, both for local listeners and for listeners abroad, was carefully controlled. Distortions of fact and timely political comments about Western "imperialism" and "decadence" crept into lectures, plays, poetry readings, and recitals. This was even more apparent in discussions on books and surveys on contemporary history, which were designed to serve the needs of current political purposes. In August 1972 radio and television stations aired shows about collaboration, castigating the members of the Council of Elders in Terezín as "Jewish henchmen of the Gestapo."[127] Another topic favored by the government "specialists" commissioned to deal with Jewish issues was the tensions between the various nationalities in Terezín; they stressed the animosity between the Zionists and the assimilated Czech Jews, between Czech- and German-speaking Jews, and so forth. Articles on this issue appeared frequently in the Czech and Slovak Communist papers.

In 1975, after the U.N. resolution equating Zionism with racism was adopted, a widespread propaganda campaign aiming to play down the issue of the Holocaust and Jewish suffering was launched in the press. In the mid-seventies the disinformation section in Prague stepped up attacks against "the main threats to peace"— American imperialists, West German militarists, and world Jewry. It disseminated rumors and invented plots linking Czechoslovak Jews, famous Jewish personalities, and former Czech citizens with fraudulent activities aimed at overthrowing the socialist order.[128] To lend credibility to the "secret" ties between Czechoslovak Jews and reactionary forces abroad, various campaigns were launched. Forged letters were circulated directing libelous charges against Jewish public and political figures, one of the initial targets being Simon Wiesenthal, head of the Vienna-based Jewish Documentation Center.[129]

In November 1976 a series of articles appeared in both Slovak and Czech newspapers under the title "The Zionist Meaning of Class [Struggle],"[130] focusing on the "aggressive policy" of Israel in its supposed effort to rule over the whole Middle East. Yad Vashem, the Holocaust Martyrs' and Heroes' Remembrance Authority in Jerusalem, was singled out for severe criticism, and several historians, including the authors of the anthology *The Jews of Czechoslovakia*, were accused of pursuing espionage work and subversive activities against the countries of the Soviet bloc.

To crown these activities, in 1986, Josef Šebesta, an official of the ministry of the interior in Prague, published *V zemi zaslíbené?* (In the Promised Land?), which described the emergence of the state of Israel as the work of imperialist agents.[131] The main objective was to denigrate the issue of the Holocaust and smear the reputations of the wartime Jewish leaders and personalities, accusing them of being Nazi collaborators.

The Period of *Glasnost*

During the mid-eighties the new Soviet policy of *perestroika* influenced all aspects of life in the Eastern bloc countries, including how the Jews, the Holocaust, and Israel were perceived. The press and other media began to handle Jewish issues in a more balanced way. Indeed, righteous Czech and Slovak individuals who rendered help to Jews began to make their deeds public and even participated in the ceremonies held in their honor at Yad Vashem.[132] Conversely, Jews who were helped began to identify their benefactors, no longer fearing adverse repercussions. The fear that prevailed within the Jewish community is exemplified by the case of the Wolf family, who were sheltered throughout the war by the gentile villagers of Tršovice (near Olomouc). Berthold Wolf, who after the war acted as cantor of the Moravská Ostrava Synagogue, for forty years hid the existence of the diary kept by his son Otto when he was seventeen, which described the plight of his strictly observant family hiding in the forest. One may surmise that Wolf was reluctant to expose his devout religious feelings or perhaps apprehensive to disclose the village folk who assisted them. Only after his death was this unique record deposited in the local archives, and it was finally made public in 1987 in Moravian magazines.[133]

In October 1987, after a lapse of forty years, a group of Slovak intellectuals in Bratislava, known later as dissidents, issued a uniquely straightforward proclamation on the fate of the Jews of Slovakia.[134] They were most probably prompted to make their statement by the ambiguously worded resolution of the General Assembly of the Slovak World Congress, an umbrella organization of Slovaks in exile, which convened in Toronto on July 3, 1987.[135] The congress claimed that the crimes against Jews were committed by "misguided individuals of the Slovak regime without the consent of the nation." The signatories of the Bratislava proclamation—among them prominent literati, academics, and artists—headed by the writer Dominik Tatarka, unequivocally condemned the deportation of Slovak Jews and the inhuman crimes perpetrated upon their Jewish compatriots, the majority of whom perished in Nazi concentration camps. The Bratislava proclamation also referred to the fact that no memorial had been erected in Slovakia to commemorate the tragedy and deplored the pitiful state of the Jewish cemeteries, synagogues, and the once famous community buildings, which were gradually disappearing. They stressed that they themselves could not be held accountable for the horrors and atrocities committed during the war but that because Slovak authorities had not issued a public condemnation, they felt obliged to speak out. Addressing themselves to the survivors, the families of the victims, and the Jewish nation as a whole, they begged forgiveness. On Christmas Eve 1990, one year after the November 1989 revolution, the Parliament and government of the Slovak Republic finally issued a proclamation condemning the deportation of the Jews from Slovakia. The wording, reminiscent of that of the dissidents' declaration of October 1987 (disseminated illegally and published abroad), referred to the deportation as "a crime committed by the state" and asked the surviving Jewish citizens for their forgiveness.[136]

□

Nazi persecution in all its aspects has been an omnipresent theme in every medium of communication in Czechoslovakia. However, the educational goals of the Communist authorities were established to further the political objectives of the regime and therefore were selectively chosen. Certain issues of the prewar period and World War II, such as the Holocaust, became taboo and were expunged from history books. The respite of the liberal period in the 1960s, ending with the Soviet takeover in 1968, was too short to afford in-depth long-range study of the proscribed subjects. Nevertheless, the sporadic output of books and articles of these years provides us for the first time with valuable material and analytical research. The Holocaust, not studied in either Czech or Slovak schools, gradually began to receive the attention of samizdat authors.

An enlightening article entitled "Učit myslet" (Teaching to think), by Eliška Hořelová, an expert on education and the author of several literary works, published in the December 1988 issue of *Kmen*, the weekly of the Union of Czech Writers, raises several important points about the distortion of modern Czech history.[137] "Thanks to the new era of *glasnost*," she asserts, after thirty-seven years October 28 (the day the First Republic was founded in 1918) is again celebrated in Czechoslovakia as a national holiday. The statesmen T. G. Masaryk, Dr. E. Beneš, and Milan Rastislav Štefánik, whose deeds and merits had been ignored for several decades, are again publicly honored as the founding fathers of the First Republic. Their extensive works and memoirs, proscribed in Czechoslovakia for more than forty years, are available again. However, textbooks have not been changed, according to Hořelová, and thus schoolchildren are still being exposed to indoctrination, learning about the postwar world order from standard texts written strictly in the Soviet Marxist vein.[138]

Czech reactions to the Holocaust fall into two different types: (1) the official reaction, influenced by Moscow and supported by the state-sponsored, and (2) the more sympathetic reaction of a large part of the population, which viewed with compassion the plight of the Jews. How could one otherwise explain the great success of Jewish writers whose novels and reminiscences gained such popularity? The suicide in 1973 of the half-Jewish novelist Ota Pavel (Otto Popper), considered the most creative writer of the postwar period in Czechoslovakia, evoked widespread expressions of empathy. A boy during the Holocaust, Pavel, who had lost his childhood and then died tragically at the age of forty-three, became a symbol for many Czechs of the suffering of the young generation both under German occupation and during the Communist regime.[139]

Throughout the years of official, overt hostility toward the Jews, covert interaction between the various Christian church organizations and the Jewish community developed, reflecting both solidarity and understanding. This rapprochement found expression in frequent articles on Jewish topics printed in periodicals issued by the Christian communities, some of these touching upon Jewish martyrdom and the Holocaust, others commemorating great Jewish figures in Czech history. Noteworthy is a piece written in 1982 by Rev. Jan Amos Dvořáček, an evangelical parson in Sternberk, addressing the issue of the "unrequited debt" Christians owed for a thousand years of persecuting the Jews. Dvořáček advocates in an ecumenical spirit a thorough revision of Christian attitudes.[140]

Two eloquent reports compiled by dissidents associated with Charter 77, the human-rights group spearheaded by Václav Havel, testify to the disastrous situation prevailing in the Jewish religious communities.[141] The "Open Letter to the Leadership of the Council of Jewish Communities in the Czech Lands," of February 19, 1989, signed by Dr. Leo Pavlát and twenty-four other dissidents, notes that the communities are in danger of extinction. The "Critique on the Devastation of Jewish Cultural Monuments and the Tacit Disregard of the Role of Jews in Czechoslovak History," of April 5, 1989, signed by the dissidents Tomáš Hradílek, Dana Němcová, and Sáša Vondra, condemns the Communist authorities' disregard of Jewish history and the Holocaust.[142]

The "Critique" further points out that in the eighth-grade history textbook, in which the subject of the occupation and World War II is taught in some detail, the persecution of the Jews is mentioned only twice, as follows: "The gradual liquidation of Jews, Slavs and other so-called racially inferior nations was an integral part of the overall German scheme to dominate the world" and "Fascism engaged in the purposeful murder of the Jewish population and members of Slavic nations in concentration camps." The same textbook provides the information that "360,000 of our citizens perished, amongst these 25,000 Communists, in prisons, concentration camps and on the battle fields." The fact that 250,000 of these victims were Jews and represented the majority of the Jewish population of the prewar republic is not mentioned.[143] The "Critique" also asserts that a plaque designed by the Czech artist Břetislav Benda and commissioned by the Council of the Jewish Communities in 1968 to be displayed on the grounds of the former trade fair buildings, from which the Jews of Prague and most of Bohemia were deported to Terezín and other concentration camps, has never been unveiled on the site. (It eventually ended up on a brick wall of the Terezín fortifications.)

Charter 77, which later grew into the protest organization Civic Forum, was instrumental in the final act, sealing the fate of Communist rule in Czechoslovakia. The November 1989 revolution brought a new era of vitality to the Jewish community. Dr. Dezider Galský, who was president of the Council of the Jewish Communities from 1980 to 1985, returned in 1989 to lead the community, initiating the first moves toward restoring the one-thousand-year-old Jewish enclave.[144] The leadership of the Council of the Jewish Communities established offices in Prague and Bratislava and embarked on a policy of revival. The jointly issued monthly bulletin *Roš Chodeš* (New Moon), edited by Jiří Daníček, who also heads Sefer (The book) publishing house, reflects the regained freedom of expression. Among the wide range of cultural activities listed on the community agenda, priority is given to the publication of books on Jewish history, religion, and culture. Significantly, the first volume to appear was *Židovské historické monumenty v Čechách a na Moravě* (Jewish historical sights in Bohemia and Moravia), by Jiří Fiedler, a non-Jew who researched the topic for many years prior to the collapse of Communism.[145] One of the academic authorities' first steps in promoting the study of modern history, hitherto suppressed for political reasons, was the creation of the Institute for Contemporary History at the Czechoslovak Academy of Sciences in Prague. One of its stated research goals is to study the fate of Czech Jewry after 1938, including the Holocaust. Indeed, the first volume the institute published was *Osud Židů v Protektorátu 1939–1945* (The fate of the Jews in the protectorate, 1939–1945).[146] The task of the institute, along with the Jewish Museum and the Terezín Memorial, will be to provide new generations of students with educational tools in a spirit of freedom and based on a new set of democratic values.

Freedom inevitably brought nationalist and separatist elements to the fore once again, mainly in Slovakia. Along with them came an upsurge of anti-Semitism. A massive and noisy demonstration advocating a separate Slovak state erupted in Bratislava on March 14, 1991, the day of the fifty-second anniversary of the establishment of independent Slovakia. On July 8, 1990, a ceremony had taken place at Bánovce nad Bebravou in which a plaque in memory of Jozef Tiso was unveiled on the wall of the Roman Catholic Teachers Institute, where he had taught before entering the government. A special Te Deum was led by the Catholic Bishop Jan Chrisostom Korec of Nitra, ironically one of the signatories of the 1987 Bratislava proclamation on the deportation of Jews. These provocative acts of Slovak separatists aroused nationwide protest.

In the ongoing polemics, *Literárny týždenník* (Literary Weekly), the organ of the Slovak writers, published an interview with František Vnuk, a Slovak émigré and a lecturer at the Technical Institute in Adelaide, Australia. Vnuk's provocative essay "A Look from the Other Side," in which he defended the wartime Slovak government's anti-Jewish stance, generated a heated debate. Among those taking issue with Vnuk were the writer Ladislav Mňačko; Jozef Šrámek, a Munich-based émigré associated with Radio Free Europe; Martin Spitzer, a Jewish ex-serviceman who lives in Adelaide; and the historian Ivan Kamenec.[147] This national debate, pressure from both the Czech and Slovak federal governments, and the intervention of several prominent public figures, led by President Havel, prompted the separatists finally to remove the plaque. On October 31, 1990, Havel traveled to Slovakia to participate in a ceremony unveiling a plaque in memory of the Jews who were deported from Dolný Kubín.[148]

Two direct results of this controversy were the establishment of an official commission of Slovak historians to assess the role of Dr. Jozef Tiso[149] and the decision to erect a memorial to the martyrs of the Holocaust in Slovakia, to be built in Bratislava. The debate on the role of the Slovak leaders in the deportation of the Jews continues unabated and is accompanied by much anti-Semitism. In Nitra and Prešov the Jewish cemeteries have been vandalized. At the same time, some positive events can be mentioned. In August 1991, after a lapse of twenty years, Ivan Kamenec's dissertation, a detailed description of the deportation of Slovak Jewry to the extermination camps, was published in Bratislava under the title *Po stopách tragédie* (In the track of the tragedy). Another noteworthy publication is Eugen Bárkány and Ludovít Dojč's *Židovské náboženské obce na Slovensku* (The Jewish religious communities in Slovakia).[150]

President Havel renewed Czechoslovakia's diplomatic ties with Israel, severed in 1967, stressing the moral dimension of this act. Shortly afterward, in April 1990, he and his entourage visited Israel and were received with great fanfare.[151] In his addresses, delivered in Jerusalem, Havel referred to his great predecessor, T. G. Masaryk, who in 1927 had been the first statesman to pay a visit to the Yishuv in Palestine.

In October 1991 the president of Israel, Chaim Herzog, paid an official visit to Czechoslovakia at President Havel's invitation.[152] President Herzog participated in the ceremonies held on the occasion of the fiftieth anniversary of the deportation of the Jews of Bohemia and Moravia, and in Bratislava he attended the cornerstone-laying ceremony for the memorial to be erected to the martyrs of the Holocaust. To mark this solemn occasion, Herzog addressed the Prague Parliament.

The year 1991 was also marked by several new publications on previously taboo Jewish topics. The most important among these are Viktor Fischl (Avigdor Dagan), *Hovory s Janem Masarykem* (Talks with Jan Masaryk); Erich Kulka, *Židé v Svobodové armádě* (Jews in the army of Svoboda); Ctibor Rybár, *Židovská Praha, Glosy k dějinám a kultuře* (Jewish Prague: Glossary to history and culture); and Miroslav Kárný, *"Konečné řešení": Genocida českych židů v německé protektorátní politice* ("The Final Solution": The genocide of the Czech Jews in the German protectorate policy).[153]

In Slovakia, the fiftieth anniversary of the first transport of Jewish girls dispatched from the city of Poprad to Auschwitz was officially marked on March 26, 1992, with the unveiling of a memorial plaque on the site by the prime minister, the minister of education, and the Israeli ambassador. On the same day, a solemn ceremony took place at the Banská Bystrica Museum of the Slovak National Uprising during which Yad Vashem awards were presented to nineteen Slovak and Czech

Righteous among the Nations who had jeopardized their lives to save their Jewish fellow citizens. In the afternoon a three-day historical conference on the topic "The Tragedy of Slovak Jews," attended by seven Israeli historians, began. For the first time this issue was openly and freely discussed in Slovakia.[154]

After the destructive years of Nazism and Communism, there is a dire need for the restoration and conservation of Jewish relics and monuments, many of which were abandoned and devastated. However, as President Havel observed, the process of revival in all spheres of cultural and social activities will take many decades. He underscored the difficulties involved in overcoming internal problems in order "to shake off the totalitarian system" and erase the consequences of its forty years of domination.[155]

NOTES

1. Five times since 1918, when the official name First Czechoslovak Republic was coined, the name has been changed owing to political events: in the wake of the Munich Dictate (1938), the German occupation (1939), the Communist takeover (1948), the Soviet invasion (1968), and more recently the persistent Slovak demand to be on a par with the Czech nation. The May 1990 resolution of the Prague parliament declared the new official designation of the state to be The Czech and Slovak Federal Republics. According to the bill passed by the Czechoslovak Federal Parliament on November 25, 1992, the Czechoslovak Federation was dissolved on January 1, 1993, into two separate republics, the Czech Republic and Slovakia.

2. The most useful surveys of the First Republic in English are Robert J. Kerner, ed., *Czechoslovakia: Twenty Years of Independence* (Berkeley, 1940); Věra Olivová, *The Doomed Democracy: Czechoslovakia in a Disrupted Europe, 1914–1938* (London, 1972); Victor S. Mamatey and Radomír Luža, eds., *A History of the Czechoslovak Republic, 1918–1948* (Princeton, 1973); and Josef Korbel, *Twentieth-Century Czechoslovakia: The Meaning of Its History* (New York, 1977).

3. The only comprehensive study of Czechoslovak Jews is the three-volume work sponsored by the New York–based Society for the History of Czechoslovak Jews: *The Jews of Czechoslovakia: Historical Studies and Surveys,* by various editors, 3 vols. (Philadelphia, 1968–84).

4. See Ruth Kestenberg-Gladstein, *Neuere Geschichte der Juden in den böhmischen Ländern, Erster Teil: Das Zeitalter der Aufklärung, 1780–1830* (Tübingen, 1969); idem, "The Jews between Czechs and Germans in the Historic Lands, 1848–1918," in *The Jews of Czechoslovakia,* 1:21–71; and Gary B. Cohen, *The Politics of Ethnic Survival: Germans in Prague, 1861–1914* (Princeton, 1981).

5. William O. McCagg, Jr., *A History of Habsburg Jews, 1670–1918* (Bloomington, Ind., 1989), 75–77; Gustav Otruba, "Der Anteil der Juden am Wirtschaftsleben der böhmischen Länder seit dem Beginn der Industrialisierung," in *Die Juden in den böhmischen Ländern, Vorträge der Tagung des Collegium Carolinum in Bad Wiessee vom 27.–29. November 1981,* ed. Ferdinand Seibt (Munich, 1983), 209–68.

6. Hillel J. Kieval, *The Making of Czech Jewry: National Conflict and Jewish Society in Bohemia, 1870–1918* (New York, 1988).

7. Oskar K. Rabinowicz, "Czechoslovak Zionism: Analecta to a History," in *The Jews of Czechoslovakia,* 2:19–123.

8. Gary B. Cohen, "Ethnicity and Urban Population Growth: The Decline of the Prague Germans, 1880–1910," in *Studies in East European Social History,* ed. Keith Hitchins, vol. 2 (Leiden, 1981), 3–26, gives the breakdown of the 1900 census for Bohemia by language affiliation as follows: Czech, 50,080; German, 40,521; other, 177. For the city of Prague it was Czech, 9,880; German, 8,230.

9. See Hugo Stransky, "The Religious Life in the Historic Lands," in *The Jews of Czechoslovakia,* 1: 340; and Gustav Fleischmann, "The Religious Congregation, 1918–1938," ibid., 278.

10. See František Langer's foreword to his brother Jiří (Mordechai Georg) Langer's book *Nine Gates to the Chassidic Mysteries* (New York, 1976).

11. See Jan Heřman, "The Development of Bohemian and Moravian Jewry, 1918–1938," in *Papers in Jewish Demography, 1969,* ed. U. O. Schmelz, P. Glikson, and S. Della Pergola (Jerusalem, 1973), 191–206; and Ezra Mendelsohn, *The Jews in East Central Europe between the World Wars* (Bloomington, Ind., 1983), 142–45.

12. Egon Hostovsky, "Jewish Participation in

Modern Czech Literature," in *The Jews of Czechoslovakia*, 1:439–53.

13. Up until 1918 the history of this enclave formed an integral part of the history of Hungarian Jewry. For succinct surveys see David Gross, "Die Juden in der Slowakei," in *Jüdisches Jahrbuch für die Slowakei* (Bratislava, 5700 [1940]), 7–21; and Robert Büchler, "Kürze Übersicht der jüdischen Geschichte in dem Gebiet der Slowakei," in *Slowakei* (Munich, 1982), 3–42.

14. See Livia Rothkirchen, "The Jews of Slovakia, 1848–1918, 1918–1938," in *The Jews of Czechoslovakia*, 1:72–124.

15. Ibid.

16. There is no comprehensive monograph on the history of the Jews of Subcarpathian Ruthenia. Only after World War II did they come to be regarded as a separate entity. Prior to 1918 their history formed part of the history of Hungarian Jewry. There are, however, several memorial books, dedicated to greater towns and their communities, published in Israel by survivors' organizations.

17. See Livia Rothkirchen, "Deep-Rooted Yet Alien: Some Aspects of the History of the Jews in Subcarpathian Ruthenia," *Yad Vashem Studies* 12 (1977), 147–91; Herman Dicker, *Piety and Perseverance: Jews from the Carpathian Mountains* (New York, 1981); and Dov Dinur, *Shoat Yehudei Russia ha-Karpatit—Uzhorod* (Jerusalem, 1983).

18. Aryeh Sole, "Subcarpathian Ruthenia, 1918–1938," in *The Jews of Czechoslovakia*, 2:125–54.

19. H. G. Wells, *The Outline of History* (London, 1951).

20. On the struggle of the Jewish leadership for recognition of its status after World War I, see Aharon Moshe Rabinowicz, "The Jewish Minority," in *The Jews of Czechoslovakia*, 1:155–265.

21. Aharon Moshe Rabinowicz, "The Jewish Party: A Struggle for National Recognition, Representation, and Autonomy," ibid., 2:253–346.

22. Josef Chmelař, *Political Parties in Czechoslovakia* (Prague, 1926); Charles Hoch, *The Political Parties in Czechoslovakia*, Czechoslovak Sources and Documents, 9 (Prague, 1936); Joseph Rothschild, *East Central Europe between the Two World Wars* (Seattle, 1974), 122–29.

23. Guido Kisch, "Linguistic Conditions among Czechoslovak Jewry—A Legal Historical Study," in *Czechoslovakia Past and Present*, ed. Miroslav Rechcígl, 2 vols. (The Hague, 1968), 2:1458–59.

24. Rabinowicz, "The Jewish Party."

25. See Stransky, "Religious Life in the Historic Lands"; Fleischmann, "Religious Congregation"; and Fred Hahn, "The Jews among the Nations in Bohemia and Moravia," in *Religion and National-*

ism in Eastern Europe and the Soviet Union (Boulder, Colo., 1987), 45, 48–49.

26. Goldstein's report in the parliamentary session was reproduced in the Prague community bulletin (see *Věstník židovské obce náboženské v Praze*, January 31, 1937).

27. Ernst Rychnovsky, ed., *Thomas G. Masaryk and the Jews*, trans. Benjamin R. Epstein (New York, 1941).

28. Avigdor Dagan, "The Press," in *The Jews of Czechoslovakia*, 1:523–31.

29. See Cecil Parrott, Foreword to Olivová, *The Doomed Democracy*.

30. See Jan Havránek, "Fascism in Czechoslovakia," in *Native Fascism in the Successor States, 1918–1945*, ed. Peter F. Sugar (Santa Barbara, 1971), 47–55; and Joseph F. Zacek, "Czechoslovak Fascisms," ibid., 56–62.

31. Victor S. Mamatey, "The Development of Czechoslovak Democracy, 1920–1938," in Mamatey and Luža, *A History of the Czechoslovak Republic*, 132.

32. See Elizabeth Wiskemann, *Czechs and Germans: A Study of the Struggle in the Historic Provinces of Bohemia and Moravia*, 2d ed. (London, 1967); and J. W. Bruegel, "The Germans in Prewar Czechoslovakia," in Mamatey and Luža, *A History of the Czechoslovak Republic*, 167–87.

33. The bibliography dealing with the various aspects of the Munich period is very extensive. A select and annotated bibliography can be found in Stanley B. Winters, "Munich 1938 from the Czech Perspective," *East Central Europe* 8, nos. 1–2 (1981), 62–96.

34. George F. Kennan, *From Prague after Munich: Diplomatic Papers, 1938–1940* (Princeton, 1968), 7. On the Jewish aspects of the Munich agreement, see Heinrich Bodensieck, "Das Dritte Reich und die Lage der Juden in der Tschechoslowakei nach München," *Vierteljahrshefte für Zeitgeschichte* 9 (1961), 143–50; and O. D. Kulka, "HaYahadut haTshechit bePros haShoah," *Gesher* 2–3 (1969), 143–50.

35. See essays in *The Jews of Czechoslovakia*, vol. 3.

36. Livia Rothkirchen, "The Czechoslovak Government-in-Exile: Jewish and Palestinian Aspects in the Light of Documents," *Yad Vashem Studies* 9 (1973), 157–99; Avigdor Dagan, "The Czechoslovak Government-in-Exile and the Jews," in *The Jews of Czechoslovakia*, 3:464–65.

37. Erich Kulka, "Jews in the Czechoslovak Armed Forces during World War II," in *The Jews of Czechoslovakia*, 3:331–448.

38. See Zdenek Lederer, "Terezin," ibid., 104–52; see also the bibliography, ibid., 152–64.

39. Hana Volavková, *The Synagogue Treasures of Bohemia and Moravia* (Prague, 1949); idem, *The Story of the Jewish Museum in Prague* (Prague, 1968).

40. Livia Rothkirchen, *The Destruction of Slovak Jewry: A Documentary History* (Jerusalem, 1961).

41. For instances of personal courage displayed by Catholic priests, see Ladislav Lipscher, "The Jews of Slovakia: 1939–1945," in *The Jews of Czechoslovakia*, 3:242, 255–56.

42. See Jirmejahu Oskar Neumann, *Im Schatten des Todes: Ein Tatsachenbericht vom Schicksalskapf des slowakischen Judentums* (Tel Aviv, 1956); Michael D. Weissmandel, *Min haMetzar: Zikhronot miShnot 1941–1945* (New York, 1960); Yehuda Bauer, *American Jewry and the Holocaust: The American Jewish Joint Distribution Committee, 1939–1945* (Detroit, 1981), 356–79; Livia Rothkirchen, "The Europa Plan: A Reassessment," in *American Jewry during the Holocaust*, ed. S. M. Finger (New York, 1984), Appendix 4–7, 1–26.

43. For the role of the Vatican, see Fiorello J. S. Cavalli, "La Santa Sede contro la deportazioni degli ebrei dalla Slovacchia durante seconda guerra mondiale," *La Civiltà Cattolica* 113, no. 3 (1961), 3–18; Livia Rothkirchen, "Vatican Policy and the 'Jewish Problem' in 'Independent' Slovakia (1939–1945)," *Yad Vashem Studies* 6 (1967), 27–53; John S. Conway, "The Churches, the Slovak State, and the Jews, 1939–1945," *Slavonic and East European Review* 52, no. 126 (1974), 85–112; Yeshayahu Jelinek, "The Vatican, the Catholic Church, the Catholics, and the Persecution of the Jews during World War II: The Case of Slovakia," in *Jews and Non-Jews in Eastern Europe, 1918–1945*, ed. Bela Vago and George L. Mosse (New York, 1974), 221–45.

44. See Randolph L. Braham, *The Politics of Genocide: The Holocaust in Hungary* (New York, 1981).

45. See above, n. 16; Rothkirchen, "Deep-Rooted Yet Alien"; Dicker, *Piety and Perseverance*; Dinur, *Shoat Yehudei Russia ha-Karpatit—Uzhorod;* and Randolph L. Braham, "The Kamenets Podolsk and Délvidék Massacres: Prelude to the Holocaust in Hungary," *Yad Vashem Studies* 9 (1973), 133–43.

46. For statistical tables regarding the survivors and the postwar Jewish revival in Czechoslovakia, see Peter Meyer et al., *The Jews in the Soviet Satellites* (Syracuse, 1953), 49–191.

47. Kurt Wehle, "The Jews in Bohemia and Moravia: 1945–1948," in *The Jews of Czechoslovakia*, 3:499–530; Yeshayahu Jelinek, "The Jews in Slovakia: 1945–1949," ibid., 531–43.

48. Vojtech Mastny, "Tradition, Continuity, and Discontinuity in Recent Czechoslovak History," in *Die Tschechoslowakei, 1945–1970,* ed. Nikolaus Lobkowicz and Friedrich Prinz (Munich, 1978), 86.

49. Rothkirchen, "The Czechoslovak Government-in-Exile," 164.

50. Ehud Avriel, *Open the Gates: The Dramatic Personal Story of "Illegal" Immigration to Israel* (New York, 1975); idem, "Prague and Jerusalem: The Era of Friendship," in *The Jews of Czechoslovakia*, 3:551–66.

51. Paul E. Zinner, *Communist Strategy and Tactics in Czechoslovakia, 1918–1948* (London, 1963), 186–89.

52. Václav Král, ed., *Lesson from History: Documents concerning Nazi Policies for Germanization and Extermination* (Prague, 1961), 119–20; Jan Tesař, "Poznámky k problémům okupačního režimu v tzv. protektorátě," *Historie a vojenství* 2 (1964), 178.

53. See Rothkirchen, "Vatican Policy," 27–53.

54. See Anton Rašla, *L'udové súdy v Československu po II. svetovej vojne ako forma mimoriadneho súdnictva* (Bratislava, 1969), 48–64.

55. Igor Daxner, *Ludáctvo pred Národným súdom 1945–1947* (Bratislava, 1961); *Pred súdom národa; proces s Dr. J. Tisom, Dr. F. Ďurčanským a A. Machom v Bratislave,* 5 vols. (Bratislava, 1947); Vilém Prečan, "Diskuse nad příspěvkem k dějinám retribuce na Slovensku," *Československý časopis historický* 10 (1962), 40–48.

56. Zinner, *Communist Strategy,* 186–89.

57. Meyer et al., *The Jews in the Soviet Satellites,* 104–9.

58. See Sari Reuveni, "Antisemitism in Hungary, 1945–1946," *Holocaust and Genocide Studies* 4, no. 1 (1989), 41–62; Eva Standeisky, "Anti-Semitic Movements in the Time of the Coalition" (paper presented at the conference "Jews and the Alignment of Forces in Present-Day Hungarian Society and Politics," Hebrew University, Jerusalem, November 4–5, 1990).

59. For details see Meyer et al., *The Jews in the Soviet Satellites,* 76–92; for a description of the circumstances of the enforced nationalization of the Prague Orion Chocolate Factory and the concern at Warnsdorf owned by Julius Beer, see Prokop Drtina, *Československo můj osud* (Toronto, 1982), 422–24.

60. See Anna Auředníčková, *Tři léta v Terezíně* (Prague, 1945); Irma Semecká, *Terezínské torso* (Prague, 1946); Mirko Tůma, *Ghetto našich dnů* (Prague, 1946); and Emil Utitz, *Psychologie života v terezínském koncentračním táboře* (Prague, 1947), published in German as *Psychologie des Lebens in Theresienstadt* (Vienna, 1948).

61. Ota Kraus and Erich Kulka, *Továrna na smrt*

(Prague, 1946), published in English as *The Death Factory* (Oxford, 1966).

62. Richard Feder, *Židovská tragedie: dějství poslední* (Kolín, 1947).

63. Friedrich Steiner, ed., *Tragédia slovenských Židov* (Bratislava, 1949), published simultaneously in Slovak and Hebrew-English versions.

64. Ota Klein, "Vliv koncentračního tábora na etický charakter židovské mládeže," in *Disertace pražské university*, vol. 2, *1945–1953, Karlova Universita v Praze* (Prague, 1965).

65. Fourteen leading party functionaries, of whom eleven were Jews, headed by Rudolf Slánský (1901–52), vice premier of Czechoslovakia and secretary general, were put on trial in 1950, charged with conspiracy against the state. Ten were sentenced to death and hanged in 1952. (Three of the Jewish defendants were sentenced only to life imprisonment and freed in the sixties.) The victims, including Slánský, were posthumously rehabilitated. See Karel Kaplan, *Die politischen Prozesse in der Tschechoslowakei, 1948–1954* (Munich, 1986); and Josefa Slánská, *Report on My Husband* (London, 1969).

66. For a perceptive survey, see Vladimir V. Kusin, *The Intellectual Origins of the Prague Spring* (Cambridge, 1971), chap. 8, "Historians Draw a Lesson," 76–77.

67. See *Československý časopis historický* 2 (1954), 565–72.

68. No comprehensive work on the fate of Transcarpathian Jewry has been published until recently. Several memorial books published in Israel and one in the United States, as well as a spate of volumes by the so-called *Landsmanschaften* (mostly in Hebrew or Yiddish), are the only available literature.

69. The major works on the Holocaust and the fate of Czech Jewry under Nazi occupation were published abroad. The first standard works on Terezín, *Ghetto Theresienstadt*, by Zdenek Lederer (London, 1953), and *Theresienstadt 1941–1945. Das Antlitz einer Zwangsgemeinschaft*, by H. G. Adler (Tübingen, 1955), appeared in England and Germany; other works appeared in the United States and Israel. *The Jews of Czechoslovakia*, vol. 3, which deals with the Holocaust, was published by the New York–based Society for the History of Czechoslovak Jewry (Philadelphia, 1984); and Ruth Bondy's *"Elder of the Jews": Jakob Edelstein of Theresienstadt* was published in New York in 1989. A number of articles and papers on Czech and Slovak Jewry were published in Israel, mainly in *Yad Vashem Studies* and *Yalkut Moreshet*.

70. Each of these authored several works, the most representative of which are the following: Norbert Frýd, *Krabice živých* (Prague, 1956); Josef

Bor, *Terezínské rekviem* (Prague, 1963), published in English as *The Terezin Requiem* (London, 1963); Arnošt Lustig, *Noc a naděje* (Prague, 1958), published in English as *Night and Hope* (Washington, D.C., 1976); František Kafka, *Krutá léta* (Prague, 1963); and Jiří Weil, *Život s hvězdou* (Prague, 1949), published in English as *Life with the Star* (New York, 1989).

71. See Ladislav Grossmann, *Obchod na korse* (Bratislava, 1962), published in English as *The Shop on Main Street* (Garden City, N.Y., 1970); and Emil Knieža, *Šiesty prápor, na stráž!* (Bratislava, 1964).

72. This memorial was designed by two renowned painters, Jiří Jon and Václav Boštík. During the 1970s the engravings had been obliterated from the walls. The authorities reasoned that this act was a necessity because of "dampness" caused by underground moisture from the Vltava River. After the November 1989 revolution, work was begun to restore the original structure and reinscribe the martyrs' names.

73. See Josef Škvorecký, *Sedmiramenný svícen* (Prague, 1964); Jan Otčenášek, *Romeo, Julie a tma* (Prague, 1959); Hana Bělohradská, *Bez krásy a bez límce* (Prague, 1962); Ladislav Fuks, *Pan Theodor Mundstock* (Prague, 1963), published in English as *Mr. Theodore Mundstock* (New York, 1968); and Jindřiška Smetanová, *Ustláno na růžích* (Prague, 1966).

74. See Ivan Dérer, *Slovenský vývoj a ľudácká zrada, fakta, vzpomínky a úvahy* (Prague, 1946).

75. Dominik Tatarka, *Farská republika* (Bratislava, 1948).

76. Hela Volanská, *Stretnutia v lesoch* (Bratislava, 1948); Katarína Lazarová, *Kamaráti* (Bratislava, 1949).

77. Several important works on the fate of Jews in Slovakia were published in Israel, Germany, and the United States. See Neumann, *Im Schatten des Todes;* Weissmandel, *Min HaMetzar;* Rothkirchen, *The Destruction of Slovak Jewry;* Akiva Nir, *Shvilim beMaagal haEsh* (Tel Aviv, 1967); Yeshayahu Jelinek, *The Parish Republic* (Boulder, Colo., 1976); Ladislav Lipscher, *Die Juden im Slowakischen Staat 1939–1945* (Munich, 1980); Emanuel Frieder, *To Deliver Their Souls: The Struggle of a Young Rabbi during the Holocaust* (New York, 1990), translated from the original Hebrew; and Gila Fatran, *Haim Maavak leHisardut? Hanhagat Yehudey Slovakia beTkufat haShoah* (Tel Aviv, 1992).

78. Imrich Staněk, *Zrada a pád: hlinkovští separatisté a tak zvaný Slovenský stát* (Prague, 1958).

79. Ladislav Mňačko, *Já, Adolf Eichmann* (Bratislava, 1961).

80. The conversation held with Willem Sassen,

a Dutch Nazi journalist, in Argentina in 1957 was published after Eichmann's capture. See Eichmann's confession in *Life,* January 9, 1961, 14–15.

81. This line of argument was espoused by several Slovak ex-diplomats and historians. See Joseph A. Mikus, *Slovakia: A Political History, 1918–1950* (Milwaukee, 1963); Joseph Kirschbaum, *Slovakia: Nation on the Crossroads of Central Europe* (New York, 1960); and Milan S. Durica, *Slovenský podiel na europskej tragédii židov* (Cologne, 1987), published in German as *Der slowakische Anteil an der Tragödie der europäischen Juden* (Munich, 1986).

82. Fraňo Tiso, "Slowakische Korrespondenz," referred to by Edo Friš in "V pozadí byl Heydrich," *Kultúrny život,* October 13, 1962, 2, 6.

83. See Rothkirchen, *The Destruction of Slovak Jewry.*

84. See Rothkirchen, "Vatican Policy."

85. Kusin, *Intellectual Origins,* 83; Josef Škvorecký's "iconoclastic" novel *Zbabělci,* published in 1958, is referred to as the novel that heralded the post-Stalinist "thaw" that reintroduced subjectivity and questioned the valor of the Czech anti-German uprising in 1945, which was glorified by Communist historiography.

86. Kusin, *Intellectual Origins,* 89–91; Pavel Tigrid, "Czechoslovakia, Twenty Years After," in Rechcigl, *Czechoslovakia Past and Present,* 1:387.

87. Kusin, *Intellectual Origins,* 90; Galia Golan, *Reform Rule in Czechoslovakia* (Cambridge, 1973), 91.

88. See above, n. 65.

89. Gordon H. Skilling, *Czechoslovakia's Interrupted Revolution* (Princeton, 1976).

90. Škvorecký's work is cited in n. 73. The others are Karel Lágus and Josef Polák, *Město za mřížemi* (Prague, 1964); and František Ehrmann, Ota Heitlinger, and Rudolf Iltis, eds., *Terezín, 1941–1945* (Prague, 1965).

91. I reviewed the catalogue of Czechoslovak dissertations, *Čsl. disertace,* published annually by the National Library, for the years 1964–69 at the University Library, Prague.

92. Ibid. For references to the first two theses, see also Yeshayahu Jelinek, "The Holocaust of Slovakian Jewry," *East Central Europe* 10, nos. 1–2 (1983), 15–16; Jan Džugas, "L'udácké riešenia 'židovskej otázky' za tzv. Slovenského štátu"; and Ivan Kamenec, "Židovská otázka v politike ľudáckej vlády na Slovensku v rokoch 1938–1945."

93. Ján Čarnogurský, "Rasové zákonodárstvo Slovenského štátu." A copy of the latter dissertation is in the Yad Vashem Archives in Jerusalem (YVA, sign. 9771).

94. See above, n. 91; and Zdeněk Jirotka, "Židovské listy v letech 1939–1944" (1967). Only Šor-

mová's paper was published as a book under the same title: *Divadlo v Terezíně 1941–1945* (Prague, 1973).

95. Jan Křen, *Bílá místa v naších dějinách?* (Prague, 1990), 22, 81–83.

96. See Hana Volavková, "Jewish Artists in the Historic Lands," in *The Jews of Czechoslovakia,* 2:491.

97. Kusin, *Intellectual Origins,* 88; Skilling, *Interrupted Revolution,* 682–83; Robin A. Remington, ed., *Winter in Prague: Documents on Czechoslovak Communism in Crisis* (Cambridge, Mass., 1969), 162–63, 187–88; Konstantin Ivanov, "Israel, Zionism, and International Imperialism," *International Affairs,* no. 6 (June 1968), 19.

98. Karl Baum, *Report on Czechoslovak Jewry,* no. 3, published by the International Council of Jews from Czechoslovakia (London, 1976), 8. See also Josef Frolík, *Špiom vypovídá* (Prague, 1990).

99. Kusin, *Intellectual Origins,* 126. For a description of the brave stance of the Union of Czech Writers and other intellectuals, see Skilling, *Interrupted Revolution,* 682–83.

100. See Remington, *Winter in Prague,* doc. 28, "Be Careful, Citizens," 189–94. The complete text was reproduced in *Rudé právo,* June 23, 1968.

101. Ludvík Vaculík, "2,000 slov k dělníkům, rolníkům, vedcům, umelcům a ke všem," *Literární listy,* June 27, 1968; Remington, *Winter in Prague,* doc. 29, 196–97.

102. The Central Council of Jewish Communities of Slovakia adopted a similar declaration a few days later. See *Věstník ŽNO,* May 6, 1968; see also "Jewish Aspects of the Changes in Czechoslovakia" in a special brochure put out by the Institute of Jewish Affairs in association with the World Jewish Congress in July 1968.

103. Korbel, *Twentieth-Century Czechoslovakia,* vii; Vilém Prečan, "A Preliminary Documentary Report on the Black Book," in *Sedm pražských dnů 21.–27. srpen 1968: Dokumentace,* ed. Josef Macek et al. (Prague, 1990), 391.

104. Eduard Vavruška, *Terezínská předkapitola* (Prague, 1967); Rabbi Richard Feder's "Naše milenium," written in a popular vein and published in twelve installments in *Věstník ŽNO* in 1968 and 1969. Feder's is the first and only concise survey of Jewish history written in postwar Czechoslovakia. A second work, Josef Bartušek's study "Tisíc let židů v českých zemích a čeština" was also written to commemorate the millennium. See *Židovská ročenka* 5730 (1969–70), 48–66.

105. Gordon H. Skilling, *Charter 77 and Human Rights in Czechoslovakia* (London, 1981).

106. Hana Volavková, "The Jewish Museum of Prague," in *The Jews of Czechoslovakia,* 3:567–83;

Markéta Petrášová, "Collections of the Central Jewish Museum 1942–1945," *Judaica Bohemiae* 24, no. 1 (1988), 23–28.

107. Hana Volavková, ed., *Dětské kresby na zastávce smrti. Terezín 1942–1944* (Prague, 1956), published in English as *I Never Saw Another Butterfly* (New York, 1959); Arno Pařík, "Symposium in Honour of PhDr. Hana Volavková," *Judaica Bohemiae* 24, no. 1 (1988), 60–61; and "Hana Volavková on Jewish Art and Monuments in Bohemia and Moravia," ibid. 25, no. 1 (1989), 31–49.

108. For a cumulative index of articles, see Vladimír Sadek and Jiřina Šedinová, eds., *Judaica Bohemiae* 26, no. 1 (1990).

109. On the impact of Moscow-initiated anti-Semitism, see Livia Rothkirchen, "State Anti-Semitism during the Communist Era (1948–1989)," in *Collected Proceedings from the International Seminar on Anti-Semitism in Post-Totalitarian Europe* (Prague, 1993), 125–36.

110. *Věstník ŽNO,* October 1973. For the repercussions and reactions, see International Council of Jews from Czechoslovakia, London, *Newsletter,* nos. 1 (January 1972), 3 (June 1973), and 4 (August 1973). In mid-1972 Benjamin Eichler, who had acted since 1955 as chairman of the Union of Jewish Communities in Slovakia, was dismissed from his post on charges that in 1968 he had organized courses for young Zionists in Yugoslavia and in Israel (see Baum, *Report,* 7).

111. For the open letter addressed by the Council of the Jewish Religious Communities to "The President of the USA," see *Věstník ŽNO,* July 1978.

112. In 1947 Rabbi Sicher returned to Prague from Jerusalem, where he had found refuge during the war, and took on the onerous task of reconstructing the decimated community. Rabbi Sicher's treatises and essays were published posthumously under the title *Volte život* (Prague, 1975).

113. See Vojtěch Cvek in *Katolické noviny,* March 14, 1976; the review by J. Výborný in *Kostnické jiskry,* March 10, 1976; and the review by M. Kanák, in *Český zápas,* March 21, 1976.

114. Miroslav Kryl, "Nový pramen k dějinám terezínského getta," *Terezínské listy* 1 (1970); see also I. M. Jedlička and S. Grossová, "Po stopách terezínských deníčků," *Reporter,* December 1, 1967, 10–14. The original diary is held in the Terezín Memorial, inv. no. 1617.

115. Ludvík Václavek, "Literární tvorba Petra Kiena," *Terezínské listy* 3 (1973), 19–24; Oliva Pechová, "Malířský odkaz Petra Kiena," ibid., 25–29.

116. Maxmilian Pergler, "Péče státu o Památník Terezín," ibid. 4 (1974), 1–3.

117. For a most informative commentary that contains vicious anti-Zionist attacks and references to Israel's anti-Arab policy, see Jiří Aleš, *Tribuna,* July 14, 1982.

118. See bibliographical entries in *Judaica Bohemiae* 26, no. 1 (1990).

119. Miroslav Kárný, "Terezínský koncentrační tábor v plánech nacistů," *Československý časopis historický* 22 (1974), 673–702.

120. For details on the achievements of Czech cinematography, see Antonín Liehm, *Closely Watched Films: The Czechoslovak Experience* (New York, 1974); and Ilan Avisar, *Screening the Holocaust: Cinema's Images of the Unimaginable* (Bloomington, Ind., 1988).

121. See "Klenot české literatury," in which František Kafka marks the tenth anniversary of Pavel's death, in *Věstník ŽNO,* April 1983.

122. See Ota Ornest, "Císař Atlantidy," *Reporter,* December 7, 1990.

123. Erich Kraus's guideline entitled "Cíle ŽNO a ŽRS," containing eighteen points, is in the possession of the author, courtesy of Mr. Kraus.

124. See Ladislav Bittman, *The Deception Game: Czechoslovak Intelligence in Soviet Political Warfare* (Syracuse, 1972), 47–69.

125. Rudolf Iltis, ed., *Nazi Dokumente sprechen* (Prague, 1964). For reviews of the books published on the finds, see *Hlas revoluce,* February 6, 1964, and May 5, 1966.

126. The books were published in Czech under the titles *Na dně byla smrt* (1964) and *Tajemství Černého jezera* (1965); see Bittman, *Deception Game,* 69.

127. Baum, *Report,* 8–11.

128. Ibid.

129. Bittman, *Deception Game,* 195–96.

130. Jiří Bohatka (believed to be the pen name of an editorial team of "specialists on the Jews"), "Třídní význam sionismu," *Tribuna,* November 17, 1976. The same article, with slight changes, appeared in Slovak six years later as "Korenie izraelskej agresie proti arabským národom, Ideologia a praxe sionizmu," *Nové slovo,* no. 35 (September 9, 1982). Among other accusations, Bohatka charged that "Israeli historians pilfered Czechoslovak archives and removed documents proving cooperation between Zionist organizations and the Nazis." See Baum, *Report,* 8.

131. Josef Šebesta, *V zemi zaslíbené?* (Prague, 1986). The historian and survivor of Auschwitz Erich Kulka, accused by Šebesta of collaborating with the Gestapo in Auschwitz, successfully sued the author in a Prague court; consequently, remaining copies of the book were recalled.

132. Since the November revolution the Department of the Righteous at Yad Vashem has re-

ceived many applications from survivors requesting recognition for Czech individuals who were instrumental in saving their lives.

133. The young diarist was murdered, along with other villagers, by the Gestapo on the eve of liberation. Only his parents and sister survived the war. See Miroslav Kárný and Ludvík Václavek, "Deník Otto Wolfa z let 1942–1943," in *Okresní archiv v Olomouci* (n.p., 1987), 31–41; and idem, "Otto Wolfs Tagebuch 1942–1943," in *Germanistisches Jahrbuch DDR-ČSSR* (n.p., 1987–88), 133–44.

134. "Vyhlášenie k deportáciam židov zo Slovenska," with its twenty-four signatories listed, was issued on the occasion of the forty-fifth anniversary of the deportations in the samizdat journal *Náboženstvo a současnost,* October 1987. The resolution was reproduced verbatim in the *Bulletin of the Slovak World Congress,* no. 77 (December 1987), 7. See also Yeshayahu A. Jelinek, "Slovaks and the Holocaust: Attempts at Reconciliation," *Soviet Jewish Affairs* 19, no. 1 (1989), 57–68.

135. *Resolution of the Slovak World Congress Concerning the Persecution of Jews during War-Time in [the] Slovak State as Adopted by the General Assembly of the Congress, on July 3, 1987, in Toronto* was distributed both in English and in Slovak. The *Bulletin of the Slovak World Congress,* no. 77 (December 1987) carried a revised version, signed by the president of the Slovak World Congress, Stefan B. Roman, and its secretary, Rev. Dušan Toth, in which the clause on "misguided individuals of the regime" was omitted. The same issue includes the text of the Bratislava resolution (see n. 134) on pp. 6–7.

136. For the text of the proclamation, see *Veřejnost,* December 21, 1990; and *Süddeutsche Zeitung,* December 22, 1990, January 8, 1991.

137. Eliška Hořelová, "Učit myslet," in *Kmen,* 50, týdenník Svazu českých spisovatelů, December 15, 1988. The author relies on an "orientation" poll conducted by a history teacher curious to find out how much young pupils know about the past of their native country.

138. Ibid.

139. See Kafka, "Klenot české literatury."

140. A summary of four articles originally published in *Kostnické jiskry* (Sparks of Kostnice) appeared in the *Informationsbulletin,* March 1982.

141. Skilling, *Charter 77.* See Vilém Prečan, ed., *Charta 77, 1977–1989: Od morální k demokratické revoluci* (Prague, 1990), 363–70. These documents were reproduced in English in Peter Brod, "Czechoslovakia: Jewish Legacy and Jewish Present," *Soviet Jewish Affairs* 20, no. 1 (1990), 57–65.

142. Brod, "Czechoslovakia."

143. Ibid.

144. There is a discrepancy between the official number of Jews in Czechoslovakia quoted and the number actually registered with the religious community. The figure of six thousand Czechoslovak Jews referred to in reports is but an estimate. See Peter Brod, "Czechoslovakia," *Institute of Jewish Affairs* (London), nos. 2–3 (April 1990).

145. Jiří Fiedler, *Židovské historické monumenty v Čechách a na Moravě* (Prague, 1991).

146. See Milena Janišová, ed., *Osud Židů v Protektorátu 1939–1945* (Prague, 1991). The volume contains studies by Livie Rothkirchenová, Eva Schmidt-Hartmannová, and Avigdor Dagan and a perceptive introduction by Milan Šimečka.

147. František Vnuk's "Pohlad z druhej strany," printed in *Literárny týždenník,* no. 14 (1990), was challenged by Ladislav Mňačko in "Otvorený list Františkovi Vnukovi," *Kultúrny život,* May 16, 1990, 3, 15. See also Jozef Šrámek, "Slovo k veci," *Literárny týždenník,* August 10, 1990, 1; and Ivan Kamenec, "Do dejín áno, na tabulu nie," *Práca,* August 4, 1990, 1–2.

148. For a coverage of the issue, see "Nie je tabula ako tabula," *Smena,* October 31, 1990, 1–2.

149. For the papers delivered at a related symposium in Častá in November 1990, see Valerian Bystrický, ed., *Slovensko v rokoch druhej svetovej vojny. Materiály z vedeckého sympozia* (Bratislava, 1991).

150. Ivan Kamenec, *Po stopách tragédie* (Bratislava, 1991); Eugen Bárkány and Ludovít Dojč, *Židovské náboženské obce na Slovensku* (Bratislava, 1991).

151. For reports on President Václav Havel's visit in Israel, see *Jerusalem Post,* April 28–30, 1990.

152. Reports on President Chaim Herzog's visit in the Czech and Slovak Federal Republics appeared in both the Israeli and the Czechoslovak press between October 14 and 20, 1991 (see *Jerusalem Post* and *Lidové noviny,* October 17–19, 1991).

153. Viktor Fischl, *Hovory s Janem Masarykem* (Prague, 1991); Erich Kulka, *Židé v Svobodové armádě* (Prague, 1991); Ctibor Rybár, *Židovská Praha, Glosy k dějinám a kultuře* (Prague, 1991), which contains essays by Daniel Mayer, Helena Krejčová, Jiřina Šedivová, Gabriela Veselá, and Arno Pařík; Miroslav Kárný, *"Konečné řešení": Genocida českých židů v německé protektorátní politice* (Prague, 1991).

154. See Dezider Tóth, ed., *Tragédia slovenských židov. Materiály z medzinárodného sympozia, Banská Bystrica* (Banská Bystrica, 1992).

155. For Václav Havel's New Year's address, see "The New Year in Prague," *New York Review of Books,* March 7, 1991, 19.

HUNGARY
Randolph L. Braham

During the immediate post–World War II period it was generally believed that the Holocaust and the subsequent establishment of the state of Israel would gradually put an end to the age-old scourge of anti-Semitism. The belief was based on the assumption that the traditional religious and the more modern secular and racial forms of anti-Semitism had been discredited by the Nazis' Final Solution. The belief proved naive in retrospect, as extremists of both the Right and the Left resumed the exploitation of anti-Semitism for their conflicting political and ideological interests. These extremists reinforced the traditional and modern components of anti-Semitism with distortions of the very elements on which the earlier assumption was based. Extremists of the Right and the Left, often enjoying the overt support of political parties and organized states, denigrated and distorted the Holocaust and identified Israel as an oppressive state in the service of Western imperialism. While the campaign to deny the Holocaust, which was referred to as an invention of the Jews, was spearheaded by the ultrarightists and neo-Nazis, the disguised anti-Semitic drive against Zionism and cosmopolitanism was championed by the Communists.

As a member of the Soviet bloc, Hungary participated in the anti-Zionist and anti-Israel campaign waged since 1948 and with increasing virulence after the Six-Day War of 1967. However, beginning with the 1970s, when the national Communist regime of János Kádár became increasingly reform-oriented, the anti-Zionist, anti-Israel campaign was toned down considerably. Although anti-Semitism was outlawed and the state publicly condemned all anti-Jewish manifestations during the Communist era, large segments of the population continued to harbor the prejudice. These segments looked upon Jews as "alien" elements who were chiefly responsible for the evils of Communism. Long suppressed, these anti-Jewish feelings were brought to the fore after the disintegration of the Soviet bloc in 1989–90 and the consequent dissolution of the Communist regimes. The political and socioeconomic dislocations caused by the introduction of marketization measures exacerbated ethnic and national tensions.

Although not as virulently as in the 1930s, the Jewish Question and the position of the Jews in Hungary emerged once again as major issues. After World War II the Jewish Question had become intertwined with the Holocaust, the phenomenon of Communist anti-Semitism, and the conflicting views on Israel. These issues were successfully exploited by nationalist-populist elements during the elections of 1989–90. Subtle references to Jews as "the others," the alien ethnic minority dominating the media and the professions, punctuated the rhetoric of several candidates and their chief advisers in the right-of-center spectrum of post-Communist politics. The politically explosive debate revolved, and continues to revolve, around the question whether Hungarian Jews are Magyars of the Jewish faith, as the establishment Jewish leaders and their Christian supporters hold, or merely an ethnic-national minority, as asserted by both Jewish and non-Jewish nationalists. The sources of the debate are intertwined with the history of the Jews in Hungary, especially after their emancipation in 1867.

BEFORE THE HOLOCAUST
The Golden Age

Following their emancipation, Hungarian Jews enjoyed a golden age that coincided with the lifespan of the Austro-Hungarian Dual Monarchy (1867–1918). A junior partner in the Dual Monarchy, Hungary had exclusive jurisdiction only over domestic affairs. The Jewish population of Greater Hungary grew relatively rapidly during the nineteenth century, increasing from 126,520 (1.8 percent of the country's total) in 1805 to 624,826 (4.4 percent) in 1880. It reached its peak in 1910, when it numbered 911,227, or 5 percent, of the total population of nearly 21 million.[1] Following emancipation, the Jews of Hungary took full advantage of their new opportunities and participated actively in the modernization of the country. Hungary's conservative aristocratic leadership, which preferred to pursue the activities of a bygone feudal era, encouraged the Jews to engage in commerce, industry, and the professions. The Hungarian attitude of benevolent tolerance toward the Jews was motivated not only by economic considerations but also by political and demographic concerns. The Hungarian ruling classes were eager to increase the percentage of Magyars in the polyglot Hungarian kingdom through the addition of the "Magyars of the Jewish faith," as the Jews were referred to in official statistics. The overwhelming majority of the Jews realized that emancipation required their assimilation and Magyarization, as stipulated by the Hungarian statesmen who championed their cause. They adopted the Hungarian language and culture with an enthusiasm that reflected not only gratitude for the economic and professional opportunities but also genuine patriotism. To the chagrin of many other national minorities, the Jews assumed a singularly important role in the process of Magyarization.

During the pre–World War I period, Hungary experienced an unprecedented level of economic development, in which the Jews played a leading, if not dominant, role. They were in the forefront of modernization, and partly because of the absence

201

of an indigenous middle class, they soon attained leading positions in industry, banking, business, and the professions. In the course of time a veritable *Interessen-gemeinschaft* (commonality of interests) developed between the conservative aristocratic regime and the Jewish economic magnates. Many members of the aristocracy were made silent partners in Jewish enterprises; in turn, many of the Jewish industrialists, bankers, and financiers were ennobled, eagerly adopting the mores and practices of the aristocracy. Of course, although they played a pivotal role in the capitalist enterprises and the professions, these Jews represented only a very small percentage of the Jewish community. Most Jews barely eked out a living as artisans, laborers, or small businessmen. They were unhindered in the pursuit of their religious life. Unable to unite after their emancipation in 1867, the community was split into three congregational factions that survived until the Holocaust. As a result of this split, many large Jewish communities had affiliates of all three congregations.[2]

The Jews of Hungary had many reasons to be grateful besides the newly won civil liberties and economic opportunities. They were above all cognizant of the protection provided by the Hungarian regime against the perennial threat of anti-Semitism. While anti-Semitic disturbances and demonstrations did occur even during this period, they were primarily local and sporadic in character. One such incident was the notorious Tiszaeszlár ritual murder case of 1882. The anti-Jewish agitations of renowned anti-Semites such as Győző (Victor) Istóczy and Iván Simonyi in the 1880s had a greater impact abroad than in Hungary.[3]

The golden age of Hungarian Jewry came to an end with the disintegration of the Austro-Hungarian Dual Monarchy in 1918 following the defeat of the Central Powers. The dismemberment of Hungary also entailed the splitting of the Hungarian Jewish community in accordance with the new political map of Europe. About four hundred thousand Jews were left in what came to be known as Trianon Hungary, and a somewhat larger number were divided between the successor states of Czechoslovakia, Romania, and Yugoslavia.

The Interwar Period

Following several interim governments, including a short-lived dictatorship of the proletariat, a counterrevolutionary regime headed by Admiral Miklós Horthy was installed in Trianon Hungary in August 1919. This new conservative nationalist regime began its rule by unleashing its fury against suspected supporters of the dictatorship of the proletariat, above all the Jews. Although the overwhelming majority of Jews had opposed the Communist dictatorship headed by Béla Kun and probably suffered proportionately more than the rest of the population, popular opinion tended to attach the blame for the abortive dictatorship to Jewry as a whole. This attitude was largely owing to the high visibility of Communists of Jewish origin in the proletarian dictatorship, and it was reinforced by the relentless anti-Semitic propaganda and anti-Jewish agitation of the counterrevolutionary forces. The terror of these forces dwarfed the excesses of the Communists in magnitude and ferocity, claiming thousands of Jewish lives.

The real strongholds of power supporting the counterrevolutionary regime were the secret and semiclandestine patriotic associations and paramilitary organizations.[4] Arrogating to themselves the power and responsibility to defend "the Magyar cause," these associations and organizations became the chief vehicle for the spread of the virulent seeds of revisionism, irredentism, and above all anti-Semitism. Following the absorption of the other major national minorities into the successor states, the Jews emerged as Hungary's most vulnerable minority group. With the transformation of the country into a basically homogeneous and ethnically integrated state, the Jews lost their statistical importance to the cause of Magyardom. As in the Third Reich, despite their patriotic posture, after the end of World War I they became convenient scapegoats for most of the country's misfortunes, including its socioeconomic dislocations. Hungary was the first country in postwar Europe to become preoccupied with the Jewish Question. In flagrant violation of the Minorities Protection Treaty, which it had approved rather willingly because of its concern for the Magyars in the successor states, Hungary adopted the first anti-Jewish legislation in post–World War I Europe. On September 22, 1920, it enacted Law No. XXV, the so-called *numerus clausus* act, which restricted the admission of Jews into the institutions of higher learning.

Although anti-Semitism was toned down under the government of Count István Bethlen (1921–32), it became a basic feature of all subsequent governments. The anti-Jewish campaign took an ominous turn with the coming to power of Gyula Gömbös (1932–36), a leader of the radical Right. A Germanophile, Gömbös was responsible for charting a nationalist revisionist course for Hungary that emulated many of the domestic and foreign policies of the Third Reich. In pursuit of his policy objectives, he encouraged the development of rightist radicalism by supporting pro-Nazi movements and press organs and by appointing other Germanophiles to top government and military positions.

The anti-Jewish campaign became institutionalized in early 1938, when the government of Kálmán Darányi announced a program for limiting the Jews' influence in the economy and the professions. With the blessing and support of the Christian churches, the Hungarian Parliament adopted Law No. XV, the so-called First Anti-Jewish Act, in May 1938. A year later it adopted the even more restrictive Law No. IV—the Second Anti-Jewish Act—which included a detailed and complicated Nazi-style definition of who was Jewish. That same year Hungary introduced the first in a series of legislative acts regulating the military-related forced labor service of Jews. In the summer of 1941 Hungary adopted Law No. XV—the Third Anti-Jewish Act—which in many respects was identical with the Nuremberg Laws.

The adoption of the major anti-Jewish laws coincided with Hungary's successful pursuit of its revisionist policies calculated to reacquire the territories it had lost under the Treaty of Trianon (1920). With the support of the Axis powers, Hungary acquired the Upper Province (Felvidék) and Carpatho-Ruthenia (Kárpátalja) from Czechoslovakia in November 1938 and March 1939, respectively, Northern Transylvania from Romania in August 1940, and the so-called Délvidék, including the Bácska, from Yugoslavia in April 1941. The territorial expansion of 1938–41 almost doubled the Jewish population of Hungary.

The World Reacts to the Holocaust

The Jewish Community on the Eve of the Holocaust

When Hungary joined the Third Reich in the war against the Soviet Union in June 1941 it had a Jewish population of 725,007. Of these, 400,981 lived in Trianon Hungary (184,453 in Budapest) and 324,026 lived in the acquired territories: approximately 68,000 in the Upper Province, 78,000 in Carpatho-Ruthenia, 164,000 in Northern Transylvania, and 14,000 in the Délvidék. In addition, there were about 100,000 converts or other Christians identified as Jews under the laws then in effect.[5] The Jews of Trianon Hungary were mostly assimilated, conservative (also referred to as Reform, Neolog, or congressional) in their religious orientation, and thoroughly middle class in character, mentality, and class attitude. In contrast, the overwhelming majority of the Jews in the territories acquired from Czechoslovakia and Romania were Orthodox, many belonging to various Hasidic sects. The Jews of Carpatho-Ruthenia were mostly Yiddish-speaking, while the Jews of Northern Transylvania and, to a lesser extent, those of the Upper Province identified themselves as Hungarian in language and culture.

During the years preceding the Holocaust, Hungarian Jewry had a well-developed network of religious, educational, health, and welfare organizations. These were generally organized by and operated under the auspices of the three major congregations then active in Hungary: (1) the Neolog, representing primarily the assimilated Jews who had adopted the modern, progressive, and innovative ecclesiastical practices spearheaded by the large Jewish community of Budapest; (2) the Orthodox, made up largely of those who rejected total assimilation and insisted on strict adherence to the traditional values and practices of Judaism; (3) the Status Quo Ante (or simply Status Quo), made up of Jews who adopted a position between those of the two major groups. A little more than 60 percent of the congregations in Hungary and the territories were Orthodox, close to 31 percent were Neolog, and the remainder were Status Quo. Each congregation was associated with a central body and, theoretically at least, operated under its guidance. The Neolog congregations were subordinated to the National Bureau of the Jews of Hungary (Magyarországi Izraeliták Országos Irodája), the Orthodox functioned under the auspices of the Central Bureau of the Autonomous Orthodox Jewish Community of Hungary (Magyarországi Autonom Orthodox Izraelita Hitfelekezet Központi Irodája), and the Status Quo operated under the direction of the National League of Status Quo Ante Jewish Congregations of Hungary (Magyarországi Statusquo Ante Izraelita Hitközségek Országos Szövetsége). The top officials of the central bodies were the recognized national leaders of Hungarian Jewry.

THE HOLOCAUST ERA

After Hungary's entrance into World War II in June 1941, the fate of Hungarian Jewry became intertwined with that of the conservative aristocratic leadership of the country. Although the Hungarian Jews were deprived of basic civil rights and liberties and subjected to harsh economic measures, most of them continued to enjoy the physical protection of the Hungarian government until the country's Occupation by the Germans on March 19, 1944. However, even during this pre-Occupation period Hungarian Jewry suffered more than sixty thousand casualties. Approximately forty thousand of these were labor servicemen deployed in Ukraine and in Serbia. In July and August 1941 the Hungarian police and gendarmerie rounded up between sixteen thousand and eighteen thousand "alien" Jews—those they arbitrarily identified as not having Hungarian citizenship—and deported them to the vicinity of Kamenets-Podolsk, where, together with some six thousand local Jews, they were murdered by the SS. This *Aktion* constituted the first five-figure massacre of World War II. In January and February 1942 Hungarian military units rounded up and killed close to a thousand Jews in Újvidék (Novi Sad) and other communities in the Délvidék. Also, a number of ultrarightist politicians and officers conspired with the Nazis in an attempt to "solve" the Jewish Question in Hungary. These maneuvers, like the anti-Jewish excesses of the military, took place without the knowledge, let alone the consent, of the responsible leaders of the government.[6] Prime Minister Miklós Kállay consistently rejected the German demands and pressures that the country adopt the Final Solution and attempted to extricate Hungary from the Axis alliance starting in the fall of 1943. It was the Third Reich's resolve to prevent Hungary from emulating Italy, which by that time had turned against its former ally, that sealed the fate of the conservative aristocratic regime and of Hungarian Jewry.

The Holocaust

The Jews of Hungary were destroyed on the eve of Allied victory, after surviving the first four and a half years of the war. The last relatively intact Jewish community in Nazi-dominated Europe was liquidated in a swift and ruthless campaign launched immediately after the German occupation. The Nazis and their Hungarian accomplices were successful in achieving their ideological objectives largely because of the confluence of several factors. For one thing, the Occupation enabled the German and Hungarian Nazi elements to unite and coordinate their anti-Jewish efforts. Foremost in this drive were the SS units attached to the Eichmann Sonderkommando and the Hungarian Nazi elements associated with László Baky and László Endre, the two under secretaries of state in the newly installed quisling government of Döme Sztójay. Although the Germans exercised dominant power, especially during the first four months of the Occupation, they permitted Hungary to retain a facade of sovereignty, which, from the rightists' point of view, had a positive impact on the attitude of the population. Influenced by the virulent anti-Semitic propaganda of the counterrevolutionary era, the Hungarian masses witnessed the anti-Jewish operations with passivity. While a relatively small number actively opposed the Nazis and some even risked their lives to save Jews, a proportionately large number of Hungarians collaborated with the Germans for ideological reasons or to advance their private economic interests.

The decisive factor in the destruction of Hungarian Jewry was the wholehearted cooperation of the Sztójay government, which was appointed on March 22, 1944, with the consent of Miklós Horthy, the regent of Hungary. Legitimacy for the anti-Jewish drive was provided by the commitments the Hungarian head of state had made during his meetings with Hitler at Schloss Klessheim on March 18 and 19, 1944. Under great pressure from the Germans and eager to safeguard the national interests of Hungary as he understood them, Horthy consented to, among other things, the transfer to the Reich of hundreds of thousands of "Jewish workers." Toward this end, the Sztójay government placed the instruments of state power—the police, gendarmerie, and civil service—at the disposal of the German and Hungarian "specialists" entrusted with the implementation of the Final Solution.

Since time was of the essence (in March and April 1944 the Soviet forces were about to cross the Dniester into neighboring Romania), the SS and their Hungarian accomplices quickly implemented their plans. The legal facade of the anti-Jewish operations was assured through an avalanche of decrees at the national and local levels. The first three major phases of the Final Solution—the isolation, expropriation, and ghettoization of the Jews—were implemented simultaneously throughout the country within less than two months. The final two phases—the entrainment and deportation of the Jews—were carried out serially in accordance with plans and schedules worked out in Budapest and Vienna in April and early May 1944. Hungary was divided into six zones of anti-Jewish operations, coinciding with the gendarmerie districts of the country. The entrainment and deportation drive began on May 15, 1944. Because of military and geopolitical considerations, the northeastern parts of the country, including Carpatho-Ruthenia, were selected as Zone I. The Jews from Northern Transylvania (Zone II) were to be deported next, followed by those from northern Hungary (Zone III), southern Hungary (Zone IV), and Transdanubia (Dunántul) (Zone V). It was in the midst of the operations in Zone VI, which included Budapest, that Horthy decided to halt the deportations, on July 7. Despite Horthy's decision, the anti-Jewish operations continued for two more days, resulting in the liquidation of the Jewish communities surrounding the capital. Thus, by July 9, 1944, all of Hungary except Budapest had become *judenrein* (free of Jews). In the countryside only the relatively few exempted Jews and the Jews working in labor service companies remained.[7]

The national leaders of Hungarian Jewry were totally unprepared for the disaster. Although they were aware of the tragic fate that had befallen the Jewish communities of Nazi-dominated Europe, they failed to take any precautionary measures. They continued to rely on the physical protection the conservative-aristocratic regime had provided during the first four and a half years of the war. Following the arrest and internment of the leaders of this regime during the first days of the Occupation, the Jewish community became totally defenseless. The Jewish Council of Budapest, the central leadership group organized by the SS, became a helpless pawn in the hands of the Nazis. While the council did what it could to avert or at least alleviate the draconic measures the Nazis and their Hungarian accomplices were imposing upon the Jews, it was basically helpless, if not harmful. A few leaders organized various rescue schemes by dealing with the SS or the Hungarians, but while they managed to save a few thousand Jews, they could not prevent or delay the implementation of the Final Solution.

After a short period of respite following Horthy's halting of the deportations, the situation of Hungarian Jewry worsened dramatically again on October 15, 1944. In the wake of Horthy's bungled attempt to extricate Hungary from the war, the ultrarightist Arrow Cross (Nyilas) Party of Ferenc Szálasi acquired power with the aid of the Germans. The ordeal of the Jews of Budapest, including the death marches to the borders of the Reich, the rampage of the Nyilas, and the horrors of the ghetto, came to an end only with the Soviet liberation of Budapest in January and February 1945.[8]

The Nyilas era was also the background for the rescue activities of the neutral countries' representatives in Budapest, including Raoul Wallenberg of Sweden and Charles Lutz of Switzerland and the small but heroic Jewish resistance movement. Wallenberg and Lutz saved thousands of Jews by providing them with protective passes, food, and shelter. Most of these Jews were placed in special "protected buildings" that were designated by the authorities as belonging to an international ghetto. Similar protection was provided for many thousands of Jews by the International Red Cross and the Nunciature of the Vatican. Many hundreds of Jews, especially children, were rescued by courageous members of Christian religious orders, who hid, fed, and protected them in their convents, monasteries, missions, schools, and institutes.[9]

The Hungarians offered practically no resistance to the Germans. The local resistance movement was almost nonexistent, late in formation, and basically ineffective. By far the most heroic chapter of resistance was written by the Halutzim, the young Jewish pioneers, who manufactured and distributed false Christian papers and, dressed in Nazi or Nyilas uniforms, saved many Jews from certain death.[10]

While Szálasi's Hungary remained an ally of Germany to the end, the country was liberated in stages by the advancing Soviet and Romanian troops.[11] The eastern parts of the country, including Northern Transylvania, were liberated in the fall of 1944, and by April 4, 1945, the last units of the German and Hungarian Nazi forces were pushed out of Hungary.[12]

THE POST-HOLOCAUST ERA
The Interim Period, 1945–1948

As the Soviet and Romanian forces advanced across Hungary, the devastation suffered by the Jewish communities during the German occupation became painfully evident. The padlocked and looted homes, shops, farms, factories, and offices; the desecrated and demolished synagogues; the pilfered libraries and educational and cultural institutions; the overturned tombstones; the eerie absence of Jews—all served as vivid reminders of the fury with which the Nazis and their Hungarian accomplices had carried out the Final Solution. The Holocaust, including the excesses of the pre-Occupation era, claimed close to 565,000 lives in Hungary. Of these, approximately 267,000 were from the areas annexed by Hungary between 1938 and 1941. Of the approximately 298,000 victims in Trianon Hungary, more than 100,000 were from Budapest.[13]

The first survivors to return to their former communities were the labor servicemen liberated within Hungary. They were followed almost seven months later

by the relatively few Jews who survived the concentration and death camps and by
the labor servicemen who had been captured and treated as prisoners of war by the
Soviet forces. In the first months of the postliberation period the returnees were preoccupied with the day-to-day problem of survival. Many of them still suffered from
severe camp-related mental and physical disabilities. The handful of survivors from
the smaller towns and villages gravitated to the larger cities, where they participated
in the reestablishment of Jewish communal organizations.[14] By 1946 the number of
active Jewish congregations seemed to be a hopeful sign for the possibility of a renewal of Jewish life in a democratically restructured Hungary.[15]

The surviving Jews of Hungary regained their legal rights under the terms of the
Armistice agreement of January 20, 1945. Two months later the Provisional National
Government (Ideiglenes Nemzeti Kormány) repealed all the anti-Jewish laws and
decrees.[16] Sadly, the survivors' hopes for the revitalization of their lives and communities were soon dashed. Their expectations for restitution and indemnification
failed to materialize because of the financial and economic ruin of the country; the
reluctance of Christians to return the apartments, properties, and enterprises confiscated or stolen from the Jews; the basic apathy of the central and local governmental authorities; and, above all, the gradual Sovietization of the political and economic system. Guided by considerations of power and social change, the leftist forces
urged the survivors to show understanding toward Christians who had benefited
from anti-Jewish activities and to refrain from "claiming privileges on the basis of
former suffering."[17] The frictions caused by the conflicting interests at a time of grave
economic dislocation led to many anti-Semitic outbursts. The campaign against
"black marketeers"—the term often became a euphemism for Jews—was exploited,
especially by Communist elements, in pursuit of narrow political objectives. Serious
anti-Semitic incidents took place in February 1946 in the working-class centers of
Ózd, Sajószentpéter, Szegvár, and Tótkomlós, and virtual pogroms broke out in Kun-
madaras in May and in Diósgyőr in July, claiming several casualties.

During the postwar transitional period Hungarian attitudes and reactions to the
Holocaust were shaped largely by the revelations emerging from the many national
and local war crimes trials and by the accounts of survivors and anti-Nazi Hungarians. The tragedy of individual Jewish communities in Trianon Hungary was exposed
in the war crimes trials held between 1945 and 1948 under the auspices of people's
tribunals in Budapest and in various county seats. Among the accused were the local
and county government officials as well as the military, police, and gendarmerie officers involved in the expropriation, ghettoization, and deportation of the Jews.[18] Details of the Final Solution in Hungary as a whole were revealed in several major trials
held in Budapest between 1945 and 1947. By far the most important of these was the
trial of the so-called deportation trio, László Baky, László Endre, and Andor Jaross,
the top leaders of the ministry of the interior.[19] These officials, who were generally
identified as the persons primarily responsible for the destruction of Hungarian
Jewry, were among 146 individuals executed for war crimes and crimes against humanity in Hungary.[20]

During this period, many literary accounts dealing with aspects of the Nazi era were published. These works were predominantly memoirs written by survivors and anti-Nazi Hungarians. Most of the accounts detailed the authors' experiences in the ghettos, concentration camps, and labor service companies.[21] Frequently, personal narratives were interwoven with accounts of the tragedy that befell particular communities. The majority of the memoirs and reports by the persons involved—former communal leaders, Hungarian statesmen and church leaders, and anti-Nazi elements, including resistance fighters—were subjective, selectively documented, and basically self-serving.[22] The same can be said of the memoirs of the former members of the Jewish councils, especially the Jewish Council of Budapest. The wartime leaders of Hungarian Jewry felt a desperate need to counter the accusations of collaboration that were leveled against them after liberation.[23] Similar concerns motivated the heads of the Christian churches, who were particularly sensitive to the accusation that not only had they supported the major anti-Jewish laws of the pre-Occupation era, but they had failed to take meaningful measures to help the Jews during the deportations. It was widely believed in postwar Hungary that the masses had been passive during the Holocaust primarily because church leaders had failed to provide moral leadership. It was largely in order to improve this negative image that the first accounts of the wartime role of the churches were published after the war. The impetus and guidelines were provided by the heads of the Catholic and Protestant Churches.[24]

The first historical accounts of the Holocaust are rather unsystematic and journalistic in approach. They are largely based on the records of war crimes trials and on the documentation prepared by the Hungarian government for the Paris peace treaty negotiations of 1946 and 1947. Despite their shortcomings, these historical accounts, most of which incorporate statistical data and reproductions of documents, have proved extremely useful and have been used extensively by those interested in the Holocaust in Hungary.[25] Perhaps the most perceptive and seminal analysis of the Jewish situation in the early post-Holocaust era is an essay by István Bibó, one of the most respected scholars and statesmen of postwar Hungary.[26] An eminent sociologist, Bibó demonstrated in an analytical fashion the responsibility of the Hungarian people and government for the tragedy of Hungarian Jewry and intimated that the postwar anti-Semitic manifestations were partially triggered by the fact that a relatively large number of Jews identified themselves with the Soviet-imposed Communist system.

The Stalinist Era

Four months after the establishment of the state of Israel in May 1948, the Soviet Union launched a campaign against cosmopolitanism and Zionism that soon engulfed the entire Soviet bloc. The start of the campaign coincided with the Stalinist transformation of Hungary, which had a devastating effect on the entire nation, including the Jewish community. The remnant Jewish communities, like the other religious denominations, were placed under the jurisdiction of a Communist Party–controlled state agency. Jewish communal life was strictly regulated, and contact between the communities as well as with foreign Jewish communities, especially those in Israel, was brought to a virtual end. Within a relatively short time, Judaism and Jewish culture were severely restricted, if not obliterated. "Bourgeois Jews," persecuted on the basis of both class and religion, were deported to penal camps. At the height of the anti-Semitic campaign in the Soviet Union, which involved, among other things, the execution of some of the best-known Yiddish artists and writers and the indictment of several highly reputable Jewish doctors for their alleged involvement in an anti-Kremlin plot in 1952, the Hungarian Communist authorities were engaged in a sinister campaign against some of the top leaders of Hungarian Jewry. Acting in complicity with the KGB, the Hungarian Communists arrested and accused these Jewish leaders of involvement in, *inter alia,* the murder of Raoul Wallenberg. The aim was obviously not only to advance well-calculated domestic political objectives but also to divert attention from the Soviet Union's responsibility for the disappearance of the Swedish diplomat.[27] The foreign-policy motivations of the anti-Jewish drive were also reflected in the criminal prosecution of Zionists and the arrest and expulsion of the director of the American Joint Distribution Committee.[28]

In the face of the Communists' anti-Jewish position and curtailment of emigration, many Jews tried to improve their chances by total assimilation and acculturation, concealing their identity and historical past even from their children. As a result, many young people of Jewish background grew up in ignorance of the Holocaust or of their religious and cultural heritage.

The drive against Zionism and cosmopolitanism was frequently accompanied by a distortion of the Holocaust. The tragedy of the Jews as a distinct historical phenomenon was usually downplayed, distorted, or at best hardly referred to even in textbooks. Although the Hungarian authorities played a crucial role in the destruction of the Jews during the German occupation era, the tendency was—and remained—to blame exclusively the Germans for this tragedy.

The Post-Stalinist Era

After Stalin's death in March 1953 the situation of Hungarian Jewry, like the fundamental attitudes toward the Holocaust, remained basically unchanged until the late 1950s. The regime of János Kádár, which was installed after the crushing of the Hungarian uprising of October and November 1956, gradually reversed the Stalinist course. The new liberal program of national Communism had a considerable impact on the remaining Jewish community of Hungary. At the time Hungary had approximately eighty thousand to one hundred thousand Jews, the second largest Jewish community in the area after the Soviet Union. Although still strictly controlled, communal life experienced a slow but steady reinvigoration, and interest in the Holocaust was rekindled among some professionals. Under the initiative of mostly Communist Jewish intellectuals in academia and archival institutions, several valuable Holocaust-related documentary collections were published under the aegis of the Jewish community of Budapest, chiefly with the financial support of the Conference on Jewish Material Claims Against Germany.[29] Along with monographs, plays, poetry anthologies, and fictionalized accounts about the Holocaust, these collections, along with numerous books and articles on the same subject published during the immediate postwar period, were listed and annotated in the first comprehensive bibliography on the Holocaust issued in Hungary.[30] During the post-Stalinist period there appeared autobiographical, fictionalized accounts of the Holocaust and several anthologies containing some of the most beautiful lyrical poems emanating from the pens of child survivors of the Holocaust.[31]

The situation for the Jewish community changed for the worse after the Six-Day War of 1967, when Hungary joined the other nations of the Soviet bloc (except Romania) in breaking diplomatic relations with Israel. The anti-Zionist campaign acquired new virulence, which was reinforced in the wake of Hungary's vote in support of the 1975 U.N. resolution proclaiming that Zionism was racism. The exacerbation of anti-Semitism and the increase in the number and severity of anti-Semitic manifestations, coupled with the pro–Palestine Liberation Organization and relentless anti-Israel bias of the government,[32] had a great impact on many Jews, especially the second generation of Holocaust survivors. Having lost faith in the ideology and the system they had once embraced for idealistic and pragmatic reasons, they began to assert their Jewish identity with increasing boldness and developed an active interest in Jewish affairs in general and the Holocaust in particular.

During the 1970s, Hungary, guided by increasingly reform-oriented Communists, emerged in the forefront of the Soviet bloc nations not only in its political and economic experimentations but also in the relaxation of its controls over the airing of controversial issues, including those relating to the Holocaust. The German occupation, the Hungarian involvement in the Axis war effort, and the wartime tragedy of the Jews were allowed to be treated with ever greater frankness, although the officially sponsored major historical works and school textbooks continued to downplay or generalize the Holocaust.[33] In contrast to the memoirs of the immediate postwar era, the new crop of personal narratives by Hungarian political and military figures tended to evaluate the country's role and performance during the war with greater conviction and objectivity.[34] The belletristic literature of this period usually treated the Holocaust in the context of Hungary's tragic involvement in World War II. Like many of the earlier publications in this genre, these works consisted primarily of autobiographical, fictionalized accounts by child survivors of the Holocaust of life in the ghettos and concentration camps.[35]

The persistence of the Jewish Question and the increasingly overt manifestations of anti-Semitism aroused the interest of several Christian intellectuals. Foremost among these was the late György Száraz, a well-known journalist and literary critic whose perceptive historical observations and honest assessment of anti-Semitism and its linkage with the Holocaust rivaled those made almost a generation before by István Bibó.[36] The wartime attitudes and reactions of the Christian church leaders, especially those of Jusztinián Cardinal Serédi and Bishop László Ravasz, were subjected to severe criticism by a number of Christian authors, including church figures.[37] Several of these documented exposés appeared, as did other Holocaust-related articles, in such influential journals as *Kritika* (Criticism), *Kortárs* (The Contemporary), and *Vigilia*, the organ of the Actio Catholica.

Publications on the Holocaust in general and the tragedy of Hungarian Jewry in particular continued to be written primarily by Jewish authors. In the second half of the 1970s and the early 1980s there appeared a relatively large number of fictionalized and semidocumentary accounts of life in the ghettos and concentration camps.[38] During the same period numerous articles and studies were published in various central and provincial journals dealing with many aspects of the Holocaust, including Jewish resistance.[39] By the early 1980s the Holocaust-related literary and documentary output lent itself to the writing of comprehensive literary and historical essays.[40] These appeared almost concurrently with the release of several films dealing with various aspects of the Holocaust in an artistically sensitive though basically trivialized manner.[41]

Hungary's literary, artistic, and scholarly output on the Holocaust, which was unrivaled in the other Soviet bloc nations in the 1970s, experienced further growth in the 1980s. But so did interest in the Jewish Question, which for many years had been relegated to the Communists' political closet. The political and socioeconomic problems of Communist-ruled Hungarian society began to agitate both Jewish and Christian reform-minded intellectuals. Jewish intellectuals were particularly concerned with the predicament of the Jewish community. A Jewish dissident group, Sálom, challenged the alleged servile position of the Jewish establishment's leadership and severely criticized its consistent alignment with the Communist regime's domestic and foreign policies. The Jewish dissidents were particularly critical of the community's press organ, the *Új Élet* (New Life), for scrupulously following the official line on Israel and the Holocaust.[42]

The debate on the Jewish Question, which was usually intertwined with discussions of the Holocaust and the phenomena of overt and covert anti-Semitism in a supposedly egalitarian Communist society, also disturbed a stratum of the Christian intellectual and governmental elite that feared its impact on Hungary's image abroad. These issues were crystallized in a series of conferences both in Hungary and abroad in which noted Hungarian scholars took part. The studies emanating from these conferences are among the most up-to-date and fully documented reference works on the subject.[43] They were complemented by collections of essays by well-known experts on various aspects of the Jewish Question in Hungary.[44] Indicative of renewed interest in Judaism and Jewish affairs was the establishment in 1987 of a Center for Jewish Studies in Budapest under the auspices of the Hungarian Academy of Sciences.[45]

Interest in the Holocaust and in Hungary's role during the Nazi era continued to grow during the second half of the 1980s, especially among Jews. This interest was partially sustained by the airing of new Western-style television documentary programs[46] and the publication of a series of interviews with both German and Hungarian *dramatis personae*.[47] Among the highlights of the late eighties was the publication in Hungarian translation of several Holocaust-related works originally published in the West.[48]

The Post-Communist Era

Hungary was in the forefront of the political and socioeconomic reforms that brought about the disintegration of the Soviet bloc in 1989–90. Led by reform-oriented Communists, the Hungarian government adopted a series of innovative domestic- and foreign-policy measures during the late eighties. Among other things, it expanded civil liberties, laid the foundations for a mixed economic system by encouraging marketization, and opened its borders with Austria. The dramatic liberalization and democratization measures that were adopted during that short period engendered fundamental systemic changes within the country, including the establishment of a multiparty parliamentary system. These changes also had two conflicting results with respect to the status of the approximately eighty thousand Jews still living in the country and public attitudes toward them. On the positive side, the new political system encouraged a resurgence of Jewish life. This resurgence was reflected in the establishment or rejuvenation of a multitude of cultural, religious, and political organizations.[49] The rising Jewish pride and national consciousness were reinforced by Hungary's reestablishment of diplomatic relations with Israel and the consequent development of economic and cultural ties. Many assimilated and acculturated Jews, especially children and grandchildren of Holocaust survivors, have reasserted their identity as Jews, eager to revive and preserve Jewish life and values. They have become particularly concerned with controversial issues that formerly were treated as taboo and have begun to confront openly the explosive issue of Communist anti-Semitism, the discriminatory policies of the interwar governments, and the many ramifications of the tragedy that befell the Jews during the Nazi era.

Although the government's democratization measures encouraged the development of basic civil liberties, they also brought to the surface long-suppressed ethnic and national animosities, including anti-Semitism. The political stresses and economic dislocations engendered by the restructuring of Hungarian society revived the Jewish Question and anti-Semitism as convenient instruments of domestic politics. The nationalist-populist reaction to forty-five years of Soviet-guided Communism in some cases acquired a xenophobic, anti-Jewish coloration. While extremist elements of the Right still operate only on the outer fringes of domestic politics, in the vein of the Nazis they have blended anti-Communism and anti-Semitism into a potentially explosive mixture.

The anti-Semitic exploitation of the linkage between Jews and Communism is deeply rooted in the history of the twentieth century. For one thing, a proportionately large number of secular Jews embraced Communism in the mistaken belief that it offered a solution to the age-old scourge of anti-Semitism. This was particularly true during the Nazi era, when Hungary was allied with the Third Reich. As had happened in 1919, many Communists of Jewish origin took highly visible leadership positions in the Moscow-dominated Communist regime after World War II. Although these leaders were largely purged from leading central and local party and state positions and the Jews suffered perhaps more than any other group under the Communists after 1948, when Hungary joined the other Soviet bloc nations in a vicious anti-Zionist and anti-Israel campaign, many Hungarians continue to cling to this nefarious linkage theory. A major source of the bigotry stems from the differing, if not diametrically opposed, perceptions by Jews and anti-Communist Christians of the military and political consequences of the Nazi defeat. Although it was natural for all surviving Jews, as well as anti-Nazi Hungarians, to look upon the Red Army as liberators from the long nightmare of Nazism, many Hungarians looked upon the Soviet forces as conquerors and oppressors of their nation.

The alleged linkage between Communists and Jews and the general Western liberal orientation of Jewish intellectuals were skillfully exploited during the elections of 1990, the first free elections held in Hungary in more than forty years. During the political campaigns, several prominent writers supporting the Hungarian Democratic Forum (Magyar Demokrata Fórum), the right-of-center party in Hungary's new political spectrum, successfully exploited these perceptions, which were widely held in the smaller towns and in the countryside. References to "alien" elements controlling the media and playing a disproportionately prominent role in academia and the professions in the capital—a clear reference to Jews—were subtly interwoven with discussions of the political and socioeconomic issues troubling the post-Communist society.[50] Although the leaders of the party, including József Antall,[51] distanced themselves from these views and rightly rejected the accusations of anti-Semitism that were leveled against them, they benefited from the campaign by gaining the plurality they needed to form democratic Hungary's first post-Communist coalition government.[52]

In the months that followed the inauguration of the Antall government in May 1990, the number and intensity of anti-Semitic manifestations increased in the wake of the socioeconomic dislocations caused by the new administration's efforts to create a market economy. In Hungary as elsewhere in post-Communist Eastern Europe, the anger of many people suffering from the ravages of unemployment, inflation, and general impoverishment has been directed against the Jews. Scapegoating has been skillfully manipulated by anti-Semitic elements, who blame the Jews for the current and past ills of the country, especially those ills that are associated with the Communist era. In contrast to the last few years of socialist rule, when anti-Semitic incidents were mostly on the order of verbal abuse of Jews at certain soccer games, more recent occurrences were ominous. They involved the desecration of cemeteries and synagogues, the distribution of Nazi-style leaflets and hate letters, and anti-Jewish incitement in newly established rightist press organs in tones reminiscent of the interwar period.[53] The government often explained its reluctance to employ effective countermeasures to safeguard the fragile democratic system, as its critics have requested, by saying that it was committed to the protection of civil liberties for all.

In the midst of these anti-Semitic incidents, the debate on Jewish identity surfaced with even greater intensity than in the recent past, revealing the considerable chasm that continues to exist in Jewish-Christian relations in Hungary. The debate continues to revolve around the question whether the Hungarian Jews are in fact Magyars, differing from their Christian counterparts only in their religious affiliation, or merely a tolerated ethnic minority. It highlights the basic shortcomings of assimilation as well as the failure of the Hungarians to come to grips with the Holocaust. These weaknesses are clearly reflected in the local and national press as well as in the official positions held by responsible political and governmental figures.

The controversy over the Jewish Question in general and the Holocaust in particular remained in the public eye through the publication of articles—and reader reactions—in both well-established and recently founded newspapers and magazines, including the *Népszabadság* (People's Freedom), the former organ of the discredited Communist Party;[54] the *Magyar Nemzet* (Hungarian Nation), once the country's most influential daily; and the lesser-known *Hitel* (Credit), edited by a former prominent figure of the Communist Party. The controversy became particularly venomous following the publication of a statement by Sándor Csoóri, one of Hungary's most celebrated poets and writers. In the second installment of his semiautobiographical series "Nappali hold" (Daytime Moon), the Kossuth Prize–winning poet stated:

> The possibility for a spiritual-psychological welding [of Jews and non-Jews] came to an end with the Soviet Republic, the Horthy era, and especially the Holocaust. Naturally there always were and will be [Jews like] Antal Szerb, Radnóti, György Sárközi, István Vas, György Harag, Ottó Orbán, György Konrád, György Faludy, and Tamás Zala, but one feels ever more resolutely nowadays that reverse assimilationist tendencies are surfacing in the country: liberal Hungarian Jewry wishes to "assimilate" the Magyars in style and thought.[55]

This statement, which implies that the Magyars are being threatened by the Jews, evoked an immediate and unusually vociferous reaction on the part of many Jewish and non-Jewish writers and intellectuals, causing quite a furor within the Hungarian Writers' Association (Magyar Irók Szövetsége).[56] The controversy continued to agitate the intellectual community[57] and became intertwined with the issue of the Holocaust as a major factor underlying Hungarian-Jewish relations. Taking advantage of the new freedoms, anti-Semites began to air views they previously dared whisper only among themselves. Their nefarious interpretations of the linkage between the Jews' suffering at the hands of the Nazis and their alleged destructive role in the postwar Communist era found ready outlets in the press. According to one representative of this group, the Jews came to power in postwar Hungary with the aid of Russian arms and throughout the Communist era waged a campaign of "holy vengeance" against Magyars in retaliation for the suffering Jews had endured earlier—"the anti-Jewish laws, the frequently mentioned 'Holocaust' that aimed at their physical destruction, and the deportation of 200,000 Hungarian Jews." The distortion of the deportation figure is coupled with the accusation that the Jews were responsible for the ills of the country and that they had, as part of their thirst for vengeance, waged a psychological and spiritual campaign against the Magyars for more than forty years.[58]

In another, not atypical article the linkage between Jews and Bolshevism and the correlation between anti-Communism and anti-Semitism are analyzed in the context of the alleged threats presented by Jewish internationalism, cosmopolitanism, and liberalism to the national integrity of the Hungarian state and nation. The polemical analysis is interwoven with a scathing condemnation of the allegedly excessive preoccupation with the Holocaust. The yearly Jewish communal events commemorating the Holocaust and the media depiction of Holocaust themes are characterized as constituting a propaganda campaign against the non-Jewish community. The author finds this to be especially objectionable in light of the passivity with which the world views the alleged current "genocidal policies" against Hungarian minorities living in Czechoslovakia (later Slovakia), Romania, and Yugoslavia. There is clearly an attempt to denigrate and distort the Holocaust by equating the physical extermination of the Jews with the cultural and political plight of Hungarian minorities living in the neighboring states, deplorable as that may be.[59]

It is difficult to determine how widely these views are shared by the population at large. One hopes that they are effectively counterbalanced by the resolute and unequivocal public condemnation of anti-Semitism by many responsible political and church leaders. Several among these leaders also took up the issue of Jewish-Christian reconciliation, confronting but not yet fully coming to grips with the Holocaust. Among the first to call for such a reconciliation was József Tornai, the noted poet. Speaking at the first national convention of the Hungarian Democratic Forum on March 12, 1989, Tornai declared that one cannot—and must not—enter into a debate about the Holocaust and that the time had come to share in the mourning for the victims. However, he dismissed the idea of an apology to the Jews, arguing that the current generation cannot assume guilt for the Holocaust any more than it can assume responsibility for the criminal acts that were committed against the Hungarian Jews by the wartime government, gendarmes, policemen, and civil servants. He assumed responsibility for the failure to take appropriate steps toward reconciliation after the Holocaust and appealed to all parties to call for a special parliamentary session for this purpose.[60]

At its historical meeting of May 10, 1989, the Hungarian Parliament heard an impassioned speech by Mátyás Szűrős, its president, about the responsibility of nations to confront their past with courage and devotion to truth. He eloquently condemned all forms of prejudice and paid tribute to the memory of the six hundred thousand Hungarian Jews and thirty thousand Gypsies who had been deported from Hungary. However, Szűrős found it necessary to generalize the Holocaust, lumping the martyrdom of those persecuted on racial grounds—and destined for total liquidation—with the suffering endured and the losses incurred by the Hungarian military during the war. He proposed that on the occasion of the forty-fifth anniversary of Hungary's liberation Parliament adopt a law providing for the commemoration of all Hungarian victims of World War II.[61] Similar sentiments were incorporated in the program adopted by the Hungarian Democratic Forum in October 1989.[62]

The discussion on Christian-Jewish reconciliation and the Holocaust continued with greater intensity after the 1990 elections. In its statement of June 12, 1990, the Synod of the Reformed Church of Hungary expressed its sorrow over the Holocaust and admitted that the church "proved to be weak in faith and in action" during the war. While the statement did not clearly acknowledge Hungary's part in the Final

Solution, it declared that in connection with Jewish-Christian relations the church would "have to proclaim again and again responsibility and repentance."[63] Similar sentiments were expressed by the newly elected leaders of Hungary during the July 8, 1990, unveiling of a monument dedicated to the Hungarian Jewish victims of the Holocaust.[64] President Arpád Göncz and Prime Minister Antall were both forthright and eloquent in their denunciation of anti-Semitism and their commitment to the welfare of the Jewish community. They used words never before heard from Hungarian government leaders to commemorate the martyrdom of the Jews, identifying the Holocaust as a most shameful event in history.[65]

Encouraging as the developments of the post-Communist period may be, the foundation for the much desired Christian-Jewish reconciliation is far from complete. Historical truth and the evolving democracy require that the Holocaust be confronted courageously and honestly. The linkage between the Holocaust and anti-Semitism has been proven beyond doubt. Just as unbridled anti-Semitism in the 1930s paved the way for the success of the Final Solution, the failure honestly to confront the Holocaust may once again encourage the spread of virulent anti-Semitism, with all its horrible social consequences, in the post-Communist era.

The lay and ecclesiastical leaders of Hungary, like those of the other countries formerly dominated by the Third Reich, appear to be equivocating about the country's role during the Nazi era. They are reluctant or unwilling to admit Hungary's involvement in and partial responsibility for the Holocaust of Hungarian Jewry. The tendency is still to blame almost exclusively the Germans, emphasizing mainly—and correctly—that the Hungarian Jews had enjoyed the protection of the Kállay government until the German occupation of March 19, 1944, when most of its members, along with many other anti-Nazi Hungarians, were also interned. This, however, is only part of the historical truth, for it ignores or minimizes the fact that the anti-Jewish operations were planned jointly by German and Hungarian Nazis and carried out almost exclusively by the instruments of Hungarian state power—the gendarmerie, the police, and the civil service. The historical evidence clearly indicates that Hungarian Jewry would have survived almost intact had the Germans not occupied the country. But it also reveals that without the full and enthusiastic support of the quisling Hungarian authorities, the Germans would have been unable to implement their ideologically defined racial goals.

A relatively small number of Hungarians recognize this historical reality. Many others, while acknowledging the tragedy that befell Jewry, attempt to absolve Hungary of any major responsibility for the Holocaust. Still others, thankfully only a few on the lunatic fringe of Hungarian politics, emulate their "revisionist" counterparts the world over by denigrating or actually denying it.

The drive to whitewash the historical record of the Nazi era gained momentum after the collapse of the Communist regime in 1989–90. The first group of history cleansers encompasses those, including leading governmental figures, who place almost exclusive responsibility for the Holocaust on the Germans. Others in this group, while admitting that *some* Hungarians were involved in the anti-Jewish drive, attempt to whitewash the Horthy era by placing primary blame on "a few ideologically misguided, lawless, or overzealous ultra-rightists."[66] Still others unwittingly strive to generalize or dejudaize the Holocaust by amalgamating the losses of Jewry with those incurred by the Hungarian military and civilian population during the war. Finally, there are those who try to unburden the national conscience by emphasizing almost exclusively the positive record: the help provided to the refugees, the physical protection of the Jews until the German occupation, and the rescuing of the Jews of Budapest.

On the lunatic fringe there are the new and old "revisionists," who are involved in an obscene campaign to denigrate or deny the Holocaust. Others in this group insist that the wartime suffering of the Jews was matched, if not exceeded, by the pain inflicted by the Jews during the Communist era in Hungary. A slightly different version of the same proposition is advanced by those who identify the contemporary critics of fascism as Communists.[67] Finally, there are those who claim that Hungary's aggressive war was in fact a legitimate and justified war against Bolshevism[68] or clamor for the rehabilitation of those involved in the anti-Jewish drive as law-abiding patriotic citizens.[69] A major objective of all these apologists of Hungary's role during the Nazi era is to whitewash some of the most unspeakably shameful pages in Hungarian and Hungarian-Jewish history.

The tendency to disclaim responsibility for the Holocaust, blaming it exclusively on the Germans, came to the fore during the 1992 debate on possible reparations for the surviving remnant of the Holocaust survivors.[70] The shifting of blame is often coupled with the highlighting of the positive facets of Hungary's history in 1944, reflected in the survival of the Jews of Budapest. This was dramatized during the September 1993 reburial of Horthy's remains in Hungary, an ostensibly private family affair that was transformed into a nationalist political event.[71]

These negative manifestations notwithstanding, post-Communist Hungary has made relatively great strides toward coming to grips with the tragedy of its Jewish community. It decided to make some reparation to the surviving remnant of Hungarian Jewry and passed a law on the rights of ethnic and national minorities. But while the Hungarian government has been forceful in condemning anti-Semitism and eloquent in paying tribute to the victims of the Holocaust, up to the end of 1993 at least it failed to follow the lead of many other European states in making denial of the Holocaust a crime.

Hungary has also taken the lead in advancing parliamentary democracy following the dismemberment of the Soviet bloc and the dissolution of the Communist system in 1989–90. Although it made considerably more progress than most other countries in east-central Europe, Hungary too still lags in the achievement of a genuinely pluralistic and tolerant society. Progressive Hungarians realize that their country's evolution in this direction requires not only a delegitimization of the use of prejudice as a political force but also an honest confrontation of the past—a national, collective commitment to historical truth. This idea was splendidly summarized by Mátyás Szűrős in his historic speech in the Hungarian Parliament:

A selective memory would rather evoke beautiful days, heroic eras, successes, triumphs. And we can proudly admit that we have such in our past. But neither must we hide our mistakes, defeats, dramas, and fateful tragedies. We know that there are no infallible nations with a cloudless past. One can differentiate only between those that deny their mistakes or sins and those who, on the contrary, standing before the tribunal of history with their heads held high, accept their past in its totality, becoming capable of self-examination and of stating the whole truth so that their future will not be infected or endangered by silenced sins, by unpaid debts.

The past must be admitted; there can be no absolution! The soul of a whole nation must not be burned by the glowing embers of silence about such harrowing events and uncleared questions. An unrevealed past breeds prejudice. The only way for a nation to be tolerant of otherness is to be free, independent, and clear-eyed about itself.[72]

Gyula Horn, who was elected prime minister in the wake of the May 1994 elections, went even further in coming to grips with the Holocaust. On the occasion of the fiftieth anniversary of the Holocaust, he stated that

> it would be self-delusion if anyone were to place the responsibility for the genocide in Hungary exclusively on Nazi Germany. The historical experience of fifty years is perhaps sufficient time for Magyardom to confront itself courageously and honestly. . . . We must thus unanimously declare: we owe a historical apology. Those who lived at that time as well as those who only inherited the practice of guilty silence. Yes: We owe an apology for the destruction of 600,000 of our compatriots, for the forceful removal and torturing of several tens of thousands.[73]

Also on the occasion of the fiftieth anniversary of the Holocaust, the Hungarian Catholic Bishops' Conference and the Ecumenical Council of the Churches of Hungary (A Magyar Katolikus Püspöki Konferencia és a Magyarországi Egyházak Okumenikus Tanácsa) issued a joint declaration, stating, among other things, that

> we hold that the destruction of the lives of hundreds of thousands merely because of their origin was the greatest shame of the twentieth century. . . . On the occasion of the anniversary we must declare that responsibility for this tragedy must be borne not only by the representative of irrational evil but also by those who, though they identified themselves as members of our churches, because of fear, cowardliness, or opportunism failed to raise their voices against the mass humiliation, deportation, and murder of their Jewish fellow men. For these failings that took place during the catastrophe fifty years ago we beg forgiveness before God.[74]

Although the declaration failed to identify the responsibility of the Christian churches for the anti-Semitic climate that prevailed in Hungary during the years 1919–44, it represents a long step forward in coming to grips with the Holocaust, laying the foundation for a possible genuine reconciliation. It is left for future generations to determine how well Hungary is able to live up to the ideals and aspirations so eloquently expressed by the current generation of statesmen and clergymen.

NOTES

This essay was completed in 1991.

1. Greater Hungary included Transylvania and Croatia-Slavonia. The latter territory had been constitutionally affiliated with the Hungarian crown since 1102. The Hungarians constituted a minority in the polyglot kingdom of the pre–World War I era. It was only with the aid of the Jews, who identified themselves as Magyars of the Israelite faith, that the Hungarians could claim a slim majority of 54.4 percent.

2. For some details on the three congregations, see below.

3. The case revolved around the accusation that József Scharf, an employee of the Jewish community of Tiszaeszlár, had killed Eszter Solymosi, a fourteen-year-old local Christian girl, for ritual purposes. The charges against Scharf were dismissed after a sensational trial that revealed that the girl had died of drowning. Istóczy and Simonyi exploited the case by calling in Parliament for the expulsion of the Jews. For further details, see Péter Ujvári, ed., *Zsidó lexikon* (Budapest, 1929), 897–99.

4. The oldest among these, as well as the most bloodthirsty, was the Association of Awakening Magyars (Ébredő Magyarok Egyesülete), which was founded in 1917. One of the most important associations was the Hungarian Association for National Defense (Magyar Országos Véderő Egyesület, or MOVE), which was formed after World War I by right-wing military and civilian elements.

5. Randolph L. Braham, *The Politics of Genocide: The Holocaust in Hungary* (New York, 1981), 76–78.

6. In late 1942 a number of top Hungarian military and political figures approached various German officials, including Dieter Wisliceny, a leading member of the Eichmann Sonderkommando, to bring about the gradual "solution" of the Jewish Question in Hungary. For details, see ibid., 274–84.

7. For details, see ibid., 528–690.

8. For details, see ibid., 820–84.

9. Ibid., 1045–53, 1056–1141.

10. Ibid., 987–1011.

11. Romania had committed its forces to the war against the Nazis after changing sides on August 23, 1944.

12. For details, see Braham, *Politics*, 820–84.

13. Ibid., 1143–47. See also László Varga, "The Losses of Hungarian Jewry," in *Studies on the Holocaust in Hungary*, ed. Randolph L. Braham (New York, 1990), 256–65.

14. According to the census of 1941, Hungary had a Jewish population of 725,007, as well as approximately 100,000 converts from Judaism who were identified as Jews under the racial laws then in effect. Of these, 255,500 survived the Holocaust: 190,000 were from Trianon Hungary (144,000 in Budapest) and 65,500 were from the areas acquired by Hungary during the years 1938–41.

15. In 1946 Hungary had 102 Neolog congregations, compared with 219 in 1930. During the same period the number of Orthodox congregations declined from 436 to 146, and the number of Status Quo congregations, from 54 to 15. The memberships of these congregations were, of course, much smaller than before the war.

16. On decree 200/1945.M.E., see *Magyar Közlöny* (Budapest), March 17, 1945.

17. Statement by József Darvas, the noted populist writer and leader of the National Peasant Party, reprinted in *Szabad Nép* (Budapest), March 25, 1945.

18. Trials relating to the Holocaust in Hungary in general and to the former Hungarian-annexed territories in particular were also held between 1945 and 1947 in Cluj (Kolozsvár), Romania; Bratislava, Czechoslovakia; and Novi Sad (Újvidék), Yugoslavia.

19. The scope and jurisdiction of the people's tribunals were specified in decree 81/1945.M.E., adopted by the Provisional National Government on January 25, 1945, in compliance with Article 14 of the Armistice agreement of January 20, 1945. The decree provided for two types of courts: people's tribunals *(népbíróságok),* lower trial courts to function in every court seat, and the National Council of People's Tribunals (A Népbíróságok Országos Tanácsa), to function as a court of appeal. The people's tribunals were superseded by regular courts on January 1, 1952, under Law No. III of 1951.

20. In Hungary as a whole, 322 individuals were condemned to death. However, only 146 of these sentences were carried out; the rest were commuted to life imprisonment. There is no information on when and how many of these people were eventually rehabilitated under the amnesty programs of the Communist regime. For details on the Hungarian war crimes trials, see Braham, *Politics,* 1163–68. See also Eugene (Jenő) Lévai, "The War Crimes Trials Relating to Hungary," in *Hungarian-Jewish Studies,* ed. Randolph L. Braham, 3 vols. (New York, 1966–73), 2:253–96.

21. For a listing of these accounts, consult Randolph L. Braham, *The Hungarian Jewish Catastrophe: A Selected and Annotated Bibliography* (New

York, 1984), hereinafter cited as Braham, *Bibliography*.

22. Many of these were published outside of Hungary. See, e.g., Nikolaus von [Miklós] Horthy, *Ein Leben für Ungarn* (Bonn, 1953); Nicholas [Miklós] Kállay, *Hungarian Premier: A Personal Account of a Nation's Struggle in the Second World War* (New York, 1954); and Dezső Sulyok, *A magyar tragédia* (Newark, N.J., 1954). Among the most honest of memoirs was the one by Vilmos Nagybaczoni Nagy, the former minister of defense, who was recognized as a Righteous Gentile by Yad Vashem for his efforts to protect the lives and interests of Jewish labor servicemen during his tenure in 1942–43. See Nagy's *Végzetes esztendők, 1938–1945* (Budapest, 1946).

23. The accounts by the leading members of the Central Jewish Council of Budapest were published in English translation. See Braham, *Hungarian-Jewish Studies,* vol. 3.

24. A circular (No. 3480/1945) calling for the preparation of a book in several languages to document the "positive" role of the Catholic Church was issued under the signature of Cardinal József Mindszenty, the prince primate of Hungary, on November 3, 1945. Bishop László Ravasz, the controversial head of the Reformed Church of Hungary, was reportedly motivated by similar concerns when he encouraged Reverend Albert Bereczky to document the "positive" wartime role of the Protestant churches. On the background of Bereczky's book, *Hungarian Protestantism and the Persecution of the Jews* (Budapest, [1946]), which is also available in a Hungarian edition, see Sándor Szenes, "'Saving People Was Our Main Task . . .': An Interview with Reverend József Éliás," in Braham, *Studies on the Holocaust in Hungary,* 1–64. The positive role of the Catholic Church is detailed in, among others, Antal Meszlényi, ed., *A magyar katolikus egyház és az emberi jogok védelme* (Budapest, 1947). For other references, see Braham, *Bibliography,* 281–95.

25. Foremost among the early histories are the books by Jenő Lévai, a well-known Jewish journalist who survived the Holocaust in Budapest and served as an adviser on Jewish matters to the Hungarian delegation to the peace conference. A prolific author, Lévai wrote many books, including the *Black Book on the Martyrdom of Hungarian Jewry* (Zurich, 1948) and *Zsidósors Magyarországon* (Budapest, 1948). For references to his other books, consult Braham, *Bibliography.* Another major source is a work by Ernő Munkácsi, the former executive secretary of the Jewish community of Pest: *Hogyan történt? Adatok és okmányok a magyar zsidóság tragédiájához* (Budapest, 1947).

26. See István Bibó, "Zsidókérdés Magyarországon 1944 után," *Válasz* (Budapest), 8 (October–November 1948), 778–877. Reproduced in several collections, the essay evoked a heated intellectual debate in Hungary and abroad. For references relating to this debate, see Braham, *Bibliography,* 426–28.

27. Among those arrested in 1952–53 were Lajos Stöckler, the former head of the Nazi-imposed Central Jewish Council and postwar leader of the Hungarian Jewish community, and Dr. László Benedek, director of the Jewish Hospital. For an exposé of this episode, see the series of articles by Mária Ember in *Magyar Nemzet* (Budapest), May 26, June 11, July 13, 21, 28, and August 10, 1990.

28. The Joint Distribution Committee office in Budapest was closed in 1953. Although the American welfare organization continued to do its best to help the Hungarian Jewish community, it could not reopen its office until after the Communists were ousted from power in 1989–90.

29. Most valuable among these were the first two volumes of a series of document collections titled *Vádirat a nácizmus ellen,* edited by Ilona Benoschofsky and Elek Karsai. Published in 1958 and 1960, respectively, these were followed by a third volume, published in 1967 under the editorship of Karsai. The history of the labor service system and the tragedy of the labor servicemen were documented in two volumes edited by Karsai entitled *"Fegyvertelen álltak az aknamezőkön . . ." Dokumentumok a munkaszolgálat történetéhez Magyarországon* (Budapest, 1962).

30. Arthúr Geyer, ed., *A magyarországi fasizmus zsidóüldözésének bibliográfiája, 1945–1958* (Budapest, 1958).

31. The first major literary work of the post-Stalinist era was Imre Keszi's *Elysium* (Budapest, 1959), followed by Gyula Fekete's *Az orvos halála* (Budapest, 1963). Among the anthologies, see Magda Székely, *Kőtábla* (Budapest, 1962); and Judith Tóth, *Tűzfalak* (Budapest, 1963).

32. The Palestine Liberation Organization office in Budapest was granted official diplomatic status during Yasir Arafat's visit to Hungary in February 1982.

33. See, e.g., György Ránki, ed., *Magyarország története, 1918–1919, 1919–1945* (Budapest, 1976). Ránki pays more attention to the Holocaust in his *1944. március 19* (Budapest, 1978).

34. See, e.g., Gyula Kádár, *A Ludovikától Sopronkőhidáig* (Budapest, 1978); and István Nemeskürty, *Requiem egy hadseregért* (Budapest, 1972).

35. See, e.g., András Mezei, *Kezdetben* (Buda-

pest, 1970); and Mária Ember, *Hajtűkanyar* (Budapest, 1974).

36. See György Száraz, *Egy előítélet nyomában* (Budapest, 1976).

37. Foremost among these were Father György Kis, an outspoken Catholic priest, and Reverend József Éliás, the former executive officer of the Good Shepherd Committee (Jó Pásztor Bizottság), both of Jewish origin. Their critical views of Cardinal Serédi and Bishop Ravasz, respectively, were included in interviews with journalist Sándor Szenes published in *Befejezetlen múlt. Keresztények és zsidók, sorsok* (Budapest, 1986), 29–103, 263–310.

38. The most well received among these were György Moldova, *A Szent Imre-induló* (Budapest, 1975); Imre Kertész, *Sorstalanság* (Budapest, 1975); Ervin Gyertyán, *Szemüveg a porban* (Budapest, 1975); Pál Bárdos, *Az első évtized* (Budapest, 1975); Ágnes Rózsa, *Nürnbergi lágernapló, 1944–45* (Budapest, 1978), originally published in Bucharest in 1971; and László Gerend, *Kiüzettünk városunkból* (Budapest, 1982).

39. For example, an interview by András Mezei, the noted poet and writer, with David Gur, a former member of the Jewish resistance group in Budapest who settled in Israel after the war, was published in *Műhely* (Győr), 4 (1981).

40. See Braham, *Bibliography,* 19–21.

41. The best-known among these, which were also shown in the West, are *25 Fireman's Street* (1973); *Confidence* (*Bizalom,* 1980); *Mephisto* (1981); *Temporary Paradise* (*Ideiglenes Paradicsom,* 1981); and *The Revolt of Job* (*Job Lázadása,* 1983). For a critical review of Holocaust-related films, see Annette Insdorf, *Indelible Shadows: Film and the Holocaust,* 2d ed. (New York, 1989).

42. The Jewish dissidents detailed their antiestablishment views in a series of articles and open letters, some of which were also published in the *Menóra* of Toronto. One of the top leaders of Sálom was György Gadó, a very gifted writer and political analyst. In 1990 Gadó was elected to the Hungarian Parliament as a representative of the Alliance of Free Democrats (Szabad Demokraták Szövetsége), a left-of-center party. For the text of some of the most revealing open letters issued by the dissidents, see *Menóra,* February 24, October 26, 1984.

43. A major conference was held under the auspices of the Institute for Holocaust Studies of The City University of New York and the Holocaust Institute of Haifa University in March and May 1984, respectively, on the occasion of the fortieth anniversary of the Holocaust in Hungary. Among the participants were noted historians and literary figures from Hungary, including Iván Berend, Gyula Juhász, Elek Karsai, András Kovács, György Ránki, and György Száraz. See Randolph L. Braham, ed., *The Holocaust in Hungary: Forty Years Later* (New York, 1985). A related conference was held that same year in Budapest. See Sándor Orbán, ed., *Magyarország 1944-ben* (Budapest, 1984).

44. See esp. Péter Hanák, ed., *Zsidókérdés, asszimiláció, antiszemitizmus* (Budapest, 1984); and Viktor Karády et al., eds., *Zsidóság az 1945 utáni Magyarországon* (Paris, 1984).

45. Established under a grant from the New York–based Memorial Foundation for Jewish Culture, the center began its academic functions in the fall of 1988, under the leadership of Dr. Géza Komoróczy, a professor of Near East studies at the University of Budapest.

46. One of the most popular programs was—and continues to be—*A Hét,* Hungary's version of *60 Minutes.* The author appeared on this program twice during the late 1980s, discussing various aspects of the Holocaust in Hungary.

47. Among the most influential works based on such interviews were Péter Bokor's *Végjáték a Duna mentén: Interjúk egy filmsorozathoz* (Budapest, 1982); and Szenes's *Befejezetlen múlt.*

48. Among these was Randolph L. Braham, *A Magyar Holocaust,* 2 vols. (Budapest, 1989); an abbreviated version was issued in 1990.

49. Among the first of these associations were the Magyar-Izrael Baráti Társaság (The Hungarian-Israel Friendship Group), founded by András Mezei and László Rapcsányi, and the Magyar Zsidó Kulturális Egyesület (Hungarian Jewish Cultural Association), founded by antiestablishment intellectuals, including György Gadó and Endre T. Rózsa. The Hungarian Jewish Cultural Association has several subdivisions and issues a journal entitled *Szombat.* In 1990–91 several other Zionist and Holocaust-related associations were established, including the Munkaszolgálatosok Országos Egyesülete (National Association of Labor Servicemen), the Magyar Auschwitz Alapitvány—Holocaust Dokumentációs Központ (Hungarian Auschwitz Foundation—Holocaust Documentation Center), and the Holocaust Áldozatok Magyarországi Szövetsége (League of Holocaust Victims of Hungary).

50. Foremost among the nationalist-populist writers supporting the Hungarian Democratic Forum was István Csurka, founding father, party vice president, and Parliament member. In a radio talk on January 14, 1990, for example, he appealed to Hungarians to "wake up" to the dangers represented by a "dwarf minority" threatening to retake control of the country—a clear reference to the

Jewish intellectuals, including former Communists, associated with the rival Alliance of Free Democrats. In a long and controversial essay published in the August 20, 1992, issue of *Magyar Fórum,* the party's semiofficial organ, Csurka used anti-Semitic language reminiscent of the 1930s.

Csurka has used the *Magyar Fórum* to advocate his xenophobic and thinly disguised anti-Semitic views. The paper has also featured a number of clearly anti-Semitic cartoons reminiscent of those that appeared during the interwar period, as well as anti-Jewish and antiliberal diatribes by such ultranationalists as Gyula Zacsek. Csurka has championed the cause of "traditional Magyar national-Christian values" against the interests of the "Nomenklatura" (i.e., Jews and other alleged Communists), "which has ruled the country since 1945." This Nomenklatura, in his view, is associated with the left-of-center opposition parties, especially the Association of Free Democrats (SZDSZ, that is, Szabad Demokraták Szövetsége) and the Alliance of Young Democrats (Fiatal Demokraták Szövetsége). Csurka and his ilk would like to create a new national-Christian middle class, that is, one freed of "aliens," and to bring about a "Hungarian Hungary." For an overview of Csurka's populist national-Christian views, see his "Néhány gondolat a rendszerváltozás két esztendeje és az MDF új programja kapcsán," *Magyar Fórum* (Budapest), August 20, 1992.

Guided by political expediency, the Antall administration tolerated the activities of Csurka and his extremist colleagues (Gyula Zacsek, B. Izabella Király, and György Szilasy) in the Hungarian Democratic Forum for quite a long time. It was only after they proved a liability to the party—and perhaps to the image of Hungary abroad—that they were expelled early in June 1993. For some details on Csurka, see the following pieces by László Karsai: "A Shoah a magyar sajtóban, 1989–1991," in *Zsidóság–identitás–történelem,* ed. Mária M. Kovács, Yitzhak M. Kashti, and Ferenc Erös (Budapest, 1992), 63–66, and "Turultojás," *Hiány* (Budapest), November 1992, 3–6.

51. Before the organization of the Hungarian Democratic Forum, in the late eighties, József Antall served as director of the Semmelweis Museum of Medical History in Budapest. He died on December 13, 1993.

Coincidentally, just prior to Antall's appointment as prime minister, his father, József Antall, Sr., was recognized as a Righteous Gentile by Yad Vashem. As a top official of the ministry of the interior during the Kállay era (1942–44), the senior Antall helped save many thousands of Poles, in-

cluding Jews, who had found refuge in Hungary during the war.

52. The campaign was directed primarily against the Alliance of Free Democrats, whose leadership included a relatively large number of urban, Western-oriented, and liberal Jewish intellectuals.

53. Concern about the anti-Jewish manifestations of the post-Communist era and the failure of the government to counteract them was expressed by, among others, Dr. András Losonczy, former president of the Jewish community of Hungary and head of the Jewish Hospital in Budapest. See *Menóra* (Toronto), November 9, 1990. About the same time, Prime Minister Antall took advantage of his visit to the United States to downplay the danger of anti-Semitism in Hungary and to assure his audiences of his government's commitment to combat it. See *Jewish Week* (New York), November 9, 1990.

54. See, e.g., V. Domokos György, "A kisebbség és a zsarnokság," *Népszabadság,* April 29, 1990.

55. The Jewish writers and poets listed by Csoóri are among the great masters of the Hungarian language who distinguished themselves in the arts and letters. For Csoóri's controversial piece, see *Hitel,* September 5, 1990, 6.

56. Many members of the Hungarian Writers' Association, including Miklós Mészöly, its co-president, resigned in protest.

57. See especially the exchange of open letters published by Ákos Kertész and Csoóri in *Magyar Nemzet,* September 29, October 6, 1990. See also the open letter addressed by Professor Géza Komoróczy to Dr. György Szabad, the president of the Hungarian Parliament, in *Új Élet,* November 1, 1990.

58. Imre Kálmán, "Ki áhítja a bosszút?" *Úton* (Debrecen), January 11, 1990.

59. See the contribution by Rezső Döndő to the so-called Csoóri debate in *Magyar Nemzet,* October 15, 1990.

60. József Tornai, "A kiengesztelés pillanata," *Magyar Nemzet,* March 25, 1989. In its positive reaction to the Tornai speech, the newly established Hungarian Jewish Cultural Association suggested that the first day of the deportations be declared a national memorial day. See its *Hírlevél* (Budapest), no. 4 (1989).

61. Szűrős's speech, along with the texts of other speeches on this theme, is reproduced in the *Newyorki Figyelő,* June 1, 1989.

62. See *Szombat,* January 1990.

63. For the text of the declaration, see *Új Élet,* August 1, 1990. The English version is reproduced in *Christian-Jewish Relations* 23, no. 1 (1990), 43–45.

64. Built by Imre Varga, the noted Hungarian sculptor, and financed through funds collected by the Emanuel Foundation of New York, the monument was erected in the courtyard of the Dohány Street Synagogue in Budapest.

65. For excerpts from their speeches, see *Új Élet*, July 15, 1990.

66. Interestingly, the same arguments are used in Romania in the drive to rehabilitate Marshal Ion Antonescu. There too the history cleansers place almost exclusive blame for the mass murder of Jews on the Germans and "a few overzealous Iron Guardists." The historical facts are, however, that the close to 600,000 Hungarian Jews and the approximately 270,000 Romanian Jews were killed during the rules of Horthy and Antonescu, respectively. Neither the Arrow Cross (Nyilas) nor the Iron Guard was in power during the mass deportations.

67. Jenő Fónay, one of the leading figures of the right wing of the Hungarian Democratic Forum and head of the Association of Political Prisoners (Politikai Foglyok Szövetsége), for example, declared: "A person who in 1992 wants to condemn fascism is nothing else but a shameless Bolshevik hireling" (George Hodos, "Antisemitism in Hungary," *Midstream* [New York], April 1993, 25).

68. This assertion was made by General Kálmán Kéri as a representative of the Hungarian Democratic Forum in Parliament. For some details, see László Karsai, "A Shoah a magyar sajtóban," ibid., 67–69.

69. See, for example, "Azonos mércével . . . ," a letter by Barna Farkas, a former gendarmerie officer living in Canada, in *Magyar Fórum* (Budapest), May 14, 1992.

70. This view was expressed by former minister of justice István Balsai. In a June 1992 interview on the issue of reparations, Balsai emphasized that the mass killing of the Jews did not take place on Hungarian territory and that, Hungary having lost its sovereignty, the murders were not committed at the will of the Hungarian authorities (*Népszabadság*, June 2, 1992).

71. Miklós Horthy died in Estoril, Portugal, on February 9, 1957, at age eighty-eight. His remains were returned to Hungary and reinterred in his hometown of Kenderes on September 4, 1993, together with those of his wife and youngest son, Miklós Jr. Ignoring the fact that it was during his rule that close to six hundred thousand Jews lost their lives, nationalists hailed the former regent as a patriot and a champion of territorial revisionism and anti-Communism. His ostensibly private funeral was attended by nearly fifty thousand people, including seven members of the Antall government: Péter Boross, minister of the interior; István Balsai, minister of justice; Lajos Für, minister of defense; László Surján, minister of public welfare; Gyula Kiss, minister of agriculture; Tamás Szabó, minister in charge of privatization; and Béla Kádár, minister in charge of international economic relations. On the implications of Horthy's reinterment, see Randolph L. Braham, "Horthy politikai feltámadása," ibid., August 27, 1993.

72. See n. 61 above.

73. The prime minister expressed these views in a letter addressed to László Keller, the head of the Emanuel Foundation, early in July 1994 (*Új Élet*, July 8, 1994). Mónus Áron, a leading anti-Semite, sued the prime minister, arguing that his statement appeared to represent all Hungarians but that he could ask for forgiveness only in his own name. This view was rebuffed by the leadership of the Jewish community of Hungary, who said, "There are gestures in international political life and in political-social contacts in general that are merely symbolic. . . . We, here in Budapest, read Gyula Horn's letter of July 3, 1994, in this light . . . , that is, that the Hungarian government, the head of the government, and the political spirit represented by the government and the head of government do not in any way identify themselves with the processes that brought about the Holocaust. The humanist gesture of the apology does not contain, does not include, the idea of guilt, let alone that of collective guilt" (*MTI Hírösszefoglaló* [Budapest], August 11, 1994).

74. The declaration was released by Bishop Csaba Ternyák, secretary of the Hungarian Catholic Bishops' Conference. The text was published, among other places, in *Magyar Hírlap* (Budapest), November 30, 1994.

ROMANIA
Radu Ioanid

BEFORE THE HOLOCAUST

Romanian anti-Semitism in the nineteenth and twentieth centuries was extremely virulent, but unlike Germany, Poland, Russia, or Spain, Romania did not have a medieval anti-Semitic tradition. Romanian anti-Semitism was born at the beginning of the nineteenth century, with the penetration of capitalism, and quickly became a powerful movement, first among the political elites and intelligentsia and then among the lower middle class. Romanian anti-Semitism has many unique characteristics that partly explain the peculiar nature of the Holocaust in Romania.

The first Jews to settle in Romanian territory quite probably arrived at the same time as the Roman legions.[1] When the kingdom of the Khazars of southern Russia converted to Judaism during the eighth and ninth centuries, the number of Jews probably increased in the territory of what is now Romania. In 1367 a new wave of Jewish immigrants swept toward Romania in the wake of their expulsion from Hungary. The sixteenth century marks the appearance of Jewish communities in Iasi, Botosani, and Suceava, as well as the arrival in Walachia of Sephardic refugees from the Balkan Peninsula.

The history of the Romanian Principalities does not record significant anti-Semitic troubles before the nineteenth century, despite the xenophobia fostered by a long Turkish domination. Still, apart from anti-Turkish and anti-Greek sentiment, we should note the measures taken in 1579 by Petru Schiopul, prince of Moldavia, against Jewish traders in places where competition from them was especially strong, as well as the execution of nineteen Turkish Jews by Mihai Viteazul, whose rule in Walachia, Moldavia, and Transylvania ended in 1601. Also on record are certain anti-Semitic excesses incited by Greek and Bulgarian merchants in several towns on the Danube in Walachia, along with the increased intolerance toward the Jews on the part of the Orthodox Church after 1750. In general, the Jews, like the other inhabitants of the Romanian Principalities, endured the abuses of the Ottoman Empire. And since they occasionally worked as fiscal or commercial agents of that empire, the Jews awoke suspicions, touched off by their alien culture and religious behavior.

From 1648 to 1658, Poland, Ukraine, and Russia were the scene of bloody events—the revolt of Bogdan Hmielnitki, the Russo-Polish War, the invasion by Swedish troops—that prompted the Jewish communities there to emigrate. Simple people emigrated by the thousands into Hungary and Romania, their numbers rapidly overwhelming the little local Jewish colonies.[2] Polish and czarist oppression continued, and Jews steadily emigrated to neighboring countries. In 1775, when Bukovina became subject to the Habsburgs, and in 1812, when Bessarabia fell to the czar, many Jews from these two provinces decided to settle in Moldavia, where there was no danger of violent persecution.

The Sephardic Jews of Walachia who had been established for a long time, especially in the cities on the Danube, fared better than the immigrants. They were wealthier; they had lived for centuries in the Ottoman Empire, where they were not subject to systematic persecutions; and they did not elicit reactions comparable to those experienced by the emigrants in Moldavia. The Jews coming from Galicia, Ukraine, and Russia constituted a middle class of merchants, artisans, doctors, and lawyers and thus competed with the nascent Romanian petty bourgeoisie. Moldavia was also influenced by czarist anti-Semitism. The Organic Regulation of 1830, a sort of constitution imposed by the Russians, defined "the legal position of the Jews in a manner similar to that of Russia where during the reign of Nicholas I the government's anti-Semitic policies intensified considerably." "Romanian anti-Semitism was so dependent on Russian anti-Semitism that following an attempt on the life of Czar Nicholas II in 1880, Romania passed upon Russia's demand a law against the nihilists, a law that facilitated the expulsion of the Jews from Romania."[3] While it was provoked by external causes, "Romania's anti-Semitism remains a pure Romanian phenomenon and must be analyzed in terms of its specific features and not from the standpoint of what it borrowed."[4]

During the reign of Alexandru Ioan Cuza (1859–66), the first prince of the unified provinces of Walachia and Moldavia, the number of Jews rose to 130,000, or 3 percent of the population. Table 1 shows the numeric evolution of the Jewish population of Romania from 1859 to 1930.

Wealthy Romanians were clearly afraid of the growing Jewish presence in commerce and the liberal professions. As a consequence, a systematic anti-Jewish policy was inaugurated in the spring of 1867.[5] Landlords and the new bourgeoisie found the Jews to be useful as intermediaries without rights. But any attempt by the Jews to integrate was considered to represent a social danger. Even the accusations of ritual murder, unknown before, took root at the beginning of the nineteenth century.[6]

This anti-Semitism had economic, social, cultural, and political features. Unlike the later fascist brand of anti-Semitism, it rarely had racist components. Vasile Alecsandri, a prominent nineteenth-century poet and politician, accused the Jews of having "the most blindly religious fanaticism"; he considered them unassimilable and said that their power was based on "freemasonry and gold."[7] Ion Heliade Rad-

TABLE I

Jews in Romania, 1859–1930

| | POPULATION | | |
Year	Total	Jews	Percentage Jews
1859	ca. 4,500,000	130,000	2.9
1877	ca. 5,000,000	216,304	4.3
1882	ca. 5,000,000	265,000	5.3
1894	5,500,000	243,233	4.4
1899	5,956,690	269,015	4.5
1912	7,234,919	239,967	3.3
1930	18,057,028	756,930	4.2

Sources: Matei Dogan, *Analiza statistica a democratiei parlamentare din Romania* (Bucharest, 1946), 5; Federatia Comunitatilor Evreiesti, *Monografie* (Bucharest, n.d.), vol. 2.

Note: At the end of the nineteenth century and at the beginning of the twentieth, many Romanian Jews emigrated to Palestine or the United States because of discrimination and poverty.

ulescu, one of the leaders of the 1848 revolution in Walachia, presented the Jews as a major danger, because "the International Workmen's Association is in the hands of the Yids"[8] and because the Jews instigated the Commune of Paris. Like Alecsandri, Heliade Radulescu insisted on the danger represented by the Alliance israélite universelle (the first international Jewish organization, created in 1860 to defend Jews who were discriminated against), which was supposedly guilty of bringing the situation of Romanian Jews to the attention of Western powers. This theme of Jewish danger being synonymous with the Communist threat persisted into the twentieth century. D. P. Martian, a well-known nineteenth-century Romanian economist, advised authorities to integrate rich Jews into the economy but to forbid the immigration of poor Jews. The rich Jews, he said, "can always be taken in and allowed to exercise their trade freely; this is not the case of the indigent Jew, whose only collateral is his skin, which he will not be able to use for compensation."[9] Martian was likewise opposed to granting Jews civil rights.

In 1878 the signers of the Treaty of Berlin—Bismarck, Disraeli, and Andrássy—asked Romania to respect article 44 of the treaty and article 7 of its own constitution, both of which promised to grant civil rights and citizenship to the Jews (although the Jews paid taxes and served in the military, they were not yet allowed to vote). This intervention sparked violent protests and further aroused growing anti-Semitism.

The philosopher Vasile Conta was willing to accept the idea of granting citizenship to foreigners established in Romania if they would be disposed "to assimilate with the indigenous population." But at the same time he called for a ban on the "settlement of foreigners having unchristian rites: the Jews and the Mohamedans." Conta argued that one nation must contain only one race and that "the Jews are a distinct nation from other nations, being their enemy."[10]

The poet Mihai Eminescu claimed that "the Jew does not deserve rights anywhere in Europe because he is not working," because he forms a "foreign economic army," and because he is an agent of Western culture. Eminescu thought that nobody in Europe "would move one soldier out of love for the Jews." He demanded the "death sentence for people who conspired in the Alliance Israélite" and strong anti-Jewish legislation on the German model. He believed that the Jews were "a race that has the tendency to seize the real estate of the Romanians, and in the long run his country." In his view the Romanians, "the most free and tolerant people, had their head in the yoke of the most miserable and servile of the human races."[11] Even though Eminescu generally equates the concept "race" with the concept "people," the direct influence on him of some German craniologists, such as Virchow, is easy to detect.

One scientist, Bogdan Petriceicu Hasdeu, himself half-Jewish, believed that "the Jew spreads around the seeds of corruption: bankruptcy, espionage, bribery" and "sinks in avarice and is growing mouldyly in filth."[12] There was truth in the statements of C. Z. Codreanu, the leader of the Iron Guard, the most popular wartime fascist organization, that he and his movement were carrying on what had been started by Conta, Alecsandri, Heliade Radulescu, and Hasdeu.[13]

As a result of these sentiments, the efforts of Bismarck, Disraeli, and Andrássy failed. The Jews as a group did not receive the franchise: "Beside the 888 [Jewish] combatants of the Independence War, between 1879 and 1899 only 85 persons received, after heated parliamentary debates, the status of Romanian citizen, and several hundreds [did not receive the status of citizen] until the Balkan wars."[14]

Anti-Semitism was not a feature of all the political and cultural discourse of the nineteenth century. Another leader of the 1848 revolution, Nicolae Balcescu, and Prince Alexandru Ioan Cuza were not anti-Semites, and their writings were not considered recoverable by fascist ideologists. The earlier anti-Semites were not, of course, responsible for the fate of Romanian Jewry during World War II, but their writings did influence the country's fascist and right-wing intellectuals.

The best example of this legacy is provided by A. C. Cuza (1857–1944). A conservative scholar and politician, in 1910 he created the first Romanian political party to have an explicitly anti-Semitic electoral platform. After World War I he became the leader of the first large Romanian fascist party, the Liga Apararii National Crestine (League of National Christian Defense, or LANC), from which a dissident group calling itself the Legion of Archangel Michael (later the Iron Guard) emerged in 1927. In theory Cuza represented the first variety of Romanian racist anti-Semitism. Influenced by the British theorist of racism Houston Stewart Chamberlin, the French anti-Semite Eduard Drumont, and *The Protocols of the Elders of Zion,* he supported a *numerus clausus* and, later, a *numerus nullus.* Cuza considered the Jews an "inferior ethnic combination, bastards with a certain physical and moral aspect."[15] In his book *Nationalitatea in arta,* Cuza attacked the degeneration of the Jews, who were the main danger to the Romanian people and who allegedly opposed a Romanian race, which he never bothered to define. Between the two world wars, A. C. Cuza was viewed by Romanian fascists as the man who had "worked out the scientific doctrine of Romanian anti-Semitism."[16]

Belonging to the same category was Octavian Goga, an important poet and a leader with A. C. Cuza of the fascist National Christian Party, created in 1935, when the LANC merged with Goga's National Agrarian Party. For a short time in 1938 Goga served as prime minister of a strongly anti-Semitic government that enacted many laws against the Jews. In his writings Goga described the Jews as "impure secretions of Galicia" and claimed that they were invading Romania.[17] As Paul Shapiro has observed, "Goga's and Cuza's ideas survived their regime's precipitate fall from power in February, 1938. Their principles continued to exert considerable influence on Romanian politics by virtue of the altered domestic and international situations left to the National Christian Party government's successors and by virtue of the fact that the civilian bureaucracy of wartime dictator Ion Antonescu's regime was staffed with a preponderance of one time Goga-Cuzist adherents."[18]

Another prominent intellectual who served as a powerful symbolic figure for Romanian fascists was the historian and politician Nicolae Iorga. He shared Cuza's political views, maintaining that the Romanian economy was ridiculously tolerant toward the Jews.[19] He often warned his readers about the Jewish danger; however, his harsh attacks against the Jews were balanced by attempts to establish a dialogue with them. Even though the Iron Guard looked upon him as a spiritual father, Iorga was killed by the Iron Guard because he rejected the idea of a fascist dictatorship and because he was involved in the arrest of Codreanu in 1938.

From 1867 to 1913, 196 anti-Semitic laws were passed concerning citizenship, deportation, and the professions. Discrimination in schools and universities, in military service, and in commercial activities was common. Despite strong pressure from France, Great Britain, and Germany, successive governments continued to enforce these laws.

At the end of World War I Romania was united with Bessarabia and Transylvania; the result was a country with a minority population of 30 percent—mainly Hungarians, Jews, Germans, Bulgarians, and Ukrainians. Once again the Western powers pressured Romania to respect the civil rights of these minorities, and the position of the Jews underwent a change. The constitution of 1923 granted rights to the Jews, but anti-Semitism had already spread to the general population, aided by repeated economic crises and the diversionary tactics of the Liberal Party and the National Peasant Party and the fascist organizations. The lower middle class manifested its anti-Semitism by supporting a free-initiative capitalism "ethnically corrected" by the state, which was expected to suppress Jewish commerce and encourage Romanian commerce.

Romania had one of the largest Jewish communities in Europe. By 1930, 756,930 Jews lived in the country. Only Poland and the Soviet Union had more. The constitution of 1923 granted citizenship to almost all members of the ethnic minorities, a juridical situation that lasted until 1938. But even during this period the LANC, the National Christian Party, the Legion of Archangel Michael, and other political parties engaged in agitation over the Jewish Problem. During the last free elections before World War II, in December 1937, the Iron Guard received 15.58 percent of the vote, and the National Christian Party almost 10 percent. One in four votes went to the fascist anti-Semitic parties. Anti-Semitism was also part of the platforms of most of the other political parties during these elections.

THE HOLOCAUST ERA

Theorists of the LANC and the Iron Guard variously presented the Jews as "the ruling class,"[20] spies, Communists, agents of Soviet Russia, and the main enemy of the Romanian people. The Jews were considered to be responsible for the existence of alcoholism, syphilis, white slavery, abortion, divorce, homosexuality, and women's liberation.[21] Consequently, these groups proposed measures for cleansing Romania of its Jews.

In 1938 Goga argued for the deportation of all European Jews to Madagascar, in a convoy surrounded by the warships of the League of Nations, "thereby making it impossible for the Jews to escape."[22] Iron Guard ideologist Mihail Polihroniade proposed the introduction of a "state anti-Semitism."[23] In the same year another fascist theorist, Alexandru Razmerita, criticized as impractical the suggestion of an Orthodox priest that all the Jews from Romania be drowned in the Black Sea. After emphasizing that this scheme would require too many ships, Razmerita proposed a "total elimination plan" for the Jewish population. He wanted to deprive the Jews of their civil rights and to move them from urban areas to the countryside as forced laborers. The Jews would be resettled in small rural concentration camps, each with a capacity of between twenty-five and thirty inmates. Every Jew over the age of ten would be forced to work. Their identity cards would not give the Jews' names, only the names of their owners.[24]

Traian Herseni, the racist theorist of the Iron Guard, adopted the slogan "Desiudaizare, destiganizare, desfanariotizare" (Eliminate Jews, Gypsies, and Greeks) of Constantin Papanace, a fellow member of the Iron Guard who wanted to subject the Jews, Gypsies, and Greeks to racial purification. "We need eugenics laws and eugenic practices," said Herseni. "Reproduction cannot be left to chance. . . . Certain people must not be allowed to reproduce, and inferior races must be completely isolated from the [main] ethnic group. The sterilization of certain categories of people must not be conceived stupidly as a violation of human dignity but as a tribute to beauty, morality, and perfection."[25] Another supporter of eugenics was P. Tiparescu, who, under the influence of N. C. Paulescu, another leader of the LANC, wrote about "racial diseases." Tiparescu maintained that the Jews "are the most dangerous carriers of infectious diseases because of their dirtiness," though they do not infect themselves.[26] After September 1940 the government's fascist propaganda often raised the specter of Jewish espionage. A former member of the Iron Guard, Constantin Virgil Gheorghiu, wrote in 1941, after the beginning of the war with the Soviet Union, about "all the Jews, little children and old people included, [who] are spying for the Bolsheviks. . . . Day and night these deadly enemies of our country pass along information about the positions of our armies."[27] Another racist, Toma Petrescu, wrote that marriages between Jews and Romanians posed a danger to the biological health of the state: "Jews are degenerate people because they have a great number of insane individuals." He likewise claimed that "all the Jewish women married to Christians are working as spies for the foreign powers." Petrescu proposed that "all the state clerks in Romania be prohibited from marrying Jewish women [and that] the bastards born from these marriages be forcibly sterilized."[28] Ion Chelcea, a professor at the University of Iasi, proposed the same solution for the Gypsies.[29]

When the fragile political balance of post–World War I Europe was destroyed, the government felt free to repeal the laws emancipating the Jews. On January 21, 1938, royal decree 169, signed by King Carol II and Prime Minister Octavian Goga, revised the law granting citizenship to the Jews. Minister of Justice V. Radulescu cited "the invasion" of the Jews after 1918 as the primary reason for the decree. King Carol and Prime Minister Goga, in interviews with the London *Daily Herald*'s A. L. Easterman on January 6 and 10, 1938, alternately gave the figures 250,000 and 500,000 as the number of Jews considered illegal. Both numbers were highly exaggerated. Carol spoke about the necessity of denying such people any rights, but he was not in favor of deporting them. Goga, on the other hand, declared that these "500,000 vagabond people whom we cannot regard as Romanian citizens" should be deported.[30]

Another law, adopted on February 27, 1938, but not implemented until after the coup d'état against King Carol in September 1940, emphasized "the proclamation of the law of blood" and also "the juridical and political distinction between Romanians having Romanian blood and [other] Romanian citizens."[31] On December 1, 1938, Gheorghe Alexianu, the governor of Suceava District (who three years later became the governor of Transnistria), in order "to protect public property and to maintain public order and security," adopted a decree forbidding the Jewish population "to use any language other than Romanian in places of business, factories, banks, industrial establishments, professional offices, industrial and commercial enterprises, in the halls of the Palace of Justice, and all public places in general." Article 3 of this decree specified that "Jews who continue to speak some other language than Romanian on the streets and in public places will thereby prove that they are not Romanian citizens and will not be able to enjoy the privileges of Romanian citizenship."[32]

On August 8, 1940, King Carol signed another decree, number 2650, concerning the legal situation of the Jews living in Romania, which was signed as well by Prime Minister Ion Gigurtu and Minister of Justice Ion V. Gruia. On the same day, decree 2651, which forbade marriages between Jews and "Romanians with Romanian blood," was also issued. These two laws of the royal dictatorship, openly inspired by the Nuremberg Laws, are important because they remained in force and served as permanent guidelines for the fascist Antonescu-Sima and Antonescu governments. Enacted a month before the Antonescu-Sima regime overthrew the king, they clearly represented the first Romanian racial laws. During the summer of 1940, Romania lost Bessarabia and northern Bukovina to the Soviet Union, Northern Transylvania to Hungary, and two districts of Dobrudja to Bulgaria.

From August 1940 until May 1942 Romania adopted more than one hundred anti-Semitic laws, decrees, and administrative decisions.[33] The lives of the Jews during the war were profoundly affected by this legislation. Jews were also subjected to geographical discrimination. Romanian fascist authorities killed mainly the Jews from Bessarabia, Bukovina, Transnistria (the region of Ukraine between the Dniester and Bug Rivers that was occupied by Romania in 1941 and remained under Romanian administration throughout the war), and Northern Moldavia. In July 1940, before the Iron Guard came to power and while King Carol still ruled, a pogrom without precedent in the country's history was carried out by a regular unit of the Romanian army. It claimed more than one hundred lives in the town of Dorohoi in Moldavia.

After September 6, 1940, a wave of anti-Semitic legislation was enacted by the Iron Guard government led by Antonescu. Jews were expelled from all professional associations and from schools and universities. Even the Romanian Association of the Deaf and Dumb expelled its Jewish members, on November 10, 1940. Antonescu was a fanatical hater of Jews. Three weeks after taking power, he emphasized in an interview granted to the Italian newspaper *La Stampa* that solving the Jewish problem was one of the most important tasks of the new government.[34] He "was haunted by the existence of a relatively large number of Jews in the towns, particularly in Northern and Central Moldavia."[35] Not surprisingly, during Antonescu's rule (with and without the Iron Guard) the propaganda and legal discrimination turned into violence and mass murder. At the end of January 1941, during the Iron Guard rebellion led by Horia Sima against Antonescu, its former ally, 120 Jews were savagely killed in Bucharest by members of the Iron Guard. In the following month more than 50 Jews were killed by Romanian border guards at Burdujeni, on the frontier with the Soviet Union.

A new and larger wave of murders began when Romania entered the war on Germany's side in June 1941. It took back from the Soviet Union Bessarabia and northern Bukovina, which were occupied by Stalin after the signing of the Ribbentrop-Molotov pact. Ion Antonescu ordered the deportation of all the Jews from Bessarabia and Bukovina. Vice president Mihai Antonescu supervised the drafting of new laws governing the two provinces. He spoke about "the action of ethnic purification, which will be carried out by removal and isolation in labor camps, where Jews and other foreigners with doubtful attitudes will not be able to exercise their prejudicial influences."[36]

Both Antonescus considered the Jews of Bessarabia and Bukovina to be traitors, Soviet agents, or Communists. They reasoned that these Jews had been tainted after living under Soviet occupation in 1940–41 and that some of them had even happily greeted the arrival of the Red Army. In truth, the old Romanian nationalist dream of having these provinces free of Jews and other minorities seemed within reach. Thus, "between the measures of purification of Bessarabia and Bukovina, in the autumn of 1941, after the reoccupation of these provinces by the Romanian Army, the police units and the army were ordered to transfer the Jewish elements to Transnistria."[37]

Romanian troops joined in the invasion of the Soviet Union and the mass murder of the Jews in Bessarabia, Bukovina, and occupied Ukraine. Although the Holocaust in Romania was unsystematic in Old Romania (i.e., within Romania's pre–World War I borders), it was systematic in Bessarabia, Bukovina, and Transnistria, especially during the first six months of the war. In June 1941 between ten thousand and twelve thousand Jews were killed in the city of Iasi and on two death trains. German troops joined Romanian troops in the Iasi killings but did not participate in sealing more than three thousand Jews inside trains in which they perished from lack of space, food, and water. These huge pogroms were followed by many others, especially in Bessarabia and Bukovina. According to Raul Hilberg, "Repeatedly, Romanian forces on the march invaded Jewish quarters and killed Jews, and their actions took the form of atrocities rather than well-planned or well-reasoned killing operations."[38] And according to Lucretiu Patrascanu,

> The long atrocious anti-Semitic cruelties will always accuse the regime that had tolerated them; the individual and collective assassinations were transformed into a massive, systematic, and methodic extermination by soldiers and official state bodies. Thousands and tens of thousands of individuals—men, women, children, elderly people—who had been forced to cross the Dniester in winter were condemned to certain death by the cold and starvation that ravaged those totally desert regions. . . . The wave of blood and massacres that flooded the country . . . transformed thousands and thousands of soldiers, gendarmes, and civilian clerks into vulgar assassins, arsonists, and robbers "en titre" incensed against a defenseless population.[39]

Almost the entire Jewish population from the rural areas of Bessarabia and Bukovina was decimated by the Romanian and German armies during the first weeks of the war.

Before 1940 around 300,000 Jews lived in Bessarabia and Bukovina. Several sources indicate that about 130,000 retreated with the Red Army or were deported several months before. According to Raul Hilberg, more than 27,000 Jews were killed in July and August 1941 in Bessarabia and Bukovina (more than 10,000 Jews died in mass shootings in July, about 7,000 died in transit camps in August, and about 10,000 were murdered in Transnistria). "Transnistria was a prolonged disaster. All told, some 160,000 Jews had been seized for deportation in Bessarabia, Bukovina, and Dorohoi, and 135,000 of them had reached the eastern shore of the Dniester alive." Two years later, a census revealed that "of the Bessarabian, Bukovinian and Dorohoi deportees 50,741 were left (about 5,000 of them orphans)."[40]

From Old Romania 10,000 to 12,000 Jews were deported from Dorohoi district, and only 6,000 came back.[41] Another 2,000 Jews who had been political prisoners, had tried to escape forced labor, or had wanted to emigrate to the Soviet Union before the war were also deported. In Transnistria Romanian authorities were also responsible for killing "around 150,000 indigenous Jews in the Odessa area and Golta."[42] Ion Antonescu accused the Jews of being behind the resistance of the Red Army in Odessa, and he personally ordered the massacre of Jewish hostages in Odessa after a mine exploded at the Romanian army headquarters there.[43] At least 19,000 Jews were killed in Dalnic, near Odessa, the morning of October 24, 1941. During the last ten days of 1941 at Bogdanovka, in the Golta district, more than 70,000 Jews were killed on the order of Colonel Modest Isopescu, the Romanian governor of the district.

Massacred in the villages and towns of Bukovina and Bessarabia and deported through Atachi, Cosauti, and Rezina mainly to the districts of Moghilev, Yugastru, Tulcin, Berezovca, Balta, and Golta, the Jews died by bullet, fire, forced labor, starvation, and typhus. At least twenty-five thousand Gypsies were also deported from Old Romania to Transnistria. The pretense was that they were robbers and nomads. Some of them had close relatives who were drafted into the Romanian army. Forced to leave their country at the beginning of the winter with forty pounds of luggage, most of them died.

Even though Ion Antonescu personally encouraged the violence against the Jews, he sometimes granted the requests of Wily Filderman, the president of the Romanian Jewish Communities. It was because of Filderman's intervention, for example, that Antonescu reversed his decision to force all Jews to wear the yellow star. Notwithstanding this gesture, in the summer and the autumn of 1942 the decision was made to deport the Jews of Old Romania to the Nazi death camps in Poland. "On August 17, 1942, [Martin] Luther informed [Ernst] Worman, [Ernst von] Weiszacker and [Joachim] Ribbentrop that Mihai Antonescu and Marshal Antonescu had now given their consent to the deportation of the Jews and had agreed that the transports would begin to move out from the districts of Arad, Timisoara and Turda."[44]

When he discussed this subject with Gustav Richter, the German official in charge of Jewish affairs in Romania, in October and November 1942, however, Mihai Antonescu grew more and more evasive, and Ion Antonescu changed his mind. At his trial after the war, Rudolf Höss, the commandant of Auschwitz, mentioned that in 1943 he had been expecting massive transports of Romanian Jews. He testified that Eichmann had told him about "the difficult negotiations with the Romanian authorities, who wanted to exterminate the Jews inside their country."[45]

It is not clear why Antonescu changed his mind concerning the deportations of the Jews from Old Romania. Certainly, he and members of his government were no longer as confident about the future as they had been at the beginning of the war. According to Hilberg, "Opportunism was practiced in Romania not only on a national basis but also in personal relations."[46] The tougher attitude of the American authorities, who during the fall of 1942 promised to punish the perpetrators of the Final Solution in Germany and its satellites, clearly had an impact. Vasile Mares, a former minister in Antonescu's government, refused to return to the government, saying that he did not want to have bad relations with the Jews. The minister of interior affairs, General Dumitru Popescu, told Filderman, who had been dismissed from his position several months before, that he was not responsible for what was happening in Bessarabia, Bukovina, and Transnistria.[47] Perhaps Antonescu was influenced by the interventions of the Swiss and Vatican ambassadors in Bucharest; King Michael and his mother, Elena; and Balan, the Orthodox bishop of Transylvania, who was known for his anti-Semitism. It seems that the decision not to deport the Jews from Old Romania was made immediately after these appeals.[48] Probably all these factors worked together.

The Jews from Old Romania were not deported, and about 300,000 survived. Later German pressures had no effect (Romania was not an occupied country): in 1944 150,000 Jews from Northern Transylvania were deported by the Hungarians, and most of them were killed by the Germans, but the Jews from Old Romania remained unharmed.

> In Jewish matters, too, the Romanian attitude was partly opportunistic and partly something more. There were times, for example, when the Germans complained that the Romanians were exasperatingly slow. At one time, Eichmann even wanted to withdraw his expert in Jewish matters from Bucharest, on the ground that the Romanians did not follow the expert's advice. But there also were instances when the Germans actually had to step in to restrain and slow down the pace of Romanian measures. At such times the Romanians were moving too fast for the German bureaucracy. Not hasty measures but thorough ones were required by the Germans.[49]

THE POST-HOLOCAUST ERA

In March 1945 the Romanian government created a special court for the prosecution of war criminals, under the direct supervision of the Communist minister of justice Lucretiu Patrascanu. Patrascanu was one of the organizers of the coup that deposed the fascist regime. He was also one of the leaders of the Romanian Communist Party and the minister of justice during the first years after the war. The task of this People's Court was difficult. Restoring the property of the survivors was a slow and painful process. As Patrascanu himself declared, it was dangerous to alienate all the people who had profited during the war from the spoliation of the Jews. Former fascists in the military or in the civilian administration tried to resist these trials. Intimidated, fighting for survival, or caught up in the process of emigration, many Jews avoided giving testimony in the court. Also, the Romanian Communist Party often used these trials as propaganda against its political enemies.

The leaders of the Antonescu regime were brought to justice. Also prosecuted and condemned to long terms in prison were members of the civilian and military administration who organized and implemented the deportation and mass murder of the Jews in Moldavia, Bukovina, Bessarabia, and Transnistria. High- and low-ranking officers of the army and gendarmerie and civilian clerks received long prison sentences. Only Ion Antonescu; Mihai Antonescu; General C. Z. Vasiliu, the deputy minister of the interior; and Gheorghe Alexianu, the governor of Transnistria, were executed. As Jean Ancel has observed, right-wing nationalists regarded these trials "as an anti-national act, an attempt—by foreign agents and their local aides—at vengeance against the Romanian military who had shed their blood for the liberation of the two regions annexed by the Russians [in 1940] and who embodied with their deeds of bravery the long tradition of opposition to the invaders from the East, keeping alive the Romanian culture and 'spirit.'"[50]

In his memoirs Rabbi Alexandre Safran, the chief rabbi of Romania immediately after the war, mentioned that in Paris on September 11, 1946, Gheorghe Tatarescu, the minister of foreign affairs (a member of the Liberal Party who as the under secretary of state at the ministry of the interior had been involved in organizing many anti-Semitic actions), told the rabbi: "Do not forget that although we are now in Paris we belong to Romania; do not forget that we shall leave Paris, return to Romania, and meet there again." Although Rabbi Safran was strongly anti-Communist, he praised Patrascanu: "When Patrascanu became minister under the Sanatescu administration, I went to see him often to talk about Jewish problems. . . . He was the most intellectual and humane of all the communist leaders. . . . I do not think that Patrascanu dealt hypocritically with us. In contrast to other Romanian Communist leaders or to Jewish Communists like Iosif and Liuba Kishinevski and Paul Davidovici he acted quite nobly."[51]

The most important book on the Holocaust in Romania in terms of historiography, *Cartea Neagra* (The black book), was published between 1946 and 1948 in Bucharest. The author of this impressive work was Matatias Carp, the secretary of the Union of the Jewish Communities of Romania. The first edition of *Cartea Neagra* was also the last. Under Nicolae Ceausescu, who came to power in 1964, *Cartea Neagra* disappeared even from the so-called secret sections of the public libraries. (The "secret sections" of the public libraries could only be used with special permission.) *Cartea Neagra* comprises three volumes. The first volume, *Legionarii si rebeliunea* (The legionnaires and the uprising), concentrates on the large pogrom organized by the Iron Guard in Bucharest in January 1941, but it also recounts smaller pogroms and other anti-Semitic actions carried out by the Iron Guard between September 1940 and January 1941. The second volume, *Pogromul de la Iasi* (The pogrom of Iasi), describes the June 1941 pogrom, in which about ten thousand Jews died. The third volume, *Transnistria,* analyzes the fate of the Jews from Bessarabia and Bukovina, who were either killed or deported to Transnistria. This volume also deals with the fate of the Ukrainian Jews killed in Transnistria under the Romanian administration. These three volumes are chronologically arranged and altogether encompass one thousand pages. Every assertion is thoroughly documented, and many of the supporting documents, such as the Antonescu administration's order to deport the Jews, are reproduced in full.

The Jewish journalist Marius Mircu published three small books in 1945 on the main pogroms staged in the northern part of the country: *Pogromul de la Iasi* (The pogrom of Iasi), *Pogromurile din Bukovina si Dorohoi* (The pogroms in Bukovina and Dorohoi), and *Pogromurile din Basarabia* (The pogroms in Bessarabia). These books contain personal testimonies from many survivors of the massacres and deportations. The books are of genuine historical value, but they are sometimes undermined by Mircu's journalistic style and particularly by his streaks of black humor. A similar small book, important from a documentary and historical standpoint, is M. Rudich's *La brat cu moartea* (Hand in hand with death), published in 1945, which describes the horror of Transnistria.

In the postwar period the Communists quickly consolidated their power in Romania and started to "recommend" increasingly selective criteria for writing history.

Historians were told to emphasize the "positive" aspects of Romanian history. The subjects of anti-Semitism and the Holocaust disappeared from print, and the study of the fascist period became an exercise in propaganda, marked by omissions and distortions. From the early 1960s onward, Romanian historiography was openly nationalistic and xenophobic.

This trend was strongly encouraged by Nicolae Ceausescu. Because the destruction of the Jews was carried out by the fascist government under the aegis of state anti-Semitism, it is important to analyze the way in which Romanian historians have dealt with fascism and anti-Semitism. Romanian Communist historiography has been only slightly concerned with fascism, although it largely controlled Romania's political life before and during World War II. After the war, Lucretiu Patrascanu published two outstanding works on Romanian fascism: *Problemele de baza ale Romaniei* (Romania's fundamental problems) and *Sub trei dictaturi* (Under three dictatorships).[52] The first has not been reissued since 1945. In it, Patrascanu analyzes the social and cultural forces that shaped fascist ideology. Under the Ceausescu regime, Patrascanu's work was selectively published, but *Problemele de baza ale Romaniei* was simply ignored. Patrascanu's work undoubtedly contains the most profound and pertinent analysis of Romanian fascism ever written. Without denying the presence of foreign influences, Patrascanu argued that the Romanian fascist movement derived mainly from economic and political sources: the rather late perpetuation of quasi-feudal relations in agriculture, the weakness of the middle class, and the presence of strong anti-Semitic tendencies that were fomented by some political activists before World War I. He said that fascism also gained ground owing to the support of the student organizations led by A. C. Cuza and Nicolae Iorga. Patrascanu cited anti-Semitism as one of the main features of Romanian fascism. It was no accident, he pointed out, that Romanian anti-Semitism turned to genocide: "Year after year Romanian public opinion was poisoned by an enormous anti-Semitic press campaign. Lies, the calumnies, falsifications, including the most obscene demagogy—everything had been used. . . . This press campaign was not in vain: it contaminated the minds of many people and served to justify many of the cruelties perpetrated by the fascists."[53]

After 1948, fascism in Romanian historiography and political science was portrayed in a selective and flatly descriptive way. Historians equated without distinction Carol II's dictatorship, the legionary movement, and Antonescu's dictatorship. They did not even attempt to analyze the internal and external causes for the emergence of fascism and its popularity. The few studies published between 1950 and 1970 on the Romanian political regimes in power from 1938 to 1944 and on the impact of fascism were most often empty rhetorical exercises in which slogans took the place of ideas.

During the early 1970s the first attempts at a global approach to Romanian fascism were made. Two trends emerged. The first was close to the "classic" Stalinist approach of the earlier years: Romanian fascism was a fifth column of Nazi Germany and did not attract mass support. Accordingly, the Romanians who became fascist ideologues were the mouthpieces of Italy or Germany. The second trend was an expression of Ceausescu's "national-socialism." A timid but obvious rehabilitation of Antonescu started. His regime was cleansed of any fascist characteristics, and ideologues of the Iron Guard and the National Christian Party became patriots and democrats overnight.

Both of these approaches ignored anti-Semitism, and the destruction of Romanian Jewry during World War II was mentioned only in passing, and then in a very distorted way. Moreover, there was a tendency to demonstrate that, as a whole, the bourgeoisie, which was viewed as the main supporter of fascism, was not of Romanian descent. Toward the end of Ceausescu's rule the "national-socialist" trend became very explicit. In 1987 Mircea Musat, a high-ranking official of the central committee of the Communist Party who was in charge of historiography, called for the cultural rehabilitation of A. C. Cuza, the father of Romanian fascist anti-Semitism, whom he considered a "Romanian intellectual of first rank." Musat also admired Octavian Goga, whom he also described in glowing terms: "A mind blessed with every quality, Romanian in the deepest dimensions of his soul, an uncommonly gifted man, Octavian Goga represents a profound symbol of this people."[54]

The adherence to fascism of a prestigious fraction of the intelligentsia was deliberately ignored. Despite strong evidence to the contrary, even Mircea Eliade, a former Iron Guard ideologist and a famous historian of religions, denied his legionary activities and was presented as an antifascist in the media.

The Ceausescu Regime

Nicolae Ceausescu continued the policy of his predecessor, Gheorge Gheorghiu-Dej, of remaining as independent of the Soviet Union as possible. Romania was the first Eastern European country to establish diplomatic relations with West Germany and the only Communist country to condemn the Soviet occupation of Czechoslovakia in 1968. In 1967 Ceausescu refused to follow the Soviet lead and break diplomatic relations with Israel. He also cultivated relations with American Jewish organizations. He made arrangements with Israel and West Germany in which these countries literally bought the right of Jews and ethnic Germans who lived in Romania to emigrate. A certain degree of freedom of religion was granted to the Jews; at the same time, however, anti-Semitism was clearly encouraged and practiced.

In Romanian literature the destruction of the Jews was not a major theme. During the mid-1940s few writers broached this subject. Among those who did were F. Brunea-Fox, in *Jurnalul rebeliunii* (Diary of the rebellion), a description of the January 1941 pogrom of Bucharest; and Aurel Baranga, in *Ninge peste Ucraina* (It's snowing over Ukraine), about the Holocaust in Transnistria.[55] Selective censorship allowed writers such as George Calinescu, Eusebiu Camilar, Paul Alexandru Georgescu, Georgeta Horodinca, Norman Manea, Alexandru Ivasiuc, Titus Popovici, Sergiu Dan, Maria Banus, Sasa Pana, and Camil Baltazar to mention the tragedy of the Jews in their novels and shorter pieces.

The 1975 novel *Delirul* (Delirium), by Marin Preda, won plaudits and stirred some controversy abroad.[56] Michael Shafir analyzed the book in an excellent article published in 1983:

The novel "Delirium" . . . for all practical purposes rehabilitated Romania's wartime leader Marshal Ion Antonescu. Preda, however, by no means defended the Marshal's policies toward the Jews, and no trace of anti-Semitism is to be found in the book. On the contrary, in one of the more convincing passages Antonescu's peasant mother warns him against the consequences of such German inspired unchristian crimes. Whatever other opportunistic reasons determined Preda to introduce in the volume a short passage depicting the unmistakable figure of young Ceausescu, the attempt to rehabilitate Antonescu resulted from the writer's empathy for the Marshal's grasp of his patriotic duty to return Bessarabia to Romania.[57]

From their neo-Stalinist vantage points, Radio Moscow and *Literaturnaia Gazeta,* the weekly of the Union of Writers, sharply criticized Preda's description of Antonescu. Both of these critiques and the novel itself were discussed in *Die Welt* and *Der Spiegel,* which also mentioned the attempt to rehabilitate Antonescu. The Israeli historian Theodor Lavi stated that Preda did not try to rehabilitate Antonescu; two years later, however, Lavi became much more critical.[58] Michael Shafir pertinently observed that although Preda might personally be above any suspicion of anti-Semitism, works such as *Delirium* nonetheless contributed to the creation of an atmosphere that enabled anti-Semitic intellectuals to pursue their aims.[59]

In the early 1970s, after an official visit to China and North Korea, Ceausescu launched his own "cultural revolution." It stressed that Romanian culture should be less elitist and more oriented toward the masses. Under the cover of slogans such as "Democratic Culture" and "Art for All," a powerful attack was unleashed against members of the intelligentsia who were unwilling to compromise with the "socialist realism" ordered by Ceausescu. A tacit agreement was worked out between Ceausescu's ideological lieutenants, Dumitru Popescu and Eugen Florescu, and the most reactionary members of the intelligentsia. According to this scheme, the intellectuals would support Ceausescu and in exchange would be allowed to carry out openly neofascist, xenophobic, anti-Semitic, and nationalistic propaganda attacks. Structurally and ideologically this group strongly resembled Pamyat, the extreme right-wing Russian organization.

Directed by the anti-Semitic writer Eugen Barbu, the weekly magazine *Saptamana* published many chauvinistic articles by Barbu himself, Corneliu Vadim Tudor, Constantin Sorescu, and many others. Frequently they attacked Jewish Communists such as Iosif Chisinevschi, Leonte Rautu, and Mihai Roller, who in the mid-fifties had implemented in Romania the most pro-Soviet Stalinistic policies in ideology and culture.

In the mid-sixties, Ceausescu had begun establishing his own brand of national Stalinism, and he had purged the party's *nomenklatura* of almost all of its Jewish members. Thus, Barbu's attacks were motivated by pure anti-Semitism and not by the so-called Jewish influence. Other strongly xenophobic and anti-Semitic articles were published by Adrian Paunescu, the editor of the weekly *Flacara* and a poet who consistently praised Ceausescu as a genius.

The novelist Ion Lancranjan, who often wrote in the vein of the Iron Guard ideologists about the necessity of creating a "new man," launched violent anti-Semitic attacks in his articles and novels. Between 1972 and 1989 most of the literary magazines engaged in regular attacks against Jews and Hungarians. Ceausescu formally condemned anti-Semitism several times, but in fact he encouraged the anti-Semitic and xenophobic assaults of his propagandists. Nationalism provided him a powerful tool with which to accumulate personal power for himself and his family.

The Jewish reaction to these attacks was rather weak. In his speech at the commemoration of the forty-fifth anniversary of the pogrom of Iasi, Chief Rabbi Moses Rosen condemned the media's efforts to rehabilitate war criminals. The speech was published in *Revista Cultului Mozaic,* the magazine of the Romanian Jewish community. It did not attract much attention, however, for the periodical was not widely circulated.[60]

Ceausescu himself made very few direct references to the Holocaust. But one such instance illuminates the way he distorted this chapter of Romanian history.

> Immediately after the beginning of the anti-Soviet war a real pogrom was organized against the antifascist forces, during which more than 2,000 persons were murdered in Iasi. In 1943, in the ghettos and camps created in the temporarily occupied Soviet territory, 50,000 citizens of our country were interned. In one of these, in Rabnita, the Hitlerites massacred 52 Romanian Communists and antifascists in March 1944. During the Horthyist and Nazi occupation, 170,000 citizens from Northern Transylvania were sent as forced laborers to Germany or to concentration camps, and from these more than 100,000 were killed.[61]

Ceausescu does not use the word "Jew" and sharply lowers the number of victims of the pogrom of Iasi. He also fails to explain that the 50,000 "citizens" interned in "the temporarily occupied Soviet territory" (Transnistria) in 1943 represent the survivors of the at least 125,000 Jews who were deported there in 1941–42. He also ignores the fact that the victims from Rabnita were not only Communists and antifascists but also Jews.

Official historians followed this line in their few writings about the Holocaust. In 1978 a booklet entitled *Zile insingerate la Iasi* (Bloody days in Iasi) was published in Bucharest. Written by Aurel Karetki and Maria Covaci, it contains a foreword by the propagandist Nicolae Minei. Minei and Covaci were affiliated with the Institute for Historical Studies of the Central Committee of the Romanian Communist Party, and Karetki was affiliated with the University of Iasi. Their booklet was a crude attempt to diminish greatly the number of the victims of the pogrom of Iasi, to deny the responsibility of the authorities in the massacre, and to minimize the Transnistrian horrors. *Zile insingerate la Iasi* is the only study on the Holocaust published in Romania after 1948, except for books concerning the massacres and deportations perpetrated by the Hungarian authorities in Northern Transylvania. It contains a strange description of the trip of one of the death trains, which traveled from Iasi to Calarasi and killed more than fourteen hundred Jews.

> The train halted again to unload new bodies. . . . The situation of those left in the cars ameliorated. . . . They were given bread and water. . . . A commission of military physicians arrived. . . . The commission provided first aid. . . . The wounded were taken care of . . . reembarked in other freight cars. . . . They were allowed to

receive food and clothing. . . . A scene of moving humanism took place. . . . Those
who were in the train were given 50 kilograms of sugar. . . . The military unit of the
railway station donated 600 loaves of bread.[62]

An uninformed reader of this passage would think that it was describing a Red Cross
train, not a sealed death train. As Karetki and Covaci tell it, Antonescu's local and
central authorities were only "hesitant," issuing conflicting orders and decisions,
without having any real responsibility for what happened. Even the complicity of
the Romanian guards escorting the trains is ignored. According to this odd historical viewpoint, the perpetrators of the mass murders were German troops, Iron Guard
legionnaires, social outcasts, and some Romanian soldiers who disobeyed their orders. The authors quote Curzio Malaparte, a contemporary Italian war correspondent, who placed the responsibility for the Iasi massacre on SS troops.[63] Yet they neglect to quote his mention of the "detachments of soldiers and gendarmes, groups
of simple men and women, groups of long-haired Gypsies who wrangled with shrieks
of joy while stripping the bodies, lifting and turning them over and over."[64]

In his foreword to the book, Nicolae Minei completely distorted the truth when
he wrote that "Romania did not yield to the Hitlerites one single human life." He
ignored the fate of at least forty-five hundred Romanian Jews from France, Germany, and Austria who were deported to the Nazi death camps with the approval of
Mihai Antonescu in 1942. He also failed to acknowledge the tens of thousands of
Jews the Romanian administration of Transnistria handed over to the Germans
across the Bug River. Concerning Transnistria, Minei reaffirmed the claim that the
guilt belongs to the Germans and to some unfortunate Romanian initiatives. "The
deportations across the Dniester, carried out by Antonescu's authorities, did not
have as their concealed or avowed goal the extermination of the deportees. The
deaths of some of them occurred for three main reasons: the abuses committed by
certain representatives of the authorities who embezzled the funds allotted for provisions; the criminal excesses of several brutes among the guards; the intervention of
Nazi murderers."[65] This thesis was also espoused in a 1984 article by Emanuel Kinsbruner, who argued that "the Hitlerite action of general extermination of the Jews
was not carried out in Romania because of the humanitarian spirit of the masses and
the sympathy felt for the Jews even among certain official governmental bodies."[66]

Another author who wrote on the Holocaust in Romania was Oliver Lustig, a
survivor of German and Hungarian anti-Jewish policies who had been deported to
Auschwitz from Northern Transylvania. Lustig systematically compares Hungarian
fascism with the Romanian variety and finds the latter less destructive. His writings
are contradictory in the extreme. On one occasion Lustig mentions "Antonescu's
responsibility for the death in Transnistria of 70,000 to 80,000 Bessarabian and
Bukovinian Jews," figures that ignore the Ukrainian Jews who also fell victim to the
Romanian dictator.[67] On another occasion he observes that in Transnistria "the men
of the dictator Antonescu, together with those of the Gestapo, had stained their
hands with innocent Jewish blood"; however, he also says that "it is a historical reality that in the area of autochthonous state authority after the summer of 1940 the

Final Solution had not been applied and over 300,000 Jews had been saved."[68]

The confusion here is probably deliberate: "the area of autochthonous state authority after the summer of 1940" clearly does not apply to Northern Transylvania, which was occupied by Hungary until the fall of 1944, or to Bessarabia and Northern Bukovina, which were occupied by the Soviet Union from July 1940 to July 1941. But after August 1941 "the area of autochthonous state authority" did include Bessarabia, Bukovina, and Transnistria. Lustig also ignores the deaths of about twenty thousand Jews within the borders of Old Romania and reiterates the official thesis that the "traditional humaneness of the Romanian people" prevented the Germans from accomplishing in Romania what they did elsewhere.[69]

A 1986 article by D. Sandru, A. Karetki, and I. Saizu even denied that there was any anti-Semitic legislation in fascist Romania: "Although they tried to introduce a series of anti-Semitic laws, the legionnaires failed because of opposition within the cabinet itself. But since they had the ministry of the interior and the local administration under their control, they were able to take broad action against the Jewish population even though no comprehensive anti-Semitic legislation had been introduced in Romania."[70]

The scholar Gheorghe Zaharia was able to provide a franker explanation, because his studies were published in French and thus were not accessible to most Romanian readers. An article published in the early 1960s does not mention that the victims of the pogrom of Bucharest in January 1941 were Jews.[71] The author does acknowledge, however, the Romanian fascist authorities' responsibility for the Iasi pogrom in June 1941. Quoting sources from the archives of the ministry of the interior, Zaharia puts the number of victims of the Iasi pogrom at eight thousand. He mentions the deportation of thirty-eight thousand Jews from Southern Bukovina and Dorohoi and the deportation and mass murder of Gypsies, as well as the persecution of members of religious sects. He also mentions the tragic fate of the Hungarians and Romanians in forced labor units organized by Romanian and Hungarian authorities. Zaharia supplies the same information in a 1974 book about the Romanian resistance.[72]

In his two books on Romanian fascism, Aurica Simion very briefly mentions the government's anti-Semitic policies. He adopts Karetki and Covaci's revisionist theses on the Iasi pogrom and even remarks that "unlike the measures adopted in Germany and other states, the anti-Semitism practiced by the Antonescu government did not imply genocide as one of the means for solving 'the Jewish problem.'"[73] Simion adheres to the same viewpoint in an article in which he argues that in Romania "the Nazis encountered a steadfast opposition to their attempts to recruit accomplices for organizing the deportation of the Jews and other genocidal actions." The "instigators and organizers of the pogrom of Iasi," he says, "were the Hitlerites, who practically took control of the city, preventing Romanian authorities from carrying out their duties." Two lines later, however, he observes that "among the authors of the massacres, besides the German military, were legionary elements, individual Romanian soldiers who had escaped from their units and were passing through Iasi, and hoodlums."[74]

Three studies on the Holocaust in Romania, published outside the country, may be found in volume 10 of *Documents Concerning the Fate of Romanian Jewry during the Holocaust*. The first, "Problema situatiei evreilor din Romania in timpul anilor 1938–1944 in istoriografia romana" (Romanian historiography on the situation of the Jews in Romania from 1938 to 1944), written by Gheorghe Zaharia and Nicolae Copoiu, maintains that Romanian historiography on the fate of the Jews in Romania between 1938 and 1944 may be divided into two stages. The first stage came immediately after the war, when "research on the history of dictatorship and terror in Romania during World War II was marred by the characteristic traits of an epoch that bore on all levels, including the emotional one, the marks of the tragic war that had ended in 1945." The second stage began with the ninth congress of the Romanian Communist Party, when Ceausescu was confirmed as general secretary. The party "eliminated from history a whole series of mystifications, falsehoods, and exaggerations." Zaharia and Copoiu claim that "neither Romania or, still less, the Romanian people are responsible for the disappearance [from Romania] of 425,000 Israelites." The victims of the fascist terror in Romania "had first of all been the militants of the Communist Party, anti-Nazi politicians and the Jewish population." In this study Zaharia also revises his estimate of the number of Jews who died in the Iasi pogrom: He states that from September 1940 to the end of the pogrom only thirty-five hundred Jews perished.[75]

Zaharia and Copoiu claim that "during the battles that took place at the beginning of the war against the Soviet Union in those territories [Bessarabia and Bukovina]" 5,000 Jews died. They also report that of the 118,000 Jews deported to Transnistria, about 50,000 survived, the remaining 68,000 having been "kidnapped" by the Nazis. "According to documents of the time," they continue, "these people were either executed by the Gestapo or died in epidemics and from a lack of medical and preventive care." Citing Minei as a "witness of those years," Zaharia and Copoiu stress "that the Romanian state during World War II cannot be defined as a state of the Holocaust." Furthermore, one of the "infinite number of opponents of the Final Solution among the Romanian people was Ion Antonescu, who fought Hitler on this matter."[76]

The second study, "Situation of the Jews in Bessarabia, Bukovina and Transnistria in the 1941–1944 Years," by Ion Calafeteanu and Maria Covaci, is a short survey of the anti-Jewish persecutions in the named territories.[77] It emphasizes the German responsibility for all of these persecutions: "The offensive on the Southern front in Romania, against the Jewish population in Bukovina and East of Pruth," began after orders were "received from the higher command after July 3, 1941." "In these cruel actions initiated by the Eleventh German Army under the command of General Richter von Schobert, SS troops and other German military organizations" and the "Romanian military from the Third and Fourth armies" participated.[78] The deportations of the Jews from the rural areas are viewed as improvised operations: "The fact is explainable by the absence of plans elaborated in time of any preoccupation in this respect, denoting absence of clear conceptions in this problem, everything leaving the impression of a random development of events." Using the German historian Andreas Hillgruber as their source, the authors estimate the number of Jews who retreated with the Red Army from Bessarabia and Bukovina at between 100,000 and 130,000. They assign to Antonescu the responsibility for the deportations across the Dniester and the deaths of many deportees owing to endemic disease, cold, and starvation. Calafeteanu and Covaci acknowledge that during the summer of 1941, 27,500 Jews died in Bessarabia and Bukovina "due to the military operations, the crimes perpetrated subsequently [or] . . . lack of food [and] unhealthy conditions."[79] The authors consistently avoid mentioning any Romanian governmental responsibility in the destruction of the Jews.

The third study, by Calafeteanu and Simion, "The Condition of the Jews Living within the Romanian State during the Years of Military Fascist Dictatorship," contains a brief description of Romania's anti-Semitic legislation.[80] The authors maintain that Romanian fascist anti-Semitism was "moderate" and mention only 160 victims in the 1940 pogrom of Dorohoi and the Jewish and non-Jewish victims of the Iron Guard uprising in January 1941. They blame German troops and some Iron Guard elements for the massacre of Iasi. The city's authorities are mentioned only as voices of moderation or as rescuers of the Jews. The number of Jewish victims in Bessarabia and Bukovina after the beginning of the military operations is given as 4,000.[81] The groundbreaking works of Lucretiu Patrascanu, in which he refers to the Holocaust in Romania and to the direct responsibility of the fascist administration for the massacre of the Jews, were not even mentioned as bibliographical sources.

A theme that Romanian historiography has dealt with rarely, and then only with serious distortions, is the fate of the Romanian Jews living abroad. During World War II more than eleven hundred Romanian Jews living in Germany and Austria and many others living in Nazi-occupied Europe were murdered with the consent of Antonescu's regime. On August 10, 1942, Mihai Antonescu told the Germans that the Romanian government was not interested in the Romanian Jews living in France. As a direct consequence of this position, 2,716 Jews who were recognized Romanian citizens and another 242 Romanian Jews whose status was unclear were deported from France to Auschwitz, where they were murdered.[82] It is also true that the Romanian government hesitated and then changed its position on this issue. Because of this, more than four thousand Romanian Jews in France survived, and a few hundred were even allowed to return to Romania. In an article published in 1986, the historian Ion Bulei mentioned the Romanian Jews living abroad who were killed by the Nazis and the vacillation with which they were regarded by Romanian authorities. Bulei characterized Romania's anti-Semitic foreign policy of 1938–39 as "dignified, humanitarian, and constructive." He also described the "anti-Semitism of a part of the Romanian Army" as "the result of the hostile attitude of some small groups belonging to the Jewish population."[83]

Another study on the situation of the Romanian Jews living abroad during World War II was published by Ion Calafeteanu.[84] Calafeteanu mentioned the "disappearance" of five hundred Romanian Jews from Vienna and described in great detail Romania's ambiguous foreign policy on this issue. The shifting position of the Romanian authorities was prompted by the continuing diplomatic war between Romania and Hungary. In fact both fascist governments made the status of their Jewish citizens living abroad the gravamen of a dispute that was based on national prestige rather than on humanitarian concerns. The Romanians opposed the deportation of Romanian Jews from France only after they realized that Hungarian Jews were exempted from the deportations. The Hungarians protested the fact that Hungarian Jews in France had to wear the yellow star, while the Romanian Jews did not.[85] Naturally, these considerations are ignored by Romanian historians.

A typical example of how Romanian historiography deliberately ignored the Jewish tragedy during World War II can be found in Yad Vashem's 1990 *Encyclopedia of the Holocaust.* In the entry on Romania, the general survey of the country's history through the Nazi period, written by historian Cristian Popisteanu, makes no mention of the destruction of a large part of Romanian Jewry. Tellingly, the bibliography to the survey cites as a source the pseudohistorian Ilie Ceausescu, a former general and former deputy minister of the army and the brother of the former dictator.[86]

A part of the story of the Holocaust in Romania was not ignored by Romanian historians. Many newspaper articles and several books have been dedicated to the subject of the 150,000 Jews from Northern Transylvania who were deported by Hungarian authorities to the Nazi death camps in the spring of 1944. Only 15,000 of these Jews survived. This chapter of the Holocaust was used as a propagandistic tool in Romania's dispute with Hungary. In 1985 the Federation of Jewish Communities of Romania published *Remember,* a brochure commemorating the fortieth anniversary of the destruction of the Jews from Northern Transylvania. This booklet completely ignores the fate of the Jews from Old Romania, Bessarabia, Bukovina, and Transnistria who also disappeared in the Holocaust.[87]

In the same year, Mihai Fatu and Mircea Musat edited a book entitled *Teroarea Horthysto-Fascista in Nord-Vestul Romaniei* (The fascist-Horthyist terror in northwestern Romania).[88] This 335-page volume deals with the deportation of the 150,000 Jews from Northern Transylvania in fewer than 20 pages. The editors devote much more space to the 219,000 Romanian refugees who fled Northern Transylvania as a consequence of the Hungarian fascist terror. They also note that about 1,000 Romanians were murdered by the Hungarians in the occupied part of Transylvania. This book was used by the media for anti-Hungarian propaganda. The extreme right-wing weekly *Luceafarul* cited it in an attempt to demonstrate that the Holocaust in Northern Transylvania was mainly anti-Romanian rather than anti-Semitic.[89] In a long 1986 article about the Hungarian occupation of Northern Transylvania in *Almanah Luceafarul,* one of Ceausescu's propagandists, Adrian Riza, repeatedly used the term "balanced anti-Semitism" in referring to Antonescu and his policies.[90]

The execution of Nicolae Ceausescu and the collapse of his regime in December 1989 generated the hope that Romania would face its past with more candor and begin to reassess its role in the Holocaust. This has not occurred.

After Ceausescu

A multiparty political system emerged upon Ceausescu's fall. Most of the new political parties share strong nationalistic and xenophobic tendencies, exacerbated by the many uncertainties now facing the country in the wake of the dissolution of the Soviet Union. The newly independent former Soviet republic of Moldavia contains a large Romanian population, but for the time being it refuses to unite with Romania. Romania also has territorial problems with Ukraine: parts of Bessarabia and Northern Bukovina remained incorporated in the former Soviet republic, and Romania wants them back. The numerically strong Hungarian minority in Romania, which very often responds to Romanian xenophobia with its own brand of xenophobia, presents another problem. The disintegration of Yugoslavia is creating tensions between Romania and Hungary. Some Hungarian nationalists hope to acquire Transylvania from Romania and Voivodina from the former Yugoslavia, and Romanian nationalists are using this to fan anti-Hungarian hysteria.

The Jews have again fallen prey to this resurgence of nationalism and xenophobia. Today the Romanian Jewish community claims between ten thousand and fourteen thousand members, most of them elderly. A few Jews helped overthrow Ceausescu and became ambassadors, senators, or ministers in the new government. They were immediately targeted in an anti-Semitic campaign. Synagogues and Jewish cemeteries in Alba Iulia, Tirgu Mures, Galati, Oradea, Satu Mare, and Sighetul Marmatiei were vandalized.

Corneliu Vadim Tudor and Eugen Barbu, both with ties to Securitate, the feared former secret police, soon founded the extreme right-wing weekly *Romania Mare* and a political party with the same name. Other leaders of this party were Mircea Musat and several retired high-ranking army officers. The Romania Mare Party has very close relations with Iosif Constantin Dragan, a wealthy, extremely right-wing émigré, who was associated with Tudor and Barbu. Dragan controls through the publishing trust Europa Nova the weekly magazine *Europa*. He is also the honorary president of Vatra Romaneasca, another anti-Semitic and anti-Hungarian political organization. Since 1990 *Europa* has called for the rehabilitation of Ion Antonescu.

Beginning in the spring of 1990, *Europa* and *Romania Mare* published weekly attacks on the Jews, accusing them of being Communist agents and the main source of Romania's problems. Both vitriolically attacked Chief Rabbi Moses Rosen, the Jews, the Hungarian minority, the American Joint Distribution Committee, the Mossad, the CIA, and former U.S. President George Bush. These neo-fascist publications "reminded" their readers that the new authorities planned to colonize Romania with Soviet Jews. Former Prime Minister Petre Roman, whose father was Jewish and who took a strong nationalistic stand, was often depicted in graffiti and in several rallies as a "kike," even though he hurried to publish his baptismal certificate in the press.

Starting in February 1990, several newspapers joined the anti-Semitic barrage. Among them were the progovernment newspaper *Adevarul* and the opposition National Peasant Party daily *Dreptatea*. Iron Guard publications such as *Gazeta de*

Vest began serializing the writings of C. Z. Codreanu, Horia Sima, and other leaders of the Iron Guard. *Gazeta de Vest* has close ties to Miscarea pentru Romania (The Movement for Romania), which is supportive of the Iron Guard.[91] A scandal tabloid, *Oblio,* published the *Protocols of the Elders of Zion* in serial form. A denial of the Holocaust in Europe was published in *Arena Magazin,* bolstered with quotes from revisionists such as Robert Faurisson.[92]

A few Jewish journalists, such as Radu F. Alexandru in *Romania Libera* and Vasile Grunea in *Mesagerul Transilvan,* appeared isolated in their attempts to oppose the wave of anti-Semitism and denial. The distinguished historian Andrei Pippidi wrote in the opposition weekly *22* about the Holocaust and anti-Semitism in Romania and showed how propaganda has transformed the victims into perpetrators. During the fall of 1990, Senator Gelu Voican Voiculescu delivered a strong speech in the Romanian Parliament in which he asked the government to take a stand against the anti-Semitic campaign being waged in the press. Warning against the divisive character of this activity, he emphasized that for the young, anti-Semitism is an abstract notion, and he said that after the tragedy of World War II it should be considered criminal behavior.[93] Although the text of the speech was published in the progovernment newspaper *Azi,* no action was taken.

On January 21, 1991, the Parliament organized a commemoration of the pogrom of Bucharest. The president of the Senate, Alexandru Barladeanu, and Chief Rabbi Moses Rosen made speeches. The commemoration did not generate notable public interest. In the meantime, however, there unfolded a concerted campaign to rehabilitate Antonescu as a national hero and the liberator of Bessarabia and Northern Bukovina. Government and opposition forces were equally involved in this effort and equally ignored the historical truth that Antonescu was a dictator who suspended all political parties, declared war not only on the Soviet Union but also on the Western powers, and expressed his hatred for democracy many times. Streets and squares were named after him. In May 1991 the Parliament, including its few Jewish members, observed a moment of silence in his honor. President Ion Iliescu disapproved of this parliamentary initiative, but the press of both the ruling party and the opposition ignored his declaration. Two newspapers reported his words, but only to criticize him.

Chief Rabbi Rosen was a controversial figure. From the late 1940s until his death in 1994 he was the chief rabbi of Romania, and he obviously had to compromise with the Communist regime. Since the early 1960s, Romanian Jews have been able to emigrate to Israel or to the United States. A nationalistic and anti-Soviet Romania was clearly supported in Western diplomatic chancelleries. The diminishing Jewish community in Romania received a certain degree of autonomy and was allowed to benefit from American aid. Rosen, a member of Romania's rubber-stamp Parliament, acted several times as an intermediary between Ceausescu's regime and Washington while Israel purchased from Ceausescu the right of Romanian Jews to emigrate.

In June 1991 Rosen decided to commemorate the fifty-year anniversary of the pogrom of Iasi. To generate as much press coverage as possible, such figures as Nobel

Prize winner Elie Wiesel; Israel Singer, the general secretary of the World Jewish Congress; and Rabbi Arthur Schneier of the Appeal for Conscience Foundation were invited to attend. For the first time in decades, Romanians were told about the Holocaust. As Rosen noted in his speech paraphrasing Elie Wiesel, Romanian Jews were murdered twice, once in the Holocaust and a second time through denial and lies. Through high-ranking representatives, President Iliescu and Prime Minister Roman sent messages to the commemoration. The president's conventional and weak message mentioned the Iron Guard (which had a marginal involvement in the pogrom), the legendary kindness of the Romanian people, and the fact that extremist actions during World War II were rare in Romania. The prime minister's message also avoided mention of the responsibility of Antonescu's regime in the mass murder of the Jews. Senator Gelu Voican Voiculescu and the president of the Senate, Alexandru Barladeanu, delivered courageous messages.

Survivors from Romania and Israel shared their personal tragedies with the audience. In his speech Wiesel said, "I address the leaders of this country; I hope you know that your representatives have great difficulties in the world to mobilize sympathy, political and economic support for your country. Your image is not the best. You must know that. You must know that unless these antisemites are shamed in society you will suffer. You will be isolated. The world is following with astonishment, dismay and outrage." Wiesel criticized the Romanian Parliament that had paid tribute to Antonescu and was heckled by a member of the audience who denied the Holocaust.[94]

Vatra Romaneasca, the anti-Hungarian and anti-Semitic organization that was heavily supported by former Securitate officers and middle-ranking members of the Communist Party, harshly protested the commemoration of the pogrom of Iasi. A "painful moment of meditation and human solidarity has been turned by Mr. Moses Rosen into a new opportunity for an extremely violent attack against the Romanian people." The party warned that "such actions will offer arguments and pretexts for an emergence of extremism in Romania."[95] In another statement, Vatra Romaneasca further claimed that "for the time being, if one reads the works devoted to World War II, one cannot see any proof that could support the thesis launched with so much enthusiasm by Rosen. . . . We do not exclude the hypothesis of a vast anti-Romanian plot in the international press, a plot joined by certain Romanian journalists as well as Moses Rosen."[96]

The press supporting the ruling National Salvation Front did not behave much better. Shortly before the Iasi commemoration the daily *Dimineata* published an article that played down the number of the Jewish victims of the Romanian Holocaust, blamed the Jews for all the economic and political problems of twentieth-century Romania, and strongly praised Antonescu.[97] In another pro–National Salvation Front newspaper, *Adevarul,* Cristian Tudor Popescu attacked the Iasi commemoration and Elie Wiesel.[98]

There were few reasoned and enlightened responses to this campaign. An exception was Jewish literary critic Zigu Ornea's article in the weekly *Romania Literara,* which succeeded in maintaining a level of excellence even under Ceausescu. Ornea emphasized the specificity of the Romanian Holocaust and the responsibility of Antonescu.[99] Another Jewish writer, Andrei Oisteanu, wrote a chronicle of the pogrom of Iasi based mainly on the reliable Romanian *Cartea Neagra.*[100] *Expres Magazin,* after condemning Rosen as a totalitarian for trying to "impose his version of History" upon the Romanians, organized a debate on the existence of the Holocaust in Romania. The periodical published the comments of respondents on both sides of the issue.[101]

A historian with a certain amount of prestige in Romania and the United States, Dinu Giurescu, approached the subject of the Holocaust with prudence. He denied the uniqueness of the Holocaust, emphasizing that Soviet authorities deported Romanians from Bessarabia and Bukovina and that the Romanian Communist regime threw many Romanians in jail. But Giurescu also did something that other Romanian historians did not dare to do: he acknowledged that Antonescu bears the main responsibility for the deportation of the Romanian Jews; he acknowledged the mass executions; and he affirmed that more than 110,000 Jews were deported to Transnistria and that at least half of them were exterminated.[102]

Amid this flurry of recriminations, Romania's international image declined still further. The American media had extensively covered the Iasi commemoration. On July 30, 1991, a joint resolution of the U.S. House of Representatives and Senate condemned the resurgent anti-Semitism and chauvinism in Romania. The resolution mentioned that the Romanian Parliament, instead of condemning the extremist organizations and publications promulgating nationalism, ethnic hatred, and anti-Semitism, "stood a moment of silence recently for the extreme nationalist Ion Antonescu who was responsible for the murder of approximately 250,000 Romanian Jews and was executed as a war criminal."[103] It also criticized the passivity of the Romanian government and the anti-Semitic heckling of Wiesel. The government of Romania was urged to take steps against anti-Semitism, and the president of the United States was called upon to see that Romania made progress in combating anti-Semitism and in protecting the rights and the safety of its ethnic minorities. It was promised that this progress would be a significant factor in determining levels of assistance to Romania.

The reaction of the Romanian Parliament to the resolution of the U.S. Congress was symptomatic. National Salvation Front member of Parliament Petre Turlea declared that anti-Semitism should not be declared unconstitutional in the new Romanian constitution. A representative of the Liberal Party propounded that the Jews exploited Romania and that Rosen was responsible for the anti-Semitism. National Peasant Party representative C. Constantinescu Claps declared that the Parliament should answer the "ordinary calumnies and the lies from the American media which were used by the U.S. Congress." Martian Dan, president of the Parliament, made an appeal for tolerance and asked whether anti-Semitism was an issue that should be ignored.[104]

The official response was again weak. President Iliescu condemned *Romania Mare,* emphasizing that he was a dedicated antifascist. Trying to be impartial, he said, "The mistake came from the other side as well. I talked to Moses Rosen, and

I reproached him for his attempt to promote the idea that the Holocaust started in Romania. It is not the historical truth. What he stated was taken advantage of by the anti-Semites, so *Romania Mare* appeared as the people's defender."[105] When Prime Minister Roman was asked when the government would take stronger measures against the extremist publications, he answered: "You want to know when? Well, when we have a legal instrument for that."[106] On November 21, 1991, the Parliament and the Senate adopted the country's new constitution, which a popular referendum confirmed the following month. Article 30, paragraph 7, prohibits the provocation of ethnic, racial, class, or religious hatred and the incitement of discrimination. The campaigns of *Romania Mare* and *Europa,* however, continued unabated.

Very few encouraging signs have appeared since. In a biting article the journalist Cornel Nistorescu criticized the intelligentsia for its silence on the subject of the Romanian Holocaust.[107] Unfortunately, Nistorescu later showed signs of wavering from his position. A former revisionist journalist and critic of Curzio Malaparte, Mihai Pelin, completely changed his position when he stated that the Holocaust in Romania had occurred and that it had been carried out by Romanians. Other than these, few Romanians of conscience have publicly resisted the current descent into neofascism and anti-Semitism.

After the commemoration of the pogrom of Iasi, Elie Wiesel returned to the United States sad and worried: "Antisemitism hurts Romania because of the blemish it brings to the nation."[108] He wrote that in Romania

> Zhidan (Kike) was not limited to the fanatic mobs; it was shouted in the street, whispered in the train, heard in the street, in city parks, in government offices and in school courtyards too. . . . Romania's position today in the international community is visibly not the best. . . . Unless its leaders put an immediate end to this vicious, ugly and perilous antisemitic press-campaign, unless they place the fanatic hate-mongers outside the accepted norms of society, Romania runs the risk of being isolated and condemned by the international community as few others have been.[109]

But the situation has not improved. *Expres Magazin* has criticized the post–World War II war crimes trials in which many Romanians were found guilty of massacring Jews as "communist political trials" and has cast doubt on their fairness.[110] When a delegation from the Canadian ministry of justice visited Romania in an effort to find material on Romanian war criminals who had escaped to Canada, *Expres Magazin* quickly published not only the agreement the Canadians had signed with the Romanian ministry of justice but also their names, hotel room numbers, and descriptions of the way they dressed.[111]

Paul Everac, a novelist well in favor during the Ceausescu regime, launched his own xenophobic campaign. He wrote that "the Jews are making noise with the Holocaust in order to buy Romanian factories for lower prices."[112] In a book published in 1992, he described the Jews as being "merciless and intolerant." According to him, the Jews were the most important factor behind the rise of socialism and Communism, and today they are the main promoters of liberalism. Everac also wrote that the Jews create atheistic propaganda while remaining religious fanatics themselves and that they control the media and the armed forces of the United States.[113]

In the meantime, the links between the government and *Romania Mare* became obvious. In June 1992 *Romania Mare* published a photograph showing Prime Minister Stolojan and Nicolae Spiroiu, the minister of defense, drinking with Vadim Tudor at a banquet honoring *Romania Mare*. In July 1992 Mihai Golu, the minister of education, thanked Vadim Tudor for money he had donated to a high school in Brasow.[114]

The world was unwilling to isolate Romania because of its rampant anti-Semitism and xenophobia, but the problem was difficult to ignore. During the summer of 1992, at the behest of the Bush administration, various committees and subcommittees of the U.S. House of Representatives recommended that Romania be granted most-favored-nation status. In a declaration published on August 6, 1992, the Romanian government reassured the U.S. Congress that the rights of minorities would be fully respected in Romania. The day before, the Romanian ministry of foreign affairs had published a document called *Carte Blanche,* which listed all the articles from the Romanian constitution that ensure equal rights to the country's national, ethnic, linguistic, and religious minorities. The document emphasized that any "racist show is an abuse in the exercise of the constitutional right of expression and information and it is therefore the duty of the Prosecutor's Office to bring such cases before courts of law so that the measures provided by the law might be taken."[115] Despite this assurance, not one legal measure has been taken against the authors of the ongoing anti-Semitic press campaign. The failure of the Romanian government to take action was one of the reasons why the U.S. House of Representatives on September 30, 1992, rejected the reestablishment of most-favored-nation status to Romania.

On October 21, 1993, Romania was granted most-favored-nation status because Congress believed the country was making progress with its democratic reforms. Twenty-four hours later, however, a statue of Ion Antonescu was erected in Slobozia. At the ceremony, the secretary of state for culture, the chief of the district police, and the president of the viciously anti-Semitic Party of Greater Romania addressed the crowd. Fund-raising for the statue was undertaken by members of the Romanian police, which is directly controlled by the government, and by Dragan, a pro-Antonescu émigré who was close to the Ceausescu regime.

During his visit to the United States in December 1993, the Romanian foreign minister, Teodor Melescanu, was warned in writing by the U.S. State Department about the reemergence of anti-Semitism and the rehabilitation of Antonescu in Romania. Since then matters have only gotten worse. Sergiu Nicolaescu, a Party of Romanian Social Democracy senator and the former official film director of the Ceausescu regime, made the movie *The Mirror,* in which Antonescu is depicted as a martyr, and Adolf Hitler as a wise and calm politician. During the spring of 1994 one of the extremist Romanian parties, the heavily anti-Hungarian and anti-Semitic National Unity Party of the Romanians, was brought into the government. A few months later the other two extremist parties, the Socialist Work Party and the Party of Greater Romania, also entered the government. Many representatives of these three political parties are in the forefront of Holocaust denial in Romania.

In 1994 there were many government-controlled television broadcasts rehabilitating Antonescu and other Romanian war criminals. Uniformed officers of the Romanian army were involved in at least one of the programs. Other statues of Antonescu began to appear. In only one case, in Targu Mures, did the central authorities deny permission to erect such a tribute. They did so in order to avoid an ethnic clash with the Hungarians of that town. On September 26, 1994, seven anti-Semitic members of the Romanian Senate tried to block the nomination of Alfred Moses, the president of the American Jewish Committee, as U.S. ambassador to Romania by sending a letter of denunciation to Senator Jesse Helms, chairman of the Senate Foreign Relations Committee. On November 12, 1994, a statue of Antonescu went up in Piatra Neamt. A Romanian military unit paraded in front of the statue during the inaugural ceremony, and the prefect, the highest representative of the central authorities, sent a wreath in honor of the occasion. In December 1994 *The Marshal's Destiny*, a documentary made by a state-controlled film production company, was widely disseminated by a state-controlled film distributor. The film presents Antonescu as a great patriot and justifies the massacre of the Jews during his rule with the claim that the victims were Communists and Russian sympathizers.

In March 1995 several senators skillfully manipulated the elderly Rabbi Alexandre Safran, the chief rabbi of Romania during Antonescu's rule, into declaring before the Romanian Senate that Romania's record during the Holocaust was similar to those of Bulgaria, Denmark, and Finland.

The rise of extreme chauvinism and revisionism in Romania in the mid-1990s is part of a general trend affecting all of Eastern Europe. But Romania is the first Eastern European country in the postwar period to erect statues of a war criminal with the direct involvement of the government. Romanian authorities have chosen to ignore that Ion Antonescu was one of the main allies of Nazi Germany. They obviously hope that Romania can join NATO and the Western world with a war criminal among its national heroes.

The tragedy of Romania is that tolerance and civic courage are foreign to most politicians and members of the intelligentsia. The Romanians' continuing denial of their complicity in the Holocaust will never allow them to find their freedom. The hope for a more democratic political future remains tarnished by lies and distortion.

NOTES

1. "Romania," *Encyclopaedia Judaica*, vol. 14 (Jerusalem, 1971), 386.

2. Léon Poliakov, *Histoire de l'antisemitisme—Du Christ aux juifs de cour* (Paris, 1955), 282.

3. Emanuel Turczynski, "The Background of Romanian Fascism," in *Native Fascism in the Successor States, 1918–1945*, ed. Peter F. Sugar (Santa Barbara, 1971), 104, 106.

4. Lucretiu Patrascanu, *Problemele de baza ale Romaniei* (Bucharest, 1945), 171.

5. Carol Iancu, *Bleichroder et Cremiaux—Le combat pour l'emancipation des juifs de roumanie devant le Congres de Berlin: Correspondence inedite (1878–1880)* (Montpellier, 1987), 25.

6. Carol Iancu, *Les Juifs en Roumanie, 1866–1919: De l'exclusion a l'emancipation* (Aix-en-Province, 1978), 44.

7. Vasile Alecsandri, *Poetii la cirma tarii* (Iasi, 1879), 10.

8. Ion Heliade Radulescu, *Alianta Israelita* (Bucharest, 1879), 7.

9. D. P. Martian, *Proprietatea si nationalitatea si o ochire in marea chestie a jidanilor* (Bucharest, 1866), 2.

10. Vasile Conta, *Cine sint jidanii—discurs* (Bucharest, 1866), 2, 5, 11.

11. Mihai Eminescu, *Opera politica 1870–1879* (Bucharest, 1941), 103, 477, 515, 505.

12. Bogdan Petriceicu Hasdeu, *Studii asupra Judaismului,* vol. 3 (Bucharest, 1901), III.

13. Serviciul propagandei legionare, *Adevarul in procesul C. Z. Codreanu* (Bucharest, 1938), 71.

14. Carol Iancu, *L'Emancipation des juifs de Roumanie (1913–1919)* (Montpellier, 1992), 31.

15. A. C. Cuza, *Nationalitatea in arta* (Bucharest, 1915), 108.

16. *Sfarma Piatra,* April 19, 1941.

17. Octavian Goga, "Primejdia strainilor," *Porunca Vremii,* June 5, 1934.

18. Paul Shapiro, "Prelude to Dictatorship in Romania: The National Christian Party in Power, December 1937–February 1938," *Canadian American Slavic Studies* 8, no. 1 (1974), 46.

19. Nicolae Iorga, *Problema evreiasca in camera—o interpelare* (Bucharest, 1910), 82.

20. Traian Braileanu, *Sociologia si arta guvernarii politice* (Bucharest, 1940), 82.

21. Toma Petrescu, *Ni se pierde neamul—actiunea jidanilor impotriva natiei romanesti* (Bucharest, 1940), 125.

22. Octavian Goga, quoted in *Paris Soir,* January 10, 1938.

23. Mihail Polihroniade, "National Socialismul si problema jidoveasca," *Buna Vestire,* February 11, 1938.

24. Alexandru Razmerita, *Cum sa ne aparam de jidani—un plan de eliminare totala* (Turnu Severin, 1938), 65–69.

25. Traian Herseni, "Rasa si destin national," *Cuvintul,* January 16, 1941.

26. P. Tiparescu, *Rasa si degenerare* (Bucharest, 1941), 8.

27. Constantin Virgil Gheorghiu, *Ard malurile Nistrului* (Bucharest, 1941), 8.

28. Petrescu, *Ni se pierde neamul,* 33, 36, 124.

29. Ion Chelcea, *Tiganii din Romania—monografie etnografica* (Bucharest, 1944), 96.

30. *Daily Herald,* January 6 (quotation), 10, 1938.

31. Gh. Dumitras-Bitoaica, *Statutul juridic al evreilor si legislatia romanizarii* (Bucharest, 1942), 42.

32. Jean Ancel, *Documents concerning the Fate of Romanian Jewry during the Holocaust,* 12 vols. (New York, 1986), 1:48.

33. Dumitras-Bitoaica, *Statutul juridic al evreilor.*

34. *La Stampa,* September 28, 1940.

35. Jean Ancel, "The Jassy Syndrome," *Romanian Jewish Studies* (Jerusalem) 1 (1987), 42.

36. Mihai Antonescu, *Pentru basarabia si Bucovina* (Bucharest, 1941), 63.

37. Ancel, *Fate of Romanian Jewry,* 5:510.

38. Raul Hilberg, *The Destruction of European Jews,* 3 vols., rev. ed. (New York, 1985), 305.

39. Patrascanu, *Problemele de baza ale Romaniei,* 210.

40. Hilberg, *Destruction,* 768, 771, 776, 791.

41. *Procesul marii tradari nationale* (Bucharest, 1946), 42; Matatias Carp, *Cartea Neagra,* 3 vols. (Bucharest, 1946–48), 3:447.

42. Hilberg, *Destruction,* 759; Dora Litani, "The Destruction of the Jews of Odessa in the Light of Romanian Documents," *Yad Vashem Studies* 6 (1967), 135; Julius Fisher, *Transnistria the Forgotten Cemetery* (South Brunswick, N.J., 1969).

43. Carp, *Cartea Neagra,* 2:64.

44. Hilberg, *Destruction,* 785; Ancel, *Fate of Romanian Jewry,* 4:110–13.

45. Rudolf Hoess, *Le Commandant d'Auschwitz parle* (Paris, 1979), 287.

46. Hilberg, *Destruction,* 287.

47. Carp, *Cartea Neagra,* 3:240.

48. Ancel, *Fate of Romanian Jewry,* 8:560–65.

49. Hilberg, *Destruction,* 759.

50. Ancel, *Fate of Romanian Jewry,* 11:24.

51. Alexander Safran, *Resisting the Storm: Romania, 1940–1947* (Jerusalem, 1987), 242.

52. Lucretiu Patrascanu, *Sub trei dictaturi* (Bucharest, 1970).

53. Patrascanu, *Problemele de baza ale Romaniei,* 210.

54. Mircea Musat, "Post Scriptum Octavian Goga—Jurnal Politic," *Revista de istorie si teorie literara* 3–4 (1987), viii.

55. F. Brunea-Fox, *Jurnalul rebeliunii* (Bucharest, 1944); Aurel Baranga, *Ninge peste Ucraina* (Bucharest, 1946).

56. Marin Preda, *Delirul* (Bucharest, 1975).

57. Michael Shafir, "The Man of the Archangel Revisited: Antisemitic Formations among Communist Romania's Intellectuals," *Studies in Comparative Communism* 14, no. 3 (1983), 229.

58. Theodor Lavi, "Vremuri grele pentru neamullui Israel—Umilirea mortilor," *Toladot* (Jerusalem), no. 11 (1975); idem, "Cronica," ibid., no. 15 (1977).

59. Shafir, "Man of the Archangel Revisited," 229.

60. Moses Rosen, "Uitare? Iertare? Rabilitare?" *Revista Cultului Mozaic* 609 (1986), 1.

61. Nicolae Ceausescu, *Romania pe drumul construirii societatii socialiste multilateral dezvoltate,* vol. 11 (Bucharest, 1975), 570.

62. Aurel Karetki and Maria Covaci, *Zile insingerate la Iasi* (Bucharest, 1978), 101–2.

63. Ibid., 74.

64. Curzio Malaparte, *Kaputt* (Paris, 1969), 167.

65. Nicolae Minei's foreword to Karetki and Covaci's *Zile insingerate la Iasi* was reprinted as "Barbaria cu fata nazista" in *Magazin Istoric,* July 7, 1978; see pp. 43, 44.

66. Emanuel Kinsbruner, "Adevaruri dintr—o Carte Neagra," *Almanah Flacara,* 1984, 284–87.

67. Oliver Lustig, "Denaturari si falsificari care jignesc si profaneaza memoria victimelor terorii horthiste," *Romania Literara,* April 2, 1987, 11–14.

68. Oliver Lustig, "Exceptie? Da, a fost o exceptie!" ibid., November 7, 1985.

69. Oliver Lustig, "Datoria sacra a celui care a fost martor ocular al crimelor naziste," *Almanah Flacara,* 1982, 313.

70. D. Sandru, A. Karetki, and I. Saizu, "Dificultati in colaborarea Romano-Germana (1940–1944)," *Analele Institutului de Istorie si arheologie A. Xenopol* 23 (1986), 205.

71. Gheorghe Zaharia, *La Roumanie pendant la deuxième guerre mondiale* (Bucharest, 1964), 205.

72. Gheorghe Zaharia, *Pages de la resistance antifasciste en Roumanie* (Bucharest, 1974), 45.

73. Aurica Simion, *Preliminarii politico-diplomatice ale insurectiei romane din august 1944* (Cluj, 1979), 131.

74. Aurica Simion, "Situatia evreilor din Romania in anii regimului antonescian," *Almanah Flacara,* 1982, 306, 308.

75. Gheorghe Zaharia and Nicolae Copoiu, "Problema situatiei evreilor din Romania in timpul anilor 1938–1944 in istoriografia romana," in Ancel, *Fate of Romanian Jewry,* 10:478, 479.

76. Ibid., 479, 480, 483.

77. Ion Calafeteanu and Maria Covaci, "Situation of the Jews in Bessarabia, Bukovina and Transnistria in the 1941–1944 Years," in Ancel, *Fate of Romanian Jewry,* 10:483–91.

78. Ibid., 483.

79. Ibid., 483, 487.

80. Ion Calafeteanu and Aurica Simion, "The Condition of the Jews Living within the Romanian State during the Years of the Military Fascist Dictatorship" (in English), in Ancel, *Fate of Romanian Jewry,* 10:492–525.

81. Ibid., 498.

82. Serge Klarsfeld, *Memorial to the Jews Deported from France, 1942–1944: Documentation of the Deportation of the Victims of the Final Solution in France* (New York, 1983), xxxvi.

83. Ion Bulei, "Simpozion stiintific Romano-Israelian," *Anale de Istorie,* no. 3 (1986), 133–41, quotation on 141.

84. Ion Calafeteanu, "Regimul cetatenilor romani de origine evreiasca aflati in strainatate in anii dictaturii antonesciene," ibid., no. 5 (1986), 124–37.

85. Hilberg, *Destruction,* 813.

86. Israel Gutman, ed., *Encyclopedia of the Holocaust,* 4 vols. (New York, 1990), 3:1289–92.

87. Federation of Jewish Communities of Romania, *Remember* (Bucharest, 1985).

88. Mihai Fatu and Mircea Musat, eds., *Teroarea Horthysto-Fascista in Nord-Vestul Romaniei* (Bucharest, 1985).

89. "Masa Rotundă," *Luceafarul,* June 21, 1986.

90. Adrian Riza, "Fascism si antifascism pe meleaguri transilvane," *Almanah Luceafarul,* 1985, 76.

91. Paul Hokenos, in *In These Times* (Institute for Public Affairs, Chicago), June 6–19, 1990.

92. *Arena Magazin* (Satu Mare), no. 28 (1991).

93. *Azi* (Bucharest), October 27, 1991.

94. *New York Times,* July 2, 3, 1991, quotation from July 2.

95. Foreign Broadcasting Information Service (FBIS)-EUU-91-129, July 5, 1991, 27.

96. FBIS-EUU-91-135, July 15, 1991, 29.

97. Pierre W. Telleman-Pruncul, "Ion Antonescu si problema evreiasca," *Dimineata,* June 5, 1991.

98. Cristian Tudor Popescu, "Mai ginditi-va," *Adevarul,* July 11, 1991.

99. Zigu Ornea, "Martiriul evreilor din Romania," *Romania Literara,* July 4, 1991.

100. Andrei Oisteanu, "Pogromul de la Iasi," *Cotidianul,* June 26, 1991.

101. *Expres Magazin,* July 3–10, August 13–20, 1991.

102. Dinu Giurescu, "Adevaruri ce se cuvin a fi neaparat rostite," *Romania Literara,* July 11, 1991.

103. *Concurrent Resolution Condemning Resurgent Anti-Semitism and Ethnic Intolerance in Bulgaria,* 102d Cong., H. Con. Res. 186.

104. *Adevarul,* July 27, 1991.

105. Ion Iliescu, Rompress interview in *Expres Magazin,* August 15, 1991.

106. Prime Minister Roman, quoted in *Azi,* July 25, 1991.

107. Cornel Nistorescu, "Tacerea din jurul crimei," *Expres,* January 14–20, 1992.

108. Elie Wiesel, quoted in *Jewish Week,* July 18, 1991.

109. Elie Wiesel, foreword to I. C. Butnaru, *The Silent Holocaust* (New York, 1992), vi–viii.

110. *Expres Magazin,* April–June 1992.

111. Ibid., July 14–20, 1992.

112. Paul Everac, quoted in *Libertatea,* June 12–13, 1992.

113. Paul Everac, *Reactionarul* (Bucharest, 1992).

114. *Romania Mare,* July 17, 1992.

115. FBIS-EUU-92-153, August 7, 1992.

BULGARIA
Frederick B. Chary

BEFORE THE HOLOCAUST

Bulgarians pride themselves on the survival of their Jewish community during the Holocaust. Although the claim that Bulgaria was the only country in Europe where all the Jews survived is an exaggeration, it is true that more Jews lived there in 1945 than in 1939. The circumstances of this event as well as the large Bulgarian aliyah to Israel make the Bulgarian reaction to the Holocaust a special story in European and world history.

Jews actually predate the arrival of Bulgarians, both Volga Bulgars and South Slavs, into the lands now occupied by the Republic of Bulgaria.[1] The earliest Jewish evidence is the second-century synagogue at Nikopol, on the Danube. Although it is difficult to estimate the number of Jews in the Balkans in ancient and medieval times, we know from anecdotal evidence that after the Diaspora many Jews came as merchants to Constantinople and Thessaloníki and to Bulgarian cities as well.

In 685 C.E. a scion of the Turkish Bulgar tribe, of the upper Volga River, invaded the Balkans and established a kingdom based on his conquest of the South Slavic population already living there. The state grew and prospered for more than four hundred years, eventually challenging the Byzantine Empire itself for control of the peninsula. That the state had contact with the Jews and Jewish inhabitants can be inferred from the medieval documents. In 1016 the Bulgarian Empire fell to the Byzantines. At the time of the Crusades, which began at the end of the eleventh century, many Jews may have fled into the Bulgarian lands to escape pogroms in the West. A revival of commerce in the Balkans also led to the encouragement of Jewish immigration into Bulgaria.

In the chaos of the Crusades, the Bulgarians broke away from the declining Greek state and established the second Bulgarian Empire, with its capital in Turnovo. In the years that followed, the continued invasion of the peninsula by Frankish knights resulted in the feudalization of the Byzantine lands and the rise of mercantile republics such as Venice and Ragusa. The Balkans became a mosaic of small states cemented by growing mercantilism. Jews played their part throughout the peninsula, inhabiting the great cities as merchants and artisans.

By the Middle Ages the Jews were well established in Bulgaria. The fourteenth-century emperor Ivan Alexander (1356–85) divorced his first wife and married Sara, the daughter of a Jewish merchant, who upon her baptism and coronation took the name Theodora. She became the mother of a Bulgarian czar and the grandmother of a Byzantine emperor. Under her patronage the influence of the Jews in the Bulgarian Empire increased, causing in some circles an anti-Semitic backlash encouraged by the church. In 1393 Bulgaria fell to the Ottoman Turkish Empire, which by the middle of the next century controlled virtually the whole peninsula, including Constantinople, where it established its capital.

For the Jews the new empire represented a haven against growing Christian attacks, since it was Ottoman policy to tolerate Christians and Jews. In the sixteenth century many Jews expelled from the Iberian Peninsula found refuge in the great cities of European Turkey and the Greek islands. Thessaloníki, in particular, had a large and influential Jewish population; in the early twentieth century Jews were a majority in the city. The Bulgarian cities Sofia, Ruse, Plovdiv, Varna, Burgas, and others also received Spanish immigrants, so many that the Sephardic rite became the standard for all Jews in the area and Ladino, a form of medieval Spanish, became the common language of the Jews.

In the following centuries Ashkenazi Jews fleeing pogroms in Central Europe escaped to the Bulgarian lands; while some of these melded into the Sephardic community, distinct Ashkenazi communities existed in Sofia, Varna, and Ruse. Turkish policy was to manage internal affairs through a system based on the religious communities, called millets. Jewish communities in the Balkans were legally responsible to the Jewish millet, led by the grand rabbi *(haham bashi)* in Constantinople, a paid government official as well as a religious leader. Local consistories headed by a rabbi and usually a lay leader dealt with matters such as marriage, divorce, inheritance, and civil disputes between Jews and also collected government taxes. Both Ashkenazim and Sephardim fell under the rule of the Sephardic grand rabbi. For Christians, on the other hand, there were Catholic, Orthodox, Armenian-Gregorian, and Protestant millets. As in medieval times, Jews were chiefly merchants and artisans, but occasionally they held positions in the Ottoman bureaucracy.

By the nineteenth century the Bulgarian lands had become a poor backwater of civilization in the deteriorating Ottoman Empire. The sultan's authority for practical purposes hardly extended beyond the limits of Constantinople, and while other Christian nations, such as the Serbs and the Greeks, found their way to autonomy and independence, the Bulgarians remained under the power of corrupt warlords and landlords. A Bulgarian national revival slowly grew, however, and the arrival of a reform movement sponsored by the Turkish government meant the beginning of real modernization and the amelioration of the Bulgarian condition. The failure of Turkish reforms to keep pace with the growing nationalist movement and the desire for complete independence, on the one hand, and the encroachment of the great European powers into the Turkish Empire, on the other, led to the de facto independence of Bulgaria in 1878, in the wake of one of the numerous Russo-Turkish wars.

By this time the Jewish community in Bulgaria numbered about 14,500, with about 5,000 Jews living in Sofia, which was chosen as the capital of the new state.[2] There were also 8,000 Jews living in the province of Eastern Rumelia, which was not joined to Bulgaria until 1885. Altogether, Jews made up less than 1 percent of the Bulgarian population (2 million in Bulgaria and 975,000 in Eastern Rumelia). Jews in the Bulgarian lands viewed the rise of Bulgarian nationalism and the war for independence with some trepidation because of the anti-Semitism of Russia, the patron of the new Bulgaria. While they stayed aloof from the Bulgarian national movement in general, there were a few incidents in which Jews helped the revolutionaries. Some Jews, however, fled with the Turks in advance of the Russian troops. A few anti-Semitic pogroms occurred during the war, but in general the Bulgarian population respected the lives and property of minorities, including the Jews and Turks who remained, and the professional Russian military occupation forces protected all inhabitants. In a celebrated incident during the war, Jewish citizens in Sofia put out the fire started by the retreating Turkish troops. The new monarch, Prince Alexander of Battenberg, honored the community for this deed, calling them the "true sons of Maccabi."

The new Bulgarian state was a constitutional monarchy, with one of the most democratic constitutions in Europe. Bulgarian was the official nationality and Orthodoxy was the state religion, but all national and religious minorities were constitutionally protected under the law. The Treaty of Berlin, which confirmed Bulgaria's autonomous status, specifically insisted on this in all the Balkan States. The new government continued some aspects of the Ottoman system; while Jews enjoyed the civil and political rights of Bulgarian citizens, the Jewish community controlled religious and some civil matters. There were a series of Sephardic and Ashkenazic consistories, the chief one being in Sofia. The community collected taxes from the country's Jews and was supervised by the Bulgarian ministry of foreign affairs; in practice, however, the latter interfered little in the community's functions. The Grand Rabbi of Bulgaria, selected by the central consistory, was the titular head of the Jewish community. In fact, by virtue of his office, he, along with the Bulgarian bishops and the chief mufti of the Bulgarian Moslems, participated in the Constitutional Convention.

In general the Jewish community remained outside the chaos of Bulgarian politics in the period from 1878 to 1939, although a few individual Jews did play a role. However, to put the Jewish story in perspective, we should take a brief look at the events that affected Bulgaria in these years. The Bulgarians first fought from 1878 to 1885, to unite all lands. The Treaty of San Stefano, between the Russians and the Turks, signed in March 1878, provided for a Bulgaria extending from the Danube to the Aegean Sea in the south and to Lake Ohrid in the west. The Great Powers modified these borders at Berlin, however, establishing a small Bulgaria essentially north of the Balkan range and placing most of Thrace, called Eastern Rumelia, under Turkish rule, with far less autonomy, and Macedonia completely within the Ottoman Empire. Political and revolutionary societies supporting the union of these areas to Bulgaria arose in the regions and in autonomous Bulgaria as well. In 1885 Bulgaria and Eastern Rumelia declared their union, and after a victorious war against Serbia, the Great Powers agreed to this revision of the Treaty of Berlin. However, with the exception of one small part, the struggle to unite with Macedonia was not successful.

Meanwhile, Bulgarian domestic politics suffered because of the naiveté of Bulgaria's constitution. Provisions for a unicameral parliament, destined to be overwhelmingly liberal, and a conservative monarch to share power led to irreconcilable differences in the first eight years. Prince Alexander of Battenberg constantly changed his governments, leaned heavily on Russian diplomats and army officers, and even prorogued the constitution, but he could not govern in the face of the overwhelming support the largely homogeneous peasant Bulgarian population gave its popular politicians, heroes of the national revival and struggle for independence. Because of his willingness to accept the union with Rumelia and his dashing escapades leading the troops in the Serbian War, Alexander became very popular himself in 1885. However, he now fell out of favor with the Russians for his independent policies and his English connections (his brother was Queen Victoria's son-in-law, and his prime minister was the Russophobe Stefan Stambulov). St. Petersburg and its friends in Bulgaria forced his abdication.

Ferdinand of Saxe-Coburg succeeded the prince. This ruler saw Bulgaria as his personal domain and an opportunity to further his ambitions. He mistrusted the people and the politicians and managed to use a growing number of political parties and a burgeoning civil and military bureaucracy to have his way. Overshadowing all was his quest for union with Macedonia. Terrorist groups operating in the province as well as in Bulgaria began a half-century of assassination and outrage. Meanwhile, the cost of government and the exactions of the rising bourgeoisie created an unbearable exploitation of the peasantry. In response, two new popular parties appeared in the 1890s: the Bulgarian Social Democratic Party and the Bulgarian Agrarian Popular Union. The latter very rapidly became the most popular group in the country behind its stentorian leader Alexander Stamboliiski. The former, reflecting the history of contemporary socialism, split into several factions.

In 1908 Ferdinand, with the help of Austria, declared Bulgaria's complete independence from the Ottoman Empire and assumed the title King of the Bulgarians. Then, allying himself with the other Balkan States, in 1912 he declared war on Turkey to acquire Macedonia. However, disagreements among the allies in 1913 led to a second war, in which Bulgaria was defeated by Serbia, Greece, Romania, and Turkey combined. In World War I Ferdinand sided with Germany, again with the object of gaining Macedonia (now part of Serbia and Greece), but once more lost.

These losses increased the popularity of Stamboliiski, who opposed the wars and who had become prime minister in 1919. Ferdinand was forced to abdicate in favor of his son, who called himself Boris III in remembrance of the medieval monarchs by that name. Stamboliiski, who had republican ideas, bypassed the new monarch and used his overwhelming support to create a state that benefited farmers at the expense of the government bureaucracy and the old political leaders. The latter joined with the king and the Macedonians, who opposed the prime minister's concessions to the Kingdom of Serbs, Croats, and Slovenes, and brought down the government in a coup d'état in 1923. Stamboliiski was brutally murdered. Party politics returned, but not for long. Because the Macedonian terrorists had so much influence in Bulgaria, and because the Depression of the 1930s so shook the economy, another coup, this one by the military and the intellectual political circle Zveno (Link), occurred in 1934. The military government dissolved the parliament and outlawed political parties and organizations. Within a year King Boris himself took over, exercising his personal power through hand-picked leaders. Political parties did not return; but in 1938 a new parliament was elected, the candidates running without party affiliation.

During these tumultuous years the Jews of Bulgaria essentially went about their business; they performed their civic duties but did not play a prominent role in the events. In voting they tended to support the government currently in office. The Jews of Bulgaria were always a tiny minority. Table 1 gives the Jewish population at the time of various Bulgarian censuses from 1887, following the union with Eastern Rumelia, to 1934, the last census before the war.

Non-Bulgarians, mainly Turks, represented about 20 percent of the population. The Jews lived in the major cities, which were inhabited by only 20 percent of the total population. More than half of the Jews in the kingdom lived in Sofia.

Jews were chiefly artisans and merchants, as they had been since the Middle Ages. There were Greek, Armenian, and Bulgarian merchants as well. However, there was not the kind of competition among these groups that led to anti-Semitism in other lands. On the one hand, there was enough opportunity for everybody in this country, where capitalism was just beginning; on the other, the historic presence of Jewish, Armenian, and Greek merchants led to their acceptance by the Bulgarians, who were still chiefly farmers. The various nationalities generally were associated with different branches of industry. The Jews, for example, specialized in importing and exporting, particularly of tobacco. Since most of the Jews were artisans, there were few very wealthy Jews in the country. Jewish employment before World War II is shown in table 2. The 1926 census indicated that 85 percent of the employed Jews were men. A survey by the Jewish consistory in 1937 indicated that 20 percent of the Jewish population lived in poverty.

In 1878 the Jewish community in Bulgaria had differed little from the isolated Sephardic millets that existed throughout the Ottoman Empire. However, Bulgarian independence had accelerated modernization of the entire state. The French Alliance israélite universelle (AIU) took a special interest in its brethren in the Balkans and established schools for the cultural emancipation of the community. As a result, the generation that became the leaders of the early twentieth century were secular and educated in Western thought and culture. French and Bulgarian gradually replaced Ladino. In 1920 more than 97 percent of Bulgarians reported Ladino to be their native language, compared with fewer than 60 percent in the 1934 census.[3]

TABLE I

Censuses of Jews in Bulgaria

Census	Total Population	Bulgarians		Total Minorities		Jews	
		No.	%	No.	%	No.	%
1887	3,154,375	2,326,250	73.75	828,125	26.25	24,352	0.77
1892	3,310,713	2,505,260	75.67	805,453	24.33	28,307	0.86
1900	3,745,283	2,887,860	77.11	857,423	22.89	33,633	0.90
1905	4,035,575	3,210,502	79.56	825,073	20.44	37,656	0.93
1910	4,337,575	3,497,502	80.64	839,962	19.36	40,133	0.93
1920	4,846,971	3,947,657	81.45	899,314	18.55	43,209	0.89
1926	5,478,741	4,455,355	81.32	1,023,386	18.68	46,558	0.85
1934	6,077,939	5,013,409	82.49	1,064,530	17.51	48,398	0.80

Sources: Bulgaria, *Annuaire statistique* 4 (1912), 47; 29 (1937), 25, 27, 41.

Furthermore, with the coming of the twentieth century the Jews were inspired by a new idea—Zionism. Although Zionism was principally an Ashkenazic movement, it became popular among the young Bulgarians, particularly in Sofia, as the road from Vienna to Constantinople crossed through their city. Prominent Zionists, including Theodor Herzl, on their way to and from negotiations with the Turkish authorities for Palestinian land made stops in the Bulgarian capital and lectured there on the need for a Jewish homeland to enthusiastic young crowds. Maccabi physical associations, Hebrew societies, and Palestine pioneer clubs were formed. A new generational struggle also began between the so-called notables, the older generation of AIU-trained leaders, and the Zionists. After World War I the Zionists gained control of the central consistory and drove the "notable" chief rabbi Marcus Ehrenpreis to Sweden. The struggle in the consistory was long and bitter, and the ministry of foreign affairs never recognized a new chief rabbi, although Asher Hannanel acted in that capacity. Hannanel, a sympathizer with Zionism, was a decorated war hero who had served as an officer in the cavalry unit of Crown Prince Boris in World War I.[4]

Many Jews had served in the war along with their non-Jewish fellow citizens; and since the former, especially because of the work of the AIU, were better educated as a group than was the population at large, a few of them entered the officer corps. Three attained the rank of colonel. Indeed, between the Balkan Wars Jewish officers were assigned to Thessaloníki en masse in the hope that they could persuade the Jewish majority in that city to support Bulgaria if a plebiscite took place. Unfortunately for Sofia, there was no plebiscite, only a war that Bulgaria lost.

Education in Bulgaria was compulsory and free, but there was a tradition of private schools, especially religious and national schools, going back to Turkish times. The Jews had their own system, at first Sephardic yeshivas and then, beginning in the 1880s, secular Jewish schools established by the AIU. Most Jewish students attended the Jewish schools, but as time went on more Jews attended the state schools.

TABLE 2
Jewish Employment in Prewar Bulgaria

Field	1926				
	Number Employed	Self-employed		Salaried Employees	
		No.	%	No.	%
Business, banks, credit, insurance	7,373	4,665	63.3	2,708	36.7
Industry, crafts, transportation	4,729	1,736	36.7	2,993	63.3
Professional, civil service, domestic service	1,342	231	17.2	1,111	82.8
Total	13,444	6,632	49.3	6,812	50.7

Field	1934				
	Number Employed	Self-employed		Salaried Employees	
		No.	%	No.	%
Business, banks, credit, insurance	9,381	5,243	55.9	4,138	44.1
Industry, crafts, transportation	5,165	1,616	31.3	3,549	68.7
Professional, civil service, domestic service	2,582	999	38.7	1,583	61.3
Total	17,128	7,858	45.9	9,270	54.1

Source: Salvator Israel, "Bulgarskite evrei v godinite na narodna vlast" (The Bulgarian Jews in the years of people's power), in OKPOE, *Annual* 6 (1971), 117.
Note: The calculations have been corrected.

In 1907 there were forty-three Jewish schools with 5,499 students. By the 1939–40 school year there were only ten Jewish schools with 402 students, despite an almost 25 percent increase in the Jewish population. This decline reflects the modernization of Bulgaria and its Jewish community.

Jews did not generally associate with the Bulgarian population, and social intercourse between Jews and Bulgarians was rare. Few Jews participated in national politics or culture. Among the most prominent who did were the Radical Party lawyer Iosif Fadenhecht, the journalist Iosif Herbst, and the poet Dore Gabe. Probably the most famous Bulgarian Jew in the world today is Nobel laureate Elias Canetti of the Ruse community, although he did his major writing after he left Bulgaria and cannot really be considered part of Bulgarian culture. Only a handful of Jews were elected to parliament. The chief rabbi served ex officio only on those occasions when a Grand Parliament was called. On one occasion a Jewish member was not seated by the body because he was Jewish. However, in most cases Jews who did cross the line into the Bulgarian mainstream were accepted.

As indicated above, the civil and political rights of all citizens in Bulgaria, regardless of nationality, were guaranteed, and in general this principle was respected. Anti-Semitism was not unknown, however. Most often it took the mild form of certain prejudices familiar in all societies—Jews were sharp bargainers, foreigners, and so forth. Yet there were also isolated incidents of pogroms and blood libels before World War I.

The Bulgarian peasantry by and large was not anti-Semitic. Unlike in neighboring Romania, where Jews served as rent collectors for the gentry and moneylenders, usurers in Bulgaria were national Bulgarians, usually local innkeepers. Furthermore, Stamboliiski's major ideological associate, Tsanko Bakalov, was a former socialist who had a great admiration for the Jewish socialists Eduard Bernstein and Eduard David, and Stamboliiski himself was a man of democratic principles.[5] Their influence over the peasant movement in Bulgaria nipped nascent anti-Semitism, a possible anti-urban tool, in the bud. However, modern anti-Semitism imported from Vienna, Berlin, and St. Petersburg by returning students at the turn of the century began to make its appearance just as the medieval variety began to die out. Nevertheless, it was confined to a small number of extremist circles.[6]

In the 1930s the rise of Hitler and Nazism provided a new model. But because of the democratic nature of the peasant movement and the great influence that democratic socialism, liberalism, and Communism had in the country, Bulgaria was not a fit ground for fascism. The mass fascist movements that existed in Germany and Italy or in Romania and Hungary did not exist in Bulgaria. There were, however, many small genuine fascist parties and groups. The largest was the National Socialists led by Alexander Tsankov, the organizer of the 1923 coup. Despite its name and despite the fact that it was the party most favored by Germany, it was closer to Italian fascism and did not practice virulent anti-Semitism. In 1937 the Jewish journalist Buko Piti published the book *Bulgarskata obshtestvenost za rasizma i antisemitizma* (Bulgarian public opinion on racism and anti-Semitism), which contained articles and statements against anti-Semitism by fifty prominent Bulgarian political, social, and cultural leaders, including even Tsankov. Of the several avowed anti-Semitic parties and organizations, the National Union of Legions and the Defenders of the Bulgarian Spirit (Ratnitsi) were particularly dangerous. In the mid- and late thirties these groups printed anti-Semitic propaganda leaflets and newspapers and organized demonstrations and pogroms. These activities brought them into physical conflict with counterdemonstrations organized by Communist and democratic associations. The most infamous melee took place in September 1939 when Ratnitsi gangs marched through the Jewish commercial street in Sofia to protest an antifascist speech by a well-known non-Jewish Bulgarian professor. The fascists were met by antifascist students, and a riot ensued.[7]

THE HOLOCAUST ERA

When war broke out in Europe, Bulgaria, like the other Balkan countries, declared its neutrality. However, by that time the government had become more profascist and, because of economic ties, definitely pro-German. During the Depression, German trade with all countries in Southeastern Europe increased; at the same time, all of these countries adopted some form of dictatorial or semidictatorial political system. Although at the start of the war major figures in Boris's cabinet, including the prime minister and the foreign minister, had pro-Western leanings, the initial victories of Germany in 1939 and in the spring of 1940 brought the country even further into the German camp.

Change was facilitated by a domestic crisis. The minister of agriculture, Ivan Bagrianov, who stood close to the royal court if not to the king, attempted to attain power through a series of political maneuvers. He succeeded in bringing down the government with a no-confidence vote in the parliament. Boris, however, retained control by shuffling his cabinet and proroguing the parliament while seemingly holding out to Bagrianov the hope of the premiership. However, when the new parliamentary elections created an even larger progovernment majority (officially there were still no parties), Boris dismissed Bagrianov and his allies and in February 1940 gave the post of prime minister to Professor Bogdan Filov, a pro-German art historian who was then the minister of education. The new minister of internal affairs was the ex-Ratnik lawyer Petur Gabrovski. Ironically, because of the Soviet-German pact of August 1939, known members of the Bulgarian Communist Party were permitted to stand for election, and they now made up the largest group in the opposition.

With the fascist Gabrovski as minister of internal affairs, Bulgarian police officials began anti-Semitic actions even though the status of the Jews had not officially changed. They directed their first activities against the many foreign Jews who had fled in advance of German troops into Central Europe since 1938. Most of these Jews had come to Bulgaria hoping somehow to get entry visas for Palestine. In the winter of 1939–40 the Bulgarian authorities unceremoniously expelled several hundred into Turkey, where they were imprisoned in refugee camps. Others were deported via the Black Sea on unseaworthy boats, one of which sank, killing more than two hundred persons. Gabrovski also sent a lawyer in his department, Alexander Belev, to Germany to study the Nuremberg Laws.[8]

In June 1940, after the fall of France, the Soviet Union invaded and annexed Bessarabia in Romania and then offered Bulgaria cooperation in regaining Dobrudja, the province given to Romania as part of the treaty ending the Second Balkan War and a Bulgarian irredenta. In response to this offer, Boris, to avoid being indebted to Moscow, turned to Hitler, who arranged for Romania to cede territory to both Bulgaria and Hungary. All three countries became Hitler's allies and within a year joined the Three Power Pact, the basic war agreement between Germany, Italy, and Japan. Once again Bulgaria's move toward closer relations with Germany brought hardship for the Jews, many of whom were forcibly deported from Dobrudja to Romania along with Romanian nationals in an exchange of populations.

In the fall of 1940 Mussolini began his unsuccessful invasion of Greece. Hitler used this event to pressure Boris and Filov into joining the Three Power Pact in order to gain permission for German troops to march through Bulgaria to Greece the following spring. Hitler intended to have Bulgarian troops serve as an occupying force in Greek Thrace after the conquest of Greece. At the same time, the Bulgarian parliament debated the Law for the Protection of the Nation. Modeled on Germany's Nuremberg Laws, this bill's main purpose was to limit Jewish access to education, business, and the professions. The debate lasted only a few days. The opposition delegates, joined by one government member, protested, but the overwhelming majority of the government ensured its passage. Outside the chamber the debate was more furious and became a symbol of support for the government and its pro-German foreign policy. Intellectuals and progressives defended the Jews, while patriotic associations and national booster clubs supported the law.

Most of the law's provisions affected only a minority of Bulgaria's small, separate Jewish community. Most of the members of parliament wished to avoid responsibility for this law; the government spokesmen in support of it were extreme fascists whom their government allies did not even respect. In fact, the most heated debate on the law concerned, not the provisions applying to Jews, but the anti-Masonic provisions. It provoked an indecorous argument between two rival fascists, the head of the National Socialists, former premier Alexander Tsankov, who counted himself among the opposition, and a government spokesman who led a small right-wing farmers' movement. Tsankov was a former Mason, as were practically all members of parliament. There was a rumor that King Boris himself was president of the Sofia Masonic Lodge. However, following the German model, the Bulgarian politicians resigned from the order and included its prohibition in the new anti-Semitic law.[9]

The law went into effect in January 1941. It did not always apply in Bulgaria, because Bulgaria's Jewish community was small. It also contained many loopholes for the Jews because of its provisions for war veterans, converted Christians, and Jews in mixed marriages. Even Jews excluded by the *numerus clausus* sometimes received special exemptions or, because of their specialization, were drafted for government service under Bulgaria's civilian mobilization law, although the Law for the Protection of the Nation forbade Jews from serving in the military. This was true for physicians, who were greatly needed after April 1941 in Macedonia and Thrace. Despite such exceptions, the process of ghettoization began, and a number of Jews had to sell their property at a loss. Local chiefs of police could issue special regulations for the Jews, and some were drafted into labor gangs.

In April 1941 Bulgaria joined the fighting by sending troops to occupy parts of Greece and Yugoslavia, where a new government had aroused Hitler's ire by overthrowing the leaders who had signed the Three Power Pact. In June Germany invaded the Soviet Union. Although Sofia did not declare war on Moscow, the government expelled some Communist and other opposition deputies from the parliament, creating an even larger majority. In July the parliament placed an exorbitant confiscatory tax on Jewish property.[10]

In January 1942 the German government held its infamous Wannsee Conference, at which the plan for the deportation and execution of the Jews of Europe was adopted. Since Bulgaria was an ally of the Reich rather than an occupied area, the scheme called for cooperation from the Bulgarian government. In response, the Bulgarian parliament passed a law in June 1942 that enabled the ministry of internal affairs to create a special commissariat to deal with "Jewish Affairs." The commissariat had special powers to issue decrees.[11] The approval of parliament and the king, which had been necessary under the Law for the Protection of the Nation, was no longer required.

The new commissar was Alexander Belev, the lawyer who had drafted Bulgaria's version of the Nuremberg Laws. Belev issued a decree in August 1942 that placed the Bulgarian Jewish community under the heavy yoke of Nazi discrimination. Stars were required; ghettoization was completed; and Jewish movement was highly restricted. All these measures were made with the aim of deporting the community to Poland in the spring of 1943. Theodor Danneker, the expert from Adolf Eichmann's office who had worked in France, came to Bulgaria and with Belev worked out a plan to deport Bulgaria's Jews as well as those in the lands occupied by Bulgaria. The deportations were to be accomplished in stages. The first groups scheduled for removal, in March and April of 1943, included 11,500 Jews from Bulgarian-occupied Greece and Yugoslavia and 8,500 from the kingdom of Bulgaria. Temporary transfer camps were built in southwestern Bulgaria and Macedonia.[12]

The construction of these camps, as well as information leaks in the commissariat and local police departments, revealed to the Jews and sympathetic Bulgarians that deportations were about to take place. As at the time of the debate about the Law for the Protection of the Nation, public protests, including some from prominent members of the church and government, were heard again. The bishops of Sofia and Plovdiv spoke harshly against the proposed deportations. Metropolitan Cyril of Plovdiv even threatened civil disobedience if Jews from his city were deported. Most important was a letter of protest signed by forty-three members of parliament, almost all from the government faction and headed by the vice president of the body, Dimitur Peshev. Even Alexander Tsankov signed! The protests helped the Bulgarian Jews, but those from Macedonia, Serbia, and Thrace were deported to the death camps in Poland.[13]

Belev attributed the failure of the deportation plan to the influence of the Jews concentrated in Sofia, and he drew up a new plan that called for the expulsion of the Jews from the capital to cities near the Danube, from which they could be deported. In the meantime, the issue of the Jews once more became a subject of debate in the parliament because of the members' protest.[14] Furthermore, the defeat suffered by the Germans at Stalingrad caused the government to ponder the wisdom of cooperating with Berlin on this issue. The day slated for the expulsion of the Jews from Sofia, May 24, 1943, was a Bulgarian national holiday, and the large crowds inside and outside the Sofia ghetto created a great deal of confusion. Once more local Jewish leaders were able to get support from the Bulgarian community, and this time the supporters included friends at the royal court as well as Metropolitan Stefan. In the end, although the expulsion order stood, the deportations never took place. As the Germans began to lose the war, the issue became less important in Bulgaria.[15]

In August 1943 King Boris suffered a fatal heart attack. A regency council of the king's brother Cyril, Filov, and the minister of war, General Nikola Mikhov, reigned in the name of young King Simeon II. The new prime minister was the ineffective Dobri Bozhilov. In reality, Filov, who was strongly influenced by Germany, was in charge of the country.[16] But Filov and the Germans' immediate problem now was the war, not the Jewish Question. Although Bulgaria still was not at war with the Soviet Union, in 1941 it had declared a so-called symbolic war on Great Britain and the United States. Heavy Allied bombing of Sofia in the winter of 1943–44 caused the evacuation of the capital. Furthermore, the government's new minister of internal affairs discovered a vast amount of corruption in the Commissariat for Jewish Affairs, and Belev was dismissed. The new commissar was a bureaucrat, not a dedicated anti-Semite.[17]

German losses on the eastern front, Allied bombing, and growing disenchantment at home, including a burgeoning partisan movement, caused a continuous government crisis. Secret negotiations with the Allies began early in 1944. In the summer a new government was constructed under the dynamic Ivan Bagrianov. Bagrianov, rather than Filov, was now in control, and he sought a negotiated exit from the war. The United States and Britain regarded Bulgaria as part of the Soviet sphere, even though the two Slavic countries were not at war, and they refused to talk, acceding to Moscow's wishes. On September 2 the regency replaced Bagrianov with the pro-Western Kostadin Muraviev, a nephew of Alexander Stamboliiski, whose cabinet included the opposition deputy Nikola Mushanov and a number of prominent antifascists.[18] Moscow still did not agree to talks. The Red Army approached Bulgaria, and on September 5 the Kremlin declared war on the country; Muraviev broke with Berlin and declared war on Germany. On September 9 the Communist-led resistance group Fatherland Front, aided by Soviet troops, took power, and the cabinet and regency were arrested. The new government made immediate peace with the Allies and joined the fight against the Germans. All laws against the Jews were revoked, and the process of restoring them to full citizenship began.

Naturally much of the strength of the new government rested with the resistance fighters who had opposed the fascists and the government during the war years. Who these fighters were and the role of the Jews among them is a complex story. Some resisted peacefully, as members of the legal opposition, which included some members of parliament. Some actually took part in the government of September 1944 under the profascist regency. But others joined armed resistance groups, such as the Fatherland Front.

Armed resistance began in March 1941, when German troops crossed the Danube into the kingdom. The resistance was carried out by the pro-English radical wing of the Agrarian Union. Since Berlin and Moscow were still at peace at that time, the Communists did not join in. The Bulgarian Communist Party did not have a particularly large number of Jewish members, although there were some. The most prominent was the economic historian Zhak Natan. With the rise of fascism in the 1930s, more, mainly young Jews had joined. The party was divided into various factions and was in a state of disarray because of the political struggles in the Soviet Union and the Comintern purges of the 1930s.[19] The general secretary of the Comintern, after all, was the Bulgarian Georgi Dimitrov, hero of the 1934 Reichstag fire trial in Germany, in which he defended himself and his co-defendants against the charge of burning down the German parliament building. This trial was a turning point in the history of the Bulgarian Communist Party, because Dimitrov was accused by the Nazis of being the mastermind behind the fire, and not only was he able to defend himself and earn acquittal at the Leipzig trial but he successfully, albeit erroneously, passed the accusation onto the Nazis themselves. Dimitrov won international renown and consolidated his position as the leading Bulgarian Communist. The party was illegal in Bulgaria but had existed before 1934 as the front Bulgarian Workers Party. After 1934 all parties were illegal. Nevertheless, nine Communists were elected to the parliament in 1940.

With the invasion of the Soviet Union by Germany, the Bulgarian Communist Party declared a state of active resistance. The first act of sabotage carried out by the Communist resistance was the dynamiting of a fuel depot in the Danubian port of Ruse by Leon Tadzher, a Jewish Communist. In the Communist period after World War II a factory on the spot bore his name. Shortly thereafter the Communists took to the mountains to form brigades of guerrilla fighters. Prominent Communists secretly parachuted into Bulgaria from the Soviet Union or disembarked from Soviet submarines along the Black Sea coast to aid in the struggle. The total number of guerrilla fighters is a matter of some dispute, varying from ten thousand to thirty thousand. It is clear that in the first years Communist partisans were very few. In 1942, however, the Communist Party formed an alliance with other opposition parties to create the Fatherland Front. These parties included the radical wing of the Agrarians, the first active resistance group, some Social Democrats, and members of Zveno. The leaders of Zveno spent much of the war period under government surveillance, but because Zveno had many military connections, professional antifascist officers joined the resistance. In 1943 the Fatherland Front organized the Narodoosvoboditelnata vustanicheska armiia (People's Liberation Revolutionary Army), or NOVA, and its numbers as well as its successes increased. The government retaliated by creating a special, particularly cruel police force to fight the resistance, since the regular police and army units had little taste for fighting their fellow citizens. Sympathy for the resistance grew throughout the country as the war went on.

The recruits for the partisans and NOVA quite naturally came from the young. They were primarily between eighteen and twenty-five years of age and of both sexes. Also quite naturally many young Jews joined because of Nazi anti-Semitism and the new Bulgarian legislation. Altogether there were about four hundred Jewish partisans, or about eight times the proportion of the non-Jewish Bulgarian resisters based on the population figures for the two communities. More than seventy Jews died in the struggle. Besides Tadzher, prominent Jewish partisans included Violeta Iakova, who was a member of an assassination team in Sofia called the Dark Angels. Iakova shot the former minister of war, General Khristo Lukov, who in 1943 headed the anti-Semitic legionnaires and was trying to persuade Berlin to replace Boris's government with one based on his organization. Menachem Papo was also a member of a Sofia guerrilla group. The government used his capture, trial, and execution in 1943 to justify its anti-Semitic policies.[20]

On September 9, 1944, Jewish rights were completely restored, although it took some time to release Jews from the compulsory labor groups.[21] The Commissariat for Jewish Affairs, under the leadership of Natan Grinberg, a Jew, became a document-collecting and record-keeping agency devoted to preparing cases against war criminals. Jews in the Fatherland Front became members of the ruling government. Zhak Natan very soon became the director of the Bulgarian Academy of Sciences's Institute for History. Rubin Avramov was elected a member of the Central Committee of the Communist Party and later minister of culture. Bulgaria was still at war, now with the Germans, and from September 1944 to April 1945 the Bulgarian army, including Jews, fought in Yugoslavia and Hungary. An Anti-Fascist League was established by Jews and maintained close contacts to its Soviet counterpart. It was led by the non-Communist Avram Tadzher (no relation to the resistance fighter), a former colonel and a member of Crown Prince Boris's regiment in World War I.[22]

THE POST-HOLOCAUST ERA

The consistories had been maintained throughout the war and were still in charge of the Jewish community. They helped prepare the communities for postwar restoration. There were many problems. The Jews were spread throughout Bulgaria because of the expulsions of 1943. Their property had been largely confiscated under the anti-Semitic legislation. There was also a question whether the Jews would remain in Bulgaria or go to Palestine. Bulgaria was certainly unique, since a large number of its Jews survived. However, since the community was small to begin with, more Jews survived in other countries.

One of the first actions of the government regarding the Jews was to hold war crime trials for anti-Semitic activity. These trials, as well as the restoration of Jewish rights, were mandated by the armistice terms and later peace treaties with the Western Allies and the Soviets. However, the new government enthusiastically supported the measures. The Jewish trials in fact constituted only a small number of the wartime trials taking place against former government officials. Because of the nature of the Bulgarian experience in the war, there was disagreement among the Allies about who constituted war criminals, but the Fatherland Front government, especially the Communists, had no desire to be lenient. More than ten thousand persons were brought before nine special people's courts, manned by ordinary citizens rather than professional judges. More than two thousand were executed. All the regents and cabinet ministers except two, both supporters of the Allies (one had been minister of war and a Fatherland Front agent in the Muraviev government, and the other had been selected by Bagrianov as minister of agriculture but never served) were tried and sentenced. Ministers of the last pro-Western government received prison sentences, but those from the pro-Axis regimes were executed. More than one hundred members of parliament were sentenced, and sixty-seven were executed. Dimitur Peshev, whose protest in parliament on behalf of the Jews aided his case, was saved from the firing squad but did spend a number of years in prison.[23]

Considering the severity of the sentences, the accused at the Jewish trials fared well. The Seventh People's Court tried members of the Commissariat for Jewish Affairs, leaders of Jewish labor gangs, and two journalists accused of anti-Semitic propaganda. The harshest sentences were given to Belev and the governor of one of the districts where the Thracian Jews had been impounded, the only capital judgments. However, Belev had vanished, probably assassinated. Most of the other leaders of the commissariat were given sentences of two to fifteen years. Those few who received harsher sentences had, like Belev, disappeared from the country. All of the other personnel were acquitted, as were the military labor gang chiefs despite testimony of harsh treatment by the Jews. Thus, although the new government enthusiastically welcomed the integration of Jews into the country, they were not particularly interested in punishing the Bulgarians involved in persecuting Jews under the old regime.

The restoration of the Jews to full legal status, particularly with regard to property rights, presented some problems for the new government. Since the whole Bulgarian Jewish community survived the war, all the property would have to be restored. The occupied territories of course had to be returned to Yugoslavia and Greece, although Bulgaria retained the Dobrudja region acquired from Romania in the summer of 1940. There were negotiations with Yugoslavia and Greece for reparations for the Bulgarian occupation, including the deportation of the Jews and the confiscation of their property. These negotiations were complicated, however, by the tumultuous events of the postwar period—the civil war in Greece, the possibility of a union between Bulgaria and Yugoslavia, and the split between Yugoslavia and the Soviet Union and its allies. Much of the Jewish property in Bulgaria had been destroyed in the bombings or had been liquidated. The Bulgarian economy had been linked to the German economy, and with the collapse of the Axis powers the value of Bulgarian money disintegrated, and restitution would put a tremendous strain on the postwar economy. This was counterbalanced, however, by the fact that the Jews constituted a very small part of the Bulgarian population. After 1944, 40 percent of the Jews required aid. David Ben Gurion, then chairman of the Zionist Jewish Agency Executive, visited Bulgaria and promised to arrange for relief. Jewish agencies sent massive amounts of clothes, medicines, and canned foodstuffs. Aid was provided to the Jews by the United Nations Relief and Rehabilitation Agency (UNRRA), Hadassah, and the United Jewish Appeal (UJA). The Bulgarian government also readily granted Jews scholarships to Bulgarian and Soviet schools. The Bulgarian authorities used some of the aid sent to the Jews, particularly medical supplies, for all Bulgarians. When the agencies objected, the government warned that favoritism toward the Jews might cause an anti-Semitic backlash. Reports in the West in 1945 complained that, despite the government's promises, Sofia was not restoring the Jews to their prewar status quickly enough.[24]

The most important question for the Bulgarian Jews in the immediate postwar period was whether they should remain in Bulgaria or migrate to Palestine. Zionism was an important movement in Bulgaria. Although the Jews had survived the Holocaust, most were bitter over the discriminatory policies of the war period and wanted to leave. Those who wished to go found it difficult to obtain entry visas until 1948, although a number of refugee ships left from Black Sea ports and illegally transported Jews to Palestine. A significant minority, particularly former partisans and Communist Jews, wished to stay. Moreover, they opposed any Bulgarian Jews' migrating to Palestine, and the issue became a point of contention along with other fractures in the governing coalition.[25]

The first prime minister of the Fatherland Front government was Kimon Georgiev, who had been the prime minister after Zveno's 1934 coup d'état. In 1947, however, a new constitution was promulgated that changed the country to a republic, and the Communist leader Dimitrov returned from the Soviet Union to assume the premiership. The major break within the government coalition was between the Communists, who closely followed the Soviet Union, and the Agrarian Union, which was pro-West. The Communists and the Agrarians had internal divisions as well. A number of Communists were purged as "Titoist" in 1948 and 1949, and some Agrarians allied themselves to the Communist position. As the tensions grew, the smaller parties in the Fatherland Front were dissolved and their members joined the Communists or remained in the front as independents. With the exception of those who supported the Communist Party, the Agrarian leadership either fled the country or were forced from the government. Some were imprisoned or executed. The Agrarian Union remained part of the Fatherland Front until 1989 but played a secondary role in the country.

The front parties also disagreed on the question of Jewish emigration. At first the Communists and the Zvenarists, including Georgiev, wanted the Jews to remain in Bulgaria. The Agrarians and the Social Democrats supported the Jewish desire to emigrate. Bulgarian socialist newspapers extolled the virtues of Jewish socialism in the Palestine kibbutzim. The Agrarian Union donated land, material, and teachers to establish model farms for the training of young Jews who were planning to become farmers in the new land. Then, in 1947, at the start of the Cold War, the Soviet Union began to follow an anti-British foreign policy that included agitating for a Jewish homeland and promotion of an Arab-Jewish radical alliance against the British in Palestine. The Soviets hoped that a new Jewish state would be an ally of the socialist bloc. The Bulgarian Communist Party began a campaign against the restriction of immigration, and the Fatherland Front reversed its position and supported the emigration of the Bulgarian Jews. In 1948, after Israel was founded, and 1949 more than thirty thousand Bulgarian Jews left the country and settled there as part of what at that time was the second largest aliyah to the new land, smaller only than Iraq's.[26]

The Bulgarian Jews arrived just as the Palestinians were fleeing their homes, and the Jews settled mainly in Jaffa, Haifa, Ramalah, and Ako. Decades later, Rehov Yerushalaim in Jaffa looked like a street in Sofia, with Cyrillic signs on the shops and the traditional Bulgarian death notices on the walls. Table 3 shows the decline in the Jewish population in Bulgaria.

The emigration of the Bulgarian Jews had some advantages for the Bulgarians. It eased some of the strain of the reparations problem, although the Bulgarian government was still obligated by treaty to compensate the Jews. It solved a minority issue at a time when the socialist countries were beginning to use nationalism as a

TABLE 3
The Jewish Population after 1934

Census	Total Population	Jewish Population	Jews as % of Total Population
1934	6,077,939	48,398	0.80
1946	7,029,344	44,209	0.63
1956*	7,613,709	6,027	0.079
1965	8,227,868	5,108	0.062

Source: Israel, "Bulgarskite," 114–15.
Note: *About half of the postwar population lived in Sofia.

binding force. In 1952–53, the Turks, Bulgaria's largest minority, would be pressured to move to Turkey. In 1984–89 those Turks remaining in Bulgaria were forced to adopt Bulgarian nationality, and in 1989 many were forced to emigrate to Turkey.[27]

The constitution of 1947 eliminated all distinctions of religion in Bulgaria. Orthodoxy was no longer the state religion, and Bulgarians were permitted to believe or not to believe. In practice Communist Bulgaria officially embraced atheism and harassed religious institutions in various ways. Rabbi Hannanel was tried in 1962 for smuggling and speculation, though there appeared to be a basis to the charges.[28] Paradoxically, however, the Communists at the same time supported the Bulgarian Orthodox Church as a national institution. Because of their antifascist stands in the war, Metropolitans Stefan and Cyril were well respected. In 1953 the government prodded the Bulgarian church to elevate itself from an exarchate to a patriarchate with Cyril as patriarch.

The first conference of Jewish Communists took place in the capital in November 1944, and it was followed by two others in 1945.[29] In January 1945 there was also a joint conference of the Central Jewish Committee of the Fatherland Front, organized in September 1944, and the Jewish community organizations, which adopted the following resolution:

> The [Central] Jewish [Committee of the] Fatherland Front must bring up the Bulgarian Jews in the spirit of patriotism, must divert them from the Zionist ideology, must fight against racism in our economic life, for finding out and bringing to trial those who made use of the Law for the Protection of the Nation for their own personal benefit and on account of the oppressed Jewish people.
>
> The Jewish Fatherland Front in the future must hold to heart the defense of the Jewish minority, must look for the observance and precise fulfillment of the new regulations about property relations, must give a progressive direction to education and upbringing in the Jewish schools, must take [responsibility] for vocational training especially of the youth and for the productive efforts of the Jewish people's masses.[30]

In 1946 Georgi Dimitrov addressed the second conference of the Jewish Fatherland Front and Jewish People's Communities (Evreiski otechestven front i evreiskite narodni obshtini), as the Communist-led organization then called itself.[31] The Bulgarian Jewish organizations began to seek contacts with prosocialist Jews and organizations abroad. The antifascist committee was dissolved, and its functions were assumed by the national Fatherland Front. Reorganization of the minority committees of the Fatherland Front in 1948 led to changing the Jewish organization's name to simply the Jewish People's Communities.

Jewish "People's Reading Rooms," libraries that were traditionally used as centers for cultural, political, and social meetings and education, were established in Bulgaria and became very popular. In Sofia the Jews established an arts circle, a chorus, an orchestra, a drama company, a literary circle, and a night school. There was also a Jewish scientific institute. Other cities also founded Jewish cultural clubs. Credit cooperatives were reopened, and a Jewish craftsmen's cooperative was organized. In the period between 1946 and 1948 there were eight Jewish newspapers, all published in the Bulgarian language. Six of them had editorial policies linked with international Zionist political parties such as Ha-Shomer ha-Za'ir and Pa'olei Zion. There was also a Jewish cultural magazine, as well as a number of special publications. The Communist weekly *Evreiski Vesti* (Jewish News) was also established during this time.

After 1948 many Jewish schools, reading rooms, and other organizations were closed because of the emigration. The ORT (Obshchestro Rasprostraneniya Truda) Institute became a general Bulgarian school. In April 1952 the Jewish scientific institute became the Hebraic Section of the Academy of Sciences, with a collection of thirteen thousand books, including seven thousand from the sixteenth and seventeenth centuries in Hebrew and Ladino, and thirty-three hundred manuscripts, as well as a collection of ritual and household objects. Ladino and Hebrew literature in Bulgaria died out, although the study of the languages by specialists continued. Many local consistories where the Jews were few in numbers were closed. With the commencement of the Cold War between the Soviet bloc and the West, the Bulgarian community left the World Jewish Congress.

The five thousand Jews who remained in Bulgaria were generally secularized and assimilated. Although a religious community still existed, it was very small, and only a few Bulgarian cities had operating synagogues. By the 1960s there were no rabbis left in the country, but in the 1980s there was a mini–religious revival in the community and some members went abroad for religious training.[32] Many Jews married non-Jews, diluting the community still further. Evidence of overt discrimination against the Jewish community was not apparent in the Communist period, but revelations after 1989 demonstrated that some prejudices and barriers existed. Most of the remaining Jews were educated and rose to high positions in the arts, education, and journalism. Some entered government service, the Bulgarian diplomatic corps, and military officer ranks. A number of streets in Bulgaria's cities have been named after Jews, particularly those who were partisans.

In 1962 the famous Samokov synagogue, known for its murals, was designated a historic monument, and its preservation was undertaken by the Institute for Monuments of Culture.[33] In 1988 the town council of Kiustendil planned to restore its synagogue in traditional style. The Sofia and Vidin synagogues have also been designated as national cultural monuments. The synagogue in Burgas is an art gallery, and the one in Pazardzhik is a museum.[34]

At the sixth conference of the Jewish People's Communities, held in June 1957, the organization reconstructed itself as the Social, Cultural, and Educational Organization of the Jews of the People's Republic of Bulgaria. Headquartered in Sofia, it maintained branches in the appropriate provincial cities. The meeting became the new body's first organizational conference. At its second conference, in 1962, it addressed itself to linking its activity more seriously to the "construction of socialism and the struggle against Zionism."[35] All other Jewish organizations ceased functioning at that time, and the organization was funded by the state.

In January 1963 the organization's leadership decided to begin an annual publication to provide information about Bulgarian Jews who had fought for socialism and against fascism and Zionism. Bulgaria's government was attempting to broaden its contacts with the nonsocialist world, and the survival of the Bulgarian Jews during the Holocaust was a propaganda tool. The first *Annual,* however, was not published until 1966. The third conference, in 1967, resolved to carry out, in the words of Dr. Salvador Israel, the former director of the Hebraic Section of the Institute for Balkan Studies of the Bulgarian Academy of Sciences, "a more decisive and consistent campaign . . . for clarifying before world public opinion the truth about the salvation of the Bulgarian Jews during World War II."[36] The conference also resolved to promote solidarity between Bulgaria and the Soviet Union in the Jewish community and to join with Jewish groups abroad in fighting neo-Nazism. Plans were made for a scholarly symposium on the social and economic situation of the Jews in Bulgaria after 1944 and for a scholarly history of the Bulgarian Jews to be published under the auspices of the Academy of Sciences. The organization did go on to hold several symposiums on Jewish society in Bulgaria, but the projected volume was never completed. About the same time, however, the Bulgarian community in Israel began preparing its own history; written chiefly by Chaim Keshalis, a historian and Bulgarian survivor, it appeared in 1967.[37] The Bulgarian community had also published books by Benjamin Arditi, the main Jewish proponent of the view that King Boris "saved" the Jews, a view the Bulgarian government was trying to dispel.[38] The Bulgarian Jewish organization also took responsibility for the *Evreiski Vesti.* In 1969 the *Annual* began publishing an English edition as well as a Bulgarian one.

The Jewish *Annual* frequently reprinted German and Bulgarian documents that reinforced the organization's version of the survival of the Bulgarian Jews, that is, that the Bulgarian people, led by the Communist Party, saved the Jews. Many articles stress the role of the Communist Party in fighting anti-Semitism and establishing Jewish equality. Short biographies of Jewish partisans, such as Leon Tadzher, Violeta Iakova, and Menachem Papo, were also regularly featured.

In his historical article on the Jewish community in Bulgaria since 1944, Dr. Salvador Israel reported the census of the community conducted in 1965 for the Social, Cultural, and Educational Organization of the Jews.[39] His findings on employment verify that Bulgarian Jews, who had been chiefly artisans and small tradesmen before

TABLE 4
Jewish Occupations, 1965

Field	No.	% of Jews Employed
Management on a national and district level in state and cooperative enterprises and in public organizations	226	9.7
Science, education, culture and the arts	416	17.9
Accounting, planning, and trade	520	22.4
Engineering and technology	302	13.0
Medicine	145	6.3
Metallurgy	134	5.8
Clothing industry	91	3.9
Law	36	1.6
Other	449	19.4
Total	2,319	100.0

Source: Israel, "Bulgarskite," 121.

the war, were now in positions requiring higher education, principally in academia and the arts. It appears that in Bulgaria, as elsewhere in the Soviet bloc, Jews were shepherded into the golden ghettos of education and culture. Israel's analysis of the actual occupational breakdown for Jews in 1965 is shown in table 4.

Jewish literacy was always high, but by 1965 it had become almost universal. Out of the total Jewish population of 5,108, only 80 persons over seven years of age were illiterate, and these were chiefly elderly women. In 1934 a ratio of 58 to 40 Jews had considered Ladino rather than Bulgarian to be their native language; in 1965 the ratio of native Ladino to Bulgarian speakers in the Jewish community was 2.6 to 97. Israel's findings on Jewish educational levels and work status in 1965 are shown in table 5.

Jews have made contributions to the cultural life of Bulgaria, especially in the theater.[40] Boyan Danovski, the most notable Jewish member of the profession, played a major role in the development of the postwar socialist theater in the country and trained a generation of young actors. Danovski already had an established stage career before World War II. In 1945 he became a radio personality as well. However, his major roles continued to be on the stage, and he went on to become the chief director at the Ivan Vazov National Theater. He also worked as a film director and producer and has written a number of books and plays. He has been honored with the titles of National Artist and Hero of Socialist Labor. Danovski also won the Georgi M. Dimitrov Prize, which was Bulgaria's highest civilian award under the Communists.

Mois Beniesh was another well-known actor and director at the National Theater. After his rights were restored on September 9, 1944, he became a newscaster and producer at Radio Sofia, but in 1945 he turned to stage production. After study-

TABLE 5
Work Status of Jews in 1965, by School Level Completed

School Level Completed	Work Status		Total
	Working	Nonworking[a]	
University	726	95	821
Vocational	339	164	503
Secondary	514	492	1,006
Middle	592	934	1,526
Elementary	98	517	615
Some Elementary	17	223	240
No Schooling[b]	4	352	356
Unknown	29	12	41
Total	2,319	2,789	5,108

Source: Adapted from Israel, "Bulgarskite," 124.
Notes: [a]Pensioners, children, etc. [b]Includes 269 children below school age.

ing in Moscow, he returned as a director to Sofia, where he earned a reputation as an innovator. In addition to contemporary Soviet and other socialist works and Bulgarian classics, he staged Western works, including the Bulgarian performance of *The Diary of Anne Frank.* The significance of this event was noted in the review of Haim Oliver, a Bulgarian Jewish author, who wrote: "The production of *The Diary of Anne Frank* at the Ivan Vazov National Theater comes on stage in timely fashion, for those who killed Anne Frank and her dreams have started clanking their weapons again. . . . They threaten to revive fascism. The production is a warning and an ordinance that we should never forget or allow this again. The idea is very forcefully put across to us and constitutes the chief merit of that moving human document produced by Beniesh and his enthusiastic cast."[41]

The actor Leon ("Leo") Naim Konforti also made his mark on the Bulgarian stage, winning critical acclaim for roles in the Bulgarian Stefan Kostov's *Golemanov* and in Arthur Miller's *The Price.* As a comedic actor he was compared to Chaplin. In *Leipzig 1933,* one of many Bulgarian works dealing with the Reichstag fire trial, Konforti played Van der Lubbe, the Dutch arsonist who burned the Reichstag building in 1933, unwittingly enabling Hitler to consolidate his dictatorship in Germany.

Other Bulgarian Jewish actors include Joseph Rosanov, the Honored Actress Luna Davidova, Buko Davidov, Leontina (Lyoshka) Arditi, the Honored Actor Itshak Fintsi, the National Actor Grisha Ostrovski, and the National Actor Leon Daniel.[42] Luna Davidova played Lenin's mother in Yuri Yakolev's *My Son Volodya.* This role may have had particular significance because of the sensitivity of the Soviet Communist Party to persistent rumors that Lenin had some Jewish roots.[43] Davidova's acceptance as a Bulgarian actress was an indication of the integration of the Jews into postwar Bulgarian society.

The number of Jews who were employed in the cultural and artistic fields in

1965 was about 184, or 3.6 percent of the total Jewish population. This group included 22 directors of libraries, cultural clubs, and other organizations; 82 writers, journalists, and editors; 33 actors and directors; 13 composers, conductors, and concert performers; and 6 artists and sculptors. The percentage of Jews employed in these fields was higher than that of the general Bulgarian population: 2.1 percent of Bulgarians, or 175,768, worked in the arts.[44] One reason for this was that, as elsewhere in Eastern Europe, because of unofficial quotas the arts and education were areas into which Jews could enter more freely than they could other professions. Jews who work on particularly Jewish cultural forms include the artists Marko Behat and Zhak Avdala and the writers Haim Benadov, Dragomir Arsenov, Salis Tadzher, Victor Baruh, and Haim Oliver. Aside from Nobel laureate Elias Canetti, Bulgaria's most renowned Jewish author is the playwright and novelist Valeri Petrov. Some of their pieces deal with the Holocaust, such as Baruh's novel *Otvun zakona* (Beyond the law) and Oliver's history *Nie spasenite* (We were saved). There are also a number of non-Jewish Bulgarians who specialize in studying Jewish history, culture, and society.

Nevertheless, despite the integration of the Jews in Bulgarian society and the pride with which the Bulgarians point to their record in the Holocaust, some anti-Semitism lingers. For the most part, it has been manifested in the persistence of the traditional stereotypes of the Jews, such as that all Jews are wealthy or that Jews have a special talent in learning languages. Other manifestations have been hidden quotas in various government and economic departments.[45] Anti-Semitism has taken uglier forms as well. In 1974 there was an international scandal when the Bulgarians tried and sentenced to death for espionage the Bulgarian Jewish economist Heinrich Shpeter, a known dissident who had been working for the Bulgarian government abroad. International pressure ultimately led Bulgaria to allow him to emigrate to Israel.[46]

The relationship between Bulgaria and the survivors abroad, most of whom are in Israel, has played an important role in the country's affairs. Israel's forty thousand Bulgarian Jews and their Israeli-born children made up one of the largest Bulgarian emigrant communities in the Communist period. The Israeli community represented a possible source of foreign hard currency. Reparations to the Jewish community were made in Bulgarian leva, which were worthless outside of Bulgaria. As a result, they were kept in Bulgarian bank accounts, along with rents from Jewish property that were paid throughout the years. Travel from Israel to Bulgaria became quite common and continued even after diplomatic relations between the two countries were severed in the wake of the 1967 Six-Day War.

The relationship between Bulgaria and Israel has always been complicated. In 1950, when the socialist bloc began to give wholehearted support to the Arab position in the Middle East conflict, official relations between Sofia and Jerusalem cooled to the point of hostility. Yet Sofia continued to woo the Israeli Bulgarian community and to maintain cordial relations with the Israeli Communist Party, whose leaders were welcomed in Sofia even after formal diplomatic relations between the two countries were severed in 1967. In the period from 1956 to 1967 diplomatic relations between Bulgaria and Israel, though still cool, improved, and many cultural exchanges between the two countries took place. In 1962 Patriarch Cyril visited Israel.[47] In the 1980s, particularly as relations between the Soviet Union and the West improved, a rapprochement with Israel occurred. The two governments held talks in preparation for resuming formal relations, although this did not occur before the fall of Todor Zhivkov in 1989.

The history of the Holocaust in Bulgaria itself became an important issue for the Communist Party and its government. As the facts of the hideous destruction of European Jewry were revealed and the singularity of the Bulgarian community's survival became known, Bulgarian historians developed a myth of the "rescue of the Bulgarian Jews." The question of who saved the Bulgarian Jews became a political football.[48] Both the Communists and the anti-Communists proclaimed that Bulgaria was the only country in occupied Europe where the Jews survived. According to the historians of the Bulgarian Academy of Sciences, the rescue was the result of the activism of an aroused, progressive public led by the Communist Party. Bulgarian anti-Communists in exile, including many Jews, claimed that credit for the rescue should be given to King Boris. Academy historians and government spokesmen countered that in fact Boris was a leading anti-Semite, pro-German, and the chief persecutor of the Jews. Both sides published documents—some falsified, some genuine, and most taken out of context—to support their views.

Both interpretations had problems. The question of who should be given credit for rescuing the Jews is inappropriate. The failure to implement the Final Solution in Bulgaria was the result of a combination of external circumstances and internal protest. Although the Communist Party did organize protests and appeals on behalf of the Jews as part of the general antigovernment resistance, it certainly did not influence the entire population. Other independent groups protested as well. On the other hand, the opposition exaggerated the role of the king. Although the royal court did intervene on behalf of the Jews, Boris appeared to be especially vacillating on this issue. He did nothing to prevent the deportation of the Greek and Yugoslav Jews, and there seems to be little doubt that without the changes in the war or the protests he would not have protected the Bulgarian Jews. It was even questionable whether Bulgaria could claim to be the only occupied country in which the Jewish community survived. Bulgaria was not really occupied but allied, and similar stories of survival occurred, to an extent, in other countries allied to the Reich. Jews survived in Romania and Finland and even in Hungary and Italy, where Jews were deported only after the Germans occupied the latter countries. There was also the massive Danish rescue.

In the 1980s Bulgarian historians modified the account of Jewish survival. It was acknowledged that Bulgaria had not been truly occupied. The role of government opponents other than the Communist Party—the church, non-Communists, even Dimitur Peshev—was recognized, although the Communists were still regarded as the primary opponents. The role of King Boris was portrayed in a historically more accurate light. These changes undoubtedly were in reaction to the more serious historiography of a new generation of Bulgarian scholars as well as studies of the subject by foreign specialists. Also, despite years of propaganda to the contrary, the myth that King Boris saved the Jews remained widespread among Bulgarians, so that the Communist government had to more credibly document its version.

One interesting aspect of the government-supported viewpoint surfaced after Todor Zhivkov came to prominence in Bulgaria. Zhivkov, a political commissar in the partisan regiment of Sofia in 1944, rose to become the head of the Communist Party a decade later. Between 1954 and 1989 he led both the party and the country. In 1943 Zhivkov had been in the party organization in the Iuch Bunar section of Sofia, the Jewish ghetto. His official party biography stated that he had been in charge of writing pamphlets defending the Jews and urging them to join the resistance.[49]

Since during the Communist period all education and mass media in Bulgaria were state-controlled, the account of the attitude toward the Jews and the Holocaust was monochromatic. The absence of anti-Semitism in the country and the role of the Communist Party in preventing the deportation of Bulgarian Jews were stressed at all levels—in the primary and secondary schools, in the publications of Sofia University and the Academy of Sciences, and in the popular press and broadcasts.

Bulgarians began to take credit for the rescue of the Jews as soon as the war was over. General Vladimir Stoichev, a Zvenarist who was sympathetic to the Fatherland Front and well known in international dressage circles, was appointed by Sofia in 1945 to be an emissary to the United States. In March 1946, elaborating on a government statement, he told the *New York Times* that the Jews in his country survived because the Bulgarian people "defeated [the] full application" of anti-Semitic policies. Although there were "certain inconveniences in the daily life of the Bulgarian Jews [the Bulgarian people] forced the government to abandon its contract with the Germans for their export to Poland."[50] For some time, however, the story of the Jewish survival was just a small part of the historiography of Bulgaria's role in World War II. During the 1950s not much was mentioned about it. In the Academy of Sciences's *Istoriia na Bulgariia* (History of Bulgaria), published in two volumes in 1954 and 1955, there are a few references to Jews, some of which can even be interpreted as anti-Semitic. Among the more important references are the following:

> [The fourteenth-century emperor] Ivan Aleksander had children from two marriages—first from the Wallachian Theodora and later from the Jewish Sara. . . . [He left] the greater part of the state, with the capital Turnovo, to Ivan Shishman, the son of Sara.
>
> During the middle of the fourteenth century [the number of] Jewish preachers began to increase greatly in Bulgaria . . . [the Jews] played a significant role in the economic life and had their quarters in some cities, chiefly in Turnovo. Even the queen was Jewish, the second wife of Ivan Aleksander. According to the biography of Teodosi Turnovski, the Jews were insolent toward the priests, reviled the icons, denied the cult of Christ and the virgin, etc. They used rationalist arguments for their anti-Christian propaganda in order to mock the faith of the population as they represented it as unreasonable and illogical.
>
> Bogomilism [the beliefs of a Christian anticlerical sect] continued to grow, and Jewish preaching increased.[51]

The second edition, published in 1962–64, repeated these sections on the medieval period almost verbatim. On the World War II period, the first edition provided the following:

> Through the Law for the Protection of the Nation the government attempted to conceal its antinational politics, which designated the Jews as the chief culprits for the impoverished condition of the country. . . .
>
> The prospect of the complete collapse of government policies [in 1943] resulting from the emerging rout of Hitlerist Germany, the great dissatisfaction of the people toward those policies, and the growth of the armed struggle increased the fear among some sections of the governing bourgeoisie because of the expectation of punishment for their cooperation in the Hitlerist crimes. Differences between those bourgeoisie who were wavering, on the one hand, and those who were loyal to the Hitlerist forces, on the other, came out into the open. In the national assembly the policies of Filov encountered a lack of confidence on the part of a significant number of the government deputies. On March 17, 1943, forty-three national representatives, led by the vice president of the national assembly, handed a resolution to the minister-president, Bogdan Filov, in which they declared themselves opposed to the persecution of the Jews and said they wanted to discuss in the national assembly the question of the deportation of the Jews from Macedonia and Thrace. Thus the discouraged accessories, tens of deputies, who up to then supported all of these policies expressed their dissatisfaction and lack of confidence to those who were still faithful to the Hitlerist ranks.
>
> Especially characteristic was the case of the vice president of the national assembly. He rejected the government policy with which he had been in step up to this moment. Then the president of the national assembly declared on March 26, 1943, the dismissal of the vice president. Without giving him the floor, [the president] proposed the vote for [the vice president's] removal without discussion. The resolution of the forty-three deputies was an expression of doubt in the victory of Hitlerist Germany that enveloped some of the governing circles and drove them openly to impede Filov.[52]

Peshev is not even mentioned by name. The action of the deputies is seen not as a humanitarian act but as an attempt to save themselves. The second edition retained the explanation of the Law for the Protection of the Nation, but discussion of the March 1943 events was slightly, but significantly, altered.

> The evident emerging rout of Hitlerist Germany, which was inevitably linked to the complete collapse of Bulgarian monarcho-fascism; the great dissatisfaction of the people toward the government policies; and the growth of the armed struggle increased the fear among some sections of the governing bourgeoisie because of their expectation of punishment for their cooperation in the Hitlerist crimes.
>
> After the battle of Volgograd [Stalingrad], differences between those who were wavering, on the one hand, and those who were loyal to the Hitlerist forces, [on the other,] came out into the open. In the national assembly the policies of Filov encountered a lack of confidence by a significant number of the government deputies. On March 17, 1943, forty-three national representatives, led by the vice president of the national assembly, Dimitur Peshev, handed a resolution to the minister-president, Bogdan Filov, in which they declared themselves opposed to the persecution of the Jews and said they wanted to discuss in the national assembly the question of the forceful deportation of the Jews from Macedonia and Thrace. Thus the discouraged

accessories, tens of deputies, who up to then supported all of these policies expressed their dissatisfaction and lack of confidence to those who were still faithful to the Hitlerist ranks. Especially characteristic was the case of the vice president of the national assembly. He rejected the government policy with which he had been in step up to this moment.

The attempts of the government and its supporting deputies to persuade the initiator and signatories of the resolution to withdraw it met no success. Then the president of the national assembly moved on March 26, 1943, to dismiss D. Peshev. Without giving [Peshev] the floor, [the president] proposed the vote on this motion without discussion.

The resolution of the forty-three deputies was an expression of doubt in the victory of Hitlerist Germany that enveloped some of the governing circles. This led to open wrangling in their ranks.[53]

Although the second edition is a bit more moderate in tone, still nothing is mentioned about the "rescue" of the Bulgarian Jews. Published in the early sixties, the new official history reflected in its moderation Bulgaria's reopening to the non-Communist world. In the *Kratka istoriia na Bulgariia* (Short history of Bulgaria), published in 1958, the Jews are not mentioned at all.[54]

In the 1960s the government, finally realizing the story's propaganda value, began to pay more attention to it. The Hebraic Section of the Institute of Balkan Studies in the Bulgarian Academy of Sciences increased its study of the history of the Jews in Bulgaria. Special attention was devoted to the World War II era. The Hebraic Section collected documents and oral histories relating to the Bulgarian Jewish experience during the war and sent copies to archives around the world. Articles, books, and memoirs were published. In 1959 the Jewish Bulgarian director Angel Wagenstein wrote the screenplay for the moving film *Zvezda* (Stars), a joint Bulgarian–East German production, in which the actors spoke in the German, Bulgarian, and Ladino of the characters they played. The film portrayed the relationship between a sympathetic German soldier and a Jewish refugee from Greece en route to the death camps through Bulgaria. A 1970 film, *Cherveni angeli* (The Dark Angels), directed by Vulo Radev, recounted the exploits of the Sofia guerrilla group, although there was no mention of the ethnicity of the Jews in the group. The 1986 film *Eshalonut* (The Trains of Destruction), with a screenplay by Haim Oliver and directed by Borislav Punchev, was a docudrama about the survival of the Jews. Victor Baruh's *Otvun zakona* (Beyond the law), a novel about the Bulgarian Jewish wartime experience, was published in 1960 in Bulgarian and several other languages. In 1966 the Social, Cultural, and Educational Organization of the Jews established a permanent exhibit in its offices in Sofia on the survival of the Jews of Bulgaria. The exhibit consisted chiefly of photographs, artifacts, and photostats of documents and emphasized the Communist interpretation of the survival.

Also in 1966, in the first volume of the *Annual* of the Jewish organization, Astruk Kalev wrote an article entitled "Pravnoto polozhenia na evreite v Bulgariia—svobodni pravnopravni grazhdani v narodna republika Bulgariia" (The legal position of Jews in Bulgaria—Free and equal citizens in the People's Republic of Bulgaria).[55] His thesis was that before World War II, Bulgarian Jews enjoyed equal rights, but anti-Semitism and racist propaganda were also permitted. In the 1930s such un-official campaigns as, for example, the exclusion of Jews from the civil service, had been tolerated. During the war there had been anti-Semitic legislation, but since the war Jews had been completely restored to equality and, in addition, anti-Semitism and anti-Semitic literature were forbidden by law. Censors would not allow Kalev to reveal that unofficial quotas still existed. The truth came out after 1989.[56]

Later, the media began to give credit for helping to save the Jews to other persons and institutions in Bulgarian society besides the Communists. In the 1979 *Annual,* David Benvenisti, the editor-in-chief, contributed an article called "The Bulgarian Orthodox Church in the Common Struggle of the People for Saving the Bulgarian Jews from Annihilation (1940–1944)."[57] In it he gives credit to the church in general and the metropolitans Stefan and Cyril in particular, although he still stresses the major role of the Communist Party. "One can trace the hand of the party in 90% of the Bulgarian public's protests against the Law for the Protection of the Nation, against the anti-Semitic persecutions," he wrote.[58] Indeed, the first third of the article is devoted exclusively to the role of the party, not the church. However, he described the Bulgarian church as a protector of Bulgarian nationalism in the Ottoman period and a combatant for justice.

The film *Eshalonut,* which names the major historical characters, gives much of the credit for saving the Jews to many non-Communist Bulgarians, including Metropolitan Cyril; Nikola Mushanov, a former prime minister (1932–34) and a leading spokesman against the anti-Semitic legislation in the wartime parliament; and Dimitur Peshev. It shows King Boris as vacillating under rather than leading the anti-Semitic forces. The major role in saving the Jews is given to Todor Zhivkov. In line with his style of leadership, however, the Bulgarian general secretary is portrayed, not as a superhero, but as an ordinary courageous man caught up in the times. Undoubtedly to give the film credibility, he is shown to have character flaws as well as strong points. He is featured as a sensitive idealist. In the film, Zhivkov has a tender relationship with the Danons, a Jewish family in Sofia. At one point the rabbi in Sofia scolds him for not wearing his hat in the synagogue. (The rabbi portrayed in the film is not Hannanel, who had trouble with the government. Despite his crucial role in the events, he is not mentioned. The rabbi featured is Rabbi Daniel Tsion, who in 1943 was mistrusted by the Jewish consistory because of his heretical beliefs but who did play a role in the events.) The film is remarkable for calling attention to the Bulgarian Jews and the relationship between the government and the Jews despite Bulgaria's siding with the Palestinians against Israel on the international scene. The Jews of Bulgaria in general did not like the film because it portrayed them too much as victims needing outside help for their survival. The Bulgarian Jews who remained in the country after the war were mainly secularists and Communists, many of them partisans during the war. Also, the key events that delayed their deportation and led to their survival were originally initiated by the Jews themselves when they learned of the deportations from the commissariat. Therefore, the Bulgarian Jews believe that they saved themselves by actively resisting fascism.

In the introduction to the 1987 edition of the *Annual* the non-Jewish scholar

Veselin Hadzhinikolov summed up the official attitude toward the Jews in Bulgaria and Bulgaria's role in the Holocaust:

> I feel honored to have been invited to write the preface to the present volume which is but another sequel to a highly appreciated series in the history and contemporary achievement of the Bulgarian Jews who are an inseparable part of the Bulgarian people. This *Annual* has been repeatedly praised in the press by . . . eminent Bulgarian scholars. . . .
>
> All . . . have expressed their legitimate pride in the Bulgarians who were the only European people to save the Jews from the savage extermination planned by the Nazis. That phenomenon, unique in European history, is duly regarded as an indisputable evidence of the humanism of the Bulgarian people—a people who has contributed significantly to our civilization.
>
> All these eminent scholars have expressly emphasized the existing friendly relations between the Jews and the Bulgarians in the fields of science, literature, and art.[59]

Bulgaria's attitudes toward the Jews have become a source of disagreement outside of Bulgaria. Several works by Jews and non-Jews support the thesis that anti-Semitism was not prevalent in Bulgaria. The German historian Wolf Oschlies in his book *Bulgarien, Land ohne Antisemitismus* (Bulgaria, the land without anti-Semitism) advanced the argument proposed by a number of Bulgarians and Bulgarian Jews.[60] Buko Piti, who in the 1930s had expressed the idea that anti-Semitism did not have roots in Bulgaria, emigrated to Israel after the war and wrote a second work that arrived at the same conclusion. It was published in Bulgarian in Tel Aviv in 1960. Rabbi Haim Asa, a Bulgarian survivor living in Los Angeles, led an American-Jewish tour to Bulgaria in 1981 with the cooperation of the Bulgarian Foreign Office. Asa arranged the tour in honor of the Bulgarians' rescue of their Jews. In connection with this commemoration, the Bulgarian government and private American donors abroad planned to build a monument honoring the rescue of the Jews in Sofia. The work was based on a model submitted by an American sculptor, but nothing came of it.[61]

Other Bulgarian Jews abroad, however, have contested the picture of harmony between the Bulgarians and the Jews. Nissan Oren, a professor of political science at the Hebrew University, emigrated from Bulgaria to Palestine as a child. He wrote the entry on Bulgaria for the 1971 edition of the *Encyclopaedia Judaica*. He states: "Most Bulgarian political parties were steeped in anti-Semitism. The Bulgarian peasantry did all in their power to prevent Jews from acquiring land, and from time to time there were blood libels."[62] But the very next entry on Bulgarian literature was written by Dr. Salvador Israel of the Bulgarian Academy of Sciences. Israel emphasizes the Jewish influence on medieval Bulgarian literature, citing the Hebrew letters in the Cyrillic alphabet and the use of Hebrew religious texts by Bulgarian monks. In the modern period, he insists, Jews were sympathetic figures in Bulgarian literature. He writes, "Protesting anti-Semitism, . . . non-Jewish writers portrayed Jewish suffering as a tragic destiny, while others advocated a solution to the problem, either through total emancipation or Zionism." He mentions Bulgarian authors "who after World War I, regarded the Jew as a comrade in the struggle for social justice" or "wrote of the Jewish contribution to the national movement."[63] The most prominent philo-Semitic authors Israel names are Petko Slaveikov and Aleko Konstantinov. We might note, however, that while Israel refers to Konstantinov's 1921 pamphlet *We Fight On My Brother,* a polemic against police harassment of a Zionist leader, Konstantinov's celebrated 1895 cycle of stories *Bai Gan'o never-oiatni razkazi za edin suvremenen bulgarin* (The life and times of Bai Gan'o: The unbelievable tales of a contemporary Bulgarian) contains anti-Semitic statements.[64] Of course, anti-Semitic remarks can be found in the works of authors from Benjamin Franklin to Ernest Hemingway and Charles Dickens to T. S. Eliot. In Bulgaria, those who supported the Law for the Protection of the Nation could quote the national hero Hristo Botev, a nineteenth-century revolutionary poet, to muster support against the Jews. However, the defenders of the Jews had their favorite national authors as well. Israel insists that "hostile treatment of the Jew is rare in Bulgarian literature," although he refers to an unfavorable portrait of Queen Theodora by Ivan Vazov, Bulgaria's national poet. The Jewish writer Victor Baruh in his *Svatbeni sveshti* (Wedding candles) pointed to anti-Semitism in post–World War II Bulgaria.[65]

Israel also wrote the lead article in the first issue of the *Annual* of the Social, Cultural, and Educational Organization of the Jews, entitled "Istoricheskite koreni na druzhbata mezhdu Bulgari i Evreite" (The historical roots of friendship between Bulgarians and Jews).[66] That initial publication also included two important quotes. One was from Georgi Dimitrov:

> In the dark and ignominious fascist regime our people did not allow the annihilation of their fellow countrymen—the Jews. It is widely recognized that Bulgaria was the only country under fascist domination where the life of the Jews was rescued from the bestial clutches of Hitlerite butchers and cannibals.
>
> Our brethren, the Jews, should always be grateful to the noble, democratic Bulgarian people and their Fatherland Front.
>
> Now that we are building a new, democratic, free, independent, powerful, and prosperous Bulgaria, the supreme task of Bulgarian Jews cannot be other than to participate most actively and with devotion in the peaceful construction for the welfare of our common fatherland.[67]

The other quote was from Todor Zhivkov:

> The ideas of our revolutionaries in the struggle against the Ottoman Bondage were further developed and formulated by the Bulgarian Communist Party on a fresh basis along the Marxist-Leninist line of the national question. Learning from Marx and Lenin, the Bulgarian Communist Party has always carried out in respect to other nationalities in this country . . . a consistent, international policy of profound respect and recognition of their national features and rights.[68]

On the other hand, Viki Tamir, a Bulgarian Jew who left the country as a young woman after World War II, maintained in her book *Bulgaria and Her Jews: The History of a Dubious Symbiosis* that Bulgaria was one of the most anti-Semitic countries in Europe and that most Jews were happy to have escaped after the war and moved to Israel.[69] Although Bulgaria's official support for the Arab cause during the Communist period fostered bitterness and tainted the good opinions of many Israelis, including those whose families came from Bulgaria, probably most Bulgarian Jews abroad, in Israel and elsewhere, maintain more friendly sentiments than those of Tamir and Oren.

Several ceremonies and conferences have been held in Bulgaria to commemorate the Holocaust. Although reports about and references to the Jewish survival had been presented at various scholarly conferences and public gatherings before, the first commemorative session devoted entirely to the Holocaust was held in 1973 before the Central Committee of the Bulgarian Communist Party. The president of the Social, Cultural, and Educational Organization of the Jews, Dr. Iosif Astrukov, thanked the party for its role in saving the Jews.

In the 1980s two major meetings were devoted exclusively to the topic of the "rescue" of the Jews. One, in 1983, "Forty Years since the Salvation of the Bulgarian Jews," was a small, unpublicized affair sponsored by the Social, Cultural, and Educational Organization of the Jews and held in the building of the Fighters against Fascism and Capitalism. Those giving reports were mainly Jewish and non-Jewish historians and writers.[70] The second conference, in 1988, "Forty-five Years since the Salvation of the Bulgarian Jews," was quite different. It was sponsored by the Sofia Press Agency, the chief publisher and news agency in the country, and held in the National Cathedral of Culture.[71] Many of the guests were foreigners and included scholars, rabbis, statesmen, and public figures. There was a large contingent from Israel headed by Shulamit Shamir, a Bulgarian Jew and the wife of the then Israeli prime minister, who gave a speech in Bulgarian thanking the Bulgarian community for saving the Jews. Gerald Kaufman, the British Labour Party's shadow foreign minister, was also present. Some American Jews representing B'nai B'rith and the United Jewish Appeal attended. The two-day congress was covered by Bulgarian and international journalists and received much attention in the Bulgarian press and on television. The delegates were greeted by Prime Minister Zhivkov in the official residence. A new documentary film in English, *Saving the Bulgarian Jews,* was produced for the conference. It gave credit for the rescue of the Jews to all strata of Bulgarian society and acknowledged Peshev, Mushanov, and the church leaders. Unlike in *Eshalonut,* King Boris, though, was once more portrayed as an initiator of anti-Semitism rather than a passive witness of the phenomenon.

The role of the Communist Party in the rescue continued to be emphasized at the conference. Indeed, some of the participants who were learning of the Bulgarian story for the first time saw it as propaganda for the party, an impression that was reinforced by the permanent exhibit at the offices of the Social, Cultural, and Educational Organization of the Jews. The participants attended the exhibit and visited Sofia's historic central synagogue to meet the head of the religious community. However, in the context of the continuing historiography of this issue, the conference gave relatively less emphasis to the party than previous official commemorations had. Since originally this conference was to be as localized as the one of 1983, it appears that part of the purpose was preparation for renewed recognition of Israel, a subject about which the participants constantly talked, although in fact this did not occur.

Some of Shulamit Shamir's remarks in her speech at the conference follow:

> I am very happy to be visiting again the country in which I was born and where forty-five years ago during the period of fascist obscurantism the Bulgarian people fulfilled the prophecy of the prophet Isaiah who said:
>
> "And if thou draw out thy soul to the hungry, . . . then shall thy light rise in obscurity, and thy darkness be as the noonday." . . .
>
> Other people too tried to help the Jews who were persecuted by the Nazis. Other people too succeeded in partially saving Jews. But it is a historically recognized fact . . . that of all European countries trampled underfoot by the Nazi boot in the darkest period of the history of Europe and the Jewish people only Bulgaria's Jews were saved.
>
> We shall remember this forever!
>
> . . . The plans for the persecution of the Bulgarian Jews were ready and sealed. The trains were waiting at the stations to take on their human load! And then a historical miracle happened. Everybody witnessed how a whole people, intellectuals and workers, peasants and townsfolk, the church, the Holy Synod, men and women, rose to save their Jewish compatriots in the face of fascist authorities at this hellish time.
>
> This is a remarkable period in the history of the Bulgarian people and of the Jewish people.
>
> This section of their history which the two peoples share can be the basis for a strong spiritual bond.
>
> I have spent the greater period of my life in my country Israel, to which I returned in order to fight for the liberation of my people and the creation of a national home for [them]. I fought in the ranks of the underground movement for the setting up of a Jewish state.
>
> It was here in Bulgaria that I was raised to love my homeland, my country; here I learned from the history, literature, and poetry of the Bulgarian people the meaning of the word "freedom." I learned from the immortal Vasil Levski and Hristo Botev that no sacrifice in the struggle to defend one's homeland is dear enough. These [values] inculcated in me in Bulgaria were for me a source of strength in the struggle for the freedom of my people.[72]

The Sofia *Evreiski Vesti* printed Shamir's speech in its entirety.

On November 10, 1989, Zhivkov's forty-five-year reign came to an end in the wave of revolutionary change sweeping Eastern Europe. A reformist government, one that was still composed of Communists, replaced his regime. Although a significant portion of the population supported the new government and the Communist reformers, a majority most likely did not. Nevertheless, two years passed before a non-Communist government came to power. During that period the Communist Party, renamed the Socialist Party, won the first round of free and fair elections. However, the country fell into political and economic stagnation because of the nearly equal division of power between the Socialists and the main opposition coalition, the Union of Democratic Forces (UDF). The Socialists agreed to choose Zheliu Zhelev, a UDF leader, as president of the country. At the end of 1991 the UDF, with the support of the Turkish Rights and Freedom Party, was able to form a government. In the fall of 1992 Rights and Freedom withdrew its support, and a government crisis ensued that continued until the end of the year, when the Socialists again formed a government.

In November 1989 the leadership of the Social, Cultural, and Educational Organization of the Jews immediately backed the Socialist reform government. Commenting in *Evreiski Vesti,* Dr. Iosif Astrukov, the president of the organization, promised that the Jewish community would help in rebuilding Bulgaria "in a just socialist way." He referred to mistakes made in the era before November 10, but he did not go into detail.[73]

Then some members of the Jewish community staged their own revolt. At the customary New Year's party at the organization's social hall, this one to usher in 1990, young Jews staged a demonstration demanding that the organization adopt a more ethnically centered position. They demanded that Jews in Bulgaria be permitted to celebrate Hanukkah and Purim and that Hebrew be taught. They asked that the organization establish a religious committee.

At an open meeting on January 13, 1990, the Jewish organization adopted a new constitution and a new structure. The members voted out the Communist leadership and changed the group's name from the Social, Cultural, and Educational Organization of the Jews in the People's Republic of Bulgaria to the Organization of Jews in Bulgaria Shalom. The new leaders pledged to follow democratic and progressive principles and to lead an "uncompromising battle against racism and anti-Semitism, fascism and chauvinism." The members also elected a Central Jewish Spiritual Council to revive religious education and services in Bulgaria. The chairperson of this council, Iosif Levi, stated that among his main goals were the care of Jewish graves in Bulgaria and the completion of repairs to the central synagogue.[74] The Communist government had been pledging to do the latter for forty years.

Just before his ouster Dr. Astrukov defended his tenure in the *Evreiski Vesti.*[75] Revealing that unofficial anti-Semitism had existed in Bulgaria during the postwar years, even among some of the Communist and government leadership, Astrukov claimed that he and his associates had done whatever they could to ameliorate the situation of the Jews. This anti-Semitism took the form of quotas in certain professions and government departments. However, Todor Zhivkov did not hesitate to link his name with the promotion of friendly relations with Jews. In fact he had personal friendships with Robert Maxwell, publisher of a series of books on great Eastern European leaders (including Zhivkov), and Armand Hammer, both of whom visited him in Bulgaria on several occasions.

After the fall of the Zhivkov government, several incidents of outright anti-Semitism were reported in the press: the painting of swastikas and Jewish stars on public buildings and private homes, the circulation of malicious articles and propaganda, and isolated assaults.[76] However, these incidents were not widespread, and Bulgarians in general continued to remain true to their tolerant tradition. Even anti-Turkish and anti-Gypsy propaganda, a much more serious problem, made little headway in the country. The prominent Communist screenplay writer Angel Wagenstein claimed that he was being harassed in the press because he was a Jew, but both Jews and non-Jews have made it clear that his Communism and not his Judaism was the source of the criticism. Sofia reestablished relations with Israel in 1990, and a Bulgarian-Israeli friendship association was formed. The first foreign head of state to visit the new Bulgaria was Israeli President Chaim Herzog.[77]

Initially, the Jews did not plan to leave Bulgaria, but the economic plight of the country led to the emigration of about half of the community to Israel between 1989 and 1992. Those who remained, numbering between two and three thousand, continued to play a significant role in Bulgarian life. Six—three Socialists and three from the UDF—were elected to parliament. Ilko Eshkenazi was a deputy prime minister in the UDF government of 1992.

With the dwindling of the Jewish population, Shalom's role has become focused on the twin goals of attracting foreign Jewish investment to Bulgaria and preserving Bulgaria's rich Jewish archives by establishing a major scholarly center of Sephardic Judaism. In connection with the five-hundredth anniversary of the expulsion of the Jews from Spain in 1492, a public ceremony was held to open the center. President Zhelev gave the keynote address, acknowledging the contribution of the Jews to Bulgaria's history and society and reminding the audience once again of their survival during the Holocaust. But he also pointed out that Bulgarian officials were responsible for the deportation to death camps of Greek and Yugoslav Jews. This was a significant change in the official Bulgarian story of the Holocaust. In the past both Communists and anti-Communists had ignored or excused this fact. The lifting of the Bulgarian censorship after 1989 allowed the debate over Jewish survival to be openly continued in Bulgaria. The central theme then became the role of the king. The argument continues.[78]

In conclusion, we can see that the unique circumstances of the survival of the Bulgarian Jews in the Holocaust have led to unique reactions. In the period of postwar Bulgaria under Communist leadership, official attitudes were controlled and the Holocaust became a propaganda tool, along with other past national Bulgarian events, for justifying the regime in power. The Jews who remained in Bulgaria became almost completely assimilated into the society. Their cultural identity survived, but the Ladino language all but disappeared. Those Jews for the most part were considered, and considered themselves, to be Bulgarians. They served in the army officer corps, in government, and in the diplomatic service, but they were involved chiefly in the arts, education, and journalism. After 1989, however, there was a national and religious revival led by the younger members of the community, the children of those Communists and partisans who had elected to stay in the country in the postwar years. Half of these several thousand soon emigrated for economic reasons, but the few who remain continue to play an important role in Bulgarian society.

The Bulgarian Jewish communities in Israel and, to a lesser extent, elsewhere maintain for the most part fond memories of Bulgaria, which in many cases have been transmitted to the first generation born abroad. There are, however, notable exceptions. There are some Jews who criticize Communist Bulgaria because of its officially anti-Zionist attitudes and some who have no feeling for the country at all.

After 1989, however, Bulgaria became a strong friend of Israel and continued to point with pride to its record during the Holocaust. In any case, the fate of this small land during the Holocaust, that devastatingly tragic story of the twentieth century, sheds much light on its significance for the rest of the world.

NOTES

1. A good, impartial, complete history of Bulgaria still needs to be written. In the meantime, Dimitur Kosev et al., *Istoriia na Bulgariia,* published by the Bulgarian Academy of Sciences, 2d ed., 3 vols. (Sofia, 1962–64), and the academy's more recent but incomplete edition, begun in 1979, *Istoriia na Bulgariia v chetirinadeset toma,* ed. Velizar Velkov (Sofia, 1979–), are useful. For the period 1870–1920, see Richard J. Crampton's excellent *Bulgaria, 1878–1918: A History* (Boulder, Colo., 1983). For more on the Bulgarian Jews, see Saul Mezan, *Les Juifs espagnols en Bulgarie* (Sofia, 1925); and Frederick B. Chary, *The Bulgarian Jews and the Final Solution: 1940–1944* (Pittsburgh, 1972). *Yahadut Bulgariyah,* ed. A. Romano et al., vol. 10 of the *Entsiklopediyah shel galuyyot* (Jerusalem, 1967), deals with Bulgaria. The annual of Obshtestvena kulturno-prosvetna organizatsiia na evreite v narodna republika bulgariia (Social, Cultural, and Educational Organization of the Jews in the People's Republic of Bulgaria), *Godishnik* (hereafter cited as OKPOE, *Annual*), published yearly since 1966, has valuable articles. Almost all volumes are accompanied by an English translation.

2. Bulgaria, Direction Générale de la Statistique, *Annuaire Statistique 1937* (Sofia, 1937), 27.

3. Salvator Israel, "Bulgarskite evrei v godinite na narodna vlast," OKPOE, *Annual 6* (1971), 124.

4. Asher Hannanel, testimony, April 1945, Sofia, Protocols of the People's Court No. 7, vol. 3, 805–17.

5. For information on the Agrarian Union, see John D. Bell, *Peasants in Power: Alexander Stamboliiski and the Bulgarian Agrarian National Union, 1896–1923* (Princeton, 1977); and Frederick B. Chary, "Aleksandur Stamboliiski—suzdatel na selskata partiia v Bulgariia," in *Aleksandur Stamboliiski: Zhivot, delo, zaveti,* ed. Hristo Hristov et al. (Sofia, 1980).

6. For anti-Semitic incidents, see Mezan, *Les Juifs espagnols.* For tolerance, see Buko Piti, ed., *Bulgarskata obshtestvenost za rasizma i antisemitizma* (Sofia, 1937).

7. See Chary, *Bulgarian Jews,* 7–9.

8. Ibid., 36.

9. Ibid., 37–41. For the parliamentary debate, see Bulgaria, Narodno Subranie, *Stenografski dnevnitsi,* 25th Obiknoveno Narodno Subranie (here-after cited as ONS), 2d regular sess. (October 28, 1940–May 28, 1941), 1:204–60, 2:689–732, 808–10.

10. Chary, *Bulgarian Jews,* 41–55.

11. Ibid., 53–54; Bulgaria, Narodno Subranie, *Dnevnitsi,* 25th ONS, 4th extraordinary sess. (June 22–July 2, 1942), 68–96, 220–22.

12. Chary, *Bulgarian Jews,* 69–84.

13. Ibid., 90–128.

14. Ibid., 98–100; Bulgaria, Narodno Subranie, *Dnevnitsi,* 25th ONS, 4th regular sess. (October 28, 1942–March 28, 1943), 2:1157–58, 1163–70 (pages 1167–71 are missing from all copies).

15. Chary, *Bulgarian Jews,* 129–52.

16. Ibid., 152–57; Marshall Lee Miller, *Bulgaria during the Second World War* (Stanford, 1975), 135–216; Nissan Oren, *Bulgarian Communism: 1934–1944* (New York, 1971), 230–31.

17. Chary, *Bulgarian Jews,* 165–67.

18. Ibid., 175–83.

19. See Oren, *Bulgarian Communism,* 215.

20. For Jewish partisans, see Central Consistory of Jews in Bulgaria, *Evrei-zaginali v antifashistkata borba* (Sofia, 1958).

21. Chary, *Bulgarian Jews,* 178–80.

22. For the history of the Jews in postwar Bulgaria until 1970, see Israel, "Bulgarskite."

23. Chary, *Bulgarian Jews,* 178–80.

24. *New York Times,* January 20, 1945, 3; January 27, 1945, 3; March 19, 1945, 6; March 31, 1945, 13; February 7, 1947, 5.

25. Chary, *Bulgarian Jews,* 181–82.

26. Israel, "Bulgarskite," 114.

27. Huey Louis Kostanick, *Turkish Resettlement of Bulgarian Turks, 1950–1953* (Berkeley, 1957); *New York Times,* January 17, 1985, sec. 1, p. 5; August 15, 1989, sec. 1, p. 1.

28. *New York Times,* January 8, 1962, 22.

29. Israel, "Bulgarskite," 125.

30. Ibid., 127.

31. Ibid., 128. Israel's article is undocumented, and he simply states that "Georgi Dimitrov addressed the delegates with words of wisdom *[s murdi naputstvia].*" The official, detailed accounts of Dimitrov's activities do not record that he attended the conference. See Elena Savova, *Georgi Dimitrov: Letopis na zhivota i revoliutsionnata mu deinost* (Sofia, 1982).

32. An example is the case of Maxim Koen,

which gained attention in the West. Koen, the son of Communist professors, attended Yeshiva University in New York at the request of Bulgarian folklorists to relearn Sephardic chants (*New York Times,* December 3, 1988, sec. 1, p. 29).

33. Anna Roshkovska, "Sinagogata v Samakov, in OKPOE, *Annual* 3 (1968), 175–79.

34. Israel, "Bulgarskite," 132–33.

35. Ibid., 128.

36. Ibid., 43.

37. See Romano et al., *Yahadut Bulgariyah.*

38. Benjamin Arditi, *Roliata na tsar Boris III pri izselvaneto na evreite ot Bulgariia* (Tel Aviv, 1952); idem, *Yahade Bulgariyah Bishanot Hamishpat Hanatsi: 1940–1944* (Tel Aviv, 1962).

39. Israel, "Bulgarskite," 120–21.

40. See Dimitur Paunov, "Bulgarian Jews in the Bulgarian Theatre during the 30s and 40s of XXc," OKPOE, *Annual* 21 (1986), 149–73; and idem, "Pages from the History of Theatrical Art in Bulgaria (1944–1986)," ibid., 22 (1987), 267–95.

41. Haim Oliver, quoted in Paunov, "Pages from the History of Theatrical Art," 272.

42. "Honored" and "National" actor, performer, and so on, are designations awarded by the state. National Actor is the highest award.

43. See Louis Fischer, *The Life of Lenin* (New York, 1964), 2–3.

44. Israel, "Bulgarskite," 122–23.

45. Iosif Astrukov, "Istinata," in *Evreiski Vesti,* January 8, 1990, 1–2.

46. *New York Times,* June 6, 1974, 2; June 7, 1974, 14; June 14, 1974, 32; August 15, 1974, 4; August 23, 1974, 5.

47. David Benvenisti, "The Bulgarian Orthodox Church in the Common Struggle of the People for Saving the Bulgarian Jews from Annihilation (1940–1944)," OKPOE, *Annual* 14 (1979), 107.

48. Among the most prominent works are Arditi's works mentioned above; Haim D. Oliver, *We Were Saved: How the Jews in Bulgaria Were Kept from the Death Camps,* 2d ed. (Sofia, 1978); and Chaim Keshales, *Korot Yahude Bulgariyah* (Tel Aviv, 1969).

49. See, e.g., Betty Danon, "The Third Fighting Borough and Its Secretary—Todor Zhivkov (Janko)," OKPOE, *Annual* 16 (1981), 15–17. Betty Danon is a member of the Jewish family portrayed as having friendly relations with Zhivkov in the film *Eshalonut,* discussed below.

50. Vladimir Stoichev, quoted in *New York Times,* March 30, 1946, 6; May 12, 1946, 29.

51. Dimitur Kosev et al., eds., *Istoriia na Bulgariia,* 2 vols. (Sofia, 1954–55), 1:220, 224–25.

52. Ibid., 2:753, 794–95.

53. Kosev et al., *Istoriia na Bulgariia,* 2d ed., 3:404–5.

54. Dimitur Angelov et al., eds., *Kratka istoriia na Bulgariia* (Sofia, 1958).

55. Astruk Kalev, "Pravnoto polozhenia na evreite v Bulgariia: Evreite—svobodni pravnopravni grazhdani v narodna republika Bulgariia," OKPOE, *Annual* 1 (1966), 47–62. (This volume was not translated into English.)

56. See Astrukov, "Istinata."

57. Benvenisti, "The Bulgarian Orthodox Church," 87–123.

58. Ibid., 87.

59. Veselin Hadzhinikolov, introduction, OKPOE, *Annual* 22 (1987), 5.

60. Wolf Oschlies, *Bulgarien, Land ohne Antisemitismus* (Erlangen, 1976).

61. For examples of fond and bitter memories of Bulgaria by Jews, see the friendly addresses of Shulamit Shamir, the wife of the Israeli prime minister and a native of Sofia, and Abraham Melamed, secretary of the Israel-Bulgaria Society, delivered at the conference in Bulgaria on the survival of the Bulgarian Jewish community in Sofia in November 1988. Shamir delivered her speech in Bulgarian. They are reprinted in OKPOE, *Annual* 24 (1989), 225–33, 242–43. For contrast, see the unfriendly account by Bulgarian-born Israeli Viki Tamir, *Bulgaria and Her Jews: The History of a Dubious Symbiosis* (New York, 1979).

62. Nissan Oren, "Bulgaria," *Encyclopaedia Judaica,* vol. 4 (Jerusalem, 1971), 1479–91.

63. Salvador Israel, "Bulgarian Literature," ibid., 1492–94.

64. Aleko Konstantinov, *Bai Gan'o neveroiatni razkazi za edin suvremenen bulgarin* (Sofia, 1981).

65. Israel, "Bulgarian Literature," 1493; Victor Baruh, *Svatbeni sveshti* (Sofia, 1968).

66. Salvador Israel, "Istoricheskite koreni na druzhbata mezhdu Bulgari i Evreite," OKPOE, *Annual* 1 (1966), 13–45.

67. Georgi Dimitrov, quoted in OKPOE, *Annual* 1 (1966), 3.

68. Todor Zhivkov, quoted in ibid.

69. See Tamir, *Bulgaria and Her Jews.*

70. Iosif Astrukov, "The Rescue of the Bulgarian Jews—The Victory of Humanism and Internationalism," OKPOE, *Annual* 18 (1983), 11–36.

71. "A Round Table Conference 'Saving of the Bulgarian Jews 1941–1944,' which Took Place on 16–17 of November, 1988 in the People's Palace of Culture," ibid., 24 (1989), 218–71.

72. Shulamit Shamir, quoted in ibid., 225–26.

73. The events since 1989 have been printed in *Evreiski Vesti*.

74. *Evreiski Vesti*, January 22, 1990, 1–3; January 29, 1990, 1, 3.

75. Astrukov, "Istinata."

76. Incidents were reported in the various issues of *Evreiski Vesti* in 1990.

77. *Keesing's Record of World Events* 37, no. 9 (suppl., 1991), 38.

78. See, e.g., Christo Boyadjieff, *Saving the Bulgarian Jews in World War II* (Singer Island, Fla., 1989); and "Tsar Boris, koito kaza 'ne' na Hitler," in *Kultura,* September 7, 1990, reprinted in *Evreiski Vesti,* October 9, 1990, 1.

THE SOVIET BLOC

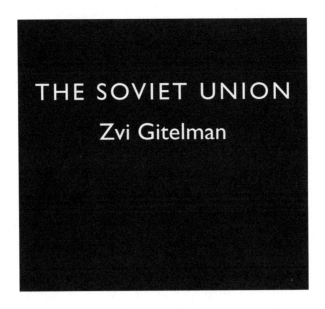

THE SOVIET UNION
Zvi Gitelman

BEFORE THE HOLOCAUST

By 1897 there were more than five million Jews living in the Russian Empire, where they constituted the largest Jewish community in the world. They were never fully accepted by the czarist authorities or by society. Until 1772 they were barred by law from residing in the empire. When the czars annexed eastern Poland in the late eighteenth century, they found themselves "burdened" by a large Jewish population that had lived in Poland for centuries. In order to prevent the Jews from "contaminating" the rest of the population, the government decreed that they could reside only in the fifteen western provinces now annexed to the empire. These provinces include roughly present-day Lithuania, part of Latvia, Belarus, and Ukraine. At the time of the first comprehensive census, in 1897, about 97 percent of the Jews lived in these areas, known as the Pale of Settlement.[1]

Other restrictions were imposed on the Jews from time to time. Under Czar Nicholas I (1825–55) young Jewish boys were drafted into the military for terms of twenty-five years, sometimes undergoing pre-induction military training in addition. The aim was not so much to beef up what was already the largest standing army in the world as it was to remove Jewish youngsters from their families and communities and thus to wean them away from their faith and their people. It is estimated that about fifty thousand Jewish teenagers were drafted in this way, and that about half of them were lost to the Jewish people. Moreover, each community was assigned a quota of recruits that it had to deliver to the authorities. Since communal leaders generally selected the children of the poor and uninfluential, this episode led to serious tensions within the Jewish communities. In the view of Marxist historians, this was the beginning of class conflict among the Jews of the empire.

A *numerus clausus,* or quota system, was imposed on Jewish aspirants to higher education and the professions. It set very low limits on the numbers of Jews who could be accepted to institutions of higher education and allowed to practice in the professions. These limitations were imposed even though the great majority of the Russian population was illiterate even as late as 1914 and the government had to import professors, engineers, agronomists, and architects from abroad to meet even the modest needs of an overwhelmingly agrarian and still essentially feudal country. Thus, at the end of the nineteenth century most Jews who sought higher education had to obtain it abroad.

An even more serious restriction was the denial to the Jews of the right to own land, the primary source of wealth in an agrarian economy. From time to time the authorities would permit some Jews to settle on land in Ukraine or in newly acquired territories, but these were exceptional cases; the vast majority of Jews became traders, craftsmen, workers in small factories and workshops, storekeepers, or simply *luftmentshn,* people without any profession, "living off the air" and making their livelihood from chance opportunities. In many communities 40 percent of the population fell into the *luftmentsh* category. In 1898 nearly 20 percent of the Jews in the Pale applied for Passover relief. In 1900 in Odessa, one of the wealthier cities in the empire, nearly two-thirds of the Jewish dead had to be buried at communal expense. At the turn of the century about a third of the Jews were dependent on relief provided by Jewish institutions.

Finally, government anti-Semitism was complemented by popular anti-Jewish sentiment. In 1881, following the assassination of Czar Alexander II, for which the Jews were held responsible, a wave of pogroms swept over Ukraine and Belorussia and reached as far west as Warsaw. Anti-Jewish laws passed in May 1882 and pogroms in 1903 and 1905 impelled nearly two million Jews to flee Russia; most of them immigrated to Western Europe and North America, with smaller numbers going to Latin America and Palestine.[2] As late as 1911 the government accused a humble Ukrainian Jew, Mendel Beilis, of murdering a Christian child in order to use his blood in Judaic ritual. High officials conspired to suppress evidence that Beilis was in no way involved in the murder, which had actually been committed by a gang of thieves. Beilis sat in prison for two years while the authorities tried to make a case against him. He was brought to trial in September 1913, and though he was acquitted, the government was still appealing the verdict up to the eve of the 1917 revolution. Thus, the czarist government was committing its resources to sustaining a medieval canard right up to its own demise.[3] This is eloquent testimony to czarism's bankruptcy and to its obsessions.

Jewish Communal Life

Perhaps because society in general shunned and isolated them, Jews in the Russian Empire turned their energies and talents inward and developed a dynamic, vibrant communal and cultural life. Religious life was especially strong in the small towns *(shtetlakh)* and villages. In most of these, Jews constituted a majority of the population. This gave them a strong sense of community and solidarity, but it also induced conformity to powerful social pressures. Although the official community organization, the *kahal,* had been abolished by the government in 1844, Jewish communities continued to regulate their internal affairs much as before. They had their burial societies, charitable organizations, educational institutions, orphanages, old-age homes, infirmaries, and other welfare institutions. In a country where four-fifths of the population could not read or write, almost all Jewish boys and girls learned to read and write Hebrew and Yiddish, and a substantial proportion could read Russian as well. The most famous yeshivot, schools of higher rabbinic learning, were in the Russian Empire, often in very small towns. By the twentieth century there were substantial numbers of Jewish students in Russian schools, as well as in Yiddish and Hebrew secular schools.

One of the remarkable achievements of Russian Jewry is that it produced two major modern literatures, Yiddish and Hebrew. Perhaps even more remarkable is the fact that two of the three "classic" Yiddish writers, Mendele Mocher Sforim and Y. L. Peretz—the other was, of course, Shalom Aleichem—were also among the creators of modern Hebrew literature. Usage of Hebrew as a living language, propagated by the Haskalah, the enlightenment movement of the mid-nineteenth century, became a plank in the platform of the Zionist movement, and Yiddish became the cornerstone of the secular culture advocated by some elements in the Jewish socialist movement. But these languages and literatures stood independently as cultural forces that attracted their own loyalists, creators, and publics. Yiddish theater emerged at the end of the nineteenth century, and the beginnings of the Hebrew theater were also in Russia. Jewish folk and cantorial music were well developed, and there were some Jewish composers and performers of classical music, though many of them had to convert to Christianity in order to be accepted. By the first decade of the twentieth century, serious study and production of Jewish music was undertaken by a society established for that purpose. In addition, a Historical-Ethnographic Society was established that carried out important research. Russian Jews made contributions in Semitics, history, sociology, ethnography, and demography.

Efforts to Protect Jewish Rights

In the latter half of the nineteenth century some Jews began to become politically active. Beginning in the 1860s and 1870s, some joined the radical youth who looked to the peasantry to rise against the czarist autocracy and liberate the entire population, including Jews, from political, social, and economic oppression. The *narodniki* (populists), who regarded the peasantry as the revolutionary class, were disappointed in the social conservatism and political inertness of this class. Jewish *narodniki* were shocked by the pogroms perpetrated largely by the peasantry, but even more so by the reactions of their fellow revolutionaries, some of whom welcomed the pogroms as a sign that the peasants were at last being activated, even though they were venting their frustrations in the wrong way. Disillusioned Jewish populists generally tended to emigrate, which meant that they had given up on Russia; to become Marxists, which meant that they had transferred their hopes from the peasantry to the proletariat; or to become Zionists, which signaled their despair of finding solutions to the Jewish Problem anywhere in the Diaspora.[4] By 1897 Russian Jewry had seen the birth of both the Jewish Labor Bund, a Marxist, secular, anti-Zionist movement oriented toward Yiddish, and Zionism, a movement with several streams—socialist, religious, culturalist—all of which saw the Jewish people in a state of their own in the future.

The Bund, which helped found the Russian Social-Democratic Labor Party, out of which the Bolsheviks and Mensheviks emerged, advocated the overthrow of czarism and the replacement of the feudal-capitalist system by socialism. This, they reasoned, would solve the Jewish Problem, which they, in contrast to the Zionists, argued needed no unique solution but would be part of the overall transformation of the world into a more just society in which ethnic and racial hatreds would be unknown.[5] The Zionists, on the other hand, believed that only a Jewish state or homeland could provide Jews with security and equal opportunity. However, they decided that as long as Jews remained in the Diaspora, their rights would have to be protected and fought for. A group of generally wealthy, educated, and privileged Jews defended Jewish rights through legal channels and associated themselves with Russian constitutionalist movements and parties. They hoped that a constitutional democracy would be sufficient to guarantee civil rights to all and equal rights to Jews. But the czarist system was unyielding, and concessions made in the aftermath of the 1905 revolution were soon withdrawn. The last czar, Nicholas II, retreated into reaction and policies that were even less enlightened than those of his predecessors.

It should be remembered that only a minority of Jews were active in any of the movements described. The need to eke out a living, isolation from the larger society, and the self-contained nature of Jewish society, which had a well-developed institutional infrastructure and was spiritually self-sufficient, enabled most Jews to live their daily lives outside the political arena. It should also be remembered that within that arena Bolshevism enjoyed little support among Jews. A census of Bolshevik Party members taken in 1922 revealed that there remained in the party only 958 Jews who had joined before 1917; in the latter year, the Bund had more than 30,000 members. The myth that Bolshevism was a "Jewish conspiracy" was based on the presence of a disproportionate number of people of Jewish origin, none of whom were practicing or committed Jews, in the upper echelons of the Bolshevik Party in 1917 and for several years afterward. The myth gained credence in 1918–21, when many Jews joined the Bolshevik Party and became Soviet officials, largely because only the Bolsheviks did not pogromize the Jews, whereas their White opponents, Ukrainian nationalists, and others systematically attacked Jews; the new regime removed restrictions on their education and employment; and some former anti-Bolshevik socialists became convinced that the world revolution was at hand and that the Bolshevik analysis of the situation was correct. Thus, by 1922, when Jews made up less than 2 percent of the population—there were about 2.4 million Jews in the country at the time—they constituted 5.2 percent of party members. That proportion declined to 3.8 percent by 1930.[6]

Open political activity by Jews became possible only with the fall of czarism in February–March 1917, when the legal impediments to Jewish equality were removed. For the first time in the history of Russia, Jews became full-fledged citizens. They greeted the revolution with great enthusiasm and set about creating a comprehensive public Jewish life. Publications, cultural groups, and political parties flourished in 1917. The Zionists, given a boost by the Balfour Declaration, wherein the British government promised the Jews a homeland in Palestine, emerged as the most popular political force among Jews.

But all the activity was brought to a halt by the Bolshevik seizure of power late in 1917. The Bolsheviks were militantly opposed to Zionism, which they saw as splitting off the Jewish workers from the rest of the proletariat and retarding the assimilation of the Jews, which they considered a progressive phenomenon to be emulated by all nationalities. Ex-Bundists and other socialists who eventually joined the Communist Party persuaded the leadership to mount campaigns against the Hebrew language, now considered the language of the class enemy—the bourgeoisie and the clerics—whereas Yiddish was the language of the "toiling masses." In the 1920s the foundations of traditional Jewish life were undermined by Communist assaults on Judaism, Hebrew, and Zionism. The Jewish religion was attacked as part of the general campaign against religion, Zionism was declared a subversive ideology and movement, and Hebrew was banned as a language of study, discourse, and publication. Religious Jews, Zionists, and Hebraists were hounded, driven underground, forced to change their ways of life, imprisoned, or exiled.

To replace traditional Jewish culture, Communists who were active in the Jewish sections *(Evsektsii)* of the party tried to devise a secular, socialist, Soviet Yiddish culture. They created Jewish schools, theaters, newspapers, journals, and research institutes that operated in Yiddish and reflected the Bolshevik ideology. Moreover, they tried to solve Jewish economic problems by settling Jews on land and making them into agriculturalists. By 1931 there were eleven hundred state-supported Yiddish schools, forty daily newspapers in Yiddish, and trade unions and even party cells operating in Yiddish. The Communists planned to settle one hundred thousand Jewish families on lands in Belorussia, Crimea, Ukraine, and Birobidzhan, an underpopulated area of the Soviet Far East.

Neither the "Yiddishization" nor the agricultural settlement campaigns succeeded. Traditional Jews considered Soviet Yiddish culture ersatz and inimical to their values. They often preferred to send their children to non-Jewish schools, where Judaism and Zionism were not attacked as frequently or as directly as they were in the Yiddish schools. On the other hand, most other Jews saw no reason for clinging to the *shtetl* culture and its language once the doors to a "higher" (Russian) culture were opened. The majority of younger Jews were quite content to trade the culture of their *shtetl* upbringing for the educational and vocational mobility offered by the drive to modernize and industrialize the Soviet Union. To build the factories and plants that would propel a backward country into the modern industrial world, millions of workers were needed. Thus, thousands of Jews moved out of the *shtetlakh* of the former Pale areas, migrating to the larger cities of Ukraine and Belorussia and to the cities of the Russian republic, especially Moscow and Leningrad, which had been off-limits to almost all Jews before 1917. They became industrial workers, technicians, engineers, economists, and factory managers. They entered universities and technical institutes and took up government posts, reaching the highest echelons of the military, the state apparatus, the police, and the party. Between 1926 and 1935 the number of Jewish wage and salary earners nearly tripled. At first Jews became blue-collar workers, but very soon they moved into the white-collar ranks. By 1939 there were 364,000 Jewish white-collar employees. In 1934–35 Jews made up 18 percent of all graduate students. By the late 1930s Jews were well established in the proletariat and in the managerial and professional strata.[7]

In achieving this mobility, they did what their relatives and ancestors who had crossed oceans had done: abandoned their traditions, changed their language to that of the majority, changed their clothes, cuisine, cultures, and social milieux. Jews were offered the opportunity to go as far as their talents and education would carry them, and they seized it eagerly. By the early 1930s it was clear that the high road to modernization was industry, not agriculture, and so most preferred to move to the cities rather than to the now collectivized farms. Birobidzhan was too far away and too undeveloped to attract any but the most politically enthusiastic or economically desperate, and a high proportion of the original pioneers made their ways back to where they had come from. Moreover, most Jews seemed to accept at face value the myth of "proletarian internationalism," which rendered ethnic identities and cultures meaningless. They were convinced that ethnicity was now irrelevant, as all peoples had overcome their mutual prejudices and were united in their commitment to "progressive" ideals. There was not much reason to settle on specifically Jewish farms or to cling to Jewish identity and culture in the urbane, cosmopolitan settings of Moscow, Leningrad, Kiev, and Odessa. Little wonder that rates of marriage between Jews and non-Jews rose precipitously in the 1930s. Acculturation, the adoption of another culture, was being followed by assimilation, the abandonment of one's original identity.

Anti-Semitism in the Soviet Union

Jews' belief that they had at last achieved equality with all others was buttressed by the explicit stand the government had taken against anti-Semitism. Lenin had denounced anti-Semitism in strong terms before and during the revolution. In the 1920s the government had published several pamphlets directed at the working class that explained that anti-Semitism was a tool of the capitalist bosses for splintering the workers and diverting them from their true class interests. Lectures and even films were used to combat anti-Jewish feelings. Anti-Semitism was clearly labeled a reactionary, antisocialist phenomenon that had no place in socialist society. It became punishable by Soviet law. Yet, there were manifestations of Jew-hatred, and they seemed to grow with time. During the New Economic Policy (NEP) period (1921–28), when some private enterprise was allowed, some Jews went back to their pre-revolutionary occupations and engaged in small-scale commerce. But "NEP-men" soon became objects of ridicule and condemnation, barely tolerated as marginal figures in Soviet society. The population was socialized to despise private trade, and some transferred this class-based animosity to an ethnic one, characterizing Jews in general as "exploiting elements." Ironically, other people held the Jews responsible for making the revolution and destroying the private economic sector, for had not Jews been prominent among those who had made the revolution? Some among those who opposed the revolution and what it stood for—for example, religious people, those ideologically opposed to Bolshevism, and those economically ruined by socialism—associated the revolution with the Jews and blamed them for the troubles it had visited upon them.[8]

When efforts were made to settle Jews on the land, there was resentment among peasants who feared that their lands would be expropriated for Jewish settlement. Just as many Russians and other non-Jews found it strange and "unnatural" that Jews should hold leading political and military positions in a country where until only recently they had been barred from such positions, some peasants looked with a mixture of resentment and amusement at the spectacle of large numbers of urban types being made over into farmers. Some were convinced that there was a plot by the Jewish-dominated government to take away their land and hand it over to the Jews. Perhaps such attitudes could be expected in a sector of the population that had no enthusiasm for socialism and was considered politically and culturally backward by the Bolsheviks. But the Bolsheviks could not easily account for the anti-Semitism that cropped up in the ranks of the proletariat. Soviet newspapers reported instances of violent anti-Semitism among workers and condemned them. Apparently, the "New Soviet man" had not yet been created and "survivals of the past," including anti-Semitism, were visible in many strata of Soviet society.

Moreover, by the early 1930s reports of anti-Semitism among the "toiling masses" and condemnations of it no longer appeared. Where once the authorities had condemned "Great Power chauvinism" (Russian nationalism) as a more serious evil than "petit bourgeois nationalism" (nationalism among the non-Russians), in the 1930s the latter came to be identified as the greater evil. This was in line with Stalin's shift in emphasis from encouraging the nationalities to develop their cultures to promoting the interests of the Russians. After all, devoting energies to the development of Ukrainian theater, Jewish literature, Belorussian music, or the Uzbek language would detract from the common, single aim of *all* Soviet peoples, namely, extremely rapid economic modernization. "Socialist in content, national in form" became the catch phrase of nationality policy. The purges of cultural and political leaders among the non-Russians made it clear to everyone that "socialist content" took precedence over "national form." Thus, the problems of particular nationalities were not a matter of great concern. Anti-Semitism was talked about less and less, but this did not mean that it had disappeared. On the contrary, it may have been spreading in the thirties, because it was no longer as widely and consistently condemned as it had been in the previous decade.

Finally, Jews were prominent in the secret police. In the early days of the revolution, Jews had joined the police partly in order to protect and revenge themselves against the White enemies of Bolshevism, who were pogromizing their people. Bolshevik leaders regarded Jews as especially trustworthy because they could not conceivably be sympathetic to a czarist restoration. It may also be that, having been deprived of power for so long, some Jews found the lure of the secret police and its nearly unlimited powers irresistible. Then, too, as an urban, educated element, Jews were more likely than many others to be recruited for such functions. Nevertheless, the visible presence of Jews in the organs of repression could not but arouse antipathy to Jews generally. Even though enormous numbers of Jews were themselves purged—not as Jews but as party members, military, governmental, and economic officials, and cultural leaders—the impression might well have been created that a disproportionate number of Jews were involved in repressing millions of Russians and members of other nationalities. These, then, were some of the proximate causes of anti-Jewish sentiments in the early Soviet period. Clearly, many of the prejudices and stereotypes of the pre-revolutionary days had survived as well, despite the Bolsheviks' assertions that they were creating a wholly new society and that any ethnic hatreds that remained were mere "survivals of capitalism."

Following Adolf Hitler's rise to power in Germany in 1933, the Soviet Union attempted to become part of a broad international "popular front" against fascism. Soviet publications and media detailed the evils of German Nazism, among them anti-Semitism. Yet, in August 1939 the Soviets signed a treaty with the Nazis. Stalin took care to remove from his post his Jewish foreign minister, Maxim Litvinov, before signing the treaty. The Soviet line had changed, and so had the domestic media's treatment of fascism, Nazism, and events in Germany. From 1939 until the German invasion of the Soviet Union, nearly two years later, little or nothing was said about the evils of anti-Semitism and what the Germans had been doing to Jews, first in Germany and then in the countries they had annexed or invaded. Thus, the Soviet population as a whole and Jews in particular ceased to hear about Nazi anti-Semitism or even to learn about the atrocities that were being perpetrated against the Jews. It appears that on the eve of the German invasion, therefore, the Soviet population was not sensitized to the problem of anti-Semitism generally nor to the specifics of Nazi policies toward Jews. Even most of the Jewish population, living as they were in a country where information was tightly controlled and where there was very little contact with foreigners, were not prepared for the horrors soon to befall them.

THE HOLOCAUST ERA

Under secret agreements attached to the 1939 Soviet-German nonaggression pact, the two powers divided much of Eastern Europe between themselves. Thus, less than three weeks after Germany invaded Poland on September 1, 1939, Soviet troops moved into eastern Poland on the pretext of liberating Ukrainians and Belorussians living in that area from the oppressive rule of the Poles. Staged referendums, conducted under the watchful eyes of the Soviet army and police, "proved" that the local population wished to join the Soviet Union and provided the legal mask for the annexation of eastern Poland to the Soviet Union, which called the territories West Belorussia and West Ukraine. Then in 1940 Soviet troops occupied the Baltic republics of Estonia, Latvia, and Lithuania. The same charade followed, with the local populations "requesting" to be admitted to the Soviet Union as republics. Of course, the "request" was granted. In 1940 the Soviet Union also acquired Northern Bukovina and Bessarabia from Romania, and in roughly the same way. Eventually, these formerly Romanian territories were divided between the Ukrainian republic and the newly created Moldavian republic.

The full panoply of Soviet institutions was installed in all these areas. Schools and cultural institutions were Sovietized, the economies were nationalized, and the Communist Party was given a monopoly of power in the political arena. Thousands of people were identified by the authorities as "class enemies" and deported to the interior of the Soviet Union or sent to prison and labor camps. These were usually non-Communists who had been politically active, religious functionaries, private entrepreneurs, including even shopkeepers, and others suspected of being potential enemies of the new regime. The Communist Party had been illegal in these areas before the coming of the Soviets, and Jews constituted substantial proportions of the underground parties. While these Communists made up only a tiny fraction of the Jewish population as a whole, their proportions in the Communist parties were larger than their proportion in the overall population. The reasons for this were that Jews were more urbanized and better educated than the rest of the population; they had not been treated equitably by the ruling powers, and some of them had sought to replace the prevailing systems with systems that did not discriminate between different ethnic groups; and some Jews had been attracted to the secular Yiddish culture promoted by the Soviets. Again, as in 1918–21 in the Soviet Union proper, the new regime relied on Jewish Communists to identify and arrest "class enemies" and "reactionary elements." Naturally, this did not endear the Jews to the local populations, who had just lost their political independence, acquired only two decades earlier, to the Communists.

It should be noted that all Jewish institutions in the newly acquired territories were also Sovietized. The same persecutions of Hebrew, Zionism, and religion that Soviet Jews had experienced earlier were now felt by Baltic, Polish, and Romanian Jews. There is also some evidence that the Soviet occupiers soon realized how unpopular Jews were in the new areas and took care not to place Jews in visible positions of authority; they even replaced some Jews who had been installed in such positions early in the Sovietization process. Some Jewish leftists in the new territories also soon realized that the purges of the 1930s had not singled out genuine enemies of the Soviet system alone and that many of their Communist colleagues across the border had been repressed unjustifiably. But by the time Jews in the new areas realized the full import of Sovietization, they were faced with the frightful dilemma of choosing between areas dominated by Romanian fascists, German Nazis, or Soviet Communists, if they had any choice at all.[9]

The acquisition of the new territories added substantially to the Soviet Jewish population. According to the 1939 census, the results of which were only recently published in full and which are today acknowledged to have been substantially falsified and distorted, there were 3.1 million Jews in the Soviet Union. In 1939–40 about 1.9 million Jews lived in the territories annexed to the Soviet Union—1.3 million in eastern Poland, 255,000 in the Baltic States, and about 330,000 in territories that had formerly belonged to Romania. Thus, when the Nazis invaded the Soviet Union on June 22, 1941, there were about 5 million Jews in the country.

The Holocaust in the Soviet Union

Perhaps as many as one-third of all the Jews killed in the Holocaust were under Soviet rule as of 1940. According to most estimates, necessarily based on fragmentary information, about 1.5 million Soviet Jewish citizens who lived within the pre-1939 borders of the Soviet Union were murdered by the Nazis and 200,000 more died in combat.[10] The rest of the victims were Jews who came under Soviet rule in 1939–40. Yet, the Soviet treatment of the Holocaust was very different from that in the West. Although they did not deny the Holocaust, most Soviet writers either ignored it or submerged it in more general accounts of the period. A preliminary survey of Soviet writings reveals that they vary significantly in the prominence and interpretations they give to the Holocaust. Most Soviet works either passed over it in silence or blurred it by universalizing it. Western assertions to the contrary, there was no consistent Soviet "party line" on the Holocaust. Some works did acknowledge and describe the Holocaust, while others discussed only some aspects of it. We can only speculate regarding Soviet motivations, but we can point with greater certainty to some consequences, intended and unintended, of the general Soviet tendency to ignore or downplay the Holocaust. In any case, as the Soviet Union and its dominating party broke up, the treatment of the Holocaust began to change.

Soviet treatment of the Holocaust had profound, if subtle, effects on both Jews and non-Jews in the Soviet Union. On the one hand, it denied Jews any particular sympathy from non-Jews. Unlike in the West, Soviet non-Jews, for the most part, felt no need to "make up" to the Jews, as it were, for any of the wrongs done to them. On the other hand, Soviet treatment aroused Jewish consciousness, as it has in the West. But it also engendered first puzzlement and then bitterness when Jews, especially younger ones, realized that a vital part of their recent history was being denied them. Hence, their worth and importance were denigrated, their particular history and culture dismissed, and their claims to being discriminated against rejected. Soviet treatment—or lack of treatment—of the Holocaust was a significant factor in the reemergence of Jewish national consciousness in the former Soviet Union. Whether the current reexamination of Soviet history now proceeding in the successor states will reopen the pages of the Holocaust and permit this chapter to be written in full will be not only interesting from an academic point of view but important socially and politically. Indications are that this is beginning to occur. In 1991 and 1992 articles began to appear in non-Jewish journals in Ukraine and Russia that described the Holocaust and raised some of the sensitive issues of complicity by local populations, Soviet suppression of discussion of the Holocaust, and the impact of the Holocaust on Jewish perceptions. In Lithuania, on the other hand, most of the discussion has centered on official pardons by the newly independent Lithuanian government of several thousand Lithuanians convicted by the Soviets of collaboration. Criticism of the wholesale pardons by Jewish and Israeli bodies evoked countercharges of sympathy for Communism, and the issue remains unresolved and highly sensitive.

Except in the popular press, few articles on Russia and Ukraine were published in 1992 and 1993. After briefly identifying the main outlines of how the Holocaust was perpetrated in the Soviet Union, I shall discuss how it was treated in Soviet writings, offer some suggestions as to why it was accorded such treatment, and examine the consequences of that treatment.

The War against Soviet Jewry

Around a quarter of a million of the Jews from the territories annexed in 1939–40 either fled to the interior, beyond the Nazi grasp, or were inadvertently saved by the Soviets from Nazi annihilation when the former deported them to Siberia and Central Asia.[11] The Soviet occupation of the western territories brought with it a tragic, fateful divergence in the perceptions and interests of Jews and non-Jews. In all of those territories anti-Semitic regimes in the 1930s had made life increasingly uncomfortable for the Jews, in many cases intolerable. America and Palestine were closed to immigration. Jews in Poland, Romania, Latvia, and Lithuania had little hope of improving their lot. The entry of the Red Army, with its Jewish officers and men and its promises of national equality and social justice, gave hope to some of the younger and more radically inclined Jews. Despite misgivings about the Bolsheviks' militant atheism, their persecution of Zionism, and their nationalization of property, many Jews welcomed the Red Army as a liberator. A resident of eastern Poland recalled that when the Red Army came, "there was a holiday atmosphere. Things changed overnight . . . the Germans would not come in and that was the most important thing."[12] Others saw the Soviets as the lesser of two evils. Another survivor from the same area commented, "When the Russians came in we were a little afraid, but not as afraid as we were of the Germans in the western part of Poland."[13]

The Poles, the Baltic peoples, and the Romanians, by contrast, saw the Red Army as an invader, one that was depriving them of their hard-won and all too brief political independence. Jews who welcomed the Red Army were seen as traitors, and all Jews were assumed to be Bolshevik sympathizers and betrayers of the lands of their birth. Little wonder, then, that when the Germans drove the Red Army out in 1941, many non-Jews greeted them as liberators from Soviet oppression and took the opportunity to wreak harsh vengeance on the traitorous Jews. In the first few days of the German occupation of Lithuania, for example, Lithuanian groups murdered between seven thousand and eight thousand Jews.

Three million German troops invaded the Soviet Union from the west, quickly encircling the main centers of Jewish population. The Nazis had long been explicit about their consuming hatred for both Bolsheviks and Jews, whom they equated with each other. Adolf Hitler wrote in 1930, "The Nordic race has a right to rule the world. . . . Any cooperation with Russia is out of the question, for there on a Slavic-Tatar body is set a Jewish head."[14] German General Von Reichenau issued an order stating that "the most essential aim of war against the Jewish-Bolshevistic system is a complete destruction of their . . . power. . . . Therefore, the soldier must have full understanding for the necessity of severe but just revenge on subhuman Jewry." General Von Manstein wrote, "More strongly than in Europe, [Jewry] holds all the key positions in the political leadership and administration . . . the Jewish-Bolshevist system must be exterminated once and for all. The soldier must appreciate the necessity for harsh punishment of Jewry, the spiritual bearer of the Bolshevist terror."[15]

Though the Nazis could not have been more explicit about their intentions, the Soviet media had draped a blanket of silence over Nazi atrocities following the Nazi-Soviet pact of August 1939. Together with older people's memories of the Germans of World War I as "decent people," this left many Soviet Jews unprepared for the mass-murder campaign conducted by four *Einsatzgruppen,* or mobile killing squads, who liquidated much of Soviet Jewry by machine gunning them in or near their hometowns. Other Jews were placed in ghettos, most of which were liquidated, along with their inhabitants, by 1941–42. Within five months, the *Einsatzgruppen,* whose officers, as Raul Hilberg observed, were largely intellectuals and professionals, had killed about half a million Jews. The *Einsatzgruppen* worked closely with the Wehrmacht, the regular German army, which, according to Hilberg, "went out of its way to turn over Jews to the *Einsatzgruppen,* to request actions against Jews, to participate in killing operations, and to shoot Jewish hostages in 'reprisal' for attacks on occupation forces."[16] The army's rationale was that the Jews were Bolsheviks who encouraged partisan warfare against the Germans, and so killing Jews was a prophylactic military measure.

The *Einsatzgruppen* numbered only about three thousand men but were supplemented by Lithuanian, Latvian, Estonian, and Ukrainian collaborators. The mobile killing squads aimed to reach as many cities as quickly as possible and to kill local Jews before they could realize what fate Hitler had planned for them. "The Einsatzgruppen had moved with such speed behind the advancing army that several hundred thousand Jews could be killed like sleeping flies."[17] These killings were often preceded by extensive torture. By war's end, perhaps two million Jewish civilians had been killed, singled out from the rest of the population for "special handling."

THE POST-HOLOCAUST ERA
Soviet Historiography of the Holocaust

Some Western observers charge that it was Soviet policy to suppress any public discussion of the Holocaust. William Korey writes of "the Soviet attempt to obliterate the Holocaust in the memories of Jews as well as non-Jews."[18] Writing in 1970, Mordechai Altshuler asserted: "The wall of silence regarding the Holocaust still stands in the Soviet Union, though here and there small cracks were observed. . . . the paucity of publications on the Holocaust of Soviet Jewry . . . and the attacks on Yevtushenko's 'Babi Yar' . . . testify to a purposeful policy of the regime to suppress the Holocaust in the Soviet Union."[19] This policy is sometimes explained as a consequence of Soviet anti-Semitism and hostility toward Jewish history and culture. Korey's explanation is more sophisticated. "Expunging the Holocaust from the record of the past was hardly a simple matter, but unless it were done the profound anguish of the memory was certain to stir a throbbing national consciousness. Martyrdom, after all, is a powerful stimulus to a group's sense of its own identity."[20] In his study of Lithuanian Jewry's resistance to the Nazis, Dov Levin pointed out that Soviet writing on World War II generally downplayed the role of Lithuanian Jews as well as other Jews. He reasoned that this was in order not to diminish the already marginal role of the Lithuanians in the resistance against the Nazis.[21]

A closer examination of Soviet writings on World War II reveals that if there existed a policy of repressing the Holocaust, it was applied unevenly at best. Nevertheless, it remains true that the overall thrust of the Soviet literature was to assign the Holocaust far less significance than it has been given in the West. One cannot entirely dismiss the possibility that this is the consequence of having large, articulate, nationally conscious Jewish populations in the West, where they are mostly free to explore Jewish history and draw whatever conclusions they wish, whereas conditions in the Soviet Union permitted neither such exploration nor such expression. Moreover, no country in the West lost as many of its non-Jewish citizens in the war against Nazism as did the Soviet Union, so that the fate of the Jews in France, Holland, Germany, or Belgium stands in sharper contrast to that of their conationals or coreligionists than it does in the East. On the other hand, in Yugoslavia and Poland, where civilian populations were decimated in no less a proportion than they were in the Soviet Union, greater public attention has been paid to the specifically Jewish tragedy of the war period. Thus, the Soviet Union did treat the issue differently from the way it was treated in most other countries, whether socialist or not, though the Soviet treatment was not uniform.

In the Soviet Union, in striking contrast to the way it has been treated in the West, the Holocaust was not presented as a unique, separate phenomenon. It was not denied that six million Jews were killed, among them many Soviet ones, nor that Jews were singled out for annihilation. But the Holocaust was seen as an integral part of a larger phenomenon—the murder of civilians, whether Russians, Ukrainians, Belorussians, Gypsies, or other nationalities. It was said to be a natural consequence of racist fascism. The Holocaust, in other words, was but one of several reflexes of fascism, which is, in turn, the ultimate expression of capitalism. Thus, the roots of the Holocaust lie in capitalism, expressed in its most degenerate form. Armed with the theory of "scientific socialism," the Soviets were able to explain in a facile way how so many were murdered. For the Soviets there was no mystery about the Holocaust.

In the West there is a vast body of literature that seeks to understand how it happened. There are cultural explanations, psychological and sociological ones, and political and bureaucratic ones. There is an extensive theological literature that seeks to confront God with the Holocaust. I know of no book published in the Soviet Union that sought to explain the Holocaust as *sui generis*. In fact, the term "Holocaust" was completely unknown in the Soviet literature. In discussions of the destruction of the Jews the terms "annihilation" *(unichtozhenie)* and "catastrophe" *(katastrofa)* were used. Only in the early 1990s did "Holocaust," transliterated from English, appear. The *Chernaya Kniga* (Black book) of Soviet Jewry, containing documentation gathered from all over the country by the writers Ilya Ehrenburg and Vassily Grossman and others, comprised twelve hundred typescript pages and was printed in Moscow in 1946. But all the copies save one were sent to storage warehouses, where in 1948 they were destroyed along with the type from which they were set. The one surviving copy had been sent abroad and as a result escaped destruction. Thus, the major work on the Soviet Holocaust was never published in the former Soviet Union, though there are Hebrew, English, and even Russian editions, the latter published in Jerusalem.[22] The Holocaust was treated as regrettable but merely one small part of the larger phenomenon that, according to the Soviets, resulted in the death of twenty million of their citizens. (In the early 1990s, in the post-Soviet media, the figure twenty-seven million came to be used.) If the Nazis gave the Jews "special treatment," the Soviets would not.

This premise translated into a policy of bypassing the Holocaust for most general audiences and addressing it in a highly ideological way for certain specialized ones. William Korey's survey has shown that Soviet elementary-school history textbooks contained no reference to Jews at all, and a thirty-page chapter on World War II in one of them had not a single reference to either Jews or anti-Semitism. The same was true of secondary-school texts and syllabuses, except for a single reference to "terrible Jewish pogroms."[23]

The controversy over the construction of a monument at Babi Yar, the site in Kiev where more than thirty-five thousand of the city's Jews were shot in the course of two days, is well known. For years no monument was placed there, and the site was prepared for housing, a park, and other uses. In 1959 the writer Viktor Nekrasov protested plans to turn the site into a park and soccer stadium, and support began to build for the construction of a memorial monument. The issue gained world attention when popular Soviet poet Yevgeny Yevtushenko published a poem, "Babi Yar," whose first line is, "Over Babi Yar there are no monuments." The poem was a sensation because it condemned anti-Semitism and made it clear that Soviet society was not free of that problem. When Dmitri Shostakovich included the poem in his thirteenth symphony, authorities banned public performances of the symphony for several years.

Clearly, they were uncomfortable with the issue of anti-Semitism as well as with the memorialization of Jewish suffering in the war. But public pressure mounted for some kind of memorial to be placed at Babi Yar. When this was finally done, the monument was a typically socialist realist monument on a heroic scale. But the inscription read, "Here in 1941–1943, the German fascist invaders executed more than 100,000 citizens of Kiev and prisoners of war." There was no reference to Jews. Similarly, Yevtushenko was roundly criticized by conservative writers, who charged that his poem slandered the "Russian crew-cut lads" who had fought the Nazis because it focused on Jews. The writer Dmitri Starikov asserted that "the anti-Semitism of the Fascists is only part of their misanthropic policy of genocide . . . the destruction of the 'lower races' including the Slavs."[24] When Shostakovich included "Babi Yar" in his symphony, Yevtushenko was forced to make two additions to the text. One line reads, "Here together with Russians and Ukrainians lie Jews," and the other, "I am proud of Russia which stood in the path of the bandits." Again, the point is not that others suffered along with Jews, which no one would dispute, but that there was nothing unique about the quality and quantity of Jewish suffering, a far more dubious assertion. The same issue arose in regard to Anatoly Kuznetsov's novel, *Babi Yar,* published in 1966. Public controversy ensued over whether Jewish travails should have been singled out from among those of all others. Kuznetsov's novel and the Jewish writer Anatoly Rybakov's *Heavy Sand* (1978) are among the very few Russian-language novels that acknowledge, even assert, a special fate for the Jews during the war.

The problem surfaced not only in regard to novels and monuments but also in connection with museum displays. For example, despite the testimony of her uncle and several others, the seventeen-year-old Jewish partisan Masha Bruskina, who was hung by the Nazis in Minsk, is still identified as an "unknown partisan" in the Minsk Museum of the History of the Great Patriotic War. Significantly, the authorities' refusal to give her name and nationality was seen by some Jews as a deliberate insult and a refusal to acknowledge Jewish heroism. A highly decorated war veteran, Lev Ovsishcher, commented, "This story explains why Jews who understand what is happening in this country feel the only correct decision is to leave." He subsequently emigrated and went to Israel, after a long struggle.[25]

An examination of strictly historical treatments of the period 1941–45, whether popular or scholarly, reveals a more complex picture. The overall tendency remained to downplay, even ignore, the Holocaust, but some striking contrasts appeared. Although some works that should logically have discussed the Holocaust ignored it completely, others touched only on selected aspects of it, and still others presented a relatively straightforward and well-rounded account.

A fairly close examination of the six-volume official Soviet history of the war reveals not a single reference to Jews. Nor do the terms "anti-Semitism" or "Holocaust" appear in the index. In the third volume, the Nazi occupation of the Soviet Union is referred to as "a regime of terror and occupation," and the *Einsatzgruppen* are mentioned, as is Babi Yar, but the word "Jew" does not appear in connection with any of these.[26] A lengthy history of Ukraine, *Istoriia Ukrainskoi SSR*, published in 1982, does not mention Jews even once, not even in connection with the Holocaust, even though Jews have lived there for centuries, have played a major role in its economy and culture, and died there in the hundreds of thousands during the Holocaust.[27] A study of wartime Estonia provides a striking, almost ludicrous contrast. In 1939 there were more than 1.5 million Jews living in Soviet Ukraine and only 5,000 in "bourgeois" Estonia. Yet, while at least two histories of Ukraine pass over Jewish history and the Holocaust in silence, the study of Estonia presents a sympathetic account of Jewish suffering during the Holocaust and an undistorted account of Jewish participation in the armed struggle against the Nazis. The Germans' robbery of art and other treasures in private Jewish hands is explicitly referred to. German documents that report "the total liquidation of the Jews" are quoted ("at the present time there are no more Jews in Estonia"). The editors comment, "Implementing their monstrous racial theories, the German fascists and their collaborators in Estonia exterminated each and every Jew and Gypsy." Collaboration by Estonians with the Nazis in the murder of Jews is also discussed frankly. The authors acknowledge that Estonian collaborators "boasted to their bosses that they had outdone the others in annihilating the Jews" and that the groundwork had been laid before the war by anti-

Semites, one of whom is quoted as saying to an audience at the Estonian military academy, "We should be happy that we have few Jews among us. We took in a good number from czarist Russia, but we look down on the Jews."[28] Unlike other studies, this one prominently features Red Army men and partisans of obviously Jewish extraction.[29]

A documentary collection on Belorussia includes, among other things, the order establishing the ghetto in Minsk; descriptions of Germans killing Jews wantonly, mass murders of Jews in the Brest-Litovsk area, and the extermination of the Jews in Pinsk; a German report on the resistance of one of the condemned men; and a photograph of Jews being herded into the Grodno ghetto. There is an explanation of the historical origins of ghettos, concluding with the observation that "the Hitlerites revived ghettos in territories occupied by them, turning them into camps for the mass annihilation of the Jewish population."[30] A pamphlet on the Ninth Fort in Lithuania, where thousands of Jews were killed, mentions several Nazi *Aktions* against the Jews. Here, however, there is a greater attempt to blur the specifically Jewish tragedy. It is said that Einsatzgruppe A entered Kaunas with "the special task of exterminating the local party and Soviet *Aktiv*, eliminating the resistance by Soviet patriots, exterminating the Jews." The order in which the victims are listed here may be significant. Even clearer is the contrast between the reproduction of a German document reporting on the "special handling" of four thousand *Jews* in the Ponary death camp and the Russian caption that reads, "The Hitlerite security police report: another four thousand *people* [emphasis added] have been killed."[31]

One of the most popular Soviet works on the war treats the Holocaust most curiously. S. S. Smirnov's three-volume work appeared in an edition of one hundred thousand, and Smirnov was a popular participant in media features on the war. In the work Smirnov refers several times to the suffering of the Jews, but he seems to go out of his way to avoid references to Jews as fighters and resisters.

> For the Hitlerites, all peoples, aside from the Germans, all nations aside from the Germanic ones, were inferior and superfluous inhabitants of this earth . . . the first among these "inferior" nations that would have to disappear were the Jews. The Germans left them no choice—this nation was to be completely exterminated. In all countries captured by the Hitlerite armies the extermination of the Jews was carried out on an unprecedented scale, with typical German planning and organization. Millions of people of Jewish nationality or with a tinge of Jewish blood became victims of mass shootings, were burned in crematoria or asphyxiated in the gas chambers and trucks. Whole neighborhoods were turned into Jewish ghettos and were burned to the ground with their thousands of inhabitants who wore the yellow six-pointed star, the compulsory badge for Jews in lands occupied by the Germans.

Smirnov goes on to say that the people of Kiev "remember how, hour after hour, endless columns of Jews passed on the way to being shot at Babi Yar. Prisoners at Auschwitz, Majdanek, Treblinka remember how thousands of groups of Jews from Poland and Hungary, the Soviet Union and Czechoslovakia, from France and Holland, passed through the gas chambers in an endless convoy of death and how piles of bodies lay at the ovens of the crematoria." He speaks of "the terrible fate of those who lived behind the barbed wire of innumerable ghettos." His generalizations are exemplified in the story of Roman Levin. "The ten-year-old Roman, who until then had been simply a Soviet boy, a Pioneer and school boy, suddenly learned that he was a Jew, and because of that they could insult him with impunity, beat him, or even kill him." Levin escaped the Brest ghetto and was hidden by a devout Polish Catholic woman, who was later shot when the Gestapo discovered her ties to the partisans.[32]

In subsequent volumes, Smirnov discusses the persecution of Jews in Ukraine and Hungary. In Ukraine the Nazis "often . . . marched groups of people, condemned to being shot, along the streets . . . on their way out of town. At first they shot groups of communists, Soviet officials and people active in civic affairs. After that along the same route they began to take Jews, whole families, young and old. After that came columns of Gypsies who were also considered an inferior nation." He reports that the Germans used a slogan: "Germans—*gut;* Jews—*kaput;* Russians—*tozhe* [also]; Ukrainians—*pozzhe* [later]." Smirnov also describes the huge concentration of Jews in the Budapest ghetto and their deportation.[33] At the same time, he assiduously avoids identifying fighters as Jews. Describing the defenders of the Brest fortress, he mentions "the Russians Anatoly Vinogradov and Raisa Abakumova, the Armenian Samvel Matevosian, the Ukrainian Aleksandr Semenenko, the Belorussian Aleksandr Makhnach, . . . the Tatar Petr Gavrilov," and even "the German Viacheslav Meyer." The one hero whose nationality is not mentioned is Efim Moiseevich Fomin. Lest there be any doubt about his nationality, he is described as "short . . . dark-haired with intelligent and mournful eyes," a political commissar from a small town in the Vitebsk area, the son of a smith and a seamstress. All these are stereotypical characteristics of the Jew. Yet, Fomin is identified only as "the renowned commissar of the Brest fortress, a hero and a true son of the Communist Party, one of the chief organizers and leaders of the legendary defense." When referring to the other heroes, Smirnov points out their nationality: Gavrilov, the Kazan Tatar; Matevosian, "of a poor Armenian family"; and Kizhevator, "the son of a Mordvin peasant."[34] Smirnov follows the same pattern in his description of Soviet partisans in Italy.[35] Why did Smirnov describe Jewish martyrdom in detail and assiduously ignore Jewish heroism? Was this in line with an official directive? Perhaps it was the compromise he reached with himself, or, more likely, with a censor. We cannot tell, of course, but the pattern is too consistent to be accidental.

Another book, published one year earlier, presents Jews in a heroic light as partisans. A character in the book, Sarah Khatskelevna Levin, and her Yiddish-speaking daughter meet "remarkable people who have not lost their courage and their human dignity" even in the Minsk ghetto. They "refused to give in without a struggle" and formed a fighting organization.[36] The sharp contrast between treatments of the Holocaust in Ukraine, Belorussia, Lithuania, and Estonia can be explained by the choices made by the writers themselves or, less likely, by a republic-level policy that differed from one republic to another or by the capriciousness of censors. It should be noted that the Holocaust is treated most openly in the Estonian volume and is avoided in the Ukrainian literature. In Estonia there is no tradition of anti-

Semitism, whereas in Ukraine there is a substantial one. Whatever the reason for the different treatments of the Holocaust, they clearly indicate the absence of a uniform, universally applied party line on the issue, though there was an overall thrust toward downplaying it or generalizing the Holocaust to include many peoples.

A Soviet study of Nazi propaganda mentions Nazi views of Poles, Gypsies, and Jews as inferior races and the fact that the Nazis played up "the Jewish origins" of the leaders of the Russian Revolution. The author does refer to the Nazis' "pathological anti-Semitism" and their claim that in the Soviet Union those who could not show Jewish origins were considered class enemies. This foreshadowed the "fate that the German racists prepared for the Jews."[37] Further details are not given, and it should be noted that this is an academic monograph, published in a relatively small edition. A documentary history of the Soviet Union that devotes an entire chapter to World War II includes no references to the Nazis' racial policy. The excerpt from the diary of Masha Rolnikaite, a Jewish girl in the Vilnius ghetto, does not mention the word "Jew."[38] The authoritative *Great Soviet Encyclopedia* admits that anti-Semitism "found its most extreme expression in fascist Germany." It states succinctly that "the Nazis carried out a policy of mass extermination of the Jews; about six million Jews were murdered in World War II."[39] Thus, Soviet audiences were generally not exposed to even the most elementary details of the Holocaust, though in the 1960s a few books were published that did provide more information.[40] Significantly, at least some were translations from other languages.

It is all the more striking, therefore, that almost every issue of *Sovietish haimland*, the Yiddish monthly that began in 1961 (originally with a circulation of twenty-five thousand, which was later reduced to seven thousand), contains material on the Holocaust—stories, poems, memoirs, factual information. Of course, this journal was published with the approval of the authorities; in fact, the initiative for publishing it probably came "from above" as part of Khrushchev's campaign to refute Western charges of official Soviet anti-Semitism. Therefore, it is not surprising that a reading of the journal shows that certain themes, serving a didactic political purpose, appear consistently: (1) gentiles frequently saved Jews in occupied territories; (2) the Jews who resisted did so for universal, not parochial, reasons; (3) there was much cooperation among all nationalities against the Nazis; and (4) the only collaborators with the Nazis were fascists, and nearly all of them now live in the West. The first theme is illustrated by documents such as a letter from a woman now living in New York who describes how a Lithuanian couple named Ruzgis, a Polish doctor named Hrabowiecka, and a Russian family named Yakubovsky saved her daughter. Short stories present Russians, especially workers, saving Jews, and wealthy Jews serving on *Judenraten* (Jewish councils).[41]

The second theme, *druzhba narodov* (friendship among peoples), is emphasized throughout. Even an account of the Warsaw Ghetto Uprising praises Soviet Yiddish writing on it because, of course, the role of Communists in the uprising is emphasized and there are fictional accounts of Red Army men sneaking into the ghetto to help the resisting Jews. The uprising is described as "an important contribution of the Jewish masses to the international struggle of the progressive forces of all peoples, led by the Soviet Union, against fascism and international reaction."[42]

A description of how Bulgarians saved Jews concludes that "the struggle of the Bulgarian people to save the Jews, under the leadership of the Communists, can in no way be separated from the general struggle of the Bulgarian people against Fascism." The struggle against anti-Semitism can be successfully conducted "only in close alliance with the progressive and democratic forces of the world."[43] The other side of this coin is seen in the resistance of Soviet authorities to the publication of Peretz Markish's novel *Trot fun doires* (Footsteps of the generations [1966]) on the grounds that its hero was a "Zionist." The portrayal of him dying wrapped in a prayer shawl was also objectionable. The objections to publishing the novel were overridden by special authorization of the Soviet Writers Union.[44] Thus, resistance to the Holocaust and to anti-Semitism had to be universalized. It had to be portrayed as part of larger progressive struggles, led by Communists.

The third theme, the cooperation of all nationalities in the struggle against the Nazis, is illustrated in the following quotation: "One of the main sources of the world-historical victory . . . was the friendship among the Soviet peoples. Against the . . . enemy, Russians, Ukrainians, Belorussians, Jews, Georgians, Armenians—the sons and daughters of all the peoples of the Soviet Union—fought shoulder to shoulder."[45] A story about a Jewish Hero of the Soviet Union, Chaim Tevelevich Diskin, points out the heroism of his two Russian comrades,[46] and another relates how Russians in Taganrog saved Jews.[47] A discussion of the proposal to build the Babi Yar monument in Kiev stresses that "people of different nationalities—Russians, Ukrainians, Jews—were attracted by the idea of putting up a monument in Babi Yar."[48]

The well-known writer Boris Polevoi claims that gentiles "stubbornly opposed the murderers of the Jews, and Jewish families were hidden."[49] An editorial comment asserts that "in the days of the Great Patriotic War, friendship among peoples, among nations, was the most powerful weapon in the struggle with the fascists."[50] Writing about the sculptor Elmar Rivosh, whose entire family was killed in Riga, Misha Lev points out that Rivosh could not have saved himself without the assistance of his friends, identified as "anonymous Latvians and Russians, Jews and Poles." A Russian woman on the "Aryan side" fed him, a Russian doctor healed him, and a Latvian friend helped him find a hiding place.[51] This is the pattern emphasized throughout the literature, whether in Russian or Yiddish.

How then can one explain collaboration with the Nazis on the part of hundreds of thousands? The fourth theme provides the answer, and it is simple: the collaborators were all ideologically deformed. "Petty bourgeois are the same all over. Whoever has might, is right, they feel."[52] All the collaborators, whether Latvian, Polish, Ukrainian, or Russian, were "bourgeois nationalists" or marginal elements, "the refuse of the Latvian people," as one article puts it.[53] Many of them, it was claimed, led anti-Soviet agitators in the West. The Soviets long denounced anti-Soviet émigrés as collaborators with the Nazis, and there is no doubt that the label fits many. Sometimes it was acknowledged that these people participated in the annihilation of the Jewish population. But more recently some called for a reassessment of Soviet émigrés. "Our compatriots abroad—until just recently we pretended they didn't exist (and if there were some abroad, they were all former Vlasovites, traitors to the homeland one and all). And yet millions of our fellow countrymen—Russians, Ukrainians, Belorussians, Armenians, Jews—live far from their native land and many of them were scarcely burdened with inexpiable guilt."[54] But the more usual pattern was to omit the Jews. "It is precisely in the West . . . that traitors on whose hands the blood of Latvians, Lithuanians and Estonians will never dry have taken refuge."[55] Of course, these discussions avoided the fundamental problem of explaining how such large numbers of people could have been so infected with anti-Semitism and/or so hostile to the Soviet regime that they participated in the Nazis' work.[56]

Also avoided was mention of anti-Semitism in the Red Army and among the partisan groups.[57] In fact, the existence of separate Jewish partisan groups was completely unacknowledged. The role of Jews in the armed struggle against the German invaders was generally downplayed, as we have seen in the work of S. S. Smirnov. Writing about Hero of the Soviet Union Chaim Tevelevich Diskin, Marshal V. Kazakov never mentions Diskin's very obvious Jewish nationality.[58] Even partisan leader Colonel Dmitri Medvedev, who accepted Jewish survivors, including women and children, into his group, never mentions the nationality of three Jewish heroes he describes, "although in his two books Medvedev rarely forgot to tell his readers whether his heroes were Russians, Ukrainians, Belorussians, Poles or Kazakhs." He also does not mention how he saved 150 Jewish women, children, and old people. The assumption is that the censors or editors deliberately omitted these items.[59] Jewish combatants are mentioned in general discussions of the armed forces,[60] and there are a few pamphlets or books published about Jewish war heroes, though the total number of biographies is very large.[61] Again, *Sovietish haimland* is different from the literature in Russian. In this Yiddish journal there is considerable fictional and non-fictional material about Jewish fighters. Jewish partisans are described in positive terms,[62] memoirs of Jewish generals and soldiers of lesser rank are often published,[63] and many Jewish soldiers, including those who gave their lives, are portrayed.[64] But the overwhelming majority of Soviet readers, even Jewish ones, had no access at all to this literature. The role of the Jews as combatants was largely ignored—even more than their role as victims—in most cases, it would seem, deliberately.

For many years it was assumed that anything published in the Soviet Union, since it had to pass official censorship, reflected policy at some level. Examination of the literature on the Holocaust casts some doubt on this assumption. Nevertheless, the published literature remains almost the only source on reactions to the Holocaust, since to date there have been no other instruments for gauging public reaction to it. Thus far, there have been no surveys of people's reactions to the fate of the Jews during the war, nor are there any measures of their knowledge of the Holocaust. However, a survey conducted among nearly four hundred Soviet Jewish immigrants in Detroit within half a year of their arrival, in 1989–91, reveals that few knew the approximate number of Soviet Jews killed in the Holocaust, though a majority cited the figure six million for the total number of Jews who died. When asked whether they had read about the Holocaust in the Soviet Union, a majority of those over the age of thirty had read some literature on the subject. The most frequently cited works were Rybakov's novel *Heavy Sand,* Yevtushenko's poem "Babi Yar," and Kuznetsov's novel of the same name. The most frequently cited source of information on the Holocaust was discussions among family and friends. Almost no nonfictional, historical sources of information were cited. One can presume that if Jews were not aware of any other sources of information on the Holocaust, non-Jewish Soviets were even less aware.

The Holocaust and the Soviet Political Calculus

Why was the Holocaust generally glossed over, suppressed, or universalized in the Soviet literature? Several possible explanations present themselves. One is that this was the result simply of anti-Semitism. The Soviets were incapable of showing sympathy for the Jews and refused to acknowledge the national tragedy. This may be too simplistic. As we have seen, there was considerable variation in the treatment of the Holocaust in Soviet works on the subject. Another explanation sees the origins of this policy in Stalin's postwar anti-Semitism. A different kind of Holocaust was being prepared after the war, as foreshadowed by mass arrests in 1948, the "anticosmopolitan campaign," the execution of the Yiddish writers in 1952, the "doctors' plot," and the building of large barracks in Siberia. To admit that Jews had just been so terribly persecuted and to signal to the Soviet public that their suffering was a matter of concern might have impeded this policy.

A third explanation has to do with the shift in the Soviet "political formula." The basis of legitimation of the Soviet regime, the legitimating myth, had moved from the revolution to World War II. After all, only a tiny minority of Soviet people remembered the revolution, but a far greater number could identify with the Great Patriotic War. Moreover, while the outcome of the revolution was not welcomed by all, no Soviet citizen could wish for a different outcome of World War II. For several decades there was a virtual cult of World War II in the Soviet Union in literature, movies, art, and television. To emphasize the Jewish role and fate would have diminished the all-union effort and experience. It is bad enough, some would have argued, that the revolution was identified with the Jews. To "give the war to the Jews" would not only be a gross distortion of history but would also erode the legitimating power of the experience and would arouse great resentment by other nationalities. Of course, this does not explain why such strenuous efforts were made to diminish artificially the Jewish fate. After all, straightforward treatment would not in any way have diminished the overall Soviet sacrifice or effort.

Soviet authorities no doubt were aware that knowledge of the Holocaust raised Jewish consciousness and retarded assimilation. It is no accident that Jewish educators in the United States emphasize the Holocaust in curricula for children and adults, especially for audiences that have less than intensive exposure to other Jewish experiences. The Holocaust is so recent, so devastating, that few can remain untouched or unmoved by it. Even the most assimilated Jew, whether in the United States or the former Soviet Union, must be in some way affected by it. The Soviets, who saw assimilation as the solution to the Jewish Question, were opposed to anything that "artificially" raised Jewish consciousness. Moreover, the Holocaust raised the troublesome question of what the non-Jews were doing during the mass murder of Jews. An "incorrect" understanding could lead one to draw equally "incorrect" conclusions about the prospects for assimilation. Indeed, in the Detroit survey, when immigrants were asked to describe the attitude of most non-Jews to the murder of Jews during the war, most thought they had been supportive of the killing or indifferent to it. The conclusion the respondents drew from that was that "there is no place for me in the Soviet Union," as many of them phrased it. Zionists have used the Holocaust to justify the "negation of the Diaspora," to argue that the world is inherently anti-Semitic and that there is, therefore, no solution to the Jewish Problem other than a Jewish state and immigration to it. Since the Soviets were opposed to this conclusion, they were wary of even dealing with the premise as raised by the Holocaust. Finally, any discussion of the Holocaust brought up the troublesome issue of collaboration and betrayal in the Soviet Union, a topic with which Soviet historiography was not comfortable and which continues to trouble the successor states. Indeed, the matter has not been thoroughly investigated in the West and remains a major source of tension between Jewish and Eastern European communities there.

Some Consequences of the Soviet Treatment of the Holocaust

The ultimate universalization of the Holocaust was the Soviet equation of fascism with Zionism and the charge of collaboration between the two. As one Soviet writer asserted, "Many facts have convincingly demonstrated the fascist nature of the ideology and policies of Zionism. Fascism is disgusting in any of its guises—its Zionist version is no better than its Hitlerite one."[65] Between the years 1975 and 1978 at least twenty-three articles in the Soviet press claimed that Zionists collaborated actively with the Nazis. A 1983 pamphlet, *Istinnoe litso sionizma* (The true face of Zionism), outlined alleged Zionist collaboration with the Nazis as it was manifested in the presence of Zionists on *Judenraten,* in Zionist attempts to negotiate with Nazis in order to save Jews, and in the Zionists' defense of war criminals.[66] In another pamphlet, published a year later, Zionism was described as "a bourgeois-nationalistic ideology, suffused with the poison of racism and chauvinism, militarism and extremism, representing a threat to all of humanity"—precisely the characteristics generally attributed to Nazism.[67]

In the late eighties some anti-Zionist works were criticized for their "inexact formulations and even incorrect assertions," including exaggerations of the linkages between Zionism and Nazism and the claim that Zionists attempted to form a "united anti-Soviet front of Hitlerism . . . [and] West European and American capitalism at the end of World War II." But there was no rejection of the Nazism-Zionism link, only an admonition to "evaluate properly the real dimensions of the cooperation among various elements in the course of historic events."[68] The legitimacy of linking Nazism and Zionism remained unchallenged. One can make such an assertion if one argues that ideology and class, not ethnicity, were what determined the behavior of the Nazis and the fate of the Jews. Nazis and Zionists were said to share class-based interests, strategies, tactics, and goals. One of the great ironies in this is that in 1947 Soviet diplomat Andrei Gromyko said at the United Nations that "during the last war, the Jewish people underwent exceptional sorrow and suffering . . . the time has come to help these people not by word but by deeds."[69] This was his explanation for the Soviet vote to partition Palestine and create a Jewish state.

More than forty years ago, then, Zionism was a justified consequence of fascism. Later it became but a variant of it. The equation of Zionism with fascism may have made Zionism comprehensible to Soviet citizens—otherwise it was as abstract as Buddhism—but it was deeply insulting to Soviet Jews. In fact, even the universalization or suppression of the Holocaust deeply injured them, because a traumatic part of their recent history was denied. Not surprisingly, it led them to ask questions about a system that did such a thing, about their neighbors, about their own fate as Jews, as the Detroit study makes clear. Many came to precisely the Zionist conclusions the regime wished to avoid. In late 1989 and through 1991, when more than three hundred thousand Soviet Jews emigrated, largely to Israel, the fear of social breakdown and "anarchy" was cited by many as the reason for their hasty departure. Not a few made specific reference to the Holocaust and said that they thought there was a realistic chance that it could be repeated, this time without a foreign invasion.

A less important, but not trivial, consequence of the Soviet downplaying of the Holocaust was that it was perceived in the West as further evidence of Soviet anti-Semitism. Moreover, the cooperation of some Jews with the Bolsheviks and the collaboration by some Baltic people, Poles, and Ukrainians with the Nazis in the persecution and murder of the Jews remain extremely controversial and touchy points in the relations between Jews and Eastern Europeans.

The dominant Soviet approach to the Holocaust, criticized by most Westerners who were aware of it, raised an interesting question. It was obviously a malicious distortion to pass over it in silence. It robbed people of an important part of their history, desecrated the memory of millions, and signaled that Jewish lives were not worth remarking on. But what about the other Soviet strategy, that of embedding the Holocaust in the larger "struggle against fascism"? Disregarding the question of historical accuracy for the moment and concentrating on the question of using the knowledge of the Holocaust to prevent future such occurrences, one wonders whether the latter aim is best served by emphasizing the Jewish catastrophe's uniqueness. Especially in a country with some anti-Semitic traditions, assigning the Holocaust to a marginal minority that was despised by some might have allowed many to dismiss it as either irrelevant to their concerns or something Jews might have "deserved." In the former Soviet Union and elsewhere, some people with very partial knowledge have expressed contempt for the Jews, who suffered much but "did not fight back," an image that one could easily derive from the Soviet literature. Perhaps the approach of some Soviet writers—discussing the Holocaust in the context of the overall Soviet struggle but pointing out those features that set the Jews apart from others—might have been most effective in the former Soviet Union and other Slavic countries in alerting readers to the dangers that face *all* people while not diminishing the Jewish tragedy. Western gentiles did not suffer nearly as much as the people of Eastern Europe did from the Nazis, and many American noncombatants hardly suffered at all. For Westerners, the Jewish tragedy stands out more starkly than for East Europeans, who witnessed the totality of the Nazi occupation. The Jewish experience is not so easily discounted in Western societies, where Jews are more accepted than in the former Soviet Union. In Eastern Europe and the former Soviet Union the Holocaust must be embedded in a larger mosaic of palpable, immediate suffering, though its unique configurations should not be blurred in that mosaic, for even in the experience of those regions the unspeakable tragedy of the Jews remains unique.

The time seems to be at hand for post-Soviet reassessments of the war, and we were told that a new, ten-volume history of the Great Patriotic War was in preparation. The previous history "no longer meets the present-day requirements of our society, in which an expansion of openness and democracy is now under way."[70] As part of *glasnost* and *perestroika,* there was a major reexamination of Soviet history in the Soviet Union. An article in *Izvestiia* explained: "The creation of an honest school course in USSR history is a task of paramount state importance."[71] Another article noted that "the public's growing interest in history is an indisputable fact. . . . Only by not concealing facts, but subjecting them to public scrutiny, thorough examination, objective analysis and impartial assessments can our historical scholarship restore its reputation."[72]

Not surprisingly, the ten-volume history of the war that was supposed to be published in 1991, the fiftieth anniversary of the Nazi invasion, became embroiled in political controversy. The chief of the team of editors responsible for the publication, Colonel-General Dmitry Volkogonov, was dismissed from that post and also left his post as director of the Military History Institute. He was attacked from two sides. In November 1990 three historians charged that the team was not properly trained, had not reviewed non-Soviet literature on the subject, and did not have access to the necessary documents. Thus, the new work would be no improvement over its predecessor, published between 1973 and 1982. The new edition, the critics said, was under the supervision of Marshall Yazov and others selected on the basis of their posts, not their abilities or knowledge, and so it was "doomed to be a repetition of its predecessors."[73]

On the other hand, the late Marshal Sergei Akhromeyev accused Volkogonov of being "clever and glib" but having a "deep antipathy for socialism," though earlier he hypocritically espoused Communism. Thus, it was no wonder that the draft of the first volume "makes it seem that Stalinism was the dominant, distinguishing feature of the prewar decades" and "relates almost nothing of the Soviet people's dedication and heroic efforts in building socialism during those years." Even after the draft of the first volume was reedited, Marshal Yazov accused Volkogonov of "giving a tendentious, anticommunist interpretation of the events preceding the start of the war." Volkogonov replied that his work in the archives made him realize that "a great deal that people ought to know is kept shrouded in secrecy." He observed that it might be possible to compile a true history of the war in twenty or thirty years, after the last of the participants had died.[74]

In 1989–90 several articles on the Holocaust appeared in the Soviet press, particularly in Ukraine. The massacre at Babi Yar and its specifically Jewish aspects were commemorated in public ceremonies. A Kiev newspaper devoted an entire page to an excerpt from Ehrenburg and Grossman's *Black Book,* referring to an earlier article in a Moscow evening newspaper that had revealed to Soviet readers the existence and fate of that documentary study.[75] In September 1988 a large gathering in Moscow commemorated the slaughter at Babi Yar, and the event was marked publicly at Babi Yar itself. Not only did police not interfere, as they had in earlier years, but scenes from the meetings were shown on television. In Minsk, Lvov, and Vilnius memorial sculptures commemorating the Jewish Holocaust were commissioned or planned.[76] In 1989 an agreement was reached between Soviet archivists and the Yad Vashem Institute in Jerusalem permitting several researchers from Jerusalem to go through some Soviet archives and microfilm German and Soviet documents pertaining to the Holocaust. At an April 1990 international congress of historians in Moscow, Dr. Yitzhak Arad, director of Yad Vashem, and one or two others delivered papers on the Holocaust period. It is highly significant that several groups of amateur historians—in Moscow, Leningrad, Minsk, Odessa, and elsewhere—have been studying the Holocaust and conducting taped interviews with survivors and non-Jews who observed aspects of the mass murder of the Jews. The great majority of these researchers appear to be people who were themselves born after the war. In the fall of 1989 several of them were invited to Israel to participate in a training seminar for Holocaust researchers, and this was done again in subsequent years.

The politicization of the Holocaust continued after the breakup of the Soviet Union. In September 1991 the Lithuanian government, having just achieved Soviet recognition of its declaration of independence, pardoned about a thousand Lithuanians who had been convicted by Soviet tribunals of collaborating with the Nazis. Jewish and Israeli circles immediately protested. Clearly, the Lithuanian motivation was political: having achieved independence, they were inclined to say everything Soviet was bad. If a Soviet tribunal adjudged a man guilty, he must have been innocent. This was not only prima facie absurd but also a foolish move politically. The Lithuanians modified their position, suspending the rehabilitations in October, and considered setting up a Lithuanian-Israeli-American commission of experts to review rehabilitation requests.[77] Although the commission was established, it had not issued any reports as of late 1993.

These incidents illustrate (1) the continued sensitivity of the collaboration issue; (2) the tendency to politicize the issue and give it contemporary significance; and (3) the very different perceptions of Jews and other peoples. In Ukraine the issue is at least as sensitive as it is in the Baltic. Ukrainian images of Jews as Communists and Jewish images of Ukrainians as fascists survive long after the war. The trial and acquittal in 1993 of John Demjanjuk in Israel, where he had been extradited from the United States on charges that he was a notorious guard at Treblinka, highlighted the issue. It is impossible to establish with certainty how many Ukrainians collaborated with the Nazis (and in what ways) and how many saved Jews, though there is no doubt that the former vastly outnumbered the latter. In Ukraine, collaboration with the Nazis took the form not only of individual acts but of organized politics. Ukrainian collaboration took six general forms. The Organization of Ukrainian Nationalists, formed in Poland (West Ukraine) before the war, split into two factions in 1940. One faction, led by Stepan Bandera (after whom a major boulevard in Lviv [Lvov] has been renamed today), declared at its second congress, in April 1941, that "the Jews . . . are the most faithful prop of the Bolshevik regime and the vanguard of Muscovite imperialism in Ukraine. . . . The Organization of Ukrainian Nationalists is engaged in a struggle against the Jews." In July 1941 Yaroslav Stetsko, head of the Ukrainian government supported by Bandera, stated that "the principal enemy of Ukraine is not Jewry but Moscow. . . . Yet the role of the Jews must not be underestimated. We are of the opinion that a struggle against the Jews of Ukraine should be undertaken according to the German methods, and so I am firm in my view that the Jews must be annihilated completely, and the German methods for liquidating the Jews should be brought to Ukraine."[78]

The second form of Ukrainian collaboration was the formation of Ukrainian armed units, which were attached to German military and police formations. The Ukrainian units included the Nachtigal and Roland battalions, and the Waffen SS division Halychyna.[79] Third, leaders of at least two Ukrainian churches blessed the German army and called upon their followers "to cooperate with the Nazi regime."[80] Fourth, when the Germans occupied West Ukraine, a wave of pogroms broke out in the major cities of Lvov, Stanislavov, Kremenetz, and elsewhere. Fifth, "During the liquidation of the ghettos in . . . 1942, the Ukrainian police was among the forces that participated in the action, and its men were responsible for shooting thousands of Jews who had been marched to sites of execution and thousands of others who tried to remain in hiding or to escape." Finally, "countless Jews were turned over to the authorities" by Ukrainians who were motivated by either enmity or greed.[81] The same was done by members of the Ukrainian Insurgent Army who encountered Jews who had fled the ghettos for the forests. In East Ukraine, which had been part of the Soviet Union since 1918–21, there apparently were fewer pogroms, but there are many German reports of individuals turning in Jews. Thus, in one way or another, whatever their motivations, tens of thousands of Ukrainians assisted the Nazis in their attempt to annihilate the Jews.

Against this background—though it was not much discussed in public—Ukrainian and Jewish groups, with the support of the Ukrainian government, organized a large-scale commemoration of the fiftieth anniversary of the massacre at Babi Yar in September 1991. The main streets of Kiev were lined with photographs of Kievan Jews who had been murdered at Babi Yar. Several days of conferences, meetings, exhibitions, concerts, and speeches were devoted to the commemoration, and a *Book of Memory* was published in a print run of seventy-five thousand copies. The media reported these events extensively, and the subject of the Holocaust generally achieved a prominence unknown in the Soviet period.

The collapse of the Soviet Union means that its former constituent parts now have to face the issue of the Holocaust individually. As they rewrite their histories, the Holocaust will again become a major issue between the Ukrainians, Latvians,

Lithuanians, Belorussians, Moldavians, Russians, and others, on the one hand, and the Jews, on the other. Revisions of history may be politicized and tendentious at first. One would hope that these would be only infantile disorders of newly won independence, though they might turn out to be symptoms of a more chronic illness.

NOTES

I am grateful to the Office of the Vice-President for Research at the University of Michigan for its financial support and to Yury Polsky and Scott Tarry for their assistance in research. Some of the material in this essay first appeared in *Holocaust and Genocide Studies* 5, no. 1 (1990), copyright 1990, Oxford University Press.

1. For an overview of the history of Jews in czarist Russia, see Salo Baron, *The Russian Jew under Tsars and Soviets* (New York, 1964); Louis Greenberg, *The Jews in Russia*, 2 vols. (New Haven, 1944); and Simon Dubnow, *History of the Jews in Russia and Poland*, 3 vols. (Philadelphia, 1916–20).

2. On czarist policies, see Hans Rogger, *Jewish Policies and Right-Wing Politics in Imperial Russia* (Berkeley and Los Angeles, 1986). On pogroms, see I. Michael Aronson, *Troubled Waters: The Origins of the 1881 Anti-Jewish Pogroms in Russia* (Pittsburgh, 1990); and John Klier and Shlomo Lambroza, eds., *Pogroms: Anti-Jewish Violence in Modern Jewish History* (Cambridge, 1992).

3. On the Beilis case, see Alexander Tager, *The Decay of Czarism* (Philadelphia, 1935).

4. On the development of political life, see Eli Lederhandler, *The Road to Modern Jewish Politics* (Oxford, 1989).

5. See Henry J. Tobias, *The Jewish Bund in Russia* (Stanford, 1972).

6. Zvi Gitelman, *Jewish Nationality and Soviet Politics* (Princeton, 1972), 105–16.

7. For a general history of Soviet Jewry, see Zvi Gitelman, *A Century of Ambivalence: The Jews of Russia and the Soviet Union, 1881 to the Present* (New York, 1988).

8. See Solomon Schwarz, *The Jews in the Soviet Union* (Syracuse, 1951), pt. 2.

9. For the period 1939–41, see Norman Davies and Antony Polonsky, eds., *Jews in Eastern Poland and the USSR, 1939–1946* (New York, 1991); and Solomon Schwarz, *Evrei v Sovetskom Soiuze* (New York, 1966).

10. Mordechai Altshuler asserts that "estimates of the number of Jewish Holocaust victims in the Soviet Union fluctuate between 2.5 million and 3.3 million" (*Soviet Jewry since the Second World War: Population and Social Structure* [New York, 1987], 4).

11. On the eastward movement of Jewish refugees, see B. Z. Pinchuk, *Yehudai Brit haMoetsot mool pnai haShoah* (Tel Aviv, 1979); Mordechai Altshuler, "Hapinui veham'nusah shel yehudim miBelorussiya haMizrakhit bitkufat haShoah (Yuni–August 1941)," in *Yahadut Zmaneinu* (Jerusalem) 3 (1986); and Schwarz, *Evrei v Sovetskom Soiuze*.

12. Z. Segalowicz, *Gebrente trit* (Buenos Aires, 1947), 96.

13. Allen Small, interview, December 14, 1986, Video Archive for Holocaust Testimonies at Yale University, interview no. T-833.

14. Adolf Hitler, quoted in Alexander Dallin, *German Rule in Soviet Russia, 1941–1945*, 2d ed. (London, 1981), 9.

15. Generals Von Reichenau and Von Manstein are both quoted in Matthew Cooper, *The Phantom War* (London, 1979), 171–73.

16. Raul Hilberg, *The Destruction of the European Jews*, 3 vols., rev. ed. (New York, 1985), 301. On the relationship between the army and the *Einsatzgruppen*, see Hans-Heinrich Wilhelm, *Rassenpolitik und Kriegfuhrung* (Passau, Germany, 1991).

17. Hilberg, *Destruction*, 295 and chap. 7, esp. 288–89. Many accounts of the tortures inflicted on the victims can be found in Ilya Ehrenburg and Vasily Grossman, *The Black Book*, trans. John Glad and James S. Levine (New York, 1981).

18. William Korey, "Down History's Memory Hole: Soviet Treatment of the Holocaust," *Present Tense* 10 (winter 1983), 53.

19. Mordechai Altshuler, "Pirsumim Russiyim biMoetsot al nos'im Yehudiyim bashanim 1917–1967," in Altshuler, ed., *Pirsumim Russiyim biVrit haMoetsot al Yehudim veYahadut* (Jerusalem, 1970), lxvi. See also "Seventy Years of Soviet Jewry," *Insight* (London), November 1987, 6.

20. William Korey, *The Soviet Cage* (New York, 1973), 90.

21. Dov Levin, *Fighting Back: Lithuanian Jewry's Armed Resistance to the Nazis, 1941–1945* (New York, 1985), xii.

22. For the English version, see n. 17 above. A Russian edition was finally published in Vilnius in 1993.

23. Korey, "Down History's Memory Hole."

24. Dmitri Starikov, quoted in Korey, *The Soviet Cage*, 109.

25. Bill Keller, "Echo of '41 in Minsk: Was the Heroine a Jew?" *New York Times,* September 15, 1987, A1, A8.

26. *Istoriia velikoi otechestvennoi voine Sovetskogo Soiuza, 1941–1945 gg,* 6 vols. (Moscow, 1962–65); see vol. 3 (1962), 438, 442, 443, 446.

27. Yu. Yu. Kondufor et al., *Istoriia Ukrainskoi SSR* (Kiev, 1982).

28. L. N. Lentzmann et al., *Estonskii narod v velikoi otechestvennoi voine Sovetskogo Soiuza 1941–1945* (Tallin, 1973), 437, 440, 449, 452, quotations on 437 and 452.

29. See, e.g., p. 330 and the pictures between pp. 448 and 449.

30. P. P. Lipilo and V. F. Romanovskii, eds., *Prestuplenia Nemetsko-fashistkikh okkupantov v Belorussii 1941–1944* (Minsk, 1965), 24–25, 28, 56–58, 231, 397.

31. O. Kaplanas, *Deviaty fort obvinaet* (Vilnius, 1964), 37–38, 40.

32. S. S. Smirnov, *Sobranie Sochinenii,* 3 vols. (Moscow, 1973), vol. 1, *Brestkaia Krepost', krepost' nad Bugom,* 331–32.

33. Ibid., vol. 3, *Stalingrad na Dnepre; Na poliakh Vengrii; Liudi, kotorykh ia videl',* 23, 32, 274.

34. Ibid., vol. 1, 227, 187, 194, 157, 44, 235.

35. Ibid., vol. 2, *Rasskazy o Neizvestnykh Geroiakh,* 131, 214–15.

36. N. Matveev, *Parol'—'Brusnika'* (Moscow, 1972). This book was published in an edition of one hundred thousand by a publishing house that has issued several books considered anti-Semitic by many. Yet, this volume favorably presents heroes of obvious Jewish nationality, such as Captain David Keimach (whose pseudonym was Dima Korneenko), a Red Army officer who worked behind the German lines; Rafael Monusovich Bromberg; and Sarah Levin. Thus, the portrayal of the Jews is not consistent.

37. Yu. Ya. Orlov, *Krakh Nemetsko-fashistkoi propagandy v period voiny protiv SSSR* (Moscow, 1985), 95, 61.

38. V. I. Vinogradov, *Istoriia SSR v dokumentakh i illustratsiiakh* (Moscow, 1981).

39. *Great Soviet Encyclopedia,* 32 vols. (Moscow, 1970; New York, 1975), s.v. "Jews." There is no "Holocaust" entry in the encyclopedia.

40. For example, F. Kral's *Prestuplenie protiv Evropy* (1963) and *SS v deistvii* (1961).

41. See, e.g., Henrikh Hoffman, "Dos iz geshen in Taganrog," *Sovetish haimland,* no. 2 (1966); Hirsh Dobin, "Der koiech fun lebn," ibid., no. 3 (1966); and Yekhiel Falikman, "Der shvartser vint," ibid., no. 8 (1967).

42. Hersh Remenik, "Der ufshtand in Varshever getto in der Yidisher Sovetisher literatur," ibid., no. 2 (1963), 150.

43. Ibid., 153. In a poem by Shmuel Halkin, the Soviet warrior Bereza comes to the ghetto to help the fighters. The Jewish fighter Ratnitsky says, "Let the people be blessed and the land from which this man came to participate in our struggle as an equal." A major study of the Warsaw ghetto mentions no such episode and points out that the Soviet Union, like the other allies, "did not come to the aid of the fighters in the ghettos." Ironically, spokesmen of the Polish Home Army believed that "the ghetto is no more than a base for Soviet Russia . . . the Russians were the ones who prepared the revolt in the Warsaw ghetto" (Yisrael Gutman, *The Jews of Warsaw, 1939–1943* [Bloomington, Ind., 1982], 408, 409, 417). A Polish Communist historian also does not mention Red Army men in the two versions of his history of the Warsaw Ghetto Uprising. See B. Mark, *Powstanie w getcie Warszawskim* (Warsaw, 1953, 1963).

44. Israel Meyer, "Dos Bulgarishe Folk hot geratevet di Yidn fun fashistisher oisrotung," *Sovetish haimland,* no. 6 (1967), 124.

45. See Esther Markish, *The Long Return* (New York, 1978), 152.

46. Valentin Tomin and Alexander Sinelnikov, "Dokumentn raidn," *Sovietish haimland,* no. 2 (1963), 158.

47. Yudl Pertsovsky, "Er hot farteidikt Moskve," ibid., no. 2 (1966); Hoffman, "Dos iz geshen in Taganrog." See also Dobin, "Der koiech fun lebn."

48. "Proyektn far a denkmol in Babi Yar," *Sovietish haimland,* no. 3 (1966), 158. The Ukrainian writer Ivan Khomenko described how his mother hid a Jewish teenage girl for nine months. He published a poem, "Di Yidishke," about the incident in ibid., no. 10 (1966). Other items emphasized the friendship among nationalities in the ranks of the partisans (letter from Avrom Hurman, ibid., no. 6 [1963], 122) and the sympathy of gentiles for the massacred Jews (letter from Piotr Bulakh, ibid., no. 3 [1964], 156–57).

49. Boris Polevoi, "Doktor Vera," ibid., no. 3 (1967), 46.

50. *Sovietish haimland,* no. 5 (1965), 3.

51. Misha Lev, "Der Riger Manuskript un zein autor," ibid., no. 5 (1962), 37.

52. See Iosif Yuzovsky, "Faran in Varshe a denk-mol," ibid., no. 4 (1967), 132.

53. M. Vesterman, "Zeit vachzam!" ibid., no. 2 (1963), 156–57.

54. "There's No Turning Back," *Pravda,* August 24, 1987, translation in *Current Digest of the Soviet Press (CDSP)* 39, no. 34 (1987), 1.

55. Gennady Vasilev, "Journey to Russian America," *Pravda,* November 16, 1987, translation in *CDSP* 39, no. 46 (1987), 21–22.

56. Yu. Kirilchenko, "Touchstone of Ill Will," *Pravda,* August 23, 1987, translation in *CDSP* 39, no. 46 (1987), 2.

57. One result of *glasnost* was the possibility of opening up this issue. As one article put it, "Ignorance of history is kindling wood for the bonfire of fervent nationalism. But one has to admit that in the Baltic republics textbooks . . . suffer from a lack of objectivity and, with incomprehensible diffidence, pass over in silence, to put it bluntly, tragic periods in the life of Latvia, Lithuania and Estonia. . . . Anti-Soviet propaganda takes skillful advantage of this, filling the blank spots in the textbooks with malicious fabrications and fanning national enmity" (O. Meshkov et al., "In a Foreign Voice," *Pravda,* September 1, 1987, translation in *CDSP* 39, no. 34 [1987], 7).

58. V. Kazakov, "Der goirl fun a held," *Sovietish haimland,* no. 12 (1966), 12, translated from *Sovietskaia Rossiia,* September 24, 1966.

59. Reuben Ainsztein, *Jewish Resistance in Nazi-Occupied Europe* (London, 1974), 373.

60. See, for example, G. A. Kumanev, ed., *Istochniki pobedy Sovetskogo naroda v velikoi otechestvennoi voine 1941–1945* (Moscow, 1985), 187, 194, 197.

61. Among the biographies listed in one Western bibliography are four on Jewish heroes (two on Lev Dovator, a cavalry commander killed in the battle of Moscow). At least one other biography, a second one of General David Dragunsky, has appeared since. See Michael Parrish, *The U.S.S.R. in World War Two,* vol. 2 (New York, 1981). The later biography of Dragunsky is V. Z. Krivulin and Yu. I. Pivovar, *I eto vse v odnoi sud'be* (Moscow, 1986).

62. Serafim Alekseev, "Di operatsie in Adamov," *Sovietish haimland,* no. 2 (1963), 145: "The Jewish fellows distinguished themselves by their discipline, courage, steadfastness."

63. See, e.g., Guards Lt. Gen. Hirsh Plaskov, "Frontovnikes," ibid., no. 5 (1966), 71–73. Plaskov wrote about several heroic Jewish soldiers.

64. See, e.g., Shire Gorshman, "Zol feln a hor," in ibid., 77–85.

65. A. I. Epshtain, ed., *Nash otvet klevetnikam* (Kharkov, 1976).

66. R. M. Brodskii and O. Ia. Krasivskii, *Istinnoe litso sionizma* (Lvov, 1983), 34–39.

67. L. E. Bernshtein, *Antikommunisticheskaia sushchnost' ideologicheskikh kontseptsii sionizma* (Kiev, 1984), 33.

68. L. Ia. Dadiani, S. I. Mokshin, and E. V. Tadevosyan, "O nekotorykh voprosakh istoriografii proletarskogo internatsionalizma," *Voprosy istorii KPSS,* January 1987, 76.

69. Andrei Gromyko, quoted in Yaacov Ro'i, *Soviet Decision Making in Practice* (New Brunswick, N.J., 1980), 70.

70. S. Bugayev, "History Covered with Glory," *Krasnaia Zvezda,* August 15, 1987, translation in *CDSP* 39, no. 33 (1987), 18. See also Yury Perechnev, "Ten Volumes on the War," *Moscow News,* September 20, 1987, translation in *CDSP* 39, no. 50 (1988), 7.

71. V. Svirsky, "History Passes Over in Silence," *Izvestiia,* July 21, 1987, translation in *CDSP* 39, no. 29 (1987), 6.

72. Yury Orlik, "Treat History with Respect," *Izvestiia,* August 8, 1987, translation in *CDSP* 39, no. 32 (1987), 9–10.

73. See V. Dashichev, V. Kulish, and A. Mertsalov, "History of the War: Yet Another Version?" *Izvestiia,* November 19, 1990, translation in *CDSP* 42, no. 46 (1990), 27.

74. Maj. Gen. V. I. Filatov, interview in *Voenno-Istorichesky Zhurnal,* no. 4 (April 1991), translation in *CDSP* 43, no. 17 (1991), 17.

75. "'Chernaia Kniga' sushchesvuet," *Vechernii Kiev,* September 29, 1989.

76. See the documents and testimonies in Sima Ycikas, "Lithuanian-Jewish Relations in the Shadows of the Holocaust," *Jews and Jewish Topics in the Soviet Union and Eastern Europe,* no. 1 (11) (1990), 33–66.

77. Henry Kamm, "Lithuania Halts the Reversal of War-Crimes Convictions," *New York Times,* October 17, 1991.

78. Stepan Bandera and Yaroslav Stetsko, quoted in Shmuel Spector, "The Attitude of the Ukrainian Diaspora to the Holocaust of Ukrainian Jewry," in *The Historiography of the Holocaust Period,* ed. Yisrael Gutman and Gideon Greif (Jerusalem, 1988), 277, 278.

79. A recent article is Basyl Dmytryshyn, "The SS Division 'Galicia': Its Genesis, Training, Deployment," *Nationalities Papers* 21, no. 2 (1993). German accounts indicate that eighty thousand Ukrainians volunteered for the division and fifty thousand were provisionally accepted. Dmytry-

shyn generally downplays what he calls (always in quotation marks) "German-Ukrainian collaboration."

80. Spector, "Attitude of the Ukrainian Diaspora," 279.

81. Ibid. Further discussion of Ukrainian collaboration can be found in Aharon Weiss, "Jew-ish-Ukrainian Relations in Western Ukraine during the Holocaust," in *Ukrainian-Jewish Relations in Historical Perspective,* ed. Peter Potichnyj and Howard Aster (Edmonton, Canada, 1988). For documentation, see also B. F. Sabrin, ed., *Alliance for Murder* (New York, 1991).

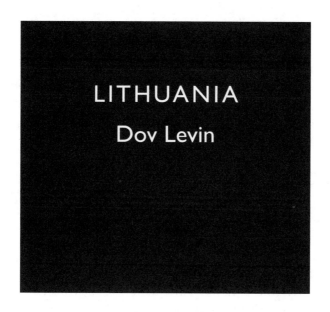

LITHUANIA
Dov Levin

Jews have lived in Lithuania since the fourteenth century, arriving shortly after the country was first constituted as a Christian monarchy (1251). The ensuing history of relations between Lithuanians and Jews is a complex story of two smaller peoples caught between much larger (and often dominating) nations—Russians, Germans, and Poles. Through the centuries of both groups' coterritorial existence, Lithuanians and Jews developed their own distinctive patterns of economic, social, and political activities while evolving equally distinctive religious, linguistic, and cultural forms. Each group tends to view the past as a struggle to survive against economic, political, and cultural-religious oppression, a struggle in which the two small nationalities sometimes found themselves on the same side, and at other times, at odds with each other.

That some of the more brutal chapters of the Holocaust were written on Lithuanian soil and, consequently, only a tiny remnant of prewar Lithuanian Jewry remained in 1945 has left an indelible mark that has colored all subsequent responses and developments. To Lithuanian Jews the Holocaust represents the sudden, devastating defeat and virtual end of their struggle to survive as a viable minority in Lithuania. To Lithuanians, on the other hand, the Holocaust often represents no more than an episode that, in the framework of their own historical struggle, pales in significance in comparison with the dissolution of their hard-won national independence by the Soviet Union in 1940. However, the renewal and recent success of their efforts to restore their lost national sovereignty has prompted them to confront anew the catastrophic legacy of the 1940s, because in order to create a new Lithuania, they must purge the traumas of the past.

BEFORE THE HOLOCAUST

Jewish communities in Lithuania grew and flourished under the liberal charter of religious freedom and permission to engage in manual trades and commerce granted in 1388 by Grand Duke Vytautas. Despite subsequent setbacks—commercial, professional, and residential restrictions—Lithuania became a significant center of Jewish population. In the seventeenth century the major Jewish communities in Lithuania were sufficiently well established to form a national federation (Va'ad medinat lita) for maintaining civil and religious order, internal taxation, and collective representation vis-à-vis the Lithuanian and Polish authorities. (The Lithuanian Grand Duchy, which included extensive parts of present-day Poland, Belarus, and Ukraine, was linked politically to the Polish Commonwealth by the Union of Lublin in 1569.) Inhabiting mainly the large and small towns, Jews interacted more intensively with the urban population, which was ethnically Polish to a large extent, and with the gentry and aristocracy who employed them and less so with the ethnically Lithuanian and Belorussian agrarian population.

By 1795, in the third partition of Poland, most of Lithuania was annexed by Russia, the remainder being taken over by Prussia. Both absolutist regimes proceeded to curtail the internal autonomy of the Jewish communities, even as they pursued, respectively, centralistic "Germanizing" and "Russifying" policies vis-à-vis Poles, Lithuanians, and Jews alike. Under Russian administration Lithuania became part of the Pale of Settlement, the western border zone to which Jews were restricted by statute.

Despite this and a host of other oppressive aspects of the czarist regime, the Lithuanian provinces remained a vital center of Jewish religious, cultural, and intellectual life. In the course of the nineteenth century Jewish population soared, increasing to some 260,000, even though many hard-pressed Jewish families began to migrate south in this period and, increasingly after 1870, thousands began to find new homes in Western Europe, North America, South Africa, and elsewhere. In 1897 Jews made up 13 percent of the population in the Lithuanian provinces (gubernii) of the Pale—Vilna, Kovno, Suvalk, and a small area of Kurland—and 43 percent of their urban population.[1] In Lithuania, as elsewhere in the Pale, rapid population growth, steady urbanization, sluggish economic development, continued discrimination, and outbreaks of violence fueled the development of Zionist as well as underground social-revolutionary activities among younger Jews at the end of the nineteenth century.

The Yiddish-speaking Jews continued to live as a well-defined national minority, occupying their own urban niche in the local economy and interacting minimally with the rural Lithuanian population. Nevertheless, democratic Jewish and Lithuanian political parties cooperated on a number of occasions to elect representatives to the Russian State Duma (the national assembly established after 1905). During World War I Jewish leaders in Lithuania and abroad maintained close and supportive contact with Lithuanian statesmen. Jews figured prominently, in the international arena and at home, in securing and consolidating Lithuanian independence.[2]

When, therefore, the Lithuanian national council, the Taryba, proclaimed the independent state of Lithuania on February 16, 1918, Lithuanian Jewry could feel the hope for a new era of cooperation between their two newly liberated peoples. Jewish civil and group rights, along with those of other minorities in Lithuania, were clarified in Article 4 of the declaration (May 12, 1922) of the Lithuanian delegate to the League of Nations on the eve of the country's admission to that body, as follows:

> All Lithuanian nationals shall be equal before the law, and shall enjoy the same civil and political rights without distinction as to race, language or religion. Differences of religion, creed or confession will not prejudice any Lithuanian national in matters relating to the enjoyment of civil or political rights, as, for instance, admission to public employments, functions and honours, or the exercise of professions and industries. No restriction will be imposed on the free use by any Lithuanian national of any language in private intercourse, in commerce, in religion, in the press or in publications of any kind, or at public meetings.[3]

These rights were largely implemented during the term of the Constituent Diet (1920–22), which included six Jewish members. In their everyday lives, the Jews and their institutions enjoyed broad national autonomy, particularly in the educational and cultural fields.

Such freedoms did not come without struggle. Between 1918 and 1920 Lithuania fought its War of Independence, contending variously with Soviet and Polish efforts to acquire its territories. In 1920 Polish forces successfully captured the Lithuanian capital, Vilnius (Vilna or Wilno), and the surrounding towns and annexed them to Poland. As a result, Lithuania's second largest city, Kaunas (Kovno), became the temporary capital. On the other hand, Lithuania annexed the harbor of Memel (Klaipeda) and its environs from Germany in 1923, according to the terms of the Versailles Treaty. Independent Lithuania therefore comprised a territory of 21,489 square miles and a population of 2,421,570, of whom 84 percent were Lithuanian; 7.6 percent (or 153,746) were Jews; 2.7 percent, Poles, Russians, and Belorussians; 1.4 percent, Germans; 0.7 percent, Latvians; and 0.5 percent, other.[4]

During this period Jews served in senior governmental and municipal posts, with some attaining officer's rank in the armed forces and the police. "In Kovno alone, there were during the mid-1930s 542 Jewish veterans of the Lithuanian War of Independence. Of these individuals, 182 had participated in the battles, 10 had been wounded, and 32 had been decorated (6 of these with the highest order 'Vytis'). There were 56 officers (including NCOs)."[5] However, as Lithuania consolidated itself politically and the large Jewish population of Vilnius remained outside Lithuania, thus keeping the number of Jews substantially lower than their total at the end of World War I, Jewish support was no longer as important as it had appeared to be in 1918–19. This, combined with growing economic competition between Jews and the newly urbanizing Lithuanians, which compounded popular anti-Semitism among a portion of the populace, brought about a steady deterioration of Jewish-Lithuanian relations.

The democratic system instituted at the time of independence did not last very long. In 1926 a military coup brought the fascist movement to power and abolished the democratic constitution. Three years later the fascists were themselves overthrown by a new nationalist regime that was to rule Lithuania until 1940.[6]

Ugly incidents sometimes underscored the fragility of the Jews' position. During the Lithuanian War of Independence, for example, in which thousands of Jews, many of them volunteers, actively participated and dozens lost their lives, Lithuanian troops staged pogroms in Panevežys (Ponevezh) and other places.

Yet, in spite of such occurrences, which were relatively rare in Lithuania, and in spite of irksome and disappointing discriminatory policies, the Jews of Lithuania were fully aware that they were better off than the Jews of neighboring countries. It is, therefore, easy to understand their general inclination to serve in the armed forces and in such patriotic associations as the Vilnius Liberation Committee. Hebrew high-school pupils in Kaunas had volunteered to serve in the Lithuanian "sharpshooter units" against the Polish legions' assault on Vilnius. The Association of Jewish Veterans of the Lithuanian War of Independence, founded in 1933, had more than three thousand members in over thirty branches. Its Lithuanian-language newsletter, *Apžvalga* (Review), repeatedly stressed the Jewish contribution to Lithuanian independence and development. At the same time, it tried to "serve as a central address for Lithuanian Jewry" in the absence of a recognized general Jewish representative body.

The extensive Hebrew-language educational system survived the demise of other aspects of Jewish national autonomy, such as the short-lived ministry for Jewish affairs, and it set Lithuanian Jewry apart from most other interwar Jewish communities, with the exception of the Jewish Yishuv (community) in Palestine. Yiddish continued to be the daily vernacular of the overwhelming majority of Jews: six daily newspapers and a number of weeklies and other periodicals were published in Yiddish. Lithuanian Jewry was also distinguished by its yeshivot (Orthodox rabbinic academies), some of the most prominent of which were the yeshiva at Slobodka (or Vilijampolė, a Kaunas suburb) and those at Telšiai (Telsh), Ponevezh, and Kelmė (Kelm).

The strong national and religious character of Jewish life was reflected in the Jewish community's political and ideological development as well. In 1938 there were 215 registered Jewish institutions and organizations (28 percent of the country's total), including 78 mutual aid associations, 45 cultural and athletic associations, 43 social-welfare organizations, and 16 related to labor, commerce, manual trades, and the professions.

The 1923 census, the first and only one taken in independent Lithuania, showed that two-thirds of the Jewish population lived in the cities, constituting 32 percent of all urban dwellers, the rest residing in two hundred smaller communities. Jews constituted an overwhelming majority of the mercantile class. But in the wake of government policies aimed at encouraging new, Lithuanian-run cooperatives, and because of the concentration of import-export activity in the hands of state companies, the Jews' role in both wholesale and retail trade gradually declined through the 1930s. Official harassment, which peaked with the outbreak of World War II, made Jewish participation in industry, manual trades, commerce, and the free professions increasingly difficult; at the same time, quotas against Jewish students were introduced in universities and technical institutes.

Under the constitution adopted in 1938, the last vestiges of the minority-rights legislation of 1920 were omitted. Farmers and urban economic organizations launched a "Lithuania for Lithuanians" campaign, demanding the expulsion of Jews who had entered the country since 1918 and advocating that Jews be barred from selling beer, flour, grain, flax, and seed; that Jews be prohibited from operating restaurants, cafés, and hotels; that Saturday, the traditional Jewish day of rest, be declared the official market day and that all trade be prohibited on Sunday (in contrast to all historical precedent); and that kosher meat slaughtering be banned. A number of restrictive measures were indeed put into effect, despite official assurances to the Jewish community. A rash of physical assaults against Jews, hitherto a minor aspect of Lithuanian-Jewish relations, also took place at this time.

Although these events served to divide Jews and Lithuanians, they also promoted the efforts that were made to foster closer ties between them. A Lithuanian-Jewish Friendship Society (Geselshaft far dernenterung tsvishn litviner un yidn), headed by Professor M. Biržiska, was founded; its members included liberal intellectuals, writers, and progressives from both communities. Unfortunately, given the social and political trends outlined above (similar to antidemocratic and antiminority trends in neighboring Poland and Latvia), as well as the influence of the dominant racist ideology in nearby Germany, the effectiveness of this and other organizations (e.g., the Association of Jewish Veterans) was severely undermined.

THE HOLOCAUST ERA
Under Soviet Occupation

On the eve of World War II, the Ribbentrop-Molotov treaty between Germany and the Soviet Union, in August 1939, divided Poland between the two countries and placed Lithuania in the Soviet sphere, enabling Stalin to demand that Soviet military bases be established in the country. The return of Russian domination a mere twenty years after the coming of independence was a severe blow to the Lithuanians. With the outbreak of war, the Soviets, however, also returned the Vilnius district to Lithuania. This act increased the Jewish population of Lithuania by 100,000, which included some 15,000 war refugees from German-occupied Poland, bringing the total Jewish population to 250,000.

After the Red Army left Vilnius at the end of October 1939 and the Lithuanians took over the city, the situation for the Jews did not improve. With the encouragement of the Lithuanian police, a pogrom was staged in the city that resulted in the killing of one Jew and the wounding of nearly two hundred.[7] Attacks against Jewish students increased at Kaunas University, and cases of arson and vandalism directed against Jews spread to other locations.[8] That these attacks appeared to occur in various places simultaneously implied that the activities were deliberately organized, probably by extreme right-wing groups associated with Nazi Germany.[9] Despite such outbreaks of violence, Lithuanian Jews, including those in the Vilnius district, demonstratively participated in celebrations of Lithuania's Independence Day on February 16, 1940. The Lithuanian newspaper in Vilnius, *Vilniaus Balsas,* reported that overcapacity crowds of more than ten thousand Jewish residents gathered for celebrations and special festive prayers.[10] With the country's sovereignty already severely compromised by the Ribbentrop-Molotov treaty and the threat of further pressure during wartime, from either Nazi Germany or Soviet Russia, Jews had as great a stake in Lithuanian independence as other citizens did.

In June 1940 Soviet troops occupied Lithuania, paving the way for the country's formal annexation as a Union Republic (SSR). Along with the concurrent occupation of Latvia, Estonia, Bessarabia, and parts of eastern Poland, the Soviet annexation of Lithuania completed Stalin's prewar plans for expansion into Eastern Europe. At the same time, it seemed to rule out for the moment the possibility of a German incursion, with all that such a prospect entailed for Jews.

Between these two alternatives Lithuanian Jews had no real choice, and some Jews played a significant though by no means exclusive role in the Sovietization of Lithuania, taking managerial and official jobs shunned by some Lithuanians. The genuine interests of both groups were clearly in conflict. Consequently, the Jews would later bear the brunt of the anger of patriotic Lithuanians.

Ironically, Jews suffered disproportionately from the nationalization policy introduced under the new Soviet regime, as most of the nationalized businesses and other property belonged to Jews. Of the 986 plants that the state took over, 560, or 57 percent, were owned by Jews. Jews also owned 1,320 (83 percent) of the 1,595 businesses that were nationalized, along with their other assets and bank accounts. The agrarian reforms also hit Jewish landowners harder than others, because the authorities contended that the Jews did not work their lands and thus were not entitled to retain them. Furthermore, many Jewish shopkeepers, upon whom heavy taxes were imposed and who were subjected to severe restrictions in obtaining merchandise, had to close their shops, while others were banished from the big cities to the small towns or assigned to forced labor on public-works projects.

Just a few weeks after the Red Army entered the country, the editors of all Jewish newspapers were dismissed, most of the papers were closed down, and new editors were appointed for those papers that remained in operation. The Hebrew libraries were liquidated, and the Yiddish libraries were absorbed by the municipal libraries. All Jewish schools were placed under the aegis of the Commissariat of Education, and before the beginning of the 1940–41 school year all teachers who were not automatically disqualified as "undesirable" (because of their Zionist or other anti-Soviet political affiliations) were obliged to undergo a special "retraining" course in Soviet educational methods. Yiddish, considered to be the language of the proletarian masses, became the language of instruction in Jewish public schools, replacing Hebrew, which the Communists had long considered to be tainted by bourgeois nationalism. In the university, Semitic studies, which included Hebrew-language courses, were replaced by a Yiddish-language department. All Hebrew-language schools and the yeshivot, including the most famous ones, at Slobodka and Telsh, were closed.

On the other hand, discriminatory policies that had been instituted in interwar Lithuania no longer applied. *Numerus clausus* restrictions that had kept some Jews out of higher-education institutions in the 1930s were abrogated by the new regime. Since all education was now free and the quotas had been rescinded, young Jews flocked to the universities and technical schools in unprecedented numbers. Both Vilnius and Kaunas now had state-supported Yiddish theaters. Such benefits of the new regime were offset, however, by the fact that Sunday was declared the official day of rest and Saturday, the Jewish Sabbath, a mandatory workday.

Jewish participation in the political life of the country increased, in contrast to the situation obtaining under the nationalist Lithuanian regime of the 1930s, in which Jews routinely had been frozen out of public office and the civil service. Two Jewish commissars served in the new government. As of January 1, 1941, 479 members of the Lithuanian Communist Party (out of a total of 3,138, i.e., 15.2 percent) were Jewish.[11] A relatively large number of Jewish administrators and other specialists were involved in implementing the new economic policies.

The domination of the country's political and cultural life by the Communists ruled out any activities by individuals or groups that were considered unreliable, hostile, or dangerous. Harsh measures against all such elements—the liquidation of all national, cultural, and economic organizations in Lithuania, including, of course, the Jewish ones—were coordinated with the Communist Party's minorities bureau, headed by Genrikas Ziman (Zimanas). A number of Jewish and non-Jewish leaders who refused to cooperate with the authorities or join the Party were arrested and deported to Siberia. Among the Jews classed as "ideologically dangerous," "anti-Soviet," and "counterrevolutionary" were leaders and members of Zionist and Bundist (democratic socialist) organizations and of such paramilitary groups as the Jewish war veterans, the Zionist Revisionists, and their youth organization, Betar.[12] Then, on June 14, 1941, just a week before the German invasion, thirty-five thousand people from all over Lithuania, including seven thousand Jews, were arrested and deported to Siberia.[13] Those expelled, including Party and organizational activists, factory owners, and even small shopkeepers, were taken on freight trains to various labor camps in the far north of Russia and put to work under extremely harsh conditions. Many of them died of exposure, hunger, and disease.

Thus, willingly or unwillingly, whether victims, beneficiaries, or executors of Sovietization, Jews and other Lithuanian citizens lived for a year and seven days under a regime that decimated the existing elites and drastically altered social, political, cultural, and economic conditions in the country.

Jewish Reactions to the Soviet Regime

During the first few months of the Soviet takeover, the Jews' reactions were varied. Some among them felt relief that they had been spared the terrifying prospect of Nazi domination and viewed Soviet rule as the lesser of two evils. Others were motivated by ideology or social consciousness to welcome the new social order. Still others hoped the new government would be more equitable and flexible in its treatment of minorities than the previous government had been. Some were actually opposed to the Soviet presence, fearing arrest and persecution.

As the Soviet regime settled in and began to clash with greater frequency with traditional Jewish values and institutions, initial enthusiasm and optimistic hopes waned. At the same time, the German threat and Jewish fears of Lithuanian reprisals reinforced the tendency to view the Soviet regime as better, on the whole, than a German occupation. Jews were thus inclined to accept and adapt to the new circumstances or at least to avoid clashing openly and provocatively with the authorities.

That being the case, many Jewish activities were carried on clandestinely. Hebrew books were secreted before Soviet authorities could seize them. Some Jews risked publishing Hebrew-language bulletins. Jewish education continued underground, teaching the forbidden Hebrew language and literature and Jewish history. Other Jews sought to cross the Baltic and escape to Palestine.

Tensions between Jews and Lithuanians

Even though the majority of Lithuanian Jews were as adversely affected by Sovietization as was the general population, many Lithuanians identified the Jews with the despised Soviet regime. While in independent Lithuania virulent Jew-hatred had not been a mass phenomenon, a degree of anti-Semitism having been more a feature of economic and professional competition than an endemic popular attitude, in the new situation anti-Semitism came to the fore and tainted Lithuanian-Jewish relations. Lithuanians saw Jewish militiamen as collaborators and traitors, especially if they participated in arresting anyone deemed a patriotic Lithuanian. The rise of several hundred Jews to managerial positions in businesses that had previously not hired Jews was the occasion for further tension. Open enthusiasm for the Soviet regime displayed by young Jews, who, as one prominent Jew suggested, "did not always behave with the necessary tact,"[14] only exacerbated anti-Jewish antipathy. Lithuanians either failed to note or refused to acknowledge that the percentage of Jews deported to Siberian labor camps and other remote parts of Russia was at least three times greater than that of the Lithuanian population.[15] Jews as a group bore the blame because the committees responsible for the roundups had included several Jews.

Though they were limited to verbal threats of revenge (actual violence being impossible under the strict regime imposed by the Soviets), patriotic anti-Soviet Lithuanians were able to form a nationalist underground, the Lietuviu Aktyvistu Frontas (Lithuanian Activist Front), or LAF. With the financial support from Nazi intelligence services and drawing upon sympathizers among the local population, the LAF carried out acts of subversion and agitation explicitly directed against the Jews in anticipation of war between Russia and Germany. A proclamation issued by the LAF in the early summer of 1941 read as follows: "Lithuanian brothers and sisters: The time has come to make a final accounting with the Jews. . . . The old rights of sanctuary granted to Jews in Lithuania by Vytautas the Great are abolished forever and without reservation. Hereby all Jews without any exception are strictly ordered to immediately leave Lithuania." The statement ended with a call to the Lithuanian people: "At the designated time seize [the Jews'] property so that nothing will be lost."[16]

The Nazi Occupation

Realizing that these were no idle threats, some Jews managed to escape to Russia before the Soviet-German war broke out. Once the war began, on June 22, 1941, and prior to the arrival of Wehrmacht units, outrages were committed against Jews by Lithuanians in at least forty communities. In twenty-five communities women were raped; in thirty-six, rabbis (who certainly were the least likely to be suspected of harboring Communist sympathies) were brutally tortured.[17]

In Kaunas a communiqué issued by J. Bobelis, a colonel in the Lithuanian army, helped foment the rioting. Issued a day before the entry of German forces, the communiqué assumed an unequivocally pro-German position and depicted the Jews as the common enemy of both Germans and Lithuanians.[18] Lithuanian gangs perpetrated massacres in Kaunas, killing and sadistically torturing Jewish inhabitants at several locations around the city, as attested to later by Lithuanian witnesses.[19] Intellectuals and publicly known figures were among those who helped to instigate these rampages or who actively participated in them. Unlike the pogroms in Russia and Ukraine at the turn of the century, which had been organized mainly by the anti-Semitic and archconservative political vigilantes known as the Black Hundreds, in Lithuania, especially in the smaller towns, Jews were actually murdered by former neighbors, classmates, and customers.[20]

On the night of June 25, 1941, about 1,200 men, women, and children were brutally massacred in the Kaunas suburb of Slobodka by armed Lithuanians who called themselves partisans. They ransacked or burned about sixty Jewish homes, over the course of several nights killing 2,300 more Jews. Jews in Kaunas, Vilnius, Šiauliai (Shavli), and elsewhere were rounded up by Lithuanian paramilitary squads. Most of those seized were held in prisons or other locations that later served as mass-extermination sites, such as Paneriai (Ponary) in the Vilnius countryside, the Kužiai woods near Šiauliai, and the Ninth Fort at Kaunas.

Then, with the arrival of the German army, the wave of murders swelled, partly because of quiet support lent by the special German mobile killing units, the *Einsatzgruppen*. One such unit, Einsatzgruppe A, was sent ahead of the invading forces so that the resulting massacres would, in the words of one of the unit's commanders, "appear as though the local population initiated the first incidents as a natural reaction against the oppression suffered at the hands of the Jews for decades."[21]

Actually, as German supervision and implementation of anti-Jewish activity grew more methodical, random violence and pillage by bands of avenging Lithuanians decreased. Lithuanians were soon accepted, however, as auxiliaries attached to German units, especially the *Einsatzgruppen*. Among such auxiliaries were a substantial number whose relatives or families had been murdered or exiled by the Soviets.

One of the *Einsatzgruppe* units, Einsatzkommando 3A, began a systematic, countryside program of mass slaughter on July 3, 1941, according to a prearranged timetable. Upon arrival at their destination, the liquidation units seized the already traumatized Jews and marshaled them into synagogues, market squares, or large estates. From these locations, the Jews were then forced to move on in groups of five hundred to isolated killing sites. They were driven into already prepared pits or trenches, sometimes forced to undress, and then shot by firing squads using light or medium arms, sometimes firing incendiary bullets. When their task was completed, the units moved on to a new location to repeat the operation.[22]

In this manner, the majority of Jews in the countryside were murdered during July and August of 1941. Most of the Jews in the large cities were first herded into ghettos before they were murdered in a series of similar *Aktionen* between September and November. The scale of these operations is indicated by the "great *Aktion*" that took place in Kaunas on October 28, 1941, in which 10,000 Jews were annihilated. By the end of December 1941 about 180,000 (approximately 72 percent) of Lithuania's Jews had been wiped out by various means. Only some 40,000 remained, most of them concentrated in the large ghettos—16,000 in Kaunas, 17,000 in Vilnius, 4,700 in Šiauliai, and 2,000 in Svenčionys (Svencian).[23]

Attempts to Save Jews and Armed Struggle

Jewish appeals for help from gentile leaders and reputedly liberal-minded public figures were unsuccessful. One egregious example involved Dr. Jurgis Žilinskis, the local head of the Red Cross. When asked by Jewish mothers for assistance in locating children who had been lost during the confusion of the first days of the invasion, Žilinskis is said to have turned them down with the retort that "he who rejoiced in the past will now be the one to mourn."[24]

Bishop Vincentas Brizgys warmly received a delegation of Jews, but when he was asked to intervene with the German authorities, he replied: "By doing so I could endanger the Catholic Church in Lithuania, and I cannot assume such a responsibility."[25] When members of the delegation suggested that he might at least circulate a letter among his flock to urge them not to participate in the massacres, he replied: "The Church cannot help you. I personally can only weep and pray."[26] Yet Brizgys and other prominent clergymen were among a group of public figures who sent congratulatory telegrams to Hitler.[27] As far as we know, only three individuals appealed publicly to the German authorities on the Jews' behalf, but this effort came only after most Jews in the country had already died.[28]

Most of the attempts to aid Jews coincided with a later stage of the war. The losses sustained by the Germans at Stalingrad and on other fronts during 1943, as well as the Germans' continuing refusal to restore an independent Lithuania, created the conditions for a reassessment of the general Lithuanian position. It may be that these factors, along with genuine acts of human conscience, were responsible for help that was extended to the surviving Jewish population at that time. Aid and rescue efforts on the part of Lithuanians were usually prompted by Jewish appeals, but there are recorded cases in which the initiative came from Lithuanians, who encouraged Jews to escape from the ghettos and then provided food and shelter.

Gentile Lithuanians helped Jews for a variety of reasons, some of which remain unclear. Most of those who helped Jews had very limited financial resources—poor farmers, laborers, and the like—some of whom may have been motivated by pecuniary reward. Some were former housekeepers in Jewish homes who rescued the children they had once cared for. Some were doctors and clergymen. It is unclear whether missionary or humanitarian concerns came foremost, for example, in the case of the Rev. Dr. Bronius Paukštys, who rescued many Jewish children and had them baptized. Brother Gotautas, on the other hand, a monk who did much to save Jews, justified the activities for which he risked his life in explicitly ethical-humanitarian terms: "The world should know that there are decent people among the Lithuanians."[29]

A librarian at the University of Vilnius, Ona Šimaitė (Shimaite), formerly active in the Social Revolutionary (S.R.) movement, not only rescued Jews but also hid Jewish cultural treasures, books and manuscripts belonging to Jewish institutions in Vilnius. She was also instrumental in forming a committee of sympathetic Lithuanians for the rescue effort. Although she was apprehended and brutally tortured by the Gestapo, she refused to disclose the whereabouts of Jews in hiding.[30]

Organized rescue was also undertaken by groups established under antifascist (i.e., Communist or pro-Communist) auspices as well as by church- and civic-related groups. Although these activities were of tremendous symbolic and moral significance, their effectiveness was of necessity limited by the fact of their late commencement. In both absolute and relative terms, few Jews were rescued in Lithuania by non-Jews (Lithuanians, Poles, and Russians), the total being at most about one thousand (or 0.4 percent of the prewar Jewish population).[31]

Some eighteen hundred Jews escaped from ghettos and labor camps into the forests either with the help of Jewish underground resistance groups or by their own efforts. Most of them were absorbed by Jewish partisan units in Lithuania and Belorussia; the rest managed to maintain themselves on the run in groups of families, or "family camps."

The Jewish resistance, partisan forces, and other Lithuanian Jewish fighters numbered at least ten thousand men and women: some six thousand Jews served in the 16th Lithuanian Rifle Division of the Red Army, constituting fully half of that division; about two thousand more served in other units of the Soviet army or in Polish fighting forces; and more than two thousand were affiliated with resistance organizations in the ghettos and labor camps or served with the partisans.[32]

Of the Jews who remained captive under the German occupation in late 1944, many were annihilated by the Germans before the arrival of the advancing Soviet army. Other surviving Jews were removed to concentration camps in Germany; some of these lived to see the day of liberation following the German surrender, May 9, 1945.

THE POST-HOLOCAUST ERA

The total number of Lithuanian Jews who survived under German occupation is estimated to be about eight thousand. Some seventeen thousand others, refugees living on Soviet territory or serving with the Red Army, also escaped death. Thus, about twenty-five thousand, or 10 percent of the prewar Jewish population, survived the war. Those eight thousand still living on Lithuanian soil represented only 4 percent of the prewar Jewish population.

With the German retreat, many Lithuanians who had cooperated with the Germans, had murdered Jews, or feared the return of Soviet rule for other reasons fled westward. Some of them lived in displaced person (DP) camps set up by the Allies in Germany and later emigrated to such countries as the United States, Canada, England, Australia, and Brazil.

Shortly after Soviet authority was reestablished in Lithuania, Jews also began leaving the country, legally or illegally. Those leaving were motivated by a horror of remaining in a place that had become a vast Jewish cemetery, by a desire to live in Palestine, or by a wish to join relatives across the Atlantic. Despite this exodus, the number of Jewish survivors living in Lithuania increased. In addition to the local survivors themselves, they included refugees, liberated concentration camp inmates returning to search for relatives, demobilized soldiers, and former expellees returning from the Russian interior.[33]

By the 1950s the émigré Jews from Lithuania were living mainly in Israel, the United States, Canada, and South Africa, and smaller numbers were to be found in Latin America. For those remaining in Soviet Lithuania, further emigration was, for the most part, blocked.

Survivors' Activities in Postwar Lithuania

For most of the survivors, their immediate tasks included a search for family members. Four days after liberation, 265 Jewish survivors in Kaunas gathered at the site of the Ohel Yaakov Synagogue. Similar gatherings took place in Vilnius and elsewhere. Brothers, sisters, close relatives, and friends, some of whom had not known of the others' survival until that moment, found each other at these emotion-laden reunions.[34] Although the fortunate few who found their relatives alive were the exceptions, among the happy ones were parents and relatives of babies and children who had been smuggled out of the ghettos during the war and hidden by non-Jewish families. (There are cases on record of parents who risked their lives to recover their children and three known cases in which people were actually killed while trying to retrieve Jewish children.)[35]

Many among the survivors harbored a strong desire to see their former tormentors punished. Desire for justice was particularly felt among the partisans, who had already fought to avenge their murdered brethren, and among others who had fled to the forests and knew exactly who the murderers were and where to find them. The survivors were instrumental in compiling lists of war criminals for the authorities.[36] Other Jews expressed their desire for vengeance by enlisting in the Red Army as well as in police (militia) and other armed units. Violent clashes took place between Jews in uniform and Lithuanian civilians who were suspected of collaboration with the Germans or who expressed dismay at the survival of "so many" Jews—a phrase quoted by various witnesses.[37]

Another phase of activity involved the establishment of a new institutional infrastructure. On August 5, 1944, for example, ghetto survivors in Kaunas elected a four-man council, the first reconstituted civic institution in that city. Social-welfare activities were uppermost on the agenda of this council, which set up a soup kitchen. Although it was not an official agency, the council was considered by government and city authorities to be the representative of the Jewish survivors. The council's office quickly became a central meeting place, the venue for exchange of information, distribution of letters, and the search for missing relatives. A week after the council was established, a congregational board was also set up to supervise religious services. This board was recognized de facto as the body responsible for maintaining the synagogues and cemeteries and for handling religious matters generally, such as provision of kosher meat. Similar boards were established in Vilnius and Šiauliai.

Because of Soviet-imposed restrictions, however, the religious boards were barred from operating in areas now deemed outside their purview, whether educational, social, or cultural. As a result, ad hoc groups were formed almost immediately to undertake activities in these other areas. In time these groups took on a more official character.

Such tasks as searching for relatives, retrieving children, and honoring and perpetuating the memory of the dead required official authorization, organizational machinery, and a more permanent workforce. It soon became evident that volunteers would not suffice. Generally speaking, the establishment of these embryonic institutions and the efforts to maintain them were undertaken by both those who wished eventually to leave the "land of slaughter" and those who chose to remain. The latter often included Communist Party activists or those close to the Party.

Particularly notable among the survivors' achievements was the Jewish school system. Schools for Jewish children were established following the approval by the Central City Office of Education and the Communist Party of a petition submitted by the survivor community. The petition had pointed out the special psychological needs of Jewish children, who in the aftermath of their ordeal were better off in the security of a Jewish environment. Such schools were established in both Vilnius and Kaunas in the fall of 1944 and functioned in Yiddish. They comprised a kindergarten and four elementary grades, and they functioned as orphanages-cum-boarding schools, where children could live on the premises. The schools were closed by the Soviet authorities within several years, however, the final year in Vilnius being 1948–49 and in Kaunas, 1950–51. (These schools represented the last Yiddish-language public schools in the entire Soviet Union, and their closure brought an end to Jewish education there.)[38]

The urge to preserve the memory of the past formed the basis for another type of activity. The task of commemoration began with the writing of memoirs and the collecting, recording, and processing of documentary material. A small group of survivors from Vilnius engaged in gathering all the material they could find relating to Jewish life in the city, formerly known as the "Jerusalem of Lithuania," which they hoped to deposit in museums, archives, and libraries for preservation, exhibition, and research. These efforts included the attempt to revive the old Vilnius-based Jewish Research Institute, YIVO, formerly a focus of academic and cultural activity.[39]

The Jewish State Museum opened in Vilnius in mid-1945 and operated for about four years, until it too was closed by the Soviet authorities. Evidently, much of the material it housed was subsequently stored in academic institutions, libraries, and book depositories of the Lithuanian SSR, where it was inaccessible to scholars and other interested persons.

Interaction between Survivors and the Local Population

By all appearances, in the immediate aftermath of the German retreat Lithuanians treated the Jewish survivors well. Statements of regret and sympathy for Jewish suffering during the Nazi occupation were frequently made. Characteristic of this phenomenon was a very moving article by a Lithuanian professor published in the official Soviet Lithuanian newspaper, *Tarybų Lietuva,* in January 1945.[40]

Yet, as time went on, the publication of such articles and other expressions of contrition dramatically decreased. In line with Soviet policy elsewhere, condemnation of fascist atrocities was severed from direct and explicit mention of the Jewish identity of most of the victims, apparently as part of a consistent Soviet "pacification" effort aimed at consolidating the new regime's base among the local, non-Jewish, inhabitants.

At about this same time, Lithuanians who had collaborated with the Germans began to reassert themselves. Some who had hidden out in the forests or in small villages when the Red Army entered the area were involved in ongoing acts of terror and even murder of officials of the reconstituted Soviet government, of Jews returning to claim property,[41] or of fellow Lithuanians known to have given asylum to Jews.[42] They were joined by growing numbers of compatriots who had escaped Germany on the eve of the Soviet reoccupation of the country and were now returning.[43]

Continuing enmity between Jews and Lithuanians was also expressed in acts of revenge against those who had participated in the murder of Jews. There were Jewish survivors who were arrested for taking the law into their own hands to settle accounts with the murderers, and other Jews served in an official capacity, with the police or other units (some dubbed "destruction squads"), and hunted down Nazi collaborators.[44]

With time, however, the authorities seemed less willing to recognize the guilt of those named as former collaborators; similarly, they were reluctant to pursue Jewish claims relating to cemeteries, lost property, sacred Jewish objects, or books hidden during the war in the courtyards of gentile homes. Once the populace realized that the new authorities held a rather ambivalent attitude toward the Jews, they no longer felt intimidated with regard to their own failure to return Jewish property.[45] Responding to a rash of violence and threats against Jews in outlying districts, the authorities themselves proposed that Jews be relocated to the big cities.[46]

This troubled aftermath undoubtedly intensified the trauma felt by survivors during those years and encouraged those who had made up their minds to leave the country. An émigré from Kedainiai vented his bitterness as follows: "I did not look back when I left you, city of my birth. May the murderers [who live there] be damned. I can take some comfort in knowing that you will have to live under [foreign] occupation forever. Lithuania will never be independent again. The sickle of Russia has trampled you. May it crush you, so help me God."[47]

Soviet Lithuania and Policy Issues Related to the Holocaust

The aftermath of the Holocaust made itself felt in relations between Jews, Lithuanians, and the new Soviet Lithuanian regime at all levels—in the Party, the army, and local and national government. The situation was complicated by the general opposition of the populace to the reimposition of Soviet rule. In attempting to reduce that opposition, the regime became a new factor in determining Jewish-Lithuanian relations. On the one hand, Jewish survivors and refugees returning from Russia could, because of their recent fate, become a useful source of support and stability for the authorities (as in 1940–41). On the other hand, the identification of the regime with the small Jewish minority could also turn into a major obstacle, preventing the Lithuanian population from reconciling itself to Soviet rule. The Soviet Lithuanian authorities pursued policies that were sometimes contradictory but generally disposed to overcoming local opposition as quickly as possible.

It was in this context that acute differences arose between the authorities and the Jews over the treatment of the Holocaust and related issues. Although many war criminals were eventually arrested and tried, the authorities generally avoided dwelling on the widespread nature of Lithuanian wartime collaboration with the enemy. At the same time, the special fate of Jews under Nazi occupation was obscured, the victims being referred to obliquely as "Soviet citizens," "peaceful residents," or "foreign nationals," with whom all antifascist Lithuanians could identify.[48] At least once a year the authorities granted permission to the survivors to gather for memorial meetings to honor the dead. At these events they were expected to stress the general Soviet struggle against fascism, a struggle in which the Jewish role had, to be sure, been significant but not (in official eyes) of special character. In the course of time, as memorials were erected in communities where mass murders had taken place, these referred, again, to anonymous "Soviet citizens." Yet the survivors could not help but be pleased by guilty verdicts handed down by Soviet courts against war criminals.

Only one book on Jewish anti-Nazi resistance appeared (in Yiddish) in the early postwar years.[49] Thereafter, in the final five years of Stalin's rule (1948–53) the general crackdown on Jewish cultural and religious life throughout the Soviet Union also forced Jews in Lithuania to engage in memorial activities clandestinely. Nothing of substance could be published about the Holocaust. Emigration was impossible.

In the post-Stalin period, the situation improved in many respects. Under a repatriation treaty signed by Moscow and Warsaw dealing with former Polish citizens residing in the Soviet Union, several hundred Jews from Soviet Lithuania, former residents of Polish-held Vilnius, were permitted to emigrate to Poland. Many of these Jews continued on to Israel, where they resettled. Jewish survivors who remained in Lithuania concentrated their efforts on improving the welfare of their own families. As solid citizens, they hoped that cooperation with the regime would help them prosper.

Relatively favorable economic conditions in Lithuania at that time attracted Jews from other parts of the Soviet Union, leading to a significant growth in numbers. According to the 1959 census figures on nationality groups, there were 24,672 Jews in Lithuania (0.9 percent of the total population of the Lithuanian SSR).[50] Only about half of these were Lithuanian Jews who had survived the Holocaust; the rest were new immigrants.

Another sign of improving conditions at this time was the renewed publication of books and articles containing references to the Holocaust. This was true throughout the Soviet Union, and it applied in Lithuania as well. Between 1960 and 1963 the official academic printing house of Lithuania published a series of pamphlets collectively titled *Faktai Kaltina* (The facts accuse), which contained eyewitness accounts and documents bearing on the annihilation of Jews and Communists during the Nazi occupation. The two-volume work *Masines Žudynes Lietuvoje, 1941–1944* (Mass murders in Lithuania, 1941–1944) provided German and Lithuanian documentation on the murder and torture of Jews, including the names of victims and perpetrators (some of whom had been high-ranking Lithuanian military officers).[51] In 1961 a collection of articles was published in Russian and then in English as *The Hitlerite Occupation of Lithuania.*[52]

These and other publications represent a small portion of hundreds of books and articles on the war that appeared in Soviet Lithuania during the 1960s and 1970s.[53] Such publications were careful to avoid blanket statements attributing guilt to the Lithuanian people as a whole, emphasizing instead that the Lithuanian people fought the German occupation. These works are not free of tendentious historiography; some of them ignore completely the question of collaboration, choosing instead to deal with partisan units and other forms of resistance. Others focus accusations of collaboration and war crimes on "bourgeois nationalists," whereas the record shows that among the perpetrators of anti-Jewish atrocities were public figures, former Lithuanian army officers, and political officials, most of whom had lost their jobs and their property under the initial Sovietization in 1940–41. Nevertheless, despite their flaws, many of these works give an accurate picture of the extent of the annihilation of the Jews in Lithuania during the war.

Attention was also focused on the Holocaust because of war crimes trials that took place in Lithuania during the 1960s. The trials involved former members of the Lithuanian Battalions of the Auxiliary Police, who served during the Nazi occupation. Those tried had participated in the mass murder of Jews and members of other nationalities not only in Lithuania itself but also in Belorussia and in Poland.

Among those found guilty (in absentia) and sentenced to death in 1962 were two high-ranking officers: Major A. Impulevičius, former commander of the 2d (later 12th) Police Battalion, who had taken an active role in the slaughter of Jews in Kaunas during the initial phase of the Nazi occupation; and Major Mečys Paškevičius, who had overseen the execution of hundreds of Jews in Ukmerge and Kaunas during the second half of 1941. Impulevičius had emigrated to the United States (where he changed his name to Impulionis) and obtained American citizenship in 1964, two years after the Lithuanian court passed its sentence and requested his extradition from the American government.[54] Paškevičius also found asylum in the United States after the war. Known as the "butcher of Kovno" for acts of murder he committed with his own hands, he changed his name to Mike Pascar when he obtained his American citizenship in 1962.[55] Neither of these men was extradited to Lithuania. (Other Lithuanians living in the United States were later investigated by the Office of Special Investigations [OSI] of the U.S. Justice Department in the late seventies and eighties.)[56]

Since war crimes trials in Lithuania involved charges against émigrés living abroad, and since free discussion and memorialization of the Holocaust were fully possible only outside Lithuania—in the Lithuanian and Lithuanian Jewish émigré communities—"Lithuanian" reactions to the Holocaust took place not only within the Lithuanian SSR but wherever the Lithuanian diaspora existed.

In Israel, the Association of Lithuanian Jews, which has been in existence since 1945, has been responsible for organizing annual commemoration activities, the erection of a monument to the Lithuanian Jewish victims of the Holocaust, and the publication of a massive, four-volume history of Lithuanian Jewry before and during the Holocaust.[57] The association also maintains an archive in its Tel Aviv office. Smaller groups of survivors have commissioned *yizkor* (memorial) books devoted to the Jewish communities in their old hometowns. For the community of Vilnius alone, twenty such books have been published.

The centers of non-Jewish Lithuanian émigré activity have been in the United States and Canada. Lithuanian immigrants in the West were considered political refugees, forced to leave their homeland because of the Soviet occupation and totalitarian rule. They waged a tenacious campaign against Soviet domination of their country, a campaign that was buttressed by the maintenance of independent Lithuanian consulates in the United States.

Heated polemics periodically flared up between the Lithuanian and Lithuanian Jewish émigré communities against the background of events in Lithuania in the 1940s. Thus, the conflict begun years before between the two groups was perpetuated abroad for many years. Jewish survivors from Lithuania issued a broad indictment against Lithuanian participation in the mass murder of Jews in a group statement issued in April 1947 in Munich.[58] From then until 1949 the group gathered documentation of the atrocities committed in Lithuania and published some of these materials. The documents were then transferred to Israel and subsequently housed in the archives of Yad Vashem in Jerusalem.

Lithuanian émigrés responded to the charges by denying the extent to which

Lithuanians were involved in anti-Jewish atrocities, by exaggerating the extent of rescue activities undertaken by Lithuanians to save Jews, and by setting up a kind of "symmetry" between Jewish collaboration with the Soviet occupiers and Lithuanian collaboration with the Nazis.[59] Lithuanians could not help but regard the Soviet reoccupation of their country as an unmitigated disaster, while Jewish survivors continued to associate the arrival of the Red Army with a period of liberation. This situation echoed the controversial situation facing the two groups in the summer of 1940.

The basic response to war crimes trials in Soviet Lithuania and attempts to have those found guilty extradited from the West was that Soviet documentation was suspect and politically motivated. Some of those who have actively campaigned against the activities of the OSI have sought to elicit support from the wider Lithuanian immigrant community, implying that any prosecution of individual defendants is actually an attack on the integrity of the entire émigré community.[60]

Changing Realities and Attitudes in Lithuania since the 1960s

Relations between Jews and Lithuanians in Lithuania itself gradually stabilized, becoming almost normal by the late sixties. That is attributable to a number of factors. The Soviet authorities eventually arrested and tried hundreds of people accused of taking part in the killing of Jews. The government also issued public statements condemning anti-Semitism and fascism or commemorating the victims of the Holocaust. The younger generation was taught to abhor the atrocities of the Nazi regime and those who had perpetrated them.

After 1967, in the wake of the Six-Day War in the Middle East, a Jewish emigration and protest movement developed in the Soviet Union, and Lithuania was one of its first centers. Emigration was selectively permitted by the Soviet regime under the heading of family reunification beginning at the end of the sixties and increasing in volume until 1979; thereafter it was blocked until the last years of the Soviet regime, under Gorbachev, when emigration reached unprecedented levels. Most of the Jewish emigration from Lithuania, totaling 10,704, occurred from 1969 to 1978.[61] In the context of shared anti-Soviet antipathies and in a period of growing Jewish emigration, evidence of a certain rapprochement between the Jews and the majority population was discernible. The interests and concerns of Jewish and non-Jewish Lithuanian citizens clearly coincided to a greater extent than previously. The turn of events in the Middle East, in which Israel was pitted against Soviet client-states, added yet another dimension to the sympathy accorded by some Lithuanians to their Jewish compatriots.[62]

Whether this sympathy went beyond the utilitarian level of pragmatic self-interest (Jewish emigration, for example, created vacancies for Lithuanians in housing and employment) and shared nationalist concerns (e.g., the promotion of Lithuanian, Hebrew, and Yiddish culture at the expense of Russian-language education and culture) is difficult to judge. Clearly, however, the period from the late sixties to the late seventies represented a turning point in the temper of Jewish-Lithuanian relations.

These subtle changes began to take on added significance in the third decade after Stalin's death, as the processes that led to the fragmentation and demise of the Soviet Union gathered force. The new trends favored decentralization and freer expression (*perestroika* and *glasnost*). Under the presidency of Mikhail Gorbachev, not only did Jewish emigration resume but it became possible for Jews in the various Soviet republics to develop their own cultural and educational institutions and media—freedoms that had been unheard of for decades in most of the Soviet Union. These new trends affected the remaining twelve thousand Jews in Lithuania (0.3 percent of the population),[63] where no Jewish institutions or free forms of expression had existed since before World War II.

One of the focal points for Jewish identity and group expression in Lithuania as elsewhere in the Soviet Union was the memory of the Holocaust. As a factor that set Jews apart from other nationalities, the genocide committed against the Jews during the war became central to Jewish consciousness, even among Jews who had not lived through the experience. At the same time, by evoking the special Jewish aspects of the Great Patriotic War, as the Soviet-German war was known in Soviet parlance, Jews and non-Jewish sympathizers were engaging in an act of protest against the regime's thirty-year conspiracy of silence, which had kept the lid on frank public discussion of Holocaust-related issues. This form of protest has to be regarded as part of much wider social phenomena in the Soviet Union at that time, prominently featured among which were demands for a new, more honest accounting about the past.

By the end of 1987 and early 1988, articles began to appear in the Lithuanian press (in Lithuanian-, Russian-, and Polish-language newspapers alike) severely criticizing past sins of both omission and commission in reference to the memory of the Holocaust: the official silence about the Jewish contribution to the war effort; the omission of specific references to the Jews as the chief victims of the Nazis; the failure to mark mass graves properly; and desecrations of mass-grave sites in more recent years.[64] A veteran officer of the 16th Lithuanian Rifle Division publicly charged that a television documentary on the combat record of the division was patently discriminatory, since Jews, who had made up 50 percent of the division, were passed over in silence in the listing of the various nationality groups represented among its troops.[65] Proposals were aired to erect monuments in memory of the Jews who had perished in Vilnius during the war.[66]

It was also at this time (late 1987) that an ad hoc group called the Jewish Cultural Society of Lithuania (JCSL) sought to establish a new Jewish museum in Vilnius like the one that had existed there until it was closed by the Soviets in 1949. The original museum had housed a display depicting the Lithuanian Jewish struggle against the Nazis. The new Jewish State Museum of Lithuania, which opened in 1988, featured an exhibit of the works of Jewish artists in prewar Lithuania. The theme was suited to those who wished to stress the cultural vitality of Lithuanian-Jewish coexistence before the Holocaust and the contributions of Jewish artists to the Lithuanian cultural heritage.

In the spring of 1988, to mark Victory Day (May 9), the JCSL also organized a public memorial service at the mass-killing site in the Ponary Forest. The service was attended by both Jewish and non-Jewish residents of Vilnius. Another newly established Jewish association based in Vilnius, called Tekuma (Renaissance), aimed at consciousness-raising among the Jewish population, organized a public gathering to mark the anniversary of the establishment of the Vilna Ghetto in 1941. The meeting was attended by over a thousand people, some of whom also signed a petition calling upon the authorities to put up a suitable plaque to mark the site of the ghetto. The petition also asked that the existing Lithuanian and Russian plaque at Ponary honoring the memory of the "Soviet citizens" who had been killed there be emended "to accord with the truth" (i.e., that seventy thousand of the one hundred thousand victims were Jews and that they were killed by the Nazis and their local henchmen). In addition, the petition sought the restoration in Vilnius of former street names with Jewish associations to stress the historical presence of the Jews in that city.[67]

Further assemblies took place in Vilnius in September 1988, forty-five years after the annihilation of the Vilna Ghetto in 1943, and in Kaunas in October of the same year to commemorate the "Great *Aktion*" of October 29, 1941. Participating in the latter event were hundreds of Jewish survivors, the mayor of Kaunas, the first secretary of the Communist Party of Lithuania, and senior representatives of the new Lithuanian nationalist movement, Sajudis. These events received favorable coverage in the local press. According to one account that appeared in the Komsomol (Young Communist League) newspaper, *Komjaunimo Tiesa*, "Russians, Lithuanians [and] Poles together gave witness to the survival of the Jewish people": "Once Vilnius was the center of Jewish culture in Europe, a fact about which it has not been suitable to speak until now. . . . Now the Jews are asking that a monument be erected. . . . Why should it be necessary to have to beg the authorities in such a case as this to properly mark the memory of the victims?"[68]

The encouraging responses elicited by the Jews' organizational initiatives prompted further activity, including plans for research and study of the Holocaust in Lithuania in conjunction with the U.S. Holocaust Memorial Council in Washington, D.C. The JCSL also helped to organize two groups of former ghetto resistance fighters, partisans, and war veterans. By January 1989 the JCSL was to receive official recognition by the Vilnius municipality as a body representing the Jewish population in Vilnius.[69]

During that final pre-independence period, the cause of secession from the Soviet Union and national sovereignty for Lithuania was spearheaded by the Sajudis movement. Its "parliament" effectively replaced the Communist Party and state organs as the most crucial arena for political activity. Two officers of the JCSL were members of the Sajudis parliament. Together with two other Lithuanian Jewish intellectuals, they issued a statement in August 1988 that clearly showed where their sympathies lay. They denounced the Soviet authorities' closure of Jewish institutions in Lithuania after 1948, referred to newly published evidence of Stalin's plan for a mass deportation of Jews to Siberia during the final months of his life, and decried the "posthumous ethnicity" to which Jews were relegated under Soviet domination. The statement came in response to an attempt by the Communist old guard to alienate the Jews from the Lithuanian national movement: Party hardliners had sought to draw a link between the racist Lithuanian nationalists of the 1940s and the new national movement of the 1980s.[70]

The JCSL was formally organized in March 1989, whereupon it received a congratulatory message from Vytautas Landsbergis, head of Sajudis (and now president of Lithuania), and signed as well by thirteen members of the Sajudis parliament. After noting the generally friendly course of relations between Lithuanians and their Jewish neighbors until the era of World War II, the message went on to state:

> We will never agree to the anti-Semitic statements that the Jews, as a people, ever sought the destruction of Lithuania or to cause her harm. [By the same token,] we are not able to agree to the accusation that the entire Lithuanian people murdered the Jews. There were many instances, some recorded and publicized, that in spite of the danger to their lives, Lithuanians hid and saved Jewish children and entire families. . . . We stretch out our hand to you in the belief that in the future our peoples will understand each other better and . . . we will march together on the path of justice and humanity.[71]

The message followed a group declaration signed by some fifty Lithuanian intellectuals associated with the new currents in public life. Their declaration, entitled "On the Relations between Lithuanians and Jews," addressed itself explicitly to the wartime atrocities. Acknowledging that "terrible acts" committed by Lithuanians had taken place at a time of brutal violence and in the absence of real freedom in the country, the signatories went on to say that the circumstances had not justified what was done. Although only "the dregs of society committed these despicable acts, initially on their own and later, when they were recruited by the Nazis," and even though these people could not be equated with the Lithuanian nation as a whole, yet there remained "a feeling of guilt that in the tragic reality [of the events], the Lithuanian people did not come to the aid of the Jewish people." Moreover, while other European nations (e.g., Germany) had had the opportunity to express remorse since the end of the war, "the Lithuanians did not even have such an option, because of their demoralization under occupying forces and totalitarian regimes."[72]

This pair of remarkable documents seemed to presage a historic change in the dialogue between Lithuanians and Jews and undoubtedly helped many Lithuanian Jews to identify positively with the leaders of the emerging new Lithuania. Indeed, these unpublished, semiofficial statements were soon followed by public declarations that were even more explicit in terms of recognizing the justice of Jewish claims. On May 8, 1990, the Supreme Council of the Lithuanian Republic issued a statement, signed by President Landsbergis, in which the Supreme Council "unreservedly condemn[ed] the genocide committed against the Jewish people during the years of the Hitlerite occupation in Lithuania and state[d] with sorrow that among the henchmen who served the occupying power there were also citizens of Lithuania." The statement ended with a specific instruction to all state offices, public organizations, and citizens "to create the most favorable conditions for the Jews of Lithuania, as well as for the other ethnic communities, to restore and develop their cultural, educational, scientific, religious and other institutions. . . . The Republic of Lithuania shall tolerate no phenomena of antisemitism."[73]

Problems in perception and communication continued to arise, however, in relation to the Jewish role in 1940–41. Some of the new Lithuanian leadership continued to adhere to a form of the "symmetry" theory, asking for a parallel Jewish acknowledgment of partial responsibility for the deportation of Lithuanians by the NKVD (the Soviet security police) in exchange for a Lithuanian admission of partial responsibility for the Jewish tragedy.[74] Apparently many Lithuanians still harbor the belief that the deportations were largely handled by Jewish functionaries and disregard the fact that Jews figured disproportionately among those sent into exile.

An unfortunate side effect of anti-Soviet assertiveness in Lithuania has been the desire to "disown" celebrated Communists or pro-Communists who fought the Nazis and were formerly treated as heroes. Thus, to give one example, the Vilnius municipality decided to change the name of a street that had once honored the memory of Sonya (Sheyna) Madeisker, a Jewish partisan leader.[75] Unfortunately, such actions appear to imply that Jews and anti-Nazi resisters generally do not have the right to be considered genuine Lithuanian heroes.

Complicating the renewed debate of these issues has been the reemergence of spokesmen for the extreme anti-Semitic nationalists, figures such as Alexandras Bendinskas, the former leader of the pro-Nazi LAF who was later imprisoned for his role in massacring Jews in Kaunas. After his release from prison, and under the conditions of free speech introduced in the *glasnost* years, Bendinskas publicized his own version of the events, claiming that only Communist police officials were murdered and that they just happened to be Jews.[76]

In sum, by the eve of Lithuanian independence, the nation's record during the period of the Holocaust had become a vital part of public discourse. In charting a course for the new Lithuania it had become necessary to deal with the unfinished business of the old Lithuania.

Independent Lithuania Redivivus

The path to renewed independence involved a rollback of the consequences of Soviet domination in every sphere. Even before sovereignty became a reality, independence had to be *seen* to function. Part of the effectiveness of Sajudis in demonstrating that new priorities and a new national modus vivendi existed in Lithuania lay in its support for Jewish cultural activities and its stated desire to reach a new accommodation with the Jewish people. This necessarily involved dealing with the grim legacy of the Holocaust.

In that respect, the rhetoric employed by Lithuanian officials, journalists, and others has been the rhetoric of reconciliation for the sake of a common future. Most hopeful, perhaps, has been the identification of the new nationalism with humanistic ideals and an explicit distancing of the regime from the perpetrators of anti-Jewish crimes. In July 1991, Lithuanian Prime Minister Gediminas Vagnorius spoke at the dedication of a monument to the Jews killed in Ponary, in the presence of an official delegation from Israel's Knesset. Vagnorius noted that "sadly, today we also experience great shame, for among those who violated human dignity and raised their weapons against peaceful Jews, were some of our fellow countrymen. And I want to apologize for them. We express wholehearted regret for those individuals—splinters from our community—whose actions cast a shadow of evil over the entire Lithuanian nation."[77] Nevertheless, there is, for the most part, a disturbing unwillingness on the part of many Lithuanians to abandon the defensiveness of the "symmetrical formula" and to face the record of the 1940s without flinching.[78]

Thus, a new memorial plaque was indeed unveiled at Ponary on June 22, 1991, but the inscription that notes the guilt of "Nazis and their local henchmen" appears only in Yiddish and Hebrew, not in Lithuanian or Russian, apparently at the behest of the Lithuanian authorities.[79]

Controversy erupted anew in September 1991 after the Lithuanian government enacted legislation to rehabilitate Lithuanian citizens who had been tried and imprisoned by the Soviet authorities. Somewhat belatedly, Lithuania agreed to a screening procedure that would prevent the rehabilitation of war criminals.[80] The effectiveness of such screening remains to be seen.

In the meantime, Jewish emigration from Lithuania has continued apace under a free emigration policy. Whereas only 1,201 Jews emigrated from Lithuania from 1979 to 1988, the years of the Soviet government's shutdown of previous emigration levels, 5,300 Jews emigrated from 1989 to 1991, and in the first five months of 1992 an additional 255 Jews left the country. Given such figures, the Jewish population remaining in Lithuania probably numbers fewer than 7,000.[81]

Holocaust-related issues figured prominently in the Lithuanian press during 1991–92. Given focus by the Ponary monument and the rehabilitation law, discussion of the Holocaust appeared in the form of news articles and editorials, personal reflections by those who had gone through the war, and reactions expressed in letters to the editor. According to a detailed review of the Lithuanian press, several main themes dominate much of what was published:

Idealization of the past. Jews lived comfortably in Lithuania for over six centuries, enjoying civil liberties and complete cultural autonomy in an environment of friendly relations with their non-Jewish neighbors. Pogroms certainly never took place.

Symmetry between Jewish and Lithuanian behavior during World War II. Jews helped in the Sovietization of the country in 1940–41 and collaborated in the arrest and deportation of Lithuanians. When the tables turned, Jews were punished by Lithuanians. On the face of it, both sides should agree to take their share of the blame and go on from there.

Tendentious exaggeration or distortion of proportions. Nazi collaborators were the exceptional few, while rescuers of Jews, with the same names being mentioned repeatedly, reflected a broad national consensus.

Reciprocity in punishment of war criminals. Israel is harboring former KGB officials who ought to be tried for crimes committed against Lithuanians.

Euphoria about the present and utopian optimism for the future. Today there is nothing to prevent both the Lithuanian and the Jewish peoples from developing friendly relations. Although 220,000 victims of the Holocaust cannot be brought back to life, their memory can be properly enshrined, and new Jewish cultural insti-

347

tutions may be established. As for the immediate future, perhaps Jews around the world will be able to help Lithuania politically and economically to strengthen the country's independence and development.[82]

□

Fifty years after the Holocaust, the past continues to haunt both Jews and Lithuanians. Nevertheless, the passage of time is apparently beginning to have a mitigating effect on the passions that the subject once aroused. That is because the generation that experienced the events firsthand is passing from the scene. Jewish Holocaust survivors are a minority among Lithuanian Jews, especially today. They number less than eight hundred altogether. To the extent that it is possible, the younger generation wishes to put the past behind it. It is not coincidental that the head of the JCSL, Emanuel Zingeris, is a young man; nor is the fact that during the critical months when Western political support was deemed vital for Lithuania's stand against continued Soviet domination, this young man served as head of the foreign affairs committee of his country's parliament.

By the same token, it is noteworthy that almost half of the Jews living in Lithuania in recent years were born outside Lithuania (in Russia, Belorussia, and Ukraine) and that many others spent the war years together with fellow Lithuanians either deep in the Russian interior or in the Lithuanian Division in the Red Army. They did not personally witness the events that took place in 1941–42. Jews who returned to Lithuania after the war had sometimes developed friendly relations with their Lithuanian comrades in the army and in Soviet labor camps. A certain proportion are even linked by family ties, especially in the younger generation.

In sum, while the emotionally laden subject of the Holocaust continues to rankle, the shrinking of the Lithuanian Jewish population overall and attrition among the survivor generation in particular point toward the subject's diminishing importance as time goes on. This suggests that the future handling of problems relating to the Holocaust of Lithuanian Jewry, from the writing of history to the return of property, will be done with more understanding, less bitterness, and possibly a measure of consensus among those involved. In such an atmosphere, it will be easier to attempt a more balanced reassessment. None of this, however, offers comfort for the fact that six hundred years of Jewish life in Lithuania were utterly destroyed by the Holocaust, with a terrible and irredeemable finality.

NOTES

My thanks to Dr. Eli Lederhendler of the Institute of Contemporary Jewry of the Hebrew University for his help in revising an earlier draft of this article; and thanks to Mr. David Silberklang for his editorial assistance.

1. Yaakov Lestchinsky, "Hakalkala vehademografia shel yahadut lita (1919–1939)," in *Yahadut lita*, 4 vols. (Tel Aviv, 1959–84), 2:91. Cf. *Evreiskaia entsiklopedia*, 16 vols. (St. Petersburg, 1905–13), 5:

557–65, 9:580–83, 14:604–5. Particulars on the lives of Jews in Lithuania from the time of their earliest settlement until World War II may be found in the first two volumes of *Yahadut lita*.

2. An outstanding example is Shimshon Rosenboym, who was instrumental in the negotiations over establishing an independent Lithuania and who served as deputy foreign minister in the new

Lithuanian government (see *Yahadut lita,* 2:71 n. 7).

3. The English text appears in ibid., 2:60.

4. *Lietuvos gyventojai 1923 rugsejo 17 d. surašymo duomenys* (title also given in French: *Population de la Lithuanie donees du recensement du la 17 septembre 1923*), published by the Lithuanian government (Kaunas, 1924).

5. *Tremtinys,* November 21, 1992, 78.

6. For background information on Lithuania until the end of World War II, see Thomas Chase, *The Story of Lithuania* (New York, 1946); and Alfred E. Senn, *The Emergence of Modern Lithuania* (New York, 1959).

7. For additional details, see Jewish Telegraph Agency (JTA), *Daily News Bulletin,* November 3, 1939. Cf. *Forwards* (New York), November 2, 1939, 1.

8. Concerning assaults on Jewish students at Kaunas University (Vytautas the Great University) and the degrading public statement issued by the rector, Prof. Stasys Šalkauskis, see the campus newspaper, *Studentų dienos,* November 15, 1939.

9. A document of the German foreign ministry that fell into American hands after the war and was submitted to the Nuremberg Tribunal (NG-4041) indicates that at the end of the 1930s German authorities provided funds to Lithuanian nationalist supporters of Augustinas Voldemaras, a Lithuanian statesman and the first prime minister, to encourage them to stage pogroms but refused to give them arms. The document's original serial number at the German Security Department (RSHA) was AZ 11 1123. It was not used in the Nuremberg trials, however, and was not published among the Nuremberg papers (see Sara Neshamit, "Mismakh 'al kishrei hafashistim halitaim 'im haraikh hashlishi," in *Dapim leheker hashoa vehamered,* 2d ser., vol. 2, ed. Zvi Shner and Shlomo Derech [Tel Aviv, 1973], 259–64).

10. The participation of Jews in Lithuanian Independence Day celebrations in February 1940 was described as follows in the *Vilniaus Balsas,* February 20, 1940: "In the Mildos cinema more than three thousand Jewish residents of Vilnius gathered for the celebration and over one thousand had to be turned away. . . . On that same day members of the Jewish community gathered in the Choral Synagogue for festive prayers. Rabbi Fried spoke, and the choir sang the Lithuanian national anthem. The Jews prayed for the independence of Lithuania. Approximately eight thousand people were at the synagogue. Several thousand were turned away because of lack of space."

11. See the entry "Lietuvos komunistu partija,"

in *Mažioji Tarybine Lietuviškoji Enciklopedija,* ed. J. Matulis, vol. 2 (Vilnius, 1966), 386.

12. Photostats of the forms used by the Soviet security policy (NKVD) for the arrest of Jewish "counterrevolutionaries" were published in the *Lithuanian Bulletin* (New York), October–November 1945.

13. Even if we accept the maximum estimate that the number of Lithuanians arrested or deported indeed reached thirty thousand, then that would be the equivalent of 1 percent of the total population. The seven thousand Jews similarly treated, however, represented almost 3 percent of the Jewish population in the country. For details, see Dov Levin, "Arrests and Deportations of Lithuanian Jews to Remote Areas of the Soviet Union, 1940–1941," *Crossroads* 11 (1984), 67–101.

14. Leyb Garfunkel, *Kovna hayehudit behurbana* (Jerusalem, 1958), 25.

15. See Romuald J. Misiunas and Rein Taagepera, *The Baltic States: Years of Dependence, 1940–1980* (New York, 1983), 61; cf. Garfunkel, *Kovna hayehudit behurbana.*

16. The full text of this proclamation may be found in B. Baranauskas and E. Rozauskas, eds., *Masines Žudynes Lietuvoje: 1941–1944,* 2 vols. (Vilnius, 1965–73), 1:49–50, hereinafter cited as *Mass Murders in Lithuania.*

17. These minimal data were calculated on the basis of evidence collected from Lithuanian communities, as published in *Yahadut lita,* 4:237–373.

18. The statement urged that Jews be killed in large numbers in reprisal for their anticipated resistance to the German forces, one hundred Jews for every German killed.

19. For a description of one such event, in the Lietukis garage in Kaunas, by Lithuanian witnesses, see *Mass Murders in Lithuania,* 1:231–32; cf. "Die Morder Werden noch gebraucht," *Der Spiegel,* April 23, 1983, 123–26.

20. Eyewitness accounts by both Lithuanians and Jews attesting to these circumstances include that of Elena Kutorgienė, a Lithuanian ophthalmologist (later honored by Yad Vashem as one of some 120 Lithuanian "Righteous Among the Nations"), in her diary, selections from which appeared as "Kaunaskij dnievnik, 1941–1942" (A Kaunas diary, 1941–1942) in *Druzhba narodov,* no. 8 (1968). Critical passages that were not published in the Russian version are quoted by Ona Šimaite in her article "Litviner un yidn be'es der nazi okupatsye," in *Lite* (New York) 1 (1951): 1661–71. Cf. Elena Kutorgienė, "Yoman kovna (1941–1942)," *Yalkut moreshet,* no. 17 (1974), 31–72; *Yahadut lita,*

4:344; and Sheina Sachar-Gertner, *The Trees Stood Still* (Framingham, Mass., 1981), 3.

21. The quotation is from a report by the commander of Einsatzgruppe A, Franz Stahlecker, accompanied by statistics and dated October 15, 1941 (Nuremberg Trials doc. no. L-180). Cf. Raul Hilberg, *Documents of Destruction* (Chicago, 1971), 46–57.

22. Many details and horrific descriptions are to be found in *Yahadut lita,* 4:237–373; *Mass Murders in Lithuania,* vols. 1 and 2; B. Baranauskas and K. Ruksenas, comp. and ed., *Documents Accuse* (Vilnius, 1970); and Hilberg, *Documents of Destruction.*

23. According to the protocol of the Wannsee Conference, dealing with the Final Solution (January 20, 1942, Nuremberg Trials doc. no. 2586-6), thirty-four thousand Jews remained at that time in Lithuania. This number is presumably the total for the three large ghettos, Vilnius, Kaunas, and Šiauliai, without Svenčionys or the smaller labor camps.

24. Eliezer Yerushalmi, *Pinkas shavli: yoman migeto shavli, 1941–1944* (Jerusalem, 1958), 35.

25. See the testimony of one of the members of the delegation in Garfunkel, *Kovna hayehudit behurbana,* 41. On Bishop Brizgys, see Dov Levin, "Bryzgys, Vincentas," in *Encyclopedia of the Holocaust,* ed. Israel Gutman, 4 vols. (New York, 1990), 1:246–47.

26. Quoted from the reminiscences of one of the members of the delegation, Jacov Goldberg, "Bletlekh fun kovner eltestenrat," in *Fun letsten khurbn* (Munich), no. 7 (May 1948), 39.

27. Others who signed the telegram were Archbishop J. Skriveckas, former Lithuanian president Dr. K. Grinius, and the former mayor of Kaunas, J. Vileišis (see *Mass Murders in Lithuania,* 1:53).

28. A memorandum was sent by Reverend H. Krupavičius, Prof. J. Alekna, and former president Grinius. "Of the 2,300 words contained in the memorandum, only eight (!) deal with the Jews, stating that the Lithuanian people does not look with approval upon the 'measures' being taken in relation to the Jews of Lithuania" (L. Garfunkel, "Heshbonenu 'im halitaim" [Our account to settle with the Lithuanians], in *Yahadut lita,* 4:51).

29. Sofija Binkiene, *Ir be ginklo kariai* (Vilnius, 1966), 166.

30. On Ona Šimaitė's activities, see Dina Abramowicz, "Vilner geto bibliotek," in *Lite,* 1: 1671–78; and Šimaitė, "Litviner un yidn be'es der nazi okupatsye."

31. This was the conclusion reached after a comprehensive study conducted by Sarah Neshamit,

"Rescue Attempts in Lithuania during the Nazi Occupation (June 1941–August 1944)," in *Rescue Attempts during the Holocaust,* ed. Israel Gutman (Jerusalem, 1976), 329. The estimate, which is on the high side, is based on analysis of Binkiene, *Ir be ginklo kariai,* and of a considerable number of books, articles, and documents, including data on actual cases in which Jews were rescued in the Baltic countries during the Holocaust.

32. For details on the armed resistance of Lithuanian Jewry against Nazi Germany, see Dov Levin, *Fighting Back: Lithuanian Jewry's Armed Resistance to the Nazis, 1941–1945* (New York, 1985).

33. For details on this period, see Dov Levin, "Livtei shihrur," *Shvut* 2 (1974), 55–73.

34. Rabbi Ephraim Oshry, *Khurbn lite* (New York, 1951), 262.

35. Among the representatives of the Jewish community council active in retrieving children was the spiritual leader of the community, Rabbi Ephraim Oshry. Those who were murdered while engaged in this activity included Shmuel Feifert, Y. Popel, a former officer in the Lithuanian Division of the Red Army, and Leyb Yuniski, a former partisan. See the testimony of S. Tiger, Yad Vashem Archives (YVA) 1660/31-6; testimony of Y. Burgin, Oral History Division of the Institute of Contemporary Jewry of the Hebrew University (OHD), 40–41; *Yerushalayim delita,* November 11, 1991; and "Shmuel Feifert, der held un koydesh," *Gahelet: Association of the Lithuanian Jews in Israel,* January 1992, 23.

36. Throughout the war, Aba Weinstein (Gefen) roamed about, armed, in villages in southern Lithuania gathering and recording information on anti-Jewish massacres. He later submitted to the Soviet authorities a detailed list of some one hundred Lithuanians from the area of the town of Simnas who had participated in the murder of Jews. It was on the basis of this list that murderers of Jews were apprehended. See Aba Gefen, *Unholy Alliance* (Jerusalem, 1973), 61–63.

37. This expression is cited in numerous sources, such as the testimony of Ovadia Yochelson, OHD, 6; cf. Ruzhka Korczak, *Lehavot baefer* (Merhavia, 1965), 302.

38. On the establishment of the schools and the education activities of the survivors see Dov Levin, "Haperek haaharon shel batei hasefer hayehudiim hamamlakhtiim bevrit hamo'atsot," in *Yahadut mizrah eiropa bein shoa letekuma,* ed. Benjamin Pinkus (Beersheba, 1987), 88–110.

39. Shmerke Katcherginsky, *Tsvishn hamer un serp* (Paris, 1949), 39. The book also contains

Katcherginsky's diary for July 15–September 21, 1944 (pp. 32–42).

40. R. Mironas, "Netolimos praeties gedingi vaizdai," *Tarybų Lietuva,* January 5, 1945. Mironas blamed himself for failing to raise his voice publicly. His last sentence reads: "At that time there were, unfortunately, so many scum and so few truly human beings."

41. The head of the Gel family, for example, was murdered in this manner in the town of Josvainai. See M. Karnovski, "Shtei pegishot," in *Keidan: sefer zikaron,* ed. J. Chrust (Tel Aviv, 1977), 283.

42. One of these was Jonas Paulauskas from Panemune, near Kaunas. In 1987 his widow visited Israel and received from Yad Vashem, the Holocaust Martyrs' and Heroes' Remembrance Authority, her husband's certificate as one of those recognized as "Righteous among the Nations."

43. For more details on the military activities of the Lithuanian nationalists in Soviet Lithuania during the period 1944–52, see V. Stanley Vardys, "The Partisan Movement in Postwar Lithuania," *Slavic Review* 22, no. 3 (1963), 499–522.

44. See Gefen, *Unholy Alliance,* 60–66.

45. Ruzhka Korczak, "Bema'avak 'al yehida yehudit lohemet," in *Sefer hapartizanim hayehudim,* ed. M. Gefen et al. (Merhavia, 1958), 159.

46. Ibid. Cf. Leah Tsari, *Mitofet el tofet: sipura shel Tzivya Vildstein* (Tel Aviv, 1971), 83: The people's commissar for security is quoted as saying to a Jewish delegation made up of Lt. Col. I. B. Rebelsky, Dr. Benjamin Bludz, and Zivya Vildstein, "What do you want me to do, Comrade Vildstein? Post a policeman next to every house?"

47. Karnovski, "Shtei pegishot," 285.

48. The ethnically neutral terminology appears, for example, in an official document issued on December 20, 1944, by the Extraordinary State Committee on Crimes Committed by the German Fascist Invaders of the Lithuanian Socialist Republic. See *Hiterlinė Okupacija Lietuvoje,* a compilation of documents published by the State Publishing House for Politics, Science, and Literature (Vilnius, 1961), 429–44. The Jews are mentioned just once in this collection, in connection with those murdered at the Ninth Fort in Kaunas, *after* a list that includes Russians, Ukrainians, Belorussians, Lithuanians, and Poles (433).

49. Meir Yellin and Dima Gelpern, *Partizaner fun kaunaser getto* (Moscow, 1948).

50. *Itogi vsesoiuznoi perepisi naselenia 1959 goda* (Moscow, 1962–63).

51. See Baranauskas and Rozauskas, *Masines Žudynes Lietuvoje.*

52. *Hiterlinė Okupacija Lietuvoje.*

53. See, e.g., E. Rozauskas, ed., with B. Baranauskas and K. Ruksenas, comps., *Nacionalistu talka hitlerininkama* (Vilnius, 1970).

54. The outrageous conduct of the 12th Police Battalion prompted the German commander occupying the city of Slutsk to request that the battalion's men be redeployed elsewhere. In an *Aktion* against the Jews of Slutsk on October 27, 1941, the Lithuanians fired at their victims indiscriminately, killing Christian Belorussian bystanders. The German commander claimed that the Lithuanians had stained the honor of Germany and that he had been forced to imprison two Lithuanians who, in the midst of the *Aktion,* had engaged in pillage. For these details, see the Nuremberg Trials doc. no. PS-1104. On Impulevičius, see Chaim Shoshkes, "Litvishe yidn baklogn zikh un di nazis lebn fray in amerike," *Naye yidishe tzaytung* (Munich), January 1, 1963.

55. "Raiti et hakatsav mikovna shover rashim shel yehudim," the testimony of a Holocaust survivor, in *Ma'ariv,* June 28, 1978.

56. There are many details on suspected war criminals in Vytautas Žeimantas, *A Call for Justice* (Vilnius, 1986). The OSI was established as a section within the U.S. Justice Department. Its work focused American public attention on the role of Eastern European Nazi collaborators. Among 350 suspected war criminals against whom investigations were opened there were scores of Lithuanians, including J. Kungys, accused of organizing the massacre of Jews in Kėdainiai; B. Kaminskas, for atrocities in Kražiai; A Virkutis, jailkeeper at Šiauliai; L. Kairys, an SS man at the death camp at Treblinka; Lt. J. Juodis, Lithuanian Police Battalion, for killings in Lithuania and Belorussia; Father Jankauskas, a priest who organized the killings in the town of Škuodas; and K. Palciauskas, mayor of Kaunas under the Nazi occupation, who helped to create and administer the ghetto and to confiscate and redistribute Jewish property.

57. *Yahadut lita.*

58. See *Unzer veg* (Munich), July 7, 1947.

59. For discussion of these issues by Lithuanians, see V. Domeika, "Per dideli kaltinimai lietuviams," in the Lithuanian-American journal *Teviskės Žiburiai,* June–July 1982; A. Kalnius, "Valila dziaugtis valia ir liudeti," ibid., September 16, 1982; Juozas Prunskis, *Lithuania's Jews and the Holocaust* (Chicago, 1979); Danielus Ralys, *The Chosen People: A Look Into the Past* (Toronto, 1986); and J. Vaičeliunas, "Kur filimo pradžia?" in the Brooklyn, New York, Lithuanian weekly *Darbininkas,* June 23, 1978.

60. For hostile responses to OSI investigations,

including on the part of the group called Americans for Due Process, see, e.g., the Chicago Lithuanian-American daily *Draugas,* January 31, 1985; and the Cleveland weekly *Dirva,* July 29, 1982. Cf. Silvia Kučenas, "OSI Collaborators with KGB," *Lituanus* 30, no. 1 (1984), 82–90; and *Darbininkas,* December 7, 1984.

61. Data are quoted from a communication received by the author from the Lithuanian Republic's Department of Statistics, dated June 22, 1992.

62. From anecdotal information, Lithuanian Jews who immigrated to Israel after 1967 described the jubilant reactions of Lithuanians to Israel's victory over the Arab countries. At farewell parties given for Jews about to leave for Israel, Lithuanians reportedly congratulated the Jewish people on their independence and expressed the hope that soon their own desires for independence would also be realized.

63. Census data for 1989 are based on the Lithuanian Department of Statistics report cited in n. 61.

64. See, e.g., D. Dvilinskaite-Laukiene, "To Protect Humanity," *Literatura ir menas,* December 12, 1987. (This reference and those in nn. 65 and 68 are cited on the basis of an English-language digest of the Lithuanian press, published in S. Atamukas, ed., *The Chronicle of the Jewish Cultural Society of Lithuania* [Vilnius, 1989], which renders only the articles' titles in English and does not supply page references.)

65. E. Jatsovskis, "Let's Honor the National Feeling of All Nations," *Sovetskaia litva,* January 6, 1988 (see above, n. 64).

66. R. Kalitis, "Laiškas redaktoriui," *Gimtasis kraštas,* no. 8 (February 1988).

67. G. Adomaityte, "Žydai," *Komjaunimo tiesa,* July 12, 1988.

68. J. Daunoravičiute, "The First Breath of Rebirth," ibid., September 27, 1988 (see above, n. 64).

69. These details on the organizational activities of the JCSL during the years 1987 to 1989 are found in the organization's newsletter, *The Chronicle,* covering the period October 1987–February 1989. Cf. Daniel Mariaschin, "Searching for Vilna," *Jewish Monthly,* June–July 1989, 18–22.

70. The statement was signed by Yankl Yosade, D. Judelevicius, Grigory Kanovičius, and Emanuel Zingeris and was published in *Gimtasis kraštas,* August 18–24, 1988. For an English version see *ELTA Information Bulletin,* no. 359 (November 1988), 18–19.

71. A copy of this document, which is unpublished and probably has not been widely distributed, was acquired from a Lithuanian journalist in the West. It is now in the archives of the Center for Research and Documentation of Eastern European Jewry at the Hebrew University of Jerusalem.

72. The document was not published. A copy was acquired abroad and is now at the Center for Research and Documentation of Eastern European Jewry at the Hebrew University of Jerusalem.

73. *ELTA Information Bulletin,* no. 380 (June 1990), 11.

74. Letter dated April 17, 1989, from a noted Jewish journalist in Lithuania, one of the veteran members of the Communist Party and an activist in the JCSL. The letter is located at the Center for Research and Documentation of Eastern European Jewry at the Hebrew University of Jerusalem.

75. See R. Konstantin, "Ar teisingas priimtas sprendimas?" *Respublika,* October 9, 1990.

76. Alexandras Bendinskas, "Mirtis lietukio garaže," *Gimtasis kraštas,* August 10–16, 1989. Cf. Chaim Finkelstein, "Mirtis lietukio garaže," ibid., October 24–30, 1989; and Charles Hoffman, "Lithuania Welcomes a War Criminal," *Jerusalem Post,* October 24, 1989.

77. The statement was released by the Lithuanian Information Center, New York, July 9, 1991.

78. One exception is Lithuanian historian Saulius Sužiedelis. See two of his critical articles on Lithuanian historiography: "1941 metu sukilimo baltosios demės," *Akyračiai* (Chicago), nos. 233 (October 1991), 7, 234 (December 1991), 8–9, and 235 (January 1992), 9–10; and "Penkiašdesimčiai matu praejus: lietuviu tautos sukilimo ir laikinosios vyriausybes istorijos interpretaciju disonansai," *Metmetys,* no. 61 (1991), 149–72.

79. See *Yerushalayim delita,* September 11, 1990; "Can Lithuania Face Its Past?" *Jerusalem Report,* August 1, 1991, 48; and Aba Gefen, "An Intolerable Perversion of History," *Jerusalem Post,* June 9, 1991.

80. On the rehabilitation controversy, see "A Letter from Vilnyus: Plea for Help," *Long Island Jewish World,* December 14, 1990; "Lithuania Starts to Wipe Out Convictions for War Crimes," *New York Times,* September 5, 1991, A1, A11; "120 Nazi Criminals among 'Rehabilitated' Lithuanians," *Jerusalem Post,* September 6, 1991; "Lithuania Asks Israelis to Help on War Crimes," *New York Times,* September 11, 1991; and "An Unpardonable Amnesty," *Newsweek,* September 16, 1991, 16. In a letter to Speaker of the Knesset Dov Shilansky, December 16, 1991, President Landsbergis agreed to the formation of a joint special commission (a copy of the letter is in the author's possession).

81. Lithuanian Department of Statistics (see above, n. 61).

82. On the press digest, see above, n. 64. Examples of press items that bear out the general description are J. Sabaliauskas, "Gyvenkime kaip broliai," *Šiauliu naujienos* (Šiauliai), January 20, 1991; Matas Krygeris, "Hitleriniu deportaciju užmirsti," *Tiesa* (Vilnius), March 27, 1991; Leonas Žalys, "Istieskim vienas kitam ranką," *Kauno tiesa* (Kaunas), April 13, 1991; Vygantas Vareikis, "Tragiskas lietuvos birželis," *Mažioji Lietuva* (Klaipėda), June 26, 1991; Antanas Paulauskas, "G. Vagnorius atsipraše, kas atsiprašys uz G. Zimaną," *Gimtasis kraštas* (Vilnius), July 25, 1991; Rytas Staselis, "Ko zydai nori," *Mažioji Lietuva* (Klaipėda), September 19, 1991; Grigorius-Hiršas Fišas, "Teismas ir tik teismas ir niekas kitas," *Respublika* (Vilnius), September 24, 1991; Vilius Kavaliauskas, "Žingsniai skustuvo asmenimis—apie New York Times straipsnį," *Lietuvos rytas* (Klaipėda), October 10, 1991; Letas Palmaitis, "Esu žudikas," *Liberalia,* October 10, 1991; Ruta Grinevičiute, "Tiesos pajeskos ar pretekstas tarptautiniui skandalui?" *Lietuvos rytas* (Kaunas), October 24, 1991; Eusejus Jacovskis, "Žydo trys keliai," *Respublika* (Vilnius), November 5–6, 1991; Emanuelis Zingeris, "Atvirumo testas," *Lietuvos aidas* (Vilnius), November 15, 1991; Vytautas Anulionis, "Kas užnuodi jo tarpusavio santykius?" *Panevežio balsas* (Panevezys), November 21, 1991; S. G., "Tai nežmoniška," *Kauno tiesa* (Kaunas), November 26, 1991; Antanas Petkus, "Ar tai ne šovinizmas?" *Opozicija* (Vilnius), January 3–6, 1992; and Gintautas Jonaitis, "Nužudytieji neatleis," ibid., June 25, 1992.

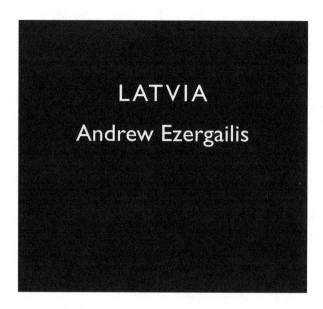

LATVIA
Andrew Ezergailis

In Latvia, as in the other countries that were occupied by the Soviet Union, the study of the Holocaust is in its infancy. It is about thirty years behind Western scholarship. Although the memoir literature about the Holocaust in Latvia is sizable, to date, with the exception of Dr. Gertrude Schneider's study *Journey into Terror: Story of the Riga Ghetto,* there is no scholarly book-length work devoted to the subject. The most elementary facts about the Nazi atrocities in Latvia still need to be clarified.

BEFORE THE HOLOCAUST

Jewish history in Latvia is tied to the expansion of the Polish-Lithuanian state into Kurzeme and Latgale in the sixteenth century. Five territories by the Baltic Sea were inhabited by Latvians: Kurzeme, Zemgale, Sēlija (all three of which came to make up the Duchy of Kurland), Vidzeme (Livonia), and Latgale (also known as Polish Livonia or Inflantia). It was only in 1918 that the territories coalesced under one Latvian flag with Riga as the capital. The number of Jewish inhabitants in Latvia peaked in the late decades of the Romanov empire. The numbers fell precipitously during World War I, escalated during the period of independent Latvia, and decreased again as World War II approached (see table 1).

From about 1500 to 1800, Jewish settlement in Latvia developed unevenly, depending on the goodwill and the needs of local nobility and the power of merchants to exclude Jews from establishing new residences. As long as the power of the Livonian (Teutonic) Order lasted, Latvian lands were not opened for Jewish residence or settlements. But soon after the collapse of the order in 1561, when Kurzeme (Kurland) became a duchy under the Polish crown, the influx of Jews into that province quickened, because residence requirements were lifted. The first Jewish presence in Latvia is traceable to the early sixteenth century in Jelgava, the capital of the Duchy of Kurland, where some Jewish grave sites dating to that period have been identi-

TABLE I
Jews in Latvia, 1897–1989

Year	No. of Jews	Jews as % of Total Population
1897	142,315	7.40
1914	185,000+	—
1920	79,368	5.13
1925	95,474	5.33
1930	94,388	5.00
1935	93,479	4.79
1939	86,422[a]	4.40
1941[b]	66,000[c]	—
1943	12,964[d]	—
1959	36,600	1.80
1970	36,700	1.60
1979	27,800	1.10
1989	23,000[e]	0.9

Notes: [a] Whether the Jewish population increased or decreased just prior to World War II is not clear. Inasmuch as Latvia was used as a point of transit by many Jews fleeing the Nazi onslaught in Europe, one would assume it would have increased; on the other hand, the gathering war clouds in Eastern Europe would have been a significant cause for leaving Latvia. The figure 86,422, taken from the authoritative study by J. Rutkis, *Latvijas Ģeogrāfija* (Stockholm, 1960), 448, is the lowest of the available estimates. See also "The Jews of Latvia," Records of the U.S. Department of State, Washington, D.C., ca. 1942, film M1177, roll 17, frames 0340 ff. A version of this document is located in the YIVO Archives, New York, Baltic Countries, folder 1.17. In this memodrandum the count is raised to 95,000, an increase of about 1,500 over the 1935 figure. The Nazi statisticians set the number at 89,000. See also Dov Levin, "Arrest and Deportation of Latvian Jews by the USSR during the Second World War," *Nationalities Papers* 16, no. 1 (1988), 50–70. Levin says that at the time of the Soviet occupation there were 10,000 Jews in Latvia.

[b] July.

[c] This number represents the Jews trapped by the Nazis in Latvia. As all Jewish population figures during the war and the Holocaust must be, it is an estimate. It takes into consideration that about 5,000 Jews were deported by the Soviets to Siberia on June 14, 1941, and that another 15,422 fled Latvia in advance of the German forces to the interior of Russia. The Nazi security police (SD) number for Jews trapped in Latvia was 66,000 (Nuremberg Trials doc. no. L-180).

[d] By 1943 the great majority of the Jews of Latvia had been killed. The figure 23,000 is cited by Rutkis; it represents Jews in the Riga ghetto and includes the 7,784 Jews deported from Germany and Austria and 276 from Lithuania. In 1943 there was a census in Latvia, but the Latvian census takers were not permitted to enter the ghetto. Rutkis has derived this figure from German documents (*Latvijas Ģeogrāfija*, 448).

[e] *Literatūra un Māksla*, October 14, 1989. The sharp drop in the number of Jews during the recent decades is the result of emigration to Israel. Today the number of Jewish residents in Latvia may be as low as 17,000.

TABLE 2
Jews in Riga, 1824–1979

Year	No. of Jews	Year	No. of Jews
1824	513	1925	39,459
1867	5,254	1930	42,323
1881	14,222	1935	43,672
1913	33,651	1979	23,570
1920	24,725		

fied.[1] It was also the Polish rule over Latgale, the southeastern part of Latvia, that facilitated Jewish settlements there. After the first partition of Poland in 1772, Latgale became part of the Russian Empire, and soon thereafter the laws of the Pale, with all of their benefits and shortcomings, were extended to Latgale. Many Jews settled in Latgale after the Chmielnicki massacres and the Cossack raids between 1648 and 1653.

The first evidence of Jews in Riga is a statement in a ledger dating from 1536 that begins, "From the Jew Jacob, received for sale and also sold to him. . . ."[2] But since Riga, along with the province of Livonia, came under Swedish rule, the liberal residence rules under the Polish crown did not apply. Only with time did the Swedish-dominated regions become more accessible to Jewish merchants. Livonia and Riga passed into Russian hands after the Peace of Nystadt in 1721, but this transfer did not have an immediate impact on Jewish residents.

Riga, being a major harbor on the Baltic and a commercial outlet of the Russian Empire, was the most desirable place of residence for Jews from Lithuania, Kurzeme, and the East—Latgale and Belarus (the Reisen Jews). The exclusionary laws of the Russian Empire and the jealously guarded privileges of the German merchants in the cities kept the number of Jewish residents low. As late as 1824 there were only about 513 Jews in Riga, but following the lifting of the strict residence laws in the 1840s, the number began to grow rapidly: there were 5,254 in 1867; 14,222 in 1881; 33,651 in 1913; and 43,672 in 1935 (see table 2).[3] During the period of Latvia's independence, all regions of Latvia lost Jewish inhabitants except Riga, where they increased.

Through the centuries, Latgale was the most hospitable of the Latvian territories to Jewish settlement. Daugavpils (Dvinsk) became one of the important centers of Jewish culture and learning in Eastern Europe. By the beginning of the twentieth century, Jews made up the majority of inhabitants in several Latgale towns and villages. In comparison with the Jews of Kurland, who over the centuries had become Germanized and cut off from Jewish cultural life, the Jews of Latgale were in touch with the cultural currents sweeping through Poland and Belarus. In their religious persuasion the Jews of Latgale were Hasidic. They were influenced more by Russian culture, an influence that intensified after the imposition of Russification in the late nineteenth century, than by German culture.[4]

TABLE 3
Jewish Residents by District in Latvia, 1935

District	No. of Jews		% of Jews in Latvia	% of Total Population in Latvia
	By Nationality	By Faith		
Riga	43,672	43,558	46.72	11.34
Vidzeme	2,458	2,460	2.63	0.60
Kurzeme	12,012	12,002	12.85	4.11
Zemgale	7,363	7,382	7.88	2.46
Latgale	27,974	28,004	29.92	4.93
Total	93,479	93,406	100.00	4.79

Source: A. Maldups, ed., *Latvija Skaitļos* (Riga, 1938), 67–69, 71.

Vidzeme (Livonia) was fully opened for Jewish residence only during the period of Latvia's independence, and thus the Jewish population there was minimal. In 1935 only 2,458 lived in Vidzeme.

The Jews of Latvia divided into two general sects: the Mitnagdim, followers of the letter of the law without fidelity to any rabbinic dynasty, whose roots were in Prussia and northern Lithuania, inhabited the provinces of Kurzeme, Zemgale, and Vidzeme; and the Hasidim, followers of a rabbinic dynasty, lived in Latgale. In addition to Yiddish, the former spoke German, the latter Russian. Riga was the melting pot of Latvia's Jewry, where the Mitnagdim and Hasidim met.[5]

The Jewish community of Latvia was pluralistic in the extreme, not only culturally and religiously but also socially and economically. Some of the richest and some of the poorest people in Latvia were Jews. Modern ideologies, Social Democrats (Bundists), and Zionism contributed more divergences. For example, there was a conflict between those Latvian Jews who favored sending their children to Hebrew schools (preferred by the Zionists) and those who favored sending their children to Yiddish ones (preferred by the Bundists). For the great majority of Jews, the cultural life, though highly variegated, until the end remained centered around synagogues and *minyanim* (see table 3).[6]

Latvian-Jewish Relations before 1914

Our knowledge of Latvian-Jewish relations prior to 1900 is fragmentary. Latvia appears not to have been a society saturated with anti-Semitism. The historical record reveals no pogroms or desecrations of synagogues. While the independence of Latvia lasted (until the Soviet occupation in 1940), there were no anti-Jewish laws, and Jews from Europe found refuge in Latvia. Inasmuch as the great majority of Latvians were rural and the Jews were urban, Jewish-Latvian contacts over the centuries were few, being restricted to marketplace encounters and visits of Jewish peddlers and itinerant craftsmen to Latvian farmsteads. The Jew as a peddler and tailor has left perhaps the most deep-seated impression on Latvian peasantry. Surprisingly, the Jew as a buyer of crops and livestock, a position that could arouse envy and resentment in farmers, has not found much room in the Latvian collective memory.[7] The Jews and Latvians were separated socially and physically, which prevented them from developing great animosities or friendships.

What the Jews have thought of Latvians over the centuries has not been made available in a scholarly or literary form.[8] Latvians, however, have commented extensively about the Jews in their midst in folk songs and literature. In both genres the Jew represents a figure of curiosity, if not always admiration. Understanding the meaning of Latvian folk songs is difficult, for the songs tend toward a formulaic use of words (into which the name of any ethnic group could be plugged in) and alliterative verbal designs. If one is searching for signs of anti-Semitism, the folk songs are ambiguous sources.[9] Most of the literary and dramatic portrayals of Jews date from the early twentieth century. They tend to be even-tempered and friendly toward the Jews. The most fully developed accounts of Jewish social life occur in J. Janševskis's novels *Dzimtene* (My country), *Mežvidus ļaudis* (The people of the forest), and *Bandava*.[10] Numerous Latvian writers have written short stories about Jews. A representative selection of them, from which the study of the Jew in Latvian literature can begin, is found in K. Tolmans's Hebrew-language anthology, *The Jew in Latvian Literature* (1938). The stories deal almost exclusively with the itinerant Jew within peasant society, and with one exception they would not be judged anti-Semitic even today.[11] In these stories Jews are treated with condescension at times but also with sympathy and, frequently, pity, for they are seen as lonely travelers who are forced to live a life away from their families and their people. Some of the stories have a comic premise, which makes it more difficult to evaluate them for their philo- or anti-Semitic content.

The itinerant Jew was a familiar character in Latvian drama, employed by playwrights from Stender the Younger (1744–1819) to the turn-of-the-century master of Latvian theater, Rūdolfs Blaumanis. The play *Icigs Mozes* (Isaac Moses [1874]), by Juris Alunāns, in which a Jewish merchant is the central character, is considered to be a pivotal depiction of a Jew and to have led to Blaumanis's more versatile use of the Jew.[12] Although the Jews' roles in Latvian plays were usually to add merriment through gesture and accent, they frequently also contributed a more somber note, communicating a human truth or a secret of social relationships.

One hostile portrait of the Jew, anti-Semitic almost in a medieval mold, is to be found in Andrievs Niedra's novel *Kad mēness dilst* (When the moon is waning), published in 1902. In the novel Niedra depicts an old bearded Jew who, to avenge wrongs committed against him and his sons, engages in the ritualistic murder of Christians.[13] How much influence this kind of portrayal, by a very popular writer, may have had, is difficult to assess. Niedra's works were forbidden in Soviet Latvia, as they were under Kārlis Ulmanis's regime in the 1930s.[14] The Jew as a stock figure in Latvian literature or as an individuated character almost vanished with the Holocaust.

The Jews in Independent Latvia

From 1900 to 1917 Latvians were engaged in a revolutionary struggle. In Latvian history books, especially those with Social Democratic leanings, this period is portrayed as a period of fraternal Latvian-Jewish struggle against the autocracy. Latvian-Jewish relations were stormier in the years 1918 to 1921, the period of Latvia's War of Independence. In late 1918, as the German forces withdrew from the Baltic after the armistice, the Red Army entered Latvia. On November 18, 1918, the liberal Latvian leadership declared an independent Latvia. At first the war had the character of a civil war, with the Latvian liberal forces fighting the Latvian Red *strelki*. However, the Communist effort collapsed in May 1919, when difficulties at home forced the Russian forces to retreat. Soon afterward, the Latvian army had to battle German Free Corps forces, who in conjunction with the Baltic Germans desired to obtain dominance in the Baltics. With the signing of the peace treaty between Russia and Latvia in 1920 the hostilities ended.

The tension of this period, which sometimes erupted into street violence, has been documented by both Latvians and Jews. Dr. Max Laserson, one of the most important Jewish politicians in Latvia during the 1920s, cited "minor" assaults in Bastejkalns Park and in the provinces, "particularly in Rēzekne [Rezhitza]."[15] Frida Michelson told a more violent tale in *I Survived Rumbuļi* (1979), her book about her Holocaust experiences. She noted that her relatives, from the town Varakļāni, in Latgale, experienced a pogrom at the hands of Latvian soldiers in 1919: "We still remembered the atrocities of 1919 after the occupation of Varakļāni when the Latvian soldiers were given thirty minutes to do as they pleased. Murder, rape, and robbery reigned for those thirty unforgettable minutes."[16]

In 1920 a company of soldiers on leave from the eastern front for no apparent reason began chasing Jews out of a park in Riga, shoving some into the canal. The prompt appearance of President Ulmanis and Minister of War General Kārlis Balodis in the regimental headquarters put an end to the disturbance, and the offending company was ordered back to the front.[17]

However many such incidents occurred, they all seem to have been isolated. Although questions were raised about them in the Constituent Assembly, no case came before a court of law. The government of Latvia was operating under democratic procedures, and it was mindful of Latvia's international position, that is, that Latvia had not yet obtained full diplomatic recognition from Western powers. And the Social Democrats, who considered the leftist Jews to be their allies, likewise would not have countenanced pogroms.

Jews fought in the War of Independence against the Bolsheviks and the Germans, some earning the *Lāčplēsis* (Bearslayer) medal, the highest Latvian award for valor.[18] There existed an Association of Jewish War Veterans, and Zigfrīds Meirovics, the first foreign minister of Latvia's republic, was half-Jewish. To what degree Jews shared in the land reforms of Latvia (the partitioning of the German baronial estates) is not clear; to the war veterans, at least, land was distributed without prejudice.[19]

Although during the early years of Latvia's republic the Jewish-Latvian relationship can be described as tense, it was also during this time that the constitution of Latvia's republic was written. Jewish deputies freely participated in the development of this document, which was adopted in 1922. The Latvian constitution was unique in that it not only conferred a full spectrum of civil rights on all citizens but also conferred rights on all minorities as such. Each minority was sovereign and autonomous within the Latvian republic. Laserson, who was a participant of the Constituent Assembly, explained its importance: "The fact that these minority rights were conferred not upon the individual members, but on the nationality as a whole is particularly noteworthy in view of the fact that Latvia was the first European state to adopt such a law after the World War."[20]

In practical terms, this ethnic autonomy meant that Jews could pursue their cultural and economic life in a free and uninhibited manner. The state of Latvia guaranteed them the right to establish schools in their own languages (Hebrew and Yiddish),[21] not to mention religious rights[22] and the rights of free speech and assembly. The republic of Latvia, although strongly socialistic in its social policies, was capitalistic economically. No Jewish writer of liberal or bourgeois inclinations has described Latvia's constitution as deficient or prejudicial toward Jews.[23] This brand of latitudinarianism was, and still is, unique to the constitutions of the three Baltic states. This extended internal autonomy had no Western model; it was an outgrowth of the Russian revolutionary experience.[24]

Jews participated fully in the political life of the republic of Latvia. To the Constituent Assembly the Jews sent eight deputies; to the first Saeima (Latvia's parliament), six; and to the second and third, five. But in the fourth their representation, due to a splintering of the Jewish vote, fell to three. Jewish political opinions and parties, unlike those of the Germans, who tended to vote along ethnic lines, ranged over the whole political spectrum. In independent Latvia some of the most distinguished Jewish political personalities were Dr. Noah Maisels, representing the Bund; Dr. Jacob Hellmann and Dr. Laserson, representing the Zionists; Rabbi Mordechai Nurock, representing the Mizrahi Party; and Mordechai Dubin and Dr. Shimon Wittenberg, representing Agudat Israel.[25] The most significant contribution of the Jews to the new Latvian state, though, was in the realm of economics. Their commercial and banking contacts abroad helped the republic recover from the devastation after the war.[26]

When a more detailed history of Jewish-Latvian relations is written, perhaps some as yet unperceived reason for the tragedy of 1941 will be made clear. But so far, Latvian and most Jewish writers have portrayed those relations during the period of Latvia's independence as tending more toward the idyllic than the menacing. Some Jewish writers have detected anti-Semitism in the exclusion of Jews from civil-service and military appointments in Latvia.[27] If the Jews felt excluded from the affairs of the state, there is every reason to say that there was anti-Semitism in Latvia. At the same time, it must be noted that Latvian anti-Semites attacked the state and its parliament for being in the pocket of the Jews.

But there is no reason to portray the relationship too idyllically: there was little contact between the two peoples. They lived like oil and water, separated by tradition, religion, and language. The 1922 constitution, although it embodied a high ethical standard and a respect for human diversity, at the same time fossilized the two peoples into separate compartments, prohibiting them from viewing each other as anything but the "other."

In 1934 the Latvian republic underwent a major change. President Kārlis Ulmanis, who as the leader of the Farmers Union Party represented the center of Latvia's politics, carried out a military coup against the Saeima. He suspended the constitution of 1922 and banned all political parties, including his own Farmers Union Party. The Jewish situation under Ulmanis from 1934 to 1940 was far from simple. He did not attack Jewish cultural autonomy or select Jewish entrepreneurs for special punishment. That there was no overt anti-Semitism, and no anti-Jewish legislation was passed, does not mean that Ulmanis did not create a situation that set some Jews on edge, making them angry and fearful for their future. After all, Ulmanis closed down about 95 percent of the press. In 1934, prior to Ulmanis's coup, there were fourteen Yiddish newspapers; by 1937 there were only two.[28] Certainly no leftist or Social Democrat had any reason to like Ulmanis, for their parties were banned and some of their leaders incarcerated.[29] Since the ascension of Stalin and especially since the purges, Communism in Latvia had been on the wane, but Ulmanis, by his antiparliamentary, antisocialist putsch, came to be the biggest Communist-maker in Latvia since czarist Russia's ministers of the interior Pobedonestsev and Plehve, the great Russifiers. Ulmanis drove the leftists of Latvia—Latvian, Jewish, or Russian—into the arms of Communism.[30]

Conservative religious Jews liked Ulmanis. The social, educational, and religious privileges that the 1922 constitution guaranteed to Latvia's minorities were, in general, preserved by him, although in an altered form. The Agudat Party, the political organization of religious Jews, was the big winner. "With the advent of the authoritarian regime, which turned over the Jewish schools system to the Agudat, religious observance was definitely encouraged by the state, whereas pronounced antireligiosity was bound to be considered characteristic of leftism."[31]

Ulmanis's political and social policies alienated the leftist Jews, and his economic policy antagonized the propertied Jews. To what degree Ulmanis's economic policies were anti-Semitic has been debated since the 1930s. There is no doubt that some Jews suffered under his program of Latvinizing Latvia's economy, to the detriment of the country. But it is doubtful that his policies were specifically anti-Jewish, for all large property owners, including Latvians themselves, lost their businesses. All had their property rights infringed upon.[32] Ulmanis's plan was not to nationalize property but to buy out certain categories of large enterprises. In the thirties this policy was seen and supported more in terms of anti-Germanism than in terms of anti-Semitism.[33] Ulmanis was a follower of Mussolini, and his economic rearrangements in a rough way followed those of the Italian dictator. (See tables 4 to 6.)

Numerous statistical tables can be adduced to testify about the standard of living the Jews enjoyed in independent Latvia. Much of that evidence has been summarized in the 1942 memorandum to the U.S. Department of State, "The Jews of Latvia." This memorandum contains numerous statistics about Jewish property, health care, and education. The statistics show that the Jews enjoyed a high standard

TABLE 4

The Occupational Distribution of Employed Jews in Latvia, 1935

Field	No. of Jews	% of Total No. of Employed Jews
Agriculture	457	1.11
Industry	11,838	28.74
Trade and commerce	20,021	48.63
Communications	903	2.19
Public administration	610	1.48
Professions, education, art, etc.	3,046	7.40
Public health, hygiene	1,642	3.99
Domestic service	838	2.04
Other	1,819	4.42
Total	41,170	100.00

Source: "The Jews of Latvia," Records of the U.S. Department of State, Washington, D.C., ca. 1942, film M1177, roll 17, frames 0340 ff.

TABLE 5

Industrial Enterprises in Latvia, by Size of Enterprise, 1935

No. of Workers	Total No. of Enterprises in Latvia	Jewish-owned Enterprises		
		No.	% of Total Enterprises	% of Jewish Enterprises
0–4	46,404	4,627	9.97	92.62
5–9	833	193	23.17	3.86
10–49	369	93	25.20	1.86
20–49	224	56	25.00	1.12
50–99	61	17	27.87	0.34
100 and over	30	10	33.34	0.20
Total	47,921	4,996	10.43	100.00

Source: See table 4.

of living, if not the highest of any ethnic group in Latvia. Education and health-care statistics reveal that in no sense were Jews treated as inferior to the other groups.

The literature about Jewish education in Latvia is lengthy and polemical. The following extract from a U.S. Department of State document is offered as a summary of the situation of Jewish schools in Latvia under Ulmanis.

Before the establishment of the Ulmanis regime, the educational facilities for Jews were provided as part of the minority set-up of the country. Schools in which Yiddish or Hebrew was the language of instruction were maintained by the municipalities or the state, and there was a Jewish Department under the Ministry of Education. Under Ulmanis the Jewish schools were affected by a law promulgated on July 24, 1934, abolishing the minority school departments and substituting individual

TABLE 6
Industrial Enterprises in Latvia, by Industry, 1935

Industry	Total No. of Enterprises in Latvia	Jewish-owned Enterprises		
		No.	% of Total Enterprises	% of Jewish Enterprises
Mines, quarries	30			
Ceramics, stone production	790	30	3.80	0.60
Metallurgy, mechanics	6,545	646	9.87	12.93
Chemicals	290	87	32.00	1.74
Leather	798	135	16.92	2.70
Textiles	1,317	77	5.85	1.54
Lumber	6,346	198	3.12	3.96
Paper	72	31	43.05	0.62
Graphic arts	755	128	16.95	2.56
Food	4,075	343	8.12	6.87
Clothing, shoes	18,947	2,967	15.66	59.39
Building	7,923	353	4.46	7.07
Public utilities	33	1	3.03	0.02
Total	47,921	4,996	10.43	100.00

Source: See table 4.

officials ("referents"). The Jewish schools of all types were turned over to the Agudath Israel which did its best to transform them, with the help of state machinery, into Orthodox schools. A number of Jewish parents who disliked this return to religious schooling reminiscent of the Heder (Hebrew school), preferred to transfer their children to Lettish schools. Nevertheless it must be emphasized that the right of the Jews to have their own tax-supported schools in their own languages (Yiddish or Hebrew) was maintained even under the dictatorship, but a number of Jewish schools were closed for reasons of "economy" or "efficiency" in the general course of school reforms. In 1932 the total number of Jewish schools was 122, in 1939 it had fallen to 77. The corresponding figures for Lettish schools in these two years were 1,679 and 1,672.

Elementary Schools: Of the 1,904 elementary schools in existence in the country in the academic year 1937–1938, 62 (3.3%) were Jewish (Yiddish or Hebrew was the language of instruction). They were attended by 9,715 (4.2%) children out of the total of 213,533 children of school age. Since there were 11,372 (4.87%) Jews by nationality in the elementary schools that year, only 1,657 Jewish children attended Lettish schools.[34]

THE HOLOCAUST ERA
Anti-Semitism in Latvia

Although the period of the republic, from 1919 to 1934 or even 1940, could be generally characterized as philo-Semitic, hostile, anti-Semitic viewpoints were expressed occasionally in Latvia's press and Saeima.[35] Latvia's first anti-Semitic organization,

Nacionālais klubs (The National Society), made its appearance in the early years of the republic,[36] and a party with a strong anti-Semitic undertone, the right-wing National Christian Society, led by Dr. Gustavs Reinhardts, had a voice in the Saeima. Some observers saw the appearance of anti-Semitism as originating in the insecurity of the Latvian intellectuals during the period of the early republic, a feeling that subsided in the mid-twenties. In general, we can trust Laserson's conclusion that within the Saeima, Jews as such never became a major issue. In the conflicts between the Latvian majority and the minorities, the Germans were always the primary target.[37]

In the late twenties, with the rise of fascism in Europe, a more clearly articulated anti-Semitism surfaced, this time in the form of party named Ugunskrusts (Firecross), soon to become Pērkoņkrusts (Thundercross). This organization was the one to introduce the slogan "Latvia for Latvians," thus placing itself at odds with the multiethnic nature of Latvia as defined and protected by the constitution of 1922.[38] Anti-Semitism in Latvia was found mostly among the urban and educated classes, and though Pērkoņkrusts had a small membership, it is said to have exercised considerable influence among university students, especially within fraternities.[39] Pērkoņkrusts was not an electoral success. Although it was an anti-Semitic organization, anti-Semitism was not its exclusive preoccupation: it was also vociferous about the Germans. In the early 1930s, when support for the Nazis began to grow among the Baltic Germans, the anti-German aspect of Pērkoņkrusts's ideology attracted even greater attention than its anti-Semitism did.[40]

In 1934 Ulmanis outlawed Pērkoņkrusts, imprisoning many of its leaders. The organization continued to operate underground, but its influence and membership diminished. In 1937 its leader, Gustavs Celmiņš, was exiled. At first Celmiņš lived in Finland, married a relative of Mannerheim's, and fought on the Finnish side of the Winter War of 1939 and 1940. In the spring of 1941 Celmiņš was in Germany, engaged in the service of the Abwehr, and in June 1941 as a *Sonnderführer* he returned to Latvia.

Pērkoņkrusts had its final hour during the early weeks of the German occupation, in July and August 1941, but it is not easy to assess its influence in 1941. No group of Latvians has been mentioned with greater frequency than has the Pērkoņkrusts as being a main participant in the Holocaust killings. The truth of the matter, however, is that the participation of the Pērkoņkrusts was only peripheral. There is no doubt that some Pērkoņkrusts members belonged to the killing troops, but they were only a few among many.[41] Before the organization could start playing a significant role, the members had to reassemble after years of persecution. And by mid-August 1941 the Nazis began again to persecute the organization, although numerous individuals stayed to work for the Nazi cause.

Pērkoņkrusts's responsibility in the Holocaust is an indirect one in that it provided a background of anti-Semitism in Latvia, giving it an intellectual and social respectability. The group's educational efforts during the last years of the Saeima cannot be overestimated. In 1941 Pērkoņkrusts members were the major purveyors of anti-Semitic literature, for most of the press during the Nazi occupation was under their control. It is true that Pērkoņkrusts hoped to play a major role during the German occupation, but the Germans only used the organization, placating it with false promises. Pērkoņkrusts did not fail because of a lack of trying but rather because its members were Latvian nationalists and because the Nazified Baltic Germans remembered the early thirties, when Pērkoņkrusts had been anti-German and had ridiculed the Nazis. Celmiņš returned to Latvia and began an underground life in 1941. He fought the Germans, was arrested in 1943, and ended up in a concentration camp in Germany.[42]

What of anti-Semitism under Ulmanis? Ulmanis was not an anti-Semite, and he was unique among the fascist leaders of Europe in his prohibition of anti-Semitic writings. "With the strengthening of the Ulmanis regime this kind of publication disappeared."[43] Latvian participation in the killing of the Jews cannot be ascribed to the presence of anti-Semitic literature. Latvian anti-Semites disliked Ulmanis and considered him to be a Jewish agent. According to J. Dāvis, the well-known writer, translator, and publisher of anti-Semitic literature in Latvia, Ulmanis personally told him that all of his writings would be destroyed if he continued.[44]

Anti-Semitism could exist, of course, without being overt and without being fostered by the state. One can indeed make the case that there was plenty of social or private and institutional or systemic anti-Semitism. The civil-service situation under Ulmanis did not improve and perhaps got worse. Jews could pledge Latvian student fraternities but could not gain full membership. It was difficult for Jews to gain entrance to the military academy. It has been said, although never proven, that in some university departments there were hidden quotas. Entrance into the university was based on tough, competitive examinations, and the Jews had no problem passing them. Thus the percentage of Jews in the university was much larger than the percentage of Jews in the total population.[45] Many bourgeois Jews studied abroad; the Latvian institutions of higher learning were not always their first choice.

The most fateful of all of Ulmanis's policies was the smothering of the press. Ulmanis's censors took the position that for diplomatic reasons newspapers in Latvia should tread carefully on the sensibilities of Stalin and Hitler. Consequently, the Latvians had no dependable way to learn about the impending dangers. The press was not allowed to report fully about the Winter War in Finland or about the German atrocities in Poland. To some degree the Jews, due to their family contacts in Poland, knew more about German crimes than did the Latvians. In fairness to Ulmanis, it must be said that until 1940 he kept the door open to Jewish refugees from Germany and Austria, even after numerous other countries of Europe, including Sweden, had ceased to do so.[46]

Jews under the First Soviet Occupation

The Soviet occupation of 1940 was the beginning of the end of Jewish religious and cultural life in Latvia. All Jewish schools and many social institutions were closed. The Communists had no use for the Jews as capitalists, Zionists, socialists, or religious believers. Although the Soviets have boasted that they liberated the Latvian Jews from prejudice and social inequality, the propaganda cannot disguise the fact that the undermining of Jewish social and religious institutions began with the Sovi-

etization of Latvia, about one year before the Nazi occupation. The Soviets imprisoned numerous Jewish political and social activists and deported to Siberia about
five thousand other Jewish citizens, a number that represents a much higher rate of
suppression than that suffered by the Latvians themselves. After the Hitler-Stalin
pact most Jews held no illusions about the Soviets.[47] Nazi propaganda notwithstanding, they had no special affinity for Communism. In fact, the Jews had every
reason to mistrust the Soviets. In spite of information about Hitler's policies toward
the Jews, the overwhelming majority of Latvia's Jews did not opt to flee to the Soviet
interior in July 1941.

Even today the contrary view persists that the Jews of Latvia, instead of being
victims of Communism, were Communism's closest allies and as such the victimizers of non-Communists in general and Latvians in particular. This view was the cornerstone of Heinrich Himmler's anti-Semitism[48] and it gained great currency in
Latvia during the Nazi occupation. The widespread belief in it was significant, even
crucial, to the Nazis in organizing Latvian help in the killing of Jews in 1941. However, no reasonable analysis of the facts supports this view. Four specific assertions
of Himmler's propaganda campaign particularly pertain to Latvia and the Soviet occupation of 1940.

1. *It was Jews, or mainly Jews, who welcomed the Red Army tanks in Latvia, especially on the square of the Riga railroad station.* Although many observers, including
Jews, have testified that indeed there were Jews among the pro-Soviet demonstrators,[49] the available evidence does not allow one to conclude that the welcoming
party was a Jewish group.[50] The crowd was made up of Russian speakers, among
them many in high hip boots, a type of footwear peculiar to Russians in Latvia.
Regardless of the composition of the crowd, which for a metropolis of Riga's size was
not a big one, the demonstration was a staged event. Andrei Vyshinskii (the one of
the Moscow 1930s show trials fame), who coordinated the occupation of Latvia,
could not depend on spontaneity, and there is no reason to think that he did. To
swell the crowds, a whole ship of demonstrators was sent in from Leningrad, and
other supporters came by rail. To the degree that there was spontaneous participation in the demonstrations, whether by Russians, Latvians, or Jews, some explanation must be sought in the policies of Ulmanis, his antileftism and the driving of the
radicals underground.[51] For the Communist underground there was every reason to
consider Ulmanis a tyrant and to welcome the Soviets.

2. *During the Soviet occupation the Jews were in control of Latvia's administrative
and legal apparatus.* Observers agree that indeed, especially in comparison with the
situation under Ulmanis, the Jews gained some visibility in the administrative structure, but there is no reason to think that the Jews exceeded their proportional number. The increased Jewish presence was only felt in the cities, especially Riga. In the
countryside there was no increase in the number of Jewish judges or administrators.
On the national level there were no Jewish administrators.[52] Numerous observers
have noted that in the period following the Ribbentrop-Molotov pact, anti-Semitism
intensified throughout the Soviet Union.[53]

3. *The Jews were especially active in the great deportation of Latvians on June 14,*

1941, when about 15,000 citizens were shipped to Siberia.[54] This assertion, though frequently repeated, has not been substantiated by any statistical evidence and is based only on the most coincidental observations.

4. *Jews controlled the Cheka in Latvia.* This has been the most pernicious and most frequently repeated accusation made since the Nazis occupied Latvia. The evidence to support the claim rests on flimsy grounds and, in the best of cases, on statistically insignificant numbers. The head of the Cheka in Latvia was Alfons Noviks, a Latvian from Latgale. It is true that Semyon Shustin, who was sent by Moscow to oversee Latvia's Cheka and who seems to have outranked Noviks, was a Russian Jew. His name is always mentioned as proof of the Jewish domination of the Cheka, and the anti-Semitic literature assigns to him most, if not all, of the Communist crimes in Latvia. In addition to Shustin, proponents of this theory cite a half-dozen other Jews who served in the various branches of the Cheka in Latvia. During the Nazi occupation, an Anti-Semitic Institute was established for the purpose of proving Jewish crimes in Latvia. This institute, although it had many opportunities, never issued a report of its findings. The most lurid of rumors is the story about the "ever-present" Jewish female doctor, who either pulled off people's nails or castrated Latvian men.[55]

In summary, we must conclude that the four assertions of the Nazis' propaganda have not been proven. In fact, to date they have not been subjected to serious inquiry. If any nationality dominated Latvia in 1940 and 1941, it was the Russians, not the Jews.[56]

A topic that still requires examination and analysis is Stalin's nationality policy after the Ribbentrop-Molotov pact and during the occupation of the Baltic States. Evidence suggests that part of the occupation strategy was to acerbate tensions between nationalities. The relations between Latvians and Jews were far worse after the Soviet occupation. The degree to which Latvian-Jewish relations worsened during Soviet rule is the degree to which the Soviets must share in the consequences of the Holocaust in Latvia.

The Holocaust

The Nazis killed about 69 percent of Latvia's Jews: approximately sixty-five thousand out of the ninety-four thousand Jews living in Latvia in 1935, when the last full census was taken. About five thousand Jews were deported by the Soviets to Siberia in June 1941, and an equal number perhaps had emigrated before the war. An additional eighteen thousand fled the advancing Nazi forces and hid in the interior of the Soviet Union during the occupation. The number of Jews trapped in Latvia in 1941 was about sixty-six thousand (the German figure was seventy thousand). It is certain that at least fifty-nine thousand of Latvia's Jews were killed in 1941. Approximately five thousand were transported to Germany in 1944; many of these died in the death marches of the winter of 1945. Perhaps two hundred Latvian Jews survived by hiding with gentiles.

The destruction of the Jews of Latvia began with the first days of German occupation in late June and early July 1941. Latvia fell within the scope of Einsatzgruppe A, which was under the leadership of General Walther Stahlecker. To expedite the killing of Jews, Stahlecker organized special Latvian units. The largest and most significant unit formed was the Arājs Kommando. This kommando alone was responsible for murdering perhaps thirty thousand Jews and aided in the massacre of many thousands more. There were two great waves of massacres in Latvia, the first from July to October 1941, when approximately thirty thousand Jews from Latvia's small towns were killed, and then the big actions of November and December 1941, when most of the Jews from the Riga, Daugavpils, and Liepāja ghettos were liquidated. In these later actions, about twenty-nine thousand people were killed. The biggest massacres took place on November 30 and December 8 at Rumbula, when about twenty-four thousand Riga Jews were killed. In 1942 approximately seven thousand Jews from Riga, Daugavpils, and Liepāja remained alive as slave laborers.

In late 1941 the Germans were considering developing the Ostland region as a killing center for European Jews. As a part of that plan, about twenty-one thousand people were brought to Latvia and housed in the Riga ghetto and other camps. About ten thousand of these "foreign" Jews were killed during the early months of 1942. In 1943, before the closing of the ghetto, about ten thousand "foreign" and five thousand Latvian Jews were still alive. From 1942 to the autumn of 1944, when the survivors were deported to Germany, the Jews were scattered throughout Latvia, the largest contingent, numbering about two thousand, housed in the Mežaparks (Kaiserwald) concentration camp. In the late summer of 1944, as Red Army forces reoccupied Latvia, the Germans transported the surviving ten thousand or so Jews to Germany, the majority going to Stutthof, a concentration camp in Prussia. The last and final agony that the Jews from Latvia had to endure was the death marches of the winter of 1945, when the Red Army approached the Stutthof area.[57]

THE POST-HOLOCAUST ERA

World War II caused a great dispersal of Latvia's inhabitants. The conquering Soviet Union did not allow the antebellum conditions of life to be reestablished. The Nazi dictatorship was exchanged for the Soviet one. The Soviets even more than the Nazis demanded that the society be subjugated to the state. Although Latvia was named a sovereign republic in the Soviet constitution, in reality Moscow governed it as a colony, with no local rights or privileges. The rights of individuals and of ethnic groups were de facto annulled. The property confiscated from the Jews by the Nazis was not returned to them by the Soviets. Even so, the Soviets were not the Nazis. The Subcommittee on Europe of the U.S. House of Representatives Committee on Foreign Affairs summed up the difference: "Nobody in a responsible position has ever dared to compare the Soviet Government's treatment of the Jews with the practice of the Nazis. But it is still true that there exists a spirit of terror and attack upon the very spiritual existence of the Soviet Jews which, while entirely different and less obvious in nature than was [sic] the Nazi persecutions, may be no less painful for the souls of the individuals and no less disastrous for the survival of the Jewish community in the Soviet Union."[58]

Whatever the comparisons between the Nazis and the Soviets, it is true that many Latvian Jews were saved from the Nazis by the Soviets. Even those five thousand Jews who were deported to the gulag on June 14, 1941, if they did not die in the Siberian exile, ironically survived the Holocaust because of the Soviets. Yet it is also true that during the early days of the war NKVD troops closed numerous border posts between Latvia and the Soviet Union, preventing thousands of Jews from escaping the Germans.

The Holocaust Remembered in Latvia

Of the twenty-five thousand Latvian Jews who survived the Holocaust, about twenty thousand found themselves behind the Iron Curtain after the war. The majority had fled the advancing German forces in 1941 and hidden in the Soviet Union. The first Jews to return to Latvia were those who fought in the partisan and Red Army forces, especially the Latvian Strelki 130 Corps. Beginning in late 1944 the Jewish refugees from the Soviet interior began to trickle back to Latvia. The last to return were the 1941 deportees to Siberia, who were released from the gulag by General Secretary Nikita Khrushchev in 1956.

Those Jews who had survived the Holocaust in Latvia and came out of their hiding places after the arrival of the Red Army were given a special survivor status, but only for a brief period. Then a web of suspicion began to be spun around them; some were even accused of collaborating with the Nazis. The survivors were interrogated by NKVD agents, and some were incarcerated and deported to Siberia.[59] As the Stalinist regime hardened, the persecution of Jews continued and intensified. Attempts to extinguish Jewish consciousness in the Soviet Union began with the end of the war. In numerous ways, the Soviets communicated that the "authentic Jew," as Jean-Paul Sartre defined the term in 1945, was not acceptable to the regime.[60] Until the time of Mikhail Gorbachev, the policy of Kremlin leaders was to Russify and Sovietize the Jews.[61] The cultural secretary of the Latvian Communist Party, Viktors Krūmiņš told a group of Jews who wished to start a Jewish choir in Riga that "your [Jewish art] will cause more harm than good. . . . You will artificially slow down the natural assimilation of Jewish children."[62]

This anti-Jewish policy was pervasive and constant, yet there were some periods in which it was applied more vigorously than others: (1) the late 1940s and early 1950s, culminating in the Doctors' Plot of 1953; (2) from 1959 through the early 1960s; and (3) the early 1970s, leading to the Riga trial of 1971. The irony is that from the viewpoint of Soviet nationalities, Khrushchev's de-Stalinization did not bring about a liberalization in relations between the nationalities. Especially in Latvia, because of the rise and suppression of the "national" Communists, a heavy-handed Russification program was initiated in 1959. The purge of the Latvian Communists in the same year was also felt by the Jews.

The attempt to diminish, even extinguish, the memory of the Holocaust that began in 1945 is revealing of the Kremlin's thinking about the Jews and their fate under the Nazis. The Nazi atrocities were not denied; quite to the contrary, on a certain level they were exaggerated and propagandized. But it was all done in generalities, without detail, and, in the best of cases, with shoddy scholarship. Jews as Jews had no place among the victims of Nazism, and they were submerged in the general victimization of the Soviet people.

No Jewish cultural institutions in Latvia survived the Nazis. Most of the synagogues had been destroyed, and the few that remained lacked worshipers. Even the Old Jewish Cemetery, near the Riga ghetto, where hundreds if not thousands of Jewish victims from the ghetto were buried, was in shambles in 1944. Soon after that it was vandalized, its fence destroyed, and in the 1950s it was converted into a shady park, with no evidence left that it had once served as a Jewish burial ground. Jewish communities in small towns had vanished completely.

Although general Soviet policies and attitudes toward the Jews affected the Jews in Latvia, both those surviving and those returning, some local peculiarities distinguished the Latvian Jews from the Soviet Jews. The Latvian Jews, in spite of the devastation, were "truer" Jews after the war than the Soviet Jews. The returning Jews carried back to Latvia much of their prewar Jewish culture. They were more cosmopolitan, having a good command of German or other European languages, and they were anti-assimilationist. Many of the secular Riga Jews, unlike those in Moscow and Leningrad, still knew Yiddish and Hebrew, which they had studied in prewar Latvian schools.[63] They were likely to have had some acquaintance with Zionism[64] and to have spoken Yiddish at home. This linguistic adroitness of the Jews survives today. It is not surprising, therefore, that in the 1960s the Jews of Riga played a key role in the awakening of Jewish consciousness in the whole Soviet Union. This awakening began after Stalin's death, and in Latvia it is very much associated with the Sinai campaign, the Six-Day War, and the trial of Eichmann. The roots of the awakening go back to the mid-fifties, when some samizdat Zionist literature began to circulate.[65] In 1970 a Jewish underground group in Riga published the first Jewish samizdat periodicals, *Iton Alef* and *Iton Bet*. Although the two publications were duplicated in small numbers, they reached Jews in many parts of the Soviet Union. A third periodical, *Iton Gimel*, was confiscated, and the compilers were arrested and charged with dissemination of "Zionist and anti-Soviet materials." They were tried in the Riga trial of 1971.[66]

From the end of the war the Soviets placed limits on the memory of the Holocaust. In 1944 a special commission to investigate the crimes of the Nazis was convoked, and Jewish survivors submitted their personal stories. The killing of Jews, the sites, and numbers were documented, if inaccurately, but all the information was placed in a special section of the Latvian State Archives. Until 1989 the archive had been seen by very few scholars and Party functionaries.[67] Nothing of significance about the Holocaust was published in Soviet Latvia. Even German atrocities in general received limited coverage. Only in the very early period of Soviet occupation, before the war had ended, was some press attention given to the crimes committed under the Nazis, but this coverage suddenly ceased around April and May 1945.[68] Thereafter, the Holocaust and German atrocities in general received haphazard coverage,[69] and when they were discussed, it was for propaganda purposes, with no details being given about specific crimes. The fact that Jews were killed by the Nazis was not denied, nor was it affirmed. Even to mention the Rumbula killings in the press was prohibited.[70] Frida Michelson, a fashion designer from Riga, wrote a book about her miraculous escape from the Rumbula massacre and wanted to have it published in Latvia. It was printed in a limited edition, but its distribution was prohibited. *I Survived Rumbuļi* was finally published in 1979 in New York.[71] As the Yad Vashem collection shows, memoirs about the Holocaust in Latvia have been written, but so far none have been published in Latvia.[72]

On the other hand, it must be noted that Latvia's Nazi victims are honored with one of the largest assemblages of monuments in the world at Salaspils, the site of a concentration camp, near Riga. The selection of the Salaspils camp site for a memorial garden, however, slighted the Jewish victims. The Salaspils camp, although a brutal one, was neither a killing camp nor a Jewish camp.

To summarize the Soviet reaction to the Holocaust in Latvia, we can say that it underwent four stages:

1. *The postwar phase, the period of the Nuremberg trials.* Nazi atrocities, horrible as they were, were blown out of all proportion, the number of victims doubled and tripled. We can only presume that this was done to obtain a larger share of reparations from defeated Germany. In the case of Latvia, the word "Jew" was avoided in official Soviet documents, even those issued by the special investigative committee and those submitted to the Nuremberg trials. For example, Nuremberg document USSR-41, which sums up Nazi atrocities in Latvia, mentions no Jews but states that about 250,000 civilians were killed. That number is about two and one-half times the actual number of Nazi civilian victims in Latvia.[73]

2. *The KGB phase, which began in 1961.* For the first time Soviet publications appeared with specific details about the killing of the Jews in Latvia, but these publications were intended for external use only. A series of publications appeared about the Nazi atrocities in Latvia, and though these pamphlets were printed in Riga, they could not be purchased in the city. They were distributed worldwide through Soviet embassies, sent to Latvian émigrés, and deposited in Western libraries. The pamphlets concentrated on the role Latvian collaborators played in the killing of the Jews. Some of the pamphlets contained detailed descriptions about the atrocities, but as several war crimes trials have shown, the information was not accurate. In retrospect, it appears that the purpose of this "openness" was to limit the influence of émigré Latvians abroad, especially those living in the United States.[74]

3. *The phase of limited cooperation.* In the 1970s Soviet authorities began to help the war crimes prosecutorial offices of Germany, the United States, and other countries by obtaining evidence and witnesses from Latvia.[75] The documents the Soviets released were incomplete, and most of them had been sanitized. The information passed to Western prosecutors was prepared by the KGB in Latvia and then sent to Moscow, where it was screened. The reason for this cooperation is not yet known, but inasmuch as it started with Germany, it may have had some connection with the Ostpolitik.[76]

4. *The openness phase, which began under Gorbachev around 1989.*[77] Since Latvia gained its independence in August 1991, there appears to be no limit to the cooperation of those in control of the Latvian archives. All the archives in Riga are open,

although use of the ex-KGB facility requires special permission from the general prosecutor of Latvia.

The openness came gradually. In 1988 a Jewish cultural society was established in Riga. In the spring of 1989 the first issue of a Russian-language Jewish magazine, *The Jewish Cultural Bulletin,* was published. A memorial stone was placed on the site of the Gogol Street synagogue.[78] A memorial plaque now marks the house of Žanis Lipke, a Latvian worker who saved dozens of Jews.[79] In the fall of 1989 a Jewish school, with classes taught in both Yiddish and Hebrew, reopened in Riga. On October 26, 1989, the Latvia-Israel Friendship Society was founded.[80] Today the spectrum of Jewish cultural activities is broad, limited only by resources and initiative. Ad hoc flights take place between Riga and Tel Aviv, and regular air traffic is planned.

Even though Jewish cultural life during the postwar years was suppressed, there was some underground activity. Perhaps the most significant development among Riga Jews was the reclaiming of the killing grounds of Rumbula in the 1960s.

The Reclaiming of Rumbula

The news about Eichmann's arrest and trial in 1961 reanimated Latvian Jewish memories of the Holocaust. Although there are more than sixty mass graves of Jews in Latvia, the major killing ground was Rumbula, a sandy knoll covered with shrubbery and pine trees where as many as twenty-five thousand people were murdered on November 30 and December 8, 1941. Since the war the grounds at Rumbula had been neglected and were overgrown. The area was difficult to locate. In 1961 a group of young Riga Jews began to search for it.[81] They found burned bones and other remains from the massacre.[82] The grounds were in an especially disorderly condition because in 1943 the Nazis had partially disinterred the victims to burn them. Rumbula galvanized the young Jews of Riga; in spite of official warnings to keep away from the site, it became a weekly gathering place. To divert attention from the Rumbula activities, Communist officials in 1962 organized a ceremony to memorialize Nazi victims at Biķernieki, another area in Riga where thousands of Jews were killed. But unlike Rumbula, Biķernieki was a place where thousands of gentiles were also murdered. At the ceremony the speeches mentioned only "Nazi victims." Jews were not acknowledged. Instead of quieting the movement, this snub provided greater impetus to the activities at Rumbula. In 1963 as many as five hundred young Jews worked weekly with shovels, pails, and wheelbarrows to clean up the grounds. Today Rumbula looks like a small shady park within a forest of gnarly pine trees. Neat paths and raised mounds indicate the location of the mass graves. At the entrance to the grounds stands a modest stone marker adorned with a hammer and sickle in the upper righthand corner and an inscription in Latvian, Russian, and Yiddish that reads, "To the Victims of Fascism 1941–1944." Among Riga Jews this monument is known as the "Aryan Compromise." There are many things they dislike about the monument. The Jews wanted the inscription to be in Yiddish alone and did not want it to be accompanied by a hammer and sickle. They also wanted the marker specifically to commemorate the killing of the Jews at Rumbula in 1941, not all the victims of fascism from 1941 to 1944.

Other attempts to raise a monument at Rumbula were made before the "Aryan Compromise." In the early 1960s a barbed-wire Mogen David was constructed, but that was prohibited. Then in 1963 "The Jew," a four-meter-high plywood statue painted in black and white, was placed on the site. Based on the design of Jewish artist Joseph Kuzkovsky, it depicted a man with a raised fist, seemingly climbing out of the earth. The Rumbula hillock, less than one hundred meters from the Riga-Moscow railroad line, attracted much attention, especially with this statue marking it. Authorities began to question the significance of the raised fist of the Jew. There was ambiguity in the gesture. After it had stood there for about six months, it disappeared one night. Only the heavy tracks of a truck were left behind.[83] Then the Jews proposed a stone slab inscribed "To the Victims of Fascism, 1941" in Yiddish. It too was rejected, and the "Aryan Compromise" was reached.

The Latvian Reaction

The reaction in Latvia to the Holocaust is impossible to reconstruct. The Soviet Union banned the airing of Holocaust issues in Latvia while the country was under its control, between 1944 and 1991. The Holocaust was not on the agenda of the Soviet press or educational system. Consequently, knowledge of the Holocaust is skimpy to nonexistent, especially among the young. There was no full treatment of the Holocaust in either history, fiction, or film, though the war itself received considerable attention Soviet-style. With the advent of *perestroika* and *glasnost,* the intelligentsia leaped forward to welcome and foster the Jewish cultural revival. To what degree the general population supported this effort is unknown. In the press no objection has been voiced about the Jewish cultural rebirth. Today nothing impedes the discussion of the Holocaust in the press or in academic journals. This does not mean that anti-Semitism has vanished: it still exists below the surface. There are no anti-Semitic periodicals, although one can encounter articles with anti-Semitic undertones. Among the Latvians there is no known organization similar to the Russian Pamyat, although among the Russians in Latvia a branch of Pamyat is said to exist and in the Russian-language kiosks anti-Semitic literature is available.

During the years since the war only two small volumes of scholarship have been published about the Holocaust, and they deal with it only partially: a document collection, *Mēs apsūdzam* (We accuse),[84] and an anthology of reminiscences, *Salaspils Nāves Nometnē* (Within the Salaspils death camp).[85] We may also include *Tiesas prāva* (The court trial), which contains a description and fragments of the transcript from the Jeckeln trial of 1946.[86] To some degree the Holocaust has served as a backdrop, without its being dealt with in details, for Soviet studies on World War II. For example, bits of information about the Jewish tragedy can be found in the work of academician Vilis Samsons, who has concentrated on the Latvian partisans during World War II,[87] and other studies about Communist resistance and World War II.[88]

In belles-lettres, too, the atrocities, though never fully explored, have served as a backdrop. At least on the level of folklore, the figure of *Žīdu šāvējs* (Jew shooter) makes a shadowy appearance every so often.[89] Frequent references to the German atrocities can be found in the late Ojārs Vācietis's poetry. Especially noteworthy is the poem "Rumbula," in which he directly confronts the atrocities. It dates from the early 1960s, when the Jews of Riga were reclaiming the site. An unrecognized masterpiece of Latvian postwar literature,[90] it is perhaps one of the greatest Holocaust poems in the world.

I walk past the forest's eyes,
My shoulder feels the swish of the lashes of the pines.
Under my feet a mound of earth sighs.

Those are the only sounds.
And I stop,
To stop all sound.

And no longer can I hold
the dam.
That my sight broke down.

The wood is full of shrieks,
The wood is full of shrieks.

The shudders cleaving on the pine trees,
Bark made craggy by the
Horror.
Shriek

The dirt that covered those interred alive—
Those mounds that kept quivering until the dawn.
Shriek
My pulse is pounding
and cuts this forest—
in the name of birches that will grow tomorrow,
in the name of children that will come tomorrow,
in the name of lips that will not shriek,
in the name of words that refuse to die.

And now I shriek,
I curse the forest:
—Such as you, we do not need you now!—

Like a green crater the forest besieges me.
A green and angry voice
Like a current passes through me:
—Thou shalt not promenade by my eyes!
Thou shalt not flirt
before my lashes!
Thou shalt not find solace
in my mounds!—

So all forests aren't like this,
I stand and shriek in Rumbula—
A green crater in the midst of grainfields.

Every man who has entered me
Becomes my tongue,
My flame.

You come in me
And shriek!

Other than in these few exceptions, one could say, the Jew does not exist in Soviet Latvian literature. In other media there are just as few examples. In 1965, for example, dramatizations in Latvian and Russian of Leons Briedis's stories "The Star of David" and "The Little Apple Tree" were broadcast on the radio.[91]

Latvian Jews outside of Latvia

Many Latvian Jews have left Latvia. Wherever they have emigrated, whether to Israel, Europe, the United States, or South Africa, they have maintained a consciousness of their origins. It is perhaps precisely because of the Holocaust that this consciousness has been maintained. One must also include among the Latvian Jews those European Jews who were transported to and survived in Latvia, because they have made important contributions to the memory of the Holocaust in Latvia. These Jews have contributed to the memory in two visible ways, by organizing societies and by writing books. There are four Latvian Jewish societies in the world: the Association of Latvian and Estonian Jews in Israel, in Tel Aviv (president, Zvi Segal, now deceased); the Jewish Survivors of Latvia, in New York (president, Steven Springfield); the Society of Survivors from the Riga Ghetto, also in New York (president, Lore Oppenheimer); and the Association of Latvian Jews in South Africa (Johannesburg; chairman, Jack Efrat).[92]

Several important reminiscences about the Holocaust in Latvia have been published in the West. In terms of immediacy, no other book about the Holocaust can compete with Max Kaufmann's *Die Vernichtung der Juden Lettlands* (The destruction of Latvia's Jews), published in 1947.[93] The most valuable part of the book is the story of Kaufmann's own experiences, which began with the Nazis' entrance into Riga and included his transport to Buchenwald in August 1944 and participation in the death march to Sachsenhausen, from which he was liberated on May 1, 1945. He survived the shootings of November and December 1941 as a working Jew. His tale of horrors mainly involves the Riga ghetto and the Mežaparks (Kaiserwald) concentration camp. But as part of a work detail, he saw many other camps and work details throughout Riga and its environs. It is a large work, and Kaufmann purports to give evidence about numerous other locales in Latvia, but in general his information about events that he did not witness is thin.

A book of special interest is Frida Michelson's *I Survived Rumbula*.[94] Michelson wrote the book in Russian after the war, but it was confiscated by the authorities, and she had to rewrite it after she emigrated to Israel. During the second big action, in December 1941, Michelson was taken to the killing field of Rumbuļi. Desperate to save her life, she fell on the ground near the pits and had the good fortune to be covered with the shoes taken from the victims as they were herded past her. At night she got up from under the shoes and walked away to tell her story. Her book is important for the information she provides about the first days of the Nazi occupation of Latvia, life in the ghetto during the period of the actions of November and December 1941, the killing operation itself, and her life in hiding during the years of persecution.

Gertrude Schneider has edited two volumes of reminiscences, *Muted Voices: Jewish Survivors of Latvia Remember* and *The Unfinished Road: Jewish Survivors of Latvia Look Back*.[95] Both are collections of the personal narratives of Latvian and German Jews about their experiences in Latvia. Bernard Press's *Judenmord in Lettland, 1941–1945* (The murder of Latvia's Jews, 1941–1945) is in part reminiscences and in part the product of research from secondary sources. The author and his father were saved by a Latvian family in Riga.[96]

Josef Katz, the author of *One Who Came Back*,[97] was a tough Hamburg Jew who, as a member of a work detail, like Kaufmann, had an opportunity to range far from Riga, on one occasion going to Liepāja and on another going as far as the environs of Leningrad. He arrived in Riga in December 1941, when all of the big *Aktionen* in Latvia were over; therefore, unlike Kaufmann, he has little to tell us about the killing operations themselves. His book is indispensable, however, for learning about Jewish life, the threats and cruelties, in the "quieter" period from 1942 to 1944. Reminiscences of smaller scope include Betty Happ's *Bortom All Mänsjklighet* (At the bottom of humanity [1945]); Jeanette Wolff's *Sadismus oder Wahnsinn* (Sadism or insanity [1946]); H. Sherman's *Zwischen Tag und Dunkel* (Between day and night [1984]); A. Levin's *Chortu Cherez Zubi* (Between the teeth of the devil [1986]); and Isaac Levinson's *Untold Story* (1989).[98]

A work of a different ilk is *Journey into Terror,* by Gertrude Schneider.[99] Schneider was a girl in her early teens when she, her parents, and her eleven-year-old sister were transported from Vienna to Riga. *Journey into Terror* is a memoir largely based on her diary, which she fortified with research and interviews with fellow survivors. At this writing her book is the only published history of the Riga ghetto. The special strength of her book is the information she brings together about the social and cultural life in the ghetto (which was later transplanted to the Mežaparks [Kaiserwald] camp) and the data she provides about the Jewish transports from the Reich to Latvia. Without her effort, our knowledge about the Holocaust in Latvia would be considerably diminished.

On the scholarly level, the most diligent writer about the Holocaust in Latvia and related topics is Dov Levin of the Hebrew University in Jerusalem. Most notable are his Hebrew-language works *Im hagav at Hakir* (With the back against the wall [1978]), about the Latvian Jewish resistance against the Nazis, and his *Pinkas Hakehillot* (Encyclopedia of Jewish communities [1988]). His articles "Jews and the Sovietization of Latvia, 1940–41" and "Arrest and Deportation of Latvian Jews by the USSR during the Second World War" are also indispensable.[100] One must also mention *The Jews in Latvia*.[101] An anthology of articles published by the Association of Latvian and Estonian Jews in Israel, it is an important study of Jewish history in Latvia. It is especially valuable for the information it provides about Jewish life in Latvia and Latvian-Jewish relations before World War II.

Latvians in Emigration

The non-Jewish Latvians in emigration have written more about the Holocaust in Latvia than they themselves realize. It is true that there is not a single work that would give us any full understanding of the tragedy. Nor is there a work that would tell us half of the story or, for that matter, even one-fifth of it. But there are bits and pieces.

The reasons for the failure of the first generation of emigrants to tell the story of Nazi atrocities directly and forthrightly are complicated and involve a number of factors. By and large, the Latvians and Jews in Latvia did not live as an integrated society. In emigration the relations, such as they were, were almost completely severed. Practically, there was no dialogue between the Latvian emigrants and the Jews. Latvian-Jewish writings and books found no echo in the Latvian emigration press. Furthermore, the information about the Holocaust in Latvia is far from easily accessible. The dearth of sources is to a great degree the doing of the former Soviet Union, which treated the killing of the Jews as a propaganda and foreign-policy issue. The Soviets did not make the information available to anybody, not even to their own scholars. Only in the mid-1970s, beginning with the Arājs trial in Hamburg, Germany, and the trials of other Latvian war criminals in the United States, did the study of the Holocaust in Latvia become possible. Latvian emigrants also did not know how to approach the subject. They did not know how to apportion the guilt, for they did not feel that the killing of Jews was in any way their doing. Émigré Latvians repeatedly asserted that while the state of Latvia existed Latvian-Jewish relations were good, if not exemplary, and that what happened thereafter was the doing of the occupying powers.[102] The emigrants felt that to discuss the subject of the Holocaust would mean to assume some kind of collective guilt. They themselves have been so enwrapped in their own grief, the loss of their homeland, and the fight against Communism that they have failed to become acquainted in any full sense with the Nazi assault on Europe's Jews.

Since the beginning of the emigration, some of the opinion makers, especially in the editorial offices of the emigration press, have been people who were active during the Nazi occupation, many of them working for *Tēvija,* published by the SD, the security service of the SS, during the Occupation. To what degree these editors were guilty of war crimes is not clear, yet it seems beyond doubt that they have been crucial in suppressing a free debate about German atrocities.[103] Those Latvians who were direct participants in the atrocities, as collaborators and killers, and who could write with authority on the subject for obvious reasons are not likely to offer treatises and memoirs on the subject.

Émigré Latvians have written voluminously about the German occupation in histories, memoirs, polemics, and novels. In fact, they have written about everything that occurred in Latvia except the killing of the Jews, Gypsies, Communists, and Russian prisoners of war. From the émigré writings we can learn a great deal about the German administrative structure in Latvia and the Latvian participation within it. Among these works are publications by Žanis Unāms, *Melnā vara* (The black power [1955]) and *Zem Barbarosa Šķēpa* (Under the sword of Barbarossa [1975]);[104] Oskars Dankers, *Lai vēsture spriež tiesu* (Let history judge [1965]);[105] Ādolfs Blāķis, *Medaļas otrā puse* (The other side of the medal [1956]);[106] Boris Zengals, *Dienās Baltās Nebaltās* (During good and evil days [1949]);[107] and Gustavs Celmiņš, *Eiropas Krustceļos* (At Europe's crossroads [1947]).[108] A work of special distinction that clarifies the economic issues of the Occupation is Arnolds Aizsilnieks, *Latvijas Saimniecības vēsture, 1914–1968* (The economic history of Latvia, 1914–1968 [1968]).[109]

Many publications detail the origin of the Latvian military units, from the partisan groups fighting at the time of the German takeover of Latvia to the Schutzmannschaften (Police Guards) and the Latvian SS Legion. The body of military literature is immense; among the most important works are Arturs Silgailis's *Latviešu Legions* (Latvian legion [1962])[110] and the multivolume *Latviešu Karavīrs Otrā Pasaules Karā Laikā* (The Latvian soldier in World War II [1970–82]).[111] The World War II literature is also rich in fiction and memoirs. There are several periodicals that print war reminiscences on an ongoing basis. Among these are *DV Mēnešraksts* (DV Monthly), *Kara Invalīds* (War Invalid), *Latvija Amērikā* (Latvia in America), and *Treji Vārti* (Three Gates). A distinguished book of memoirs is the first volume of Vilis Hāzners's *Varmācības Torņi* (Towers of tyranny [1977]).[112] *Mana atbilde* (My answer [1982–85]), the memoir of the defiant Kārlis Siljakovs, the chief of the Liepāja political police during the Occupation, tells less than promised but even so contains many important facts about police work during the Occupation.[113] One can also find some telling things about the brutalities of the Nazi occupation in theologian Kārlis Kundziņš's *Laiki un Likteņi* (Time and fate [1955])[114] and Arvīds Dravenieks's *Es atceros: Latvijas skolas un skolotāji* (I remember: Latvian schools and teachers [1970]).[115]

From the scholarly point of view, the most diligent writer about the seamy side of the Occupation has been Haralds Biezais. Biezais concentrates mostly on the quisling issue, the high number of civilian and military collaborators, but he tells a great deal about the Nazi atrocities as well.[116] The most direct analysis of the Holocaust in Latvia can be found in my recent work, especially the article "Arāja komanda."[117] Edgars Andersons was near completion of his work *The Third Front,* about the Latvian resistance during the German occupation, at the time of his death, in 1989; the completed parts are slated for publication.

Although the contacts between Latvians and Jews in emigration are few and writers dealing with the Holocaust have been in short supply, there are some exceptions. Notable is the leader of the Latvian Social Democratic Party in exile, Dr. Bruno Kalniņš. In a 1960 article in his *Brīvība* he unambiguously condemned anti-Semitism and asked for openness about the killing of the Jews in Latvia. He called forcefully for an end of the defense of Latvian war criminals in the emigration press.[118] The second noteworthy exception is Kārlis Kalniņš, who, under the pseudonym Charles Collins, published a mimeographed pamphlet, *Latvian-Jewish Relations,* in 1949.[119]

Writers of fiction have been more forthcoming about the Holocaust than have scholars and politicians. Valentīns Pelēcis, in his reminiscences *Mālenieša pasaule*

(The world of Maliena [1971]),[120] briefly relates how he witnessed the internment of the Jews of Alūksne and the killing of some Communists in his native *pagasts* (township) of Mālupe. Eduards Freimanis powerfully and directly confronts the killing of the Jews of Kuldīga in two of his novels, *Ticība* (The faith [1978]) and *Visādais Jēpis* (All kinds of clods [1990]).[121] In both of these novels the killing operations are described in detail. In *Ticība* the killer is the first-person narrator, and in *Visādais Jēpis* the killing operations are described by an omniscient narrator. The descriptions, especially in the second novel, are stark and make no compromises to national "honor" and related issues. A full account of the killing of the Jews in Krustpils is portrayed by Gunārs Janovskis in *Pilsēta pie upes* (City by the river).[122] Uldis Ģēr-manis, in his autobiographical novel about the German occupation, *Pakāpies Tornī* (Climb up in the tower [1989]), incorporates his friend Valdis Čoks, a member of the Arājs Kommando, into the story and provides some psychological insights about the Latvian participants in the killing units.[123] The Holocaust is also touched upon by Richards Rīdzenieks in *Zelta motociklets* (The golden motorcycle [1976])[124] and by Arnolds Apse in *Klostera kalnā* (On the cloister mountain [1964]).[125]

Dramatic works that have explored the Holocaust include Aivars Ruņģis's play *Salaspils,* a highly stylized piece that portrays Latvia's entrapment by its powerful neighbors.[126] It does not, however, highlight the Nazi atrocities committed in Latvia's most notorious concentration camp. Another play worthy of mention is *Pēdējā Laiva* (The last boat [1970]), by the Latvian master playwright Mārtiņš Zīverts, in which a Jewish woman is helped by two Latvians to escape across the Baltic Sea to Sweden.[127] The life of a literary person and her limited encounters with the SD during the Occupation are recorded by Zenta Mauriņa in *Dzelzs Aizbīdņi Lūst* (The iron bolts crack [1960]).[128]

Since the Holocaust the relations between Latvians and Jews in emigration have been poor; consequently the remembrance of the Holocaust in Latvia leaves much to be desired. There has been practically no meeting ground between the two peoples. Given the involvement of numerous Latvians in the atrocities, the relations between the Latvians and the Jews would have been difficult to repair under the best of circumstances. There is no reason to believe that the state of Latvia, had it been reestablished, would have differed in its attitude toward the Holocaust from the Western democracies of France, Belgium, and Scandinavia. It is true that the Latvian leadership in emigration has made no effort to answer the Latvian Jews' questions about the Holocaust. Yet the Soviet occupation of their country made it difficult, if not impossible, for Latvians to come to terms with the Holocaust, which even free societies have had problems doing. The Soviets had no interest in freely debating the Holocaust or in allowing access to their archives so that the facts could speak for themselves. By controlling the debate and the archives, the Soviets used the Holocaust to drive wedges between the Jews and the Latvians. The Latvians in emigration even today have not been able to free themselves from "debating" the agenda the Soviets set for them.

Jewish and Latvian relations began to assume a normal course of development with the emergence of *perestroika* and *glasnost*. This has continued in liberated Latvia. Today Jews are active in all social and political spheres. In addition to their participation in music, theater, and science, in which Jews have been active since 1945, they have also obtained the right to participate in politics. Today they serve in Latvia's parliament and government. Especially notable is the development of the Jewish Cultural Society of Latvia. No longer do the Jews need to send their children to Latvian or Russian schools as they had to do under the Soviets. The liberation of Latvia gave the Jews the opportunity to reclaim their old cultural center, which today houses part of the Jewish school and the archives of Latvian-Jewish history. The Jewish school in Riga has been open since 1989; it educates more than six hundred pupils a year, providing classes from kindergarten through high school. The rebirth of Jewish cultural life in liberated Latvia was noted by Mihails Levins, the secretary of the Latvia-Israel Friendship Society, at its founding session in 1989: "Certainly, the determining factor in the founding of our Society is the rebirth of the Latvian people. Without that our society could not be possible."[129]

On September 19, 1990, the Latvian government passed a resolution "On the impermissibility and condemnation of genocide and anti-Semitism in Latvia." A partial translation of the resolution, which was signed by Latvian president Anatolijis Gorbunovs and secretary I. Daudišs, follows.

> Since 1940, when the state of Latvia was liquidated, waves of genocide have rolled over the Republic. All peoples living in the Republic have been its victims, but especially the Jews.
>
> In the name of the Latvian people, the Supreme Council of the State announces that it condemns the genocide of the Jews unconditionally, and that more than eighty thousand Latvian Jews and no fewer than two hundred thousand Jews brought in from Europe, were killed, among them women and children.
>
> It must be noted with especially deep regret that among those who helped to carry out the terror started by the occupiers were citizens of Latvia. There is not, and cannot be, any justification, nor can there be statutes of limitation for the sanguinary genocide against the Jews as a crime against humanity.
>
> The Republic of Latvia assumes the responsibility for perpetuating the memory of the Jewish victims, as well as the safeguarding of the memory of those citizens who, risking their own lives, attempted to save the lives of fascism's victims.
>
> The Latvian people are following the national rebirth of the Jews in their historical homeland in Israel with satisfaction and congratulate the state of Israel for its attainments in culture, economy, and science. We hope that our erstwhile compatriots in Israel will maintain many-sided contacts with Latvia.
>
> The Jews are one of the oldest traditional minorities in Latvia. Over many centuries they have invested in Latvia's economy and enriched its culture, sciences, and medicine. The Jewish minority is recognized as a fully legal component of Latvia's Republic.
>
> The Supreme Council of Latvia's Republic invites all local and central state agencies, social organizations, and citizens to create favorable conditions for the rebirth of Jewish culture, education, sciences, religion, and the development of their cultural autonomy.
>
> The Supreme Council of Latvia declares that the state of Latvia will shun all expressions of anti-Semitism and national discrimination as being incompatible with the traditions of our nation.[130]

Since Latvia gained its independence in August 1992, the relationship between Latvians and Jews has been friendly, although not without suspicions. The development of Jewish culture, especially in education, in spite of Jewish emigration from Latvia to Israel, has continued. On November 29, 1992, a Holocaust memorial was opened on the site of the Gogol Street synagogue in Riga, which was burned on July 4, 1941. The memorial consists of a statue by Russian sculptor Ernst Neizvestny and an excavated wall of the synagogue's basement. Although there has been no overt anti-Semitism, Latvia's Jews, especially the Holocaust survivors, have viewed with apprehension the rebirth of a variety of prewar organizations with erstwhile fascist connections, such as the Aizsargi (Land Guard). The Holocaust has not been forgotten, and the wounds have not fully healed.

NOTES

1. For information about the earliest Jewish settlements in Latvia, see *Literatūra un Māksla*, a Latvian literary weekly, of November 25, 1988, which was devoted to the Jews of Latvia; and Mendel Bobe, "Four Hundred Years of the Jews in Latvia: A Historical Survey," in *The Jews in Latvia*, ed. Mendel Bobe et al. (Tel Aviv, 1971), 21–77. For an analysis of Jewish gravestones in Latvia, see Gedalje Moreins, "Ēbreju kapakmeņi Latvijā," *Māksla*, no. 6 (1988), 42–43.

2. Bobe, "Four Hundred Years," 21.

3. For the numbers of Jewish residents in Riga, I have mostly used the data from J. Rutkis, *Latvijas Ģeogrāfija* (Stockholm, 1960), 448–51; and M. Skujeneeks, *Latvija, zeme un eedzī votāji* (Riga, 1927), 307–11. See also Mendel Bobe, "Riga," in Bobe et al., *Jews in Latvia*, 243–61.

4. Abraham Godin, "Jewish Tradition and Religious Life in the Latvian Communities," in Bobe et al., *Jews in Latvia*, 217–29.

5. See the memorandum "The Jews of Latvia," Records of the U.S. Department of State, Washington, D.C., ca. 1942, film M1177, roll 17, frame 0340 ff., 1–26. This document contains very detailed sociological information about Latvian Jews, especially on the period between the world wars. A draft of this memorandum, which in some particulars differs from the copy in the Department of State, is in the YIVO Archives in New York, Baltic Countries, folder 1.17.

6. In Latvia there were no Jewish kehillah organizations. According to "The Jews of Latvia," however, "In Riga there was an institution known as the Jewish Kehillah, which registered births, marriages and deaths as an agent of the municipality, but this Kehillah was considered a private institution, not a public corporation" (2).

7. An exception is H. Biezais, *Saki tā kā tas ir* (Lansing, Mich., 1985), 59–60.

8. Jewish thinking about the Latvians must have been extensive after the development of the Jewish press during the early decades of this century.

9. Out of twelve volumes of Latvian folk songs, about 150 four-line stanzas mention Jews. In general, the Jew is treated as a stranger in the songs. But there are indications of more intimate social relationships. The celebration of nuptials with Jews is frequently encountered. If the folk songs are any indication, intermarriage with Jews was not an infrequent occurrence. Fear or hatred of the Jew is not expressed in the songs. The songs frequently feature caricatures of Jews, but they also portray Jews with positive attributes, such as charity.

10. There are numerous editions of Janševskis's works. *Dzimtene* was originally published in 1923–25, *Bandava* in 1928, and *Mežvidus ļaudis* in 1929–30.

11. K. Tolmans, ed., *The Jew in Latvian Literature* (Riga, 1938). See an article about this book in *Atbalss* (Riga), no. 3 (1985), 3. The exception is the story "Mūžīgais žīds," by Jānis Poruks.

12. Viktors Hausmanis, *Ādolfs Alunāns* (Riga, 1988), 63.

13. Andrievs Niedra, *Kad mēness dilst* (Riga, 1902).

14. Only now has Niedra been fully rehabilitated, and his works are being reprinted in Latvia.

15. Max Laserson, "The Jews and the Latvian Parliament, 1918–1934," in Bobe et al., *Jews in Latvia*, 119. Laserson, a liberal, emigrated to the United States after the Ulmanis insurrection and ended his career as a professor of law at Columbia University.

16. Frida Michelson, *I Survived Rumbuļi* (New York, 1979), 31. Michelson's story is the most ex-

treme on record, and inasmuch as she only heard it from her relatives, the part about murder and rapes may be exaggerated. A pogrom in Kurzeme perpetrated by Latvian officers of the Balodis Brīgade is noted in Marģers Vestermanis, "Cilvēcībai bija jāklusē," *Literatūra un Māksla,* November 25, 1988, 7. Vestermanis's account still needs to be substantiated by a second source.

17. A. Ezergailis, ed., *Ezergaiļa Grāmata* (Ithaca, N.Y., 1988), 226.

18. Edgars Andersons, "Trīs Bezvalsts Tautas Latvijā," *Treji Vārti,* no. 94 (1983), 11.

19. M. Laserson, "Jewish Minorities in the Baltic Countries," *Jewish Social Studies* 14, no. 3 (1941), 280, as cited in Charles Collins [Kārlis Kalniņš], *Latvian-Jewish Relations: The Tragic Plight of Latvians and Jews under Nazi Occupation of Latvia* (Esslingen, West Germany, 1949). Laserson was a member of the Central Land Distribution Committee, and consequently he speaks on the matter with authority. It must be noted, however, that only 2 percent of the Jews lived in the country.

20. Laserson, "Jewish Minorities," 276.

21. For a history of Jewish schools in the free state of Latvia, see Z. Michaeli, "Jewish Cultural Autonomy and the Jewish School System," in Bobe, *Jews,* 186–216. It must also be mentioned that the Jews were not mandated to attend Jewish schools. They could attend any school they wished. For many Riga and Liepāja Jews the preference was to attend German schools. Some specialty Latvian schools, such as the French lycée and the English Institute, were also in high demand among Jews.

22. Godin, "Jewish Tradition and Religious Life."

23. Laserson, "The Jews and the Latvian Parliament," 94–185.

24. The principle of cultural autonomy derived from the principle of political autonomy. For a discussion of this question, see Karl Aun, "The 1917 Revolution and the Idea of the State of Estonia," in *Die Baltishen Provinzen Ruslands Zwischen den Revolutionen von 1905 und 1917,* ed. A. Ezergailis and G. von Pistohlkors (Cologne, 1982), 287–94.

25. Andersons, "Trīs Bezvalsts Tautas," 12.

26. The Jewish contribution to Latvia's economic life is a matter of great pride to Latvia's Jews, and this effort was appreciated by Latvians except in anti-Semitic circles. Even Ulmanis is reputed to have been grateful to the Jews for their commercial astuteness.

27. See Bernard Press, *Judenmord in Lettland, 1941–1945* (Berlin, 1988), 23. The title on the title page reads *Judenmord in Riga.* Press's view represents a post-Holocaust assessment of the problem,

and from the democratic and egalitarian point of view he is correct about the unfairness of distribution of civil-service jobs. All nationalities, especially the Germans, were equally excluded from the positions. One may also note that there was a great deal of corruption in the distribution of civil-service jobs in Latvia. They were meted out by patronage, frequently through fraternities, and even Latvians themselves had a hard time obtaining a government job. To say that anti-Semitism did not influence government hiring practices would be wrong, yet to see these hiring practices as a high point of Latvian anti-Semitism is equally wrong. For a general assessment of the Jewish relationship with Latvia's government, see also "The Jews of Latvia": "There is little to be said about the attitudes of the Latvian government towards the Jews before the establishment of the authoritarian regime. The government scrupulously fulfilled its obligations as to maintaining the Jewish schools. No limitations were imposed upon the Jews in the political field, or for that matter, in the field of free business enterprise. There were limitations, to be sure, as to Jewish participation in officialdom and as to government orders to private business firms. Even more restricted was the admission of Jews to the Latvian University where rigorous entrance tests in the Latvian language were used to keep away a considerable portion of Jewish applicants. As to Jewish professors, only two were admitted to the faculty of the university during the whole time of Latvian independence" (24).

28. "The Jews of Latvia," 12.

29. Bobe, "Four Hundred Years," 72.

30. That Ulmanis's ban of the leftist parties prompted many leftists to embrace Communism is very powerfully demonstrated by Kārlis Siljakovs in *Mana atbilde,* 2 vols. (Lansing, Mich., 1982–85), 2:206.

31. "The Jews of Latvia," 3.

32. Ulmanis's foreign ministry fended off charges of anti-Semitism or any other kind of discrimination with the following argument: "The situation for Jews in Latvia is not worse than that of any other minority. The Jewish citizens enjoy equal rights with other citizens of Latvia, and their activities in no way are infringed upon, as long as they do not engage, as individuals or in organizations, in hostile acts against the state" (letter to Alfred Feldmanis, ca. 1934, box 6, Feldmanis Archive, Hoover Institution of War, Revolution, and Peace, Stanford University, Stanford, Calif.).

33. It is, however, true that the only thing that the anti-Semitic circles of Latvia liked about Ulmanis was the Latvianization of the economy,

which they understood as an infringement of Jewish influence in Latvia.

34. "Jews of Latvia," 18.

35. A history of the Saeima from the minority viewpoint has not yet been written. For information on the tensions between the Latvian majority and minorities in the Saeima, see Bobe, "Four Hundred Years," 62–71; and Adolfs Šilde, *Latvijas vēsture, 1914–1940* (Stockholm, 1976). See also Andersons, "Trīs Bezvalsts Tautas," 12.

36. Brief descriptions of the Nacionālais klubs and other nationalistic organizations and their contacts with European fascists can be found in Edgars Andersons, *Latvijas vēsture, 1920–1940: Ārpolītika,* 2 vols. (Stockholm, 1982–84), 1:395–432, esp. n. 1.

37. Laserson, "The Jews and the Latvian Parliament," 124–25.

38. The first abbreviated translation of *The Protocols of the Elders of Zion* was published in 1923; the second, also abbreviated, appeared in 1933; and the full edition came out in 1942, after first being published in the newspaper *Tēvija* in 1941.

39. See Šilde's discussion of Pērkoņkrusts in Šilde, *Latvijas vēsture,* 562–64. The circulation of Pērkoņkrusts's newspaper at times reached fifteen thousand, which was considered very high for a newspaper of an upstart party.

40. Pērkoņkrusts's publications of the early 1930s, *Ugunskrusts* and *Pērkoņkrusts,* are indispensable for understanding anti-Semitism in Latvia in particular. In the early 1930s the Latvian National Socialist Party, closely related to Hitler's Nazis, came into existence. In 1933 it had only eighty members (Šilde, *Latvijas vēsture,* 564). The background and history of Pērkoņkrusts, from the party's perspective, is well documented in Ādolfs Šilde, *Ardievas Rīgai* (New York, 1988), 68–122; and Haralds Biezais, "Gustavs Celmiņa Pērkoņkrusts dokumentu gaismā," *Treji Vārti,* nos. 127–28 (1989).

41. The Pērkoņkrusts member with the highest standing in the SD apparatus was Feliks Rikards, but his assignment was to keep a file on Latvians, not to participate in the killing of Jews.

42. Gustavs Celmiņš, *Eiropas krustceļos* (Esslingen, West Germany, 1947).

43. See "The Jews of Latvia." The last anti-Semitic pamphlets in independent Latvia were written, translated, and published in the early 1930s. For a review of anti-Semitic literature in Latvia, see ibid., 22–24. The sentence quoted in the text comes from the YIVO version of the document, Baltic Countries, folder 1.17, doc. 38-1a.

44. J. Dāvis, *Latvijas nostāja žīdu jautājumā,* Anti semītiskā literatūra, no. 10 (Riga, 1943), 7.

45. On the anecdotal level, during the 1930s a story was told about the Jew who could not be kept out of the university, regardless of the barriers the guardians of "high standards" might construct against him. If he failed once, this mythic Jew would tenaciously return for a second or third attempt to gain admittance. One mythic professor in the Latvian Language Department had a method of success in flunking a Jew that was foolproof. After the Jew had successfully navigated through all of the perils of morphology, syntax, and conjugations, the professor would snag the candidate on pronunciation by asking the Jew to pronounce the name of the literary character "Biezumbozums." This Cerberus of Latvian linguistic purity would triumph because supposedly no Jew could ever master the falling, rising, and inflecting intonations of the word.

46. See "The Jews of Latvia," 3, 25. The author of the memorandum attributes Ulmanis's generosity to the influence of Mordecai Dubin, the Aguda leader, with whom Ulmanis had a close relationship. According to this author, however, visas to Polish Jews were stopped in 1939. For the situation in Sweden at the same time, see Steven Koblik, *The Stones Cry Out* (New York, 1988).

47. See Press, *Judenmord in Lettland,* 33–35.

48. While the Jewish-Communist nexus probably existed in Latvia before the German occupation, finding it would require a deep search. Not even Dāvis, the publisher of anti-Semitic pamphlet literature, dwelled on the Jewish-Communist connection in the 1930s.

49. A. Levin, *Chortu cherez zubi* (Jerusalem, 1986), 5–6.

50. Dov Levin has perceived sporadic Latvian-Jewish confrontations in Riga and elsewhere in Latvia in June 1940. See "The Jews and the Sovietization of Latvia, 1940–41," *Soviet Jewish Affairs* 5, no. 1 (1975). He cites a variety of newspaper accounts and personal testimonials. The question needs to be investigated further. Aivars Stranga has been somewhat supportive of Levin's view. See Ilga Gore and Aivars Stranga, *Latvija: Neatkarības mijkrēslis. Okupācija, 1939–1940* (Riga, 1992), 157ff.

51. It has also been frequently said that in 1940 the Jews, fearing the Nazi occupation of Latvia, preferred the Russians as the lesser evil.

52. See Levin, "The Jews and the Sovietization of Latvia."

53. See Yehoshua Gilboa, *The Black Years of Soviet Jewry, 1939 to 1953* (Boston, 1973).

54. Estimates of the number of people taken to Siberia on June 14, 1941, are presently under revision. The most frequently mentioned number is fourteen thousand. But this number was determined

during the Nazi occupation, and it is known that the statisticians were prohibited from counting Jews. Thus, the true number of deported Latvian citizens may reach about nineteen thousand.

55. The paucity of proof for the reputed Jewish control of the Cheka in Latvia is especially evident from the Nazi-era publication *Baigais gads,* ed. Paulis Kovaļevskis (Riga, 1943), and from an English-language synopsis, *We Accuse the East, We Warn the West* (Germany, 1948).

56. The most authoritative work on the Bolshevik occupation is Alfrēds Ceichners's *Latvijas Boļševizācija, 1940–1941* (Lansing, Mich., 1986). It is noteworthy that this work, which was written in 1944, during the Nazi occupation, is almost completely free of anti-Semitic assertions.

57. For statistical estimates of the number of Jews during the last stages of the Holocaust I must thank Dr. Gertrude Schneider. See also her book *Journey into Terror: Story of the Riga Ghetto* (New York, 1979).

58. House Committee on Foreign Affairs, Subcommittee on Europe, *Soviet Jewry* (Washington, D.C., 1972), 135.

59. See Michelson, *Rumbuļi,* 225–32.

60. Jean-Paul Sartre, *Anti-Semite and Jew* (New York, 1965).

61. For books about Jewish life in the Soviet Union, see especially Nora Levin, *The Jews in the Soviet Union since 1917: Paradox of Survival,* 2 vols. (New York, 1988); Leonard Schroeter, *The Last Exodus* (New York, 1974); Alla Rusinek, *Like a Song, Like a Dream: A Soviet Girl's Quest for Freedom* (New York, 1973); William Korey, *The Soviet Cage* (New York, 1973); Yehoshua Gilboa, *A Language Silenced: The Suppression of Hebrew Literature and Culture in the Soviet Union* (New York, 1982); idem, *The Black Years;* Gregor Aronson et al., *Russian Jewry, 1917–1967* (New York, 1969); Mordechai Altshuler, *Soviet Jewry since the Second World War: Population and Social Structure* (New York, 1987).

62. David Garber, "Choir and Drama in Riga," *Soviet Jewish Affairs* 4, no. 1 (1974), 40.

63. Schroeter, *Last Exodus,* 61. See also, e.g., Levin, *The Jews in the Soviet Union since 1917,* 2:599–614; Rusinek, *Like a Song,* 251–56; Vladimir Lazaris, "The Saga of Jewish Samizdat," *Soviet Jewish Affairs* 9, no. 1 (1979); Garber, "Choir and Drama in Riga," 39–44; and Mordecai Lapid, "The Memorial at Rumbuli: A First Hand Account," *Jewish Frontier,* June 1971, 10–19.

64. It was the revisionist Zionism inspired by Vladimir Jabotinsky that the Jews of Latvia found attractive after the war. See Schroeter, *Last Exodus,* 62, 272.

65. Among the samizdat literature that was circulated were writings by Jabotinsky, the historian Simon Dubnov, and *Exodus* by Leon Uris. *Exodus* enjoyed a great popularity.

66. Lazaris, "The Saga of Jewish Samizdat," 7–8.

67. In the summer of 1989 I was permitted to investigate the archive of the special commission, which is located in the Latvian State Archives. I found the archive to be in good order, although the data in the files, from the grass-roots findings to the overall conclusions, were tainted with propaganda. The archive is organized by district and then by city and *pagasts* (township). The quality of the information is uneven, some districts' reports being very carefully prepared, others being slipshod and hastily compiled. The information is not always reliable; it is full of unsubstantiated figures, especially concerning the number of Nazi victims. But in most cases there is enough information to separate the wheat from the chaff. Most of the killing grounds have been charted, and the archive even contains lists of Jewish victims from some of the smaller towns.

68. The fate of the coverage of the Holocaust in Latvia to a high degree parallels the fate of Ilya Ehrenburg and Vasily Grossman's *Black Book.* During the war, while Stalin needed the help of the Jews, Ehrenburg and Grossman were encouraged to collect information about the Nazi killings of Jews, but once the war ended their effort was arrested. *The Black Book* that eventually was permitted to appear was only a shadow of the one planned. The manuscript was cut several times. A fuller version of the manuscript that was finally published in the Soviet Union was carried out to the West and published in 1981. For the history of *The Black Book,* see Joseph Kermish's introduction to the 1981 edition, published in New York.

69. One small exception in 1946 was the trial of General Friedrich Jeckeln and others in Riga. See "Tiesas prāva par vācu fašistisko iebrucēju ļaundarbībām Latvijā," *Cīņa,* January 29–February 5, 1946. For an overview of Holocaust coverage between 1940 and 1960, see *Latvijas PSR 1940–1960 Literatūras Rādītājs* (Riga, 1961).

70. The first article after 1945 to tell the Rumbula story briefly was I. Rodinov, "Rumbulas traģēdija," *Rīgas Balss* (Riga), November 30, 1959. The publication of this brief article was connected with numerous difficulties caused by the censors.

71. Michelson, *Rumbuļi.* The first break came only in 1988 with two articles about the Holocaust, one by Marģeris Vestermanis, "Cilvēcībai bija jāklusē," and the other by A. Ezergailis, "Arāja ko-

manda," *Zinātņu Akadēmijas Vēstis,* no. 10 (October 1988). The latter, with some changes, was republished in *Cīņa,* May–June 1989.

72. About the Jewish difficulties under the Soviets, see also Ruta Marjaša, "Ebreji Latvijā," *Atmoda,* February 20, 1990.

73. Nuremberg Trials doc. no. USSR-41, submitted to the Nuremberg war crimes trials, contains the Soviet summary of Nazi atrocities in Latvia.

74. The most broadly distributed pamphlet was *Daugavas vanagi?* The positive consequence of these pamphlets, though they were written in a propagandistic vein and contain much false information, was that a number of Western countries started investigations of war crimes. For my analysis of the Soviet KGB phase, see "War-Crimes Evidence from Soviet Latvia," *Nationalities Papers* 16 (1988), 209–24.

75. The problems with war crimes evidence from Soviet Latvia are discussed in Ezergailis, "War-Crimes Evidence from Soviet Latvia," and idem, "Latviešu kara noziedznieki Amērikas tiesās," *Izglītība,* August 1991.

76. On another level, the cooperation was a result of the KGB phase, because the cases prosecuted in the Western courts frequently concerned collaborators exposed in the pamphlets.

77. This new Soviet attitude was acknowledged already in 1989 by Samuel Norich, the director of YIVO: "Jewish societies now exist in two dozen cities of the Soviet Union and have received particular encouragement in Lithuania, Estonia and Latvia, and . . . all these developments had taken place in the last year and a half. . . . The first meeting of Soviet Jewish organizations was held in Rīga, Latvia, last May. Plans are being made for a conference and cultural festival in Vilnius next August to commemorate seven centuries of Jewish life in the city." See "Rejoining the Chapters of Yiddish Life's Story," *New York Times,* August 30, 1989, C15.

78. The stone was placed on the site of the Gogol Street synagogue on July 4, 1989. In 1992 a more elaborate memorial was opened on this site.

79. The heroism of Žanis Lipke, who died in 1986, has been noted in a variety of ways: a tree was planted in his name in the park of the righteous gentiles in Jerusalem, a monument was unveiled on his gravesite in May 1989, and there are plans to convert Lipke's house into a museum. The fullest account of Lipke's deeds is found in David Silberman, "Jan Lipke: An Unusual Man," in *Muted Voices: Jewish Survivors of Latvia Remembered,* ed. Gertrude Schneider (New York, 1987), 87. The essay

has also been published in Latvian in *Apskats,* nos. 1 and 2 (1989).

80. *Literatūra un Māksla,* October 28, 1989, 3. The establishment of the Latvia-Israel Friendship Society had a diplomatic dimension, for it was the first direct contact between Israel and the Soviet Union. The amicable relationship between the Jews and Latvians today has not slowed the emigration of Latvian Jews to Israel. Although the activities of Pamyat' in Latvia are not much in evidence, the specter of anti-Semitism that the organization has raised has prompted many, especially the young, to leave Latvia for Israel. This question is discussed by Ruta Marjaša, "Ebreji Latvijā." See also *Horozonts,* no. 12 (1989).

81. Lapid, "Memorial at Rumbuli," gives the most detailed description of the Rumbula episode. Schroeter, in *Last Exodus,* bases his version on an interview with Leah Bliner, a Riga Zionist activist.

82. Lapid, "Memorial at Rumbuli," 10–19.

83. Schroeter, *Last Exodus,* 69; Lapid, "Memorial at Rumbuli," 16.

84. Latvijas PSR Ministru Padomes Arhīvu pārvalde, *Mēs apsūdzam* (Riga, 1965). Actually the documents in this volume were selected by Marģeris Vestermanis. Among the Holocaust books, one can also include Vestermanis's *Tā rīkojās vērmahts* (Riga, 1973). Even this volume was abbreviated and changed by the KGB watchdogs and did not come out as intended (Vestermanis, interview by Ezergailis, June 1989, Riga).

85. K. Sausnītis, ed., *Salaspils Nāves Nometnē* (Riga, 1973).

86. *Tiesas prāva: Par vācu-Fašistisko Iebrucēju Laundarbiem Latvijas, Lietuvas un Igaunijas PSR Teritorijā* (Riga, 1946).

87. Vilis Samsons, *Kurzemes partizāņi* (Riga, 1959); idem, *Kurzemes Meži Šalc* (Riga, 1974). *Kurzemes Katlā* (1969) is an earlier version of *Kurzemes Meži Šalc.* Among his other works the more significant are *Partizāņu Kustība Ziemeļlatvijā Lielajā Tēvijas Karā* (Riga, 1950), *Deviņpadsmitais—Sarkano Partizāņu Gads* (Riga, 1970), and *Cauri Puteņiem* (Riga, 1983).

88. Works in which the Nazi atrocities are touched upon are Latvijas PSR Zinātnu Akadēmija, Vēstures Institūts, *Latviešu Tautas Cīņa Lielā Tēvijas Karā (1941–1945)* (Riga, 1966); Latvijas KP CK Partijas Vēstures Institūts, *Reiz Cēlās Strēlnieks Sarkanais,* vol. 2 (Riga, 1971); J. Dzintars, *Neredzamā Fronte* (Riga, 1970); and Alfrēds Raškevics and Olga Spoģe, *Avangardā Komunisti* (Riga, 1978).

89. These references can be found in the works of Regina Ezera and many others.

90. Ojārs Vācietis, "Rumbula," *Elpa* (Riga), 1966, also reprinted in *Kopoti raksti* (Riga) 1 (1988), 394–95; the translation is mine.

91. Lapid, "Memorial at Rumbuli," 10–19.

92. The Association of Latvian and Estonian Jews in Israel maintains a museum and has published a noteworthy book on the history of Latvian Jews, *The Jews in Latvia* (see above, n. 1). The Jewish Survivors of Latvia publishes a newsletter titled *The Latvian Jewish Courier*. The Society of Survivors from the Riga Ghetto has collected and maintained large documentary archives devoted to the Riga ghetto. See Henry R. Huttenbach, comp., *Introduction and Guide to the Riga Ghetto Archives Catalogue* (New York, 1984).

93. Max Kaufmann, *Die Vernichtung der Juden Lettlands* (Munich, 1947).

94. Michelson, *Rumbuḷi.* Her story is also recorded in Ehrenburg and Grossman, *The Black Book.*

95. Schneider, *Muted Voices;* idem, *The Unfinished Road: Jewish Survivors of Latvia Look Back* (New York, 1991).

96. Press, *Judenmord in Lettland.*

97. Josef Katz, *One Who Came Back* (New York, 1973).

98. Betty Happ, *Bortom All Mänsjklighet* (Stockholm, 1945). This book, written under a pseudonym, tells, among other things, about the author's sexual relationship with the commander of the camp Krause. Jeanette Wolff, *Sadismus oder Wahnsinn* (Dresden, 1946), republished as *Mit Bibel und Bebel* (Bonn, 1981). Levin, *Chortu Cherez Zubi.* Isaac Levinson, *The Untold Story* (Johannesburg, 1959).

99. Schneider, *Journey into Terror.*

100. Dov Levin: *Im hagav at Hakir* (Jerusalem, 1978); *Pinkas Hakehillot* (Jerusalem, 1988); "Jews and the Sovietization of Latvia"; "Arrest and Deportation of Latvian Jews by the USSR during the Second World War," *Nationalities Papers* 16, no. 1 (1988).

101. Bobe et al., *Jews in Latvia.*

102. The fullest discussion of this problem is to be found in ibid. For the Latvian point of view, see Andersons, "Trīs Bezvalsts Tautas," 9–16. See also J. Lejiņš, *Latvian-Jewish Relations* (Toronto, 1975).

103. Many authors who have been critical of the happenings in Nazi-occupied Latvia have had to self-publish or publish with small-circulation presses. Among the authors who found little or no possibility of publishing in the emigration press, one can mention Miķelis Valters, Ādolfs Blāķis, and Žanis Unāms. During the very early years of emigration, perhaps only *Jaunais Vārds,* published in Stockholm from 1944 to 1952 and edited by Dagnija Šleiers,

was in the full sense a democratic centrist newspaper.

104. Žanis Unāms has written a whole series of treatises and articles critical of Latvian leadership during the German occupation. The most important of them are *Melnā vara* (1955) and *Zem Barbarosa Šķēpa* (Lansing, Mich., 1975).

105. Oskars Dankers, the chairman of the Council of Self-Administration during the Occupation, wrote two books highly defensive of his position under the Nazis that reveal less than they conceal: *Lai vēsture spriež tiesu* (Toronto, 1965) and *No Atminu pūra* (Toronto, 1973), a collection of articles that includes a number of Dankers's speeches. His wife, Irma Dankers, in her hefty memoir, *Daudz Tu man Soliji . . .* (Lansing, Mich., 1982), chooses to write about the happier days of her family's life, before and after the war, reducing the coverage of the war years to about half of a page.

106. Ādolfs Blāķis, *Medaḷas otrā puse* (Buenos Aires, 1956).

107. Alfrēds Valdmanis, another collaborator, has not actually written his memoirs, but it is thought by many who knew Valdmanis that Boris Zengals's *Dienās Baltās Nebaltās* (Geneva, 1949), a boastful little book, is in effect a Valdmanis memoir. Some insight about Valdmanis's career can also be gleaned from his letters to Edgars Andersons in "Atmiņās kavējoties," *Treji Vārti,* nos. 95–98 (1983).

108. Gustavs Celmiņš's memoir, *Eiropas krustceḷos,* deals almost exclusively with his experiences in German concentration camps.

109. Arnolds Aizsilnieks, *Latvijas Saimniecības vēsture, 1914–1968* (Stockholm, 1968). Aizsilnieks is also informative about Ulmanis's economic policies regarding Jewish business establishments.

110. Arturs Silgailis, *Latviešu Legions* (Copenhagen, 1962). An abbreviated version of this work has also been published in English as *Latvian Legion* (San Jose, 1986).

111. Osvalds Freivalds et al., eds., *Latviešu karavīrs Otrā Pasaules kara laikā,* 8 vols. (Toronto, 1970–82).

112. Vilis Hāzners, *Varmācības Torņi,* vol. 1 (Lincoln, Nebr., 1977). Hāzners was accused by the U.S. Justice Department of participating in the killing of Jews in 1941, a charge of which he was acquitted. Since the acquittal he has put together a volume of court documents and published it as the second volume of *Varmācības Torņi* (1985).

113. Siljakovs, *Mana atbilde.*

114. Kārlis Kundziņš, *Laiki un Likteņi* (Minneapolis, 1955).

115. Arvīds Dravenieks, *Es atceros: Latvijas skolas un skolotāji* (New York, 1970).

116. Haralds Biezais, *Latvija kāšu krusta varā* (Lansing, Mich., 1992). See also idem, "Pateicība Hitleram," *Treji Vārti,* no. 95 (1984), 8–9; and idem, "Nacionālie Partizāņi," *Kara Invalīds,* no. 29 (1984), 12–22.

117. See also A. Ezergailis, "Latvia," in *Encyclopaedia of the Holocaust,* ed. Israel Gutman, 4 vols. (Jerusalem, 1990); idem, "War-Crimes Evidence from Soviet Latvia" and "Anti-Semitism and the Killing of the Jews of Latvia," in *Anti-Semitism in Times of Crisis,* ed. Sander Gilman and Steven Katz (New York, 1991).

118. Bruno Kalniņš, "Latvieši un žīdi," *Brīvība* (Stockholm), no. 7 (1960), 1.

119. Collins, *Latvian-Jewish Relations.* See also Frank Gordon, *Latvians and Jews between Germany and Russia* (Stockholm, 1990).

120. Valentīns Pelēcis, *Malēnieša pasaule,* vol. 3 (Minneapolis, 1971), 147–57.

121. Eduards Freimanis, *Ticība* (Lincoln, Nebr., 1978); idem, *Visādais Jēpis* (Toronto, 1990).

122. Gunārs Janovskis, *Pilsēta pie upes,* serialized in the newspaper *Laiks* (Brooklyn), 1990–91.

123. Uldis Ģērmanis, *Pakāpies Tornī* (New York, 1989).

124. Richards Rīdzenieks, *Zelta motociklets* (New York, 1976).

125. Arnolds Apse, *Klostera kalnā* (Stockholm, 1964).

126. See Aivars Runģis, "Salaspils," in Runģis et al., *Trīs Lugas* (Ann Arbor, Mich., 1980).

127. Mārtiņš Zīverts, *Pēdējā Laiva* (Sydney, 1970).

128. Zenta Mauriņa, *Dzelzs Aizbīdņi Lūst* (Toronto, 1960).

129. Mihails Levins, quoted in *Literatūra un Māksla,* October 28, 1989, 3.

130. Press release, Supreme Council of Latvia, September 19, 1990. The number of Jewish victims mentioned in the resolution was picked up from Soviet propaganda. The number of Latvian Jews killed during the Occupation was closer to seventy thousand than to eighty thousand, and the number of those brought in from Europe was closer to twenty thousand than to two hundred thousand.

THE AXIS POWERS

WEST GERMANY
Andrei S. Markovits
Beth Simone Noveck

One of the most curious characteristics of contemporary German-Jewish relations is their surprising surface "normalcy." Nonetheless, despite the absence of large numbers of Jews in Germany today, anti-Semitic incidents have persisted since the Holocaust. Indeed, the 1990s witnessed an increase in these troublesome episodes throughout the Federal Republic. In spite of the apparent success of the postwar economic miracle in West Germany and democracy's unquestionable durability in the Federal Republic of the postwar period, there is no denying that culturally and psychologically, indeed legally, the Bundesrepublik is the successor state of the Third Reich. Hence, whether one views the Nazi period as an inexplicable anomaly or as the logical culmination of Germany's historical development, there can be no analysis of modern German politics without reference to the Holocaust.

BEFORE THE HOLOCAUST

The precarious relationship between Jews and Germans has a long history. Despite centuries of Jewish settlement and cultural participation in Germany, anti-Semitism has been an ever-present specter. Only periodically symbiotic, the German-Jewish relationship was marred by violence perpetrated against the Jews in the Middle Ages. Clearly, modern anti-Semitism in Germany, as elsewhere, has had its own particular causes. Emancipation did not free German Jews from historical stereotypes that falsely accused them of blood libels and host defilement and branded them as magical and usurious outsiders. Modern anti-Semitism has been fueled by this "conception of the Jew which has nothing to do with facts or logic," but is rooted in a long tradition of hatred and persecution.[1] The horror of the Holocaust had its foundation in the earliest history of the German-Jewish experience.

The first evidence of Jewish settlements in Germany dates to the time of Emperor Constantine, in the fourth century, when merchant families followed the trade routes of the Rhine and established themselves in Cologne, Trier, Mainz, Worms, and Speyer.[2] During the Middle Ages, as a result of both persecution and financial opportunity, the Jews migrated north- and eastward. They not only became successful members of the growing urban populations but also brought the scholarly and spiritual culture of their ancestors with them, erecting yeshivot, centers of learning, that rivaled those in Jerusalem in their level of piety and academic achievement.[3] It was in these communities that the study of the Bible and the Talmud flourished during the early Middle Ages. The legendary Bible and Talmud commentator Rashi, for example, left his native Troyes to study in both Mainz and Worms.

But the Jews' privileged status was short-lived, for the First and Second Crusades (in 1096 and 1146) visited upon them widespread massacres and forced conversions. During these early years, wherever their persecutors had left a remnant, the local Jews formed cohesive and self-sustaining religious communities, their suffering even fostering cultural development. In the course of the thirteenth, fourteenth, and fifteenth centuries anti-Semitism ran rampant. In the late 1300s all the Jews in Erfurt were systematically killed. Every Jew in Mainz who had not converted to Christianity was burned at the stake, his property repossessed by church or town.[4] Even where royal or papal decree forbade it, defiant crowds, driven mad by the ravages of the plague, fanaticism, and superstition, slaughtered entire communities of Jews. Fifteen Jews in Germany during the fourteenth century and ten in the fifteenth were accused of blood libels and executed, higher numbers than for any other European country.[5] Only with the devastation of the Thirty Years' War, in the seventeenth century, did the Jews receive a reprieve, the persecution of the Jews receding temporarily during the conflict between Catholics and Protestants.

The medieval German came to conceive of the Jew as an embodiment of evil. The extra-civilian status of Jews, who were only accorded partial civil rights, made them outsiders in a close-knit gentile social order. The "differentness" of the Jews seemed markedly antithetical to German communal culture. And the church played a major role in constructing an image of the Jew as "Christ-killer" and demon. This conception of the Jew as the "other" was indelibly carved into the collective consciousness of most gentiles through the perpetuation of such myths and the regular occurrence of massacres. The usurious rates of interest that local lords had compelled Jewish moneylenders to charge—in excess of 170 percent at times—also fueled popular resentment. Perhaps the most significant factor in the early development of anti-Semitism in Germany was the precarious relationship that developed between the crown, nobles, and Jews.

The Holy Roman Emperors and later the German kings had invited Jews to settle in proscribed areas in order to promote commerce and trade. This rendered them wards of the crown and thus objects of contempt and scorn from local lords and nobility, who resented the power of the central monarch. The political and economic rights of the Jews became, in fact, closely tied to the relative power of the king.[6] Until the late nineteenth century, the loose confederation of German states constantly vied for territory and power with the central authority. In this struggle

Jews became the pawns between the powerful nobles and the weak emperor. This instability of the Jews' position in German society has probably furnished the most salient and lasting historical legacy of early Jewish history in Germany.

The Age of Enlightenment: The Road to Emancipation

In the eighteenth century, when the danger of the persecutions of the Middle Ages had subsided, Jewish life began to flourish once again in Germany. The spread of the ideals of tolerance from the French Enlightenment to humanist intellectuals such as Immanuel Kant and Gotthold Ephraim Lessing in Germany in the 1780s marked the starting point of the movement for Jewish emancipation. Political equality, however, was not readily achieved by the Jews. It was more than eighty years before they attained emancipation and some semblance of formal equality. Even when this was accomplished, in 1869, far later than for their coreligionists in France or England, all but the wealthiest German Jews continued to live under extremely difficult social and economic conditions.[7]

While some leaders of the Enlightenment, such as Voltaire and Diderot, were hostile to Jews, there were several advocates of Jewish emancipation during the last decades of the eighteenth century. Christian Wilhelm Dohm, the Prussian councilor, wrote a plea in 1781, at the request of Moses Mendelssohn, the great Jewish humanist, urging that civic rights be granted to the Jews. In 1787 Count de Mirabeau, an admirer of Mendelssohn, published a tract entitled *Moses Mendelssohn and the Political Reform of the Jews* (1787), in which he showed the absurdity of the prevalent anti-Semitism. Moreover, he suggested that the most appropriate way to make Jews "better men and useful citizens" was to "banish every humiliating distinction, and open to them every avenue of gaining a livelihood." Mirabeau's views were supported by the liberal cleric Abbé Henri Grégoire, who in his essay *On the Physical, Moral and Political Regeneration of the Jews* blamed Christian society for whatever faults the Jews may have. "In their place would we not be worse?" asked Grégoire.[8]

The Enlightenment's regard for the individual and contempt for religion not only increased tolerance on the part of the Germans but also encouraged the Jews to prefer the newly acquired liberal and secular German *Weltanschauung* to the traditional ways cultivated by centuries of isolation. Moses Mendelssohn epitomized this readiness of the Jews to absorb the riches of German culture, language, literature, and philosophy, from which they had been excluded. Jewish emancipation moved with the general tide of human freedom, dignity, and natural law promulgated by the Enlightenment and the French Revolution.

In 1782 the Habsburg Emperor Joseph II issued his Edict of Tolerance. His interest in "philosophical morality" and the values of the Enlightenment extended to his treatment of the Jews.[9] The edict opened a narrow window of educational opportunity for the Jews, yet it was so hedged by conditions that it had few practical implications for genuine improvements in the daily lives of German Jews. In Frankfurt, for example, the laws of 1616 still prevailed, forbidding Jews to walk on the avenues and promenades.

In the course of the Napoleonic wars, measures for the emancipation of the Jews were finally taken in several German states. Napoleon appointed his brother Jerome king of Westphalia, and the latter granted Jews complete equality, including the right to hold office and enter the professions (1808). Equality was also given to the Jews in the Grand Duchy of Frankfurt. The Jews had to buy this basic right from the city's financially desperate archduke for twenty times the normal annual tax. In 1811 the Jews of Hamburg received citizenship and the Jews of Bremen were granted residence status, and in the Domain of Mecklenburg they were even allowed to marry gentiles.[10]

In Prussia anti-Semitism persisted. However, following the decisive defeats at the hands of the Napoleonic armies, Prussia modernized its political system, a process that included, in 1812, granting the Jews full citizenship. Among other improvements, Jews no longer had to pay special taxes; nor were they required to live in specially designated slum areas. However, they still were not allowed to hold public office.

The downfall of Napoleon in 1814 represented a considerable setback for the Jews: many of the rights granted them during the Napoleonic period were withdrawn. Even though Prince Karl August von Hardenberg and Baron Wilhelm von Humboldt, leaders in Prussia's political and social modernization, made every effort at the Congress of Vienna to retain Jewish rights, they encountered strenuous opposition by the other states that made up the German Confederation. A compromise clause proposed that "the rights already granted [to the Jews] 'in' the confederated states were to remain in force." One shrewd delegate, however, replaced the word "in" with "by," thus revoking the rights granted the Jews "by" all those states that had been forced to do so under French occupation. In Prussia, where these rights had been offered under the aegis of Prussian sovereignty proper, the conservative *Zeitgeist* mirrored the attitudes of the other German states. There too, many of the rights offered the Jews by the Edict of 1812 were severely proscribed. These infringements on Jewish rights were frequently accompanied by medieval-style anti-Jewish riots. Particularly heinous were the so-called Hep-Hep pogroms in 1819, named for a rallying call made popular by the growing student movement.

Unsuccessful in achieving political unity, the Germans after 1806 turned inward and backward to their conservative past, opposing the concepts of progress and Enlightenment and adopting a *völkisch* notion of the state. During the first quarter of the century, when the German national ethos was being formulated, philosophers and poets like Johann Gottlieb Fichte, Ernst Moritz Arndt, Johann Gottfried Herder, and the historian Christian Friedrich Ruhs developed the *völkisch* idea of nationalism. According to this concept, Germans were more than a people linked by political arrangements, common traditions, and cultural heritage: they were united foremost by a transcendental essence that was the source of their creativity and individuality. According to this theory, German unity was to serve as a way of preserving the *Volk* and its natural qualities. In the German nation the Jews would by definition remain, as they had been in the Middle Ages, outsiders without the rights of citizenship. The *völkisch* concept of the state defined Jews de facto as the "other."

The Jews, anxious to be accepted as equals, were embittered by the retrogression. Many emigrated to the United States, and others sought in baptism the passport to personal advancement. In fact, between 1812 and 1845, 3,370 conversions occurred, among them that of the renowned poet Heinrich Heine.[11] The equality of Jews in German society was further hindered by the persistence of deep-rooted popular prejudices against them. Even the friends of the Jews were divided into two camps: those who demanded assimilation as a precondition to emancipation and those who envisioned emancipation as the best route to assimilation.

Although their struggle for rights was stalled, Jews, along with the rest of the middle class, did not cease to make economic progress within Germany. With the growth of cities in the modern era of manufacturing and protoindustry at the end of the nineteenth century, most German Jews and their newly arrived Eastern European compatriots flocked to the larger cities—Frankfurt, Berlin, Leipzig, and Hamburg. In the previous century small Jewish communities had dotted the countryside; now Jewish bankers, merchants, and businessmen formed a prosperous, state-protected arm of the growing urban middle class. Their economic success led them from isolation toward a semblance of absorption in the economy. This limited toleration, of course, did not mean that they were accepted by Germany's general population.

From Emancipation to Assimilation, 1869–1914

On July 3, 1869, the Reichstag of the North German Confederation at last confirmed equality for Jews in the northern states of Germany. National unification in 1871 expanded this emancipation to all Jews in Germany. Jews were given full citizenship, including all civil and political rights accorded to non-Jews, but not the right to hold public office. Moreover, for all practical purposes Jews were still excluded from the highest officer corps and from university professorships.[12]

Jews ardently applied themselves to those areas where they were allowed. They became important patrons of the arts. With great rapidity, successful Jews adapted themselves to the world of German high culture. They adopted the refinements, manners, tastes, and conventions of the Mandarin German elite, whose world they soon regarded as their own.[13] Thus began the metamorphosis of Jews in Germany into German Jews. The 1876 Prussian Austrittsgesetz, or Law of Withdrawal, allowed the Jews to withdraw from their religious community without undergoing conversion, facilitating what they had hoped would lead to painless assimilation.

The process of Germanization begun by the Jews, however, represented more than assimilation. It led to an inadvertent self-destruction through an obsessive preoccupation with conformity. Even in purely quantitative terms the number of Jews in Germany—512,158, or 1.25 percent of the population at its apex in 1871—diminished. Conversion, mixed marriage, assimilation, emigration, and the low birth rates all led to a considerable decrease in the percentage of Jews in the general population, a trend mitigated only by the influx of thousands of Eastern European Jews during the nineteenth century.[14] The Germanness of Jewish cultural life in the late nineteenth century was not simply an attempt to hide Jewishness; it was the result of a resolute pride in the tradition of German arts and letters.[15] Most German Jews felt proud to be German, to be members of a culture they genuinely perceived to be superior to any other.

Jews filled the theaters and opera houses, not only because they loved the arts but also because sitting among gentiles in an audience gave the Jews a sense of integration and acceptance.[16] Their participation helped shape German culture. As Frederic Grunfeld commented:

> For well over a half a century the confluence of these two intellectual traditions, the German and the Jewish, produced such an outpouring of literature, music and ideas that had it not been for its infamous finale, the cultural historians would now be writing of it as a golden age second only to the Italian Renaissance. It was a time of great poets and painters, of composers, philosophers, scholars, critics: of Expressionism, Dadaism and a new sense of compassion in the arts.[17]

Ironically, their presence among the cultural elite also set the Jews apart from the rest of society, isolating them in the upper middle class. Their conspicuous position was further exacerbated by the fact that those who intermarried tended to depart from Jewry, leaving those who remained faithful to it ever more distinct.[18] Thus it was during the late nineteenth and early twentieth centuries that Jews became sufficiently emancipated to be objects of envy while remaining sufficiently insecure to succumb to the growing wave of anti-Semitism and *völkisch* racism.

Those who stayed within the fold created an extensive array of Jewish institutions, both religious and social organizations. It was in nineteenth-century Germany that neo-Orthodoxy, following Samson Raphael Hirsch, and the Reform movement, under the leadership of Abraham Geiger, emerged. Zionist politics, especially after the death of Theodor Herzl, moved its center from Vienna to Germany. Newspapers, synagogues, cultural societies, and houses of study arose, populating the cities with the ziggurats of European Jewish renaissance. The Jews' political integration allowed even the religiously active Jews to mold their Jewishness in the image of the larger German culture.[19] Jewish scholarship was "Germanified" and paralleled trends in theme and style that developed in German secular *Wissenschaft.* Not surprisingly, Heinrich Graetz modeled his monumental six-volume *History of the Jews* after the seminal works of Otto Rank and Jakob Burckhardt.[20]

The peculiarity of Jewish emancipation in Germany was that the Jews were given not so much the freedom to be Jews as the freedom to be Germans. Jews could at long last participate in German life and culture as long as they left their cultural baggage—their Jewishness—behind. This phenomenon represented a conception of individual, not collective, freedom that was typical of the Enlightenment. Jews could be citizens as individual Germans but not as collective Jews. Such discrete integration was desired by all but a small minority of German Jews who, after centuries of persecution, desperately wanted their social status to mirror their economic success. Understandably, Jews yearned for acceptance. As Ismar Schorsch so clearly described it, the German Jew "had not failed to grasp the message that his admission into society demanded the suppression of every external trace of Jewishness. To fight anti-Semitism at the end of the century inevitably required a public affirmation of Jewish identity. But such a display of Jewishness was precisely what the extended battle for equal rights had conditioned Jews to fear and loathe."[21]

However, the Jews' desire to assimilate into German culture and to use this process of *Eindeutschung* (Germanization) to become bona fide Germans was not reciprocated by German society. The Germans continued to resent and despise the separateness and alleged racial difference of Jews. Since Jews were disproportionately grouped into the two extremes of the German social order, overrepresented both at the top by virtue of their economic success, which made them members of the upper middle class, and at the bottom by the immigrants from Europe's impoverished East (the so-called *Ostjuden*), their cultural behavior and very existence remained distinct.[22] Hence, whereas the Jews successfully assimilated German culture into their own lives, they in turn were never assimilated into German society.[23] To the contrary: the secularization and partial integration of the Jews in nineteenth-century Germany was explicitly countered by a secularization of the religious anti-Semitism of the Middle Ages and the rise of a new and insidious variant of politically motivated hatred of the Jews, known as political, or "modern," anti-Semitism.

The Rise of Political Anti-Semitism, 1914–1933

The spread of this new form of anti-Semitism, based on political as well as racial prejudice, ironically paralleled the long-awaited full integration of the Jew into German political and social life after 1870. These centrifugal tendencies in greater German society in turn were mirrored within the Jewish community itself via internal divisions between eastern and western, Zionist and anti-Zionist Jews.[24]

Political anti-Semitism was not restricted to the far Right or to the extreme Left of the political spectrum. Instead it had its origins in Germany's rapid industrialization and the evolution of its party politics in the late nineteenth century. The decline of liberalism in an increasingly conservative political climate accentuated the Jews' precarious position and marginalized them further.[25] Although not all Jews were liberals, they were collectively influenced by liberal thought, for it was liberalism, in Germany and elsewhere in Europe, that had brought them emancipation.

The German chancellor Otto von Bismarck, who had forged German unification in 1871, epitomized the conservatism of much of the Prussian aristocracy, which feared the growth of the working class and resented the liberal ideals of the Enlightenment. Bismarck's politics of social fragmentation, which were meant to weaken Germany's Catholics and coerce the working class into submission, also had adverse effects on the Jews. Coupled with rising anti-Semitism as a consequence of the economic crash of 1873, political anti-Semitism developed into a mainstay of German reactionary politics and culture when it found its way into respectable circles of bourgeois society.

Parallel to the anti-industrial sentiments of Germany's conservative politicians was the popularity among intellectuals and the bourgeoisie of Romanticism in reaction to the classical humanism of the late eighteenth century. German unification had been accompanied by a glorification of German nationalism and pan-Germanism, an idealization of the *Volk* and an extolling of the idyll of an allegedly disappearing natural landscape. This romanticization of Germany's unspoiled past was accompanied by the rhetoric of fanatical anti-Semitism, much of it imported from neighboring Austria, where, because of multinational tensions within the Habsburg monarchy, it attained a particular virulence with a decidedly racist tinge.

The continued social mobility and economic advancement enjoyed by many Jews created further tension in an already hostile environment.[26] In spite of the Jews' legal freedom and formal equality, the price for complete social acceptance was still assimilation. They thus continued to shed the external trappings of their ethnic heritage. Nonetheless, the paradoxical and ultimately tragic situation emerged in which the more the Jews sought assimilation, the more they met with ostracism. Individually, some Jews were "rewarded" for their endeavors by becoming fully accepted Germans. The high rate of intermarriage between Jews and gentiles (64 Jews out of 100 took non-Jewish spouses) also lends credence to their manifest integration into German society. Collectively, however, the gulf between Germans and Jews increased at a steady, irreversible pace. Nothing stopped this development, not even intra-Jewish discrimination in which German Jews asserted their Germanness by looking down on their coreligionists from Russia, Romania, Poland, and Hungary.

Attracted by the economic prosperity and relative safety of Germany compared with the situation in their massacre-ridden homelands, the *Ostjuden*, particularly after the pogroms of 1891, arrived in Germany by the thousands every year. Of the 567,884 Jews in Germany in 1890 (1.15 percent of the German population), 22,000 were foreign. By 1915 the percentage of Jews in the population had dropped to 0.9 percent (or 564,379), among whom almost 20 percent were foreign Jews.[27] Of course, Jews were still only a minority within the massive wave of immigration moving across Europe en route to America. Germany could not regulate this human onslaught, particularly of such "undesirables" as Eastern European Jews, at its borders. It was feared that these newcomers would place an unnecessary strain on the German economy. This general aversion to the newcomers by the indigenous population manifested itself in a particular disdain for their outward appearance. German anti-Semites were not the only ones to find the dress and demeanor of the *Ostjuden* "unappetizing"; German Jews did too.

By the early twentieth century anti-Semitism had experienced a transformation. While, on the one hand, the explicitly anti-Semitic one-issue parties of the latter part of the nineteenth century had disappeared, on the other hand, anti-Semitism had attained a greater degree of normalcy in all aspects of German life. Hardly any of the German political parties, including both parties of the Left, the German Social Democratic Party (SPD), and, after 1918, the German Communist Party (KPD), as well as numerous new parties proliferating in the instability of Weimar, remained free of at least some kind of anti-Semitism. Even the German Democratic Party (DDP), once a defender of the Jews against reactionary and nationalist intolerance, had distanced itself from Jewish causes in its self-destructive conversion to German nationalist sentiment. By the end of the Weimar Republic, Jews qua Jews had lost all advocates among Germany's parties and interest groups.[28]

Oddly enough, this insidious disenfranchisement of Jewish advocates paralleled a certain spiritual and religious rejuvenation in Jewish communal life. The Reform movement flourished, attracting the largest segment of Jewish membership. Among practicing Jews, the social aspect of Jewish life diversified and prospered. The Centralwohlfahrtsstelle, or Central Welfare Agency, and other social welfare organizations ran hospitals, nursing homes, schools, and libraries. Jewish academic societies, Zionist and youth fraternities, and religious groups such as B'nai B'rith prospered. All-purpose organizations such as the Centralverein deutscher Staatsbürger jüdischen Glaubens (Central Association of German Citizens of Jewish Faith), which published its own newspaper, boasted a membership of many thousands. Other periodicals of Jewish content, among them Martin Buber's *Der Jude,* also appeared in wide circulation.

In terms of their class composition, German Jews remained overrepresented in the middle class, particularly in the trading and commercial sector.[29] They were almost exclusively urban, concentrated in Germany's major cities, such as Berlin and Frankfurt. They were vastly overrepresented in the country's so-called free professions, consisting mainly of lawyers, doctors, journalists, and academics. Jews were especially prominent among the latter, furnishing, for example, eleven of forty German Nobel prize winners before 1933.[30] German Jews prospered economically at the turn of the century and suffered considerably during World War I and the economic vagaries of the Weimar Republic. Contrary to the anti-Semitic propaganda of the time, which depicted Jews as beneficiaries and profiteers from the war and its aftermath, Jews were no different from the rest of German society: the rich upper echelons had profited at the expense of the vast majority of middle- and working-class people. Despite the exaggerated resentment of the Jewish haute bourgeoisie and disdain for the poorer foreign Jews, one hundred thousand Jewish men had fought on Germany's side, in World War I, of whom twelve thousand had died.[31] Although the Jews had proved that they were reliable and law-abiding citizens as well as patriotic Germans, they were constantly accused of being inherently unable to be committed Germans.

Germany's defeat in World War I, its self-perceived humiliation in the Versailles Treaty, and the tremendous economic shocks experienced during the immediate postwar period only served to intensify the political witch hunt for an appropriate scapegoat. Although one in six Jews had fought in World War I, the "stab-in-the-back" legend—that the liberal Jewish press and mercenary Jewish war profiteers had sabotaged the war effort and willfully caused Germany's defeat—attained legitimacy. An array of theories and distortions circulated regarding an alleged Jewish capitalist-Bolshevik-liberal-Zionist conspiracy against the German people. Anti-Semitism became de rigueur in German politics.

The economic and political disabilities of the Weimar regime ripened the fruits of fascism that had long been growing in Germany. Nationalist sympathizers saw Jews as the creators of the despised Weimar system.[32] Between 1923 and 1932, 128 Jewish cemeteries and 50 synagogues were desecrated; in the early 1930s, during the worldwide depression, physical attacks against Jews increased, especially by right-wing students. By this time the Nationalsozialistische Deutsche Arbeiterpartei (NSDAP) had already attracted more than six million voters on its way to becoming Germany's strongest party by 1932 and its only party by 1933.[33] Under the Nazi dictatorship the Jewish Question became an obsession.

THE HOLOCAUST ERA

The circumstances of the Jews' annihilation within the Reichsprotektorat were different from those in Eastern Europe. Germany, although the ideological center and primary perpetrator of the Final Solution, was not the site of the horrors now associated with the term "Holocaust." In fact, a large percentage of Germany's Jews, who were wealthier and more mobile than their Eastern European compatriots, were fortunate enough to have left during the 1930s, after the enactment of racially restrictive and discriminatory legislation. Thousands of German Jews emigrated to Palestine, North and South America, and those parts of Europe not yet under Nazi control. Some 8,000 even found safe passage to China. Of the estimated 503,000 Jews in Germany in 1933 (this figure does not include thousands of nonaffiliated people of Jewish descent who were considered Jews under the Nuremberg Laws), 315,000 had emigrated by 1939. According to the census of that year, however, 234,000 Jews were still living in Germany.[34]

On April 1, 1933, the Nazi party organized the first large-scale anti-Jewish demonstration and boycott. In the same year the designation "non-Aryan" was adopted. The September 1935 Nuremberg Laws deprived Jews of citizenship, prohibited marriage and sexual relations between Jews and non-Jews, and defined those of Jewish descent, regardless of their personal identification with Judaism, as Jewish. The Law Respecting Reich Citizenship declared Jews to be non-Germans.[35]

The 1930s remained, however, a relatively stable and even prosperous time for Jews. The beginnings of persecution even encouraged a continued flourishing of Jewish life and community activities. Anti-Semitic hostilities in Germany's small and medium-sized towns drove the few Jews in those communities to the denser cities, where there already existed a critical mass of their coreligionists. This increased density of the Jewish population in a few German cities intensified Jewish communal life, at least for a short time. Jewish schools and newspapers emerged to fill the void left by the exclusion of Jews from German cultural life. Community leaders opened agricultural training centers to prepare emigrants for Palestine, thus boosting the Zionist cause.

On August 17, 1938, the Nazis compelled all Jews to adopt distinctly "Jewish" names, such as Sara or Israel. The beginning of the end for the Jews, however, was Kristallnacht, on November 9, 1938, the Hitler regime's officially sanctioned and well-orchestrated pogrom in which ninety-one Jews were murdered and three hundred were arrested and seventy-five hundred Jewish-owned businesses were burned and vandalized.[36] After 1938, Jews were no longer allowed to attend mixed schools, the theater, or movies, to possess driver's licenses, or to own businesses. By this time only about 15 percent of the Jews were still gainfully employed; the rest survived on other sources of income or the organized welfare support of the Jewish community. By mid-1941 all escape routes from Germany had been sealed. Many Jews had been deported to detention and concentration camps. On September 1, 1941, the Nazis forced all Jews over the age of six to wear the medieval yellow *Jude* badge. Within the next two months the regime began to transport Jews to ghettos in Eastern Europe and to confiscate the property they were forced to abandon. Others were shipped to the concentration camps, particularly to Auschwitz. Of the 139,606 inmates in Theresienstadt, 43,103 were from Germany. Because the elderly and female populations were less mobile than the male, they were left behind to suffer disproportionately at the hands of the Nazi machine.

In 1942 all Jewish educational institutions were closed. One year later the last of nearly 3,000 Jewish communal and religious organizations in Germany were absorbed into the central Reichsvereinigung (Imperial Association). By that time few Jews remained in Germany. An estimated 14,500 Jews, mostly the spouses of non-Jews, survived the war unharmed in Germany. Another 9,000 managed to do so underground. Still, the Nazis murdered somewhere between 160,000 and 180,000 German Jews. At most, 8,000 survived the transports, camps, and death marches. Among this number were a few slave laborers who had been brought back from the camps to work in German munitions plants. An estimated 800 German Jews also survived the war as patients interned in the Jewish hospital of Berlin.[37] In spite of the unspeakable atrocities committed against the Jews of Europe, it would seem that Heinrich Himmler and Reinhard Heydrich, the masterminds of the *Endlösung* (Final Solution), harbored a certain reluctance to round up German Jews on German soil.[38] Their minions occasionally showed lenience toward "their own" Jews, a trait that was woefully absent in their treatment of the *Ostjuden*.

Although the majority of the German Jewish population escaped death through emigration, the rich cultural heritage of fifteen hundred years of Jewish participation in the shaping of German history had ended. Gone were the networks of organizations, the communal institutions, the newspapers, theaters, law offices, shops, and publishing houses. The Holocaust destroyed a unique cultural symbiosis whose achievements rival other such singularly creative periods in the history of civilization.

THE POST-HOLOCAUST ERA

Germans refer to 1945 as *Stunde Null*, a historical tabula rasa created by the end of the war and the reestablishment of democracy in the Federal Republic.[39] But a number of German as well as foreign critics have questioned the validity of this tabula rasa. They point to the many continuities between the Nazi regime and the Federal Republic and to the failure, as well as the refusal, of many Germans to come to terms with the past. The democratic values and economic successes of postwar Germany, the critics argue, have been built, not on the bedrock of reconciliation, but on a swampy mire of national guilt and confusion over the events of the Holocaust. A mature *Bewältigung der Vergangenheit* (coming to terms with the past) has never occurred in West Germany, because the initial response to the Holocaust in 1945 was to repress and forget it rather than confront it in an honest and collective manner. Moreover, it is important to remember that it was not the Germans but the victorious Allies who were responsible for the end of the Holocaust and the return to a parliamentary democracy. Unlike fascism in Italy and Spain and Bolshevism in the former Soviet Union and Eastern Europe, National Socialism was not defeated endogenously. Its demise was imposed, a construct that has already led to certain peculiarities in Germany's postwar history and is certain to yield many more in the future now that West and East Germany have reunited.

The German reaction to the Holocaust can be divided into three periods.[40] The first, from 1945 to 1949, was characterized primarily by a continued clinging to Nazi ideology and anti-Semitism in West Germany and the very gradual reabsorption of those surviving victims displaced by the war. It was only under the aegis of Konrad Adenauer's administration after 1949 that the second period, one of *Versöhnung* (reconciliation) began. *Wiedergutmachung* (reparation and restitution), the denazification trials, the rewriting of textbooks, the treatment of the Holocaust by German writers and artists, the building of relations with the new state of Israel—all these were highlights of the problematic *Bewältigung der Vergangenheit* after 1949, which culminated in the opening of official diplomatic relations with Israel in 1965. After the Six-Day War in 1967, which marked the beginning of the third era, German-Jewish relations took a pronounced turn. Suddenly the political Right, whose moderate faction had maintained a silent philo-Semitism and whose more radical wing still issued anti-Israel statements bordering on anti-Semitism, rejoiced at Israel's defeat of the Arabs. Israel's bravura and victory signaled to the German conservatives a release from the burden of guilt, for the Jews were no longer the perennial victims. The student Left, however, who now constituted the vanguard of what was to be known as the New Left, reversed from being the most outspoken supporter of German-Jewish and German-Israeli relations to criticizing harshly what it perceived to be a brutal repression of the Arabs at the hands of Israel. The transformation of the constellation of internal political alignments in the late 1960s affected the way members of the Left and the Right viewed the past.

Gradual Transition: The First Period, 1945–1949

Estimates of the number of Jews left in displaced-person (DP) camps in the Allied zones at the end of the war verge on one hundred thousand. Jewish DPs were collected at these camps, under the guidance of the United Nations Relief and Rehabilitation Administration (UNRRA), for return to their original countries. But many Jews could or would not return to places scarred by nightmares of destruction, and their numbers swelled the population of the DP camps.[41] The Harrison Report of the summer of 1945 revealed, however, that these victims of Nazi persecution lived in conditions hardly better than those their torturers had imposed on them in the concentration camps. They were watched by German guards, fed a diet of black bread and coffee, forbidden to leave the camps, and confined to inhumanly small living quarters. For thousands of displaced German and Eastern European Jews in the occupied territories of Germany the Holocaust did not end with V-E Day. Anti-Semitic excesses continued, especially in Poland, where Europe witnessed its last full-scale pogrom against Jews in the town of Kielce in the summer of 1946, forcing thousands to flee to the DP camps of Germany.

In the fall of 1945, reforms alleviated the misery in the camps for the "victims of fascism," as the Jews were ambiguously called by the Berlin Allied administration.[42] But the influx of Eastern European refugees only intensified the plight of the DPs. Demoralization rose as time passed, and Palestine remained closed to Jewish immigration by the British. Persistent anti-Semitism and the fragile physical and psychological state of Jewish DPs raised serious doubts whether a Jewish community could ever be rebuilt in Germany. On April 30, 1946, an estimated 74,000 displaced Jews were living, interned or free, in postwar Germany.

Despite the abysmal situation in which these people found themselves, they began to reconstitute something akin to what might be called Jewish life in Germany. Organizations were founded, newspapers started, and religious activities initiated. Among the new organizations was the Central Committee for Jewish Liberatees in Germany, which fought for the emigration and resettlement rights of DPs and provided them with agricultural training for life in the Holy Land. At the end of 1946 only 15,000 of the 500,000 German Jews in the prewar community still remained in Germany. This figure included half-Jews as well as those Jews who had already converted to Christianity. The 1946 census estimated that of a total German population of over 65 million people only 156,705 were of Jewish origin, most of them still living in DP camps. Thus, for example, of the 3,000 prewar Jews in Karlsruhe only 90 remained; of 10,000 Jews in Frankfurt 600 were left. Most telling of the destruction wrought by the Holocaust was the fact that in all of Germany only one rabbi remained after the war.[43]

During the subsequent years organizations emerged that attempted to bridge the gap between Jews and Christians. These organizations condemned and investigated the Holocaust for the first time. They also cared for its victims and drafted proposals and claims for restitution. At the same time, acts of anti-Semitism, especially the desecration of Jewish cemeteries, continued. Nonetheless, the election of Konrad Adenauer as the first chancellor of the newly formed Federal Republic began an era in which the German government initiated various measures that became the modest beginnings of a collective restitution by the German people for crimes they had committed against the Jews. Concentrating mainly on monetary compensation, this effort became known as *Wiedergutmachung*. Ultimately, *Wiedergutmachung* amounted to little more than a monetarization of German culpability and guilt.

Versöhnung: The Second Period, 1949–1965

Denazification. The four years immediately following the war left the occupying powers in charge of Germany's public affairs. This period marked the nominal beginning of the "reckoning with the past," primarily through efforts at denazification. With the onset of the Cold War and its exacerbation by the Berlin blockade, the Western powers, led by the United States, deemphasized denazification, stopping it in many instances before it even began. The Cold War had created a new enemy for the West that was more formidable and immediate than a vanquished and wholly discredited Third Reich. It was in this context that reparation and restitution emerged as options for Germany to atone for its war crimes. Both alternatives were seen not only as morally imperative by the leadership of the victors and the vanquished but also as pragmatically expedient to the reintegration of Germany within the West. The political and psychological dynamic of the postwar period was an ambiguous one of, on the one hand, coming to terms with a shameful past and, on the other hand, redefining, collectively and individually, the character of a new, untainted republican culture.

Denazification efforts can be said to have begun with the Nuremberg tribunal, established on November 20, 1945. This special court, presided over by the Allied victors, continued to mete out justice for crimes against peace, war crimes, and crimes against humanity until October 1, 1946. Hitler, Himmler, and Goebbels had all committed suicide after the Allied victory in May 1945, but ten other top Nazi officials were condemned to death and three to life imprisonment at the Nuremberg trials.[44] Göring took poison after receiving his death sentence, and Hitler's top aide, Martin Bormann, was condemned *in absentia.* Between October 1946 and April 1947 twelve U.S. tribunals indicted 185 high Nazi officials in the so-called Landsberg and Dachau cases.[45] Friedrich Flick, one of the most infamous members of Himmler's inner circle, received a sentence of twenty-seven years' imprisonment. However, the I.G. Farben directors, representing the huge conglomerate that not only produced the Zyklon B that was used to gas millions of people but also profited from the use of thousands of prisoners of war and Jews as slave laborers, received only light sentences.

Concomitant with Nuremberg were attempts by the Allied regional administrations to root out Nazi offenders. On March 5, 1946, Bavaria, Baden-Württemberg, and Hesse all adopted laws "concerning liberation from Nazism and militarism." Questionnaires were sent to every member of the population in an effort to denazify postwar society. Clearly, such a method, which relied on Nazis to abide by an "honor system" and confess crimes for which they felt no remorse, represented a futile administration of justice.

In some respects the external imposition of justice and the ensuing controversial legal debates over the criteria used to select and handle the cases at Nuremberg may have had the unfortunate consequence of vindicating Nazi apologists and circumventing the German people's own direct confrontation with their criminals. As a result of Germany's occupation and the absence of any native statelike structures, the authorities never established an indigenous *German* judicial mechanism that could work in conjunction with the Allied system. While we might argue with the benefit of hindsight that the establishment of such an internal structure could have been helpful to the subsequent process of reparation to the Jews and the Germans' coming to terms with their past, it should be pointed out that conditions at the time probably could not have countenanced the formation of such German courts. Whereas elsewhere in Europe former fascists and Nazis were often attacked and most certainly ostracized by the population, neither happened in Germany. We know of no instances during this time period of the German public's turning against a German citizen because of his or her active involvement with the Nazi regime.

In fact, the abolition of the death penalty in the Basic Law of the Federal Republic represented a reaction to denazification, which was perceived by many Germans as a violation of German sovereignty and an affront to Germany's political maturity. It is important to add in this context that neither the United States nor its European allies ever demanded that the Germans engage in a strict coming to terms with their past. The onset of the Cold War had deflected their attention away from the Federal Republic and toward the East, thus encouraging a premature abandonment of denazification. There is a clear correlation between the decline of Nazi trials in late 1947 and 1948 and the escalation of tensions between the West and the Soviet Union. The Allied powers wanted both to appease the German political leadership and to rehabilitate the German image as quickly as possible in an effort to establish the Bundesrepublik as an ally for the West in its increasingly bitter conflict with the Soviet-led East. The United States even went so far as to push for the rearmament of Germany. All of these measures necessitated a leniency in the treatment of ex-Nazis. One could legitimately point to the ineffectual handling of denazification as one of the prime causes for the continuity between the Third Reich and the Federal Republic, as well as for the Germans' failure to come to terms with their wartime deeds.

Throughout, the dilemma persisted whether to emphasize denazification or rebuilding the postwar economy rapidly. This conflict was alleviated to some extent by the regional relativization of the definition of "Nazi."[46] Instead of creating a generally acceptable definition of Nazism, the federal government empowered each of the federal states to arrive at its own definition of the term, which meant that the process of dealing with Nazis and the Nazi past remained within the purview of the states. This approach facilitated the displacement of the responsibility for the war and the Holocaust onto the nonexistent government of the Third Reich, in whose absence individuals were left to approach these issues as they chose. Furthermore, by in effect pronouncing every person either a guilty participant or an innocent bystander, the denazification trials acted to exonerate all those who were not legally punished, thereby eliminating gradations of responsibility and moral guilt.

In fact, a vast majority of those who were subjected to the process of denazification returned to normal society fully integrated, without any stigma or harm.[47] In no way did denazification represent a cleansing of Nazis from public life. Instead, it guaranteed the alleviation of any collective or individual responsibility via the efficient legal reintegration. Ultimately, denazification failed abysmally to force the German public to confront the evil of National Socialism and its contribution to twelve years of criminality, which implicated many Germans in addition to the Nazi leadership and those actively engaged in the machinery of murder.

German Reparations and Restitution. Denazification served as a forerunner to the reparations agreement, the first major effort on the part of the new German government to atone, at least in part, for the actions of its predecessor, the National Socialist regime. The story of the reparations agreement between Germany and the new state of Israel was one of complicated motives and outcomes. Driven partly by moral considerations but much more by pragmatic concerns and the logic of Realpolitik, Jews and Germans regarded reparations as imperative for the restoration of normalcy as well as—particularly in the case of the latter—for the reestablishment of their legitimacy in the international order. But numerous moral and political conundrums rendered the process and debate of *Wiedergutmachung* quite problematic. On the one hand, a treaty with the Jewish victims, represented by Israel, placed a compelling obligation on the Federal Republic, the successor state of the Third Reich. On the other hand, the exclusive negotiating by Jews aroused resentment against Israel and Germany on the part of those non-Jewish victims who were excluded from the Luxembourg Reparations Agreement. Reparations, however, represented an indispensable step for the Germans toward erasing their image as inherently evil people. Restitution was essential to convincing the world of the establishment of a *new* Germany. Yet, many victims of Nazism and people around the world took offense at the idea of Germany "buying" its redemption with blood money. Reparations were supposed to represent an entreaty for forgiveness on the part of the German people. Above all, they were meant to be gestures of goodwill toward the Jews. However, the efforts of the Adenauer government stood in opposition to the opinion of the majority of the German people, who were not in favor of reconciliation with the Jews and Israel and felt no responsibility for the atrocities committed by the Third Reich. At the same time, most Israelis, who saw no difference between the Third Reich and the Federal Republic, were repelled by the idea of negotiating directly with their former torturers.

In the immediate postwar period a profound silence about the horrors of the Holocaust prevailed not only in Germany but also among a stunned global population. Neither the Jews nor the Germans, whether for reasons of guilt, horror, or confusion, made any official statements about the events that had just transpired. Perhaps one was waiting for the other to make a first gesture. Although 10,000 German physicians received Alexander Mitscherlich's report *Medizin ohne Menschlichkeit* (Medicine without humanity), which detailed the medical trials at Nuremberg, not a single response was heard. Many Germans adopted psychological defense mechanisms to resist coming to terms with the past, such as denial of the Nazi atrocities and projection of blame onto Hitler, the SS, the SA (storm troopers), or some abstract, vanished arm of government. Peter Märthesheimer commented that the Germans' failure to "master the past" or explain their own idealization of Hitler led to the "psychopathology of a whole nation." In 1945, he said, "these people put their soul on ice."[48]

Curiously, the uniformity of silence did not reflect a common view of the Holocaust. Although some sense of guilt and complicity existed on the part of the populace, anti-Semitism remained strong after the war and, according to surveys conducted between 1949 and 1952, even increased.[49] Whatever the variety of individual perceptions, silence was the only response during the 1940s and early 1950s to the question how this could have happened in Germany. The banal rhetoric of *Wiedergutmachung* did little to break this wall of silence and genuinely confront the repressed guilt, rage, and despair of Germans after the Holocaust.

German reparations to the victims of National Socialism began under Allied direction on November 10, 1947, when Law 59, providing for the reimbursement of concrete wealth illegally confiscated from the Jews by the Nazis, was passed in the American Zone. This decree covered all those possessions expropriated by the Nazis in the course of their Aryanization of the economy. The reparations included, when possible, the return of the goods in question. Reparations began, however, with redressing wrongs for destroyed property. Many claims were adjudicated by German judges who deliberately attempted, for anti-Semitic reasons and because of resentment against the Allied forces, to hinder the return of stolen properties. Law 59 was, after all, not German, and only among a minority of the judges could one find a genuine sense of contrition and a readiness to right the wrongs of the past.[50]

The Allied provisions for reparations were only partial, barely redressing a small portion of the injustices suffered. Offenses against life, health, freedom, and professional potential found no compensation under the law. Furthermore, Law 59 was uneven in its geographical distribution, leading to the gross undercompensation of some of the neediest victims. The American measures aroused much latent resentment against the Jews that had persisted after the fall of the Third Reich. Nonetheless, by the mid-1950s the majority of claims brought forth under the American occupation had been settled.

In 1951, when forty-seven nations declared the end of their war on Germany, Israel continued to withhold its approval of this collective peace accord, arguing that the German leadership had as yet failed to denounce Hitler's war against the Jews. This Israeli position prompted many Germans to oppose the reconciliation with the Jews and Israel. But Erich Lüth, one of the founders of the Peace with Israel movement in 1951, stated:

> We are the ones who must begin! We must say: We ask Israel for peace. . . . We must set an example, which at the same time should be a sign that we are prepared to wage the struggle against the remnants of anti-Semitism with the same passion and uprightness with which we will fight any new anti-Semitism. We must link this call for peace . . . with an expression of grief for the six million innocent victims and of thanks for the incalculable good which the Jews have done in the service of mankind and in Germany.[51]

This statement broke the floodgates of pent-up emotion. A lively debate ensued in newspaper columns and letters to the editor welcoming or denouncing the Peace with Israel initiative. Probably a sign of the more activist *Zeitgeist* regarding this sensitive issue, Chancellor Adenauer broke the government's silence with a bold statement before the Bundestag on September 27, 1951:

> The Federal Government and with it the great majority of the German people are aware of the immeasurable suffering that was brought upon the Jews in Germany and the occupied territories during the time of National Socialism. . . . Unspeakable crimes had been committed in the name of the German people, calling for moral and material indemnity. . . . The Federal Government is prepared, jointly with representatives of Jewry and the State of Israel . . . to bring about a solution of the material indemnity problem, thus easing the way to the spiritual settlement of infinite suffering.[52]

There is no doubt that moral considerations, perhaps even more than the dictates of Realpolitik, were the motivating force behind Adenauer's intentions. As he frequently noted in his memoirs, his dealings with Israel were based primarily on a pressing moral obligation.[53] It would be safe to argue that Adenauer's anxiousness to forge links with Israel represented in part a collective desire by some Germans to release the psychological turmoil restrained since the war. However, many in Israel expressed reluctance to negotiate reparations directly with Germany. Why should the victims be asked to beg before their oppressors? The Israelis requested that any talks be arbitrated by Allied mediators, who refused this role. Conversely, it also seemed that the hostility the Israelis and world Jewry felt toward the Germans perhaps drove them to negotiate directly with the Germans instead of to shy away from them.

In retrospect, it is clear that the evolution of direct negotiations between Israel and Germany stemmed not only from pragmatic considerations but also from a strong moral and psychological symbiosis. Each needed the other in order to pay a heavy moral debt that weighed on them both—on Germany to pay compensation and on Israel to demand it—and to break the silence and begin the painful process of coming to terms with the past. *Wiedergutmachung* offered each side the opportunity to reestablish and redefine its relations with the other, in effect to write the history of German-Jewish relations before the accounts of the Holocaust had faded.

In spite of Chancellor Adenauer's desire for a reparations agreement, many, including finance minister Fritz Schäffer, had hoped that the Federal Republic would save money by relying on the already existing regional *Länder* laws instead of on a comprehensive national policy. This lack of ideological commitment to reparations was further evidenced by the reinstatement of former Nazi Party members in the civil service on May 11, 1951, as sanctioned by Article 131 of the Basic Law. Since denazification was never implemented with the thoroughness and rigor necessary for it to be successful, it ultimately proved to be a fiasco. In 1949 there were still 14,443 former NSDAP members among Bavaria's 49,121 civil servants. Indeed, in the state of Lower Saxony the number of former NSDAP members among the state's judges and judiciary officials *increased* between 1945 and 1949. By contrast, few who had been politically persecuted and racially discriminated against had been restored to their former positions after the end of the war.[54]

Though they began on shaky foundations, the *Wiedergutmachung* treaty negotiations proceeded, if slowly. Israel demanded money from the Bundesrepublik to facilitate the absorption of the half-million Jews who had fled to Palestine during the Third Reich. At the same time, reparations were to serve the more general purpose of building a homeland for persecuted Jews. Because of his moral convictions, Adenauer felt compelled to respond to the Israeli demand. At secret meetings in Paris in April 1951 Israel stipulated two conditions for negotiating with Germany: a declaration of guilt and a condemnation of the Nazi atrocities and the acceptance of the Israeli terms of discussion. These demands were to be the price for Israel's presence at the bargaining table and its promise to spare the German state embarrassment in the global community. For this reason Adenauer sent two respected anti-

Nazi and proreparation leaders, Franz Böhm and his deputy Otto Küster, to handle negotiations with Israel.

In December of the same year World Jewish Congress president Nahum Goldmann, arguably the most important diplomatic catalyst in bringing about the reparations agreement, requested $1 billion (4.2 billion DM) to pay for reconstruction on behalf of Israel. Hermann Josef Abs, Adenauer's finance minister, feared that to commit such an enormous sum would endanger the international financial community's confidence in Germany. On May 19, 1952, Abs offered Israel payment in the amount of 100 million marks over four years, with a possibility of renegotiation for additional payments thereafter. The Israelis took this suggestion as an insult. Germany's miraculous economic turnaround had already begun, and the Israelis were angered by the German government's haggling over terms the Israelis perceived as moral imperatives. The negotiations foundered and their future seemed uncertain. Mutual recriminations—that the Germans were trying to save money at the expense of their victims and that the Israelis were using these same victims to profit from German guilt (*Guiltgeld*)—proliferated on both sides. Küster resigned.

Recognizing the importance of negotiations with Israel for Germany's position in the world, particularly in relation to the United States and its vocal, organized Jewish community, Adenauer impressed upon his cabinet the need to continue the talks. The charter of February 26, 1952, which officially released the Germans from their "occupied" status and established, in effect, the uncontested sovereignty of the Bundesrepublik, called explicitly for greater attention on the part of the German government to facilitating restitution for the victims of Nazism. Böhm resumed his contact with Goldmann and renewed the negotiations with the offer of 3 billion marks. On September 10, 1952, Adenauer, Goldmann, and the Israeli foreign minister, Moshe Sharett, signed a treaty in Luxembourg stipulating the payment of 3.5 billion Deutsche marks by the German government to the Jewish community, of which 3 billion were to go to Israel and 500 million to the Conference on Jewish Material Claims against Germany, the umbrella organization of world Jewry for victims outside Israel.

The Luxembourg Conference represented the first concrete institutional attempt at rebuilding the fragile relationship between Germans and Jews in the post-Holocaust world. Paradoxically, in 1951 and 1952 Israel and Germany needed each other for moral, psychological, and political reasons. Only Israel, representing the most obvious manifestation of post-Holocaust Jewry, could grant Germany the political rehabilitation and spiritual forgiveness it so much needed. At the same time, only the Jews' direct confrontation with their former oppressors and murderers could bring about their collective reaffirmation following the trauma of the Holocaust.

While morality was certainly a key factor in shaping German and Israeli psychology, it was the exigency of Realpolitik that compelled both parties to come to an agreement in the Luxembourg Treaty. Had morality alone been the impetus, the negotiations would have proceeded more smoothly. Instead, the coexistence of morality and pragmatism among the motivating factors was evidenced by the meandering process of the negotiations. The greater the Allies' warmth toward Germany, the weaker the German commitment to *Wiedergutmachung* became.[55] The ambivalence on both sides, while the product of real political pressures, tainted even this well-intentioned effort and bankrupted its potential healing powers.

Although it may have started the restitution process, morality did not govern its outcome and policy in the early 1950s. The Germans needed to revive and restore their political standing in the world, while the Israelis desperately required economic assistance. In order to improve their image and expedite their acceptance into the community of Western nations, the Germans needed to appease the United States. This included neutralizing the opposition of American Jews to all things German, including improved German-American relations. The increasing pressures of the Cold War made the West, especially the Americans, eager to accept Germany. One could, of course, interpret Luxembourg as an act of goodwill, a gesture of material sacrifice attesting to a German commitment to the ideals of democracy and support of a new world order. In a similar vein, one could also interpret the reparations agreement as proof of the Germans' unwillingness to travel the hard road of penitence and contrition.

The numerous pressures facing Israel—Arab hostility, economic instability, the burden of providing for hundreds of thousands of refugees—encouraged the young nation to accept funds from an increasingly prosperous Germany. While the Israeli leadership rightly believed that accepting this money for the creation of a homeland and for the restitution of the wrongs perpetrated by the Germans on the Jewish people had a moral dimension, the pressing reality of providing for the needs of Holocaust survivors was also a very real concern. Both sides resisted any psychological confrontation with the guilt for the Holocaust. Against this background the new beginning for German-Jewish relations emerged.

Yet, while it was positively redefined in this era, the relationship between Germans and Jews was rebuilt on hollow foundations. The hesitance of both sides during the painful negotiation process tarnished the effort. Various expressions of Israeli contempt for Germans as well as German industrialists' concern over how the Luxembourg Treaty would affect their business with the Arabs tainted the gesture of mutual goodwill. Like the denazification efforts, *Wiedergutmachung* avoided more confrontation with the past than it engaged. It led to an acknowledgment of German responsibility on an instrumental level rather than to an act of genuine collective contrition.

One cannot help but be somewhat puzzled by the fact that Israel helped Germany regain its international legitimacy and thus its national composure. After four years in which Germany's official state policy was to systematically annihilate the Jewish people, followed by six years of virtually complete silence regarding this matter on the part of Germans and Jews, both Israel and Germany "simultaneously concluded that they could not prosper without each other. Despite the horrors of the past relationship of their peoples, the two countries needed each other—and uniquely each other."[56]

Throughout the 1950s and early 1960s, Germany and Israel avoided any official contacts on the state level that could be construed as public legitimation of each other's existence as political entities. Activity increased substantially, however, in the areas of trade and commerce. The Israelis established a trade union office in Cologne, while the Germans extended loans to Israel for various developmental projects. Germany purchased Israel's new status symbol, the Uzi submachine gun, in large quantities, and Israel imported cars and ships from the Federal Republic.

The years 1952–65 also witnessed an array of cultural exchanges between the two countries, mainly in the arts, music, and science. Youth and student exchanges attained particular importance, with many German young people traveling to Israel in an attempt to atone for the crimes committed against the Jews by their parents. Union members visited one another's organizations, and it became almost de rigueur for young German intellectuals who were part of, or close to, the labor movement to pay a visit to one of Israel's many kibbutzim. Yet it was not until May 12, 1965, after very difficult and protracted negotiations, that the two countries finally established full diplomatic relations.[57]

In 1966, the year before his death, Adenauer visited Israel for the first time, but not without incident from anti-German protesters. In the same year, conservative German newspaper magnate Axel Springer donated $900,000 (3.6 million DM) to the Jerusalem Art Museum. Increased Middle East tensions in 1967 drew Israelis closer to German sympathies. The outbreak of the Six-Day War in June 1967 between Israel and its Arab neighbors was greeted with an explosion of popular approval in Germany for the Israeli cause. A survey during the summer of 1967 indicated that 59 percent of Germans harbored decidedly pro-Israel sympathies, while only 6 percent were pro-Arab (27 percent declared themselves to be neither for nor against, and 8 percent registered as undecided).[58] The war represented a show of might uncharacteristic of Jews, whom the Germans had seen as the perennial victims. The Germans were "prouder" than other Europeans over the victory of the Israelis. Now the world could no longer say that the Germans had robbed the Jews of all their strength. The victims had become the victors.

The late sixties were a time of excellent German-Israeli relations. Germany alone within the European family of nations supported the associate membership of Israel in the European Economic Community (EEC). Israeli and German educators agreed at a major conference in 1967 to revise the images of each other that their respective countries' textbooks provided.

Die Schuldfrage, the Question of Guilt: German Intellectuals Confront Their Past. In the period between the end of World War II and the founding of the new Federal Republic, Germany's political, administrative, and economic elites remained silent on the Holocaust. German writers and intellectuals, however, did not. Immediately following the fall of the Reich an open dialogue commenced among writers over the question of German guilt and the process of assessing the past, particularly the role of the humanist intellectual during the era of National Socialist barbarism. It would not be an exaggeration to say that the Holocaust and the legacy of German anti-Semitism have to this very day provided *the* central theme framing discourse among the Federal Republic's literati and intellectuals. The artist's treatment of the past, which became an issue for German intellectuals in the postwar period, has been as closely linked to contemporary political concerns as it has been informed by the Holocaust.

Numerous creative spirits incorporated the lessons of the Holocaust into their works, which are too copious to list. Although they represent individual attempts at reconciliation and explanation, the works of authors like Hermann Hesse, Heinrich Böll, Carl Zuckmayr, Erich Fried, or Rolf Hochhuth influenced the multitudes who read them in Germany and abroad. More than that, an examination of the works of such creative individuals has the additional value of illuminating the substantial changes that their ideas brought to the political culture of the time. In postwar Germany, intellectual debate probed the Gordian knot of anti-Semitism, catalyzing a discourse on the Holocaust.

"Silence concerning some massive event is possibly the most explicit narrative of all," wrote Holocaust survivor and historian Saul Friedländer.[59] An uncharacteristically taciturn period in German literature marked the immediate postwar years. "People were filled with silence," another survivor noted. "Everything that happened was so inconceivable, that the witness even seemed like a fabricator to himself. . . . [I]ts essence will always remain within that sphere which no expression can encompass."[60] This "literature of silence" was created partly by the emigration and wholesale slaughter of German intellectuals. The absence of literature is perhaps the best and most appropriate representation of the Holocaust in art. However, this aside, the profundity of the silence among those writers who did survive rested on their using this hiatus to prepare a response and formulate an approach, both personal and literary, to the events of the immediate past. While we will attempt to outline the general history of German literary reaction to the Holocaust, it is important to recognize that for every representative of one artistic position, there have existed many advocates of the opposing view. The literary reaction to the Holocaust is one of dialogue and disagreement among intellectuals involving the use of symbolism or realism, individual or collective confrontation with the past, and the controversy of guilt versus responsibility. There has never existed a consensus on *how* to treat the Holocaust. Nonetheless, there has been a universal preoccupation with adopting the metaphors of the Holocaust in some way, if only to discredit its literariness.

Tracing the history and pattern of reactions to the Holocaust among postwar German writers is, in and of itself, an exercise in historical sleuthing. One must delve into the evolution of the intellectual response to the dilemmas posed by writers both as intellectuals and as Germans. An extensive body of secondary literature exists on the topic of exile writers and the reaction to the Holocaust among émigré intellectuals after the war. We will limit our focus here, however, to the literature written in German and, almost exclusively, by those artists writing from "inner exile" within Germany. This group's work had an immense impact on the German public and thus played a decisive role in shaping its view of the Holocaust.

The late 1940s were by no means devoid of attempts to grasp the lessons of the Holocaust. The American occupiers had begun the debate over the guilt and responsibility of the German people through their attempts at denazification. Their reeducation efforts were furthered by the government-sanctioned production of morally challenging and appropriate propaganda. Alfred Döblin, author of the novel *Berlin Alexanderplatz,* wrote one such piece, *Der Nürnberger Lehrprozess* (The Nuremberg instructional process [1946]), under the pseudonym Hans Fiedeler. One of the best satirical records of this reeducation, or *Umerziehung,* was provided by the conservative East Prussian nobleman Ernst von Salomon in his autobiographical novel *Der Fragebogen* (The questionnaire [1951]). It followed in form (and parodied the inanity of) the Allies' 131-question survey, distributed in their largely futile efforts at denazification.

The occupying forces and German writers in exile asked for an accounting from those writers who had published under Hitler. They challenged those who had stayed to come to terms with their country's behavior. Thomas Mann declared in a May 8, 1945, BBC German-language broadcast that

> the thick-walled torture chamber into which Hitlerism had transformed Germany has been broken open. Our disgrace lies before the world, in front of the foreign commissions before whom these incredible pictures are presented and who report home about this surpassing of all hideousness that men can imagine. "Our disgrace" German readers and listeners! For everything German, everyone that speaks German, writes German, has lived in Germany, has been implicated by this dishonorable unmasking.[61]

This overwhelming sense of guilt was palpable among the exiles. "I, as a German-born person and soul," wrote Thomas Mann in a letter to Ewald Vetter in Germany, "deeply and painfully feel my own participation in German guilt, in German responsibility for everything that Germany, as a *nation,* in its delusion and delirium did to the world."[62] It was the intensity of the world's gaze upon Germany and the accusations of such émigré intellectuals as Mann that prompted a confrontation with the question of German guilt and broke down the wall of literary reticence.

The most controversial and provocative challenge to German intellectuals of the immediate postwar era came from the renowned philosopher Karl Jaspers in a series of lectures entitled "Die Schuldfrage" delivered at Heidelberg University in 1945–46. The lectures were published under the same title in 1946. In the same year, Jaspers, along with Werner Krauss and Alfred Weber, published the first German periodical licensed by the military authorities. Called *Die Wandlung* (Metamorphosis), its stated purpose was worded as follows:

> To be able to speak freely with one another is the first task in really being able to speak freely. That is hardly simple. None of us is a leader, none is a prophet who can say with certainty what really exists and what ought to be done. All "Führers" were incurable phantoms. They robbed us of our freedom, first inwardly, then outwardly. But their existence was possible because so many people no longer wanted to be free, to be responsible for themselves. Today we have the legacy of this abdication. We must venture once again to be responsible, every man for himself.[63]

Jaspers's work could be characterized as an attempt to define a moral path in Germany between the sweeping generalizations of *Kollektivschuld* (collective guilt) on the one hand and the seemingly pervasive amnesia on the other. It was moral and not political or judicial guilt that presented the profoundest difficulty, according to Jaspers. Moral responsibility had to be felt by the individual in question; guilt should not be imposed on another. At the same time, Jaspers argued that one could never make a criminal morally responsible without making him or her aware of his or her transgressions. While Jaspers's paradigm of political, juridical, metaphysical, and moral levels of responsibility did not refer directly to the details of the Final Solution, it did force the opening of debate on the Holocaust among the Federal Republic's intellectuals.[64] Much of the subsequent literature represented a reaction, a rejection, or an extended reworking of Jaspers's pioneering efforts.

The Holocaust presented a singular dilemma to the generation of young writers who were just coming into their own in the 1940s and 1950s and could not empathize with the accusations of collective guilt. While 1945 represented the beginning of a positive economic and political tabula rasa for many Germans, for writers a blank slate demands inscription. The Holocaust and its intellectual consequences were the formative forces leading to the creation of the Gruppe 47, a group of writers who convened in the fall of 1947 under the leadership of Hans Werner Richter. In *Scorpion,* the Gruppe's journal, Richter exhorted young writers not to allow themselves to be drawn back into an imaginary, romantic world but instead to confront the past via a modern, vernacular, living German.[65]

While the chaos of the postwar period fostered the creation of some epic German fiction, such as Hermann Broch's *Der Tod des Vergils* (The death of Vergil [1945]) and Elisabeth Langgässer's *Das unauslöschliche Siegel* (The inextinguishable mark [1946]), plays by Bertolt Brecht, and the lyrical poetry of Paul Celan, the younger generation represented by Gruppe 47 sought new models and forms for expressing the emotional excesses of the Holocaust.

The horrors of the Nazi period forced young intellectuals to reexamine and reject the German literary tradition. In the postwar period, German writers faced a crisis of language in which the inadequacy of words was painfully obvious. Young writers could not return to literary styles tainted by the Nazi experience. A romanticization of old themes would have implied a continuity with a past from which this group of Germans, at least, needed to break. At the same time, however, any attempt to represent adequately the horrors of the Holocaust was a recipe for madness because of the impossibility of the task and because of the mind-boggling nature of the truth.

For these intellectuals, the Holocaust completely delegitimized and discredited the German language, which had become the tongue of oppression and genocide. Unable, however, to change completely the building blocks of their craft, members of Gruppe 47 experimented with innovative approaches to their art, such as surrealism and existentialism. Drawing inspiration from authors such as Franz Kafka, William Faulkner, and Ernest Hemingway, writers like Wolfgang Borchert, Erich Fried, and Ilse Aichinger approached the "truth" of the Holocaust through the imaginary, the surreal, the fantastic, and the lyrical. Once these young writers abandoned their silence, many of them discovered in fiction the ideal medium through which to synthesize the unfathomable disaster of Hitler's reign. The infusion of the imagination into the historical narrative allowed the individual to break away from collective guilt and make an independent statement free from political hypocrisy and historical inaccuracy. This was what Heinrich Böll called "the aesthetics of the humane."[66]

Another difference between those who entered their creative prime after the war and the generation of intellectuals who worked during it was the latter's use of a strongly philo-Semitic stereotype: the Jew as the pure, good, and sacrificial victim. Older émigrés in particular showed a greater propensity toward philo-Semitism. This generational difference in perception was owing to the fact that the younger writers felt relatively free to redefine the meaning of the Holocaust, while those who had lived through it as adults still felt compelled to do honor to the memory of the victims. Karl Jaspers's student and protégé Hannah Arendt, though herself in exile, had led this change in approach through her reporting of the Eichmann trial, which was published as a controversial volume entitled *Eichmann in Jerusalem*.[67] The ideas of the banality of evil and the sin of apathy, which were central to Arendt's analysis of Eichmann as the quintessential representative of the Nazi regime, gradually transformed the metaphor "Jew as victim" to "artist as victim" in postwar German literature. This led to an emphasis on persecution in general, not just on the singularities of the Holocaust. Few writers of the postwar generation in Germany set their fiction in the concentration camps, or dealt with the day-to-day events in these hellish institutions, despite the numerous possibilities for such depictions and their undoubted poignancy. Rather, the theme of the Holocaust became universalized in such works as Martin Walser's *Der schwarze Schwan* (The black swan [1964]), which focused on the attitudes of the Holocaust *perpetrators* during the period of economic rebuilding after the war.

Two writers whose careers were defined and built around a confrontation with and universalization of the Holocaust were leading members of Gruppe 47: Heinrich Böll and Günter Grass.[68] Böll's first stories focused mainly on the devastation of the war as depicted by first-person narrators, usually army privates. By re-creating the horrors and destructiveness of the war, Böll attempted to initiate a process of reflection. Many of these stories, written in Germany in the late 1940s and early 1950s and published in English under the titles *Adam and the Train* (1974) and *Stories* (1986), acknowledged in a Kafkaesque manner the futility of war and the inevitability of death.

Böll's fiction expressed his contempt for the creators of the Federal Republic's so-called economic miracle: to be "denazified a bit—the way you go to the barber to get rid of that tiresome beard," without acknowledging the moral burdens of the past, was to base economic renewal on hollow ethical foundations. According to Siegfried Mews, Böll's predilection for protagonists of less than heroic proportions who were unable to cope with postwar guilt on anything but a personal and self-absorbed level—"as an existential crisis rather than a political phenomenon"—"lends to his texts of the 1940s and early 1950s the quality of authentic record of his generation's shattering experiences rather than that of politically committed or polemically critical literature."[69]

To Günter Grass, author of the Danzig Trilogy (*The Tin Drum* [1959], *Cat and Mouse* [1961], and *Dog Years* [1963]), the very act of narration was an evocation and perpetuation of a world otherwise lost. In a highly unconventional style, Grass posed the question of the individual's responsibility as it applied to Oskar Matzerath, the hideous, dwarfed, boastful narrator of *The Tin Drum,* and, by extension, to the whole of postwar German society. Grass, very much in reaction to German literary tradition and because of the Holocaust, rejects the notion that citizen and artist were somehow separate. He regularly uses his popularity to attract attention to political causes, especially those of German Social Democracy.

Both Böll and Grass experimented with varying degrees of political moralizing in their fiction. There is no doubt, however, that the meteoric rise of the political novel in postwar Germany had its origins in the dissatisfaction with both the Third Reich and the government of Konrad Adenauer and his allies. Yet, paradoxically, these politically engaged and morally conscious intellectuals wrote about the horrors perpetrated by the Third Reich without mentioning the Jews in particular. These stories were immensely successful in decrying cruelty and murder on a universal level without addressing the Holocaust's uniqueness. In a sense, these authors omitted the specific plight of the Jews, thus rendering their accounts of Nazi brutality *judenrein.*

The West German literature of Holocaust reaction can be divided into three distinct categories.[70] The first category is survivor memoirs, the most notable example of which is *Jenseits von Schuld und Sühne* (At the mind's limits [1966]) by Jean Améry, written after the Auschwitz trials in Frankfurt. This book and Améry's later work echo an identical theme, spelled out in its subtitle, *Bewältigungsversuche eines Überwältigten* (An overwhelmed person's attempt to overcome). Améry's tragic characters try in vain to forget their harrowing experiences.

The second category is represented by a group best described as "witnesses through imagination," those writers who either were too young to experience the Holocaust or were in hiding or in exile. Prominent members of this group include Peter Handke, Ilse Aichinger, and Hubert Fichte. The artistic dilemma of these authors lay in how to represent with adequate gravity and seriousness a trauma that for them at least was more imaginary than real. They struggled as concerned intellectuals to continue the legacy of the past. The task of representing the Holocaust and the truth of its horrors presented a formidable challenge. As we have seen, many postwar writers translated the Nazi legacy into a universal metaphor of suffering in which the victims as well as the persecutors became theoretically interchangeable. The danger in this, of course, lay in the possibility of relativizing a singular event and in denying the existence of any victims at all.

Yet deliberate revisionism was rarely the case among writers of fiction, many of whom felt constrained by the necessity to write and rewrite the morals of the Holocaust. These "witnesses" became, in the words of Hans Magnus Enzensberger, hostages of the *Bewusstseinsindustrie* (consciousness industry). They had discarded the generalizing condemnation of the immediate postwar period's collective guilt and experimented with new, even postmodern, literary forms, linguistic constructions, and styles of narration as a form of conceptual replacement.

The third category of Holocaust literature had its origins in the captivity to conscience, or "narcissism of guilt," a hypocritical, self-righteous confrontation of the past. This narcissism ranged from the collective guilt expressed in 1945 to the doubts expressed in the late 1960s over the sincerity of this uniform remorse. It included the whole spectrum of attitudes that sought to monopolize the politics of guilt consciousness. In 1960 Helmuth Heissenbüttel published a captivating work, *Kalkulation über das was alle gewusst haben* (Calculation about that which everybody knew), in which he suggested that the entire German social system, not just Hitler, represented the embodiment of evil.

The literature of writers such as Heissenbüttel, Grass, and Walser often met with resistance from the general public, which focused on the glories of the German resistance, the heroism of the righteous few, and stories of survival rather than the banality of evil. The central dilemma in the German literary treatment of the Holocaust has been the rift between the unacceptability of silence and the impossibility of literary dialogue on the topic. Where literature risks turning real suffering into metaphor, silence offers no outlet to express pain. The telling of the tale keeps it alive at the same time that it fulfills the obligation of recitation necessary for moral penance. This tension between silence and representation, however, disintegrated in the 1970s, when both the cultural and the political spheres were transformed by student protest and the advent of a radical German Left. By then many of the survivors had died and their influence had diminished in intellectual and literary circles. There arose at this time a literature that began to glorify Hitler and express longing for the thrills of National Socialist imperialism and self-declared supremacy.

Throughout the evolving debate over the literary and artistic representation of the Holocaust, however, one fact stands out dramatically. In the whole corpus of German Holocaust literature the presence of the Jews as characters remains all too conspicuously and painfully absent. Regardless of the enormous intellectual conundrums presented by the lessons of the Holocaust, the neglect of the Jews highlights the failure even of intellectuals to achieve a successful coming to terms with the past. To ignore the Jews in Holocaust literature in favor of abstractions is a poststructuralist error that is all too carelessly committed by German authors.

Historical Treatment of the Holocaust. All writing about the Holocaust, including history, is inadequate. As with fiction, the writing of history has inevitably demanded that scholars select facts. Not surprisingly, the attempt to record and explain accurately National Socialism and the Holocaust has caused major debates and rifts among German historians, most notably between the "structuralists/functionalists" and the "intentionalists," to be explored in further detail below.[71] First, let us look at the key works in the history of Holocaust interpretation since 1945.

In the immediate postwar years, the major works on World War II were neither written in German nor authored by German historians. Moreover, these treatises typically omitted events of the Holocaust, focusing instead on the diplomatic and military aspects of the war. Many books, such as Alan Bullock's *Hitler* (1952), concentrated on the complicity of the Weimar Republic in the ascendance of Hitler. Rather than dealing with the Jews, these studies debated such topics as totalitarianism, fascism, and Hitlerism. Archival documentation on Jews served only as secondary corroborative evidence for tracing the rise of Hitler.

The first systematic collection of documents on the Third Reich was published by Swiss historian Walther Hofer in 1957. Exiles such as Hannah Arendt, Paul Massing, and Fritz Stern wrote about the Holocaust from abroad. The common denominator among these early histories of the Holocaust and World War II was the desire to unravel the background of Nazi Germany and to expose the latent forces in the Weimar Republic that allowed Hitler to attain power.

Hardly anything of note on the topic appeared in Germany until 1960, when Wolfgang Scheffler's *Judenverfolgung im Dritten Reich* (The persecution of the Jews in the Third Reich) was published. This concise history of the Third Reich marked the first effort to detail the Jewish response to Hitler while depicting the internal organizational life of the Jews in the 1930s. *Die Nationalsozialistische Machtergreifung: Studien zur Errichtung des totalitären Herrschaftssytems in Deutschland, 1933–34* (The National Socialist ascendance to power: Studies on the establishment of totalitarian rule in Germany, 1933–34 [1960]), by Karl Dietrich Bracher, Wolfgang Sauer, and Gerhard Schultz, stressed the unique role of anti-Semitism in the Nazi ideology. The authors agreed that following Hitler's ascent to power, "the persecution of the Jews was not only systematically organized and propagated, but that it also became a guiding principle of Nazi domestic policy."[72] This work, as well as Martin Broszat's *Die Nationalsozialistische Weltanschauung: Programm und Wirklichkeit* (The National Socialist worldview: Program and reality [1960]), which suggested that anti-Semitism was the one constant and unchanging element of National Socialism, marked the acknowledgment by German historians of the Holocaust's centrality to the definition of the National Socialist experience. Subsequently, even such popular reference works as the *World History in Maps, Dates, and Pictures* (1970) and the *Big Lexicon of the Third Reich* (1985), both published by the renowned Munich publisher Piper, named anti-Semitism as a key ingredient in National Socialist thought and action.

The plethora of research concerning the ideological aspects of National Socialism stemmed not only from an increasing public awareness and a willingness to confront the horrors of the Holocaust through the late 1950s and 1960s but also from the discovery of documents from the earliest and final stages of Hitler's career. Vast quantities of archival material gave historians the resources to synthesize the ideological and political components of Nazism.

Ernst Nolte (later to become a revisionist of National Socialism and by the early 1980s the most pronounced "relativizer" of the Holocaust) in the 1960s pioneered a structural explanation of anti-Semitism. He saw it as providing the major link to other aspects of Hitler's far-reaching political goals. In various scholarly articles and in his major work, *Der Faschismus in seiner Epoche* (1963), published in English as *Three Faces of Fascism,* Nolte described the German variant of fascism as a two-pronged ideological attack against the Judeo-Christian tradition on the one hand and the liberal-Western and Bolshevik-Marxist creeds on the other. Nolte labeled this the "theoretical" and "practical" justification for Nazi rule, and both aspects, according to him, had their roots in earlier forms of anti-Semitism and thrived under the Nazi "legal" system.

In the late 1960s and early 1970s dozens of publications analyzing the Nazi regime and its plan for the destruction of the Jews appeared. Most of these studies, often neo-Marxist in their intellectual orientation, dwelt on the contradictions and competition between various groups in the Nazi state and party.[73] It was in the interplay of these institutional structures that most of these authors sought explanations for the Nazis' Final Solution. In addition, respected though not widely adopted theses linked anti-Semitism to Hitler's Kulturkampf and sought to analyze how the symbiosis of the two pernicious ideologies prepared the way for the invasion of other nations. Eberhard Jäckel, in a thorough study of Hitler's rhetoric, *Hitlers Weltanschauung: Entwurf einer Herrschaft* (Hitler's worldview: Framework for domination [1969]), demonstrated how Hitler's concept of Lebensraum and his anti-Semitic policies complemented one another ideologically and politically.

The works of Nolte, Helmut Krausnick, Andreas Hillgruber, Jäckel, Martin Broszat, and Karl Dietrich Bracher, though fundamentally different in their epistemology and methodology, nevertheless constitute a common historiographic approach. They all elevated the Holocaust to one of the central elements of National Socialism, in contrast to earlier scholarly works, which had viewed Hitler as the most important, sometimes even the sole, reason for the creation of the Third Reich and had seen Hitler's anti-Semitism as a bizarre aberration. Until the mid-1980s, when revisionist approaches began to proliferate, this view of the centrality of the Holocaust dominated German historiography.

Two large methodological groupings emerged in this diverse and sophisticated body of work. The first, preoccupied primarily with explaining the Holocaust as a clearly intentional act by the Nazi elite, had come to be known as "intentionalist." Brilliantly embodied in the writings of Bracher and Jäckel, intentionalism anchored Nazi behavior in Hitler's and his cohorts' deeply felt anti-Semitism, which they had formulated well before their ascent to power; once in power, they had put into practice what their intentions had been all along.

In contrast to the intentionalists, the "structuralists" refused to concentrate on particular individuals in their explanation of the Holocaust. Instead, they focused on the more abstract interaction of structures, institutions, and bureaucracies of Hitler's government. Because they concentrated on analyzing the "functions" of these structures, that is, what role each structure assumed in the regime's continuation, they became known under the collective sobriquet "functionalists."

The "structuralist" and "functionalist" views were potentially more damning than that of the "intentionalists," because they blamed the atrocities of the Holocaust on the structures and functions of an entire country rather than on the intentions of an elite minority. However, even their interpretation was inadequate. The refusal to blame agents, actors, and their intentions rendered responsibility abstract, indeed apolitical. Everything was explained by functional inevitability instead of being attributed to concrete political actions and real individuals.

The monumental two-volume *Anatomie des SS-Staates* (*Anatomy of the SS State* [1965]), authored by Hans Buchheim, Broszat, Hans-Adolf Jacobsen, and Krausnick, was an early precursor of the structural and systemic approach to the study of the Holocaust. Between 1969 and 1971 functionalists Martin Broszat and Hans Mommsen rejected what they considered to be the overly rationalized and personality-centered history of the intentionalists for analyses that emphasized "internal contradictions" and the "chaotic" decision-making apparatus within the Nazi state. These scholars viewed the Holocaust, not as the result of profound intent, but as the unpredicted outcome of a system run amuck. In 1972 Uwe Dietrich Adam published *Judenpolitik im Dritten Reich* (Jewish policy in the Third Reich), a comprehensive functionalist analysis of the war that assessed the tensions within German society to be as responsible for the Holocaust as Hitler.

Sebastian Haffner's structuralist *Anmerkungen zu Hitler* (The meaning of Hitler [1978]) inverted Eberhard Jäckel's theory of the complementarity of the Nazis' quest for Lebensraum and their implementing the Final Solution by proposing that these two concepts were fundamentally opposed to each other. The former set nation against nation, he said, whereas the latter coalesced all nations against the Jews. According to Haffner, when Lebensraum began to fall short of Hitler's expectations, he turned to the Final Solution in the second half of 1941.

Few social histories of the Holocaust have been published in Germany, and they appeared belatedly. Thus, only in the 1970s and 1980s did German scholars begin to research the question of Jewish resistance against the Nazis. Volker Dahm wrote about the history of the Jewish publishing house Schocken Verlag in 1982, and in the same year Monika Richarz published a testimonial history of Jewish life in the Weimar Republic and the Third Reich. Except for these first-rate scholarly efforts and a few less prominent monographs, the internal workings of the Jewish community and its relationship to the Nazi regime have remained untreated by German academics.

It should be noted that while the functionalists/structuralists and intentionalists represented two different interpretations of the causes and events of the Holocaust, both condemned the Nazi perpetrators.[74] This was not the case in the Federal Republic of the 1980s. The disagreements between intentionalists and functionalists/structuralists reflected the impulse toward polarization that has characterized German historiography.[75] The intentionalists, who had fought to stem the tide of apologia and national amnesia of the immediate postwar era, felt threatened by the analyses of functionalist historians, which they perceived as undermining their efforts. Unlike the gradual shifts in Holocaust studies among non-Germans, in Germany the struggle between intentionalists and structuralists/functionalists led to bitter controversies, reflecting the emotionally charged significance of the Holocaust for Germany.

The Treatment of the Holocaust in Textbooks. Perhaps even more influential in forming attitudes and perceptions about the Holocaust has been its presentation in textbooks used in elementary and secondary education. Ultimately, textbooks have a long-term impact on a population's view of a topic as sensitive as the Holocaust. President Richard von Weizsäcker put it succinctly: "Young people are not responsible for what happened then; but they are responsible for what will be made of it in history."[76]

The challenge facing German primary- and secondary-school teachers has been how to educate students about the events of World War II while maintaining a positive connection between the past and the present. During the 1950s, history textbooks dealt with the Holocaust inadequately, and many social studies teachers avoided the topic altogether. The Holocaust was too controversial, many teachers claimed, for a crowded curriculum in which the twentieth century had been accorded too little attention as it was.

The real push to teach the Holocaust in Germany's schools began in the early 1960s after a rash of anti-Semitic graffiti prompted politicians to supplement the social science curriculum with materials combating the cultivation of fascist and undemocratic sentiments.[77] Teaching the history of the Third Reich became mandatory for the curricula of all types and levels of schools in 1961. Students who wanted to complete high school were required to study the Holocaust. Textbooks were rewritten, and more political science and history teachers were employed.

In spite of these formal requirements, Holocaust education has by no means received uniform treatment in Germany's primary and secondary schools. The subject has been much more frequently and more thoroughly discussed in the Federal Republic's elite gymnasia than in the less academically oriented *Hauptschulen.* Entries to the German President's History Essay Contest for schoolchildren, for example, have usually come from the college preparatory students in gymnasia (56.8 percent) rather than from the students at *Hauptschulen.*[78] As the 1990 film *The Nasty Girl* demonstrated, the "confrontation with the past" has been far from thorough or even adequate in many German classrooms.

Yet, as Peter Dudek, a German educational specialist, has written, "Auschwitz is not material that can be handled with the same curriculum-planning strategies by which the quadratic equation and hexameters are modeled into learning material."[79] Two German high-school teachers, Birgit Wenzel and Dagmar Weber, conducted a study of history textbooks commonly used in all types of German schools to teach the Holocaust.[80] They found that while a majority of the textbooks covered the major events of the Holocaust, most neglected to convey the qualitative significance of the tragedy. One of the major problems, they said, was the texts' depersonalized presentation of events. An array of numbers and statistics, instead of stories of personal experiences, formed the core of these texts. Yet another problem was the overemphasis on Hitler's personality and the Nazi elite, with little explanation given of National Socialism and its causes. Moreover, the persecution of the Jews was never presented in the larger historical context of German and European anti-Semitism.

Wenzel and Weber's study offered six suggestions for improving the Holocaust curriculum in German schools. First, a mere listing of facts and statistics had to be avoided. Second, the victims of National Socialism should not be portrayed as faceless and anonymous; rather, the fate of individuals with whom students could empathize should be an integral part of Holocaust education. Third, the roles played by judges, bureaucrats, and leaders of industry and of the economy in the rise of National Socialism and the success of the Nazi machine needed to be explained. Teachers must address the German people's passivity and inaction during the war, central to the German dilemma of coming to terms with the past. Fourth, the history of the Holocaust should not be monocausally presented and thereby depicted as inevitable. Fifth, the Holocaust should be used to combat present-day anti-Semitism and hatred of foreigners and teach the responsibilities of citizens in a democracy. Finally, homework and class assignments should focus less on the memorization of facts and more on analysis and interpretation. Pictures as well as interviews with survivors should also play a vital role in the study of the Holocaust.

These suggested reforms reveal some of the disturbing lacunae in Holocaust education in the Federal Republic. Even the government-sponsored exhibit "Questions on German History, 1800 to the Present," which has been displayed in Berlin continuously since 1971, is conspicuously meek on the Holocaust. It provides a statistical table on the number of people murdered and several uncaptioned photographs of the concentration camps, but little else. It includes no background on Germany's Jews nor any history of German anti-Semitism. Within the one room allotted to the Third Reich, neither the word "Holocaust" nor the term "Final Solution" is to be found. The exhibition portrays the Hitler period mainly as the unfortunate interlude of an unsuccessful and overblown military regime. In the extensive exhibition catalogue, which comprises several hundred pages, only two and a half pages deal with National Socialism, anti-Semitism, and the Holocaust. As in the exhibit itself, pictures of concentration camp victims appear without explanation. Kristallnacht is mentioned only in an appendixed historical chronology. Not one of the multicolored charts designed to explain the political evolution of the Federal Republic mentions the Holocaust.

That an officially sponsored exhibit entitled "Questions on German History" should ignore the most perplexing and troubling one of all is yet another illustration of Germany's avoidance of this painful topic and its failure to confront it with honesty and vigor. Of course there are monuments in Germany erected in memory of the Holocaust. It was exactly twenty years after the end of World War II—May 9, 1965—before Dachau, one of the Third Reich's most notorious concentration camps, was opened as a memorial. Approximately three hundred thousand people visit the camp each year. During the 1980s many plaques and other mementos memorializing the Holocaust were erected on the local level. As of 1996, however, Germany did not have a national monument to the victims of the Holocaust. Instead, these can be found with increasing frequency in American cities.

The Auschwitz Trials. The Auschwitz trials, held in Frankfurt from 1963 to 1968, had a key part in the evolution of West Germany's reaction to the Holocaust. The result of five and a half years of preparation, including the gathering of over four hundred witnesses, these proceedings to prosecute members of the SS who had run the Auschwitz concentration camp grew into a major media spectacle. Journalists from around the world attended the trials and reported the horrors recounted by survivors who had come to testify from the United States, Israel, and Eastern Europe.

Not one of the twenty-three defendants (twenty-two Waffen SS and one camp trustee, or *kapo*) had actually violated the laws of the National Socialist state. Nonetheless, the defendants—doctors, guards, and supervisors of the gas chambers—were to stand trial for crimes committed against the statutes of the Federal Republic and against the foundations of morality. Twenty years after the war, they came before the Frankfurt Court of Assizes on charges of murder and torture of an unascertainable number of human beings.

The first and longest of the trials began on December 20, 1963, and ended on August 20, 1965. Two other proceedings lasted about nine months each. All remained unpopular among the German public. To uncover such a horrible past by singling out a handful of seemingly peaceable, bourgeois family men with no criminal records seemed an unnecessary witch hunt to most Germans. Opinion polls consistently revealed that a decisive majority of the Federal Republic's population opposed the trials.[81]

Yet for those who had suffered at the hands of the Nazis, especially the Jews, the Auschwitz trials were vital for the very reasons that made them threatening and distasteful to Germans. Documenting and publicizing the atrocities of Auschwitz were as important functions of the court as the rendering of justice. In a sense, then, the Frankfurt Auschwitz trials succeeded not because they meted out justice but because they publicized a hitherto well-guarded secret. Truths about National Socialism and the mass murder implemented by Hitler's SS and *Einsatzgruppen* became public knowledge. Among other immediate ramifications, the trials inspired many artists to express their reaction to the accounts of the survivors and sparked a new wave of Holocaust fiction. Martin Walser's drama *Der schwarze Schwan,* about the impact of the Holocaust on the Federal Republic's second generation, was one such work. Rolf Hochhuth's *The Deputy* (1964), about the passivity of the pope concerning the extermination of the Jews, also premiered in Berlin at this time. Peter Weiss, deeply moved by the testimonials at Frankfurt, adapted the trial into a drama and eleven-song verse cycle, *Die Ermittlung* (The investigation [1965]), which was later performed as an oratorio.

In the first trial, six of the defendants were sentenced to life imprisonment, the maximum punishment permitted by the Federal Republic's constitution, the Basic Law. Three were acquitted. Ill health accounted for the release of two more of the accused. All of the remaining defendants received prison terms ranging from 3.5 to 14 years. While the life sentences truly meant life imprisonment without parole, the other sentences were lenient considering the enormity of the crimes committed.[82] It was at this trial that the West German public witnessed the widespread—and successful—usage of *Befehlsnotstand* (just following orders) as a defense strategy. This cynical abdication of individual responsibility was likely to appeal to most Germans, because it also exonerated them from their complicity in the worst crime in human history.

Rebuilding the Community. The 1950s and 1960s marked the height of the Cold War in Germany. While tensions between East and West Germany attained crisis proportions, the Federal Republic was in the midst of its "economic miracle." Unemployment reached such low levels that the Federal Republic had to import almost one million foreign workers, mainly from Greece, Italy, and Turkey, to fill jobs the Germans had the luxury to reject. While this multiethnic and multicultural infusion was to sow the seeds of a new and pernicious racism and xenophobia in Germany, this period also witnessed a particularly heightened and heretofore unprecedented sensitivity toward Jews on the part of certain German institutions, particularly religious ones.

The Council of Societies for Christian-Jewish Cooperation, founded in 1949 under American aegis, instituted an Annual Brotherhood Week to be commemorated every March with activities and lectures on Jewish themes all over Germany. Heinrich Böll and Paul Schallück founded a library of German Jewish history in Cologne. Government and religious community leaders worked together to erect a new synagogue in Berlin in 1959 on the site of the magnificent Fasanenstrasse temple, which had been destroyed by the Nazis on Kristallnacht.

A synagogue desecration in Cologne in 1959 set off a rash of similar incidents, and the acts were greeted by a general public outcry condemning the vandalism. In several communities, schoolchildren and boy scouts volunteered to clean up desecrated cemeteries. Groups like Drei Ringe (Three Rings), made up of Protestant, Catholic, and Jewish students, made the promotion of interfaith cooperation their central purpose.[83] This demonstration of idealism among certain youths was an exception in a period when Germany's young people, like those in other parts of Western Europe and the United States, appeared to be increasingly skeptical of all ideologies, feeling equally apathetic about Nazism, Communism, and democracy. However, Nazism, although thoroughly discredited and delegitimized, did not vanish completely.

In 1961 the West German Institute of Opinion Research reported that only 5 percent of the German population "would vote for a man like Hitler"; in comparison, 15 percent had responded in this way in 1954.[84] Political leaders and the media all condemned Hitler and National Socialism as well as contemporary signs of emergent neo-Nazism. Although there were still those who publicly expressed admiration for the "achievements of Nazism," almost all established political and cultural leaders warned of the moral dangers of forgetting the past.

Also in 1961, a new synagogue was dedicated in Bremen, and the historic Rashi synagogue in Worms was rebuilt. In February of the following year, services were held again in the two-hundred-year-old synagogue in Ansbach, Bavaria, even though no Jews lived there any more. Hundreds of thousands of Germans flocked to the

"Monumenta Judaica," a vast exhibition in Cologne describing two thousand years of Jewish history along the Rhine. The length of the exhibition's stay had to be extended to accommodate all the visitors. Even though there were few Jews left in Germany, Jewish culture was, to some extent, revived by the Germans during the 1960s.[85]

At that time, unofficial population estimates placed the number of Jews in West Germany at 30,000 to 40,000, in seventy-two communities, the largest of which was Berlin. Between 1945 and 1961 some 12,000 Jews returned to Germany.[86] While the death rate remained higher than the birth rate, immigrants created a steady, if small, increase in the Jewish population during the 1960s. The high rate of intermarriage impeded a more substantial growth of the Jewish community, as did the relatively advanced age of its members. The average age of Jews living in Germany in 1964 was 46.1. A 1966 survey indicated that only 35 percent of the Jews were employed. An additional 25 percent were already pensioners, while 40 percent remained unemployed and were supported by their families. Even by the mid-1960s no Jews held top managerial posts in any branch of the economy.[87] Under the auspices of the Zentralwohlfahrtsstelle der Juden in Deutschland, the main umbrella organization for Jewish welfare, social services flourished within the Jewish community. Jewish loan societies and clubhouses for Jewish youth, for example, opened in several cities. An absence of ordained rabbis and a shortage of religious teachers in the late 1950s and their only minimal presence in the 1960s prompted the active participation of lay members of the small community.

Several major war crimes trials during this period also drew the attention of Germans to the fate of the Jews. Ninety-five percent of the population professed to be aware of the Eichmann trial in Jerusalem, which had attracted worldwide interest in 1961. Fewer followed the Auschwitz trials in Frankfurt. The Treblinka trial (1964–65), the Krumey-Hunsche trial over the deportation of Hungarian Jews (1964–65), and the Tarnopol trial of the SS men responsible for the massacres in Lvov, to name only a few, all conveyed the Holocaust's enormity to an apathetic, skeptical, and often hostile public.

The Verjährungsdebatte. The *Verjährungsdebatte,* the debate over the extension of the statute of limitations for Nazi war crimes, began in the spring of 1965.[88] If the statute had been allowed to expire, it would have put an end to any additional trials against war criminals. While eighty thousand cases had already been processed by this time, another fourteen thousand were still pending. After much impassioned debate, the Bundestag voted 364 to 96, with 4 abstentions, to extend the term of permissible prosecution. This move in favor of extending the statue of limitations won the support of the Left and Center, comprising the Social Democratic Party of Germany (SPD), the Free Democratic Party (FDP), and, surprisingly, the liberal factions of the Christian Democratic Union (CDU). As expected, the Social Democrats were the most reliable advocates of the Jewish cause. The Social Democrats received support from the Free Democrats, who, though on the other side of the political aisle, were allied with them in this crucial campaign. Even some "liberal" members of the CDU, whose party, together with the FDP, formed the ruling coalition at the time, opposed the *Verjährung,* the statute of limitations.[89] As a result the trials continued. Of 176 defendants tried by 1976, 26 received life sentences, 96 faced shorter prison terms, and 54 (30 percent) were acquitted.[90] The *Verjährungsdebatte* continued amid controversy well into the 1970s. In 1979, after the airing of the television series *Holocaust,* the statute of limitations was finally abolished altogether.

The extension of the statute of limitations boded well for German-Jewish reconciliation. In 1965 the West German federal ministry of the interior reported a decline in anti-Semitic incidents, membership in left- and right-wing extremist parties, and the circulation of anti-Semitic periodicals.[91] Nonetheless, cemetery desecrations continued, most ironically in places like Bremen, where only seventy-three people out of a population of seventy-three thousand were Jewish. Nationalist sentiments were on the rise following the electoral successes of the right-wing German Nationalist Party (NPD) in many regional parliaments. While the NPD did not officially endorse anti-Semitism, its membership undeniably contained significant numbers of old and new Nazis. Throughout the 1960s, conflict between Jewish leaders and the local politicians in Oberammergau created an unpleasant source of tension. The script of the passion play traditionally performed at Oberammergau once every decade contains overtly anti-Semitic references to Jews.

In 1967 unemployment in Germany doubled from the previous year. Although economic conditions worsened, which traditionally meant a precarious time for any Jewish community in Europe, Christian-Jewish relations became stronger, in large part due to the overwhelming public support for Israel during the Six-Day War. Germans were proud to see the Jews, the perpetual victims, assert themselves and become victors. By January 1, 1967, the German government had paid 31.3 billion DM ($8 billion) in restitution to Israel and the Jews, including indemnification payments to individuals persecuted under Hitler.[92] Of course, many claims remained unfulfilled. No matter how substantial the sum appears, it could never even approximate a just level of atonement for the crimes committed by the Nazis against the Jews. Yet, at the end of the sixties it seemed that certain bonds of goodwill had been forged between the German and Israeli governments.

Changing Attitudes: The Third Period, 1967 to the Present

Israel and the German Left. In the 1960s the positive relationship between the Jews and the German Left, in particular, was fostered by the Left's fervent antifascism and concomitant anti-Nazism. However, partly in opposition to this old Left, its post-1968 successor, the so-called New Left, used antifascism to displace the Jewish Question from its prominence among paradigms of historical analysis. Through the Marxist-Freudian lens of the New Left, all fascists, whether Nazis or Americans in Vietnam, appeared in the same hue. Ironically, the intensity of the New Left's antifascist convictions furthered the marginalization of the Holocaust in German discourse. Whereas the student movement had sympathized with Israel in reaction to the students' fathers' generation, the New Left's sympathies drifted increasingly toward the Arab viewpoint after the Israeli victory in 1967. This identification with Palestinians against their supposed imperialist oppressor (Red Army Faction terrorists often linked their cause with Arab activities) represented to many not a genuine rejection of Israel but rather a symbolic displacement of blame on the "victim."[93]

The New Left's conflation of fascism and Nazism, part of a larger historical debate over whether to interpret National Socialism as fascist or totalitarian, minimized the uniqueness of the Holocaust and helped accentuate the Left's rapidly growing hostility toward Israel, which had become an integral part of its credo and identity. Members of the Left disrupted speeches made by the Israeli ambassador, and everything Israeli was vilified; conversely, all things Arab, especially Palestinian, were extolled.[94]

Instead of continuing to wear the formerly fashionable kibbutz hat, members of the German Left began to drape themselves ceremoniously in the checkered scarf of the Palestinian fedayeen, creating a milieu in which Israel became *the* enemy. By the early 1970s a number of radical leftists were receiving extensive training in guerrilla warfare in camps administered by the most radical and uncompromising factions of the Palestine Liberation Organization (PLO), notably the Popular Front for the Liberation of Palestine (PFLP) and the Democratic Front for the Liberation of Palestine (DFLP). Those familiar with this atmosphere should not have been shaken when Germans could once again participate in the selection of Jews from non-Jews, as happened during the 1976 hijacking of an El Al plane to Entebbe, Uganda.[95]

Why did the New Left fail to address the Holocaust while remaining obsessed with the trauma of the Weimar period, during which internecine conflict between Communists and Social Democrats predominated? The Left's amnesia resulted in part from its ritualized adherence to a simplistic Marxist model through which it repeatedly reground the past. It also resulted from a preoccupation with other issues at the time: the question of German unification, relations with the countries in Eastern Europe and the Soviet Union operating under "real existing socialism," and America's involvement in Vietnam.

One of the most salient dividing lines between the old Left and the new was the position taken on Israel. The old German Left's support of Israel was tantamount to a *Glaubensbekenntnis,* a declaration of faith, and a basic tenet of its dominant social democratic expression. For the New Left, however, Israel became the new bogeyman, the neighborhood bully who had to be opposed by all progressives and their allies.

The New Left professed to differentiate between Jews and Israelis, embracing the cause of the former and vilifying that of the latter. It saw nothing contradictory in attacking Israel while rallying on behalf of various Jewish causes in the Federal Republic. This ideological stance stemmed in large part from the New Left's unwillingness to come to terms with the Holocaust's role in German history. As long as it continued to speak only about fascism in a generic sense instead of National Socialism in a very particular one, it maintained the view that anti-Semitism and the Holocaust were merely ancillary to fascism rather than integral parts of National Socialism. Thus, for the New Left, Auschwitz always remained a secondary manifestation of fascism.

The New Left's animosity toward Israel had other roots as well. The Six-Day

War metamorphosized Israel into the darling of the Right. Gone were the days when Germans were haunted by the ghosts of the past. Reminiscent of the German army's heroes, Moshe Dayan (the new "Desert Fox") and his generals destroyed a numerically superior enemy in a matter of days. To the right-wing Springer Press, publisher of many newspapers, including the mass-circulation daily *Bildzeitung*, Israel was a much-admired and even welcomed hero. This, of course, was the same organization that mocked the student Left in its flagship papers, denouncing its views, activities, and leaders and exhorting the police and the public to oppose the students with all possible means, including violent ones. The fact that Israel's most vociferous friend was the New Left's most uncompromising enemy did not endear Israel to the New Left. The Left held the view that everything Israeli had to be reactionary, because Israel was approved by the most emphatically conservative voice in the Federal Republic.[96]

Like the Left, the conservatives differentiated between Jews and Israelis. The Right's view of the two groups was a mirror image of the Left's: if the latter disliked Israelis and favored Jews, the former did just the opposite. The Right's traditional dislike of Jews reemerged once again during the so-called Hitler Wave, which swept across Germany in the mid-1970s. Films, books, records, plays, and various paraphernalia attempting to justify and, in some cases, even glorify National Socialism and especially Hitler proliferated. Among the most notorious contributions to this trend were Helmut Diwald's *Geschichte der Deutschen* (History of the German people [1976]), which omitted virtually all mention of the Holocaust, and Joachim Fest's generally favorable biography of Hitler, *Hitler, eine Biographie,* published in 1973 and subsequently made into a documentary. Fest minimizes the Holocaust to the point of de facto denying its existence. A rock opera performed in Hamburg extolled Hitler's charismatic power and portrayed him positively as an offbeat, campy character. Hans-Jürgen Syberberg's films on Hitler (*Hitler ein Film aus Deutschland* [1979] and *Parsifal ein Filmessay* [1982]), though artistically original, also whitewashed and even praised Hitler as a leader and a German. However influential some of these works were, none of them approached the immense impact made by *Holocaust,* a Hollywood-style television series, on the perception of the Holocaust in Germany.

Holocaust. The airing of the American-made television docudrama *Holocaust* during the week of January 21, 1979, captured the German nation's rapt attention.[97] More than one hundred previously televised documentaries and educational programs on Germany's Nazi past had attracted only a handful of viewers. The much-maligned Hollywood melodrama, however, succeeded where the others had failed: it pricked the conscience of many Germans and catalyzed a public debate on an unprecedented scale.

Few people expected such a positive and overwhelming reaction. Efforts to bring the film to a German audience had been fraught with difficulties. Following *Holocaust*'s controversial and commercially successful American showing in April 1978, WDR, the largest of the West German regional television networks, paid one million DM ($550,000) to secure broadcasting rights. This fee was second only to the 1.3 million DM ($750,000) WDR had paid for *Roots*. WDR's initial intention of airing the film jointly with the eight other regional, publicly supported networks ran into immediate difficulty. Four of the eight refused to air the film nationally and simultaneously on ARD, the most highly watched "First Program." They justified their decision by saying that *Holocaust's* cinematic merits, historical accuracy, and suitability for the German viewing public were questionable.[98] Minor discrepancies, such as an American ring to a German telephone and an inaccurate depiction of SS uniforms, became part of a larger political disagreement that reflected party loyalties and divergent views regarding the past and its implications.

A compromise solution relegated the simultaneous showing of *Holocaust* to a regional channel (the "Third Program"). Demoting the film to the "intellectual ghetto" of the "Third Program" represented more than a symbolic act. Like American Public Television, this channel's viewing audience remains small in number. Furthermore, the air time, from 9:00 P.M. to 12:00 A.M., presented another obstacle to attracting a large audience. It is in this context that the viewer ratings were nothing short of sensational: more than 40 percent of all German television viewers—roughly 15 million people—watched the program every night. Over 35,000 telephone calls (four times the number reported by NBC during the film's American showing) were received by the stations, and a comparable number of letters and telegrams poured in. The 20,000 information booklets published by the government to accompany the show disappeared in an avalanche of 255,000 orders. Most of the requests came from people under thirty-five, an age group particularly interested in this period.[99]

The controversy following the acquisition of *Holocaust* by WDR demonstrates that the film's subject matter touched a raw nerve. Three days prior to the airing of the film's first segment, during the showing of a preparatory documentary entitled *Final Solution,* two television transmitters were bombed by neo-Nazi groups. Letters and editorials in some of the country's conservative newspapers critiqued the film's kitsch and American Hollywood sentimentality. Many criticisms echoed a desire to forget finally the past and refrain from making the Germans the sole culprits for World War II and its atrocities. They were also concerned that the Federal Republic's international image would be tarnished.[100]

In marked contrast to these views, most liberal and Left-leaning periodicals wholeheartedly supported the film's showing. Many members of the governing Social Democratic Party, including Chancellor Helmut Schmidt, regarded the event as a healthy step in the Federal Republic's political development.[101] The Trade Union Federation (DGB) and each of its seventeen constituent unions issued strongly worded statements in support of the program.

When *Holocaust* was finally broadcast in four segments, each part was followed by a two-hour-long panel discussion in which distinguished German and international academics explored issues presented in the film in the present German context. Although the panels differed in their modes of analysis and presented often contradictory opinions in their attempts to explain the horrors of National Socialism, they nonetheless contributed intellectual insights of rare quality.[102]

No medium can ever fully convey the horrors of the Holocaust. All the panel experts emphasized that the film's explicit brutality never came close to the reality. Yet the film did disseminate valuable, if flawed, information to the widest possible public. In Germany the critical drawbacks of *Holocaust* were precisely what enabled its success. Hollywood's simplification allowed a large segment of the German public to experience the destruction of the Jews. For a large number of Germans, Mrs. Weiss's final walk to the gas chambers, even though she was in unrealistically good health and in full possession of her long hair, expressed more about Auschwitz than the most authentic documentaries had done.[103]

The movie's American origins gave it a creative freedom no German production could have enjoyed. *Holocaust*'s historical naiveté, empirical inaccuracy, and emotionalism—prerequisites for a popular success of this dimension—would have been morally inexcusable, politically unfeasible, and historically impossible in a German film. A German-made *Holocaust* like the American one would have been rejected not only by the Germans themselves but by the rest of the world as well, especially the Jews. Since a similar German production remained impossible in 1979, *Holocaust* provided Germans with a popular educational tool.

Despite numerous noble attempts to examine particular aspects of the Nazi era, the Holocaust had remained largely taboo in the Federal Republic before the showing of *Holocaust*. As a result, one encountered great ignorance about the genocide along with extensive detailed knowledge of the war on the part of those individuals who directly experienced National Socialism. For example, viewers who could give sophisticated clarifications of the differences between the Wehrmacht, the *Einsatzkommandos,* and the Waffen SS displayed a shocking lack of knowledge about the Holocaust. While some viewers provided valuable corroborative historical documentation from personal collections—one former SS officer sent in his private pictures of a burning synagogue filled with Jews to confirm the accuracy of a similar scene in the movie—others still could not quite fathom how Germans could have committed such crimes.[104]

The question that many Germans were unable to articulate was now undeniably answered for all of Germany: the Holocaust did in fact happen. *How* it happened was not as easily answered. The discussions proliferating in restaurants and train stations represented an important milestone in the lengthy and painful process of finding an answer. Individuals who until then had remained silent about the *Endlösung* began to discuss *Holocaust,* not only as a film but as a tragic and integral part of German history. Although no single word or expression could do justice to events of this magnitude, the linguistic adoption of the English term "Holocaust," in lieu of the German *Endlösung,* seemed significant. The former connoted a particular human tragedy, whereas the latter merely reiterated the bureaucratic euphemism of the Nazis.

Questions such as who willingly helped the Jews or looked the other way and who resisted or collaborated with the Nazis provided for the first time the basis for a comprehensive evaluation of Nazism's implications for the twentieth century. A variety of approaches became evident in public debate. Discussions focused on themes ranging from the temporal and cultural manifestations of cruelty to the particular formations of German authority patterns that culminated in a frequently servile demeanor toward the state. Most important, demands were voiced for a series of German-made documentaries and dramatic presentations explaining the role of the Jews in modern German history and showing their contributions to German culture.[105]

The movie and its aftermath had surprisingly tangible effects on Germany's public debate. When four out of eleven defendants in the Majdanek trial, one of the country's last trials of camp guards and their accomplices, held in Düsseldorf in the late 1970s, were acquitted, an unusual display of public outrage ensued. On July 4, 1979, in the continuing debates over the expiration of the statute of limitations on war crimes, 355 members of the Bundestag—all but one of the SPD delegates, supported by a smattering of CDU and FDP politicians—voted against the expiration, thus making further prosecution of Nazi war criminals possible. (For over a century German law had prohibited prosecution for the crime of murder after thirty years.) Since the constitution of the Federal Republic was adopted in 1949, December 31, 1979, would have been the last date for prosecution.

Until the screening of *Holocaust*, the German public remained relatively indifferent to the debate concerning the statute of limitations. Between 1945 and 1949 the Allies had found 5,000 people guilty of war crimes; during the next thirty years (1950–77) only 1,204 were convicted.[106] The Germans generally resisted judicial efforts to unveil the past and to conduct trials for crimes they preferred to forget. Remarkably, however, the series awakened a consciousness that involved all the political parties, putting the Right on the defensive. No other book, film, or event was mentioned by those fighting against the expiration of the statute of limitations as more influential than *Holocaust*.

The series was also broadcast at a time of growing public criticism of the failure of the republic to fulfill some of its own basic principles of justice. Of particular importance in this context were the two Russell tribunals, held in Frankfurt in 1978 and Cologne in 1979. These proceedings investigated the alleged human-rights violations committed by West Germany in its zeal to fight terrorism. The state's security checks at this time were so excessive that they erroneously implicated innocent people and ruined many a person's career. The executive order enabling such stringent measures was entitled "Basic Principles on the Question of Anti-Constitutional Personnel in the Public Service," popularly known as the "Decree against Radicals" *(Radikalenerlass)* and known by its opponents as the "Ban on Careers" *(Berufsverbot).*[107] The order gave the state executive powers to check public servants' political "reliability" and assess their political preferences. Directed mainly against the radical Left, this order intimidated many people and deterred many from entering public service. The order was deployed very unevenly in the Federal Republic's states, more stringently in those governed by conservatives and more leniently in those led by Social Democrats. Most important, the order created an atmosphere of apprehension and intimidation rather than leading to actual arrests and prosecution. The decree remained on the books until 1990.

Despite its flawed nature, and in some ways because of it, *Holocaust* sparked a long-delayed confrontation with the past. The film provoked an unprecedented level of frankness about the Germans' Nazi past, drawing the widest possible audience into the debate.

The *Wende nach Rechts:* Trends of the 1980s

German-Jewish relations during the 1980s reflected the generally increasing conservatism of the Bonn administration. One faux pas followed another in the efforts of Chancellors Helmut Schmidt and Helmut Kohl to normalize Germany's past and improve relations with Israel. Against the wishes of his own Social Democratic Party, Schmidt fought in parliament to sell some of Germany's Leopard tanks to Saudi Arabia. Defending his position in the late 1970s, he insisted that Germany must act according to its interests and not according to its past. In his view, Menachem Begin, whom Schmidt was known to dislike, abused his position as an Eastern European Jew by trying to influence Schmidt, making him feel guilty as a German for the crimes of the Holocaust. In the end, Schmidt's effort proved unsuccessful: the Federal Republic did not sell its tanks to Saudi Arabia.[108]

The issue of guilt's influencing Germany's leadership reemerged once again in January 1984, during Helmut Kohl's visit to Israel. In a much criticized speech, Kohl exempted himself and his generation from responsibility for the Holocaust by virtue of having been born too late to participate in the Nazi regime ("Gnade der späten Geburt," the grace of a late birth). During the same trip, Kohl's spokesman, Peter Boenisch, clad in a full-length, black SS-type leather coat, told his Israeli hosts upon his arrival at Ben Gurion Airport that Jews should not always confront Germans with Auschwitz.[109]

During December of the same year, a delegation from the Green Party visited the key participant countries in the Middle East conflict on a fact-finding mission. As a party interested in Third World liberation movements in general, the Greens frequently made exploratory journeys to gather data for their advocacy of these movements. They were also the most salient successors to the German New Left, which, as noted above, had assumed a particularly virulent anti-Israel stance since the late 1960s. In their report on the mission, Israel received the harshest criticism, while abuses committed by the other countries were barely mentioned. Indeed, it became known that some of the position papers voicing this criticism had in fact been written in West Germany prior to the delegation's departure, which made it clear that its mission had been less the amassing of new information than the condemnation of Israel.[110] To their credit, however, the Greens were the only political party to condemn the Bitburg Affair, which occurred a few months later.

In the spring of 1985 the Bundestag passed the "Auschwitz lie" law, by which the SPD and the Greens succeeded in making it criminal to claim that Auschwitz never existed. This act, however, was severely diluted by the CDU and its conservative allies, which linked the law's passage to the passage of a law that made it equally criminal to deny that Germans were expelled from the German Reich's former eastern territories. The law as it stands thus equates the denial of Auschwitz with denial of the expulsions of Germans from Eastern Europe.[111]

Bitburg. Few incidents better symbolized the continuing tensions between Germans and Jews than the controversy surrounding Bitburg. This incident occurred during a decade in which Germans were attempting to normalize their past. The controversy began in June 1984, when Chancellor Kohl was barred from participating in Allied ceremonies commemorating the fortieth anniversary of the D-Day landings on the beaches of Normandy. Kohl was deeply hurt by this exclusion from the inner circles of the Atlantic Alliance. Had Germany's loyalty to NATO and the United States during the past forty years been for naught, he asked? Were the memories of World War II so powerful that Germany, NATO's most faithful ally, was still viewed with suspicion? What would it take for Germany to be accepted as a fully rehabilitated and legitimate member of the Western community of nations?[112]

Kohl paid U.S. President Ronald Reagan a visit in November 1984 and expressed his great indignation (some sources claim that Kohl cried in Reagan's presence).[113] Kohl urged Reagan to visit a German military cemetery in an act of reconciliation during the president's forthcoming trip to the Federal Republic in May 1985. To keep things balanced, Kohl also suggested that Reagan stop over in Dachau.

When, in February 1985, the president's advance team approved his trip to the German military cemetery Kolmeshöhe in Bitburg, the favorable camera angles, the photogenic background, and its proximity to a U.S. air base far outweighed the fact that forty-nine members of the Nazis' dreaded Waffen SS lay buried there.[114] One month later, Reagan announced at a White House news conference that he would not visit a concentration camp during his trip to Germany lest he reawaken memories that were better left alone and potentially detrimental to the current excellent relationship between Germans and Americans. A month after that, the White House announced that President Reagan, accompanied by Chancellor Kohl, planned to lay a wreath at the military cemetery in Bitburg.

Reagan and his administration were immediately confronted with massive demonstrations from Jewish groups, veterans' organizations, and outraged citizens. Fifty-three U.S. senators "strongly urged" the president to cancel his visit to Bitburg and attend instead "an event commemorating the Holocaust."[115] This was followed by a voice vote in which 85 senators exhorted the president to "reassess his planned itinerary."[116] In the House of Representatives, 257 members wrote a letter to Chancellor Kohl asking him to release the president from his commitment to visit the Bitburg cemetery.[117] Elie Wiesel appealed to Reagan, saying, "That place [Bitburg], Mr. President, is not your place. Your place is with the victims of the SS."[118] The president was visibly moved but continued to stand by his decision to visit the cemetery. His only concession was to reinstate Kohl's original balanced plan: in addition to visiting Bitburg, he would also go to Bergen-Belsen.

The reactions to the Bitburg Affair in Germany were quite different. The entire center Right of the country's political spectrum rallied around Kohl.[119] Alfred Dregger, the CDU's parliamentary floor leader, wrote a letter in response to the one written by the fifty-three senators in which he warned that he would regard a cancellation of President Reagan's trip to Bitburg as an "insult to my brother and his fallen brothers-in-arms."[120] The press, from Germany's most prestigious daily newspaper, the *Frankfurter Allgemeine Zeitung,* to the mass-circulation weekly *Quick,* marveled at the supposedly immense powers of the American Jewish community, which almost succeeded in changing the president's original plans. Jews were accused of continuing a vendetta against the peace-loving Germans, which many interpreted as another example of the Jewish inability to forgive.

The German Bundestag voted 398 to 24 in favor of Reagan's visit to Bitburg, rejecting the Green Party's motion (to whom those 24 votes belonged) to have the visit canceled. Making matters worse was the center Left's almost complete silence on the issue. Even though the Greens mobilized at the last minute and introduced this motion in the Bundestag, they failed to rally their otherwise vocal and committed supporters to oppose the planned visit, which took place on May 5, 1985. Another example of the Left's poor strategy was the fact that the Greens went to Auschwitz on the day of Kohl and Reagan's visits to Bergen-Belsen and Bitburg. Thus, there were virtually no German leftists or liberals actively supporting the handful of Jewish demonstrators outside the gates of the Bitburg cemetery and the Bergen-Belsen concentration camp.[121]

Three days later, at a ceremony commemorating the fortieth anniversary of V-E Day, Federal Republic President Richard von Weizsäcker delivered a moving reconciliatory speech. "All of us," Weizsäcker said, "whether guilty or not, whether old or young, must accept the past. We are all affected by its consequences and liable for it. . . . We must understand that there can be no reconciliation without remembrance."[122] This sentiment was not shared by the general public. A year later, public-opinion polls showed that barely 12 percent of the West German public agreed with Weizsäcker about the importance of remembrance.

Rainer Werner Fassbinder's Der Müll, die Stadt und der Tod. A second unpleasant incident complicating German-Jewish relations occurred in the fall of 1985. Günter Rühle, the director of the Frankfurt Kammerspiele theater, decided to produce Rainer Werner Fassbinder's provocative play *Der Müll, die Stadt und der Tod* (Garbage, the city, and death).[123] Many, particularly a very vocal Jewish community, objected to the production of an overtly anti-Semitic play.[124] A prominent character in the story, the Rich Jew, uses various unsavory schemes to destroy Frankfurt in his unstoppable quest to make money and modernize the city in his image. The play not only contains an anti-Semitic monologue, which begins with the words, "He sucks us dry, the Jew," but also thematizes the traditional anti-Semitic prejudices: the Jew as modernizer who in his wanton lust for profit destroys German values and tradition; the Jew as a rootless cosmopolitan devoid of loyalties; and the Jew as a being whose essence is profoundly alien to the German people.

Other critics wondered why the play was chosen to be performed at this juncture in German history. Fassbinder had written *Der Müll, die Stadt und der Tod* in

1975, and it had been publicly available since early 1976. A loose alliance of Frankfurt's literati and the left-wing intelligentsia agreed with Günter Rühle that it was high time to abandon the *Schonzeit* (no-hunting season) on the Jews, which they thought had defined West Germany's public discourse for far too long.[125] After all, the most basic characteristics of any successful liberal democracy were complete artistic freedom and free speech. The Holocaust simply could not be used to protect the Jews indefinitely. Such excessive consideration undermined the fundamentally democratic character of the Federal Republic. Curiously, it was the country's Right—certainly no friend of the Jews—that argued against the play's performance, though mainly on the grounds of its tastelessness and sensationalism rather than its blatant anti-Semitism.

On the opening night, October 31, 1985, just before the play was to begin about thirty members of the Frankfurt Jewish community occupied the stage and unfurled a banner that read "subventionierter Antisemitismus" (subsidized anti-Semitism). Engaging in a debate with the audience, the actors, and the theater management, the protesters held their ground and succeeded in stopping the performance. Fearing further disruptions, Rühle reluctantly canceled all other scheduled performances of *Der Müll, die Stadt und der Tod.* For the first time in the Federal Republic, Jews had participated in a protest qua Jews. They had not relied on the German state or on their Jewish institutions to protect their rights. They had taken matters into their own hands to change a local situation that affected their lives.

Historikerstreit. In the year following Bitburg, the *Historikerstreit* (Historians' Debate) erupted. In this war of words many prominent historians debated the significance of the Holocaust and its causes.[126] The often vituperative and politicized discussions were widely publicized and spilled over into the mass media. That historians challenged traditional assumptions about the Jewish genocide, even by proposing revisionist theories, was hardly novel. That this move toward normalization and relativization of the Holocaust came on so forcefully and aroused such acrimonious tension in the respectable scholarly community was.

The debate revolved around the publications of two respected historians, Andreas Hillgruber, a Cologne historian, and Ernst Nolte, a philosopher of history who had previously written on the rise of fascism, and the reaction to their work by the liberal Frankfurt social philosopher, Jürgen Habermas. Hillgruber's short treatise *Zweierlei Untergang* (Two kinds of destruction) juxtaposed the Nazi genocide with the slaughter of the German civilian population in East Prussia at the hands of the Soviet army. The tone and approach of the essay, Habermas pointed out, were clearly sympathetic with the Germans.[127] While not exactly invalid, Hillgruber's equation of victim and perpetrator smacked of apologist leanings.

Whereas Hillgruber's relativization of the crime of the Holocaust could have been discounted as an ambiguous error in judgment, Nolte's article "Die Vergangenheit, die nicht vergehen will" (The past that will not pass away), in the conservative *Frankfurter Allgemeine Zeitung,* clearly and unapologetically sought to normalize the Holocaust within the framework of twentieth-century history.[128] Nolte found the roots of the Final Solution in the mass exterminations perpetrated by the Bolsheviks. Hitler, Nolte argued, was driven to killing the Jews by his own fear of what the Russians might do to Germany if they were victorious. To explain Hitler's anti-Semitism, Nolte pointed to Chaim Weizmann's declaration at the Zionist World Congress in 1939 that Jews should fight on the side of the English. While the racism of the Nuremberg laws could have been the result of any authoritarian regime, wrote Nolte, the Holocaust stemmed from the "Asiatic threat" the Jews posed to a people so conditioned by the horrors of Bolshevism.

Habermas reviled Nolte's attempt to relativize the past into neatly categorizable and discrete phenomena of modern history. He, along with other historians, such as Hans-Ulrich Wehler, Jürgen Kocka, Eberhard Jäckel, Hans Mommsen, and Wolfgang Mommsen, refuted the notion that the gulag played more of a role in German history than did Auschwitz. They criticized what they saw as Nolte's extreme intellectualization and utter distortion of the German past.[129]

The *Historikerstreit* represented more than a disagreement over methodology among historians. The issue tended to divide intellectuals along political boundaries. The belief that the Holocaust could be streamlined into the normal course of German history reflected the desire of conservative thinkers to silence the repeated attempts to rework the past in order to revive a sense of German nationalism, which the blot of the Holocaust thwarted. These conservatives were generally readers of the *Frankfurter Allgemeine Zeitung* and members of the CDU or its Bavarian affiliate, the Christian Socialist Union (CSU). Habermas's supporters, on the other hand, belonged mainly to the Social Democratic, the Green, or the Liberal Party and read *Die Zeit*.

Despite the publicity and posturing, the *Historikerstreit* marked no real turning point in the historiography of the Holocaust. Revisionism had long been practiced by historians at both ends of the political spectrum. What the *Historikerstreit* did do was mirror the larger political dispute over questions of national identity and the role of the Nazi past in the democratic present.[130] The *Historikerstreit* reflected the shift to the right in the political climate in Germany as well as Western Europe and the United States during the 1980s. In 1982 the Social Democrats were replaced by a coalition government of Christian Democrats and Liberals following a campaign that advocated a return to "traditional German virtues" and, at the same time, the creation of a new national identity. This trend had already started under the coalition government of Helmut Schmidt and Hans Dietrich Genscher in 1980, when a policy of normalization was adopted in Germany's relations with Israel and the rhetoric of contrition was dropped.[131]

In the years since the *Historikerstreit,* two younger scholars, Götz Aly and Susanne Heim, have reshaped the debate with a novel and provocative thesis.[132] Aly and Heim suggest that lower-level technocrats and social planners in Hitler's bureaucracy calculated that in overpopulated and underdeveloped Eastern Europe the elimination of the backward Jewish poor would facilitate the expansion of the German Reich. These planners articulated this vision to their superiors, who combined it with their ideological anti-Semitism and transformed these economic motivations into what became the Final Solution.

The centrality of the Holocaust, one of the most basic and accepted tenets in postwar German historiography,[133] was abandoned in the 1980s. Heim and Aly's analysis of the Holocaust hails, in good part, from the structuralist/functionalist epistemology, but interpretations such as theirs represent a departure from the traditional understanding of National Socialism and a turn toward revisionism.[134] The changing political climate subtly yet unmistakably welcomed a revision of the German past. Equally important was the passage of time since the Holocaust. After forty years, Germans wanted to put the war behind them.

Historians like Nolte, Hillgruber, and Golo Mann robbed the Holocaust of all particular meaning by equating it with other so-called similar events. The intention was to *relativize,* rather than to *universalize,* the Holocaust. Auschwitz, these historians contended, should no longer be regarded as any different from the bombing of Dresden or Hiroshima. The Jewish victims of National Socialism were in no way different from the German or Japanese victims of Allied bombing or the Soviet victims of Stalin's gulags. This debate gave notice to the fact that the Holocaust's place in the Federal Republic's history and political life had changed.

The 1990s

The fall of the Berlin Wall on November 9, 1989, heralded the end of the two Germanies, a divided Europe, and the entire post-Yalta order. Ironically, Germany's most triumphant day since World War II occurred on the fifty-first anniversary of Kristallnacht, one of the darkest nights in the history of German Jewry. German unification less than one year later, on October 3, 1990, marked the beginning of the transition from the Bundesrepublik to Deutschland. It also marked the beginning of a new chapter in German-Jewish relations.

Since unification 28,000 registered Jews in the united Germany (compared with 500,000 in 1933), in addition to an estimated 20,000 to 30,000 unaffiliated Jews, have been counted.[135] As in the 1930s, the contemporary German-Jewish community is concentrated in a few major cities. Berlin, with 8,000 Jews, and Frankfurt, with 5,000, are the two largest centers of Jewish communal life. More than half of these Jews hail from the former Soviet Union. Nonetheless, the positions of leadership within the Jewish community continue to be dominated by native German Jews or, as in the case of Ignaz Bubis, the head of the Jewish community in Germany, by East European Jews who have made West Germany their home since the late 1940s. Munich boasts an additional 4,000 Jews; Düsseldorf and Hamburg have slightly more and slightly fewer than 1,500, respectively. Several dozen Jews still live in the cities of Dresden, Leipzig, and Erfurt.

Even before the influx of Soviet Jews to Berlin and Frankfurt in the late 1980s and early 1990s, immigrant Jews from Eastern Europe were in the majority in these communities. Their children tend to be well-educated. Most have received at least a high-school diploma, and many have earned a university degree. The majority are self-employed. Rates of intermarriage are among the highest in the world, calculated at 65 percent in 1985. Nonetheless, Jews in Germany maintain cohesive political and religious organizations. All Jews, be they Reform, Conservative, or Orthodox, are organized into one central community. The Zentralrat der Juden in Deutschland (the Central Council for Jews in Germany) continues to serve as the political advocate for Jewish causes.[136]

The continuing search for a German identity in relation to the Holocaust and to the Jews was highlighted in the Germans' sustained and passionate reaction to the Gulf War in early 1991. The fact that this war engendered such fierce reactions in Germany indicates that the subject of the debate, the appropriateness of the Gulf War, couched other, more urgent and personal concerns, namely, the role of German identity, memory, and history, in a profoundly altered European and global context.

Basically, Germans divided into two camps, conveniently, though somewhat glibly, labeled "pacifists" and "bellicists."[137] A telling sign of the complexity of the Gulf War and its relation to German identity formation was that neither group conformed to the conventional political cleavages dividing German society. Thus one could not identify the pacifists as leftists and the bellicists as rightists. The pacifists believed that Germany's singularly violent past rendered *any* war, regardless of its reason and circumstance, illegitimate and criminal. Germans had been particularly "stricken" *(betroffen)* by wars and could claim a moral superiority in denouncing them. The pacifists thus concluded that no matter how evil Saddam Hussein and his regime might be, war as an option was not warranted. Given these beliefs, they were solidly opposed to the actions of the United States and, by extension, Israel. Pacifist Hans-Christian Stroebele, one of the Green Party's leading figures, argued in an interview for the *Jerusalem Post* that "the Iraqi missile attacks are the logical, almost compelling consequence of Israeli policies" and that Israel was at fault because of its past treatment of the Palestinians and the Arab states, including Iraq.[138] Even though Stroebele was forced to resign his leadership position in the Green Party because of these statements, the fact that he uttered them and that they received support in the pacifist camp reveals much about German attitudes toward Israel and the Jews.

In contrast, the bellicists were moved by a completely different reading of German history. To them, the lesson was not "no more wars" but "no more fascism." German history taught the world never to appease dictators, especially fascist aggressors like Saddam Hussein. The bellicists were pro-American, pro-Western, pro–liberal democracy, and pro-Israel. While far fewer in number than the pacifists, the bellicists made their presence felt in prestigious newspapers and journals and in speeches in the Bundestag and other forums. Such leading intellectuals as Jürgen Habermas, Wolf Biermann, Hans Magnus Enzensberger, and Peter Schneider supported Israel. While the presence of such intellectual and political pluralism was testimony to the democratic liveliness of the new Germany, it was disturbing that thousands of mostly young people and many leading politicians and intellectuals supported a regime whose openly expressed desire was the unconditional annihilation of Israel.

The 1990s witnessed a number of interesting developments in the unique and complex relationship between Germans and Jews. Following the *Historikerstreit,* the Bitburg Affair, the Fassbinder incident, and the Gulf War, one would have surmised that a general tendency toward the negative would continue, with very little positive to report. This has not been the case, even though the tally is mixed.

On the positive side, one would have to begin with the success that Steven Spielberg's Oscar-winning movie *Schindler's List* enjoyed among the Germans. The film's release in Germany was a major media event. Virtually all of the country's leading newspapers, news weeklies, and periodicals featured the film, its topic, and its director on their front pages. Lengthy articles on virtually every aspect of the film's content and form filled the pages of German publications for weeks. And in notable contrast to *Holocaust,* when the country's high-brow critics as well as many of its citizens used their entrenched anti-American sentiments to dismiss the film as Hollywood pulp, thereby once again avoiding a painful confrontation with Germany's Nazi past, *Schindler's List* engendered few such obvious cop-outs. There were, of course, a number of negative voices directed against the film, but they were all but drowned in the critical accolades. Most important, the German public voted with its feet and its pocketbooks: on a per capita basis, *Schindler's List* enjoyed its greatest success in Germany, far outdistancing any other European country and rivaling the film's popularity among the American movie-viewing public. To be sure, part of this particular film's attraction for German audiences lay in the fact that the film's hero was a "righteous German," certainly a welcome sight for many Germans.

Special mention should also be made of the construction of the Jewish Museum within the City of Berlin Museum that is expected to open its doors to the public in mid-1997. The Jewish Museum is to be a major statement of Jewish life in Berlin, past and present. Its exhibits will feature all aspects of Jewish life in the city and within the larger context of German and European history. Designed by the architect Daniel Libeskind and under the curatorship of Amnon Barzel, the Jewish Museum promises to be one of Berlin's most distinguished cultural landmarks and lively places of learning.

Most positive, perhaps, has been the growth of an awareness of Jewish culture to a degree that had been unprecedented among Germans of the post-Holocaust era. It is not uncommon to see relatively large audiences of German young people attend a concert of Klezmer music. Readings of Yiddish literature and poetry have proliferated not only in large cities such as Berlin and Frankfurt, but also in university towns such as Heidelberg and Oldenburg. Even with virtually no Jews around them, a small but respectable number of educated Germans has begun to acquaint itself with things Jewish other than the Holocaust.

On a more mixed note, the endless discussions and recriminations surrounding the construction of a Holocaust monument in Berlin have yet to give way to the actual design and erection of such an edifice. It seems certain that some kind of monument in memory of the Holocaust will be built in Germany's capital, but nobody knows for certain according to whose design, at which location, under what aegis, and favored by which coalition of rivalrous people. The fact remains that fifty years after the industrial annihilation of much of European Jewry at the hands of the Nazis, the one place in the world that should have a monument to remember the victims of this crime as of yet has none.

On the negative side, particularly troubling has been the growing number of right-wing rallies and neo-Nazi marches held in Germany's cities in the 1990s. While there has been a significant rise of xenophobia and right-wing aggression in much of Central and Western Europe, most notably in France, Spain, Sweden, Italy, and Austria, its presence in Germany is especially upsetting. Neo-Nazi skinheads and their right-wing allies have killed foreigners, attacked them in their homes, and generally engaged in behavior reminiscent of the Weimar Republic's wanton gangs of fascists.

But, once again, the reactions have been mixed. On the positive side are the huge candlelight vigils held by ordinary citizens in virtually every German city and town which demonstrated impressively that millions of Germans actively oppose racism and the right-wing violence associated with it. On the other hand, the German government's reaction to this violence lacked the zeal and thoroughness with which it pursued left-wing radicalism of the 1970s. Somewhat reminiscent of the situation in the Weimar Republic, German authorities once again exhibited a certain lenience and nonchalance toward right-wing radicalism and terrorism that they would never allow the Left. Indeed, not until it became obvious that these right-wing incidents developed into a liability for Germany's reputation in the world of international business did the government take appropriate steps to prosecute the perpetrators and to combat right-wing radicalism more proactively. While it is certain that these neo-Nazi incidents will not threaten the democratic fabric of Germany, these activities do represent the fringes of a much larger political right and a growing rightward drift that accords this political grouping a respectability and a legitimacy it never possessed in the old Federal Republic. The threshold of the politically acceptable in regard to the German Right and Germany's Nazi past has been substantially lowered in the Berlin Republic.

□

The singularity of Auschwitz has rendered the relationship between Germans and Jews unique. Neither group will ever relate to any other ethnic group, nation, or culture in quite the same way that these two groups relate to each other. This is not to say that German-Jewish relations of the past fifty years have been particularly bad. Quite to the contrary, they seemed rather good. But such descriptions miss the point when the subject is German-Jewish relations. Auschwitz made these relations unmeasurable by the conventional methods of the social sciences and indescribable by the methods of the humanities and history. While comparative data on the presence of anti-Semitism in contemporary Europe are extremely helpful in gauging the persistence (and reemergence) of this age-old prejudice in all societies, Auschwitz has rendered the German numbers beyond comparison with their equivalents in

Poland, France, Britain, or Greece. German-Jewish relations are so derivative of Auschwitz that they remain beyond comprehension. It is this, of course, that makes them unique.

Because of the effectiveness of Auschwitz, German-Jewish relations are largely memory-based. The fact is that many of today's Germans have never met a Jew. The already difficult process of dealing with the past is confined to the realm of thought and memory, virtually never to current experience. Germans "experience" Jews in films, monuments, museums, newspapers, and books, hardly ever at the movies, the grocery store, school, or the dentist's office. Hence, for Germans, Jews often are not real beings. Rather, they are the creatures of the Germans' imagination and enormous guilt. Conversely, Jews do not really experience contemporary Germans. The Jews' trauma has been so lasting that most of the time they still find it impossible to separate Germans from Nazis. Jews often construct a reality in which Germans are gauged, not by their contemporary actions, but by their traumatizing history. This is the only explanation for the fact that most Jews dreaded Germany's unification, even though it meant the destruction of the German Democratic Republic, which had fostered anti-Semitic propaganda and supported regimes favoring the annihilation of Israel. A particularly pernicious aspect of this relationship has been its zero-sum character: what the Germans are desperate to forget, the Jews want permanently remembered. Such an arrangement does not represent a particularly auspicious foundation for a healthy and mutually supportive relationship between two individuals, let alone two nations. And yet a relationship, however flawed and unique, has developed over the past half-century.

Not only has German unification brought an end to the post-Yalta European order, it has changed the nature of the relationship between Germans and Jews. To be sure, the changes in this relationship may not all be bad for either the Germans or the Jews, but things will most certainly be different. Henceforth, German politics will not be confined to the Realpolitik of two middling countries dictated by Cold War logic. Instead, German politics will develop into a powerful instrument commensurate to the hegemony the new Germany already wields in a Europe of constant flux. The changing nature of Germany's European presence, its accumulation of power, and the passage of time will all contribute to forces that will erode the "special" nature of the old Bundesrepublik's relationship with the Jews. But no matter how concerted the German effort toward normalization of this relationship, Auschwitz's indelible character will guarantee its continued uniqueness for Jews and Germans.

NOTES

1. Joshua Trachtenberg, *The Devil and the Jews: The Medieval Conception of the Jew and Its Relation to Modern Anti-semitism* (Philadelphia, 1943), 3.

2. Franz Böhm and Walter Dirks, *Judentum: Schicksal, Wesen und Gegenwart*, 2 vols. (Wiesbaden, 1965), 1:158.

3. Adolf Altmann, *Das früheste Vorkommen der Juden im Deutschland: Juden in römischen Trier* (Trier, 1932).

4. See Heinrich Graetz, *History of the Jews*, vol. 4, *From the Rise of the Kabbala (1270 C.E.) to the Permanent Settlement of the Marranos in Holland (1618 C.E.)* (Philadelphia, [1894], 1949), chap. 4.

5. R. Po-Chia Hsia, *The Myth of Ritual Murder:*

Jews and Magic in Reformation Germany (New Haven, 1988), 3.

6. Böhm and Dirks, *Judentum,* 160.

7. H.G. Adler, *The Jews in Germany from the Enlightenment to National Socialism* (Notre Dame, Ind., 1969), 22. For example, the Jews paid tolls whenever they crossed the borders of one of Germany's three hundred principalities; they paid a head tax and a tax upon the marriage of each child, and in some areas only the firstborn was allowed to marry; and in 1769 the "export of china" tax was introduced, whereby every time a Jew entered into a civil contract, he was required to purchase up to three hundred thalers' worth of royal-manufacture china, for sale abroad at tremendous cost.

8. See Simon Noveck, ed., *Great Jewish Personalities in Modern Times* (Washington, D.C., 1960).

9. Graetz, *History of the Jews,* 4:357.

10. Ibid., 504, 513.

11. Adler, *Jews in Germany,* 4.

12. See, e.g., Peter Gay's description of the case of Georg Simmel in *Freud, Jews, and Other Germans* (Oxford, 1978), 120–26.

13. See Fritz K. Ringer, *The Decline of the German Mandarins* (Cambridge, 1969).

14. Adler, *Jews in Germany,* 5; the Jewish birth rate was half that of the general population.

15. See Gay, *Freud,* chap. 2.

16. Jacob Katz, "German Culture and the Jews," in *The Jewish Response to German Culture,* ed. Jehuda Reinharz and Walter Schatzberg (Hanover, N.H., 1985), 90.

17. Frederic Grunfeld, quoted in Lily Gardner Feldman, *The Special Relationship between West Germany and Israel* (Boston, 1984), 29.

18. Ibid.

19. See the section on German Jewish thinkers in Simon Noveck, ed., *Contemporary Jewish Thought* (Washington, D.C., 1985), 129–292.

20. See Peter Gay, *Style in History* (New York, 1974).

21. See Ismar Schorsch, *Jewish Reactions to German Anti-Semitism, 1870–1914* (New York, 1972).

22. As one would imagine, Jews were disproportionately represented in law, journalism, medicine, trade, and other independent professions in business and commerce. At the beginning of the century they were also paying a disproportionately large share of income tax, reflecting an obvious prosperity (see ibid.).

23. Katz, "German Culture," 86.

24. Monika Richarz, *Jüdisches Leben in Deutschland: Selbstzeugnisse zur Sozialgeschichte, 1918–1945,* 3 vols. (Stuttgart, 1982), 13.

25. Concepts like *Rasseneigentümlichkeit,* or the racial particularity of Jews, as defined by Georg von Schönerer, the rabid Austrian political demagogue, were quickly snatched up in Germany.

26. Peter Pulzer, "Jews and the Crisis of Liberalism," in *German Jewry and Liberalism* (Sankt Augustin, West Germany, 1986).

27. See Jack Werthheimer, *Unwelcome Strangers: East European Jews in Imperial Germany* (New York, 1987), 185; and Richarz, *Jüdisches Leben in Deutschland,* 3:14.

28. Peter Pulzer, *The Rise of Political Anti-Semitism in Germany and Austria* (New York, 1964), 119. See also George L. Mosse, "German Jews and Liberalism in Retrospect," in *Leo Baeck Institute Year Book XXXII* (London, 1987); and Pulzer, "Jews and the Crisis of Liberalism."

29. Böhm and Dirks, *Judentum,* 259.

30. Leo Sievers, *Juden in Deutschland* (Hamburg, 1977), 212.

31. Adler, *Jews in Germany,* 114.

32. Feldman, *Special Relationship,* 23.

33. See Adler, *Jews in Germany,* chap. 17.

34. See the tables in Richarz, *Jüdisches Leben in Deutschland,* 3:53, 59.

35. In 1933 the Cultural Association for Jews, in which Jewish intellectuals would increasingly be ghettoized and marginalized, was founded. What is of significance here is the implied attack against the use of the German language by Jewish writers and the propagation of the idea of language as a reflection of race. Jewish cultural productions were increasingly considered to be racially defined. One could supposedly recognize on sight a poem, painting, or symphony by a Jewish artist (see Sander L. Gilman, *Jewish Self-Hatred: Anti-Semitism and the Hidden Language of the Jews* [Baltimore, 1986]).

36. Richarz, *Jüdisches Leben in Deutschland,* 3:57.

37. Gerald Reitlinger, *The Final Solution* (Northvale, N.J., 1987), 66.

38. Ibid., 157.

39. See Andrei S. Markovits, "Germans and Jews: An Uneasy Relationship Continues," *Jewish Frontier,* April 1984, 14–20.

40. Judith Miller adopts this periodization in her book *One, by One, by One: Facing the Holocaust* (New York, 1990), 38.

41. *American Jewish Year Book, 5707 (1946–7),* vol. 48, ed. Harry Scheiderman and Julius B. Maller (Philadelphia, 1947), 302.

42. Ibid., 45.

43. Ibid.

44. See Alfred Grosser, *Germany in Our Time,* trans. Paul Stephenson (New York, 1970), chap. 2.

While this is a good account, Grosser's narrative tends to be rather apologetic toward these men.

45. See Thomas Alan Schwartz, *America's Germany: John J. McCloy and the Federal Republic* (Cambridge, Mass., 1991). This excellent biography offers a good chronology of the period of U.S. occupation after the war.

46. Lutz Niethammer, *Entnazifizierung in Bayern* (Frankfurt, 1972), 118.

47. Ibid.

48. Peter Märthesheimer, cited in Feldman, *Special Relationship*, 34.

49. See Feldman, *Special Relationship*, 35.

50. Heinz Düx, "Härtefälle: Erfahrungen eines Richters mit der Wiedergutmachung," in *Vor der Gnade der geschenckten Nation*, ed. Hajo Funke (Berlin, 1988), 175.

51. Erich Lüth, cited in Feldman, *Special Relationship*, 37–38.

52. Konrad Adenauer, cited in Feldman, *Special Relationship*, 40.

53. See Konrad Adenauer, *Erinnerungen*, vol. 2 (Stuttgart, 1965), 132, 138, 140 f., 158.

54. Christian Pross, *Wiedergutmachung* (Frankfurt am Main, 1988), 54.

55. Feldman, *Special Relationship*, 60.

56. Ibid., 49.

57. See Michael Wolffsohn, *Eternal Guilt* (New York, 1993); Inge Deutschkron, *Bonn and Jerusalem: The Strange Coalition* (Philadelphia, 1970); and Ralf Vogel, ed., *Der Deutsch-israelische Dialog: Dokumentation eines erregenden Kapitels deutscher Aussenpolitik* (Munich, 1987–90).

58. Feldman, *Special Relationship*, 218.

59. Saul Friedländer, "Historical Writing and the Memory of the Holocaust," in *Writing and the Holocaust*, ed. Berel Lang (New York, 1988), 67.

60. Aharon Applefeld, "After the Holocaust," in Lang, *Writing and the Holocaust*, 86.

61. "Der dickwandige Folterkeller, zu dem der Hitlerismus Deutschland gemacht hatte, ist aufgebrochen, und offen liegt unsere Schmach vor den Augen der Welt, den fremden Kommissionen, denen diese unglaubwürdigen Bilder vorgeführt werden, und die zu Hause melden, dieses Übertreffen an Scheusslichkeit alles, was Menschen sich vorstellen können. 'Unsere Schmach' deutscher Leser und Hörer! Denn alles deutsche, alles was deutsch spricht, deutsch schreibt, auf deutsch gelebt hat, ist von dieser entehrenden Blossstellung mitbetroffen" (Thomas Mann, cited in *Das 20. Jahrhundert: Von Nietzsche bis zur Gruppe 47, Marbacher Katalog des Schiller Nationalmuseums*, no. 36 [Marbach, 1980], 301).

62. Ibid.

63. "Da wir frei miteinander reden können, ist die erste Aufgabe, wirklich miteinander zu reden. Das ist keineswegs leicht. Niemand von uns ist Führer, keiner ist Prophet, der endgültig sagte, was ist und was zu tun sei. Alle 'Führer' sind unheilvolle Phantome gewesen. Sie haben die Freiheit geraubt, erst innerlich, dann äusserlich. Aber sie waren möglich, weil so viele Menschen nicht mehr frei, nicht mehr selbstverantwortlich sein wollten. Heute haben wir die Folge dieses Verzichtes. Wir müssen wieder wagen, verantwortlich zu sein, jeder für sich" (ibid., 309).

64. Jean-Paul Bier, "Paradigms and Dilemmas in the Literary Awareness of West Germany, with Regard to the Persecution and Murder of the Jews," in *Comprehending the Holocaust*, ed. Asher Cohen, Joav Gelber, and Charlotte Wardi (New York, 1988), 286–87.

65. Hans Werner Richter, cited in *Das 20. Jahrhundert*, 312.

66. Siegfried Mews, "Moralist versus Pragmatist? Heinrich Böll and Günter Grass as Political Writers," in *Coping with the Past*, ed. Kathy Harms, Lutz R. Reuter, and Volker Dürr (Madison, Wis., 1990), 140–54.

67. Hannah Arendt, *Eichmann in Jerusalem* (New York, 1963); see also Susan E. Cernyak-Spatz, *German Holocaust Literature* (New York, 1985).

68. For data on Böll's and Grass's contributions to the developing treatment of the Nazi past, we are indebted to Mews, "Moralist versus Pragmatist?"

69. Ibid., 143.

70. This typology is a modification of the work of Jean-Paul Bier in "Paradigms and Dilemmas."

71. The terms "structural" and "functional" are not to be confused with the famous sociological school of "structural functionalism" represented by the writings of Talcott Parsons, Robert Merton, and Marion Levy.

72. Cited in Otto Kulka, "Major Trends and Tendencies in German Historiography on National Socialism and the Jewish Question," in *The Historiography of the Holocaust Period*, Proceedings of the Fifth Yad Vashem International Conference (Jerusalem, 1988).

73. Kulka, "Major Trends and Tendencies."

74. This point is made by Friedländer in "Historical Writing."

75. See Christopher R. Browning, "Approaches to the 'Final Solution' in German Historiography of the Last Two Decades," in Yehuda Bauer, Alice Eckhardt, et al., eds., *Remembering for the Future: Working Papers and Addenda*, vol. 2 (Oxford, 1989), 71. See also Browning, "Beyond 'Intention-

alism' and 'Functionalism': The Decision for the Final Solution Reconsidered," in Browning, *The Path to Genocide: Essays on Launching the Final Solution* (Cambridge, 1992), 86–121.

76. Richard von Weizsäcker, "The 8th of May, 1945—Forty Years After," in *A Voice from Germany: Speeches by Richard von Weizsäcker,* trans. Karin von Abrams (New York, 1987), 43–60, quotation on p. 50.

77. See H.-F. Rathenow and N. H. Weber, eds., *Erziehung nach Auschwitz* (Pfaffenweiler, 1989).

78. Peter Dudek, "Curriculare Folgen von Lehrplänen des Holocaust in deutschen Sekundarschulen," in ibid., 117.

79. Ibid., 114.

80. Birgit Wenzel and Dagmar Weber, "'Auschwitz' in Geschichtsbüchern der Bundesrepublik Deutschland," in Rathenow and Weber, *Erziehung nach Auschwitz.*

81. *American Jewish Year Book, 1965* (Philadelphia, 1965), 410; *1966* (Philadelphia, 1966), 348.

82. *American Jewish Year Book, 1966,* 347, 350.

83. *American Jewish Year Book, 1961* (Philadelphia, 1961), 260–61, 271.

84. Reported in *American Jewish Year Book, 1962* (Philadelphia, 1962), 344.

85. *American Jewish Year Book, 1962,* 354; *1963* (Philadelphia, 1963), 337; *1964* (Philadelphia, 1964), 254.

86. *American Jewish Year Book, 1962,* 353; *1963.*

87. "Jews in the German Economy," survey conducted by a German monthly economic journal, *Capital.* The results of the survey were published in the *American Jewish Year Book, 1967* (Philadelphia, 1967), 365.

88. *American Jewish Year Book, 1965,* 409; *1966,* 350–51. Starting in 1966, the *American Jewish Year Book* featured a regular section on the *Verjährungsdebatte* for as long as the controversy persisted.

89. Richard H. Kreindler, "The War Crimes Debates: The Evolving Relationship between the Nazi Past and Contemporary German Politics" (B.A. honors thesis, Department of Government, Harvard College, 1980). The three main political parties in the Federal Republic have been the CDU-CSU, the SPD, and the FDP. The CDU (with its Bavarian counterpart the Christian Social Union [CSU]) has, with the exception of 1972, been the strongest party in Germany, led by Chancellors Konrad Adenauer, Ludwig Erhard, and Helmut Kohl. The party has advocated largely conservative policies and has occupied the center Right of the political spectrum in the Bundesrepublik. Germany's oldest party, the Social Democrats, has been the prototypical European Social Democratic party, pursuing center Left policies largely favoring the working class, both its traditional and its new members. The FDP, too, is typical of European liberalism. Staunchly pro-market in its economic outlook, the FDP has consistently advocated individual-oriented social and cultural policies that would be categorized as liberal in the American sense.

90. *American Jewish Year Book, 1967,* 355–56; *1970* (Philadelphia, 1970), 449–50.

91. See the *American Jewish Year Book* for the late 1960s and early 1970s. The *Yearbook* stopped running its regular section on anti-Semitism from 1969 until the mid-1970s.

92. See Pross, *Wiedergutmachung;* and Rolf Theis, *Wiedergutmachung zwischen Moral und Interesse* (Frankfurt, 1989).

93. Susanne Heenen, "Deutsche Linke—Linke Juden und der Zionismus," in *Die Verlängerung von Geschichte: Deutsche Juden und der Palästinakonflikt,* ed. Dietrich Wetzel (Frankfurt, 1985), 109.

94. See Martin W. Kloke, *Israel und die deutsche Linke: Zur Geschichte eines schwierigen Verhältnisses* (Frankfurt, 1990).

95. Ibid. See also Andrei S. Markovits and Philip Gorski, *The German Left: Red, Green, and Beyond* (New York, 1993), 76.

96. Markovits, "Germans and Jews."

97. See Andrei S. Markovits and Christopher S. Allen, "The German Conscience," *Jewish Frontier,* April 1979, 13–17. See also Friedrich Knilli and Siegfried Zielinski, eds., *Holocaust zur Unterhaltung* (Berlin, 1982).

98. Jeffrey Herf, "The 'Holocaust' Reception in West Germany: Right, Center and Left," *New German Critique,* no. 19 (winter 1980), 37.

99. Andrei S. Markovits and Rebecca S. Hayden, "'Holocaust' Before and After the Event: Reactions in West Germany and Austria," ibid., 59, 64.

100. Ibid., 60, 62, 65, 71.

101. Herf, "The 'Holocaust' Reception," 38.

102. Markovits and Hayden, "'Holocaust' Before and After the Event," 63–64.

103. Ibid., 65. For opinion-poll data on what the Germans actually learned from watching the program, see 66–67.

104. Ibid., 63. See also Knilli and Zielinski, *Holocaust zur Unterhaltung,* 223–92.

105. Ibid., 63, 72–74.

106. Herf, "The 'Holocaust' Reception," 35.

107. See Gerard Braunthal, *Political Loyalty and Public Service in West Germany: The 1972 Decree against Radicals and Its Consequences* (Amherst, 1990).

108. Regina H. E. Cowen, *Defense Procurement in the Federal Republic of Germany* (Boulder, 1986), 257–71; Andrei S. Markovits and Beth Simone Noveck, "The Fassbinder Scandal," in *Yale Handbook of Jewish Writing in Germany*, ed. Sander L. Gilman and Jack Zipes (New Haven, forthcoming). See also Helmut Schmidt, *Menschen und Mächte* (Berlin, 1989), 127, on Schmidt and Begin.

109. "Einen schönen Salat hat man euch serviert," *Der Spiegel*, January 30, 1984, 27–28; see also Markovits and Noveck, "The Fassbinder Scandal," 2.

110. "Auf deutsch geflucht," *Der Spiegel*, December 31, 1984, 57. For the party's reactions to the events and the story, see "Pflanzen und Wurzeln," ibid., February 11, 1985, 23–24.

111. "Ins Irrenhaus," ibid., March 18, 1985, 132; Sebastian Cobler, "Die Strafjustiz als Selbstbedienungsladen," ibid., April 29, 1985, 34–37.

112. The standard works on Bitburg include Geoffrey Hartman, ed., *Bitburg in Moral and Political Perspective* (Bloomington, Ind., 1986); and Ilya Levkov, ed., *Bitburg and Beyond* (New York, 1987). For a full chronology of events, see Hartman, *Bitburg*, xiii–xvi. See also James Schwartz and Peter Alsberg, "A Visit to Bitburg: A Chronology," *Washington Post*, May 1, 1985, A13.

113. Bernard Weinraub, "Guiding Reagan: Friendship and Fear," *New York Times*, April 27, 1985, A4.

114. David Hoffman, "Mistakes in Two Capitals Said to Have Led to Bitburg Outcry," *Washington Post*, May 1, 1985, A13.

115. Gerald M. Boyd, "53 in Senate Ask Reagan to Cancel Cemetery Visit," *New York Times*, April 18, 1985, A11.

116. "82 Senators Urge Reagan to Cancel His Cemetery Visit," ibid., April 27, 1985, A1. The figure was later revised to eighty-five to reflect the senators' final position.

117. James M. Markham, "House Fails to Sway Kohl on Bitburg," ibid., A4.

118. Hartman, *Bitburg*, 243; see also Levkov, *Bitburg and Beyond*, 22–29.

119. See, e.g., the summary in William Drozdiak, "Dispute over Cemetery Visit Angers Many West Germans," *Washington Post*, April 28, 1985, A1.

120. See Hartman, *Bitburg*, xv. Boenisch also weighed in vociferously in favor of the Bitburg visit (see, e.g., James M. Markham, "Kohl Aide Says Switch on Bitburg Would Harm US-Germany Ties," *New York Times*, April 25, 1985, A19).

121. James M. Markham, "Bonn Unswayed by House Plea on Cemetery Visit," *New York Times*, April 27, 1985, A4; Bernard Weinraub, "Reagan Joins Kohl in Brief Memorial at Bitburg Graves,"

ibid., May 6, 1985, A1; Weinraub noted the sparse "handful of demonstrators" at the concentration camp in the story's continuation on p. A9. See also Michael Dobbs, "Camp Survivors, Protest Groups Absent at Visit," *Washington Post*, May 6, 1985, A1.

122. Weizsäcker, *A Voice from Germany*.

123. Rainer Werner Fassbinder, *Der Müll, die Stadt und der Tod* (Frankfurt am Main, 1981).

124. See Markovits and Noveck, "The Fassbinder Scandal." See also Janusz Bodek, *Die Fassbinder-Kontroversen: Entstehung und Wirkung eines literarischen Textes* (Frankfurt, 1991); Heiner Lichtenstein, ed., *Die Fassbinder Kontroverse oder das Ende der Schonzeit* (Königstein im Taunus, 1986); Andrei Markovits, Seyla Benhabib, and Moishe Postone, "Rainer Werner Fassbinder's *Garbage, the City, and Death*: Renewed Antagonisms in the Complex Relationship between Jews and Germans in the Federal Republic of Germany," *New German Critique*, no. 38 (fall 1986), 3–27.

125. Markovits and Noveck, "The Fassbinder Scandal," 13.

126. A sizable literature exists in English and in German on the Historians' Debate. For the participants' own articles and letters, see *Historikerstreit* (Munich, 1987), which was published in English as *Forever in the Shadow of Hitler?* (Atlantic Highlands, N.J., 1993). See also some of the works by principal participants in the controversy, including Jürgen Habermas, *The New Conservatism*, ed. and trans. Shierry Weber Nicholsen (Cambridge, Mass., 1989); Ernst Nolte, *Das Vergehen der Vergangenheit* (Berlin, 1987); and Hans-Ulrich Wehler, *Entsorgung der deutschen Vergangenheit?* (Munich, 1988). British and American scholars have offered some of the ablest analysis of the *Historikerstreit*. See, e.g., Peter Baldwin, ed., *Reworking the Past: Hitler, the Past, and the Historians' Debate* (Boston, 1990); Richard J. Evans, *In Hitler's Shadow* (New York, 1989); and Charles S. Maier, *The Unmasterable Past* (Cambridge, Mass., 1988).

127. *Historikerstreit*, 62–76; *Forever in the Shadow of Hitler?* 34–44.

128. *Historikerstreit*, 39–47; *Forever in the Shadow of Hitler?* 18–22. The article first appeared in the *Frankfurter Allgemeine Zeitung*, June 6, 1986.

129. Wehler, *Die Entsorgung; Historikerstreit*, 115–22, 132–42, 156–88, 300–322; *Forever in the Shadow of Hitler?* 74–78, 85–92, 101–24, 202–15.

130. Baldwin, *Reworking the Past*, 27.

131. Ibid., 60.

132. Götz Aly and Susanne Heim, *Vordenker der Vernichtung* (Hamburg, 1991).

133. Some non-German scholars, such as Lucy Dawidowicz, would argue that the Holocaust had

been trivialized by German historians. See, for instance, Lucy Dawidowicz, *The Holocaust and the Historians* (Cambridge, Mass., 1981).

134. Aly and Heim, *Vordenker*.

135. See *American Jewish Year Book, 1992* (Philadelphia, 1992), 66–68. See also Micha Brumlik, *The Situation of the Jews in Today's Germany*, the 1990 Paul Lecture at Indiana University (Bloomington, Ind., 1991).

136. Ibid.

137. For a more detailed discussion of the Gulf War and German political culture, see Markovits and Gorski, *The German Left*, esp. 136–37.

138. Hans-Christian Stroebele, cited in Henryk Broder, "Unser Kampf," *Der Spiegel*, April 29, 1991.

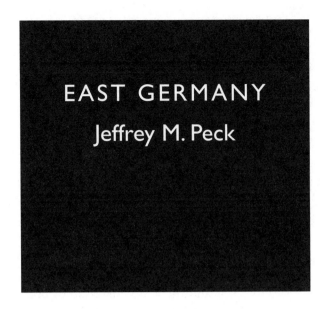

EAST GERMANY
Jeffrey M. Peck

To describe the months from November 1989 to October 1990 as revolutionary for the East Germans as well as for the Jews would be an understatement. In 1988 no one, whether East German citizens, their politicians, or scholars, could have imagined that such a transformation—the fall of the Wall, the dissolution of East Germany, the reunification of Germany—would take place. For professional observers of the German Democratic Republic (GDR) it has meant giving in to the swift course of history and acknowledging its reinterpretation in the light of constantly changing political events. Although the drama is over, the understanding of these events is still contested, and the social, economic, and psychological status of former GDR citizens, including the Jews, is still uncertain.

On February 9, 1990, the prime minister of the newly reorganized East German government made a dramatic announcement. He stated that his government recognized "the responsibility of the entire German people for the past" and was prepared to "provide material support" for those persecuted in the past.[1] A few months later, on April 12, as the country's first democratically elected government was installed, the East German Parliament formally announced its people's "responsibility as Germans in East Germany for their history and their future." It went on, "We ask the Jews of the world to forgive us. We ask the people of Israel to forgive us for the hypocrisy and hostility of official East German policies toward Israel and for the persecution and degradation of Jewish citizens also after 1945 in our country."[2] As East Germany prepared the way for its own demise, the end of its unwillingness to share in the legacy of the Nazi Third Reich marked a turning point for East Germany's response to the Holocaust.

For the East German government, the establishment of the German Democratic Republic on October 7, 1949, out of the former Soviet Occupied Zone was the beginning of a new socialist, antifascist Germany. The legitimacy of the territory (which became the GDR) was officially based on its previous "occupation" by Nazism. This meant that the GDR, although obviously not even in existence during the war, in retrospect understood itself to be in radical opposition to Nazism politically and ideologically. Thus, the GDR was not responsible for the crimes committed by the Nazis. The Nazis had persecuted, imprisoned, and killed its Communist leaders for their widespread resistance. These men inculcated antifascist ideology into the population, who accepted it as a state doctrine that assuaged their guilt and victimization by the Nazi state. For Jews who returned to the GDR, it alleviated their misgivings about returning to the land of their murderers.[3]

East Germany's liberation by the Soviet Union played a significant role in this formulation of the GDR's history. As Eve Rosenhaft points out, "The activities of the resistance are acknowledged as having laid the foundation for the new order. . . . In the formal celebration of the resistance, the Communist opposition to Hitler has a special place, because it embodies the link between native antifascism, the Soviet Union as liberator and protector, and the first generation of political leaders in the GDR; its activities confirm the historical claim to leadership of the Socialist Unity Party (SED), the . . . German Communist Party's successor and state party, and thereby testify to the legitimacy of the political system in which it has a key position."[4] In fact, this antifascist model not only dominated historiography in the GDR about World War II but also neutralized the unique situation of the Jews under Nazism and the role of the Holocaust. The GDR's Communist leaders had indeed fought against the Nazis and, like the Jews, had been persecuted and jailed. However,

> the plausible construction of a continuous tradition of revolutionary socialist and communist opposition which informs the celebration of the resistance as national heroes disguises a process by which some aspects of the resistance have been selected and instrumentalized at the expense of others. In practice, this meant . . . the experiences of certain members of the communist movement were accorded a greater weight than others, in spite of their common suffering and indeed their common heroism.[5]

Thus, the East German government saw itself as relieved of responsibility for Nazi crimes: the government and, by extension, the citizens of the GDR were the antifascist resistance fighters and victims as well. Some Jewish resistance fighters, such as the well-known Herbert Baum group, a monument to whom stands in the East Berlin Jewish Weissensee cemetery, were recognized.[6] Ignoring the dimensions and the uniqueness of the Holocaust and rejecting material compensation to Jews resulted from an ideology that subsumed distinctions not only between antifascist and Jew but also between the leadership of the state and its citizens, who were not necessarily direct victims of fascism. While the ideology of antifascism, at least in the early years of the GDR, was based on hope for a new state formation that would eradicate the ills of capitalist society, GDR leadership was blinded to how antifascist party doctrine covered up ambiguities in the system, such as its attitude toward the Holocaust. Even more, it put the GDR, its system, and its leaders on a moral high ground, allowing them to criticize the Germans "over there," that is, in the Federal

Republic. Although the East German statement in 1990 was largely a symbolic gesture, it legitimized the country (even in its final days) as responsible for its deeds. It also made the idea of a reunified Germany that accepts responsibility for its crimes more palatable to world Jewry and to Israel.

After democratic elections in the GDR in March 1990, monetary union with West Germany, the acceptance of German membership in NATO by the Soviets, and the guarantee of the Oder-Neisse border with Poland in July, unification was achieved on October 3, 1990. All-German elections followed in December. The official disappearance of East Germany, however, does not make its response to the Holocaust a moot issue. The forty-year history of the GDR was not erased with the declaration of reunification, especially in the light of last-minute attempts of the GDR to recognize its responsibility and hypocrisy toward Israel and the Jews. The unification of the two Germanies into the strongest economic and political power in Europe raises questions not only about the place of Jews in a new Germany but also about the rise of anti-Semitism, racism, and xenophobia in the former GDR and in the West during the transition period before reunification. It is significant that the West questions as well the GDR's self-image as an antifascist state in the years since the war. It is ironic that since the disappearance of the GDR, its identity has become an even more gripping subject of reflection.

The history of East German responses to the Holocaust closely parallels the GDR's postwar history, its relation to German identity, and its association with its ever-dwindling number of Jews. These parallels remind us how political histories often coincide with individual life stories, especially in the GDR, a "new" country to which Jews were drawn for political and ideological reasons. Events significant for the state's self-understanding, as well as for the personal life stories of GDR citizens, such as the founding of the GDR (1949), the Workers' Uprising (1953), and the building of the Wall (1961), are often linked through parallel narratives that construct political and personal identities by structuring such significant events into meaningful "stories."[7]

Such a history forces us to examine how the positive and negative influences of the GDR's policy toward the Jews and its attitude toward anti-Semitism figure into a new German relationship to the past and the deeds of the Nazis. Programmatic GDR state doctrine against anti-Semitism, racism, or xenophobia seems to have had little effect on either the GDR's own citizens or those in the former West Germany, since Jewish cemeteries continue to be desecrated and foreigners have been brutally attacked and even murdered. In a country such as the GDR, which saw itself as the bulwark against such tendencies, the issue of anti-Semitism and the Holocaust is especially problematic. Thus, we must look specifically at the Holocaust and its special status in the GDR, since the Holocaust occurred before its founding. We must, however, also address the historical and political discourse around the GDR's interpretation of fascism that was used to include or exclude the issues that emanate from the question. Some of these points are the GDR's relation to its Jews after the Holocaust, the influence of Stalin's policies toward the Jews, the GDR's problematic relationship with Israel, its official policy against anti-Semitism, and its attitudes toward the growth of right-wing extremist anti-Semitism at home and in the Federal Republic. I will pursue all of these questions as I review the development of the GDR and its response to the Holocaust from its beginnings as an "occupied" zone (both by the Nazis and by the Soviets), through state formation, purges, relaxation and reconciliation toward its Jews, and its increasing move into international politics, the last bringing it closer to rethinking its relationship to the Holocaust.

The East German responses to the Holocaust in the late 1980s and early 1990s were strongly colored by such events as the fifty-year commemoration of Kristallnacht[8] on November 9, 1988, the collapse of the Wall exactly one year later, the celebration of the fortieth anniversary of the GDR on October 7, 1989, and unification on October 3, 1990. The proximity and coincidence of these dates added a symbolic historical weight to the events and German responses to them, since dates such as these mark memorable (in the word's literal sense) moments that fashion the state's and its citizens' histories.[9]

The dates marking the unofficial end (or beginning of the end) of the GDR and the anniversary of Kristallnacht cannot be ignored. Coincidental as the fact that the two events occurred on a November 9 might be, many Jews feared that the dramatic events surrounding the fall of the Wall would overshadow the memory of Kristallnacht. They had good reason for their apprehension, for until late 1988 "the place and historical development of Jews in Germany was clearly not at the center of special historical discussions such as the revolutionary workers' movement or revolutions in German history."[10]

This statement begins an important article on GDR Holocaust research by Walter Schmidt, a well-known GDR historian. The piece, entitled "Jewish Inheritance of German History as Part of Understanding Inheritance and Tradition in the GDR," was published in 1989 in the party-controlled *Zeitschrift für Geschichtswissenschaft* (Journal for Historiography) in a special issue celebrating "the fortieth anniversary of the founding of the GDR." This article represents the GDR's liberalization of its official policy toward the Holocaust and its historiography. In it the author makes a concerted effort to rectify the neglect by GDR historians of such topics as Jewish culture, the persecution of the Jews, and the Holocaust. In the late 1980s the party line revealed an increasing willingness to acknowledge Jewish life and the Holocaust. This change was particularly apparent in the 1988 commemoration of Kristallnacht, which Erich Honecker, the GDR head of state, and other high party officials and international Jewish dignitaries attended. Ironically, just as the party's attitude was softening on the Holocaust and the Jewish Community[11] as a way of improving relations with the United States, the country collapsed. While the small GDR Jewish Community had welcomed this new openness from the leaders of the GDR, even if it was based on ulterior motives, they now faced a different kind of dilemma. After the Wall came down and reunification became imminent, they were uncertain what a reunified Germany and a reunified Jewish Community would mean for them.

At the end of the forty-year history of the GDR, those who thought of it as "the better Germany"[12] were forced to reevaluate their relationship to this short-lived state and reassess its attitudes toward the Nazi period and the Holocaust. Prompted by the creation of a "new" Germany after reunification, the Jews in the GDR had to reconsider their relationship to what in 1949 also had been seen as a "new" Germany, one that had tried to deny its connection to twelve years of German history. Dealing with how the Holocaust was viewed in the GDR highlights the role of the Jews in a Germany that saw itself as offering an alternative view of the German past and hope for a different future.

An examination of the beginnings of the GDR and the situation of the Jews after the collapse of the Nazi regime in 1945 in the Soviet Occupied Zone will help us to understand this development. The Iron Curtain began at the western boundary of the Soviet Occupied Zone and extended eastward to the source of Communist power itself, the Soviet Union. The fact that Jews may have been living in this area was a source of discomfort to the world Jewish community in the years after the war, although the status of Jews in all of Germany was regarded as temporary. It was believed that they should and would leave the country that had tried to annihilate them. In 1945 in the three western zones and Berlin there were approximately 68,460 Jews, of which only 15,000 were German Jews. Jews who wished to return from exile in 1945–46 were not welcomed by Western authorities, although the Soviet Zone invited and received refugees who were Communists.[13] In 1946 there were 3,100 practicing Jews in the Soviet Zone and 1,800 in the Soviet sector of Berlin and 2,500 of Jewish descent who were not members of the Jewish Communities.[14]

But numbers tell only part of the story, since the Jews who survived and found themselves in the Soviet Zone after the war or who chose to return were considered part of the general category "victims of fascism." They were not accorded special status, granted the material restitution that Jews were in the West, or recognized as having suffered more profoundly than Communists or other "resistance fighters." Along with other official victims, however, they were given some special benefits. They received high priority in the allocation of housing, free travel in the country, and priority access to higher education for themselves and their children. Furthermore, when they retired, five years earlier than other GDR citizens, they received a pension of six hundred marks per month. Other benefits included a three-week stay at a health spa every two years.[15] From the GDR's point of view, it was indeed compensating its own Jewish citizens but not those Jews living in Israel or elsewhere who had also been persecuted by the Nazis.[16] The ideology of antifascism did not grant the few Jews in the GDR who returned or survived much recognition as Jews.

Elaborating on the limitations that antifascism imposed on the GDR's official thinking, American historian Konrad Jarausch discussed GDR historians' official interpretation of the Third Reich, a position most loyal GDR citizens would have supported:

> As the guardians of the moral flame, East German historians of the Third Reich played a special but problematic role. In their public statements, they upheld antifascism as a noncommunist justification for the independence of the GDR and as cement for the progressive consensus, ranging from proletarian underground to bourgeois resistance. In their academic research they sought to uncover the economic and political mechanisms behind the Nazi dictatorship so as to prevent its recurrence. However,

these related efforts were hampered by a narrow ideological definition of National Socialism as fascism, characterized as state monopoly capitalism.[17]

Regarding the Holocaust, Jarausch declared, "In contrast to reluctant GDR references to the persecution of the Jews as a result of material envy and mass manipulation, the holocaust raises troubling general questions, since it demonstrates that race hatred can supersede class struggle. . . . In countless particular cases western scholars have been able to point out that the ideologized Marxist conception oversimplifies crucial contradictions of the German past."[18] Antifascism dominated the thinking of the government and of those whose job it was to chronicle the history of Germany. While on the one hand the GDR worked hard to claim the German past for its own progressive and socialist tradition, on the other hand the twelve years of the Nazi regime, which were an important and complicated piece of that past, were reduced in antifascist rhetoric to "state monopoly capitalism" and dissociated from the GDR.

One of Jarausch's most significant points was the connection between the outbreak of anti-Semitism and xenophobia among the citizens of the former GDR and the ideology of antifascism. "By pinning the blame on monopoly capitalists," he said, "the Comintern definition of fascism indirectly absolved the majority of the population from confronting its own complicity. The economic reductionism of attributing Hitler's power to an expropriated bourgeois class did not engage the racial dimension of anti-Semitism and insufficiently inoculated youths against xenophobia."[19] The intensity of attacks on foreigners, which began most dramatically in the eastern German Saxon town of Hoyerswerda in September 1991 and were repeated in Rostock and other cities, testify to the dangers of a state ideological program that loses track of the ideals it is supposed to defend.

The Jews and the Holocaust are equally absent from GDR textbooks. According to the sociologist Robin Ostow,

> In the history textbooks of the GDR there is no Holocaust, no Shoah. These words never appear. . . . Germans play a central role in Jewish history of the 1930s and 40s. But in the historical narrative of the German Democratic Republic (1949–1990), from 1933 to 1945 Europe was the site of a major struggle between the "Fascist Dictatorship" and the "Antifascist Resistance." The "German people" appears largely as a rather malleable and gullible human mass which was subjected to the Fascist Dictatorship, but was ultimately freed by the Antifascists. Jews, to the extent that they appear at all, serve as an example of Fascist terror, and—sometimes—resistance.[20]

School textbooks are perhaps the best propaganda tool for educating the young in every society to the ideals and philosophies of the state. Ostow examined "seven different editions of the history text used in GDR schools" and found that the forty to fifty pages covering the years 1933–45 "relate the fate of Jews in Europe and parts of the Soviet Union in approximately three entire paragraphs, and scattered shorter references to Jews as one of the many groups to suffer and die in the Fascist terror." Often identified with the ownership of property, the Jews were portrayed in the texts "as an elite of proprietors and bourgeois imperialists; a group distanced from the life and political traditions of the GDR." Ostow concluded that for the GDR, Jews "are an alien and elusive non-GDR category. . . . [They] are searched for and imagined: they are neither understood nor integrated into the historical scheme, and they remain a mystery in the end."[21]

Although the Jews did not figure as prominently in antifascist discourse as the extent of their suffering warranted, anti-Semitism was still to be fought. This contradiction reveals the inflated terminology of antifascism, which officially condemned attacks on Jews and simultaneously underplayed their persecution. Thus, the official newspaper of the SED, *Neues Deutschland,* on September 14, 1947, reported that "the complete destruction of anti-Semitism was a national duty. . . . Every concession to tendencies hostile to Jews betrayed national interests, which were in themselves contrary to Marxist concepts. Anti-Semitism and race hatred must be considered a national offense in all Germany." West Germany, *Neues Deutschland* recommended, "should follow the example set by the DDR, where race hatred was outlawed and punished."[22] While it is true that anti-Semitism became illegal in the GDR when it was codified in the *Strafgesetzbuch* (Criminal law book), at the inception of the state, and under Article 1 of the 1950 Law for the Protection of Peace, the desecration of Jewish cemeteries still took place sporadically. For example, in May 1950 vandals toppled sixteen monuments in the Weissensee cemetery. The Berlin Jewish Community logged a protest with the East Berlin city government, and Friedrich Ebert, the mayor of East Berlin, ordered such acts to be punished.[23]

To protect and represent those then living in Germany who had been persecuted in the Nazi period, Vereinigung der Verfolgten des Naziregimes (VVN, the Union of Persecutees of the Nazi Regime) was established in 1947 in Berlin. It had existed in other parts of Germany since 1945 "to protect the economic and political interests of victims of Nazi rule"[24] and of course included Jews among its members. The *American Jewish Year Book* of that year reported, however, that "a controversy arose in the German-Jewish press as to whether Jews should continue membership in the VVN, since certain groups charged that the Union was a Communist front organization."[25] The VVN was founded, according to scholar Jerry Thompson, "to coordinate the efforts toward restitution in all of Germany. The VVN's duty . . . was to represent the interests of the people persecuted by the Nazis, to gain just restitution, and to prevent the return of a totalitarian government." Thompson added that "in the Soviet Zone the VVN was a tool of the S.E.D. throughout its existence." This was especially evident between 1950 and 1953. In 1953 the VVN was replaced by the Komitee der antifaschistischen Widerstandskämpfer (Committee of Antifascist Resistance Fighters), which, according to Thompson, "also followed the S.E.D. line."[26] Robin Ostow pointed out that this new organization, "which had a less Jewish character, distinguished the passive 'Victims of Fascism'—including Jews as such—from the active 'Resistance Fighters' who were awarded more generous benefits and privileges. . . . The Committee first agreed to consider abolishing this distinction in December 1989, after the fall of the Honecker regime."[27]

Between 1947 and 1949, Jewish life had reestablished itself with the help of organizations like the VVN. Jewish Communities were reconstituted in various cities, and the American Jewish Joint Distribution Committee (JDC) supplied food to twelve hundred German Jews.[28] In 1949, after the division of East and West Germany, there were eight thousand Jews in the newly formed GDR.[29] From 1949 onwards these Jews noticed changes in official attitudes toward them, often prompted by Soviet orders. Prominent Jewish returnees to the GDR like Gerhart Eisler, who while in American exile was a Communist organizer and had been imprisoned and escaped, were under arrest by 1950. Jews were attacked for their cosmopolitanism, and those who had been in the West during the war were considered especially suspicious. The "anti-Jewish purge . . . was primarily directed against Jewish solidarity as a possible source of dangerous links with the West. It was aimed chiefly at Jewish officials in the Communist Party and the . . . VVN . . . and at community leaders."[30] Jewish refugees from the GDR reported that "the first symptoms [of Soviet influence] were the steady decline in the number of Russian officers of Jewish origins who occasionally came to attend their services, and the replacement of a Jew by a non-Jew as Soviet liaison officer to the Jewish Communities in 1951."[31] Informants were also enlisted, and the mail of Jews was checked. Questions of restitution, which were being directly addressed by the West German government (not without great disputes and disharmony in the ranks of Konrad Adenauer's own party), were dismissed in East Germany, which maintained that "fascism had been eradicated in the GDR" and that therefore there was no need for material restitution.[32]

Tensions culminated in the events of 1952–53. These events are of particular importance in that they represent a turning point in the GDR's relationship to the Jewish Community. They also indirectly affected its acknowledgment of responsibility for the Holocaust. The debate over reparations and restitution of Jewish property, the Slansky trial in late 1952 and the subsequent anti-Zionist campaign, and the Moscow Doctors' Plot in January 1953 revealed the extent of anti-Semitism in the Soviet sphere. The latter two events took place outside the GDR and illustrate the impact of Soviet policy on its satellites.

As a hard-line, Moscow-oriented Communist, the Jew Rudolf Slansky may have seemed above reproach. But on November 20, 1952, Slansky and thirteen other Czechoslovakian Communists were brought to trial for "criminal acts of espionage, sabotage, betrayal of military secrets, and high treason." The fourteen defendants were also accused of trying to overthrow the Czechoslovakian People's Democracy through their participation in an international Zionist conspiracy.[33] Slansky's indictments multiplied: he was a Trotskyite, a Zionist, a lackey of Western imperialism, a bourgeois nationalist, a cosmopolitan, and a procurer of jobs for Jewish friends. Ultimately, Slansky and his fellow defendants were forced to admit their guilt; eleven were sentenced to hang and three to life imprisonment. The Jews were being blamed for economic problems and were used to deflect the population's anti-Communist or anti-Soviet feelings.[34]

In the Doctors' Plot in the Soviet Union, the seven doctors who were Jewish (out of the nine charged) were accused of sabotaging the medical care of high Soviet officials. They supposedly had been encouraged by the JDC. Before show trials could be staged, Stalin died. Later investigations proved that the accusations were untrue and without legal basis. The accused were exonerated of all crimes. The plot was part of another effort by Stalin to purge the top Soviet leadership.

Both cases, however, stirred up animosity toward the Jews in the GDR and all of Eastern Europe. Anti-Jewish measures in the GDR between November 1952 and March 1953 resulted in the flight of five hundred Jews, including most of the old Community leadership, out of an estimated Jewish population of seventeen hundred to eighteen hundred in East Berlin and nine hundred in the former Soviet zone.[35] The SED published a report on the Slansky trial that was published in *Neues Deutschland* on January 4, 1953. The article warned about agents of "American imperialism,"[36] such as Communists like Paul Merker, who had spent time in the West as an émigré, and agencies like the JDC. Merker, although not Jewish, strongly supported the Jewish cause.[37] He had been expelled from the Central Committee of the SED in 1950 and was accused of encouraging Jewish victims to join Jewish organizations in order to receive relief packages from the JDC and to demand restitution. In this climate, concluded the historian Konrad Kwiet, "any serious study or discussion of anti-semitism and the destruction of the Jews was bound to appear ill-advised."[38] Thus, the Soviet-influenced GDR policy on the Jews was definitely related to the government's lack of interest in the writing of official Holocaust histories.

The issue of reparations also contributed to the hostility toward Jews in the GDR. In 1952 the Allied restitution laws of 1945 were dismissed in the GDR. In the same year West Germany agreed to pay reparations to Israel.[39] Government spokesmen such as Albert Norden, himself a Jew, declared that the reparations agreement was "completely unjustified."[40] Jews who had suffered under National Socialism wanted compensation for lost and confiscated property, much of which was now nationalized or in other people's hands. For the GDR, where in official terms anti-Semitism and fascism had been completely destroyed, it was not necessary or appropriate to give special monetary restitution to the Jews. They were receiving benefits as members of the VVN and, more importantly, were living in an antifascist state whose laws protected them from persecution and violence. A Jewish citizen could live in the GDR as safely as any other citizen. Ultimately, however, the suspicions against Jews, especially those who had lived in the West during the war, provoked the dismissal of the last remaining Jews from party leadership. And in 1953 the VVN was dissolved, to be replaced by the new Komitee der antifaschistischen Widerstandskämpfer (Committee of Antifascist Resistance Fighters), whose Jewish members numbered only one in twenty.[41]

In part because of Stalin's death and the departure of anti-Communist Jews for West Berlin, the public campaign and purges against Jews subsided in 1953. Robin Ostow reported that "by mid-June 1953 the stream of Jewish refugees from the GDR to West Berlin abated, and within the GDR there was an abrupt change of policy; the measures against Jews ceased and the rehabilitation of the Jews and their Communities began."[42] The GDR made a number of efforts to publicize its positive attitudes toward its Jewish citizens. The beautiful Rykestrasse synagogue in East Berlin was renovated with government funds, and High Holy Day services were held. In

October a monument was unveiled at the Weissensee cemetery in East Berlin, which was being cared for by the Jewish Community. Far from being a persecuted minority, the Jews in the GDR seem to have become a "protected species." During 1956, Ostow noted, "many Jewish government officials and artists who had been purged in the early 1950s were rehabilitated."[43] In April 1955 Albert Norden had, in fact, been appointed a member and one of the secretaries of the SED Central Committee. Paul Merker was partly rehabilitated. The Central Committee declared that it had been wrong to send him to prison and released him in the spring of 1956, admitting that the charges against him had been "chiefly of a political character."[44]

The GDR began to take a more relaxed attitude toward its Jewish citizens. Thompson goes so far as to call the Jews the GDR's "museum pieces," since the attention paid to the small community and the efforts to maintain its synagogues and cemeteries were intended to show the world how antifascism contributed to the religious and personal well-being of Jews. In 1960 Soviet officials were present at the dedication of a monument at the site of the Ravensbrück concentration camp. However, "Jews were mentioned only incidentally." East German propaganda efforts shifted to denouncing anti-Semitism in West Germany. Both Germanies intensified their campaigns, accusing each other of having Nazis in high government posts. As far as the GDR was concerned, it had officially eradicated Nazism by, among other things, instituting laws that protected human rights and peace and prosecuted Nazis. In fact, "a total of 12,087 people [were] convicted of crimes against humanity by GDR courts." In West Germany, ex-Nazi officials, such as Hans Globke, Adenauer's chief aide from 1950 to 1963, and Hans Filbinger, the minister-president of Baden-Württemburg and a former Nazi judge who had pronounced death sentences, were discovered in high government posts. The West German federal government seemed reluctant to punish ex-Nazis. The GDR also worked toward establishing diplomatic contacts with Egypt, and this move was coupled with the GDR's criticism of West Germany's reparations agreement with Israel as an act hostile to the Arab countries.[45]

During the years following this period, the Jewish Community appeared to be left to its own resources. Although there was no rabbi in the GDR, Dr. Martin Riesenburger, who staunchly supported the GDR, served as the spiritual leader and officiated at religious functions. He was criticized as the "red Rabbi" by Jews in West Berlin, with whom the GDR Community had little contact. In 1952 he warned the Jewish Community not to accept food packages from the West, since "they will entice people to take a path toward destruction."[46] In the official newsletter of the Association of Jewish Communities in the GDR, the *Nachrichtenblatt,* which began regular publication in March 1961, Riesenburger proclaimed in an article entitled "Unsere Heimat ist hier, in der DDR" (Our homeland is here, in the GDR) that "we Jews have always had a homeland where we find a home in the hearts of people. Our homeland is here, in the GDR, where the brown [Nazi] past was absolutely conquered."[47] When Riesenburger died in 1965, he was eulogized in the English-language *GDR Review,* and Walter Ulbricht, the GDR's highest-ranking statesman, sent his widow a revealing letter of condolence:

During the years of cruel persecution of upright anti-fascists and the mass murder perpetrated on Jewish citizens, chief Rabbi Dr. Martin Riesenburger never wavered, but continued to give counsel and aid to the members of his constantly menaced community. It was above all the knowledge and experience gained during this dark era of nazism which caused chief Rabbi Dr. Martin Riesenburger, after the defeat of fascism to take his place on the side of all anti-fascist and democratic forces and help eradicate for ever the evil spirit of fascism and militarism. With all the weight of his personality he warned to the last against the danger of admitting to positions of influence in West Germany the mass murderers of Jews, and he insisted on their removal from public offices.[48]

In the *GDR Review* Heinz Schenk, the head of the East Berlin Jewish community, also emphasized the religious freedom of the Jews in the GDR and their observance of rituals and traditions. He even cited the existence of a kosher butcher shop in Berlin. He said that "the Jewish citizens of the GDR have found here a real home where they are allowed to live in peace, security, and complete equality,"[49] and he claimed that "there is no anti-semitism here."[50]

In the 1960s, a decade that began with the building of the Berlin Wall in 1961, historical research in the GDR began to address the Holocaust, since it was "at the beginning of this decade that GDR historiography was constituted as an independent *[selbständige]* social science discipline." Historian Walter Schmidt pointed out that while up until this time the social sciences, including history, did not attend to the Holocaust sufficiently, the Holocaust was a subject of great interest in the public sphere in "popular literature, art, painting, film, journalism, radio, and television."[51] Schmidt's assertion here typified the dilemma he and other more "progressive" GDR historians found themselves in during the late 1980s when reviewing the unsatisfactory attention given to the Jews in antifascist historiography from the 1960s onward. On the one hand, Schmidt was critical of the lacunae in GDR historiography on this topic; on the other hand, he made an effort to give credit to anyone, in this case, writers, filmmakers, and journalists, who had addressed the Holocaust. He named, for example, the second film of the GDR film company DEFA, *Ehe im Schatten* (Marriage in the Shadows [1947]), about "the fate of the Jewish actress Meta Wolff and her gentile colleague Joachim Gottschalk, whose lives ended together in common suicide under the fascistic racial madness."

Schmidt wanted to be both critical and supportive of the GDR's relationship to the Holocaust, even if the work was not primarily scholarship. In typical fashion, as he reviewed popular literature in the GDR from 1945 to 1948, he criticized the Western zones, "where trivial literature *[Trivialliteratur]* and authors of the 'inner emigration' dominated." In the Soviet Occupied Zone, however, he found that "the publication of [the] antifascist literature of exiles played a great role in [the GDR's] coming to terms with fascism and the resistance fight." It should not be forgotten, he proudly added, that many of these authors, such as Anna Seghers, Arnold Zweig, and Stefan Heym, "without whom GDR national culture would be unthinkable," were of "German Jewish background." Seghers, who spent the war in Mexico, was a prolific writer, best known for her novel *The Seventh Cross;* Zweig returned from

Palestine to assume a prominent position in GDR literature; and Heym returned to Germany with the American army and remained in the GDR as a critical yet dedicated Communist, becoming prominent with the publication of his novel describing the 1953 workers' uprising, *Five Days in June*. These writers had "dedicated their artistic work to antifascist resistance and often to the fate of the Jews, their sufferings and their resistance."[52]

Corroborating the ambivalent and ambiguous reaction in the GDR to Nazi persecution and the role of the Jews, Konrad Kwiet, in his seminal article "Historians of the German Democratic Republic on Antisemitism and Persecution," stated that until 1961 there was an increase in books on contemporary history, the antifascist resistance, and World War II. However, anti-Semitism and the Holocaust did not receive much attention. Established historiography covered the Holocaust only within the framework of fascist crimes and antifascist resistance.[53]

According to Kwiet, the rise of anti-Semitism in the Federal Republic and the Eichmann trial in 1961 drew attention in the GDR to "a topic that had been hitherto treated somewhat casually."[54] An international conference was held in East Berlin in 1961 for the "purpose of taking the Eichmann trial in Jerusalem as a point of departure for bringing scientific proof of the anti-democratic and barbarous nature of German imperialism." The main speaker was the economic historian Jürgen Kuczynski, himself of Jewish background, whose presentation was entitled "Barbarity—The Most Extreme Manifestation of Monopoly Rule in Germany."[55] Despite the paper's title, Kuczynski dealt with anti-Semitism and the persecution of the Jews in a few sentences.[56] For Kwiet this conference proved that "the GDR had fallen far behind in the study of anti-Semitism and the Holocaust." Quoting from the official conference report, Kwiet emphasized, "It was not so much the contributions of German participants but rather the remarks of Polish and Czechoslovak guests which 'revealed wide-ranging knowledge of the field and gave fresh impulses to the discussion.'"[57]

According to historians from the West and the East, the years 1966–67 marked the beginning of a period in which more attention was given to what Walter Schmidt called "the first independent historical research on the topic."[58] The 1966 publication *Kennzeichen J. Bilder, Dokumente, Berichte zur Geschichte der Verbrechen des Hitlerfaschismus an den deutschen Juden* (Marker J. pictures, documents, reports regarding the history of the crimes of Hitler fascism on the German Jews), edited by Helmut Eschwege, was even described by Kwiet as "the first comprehensive documentation on the persecution and destruction of the German Jews."[59] Eschwege was joined in this endeavor by Arnold Zweig, who wrote the foreword, Rudi Goguel, who wrote the introduction, and Klaus Drobisch, who collected facts and dates. Goguel and Drobisch later joined W. Mueller and H. Dohle to produce another significant volume in 1973, *Juden unterm Hakenkreuz. Verfolgung und Ausrottung der deutschen Juden, 1933–1945* (Jews under the swastika: Persecution and genocide of German Jews, 1933–1945), which was praised by scholars from both sides of the Iron Curtain. While from the GDR perspective the book was "the first comprehensive

Marxist account of the persecution and destruction of the German Jews," in the West it was considered comprehensive but also a justification of the GDR's refusal to make restitution to the Jews.[60]

As far as the GDR was concerned, life in an antifascist socialist state that protected its Jewish citizens from anti-Semitism was restitution enough. For Kwiet the book reflected "a serious endeavor to catch up and gradually close the gaps in the state of GDR research in the field of anti-Semitism and the persecution of the Jews, while at the same time broadening the topic to include patterns of Jewish behavior and tracing inner-Jewish developments from the foundation of the *Reich* to the final deportations in 1943." Kwiet criticized the book for being based almost exclusively on previously published sources and for its lack of any material from GDR archives. Kurt Pätzold's *Faschismus. Rassenwahn. Judenverfolgung* (Fascism, the madness of racism, and Jewish persecution), which was completed as a dissertation in 1973 and published in 1975, also attracted attention. Kwiet praised Pätzold for his "rich documentation" and "an empirically sound reconstruction of the beginnings of the Nazi policy on the Jews." Yet, he added, "positive as Pätzold's contribution is, he cannot, any more than his colleagues, evade the obligation of responding to the demands of anti-Zionist propaganda. This starts at the precise point where the antifascist resistance is introduced into the narrative." Kwiet concluded his survey of GDR historiography by declaring emphatically that "working within strict methodological rules and inhibited by ideology, GDR historians are precluded from arriving at independent assessments. Not one of the authors . . . has really come to grips with the complex problem of German-Jewish co-existence. There is little indication that we shall see any improvement in the near future."[61]

In 1978, soon after Kwiet published his essay, the commemoration of the fortieth anniversary of Kristallnacht generated increased interest in the Holocaust. This was reflected in books, brochures, and articles in magazines, journals, and newspapers. Governmental officials participated in commemorations and religious services in large cities and smaller towns. A ceremony was held at the Sachsenhausen concentration camp, and an exhibition entitled "The Fortieth Anniversary of 'Kristallnacht'" was launched at the Museum for German History. Members of the Free German Youth, the most significant organization in the GDR for educating and integrating the young into the party and socialist society, gathered at neglected Jewish cemeteries and worked to clean them up.[62]

But even with this attention to the Jews and the Holocaust, a deficit still existed in the work done on these topics in the GDR. Just as historical scholarship began to move in the late 1970s toward correcting this deficit, Jews in the GDR seemed to be finding their place. At the celebration of the thirtieth anniversary of the Liberation, on May 8, 1975, GDR Jewish community leaders stated that for the first time in the history of Germany, Jews were "fully equal in all fields of communal life"; that the work of the Jewish communities was "made possible and promoted by the generous support of the state." The president of the People's Chamber, Horst Sindermann, said that this day represented "the capitulation of the military forces of German monopoly capital." A monument was also dedicated in Dresden at the site of a synagogue burned in 1938, and a Jewish calendar for the year 5736 was issued by the Association of Jewish Communities.[63]

In 1976 the president of the East Berlin Jewish Community, Dr. Peter Kirchner, reaffirmed the Jews' relationship to the GDR when he spoke against the Brussels World Jewish Congress on Soviet Jewry. He did not want Jews in socialist countries to be identified with such a "conscious provocation," since they had "equal rights in all matters."[64] However, the GDR itself took a giant step toward détente in 1976, two years after establishing diplomatic relations with the United States. It offered the Conference of Jewish Material Claims Against Germany $1 million to compensate survivors from the territory occupied by the GDR who were living in the United States. Although the money was rejected because it was viewed by some as "an insult"[65] and by others "as unacceptable because it did not apply to Jewish victims of Nazism as a whole,"[66] the offer marked the first time that the GDR had recognized its responsibility for compensating the Jews for the Holocaust.[67]

The forty-year anniversary of Kristallnacht in 1978 and the thirtieth anniversary of the founding of the GDR in 1979 marked important moments in the history of GDR German Jews. For the GDR Jews, these dates were special occasions for remembering and strengthening their dual identities, since with each event Jewish citizens and the state reminded each other of their mutual commitment. For the Kristallnacht anniversary, Erich Honecker, secretary general of the SED, sent the following message to Helmut Aris, a leader of the Jewish Community:

> It is my desire to assure you and all members of the Jewish communities in the German Democratic Republic of our vigilant remembrance of the victims and their measureless sufferings. In doing so, I am mindful of the fact that our socialist state of workers and peasants has forever cut the ground from under any reactionary forces. As a secure home of humanitarianism and progress, our state guarantees all citizens equal participation in the life of society. . . . By building socialism, our nation, as master of its fate, shapes its new life. In this process, citizens of the Jewish faith have an active share. They have equal rights in the German Democratic Republic, and enjoy equal respect. As they practice their religion and cultivate their tradition, they may continue to count on the full understanding of our state and our society.

Aris viewed Honecker's words as "renewed confirmation of the great solicitude the German Democratic Republic bestows on the work of the Jewish Communities." His words gave Jewish citizens "an incentive and an obligation to continue working for the well-being of our socialist homeland, for peace and for understanding among nations."[68] During these events some discussion took place among Christian church leaders as to Christians' involvement in the persecution of the Jews, and one bishop was still concerned about the presence of fascist thinking and anti-Semitism in GDR youth. But another Christian leader, Manfred Stolpe, cautioned that one should not exaggerate their significance. The East Berlin weekly *Die Weltbühne* also dismissed anti-Semitism as a problem. Although the GDR spoke out forcefully against Israeli policies, it was "never against Israel or the Jews."[69] Anti-

Zionism was not anti-Semitism, according to the magazine. The GDR's continuing prosecution of ex-Nazis and its anti-Israel, pro-Arab policies remained significant issues in its propaganda war with the West.

On the occasion of the GDR's thirtieth anniversary, the Federation of Jewish Communities declared in similar tones its commitment to the GDR. In its formal statements, the federation stressed that the GDR offered Jews "life in security and safety," "unqualified equality," "religious freedom guaranteed by our constitution," and "a home . . . in which we are fully integrated." "We live free and undisturbed; antisemitism and race agitation are strictly punished here. . . . We see that in some parts of the world, particularly in the Federal Republic of Germany, fascism and agitation for war boldly raise their heads, with antisemitism following in their wake. . . . We citizens of the Jewish faith are loyal citizens of our German Democratic Republic."[70] The harmony between the state and the Jews was praised by both sides, but in fact the Jewish population was very small, with fewer than eight hundred mostly aged members. Ninety percent of them were recognized as victims of Nazi persecution or anti-Nazi fighters. As such they received honorary pensions, and as Aris stated, "there were practically no poor Jews."[71] Ironically, in this same year the GDR ministry of culture would not air the American television production *Holocaust,* since from its point of view the program did not show the whole truth about Nazism. Of course, since most GDR citizens could receive Western broadcasts, they could watch it when it aired in West Germany.[72]

A number of other anniversaries and celebrations in the next few years drew attention to the Jews in the GDR and illustrated the connections between the state, the Jewish Community, and the Holocaust. Commemorative events were organized to celebrate, for example, the births of Moses Mendelssohn and Albert Einstein, both of whom were considered great progressive Jewish thinkers. The traditional memorial day for the victims of fascism was observed in East Berlin with demonstrations attended by thousands of people, including leading politicians.[73] Memorials were established at the concentration camps of Nordhausen, Ravensbrück, and Buchenwald. In September 1980 the Weissensee cemetery in East Berlin celebrated its centennial anniversary, and not only GDR Jewish leaders but also East German governmental officials and West Berlin Jewish leaders attended the event. The Jewish Community even issued a publication entitled *Jewish Cemeteries in Berlin.* The state, in fact, supported the upkeep of the four main Jewish cemeteries in East Berlin and more than one hundred Jewish cemeteries in the country, a burden the Jewish Community could not bear alone. In the early 1980s, as before, the annual anniversary of Kristallnacht provided the GDR Jews the opportunity to announce that "the legacy of all the victims of fascism, including Jewish citizens, has been fulfilled in the GDR. The policy of our state guarantees that a *Kristallnacht* cannot happen again."[74] Christian church groups were formed to promote Christian-Jewish relations.

The relationship between the GDR and its Jews became more complicated, however, in 1982, after the Israeli invasion of Lebanon. The government's hostility toward Israel put the Jewish Community in a bind. On the one hand, the group criticized Israel by supporting public opposition to the Begin government within Israel;

on the other hand, Peter Kirchner, the president of the Community, emphasized that the negative attention in the GDR media toward Israel promoted anti-Semitism. He stated, "If young people are fed almost daily, for political reasons, negative data about Israeli Jews, they can hardly avoid applying this negative description to the Jews in their environment as well."[75] Anniversaries such as that of the deportation of Berlin Jews to Auschwitz, the forty-fifth anniversary of Kristallnacht, the thirty-fifth anniversary of the GDR, and the fortieth anniversary of the Stauffenberg plot against Hitler's life were commemorated against the backdrop of anti-Israel declarations. In 1985, at the fortieth anniversary of the defeat of the Third Reich, Sindermann honored the war dead, including the "six million Jews who died as a result of criminal Fascist policy."[76] Christian churches made special efforts to pay tribute to Jewish war victims. The Jews were slowly making their way into GDR antifascist discourse, and the churches would become a major force in creating a forum for discussion about Jewish topics and for political activism among a populace that was becoming increasingly frustrated with the government.

In 1987 three major Holocaust-related events occurred in the GDR. American Rabbi Isaac Neumann, from Champaign, Illinois, arrived to serve the East Berlin Jewish community. A Polish Jew who had survived the camps, Rabbi Neumann's visit came about through the cooperation of the GDR, the U.S. State Department, and the American Jewish Committee. However, hopes of a long tenure in the GDR were cut short after eight months because of disagreements between Rabbi Neumann and the Jewish Community over religious matters and his commitment to living in the GDR. Second, Rabbi Israel Miller of the Jewish Claims Conference visited Dresden and East Berlin and met with Honecker "to discuss restitution payments by the East German government to Jews who lived or owned property in what is now the German Democratic Republic."[77] These meetings resulted a year later in the offer of a "humanitarian donation" of $100 million to Jewish survivors of the Holocaust, which was ultimately rejected. Third, Henry Schmidt, a former Nazi who had led the Dresden Gestapo and SS, was tried for his crimes and sentenced to life imprisonment. At the same time, dissatisfaction with the government began to surface. There were demonstrations, requests to leave the GDR, and resignations from the SED. Anti-Semitic harassment was also on the rise. In one incident, skinheads attacked members of the audience at a church-sponsored rock concert; the police did not respond quickly.[78]

The year 1988, a very significant one in GDR history, included the fiftieth anniversary of Kristallnacht. During October and November many articles about Jews appeared daily in the newspapers. Robin Ostow reported that "privately, many Jews and non-Jewish antifascists expressed fears that the massive commemorations in November and the sudden priority given to Jewish projects—in a country where shortages of basic commodities were a fact of life—could cause jealousy among less privileged groups and strengthen anti-Semitic tendencies."[79] In October the president of the World Jewish Congress, Edgar Bronfman, visited the GDR at the invitation of Minister of Foreign Affairs Oskar Fisher. Bronfman met with Erich Honecker, members of the Free German Youth, and young members of Berlin's Jewish Community. Bronfman paid tribute to Nazi victims buried at the Jewish cemetery in Weissensee and viewed the memorial stone on Grosse Hamburgerstrasse.[80]

A small booklet entitled *Beware Lest the Nightmare Recur* was published in a number of languages by the Association of Jewish Communities in the GDR. The title referred, of course, to the Holocaust, although it pointed portentously to the fear surrounding the rise of antiforeigner sentiment. The booklet included accounts of events at a reception held in the GDR's Council of State building on November 8 during a special session of the Volkskammer (People's Chamber). Erich Honecker spoke about the role of the Jews in Germany and their suffering at the hands of the Nazis. He stated dramatically at the end of his speech that "our commemoration of the victims of Nazi savagery prompts me to emphasize once again that the eight associated Jewish Communities in the GDR, indeed all citizens of Jewish faith, will continue to enjoy the full support and encouragement of the socialist state. The reconstruction of the New Synagogue in Berlin's *Oranienburger Strasse* will serve as a symbol to the world, as a reminder and warning."

Honecker concluded his speech by conferring awards of merit on "eminent figures of the world Jewish movement" and presenting to the library of the Jewish Community in Berlin "a collection of 543 valuable historical books from past centuries which were rediscovered in Berlin libraries."[81] Honecker was joined by Sindermann and by prominent members of the GDR Jewish Community, such as Friedrich Broido, chairman of the Jewish Provincial Committee of Mecklenburg, and Sigmund Rotstein, president of the Association of Jewish Communities in the GDR.[82] International guests included Heinz Galinski, chairman of the Central Council of Jews in Germany, rabbis from the United States, Romania, and Hungary, and Gerhart Riegner, co-chairman of the World Jewish Congress. As noted in the booklet, more than fifty events took place during 1988 in commemoration of Kristallnacht. The speeches given by Honecker and the Jewish GDR leaders at these events were peppered with such ideology-laden phrases as "antifascism," "the glorification of the working class," and "the evil of West German imperialism."

The commemorations of 1988 focused not only on the Holocaust but also on the future of the GDR Jewish Community and its place in world Jewry. As Honecker mentioned in his address, plans were made for the reconstruction of the synagogue on the Oranienburgerstrasse, and an international board of trustees was established to promote the New Synagogue. On November 10, 1988, the Centrum Judaicum Foundation was created to "become an international meeting centre concerned with the preservation of Jewish culture and tradition, research into the antifascist resistance struggle and memory of the victims." This "Jewish Museum to be established in the New Synagogue would work under the patronage of the GDR's National Council for the Cultivation and Dissemination of German Cultural Heritage."[83] Sigmund Rotstein reiterated, "We have set ourselves the task of rebuilding and equipping this synagogue as a commemorative centre, a meeting house, a place of prayer, remembrance and recollection, and as a research centre. . . . The New Berlin Synagogue . . . will cultivat[e] and publiciz[e] the accomplishments of Jewish culture, arts, literature and science, past and present, worldwide."[84]

While these gestures can be interpreted as political propaganda, especially in light of the GDR's very small Jewish population, one can also acknowledge the commitment of the government to recognizing its Jewish citizens and their achievements. Historians also addressed the accomplishments of well-known GDR Jews, although they could be faulted for doing this to deflect attention from the GDR's neglect of the Holocaust. Schmidt sounded suspiciously compensatory and defensive when he described German interest in Jewish achievements: "Aside from [concentration camps and pogroms] Jewish culture and tradition in Germany and the participation of citizens of the Jewish faith and Jewish background in German history, economics, science/scholarship, and culture in the battle for social progress in Germany are much less, too less, often not at all known." However, Schmidt pointed out proudly, "In 1988 the role of the Jews in German history and their participation in economics, science/scholarship, and culture was the subject of special scholarly events for the first time." In one, organized by the Central Institute for History of the Academy of Sciences, "an interdisciplinary colloquium addressed the role and place of Jews in the political and intellectual conflicts of German history in the twentieth century."[85]

At this particular conference the participants discussed the role of Jewish scholars in German history. But keeping the event firmly rooted in conventional GDR historiography, they also focused on the battle of the revolutionary German workers' party against anti-Semitism and Jewish persecution. They also surveyed the artistic, political, and intellectual accounts of anti-Semitism and fascistic Jewish persecution in the GDR.[86]

Many more events were held during that year. In January the theological department of Humboldt University began a lecture series that culminated on November 7 and 8 with an international seminar entitled "Remember for the Future." In attendance were such prominent figures as Gerhart Riegner and Rabbi Norman Solomon from Birmingham, England. On April 1 the exhibition "We Must Never Be Allowed to Forget" opened. It dealt with the lives of Protestant ministers of Jewish origin. The Historical Society of the GDR and the Committee of Antifascist Resistance Fighters held a symposium concerning Kristallnacht on April 28. On June 2 the exhibition "All Because They Were Jews" opened in Eberswelde, and a memorial stone was unveiled on the site of the town's former synagogue.

The long list of events marking Kristallnacht in 1988 included cultural, artistic, historical, and political commemorations, one of the most prominent being an exhibition that opened on October 16 at Berlin's Ephraim Palace. It was organized by the ministry of culture and the state secretary for religious affairs in cooperation with the Association of Jewish Communities in the GDR. The exhibition documented, in the words of Erich Honecker, "the unforgettable contributions of Jewish people to the historical, cultural, and scientific heritage of the German people. The history of the Jewish Community in Berlin is traced from its founding in 1671 to the present day."[87] Many memorial stones were laid at the sites of concentration camps and destroyed synagogues. Films about the Jews during the Nazi period were shown. Special services were held in Christian churches. The prolific activities commemorating the fiftieth anniversary of Kristallnacht took place all over the GDR. Many of these events attracted West Germans and international visitors from the Jewish community to the GDR for the first time.

Particularly noteworthy are the many publications that appeared in the late 1980s, for example, *Pogromnacht 1938,* by Kurt Pätzold and Irene Runge. Pätzold was one of the GDR's leading scholars on fascism and the Third Reich, and Runge, a sociologist at Humboldt University, was the spokesperson for the East Berlin Jewish Community and was very active in organizing young GDR Jews in the Community. The book explores the *Alltagsgeschichte,* or everyday history, of individual lives and the issues of guilt and responsibility during the days between November 7 and 18, 1938.[88] Also important were Ludwig Geiger's *Geschichte der Juden in Berlin* (History of Jews in Berlin), which had an introduction by Hermann Simon, director of the Centrum Judaicum Foundation, and Rudolf Hirsch and Rosemarie Schuder's 1987 book *Der gelbe Fleck. Wurzeln und Wirkungen des Judenhasses in der deutschen Geschichte* (The yellow mark: Roots and repercussions of hate toward the Jews in German history).[89] The latter volume, 750 pages long, chronicles the history of anti-Semitism in an effort to understand how such hostility developed ultimately into a political program and the Final Solution. Such works were complemented by shorter monographs on Jewish museums, cemeteries, and holidays, as well as by studies of Jewish Communities in smaller GDR cities.

There is, in short, a wealth of studies on the Jews in German history, anti-Semitism, and fascism. Studies on the Holocaust are markedly fewer in number. Schmidt admitted that "the research that has been addressed here has not in any way been able to eliminate the enduring deficit. There still is a great deal to do in order to expand and deepen the historical image of socialist society in the GDR and the essential contribution of Jewish participation in the social life in the centuries of German history from the Middle Ages to the present."[90]

The fact that most of the Jews in the GDR were Communists or closely affiliated with the Communist Party is central to understanding the GDR response to the Holocaust. The smallness of their numbers (250 to 300 Jews in East Berlin and about 250 more scattered among eight very small Communities) made the position of the Jews in the GDR's final years extremely complex. On the one hand, especially after November 9, 1988, there seemed to be almost philo-Semitic, enthusiastic attention paid to a relatively small group of people. On the other hand, most of the Jews or their children, often having returned to the GDR from abroad, were committed to the GDR and its policies. The Jewish Community itself, to which many of these Jews did not belong, played a highly symbolic role. The GDR's recent attention to "its Jews" publicized its commitment to combating anti-Semitism, which had grown in the Federal Republic.

On October 9, 1989, a month before the Wall fell, *Neues Deutschland* printed a small article, "Grüsse Jüdische Gemeinden zum 40. Jahrestag der DDR. Andenken an Opfer des Faschismus wird wachgehalten" (Greetings from the Jewish Community on the occasion of the Fortieth Anniversary of the GDR: Remembrance of the victims of fascism stays alive). In it, the president of the Jewish Communities in the

GDR declared that "especially for the Jews, the founding of the GDR for the first time in German history represented a turning point that provided a peaceful future for secure social relations."[91] Although this was clearly the official line of the Jewish representatives, the Jews had indeed achieved a fairly secure position in GDR society.[92]

Therefore, the destruction of the Wall was not received with unbridled optimism by the Jewish Community. In December 1989 many East Berlin Jews were disappointed and even shocked to find themselves excluded as "foreigners," as somehow not belonging to the German people. Signs at political rallies supporting reunification, while not overtly anti-Semitic, brought back memories of German nationalism that made Jews feel very uncomfortable. The chants of demonstrators shifted from anti-GDR slogans such as "Wir sind das Volk" (We are *the* people) to "Wir sind ein Volk" (We are *one* people). The euphoria that erupted at the opening of the borders and the toppling of the Stalinist Honecker regime quickly was transformed for many Germans into hope for a future "Fourth Reich," in which they could again be proud of their national identity. Some GDR Jews began to inquire about getting back the foreign passports they had given up after reemigrating to the GDR. They felt that life in a reunited Germany might be less pleasant for them than life under the previous regime.

The East Germans' overwhelming desire for reunification, however, was proven by the March 1990 elections. In the same month, the newsletter of the East Berlin Jewish Community openly criticized the Honecker regime, while praising the peaceful revolution in the GDR, which was a first for all Germans. The editors focused particularly on the GDR's exaggerated claims that anti-Semitism did not exist and cited the reasons for its increasing appearance. They listed a number of factors, such as the forced antifascism and an unsuccessful school policy of arrogantly making antifascism the declared Communist state doctrine. This approach made it very difficult for the Holocaust to be understood as rooted in anti-Jewish attitudes. In addition, the media were consistently anti-Zionist and were seen as anti-Semitic by many young people. In the press Israel was presented as an "inhuman state."[93]

Uncertainty and concern about the future heightened for GDR Jews after the election. Numerous anti-Semitic incidents occurred, such as desecrations of cemeteries and the appearance of anti-Jewish slogans. They were often part of a broader antiforeigner movement. Some black African and Vietnamese immigrants were brutally attacked by skinheads. At the Alexanderplatz in East Berlin, skinheads formed themselves into a swastika as police looked on.[94] While police inaction can be better read as impotence against a populace that had had too much police intervention in their lives, Prime Minister Hans Modorow remarked that "there is some basis for fears about a resurgence of nationalism, racism and anti-Semitism in East Germany as the two Germanies move toward union." Modorow conveyed this message in response to a letter sent him by Rabbi Marvin Hier of the Simon Wiesenthal Center for Holocaust Studies in Los Angeles. Hier had written to the leaders of both Germanies and asked "how they would preserve the memory of Nazi crimes as a warning to the future."[95]

Unification came on October 3, 1990, accompanied by great celebration. A few weeks before unification, Jewish High Holiday services in the East Berlin Ryke-strasse synagogue brought the East and West Berlin Jewish Communities together as they had not been for over thirty years. Even more significant and symbolic was the first public event marking the unification of the two Jewish Communities. On October 29, 1990, the main cupola of the Oranienburgerstrasse synagogue was put into place. All attention, especially from the media, was on Heinz Galinski, the former head of the West Berlin Jewish Community and at that time the leader of the entire West German Community. He was, in effect, the most important Jewish figure in the new Germany. Members of the two Communities mixed freely with each other, although not without tensions.

GDR Jews realized that when they became citizens of the Federal Republic of Germany their voices might not be heard. A massive exhibition, "Patterns of Jewish Life," was mounted in Berlin at the famous Walter Gropius Building near the fallen Wall. It opened on January 12, 1992. While *New York Times* correspondent John Rockwell reported that the exhibition "fascinates its German viewers," he also noted that "the main source of criticism has been the Jewish organizations in the eastern part of Berlin. . . . Jewish organizations [there] compete with the official group in the west, and reflect larger East Berlin resentments about the supposedly domineering predilections of the West Berliners, Jewish and non-Jewish alike." Rockwell added that problems also arise from "tensions between German-born Jews and recent immigrants from Eastern Europe." He also mentioned the "philo-Semitism" sweeping Germany, saying that "some observers have expressed doubts about the current wave, . . . that it is a mere sop to the past, a way of avoiding guilt through neatly sequestered scholarly exhibitions."[96]

The year after the unification of the two Germanies and the two Jewish Communities, former GDR Jews realized that the rapid transformations in their lives had brought not only welcomed new freedoms, such as travel, but also economic burdens with dire social consequences. While consumer goods were now accessible, many East Germans were frustrated by their inability to buy even some of the necessities they had taken for granted under the socialist system. Compounded by layoffs and firings, unemployment promoted a general disorientation and political disaffection. Such economic hardships fueled xenophobia; foreigners were seen as threatening the employment security of former GDR citizens, who were becoming increasingly insecure, both financially and psychologically. The attacks in September 1991 in Hoyerswerda, in which skinheads threw stones and Molotov cocktails at foreigners, worried the Jews.

In January 1992 the German magazine *Der Spiegel* devoted two articles to the issue of Germans and Jews. In the first (January 13), the topic was the attitudes of Israeli Jews and Germans toward each other. In the second (January 20), attention was given to the question of German anti-Semitism, the parallels between the Jews and the Turks as foreigners, and right-wing movements. The second article announced that "every eighth German is anti-Semitic." The statistical analyses showed that while few people were willing to say directly that they were anti-Semitic, other

responses indicated those tendencies. Perhaps most interesting were the comparisons of East and West Germans' attitudes, which revealed that the former were less
anti-Semitic, less right-wing, and less xenophobic. In August 1992, however, Rostock, in eastern Germany, was the scene of an attack on a hostel for foreigners. The
murder of Turkish residents in the West German town of Mölln in November 1992
and later in Solingen in May 1993 illustrated that right-wing violence was not only
a product of eastern Germany. Local elections in April 1992 reflected an increase in
voter support for far-right parties in western Germany. Far-right parties captured 11
percent of the vote in Baden-Württemburg and 6 percent in Schleswig-Holstein.
When asked about his party's policies, Gerhard Frey, the head of the German People's Union, stated, "We are not unfriendly to foreigners. We are friendly to Germans."[97] Increasingly, the fate of Jews in the new Germany was perceived as linked
to the future of other, more numerous and more visible minorities.[98]

In the GDR both historians and Jews were trapped between wanting to give the
Jews and the Holocaust a greater role in the official version of the twelve years of
Nazi domination and accommodating the ideology of antifascism. The history of
the GDR and its Jews is riddled with complications and ironies. The forty-year
anniversary of the GDR came only one month before the Wall came down on
November 9, 1989. That date marked the end of an era in the political history of
both Germanies as well as the beginning of the systematic persecution of the Jews
in Germany fifty-one years before. After November 9, 1989, nothing was the same.
The events of the year leading up to November 1988 proved that the GDR was committed to making the fate and history of its "Jewish fellow citizens" its own, albeit
often for self-serving reasons. The many Jews who returned to the GDR after the
end of the war were dedicated to rebuilding what they had hoped would be a different and better Germany than the one they had escaped from. This experiment in
large part failed, as was demonstrated by the overwhelming support in the GDR for
reunification.

In the united Germany violent attacks against refugees and asylum seekers continued to increase. Six hundred were reported in the first three months of 1992 alone.
In July 1993 the liberal German political asylum law was changed in order to stem
the flow of refugees and thus to curb right-wing violence against foreigners by eliminating the source of the tensions. Critics like Jürgen Filjakowski of the Free University of Berlin reject the assumption that aggressive xenophobia and attacks on
foreigners are, as the revised law implies, the fault of those non-Germans seeking
asylum.[99] Overall statistics for 1993 show that "right-wing acts of violence . . .
dropped slightly," although "there were still 1,609 stabbings, beatings, arson attacks
and the like against foreigners that took the lives of 7 people in 1993." One synagogue in Lübeck was bombed. In April 1994 a *New York Times* report noted that
"prosperous western German states, not the formerly Communist eastern areas now
afflicted by unemployment, had the highest per capita incidence of racial violence
in 1993."[100] In fact, a poll conducted in January 1994 for the American Jewish Committee by the respected Emnid Institute showed that former East Germans are less
likely "to express negative attitudes toward Jews." Nineteen percent of former East

Germans, compared with 44 percent of former West Germans, agree that Jews are exploiting the Holocaust. Only 8 percent of former East Germans, in comparison with 24 percent of former West Germans, feel that Jews have too much influence in German society.[101]

The divergence would seem to show that GDR anti-fascist ideology, as programmatic as even the Jews themselves found it, did indeed have some effect. Rabbi Andrew Baker of the American Jewish Committee commented that "such disparities may reflect the anti-fascist ideology of communist East Germany, which tended to absolve eastern Germans of Nazi-era crimes and stressed the Nazi victimization of Jews."[102] The poll also indicated that Germans have even greater hostilities toward other minorities: Gypsies, Arabs, Poles, and Turks, in that order. One can only hope that in the new Germany all Jews and "foreigners" will be protected from persecution and that Jewish fears about a reunified Germany can be laid to rest.

NOTES

This essay was completed before the archives of the former GDR became available. Therefore I am appreciative of comments on this article by Dr. Angelika Timm of Humboldt University, who drew from primary sources in her own work on this topic. Dr. Timm's work was presented at a workshop sponsored by the American Institute for Contemporary German Studies and the German Historical Institute, Washington, D.C., which was funded by the Volkswagen-Stiftung Program in Post-War German History.

1. Ari L. Goldman, "East Berlin Moves to Pay Reparations to the Jews," *New York Times,* February 9, 1990, A10.

2. "Excerpts From East Berlin Statement of Apology," ibid., April 13, 1990, A5.

3. See *Sojourners: The Return of German Jews and the Question of Identity* (Lincoln, 1995), based on interviews with GDR Jews who returned from exile to the GDR by John Borneman and me in East Berlin in August, September, and December 1989 and by me in the fall and winter of 1990–91. These interviews also form the basis of a video documentary.

4. Eve Rosenhaft, "The Uses of Remembrance: The Legacy of the Communist Resistance in the German Democratic Republic," in *Germans against Nazis: Essays in Honour of Peter Hoffmann,* ed. Francis R. Nicosia and Lawrence D. Stokes (New York, 1990), 371. Rosenhaft emphasizes that the German Communist Party was "the only major political party in Germany that attempted to maintain a coherent organizational structure during the Third Reich and to mobilize popular resistance through illegal activity" (369). This legacy was regarded differently in the divided Germanies after the war: it was "an

object of cultivated oblivion" in the West, while it was cause for "pious celebration" in the East.

5. Ibid., 371–72.

6. For further discussion, see Eric Brothers, "On the Anti-Fascist Resistance of German-Jews," *Leo Baeck Institute Yearbook XXXII* (London, 1987), 369–82. Brothers points out at the start that not enough work has been done "on the group's specific activities between 1933 and 1941." He acknowledges Margot Pikarski, a GDR scholar, who "places Herbert Baum and his comrades in the midst of the different groups and individuals, Jews and non-Jews, who engaged in active resistance in Berlin, mostly under the direction of the *Kommunistische Partei Deutschlands* (KPD)." He said that Pikarski "does not promote the Baum group as Jewish, but the persecution of Jews, membership in Jewish and Zionist youth groups, and aspects of Jewish descent and heritage are covered in her work" (370; see also Konrad Kwiet and Helmut Eschwege, *Selbstbehauptung und Widerstand. Deutsche Juden im Kampf um Existenz und Menschenwürde 1933–1945* [Hamburg, 1984]).

7. For further detailed analysis of this connection, see John Borneman, *Belonging in the Two Berlins: Kin, State, Nation* (Cambridge, 1992).

8. The term *Pogromnacht* is being used in Germany today.

9. For an important discussion of November 9 and the problem of memory, see Elisabeth Domansky, "Kristallnacht, the Holocaust, and German Unity: The Meaning of November 9 as an Anniversary in Germany," *History and Memory* 4, no. 1 (1992), 60–94; and idem, "Die gespaltene Erinnerung," in *Kunst und Literatur nach Auschwitz,* ed. Manuel Köppen (Berlin, 1993), 178–96.

10. Walter Schmidt, "Jüdisches Erbe deutscher

Geschichte im Erbe- und Traditionsverständnis der DDR," *Zeitschrift für Geschichtswissenschaft* 37, no. 8 (1989), 692. This and all other translations from the German are my own.

11. I use the term "Jewish Community," with a capital *C,* to refer specifically to those Jews in the GDR who were officially members of the Community *(Gemeinde)* and had a more traditional religious orientation. They viewed themselves as belonging to this group and were officially affiliated with a synagogue. Outside of the Community were Jews who were atheists or did not feel they could identify with stricter Jewish laws. In 1987 a new group was founded that brought some of these people, many of them children of party functionaries who knew little of their Jewish ancestry, into the synagogue and to Community-related activities. Robin Ostow reported that only 15 percent applied to join the Community. "But the existence of the group meant that there was now an interested Jewish public around the Jewish community, this public consisting largely of writers, state and party functionaries, intellectuals, and artists, people whose ideas inevitably found their way into the political culture of the East German state" ("German Democratic Republic," *American Jewish Year Book, 1989* [Philadelphia, 1989], 351).

12. See the two-part article "Das bessere Deutschland," *Der Spiegel,* April 8 and 15, 1991, about these people. This group included dedicated Communists, some of whom were Jews who returned from emigration or survived the Holocaust, or those otherwise committed to building a different, more progressive Germany.

13. Jerry E. Thompson, "Jews, Zionism, and Israel: The Story of the Jews in the German Democratic Republic since 1945" (Ph.D. diss., Washington State University, 1978), explains that those who wanted to return to the West in 1945–46 were "rejected by Western occupation authorities, who saw no point in intensifying the problem of housing and food shortages for sixty million Germans by inviting in a few hundred, or a thousand, German Jews" (12).

14. For more detailed figures and discussion, see ibid., 10, 56. Since Thompson's dissertation is one of the very few extensive studies on this topic, I follow it quite closely, especially as regards Thompson's primary source material. See also Richard L. Merritt, "Politics of Judaism in East Germany," an unpublished manuscript in the author's possession; and especially the work of Robin Ostow, e.g., *Jews in Contemporary East Germany: The Children of Moses in the Land of Marx* (London, 1989).

15. These benefits are emphasized as part of the GDR's antifascist program in an article by two GDR academics and an American sociology professor who lived in the GDR: Hanna Behrend, Joan Ecklein, and Frederike Hajek, "Antifascism in the Two Germanies: The Case for the GDR," *Radical America* 23, no. 4 (June 1991), 65–79. This article is especially interesting because these authors want to make an evenhanded case for the GDR's program of antifascism while also criticizing its faults, especially Stalinization. In their article, written just after unification, they claimed that they would "compare the antifascist records of East and West Germany in detail and try to assess what this complex history of denazification will mean for a united Germany" (65).

16. I draw the reader's attention to a small but important collection of essays, *Holocaust and* Shilumim: *The Policy of* Wiedergutmachung *in the Early 1950s,* ed. Axel Frohn, German Historical Institute Occasional Paper No. 2 (Washington, D.C., 1991). Aside from emphasizing the use of the Hebrew term *shilumim* instead of "payment," "restitution," or *Wiedergutmachung,* this series of articles details West and East German material payment to Jews and Israel, as well as America's special role in the process.

17. Konrad Jarausch, "The Failure of East German Antifascism: Some Ironies of History as Politics," *German Studies Review* 14, no. 1 (1991), 85. For an extensive analysis of East German historiography, see Andreas Dorpalen, *German History in Marxist Perspective: The East German Approach* (Detroit, 1985); and Georgi Verbeeck, "Marxism, Antisemitism, and the Holocaust," *Leo Baeck Institute Yearbook XXXV* (London, 1990), 385–97, esp. 391–95.

18. Jarausch, "Failure of East German Antifascism," 90.

19. Ibid., 94.

20. Robin Ostow, "'The Persecution of the Jews by the Fascists': GDR Textbook Examples of Terror and Resistance in Presocialist Europe," unpublished manuscript in the author's possession, 1. Angelika Timm disputes Ostow's point.

21. Ibid., 10.

22. Thompson, "Jews, Zionism, and Israel," 69.

23. Ibid., 77.

24. Boris Sapir, "Germany and Austria," *American Jewish Year Book, 1948–49* (Philadelphia, 1949), 378.

25. Sapir, "Germany and Austria," 378.

26. Thompson, "Jews, Zionism, and Israel," 68.

27. Ostow, "Persecution of the Jews," 8.

28. Sapir, "Germany and Austria," 377.

29. Thompson, "Jews, Zionism, and Israel," 75.

30. Joseph Gordon, "Eastern Germany," *Amer-*

ican Jewish Year Book, 1954 (Philadelphia, 1954), 268.

31. Ibid., 270.

32. In his contribution, "A Participant's Response," in *Holocaust and* Shilumim, Saul Kagan, executive director of the Conference of Jewish Material Claims Against Germany, tells of his meeting with Erich Honecker in June 1987. Since 1975 Kagan's group had been trying to get action from the GDR on the reparations issue. Among Honecker's responses, Kagan reports, were: "We are the anti-fascists," "The Nazis are *drüben*" ("over there," referring to the West), and "We have provided pensions or *Renten* to the anti-fascists residing in the GDR." Kagan also added that Honecker mentioned the help East Germany gave to the small *Kultusgemeinde* (Jewish Community) (55).

33. Thompson, "Jews, Zionism, and Israel," 113.

34. Ibid., 119.

35. Gordon, "Eastern Germany," *American Jewish Year Book, 1954,* 268.

36. Ibid., 269.

37. See Jeffrey Herf, *East German Communists and the Jewish Question: The Case of Paul Merker,* German Historical Institute Occasional Paper No. 11 (Washington, D.C., 1994).

38. Konrad Kwiet, "Historians of the German Democratic Republic on Antisemitism and Persecution," *Leo Baeck Institute Yearbook XXI* (London, 1976), 180.

39. See the discussion in Axel Frohn, "Introduction: The Origins of *Shilumim,*" in *Holocaust and* Shilumim, where he states that "in the Luxembourg Agreements of September 10, 1952, the Federal Republic of Germany consented to global payments to Israel. This was considered as some kind of collective payment from the German people to the Jewish people insofar as the latter was represented by the State of Israel. . . . On March 12, 1951, the Israeli government sent a note to the four powers which had occupied Germany after World War II and demanded German payments of 1.5 billion dollars for the integration of 500,000 Jewish refugees (three thousand per person). One billion dollars were claimed from the Federal Republic and 500 million from the GDR. The Soviet Union never replied to this note, and the GDR never paid any amount" (1–3).

40. Joseph Gordon, "Eastern Germany," *American Jewish Year Book, 1955* (Philadelphia, 1955), 403.

41. Gordon, "Eastern Germany," *American Jewish Year Book, 1954,* 270. Compare the discussion in Behrend, Ecklein, and Hajek, "Antifascism in the Two Germanies."

42. Ostow, *Jews in Contemporary East Germany,* 5, 6.

43. Ibid., 6.

44. Lotte Lowenthal, "East Germany," *American Jewish Year Book, 1957* (Philadelphia, 1957), 297.

45. E. M. Orland, "East Germany," *American Jewish Year Book, 1960* (Philadelphia, 1960), 248; Behrend, Ecklein, and Hajek, "Antifascism in the Two Germanies," 69.

46. Martin Riesenburger, "Letter," *Newsletter,* 1952, 1.

47. Martin Riesenburger, "Unsere Heimat ist hier, in der DDR," in *Nachrichtenblatt,* December 1963, 18, reprinted from *Neue Zeit,* November 13, 1963.

48. Heinz Schenk, "Jewish Citizens and Their Religious Communities in the GDR," *GDR Review* 9 (1965), 9. The article is introduced with the comment that it was inspired by foreign readers' requests for information "on the activities and the position of Jewish communities in the public life of the German Democratic Republic." Schenk, chairman of the Jewish Community of Democratic Berlin, "kindly consented to deal with the various problems raised by the readers" (7).

49. Ibid.

50. Heinz Schenk, in *Nachrichtenblatt,* quoted in Hans Lamm, "East Germany," *American Jewish Year Book, 1966* (Philadelphia, 1966), 365.

51. Schmidt, "Jüdisches Erbe deutscher Geschichte," 699.

52. Ibid., 697–98.

53. Kwiet, "Historians of the German Democratic Republic," 181.

54. Ibid., 184.

55. Ibid., 185. Kwiet cites here the conference report by H. Heitzer published in the *Zeitschrift für Geschichtswissenschaft,* 1961.

56. Ibid., 185.

57. Ibid., 184.

58. Schmidt, "Jüdisches Erbe deutscher Geschichte," 700.

59. Kwiet, "Historians of the German Democratic Republic," 188.

60. Schmidt, "Jüdisches Erbe deutscher Geschichte," 701.

61. Kwiet, "Historians of the German Democratic Republic," 192, 198.

62. Schmidt, "Jüdisches Erbe deutscher Geschichte," 702–3.

63. Friedo Sachser, "German Democratic Republic," *American Jewish Year Book, 1977* (Philadelphia, 1977), 452.

64. Friedo Sachser, "German Democratic Re-

public," *American Jewish Year Book, 1978* (Philadelphia, 1978), 424.

65. Frohn, "Introduction: The Origins of *Shilumim,*" 3.

66. Sachser, "German Democratic Republic," *American Jewish Year Book, 1978,* 424.

67. Ibid., 235.

68. Sachser, "German Democratic Republic," *American Jewish Year Book, 1980* (Philadelphia, 1980), 235.

69. Ibid., 236.

70. Sachser, "German Democratic Republic," *American Jewish Year Book, 1981* (Philadelphia, 1981), 232.

71. Ibid., 233.

72. Ibid., 233–34.

73. Ibid., 233.

74. Sachser, "German Democratic Republic," *American Jewish Year Book, 1984* (Philadelphia, 1984), 210.

75. Ibid., 211.

76. Sachser, "German Democratic Republic," *American Jewish Year Book, 1987* (Philadelphia, 1987), 261.

77. Robin Ostow, "German Democratic Republic," *American Jewish Year Book, 1989* (Philadelphia, 1989), 349.

78. Ibid., 350.

79. Ostow, "German Democratic Republic," *American Jewish Year Book, 1990* (Philadelphia, 1990), 374.

80. Erich Honecker, "Pledged to a Policy of Humanitarianism, Peace, and International Understanding," in *Beware Lest the Nightmare Recur: Remembrance of the Nazi Pogrom in the Night of 9 November 1938,* a documentary account published by the Association of Jewish Communities in the GDR (Berlin, 1988), 32. For a lengthier and more critical analysis of this speech, see Robin Ostow, "Imperialist Agents, Anti-Fascist Monuments, Eastern Refugees, Property Claims: Jews as Incorporations of East German Social Trauma, 1945–1994," in *Jews, Germans, Memory: Reordering Jewish Life in Germany,* ed. Y. Michael Bodemann (Ann Arbor, Mich., 1995).

81. *Beware Lest the Nightmare Recur,* 13.

82. Rotstein's contribution was appropriately titled "We Enjoy Respect and Esteem in This Country."

83. Honecker, "Pledged to a Policy of Humanitarianism," 74.

84. Sigmund Rotstein, "Appeal by the President of the Association of Jewish Communities in the GDR (4 July 1988)," in *Beware Lest the Nightmare Recur,* 73.

85. Schmidt, "Jüdisches Erbe deutscher Geschichte," 711.

86. Ibid.

87. Honecker, "Pledged to a Policy of Humanitarianism," 92.

88. Kurt Pätzold and Irene Runge, *Pogromnacht 1938* (Berlin, 1988).

89. Ludwig Geiger, *Geschichte der Juden in Berlin. Festschrift zur zweiten säkular-feier* (Berlin, 1871; reprint, with an introduction by Hermann Simon, Leipzig, 1988); Rudolf Hirsch and Rosemarie Schuder, *Der gelbe Fleck. Wurzeln und Wirkungen des Judenhasses in der deutschen Geschichte,* 2d ed. (Berlin, 1989).

90. Schmidt, "Jüdisches Erbe deutscher Geschichte," 712–13.

91. "Grüsse Jüdische Gemeinden zum 40. Jahrestag der DDR. Andenken an Opfer des Faschismus wird wachgehalten," *Neues Deutschland,* October 9, 1989, 9.

92. See Borneman and Peck, *Sojourners.*

93. *Nachrichtenblatt,* March 1990, 2.

94. Two such instances are mentioned in David Binder, "Violence by Skinheads Startling East Germans," *New York Times,* August 21, 1990, A2.

95. "East Berlin Premier, In Letter to a Rabbi, Sees Some Nazi Peril," ibid., March 13, 1990, A18.

96. See John Rockwell, "Exhibition Evokes Past Jewish Life and Grips Its German Viewers," ibid., March 30, 1992, C1, C11.

97. Stephen Kinzer, "Far Right Gains Sharply in German State Elections," ibid., April 6, 1992, A1, A6.

98. For a detailed discussion of the relationship of Jews to other minorities in Germany since reunification, see Jeffrey M. Peck, "The 'Ins' and 'Outs' of the New Germany: Jews, Foreigners, Asylum Seekers," in *Reemerging Jewish Culture in Germany: Life and Literature since 1989,* ed. Sander L. Gilman and Karen Remmler (New York, 1994), 130–47.

99. See Jürgen Filjakowski, *Aggressive Nationalism, Immigration Pressure, and Asylum Policy Disputes in Contemporary Germany,* German Historical Institute Occasional Paper No. 9, with comment by Jeffrey M. Peck (Washington, D.C., 1993), 7–33.

100. Stephen Kinzer, "Attacks Drop Slightly," *New York Times,* April 19, 1994, A6.

101. Emnid Institute, "Current German Attitudes toward Jews and Other Minorities: A Survey of Public Opinion," conducted for the American Jewish Committee, January 12–31, 1994, typescript.

102. Rick Atkinson, "Poll in Germany Finds Many Hostile Toward Foreigners, Jews," *Washington Post,* March 8, 1994, A14.

AUSTRIA
Bruce F. Pauley

Despite its small size, Austria was a major factor in the Holocaust as well as in Holocaust-related events in the years following World War II. Although the republic of Austria that was created in 1918 could boast little more than thirty-two thousand square miles and scarcely 6.5 million inhabitants, its Jewish population was fairly large. The country's 220,000 Jews represented three and a half times the proportion of the total population that the 550,000 Jews in Germany did. For Vienna alone the numbers were even more significant. In the 1920s over 200,000 self-professed Jews lived in the Austrian capital, making it the sixth-largest Jewish community in the world, after New York, Warsaw, Chicago, Philadelphia, and Budapest, and well ahead of Berlin's 173,000.

Size alone, of course, does not begin to explain the importance of Austria's Jewish population in the modern world. No other group in Austria between 1848 and 1938 produced as many original thinkers.[1] Such figures as Sigmund Freud, Ludwig Wittgenstein, Arnold Schoenberg, Hugo von Hofmannsthal, Arthur Schnitzler, Karl Kraus, Stefan Zweig, Fritz Kreisler, and Gustav Mahler, to name only a very few, immeasurably enriched the culture not only of Austria but of the world. The expulsion of Vienna's Jews has to some extent provincialized the Austrian capital and lowered its cultural standards.[2]

The Emancipation of Austrian Jewry and the Anti-Semitic Reaction

The rise of Austria's Jews to cultural and economic prominence is very recent. Although Jews lived in Austria as early as the tenth century, they were expelled or forcibly converted to Christianity in 1421 and again in 1670. In the early 1780s Emperor Joseph II freed them from numerous medieval restrictions related to economic activities, education, and military service; but many of these freedoms were taken away by his successors and were not restored until the revolutions of 1848. Emperor Franz Joseph revoked some of these newly granted rights the next year, including the right to purchase land or hold public office, but Austria's defeat by France in the Italian War of 1859 led to a series of constitutional reforms during the next eight years, many of which directly affected Jews. Franz Joseph's edict of January 12, 1860, again permitted them to own land, enter a profession of their own choosing, settle in parts of the monarchy previously forbidden to them, testify against Christians, and employ Christian servants. All remaining laws that discriminated against Jews were removed by the new constitution of December 21, 1867, following Austria's defeat by Prussia and the creation of the Dual Monarchy with Hungary. Thanks in large measure to this new constitution and to the benevolence of Franz Joseph, Austria's Jews came to regard the last half-century of the Habsburg monarchy as a golden era in their history.[3]

As early as the 1850s and 1860s Jews took advantage of their new freedoms by establishing woolen factories in Bohemia and Moravia; in Hungary they founded the silk industry. Throughout the monarchy they played an important role in the building of steel mills and railroads. Near Vienna they were instrumental in building factories that produced silk, cotton, woolens, laces, and leather, as well as the only factory in Austria that made chocolate. They also founded many of the capital city's more important banks.

It was in the academic professions, however, that Jews made the greatest progress after 1867. Poor Jewish immigrants in Vienna from Austria's eastern provinces were far more likely to send their children, especially girls, to elite middle schools than were gentiles of comparable social position. By 1913 no fewer than 35 percent of all *Gymnasien* students in Vienna were Jewish, making Jews more than three times as likely to attend these schools as Christians. The situation at the University of Vienna on the eve of World War I was scarcely different, as Jews made up more than 27 percent of the enrollment. Armed with their higher education, Austrian Jews now entered such free professions as law, teaching, journalism, and medicine in large numbers; in some fields, such as medicine, they became an absolute majority in Vienna.

Franz Joseph also assured Jews that they would be treated with complete equality in his beloved army, and he proved it by appointing one Jew to the highest rank in the army and another as the chief officer on the army's medical staff. By 1914 Jews were actually overrepresented among the army's officers, especially its reserve officers, because of the need for educated young men with linguistic skills. Although Jews made up only about 4.5 percent of the Dual Monarchy's population in 1900, they made up 8 percent of the army's officers, making Austria-Hungary the only country in the world with such an overrepresentation. In fact, prior to the establishment of the Israeli Defense Force no army even came close to having as many Jewish officers as Austria-Hungary's.

Until at least 1880, and to a lesser extent even later, Jews tended to acculturate into the German-Austrian nationality and were considered German-Austrian by the non-Jewish German-Austrians and the national minorities of Austria. In the meantime, Jews in the Hungarian half of the monarchy increasingly identified with the dominant Magyar nationality. In both cases, members of national minority groups who felt oppressed, especially the Czechs, regarded Jews as accomplices in their oppression, an opinion that could also be found in Hungary.

The incredibly long reign of Franz Joseph (1848–1916) witnessed not only increasing rights for Jews, including the right to hold public office, but also a broadening of the franchise. The sudden rise of political anti-Semitism in Austria after 1882 was a result of the partial democratization of politics. Two Viennese politicians in particular tried to appeal to the new voters. The pan-German racist Georg von Schönerer attracted votes by using anti-elitist, anti-individualistic, and anti-intellectual demagoguery. While Schönerer was much admired by Adolf Hitler for his racial anti-Semitism, Hitler, who lived in Vienna from 1907 to 1913, also criticized Schönerer for his open attacks on the Roman Catholic Church, which alienated many potential followers.[4]

Dr. Karl Lueger was the founder of the Christian Social Party and the mayor of Vienna between 1897 and 1911. Another Hitler favorite, Lueger was described by the Nazi leader as "the greatest German mayor of all times."[5] Like Schönerer, Lueger used anti-Semitism to appeal to the same unstable elements of the population: artisans and university students. And like Schönerer, he favored political platforms that denounced the emancipation of Jews. However, the similarities ended there. Lueger, in sharp contrast to Schönerer, was pro-Catholic and pro-Habsburg. He hoped to unite all Christians and all the nationalities of the monarchy against a common Jewish enemy.[6]

Anti-Semitism was rife in Vienna and the remainder of the Austro-Hungarian monarchy during the last two decades of the nineteenth century, a time known then as the Great Depression. But the return of prosperity, which coincided with Lueger's advent to power in 1897, greatly diminished the virulence of the prejudice. Moreover, Lueger's anti-Semitic bark turned out to be much worse than his bite. World War I, however, brought a resurgence of anti-Semitism, especially in Vienna, which was forced to absorb 125,000 Jewish refugees from Galicia and Bukovina who were fleeing the czar's army.[7] This veritable population explosion, which temporarily increased the city's Jewish population by 75 percent, consisted mainly of penniless peddlers, artisans, and cattle dealers, who only added to the already serious prewar shortage of housing and the wartime shortages of food and fuel. Even though all but about 20,000 of these refugees returned to their homes during or immediately after the war, anti-Semites continued to blame them for all manner of ills, especially during the early years of the new Austrian republic.[8]

The Jewish Community in Austria: Demography and Occupations

Although Vienna's Jewish population remained the third largest in Europe until the 1930s, contrary to the fantasies of anti-Semites, the size of the community steadily and rapidly declined during the entire First Austrian Republic (1918–38). The highest number ever recorded in an official census occurred in 1923, when 201,513 Jews, or 10.8 percent of Vienna's shrunken population of 1,868,000, were counted. Another 18,695 Jews, well under 10 percent of Austria's total Jewish population, lived in the other eight federal states; thus Jews made up 3.37 percent of the country's population. After that the number of Jews in the Austrian capital declined to 176,034 in 1934 and to just under 170,000 on the eve of the German annexation in 1938. Except for Lower Austria, where there was a slight increase in the Jewish population, the number of Jews declined in the Austrian provinces even more rapidly than in the capital. By 1938 there were only 185,000 registered Jews in the entire country, a decline of 17 percent in just fifteen years.[9] This drastic diminution resulted from the sudden cessation of immigration from the eastern provinces of the Austo-Hungarian monarchy and from an extremely low birthrate. As early as 1925 there were only 8.5 live Jewish births in Vienna per 1,000 people, fewer than half as many as were needed to maintain a stable population.[10]

Not only was Austria's Jewish population concentrated in Vienna, but 60 percent of Vienna's Jews lived in just four of the city's twenty-one districts, 75 percent in eight districts. This pattern made it easy for Jews to socialize with one another and made a complete assimilation into the general population much less likely.[11] Nevertheless, there was a rapid integration of Jews into German-Austrian culture after their emancipation in 1848, along with a relatively high rate of Jewish conversion to Christianity or at least to a "confessionless" status. And the large number of Jewish-Christian marriages also contributed to a declining sense of Jewish identity, though certainly not to its disappearance, in the late nineteenth and early twentieth centuries.[12]

The high profile of Vienna's Jews in certain parts of the city was increased by their economic activities. Although anti-Semites often grossly exaggerated the percentage of Jews in certain fields, there is no doubt that they dominated the free professions. According to one Jewish calculation made in 1936, 62 percent of all Viennese lawyers were Jewish, as were 47 percent of all physicians and almost 29 percent of the city's university instructors. Vienna, in fact, had a higher percentage of Jewish lawyers and physicians than any other city in Europe.[13]

Two areas in which the anti-Semitic stereotype of the rich Jew contained an element of truth were banking and big industry. Fully 60 percent of those engaged in finance and industry, or about six times as many per capita as gentiles, were Jewish.[14] Although most were wealthy, they were also among those who suffered the most catastrophic losses during the Depression of the 1930s, when ten of the twelve Austrian banks that failed were Jewish-owned.

Further down the social scale were businessmen. The Nazis estimated just after they took power in 1938 that Jews owned 36,000 of the 146,000 business enterprises in Vienna, or 25 percent, which was about three times their percentage of the city's population. The great majority of these businesses, however, were small, old-fashioned, family-run operations. The large number of Jewish businesses helps explain why some 45 percent of all Viennese Jews, compared with just over 28 percent of non-Jews,[15] were self-employed. Even lower on the social totem pole were Jewish tailors, money changers, and peddlers, most of whom were recent immigrants from Eastern Europe. Almost too few to be counted were Jewish peasants, all 760 of them, who in 1934 accounted for just 0.7 percent of Jewish employment. Anti-Semites, completely ignoring the laws that prevented Jews from owning property in Central Europe before 1848, regarded the virtual absence of a Jewish peasantry as particularly damning.[16] Finally, of the more than 160,000 civil servants employed by the Austrian government in 1935, only 682, or 0.28 percent, were Jews, the result of a centuries-long tradition in Austria and other European countries of excluding Jews from government service.[17]

Another area of the economy in which Jews were heavily involved was the press. It is a fact that the creation of the liberal Viennese press, like much of the metropolitan press in Germany, was to a large extent a Jewish achievement. Jews wrote the leading articles, advertisements, essays, and business news; they were also highly influential in the publication of books and magazines. However, far from supporting specifically Jewish causes, the liberal Jewish-owned and -edited newspapers of Vienna actually avoided even mentioning Jewish topics such as Zionism or Palestine.[18]

Varieties and Causes of Anti-Semitism in the First Austrian Republic

The new Austrian republic founded in November 1918 inherited the anti-Jewish prejudices that had become well established in the monarchy. The Roman Catholic Church, with its long tradition of anti-Judaism, maintained its strong influence, particularly with the peasantry. It also appears plausible that Jews in the First Republic, as the only remaining sizable minority after the downfall of the monarchy, assumed the position of scapegoats held earlier by Czechs, Hungarians, Italians, and other national minorities.

The economic and political dislocations of the war that fueled Austrian anti-Semitism continued after 1918. The new state, whose population was only about one-quarter the size of the prewar population of just the Austrian half of the Dual Monarchy, was cut off from the sea as well as from its prewar markets and sources of raw materials. Although a modicum of prosperity returned between 1924 and 1929, a period in which anti-Semitism lessened but did not disappear, most years of the First Republic were marked by inflation, depression, and high unemployment.

Despite the democratic institutions and civil liberties of the First Republic, it was during this period that anti-Semitism enjoyed its most luxuriant expressions. Freedom of speech and freedom of assembly also meant freedom to shout anti-Semitic slogans and to hold anti-Semitic demonstrations. If there was a connection between democracy and anti-Semitism, there was also a parallel between anti-Semitism, education, and religiosity. Thus rank-and-file socialists, who rarely had more than an eighth-grade education and were atheists, were far less likely to be anti-Semitic than were regular churchgoers and holders of academic degrees. On the other hand, while democracy may have made the expression of anti-Semitic sentiments easier, it was not the *cause* of anti-Semitism. On the contrary, anti-Semites were the enemies of democracy.

Anti-Semitism could be found in all the major political parties of interwar Austria, in thousands of private organizations, and in all social classes and age groups. It was among young people, however, particularly university students, that the prejudice was usually the strongest. Already converted to Schönerer's racial anti-Semitism of the 1880s, "Aryan" students after World War I more than ever feared the economic competition of Jewish students for extremely scarce positions in the professions and business. Student anti-Semites did not content themselves with mere verbal abuse; organized beatings of Jewish students, which had been rare before the war, became commonplace during the First Republic.[19]

The categories of anti-Semitism in interwar Austria remained the same as in the late nineteenth century: religious, economic, social, and racial. The divisions between these categories, however, were not clear. Economic and social motivations could be found in every form of Austrian anti-Semitism. Religious anti-Semitism was, of course, most closely associated with Catholics in their Christian Social Party, but it was by no means eschewed by the country's other bourgeois parties. Even the Social Democrats might be accused of religious anti-Semitism, except that in their case the distrust was of all religions, not just Judaism. Racial anti-Semitism was most frequently found in the pan-German parties, including the Grossdeutsche Volkspartei (Greater German People's Party), part of the paramilitary Heimwehr, or Home Guard, and of course the Austrian Nazi Party, but some of the more extreme Catholics came close to anti-Semitism in their refusal to accept baptized Jews as full-fledged Christians for up to three generations.

The most moderate anti-Semites in Austria were the Marxist parties: the Social Democratic Workers' Party (SDAP) and the tiny Communist Party. Confining their anti-Semitism to verbal abuse, they were also the only parties that had no specifically anti-Semitic program and that directed their wrath exclusively against capitalists, especially Jewish capitalists; the latter could be salvaged by abandoning their "exploiting" ways. The Marxists also occasionally opposed anti-Semitism as an anti-leftist snare.

For Austrian Marxists the Jewish bourgeoisie represented a conservative social force that blocked the socialists' goals of nationalizing industries by upholding the economic and social status quo. Ironically, Catholics in Austria (as well as in other countries, including the United States) saw them in exactly the opposite light. For them, Jews were revolutionaries, or at least extreme modernists, who were determined to secularize society by undermining the Catholic faith and traditional Christian values.

Catholic anti-Semitism was the middle-of-the-road variety in interwar Austria, although it encompassed both moderate and extreme forms. Catholics usually "limited" their demands to the reduction of Jewish "influence," though some favored the expulsion of Jewish newcomers. And they considered Jews redeemable only if they converted to Catholicism. No member of the church's hierarchy or leader of the Christian Social party approved of anti-Semitic pogroms, but nearly all of them appear to have supported some kind of legislation limiting the influence of Jews in Austria's cultural life, and many also favored restricting their numbers in Austrian universities. A nostalgic longing to reverse the emancipation of Jews and return them to their medieval spiritual and even physical isolation was unmistakable.

The most infamous of the anti-Semitic organizations of Austria undoubtedly was the National Socialist German Workers' Party, or NSDAP. But if we look beyond the Nazis' popular reputation, we discover that their ideas and methods of propaganda were in no respect completely novel. It is even doubtful whether their Jewish policy prior to the Anschluss was much more extreme than that of the Antisemitenbund, or League of Antisemites, a private umbrella organization that flourished in the early 1920s and again between 1936 and 1938. The same could be said of the Workers' Association of the Christian Social Party or some elements of the Greater German People's Party. Only in their greater willingness to use violence against Jews did the Nazis differentiate themselves to some extent from other Austrian anti-Semites.[20]

The Jewish Community and the Defense against Anti-Semitism

Oddly enough, scholars have devoted far more attention to anti-Semitism than they have to the victims of that prejudice. This is particularly true of the Jews of Austria and most especially for the interwar years. Judging from their propaganda and even from their private comments, Austrian anti-Semites knew little about the people they were so quick to condemn.

A single, monolithic Jewish community of Austria existed only in the fervid imagination of anti-Semites. In reality, there was not one Jewish community but several. There were, to begin with, well-assimilated or at least well-acculturated Jews whose ancestors generally had come from the Bohemian crownlands of the Austrian Empire or from Hungary. They almost always adhered to Reform Judaism if they were still observant at all. They tended to be upper-middle-class businessmen or professional people and were deeply devoted Austrian patriots. In contrast to these *Westjuden* were the more recent immigrants from Galicia or Bukovina. Consisting largely of peddlers, small businessmen, or industrial workers, they too spoke fluent German. Nevertheless, these *Ostjuden* were much less assimilated than the *Westjuden,* at least for a generation or two. Younger immigrants from the East tended to be either Zionists or socialists, whereas the older generation often still clung to the Orthodox faith and, even more than the Zionists, shunned assimilation.

Only when these basic divisions are understood can the reader appreciate how bitterly divided the Jewish community was in Austria and why it was utterly incapable of presenting anti-Semites with a united front. The Jews of Austria, in fact, were split into at least as many acrimonious political factions as the gentiles, who outnumbered them by a thirty-to-one ratio. Their religious, political, and economic differences colored the way they interpreted events not only in Austria but in neighboring Germany as well. Only after Adolf Hitler came to power in Germany in January 1933 could Austrian Jews finally agree on something: the need to support the federal government of chancellors Engelbert Dollfuss and Kurt von Schuschnigg, who were at least willing to protect Jews from the worst manifestations of anti-Semitism, especially from physical violence.

The factionalism in the Jewish community in Vienna produced bitter rivalries within the Israelitische Kultusgemeinde (IKG, or Jewish Communal Organization) and widely differing interpretations concerning the rise and triumph of nationalism in Germany.[21] Nor was there a great deal of cooperation between Austrian Jews and the few Christians who were willing to help them. To a large extent the various Jewish factions regarded their ideologies as providing the best protection against anti-Semitism, at least in the long run. Liberals belonging to the Union of Austrian Jews, with their philosophy of cultural but not religious assimilation, were convinced that anti-Semitism would disappear as soon as Jews were fully integrated socially and economically into Austrian society and Christians had become convinced that the Jews were unequivocally patriotic Austrians. Jews could also defend themselves by uniting with progressive and liberal elements of other political parties. This policy would require decades, if not centuries, to be fully implemented, however. Unfortunately, the Unionists' philosophy was also something of a handicap in combating anti-Semitism. Their desire to blend into Austrian society made them reluctant to do anything that might emphasize their Jewishness.[22]

Jews who belonged to the Social Democratic Party and who fully accepted its Marxist philosophy were likely to hold views on the question of self-defense somewhat similar to the Unionists'. Marxism taught that the Jews would eventually disappear in the classless society of the future. A self-conscious expression of Judaism was therefore simply not compatible with socialism.

The Zionists thought that anti-Semitism would end only after the Jews had established their own autonomist society, thus removing all sources of conflict with Christians. Until that day anti-Semitism would continue to exist. Moreover, Zionists' belief in an ultimate emigration to Palestine, even if that day might be in the indefinite future, fostered a more ambiguous commitment toward Austria, although they were far from being disloyal citizens. Their philosophy, however, produced a somewhat fatalistic attitude toward anti-Semitism and a tendency to ignore all but the most outrageous manifestations of the prejudice.

Like the Zionists, Orthodox Jews also believed that a partial withdrawal from Austrian politics and culture represented the best means of combating anti-Semitism. Their belief that they were "the most worthwhile element representing the real Judaism"[23] virtually precluded cooperation with other Jewish factions. They viewed religion as the primary means for combating anti-Semitism. The inner strengthening of religious belief and following the laws of Orthodox Judaism would win the respect of non-Jews, including anti-Semites. The past and present suffering of the Jewish people had been beneficial, they believed, because it had helped them to "purify their souls" and "to understand God's word and way."[24]

The defense strategy favored by the Union of Austrian Jews and the IKG, especially during the years up to 1932, when the latter was controlled by the Unionists, was *shtadlanut,* or lobbying behind the scenes with government officials for the enforcement of Austrian laws, and issuing formal protests. The Unionist leaders of the IKG, many of whom were lawyers, hoped that their grievances could be resolved through normal legal channels, that is, police authorities, law courts, and district attorneys. Formal declarations and personal remonstrances to government officials were also employed. For example, the IKG frequently adopted resolutions demanding that the government stop the violence at Austria's universities. It also protested anti-Semitic posters, pamphlets, newspapers, and books, as well as certain laws. The results, however, were mixed, especially with regard to academic anti-Semitism. Usually government officials replied that existing laws made it impossible for them to do anything; this was especially true with regard to academic autonomy.[25]

Austria's Jews were very much aware of their own disunity; most of them believed that they could better defend themselves against anti-Semitism if they were united. Consequently, appeals were made for Jewish unity time and again by nearly every Jewish faction in the First Republic. The problem, however, was that nearly every group wanted unity only on its own terms; Jews were supposed to give up their ideology and identity and join the group making the latest call for unity.

Probably the most impressive Jewish means of self-defense in interwar Austria, and also the most nonpartisan, was the Bund jüdischer Frontsoldaten, or League of Jewish Front Soldiers. Founded in Vienna in the summer of 1932, shortly after the Austrian Nazis' great electoral breakthrough in local elections in April (when they won nearly 17 percent of the vote), the organization declared in its statutes that its purpose was "to protect the honor and respect of the Jewish people living in Austria."[26] The Bund was supposed to be *überparteilich,* or nonpartisan. By deliberately avoiding partisan politics and emphasizing military virtues like discipline, obedience, and physical fitness, it hoped to overcome the chronic divisiveness of the Jewish community in Austria. Starting in January 1933 it had its own newspaper, the *Jüdische Front,* and by February 1934 it had some eight thousand members in Vienna, Graz, Linz, and Baden bei Wien, including the Zionists and assimilationists, making it the largest single Jewish organization in Austria apart from the IKG in Vienna.[27]

The Jewish Front Soldiers had a number of ways of defending Jews against anti-Semitism. First and perhaps foremost, it sought to provide physical protection against sometimes brutal Nazi attacks. Like the Union of Austrian Jews, it would also respond to false accusations against Jews. Likewise resembling Unionist activities were direct complaints and open letters to high government officials about anti-Jewish violence at state institutions of higher learning or anti-Semitic speeches and publications. The Bund even organized protest rallies.[28]

Fortunately, there were also some Christians who attempted both to analyze the causes of anti-Semitism and to fight it. Probably the most famous of these people were the Austrian noblemen Count Heinrich Coudenhove-Kalergi and his son Richard. Their two-part book, translated into English as *Anti-Semitism throughout the Ages,* first published by the father in Berlin in 1901, was brought up to date by the son and republished in Vienna and Zurich in 1935. It was the only major work published in Austria during the interwar period that dealt objectively with anti-Semitism. The authors identified several critical features of the phenomenon: its link with anti-Marxism; the impact of the bad economic situation in Europe following World War I; the irrational nature of anti-Semitism; and the special fear and hatred anti-Semites felt toward secular, assimilated Jews, whose ideas seemed to threaten their traditional ideas and economic states.

Another outspoken critic of anti-Semitism in interwar Austria was Wilhelm

Boerner. Some of his arguments, outlined in a booklet called *Antisemitismus, Rassen-frage, Menschlichkeit* (Anti-Semitism, racial question, humanism), published in Vienna in 1936, resembled those of the Coudenhove-Kalergis. Boerner regarded the religious, economic, and racial arguments used against Jews as no better than crude generalizations. He denied that there were any constant Jewish racial characteristics and therefore rejected the idea that there was a real "Jewish race." He said that certainly there was no scientific proof that Jews were inferior, and he praised Jewish success in cultivating internationalism in the modern world.[29]

Incisive as Boerner's ideas were, he was far from being the most prominent critic of anti-Semitism in interwar Austria. The most courageous opponent of both anti-Semitism and Nazism that Austria, or very likely the whole of Central Europe, produced in the 1930s was a previously unknown and politically inexperienced young woman by the name of Irene Harand. A less likely heroine is difficult to imagine. Born in 1900, for a decade after World War I she lived the life of a conventional middle-class housewife, far removed from the turmoil of Austrian politics. She was, however, profoundly distressed by local examples of church-sanctioned intolerance.[30]

Soon after the Nazi electoral victory in Germany in September 1930, Harand appeared at a Catholic political meeting and warned about the growing menace of the Nazis, but she was rudely rejected by the conservative audience. Far from being intimidated, however, she wrote a brochure in March 1933, shortly after Hitler came to power, entitled *So oder So? Die Wahrheit über den Antisemitismus* (Either this or that? The truth about anti-Semitism). She printed and distributed fifty thousand copies at her own expense. In August of the same year she established her own weekly newspaper, *Gerechtigkeit* (Justice), which by December 1936 had twenty thousand readers in thirty-six countries. In 1935 Harand also wrote *Sein Kampf: Antwort an Hitler* (His struggle: An answer to Hitler), a 347-page rebuttal to the ideas Hitler had laid out in *Mein Kampf*.[31]

In October 1933 Harand and her Jewish collaborator, Moritz Zalman, founded the World Organization against Racial Hatred and Human Need, popularly known as the Harand Movement. It eventually had nearly forty thousand members, including six thousand outside of Austria. Branches of the organization were established in twenty-seven countries. To encourage the growth of her movement, Harand traveled all over Austria and other parts of Europe and even to the United States, giving public speeches, often several a week, against anti-Semitism and Nazism.[32] Her commitment to fight anti-Semitism arose essentially from her conviction, repeated at the top of every issue of *Gerechtigkeit* and in all of her other publications, that anti-Semitism was harmful to Christianity.

The Austrian Jews and the Austrian Government on the Eve of the Anschluss

The record of the republican government of Austria was less admirable vis-à-vis anti-Semitism than that of Franz Joseph's administration. Caught between its desire to appease Western opinion by distancing itself from Nazi policies and domestic and German pressure to limit Jewish "influence," the Austrian government chose a middle position, tolerating the political and economic anti-Semitism of middle- and lower-level officials while not promoting it at the highest levels. Chancellors Dollfuss and Schuschnigg assured foreigners and Jews that they opposed anti-Semitism and were in favor of equal rights for Jews, but they often tolerated newspapers and organizations that specialized in hatemongering as long as they had no known connections with the Austrian Nazi Party. Dollfuss did organize a security force in the summer of 1933 to protect Jews at Austrian universities and outlawed the Nazified Deutsche Studentenschaft (League of German Students). Most important of all, in June 1933 he outlawed the Austrian Nazi Party itself, much to the relief of Austria's Jews.[33]

Austrian Jews fared considerably worse under Schuschnigg, whose administration after July 1934 coincided with the growing power of Nazi Germany and the increased willingness of the Western democracies to appease Hitler. Jews were gradually eased out of Austria's cultural life. They had no influence in the ministry of education, and the various art associations had long been "Aryan." By 1935 no publishing houses were open to Jewish authors. At the state theaters only Jewish actors with an international reputation were allowed to perform. There were still many Jewish journalists in Vienna after 1934, but they dealt mainly with nonpolitical subjects, such as sports and art. Austrian films were produced without Jews so that they could be shown in Nazi Germany.[34]

By the beginning of 1938 the status of the Jews of Austria was in some respects similar to that of the Jews in Nazi Germany. To be sure, there were no headline-catching denunciations of Jews from the highest government offices, no Jewish books were burned, and no physical assaults on Jews were permitted, let alone encouraged, by the government. However, the government did tolerate the verbal abuse of Jews by newspapers and private organizations. Many Jews, especially physicians, lost their government-paid jobs, and most others found themselves more socially isolated than ever. The government's official umbrella organization, known as the Fatherland's Front, segregated Jewish children in its Jungfront (Youth Front); some schools were at least partially segregated; and even the Boy Scouts had separate sections for Jews.[35]

An important difference in the treatment of German and Austrian Jews after 1934 was that discrimination in Austria was quieter and did not attract much worldwide attention. The Austrian Jews themselves referred to it as "rubber-soled anti-Semitism."[36] The Austrian government and economy, unlike those of Germany, were not nearly strong enough to defy world public opinion or a boycott. However, an even greater distinction between Austria and Nazi Germany was that in the former there was no systematic attempt by the government to pauperize the country's entire Jewish population or to force its emigration. At its worst, the Austrian government followed rather than led public opinion and did at least protect Jews from violence. Consequently, Austrian Jews confidently continued to look to the government for protection almost literally up to the eleventh hour of the eleventh day of March 1938.

THE HOLOCAUST ERA
Austria's Jews and the German Annexation

In the final six weeks of the First Austrian Republic two Jewish attitudes remained constant: support for Chancellor Kurt von Schuschnigg and confidence that Austria would remain independent. Even the most ominous news never shook these beliefs for long.

Although Adolf Hitler had made it absolutely clear on the first page of *Mein Kampf* that his ultimate goal was to annex Austria, the practical realities of German military weakness and the strong opposition to any such move by Britain, France, Italy, and Czechoslovakia induced Hitler to scale back his ambition regarding Austria to an interim policy of *Gleichschaltung,* or coordination. Austria was to have a Nazi government that would fully cooperate with the Reich in political, military, social, and economic affairs until a full-fledged annexation could be safely consummated. Hitler apparently saw that time rapidly approaching when he called his famous "Hossbach Conference" in November 1937, at which he discussed possible foreign-policy options with the top military and political leaders of the Third Reich. One initiative that the Führer mentioned specifically was the takeover of Austria.

In late February Schuschnigg had his infamous meeting with Hitler at Berchtesgaden, in which the Austrian chancellor made a number of concessions, the most important of which was granting an amnesty to imprisoned Austrian Nazis. But even this development failed to alarm Jewish opinion makers. The *Jüdische Presse,* the mouthpiece of Jewish Orthodoxy, said that fears of a Trojan horse arising from the meeting were highly exaggerated. The Unionist organ, *Die Wahrheit,* thought that the only purpose of the Berchtesgaden meeting was to restore peace between Germany and Austria. The Germans had assured Schuschnigg that they would not intervene in Austrian affairs and would not support the Austrian Nazis.[37] Schuschnigg himself sought to quiet Jewish fears by telling a group of Jewish industrialists that there would be no further changes in the Austrian government.[38]

Never were the Austrian Jews more solidly behind the Austrian government, and never were they more united, than after Schuschnigg announced on March 9 that a plebiscite on the question of Austrian independence would be held four days later. Following the meeting at Berchtesgaden, Schuschnigg was far more forthright with Dr. Desider Friedmann, the president of the Israelitische Kultusgemeinde, than he was with the press or with foreign diplomats. The chancellor described in detail Hitler's ravings and threats. Schuschnigg asked Friedmann to travel abroad and do what he could to bolster the sagging Austrian schilling, perhaps by reassuring worried foreign governments about Austria's stability. Then on March 10 and 11 Dr. Friedmann presented Schuschnigg with two checks with a total worth of 800,000 schillings, or about $120,000 in the currency of that time, to defray some of the costs of his plebiscite campaign. After the Anschluss the Nazis ransacked the headquarters of the IKG and discovered a list of contributors to this fund. The Jewish community was fined a sum equal to this amount, and Friedmann and other IKG officials were arrested.[39]

Arrests and "Aryanization"

The fate of the officials of the IKG was representative of the plight of thousands of Austrian Jews immediately after the German invasion and annexation of Austria, which began on March 12, 1938. The optimism to which most Jews had clung in the last years and months of Austria's independence nearly vanished, although wishful thinking never entirely disappeared.

The change in the political atmosphere from the Schuschnigg regime to the Nazi dictatorship was incredibly swift and dramatic. One Austrian émigré recalled fifty years later that when she entered a cinema at five o'clock on the afternoon of March 11, Vienna was festooned in red-and-white Austrian flags, but that when she emerged from the theater two hours later the city was bedecked with red-white-and-black swastika flags. Another Jewish émigré remembered feeling as though she were suddenly surrounded by enemies who wanted her dead. On the other hand, still other refugees recounted years later how their fathers had advised their anti-Nazi employees to wear swastikas on their lapels as a security measure. Still other refugees' fathers had been confident that their war record would protect their family.[40]

The first few days following the German annexation saw a major outburst of plundering and brutality perpetrated against the Jews. Only rarely were these acts committed by German Nazis, and still less often by German soldiers; rather it was the Austrian Nazis and even non-Nazis who now released the hatred against the Jews that they had repressed, especially since the outlawing of the Nazi Party in 1933. With the blessings of the new Nazi government, anti-Semitism now became a patriotic virtue and crypto-anti-Semites could freely display their long-pent-up prejudices. The anti-Jewish fury took a wide variety of forms. On the first night of the Nazi takeover, March 11–12, numerous Viennese, especially unemployed Nazi storm troopers (Sturmabteilung, or SA), invaded thousands of Jewish homes, pulling people out of their beds and stealing their money and jewelry.[41] Nazis ordered Jewish women to dress in their best clothes and scrub pro-Schuschnigg slogans off sidewalks with their bare hands or with toothbrushes; Jewish children were forced to write the insulting word *Jud* on the windows of their fathers' shops. Other petty tortures included forcing actresses from the Theater in der Josefstadt to clean SA toilets; more fortunate Jews cleaned cars. Hitler Youths pulled Orthodox Jews around by their beards; Jews in the working-class district of Leopoldstadt were forced to call each other insulting names; and Jews at the Praterstern were compelled to lie down and eat grass.[42]

During the 1930s Nazi sympathizers had not tried to purchase Jewish property, because they thought they would someday get it for free. Now gangs of Nazis invaded Jewish department stores, humble Jewish shops in the Leopoldstadt, the homes of Jewish bankers, and the apartments of middle-class Jews to steal money, art treasures, furs, jewelry, and furniture. Some Jews were robbed of their money on the street. All automobiles owned by Jews were confiscated immediately. Jews who complained to the police about the thefts were lucky if they escaped arrest or physical violence. Beginning about a week after the Anschluss, bargain hunters could buy Jewish possessions at nominal prices when word got around that a particular Jewish family was desperate for money.[43]

The economic spoliation of the Jews was especially popular with broad sections of the Viennese public. The *Sozialistische Kampf,* an Austrian Socialist newspaper published by exiles in Paris, reported with considerable horror the violence and humiliations perpetrated against the Jews in the spring of 1938 but acknowledged that although workers had not taken part in these actions, they did approve of measures taken against "unloved Jewish department stores and individual capitalists." The petite bourgeoisie approved of the economic campaign against all the Jewish classes but rejected the violence.[44]

Many Jews, especially prominent ones who were in great danger, attempted to flee to Czechoslovakia. However, a train carrying a large group of refugees, both Jewish and gentile, was halted at the Czechoslovak border, and all the passengers were ordered by the Czech minister of the interior to return to Austria. Other Viennese Jews were more shrewd and took trains to Berlin, where they resided for several days or weeks in comfortable and secure hotels. These Jews were amazed at how much better they were treated in Berlin than in Vienna. Later, other Viennese Jews were even more surprised when they discovered that in Berlin they could shop in almost any store or attend the cinema long after they had been banned from these activities in Vienna.[45]

Outright violence against Austrian Jews ended a week or so after the Anschluss and did not resume until October; however, the persecution of Jews was actually just beginning. For example, on April 1, 1938, 60 of the 154 political prisoners sent from Austria to the Dachau concentration camp in Bavaria were Jewish; they were released early on if they promised to emigrate from Austria immediately. Between April 23 and 25 a boycott of Jewish stores in Vienna took place. SA men stood in the entrances of Jewish shops, and Christians who entered the stores were arrested and forced to wear signs identifying them as "Christian pigs." In May there began a new wave of arrests, this time of members of the Schuschnigg government, along with many Jews who had held some kind of political or cultural position; the result was that another 5,000 people, 2,000 of them Jews, were sent to Dachau. Those arrested had long been on the blacklists of the Austrian Nazis.[46]

Within a few hours or at most a few days of the Nazi takeover all Jewish actors, musicians, and journalists lost their jobs. By mid-June 1938, just three months after the Anschluss, Jews had been more thoroughly purged from public life in Austria than they had been in the five years following Hitler's takeover in Germany.

Jews were also excluded from most areas of public entertainment and to some extent even from public transportation by the early summer of 1938; similar rules were not imposed on German Jews until November. Austrian Jews were also subjected to all kinds of personal insults and indignities that were not the result of official Nazi legislation. If a gentile streetcar passenger did not like the looks of a Jewish fellow passenger in the summer of 1938, he could have the trolley stopped and the Jew thrown off. The number of coffeehouses and restaurants that would not serve Jews grew from one day to the next. All of the public baths and swimming pools were closed to Jews. Park benches all over the city had the words *Juden verboten* stenciled on them. Jews were not admitted to theater performances, concerts, or the opera. Numerous cinemas posted notices saying that Jewish patronage was not wanted. Sometimes Jews were ejected from a motion picture theater in the middle of a showing if gentiles complained about them. SA men at times even stood at the last tramway stop in the suburb of Neuwaldegg in order to prevent Jews from strolling in the nearby Vienna Woods.[47]

Austrian Nazis raced ahead of their German *Parteigenossen* in their zeal to Aryanize. By May 1939 only 6 percent of the Viennese Jews were still employed, compared with 30 percent in Berlin. The Nazis segregated Jewish pupils and teachers and prohibited Jewish professionals from having gentile clients. The same was true of their plans, which were never actually implemented, for interning Jews in concentration camps near Vienna.[48]

The "achievements" of the Austrian Nazis did not go unnoticed by leading German Nazi Party institutions and members. Only six weeks after the Anschluss the official SS journal, *Das Schwarze Korps,* noted with some envy that the Austrians had managed to do almost overnight what the Germans had failed to do after several years. The Austrians could even organize anti-Jewish boycotts without any supervision. None other than Hermann Göring complained in the fall of 1938 that the "de-Jewification" of the economy in Germany was not progressing as rapidly as in Austria. Austrian methods were therefore introduced into the *Altreich* in 1939. The Nazis' official newspaper, the *Völkischer Beobachter,* also noted that whereas in northern Germany it was the duty of the party to educate the people about the Jewish danger, in Austria the duty of the party was to preserve the purity of the movement by restraining overly exuberant radicalism.[49]

To some extent Austria indeed served as a model for the rest of the Third Reich in the persecution of the Jews. Certainly Nazi officials from Germany found the enthusiasm of their *Parteigenossen* in Austria a useful tool with which to shame their German comrades into a more energetic implementation of Nazi goals. However, Aryanization had already begun to speed up rapidly in Germany by 1937. Aryanization (and also emigration) measures carried out by Austrian Nazis only slightly accelerated trends already well under way in the *Altreich.*[50]

The November Pogrom

Essentially the same thing can be said about Kristallnacht. The November Pogrom in Vienna, far from being a turning point, merely completed the economic destruction of the Jewish community in Vienna as well as in other cities of the Third Reich. Nazi outrages against Austrian Jews, which had abated during the summer of 1938, began again in early October, when numerous Jews were hauled out of their beds by Nazi functionaries and told to go to the nearby Danube canal, where nonexistent boats presumably were waiting to take them to Palestine. The Gestapo later admitted that it was all a "mistake." In the middle of the month some Jewish religious places and stores were damaged.[51]

Although the Nazi instigators of the pogrom wanted it to appear like a spontaneous popular outburst of indignation aroused by the assassination of a German diplomat in Paris by a Jewish refugee from Poland, the pogrom was actually carefully planned. Two days before the "action," the Vienna edition of the *Völkischer Beobachter* carried an article describing the location and appearance of the Jewish temples in the city. The SS and Hitler Youth (including the League of German Girls), which were the principal perpetrators of the pogrom in Vienna, ordered their members, especially those between the ages of fourteen and thirty, to leave their uniforms at home and not to plunder. The police were instructed to protect the property of non-Jews and foreign Jews.[52]

Probably no one in Vienna was fooled into thinking that the pogrom was really spontaneous in its origins. Nevertheless, there were elements of spontaneity that the instigators themselves probably had not envisioned. Not only were all but one of the twenty-four temples and synagogues, as well as seventy prayer houses, in Vienna—in addition to the few Jewish religious houses that existed in the provinces—destroyed by fires started by hand grenades, but they were also plundered, and sacrilege was committed against their sacred contents. Over four thousand Jewish shops were looted, and their inventory was partially or sometimes completely destroyed; afterward they were closed, their doors and windows sealed by the police. On some streets so many shops were closed that a work day looked like a holiday. Nearly two thousand Jewish apartments in the inner city alone were Aryanized by the SA; in the process a great deal of furniture was destroyed as the looters searched for silver, jewelry, and other valuables. Men who tried to defend their homes against the looters were sometimes beaten to death. Several hundred Viennese Jews committed suicide during the night of burning and looting and in the following few days; another twenty-seven were murdered, and eighty-eight were seriously injured. Over sixty-five hundred Jews in Vienna and about twelve hundred in the rest of Austria were arrested. Thirty-seven hundred of these people were sent to Dachau.[53]

Many of the actions carried out by the SA against Jews were nothing less than pure sadism. Jewish men who were arrested were placed in schools, prisons, and even the Spanish Riding School (next to the Habsburg Hofburg Palace) and forced to do calisthenics and to stand while going without food and sleep. Some Jewish women were forced to strip and perform lesbian acts with prostitutes for the entertainment of storm troopers. Other Jewish women were forced to dance naked. One Gestapo agent in Vienna later reported that he and his colleagues had difficulty preventing crowds from manhandling still more Jews.[54]

Many historians believe that the November Pogrom was even more severe in Austria than in the *Altreich*. The only evidence to support this contention is anecdotal. Two things are reasonably certain, however: Kristallnacht was at least as brutal in Austria as elsewhere in the Third Reich; and the events of November 10 and 11 proved that the robbery and murder of defenseless Jews would not cause a collective protest. The Nazi government therefore had little to fear from the Austrians when it decided to accelerate the process of destroying what remained of the Jewish community.[55]

The housing situation for Jews after the November Pogrom can only be described as appalling, although far worse conditions awaited those Jews who were eventually deported to concentration camps in Poland. Jews were sometimes notified by a piece of paper on their front door that they had only a few days or even hours to move out of their apartment. And leaving their own apartment was the first of as many as six moves they had to make between 1940 and 1942. By 1940 up to five or six families were living in a single apartment; the married and unmarried, young and old, and people of both sexes were all living in one room without plumbing or cooking facilities. Telephone calls could be made only from a central office.[56]

Legal Discrimination

The Nazis created special laws that were intended to segregate Jews completely from the rest of society and to make them want to leave Austria as soon as possible. Although the laws became really severe only after the beginning of World War II in September 1939, some were first introduced immediately after the Anschluss. By the end of Nazi rule in 1945 approximately 250 anti-Jewish laws had been enacted in the former Austrian territories.[57]

One of the first such discriminatory laws to be enacted was a *numerus clausus* (or cap on enrollment) for Jewish university students. Introduced on April 24, 1938, it fulfilled one of the oldest and most cherished demands of Austrian anti-Semites. Only 2 percent of the students at Austrian universities could be Jews, a figure considerably below the 2.8 percent of religious Jews in the country in 1934 and far below the percentage of "racial Jews" that pan-Germans had always cited when speaking of Jewish "domination." After December 8 even the few remaining Jewish students were excluded from the universities. In some cases unqualified gentile professors replaced world-famous Jewish scholars who had been dismissed. Also in April 1938, the sixteen thousand Jewish primary and secondary pupils in Vienna were placed in segregated classes, and they were later forced to transfer to eight purely Jewish schools, often far from their homes. At the end of the school year in 1939 they were no longer allowed to attend even these public schools.[58]

Other forms of discrimination also proliferated in 1938 and 1939. After July 2, 1938, Jews were allowed to enter only certain public gardens and parks, and none at all after September 1939. At the end of September 1938 Jewish physicians and lawyers were forbidden to have gentile clients. Only about fifty Jewish lawyers were able to make a living even briefly under these circumstances. After October 5 Jews were not permitted to enter sports stadia as spectators. Shortly after the November Pogrom Jews were not even allowed to appear in public during certain times of the day. After January 1939 they could not use sleeping or dining cars on railroad trains.[59]

By far the harshest anti-Semitic laws were introduced just before and during World War II, when they developed a kind of dynamic of their own that went far beyond the previous "moderate" steps. On the eve of the war, in August 1939, the Nazis requisitioned all rare metals and jewelry except wedding rings, watches, and table service for two people. On September 25, shortly after the outbreak of the war, Jews were forbidden to go out after 8:00 P.M. and were not allowed to listen to the radio or to visit any public places (although there were few that were not already closed to them). The purpose of the curfew was to facilitate mass arrests, which always occurred at night. In 1942 the few Jews who still remained in Vienna could not use public transportation without police permission; and they could not go to "Aryan" barbershops or buy newspapers or magazines. In April 1942 non-Jews who were married to Jews had to move to Jewish housing. In November Jews had to surrender all of their electrical appliances.[60]

Emigration and Deportation

Whereas German Jews had, until Kristallnacht, often hoped that they might remain in Nazi Germany indefinitely, albeit with an inferior legal and social status, most Austrian Jews were disabused of any such illusion soon after the German annexation. Hermann Göring announced in March 1938 that Vienna had to be a German city once again and that this would be accomplished by eliminating Jews from the city's economy. A month later, the *Völkischer Beobachter* declared that this task had to be completed within four years, a goal that was in fact reached. Most Viennese Jews wasted no time in helping Göring to realize his dream. They stood outside the consulate of every possible host country in lines that sometimes stretched for miles and were subject to constant attack by anti-Semites. Some Jews, however, were reluctant to sell their property and emigrate, because they hoped that property values would somehow improve. Others waited too long to apply for visas. Still others—estimated by Jewish leaders as constituting one-third of all Austrian Jews—were simply too old, sick, or settled in their ways to contemplate emigration.[61]

In Vienna only 3 of 450 Jewish organizations survived the takeover: the IKG; the Pal-Amt (Palestine Bureau), a Zionist umbrella organization; and the League of Jewish Front Soldiers.[62] The IKG was closed on March 18, 1938, but was reopened on May 2, 1938, in order to provide welfare and to facilitate emigration (and later deportation). More than forty-two thousand Jews enrolled in its courses, which trained people in the skills they would need in their new homelands. Young Jewish women had comparatively little trouble finding work as domestic servants, particularly in Britain, in 1938 and 1939. They hoped to bring the rest of their family to join them once they were settled, but often their loved ones perished in extermination camps instead.[63]

Obtaining an immigration visa was probably the most difficult obstacle for an Austrian Jew trying to escape from the Third Reich. Neighboring countries such as Czechoslovakia, Hungary, and Switzerland required Jews to have a visa merely to cross their borders. Switzerland also insisted that German Jewish passports be clearly identified with the letter *J*. The worldwide depression only made potential host countries all the more reluctant to accept penniless Jewish refugees.

Once an immigrant's visa had been obtained, there were still other roadblocks to overcome before a Jew could leave Austria. The Nazis hoped to export anti-Semitism and enrich the Third Reich by allowing only penniless Jews to leave the country. Therefore, in sharp contrast to German Jews, who had been allowed to take a large part of their wealth with them in 1933, Austrian Jews in 1938 were permitted to take only thirty marks (later reduced to only ten) in German and foreign currency when they left Austria. This problem could be surmounted only with the aid of Jewish organizations abroad. The American Jewish Joint Distribution Committee, the Jewish Agency for Palestine, and the Central British Fund for Refugees set up soup kitchens for Jews while they remained in Vienna and paid all the costs of Jewish emigration. Unfortunately, such aid ended in 1941 with the entry of the United States into the war. The Third Reich was able to make a profit of $1.6 million by the end of November 1939 from the emigration of Austrian Jews alone. Still more difficulties were caused by fake travel agencies, which swindled desperate Jews.[64]

With so many obstacles to overcome, emigration from Austria after the Anschluss was at first slow; only 18,000 Jews left in the first three months following the German annexation, compared with 32,000 during the next three months. By the end of November 1939 over 126,000 had escaped, including 80 to 90 percent of the Jewish intelligentsia. Having been the first to lose their jobs, they had the most time to emigrate and the least difficulty in obtaining immigrant visas.[65] Only 66,000 Jews remained in Vienna, along with another 30,000 "racial" Jews. During the next two years only 2,000 more managed to get out of the country before legal emigration was ended in November 1941. A plurality of the departing Austrian Jews, 30,850, moved to Great Britain. The 28,615 who went to the United States probably constituted the largest single influx of talent in American history even before the arrival of another 17,000 Austrian Jewish refugees between 1945 and 1954. However, the United States, which already had very limited nationality-based immigration quotas, virtually closed its doors to further immigration in July 1940. China accepted 18,124 refugees, most of whom settled in Shanghai. Palestine received 9,195. Smaller numbers emigrated to eighty-five other countries all over the world.[66]

Austrians were involved not only in planning the administering the deportations but also in operating the death camps. By far the best known of these Austrians was Adolf Eichmann, who in October 1939 was put in charge of Jewish deportation for the entire Reich.[67] Austrians made up 80 percent of Eichmann's staff. Three-fourths of the commandants and 40 percent of the staff who actually operated the death camps were also Austrians. Odilo Globocnik, who had joined the Austrian Nazi Party in 1920 and who became the gauleiter of Vienna for a time shortly after the Anschluss, exercised supervision over Treblinka, Sobibor, and Belzec, three concentration camps whose only purpose was to kill Jews as expeditiously as possible and where, in fact, two million Jews were murdered. The commandment at Treblinka, the largest of these three camps, was likewise an Austrian, Franz Stangl. The concentration camp of Mauthausen, near Linz, which by early 1945 had more than 84,000 inmates in forty-nine satellite camps, was by far the harshest of all the camps inside the prewar territory of the Third Reich. The prisoners were worked to death in quarries within a few months. However, relatively few Austrian Jews were sent there. Simon Wiesenthal, the internationally renowned hunter of Nazi war criminals, has estimated that Austrians were directly or indirectly responsible for the deaths of three million Jews during the Holocaust. Austrians also made up 13–14 percent of the SS, even though they made up only about 8 percent of the population of the Greater German Reich.[68]

When the deportations from Austria were to begin in earnest, it was again an Austrian, Eichmann's deputy, SS Captain Alois Brunner, who issued the order in late September 1941, three weeks before a similar decision was made for Jews in the *Altreich*. Would-be deportees were seized in the middle of the night and given only three or four hours to pack their bags. Only people with permission to emigrate, war invalids, people working in essential industries or for the IKG, "part Jews" (*Mischlinge*), and baptized Jews were temporarily exempted. In the end, only the last two categories escaped deportation, although in all special cases much depended on the mood of local SS men.[69]

By the time World War II ended, in May 1945, a total of 65,459 Austrian Jews, or slightly more than half as many as the 128,500 who successfully escaped by emigration or other means, had been killed in one way or another. Some 2,142 who survived had been in concentration camps, and around 6,200 survived because they were married to Christians or had been baptized before 1938, or both. Of those who survived as "U-boats" (in hiding), 700 were hidden by friends in Vienna. This should be compared with the 5,000 Jews who were hidden by righteous gentiles in Berlin, which had had a considerably smaller prewar Jewish population, no doubt a testimony to Berlin Jews' greater integration into gentile society.[70]

Cardinal Innitzer and Catholic Assistance to Baptized Jews

That so many baptized Jews survived the war in Austria was largely due to the efforts of the Sudeten-born pan-German Theodor Cardinal Innitzer of Vienna. In 1940 he started a welfare agency that fully supported 300 Jewish Catholics and partially assisted another 100. In 1941 he personally opposed converted Jews' having to wear special identification and to their being required to attend separate church services for Jewish converts. He felt these measures were unwarranted concessions to Nazi racial theories. His opposition to both endeavors was unsuccessful, however. He did obtain money from the Vatican to help about 150 Jewish Christians escape to North and South America by way of Portugal and Spain. Perhaps most important of all, in April 1943 he informed Pope Pius XII that the Nazis were planning to dissolve "legally" all mixed marriages between Christians and Jews; the Jewish partners would then be deported to the East, Innitzer said, where they would face an uncertain future. The Vatican in turn succeeded in persuading the Nazi government to suspend its program. But Innitzer, like the rest of the Catholic hierarchy of Austria and Germany, did not extend his assistance to religious Jews or those who were not married to Christians.[71] Of course, he may simply have believed that Jewish converts were the only ones he had any hope of saving.

THE POST-HOLOCAUST ERA

On the eve of the Anschluss, 185,000 Jews (not counting the 34,500 classified as Jews by the Nazis in their Nuremberg Laws of 1935) lived in Austria. The country's Jewish population was little more than 11,000 shortly after the war. In the mid-1990s just 7,500 Jews were registered with the Israelitische Kultusgemeinde in Vienna, and an equal number lived in Vienna but did not belong to the IKG. Of this remnant, about 1,600 had lived in Austria before the war. At most only 12,000 to 15,000 Jewish émigrés ever permanently returned to their former homeland, although another 18,000 to 22,000 returned for long stays; the remainder had no desire to return to the scene of so many painful memories. The exceptions typically were around forty years of age, mostly baptized, married to gentiles, and reluctant to learn a new language in a foreign land, or they entertained (naive) hopes of recovering their businesses. The Austrian government, for its part, issued no blanket invitation for the refugees to return until after Kurt Waldheim became president in 1986. Indeed, the government placed difficulties in the way of the returning refugees, particularly if they had acquired a new citizenship since leaving Austria. (Dual citizenship for former Jewish refugees was not permitted until 1993.) The postwar Jewish newcomers were mostly Hungarian, Polish, Romanian, or, more recently, Russian immigrants. As before the war, over 90 percent of Austrian Jews in the 1990s lived in Vienna. Graz, with just ninety Jews, had the second-largest community. Those few who did return often enjoyed financial success because of family and international connections, tradition, and education (especially knowledge of foreign languages) and rarely had direct encounters with anti-Semitism. However, generalizations about the Jewish community are difficult to make because, just as before the war, it is very diverse socially, economically, and religiously.[72]

Anti-Judaism in Public-Opinion Polls

One might suppose that the virtual disappearance of Austria's Jewish population would have been accompanied by the disappearance of anti-Semitism. However, neither the minuscule number of Jews nor knowledge about the Holocaust—which at first was viewed by Austrians as crude Allied propaganda—eliminated anti-Jewish attitudes, especially in the early years following World War II. A public-opinion survey conducted in 1946 by Americans in their zone of occupation revealed that 44 percent of the Viennese, 50 percent of the Salzburgers, and 51 percent of the Linzers believed that although "the Nazis had gone too far in the way they dealt with the Jews, something had to be done to place limits on them."[73] Another survey conducted in the same year showed that 46 percent of the respondents opposed a return of those Jews who had survived the slaughter, compared with just 28 percent who favored their return. In 1973, 21 percent still opposed their repatriation, the same percentage that favored it. Even Social Democratic politicians, who had been among the least anti-Semitic people in the First Republic, were not anxious to see too many Jews, including their own former leaders, come back to the country. It is not certain, however, whether this feeling was because of resentment against émigré Jewish leaders for sitting out the war in safe havens (even though this was hardly their choice) or because of the exiled leaders' Jewish background.[74]

As the above statistics show, the continued existence of anti-Semitism can easily be demonstrated in public-opinion surveys conducted since the early postwar years. All of them have shown that anti-Semitism remains stronger in Austria than in Germany, France, or the United States. For example, in polls conducted in 1986, 60 percent of the Austrians surveyed said they thought that all Jews ought to move to Israel. Only 44 percent of the Germans agreed with that statement, 35 percent of the French, and just 13 percent of the Americans. Sixty-three percent of the Austrians said they would not want to live next to a Jew, compared with 48 percent of Germans, 15 percent of the French, and 9 percent of Americans.[75] In general the surveys have shown that about 75 percent of all Austrians privately articulate at least some anti-Semitic views, about 20 to 25 percent have fairly strong anti-Semitic opinions, and about 7 to 10 percent can be described as extreme anti-Semites.[76] A poll conducted in 1970 revealed that 35 percent of the respondents would not marry a Jew; 45 percent thought that Jews acted only out of self-interest; and 21 percent thought it would be better if there were no Jews in Austria.[77]

Polls conducted during the 1970s revealed a strong skepticism about the Holocaust and a hostile attitude toward paying reparations to Jewish victims. In 1973, 38 percent rejected the notion that six million Jews had been gassed (the question was poorly phrased, since not all Jews had been killed by gas), and 67 percent rejected the idea that Austrians had any special obligations toward Jews because of crimes committed against them; only 5 percent favored such payments. A poll conducted three years later showed that 56 percent of those asked believed that the Jews were partially responsible for their own persecution; 83 percent thought there should be no more war crimes trials; and 85 percent felt that the past ought to be closed.[78]

Another interesting revelation of the public-opinion polls is the striking similarity between the political anti-Semitism of the First and Second Republics. A 1989 poll showed that the Socialist Party (SPÖ) still had the fewest hard-core anti-Semites, with 6.5 percent, followed by the conservative Austrian People's Party (ÖVP, the successor to the Christian Social Party), with 8 percent. On the other hand, 35.5 percent of the members of the Freedom Party (which might be considered the successor to the Greater German People's Party) were extreme anti-Semites; according to an earlier poll, conducted in 1970, they made up about half of all the extreme anti-Semites.[79]

A public-opinion poll on Austrian anti-Semitism conducted in 1991 by the Gallup Institute of Austria and sponsored by the American Jewish Committee revealed that anti-Semitism may have actually increased since 1989. For example, 19 percent of those questioned said that Austria would be better off with no Jews, compared with 13 percent in 1989. Fifty-three percent said it was time to end the discussion on the Holocaust, and 32 percent thought that Jews were exploiting the whole subject. Fifty-six percent said that the Austrian government should no longer prosecute war criminals. On the other hand, only 6 percent said that they would refuse to shake hands with a Jew, compared with a 1987 figure of 7 percent. In addition, only 34 percent of those polled still clung to the idea that Austria had been simply a victim of Nazi aggression in 1938, while 39 percent believed that Austria had been an accomplice. When pollsters broached that topic in 1987, just prior to the fiftieth anniversary of the Anschluss, 48 percent believed that Austria had been a victim and 24 percent thought it had been a participant.[80]

Polls taken under very different circumstances in 1979 also revealed the persistence of anti-Semitism in Austria. The showing of the American-made television miniseries *Holocaust* in Germany and Austria was accompanied by a great many public-opinion polls, telephone calls to television stations, television talk shows, and letters to editors. Perhaps because the program received so much publicity in Germany, it was viewed by an even higher percentage of Austrians when it was shown in their country six weeks later. Close to half of all Austrians viewed the program during the four consecutive evenings it was shown. Proportionately, twice as many Austrians (8,227) as Germans phoned television stations to express an opinion about the show. A breakdown of the calls revealed that 49 percent were positive and 39 percent were negative; 8 percent were hostile, which approximately reflects the number of hard-core anti-Semites in the Alpine republic. Whereas prior to the broadcast 72 percent of the Austrians had believed that Jews were murdered en masse by the Nazis, 80 percent thought so by the end of the program. Forty-seven percent of all Austrians had wanted to forget the Holocaust before the broadcast, a figure that fell to 42 percent after the program. Before *Holocaust* aired, 17 percent of all Austrians had wanted the prosecution of Nazi criminals to continue; four days later this figure was 24 percent. A follow-up survey five months later, however, indicated that that figure had returned to its pre-broadcast level. But public awareness of the Holocaust had increased. Before the film 44 percent of all Austrians had believed they shared a responsibility for Nazi atrocities with the Germans, whereas afterward that figure rose to 50 percent, with younger and better-educated Austrians being willing to assume more responsibility.[81]

Compensation and Denazification

Probably in response to these popular feelings, the Austrian government, until the 1990s at least, has not been anxious to compensate those former Austrian Jews who lost their homes, jobs, and property after the Anschluss. Indeed, the very idea that Austrian Jews had been victims of outrages committed by other Austrians contradicted the carefully nurtured half-truth that the country as a whole had been a victim of German aggression in March 1938, an idea enshrined in the Moscow Declaration the Allied Powers issued in November 1943 as a means of encouraging Austrian separatism from the Third Reich. A victims' welfare law enacted by the Austrian parliament in 1945 and amended twenty-eight times thereafter at first recognized only members of the wartime Austrian resistance movement as victims. Not until 1961 were Jews recognized as victims, and then only if they had remained hidden in Austria during the war under "inhumane" circumstances. Not until 1969 were Jewish refugees recognized as victims.[82]

The Austrian press was almost unanimously opposed to the negotiations over reparations that took place between representatives of the Austrian government and the Jewish Claims Committee during the 1950s and early 1960s. Even in the 1990s *Wiedergutmachung* (reparations) is a dirty word as far as the Austrian public is concerned. Therefore, the history of the attempts by Jews to gain compensation is a long and torturous one. The issue remains not fully resolved.[83]

Apart from the political unpopularity of compensating Jewish victims of Nazism, the other fundamental difficulty has been the unwillingness of the Austrian government to consider itself a successor to the Third Reich. To a certain extent this policy was at the outset part of a perfectly understandable effort to legitimize the Second Republic by putting as much distance between Austria and Germany as possible. Consequently, the Austrian government, which from 1945 to 1966 was a coalition of both major parties, the People's Party and the Social Democratic Party, at first rejected any responsibility for reparations, saying that Austria had been an occupied country between 1938 and 1945. The coalition would not have been able to function if the Social Democrats had reminded the ÖVP of the Christian Social anti-Semitism during the First Republic or if the ÖVP had referred to the interwar nationalism of the socialists. Therefore they agreed that it was the Germans rather than the Austrians who were accountable for the suffering of the Austrian Jews. The Federal Republic of (West) Germany had the opposite motivation. By accepting the role of successor to the Third Reich, it hoped to strengthen its claim to speak for all Germans on both sides of the Iron Curtain and therefore fully cooperated with the Jewish Claims Committee. Chancellor Konrad Adenauer also realized as early as 1950 that reparations would be an important factor in the international rehabilitation of West Germany, an early end to the occupation, and better relations with the United States. On the other hand, having no desire for a new Anschluss with Austria, the Federal Republic refused to accept responsibility for illegal or violent acts committed against Austrian Jews by Austrian citizens.[84]

It is extremely unlikely, however, that political legitimacy was the only factor prompting the Austrian government to reject responsibility for Jewish property losses, which, according to Nazi-compiled statistics, had amounted to $1.2 billion. The new owners of the "Aryanized" property, like the owners of confiscated Jewish property in Poland and other Eastern European countries, had no desire to return it to its original owners (if they were still alive). They exercised enormous pressure on the Austrian government to limit any possible restitution. At first the Austrian government took the wildly exaggerated view that 50 percent of the Austrian Jews in 1938 had been baptized and therefore could not be represented by a Jewish organization. Only in 1953, after pressure had been put on the Austrian government by the U.S. State Department, the British Foreign Office, and world public opinion, did the Austrian government consent to negotiate with the Committee for Jewish Claims on Austria, a coalition of the Jewish communities of Austria and twenty-three international Jewish organizations. Even then the Austrians agreed only to a moral, not a legal, responsibility for making compensations, a position it continued to subscribe to in the 1990s. After nine years of negotiations the Austrian government settled on a sum of $22 million for Jewish survivors plus 10 percent to cover administrative costs, compared with the $822 million agreed to by the West Germans, not counting the $52 billion Bonn had given to Israel by 1990. Jews who had lost land in 1938 (a relatively small number, since Jews were not large landowners) received only two-thirds of its actual value; those who had lost property were awarded only one-fourth of its real value. Left completely uncompensated were the almost total loss of income the Jewish refugees had suffered during the first two or three years following their departure from Austria, interrupted educations, lost promotions, illnesses induced by the persecutions, and, of course, the lives of sixty-five thousand murdered Jews.[85]

The Austrian government has been particularly opposed to making lump-sum payments to any international group of victims. On the other hand, in recent years it has been more forthcoming with regard to pensions for individual Jews now living abroad and especially in assisting the tiny Jewish communities remaining in Austria. In addition to the modest one-time payment of between $250 and $500 granted in 1988 by the Austrian government to Jewish victims of the Anschluss all over the world on its fiftieth anniversary, in 1990 the government approved a "48th Social Insurance Amendment," which will eventually amount to $165 million in social insurance benefits to Jews who were between the ages of six and fourteen in 1938. Another $30 million will be paid to assist homes for elderly Jews living in Austria, the United States, Israel, and other countries. Rabbi Miller, the president of the Austrian claims committee, described the agreement as a "major achievement."[86] Although the Austrian record on restitution is not nearly as generous as West Germany's or as good as Jewish survivors would wish it to be, it has been infinitely better than that of the former German Democratic Republic, which until 1989 did not even respond to Israel's appeals for reparations.[87] Nor have other Eastern European governments been any more eager to admit that many of their citizens were active collaborators in the Holocaust.

Another source of enormous aggravation for Jews in Austria and abroad has been the Austrian record on denazification. It should be remembered, however, that the task of prosecuting former Nazis in Austria was at first shared between the Austrian government and the four occupying powers, who thought that only those Nazis who had joined the Austrian Nazi Party before the Anschluss, when it was still illegal, or who had held important positions after 1938 ought to be punished. However, since the end of the Allied occupation in 1955 the record of the federal and state governments in Austria for trying Nazi criminals has been weak. Victims of Nazism, especially those who were forced to leave their homes and jobs and emigrate, were incensed by the Austrian government's restoration of the property of former Austrian Nazis in 1952, before the victims themselves had been compensated. By contrast, a Jewish refugee wishing to recover an apartment inhabited by someone who had joined the Austrian Nazi Party after the Anschluss could do so only by first finding that person alternative housing. Still worse was the granting of amnesty to 90 percent of the former members of the Nazi Party in 1948 and to nearly all the others, including the Gestapo and the SS, by 1957.[88]

Many Austrians and even non-Austrians have argued that excluding 500,000 former Nazis (or upwards of a million counting relatives) from the franchise indefinitely might somehow threaten democracy. What is certain is that these newly enfranchised voters had substantial influence, because they often held the balance of power between the two major parties, the People's Party and the socialists. Although the government instituted proceedings against 137,000 accused war criminals, only 28,000 were brought to trial; of these, just 13,600, or 10 percent, were found guilty and 28 were executed. Of those who suffered capital punishment, all but 4 had been guilty of ordinary murders unrelated to the Holocaust. Another 100,000 civil servants were dismissed but otherwise escaped prosecution. That more former Nazi Party members did not lose their jobs was the result of Allied fears that Austria's war-torn economy could not be restored if a large part of its population was either imprisoned or barred from the labor force. The success of the IKG in Vienna in suing anti-Semites has been no better than that of the government; it has lost twenty court cases of documented attacks on Austrian Jews.[89]

Critics of the Austrian denazification record, especially in the United States and Great Britain, should be aware that their postwar governments considered it counterproductive to dwell on Austria's Nazi and anti-Semitic past at a time when Soviet communism was rapidly engulfing east-central Europe. From 1946 on, the American policy toward Austria was based on the idea that Austria was the "first victim" of Nazi aggression. The very real differences between the American and Austrian governments over the issue of compensation for Jewish victims were therefore kept out of the public's view because of the Cold War. This factor alone, of course, limited the amount of pressure the United States could put on Austria. Consequently, foreign pressure to make restitution to the Jews steadily declined after early 1947, whereas domestic pressures against such compensation correspondingly increased. The United States, joined by its Western allies, Britain and France, did not press the issue of reparations, because it wanted a stable Austria; the Soviet Union likewise was not insistent, because it wanted a neutral Austria. The anti-Communist ideology of the Cold War was easy for many Austrians to accept because it had been a cardinal feature of Nazi dogma as well as of the ideologies of all the non-Communist parties in interwar Austria.[90]

The Kreisky Era

Despite the mixed findings of the public-opinion polls and the foot-dragging of the Austrian government on denazification and restitution, at least as early as the late 1960s and the 1970s there were some indications that Austrian views of Jews were becoming more positive. The Arab-Israeli Six-Day War of 1967 showed Austrian newspapers decidedly on the side of Israel even though they had generally favored the Arab side in the war of independence in 1948. In 1967 the Austrian newspapers blamed the war on the Arabs and described the Israelis as a small and desperate people who had frequently been persecuted in the past. The Egyptian president, Gamal Abdel Nasser, was often compared to Hitler.[91]

Further evidence of a change in attitude came with the socialist administration of Bruno Kreisky between 1970 and 1983. Kreisky was the first person of Jewish origin to become the leader of a German-speaking country, despite the campaign poster of his People's Party opponent, Josef Klaus, which appealed to the country to vote for a "real Austrian," thus implying that Kreisky was somehow less than a true native.[92]

Kreisky's views of his own Jewishness, however, as well as his attitude toward other Jews and the Jewish state, were complicated, to say the least, as were the reasons for his unprecedented popularity. As a sixteen-year-old he had had his name officially removed from the rolls of the Viennese IKG. Thereafter he had not practiced Judaism or made Jewish concerns part of his intellectual framework. This attitude was revealed in his first (minority) government, in 1970, when he appointed four former members of the Nazi Party to his cabinet (of eleven), including a former Waffen-SS officer whose unit had engaged in documented atrocities against civilians. Although ex-Nazis had previously held positions of responsibility in the Austrian government, this was the first time that they had been appointed to cabinet posts.[93]

Kreisky's views on Israel and the Palestine Liberation Organization (PLO) were also controversial, although they appear much more enlightened and farsighted today than they did at the time. As a typical socialist, he had never been a Zionist, which would have offended his senses of Austrianism and raised in his mind the specter of dual loyalties; nevertheless, he was sympathetic to the Jewish state and was well informed about its domestic politics. As a first step in defusing Arab-Israeli tensions, he gave the Arabs an opportunity to state their case to the Socialist International. Thereafter he favored the creation of an independent Palestinian state. To increase the respectability of the PLO and to enable it to enter into serious diplomatic negotiations with the Israeli government, he granted it limited diplomatic status in its dealings with international organizations in Vienna. In 1979 he became the first Western head of government to officially receive PLO chief Yassir Arafat and did so with an affectionate embrace. For these and other actions (such as receiving Libyan leader Colonel Muammar al-Qaddafi) Kreisky earned the condemnation of the Israeli media, which regarded him as a renegade Jew, and severe criticism from much of the American press. Although the chancellor's intent was to end the continuous state of war between Israel and its neighbors, he failed to see how offensive many of his words and actions were to Jews and how comforting they must have been to Austrian anti-Semites. By the end of 1975, in fact, Kreisky had been turned into a veritable honorary "Aryan" in the eyes of Austrian German nationalists, who strongly approved of the chancellor's repudiation of specifically Jewish concerns.[94] Nevertheless, it is difficult to imagine a Jew of any political persuasion becoming a chancellor in the First Republic, let alone holding that position for thirteen years.

The Waldheim Affair

Whatever progress had been made in combating anti-Semitism seemed to be undone by the international uproar accompanying the presidential campaign of Kurt Waldheim in 1986. Any detailed discussion of whether Waldheim was a war criminal or an anti-Semite lies well beyond the scope of this study; in any event it has already been thoroughly explored by historian Robert E. Herzstein. Herzstein argues in his book *Waldheim: The Missing Years* that the former secretary general of the United Nations was not a war criminal according to the Nuremberg definition of the term but a facilitator. Above all he was a careerist who had never actually lied about his wartime past but had neglected to mention the more embarrassing aspects of it. His 1944 doctoral dissertation, on the German political theorist Konstantin Frantz, contained no anti-Semitism even though it would have been politically advantageous for him to resort to it. Waldheim, in short, was more clever and ambitious than evil, and like many other people of his generation, he simply wanted to forget "the awkward baggage of his past."[95]

There is no clear evidence that Waldheim personally exploited anti-Semitism during the presidential campaign in the spring of 1986. On the other hand, he was quoted by *Le Monde* as complaining that the international press was dominated by the World Jewish Congress (WJC). Waldheim also did not unambiguously oppose the anti-Semitic undertones of some of his supporters; in fact, he denied that there were any such biases. Pro-Waldheim newspapers described the WJC as powerful and dangerous, and 85 percent of the Austrian electorate believed that the WJC was interfering in Austria's internal affairs. Leading officials of Waldheim's People's Party, such as Alois Mock, therefore demanded several times that "Jewish circles" stop interfering in the campaign. Waldheim was criticized for not denouncing anti-Semitism until after the first election in May, and not vigorously until after the runoff election the next month, when he promised to oppose discrimination against Jews and said that he would welcome a historical commission to investigate his wartime activities. The *New York Times,* which devoted no fewer than 126 articles to the affair between March 4 and June 15, described his apparent nonchalance about his military assignments in the Balkans as "staggering." The *Times* was also critical of Waldheim for not being repentant about Austria's Nazi and anti-Semitic past. On the other hand, contrary to popular belief in Austria, it never accused him of having committed war crimes. Waldheim's attempts to brush off accusations against him as having been caused by "some interest groups in New York" could be interpreted as having anti-Semitic overtones.[96]

The Waldheim campaign, along with the placement of the Austrian president on the infamous Watch List in the United States, clearly led to a revival of Austrian anti-Semitism, as the public-opinion poll of January 1989, mentioned above, showed. During the campaign mass-circulation newspapers were filled with anti-Semitic (as well as anti-American) commentaries. One study by two Austrian researchers, in fact, revealed that a third of the 177 sampled articles from two mass-circulation dailies, the *Kronenzeitung* and *Die Presse,* published during the campaign contained anti-Jewish references. Sixty to seventy hate letters were sent to the IKG, some of them threatening violence if Waldheim lost. Other recipients of such mail were anti-Waldheim journalists; Waldheim's Socialist opponent, Kurt Steyer, who was accused of being part of a Jewish conspiracy; Orthodox Jews, who were told to get out of the country; and even a gentile critic of anti-Semitism, the historian Gerhard Botz. Eighty-five percent of the Austrian public was especially outraged over charges leveled against Waldheim and Austria by the WJC and its leader, Edgar Bronfmann. Because most of the American criticism of Waldheim originated with Jewish organizations, it appeared to many Austrians that the whole controversy was an American Jewish plot. On the other hand, Waldheim's evasive responses to the allegations only deepened the mistrust of his accusers.[97]

The Austrian reaction to the Waldheim affair, however, was far from uniform, and, in fact, the controversy divided the country more than any other issue faced by the Second Republic.[98] Many Austrians, accustomed to thinking of themselves as "victims" for more than forty years, were ill-prepared for the controversy. If the international focus on the Waldheim campaign caused some anti-Semites to vote for the former U.N. official, there is evidence that an equal number of Austrians voted against him merely because of his unwillingness to be forthcoming about his military activities in the Balkan Peninsula during World War II. An even larger number of Austrians voted for him as a protest against the incumbent socialist government. It is also significant that an independent candidate and former member of the Free Democratic Party, Otto Scrinsi, who had been an SA *Sturmführer* in the Third Reich, was able to win only 1.2 percent of the national vote. It should likewise be recalled that the initial accusations against Waldheim were leveled by the popular Austrian magazine *Profil*.[99] Austria's intelligentsia were almost unanimously opposed to Waldheim. A petition with fifteen hundred of their signatures called for his resignation in February 1988. At the same time, many intellectuals made a similar demand in speeches at several large anti-Waldheim demonstrations in front of St. Stephen's Cathedral in the center of Vienna.[100]

Austria's small Jewish population, and indeed the Jews of the entire world, were divided by the episode. Many distinguished Jewish families in Austria steadfastly supported Waldheim. Even the anti-Waldheim Austrian Jews did not feel threatened enough by the rise of anti-Semitism to leave the country. Paul Grosz, president of the IKG in Vienna, criticized Bronfmann's attempts to block Austria's admission into the European Community. An Israeli scholar, Shlomo Avineri, was also scathing in charging the WJC with upsetting the delicate balance of Jewish life in Austria without adequately consulting the Jewish community in advance. He said that the policy of the WJC had been unnecessarily confrontational and more concerned with passing judgment than with presenting evidence.[101]

Simon Wiesenthal also accused the WJC of stirring up anti-Semitism in Austria. He told one Austrian historian that "to make a collective threat [to keep Austria out of the EC] is indefensible, particularly when it comes from a Jew whose people have themselves been the victims of collective threats for two thousand years. . . . Guilt is always an individual thing. It is never collective."[102] Wiesenthal denied that Waldheim was a war criminal, although he found it hard to believe that Waldheim knew nothing about the deportation of Jews from Salonika, Greece. Consequently, he called on Waldheim to resign from his position after an international commission of historians cleared the president of any criminal acts. Wiesenthal's qualified defense of Waldheim prompted a furious attack on the famed Nazi hunter by the WJC's chief investigator of the Waldheim affair, Eli Rosenbaum, who accused Wiesenthal of "betrayal" because he allegedly wanted to cover up the fact that he had failed to inform the Israeli government of Waldheim's controversial wartime career, a charge that Wiesenthal indignantly denied in a letter to the *New York Times*.[103]

Probably the most important outcome of the Waldheim affair was the worldwide publicity given to Austrian anti-Semitism and Austria's role in the Holocaust. President Waldheim's unwillingness to face his own past became symbolic of the whole country's amnesia. The specifically Austrian roots of anti-Semitism and the survival of the phenomenon in the Second Republic were widely discussed on both sides of the Atlantic. Austria's status as the "first victim of Nazi aggression" was now a thing of the past, at least internationally, and to a considerable extent, domestically as well.[104]

Austrian Schoolbooks and the Holocaust

That so many Austrians reacted with shock and resentment to the allegations made against Kurt Waldheim can be blamed to a large extent on the country's history textbooks and curricula.[105] Of course, history schoolbooks in all countries, including the United States, are not known for being critical of their own country. This is not to suggest that the Austrian texts have done anything but denounce the Holocaust, anti-Semitism, and National Socialism. Nevertheless, the descriptions and explanations for these phenomena tend to reinforce the long-held view that Austrians had little, if anything, to do with their origins and manifestations. This conclusion is drawn from the author's examination of eight of the textbooks most commonly used by students between the ninth and twelfth grades, which were written between 1972 and 1991. The textbooks say nothing about the separate Austrian origins of National Socialism, sixteen years before the birth of the German Nazi Party in 1919. The growth of the Austrian Nazis in 1932 is mentioned in some of them, but the only explanations given are high unemployment and clever Nazi propaganda. The same reasons are cited for the enthusiastic reception with which the Austrians greeted the German annexation in 1938. Nothing is said, however, about the virtual Nazi takeover of the province of Styria several days before the Anschluss, which persuaded Chancellor Schuschnigg to call for his ill-fated plebiscite.

Homegrown anti-Semitism is almost equally ignored by the Austrian textbooks. One book does mention Georg von Schönerer and Karl Lueger, who were active while the young Hitler was living in Vienna.[106] However, anti-Semitism is not cited in connection with the rise of the Austrian Nazis, nor is the anti-Jewish plundering and brutality by Austrian anti-Semites following the annexation of Austria. Although some of the books mention Kristallnacht and all of them discuss the Holocaust, none deals with the participation of Austrians in these events.

Two Austrian scholars, Peter Malina and Gustav Spann, have noted the tendency of Austrian textbooks to blame crucial events on Hitler rather than his followers. The passive voice is frequently used to describe the stages of the Holocaust, as though events happened spontaneously, without individual involvement or responsibility. The same writers also criticize Austrian textbooks for exaggerating the significance of the Austrian resistance while ignoring the fact that incomparably more Austrians actively supported the Nazi regime or collaborated with it almost to the end of the Third Reich. Likewise, denazification and right-wing extremism after the war are virtually ignored.[107]

A textbook published in 1991 should be cited for its attempts to engage readers in serious discussions about Nazi crimes. Although it neglects Austria's unique role in the Holocaust, *Die Geschichte unserer Zeit* (The history of our times) cites the achievements of German and Austrian Jews and asks students to discuss Hitler's "racial madness" and talk about Hitler's view that Jews were inferior. Students are asked to explain the rise of anti-Semitism, discuss the Nuremberg Laws, explore why so few Germans and Austrians helped the Jews, and think about how the catastrophes of Kristallnacht and the Holocaust might be avoided in the future.[108]

The deficiencies of Austrian textbooks have also been noted by Minister of Education Dr. Hilde Hawlicek, who has publicly argued that these books need to deal more explicitly with the problems of anti-Semitism, racism, violence, and inequality. Not satisfied with exhortations alone, since 1989 her ministry has been partially responsible for editing several books intended for secondary schools that deal specifically with Nazism, World War II, and the Holocaust. For example, *Österreicher und der Zweite Weltkrieg* (Austrians and the Second World War) credits the Allies, not the one hundred thousand members of the Austrian resistance, for the liberation of Austria and admits that "not a few Austrians were willing helpers of the Nazi terror and facilitated the destructive machinery of the system through their expertise and energetic support."[109] Another book, edited by both the ministry of education and the Documentation Center of the Austrian Resistance, contains several articles that attack efforts to deny or belittle the Holocaust.[110] A third book published for students with the support of the ministry contains chapters on Holocaust memorials and efforts to preserve the remains of Nazi concentration camps in Austria, such as Mauthausen.[111]

Austrian schools, however, are not mandated to cover Nazism or the Holocaust; until the early 1980s there was no systematic effort on either the national or the state level to include units on Nazism and the Holocaust in the history curriculum. By contrast, West Germany had had such units since the early 1970s. Moreover, there is considerable evidence, albeit strictly anecdotal, that many Austrian teachers and principals at the secondary level actually avoid these embarrassing and controversial subjects for fear of outraging parents and creating a sense of "national guilt" within a generation born long after the Holocaust.[112]

Educating the Austrian public about anti-Semitism will not be easy, because there is strong resistance to it. In 1988 over half of all Austrians said they had not changed their attitudes after the many activities commemorating the fiftieth anniversaries of the Anschluss and Kristallnacht. Fully 65 percent, moreover, did not want to hear any more about the persecution of Jews. This attitude may have been the temporary result of overexposure to the subject.[113] Such a view is supported by the fact that, as indicated above, Austrian opinions about the "victim" theory have changed considerably since 1988.

Renewed Efforts to Commemorate the Holocaust Years and Combat Anti-Semitism

If on balance the Waldheim campaign reawakened anti-Semitism, it also caused many Austrians to take a hard look at their Nazi and anti-Semitic past and to improve relations between Jews and gentiles. These efforts were by no means without precedent. As early as 1955 an organization called Action against Anti-Semitism was founded to fight anti-Semitism by sponsoring special exhibitions and awarding a literature prize for works that furthered understanding between Jews and non-Jews.[114] In 1985 a Liga der Freunde des Judentums (League of the Friends of Jewry) was founded to investigate anti-Semitism by organizing a thorough public-opinion poll of the prejudice and then publishing a series of booklets describing the past and present cultural and economic achievements of Austrian Jews.[115]

However, the Waldheim affair undoubtedly gave a new urgency to the fight against anti-Semitism. In June 1987 Chancellor Franz Vranitzky gave a speech to Parliament warning that anti-Semitism had to be stopped or Austria would face international isolation. On the fiftieth anniversary of the November Pogrom, both the chancellor and President Waldheim gave speeches denouncing anti-Semitism; the chancellor even pointed out that Kristallnacht had not been an isolated incident in interwar Austria. In July 1988 the People's Party also passed a resolution condemning anti-Semitism.[116]

The negative international publicity accompanying the Waldheim affair doubtless also encouraged governmental institutions in Austria to improve their relations with Jews throughout the world. Memorial plaques have been placed at the sites of some synagogues. City, state, and federal governments have joined with the IKG of Vienna to restore synagogues in St. Pölten and Innsbruck, and a private interdenominational organization dedicated to the restoration of Austrian Jewish cultural artifacts has been founded. Austria has served as a temporary host for around three hundred thousand Jewish emigrants from the Soviet Union, or more than 90 percent of those seeking new homes in Israel and the West, although the cost of their stay has been paid for by international Jewish organizations. No incidents have resulted from this program, and a few hundred Soviet Jews have made Vienna their home. Public money was spent on a Jewish museum in the Netherlands that opened in 1987.[117]

A major effort to improve Austrian-Jewish relations was the opening of a new Jewish museum in Vienna. The first Jewish museum in Europe was founded in the Austrian capital in 1896 but was completely destroyed by the Nazis in 1938. A new provisional museum, conceived during the dark days of the Waldheim affair and located in the city's only surviving synagogue, on the Seitenstettengasse in the city's center, was opened in March 1990 through the financial support of the municipal and federal governments. A new, much more spacious location for the museum was found in an eighteenth-century palace on the nearby Dorotheergasse. It was opened with great fanfare by the Austrian president, Thomas Klestil, Chancellor Vranitzky, Mayor Dr. Helmut Zilk of Vienna, and Teddy Kollek, the Vienna-born former mayor of Jerusalem, in November 1993. The site has space for four exhibits and will host symposia dealing with the profound Jewish influence on Viennese life and culture. The history of Austrian Nazism and anti-Semitism will be included in the museum's permanent exhibits, as will surviving objects of the pre-Anschluss museum. The new museum is intended to be a study center where Jewish and gentile ideas can be exchanged. For his role in opening the museum as well as for "helping to bring about an atmosphere of tolerance, liberalism, and solidarity with the weaker segments of society" Mayor Zilk was awarded a gold medal by the Federal Association of Jewish Religious Communities in December 1990. (In 1993 Mayor Zilk also made it possible for Vienna's schoolchildren to see Steven Spielberg's movie *Schindler's List* free during school hours in three theaters.) Another Jewish museum was opened in Hohenems, in the westernmost state of Vorarlberg, in April 1991, thus making three such museums in Austria, counting one founded in 1982 in Eisenstadt, in the eastern state of Burgenland.[118]

The fiftieth anniversaries of the German annexation of Austria and the November Pogrom provided the occasions for numerous international scholarly conferences in Austria. In contrast to the major commemorations that had occurred every decade from 1948 to 1978, Austria was no longer portrayed almost exclusively as a mere victim of German aggression, but to a considerable extent as an active and willing participant. An exhibition on the November Pogrom shown at the Museum for the History of the City of Vienna in the winter of 1988–89 was unrelenting in unmasking the brutality of that event. Also in 1988, the Federal Press Service of Austria published an English-language pamphlet called *Resistance and Persecution in Austria, 1938–1945*, in which it was openly admitted that Austrian Nazis had been primarily responsible for the excesses committed against Jews after the Anschluss and that too many Austrians had been silent onlookers during that persecution.[119] Unfortunately, these conferences, exhibits, and publications received little attention outside Austria. At least one American newsmagazine portrayed the Austrians as still deliberately ignoring their Nazi past.[120]

In June 1991 a new controversy erupted in Austria when Jörg Haider, the leader of the right-wing Freedom Party and governor of Carinthia, made a comment supporting the employment policies of the Third Reich. Chancellor Vranitzky responded with the strongest denunciation yet of Nazi Germany and the role played by many Austrians in the Holocaust. The chancellor's comments were made in a speech to Parliament in July 1991:

> We must also not forget that there were not a few Austrians who, in the name of [the Third Reich] brought great suffering to others, who took part in persecutions and crimes of this Reich . . . [some of whom were] in prominent positions. Our citizens cannot distance themselves even today from a moral responsibility for these deeds. Much has happened in the past years to rectify as much as possible the damage and to ameliorate the suffering. Much still remains, and the federal government will continue to undertake all within its power to help those who have not been helped until now, or who have been insufficiently helped, or whose moral and material claims have not been taken into consideration.[121]

The Austrian chancellor made a similar but more detailed speech at the Hebrew University in June 1993. This was followed in November 1994 by the first visit by an Austrian president to Israel. President Klestil admitted to the Knesset that Austrians had spoken far too often about being the first victims of Nazi aggression and not often enough about the many Austrians who had served the Nazi dictatorship. In the name of the republic of Austria he bowed before the victims of the Holocaust.[122]

The conferences and special exhibitions of the fiftieth-anniversary year represented a promising development in enlightening the public about the history and surviving elements of Austrian anti-Semitism. In 1988 the Institute of Contemporary History at the University of Vienna published a collection of documents about Jews and anti-Semitism in Austria between 1918 and 1938.[123] In May of the same year an Institute for Austrian-Jewish History opened in the restored synagogue of St. Pölten in Lower Austria.

A very concrete way of recognizing Austria's role in the Holocaust is Projekt Gedenkdienst (literally, "remembrance service project"). It is the product of a fifteen-year campaign by Andreas Maislinger, a professor of political science at the University of Innsbruck, who wrote hundreds of letters to the chancellor, the minister of the interior, and the foreign minister, published magazine articles, and appeared on a number of radio talk shows. Finally, in 1991 the Austrian government approved a law that makes it possible for Austrians to fulfill their one-year military obligation through a year of service at Holocaust memorials around the world. In 1994 there were three volunteers serving at Yad Vashem in Jerusalem and one each at Theresienstadt in the Czech Republic, the Anne Frank Foundation in Amsterdam, the Auschwitz-Birkenau Museum in Poland, and the United States Holocaust Museum in Washington, D.C. The volunteer in Washington was responsible for giving guided tours of the museum to visitors from Austria, translating German-language documents and videotapes for the museum's research institute, and preparing Holocaust educational materials for Austrian schools. For these and similar services each volunteer received $8,500 from the Austrian government.[124]

The federal and local governments have not been alone in their efforts to educate the Austrian people. Private individuals, including playwrights, have also done their part. Almost certainly the most direct criticism by an Austrian dramatist of the indifference shown by Austrians during the Holocaust is the play *Kein schöner Land* (No Beautiful Country) by Felix Mitterer. The work was first performed for a large, appreciative audience in Innsbruck in April 1987. It takes place immediately following the Anschluss and was inspired by the story of a Jew named Rudolf Gomperz, who lived in the Tyrolean town of St. Anton. Gomperz had been instrumental in bringing tourism to St. Anton. He was a respected citizen until everything changed after the takeover. The names, professions, and to some extent the actual events were altered in the play, but the religious anti-Semitism, opportunism, cowardice, collaboration, and political delusions of the time were faithfully retained. In a final ironic twist following the last act, the "mayor" of the town steps in front of the curtain and tells the audience to forget the past: they should honor the fallen soldiers, "who were only doing their duty" (the exact words of Kurt Waldheim). No one should make any accusations against anyone else, because no one realized that they were being misled by a crazy person who was exploiting their idealism.[125]

Prospects for the Future

Despite the checkered record of the Austrian government toward anti-Semitism since the founding of the Second Republic and the persistence of anti-Semitism in the general population, there are signs of change. The relatively low incidence of anti-Semitism among the young and the intellectuals at the beginning of the 1990s was just one reason to believe that Austrian anti-Semitism was likely to decline in the future. At any rate, it is extremely improbable that Austria will ever experience again the passionate, violent, and nearly universal anti-Semitism that existed between 1914 and 1945.

Almost none of the conditions that made interwar anti-Semitism and the Holocaust possible still exist today. Contemporary Austria is a far more secular country than it was a half-century ago. Secular trends in art, literature, and popular entertainment, which were regarded as shocking to conservatives in the First Republic and were habitually associated with Jews, are now taken for granted. The Roman Catholic Church had taken the lead in denouncing these trends and blaming them on Jews; it had also continued to propagate the doctrine that Jews were collectively responsible for the "murder of God." However, in 1967 Franz Cardinal König of Vienna announced that the Austrian church would implement the Ecumenical Council Vatican II by absolving the Jews of deicide and purging all references to the Jews' being responsible for the crucifixion.[126] The prohibition by the Austrian church against clerics taking an active role in politics is likely to eliminate another source of conflict that poisoned the political atmosphere of the First Republic. Furthermore, the church has played a leading role in the Second Republic in educating the faithful about the Holocaust and the evils of anti-Semitism.

Austria's intellectuals, who strongly influence public opinion, also have been very active in the campaign against anti-Semitism. Cynics might say that this is because such intellectuals no longer face any competition from Jews. An equally valid argument, however, is that the vast majority of Austria's active intellectuals belongs to a generation that was in no way associated with the Holocaust and does not feel subject to the taboos that dominated the first two postwar decades.[127] Whatever the causes, the fact is that the academicians of the 1990s are relatively free of anti-Semitism, in sharp contrast to those of the First Republic, who were among its staunchest proponents. Austrian scholars such as Erika Weinzierl, Gerhard Botz, Anton Pelinka, Ernst Hanisch, Gerhard Jagschitz, John Bunzl, Jonny Moser, Bernd Marin, and Andreas Maislinger, to name only a few, have written numerous books and articles on the various aspects of Austrian anti-Semitism and the Holocaust.[128]

Although anti-Semitism can survive even in places where no Jews live, there is no doubt that anti-Semitism was strong in interwar Vienna in part because of the large Jewish population, which had grown still larger during World War I. At a time when food, fuel, and housing were in desperately short supply for everyone and the non-Jewish intelligentsia competed with large numbers of Jews for a small number of professional positions, the size of the Jewish population did make a difference, even though it was never as large as rabid anti-Semites imagined.

Therefore, most of the foundations of Austrian anti-Semitism have been undermined. Secularism has largely eliminated religious and cultural anti-Semitism, and the decimation of the Jewish population has removed the cause of economic anti-Semitism. Racial anti-Semitism has been discredited by its close association with Nazi atrocities. What remain in Austria are old stereotypes, especially concerning alleged Jewish financial power and control over the mass media. Even so, there is reason to believe that with time and education these views will gradually disappear, although the process is likely to be a lengthy one.

NOTES

Portions of this essay have been reprinted from *From Prejudice to Persecution: A History of Austrian Anti-Semitism* with permission of the University of North Carolina Press.

1. William M. Johnston, *The Austrian Mind: An Intellectual and Social History* (Berkeley, 1972), 23.

2. Friedrich Heer, "Judentum und österreichischer Genius," in *Land im Strom der Zeit: Österreich gestern, heute, morgen,* ed. Friedrich Heer (Vienna, 1958), 295.

3. Erika Weinzierl, *Zu wenig Gerechte: Österreicher und Judenverfolgung, 1938–1945* (Graz, 1985), 19; Max Grunwald, *History of Jews in Vienna* (Philadelphia, 1936), 401.

4. Peter G. J. Pulzer, *The Rise of Political Anti-Semitism in Germany and Austria,* 2d ed. (Cambridge, Mass., 1988), 295; Adolf Hitler, *Mein Kampf* (Boston, 1943), 110.

5. Hitler, *Mein Kampf,* 55.

6. Pulzer, *Political Anti-Semitism,* 167, 207; Menachem Z. Rosensaft, "Jews and Antisemites in Austria at the End of the Nineteenth Century," *Leo Baeck Institute Year Book* 21 (London, 1976), 75, 81–82; Robert S. Wistrich, *The Jews of Vienna in the Age of Franz Joseph* (Oxford, 1989), 229; Carl E. Schorske, *Fin-de-Siècle Vienna: Politics and Culture* (New York, 1980), 133, 140.

7. Grunwald, *History of Jews in Vienna,* 367, 370; Weinzierl, *Zu wenig Gerechte,* 22.

8. For details, see Bruce F. Pauley, *From Prejudice to Persecution: A History of Austrian Anti-Semitism* (Chapel Hill, N.C., 1992), 65–72, 79–86.

9. Herbert Rosenkranz, "The Anschluss and the Tragedy of Austrian Jewry," in *The Jews of Austria,* ed. Josef Fraenkel (London, 1967), 486–87; *B'nai-Brith—Mitteilungen für Oesterreich* (Vienna), January–February 1937, 58; Herbert Rosenkranz, *Verfolgung und Selbstbehauptung: Die Juden in Österreich* (Vienna, 1978), 13.

10. *Bericht der Israelitische Kultusgemeinde Wien über die Tätigkeit in der Periode 1933–36* (Vienna, 1936), 119.

11. Leo Goldhammer, *Die Juden Wiens: Eine statistische Studie* (Vienna, 1927), 63; Marsha Rozenblit, *The Jews of Vienna, 1867–1914: Assimilation and Identity* (Albany, N.Y., 1983), 3.

12. Rozenblit, *Jews of Vienna,* 32, 127; Hans Tietze, *Die Juden Wiens: Geschichte, Wirtschaft, Kultur* (Leipzig, 1933), 205; Wolfdieter Bihl, "The Jews of Austria-Hungary (Austria), 1848–1918" (paper presented at an international symposium, "The Jews of Austria," Center for Austrian Studies, University of Minnesota, May 1986), 4; Ivar Oxaal, "The Jews of Young Hitler's Vienna: Historical Sociological Aspects," in *Jews, Antisemitism, and Culture in Vienna,* ed. Ivar Oxaal et al. (London, 1987), 32.

13. Sylvia Maderegger, *Die Juden im österreichischen Ständestaat, 1934–1938* (Vienna, 1973), 220, 382; Hellmut Andics, *Der ewige Jude* (Vienna, 1969), 241.

14. Steven Beller, "Class, Culture, and the Jews of Vienna, 1920," in Oxaal et al., *Jews, Antisemitism, and Culture in Vienna,* 49; John W. Boyer, *Political Radicalism in Late Imperial Vienna: Origins of the Christian Social Movement, 1848–1897* (Chicago, 1981), 80.

15. Gerhard Botz, "'Ausmerzung': Von der Ächtung zur Vernichtung: Steigerungsstufen der Judenverfolgung in Österreich nach dem 'Anschluss' (1938–1942)," *Journal für Sozialforschung* 28 (1988), 19; Goldhammer, *Juden Wiens,* 56.

16. Eva G. Reichmann, *Hostages of Civilization: The Social Sources of National Socialist Anti-Semitism* (Boston, 1951), 46–47.

17. *Gerechtigkeit* (Vienna), October 31, 1935, 1.

18. Tietze, *Die Juden Wiens,* 210; Paul Johnson, *A History of the Jews* (New York, 1987), 481.

19. For details, see Pauley, *From Prejudice to Persecution,* 89–99, 121–30.

20. Pulzer, *Political Anti-Semitism,* xvi; Roderick Stackelberg, *Idealism Debased: From Völkisch Ideology to National Socialism* (Kent, Ohio, 1981), 156.

21. For details, see Pauley, *From Prejudice to Persecution,* 221–41; and Harriet Pass Freidenreich, *Jewish Politics in Vienna, 1918–1938* (Bloomington, Ind., 1991).

22. *Die Wahrheit* (Vienna), January 1, 1927, 3, and March 25, 1927, 1; Irene Harand, *So oder So? Die Wahrheit über den Antisemitismus* (Vienna, 1933), 20.

23. *Jüdische Presse* (Vienna), December 9, 1932, 1.

24. Ibid., March 24, 1933, 1.

25. *Die Wahrheit,* May 13, 1932, 1; *Wiener Morgenzeitung* (Vienna), March 15, 1923, 1; *Der eiserne Besen* (Vienna), January 23, 1932, 1; *Der Stürmer* (Vienna), September 2, 1933, 1; *New York Times,* September 28, 1934, 9; Avshalom Hodik, "Die Israelitische Kultusgemeinde, 1918–1938," in *Juden*

in Österreich 1918–1938, ed. Avshalom Hodik et al. (Vienna, 1982), 27, 30; *Bericht der Israelitische Kultusgemeinde Wien über die Tätigkeit in der Periode 1929–1932* (Vienna, 1932), 14.

26. O. Braudi to the federal chancellery, Vienna (hereinafter cited as BKA), Generaldirektion für die öffentliche Sicherheit, November 4, 1932, BKA Inneres 1932, carton 32, doc. 231208, 3.

27. *Jüdische Front* (Vienna), May 1, 1935, 1, and April 17, 1936, 3; Maderegger, *Juden im Ständestaat,* 56.

28. *Die Stimme* (Vienna), October 6, 1932, 2; *Die neue Welt* (Vienna), August 5, 1932, 2; *Jüdische Front,* May 1, 1937, 3, and May 15, 1937, 1.

29. Wilhelm Boerner, *Antisemitismus, Rassenfrage, Menschlichkeit* (Vienna, 1936), 16–17.

30. John Haag, "A Woman's Struggle against Nazism: Irene Harand and *Gerechtigkeit,*" *Wiener Library Bulletin* 34, nos. 53–54 (1981), 66.

31. *The Anti-Nazi Economic Bulletin,* December 1936, 8, Dokumentationsarchiv des österreichischen Widerstandes (hereinafter cited as DÖW), doc. 11059, folder 3a, p. 74. *Stimme,* November 3, 1933, 3; *Gerechtigkeit,* March 14, 1936, 1, and August 12, 1937, 1.

32. *The Anti-Nazi Economic Bulletin,* December 1936, 8, DÖW, doc. 11059, folder 3a; Oscar Leonard, "Anti-Semitism Disgraces Christianity," DÖW, doc. 11059, folder 4; *Gerechtigkeit,* March 14, 1935, 1.

33. *Die Reichspost* (Vienna), August 31, 1933, 1; *Die Wahrheit,* June 2, 1933, 1, and June 23, 1933, 1.

34. *Neue Welt,* October 30, 1934, 1, and November 3, 1935, 1; Heinz Gstrein, *Jüdisches Wien* (Vienna, 1984), 52.

35. George Clare, *Last Waltz in Vienna: The Rise and Destruction of a Family* (New York, 1980), 42, 126.

36. *New York Times,* March 30, 1936, 3.

37. *Jüdische Presse,* February 11, 1938, 1; February 18, 1938, 1; February 25, 1938, 1. *Die Wahrheit,* March 4, 1938, 1.

38. *New York Times,* February 20, 1938, 1.

39. Hugo Gold, *Geschichte der Juden in Wien: Ein Gedenkbuch* (Tel Aviv, 1971), 74; Leo Landau, "Zu Wien von 1909 bis 1939," doc. 0-1/244, Yad Vashem Archives, Jerusalem, 9; Jonny Moser, "Die Katastrophe der Juden in Österreich, 1938–1945—Ihre Voraussetzungen und ihre Überwindung," *Studia Judaica Austriaca,* vol. 5, *Der gelbe Stern in Österreich* (Eisenstadt, 1977), 107.

40. Hedi Goldfarb, December 2, 1988, Felix Pollack, December 6, 1988, and Sylvia and Ernest Rapp, December 7, 1988, all interviewed by the author in Longwood, Fla.; Lillian Axel to the author, March 14, 1989, 6.

41. Herbert Rosenkranz, "Entrechtung, Verfolgung, und Selbsthilfe der Juden in Österreich, März bis Oktober 1938," *Österreich in Geschichte und Literatur* 22 (March–April 1978), 376; G. E. R. Gedye, *Fallen Bastions: The Central European Tragedy* (London, 1939), 303, 308.

42. William L. Shirer, *Berlin Diary: The Journal of a Foreign Correspondent, 1934–1941* (New York, 1979), 110–11; *Der Sozialistische Kampf* (Paris), June 16, 1938, 45.

43. Gedye, *Fallen Bastions,* 303–4; Helen Hilsenrad, *Brown Was the Danube* (New York, 1966), 245, 281.

44. *Sozialistische Kampf,* June 16, 1938, 45.

45. Gedye, *Fallen Bastions,* 301; Clare, *Last Waltz in Vienna,* 208–9.

46. Weinzierl, *Zu wenig Gerechte,* 29; Norman Bentwich, "The Destruction of the Jewish Community in Austria," in Fraenkel, *The Jews of Austria,* 470; *Sozialistische Kampf,* June 16, 1938, 45; Gold, *Geschichte der Juden in Wien,* 84.

47. *Sozialistische Kampf,* June 16, 1938, 44–45; Jonny Moser, "Österreichs Juden unter der NS-Herrschaft," in *NS-Herrschaft in Österreich, 1938–1945,* ed. Emmerich Talos, Ernst Hanisch, and Wolfgang Neugebauer (Vienna, 1988), 191; Carl Flick, interview by author, Orlando, Fla., December 5, 1988.

48. Gerhard Botz, "The Jews of Vienna from the Anschluss to the Holocaust," in Oxaal et al., *Jews, Antisemitism, and Culture in Vienna,* 190; Hans Safrian and Hans Witek, eds., *Und Keiner war Dabei: Dokumente des Alltäglichen Antisemitismus in Wien, 1934* (Vienna, 1988), 98; Gerhard Botz, *Wohnungspolitik und Judendeportation in Wien 1938 bis 1945* (Vienna, 1975), 122.

49. George E. Berkley, *Vienna and Its Jews: The Tragedy of Success, 1880–1980s* (Lanham, Md., 1988), 306; Gerhard Botz, *Wien von "Anschluss" zum Krieg: Nationalsozialistische Machtübernahme und politisch-soziale Umgestaltung am Beispiel der Stadt Wien, 1938/39* (Vienna, 1978), 330–31; Safrian and Witek, *Keiner war Dabei,* 40.

50. Avraham Barkei, *Von Boykott zur Entjudung; Der wirtschaftliche Existenzkampf der Juden im Dritten Reich, 1933–1943* (Frankfurt am Main, 1988), 68, 71, 73, 87, 123, 139.

51. Botz, *Wien von "Anschluss" zum Krieg,* 397.

52. Ibid., 398, 400; Rosenkranz, "Anschluss," 496; Gold, *Geschichte der Juden in Wien,* 89.

53. Rosenkranz, "Anschluss," 496–97; Gold, *Geschichte der Juden in Wien,* 78; Botz, *Wien von "Anschluss" zum Krieg,* 402. Weinzierl (*Zu wenig*

Gerechte, 63) estimates that 4,600 Austrian Jews were sent to Dachau.

54. Rosenkranz, "Anschluss," 496–97; Berkley, *Vienna and Its Jews,* 278–79, 311.

55. For a recent comparison of Kristallnacht in Vienna and other parts of Germany, see Günter Fellner, "Der Novemberpogrom 1938: Bemerkungen zur Forschung," *Zeitgeschichte* 15 (November 1988), esp. 37, 44. See also Botz, "Ausmerzung," 25, 29; Weinzierl, *Zu wenig Gerechte,* 69; Sarah Gordon, *Hitler, Germans, and the "Jewish Question"* (Princeton, 1984), 175; and Berkley, *Vienna and Its Jews,* 310–11.

56. Botz, *Wohnungspolitik,* 57, 89; idem, *Wien von "Anschluss" zum Krieg,* 459; Rosenkranz, "Anschluss," 509.

57. Weinzierl, *Zu wenig Gerechte,* 36.

58. Ibid., 32; *Sozialistische Kampf,* June 16, 1938, 46; Botz, "Jews of Vienna from the *Anschluss* to the Holocaust," 190; Flick interview.

59. Berkley, *Vienna and Its Jews,* 324; Weinzierl, *Zu wenig Gerechte,* 35; Friedrich Kubl, "Geschichte der jüdischen Advokaten und Rechtsgelehrten in Österreich," in Gold, *Geschichte der Juden in Österreich,* 123; Safrian and Witek, *Keiner war Dabei,* 160; Botz, *Wien von "Anschluss" zum Krieg,* 244.

60. Rosenkranz, "Anschluss," 502, 506, 519; Weinzierl, *Zu wenig Gerechte,* 37–38, 41–43.

61. Bentwich, "Destruction of the Jewish Community," 468; Erika Weinzierl, "Schuld durch Gleichgultigkeit," in *Das Grosse Tabu,* ed. Anton Pelinka and Erika Weinzierl (Vienna, 1987), 183; Kultusgemeinden of Austria, minutes of August 7, 1938, doc. A/W 2819, 2, Central Archives for the History of the Jewish People, Jerusalem.

62. Rosenkranz, "Anschluss," 486–87.

63. Hodik, "Israelitische Kultusgemeinde," 33; Weinzierl, *Zu wenig Gerechte,* 51; Botz, *Wohnungspolitik,* 71; Goldfarb interview.

64. Botz, *Wien von "Anschluss" zum Krieg,* 254; Oskar Karbach, "The Liquidation of the Jewish Community of Vienna," *Jewish Social Studies* 2 (1940), 273; Botz, *Wohnungspolitik,* 101; Rosenkranz, "Anschluss," 469, 490.

65. Botz, *Wien von "Anschluss" zum Krieg,* 250–51; Siegwald Ganglmair, *Resistance and Persecution in Austria, 1938–1945* (Vienna, 1988), 43; Clare, *Last Waltz in Vienna,* 200.

66. Botz, "Jews of Vienna from the *Anschluss* to the Holocaust," 195; Dutch [Otto Deutsch], "Seeds of a Noble Inheritance: The Influence of Austrian Jewish Emigration upon the Anglo-American World," in Fraenkel, *The Jews of Austria,* 179; Botz, *Wohnungspolitik,* 68; Weinzierl, *Zu wenig Gerechte,* 52; *New York Times,* May 23, 1958, 22; F. Wilder-

Okladek, *The Return Movement of Jews to Austria after the Second World War: With Special Consideration of the Return from Israel* (The Hague, 1969), 36; Rosenkranz, "Anschluss," 510, 514.

67. Berkley, *Vienna and Its Jews,* 312; Rosenkranz, "Anschluss," 500, 517.

68. Simon Wiesenthal, interview, in *1938 . . . and the Consequences: Questions and Responses,* ed. Elfriede Schmidt (Riverside, Calif., 1992), 301; Paul Lendvai, "The New Austria and the Old Nazis," *Commentary* 44, no. 3 (1967), 83; Yitzhak Arad, *Belzec, Sobibor, Treblinka: The Operation Reinhard Death Camps* (Bloomington, Ind., 1987), 184, 186; Gordon J. Horwitz, *In the Shadow of Death: Living Outside the Gates of Mauthausen* (New York, 1990), 19; Berkley, *Vienna and Its Jews,* 315, 317; Botz, "Jews of Vienna from the *Anschluss* to the Holocaust," 202.

69. Rosenkranz, "Anschluss," 517, 519; Gold, *Geschichte der Juden in Wien,* 102.

70. Erika Weinzierl, "Die Stellung der Juden in Österreich seit dem Staatsgrundgesetz von 1867," *Zeitschrift für die Geschichte der Juden* 5 (1968), 94; Berkley, *Vienna and Its Jews,* 320; Weinzierl, *Zu wenig Gerechte,* 88; Rosenkranz, "Anschluss," 526.

71. Herbert Rosenkranz, "Bemerkungen zu neueren Arbeiten über das Problem der Judenverfolgung und des Antisemitismus in Österreich," *Österreich in Geschichte und Literatur* 22 (March–April 1978), 92–94, 96; Erika Weinzierl, "Österreichische Katholiken und die Juden," in *Ecclesia semper reformanda,* ed. Erika Weinzierl (Vienna, 1985), 362–65; Gordon, *Hitler, Germans, and the "Jewish Question,"* 248–49; Berkley, *Vienna and Its Jews,* 326–27.

72. *New York Times,* May 3, 1981, sec. 6, p. 127; Albert Sternfeld, *Betrifft Österreich: Von Österreich betroffen* (Vienna, 1990), 81; Ruth Wodak and Rudolf de Cillia, "Judenfeindlichkeit im öffentlichen Diskurs in Österreich," in *Sprache und Antisemitismus: Ausstellungskatalog* 43 (March 1988), 5; H. A. Kraus, "Austria's Future Jewish Problem," January 24, 31, 1947, in *Understanding Austria: The Political Reports and Analyses of Martin F. Herz, Political Officer of the U.S. Legation, 1945–1948,* ed. Reinhold Wagnleitner (Salzburg, 1984), 118; Brigitte Bailer, *Wiedergutmachung Kein Thema: Österreich und die Opfer des National-sozialismus* (Vienna, 1993), 40; Dieter A. Binder, "Das Schicksal der Grazer Juden 1938," in *Historische Jahrbuch der Stadt Graz,* 1988, 228; Helga Embacher and Michael John, "Remigranten in der österreichischen Wirtschaft nach 1945: Wiederaufbau und Wirtschaftswunder am Beispiel der Provinz," in *Österreichisch-Jüdisches-Geistes-und Kulturleben,* ed.

Liga der Freude des Judentums, vol. 4 (Vienna, 1992), 60, 65, 69, 71.

73. Hilde Weiss, *Antisemitische Vorurteile in Österreich? Theoretische und empirische Analysen* (Vienna, 1984), 127.

74. Oliver Rathkolb, "Zur Kontinuität antisemitischer und rassistischer Vorurteile in Österreich, 1945/1950," *Zeitgeschichte* 16 (February 1989), 176. On the attitude of socialists toward their former Jewish leaders see Robert Schwarz, "Antisemitism and Socialism in Austria, 1918–1962," in Fraenkel, *The Jews of Austria,* 453–55.

75. John Bunzl, "'Austrian Identity' and Antisemitism," *Patterns of Prejudice* 21, no. 1 (1987), 6.

76. Bernd Marin, "Antisemitism before and after the Holocaust: The Austrian Case," in Oxaal et al., *Jews, Antisemitism, and Culture in Vienna,* 221.

77. Erika Weinzierl, "Religious Antisemitism," in Weinzierl, *Ecclesia semper reformanda,* 18.

78. Barbara Kaindl-Widhalm, *Demokraten wider Willen? Autoritären Tendenzen und Antisemitismus in der 2. Republik* (Vienna, 1990), 105, 205.

79. Christian Haerpfer, *Anti-Semitic Attitudes in Austrian Society, 1973–1989: A Study for the Liga der Freunde des Judentums* (Vienna), July 1989, 7-8; Anton Pelinka, "SPÖ, ÖVP, and the 'Ehemaligen': Isolation or Integration?" in *Conquering the Past: Austrian Nazism Yesterday and Today,* ed. Fred Parkinson (Detroit, 1989), 267.

80. *Wiener Zeitung* (Vienna) (hereinafter cited as *WZ*), reprinted in *Der Österreich Bericht* (hereinafter *ÖB*), no. 249 (October 25, 1991), 1.

81. Andrei S. Markovits and Rebecca S. Hayden, "'Holocaust' Before and After the Event: Reactions in West Germany and Austria," in *Germans and Jews since the Holocaust: The Changing Situation in Germany,* ed. Anson Rabinbach and Jack Zipes (New York, 1986), esp. 237, 241–44.

82. Bailer, *Wiedergutmachung,* esp. 135–36, 146, 154.

83. Gustav Jellinek, "Die Geschichte der österreichischen Wiedergutmachung," in Fraenkel, *The Jews of Austria,* 399; *Oberösterreichische Tagesblatt* (Linz), reprinted in *ÖB,* no. 33/189 (August 8, 1987), Kulturbeilage.

84. Jellinek, "Wiedergutmachung," 426; *Die Presse* (Vienna), reprinted in *ÖB,* no. 275 (November 23, 1988), 2; Dietmar Walch, *Die jüdischen Bemühungen um die materielle Wiedergutmachung durch die Republik Österreich* (Vienna, 1971), 14.

85. Hal Lehrmann, "Austria and the Jews: Struggle for Restitution: Minimal Justice Denied," *Commentary* 18 (October 1954), 311; Robert Knight, *Ich bin dafür, die Sache in die Länge zu ziehen: Wort-*

protokolle der österreichischen Bundesregierung von 1945–52 über die Entschädigung der Juden (Frankfurt am Main, 1988), 42, 52, 59; Berkley, *Vienna and Its Jews,* 351; Walch, *Wiedergutmachung,* 1, 5, 9–10, 229–30; *New York Times,* December 22, 1953, 16, and April 3, 1988, sec. 4, p. 16.

86. Wolfgang Petritsch to author, enclosing an article from the February 14, 1990, *New York Times.*

87. *Presse,* reprinted in *ÖB,* no. 275 (November 23, 1988), 2; Jellinek, "Wiedergutmachung," 397.

88. Robert E. Herzstein, *Waldheim: The Missing Years* (New York, 1988), 174; Dieter Stiefel, "Nazifizierung plus Entnazifizierung in Österreich," in *Verdrängte Schuld, verfehlte Sühne: Entnazifizierung in Österreich, 1945–1955,* ed. Sebastian Meissl et al. (Munich, 1986), 29, 34; *New York Times,* December 19, 1953, 2; Walch, *Wiedergutmachung,* 148; Hal Lehrmann, "Austria: Way Station of Exodus: Pages from a Correspondent's Notebook," *Commentary* 18 (October 1954), 309–10.

89. Stiefel, "Nazifizierung plus Entnazifizierung," 34; Richard L. Rubenstein, "After the Holocaust: Waldheim, the Pope, and the Holocaust," *Holocaust and Genocide Studies* 4, no. 1 (1989), 5; Helge Grabitz, "Die Verfolgung von NS-Verbrechen in der Bundesrepublik Deutschland, der DDR und Österreich," in *Der Umgang mit dem Holocaust: Europa—USA—Israel,* ed. Rolf Steininger (Vienna, 1994), 215; Gretl Köfler, "Tirol und die Juden," in *Tirol und der Anschluss: Voraussetzungen, Entwicklungen, Rahmenbedingungen, 1918–1938,* ed. Thomas Albrich et al. (Innsbruck, 1988), 179; *AZ,* in *ÖB,* no. 182 (August 8, 1987), 2; Herzstein, *Waldheim,* 174; Safrian and Witek, *Keiner war Dabei,* 197.

90. Knight, *Ich bin dafür,* 34, 50, 55; Robert Knight, "Kalter Krieg, Entnazifierung, und Österreich," in Meissl et al., *Verdrängte Schuld, verfehlte Sühne,* 46.

91. Elisabeth Hindler, "Die Entwicklung der Haltung österreichischen Zeitungen zu Israel" (Ph.D. diss., University of Vienna, 1977), 33, 99, 100. I would like to thank Dr. Helga Embacher of the University of Salzburg for making the relevant pages of this dissertation available to me.

92. Wodak and de Cillia, "Judenfeindlichkeit," 12–13.

93. Herbert P. Secher, "Kreisky and the Jews," *Contemporary Austrian Studies* 2 (1993), 10, 13–14, 19; Berkley, *Vienna and Its Jews,* 353; Richard Grunberger, "Waldheim in the Press: A Selected Survey," *Patterns of Prejudice* 21, no. 1 (1987), 9.

94. Secher, "Kreisky and the Jews," 22–26; Robert S. Wistrich, "The Kreisky Phenomenon: A Reassessment," in *Austrians and Jews in the Twen-*

tieth Century: From Franz Joseph to Waldheim, ed. Robert S. Wistrich (London, 1992), 237, 243.

95. Herzstein, *Waldheim,* 117, 215, 254, quotation on 23.

96. John Bunzl, *Der lange Arm der Erinnerung: Jüdisches Bewusstsein heute* (Vienna, 1987), 107; Eli Rosenbaum with William Hoffer, *Betrayal: The Untold Story of the Kurt Waldheim Investigation and Cover-up* (New York, 1993), 295; Richard Mitten, "Die Kampagne mit 'der Kampagne': Waldheim, der Jüdische Weltkongress und 'das Ausland,'" *Zeitgeschichte* 17 (January 1990), 178–80; Richard Basset, *Waldheim and Austria* (New York, 1989), 122. *New York Times,* March 29, 1986, 20; April 27, 1986, sec. 4, p. 2; May 5, 1986, 4; June 12, 1986, 3.

97. Maximilian Gottschlich, "Die beleidigte Nation: Der Fall 'Waldheim': Antiamerikanismus und Antisemitismus im österreichischen Printmedien," *Journal für Sozialforschung* 27 (1987), 397, 400; Rosenbaum, *Betrayal,* 399; Basset, *Waldheim and Austria,* 98, 122; *New York Times,* April 11, 1986, 12, and June 2, 1986, sec. 6, p. 16; Herzstein, *Waldheim,* 252.

98. Chancellor Franz Vranitzky, conversation with author, Vienna, February 23, 1988.

99. Judith Miller, "Erasing the Past: Europe's Amnesia about the Holocaust," *New York Times Magazine,* November 16, 1986, 35; K. R. Luther, "Austria's Future and Waldheim's Past: The Significance of the 1986 Elections," *West European Politics* 10 (July 1987), esp. 389–91; Hermann Langbein, "Darf man vergessen?" in Pelinka and Weinzierl, *Das Grosse Tabu,* 13.

100. Wodak and de Cillia, "Judenfeindlichkeit," 8; *AZ,* reprinted in *ÖB,* no. 58 (March 10, 1988), 1; *New York Times,* February 15, 1988, 1.

101. Grunberger, "Waldheim in the Press," 12; Basset, *Waldheim and Austria,* 138; Shlomo Avineri, "The Waldheim Affair: How the World Jewish Congress Blew It," *Present Tense* 14 (May–June 1987), 20, 27.

102. *New York Times,* May 17, 1986, 4; Schmidt, *1938 . . . and the Consequences,* 308–9.

103. Mitten, "Die Kampagne mit 'der Kampagne,'" 185; Rosenbaum, *Betrayal,* esp. 461; *New York Times,* September 29, 1993, A18.

104. Anton Pelinka, "Dismantling Taboos: Antisemitism in the Austrian Political Culture in the 1980s," *Patterns of Prejudice* 27, no. 2 (1993), 42–43; Rubenstein, "After the Holocaust," 9.

105. I would like to thank Almud Pelinka of Innsbruck, Austria, for sending me photocopies of the relevant chapters of the following books used in this study (cited in chronological order): Walter Göhring

and Herbert Hasenmayer, *Zeitgeschichte* (Vienna, 1972); Herbert Hasenmayer, Erich Scheithauer, and Werner Tscherne, *Aus Vergangenheit und Gegenwart* (Vienna, 1977); Werner Tscherne, Erich Scheithauer, and Manfred Gartler, *Weg durch die Zeiten,* vol. 4 (Graz, 1983); Göbhart Chvojka, *Zeitbilder Geschichte und Sozialkunde* (Vienna, 1988); Anton Ebner, Franz Heffeter, and Harald Majdan, *Gesellschaft, Wirtschaft, Kultur im Wandel der Zeit,* vol. 4 (Vienna, 1990); Michael Floiger, Ulrike Ebenbach, Kurt Tschegg, and Manfred Tuschel, *Spuren der Vergangenheit—Bausteine der Zukunft* (Vienna, 1991); Robert Kriechbaumer and Franz Watzl, *Die Geschichte unserer Zeit,* vol. 3 (N.p., 1991); and Werner Tscherne and Manfred Gartler, *Wege durch die Zeiten,* vol. 3 (Graz, 1991).

106. Floiger et al., *Spuren der Vergangenheit,* 182.

107. Peter Malina and Gustav Spann, "Der Nationalsozialismus in österreichischen Geschichtslehrbuch," in Talos, Hanisch, and Neugebauer, *NS-Herrschaft in Österreich, 1938–1945,* esp. 583–85, 595.

108. Kriechbaumer and Watzl, *Geschichte unserer Zeit,* 36, 37, 70, 72.

109. Wolfgang Neugebauer, "Widerstand und Opposition," in *Österreich und der Zweite Weltkrieg,* ed. Wolfgang Neugebauer and Elisabeth Morawek (Vienna, 1989), 30. The quotation is from Peter Malina, "Nach dem Krieg," ibid., 145.

110. Dokumentationsarchiv des österreichischen Widerstandes and Bundesministerium für Unterricht und Kunst, eds., *Amoklauf Gegen die Wirklichkeit: NS-Verbrechen und "Revisionistiche" Geschichtsschreibung* (Vienna, 1991).

111. Bundesministerium für Unterricht und Kunst, ed., *Denkmal und Erinnerung: Spurensuch im 20. Jahrhundert. Anregungen für Schülerinnen- und Schülerprojekte* (Vienna, 1993).

112. *WZ,* reprinted in *ÖB,* no. 5 (January 8, 1988); Reynold S. Koppel, "*Heikle Sache:* The Holocaust in Austrian Schools" (paper delivered at the annual meeting of the German Studies Association, Buffalo, N.Y., October 1990), 2–3, 5, 10.

113. *Presse,* reprinted in *ÖB,* no. 300 (December 22, 1988), 2; "SWS Meinungsprofile: Antisemitismus in Österreich," *SWS-Rundschau* 27, no. 1 (1987), 91. See also Heinz Kienzl, "Der Österreicher und seine Schande: Erster Versuch einer empirischen Studie über Antisemitismus," *Forum* 13, no. 154 (1966), 657.

114. *Austrian Studies Newsletter* 2, no. 3 (1990), 10; *WZ,* reprinted in *ÖB,* nos. 5 (January 8, 1988), 1 and 42 (May 15, 1991), 1. Kurt Schubert to Verlag Kremayr & Scheriau (Vienna), November 26, 1993, enclosing an accompanying unpublished re-

view of *Eine Geschichte des österreichischen Antisemitismus* by Bruce F. Pauley.

115. "Vorwort zum letzten Band der Liga-Ausgaben," in *Österreichisch-Jüdisches-Geistes-und Kulturleben*, 1.

116. *Presse*, reprinted in *ÖB*, no. 278 (November 27, 1987), 2; *AZ*, reprinted in *ÖB*, no. 147 (June 29, 1987), 1; *WZ*, reprinted in *ÖB*, no. 157 (July 10, 1987), 1; *WZ*, reprinted in *ÖB*, no. 260 (November 9, 1988), 1.

117. *Oberösterreichische Tagesblatt*, reprinted in *ÖB*, no. 33/189 (August 8, 1987), Kulturbeilage; *New York Times*, May 3, 1981, sec. 6, pp. 140, 144; *Kurier*, reprinted in *ÖB*, no. 98 (April 22, 1989), 2; Melanie A. Sully, "The Waldheim Connection," in Parkinson, *Conquering the Past*, 307; "Austria and Israel—A New Beginning," *Austria Today*, February 1993, 4.

118. Fred Hift, "New Jewish Museum in Vienna," *Austria Kultur* 3, no. 6 (1993), 8–9; *AZ*, reprinted in *ÖB*, nos. 32/186 (August 12, 1991) and 56 (March 8, 1990), 2; *Austrian Information* 47, no. 3 (1994), 8; *Salzburger Nachrichten*, reprinted in *ÖB*, no. 26/146 (June 18, 1993), 2.

119. Ganglmair, *Resistance and Persecution in Austria*, 23, 37.

120. See, e.g., *Presse*, reprinted in *ÖB*, no. 217 (September 17, 1988), 2; *Die Furche* (Vienna), reprinted in *ÖB*, no. 238 (September 30, 1988), 2; Josef Joffe, "Where Hitler Fell Down the Memory Hole," *U.S. News & World Report*, March 14, 1988, 32. See also the catalogue of the November Pogrom exhibit, entitled *Der Novemberpogrom 1938: Die Kristallnacht in Wien* (Vienna, 1988).

121. *Presse*, July 9, 1991, 1, 6; *Austrian Information* 46, no. 6 (1993), 2.

122. *Wiener-Zeitung* documentation, reprinted in *ÖB*, no. 264 (November 16, 1994), 2.

123. Aushalom Hodik, Peter Malina, and Gustav Spann, eds., *Juden in Österreich, 1918–1938* (Vienna, 1988).

124. *Furche*, reprinted in *ÖB*, no. 88 (April 8, 1993), 3; flier entitled *Gedenkdienst* given to the author by Dr. Maislinger; *Austrian Studies Newsletter* 6, no. 2 (1994), 1, 14.

125. Felix Mitterer, *Kein schöner Land: Ein Theaterstuck und sein historischer Hintergrund* (Innsbruck, 1987), 9, 85.

126. *New York Times*, August 29, 1967, 3.

127. Pelinka, "Dismantling Taboos," 40.

128. For examples see the bibliography in Pauley, *From Prejudice to Persecution*.

ITALY

Meir Michaelis

Although nearly four-fifths of the Jews of Italy survived Hitler's Final Solution, the impact of the Holocaust on Italian Jewry was profound. Since the end of World War II it has been the subject of scholarly debate, political controversy, and legal conflict. Some of the accounts by survivors have won fame throughout the Western world, most particularly Primo Levi's *If This Is a Man,* Giorgio Bassani's *Garden of the Finzi-Continis,* and Silvano Arieti's *The Parnas.*

The controversy over the Holocaust in Italy received fresh impetus at the end of 1986 when an Italian journalist, Nicola Caracciolo, conducted a series of televised interviews on aid to Jews during World War II. *Gli ebrei e l'Italia durante la guerra, 1940–45* (The Jews and Italy during the War, 1940–45) provoked sharp polemical reactions from various Italian Jews. Two years later, the fiftieth anniversary of the fascist race laws was marked by an explosion of articles, books, and pamphlets on the anti-Jewish campaign that set the stage for the Final Solution on the Italian peninsula.

Prior to Mussolini's rapprochement with Hitler, there was no "Jewish Question" in modern Italy; it is no exaggeration to say that until 1936 there was less anti-Semitism in Italy than in any of the Western democracies. Hence, before assessing Italian reactions to the Holocaust, we should explore briefly the history and character of the Italian Jewish community.

BEFORE THE HOLOCAUST
The Historical Background

Despite their small numbers, Italian Jews are of special interest to the student of Jewish history because, first, the annals of Italian Jewry span well over twenty centuries and half a dozen civilizations, and, second, emancipation for the Jews in Italy was uniquely successful. As late as 1848 there was hardly a country in Europe where the restrictions placed on the Jews were more galling, but after 1870 there was no part of the globe where Jewish equality was more real. Finally, during World War II, Italy and the Italian-occupied territories became havens of refuge for persecuted Jews, despite Mussolini's alliance with Hitler.

Until 1860 Italy was, in Metternich's famous phrase, a mere "geographical expression"; she was divided into a dozen independent states, the largest of which were the Kingdom of Naples in the south, the Papal States and the Grand Duchy of Tuscany in the center, and the Republic of Venice, the Duchy of Milan, and the Duchy of Piedmont (Kingdom of Sardinia) in the north. Smaller states, in the area between Tuscany and Piedmont, were Modena, Mantua, Lucca, Parma, Piacenza, and Genoa. After the Spanish expulsions of the Jews in 1492 and 1542, Jewish life was confined to the north of the country. The economic decline of Italy, which began when world commercial sea routes shifted during the Age of Discovery, reached its lowest point in the mid-eighteenth century. On the eve of the French Revolution the Jews of Italy were among the poorest and most disenfranchised in Western Europe.

Approximately two-thirds of the Italian Jewish population was concentrated in ten urban communities, each with more than a thousand members; the remaining third was dispersed in over sixty rural communities *(kehillot),* most of them numbering fewer than five hundred people.[1] The largest ghetto was in Rome; it occupied a whole district of the city on the Tiber and was separated by stone walls from the surrounding society. Around the year 1500 the number of Jews in Italy reached its all-time high, possibly 120,000, more than 1 percent of the total Italian population of 10.5 million, a figure that in relative terms has declined ever since. In 1600 Jews numbered 21,000 out of a total population of more than 13 million; in 1800, 34,275 out of a total of nearly 34 million; and by 1945, after the Holocaust, it had dropped to 28,445 (not including temporary residents) out of a total of nearly 46 million. In 1990 there were only 32,000 Jews out of a total Italian population of almost 58 million, just over one-twentieth of 1 percent.[2]

As early as the period of the Enlightenment (Haskalah) and the French Revolution, Jews in Italy were more integrated socially and culturally into the surrounding population than anywhere else in Europe. According to the noted Israeli historian Raphael Mahler,

> In contradistinction to their brethren in Germany, the Jews of Italy had been firmly embedded in the Italian population for many generations. They were linked to it by language, culture, and social relationships. The culture of Italian Jewry was always suffused with secular elements. In the light of Jewish historical development, enfranchisement in Italy in no way necessitated a violent clash between the ancient mode of life and a new one. What it signified was the removal of obstacles to a line of development long since marked out.

Although the legal position of the Jews in most of the Italian states worsened in the last quarter of the eighteenth century, "the Church in Italy never succeeded in implanting hatred of the Jews among the Italian population":

On the contrary, in Italy, the land of the ghettos, mutual relations between Jews and native Gentiles were more friendly than in any other country in Europe. . . . The high level of the ordinary Italian's cultural tradition, his *joie de vivre*, affable temperament, and the fact that he had intermingled with Jews for hundreds of years on the same soil, proved more powerful than any artificial barrier. Even in Rome, Church supervision was powerless to prevent Christians from visiting the homes of their Jewish friends.[3]

The emancipation of Italian Jewry came about gradually over a period of nearly ninety years. The process started in Austrian-occupied Lombardy in 1781, when the reforming Emperor Joseph II issued his Toleration Patent, which granted the Jews the right to regard themselves as permanent residents. There followed the emancipation of 1796–1815, imposed by Napoleon Bonaparte, which ended with the fall of the invader. The Restoration brought back the pre-Napoleonic restrictions throughout Italy and a full repristination of anti-Jewish legislation in Piedmont and the Papal States.[4]

In Italy the debate over emancipation did not begin until around 1830, much later than in France and Germany. The Jews prepared for full equality both through reform of their educational and charitable institutions (courses in Italian history and literature, vocational training for Jewish youth, and so on) and through active involvement in the struggle for liberation, which won them the sympathy and support of practically all the leading figures of the Risorgimento, including Mazzini, Garibaldi, and Cavour. (Cavour's private secretary, Isacco Artom, was the first Italian Jew to achieve eminence in public affairs.) Jewish participation was greatest where long-established rights had bred civic consciousness, such as in Tuscany and Lombardy-Venetia, and almost nonexistent in the Roman community, whose Jewish population was the most oppressed and abject on the peninsula. Full emancipation was granted in various localities in 1848 but was maintained only in the Kingdom of Sardinia, whose decrees were gradually extended to the rest of the country; the process was completed with the capture of Rome in 1870. Because of the juridical form of emancipation (a single legal act rather than a series of installments), the brevity of the debate on the issue (at most twenty years), and the undivided stand of the political camp (which made religious equality an integral part of its program), after the Risorgimento the new legal status of the Jewish minority was more solid and less questioned in Italy than in other European countries.[5]

From Liberalism to Fascism, 1870–1922

The years between the unification of Italy and the fascist March on Rome revealed the unique success of Jewish emancipation on the peninsula, both its positive and its negative aspects. The security, opportunities, and acceptance accorded Italian Jews were tempered by the progressive erosion of their Jewish identity: "Italy became a byword in the Jewish world for the completeness of emancipation on the one hand, for its deadly corrosive potentialities on the other."[6]

By 1900 Italy's Jews were fully integrated into the surrounding society; they played a prominent part in the political, cultural, and economic life of the country and had access to careers in diplomacy and the armed forces, avenues generally closed to them elsewhere. The first Jewish minister of war and the first Jewish prime minister in Europe were Italians: Giuseppe Ottolenghi (1902–3) and Luigi Luzzatti (1910–11). By 1905 eleven Jews were sitting among Italy's elder statesmen in the royally nominated Senate; eighteen years later the number had risen to twenty-six.

Anti-Semitism on the peninsula was a marginal phenomenon throughout the period. Even the clerical campaign against the Jews during the reign of Leo XIII (1883–1903), which was essentially an indirect counterattack on liberalism and secularization and in which about forty newspapers and periodicals took part, had little effect on the position of the Jews in Italian life.

> It never had the opportunity to coalesce with other anti-Semitic and anti-liberal currents or to pose a threat to republican institutions, as in France during the Dreyfus affair; and in contrast to the situation in the Second Reich, where anti-Semitism was a vehicle for the integration of the Centre Party into the German political establishment, the anti-Jewish campaign of Italian Catholics served only to increase the isolation of the Church from the political life of the country.[7]

The period following the Risorgimento was also marked by progressive Jewish self-extinction. Secularization increased, as did intermarriage (with its corollary of secession from Judaism), and the Jewish birth rate dropped sharply. The Jewish birth rate reached 27.6 per 1,000 births between 1851 and 1875 and then began to fall; it was 19.0 in 1876–1900, 17.0 in 1901–5, 16.1 in 1906–10, 15.2 in 1911–15, and 11.9 in 1916–20. Economically, there was a continuous embourgeoisement of Italian Jewry, which was particularly evident in Bologna, Florence, Milan, Padua, and Turin, where Jews achieved prominence in the liberal professions, banking, commerce, industry, the armed forces, and the civil service.[8]

Jewish assimilation on the peninsula was facilitated by several factors peculiar to Italy, at least in their convergence: the smallness of the Jewish nucleus (about one-tenth of 1 percent); the all but total absence of Jewish immigration from Eastern Europe; the laic ideology of the Italian state; the integration of clerical forces into the Italian political system during the first decade of the twentieth century; and, last but not least, a curious blend of general respect for individual Jews and their rights with a widespread disregard for Judaism as a religion and ethical system, a combination that subtly encouraged irreligion and apostasy among members of the Jewish community.[9]

Countercurrents of Jewish revival began to surface at the end of the nineteenth century. In 1898 Rabbi Giuseppe Sonino of Naples went to Basel to address the second Zionist congress. In the following year the Collegio Rabbinico, after a lengthy period of semi-activity, was revitalized under the direction of Shmuel Zvi Margulies, a rabbi of Galician origin, who had been appointed to the rabbinate of Florence nine years earlier. In 1901 Carlo A. Conigliani launched a Zionist periodical, *L'Idea Sionista;* in 1905 Felice di Leone Ravenna founded the Italian Zionist Federation. In 1907 the first of a new nexus of Jewish cultural societies, under the name Pro Cultura, was established by Margulies's disciples in Florence; four years later, as a result of his untiring efforts, a Jewish youth congress was held there at which the new synthesis between the Italian and Jewish cultures was taken as a basis for action. The establishment in 1911 of the new *Consorzio* (Association) of Italian Jewish communities, with cultural rather than administrative objectives, was another outcome of the revival movement. No less important than his organizing power was Margulies's personal influence: he succeeded in rallying some of the most outstanding minds of the younger generation and fostered an "integral" Judaism, which embraced Jewish observances, Jewish culture, and Jewish national solidarity. It came to be fairly widespread among the younger intelligentsia, who used as their mouthpiece *Israel*, a Zionist weekly founded in 1916 and edited by Dante A. Lattes and Alfonso Pacifici. Chaim Weizmann rightly considered *Israel* "one of the best Zionist papers of the day."[10]

Italian Jewry under Fascism, 1922–1943

During the first fourteen years of fascist rule, the legal position of the Jews remained ostensibly much as it had been, and their place in Italian life was hardly affected. Throughout this period Mussolini concentrated on fascistizing his Jewish subjects and using them as tools to advance his imperial policy in the Mediterranean and in Africa. Toward this end, in 1931 he set up the Union of Italian Jewish Communities, which was charged with the task of maintaining "spiritual and cultural contacts" with the Jewish communities of other countries. Latent tension existed between the regime and the Jews from the outset, mainly because of fascist suspicions of Jewish "separatism," but there was no attempt to create a Jewish problem in Italy and no specifically Jewish opposition to the dictatorship. If some Jews joined the ranks of the government's opponents, others were among its earliest supporters. The anti-Jewish feeling expressed in fascist circles before 1937 was purely political, not racial; its chief target was "international Jewry," not the "Jewish Italians." In the words of Luigi Villari, the leading fascist propagandist in the Anglo-Saxon countries: "Anti-Semitism among the Fascists is the result not of any dislike of the Italian Jews, who are absolutely absorbed into the nation and are good patriots, but of suspicion of the international activities of foreign Jews, especially of those representing the great cosmopolitan financial interests of Paris, London, Berlin, and New York, and of dislike of the Russian Bolsheviks, whose leaders are mostly Jews."[11]

The rapprochement between church and state after Mussolini's rise to power caused alarm among Jewish leaders. They were particularly concerned about the Gentile Law of July 1923 and the concordat concluded with the Holy See in February 1929. The former called for mandatory religious instruction in Italian schools, which meant that Jewish schoolchildren would be subjected to a heavy dose of Catholic proselytizing. The latter restored Roman Catholicism to its place as the state religion. Since the concordat lessened Mussolini's dependence on the goodwill of the pope, its long-term effects on fascist policy toward the Jews were to some extent positive. Even so, it established an inequality of religions under the law; along with the Gentile Law, it must therefore be considered the only legal setback to Jewish parity in modern Italy before the anti-Jewish laws of 1938.

Prior to his agreement with Pius XI, Mussolini was worried about the effect pro-Zionist policies might have on the Holy See; after the signing of the concordat, his relations with the Zionist movement took a turn for the better. In 1933 he called for the establishment of a viable Jewish state in Palestine, and in 1934 he described himself as a "Zionist" in a talk with Nahum Goldmann, then the Jewish Agency representative at Geneva.[12]

The concordat made it necessary to clarify the status of non-Catholics in Italy and was followed by the comprehensive Law on the Jewish Communities (comprising Royal Decree Law nos. 1,731 of October 30, 1930; 1,279 of September 24, 1931; and 1,561 of November 19, 1931). The law gave a coherent legal status to Italian Jewry and provided an economic base for its religious and cultural activities. The Jewish population was organized into twenty-six communities, each having legally vested powers, including the right to tax its members. These communities were united under a central body, the Union of Italian Jewish Communities, which henceforth represented the entire Jewish population before the government and the public. The new regulations extended the totalitarian principles of the regime to the internal affairs of Italy's Jews; even so, they won praise from Jewish leaders, who rightly saw in them a significant extension of their own power.[13]

From 1922 to 1936, and on occasion as late as 1937, the official fascist attitude toward the Jews was summarily expressed in the phrase "The Jewish problem does not exist in Italy." The spokesmen of Italian Jewry naturally hastened to subscribe to the official thesis, paying tribute to the magnanimity of the regime and blaming the manifestations of anti-Semitism and anti-Zionism on "irresponsible underlings." At first these expressions of regard for the new regime were mainly a matter of tactics; by 1932, however, even antifascist Jews had become convinced that Mussolini was as good as his word. In April of that year the Duce condemned racism and anti-Semitism in a talk with Emil Ludwig, the noted German Jewish author. Two months later he defined the concept of nation in antiracial terms. The Jews were duly impressed. In an editorial on the tenth anniversary of the March on Rome, *Israel* emphasized the "radical difference between the true and authentic fascism—Italian fascism, that is—and the pseudo-fascist movements in other countries, which . . . are often making use of the most reactionary phobias, and especially of the blind, unbridled hatred of the Jews, as a means of diverting the masses from their real problems."[14]

Assimilation continued unabated (in 1938, 43.7 percent of all married Jews had gentile spouses), but so did the Jewish revival. The Italian Zionist Federation was not banned, despite Mussolini's notorious aversion to Italians with "dual loyalties"; local cultural societies continued to be formed; *La Rassegna Mensile di Israel* (The Monthly Review of Israel), the literary supplement of *Israel*, attained a standard surpassed by few Jewish periodicals anywhere in the world; Israel, the Zionist publishing house in Florence, had an output that, though small, was of very high quality; and in 1924 and 1928, Youth Cultural Congresses were held in Livorno and Venice.[15]

However, granted the fascist ideal of the "unitary state" in matters of religious as well as political allegiance, some degree of discrimination against nonconforming elements was inevitable. No Jew ever reached a position of power in either the government or the party hierarchy; no Jew was ever admitted to the Italian Academy, although the number of outstanding Jewish scholars was high. The number of Jewish senators dwindled from twenty-six in 1923 to six in 1938. Jews continued, however, to be prominent in commerce, the liberal professions, the armed forces, and the academic world. Margherita Sarfatti, Mussolini's first official biographer and co-editor of his monthly review *Gerarchia* (Hierarchy), was Jewish, as were Ugo d'Ancona, Achille Loria, and Teodoro Mayer among his closest financial advisers. Guido Liuzzi was promoted to army commander-designate in 1928; Guido Jung, a Catholic with a German Jewish background, served as minister of finance from 1932 to 1935. Three among the major Italian publishing houses—Bemporad, Formiggini, and Treves—were in Jewish hands.[16]

The position of Italian Jewry first began to deteriorate after Hitler's rise to power. In 1933 Mussolini could not yet risk antagonizing France and England by forming an ideological bloc with the Reich. But if Hitler's anti-Semitism was a source of grave embarrassment to him, so was the anti-Hitler crusade conducted by the Jews: while his newspapers were exulting the triumph of "German fascism," the spokesmen of Italian Jewry vied with their antifascist brethren abroad in denouncing the German atrocities. Mussolini reacted by unleashing an anti-Jewish campaign—the first in the history of modern Italy—in the fascist press, most particularly in his unofficial mouthpiece, *Il Tevere* (The Tiber). His official mouthpiece, *Il Popolo d'Italia* (The People of Italy), took up the anti-Jewish theme in a more moderate way. It deplored Hitler's racist folly but insisted that not only the Germans but also the Italians had the right to defend themselves against the "Jewish peril." Since "Jewish antifascism" was increasingly being identified with Zionism, the Jewish fascists established a weekly publication appropriately named *La Nostra Bandiera* (Our Flag) to distinguish themselves from the Zionists and other "disloyal" elements.[17]

After the abortive Nazi putsch in Austria, culminating in the assassination of Chancellor Dollfuss on July 25, 1934, the Jewish problem in Italy receded into the background, overshadowed by the clash between Rome and Berlin that prompted the Duce to join the anti-German coalition with Britain and France, known as the Stresa front, in April 1935. However, once the invasion of Ethiopia was launched on October 3, 1935, the anti-Hitler front collapsed. Britain and France condemned Italy and imposed economic sanctions on the country. True, Mussolini could not change sides overnight: while taking steps to improve relations with Hitler, he continued to play the Western card for all it was worth. And in so doing, he of course took into account the Jews' alleged influence on Western policy toward Italy. He sent Jewish emissaries abroad to protest the sanctionist policy and to exploit Zionist aspirations for fascist ends. His courting of the Zionists continued until July 1936, the month in which the German and Italian secret services began to cooperate in Spain.[18]

As long as Mussolini pursued a middle course between the Western democracies and the Reich, he had no motive for attacking the Jews as such. With the beginning of German-Italian collaboration in Spain, however, there was a marked change for the worse. The overtures to the Zionists ceased; Italian propaganda in Palestine and North Africa now fed on the anti-Jewish feelings of the local Arabs. On September 12, 1936, an anti-Jewish campaign was launched by Roberto Farinacci, the fascist boss of Cremona; six weeks later the Rome-Berlin Axis was born. In March 1937 a stir was caused by Paolo Orano's book *Gli Ebrei in Italia* (The Jews in Italy), which equated *italianità* (the Italian national character, spirit, or feeling) with Roman Catholicism and contested the right of Jews to retain their own identity. Other fascist scribes went further, calling for racial measures on the German model.

On July 14, 1938, two months after Hitler's visit to Italy, Mussolini finally threw off the mask: on that day he had the press publish a statement, the "Manifesto of the Race," in which the Italian Jews were referred to as inassimilable aliens. On August 22, 1938, a new Jewish census identified 55,103 persons as being of the Jewish "race" (the census of 1931 had counted 47,825 persons of the Jewish faith). On September 5, Jewish pupils were excluded from public schools and Jewish teachers were forbidden to teach in such schools or in any scientific or academic institution (Royal Decree Law no. 1,390). Simultaneously, a Directorate-General for Demography and Race was established within the ministry of the interior and given the responsibility for coordinating racial legislation. On September 7, Jews of foreign birth, including those who had acquired Italian citizenship after January 1, 1919, were ordered to leave the country within six months (Royal Decree Law no. 1,381). For the purposes of the law, Jews were defined as persons "having two Jewish parents, even if they profess a religion other than the Jewish." The Declaration on Race followed on October 7. In it the Fascist Grand Council laid down the guidelines for the racial policy instituted in the ensuing months. A law enacted on November 17 (Royal Decree Law no. 1,728) prohibited Jews from marrying "Aryans," made it obligatory for them to declare they were Jewish, and imposed severe restrictions on their civil rights. They were banned from military service and forbidden to own a business, land, or buildings above a certain value; to hold posts in any public service; to employ "Aryan" servants; or to tutor an "Aryan" minor. The same law specified that Jews with "civil or military merits" might apply for an exemption *(discriminazione)*. They would then be allowed to employ "Aryans" and own real estate; all the other restrictions, however, would still apply. Subsequent laws progressively reinforced the anti-Jewish measures.[19]

The racial campaign and its swift translation into official policy was a crushing blow to Italian Jewry. More than four thousand sought refuge in baptism, and about six thousand emigrated. Most of those who remained, however, faced persecution with dignity. The larger communities opened Jewish schools, and various charitable organizations were set up to aid foreign Jewish refugees, who continued to enter Italy despite the race laws. The most important of these organizations, DELASEM, or the Delegazione Assistenza Emigranti Ebrei (Committee for Assistance to Jewish Emigrants), helped to save thousands of Jewish lives during the war years. The Union of Italian Jewish Communities, after undergoing a profound crisis, regained its authority in 1939 under the leadership of Dante Almansi. After Italy's entry into the war on June 10, 1940, Mussolini took a series of "security measures" against the Jews. On June 14 all Jewish bank accounts were frozen and Jews were ordered to register any stocks they owned. On the same day, the police began to round up foreign Jews as well as Italian Jews who were considered "politically dangerous." By September 1940 fifteen internment camps had been set up to hold these people. The living conditions in these camps were harsh, but they had little in common with Hitler's concentration camps and even less with his extermination camps.[20]

While Jews on the peninsula were punished for the crime of being "Semites," the term used by the fascists to stress the "racial basis" of the anti-Jewish laws, outside of Italy the Jewish issue became a test of the Duce's remaining autonomy. This eminently political consideration helps to explain why the Italian-occupied territories in France, Yugoslavia, and Greece became havens of refuge for persecuted Jews, at least until Italy's surrender to the Allies.

With the fall of fascism (Mussolini was dismissed by the king and placed under arrest on July 25, 1943) Italian racial policy lost its point. But the new premier, Marshal Pietro Badoglio, was unwilling to antagonize his ally, Germany, by repealing the anti-Jewish laws. He did not even order his prefects to ease enforcement. The Directorate-General for Demography and Race was not dissolved, the internment camps were not dismantled, and the lists of Jewish names and addresses were not destroyed. Most of these lists fell into the hands of the SS after September 8, 1943. Thus Mussolini's downfall, far from putting an end to the racial persecutions, merely set the stage for the implementation of the Final Solution on Italian soil.[21]

THE HOLOCAUST ERA

On September 11, 1943, three days after Badoglio's surrender, Field-Marshal Albert Kesselring, the commander of Army Group South in Italy, declared all Italian territory to be a theater of war under German military control. Italy was thus reduced, in Mussolini's words, "from the position of a confederated province to the worse one of a colony." This change in status had fatal results for the Italian Jews.

In any assessment of the Holocaust in Italy, one must bear in mind three basic facts. The first has to do with the geographical distribution of the Jews. Ever since the Spanish expulsions, Jewish life had been confined to the north of the country. South of Rome there were very few Jews, and these were liberated by the Allies before the end of 1943. But the expected Allied landings in the Gulf of Genoa failed to materialize, and so the area of Jewish settlement from Rome northward remained under complete German control until June 1944.

The second is Hitler's decision to restore Mussolini to power. If the creation of the Italian Social Republic had enabled the Duce to regain some measure of independence, many Jewish lives might have been saved. But since he was now virtually a prisoner, his reinstatement had the effect of facilitating the task of Eichmann's emissaries in the German-occupied part of Italy.

The third is Hitler's decision not to occupy the Vatican City. His first thought had been to capture the new government by force and occupy the Vatican; subsequently, however, under pressure from his entourage, he agreed to spare the Holy See. Of all the decisions made by Hitler after the fall of fascism in Italy, this was the only one that benefited the Jews, for it enabled the church to save a good many Jewish lives.

Even before the "liberation" of the Duce, Hitler had ordered the setting up of a political and military system that would bring under its wing any future Italian fascist administration. The German ambassador to Italy, Rudolf Rahn, had become plenipotentiary of the Reich; Himmler's adjutant, *Obergruppenführer* Karl Wolff, had been appointed commander of the SS in Italy and security adviser to the projected fascist puppet government. The border provinces Venezia Giulia and Alto Adige had been placed under German gauleiters. For the rest, Italy was divided into two zones, operational and occupied, the former coming under Kesselring's Army Group South and the latter under Rommel's Army Group B.

Immediately after the Italian armistice Hitler began to extend the Final Solution to Italy, without even waiting for the restoration of an Italian fascist regime. On September 12 Herbert Kappler, head of the Gestapo in Rome, was ordered to round up and deport the Jews of Rome; a few days later the SS initiated a series of pogroms, arrests, and deportations in northern Italy that resulted in the death of nearly four hundred Jewish men, women, and children.

The history of the Holocaust in Italy can be divided into three distinct periods. During the first (October–November 1943) the SS took advantage of the Italian power vacuum to carry out a series of autonomous, systematic actions. During the second (from December 1943 to mid-February 1944) the fascists issued a series of anti-Jewish decrees with the object of restoring a measure of Italian sovereignty. During the third (from mid-February 1944 to April 1945) the terms of the Italian-German collaboration changed radically. Eichmann's representatives began to alter the categories of Jews to be arrested specified by the Italian ministry of the interior. The clashes between the SS and the Italian fascist police, often charged with conflicting orders from their superiors, can be traced to this period.

During the first phase operations were directed by *Hauptsturmführer* Theodor Dannecker. He enjoyed complete autonomy from even the Gestapo stationed in Italy, and he was tied to no fixed headquarters. On October 16 he struck in Rome: 1,030 Jewish men, women, and children were deported to Auschwitz, only 17 of whom returned. Dannecker's *Einsatzkommando* then shifted to other cities, including Florence, Venice, Milan, and Genoa.

The fascist reaction to German interference took the form of an affirmation of autonomy rather than a helpless application of German orders. On November 14, 1943, the Fascist Party Congress at Verona endorsed a manifesto that defined the Jews of Italy as "enemy nationals" for the duration of the war. On November 30 Mussolini's minister of the interior, Guido Buffarini-Guidi, ordered the arrest and internment of all Jews resident in the Fascist Republic ("even if exempted and irrespective of citizenship") and the immediate confiscation of their property "for the benefit of the indigent refugees from enemy air attacks." On the following day, this order was broadcast over the radio, with the result that thousands of Jews went into hiding or fled the country. On December 10 the new chief of police, Tullio Tamburini, instructed the heads of all provinces to exempt certain categories of Jews from internment, including the aged, the sick, the "Aryanized," and those with "Aryan" spouses. On January 4, 1944, a law was promulgated prohibiting Jews from owning land or shares in companies and ordering the sequestration of their wealth, including liquid assets and real estate.

Buffarini's order of November 30 meant that no Jew could remain in circulation after that date, because he was liable to arrest by the local police. In the following months, in fact, arrests were organized by the central police headquarters of the Fascist Republic. The police searched Jewish households or rounded up the Jews in the style of the SS's lightning raids. The victims of these fascist Jew hunts were crowded into local jails and then interned at Fossoli di Carpi (Modena), the central concentration camp for Jews. This went on until the summer of 1944, when the terms of the Italian-German collaboration underwent a radical change.

At the end of January 1944, Dannecker was replaced by *Sturmbannführer* Friedrich Robert Bosshammer, Eichmann's adviser on Italian affairs, who lost no time in making it clear that he had no intention of respecting fascist laws designed to prevent him from making Italy *judenrein*. In vain Buffarini protested against the "illegal" deportation of Italian Jews to the East; in vain he requested the commandants of concentration camps not to hand Jewish internees over to the SS. The fate of the Jews in German-occupied Italy was no longer in his hands. By the end of February 1944 the Fossoli concentration camp was under direct German administration, becoming a *Durchgangslager* (transit camp) designed to prepare deportation convoys. Thus, after depriving the "non-Aryans" of their property and their freedom, the fascist authorities took part in handing them over to those who would deprive them of their lives. And while it is true that Mussolini did not approve of the Final Solution (as late as 1944 he told his German medical adviser that he was "not an anti-Semite" and that Hitler's treatment of the Jews "did not redound to Germany's honor"), it is no less true that he and his henchmen helped to create the conditions under which the Holocaust in Italy became possible.[22]

At the time of the Italian armistice, on September 8, 1943, there were some 44,500 Jews in Italy and Rhodes, about 12,500 of them foreigners. By the end of the war at least 7,860 of these had lost their lives, including 303 who perished on Italian soil. Of the 6,746 "non-Aryans" who were deported from the German-occupied part of the peninsula, 830 survived; of the 1,820 who were deported from Rhodes, 179 survived. In addition, between 900 and 1,100 victims have not yet been identified.[23]

THE POST-HOLOCAUST ERA

Although Italy shares with Denmark the distinction of saving the highest percentage of Jewish lives, Italian Jewry suffered a crushing blow. In the words of Cecil Roth,

> On paper, it was possible to reconstitute Italian Jewry as it had been in former days; and indeed in some places the recovery, backed by the enthusiasm of the survivors, was both remarkable and instantaneous. It was impossible, however, to bring the dead back to life, impossible to cancel the memory of the evil years, impossible to redress the broken spirits. The devastation of the antisemitic interlude had been vast.

. . . Not only had the habit of Jewish life been interrupted, but in many places its setting had disappeared—the lovely old synagogues ruined, the artistic and literary treasures despoiled, the historic archives dispersed. Such a blow could not fail to leave a lasting impression.[24]

The once proud Italian Jewry was now but a shadow of its former self. Even so, the process of recovery and reintegration started long before the final surrender of all Axis troops in Italy. The first phase of this process was initiated by the Allied military authorities as early as July 12, 1943, thirteen days before Mussolini's "resignation" and nearly twenty-two months before the collapse of Hitler's hold on the peninsula, with the abrogation of the racial laws in Sicily. It ended on October 1 of that year with the liberation of Naples by British troops. It was during this period that several thousand Jews interned at Ferramonti Tarsia and other concentration camps in southern Italy regained their freedom.

The second phase, slightly overlapping the first, began on September 9, 1943, the day after Badoglio's surrender to the Allies, when the Resistenza Armata, the antifascist resistance movement, was born. Jews had played a prominent role in the opposition to fascism since 1919; now they took their part, and more than their part, in the armed struggle against the German invader and his Italian accomplices. Two to three thousand (out of a total of thirty thousand Jews in the half of Italy under the German heel) joined the partisans. Fighting shoulder to shoulder with their gentile comrades-in-arms for the liberation of their country, they were once again Italians among Italians, an accepted and respected part of the people from which they had been excluded five years earlier. For most of them it was an unforgettable experience. Of the four Resistance leaders who ordered the execution of Mussolini in April 1945, two—Emilio Sereni and Leo Valiani—were Jews. Seven of the Jewish partisans were posthumously awarded the Gold Medal, the highest Italian decoration for valor.

The third phase in the process of recovery and reintegration began on June 4, 1944, when Rome was liberated by the American Fifth Army and the Jewish fugitives came out of their hiding places. On the following day, the Allied occupation government installed itself in the city, the anti-Jewish laws were repealed, and a ceremony was held in the main synagogue, attended by Jewish members of the Allied forces. There were indescribable scenes of jubilation as Jewish soldiers from Palestine made their first appearance. But the Roman Jews were in a sorry state. Many of the survivors had lost all their possessions, hunger was rampant, and the local Jewish leadership was in disarray. The formidable task of reorganizing the shattered Jewish community now fell to two American officers, Colonel Charles Poletti, Allied Regional Commissioner for Rome, and his Jewish aide, Captain Maurice F. Neufeld. Both Poletti and Neufeld were highly educated and gifted men, but neither of them was familiar with the complex problems of the Jewish survivors in Rome.

On July 7, 1944, a month after assuming his duties, Poletti dissolved the councils of both the Roman community and the Union of Italian Jewish Communities and forced out the two organizations' presidents, Ugo Foà and Dante Almansi, because of their "fascist past." He then appointed an "extraordinary commissioner" of

Roman Jewry, Silvio Ottolenghi, an attorney, who happened to be a more genuine fascist than either Almansi or Foà. To fill the void in spiritual leadership, Poletti reinstated the former chief rabbi of Rome, Israel Anton Zolli, who had just been dismissed from his post for deserting his flock on April 2. Zolli now retaliated by charging Foà with partial responsibility for Dannecker's *Judenaktion* of October 16, 1943, thus sparking an acrimonious controversy over Jewish collaboration and complicity in the Holocaust that has occupied scholars and polemicists ever since. Zolli's return to office met with vigorous opposition from his constituents; even so, he continued to enjoy the backing of the Allied military authorities until February 13, 1945, the day of his conversion to Roman Catholicism. His place was then taken by his predecessor, Rabbi David Prato, a much more popular figure, who had been ousted by the fascists after the promulgation of the racial laws.[25]

Dante Almansi, whose outstanding leadership had earned him the gratitude of thousands of Italian Jews during the years 1939–44, was succeeded as president of the Union of Italian Jewish Communities by Giuseppe Nathan. A banker, Nathan had never been an observant Jew, nor was he involved in the community's internecine feuds. His father, Ernesto, had been a mayor of Rome and grand master of Italian Freemasonry. Nathan accepted the post as a moral obligation, feeling himself "bound in a special way after the abominable persecutions, of which we were the victims."[26] His appointment marked the resumption of the corporate life of Italian Jewry as a whole, although another eleven months passed before the process of liberation was complete.

Meanwhile, steps were taken to restore the Roman Jewish community to its former state. On July 13, 1944, the *Bollettino Ebraico d'Informazione* (Jewish News Bulletin) was first issued. On December 7 the Zionist weekly *Israel* resumed publication. On January 15, 1945, the Italian Zionist Federation was reinstituted; and on January 26 the Rabbinical College was reopened with Zolli as its head. In 1944, when the Jew hunt in the fascist puppet republic was still in full swing, Nathan commissioned Colonel Massimo Adolfo Vitale, a gallant airman, to set up and direct the Search Committee for Deported Jews, the precursor of the Jewish Documentation Center in Milan. On April 29, 1945, the Germans signed a document providing for the unconditional surrender of all Axis forces in Italy by May 2. After twenty months of anguish, Italian Jewry was finally free to resume its rightful place in gentile society and to reconstruct itself according to its own design. Although a beginning had been made, the obstacles to recovery were still formidable.[27]

Governmental reactions to the Holocaust were shaped by a wide variety of factors, internal as well as external, positive as well as negative. Since the fall of Mussolini the positive and negative aspects of these reactions have been inextricably intertwined, with paradoxical results. The men who overthrew Mussolini in July 1943 had been his accomplices for over two decades; but at that moment they were the only ones who could replace him. Many of them, including the king, who had signed the anti-Jewish laws, had been actively involved in the execution of Mussolini's racial policy. But their involvement had been due to cowardice and opportunism, not to anti-Semitism. Having gone over to the Allied camp, they were only too eager to turn their backs on the racial legislation. Indeed, Badoglio included three "non-Aryans"—Mario Fano, Guido Jung, and Dino Philipson—in his Cabinet of Under-Secretaries in November 1943, two months before the abrogation of the anti-Jewish laws. True, their break with Mussolini was frankly reactionary in its political inspiration. While disengaging themselves from fascism, they feared the resurgence of antifascism. Given their total dependence on the Allies, however, they had no choice but to cooperate with the Resistenza in the struggle against the common enemy; nor could they refuse to initiate a program of "defascistization." On September 16, 1943, Badoglio signed an agreement with U.S. General Dwight D. Eisenhower that obliged him to disband all fascist organizations and to cancel all legislation involving discrimination on racial, religious, or political grounds. On April 22, 1944, barely six weeks before his resignation, he formed a cabinet on which sat the representatives of the six major antifascist parties, including the Communists.[28]

But while the need for an antifascist purge was universally accepted, even staunch antifascists recognized that the task of defascistization was bound to be a difficult one. For one thing, there were very few Italians who had not compromised themselves with the fascist regime. For another, the Allies, despite their determination to extirpate fascism, needed Mussolini's former associates to fight the Germans. Even the Soviet Union established diplomatic relations with the Badoglio government. Last but not least, the ideological conflicts between the various Italian factions (which grew increasingly violent after the defeat of the common enemy) prevented a unified stand on the subject of defascistization. An American memorandum entitled "Treatment of Former Fascists by the Italian Government," written six weeks before the end of the war, explained:

> Almost two years after the fall of Mussolini no far-reaching progress appears to have been made in Italian defascistization beyond the laying of a substantial groundwork. . . . Although all political factions in Italy agree on the theoretical necessity of defascistization, they have not been able to accept a common criterion for activities which identify Fascism or to agree on the method in which defascistization should be carried out. It is on this issue that the clearest indications of a fundamental split between the philosophy of the Italian right and left may be observed. On the left, the Communist and Socialist parties have demanded a thorough epuration which included not only former Fascists but whole social categories, and these parties are prepared to press their demands with increasing vigor as northern Italy is liberated. The right, on the other hand, has advocated moderation and tolerance in defascistization and has vigorously opposed many of the extreme leftist policies. . . . It seems apparent that the reasons for the deep-rooted divergencies on epuration policies are not to be found solely in the intrinsic difficulties of the epuration program, but reflect and are closely linked with the almost insurmountable political disagreement between right and left.[29]

With the cessation of hostilities and the outbreak of the Cold War, the fight against fascism inevitably receded into the background, overshadowed by the clash between Soviet totalitarianism and Western democracy. By an irony of fate it fell to

Palmiro Togliatti, the Italian Communist leader, to put an end to the antifascist purge in April 1947 when he was minister of justice in Alcide De Gasperi's six-party cabinet.

During the struggle against the German invader, antifascists had argued fiercely over the new form Italy should take after the war. For the Communists and Socialists, and the reborn Action Party, the Resistenza was a second Risorgimento, an opportunity to complete the work left unfinished in 1861. They realized that this would be a far more formidable task than the mere elimination of fascism; it would involve destroying the roots from which fascism had sprung. The second Risorgimento, like the first, disappointed its protagonists: victory over the fascist tyranny failed to bring the sweeping political and social transformation for which so many partisans had fought. True, a government fully representative of the Resistenza was formed in June 1945 by Ferruccio Parri, leader of the Action Party and chairman of the Committee of National Liberation for Northern Italy. However, social and moral revolution was not what the Allied armies, the Christian Democrats, or the Communists had in mind. Parri's six-party coalition lasted less than six months; its resignation dashed the hopes of the resistance generation. After 1945 the partisans were replaced by the regular army and police forces, just as Garibaldi's Redshirts had been replaced eighty years before. Many antifascists returning from prison or exile reached high positions in postfascist Italy, but they had to accept as colleagues men who had never opposed Mussolini.

On June 2, 1946, the monarchy was abolished, and the first general election following Liberation was held. It resulted, not in the reemergence of a liberal Italy, but in the victory of the two forces that since 1861 had been outside the liberal state, Catholicism and socialism. The Christian Democrats won 207 seats, the Socialists 115, and the Communists 104. The Action Party, with only 7 seats, suffered a mortal blow. The triumph of the Catholics marked a decisive reversal of the secular and anticlerical orientation that had been a principal component of the Risorgimento and to which the Italian Jews owed their emancipation. The champions of the secular state were understandably alarmed; it seemed to them that the disappearance of the monarchy had opened the road to a clerical republic and that the Vatican had resumed its ancient sway over Rome.

When Parri resigned in December 1945, he was succeeded by the leader of the Christian Democrats, Alcide De Gasperi, who thus became Italy's first Catholic prime minister. In May 1947, a month after the antifascist purge ended, he ejected the Communists and socialists from his coalition. This shattered what little was left of the resistance forces. In April 1948, at the height of the Cold War, a general election was fought on the single issue of resistance to Communism. This time the Christian Democrats, with all the resources of the Vatican and Catholic Action (the Catholic lay movement elevated to national prominence by Pius XI) behind them, obtained an absolute majority, with 307 seats. This massive intrusion of the church into public life signified a final defeat for the liberal and democratic heirs of the first Risorgimento and put a halt to their attempt to make Italy more secular and more egalitarian.

These developments affected the way the government reacted to the Holocaust. Given Italy's unconditional alignment with the West, the victory of clericalism over secularism, worrying though it was, could not be permitted to interfere with the rehabilitation of the Jewish minority. Measures designed to restrict Jewish influence (as distinct from Hitler's policy of genocide) were perfectly acceptable to the Holy See;[30] but they were unacceptable to the Western democracies and incompatible with democratic principles. De Gasperi, for all his loyalty to the Vatican, was a democrat, not a clerical reactionary. He made a point of sharing power with the parties of the secular Center (Liberals, Republicans, and Social Democrats) even when he was not dependent upon their votes in parliament, thus signifying his acceptance of the political heritage of the Risorgimento. It is hardly surprising, therefore, that the reinstatement of the Jews initiated by Mussolini's accomplice Badoglio continued at an accelerated pace during De Gasperi's term of office, which lasted until July 1953.[31]

The ideological conflict between the Right and the Left had no bearing whatever on the Jewish issue. The need for abrogating the anti-Jewish legislation and repairing the damage caused by the racial persecutions was universally accepted. The former fascist hierarchs, except those who had opposed the racial laws in 1938, generally maintained an embarrassed silence on the subject. The neofascist apologists generally admitted that Mussolini's anti-Jewish policy had been a deplorable error. Even Giorgio Almirante, the founder and secretary of the neofascist Movimento Sociale Italiano (Italian Social Movement), who, as chief editor of *Il Tevere* and editorial secretary of *La Difesa della Razza* (The Defense of the Race), had played a prominent role in the racial campaign, found it necessary to dissociate himself from anti-Semitism and totalitarianism.[32] There were still plenty of unrepentant fascists and Jew-baiters in postfascist Italy, but the "Jewish Question" had ceased to be a factor in Italian politics.

Italy's new rulers, however, failed to recognize the uniqueness of the Holocaust. They equated the Jewish victims of racial persecution with the gentile victims of political persecution, and the Jewish survivors of Auschwitz with the gentile survivors of German prisoner-of-war camps. For Italy's Jews the death of 7,860 non-Aryans was a unique tragedy; virtually every Italian Jewish family had lost close relatives and friends. For Mussolini's successors the Holocaust was only a minor chapter, however deplorable, in the Italian drama. Nor was this approach peculiar to the Christian Democrats; even a liberal like the world-famous philosopher Benedetto Croce, who was a member of Badoglio's second cabinet, urged the Jews not to claim any special privileges.[33]

The government also tended to minimize Italy's share of the blame for the Holocaust. Since 1938 it had been widely believed by both supporters and opponents of fascism that Mussolini's race laws were no more than an example of "scandalous German interference." After the war these views received support from Mussolini's accomplice and successor, Marshal Badoglio, who affirmed in his memoirs that the racial legislation was not only explicitly requested by Hitler but actually "imposed" by him. As for the Final Solution on Italian soil, it was the work of the German occupiers; the Italians had been powerless to prevent it. Even before the cessation of hostilities the Italian foreign ministry began to exploit the propaganda value of Italian rescue activities in the occupied territories. The other side of the picture was ignored.[34]

Also significant was the fact that a fundamental contradiction in the new constitution was not resolved. The liberal provisions of the new constitution, which guaranteed equality to all citizens "regardless of sex, race, language, religion, and political opinions," existed side by side with the repressive clauses of the fascist civil and criminal codes, which were left in force. The problem was compounded by the incorporation in toto of both Mussolini's concordat with the Vatican and his Law on the Italian Jewish Communities into the constitution, despite their manifest inconsistency with the letter and spirit of the document. Given these incompatibilities, it is hardly surprising that the constitutional ban on the reorganization of the Fascist Party "in any form whatsoever" was never enforced.[35] The negative implications of De Gasperi's victory were, of course, reinforced by the dismal failure of the antifascist purge.

Finally, despite De Gasperi's commitment to democratic principles, Catholic rule was bound to limit the role of the Jews in government and their access to official patronage, all the more so because the Christian Democrats enjoyed a longer period of unbroken political dominance—from 1945 to 1993—than any other democratic party in the world. It is worth noting in this connection that in an electoral address on May 3, 1951, De Gasperi publicly accused the Jews of unwarranted interference in Christian affairs. His successor, Amintore Fanfani, twice party secretary, three times president of the Senate, and five times prime minister between 1954 and 1983, had publicly supported Mussolini's racial policy in May 1939. In the early 1960s Ettore Bernabei, then director general of the state radio and television network, Radio Italiana (RAI), discussed with Fanfani, then prime minister, and other leading Christian Democrats ways to limit Jewish influence on the media.[36]

The Holocaust and the Recrudescence of Anti-Semitism

Since 1938 observers of the Italian scene, both gentile and Jewish, have paid tribute to the philo-Semitism of the Italian masses. Lord Perth, the British ambassador in Rome, reported in December 1938 that the anti-Jewish legislation was "almost universally unpopular in Italy, even among most Fascists" and was "generally suspected to be due to German pressure." Sir Andrew McFadyean, a prominent British Liberal, affirmed in January 1939 (in a memorandum addressed to the heads of British Jewry) that in spite of the racial campaign, anti-Semitism outside a restricted government circle was "non-existent" in Italy. Daniel A. Binchy, an eminent Catholic scholar, made the same point eleven months later: "Prudence may have compelled the observance of the letter of the anti-Jewish laws, but their spirit has never been observed and is not observed to-day. The cruel measures designed to segregate Italian Jews from the social and economic life of their fellow-countrymen have been mitigated as far as possible by the pity and consideration shown by Italians of all classes."[37]

When Hitler extended the Final Solution to the German-occupied part of Italy, many Italians quietly rallied to the support of the Jews. The following extracts from the diary of Bernard Berenson, the celebrated Jewish humanist and art historian, who was living in Florence, throw light on the resistance Eichmann's emissaries had to face:

> January 25th, 1944: . . . I am seeing friends who, unlike myself, have no drop of Jewish blood to taint their veins. They are at least as horrified over the treatment of Jews as I am, and can get it as little out of their minds. . . . The other day a parish priest of this diocese was arrested for harbouring a Jew. The Cardinal of Florence (Mgr. Elia della Costa) intervened, declaring that he himself was the culprit and requesting to be jailed in place of the priest; which, of course, resulted in the liberation of the prisoner. . . .

> September 1945: . . . [The Italian people's] sympathies for suffering, whether physical or moral, are wide and warm. . . . Nowhere else have I encountered like generosity and self-sacrifice. Marchese and Marchesa Serlupi Crescenzi were little more than acquaintances when they offered me shelter at serious risk to their peace of mind, and even to their personal safety. They took me in, and treated me not as a refugee . . . but as if it made them happy to have me, to serve me, to see to my every comfort. . . . Despite alarms and excursions, nobody in any situation gave me away. I learned afterwards that some friends deliberately avoided finding out where I was, not to run the risk of betraying it under torture.[38]

After the Holocaust the spokesmen of Italian Jewry hastened to express their wholehearted agreement with Berenson's tribute to their gentile fellow citizens. The following report published in the *American Jewish Year Book,* which deals with the period from September 18, 1944, to September 7, 1945, accurately reflects the prevailing view:

> When Rabbi Zolli spoke of the period during which the Nazis had been in control of Rome, he contrasted "the good hearts of the Italians" with the cruelty of the Germans: "The whole Italian population has been wonderful to us." Verification of this impression of the fine attitude and behavior of the Italian people and the Catholic Church came from other sources as well. From Jerusalem, the following was sent to the *New York Times:* "Many reports have been received here from Jewish military chaplains serving in Italy and from Palestinian Jewish soldiers of the sympathetic and helpful conduct of the Italian people under the Fascist regime toward persecuted Jewish inhabitants. These letters confirm that the Italians did all they could to rescue and harbor Jews fleeing from oppression and certain death, even providing false passports for them under Italian names. . . . It is also known that many Jews found refuge in the papal villa at Castel Gandolfo as well as inside the Vatican City itself.[39]

A subsequent *Year Book* report covering the year 1949 claimed that there was "rather less fear of anti-Semitism in Italy than in most other countries because the experiences of the war and the postwar attitude to the Jewish displaced persons had shown that the Italian people had a high resistance to anti-Semitism." Sergio Piperno, president of the Union of Italian Jewish Communities, affirmed in a public speech in December 1956 that the entire Italian population had stood by the Jews during the twenty months of the German occupation. In 1961 Hulda Cassuto Campagnano, a Jewish woman from Florence, stated at the Eichmann trial in Jerusalem that "every Italian Jew who survived owed his life to the Italians." In 1983 Henry Stuart Hughes, an eminent historian and an acute student of Italian Jewry, maintained that Mussolini's racial policies might be dismissed "as a mere 'parenthesis' in a national experience which overall had been quite the contrary," the basic assumption being that in modern Italy anti-Semitism had been an anemic growth, "without deep roots in popular sentiment." True, there had been anti-Jewish incidents, but "on a modest scale and contingent on events only tangentially related to Italian Judaism." A few Catholic publications "were seeking to reawaken a long-dormant antagonism," but this kind of polemic "was bound eventually to subside." "All things considered," then, "there was little evidence that . . . Italy's Jews felt personally threatened or denied public acceptance. The vast majority believed it possible to live at peace in their own country; they felt no compulsion to emigrate to Israel." In Italy as elsewhere in Europe, the Holocaust had drawn a deep gash through contemporary Jewish history. Even so, Italian Jewry remained unique: "It was not a community swollen beyond recognition, such as that in France. It was not a community reduced to a pathetic handful of survivors, such as those of Central and Eastern Europe. It was a small but quietly assured community, at ease with itself and with its non-Jewish neighbors." And as recently as 1993 a similar view was expressed by Renzo De Felice, the leading Italian authority on Jews under fascism, although by then the rise of anti-Semitism had become a source of serious concern to the Jewish community.[40]

Some Jewish activists took a less optimistic view, most particularly Colonel Vitale, director of the Search Committee for Deported Jews, who remarked in 1953 that with respect to anti-Semitism, foreigners were apt to exaggerate the difference between Italy and the rest of Europe. True, the racial laws had been abrogated and some of the material damage done by the Nazis and their fascist accomplices had been repaired; but it was no less true that the fascist poison had "left traces which are, unfortunately, firmly rooted and which nothing will destroy":

> A new notion has risen in the spirit of the Italian people: *there is a difference between Jews and non-Jews.* During my childhood and my youth, during and after the First World War, the only grudges, if any, which existed at the time, had a religious basis. The Jew was, like a Protestant, an Italian who followed a religious faith other than the one accepted by the majority. Now the Jew is thought of as belonging to another people. He is considered in a way as an *intruder* and is accused of occupying positions which should be given *to Italians.* The creation of the State of Israel has strengthened this feeling of difference, in spite of the admiration it has aroused as a political and historical event. . . . It is inevitable that this should arouse some doubts . . . as to the loyalty of the Jews to the country where they were born and where they have lived for centuries. It gives people the idea that the Jews are different . . . and that they should therefore *move out of their country.*

According to Vitale, the situation was further aggravated by the prevailing obsession with Communism, which had resulted in the failure of defascistization and the resurgence of fascism in Italy, and by the "omnipotence" of the Holy See, "at the moment the political and cultural master" on the peninsula. Every day brought "new proofs of the hostile action of the Vatican, of its ever renewed tendency to protect Germans, to oppose the State of Israel and to do nothing to prevent churches and schools from being sources of anti-Semitism."[41]

Although Vitale's account was not free from exaggeration and distortion, he correctly diagnosed several sources of friction that were to have a considerable impact on non-Jewish reactions to the Holocaust. In the ensuing years, it became increasingly clear that relations between Jews and gentiles in Italy had indeed taken a turn for the worse. In 1960 the Nobel prize–winning poet Salvatore Quasimodo denounced Jewish financial power, adding that the Jews were "a race that has never been able to feel tied to a country and a society." And in the following year certain Italian journalists and lawyers questioned the right of the state of Israel to try Adolf Eichmann. One eminent jurist, Francesco Carnelutti, compared the Eichmann trial to that of Jesus before the Hebrew Sanhedrin. A young scholar, Stefania Vaselli, wrote in *Concretezza* (Concreteness), a biweekly review published by the minister of war in Amintore Fanfani's third cabinet, that the Jews posed a spiritual and material threat to the Christian world and that their misdeeds against the gentiles had been paid for by the Nazi massacre of six million of them.

Another article attacking the Eichmann trial and its defenders, which appeared in the Catholic magazine *La Voce della Giustizia* (The Voice of Justice), sparked a legal conflict with the Jewish community. According to the anonymous author, the Jews, "by not recognizing the divine innocence of Christ, must be considered as deicides even to-day . . . the unconscious and permanent authors of the crucifixion of Christ must be deprived of the possibility to judge those not belonging to their progeny. . . . Jews are totally lacking in morality." The president of the Turin Jewish community, Ugo Levi, and more than fifty other Italian Jews sued the magazine's editor, the magistrate Giovanni Durando, under a law prohibiting the publication of calumnies against the Jewish religion and the defamation of Jewish citizens as a group. They asked for damages of five hundred thousand lire, to be paid to the Associazione Nazionale ex Deportati Politici nei Campi (National Association of ex-Deportees to Nazi Camps). For his part, the public prosecutor demanded an eleven-month jail sentence and a fine of fifty thousand lire. Durando, while refusing to divulge the name of the article's author, declared that he took full responsibility for its contents. He defended the article on the ground that it was a statement of religious principles. He claimed that he personally had nothing against Jews as individuals and that as a partisan during World War II he had saved many Jewish lives.

The court acquitted Durando on the charge of libeling the Jewish religion "because the fact in question does not constitute an offense" but found that he had defamed Jewish citizens "because of [the article's] lack of evidence" to back its claim. Durando appealed the second half of the verdict because he wanted an unconditional acquittal. The public prosecutor appealed for a reversal of the acquittal. In January 1963 the court of appeals in Genoa, declaring that "the fact does not constitute an offense," upheld the lower court's decision. In the same month, the investigation section of the court of appeals in Bologna refused a German request for the extradition of Erhard Kröger, a former SS officer who had ordered the slaughter of

2,245 Jews in Poland during World War II. After the execution of Eichmann, the chief rabbi of Rome, Elio Toaff, received a letter from a self-styled "Italian Nazi" who denounced the Jews as "assassins" and called for revenge: "Eichmann . . . shall be avenged. Sooner or later 18 million Jews will pay with their lives."[42]

The Eichmann trial was followed by two other events that contributed to the growth of anti-Semitism in Italy during the 1960s. The first was the Second Vatican Council's pronouncement absolving the Jews from the age-old charge of deicide. The council's action shocked Catholic reactionaries and disinterred the whole baggage of anti-Semitic folklore. The second was the Six-Day War and the emergence of the Palestine Liberation Organization. After the conflict, anti-Jewish graffiti increasingly included slogans extolling the deeds of the Palestinian "freedom fighters" and comparing the state of Israel to the Third Reich. In theory, it is possible to be both an anti-Zionist and a philo-Semite (liberal philo-Semites, it should be noted, have generally been hostile to the idea of Jewish nationhood). In practice, however, the anti-Zionist crusade regularly spilled over into outright anti-Semitism: "Israel has committed aggression, Israel is the State of the Jews, hence the Jews are aggressors."[43] The Yom Kippur War of October 1973 and the ensuing Arab oil embargo cast the Jewish state in an even more unappealing light. Not only had it changed from a refuge for the persecuted into a warrior nation but it had become a serious impediment to the conduct of everyday life. The effect these developments had on Italian reactions to the Final Solution was marked: if the Jews were no better (or perhaps even worse) than their erstwhile persecutors, there was no longer any reason to feel sorry for the survivors of Auschwitz and Treblinka. Naturally, there were gentiles who disagreed; but there were also Jews who felt obliged to join the anti-Israel chorus.[44]

Further manifestations of anti-Semitism on the peninsula came in 1982, at the time of the Israeli invasion of Lebanon. Enormous public demonstrations, some having nothing to do with the war, were staged, accompanied by anti-Jewish slogans, graffiti, and attacks on Jewish institutions. This outbreak was, however, short-lived, coming to a sudden halt on October 9, after a terrorist exploded a bomb on the steps of the Rome Synagogue, killing Stefano Taché, a two-year-old boy, and injuring about forty other people. The incident provoked a strong reaction from Roman Jewry, most particularly from Rabbi Toaff, who declared at a press conference that anti-Jewish feeling had by now "infected large strata of the Italian population." He had no doubt that the blame for this must be put on the numerous politicians and journalists who, instead of confining themselves to legitimate criticism of Israeli policy, had used the invasion of Lebanon as a pretext for an all-out attack on "the Jewish people as a whole."[45]

Four years later Italian soccer fans suddenly started using anti-Jewish slogans and the vocabulary of the Holocaust to annoy opponents, calling them "Jews" and threatening to send them "to the ovens." At the annual showdown between Milan's two soccer teams, Inter and Milan, in 1986, a crowd of Inter fans carried an enormous banner that read, "MILANISTI—EBREI, STESSA RAZZA, STESSA FINE" (Milan Fans—Jews, Same Race, Same Destiny). And in 1988 Inter fans hoisted a banner during the Milan-

Inter match whose message was "BERLUSCONI—BASTARDO EBREO" (Berlusconi—Jewish Bastard), referring to Milan's owner, Silvio Berlusconi, the future prime minister, who happens to be a gentile.

In April 1987 posters demanding "CANNIBALS, BEDOUINS, RABBIS, OUT OF ITALY!" were plastered on the walls of the University of Bologna on the day of a demonstration by students belonging to the neofascist Italian Social Movement. The poster depicted an African with a ring in his nose and a sign reading "AIDS" attached to his arm, an Arab with a knife in one hand and a bomb in the other, and a Jew with a hooked nose, dollars spilling from his pocket, being kicked by a hobnailed SS boot. These crude manifestations of racism could be shrugged off as the residue of an old, discredited fascist culture. The level of concern heightened, however, when Catholic publications started dusting off the vile old theme of an international Jewish conspiracy. In November 1987 *Chiesa Viva* (The Living Church), a Catholic magazine printed in Brescia, republished extracts of the notorious *Protocols of the Elders of Zion,* with a new introduction by a priest, Padre Luigi Villa. The cover of the magazine depicted Christ on the cross with a Star of David next to him. "Obviously we do not want to engage in anti-Semitism," Villa wrote, "but we continue our struggle against that minority of ultra-powerful Jews who conspire to divide the Church of Christ. We say that the Jews, although called the Chosen People in the Old Testament, have used their undeniable intellectual talents in the service of Evil, Perversion, and Mammon . . . in order to complete the Jews' ancient plan of universal domination."[46]

Also in November 1987 the editor of the economic weekly *Milano Finanza* (Milanese Finance), Paolo Panerai, wrote a cover story about three Jews who had benefited from the October 19 stock market crash. "A question of nose," the article began. "A question of hooked nose." Panerai went on to say that the Jewish financiers Carlo De Benedetti, Edmond de Rothschild, and James Goldsmith, aided by a nose for finance developed over centuries, were the first to sniff out the impending collapse. He further hinted at the responsibility of the "Jewish lobby" for the disaster. Afterward, he indignantly rejected charges of anti-Semitism, insisting that he had been praising rather than attacking the Jewish financiers. In March 1988, however, the Association of Journalists for the Region of Lombardy issued a statement condemning Panerai's use of racial characterizations. It should be noted that De Benedetti, the son of a Jewish father and a gentile mother, did not consider himself a Jew but was frequently referred to as one in the press.

Although disturbing, these incidents attracted little attention. It was the Intifada, the Palestinian uprising begun in December 1987, that suddenly brought the "Jewish Question" into virtually every living room in Italy. Once again, anger at the Jewish state was directed toward the nation's tiny Jewish minority. Anti-Semitic graffiti appeared in at least a dozen Italian cities: "Hitler was Right," "Jews to the Ovens," "Vote Yes on the Referendum to Reopen Auschwitz." Prominent Jews routinely received anonymous threatening letters and telephone calls; copies of Jewish publications mailed to subscribers were purposely damaged and even destroyed; a left-wing group bombed a Jewish bookstore in Turin. Articles dealing with the situation in Israel's occupied territories regularly condemned "Jewish misuse of the western guilt complex about the Holocaust in order to achieve purely political goals."[47]

In February 1988 Massimo Giuliani, in an article published in the weekly *Segnosette* (Seven Signs), defined Israeli policy toward the Palestinians as a "genocide, carried out by yesterday's victims," adding that he could "understand Christians who are currently reconsidering the legitimacy of the reasons for the existence of the State of Israel and the relations between the Christian and Jewish faiths." In the following month Giovanni Rulli denounced Israeli policy in *Civiltà Cattolica* (Catholic Civilization), the authoritative Jesuit monthly, affirming that "Israeli crimes" in the occupied territories were similar to those "Jews suffered when it seemed that they were all fated to perish in the 'Final Solution.'" When an elderly death-camp survivor entered a Rome hospital, a doctor, spotting the tattooed number on the man's arm, turned to him and said, "How many Palestinians have you killed to-day?"

One of the more surprising characteristics of this anti-Semitism is that much of it is coming not from the neofascist Right but from the antifascist Left. A lot of the anti-Jewish graffiti that have been found on the walls of synagogues and Jewish stores are scrawled in red spray paint, the signature of the Left, rather than the black paint of the neofascists. Using Marxist dialectics, the radical Left associates Israel with Western imperialism and Jews in general with the rise of capitalism, thus giving anti-Jewish prejudice an intellectual respectability that is lacking on the far Right.

The Intifada spurred extreme leftist organizations, chief among them Democrazia Proletaria (Proletarian Democracy), to call for a boycott of Israeli products. Some groups adopted terrorist methods. In April 1988 several Haifa grapefruits were injected with what appeared to be a dark poison. It took several days to determine that the substance was only blue dye, but the hoax succeeded in creating a brief panic. In the same month leftist university students wrecked the Israeli booth at the International Children's Book Fair in Bologna, and an unknown anarchist group set fire to the Rosa Luxemburg Bookstore in Turin. When the owner of the shop, a gentile and a prominent figure in the Radical Party, tried to organize a public debate on Israel at Turin University, leftist students threw grapefruits at the stage and shouted slogans to prevent him from speaking.

Public demonstrations against Israel's policy in the occupied territories regularly served as a pretext for attacking the Jews as such. In the words of Paolo Mieli, a prominent Italian Jewish journalist, formerly an editorial writer for the Turin daily *La Stampa* and now editor of the Milanese daily *Il Corriere della Sera,* "Demonstrations [in Rome] against Israeli policy would break up with groups of protestors marching to the old ghetto area shouting slogans and writing graffiti in the area around the synagogue. The fact that they demonstrate not in front of the Israeli Embassy but in front of the synagogue is a sign of anti-Semitism. What does the temple have to do with the occupied territories? It is as if someone blamed the Vatican for the situation in Northern Ireland." In the polemics of the Left the terms "Israeli," "Zionist," and "Jew" are often used interchangeably. Many Italian Jews complain that their gentile friends, when discussing events in the Middle East, use the plural *voi* (you) when referring to the Israelis, despite the fact that quite a few members of the Jewish community are left of Center in their politics and are themselves frequently critical of current Israeli policy.[48]

Quite apart from extremism on the Italian Left, anti-Semitism in Italy is also a product of the growing xenophobia stemming from the immigration of more than a million African, Arab, and Asian workers to the country and the influx of southern Italians to the cities of the north. The eruption of anti-Jewish feeling has been accompanied by racial incidents involving all these groups. In the northern regional elections of June 1988, a series of new local parties (the so-called leagues), running on platforms that urged measures to curb the presence of southern Italians, collected between 6 and 7 percent of the vote. "Italy, which has been a homogeneous white society for centuries, is now becoming a multi-racial one," says Tullia Zevi, president of the Union of Italian Jewish Communities. "Suddenly, in moments of economic difficulty, a defensive mechanism, the Le Pen phenomenon, is unleashed. Anti-Semitism is a kind of litmus test. We Jews who have a historical memory of persecution must take racism in general as our battle." Miriam Mafai, a journalist, draws broader conclusions: "In all of Europe, after the fall of the Berlin Wall, there is a violent reprise of the various nationalisms, of the search for exaltation of the single ethnic and religious identity that can lead to the 'ethnic cleansing' we are witnessing in the former Yugoslavia."[49]

While anti-Semitism and anti-immigrant feeling are undeniably related phenomena, their roots are profoundly different. The immigrants are an enormous presence in Italy's major cities; their physical and cultural differences stand out. The Jews, on the other hand, are an inconspicuous minority, blended into the mainstream, of which the gentile majority is generally unaware. Anti-immigrant sentiment appears to be strongest in the working-class neighborhoods in the big cities, where contact is closest and the immigrants are seen as an economic threat. Anti-Jewish sentiment, as recent opinion surveys indicate, is strongest in areas where there are no Jews at all. The vast majority of those who express hostility toward their Jewish fellow citizens have never had any contact with them. Prejudice is highest (14.7 percent) in the southern part of the country, an area from which the Jews were banished four and a half centuries ago. It used to be argued that the absence of a "Jewish Question" in modern Italy was due to the negligible size of the Italian Jewish community; today it is being argued that it may be precisely the numerical insignificance of Italian Jewry that provides the key to the current problem. "For many Italians, the Jews are no longer the family down the street that does not work on Saturday but an abstraction—figures on the television screen beating Palestinian youths."[50]

Opinion polls conducted in 1986, 1988, and 1990 by the Intermatrix and Demoskopea Research Institutes and in 1992 by Demoskopea and Astra have revealed substantial levels of prejudice against Jews and various other minorities. Of the two thousand people surveyed in 1986, 10.8 percent expressed negative feelings for Jews, 17.5 percent expressed sympathy, and 71.7 percent were indifferent. The most disliked minority was homosexuals (47.8 percent), followed by Gypsies (45.4 percent), drug addicts (41.9 percent), Arabs (26.2 percent), atheists (16.8 percent), and blacks

(11.4 percent). When asked whether they would become romantically involved with a Jew, 10.7 percent said they would not. The rate of those admitting to dislike of Jews reached 14 percent among supporters of the Left. The responses were generally based on stereotypes rather than on actual inquiry into Jewish reality; 76.1 percent of those interviewed had never knowingly met a Jew.

The main sources of information about Jews were television, radio, and movies (55.6 percent), school (34.5 percent), the press (27.0 percent), and Catholic religious instruction (21.8 percent). More than half, 52.2 percent, had no idea how many Jews lived in Italy; 20.3 percent thought, correctly, that there were between twenty thousand and one hundred thousand, while 27.6 percent believed there were between one hundred thousand and more than 2 million. Asked to give a definition of the Jews, 10.2 percent did not respond; 31.7 percent defined them as members of a religion, 28.7 percent as a race, 26.5 percent as a people, 23.3 percent as inhabitants of the state of Israel, and 14.4 percent as heirs of a tradition. On the subject of the Middle East conflict, 36.7 percent offered no opinion, while 22.9 percent put the main blame for the trouble on the Arabs, 19.1 percent on the Americans, 16.1 percent on the Soviets, 9.6 percent on the Israelis, 7.8 percent on all the parties involved, and 3.8 percent on others (Libyans, British, Palestinians). The main charges leveled against the Jews were that they identified themselves with Israel rather than with Italy (59.7 percent), they dwelt too much on the persecutions they had suffered (43.8 percent), they were stingy (40.7 percent), they looked down on the rest of mankind (33.2 percent), the erstwhile victims of persecution had themselves become persecutors (22.8 percent), they were the pioneers of racial discrimination (20.6 percent), and they were often guilty of subversive activities (19.4 percent). The respondents who thought that the Jews ought to leave Italy and go to Israel numbered 19.1 percent.[51]

Subsequent surveys, conducted after the outbreak of the Palestinian uprising, indicate that the anti-Semitism is at least partly independent of current events in the Middle East. The results of the 1988 poll hardly differed from those of the first poll. Of the nineteen hundred people interviewed, 10.6 percent said they disliked Jews, while 17.5 percent expressed sympathy for them, and 71.9 percent were indifferent. The Arabs again fared worse, despite the widespread sympathy for the Palestine Liberation Organization and the equally widespread hostility to Israel: 16.9 percent of the respondents expressed antipathy toward them, 15.3 percent sympathy. In 1990 the picture remained unchanged: 10.6 percent of the respondents again admitted disliking Jews, while 18.4 percent expressed positive feelings toward them, and 71.0 percent were indifferent to them. The Arabs still fared worse, despite the pro-Arab policy of the Italian government and the virulent anti-Zionism of the Italian media: 16.1 percent of those polled were hostile to them, 18.1 percent favorably disposed.

Of the 1,064 persons interviewed in 1992, 44.2 percent were of the opinion that the Jews, in addition to being members of a different religion, had "cultural, social, and political characteristics, which set them apart from the rest of the population"; 10.3 percent charged them with religious intolerance, 15.2 percent regarded them as aliens, 18.4 percent thought they should stop dwelling on the Holocaust, and 24.1

percent affirmed that Jews had a "special relationship with money." About 4 percent believed that the Holocaust was a myth. Other signs of anti-Semitism existed in 1992 as well: clashes between Jews and neofascist youths, desecration of cemeteries, and anti-Jewish graffiti on the walls of synagogues and public buildings ("Death to the Jews," "Jews not wanted," "Six million are few"). Jewish-owned stores in Rome were plastered with yellow stars emblazoned with the words "Zionists out of Italy."[52] Anti-Semitism was not stronger in 1992 than in 1938; but because this time it came from the people, it seemed worse.

What particularly worried Italian Jews was the impact of anti-Zionism and anti-Semitism on Italian reactions to the Jewish tragedy in World War II, for Jewish identity, in Italy as elsewhere, was largely articulated around the Holocaust. Whatever their own reservations about Israeli policy in the occupied territories, they felt bound to protest against the prevailing tendency to equate the Israelis (and, by extension, the Jews everywhere) with the SS.

Italian Jewry's Reaction to the Holocaust

When Mussolini took the anti-Semitic plunge in 1938, Italy's Jews were on the way to self-extinction; for many, if not most, of them, Judaism was a matter of faint recollection, linked to a tradition that had been dormant for at least a generation and a half. The racial persecutions, culminating in the Final Solution, compelled them to rediscover their Jewish identity. Andrea Tabet, a prominent Jewish activist in Rome, put the point well when he wrote in 1948:

> In general, Italian Jewish activities of this period (May 1946–April 1947) were characterized on the one hand by the return of normal function to communal organs through the material, administrative, and moral reconstruction of preexisting institutions and, on the other hand, by the fresh impulses and irresistible upsurge in our life resulting from American aid and from our new consciousness, born of profound tragedy, that in Europe today we can no longer be Jews in name only but must be Jews in fact. The survivors of the great cataclysm have learned that the Jewish problem, however one may seek to resolve it, is a problem that touches all Jews without exception and that it cannot be ignored as it has been in the past. . . . Italian Jewry has definitely taken a step forward in an understanding of itself.[53]

In 1961 Tabet recalled that a century earlier, with the unification of Italy, Italian Jewry had been "swept by a profound enthusiasm for the nation and the state." Jews of all social classes had participated actively in national life, and their achievement had been notable. But when they came to realize that assimilation was no antidote to prejudice, their enthusiasm evaporated. True, since the downfall of fascism the Jewish survivors had largely recovered from the moral and material injuries inflicted on them; but they still distrusted the state that had betrayed them. "For the most part, young people hesitated to put their hopes in the careers from which their fathers had been driven in 1938 and avoided precisely those occupations in which Italian Jews had formerly been outstanding. Their tendency was to accentuate their characteristics as a minority and withdraw more and more from national life, politically as well as privately. In any case, the dominant position of the Christian Democratic party sharply circumscribed the potential political role open to the Jews." Tabet still thought that "no significant anti-Semitism existed either officially or as a feeling in the population at large," despite the swastika epidemic that had spread to Italy in January 1960.[54]

In the ensuing years, however, the recrudescence of anti-Jewish feeling served to increase the distrust and accelerate the process of withdrawal. By the late 1980s Jews had all but disappeared from public life at the national level, although Italy had meanwhile undergone a process of secularization that resulted in the virtual disestablishment of the Catholic Church by the state and a drastic reduction of its influence.[55] In 1990 Jews in Italy were an inconspicuous presence (a mere thirty-two thousand in a nation of nearly fifty-eight million) and all but indistinguishable from their gentile neighbors; even so, by 1990 anti-Semitism had become the object of intense concern to Jews and gentiles alike.[56] It still is.

The reaction against assimilation (as distinct from emancipation) was accompanied by an equally strong reaction against the traditional anti-Zionism of Italian Jews. In 1898 a correspondent for the London *Jewish Chronicle* reported that 99 percent of Italy's Jews were opposed to the Zionist movement. Though probably exaggerated, this statement did reflect the nearly universal hostility that Zionism as a political and national cause encountered among the Jews of the peninsula during the liberal era. After World War I this hostility was reinforced by fascism's all-embracing ("totalitarian") claim on the individual, despite Mussolini's repeated attempts to use Zionism as a tool of his imperial policy.[57]

The forcible rejudaization of Italian Jews between 1938 and 1945 and their consequent reaction against assimilation, however, gave rise to the feeling that the Jews dispersed across the globe should have a territorial center, which could serve them as a cultural and political homeland. The founding of the state of Israel was therefore seen as a necessary and indeed inevitable response to the Holocaust. As has been noted, the appearance of Jewish soldiers from Palestine in 1944 had aroused general enthusiasm among the Jews of Rome. In March 1946 Raffaele Cantoni, a veteran antifascist and an ardent Zionist, was elected president of the Union of Italian Jewish Communities to succeed Giuseppe Nathan. In December of the same year, two Italian delegates were sent to the Zionist congress at Basel. On December 2, 1947, in celebration of Israel's declaration of independence, a crowd of more than a thousand gathered around the Arch of Titus: "From time immemorial, Jews had not walked *under* the Arch, which commemorated the destruction of the Temple and the humiliation of having been deported. Now, as though by a general tacit agreement, many . . . filed by *under* the Arch."[58]

The birth of the Jewish state in May 1948 gave rise to rejoicing in all Italian cities containing Jewish communities. There were special religious celebrations in the synagogues, and the event was discussed with enthusiasm in all Jewish circles. And while few Italian Jews felt any compulsion to emigrate to Israel, the fundraising campaign for Haganah, the Israeli defense forces, met with great success.

Zionist activities were accompanied by intense efforts aimed at combating ignorance about and prejudice toward Judaism. In Turin the Fondazione Ebraica Marchese Cav. De Levy (Jewish Marquis De Levy Foundation) was founded for the purpose of creating a better understanding of Israel among the Jews themselves and among other religious groups. With a similar purpose, Jews and gentiles in the same city cooperated in the establishment of L'Unione contro l'Intolleranza e il Razzismo (Union against Religious Intolerance and Racism), which studied and fought all forms of religious and racial prejudice, giving particular emphasis to the varieties of anti-Semitism. The union sought to attain its objectives through scientific research, cultural meetings, conferences, publications, radio broadcasts, petitions, public denunciation of intolerant acts, and educational activities directed toward creating among Italian youth a spirit of mutual understanding, respect, and solidarity. Two antiracist periodicals were published in Turin, *Fraternità* (Fraternity), the organ of the union, and *L'Incontro* (The Encounter). Together with the Association for Christian-Jewish Friendship, founded in 1950, with branches in Milan, Florence, and Rome, they carried on the fight against anti-Semitism.[59]

In the late 1940s, after the inglorious end of fascism and the worldwide reaction to the horrors of Nazism, it was natural to assume that relations between Jews and non-Jews in Italy had more or less returned to normal, despite the residual manifestations of prejudice and intolerance. In the ensuing years it became increasingly clear that this assumption was premature, if not altogether erroneous. It would be wrong to conclude, however, that Jewish reactions to the Holocaust did not have a major impact on Italian society as a whole.

After Italy's liberation from fascism, Italian scholars were in no hurry to come to grips with the recent past. Those who did study the fascist era generally focused on the antifascist opposition, most particularly on the Resistenza Armata (Second Risorgimento). It was the Union of Italian Jewish Communities that initiated the scientific study of Mussolini's dictatorship in 1960 by commissioning a young gentile historian, Renzo De Felice, to do a study of Italian Jewry under fascism. De Felice's basic assumption—that the Blackshirt movement was dead and could therefore be studied historically—represented a radical departure from conventional wisdom. The title of the resulting book, *Storia degli ebrei italiani sotto il fascismo* (History of the Italian Jews under fascism), was somewhat misleading, since De Felice's central theme was not the Jews of Italy (with whose special problems he was evidently not familiar) but the attitude of the fascist regime and the Italian people toward them. Given this unfamiliarity and the author's ignorance of German sources, it is not surprising that the eighth and final chapter of the work, which covers the period from Badoglio's surrender to the end of the war, is in many ways the least satisfactory. In a book of 634 pages, this chapter comprises a mere 47 pages, of which only 23 deal with the Holocaust. Although 7 pages are devoted to the irrelevant activities of the renegade priest Giovanni Preziosi, Mussolini's "Inspector-General of the Race," only a few lines are given to the Germans who were charged with the task of implementing the Final Solution on Italian soil.

De Felice's main conclusions are unexceptionable: Badoglio failed to abrogate the racial laws before his surrender to the Allies, his assertion to the contrary notwithstanding; Mussolini's brand of anti-Semitism was in a sense more shameful than its German model, since Hitler at least believed in the "guilt" of his Jewish victims, whereas Mussolini was well aware of their innocence; and a large share of the blame for the Final Solution in the German-occupied part of Italy has to be put on Hitler's (willing or unwilling) fascist accomplices. Genocide was firmly embedded in the totalitarian principles common to both dictatorships. On this point De Felice agrees with Piero Caleffi, an antifascist senator of Jewish extraction and a survivor of Mauthausen, who wrote in his memoirs: "Consciously or not, the fascists had been the originators *(anticipatori)* of the extermination camps."[60]

As for the place of Italy's Jews in the history of the Holocaust, De Felice casually affirmed: "The history of the Jewish people in the Diaspora is a true reflection of the history of the peoples and nations among whom they were living." This assumption was promptly challenged by Daniel Carpi, an Israeli scholar of Italian origin, who pointed out that De Felice's presumed "central theme," the Jewish community during the fascist period, remained "disconnected from the framework of general Jewish history":

> The holocaust loses its overall significance; the fact that at that time more than 8,000 Italian Jews lost their lives is diminished in importance by comparison with the hundreds of thousands of Italians who lost their lives in the Second World War. . . . But we may ask: would twenty years in the life of a tiny Jewish community, in itself socially and politically insignificant, merit so much close scrutiny were it not for the twenty fateful months (September 1943–April 1945) in which the Jews of Italy were torn away from this narrow local environment, from its laws and special ways of life and thrown violently into the whirlpool of the events and forces that were at work among the Jewish Communities throughout Europe? Did not, indeed, the holocaust mark not only the tragic end of 8,000 people, but an event of the greatest historical significance, obliging us to reconsider the whole of contemporary history in a completely new light? De Felice the historian does not touch on these problems or, perhaps, he ignores their existence. In either case the tide of events in the period of the holocaust deserves further study and evaluation.[61]

Whatever its shortcomings, De Felice's pioneering study remains basic to an understanding of the vicissitudes of the Jews under fascism; thirty-four years after its publication it is still the indispensable, standard work on the subject. It has, however, been supplemented and corrected by a wealth of scholarly monographs and papers in learned journals that cover every aspect of the Jewish tragedy in Italy.[62] Research on the deportations, originally directed by Colonel Vitale as head of the Search Committee for Deported Jews (from 1944 to 1953), was resumed nineteen years later by the Jewish Documentation Center in Milan, first by Giuliana Donati (from 1972 to 1974) and then by Liliana Picciotto Fargion (since 1979), whose 1991 *Il libro della memoria* (The memory book) is the best account available of the Final Solution in Italy. It contains not only the most complete list of the Jewish deportees from Italy and Rhodes but also the most comprehensive and accurate analysis of Italian complicity in the Jew hunt: at least 1,898 arrests (out of a total of 7,013) were carried out by the Italian police during the period under review, in addition to which the Italians collaborated with the SS in at least 312 roundups. Some Italian officials and policemen sabotaged the anti-Jewish policy they were supposed to implement, but they were the exceptions that prove the rule. Perfunctory, if not actually zealous, execution of criminal orders was the norm. Worse still, hardly any of Hitler's fascist accomplices were brought to trial after the war.[63]

Fargion's indictment of the "Italian Social Republic" was preceded by a heated controversy over the myths of the "kindly Italians" and "fascism with a human face." The debate came to a head in 1986 after Nicola Caracciolo's three-part television program about rescue activities in Italy and the Italian-occupied territories was broadcast nationally. The program included fifty-one interviews of Jewish survivors and Italian rescuers. Caracciolo, in addition to extolling the resistance of the Italian civil and military authorities to Hitler's policy of genocide, claimed that Mussolini himself had aided the Jews, albeit in an "ambiguous and contradictory manner."[64] Rosella Fubini, a Jewish activist in Turin, objected to this view and pointed out that anti-Semitism had been imposed on the Italians by Mussolini, not by Hitler, that until July 1943 Italian Jewry had been persecuted and humiliated by the fascists, not by the SS, and that the opposition of the Italian people to fascist racial policy had been confined to murmured regrets and individual acts of kindness. When Hitler extended the Final Solution to Italy, numerous Italians, especially of the lower classes, had come to the aid of the victims; but there was another side to the picture, which Caracciolo had chosen to ignore.[65] It is this other side—the collaboration and betrayal that led to the deaths of thousands—that constitutes the central theme of *Il libro della memoria*.

But what about the strident contrast between the German and Italian approaches to the Jewish issue in the Axis-occupied territories? As has been noted, this question became a test of Mussolini's remaining autonomy in the course of World War II. For Italian authorities it became a way of asserting what little freedom of action from their German masters they were able to maintain. Even so, experts on the subject agree that the Italian rescue of Jews in Yugoslavia, Greece, and France was not simply a manifestation of fascist resistance to German encroachments on Italian sovereignty; it was also a genuine expression of spontaneous humanitarianism. Commenting on the situation in Axis-occupied Croatia, Daniel Carpi pointed out that

> the initial steps taken to save the Jews were part of the general responsibility of the Italian Army in the region and a continuation of its activities to save the Serbian population. There is no doubt, however, that the Italians eventually devoted special attention to the rescue of the Jews, and for them it assumed political and moral significance far beyond their general interest in maintaining order. . . . Soldiers and civilians on all levels participated in the rescue work and almost everyone regarded the issue first and foremost as a humanitarian problem.

This was true for the other Italian-occupied territories: "In Greece, as in France and Croatia, the Italian civil and military authorities during the occupation years developed extensive activity aimed at protecting the Jews living there from the German racial persecutions and from deportation to the extermination camps in Poland."[66] These tributes to servants of the fascist regime, however well deserved, were a source of embarrassment to Italian Jews, not only because they distracted attention from the other side of the picture but also because they were exploited by neofascist apologists for their own reactionary ends.[67]

In 1978, on the fortieth anniversary of the anti-Jewish laws, the liberal monthly *Il Ponte* (The Bridge) brought out a special issue on fascist crimes against the Jews, in part a response to the resurgence of anti-Semitism on the peninsula. On the fiftieth anniversary of the anti-Jewish laws, international conferences on the subject were held in various Italian cities. The conference held in Rome, on October 17–18, 1988, which had been organized by the Italian parliament, the Union of Italian Jewish Communities, and the Jewish Documentation Center, was attended by the president of the Chamber of Deputies (Nilde Iotti), the vice president of the Senate (Paolo Emilio Taviani), and numerous renowned scholars, including De Felice. The focus was not on Italian rescuers and Jewish survivors but on the criminality of the fascist regime and the catastrophic consequences of its racial policy. De Felice pointed out that there was a special poignancy in the Italian Jewish tragedy, because Italy's Jews had been more fully integrated into the general population than their coreligionists in other countries. Michele Sarfatti, a researcher at the Jewish Documentation Center, warned against underestimating Italian responsibility for the Final Solution: although Auschwitz was the work of the Germans, the roots of the Holocaust on Italian soil lay in the totalitarian pretensions of fascism and in the anti-Jewish crusade Mussolini unleashed in 1938. Gabriele Turi, a noted student of contemporary history, recalled that the fascists had excluded the Jews from schools and universities two months earlier than the National Socialists, although they initiated their racial campaign six years later than the Nazis. Giorgio Israel, a distinguished mathematician, denounced the "treason of the intellectuals," by which he meant the reaction of Italian scholars to the anti-Jewish purge, which had been even more abject than the reaction of their German colleagues. Giovanni Miccoli, an expert on church history, reproached the Catholic hierarchy for its failure to maintain a unified or consistent stance against Mussolini's racial heresy; there was no evidence that in the period under review it had succeeded in shaking off the traditional anti-Judaism inherited from the church fathers. The only participant to pay tribute to the "kindly Italians" was Klaus Voigt, a German scholar, who described the profound difference between Mussolini's internment camps and Hitler's extermination camps.[68]

The fiftieth anniversary of the race laws also witnessed an explosion of articles, books, and pamphlets on crimes against the Jews, including a special issue of *La Rassegna Mensile di Israel* in which Italian reactions to the Holocaust after 1945 were subjected to critical scrutiny. In an introductory note, the editor, Guido Fubini, drew attention to the gap of mutual incomprehension between Jews and gentiles in Italy: while the former were determined to rescue the victims of the Holocaust from oblivion, the latter called for bygones to be bygones. This desire to forget the past was reflected not only in the failure to incorporate the study of the Holocaust into school curricula but also in the obstructionist attitude adopted by a good many members of the judiciary, which had rendered the reinstatement of the Jews more difficult and was mainly due to the retention of former fascists in key positions.

While it was true that until 1943 the fascist brand of anti-Semitism had been less atrocious than its German counterpart, that was no reason to forget or minimize fascist crimes against the Jews.[69] Fubini also read a paper at the fiftieth-anniversary international conference in Florence in October 1988 in which he compared Italian justice to the arrival of the Messiah: "He has not come, he is not coming, and he will not come; but he is on the way."[70]

As for Catholic reactions to the Holocaust, it was generally recognized that Italian priests, monks, and nuns had been in the forefront of those offering help to persecuted Jews, whatever their prejudices against the "Christ-killers."[71] The silence of Pius XII during the Holocaust, on the other hand, has been the subject of heated controversy ever since the appearance of Rolf Hochhuth's play *Der Stellvertreter;* not a few Jews agreed with De Felice that the traditional Catholic position (i.e., prejudice against the "Christ-killers") had prevented the pontiff from viewing the plight of the Jews with a real sense of outrage. Others disagreed, most particularly Michael Tagliacozzo, the leading Italian Jewish authority on the Holocaust in Rome, who pointed out that 477 Jews were sheltered in the Vatican and its enclaves during the German occupation, while another 4,238 found refuge in the numerous monasteries and convents of Rome. The silence of the pope, Tagliacozzo argued, deprived Hitler of a pretext for invading these islands of safety, with fortunate results.[72]

No one doubted that the Catholic "teaching of contempt" was a critical precondition for the Final Solution and that the age-old conflict between church and synagogue still remained unresolved. Vatican hostility toward Israel, largely shared by the Italian government, was a constant source of friction. Even so, both sides realized the need for cooperation in the fight against anti-Semitism. The following excerpts from a report on relations between Jews and Catholics in 1989 shed light on both the progress achieved and the remaining obstacles:

> In January, the archbishop of Siena . . . said that all forms of anti-Semitism had to be eradicated, "for the Jewish people is the beloved brother of the Christian people" and "is still the covenanted people." In February the Pontifical Commission "Iustitia et Pax" issued an interesting and important document on racism. . . . The document praised the role of the Jewish people in the course of history as essential to the divine plan for salvation and redemption. The commission admitted that in the Middle Ages Christians had humiliated the Jews and often accused them of crimes that were never actually committed. . . . The document further affirmed that racism had not yet disappeared and that it was based on "the rejection of differences." From this point of view, anti-Semitism still represented the "most tragic form of racism." Anti-Zionism was defined as different from anti-Semitism, "since it consists of a protest against the State of Israel and its policy"; anti-Zionism, however, often is a way to "conceal anti-Semitism, which fuels and provokes it." . . . This last passage was regarded by several Italian Jewish figures—among them Chief Rabbi Elio Toaff and UCEI President Tullia Zevi—as an important turning point in the official position of the Church on the subject. In September the Episcopal Conference of Italy (CEI; the decision-making body of the Italian Catholic Church formed by all the bishops of the country) decided to celebrate an annual day of "study and meditation to deepen the knowledge of Judaism and further advance the Catholic Church's relations with the Jewish people." . . . By contrast with all this, Pope John Paul II seemed still to express himself, at least in part, in the metaphors of an older Catholic theo-

logical tradition. In speeches delivered in August, he referred to the ancient Israelites as being "disloyal to the Covenant of Sinai." . . . "The history of the Old Covenant shows us that the commitment was often disregarded by them. The Prophets, in particular, rebuked Israel for its sins and lack of loyalty, and saw the grievances of its history as divine punishments."[73]

The pope's remarks came during the controversy over the Carmelite convent at Auschwitz and provoked a wave of sharp criticism from both Jews and Christians involved in interfaith dialogue. The Italian press, while condemning the "intemperance of the extremists" among the Jews who protested the convent, generally supported the Jewish position. Prominent Catholic figures in Italy indicated that the feelings of the Jews, the major victims of the Germans, should be respected and the convent moved elsewhere. According to a survey published by the influential Catholic weekly *Il Sabato* (The Sabbath), most of the Italian bishops agreed with this position. Prime Minister Giulio Andreotti, an ardent Catholic, proposed resettling the convent in the area of the Ardeatine Caves, near Rome, where 335 Italians, including 78 Jews, had been massacred by the SS in March 1944. The proposal was, however, rejected on the grounds that the site should not be consecrated to any one religion.[74]

It now remains to evaluate the memoirs of Jewish survivors. They are important for two reasons: first, because it is due to them that the peripheral status of the Holocaust in Italy was gradually modified, despite its near absence from Italian school curricula; and second, because some of them have had a considerable impact on public opinion. Giorgio Bassani's *Garden of the Finzi-Continis,* a novel about the persecution and deportation of a prominent family of Ferrarese Jews, offers deep insights into the essence of a world that was doomed to disappear yet refused to believe in its own imminent destruction. Silvano Arieti's *The Parnas* is a moving account of the murder of Giuseppe Pardo Roques, the venerable president of the Jewish community at Pisa, by Himmler's myrmidons. Primo Levi's *If This Is a Man,* the story of the ten months he spent at Auschwitz, has become a classic in the genre. It has made Levi the symbol of Jewish survival.

The first edition of Levi's book, published in 1947, fell into oblivion; it was republished in 1958, and from then on the interest of the public has never flagged. In Italy it has sold more than half a million copies. *If This Is a Man* has been translated into eight languages, used as a school textbook, and adapted for radio and theater. At first sight, its success may seem surprising, given the prevailing desire to forget the painful past. It should be borne in mind, however, that Levi did not intend "to formulate new accusations," but rather "to furnish documentation for a quiet study of the human mind." He chose to dwell upon episodes in which ordinary individuals revealed their pluck, their endurance, and their abiding decency. The following observations on Lorenzo, an Italian gentile, are a case in point:

> In concrete terms it amounts to little: an Italian civilian worker brought me a piece of bread and the remainder of his ration every day for six months; he gave me a vest of his, full of patches; he wrote a postcard on my behalf to Italy and brought me the reply. For all this he neither asked nor accepted any reward, because he was good and

simple. . . . I believe it was really due to Lorenzo that I am alive today; and not so much for his material aid, as for his having constantly reminded me by his presence, by his natural and plain manner of being good that there still existed a just world outside our own. . . . Thanks to Lorenzo, I managed not to forget that I myself was a man.

In another well-known passage, Levi remonstrates with a fellow prisoner, ex-sergeant Steinlauf, who is determined to maintain the habits and principles of civilized life by keeping himself clean. Why wash? demands Levi: "We will all die, we are all about to die." To which Steinlauf replies that "precisely because the *Lager* was a great machine to reduce us to beasts, we must not become beasts; that even in this place one can survive, and therefore one must want to survive, to tell the story, to bear witness. . . . We are slaves, deprived of every right, exposed to every insult, condemned to certain death, but we still possess one power—the power to refuse our consent."[75] Though Levi does not gloss over the uglier human qualities that camp life brought to the fore, he focuses on human strength and dignity. Hence his book comes as a welcome antidote to the effects produced by more horror-laden accounts.

In his last completed work, *The Drowned and the Saved,* Levi addresses himself to "the most urgent question": "How much of the concentration camp world is dead and will not return? . . . How much is back or is coming back? What can each of us do so that in this world pregnant with threats at least this threat will be nullified?" His answer was predictably pessimistic:

> The experiences that we survivors of the Nazi Lagers carry within us are extraneous to the new Western generation and become ever more extraneous as the years pass. . . . For the young people of the 1980s, they are matters associated with their grandfathers: distant, blurred, "historical." These young people are besieged by today's problems, different, urgent: the nuclear threat, unemployment, the depletion of resources, the demographic explosion, frenetically innovative technologies to which they must adjust. . . . For us to speak with the young becomes ever more difficult. We see it as a duty and, at the same time, as a risk: the risk of appearing anachronistic, of not being listened to. We must be listened to: above and beyond our personal experiences, we have collectively witnessed a fundamental, unexpected event, fundamental precisely because unexpected, not foreseen by anyone. It took place in the teeth of all forecasts; it happened in Europe; incredibly, it happened that an entire civilized people . . . followed a buffoon whose figure today inspires laughter, and yet Adolf Hitler was obeyed and his praises were sung right up to the catastrophe. It happened, therefore it can happen again: this is the core of what we have to say. . . . I do not intend to nor can I say that it will happen.[76]

In an article on the dispute among German historians, Levi took issue with those who equated the slaughter of the Jews with Stalin's purges:

> That "the gulag came before Auschwitz" is true; but one cannot forget that the aims of the two infernos were not the same. The first was a massacre among peers; it was not based on racial primacy and did not divide humanity into supermen and submen. . . . Nobody has ever reported that in the gulag there took place "selections" like those in the German *Lager,* described so often, during which, by one glance at the front and one at the back, the SS physicians (physicians!) decided who could still

work and who should go to the gas chambers. . . . It was not an "imitation" of "Asiatic" methods, it was perfectly European. . . . If today's Germany sets store by the place to which she is entitled among European nations, she cannot and must not whitewash her past.[77]

Levi believed that an accurate memory of the camps and of what went on there was essential if their reemergence was to be prevented. He wrote *The Drowned and the Saved* in order to provide an antidote to the "silent transition from falsehood to self-deception" and to "the construction of convenient truth." But although the warmth and humanity of his writing won him the admiration of his readers and made him a symbol of the triumph of reason over barbarism, he felt that he was fighting a losing battle. By the end of his life he had become increasingly convinced that the lessons of the Holocaust were destined to be lost as it took a place among the routine atrocities of history. On April 11, 1987, he committed suicide.[78]

The conversion of Italy's Jews to Zionism was a natural, indeed inevitable reaction to the fascist race laws and the Holocaust in Italy; but it was not regarded as such by the gentile majority. With few exceptions, the Italians have never had much use for Jewishness, let alone Jewish nationhood; even in liberal Italy some people worried about the specter of a Jewish "state within the state." The resurgence of anti-Semitism in postfascist Italy, however alarming, was only the tip of the iceberg; the Jews' espousal of Zionism, however platonic, and their reaction against hyperassimilation were a source of friction with Italian society as a whole.

Shortly after World War II, as staunch an opponent of fascism and racism as Benedetto Croce urged his Jewish compatriots to shed their particularism, adding that their failure to do so might give rise to further outbreaks of anti-Semitism. After the Israeli invasion of Lebanon, President Alessandro Pertini, a more militant antifascist than Croce and an equally staunch opponent of anti-Semitism, compared the Palestinians to Hitler's Jewish victims, referring to them as "the Jews of today." Subsequently, in a message to the Italian people, he contrasted "Old Testament vindictiveness" ("an eye for an eye, a tooth for a tooth") with Christian charity. Bettino Craxi, the Socialist leader who served as prime minister from 1983 to 1987, went so far as to compare Yassir Arafat to the Italian Risorgimento hero Giuseppe Mazzini. In February 1987, after signing an agreement with Tullia Zevi, president of the Union of Italian Jewish Communities, Craxi called upon the Jews to follow the example of their ancestors, who after the capture of Rome had assured the king of Italy that henceforth they would be "Italians and nothing but Italians." But times changed; the Jews insisted on their right "to be themselves."[79] After his return from Auschwitz, Primo Levi still regarded himself as an Italian among Italians, but when he spoke of the "extermination of my people," he meant the Jewish people.[80]

For the Jewish survivors and their descendants, in Italy as elsewhere, the Holocaust is still "the past that will not pass away." For their gentile contemporaries that past is now truly the past or hearsay, the term used by Levi. The trauma is not theirs. For them it is enough that the Jews have again been given social and political equality after the fall of fascism. Despite the multiplication of anti-Jewish incidents, there is still plenty of goodwill on both sides; however, the gap of mutual incomprehension has not been bridged.[81] The neofascist triumph in the parliamentary elections of March 27–28, 1994, which caused a great deal of uneasiness in Jewish circles, is likely to widen it even further.[82]

NOTES

1. R. Mahler, *A History of Modern Jewry, 1780–1815* (London, 1971), 105.

2. S. Della Pergola, *Anatomia dell'ebraismo italiano* (Assisi, 1976), 56; M. M. Consonni, "Italy," *American Jewish Year Book, 1992* (Philadelphia, 1992), 353.

3. Mahler, *History*, xxii, 14.

4. A. Milano, *Storia degli ebrei in Italia* (Turin, 1963), 338–57; C. Roth, *The History of the Jews of Italy* (Philadelphia, 1946), 421–63.

5. Milano, *Storia*, 358–69; Roth, *History*, 463–73; A. M. Canepa, "Considerazioni sulla seconda emancipazione e le sue conseguenze," *La Rassegna Mensile di Israel* 47 (January–June, 1981), 45–89; idem, "Christian-Jewish Relations in Italy from Unification to Fascism," in *The Italian Refuge: Rescue of Jews during the Holocaust*, ed. I. Herzer (Washington, D.C., 1989), 13–33.

6. Roth, *History*, 506.

7. A. M. Canepa, "Reflections on Antisemitism in Liberal Italy," *Wiener Library Bulletin* 31, nos. 47–48 (1978), 110.

8. R. Bachi, "The Demographic Development of Italian Jewry from the Seventeenth Century," *Jewish Journal of Sociology* 4 (December 1962), 172–91.

9. A. M. Canepa, "Half-hearted Cynicism: Mussolini's Racial Policies," *Patterns of Prejudice* 13, no. 6 (1979), 19.

10. C. Weizmann, *Trial and Error* (London, 1949), 356; Roth, *History*, 506–8; E. Toaff, "La rinascita spirituale degli ebrei italiani nei primi decenni del secolo," *La Rassegna Mensile di Israel* 47 (November–December 1981), 63–73.

11. L. Villari, *The Fascist Experiment* (London, 1926), 201–2.

12. Renzo De Felice, *Storia degli ebrei italiani sotto il fascismo*, 5th ed. (Turin, 1993), 98–99, 135–38.

13. Ibid., 101–8, 491–502.

14. E. Ludwig, *Colloqui con Mussolini*, 2d ed. (Milan, 1950), 71–73; B. Mussolini, "La dottrina del fascismo," in *Opera Omnia di Benito Mussolini*, ed. E. Susmel and D. Susmel (Florence, 1961), 120; "Decennale," *Israel*, October 27, 1932.

15. Roth, *History*, 513–14; De Felice, *Storia degli ebrei italiani*, 17, 591. Mussolini's attitude toward Zionism was defined by an official fascist publication as follows: "Italy's attitude toward Zionism varies, depending on whether the matter under discussion is Zionism in Palestine or the participation of Italian citizens in the Zionist movement. The latter is inadmissible" (Partito Nazionale Fascista, *L'Italia nel Mediterraneo* [Rome, 1936], 44). Translations from the Italian are the author's.

16. E. Rubin, *The Jews in Italy* (Vienna, 1936); U. Ojetti, *I taccuini, 1914–1943* (Florence, 1954), 391; De Felice, *Storia degli ebrei italiani*, 68.

17. M. Michaelis, *Mussolini and the Jews: German-Italian Relations and the Jewish Question in Italy, 1922–1945* (Oxford, 1978), 57–80, 415–17.

18. Ibid., 81–103.

19. De Felice, *Storia degli ebrei italiani*, 204–20, 259–309, 344–79, 555–56.

20. Ibid., 326–38; S. Sorani, *L'assistenza ai profughi ebrei in Italia (1933–1947). Contributo alla storia della Delasem* (Rome, 1983); C. Spartaco Capogreco, *Ferramonti. La vita e gli uomini del più grande campo d'internamento fascista (1940–1945)* (Florence, 1987); F. Folino, *Ebrei destinazione Calabria (1940–1945)* (Palermo, 1988).

21. S. Zuccotti, *The Italians and the Holocaust: Persecution, Rescue, Survival* (New York, 1987), 71–73.

22. G. Zachariae, *Mussolini si confessa* (Milan, 1948), 169–70.

23. Michaelis, *Mussolini and the Jews*, 342–406; L. Picciotto Fargion, "The Jews during the German Occupation and the Italian Social Republic," in Herzer, *The Italian Refuge*, 109–38; idem, *Il libro della memoria. Gli Ebrei deportati dall'Italia (1943–1945)* (Milan, 1991), 26–63, 791–875.

24. Roth, *History*, 552.

25. W. P. Sillanpoa and R. G. Weisbord, "The Baptized Rabbi of Rome: The Zolli Case," *Judaism* 38 (winter 1989), 74–91.

26. Ibid., 86.

27. R. Bassi, "Ricordo di Massimo Adolfo Vitale," *La Rassegna Mensile di Israel* 45 (January–March 1979), 8–21; F. Del Canuto, "La ripresa delle attività e delle organizzazioni ebraiche alla Liberazione," ibid. 47 (January–June 1981), 174–220; G. A. Shepperd, *The Italian Campaign, 1943–1945: A Political and Military Re-assessment* (London, 1968), 351–69.

28. C. R. S. Harris, *Allied Military Administration of Italy, 1943–1945* (London, 1957), 129–53, esp.

147; R. Ciuni, *L'Italia di Badoglio* (Milan, 1993), 132–33, 290.

29. Quoted in H. Woller, "Die Anfänge der politischen Säuberung in Italien, 1943–1945. Eine Analyse des Office of Strategic Services," *Vierteljahrshefte für Zeitgeschichte* 38 (January 1990), 189–90; see also L. Mercuri, *L'epurazione in Italia, 1943–1948* (Cuneo, 1988).

30. *Actes et documents du Saint Siège relatifs à la Seconde Guerre Mondiale IX. Le Saint Siège et les victimes de la guerre, Janvier–Décembre 1943* (Vatican City, 1975), 458–62 (Padre Pietro Tacchi-Venturi to Cardinal Luigi Maglione, August 29, 1943).

31. *L'abrogazione delle leggi razziali in Italia (1943–1987). Reintegrazione dei diritti dei cittadini e ritorno ai valori del Risorgimento,* ed. M. Toscano (Rome, 1988), 149–85.

32. Michaelis, *Mussolini and the Jews,* 409–10; G. Almirante, *Autobiografia di un "fucilatore"* (Milan, 1973), 56–57; "Alalà per Israele," *Panorama,* October 25, 1973, 50. Interlandi's *La Difesa della Razza,* a racist biweekly magazine, appeared from August 5, 1938, until the fall of fascism in July 1943.

33. D. Lattes, "Benedetto Croce e l'inutile martirio d'Israele," *Israel,* January 30, 1947.

34. *Relazione sull'opera svolta dal Ministero degli Affari Esteri per la tutela delle comunità ebraiche (1938–1943)* (Rome, n.d.); Roberto Ducci [Verax, pseud.], "Italiana ed ebrei in Jugoslavia," *Politica Estera* 1 (September 1944), 21–29.

35. E. Wiskemann, *Italy since 1945* (London, 1971), 9; F. Spotts and T. Wieser, *Italy: A Difficult Democracy* (Cambridge, 1986), 21, 64, 96–99, 104, 156.

36. "Italy," *American Jewish Year Book,* vol. 53 (Philadelphia, 1952), 303; De Felice, *Storia degli ebrei italiani,* 391; M. Pirani, "Il prode Ettore e il complotto ebraico," *La Repubblica,* December 2, 1992, 33.

37. Perth to Halifax, December 27, 1938, *Documents on British Foreign Policy 1919–1939,* 3d ser., vol. 3 (London, 1950), 496–97; McFadyean to Board of Deputies of British Jews, January 25, 1939, PRO, FO 371/23799/10/22; D. A. Binchy, *Church and State in Fascist Italy* (Oxford, 1970), 625–26.

38. B. Berenson, *Rumor and Reflection* (New York, 1952), 218, 443.

39. "Italy," *American Jewish Year Book,* vol. 46 (Philadelphia, n.d.), 233.

40. "Italy," *American Jewish Year Book,* vol. 51 (Philadelphia, 1950), 310; De Felice, *Storia degli ebrei italiani,* 472; G. Romano, "Una testimonianza sul 'capitolo' italiano al processo Eichmann," *La Rassegna Mensile di Israel* 28 (March–April 1962), 238–

47; H. Stuart Hughes, *Prisoners of Hope: The Silver Age of the Italian Jews, 1924–1974* (Cambridge, Mass., 1983), 55, 152–55; Renzo De Felice, "Razzismo e antisemitismo nel XIX e XX secolo," *Nuova Antologia* 127 (January–March 1993), 67.

41. M.A. Vitale, "The Jewish Question in Italy after the Fall of the Nazi-Fascist Regime," Yad Vashem Archives, 031/14-57, n.d. On the evolution of Vatican policy toward Zionism and the state of Israel, see S. I. Minerbi, *The Vatican and Zionism: Conflict in the Holy Land, 1895–1925* (New York, 1990); and idem, "The Vatican and Israel," *Political Dictionary of the State of Israel: Supplement, 1987–1993* (Jerusalem, 1993), 412–14.

42. D. Lattes, "Tu quoque, Quasimodo?" *La Rassegna Mensile di Israel* 27 (January 1961), 3–5 (reply to Quasimodo's article in *Le Ore,* December 13, 1960); *Gazzettino* (Venice), March 1961; *Concretezza,* March 16–May 15, 1961; *La Voce della Giustizia,* May 6, 1961; D. Lattes, "Italy," *American Jewish Year Book,* vol. 63 (Philadelphia, 1962), 325–26; A. Milano, "Italy," *American Jewish Year Book,* vol. 65 (Philadelphia, 1964), 241–42; "Italian Jews, Disturbed by a Spate of Anti-Semitism, Regard Neo-Fascist Sentiment as a Major Cause," *New York Times,* August 27, 1972; A. M. Di Nola, *Antisemitismo in Italia, 1962/1972* (Florence, 1973), 151.

43. Hughes, *Prisoners of Hope,* 148–49, 153; A. Stille, "A Disturbing Echo: Anti-Semitism, Fifty Years after Mussolini's Infamous Racial Laws Took Effect, Is an Issue Again," *Atlantic* 263 (February 1989), 20–29; J. Sassoon, "L'informazione deviata. Analisi delle distorsioni comunicative ricorrenti nei mass media italiani in merito al conflitto arabo-israeliano," *La Rassegna Mensile di Israel* 56 (September–December 1990), 517–29.

44. Hughes, *Prisoners of Hope,* 148; Stille, "A Disturbing Echo," 28–29. The writer Primo Levi declared after the Israeli invasion of Lebanon that it was not to "this Israel" that he was bound by "a deep sentimental tie" ("Chi ha corraggio a Gerusalemme?" *La Stampa,* June 24, 1982). As a result, a wave of sharp criticism was directed at Levi in the Italian Jewish community.

45. E. Toaff, *Perfidi Giudei fratelli maggiori* (Milan, 1987), 202.

46. Stille, "A Disturbing Echo," 24.

47. R. Balbi, "Non è questione di naso adunco," *La Repubblica,* November 20, 1987, 8; A. Goldstaub, "L'antisemitismo in Italia. Una lettura della documentazione raccolta dalla Fondazione Centro di Documentazione Ebraica tra il 1986 e il 1990," *La Rassegna Mensile di Israel* 56 (January–

August 1990), 265; Stille, "A Disturbing Echo," 20, 21, 24–26.

48. Stille, "A Disturbing Echo," 24, 26; A. Cowell, "Italy Poll Sees Rising Feeling against Jews," *New York Times,* May 11, 1992; J. Petersen, "L'unificazione tedesca del 1989–90 vista dall'Italia," *Storia Contemporanea* 23 (September 1992), 117–18.

49. Stille, "A Disturbing Echo," 26, 29.

50. A. Goldstaub and R. Mannheimer, "Gli atteggiamenti negativi verso gli ebrei. Note in margine all'indagine," *La Rassegna Mensile di Israel* 56 (September–December 1990), 387–417; S. Della Seta and M. Torrefranca, "Italy," *American Jewish Year Book,* vol. 90 (Philadelphia, 1990), 347–48.

51. Goldstaub and Mannheimer, "Gli atteggiamenti negativi verso," 405–6; A. Levi, "La conta dei razzisti," *Corriere della Sera,* November 3, 1992; M. Scialoja, "Aiuto, uno su dieci odia gli ebrei," *L'Espresso,* November 8, 1992, 22–26; T. Malaspina, "L'odio c'è? Parlarne è utile o no?" ibid., November 15, 1992, 66–69.

52. "Un anno nero. Dodici mesi svastiche, scritte, provocazioni," *L'Espresso,* November 15, 1992, 68–69; Cowell, "Italy Poll." The leading exponent of Holocaust revisionism in Italy is Carlo Mattogno, a disciple of Robert Faurisson (see C. Mattogno, *Il mito dello sterminio ebraico* [Monfalcone, 1985]). He enjoys the support of several anti-Semitic periodicals, including *Orion* (since 1984) and *Il Candido* (since 1989).

53. A. Tabet, "Italy," *American Jewish Year Book,* vol. 49 (Philadelphia, n.d.), 354.

54. A. Tabet, "Italy," *American Jewish Year Book,* vol. 62 (Philadelphia, 1961), 250.

55. Stille, "A Disturbing Echo," 28.

56. B. Cocchianella et al., *Il pregiudizio antisemitico in Italia. La coscienza democratica di fronte al razzismo strisciante* (Rome, 1984); S. Malatesta, "'Io, ebreo italiano.' Un coro di testimonianze sofferte racconta una condizione difficile: Pregiudizi, ostilità, diffidenze reciproche. Siamo un paese antisemita?" *La Repubblica,* January 7, 1986; G. Bocca, *Gli italiana sono razzisti?* (Milan, 1988), 101–10; A. Galante Garrone, "La peste razzista," *Nuova Antologia* 125 (April–June 1990), 179–81; F. Colombo, "Il silenzio della cultura genera mostri antisemiti," *La Stampa,* June 1, 1991; G. Spadolini, "Gerusalemme: Il no al razzismo," *Nuova Antologia* 127 (July–September 1992), 14–30; G. Arian Levi, "Auschwitz fa anche ridere," *Ha Keillah* (Turin), December 1992, 5; C. Vercelli, "Oltre il razzismo, sinergie e iniziative," ibid., October 1993, 20; A. Roveri, "Risposta a Ferrara lo spettro dell'anti-semitismo," *La Voce,* December 10, 1994; D. Sorani, "Ponti recisi e teste di ponte. Sulla 'svolta' del MSI," *Ha Keillah,* Feb-

ruary 1995, 10; M. Contini, "Se la storia è un lavandino," ibid., April 1995, 1, 6; "Un no a Fini dalle Organizzazioni ebraiche americane," ibid., 23; D. Voghera, "L'impossibile parificazione," ibid., 23.

57. L. B., "Zionism in Italy," *Jewish Chronicle,* August 26, 1898, 8; Canepa, "Reflections on Antisemitism," 105, 110; De Felice, *Storia degli ebrei italiani,* 159–62, 174–88.

58. A. Segre, *Memorie di vita ebraica: Casale Monferrato-Roma-Gerusalemme, 1918–1960* (Rome, 1979), 386–87.

59. "Italy," *American Jewish Year Book,* vol. 53, 303–4.

60. See above, n. 12. The book was originally published in 1961; the final chapter appears on pp. 441–86 of the fifth edition. For the quotation from Caleffi, see P. Caleffi, *Si fa presto a dire fame* (Milan, 1955), 135.

61. De Felice, *Storia degli ebrei italiani,* 87; D. Carpi, "Jews under Italian Fascism," *Jewish Journal of Sociology* 5 (June 1963), 145–46.

62. M. Leone, *Le organizzazioni di soccorso ebraiche in età fascista (1918–1945)* (Rome, 1983); M. Michaelis, "La Resistenza israelita in Italia," *Nuova Antologia* 121 (October–December 1986), 239–44; M. Sarfatti, "Bibliografia per lo studio delle persecuzioni antiebraiche in Italia, 1938–1945," *La Rassegna Mensile di Israel* 54 (January–August 1988), 435–75; R. Paini, *I sentieri della speranza. Profughi ebrei, Italia fascista e la "Delasem"* (Milan, 1988); K. Voigt, *Zuflucht auf Widerruf. Exil in Italien, 1933–1945,* vol. 1 (Stuttgart, 1989); J. Steinberg, *All or Nothing: The Axis and the Holocaust, 1941–1943* (London, 1990); A. Stille, *Benevolence and Betrayal: Five Italian Jewish Families under Fascism* (New York, 1991); G. Caravita, *Ebrei in Romagna (1938–1945). Dalle leggi razziali allo sterminio* (Ravenna, 1991); M. Michaelis, "Un aspetto ignoto del ravvicinamento tra fascismo e nazismo durante la guerra d'Etiopia in un documento inedito tedesco," *Diplomazia e storia delle relazioni internazionali. Studi in onore di Enrico Serra* (Milan, 1991), 391–410; S. Ferrari, *Vaticano e Israele le dal secondo conflitto mondiale alla guerra del Golfo* (Florence, 1991); M. Shelah, *Un debito di gratitudine. Storia dei rapporti tra l'Esercito italiano e gli ebrei in Dalmazia (1941–1943)* (Roma, 1991); F. Del Regno, "Gli ebrei a Roma tra le due guerre mondiali: fonti e problemi di ricerca," *Storia Contemporanea* 23 (February 1992), 5–69; A. Canepa, "Pius X and the Jews: A Reappraisal," *Church History* 61 (September 1992), 362–72; E. Fintz Menascè, *Gli ebrei a Rodi. Storia di un'antica comunità annientata dai nazisti* (Milan, 1992); D. Bidussa, A. Luzzatto, and G. Luzzatto Voghera, *Oltre il ghetto. Momenti e figure della cultura ebraica tra l'Unità e*

il fascismo (Brescia, 1992); L. Picciotto Fargion, *Gli ebrei in provincia di Milano: 1943/1945. Persecuzione e deportazione* (Milan, 1992); M. Shelah, "Kroatische Juden zwischen Deutschland und Italien: Die Rolle der italienischen Armee am Beispiel des Generals Giuseppe Amico, 1941–1943," *Vierteljahrshefte für Zeitgeschichte* 41 (April 1993), 175–95; P. V. Cannistraro and B. R. Sullivan, *Il Duce's Other Woman: The Never-Before-Told Story of Benito Mussolini's Jewish Mistress and How She Helped Him to Come to Power* (New York, 1993); F. Fernarotti, *La tentazione dell'oblio. Razzismo, antisemitismo e neonazismo* (Bari, 1993); K. Voigt, *Zuflucht auf Widerruf. Exil in Italien, 1933–1945,* vol. 2 (Stuttgart, 1993); M. Sarfatti, *Mussolini contro gli ebrei* (Turin, 1994); D. Carpi, *Between Mussolini and Hitler* (Hanover, 1994); M. Toscano, "L'uguaglianza senza diversità: Società e questione ebraica nell'Italia liberale," *Storia Contemporanea* 25 (October 1994), 685–712; S. Urso, "La persecuzione degli ebrei in Italia," *Studi Storici* 35 (October–December 1994), 1153–65; C. F. Delzell, "The Italians and the Holocaust," *Italian Quarterly* 32 (winter–spring 1995), 85–97; M. Molinari, *La sinistra e gli ebrei in Italia* (Milan, 1995).

63. See the sources cited above in n. 23.

64. N. Caracciolo, *Gli ebrei e l'Italia durante la guerra 1940–45* (Rome, 1986), 18. See also I. Herzer, "How Italians Rescued Jews," *Midstream* 29 (June–July 1983), 35–38; and D. Rabinowitz, "An Army of Schindlers from Italy," *Wall Street Journal,* December 22, 1993, A10.

65. R. Fubini, "La giustizia e il pietismo: Su una recente trasmissione televisiva," *Ha Keillah,* December 1986, 5.

66. D. Carpi, "The Rescue of Jews in the Italian Zone of Occupied Croatia," in *Rescue Attempts during the Holocaust Period: Proceedings of the Second Yad Vashem Conference, April 1974* (Jerusalem, 1977), 505–6; idem, "Notes on the History of the Jews in Greece during the Holocaust Period: The Attitude of the Italians (1941–1943)," *Festschrift in Honor of Dr. George Wise* (Tel Aviv, 1981), 25. Cf. M. Shelah, *Heshbon Damim* (Tel Aviv, 1986), 57–59 (with unpublished documents).

67. Picciotto Fargion, "Italian Citizens in Nazi-Occupied Europe: Documents from the Files of the German Foreign Office, 1941–1943," *Simon Wiesenthal Center Annual* 7 (1990), 100; G. Pisanò, *Mussolini e gli ebrei* (Milan, 1967); D. Sorani, "Degradazione e memoria," *Ha Keillah,* December 1993, 1.

68. *La legislazione antiebraica in Italia e in Europa: Atti del Convegno nel cinquantenario delle leggi razziali (Roma, 17–18 ottobre 1988)* (Rome,

1989), 11–15, 47–54, 57–78, 95–121, 123–61, 163–274.

69. G. Fubini, "1938–1988," *La Rassegna Mensile di Israel* 54 (January–August 1988), 9.

70. G. Fubini, "L'abrogazione della legislazione razziale e la giurisprudenza" (paper read at the international conference "Fifty Years after the Race Laws," Florence, October 6, 1988), 20.

71. De Felice, *Storia degli ebrei italiani,* 477–81; Zuccotti, *The Italians and the Holocaust,* 209.

72. M. Tagliacozzo, "Ebrei rifugiati nelle zone extraterritoriali del Vaticano," memorandum to the author, June 16, 1975.

73. S. Della Seta and M. Torrefranca, "Italy," *American Jewish Year Book,* vol. 91 (Philadelphia, 1991), 297. On July 29, 1992, the Vatican and Israel established a bilateral permanent working commission to negotiate toward eventual full diplomatic ties; finally, in 1994, Andrea Cordero di Lanza Montezemolo became the first diplomatic representative of the Holy See in Israel.

74. Della Seta and Torrefranca, "Italy," 298. In April 1993 Pope John Paul II ordered the nuns to leave Auschwitz. On the massacre at the Ardeatine Caves, see A. Ascarelli, *Le fosse ardeatine,* 3d ed. (Rome, 1974).

75. P. Levi, *If This Is a Man,* trans. Stuart J. Woolf (London, 1990), 15, 46–47, 125, 127–28, 381. For a detailed assessment of the memoirs of Holocaust survivors in Italy, see G. Romano, "La persecuzione e la deportazione degli ebrei di Roma e d'Italia nelle opere di scrittori ebrei," *Scritti in memoria di Enzo Sereni* (Jerusalem, 1970), 314–39; see also M. Sarfatti, "Bibliografia per lo studio delle persecuzioni antiebraiche in Italia, 1938–1945," *La Rassegna Mensile di Israel* 54 (January–August 1988), 472–75.

76. P. Levi, *The Drowned and the Saved,* trans. Raymond Rosenthal (London, 1992), 9, 166–67. The prevailing desire to let bygones be bygones was reflected in the negative response to *Holocaust* (1979), the NBC film for television, which was dismissed by many reviewers as an American soap opera. See, e.g., E. Toaff, "Ci si nasconde ipocriticamente dietro un giudizio artistico," *Shalom,* May 1979; and F. Antonelli, "Perché l'‘Olocausto' televisivo ha ottenuto in Italia un interesse inferiore a quello suscitato in altri Paesi," *Il Tempo,* July 2, 1979. For a violent attack on *Holocaust* by fascist extremists, see C. Cantelmo, "TV: Olocaust. Il solito polpettone," *Linea,* July 1–15, 1979, 23. The editor of *Linea,* Pino Rauti, a self-confessed pro-Nazi and anti-Semite, was secretary of the Italian Social Movement in 1990. When the neofascist movement announced its own dissolution after the fall of Berlusconi's government, he objected (C. Bohlen,

"Neo-Fascists Remodel Their Party in Italy," *New York Times,* January 30, 1995).

77. P. Levi, "Buco nero di Auschwitz," *La Stampa,* January 22, 1987. On criticism provoked by this article, see L. Monaco, "Un'accusa strumentale," *Ha Keillah,* February 1993, 8.

78. A. Galante Garrone, "Il grido di Primo Levi," *Nuova Antologia* 122 (July–September 1987), 212–27; F. Molino Signorini, "'Uomini fummo . . .' Riflessioni su Primo Levi e Jean Améry," *La Rassegna Mensile di Israel* 57 (September–December 1991), 463–77.

79. "Lettere aperte a Sandro Pertini," *Ha Keillah,* February 1984, 1–2; "Dichiarazioni del Presidente del Consiglio On. Bettino Craxi," ibid., February 1987, 4; G. Disegni, "La libertà di essere se stessi," ibid., 1–2; Sassoon, "L'informazione deviata," 524–25 (on the damage caused by Pertini and Craxi).

80. Levi, *The Drowned and the Saved,* 151.

81. A striking illustration of this mutual incomprehension is the current controversy between representative Italian Jews and the erstwhile collaborator of the Union of Italian Jewish Communities, Renzo De Felice. As has been noted, De Felice irritated Jewish critics in 1961 by treating the Holocaust as simply an aspect of the Italian drama. In 1987 he went further, claiming that the fascist regime was "immune from the accusation of genocide" and calling for the abrogation of the constitutional ban on fascism (interview by G. Ferrara, *Corriere della Sera,* December 27, 1987). To make matters worse, he explicitly denied the uniqueness of the Holocaust in the preface to the fifth edition of his book on the Italian Jews, maintaining that the crimes perpetrated by the Germans against other "inferior races" were "no less monstrous" than the extermination of the Jews (*Storia degli ebrei italiani,* 5th ed., xviii). In September 1994 De Felice was appointed president of the Central Commission for Historical Studies by Berlusconi's minister for cultural affairs, Domenico Fisichella, who is a member of the Alleanza Nazionale (National Alliance), a front for the neofascist movement (on the neofascists in Berlusconi's government, see A. Lyttelton, "Italy: The Triumph of TV," *New York Review of Books,* August 11, 1994, 25–29). However, in an interview with Pasquale Chessa in August 1995, he expressed concern over the possibility that the antifascist myths he had combated might soon be replaced by profascist ones (S. Folli, "L'otto settembre di De Felice e Bocca," *Corriere della Sera,* August 24, 1995). The interview was published in book form in September: R. De Felice, *Rosso e nero* (Milan, 1995).

82. At the congress of the Union of Italian Jewish Communities in Rome on July 3–5, 1994, the participation of five members of the Alleanza Nazionale in Berlusconi's government was denounced as a threat to democracy, and the Jews of other countries were urged to support the antifascist stand of Italian Jewry (Congresso UCEI—Luglio 1994, "Il valore della politica" and "La mozione politica," *Ha Keillah,* October 1994, 1–2 and 2, respectively). When, at the beginning of September 1995, the mayor of Rome, Francesco Rutelli, announced his intention to name a street after Giuseppe Bottai, who, as Mussolini's minister of education, had been responsible for the expulsion of the Jews from Italian schools and universities, the president of the Union of Italian Jewish Communities protested violently, as did the president of the Jewish Documentation Center in Milan (F. Giuliani, "Via Bottai, apologia del fascismo," *La Repubblica,* September 5, 1995). The protest had the desired effect (G. Gomel, "Rutelli, Bottai e gli ebrei di Roma," *Ha Keillah,* October 1995, 2).

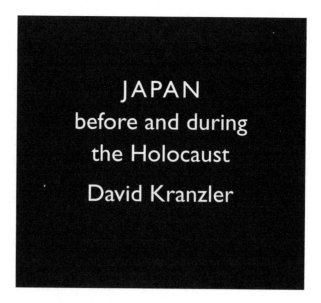

JAPAN
before and during the Holocaust
David Kranzler

While Jews have resided in Japan ever since Commodore Matthew C. Perry opened its gates to the West in 1853, they have generally remained a tiny community with a population of less than one thousand. Although the community was hardly affected during Hitler's rise to power and the ensuing war in the Pacific, anti-Semitism, in its unique Japanese form, exercised a major influence on Tokyo's policy toward the fifteen thousand stateless Russian Jews who had resided in Manchuria and North China since 1936. Most pronounced, however, was its effect upon the approximately eighteen thousand Jewish refugees from Nazi Germany, Austria, and Poland who found a haven in Japanese-occupied Shanghai during the years between 1938 and 1945.[1]

BEFORE THE HOLOCAUST

Jews in commerce are known to have visited Japan as early as the ninth century and frequently with Portuguese explorers and Dutch merchants during the "Christian Century" (1542–1639). Still, it was only after Commodore Perry's arrival that the Jews established a permanent community in Japan.[2] Although a few early merchants and adventurers reached the port cities of Yokohama, Nagasaki, and Kobe, the first permanent Jewish settler did not arrive in Yokohama until 1861. Four years later we find the first Jewish tombstone, and by 1895 the community, which had grown to about fifty families, had built a synagogue.[3] That it was not easy to maintain some of their religious customs in such an outpost is evident from the record of a circumcision performed in Shanghai on a baby boy from Nagasaki. His parents traveled five hundred miles with him in order to fulfill this important Jewish ritual.[4]

Despite steady accretions, Japan's Jewish population never grew very large. It remained under one thousand except during two brief periods, after World War I and just prior to the war in the Pacific, when it grew to several thousand. Jews in Japan were divided almost evenly between Ashkenazim and Sephardim. The former hailed primarily from Russia, Germany, England, France, and the United States, while the latter came mostly from Syria and Iraq. Among the Sephardim was Elias Sassoon, a member of the large and prosperous Sassoon clan. Because of the widespread influence of the family, the Sassoons were popularly referred to as the "Rothschilds of the East." Like their European coreligionists in the late nineteenth century, the Sassoon family served as a catalyst for the modernization of many ports in China and Japan, such as Shanghai, Nagasaki, and Yokohama. They were especially successful in Shanghai, where two branches of the family business—import and export, real estate, and finance—were opened.[5]

During the 1880s, Russian Jews developed a small but active Jewish community in Nagasaki, an important coaling and fueling station. There they set up what was probably the first *minyan* (prayer quorum) in Japan. During the Russo-Japanese War of 1904–5 the community was dissolved, and its members handed their Torah scroll over to the Jews of Kobe.[6] In the aftermath of the Russo-Japanese War and the ill-fated Russian revolution of 1905, scores of Jewish soldiers demobilized from the czar's army, including some recently released Japanese prisoners of war, settled in Japan, especially in Kobe. Among the Jewish prisoners was the highly decorated Joseph Trumpeldor, who lost his arm in the Russo-Japanese War and who later helped create a Jewish defense force in Palestine.[7]

Until the great earthquake of 1923, which devastated most of Tokyo and Yokohama, the Jewish community of Yokohama, which was Sephardic, was the center of Jewish life in Japan. Most of these Jewish residents were engaged in commerce, either independently or as representatives of American, European, or Indian firms. Following the disaster, a few Jews returned to Yokohama and reestablished their commercial enterprises, but the Jewish hub shifted about 250 miles west, to the rising port of Kobe. Until the war in the Pacific, this Jewish community comprised approximately fifty families, divided about equally between Ashkenazim and Sephardim.[8]

During the years 1917–20 the Jews of Kobe and Yokohama played an important role in helping several thousand Jewish refugees from the Bolshevik Revolution who stopped in Japan on their way to the countries in the West. In particular straits were the thousands of Jewish refugees stranded in Vladivostok, who were unable to land in Japan because they lacked the four hundred yen necessary as "show money." Crucial in resolving this situation was Jacob Schiff, head of the New York banking firm of Kuhn, Loeb, and Company and president of the American Hebrew Immigrant Aid Society (HIAS). Because he had provided much-needed financial assistance to Japan during the Russo-Japanese War, his request to Tokyo in 1917 for permission to use Kobe and Yokohama as transit centers for Jewish refugees was readily approved. HIAS established a temporary office in Yokohama, and it eventually transferred to a more permanent one in Harbin, Manchuria, where there was a large Russian Jewish community.[9]

During 1940–41 Japan allowed about 2,200 Polish Jewish refugees with dubious Curaçao visas to stay in Japan until they could obtain passage elsewhere. Although relief for the refugees in Kobe came from American Jewish relief organizations, the members of Kobe's small Jewish community were extremely helpful to their coreligionists.[10] During the war in the Pacific, Kobe's Jewish community suffered from Allied air raids, one of which destroyed both of its synagogues. After the war the center of Jewish life shifted to Tokyo, which until then had had only a small number of Jewish merchants and professionals.[11]

The Japanese knew little about the Jews: many mistakenly believed, at least until after World War II, that they were members of a Christian sect. What they did know about Jews came from the few prominent Jews with whom they came in contact. Three early Jewish settlers of Yokohama left their imprint on Japanese history. In the 1860s, Raphael Schoyer, an American businessman and president of the municipal council of Yokohama's foreign settlement, was among the first publishers to issue an English-language newspaper in Japan, the *Japan Express*.[12] He was encouraged in this pioneering venture by R. H. Pruyn, America's first envoy to Japan.[13] Schoyer was followed by Ben Fleisher, an American Jew, who in 1907 transformed his English-language *Japan Advertiser* from a four-page gossip sheet into an influential, high-quality, Western-style newspaper. Fleisher counted among his friends Jacob Schiff as well as Joseph C. Grew, the last American ambassador to Japan before the war broke out. Fleisher published and edited the *Japan Advertiser* until 1940, when Japanese militarists forced him to sell. He then returned to Philadelphia, his hometown.[14]

Although he never lived in Japan, Jacob Schiff clearly had more influence there than any other Jew before and after World War II. He and his work greatly affected Japanese policy toward the Jews, which ultimately saved the lives of thousands of European Jews during the 1930s and 1940s.[15] The Japanese did not forget Schiff and the financial backing he provided them during the Russo-Japanese War, Japan's first modern war against a Western power. Underwriting such a huge undertaking was a novel experience for this nation newly emerged from feudalism. Japan quickly found itself financially drained and sought a loan of $50 million in London, then the world's financial capital, in order to purchase a modern fleet that could counter Russia's. Since the Japanese had not yet been victorious in battle, Baron Korekiyo Takahashi, head of the Bank of Japan, found it difficult to convince skeptical European bankers of the military strength of his small nation. Schiff, however, quickly responded to Takahashi's request. Angry at the czar for ignoring his pleas to ameliorate the lot of the Russian Jews, especially following the bloody Kishinev pogrom of 1903, Schiff offered to arrange the entire loan. Three other loans were floated by Schiff in consortium with his cousin, the German banker M. M. Warburg, and English Jewish banker Sir Ernest Cassel, thus providing Japan with the desired European moral and financial support. In 1906 Schiff became the first Westerner to be honored personally by the emperor with the Order of the Rising Sun.[16]

When Italy entered the war in June 1940 and the Mediterranean Sea was closed to travel, hundreds of German Jewish refugees requested transit to Shanghai via Manchuria. Colonel Hideo Iwakura of the war ministry claimed he gave permission "on the grounds no true Japanese could deny: a debt was owed the Jews; the Jewish firm of Kuhn, Loeb and Company had helped finance the Russo-Japanese War."[17]

Later, in 1941, a U.S. delegation consisting of Bishop E. Walsh and Father James E. M. Drought visited Japan carrying a "peace proposal" approved by President Roosevelt. This mission was facilitated by a letter of introduction to the Japanese by Lewis Strauss of Kuhn, Loeb, and Company.[18]

Albert Einstein, the Nobel prize–winning physicist, made an almost equally powerful impression on the Japanese. His visit to Japan in November and December 1922, at the height of his fame, was treated almost as a state affair. Throughout his tour, which included an audience with the emperor, he was greeted with such newspaper headlines as "Giant of Science World Arrives," "Sparkles Like Brilliant Ray," and "Doctor E. Giant of Scholarship."[19] The impact of Schiff and Einstein was so strong that even in the 1960s the average Japanese, who still knew little about Jews, believed that "they must be rich and smart."[20]

Japanese Anti-Semitism

The seeds of anti-Semitism in Japan go back as far as 1877, when Shakespeare's *Merchant of Venice* was first published in the country. The ugly Jewish stereotype embodied in the character Shylock was reinforced by Christian missionaries, who regarded Jews as "Christ killers." Still, such influences touched only a very small cultured class studying Western literature and religion. It was during the post–World War I era of "Taisho democracy" that the unique Japanese form of this ancient disease gained strength.[21]

The first Japanese to study Judaism and Jewry were soldiers who picked up their knowledge incidentally, as part of their military experience. They were middle-echelon officers, many of whom were close friends and former classmates. Among them were Colonel Norihiro Yasue, Navy Captain Koreshige Inuzuka, General Kiichiro Higuchi, Colonel Maeda Mizuho, General Nobutaka Shioden, and a few dozen close friends and colleagues in military and government circles. These "experts" disseminated their unique ideology in writing and were able to shape and, to some degree, implement Japan's official policy regarding Jews.[22]

These students of Judaism began as Russian-language experts attached to the Japanese military contingent in Siberia. They were part of an allied army, along with the United States, France, Britain, and White Russian forces, that tried unsuccessfully from 1918 to 1922 to stem the tide of the Bolshevik advances in East Asia. Under the tutelage of their White Russian mentors, headed by Admiral Alexander Kolchak, a leading anti-Semite, these Japanese officers studied not only Western military tactics but also another Western product, anti-Semitism. They studied *The Essence of Radicalism* and especially *The Protocols of the Elders of Zion*. First published in 1905, the virulently anti-Semitic *Protocols* was concocted by a Russian agent in the 1890s based on a plagiarism of a still earlier satire on Napoleon III. With the help of the White Russian émigrés and men such as Admiral Kolchak, who published a special edition in Siberia, the *Protocols* quickly spread throughout the world, including East Asia.[23]

The eager but naive Japanese military men sincerely believed the claim made in the *Protocols* that in a Prague cemetery in 1888 the "Jewish Elders of Zion," who represented "world Jewry," had plotted the destruction of Christian civilization. After terrorizing the world, the leaders of Zion would then establish their empire, to be ruled by the House of David.[24] They intended to accomplish this goal by manipulating the contradictory ideologies of Communism and capitalism. Through the use of unbridled capitalism they would corner the world's gold market and destroy the global economy. Communism and Free Masonry would be used to subvert Christian society. For the believer, the sudden downfall of the Romanov, Habsburg, and Hohenzollern dynasties in 1917–18 was "proof" of this theory. Adding to the evidence was the fact that some Jews, such as Leon Trotsky, Rosa Luxemburg, and Béla Kun, figured prominently among the leadership of the successful Bolshevik Revolution in Russia in 1917 and the failed Communist coups in Germany and Hungary following World War I.[25]

The Japanese "experts" on the Jews believed also that the Jews wielded inordinate financial and political power on the international scene, especially in the United States and Great Britain. For proof of this assertion, they pointed to Jacob Schiff, the one Jew who was familiar to virtually every Japanese.[26] Throughout the 1920s and 1930s Inuzuka, Yasue, and their cohorts wrote books and articles containing such statements as in the following composite of quotations from Yasue's works:

> The Bolshevik Revolution is part of the Jewish plot. . . . Zionism seems to be the goal of the Jews, but they actually want to control the world's . . . economy, politics and diplomacy. . . . The Jewish plot must be destroyed by force. . . . The Jews are responsible for the American and European . . . control of the Chinese Nationalist Government. . . . The Jews control the American press and thereby public opinion, turning it against Japan . . . they are responsible for the immorality of the Japanese youth.[27]

Japanese Westernization

Such anti-Semitism among the Japanese, who were barely aware of the existence of Jews, can only be understood in light of Japan's painful process of modernization in the late nineteenth and early twentieth centuries. Along with industrial, technical, and military innovations came the inevitable flood of Western concepts that were in direct conflict with Japan's ancient culture and values.[28]

The liberal atmosphere in Japan during the 1920s manifested itself in socialism and other radical movements. There was great interest in Western culture. Individualism, American-style dancing, movies, and jazz became fashionable. Attitudes toward sex grew more permissive, giving rise to the *mobo* (modern boy) and the *mogo* (modern girl). Dressed in the latest Western fashions, they daringly walked down the Ginza in Tokyo holding hands. Such Western intrusions wreaked havoc in Japanese society. Especially disturbed by these changes were the ultranationalists, both military and civilian, who resented the corruption of their time-honored society and values. The ultranationalists believed in the "agrarian myth" of an earlier, more innocent age, which they sought unsuccessfully to regain.[29] The most sensitive issue was the sanctity of the family and the extended family in the form of the nation, headed by the revered emperor. Western culture's emphasis on the individual was antithetical to the Japanese concept of family.[30]

While the liberal twenties were years of theoretical anti-Semitism among a small group of Jewish experts, having no implications for Jews residing in Japan, with Emperor Hirohito's ascent to the throne in 1926 things began to change. Right-wing groups and secret societies began to proliferate. Members found outlets for their theories in journals such as *Kokusai Himitsu-Ryoku no Kenkyu* (Studies in the International Conspiracy) and in books such as Shinjun Katsui's *Yudaya-jin no inbo to heinichi mondai* (The Jewish plot and the anti-Japanese problem). At the same time, a few other writers and journalists generally presented a fair, objective portrait of Jews in their articles.[31]

A transition from theory to practice began to occur in the early thirties, especially after the rise of Adolf Hitler and the proliferation of Nazi anti-Semitic propaganda.[32] From then on, the Japanese anti-Semites focused on the alleged nefarious Jewish influence on Japanese foreign policy. If the supposedly sophisticated anti-Semites of Europe and the United States believed the Jew to be *the* cause of international and domestic problems, then the naive Japanese, but a generation removed from feudalism, were even more susceptible. To them, it appeared only logical that since Jews controlled the West, especially the United States and Britain, Jews and the West were synonymous. Thus, anti-Semitic books were given titles referring to the Jews, but the word "Jew" was mentioned nowhere in the text, which referred only to Britain and the United States.[33] For example, in *Yudaya-jin no inbo to heinichi mondai* the West (i.e., the Jews) is blamed for international opposition to Japanese policies in the 1930s. Thus, the United States, through its Jewish media and the League of Nations, censured Japan for its occupation of Manchuria and supported Chiang Kai-shek with loans in 1936.[34]

By strengthening British and American opposition to Japanese expansion, the Jews limited Japan's "righteous mission" in establishing its "New Order in East Asia." This new order involved, among other things, the unification of East Asia under the aegis of the superior Japanese and the removal of European influence. In 1937, for example, Inuzuka, under his pseudonym Kiyo Utsunomiya, declared in one of his articles that "the Jewish financiers . . . intend to drive the Japanese out of China. . . . [Moreover] the British, French and German Jews have given a loan of $200,000,000 to China . . . in order to forestall a further advance of Japan southwards . . . [as part of] an anti-Japanese plot by the Jews."[35]

Another ultranationalist, Iyataka Nakaoka, reiterated this notion by stating that "the American and British Jews . . . are trying to stop Japanese development and keep Japan out of China."[36] The war in the Pacific, known formerly in Japan as "The Greater East Asia War," was dubbed by these ideologues "The War between Japan and the Jews." They further asserted that a "Jewish invasion was creeping into our holy land" like a "frost on a chilly night" or "wind through the cracks," while Jews everywhere were "profiteers taking advantage of wars."[37]

This explains why by 1940 such books and even anti-Semitic fairs set up by ultranationalists attracted the interest of hundreds of thousands of people who knew virtually nothing about Jews. Likewise, political campaigns castigating Jews, such as those run by General Shioden, could draw tens of thousands of Japanese supporters, who only understood "Jews" to be synonymous with "the West."[38]

The Jews as Fugu

In contrast to Western anti-Semites, the Japanese, who lacked a tradition of two millennia of hatred of Jews, gave anti-Semitism a typically Japanese twist. They adopted it as merely another bit of Western knowledge, to be studied and utilized in their interests. Inuzuka encapsulated the perspective of Japanese "experts" on the Jews when he compared them to a fugu, or blowfish, a favorite Japanese dish: if the fish is handled properly, its poisonous sac removed, it is a delicacy; if treated improperly, it is lethal.[39] Thus, it came to be believed that the Jews had extraordinary power that, properly utilized, could be extremely beneficial to Japan. As Utsunomiya, Inuzuka also wrote *Yudaya mondai to Nihon* (The Jewish problem and Japan), in which he accused the Jews of controlling the League of Nations, which criticized Japan's takeover of Manchuria. Yet, as head of the Bureau of Jewish Affairs in Shanghai, Inuzuka was largely responsible for Japan's supportive policy toward the Jewish refugees and many specific efforts to help them.[40]

The Manchurian Faction

The ultranationalist political and military group that dominated Japan's policies during the 1930s and early 1940s consisted of two factions: the Control Group and the more radical Imperial Way, also known as the Manchurian Faction. While both sought to regain Japan's oldest and purest values, the former sought to assert its military and economic power by moving south into China, the Malay Peninsula, and the Dutch East Indies. The Dutch East Indies were an important source of oil for a country poor in natural resources. The Control Group was fully aware that such a move would eventually force Japan to confront the United States.

To avoid a U.S. confrontation, the Manchurian Faction focused on taking over only Manchuria, which was rich in natural resources. It was more concerned about the inevitable clash with the Soviet Union. This faction was led by Colonel Seishiro Itagaki and his good friend Colonel Kanji Ishiwara, both important staff officers in the Kwantung Army, which pushed for the Manchurian takeover. As the ideologue of the Imperial Way, Ishiwara sought a nationalist, almost spiritual, revolution based in part on his belief in Nichiren Buddhism, which would bring about a golden age of universal harmony, with Japan as its spiritual center. Ishiwara explained that "in order to build a Manchukuo [the Japanese name for Manchuria] of one people we must work with the other races to establish an ideal state. That is the real meaning of racial harmony."[41]

Although his ideas were widely influential, Ishiwara's greatest impact was on his classmates, who included Itagaki, Higuchi, Iwakura, and Yasue, all of whom became part of the Manchurian Faction. This group achieved power by the end of the 1920s and was supported by Gisuke Ayukawa, an industrialist who was not part of the *zaibatsu,* Japan's well-established big business conglomerates, of which the radicals disapproved, as well as a dozen or so other members of the Imperial Way clique. Other members included General Kiichiro Higuchi, Colonel Hideo Iwakura, Admiral Kichisaburo Nomura, Yosuke Matsuoka, Tadao Iwakawa, Sadao Araki, Nobusuka Kishi, Naoki Hoshino, Hachiro Arita, Mamoru Shigemitsu, Seihin Ikeda, and Tadao Ikawa. Most of these men had been classmates in military school. Some belonged to other ultranationalist societies, such as Genyosha (Dark Ocean Society), Toa Renmai Kyokai (East Asian League), or Nihon Keizai Renmeikai (Japan Economic Federation). Some knew each other well from financial circles. Among these men numbered a future prime minister (Arita), two foreign ministers (Nomura and Matsuoka), a minister of war (Iwakura), a head of the Bank of Japan (Ikawa), and a minister of education (Araki).[42]

They saw Japan, with the benefits of Manchuria's vast space and resources, as the leading country in an Asia free of Western influences. Japan's glorious future depended on the development and industrialization of Manchuria. This, however, required immense financial backing, which only America, dominated as it was by the rich and powerful Jews, could provide. In order to secure the billions necessary to fulfill the Manchurian development project, the faction implemented a practical application of their theory of Jewish financial power during the mid-1930s.

All assumed that if Japan treated the Jews in East Asia well, then they would be able to convince the rich and influential Jews in the United States to emulate Schiff and lend Japan the funds it needed to develop Manchuria.[43] After all, among President Franklin D. Roosevelt's advisers were such Jews as Treasury Secretary Henry Morgenthau, Jr.; presidential speech writer Judge Samuel Rosenman; professor Felix Frankfurter; and especially Rabbi Stephen S. Wise, Roosevelt's confidant. It was also believed that American Jewry, which controlled the president, would surely help mitigate America's extremely harsh and inflexible policy toward Japan.[44]

America's punitive policy was instituted after the Kwantung Army occupied Manchuria in 1931–32. Relations between the United States and Japan worsened in 1937, after Japanese forces attacked China. In 1938 the United States established a moral embargo against Japan that prohibited the exporting of scrap iron and oil, crucial to the island nation's industrial and military needs. Ultimately, America's total embargo on oil exports to Japan in August 1941 prompted Japan to go to war with the United States.[45]

Faction members further hoped that the refugees who were fleeing Hitler's Germany for East Asia, especially after Kristallnacht, in November 1938, would serve as the scientific class necessary for Manchurian development as well as valuable hostages. At the same time, a Jewish settlement in Manchuria (a Zionist state of their own?) would serve to counterbalance the Soviet Jewish "homeland" in adjacent Birobidzhan. The Manchurian Faction, dominated as it was by the Russian-trained experts on Jews, accorded far greater power than was justified to this Russian "Jewish state."[46]

Only one anti-Semite, General Nobutaka Shioden, did not espouse this theory. His notion of the Jews was not mitigated by the "pragmatic" desire to utilize them on behalf of Japan. During his trips to Germany in 1927 and 1938 he absorbed more fully the Nazi ideological goal of eliminating the troublesome Jews. In 1942 he ran for Parliament on an anti-Semitic, anti-Western platform, but he had little influence, especially before the war in the Pacific. Had he secured a commanding position, he would not have behaved as benignly toward the Jews as the anti-Semites of the Manchurian Faction did.[47]

The Four Phases of Japan's Pro-Jewish Policy

From the occupation of Manchuria until the conclusion of the war in the Pacific, one can discern four distinct periods in the development of Japan's pro-Jewish policy. The first phase, from 1931 through 1935, was on the whole one of indifference toward the Jews; the second, from 1936 until December 6, 1938, was marked by the development of a distinctly pro-Jewish policy. The third phase, from December 6, 1938, until the bombing of Pearl Harbor on December 7, 1941, can be described as the era of goodwill. And during the last phase, which covered the war years, from December 8, 1941, to August 14, 1945, Japan's posture shifted sharply, from a pro-Jewish one to one that ranged between neutrality and hostility, but even at its worst, it never approached the extremism of Japan's Nazi allies.[48]

Manchuria, China's first territory to have a sizable Jewish population, experienced a sort of golden age during the 1920s. Harbin's Jewish population numbered more than ten thousand and boasted a Jewish newspaper, a Jewish hospital, bank, and department store, two synagogues, and even a Jewish day school. With Japan's occupation of Manchuria in 1931, this golden era ended. The Japanese imposed a policy that required every business to accept a Japanese "partner," which induced several thousand Jews to move south to the freer economic atmosphere of Shanghai, Tientsin, and other cities in North China. Moreover, vicious anti-Semitism emanated from Harbin's large White Russian population, which by 1934–35 took the form of terrorism and kidnapping. The anti-Semitism found its most explicit printed expression in the pages of the scurrilous newspaper *Nash Put* (Our Way).[49]

Protests and appeals by Dr. Abraham Kaufman, the dynamic head of Harbin's Jewish community and editor of its newspaper, *Yevreskaya Zhizn* (Jewish Life), and N. E. B. Ezra, editor of Shanghai's *Jewish Messenger,* were ignored by the local Japanese authorities. Yet steps were being taken by Tokyo to improve their situation. The Japanese were sensitive to the foreign press, especially regarding Jewish concerns, which coincided with the growing desire on the part of the Manchurian Faction to make use of the "Jewish power."[50]

In 1936 Ayukawa's "Five Year Plan for the Industrialization of Manchuria," which was contingent on the underwriting of American capital, was approved by the cabinet in Tokyo. Japan's official pro-Jewish policy began to take shape. As early as 1934, undoubtedly under the influence of Ishiwara, Itagaki, and Ayukawa, who were busy designing Manchuria's future, plans were publicized advocating the settlement of at least fifty thousand German Jewish refugees in Manchuria.[51] The first act under the new policy was to give legal status and protection to the approximately fifteen thousand stateless Russian Jews living under Japanese hegemony in eight communities in North China and Manchuria. This provided some measure of protection to the Jews, but it was not the equivalent of citizenship. Then the Far Eastern Jewish Council was created. It represented all Jews under Japanese suzerainty and was headed by Kaufman. Colonel Yasue was appointed to serve as the liaison between Japanese authorities and the Jews. His first act was to close *Nash Put*.[52]

Of greater importance in bolstering the confidence of the Jews was Yasue's establishment of the Far Eastern Conference of Russian Jewish Communities. The first of these annual conferences was held in Harbin in December 1937 and was attended by a thousand delegates from eight Jewish communities. The Zionist flag flew alongside those of Japan and Manchuria, while uniformed members of Betar, the militant Revisionist-Zionist youth group, joined Japanese soldiers in standing guard. In his speech Yasue emphasized Japan's objectives of utilizing the Jewish influence in the United States and protecting the Jews in East Asia.[53] Yasue's colleague General Higuchi also spoke at the conference. Although he too had written anti-Semitic books under a pseudonym, Higuchi extolled the Jewish people and their contributions to science and economics. In line with the Zionist ideology, which he must have absorbed in his study of Judaism and the Jewish people, he blamed all the problems of the Jews on their homelessness. Thus he supported Zionism, which was very strong among the Russian Jews, in the hope of gaining Jewish support for Japan's New Order in East Asia in general and, eventually, for a "Jewish state" in Manchuria in particular.[54] Under Japanese tutelage, the Jews passed the following resolution at the conclusion of the conference, in an awkward official English rendition: "We Jews, attending this racial conference, hereby proclaim that we enjoy racial equality and racial justice under the national laws, and will cooperate with Japan and Manchukuo in building a new order in Asia. We appeal to our coreligionists."[55]

Totally unaware of the real Japanese motivation and its unique anti-Semitic perspective, the Russian Jews, represented by the industrialist Lew Zikman, did not hesitate to oblige their hosts by making contact with American Jewry. On November 22, 1938, less than two weeks after Kristallnacht, Zikman wrote Rabbi Stephen S. Wise and Cyrus Adler, head of the influential American Jewish Committee, asking them to inform American Jews of the good treatment they were receiving from Japan. Because Wise and Adler assumed that the Japanese and the Nazis were equally anti-Semitic, they responded negatively. Wise wrote, "I am in complete disagreement with your position. I think it is wholly vicious for Jews to give support to Japan, as truly Fascist a nation as Germany or Italy."[56] In response, Zikman pleaded with Wise: "In the name of the 15,000 Jews in the Far East I implore you to think of us; not to throw us upon the waves of disaster and not to take upon yourself the responsibilities of any consequences where there might be at least the minimum hopes for betterment of our situation." For obvious reasons, Wise's letter was never shown to the Japanese, whose pro-Jewish policy was officially promulgated barely two weeks later.[57]

The World Reacts to the Holocaust

On December 6, 1938, the Japanese government gave formal recognition to its by now fully developed pro-Jewish policy at a top-secret Five Ministers' Conference. It was probably prompted by the efforts of thousands of German Jews to find a haven in East Asia following Kristallnacht. The recognition came just before the second Far Eastern Conference and three weeks before Ayukawa's announcement of his Five Year Plan for the development of Manchuria. The recognition was suggested by Army Minister General Itagaki and supported by Prime Minister Prince Fumimaro Konoe, a representative of the Navy (most likely Inuzuka), Foreign Minister Arita, and Finance Minister Ikeda. As a subsequent Foreign Office document put it, "The objective of this policy plan was to treat the Jewish people well, and thereby promote introduction of foreign capital and avert aggravation of [Japan's] relationship with England and the United States."[58]

A flurry of activity in Tokyo in early 1939 to implement the pro-Jewish policy and utilize the alleged American-Jewish influence on behalf of Japan proved fruitless, but it had a profound effect on the lives of almost eighteen thousand Jewish refugees. It was the Japanese—the real power in Shanghai, especially since the onset of hostilities with China in July 1937—who permitted the German and Austrian refugees to enter the city's International Settlement without visas or papers of any kind. In fact, during 1938 and 1939, when Jews found most doors to the free world closed, even those incarcerated in Dachau or Mauthausen would be released if they possessed a boarding pass for a ship to Shanghai.[59]

These circumstances created an amazing paradox. Until Germany declared war on Russia in June 1941, Germany permitted Jews with visas to leave, and the much more benign, fascist Italy allowed them to use its ports and ships, while Japan, the third Axis power, provided them with a safe haven. At the same time, the Jewish relief organization in Shanghai, overwhelmed by the arrival of boatload after boatload of penniless Jews, tried to stop the flood of refugees. It sought help from the New York–based Joint Distribution Committee (JDC), the largest Jewish relief organization and the major source of support for most of the refugees. The JDC agreed to try to persuade the American, British, and French governments to ask Germany to prevent its Jews from fleeing to Shanghai. This appeal had no effect on Hitler, whose policy of making his country *judenrein* did not yet mean genocide; the appeal merely reinforced his notion that the democracies had as little interest in the Jews as he did.[60]

The third annual Far Eastern Conference, held in Harbin in December 1939, focused on Japan's humane treatment of the Jews. In addition to the Russian Jews who had been living in Manchuria for years, the large German refugee settlement in Shanghai already numbered about fourteen thousand. And Foreign Minister Arita agreed to plans to create a Jewish settlement, whose population was expected to number as many as three hundred thousand, in either Manchuria (suggested by Yasue) or Shanghai (proposed by Inuzuka).[61] The sensation of the 1939 conference was the speech delivered in Hebrew by Professor Setzuso Kotsuji, the only Japanese person in all of Japan who was fluent in the Holy Tongue. He was employed by the Manchurian Faction as an adviser on Jews and Judaism.[62]

On February 28, 1939, Foreign Minister Arita's pro-Jewish policy had made the headlines in the *Japan Times,* which read: "Japan Will Treat Jews Equally." The decision to publicize the policy was in response to a request in the Diet that Arita give a clear-cut enunciation of the government's stance toward the Jews. Arita's message was essentially that "the Government has decided on a positive policy toward the Jews, which aims at no discriminations against Jews."[63]

Such an official policy is doubly interesting. Besides being an Axis partner, Japan had signed the Cultural and Anti-Comintern Pacts of 1936 and 1938, respectively. The agreements were designed to end Japan's isolation in the world community and to bolster its security vis-à-vis the Soviet Union. Japan had been under a great deal of pressure from Germany to emulate its anti-Semitic philosophy toward the Jews in Japan. While the Germans did succeed in persuading the Japanese to fire the academic Kurt Singer, a German Jewish economist, in 1936, they failed to convince the Nippon Columbia Records Company, owned by Ayukawa, to eliminate all records by Jewish artists. When a Jewish executive showed his manager the list of "forbidden" Jewish violinists, which included Mischa Elman, Szymon Goldberg, Jascha Heifetz, Yehudi Menuhin, Bronislaw Hubermann, Fritz Kreisler, Joseph Szigeti, and Efrem Zimbalist, the manager replied, "Oh, I see, so-called Aryans—I think that is the word the Germans are using—are not allowed to play the violin!" Since all the outstanding violinists were Jewish, there being not a single "Aryan" on the list, the Japanese manager concluded that the Nazis would not permit Aryans to play this "Jewish" instrument.[64]

Even as late as 1940 the Germans were unable to persuade the Japanese to remove Joseph Rosenstock, the talented teacher and conductor who created the Nippon Symphony, from his post. Still, the signing with Germany and Italy of the Tri-Partite Pact on September 27, 1940, by Foreign Minister Matsuoka did have several negative results for the Jews in Japan. In the agreement Germany and Italy recognized Japan's New Order in East Asia, and Japan recognized Germany's and Italy's new roles in Europe. The Nazis convinced the Japanese to prevent the opening of the fourth annual Far Eastern Conference, scheduled for December 1940.[65] Then they subsidized and ran a fair in Tokyo at which tens of thousands of pieces of anti-Semitic literature were distributed, though few, if any, readers of this Nazi propaganda understood what a Jew was.[66]

About this same time, in November 1940, Inuzuka made an unusual government-sponsored radio broadcast in Tokyo in which he welcomed the Jewish refugees to Shanghai, a gesture that was strongly criticized by the German Embassy. Neither the Germans nor the Jews had any inkling that this man, under his pen name, Kiyo Utsunomiya, had recently published the popular, vitriolic anti-Semitic book *Yudaya mondai to Nihon,* which was highly lauded by the same German Embassy.[67]

Nor can one ignore the extraordinary fact that in the winter of 1940–41 Japan permitted the entry into Japan of more than two thousand Polish refugees who were traveling through Siberia with obviously phony Curaçao visas and eight-to-twelve-day transit visas. The refugees were allowed to stay in Kobe for from three to eight months while awaiting passage out. This enabled about half of the refugees to obtain papers to countries in the Western Hemisphere. The remainder were permitted to settle in the Japanese-occupied sector of Shanghai, where they survived the Holocaust. These life-saving papers were made available by Jan Zwartendijk, a Dutch honorary consul stationed in Kaunas, Lithuania. This amateur diplomat, who was in reality a representative of the Dutch Phillips Corporation, originally created the Curaçao visas as a means of enabling Jewish refugees who had fled Poland in 1939 to enter neutral Lithuania. Armed with these visas, the refugees took the next step and went to Sempo Sugihara, the Japanese commercial attaché in Lithuania. Although he had no official sanction, Sugihara stamped more than two thousand passports with a Japanese eight-to-twelve-day transit visa. These two visas enabled the refugees to obtain exit visas from the Russian authorities.[68]

About five hundred of the Polish refugees were the students, scholars, rabbis, and families of the Yeshiva of Mir, the only higher Talmudic academy saved intact from the Holocaust. While efforts were made to seek a haven for them in the West, they set up their *Beit Midrash* (study hall) in a quiet neighborhood of Kobe. The Japanese, who had never seen a yeshiva, let alone one in which students studied eighteen hours a day in their Talmudic singsong, sent an officer to investigate this strange phenomenon. After a few days the yeshiva was given governmental "clearance" and its members were declared "Holy idealists."[69]

With financial help from the Joint Distribution Committee, the local Jewish relief committee in Kobe, the Jewish Committee, better known as Jewcom, cared for the refugees during their months-long stay. Members of Jewcom approached the Hebrew-speaking Kotsuji, whom they remembered from the 1939 Far Eastern Conference, to seek help in extending the refugees' eight-to-twelve-day transit visas while they searched for safe havens in the West. Kotsuji visited Foreign Minister Matsuoka, the man he had reported to while an adviser to the Manchurian Faction. Matsuoka was technically head of the South Manchurian Railroad, which in reality was the ruling authority in Manchuria. After Kotsuji explained the use of "Jewish Power" on behalf of Japan, Matsuoka readily approved the extensions. Then he left on his trip to Berlin to cement the Berlin-Tokyo-Rome Axis with the Tri-Partite Pact.[70]

The refugees ultimately stayed in Kobe for three to eight months and were the recipients of much kindness and sympathy. They received donations of food, and some Japanese even gave them their own ration cards for hard-to-get bread or provided them free medical exams. About half of the refugees found homes in the United States, Canada, and elsewhere in the Western Hemisphere during the critical months before the bombing of Pearl Harbor. The remainder, including the entire yeshiva and members of a few other institutions of higher learning, found no place to go and were permitted entry into the Japanese sector of Shanghai.[71]

The attack on Pearl Harbor on December 7, 1941, ended the Japanese government's concern about the Jews, since their relationship with American Jewry lost its importance. As a secret Foreign Office document noted, "Heretofore, Japan's policy concerning the Jewish people was based on the Jewish Policy Plan which was adopted at a Five Ministers Conference on December 6, 1938. . . . [D]ue to the outbreak of the war, this necessity has been eliminated."[72] This also meant that Japanese officials, such as Shioden, who espoused the Nazi ideology became more influential. Their harsh suggestions for handling the Jews, however, were never fully implemented.[73]

While 1942 passed relatively uneventfully for the Jews, on February 18, 1943, the Japanese finally gave in to German pressure to set up a ghetto for the Jewish refugees. Even then the Japanese never used the dreaded word "ghetto," preferring the euphemism "Restricted Area." By May 18 all German, Austrian, and Polish refugees had been relocated to the Restricted Area, a dingy, treeless, two-square-mile section of Hongkew. The fact that thousands of Chinese were also crowded into this area made the incarcerated Jews feel somewhat less isolated.[74]

Not all the Jews in Shanghai were forced to live in the Restricted Area. Since the wealthy among the Sephardic Jews usually carried British citizenship, they were interned as enemy aliens along with nationals from the Allied countries. The less affluent Sephardim were either stateless or citizens of Iraq (which was not at war with Japan) and remained unmolested. Moreover, because of Japan's delicate relationship with the Soviet Union, the three thousand to four thousand stateless Russian Jews in Shanghai remained free throughout the war. The approximately fifteen thousand stateless Russian Jews living in North China and Manchuria also remained free and even prospered economically throughout the war.[75]

While the ghetto caused economic and psychological hardship, it in no way resembled its European counterpart. Japanese soldiers, with the help of unarmed Jewish auxiliary police, called *Pao Chia*, restricted access to the ghetto, but no walls or barbed wire surrounded it. The Japanese authorities generally left the community alone, allowing its cultural, religious, and educational activities to continue, and conducted no torture or shooting. Thus, while there was not much to eat, one could live in relative peace unless one needed a pass to leave the ghetto for business or medical reasons. Only then would a refugee encounter one of two men responsible for the passes. In charge of the daily and weekly passes was the tall, brutal Okura, who on the slightest pretext might throw a refugee in the typhus-ridden Ward Road jail, with dire results. The other officer, Ghoya, who dispensed the one-to-three-month passes, was a short, ugly psychopath. One minute he would slap or kick a refugee standing in line, and the next minute he would behave like a gentleman, providing the startled refugee with a better pass than he or she had requested.[76] Meanwhile, in Japan proper most of the Jews were left alone, though they were under surveillance along with other Westerners. The small Jewish population of Tokyo was required to relocate to two small resort towns in the mountains. Since Jews could no longer conduct their businesses, the poorer ones grew their own food or relied on the support of wealthier Jews.[77]

Since the ghetto restricted their economic activities, many refugees lost their sole means of livelihood. While some relief was now provided by the Russian Jewish community, many had to sell their last few possessions in order to avoid starvation. The primary source of relief funds, provided by the JDC, was cut off because of the United

States' Trading with the Enemy Act, which forbade any Jewish or other organization in the United States to communicate with the Jews in Japanese-occupied Shanghai or Nazi-occupied Europe. This even included the American transfer of Swiss francs through neutral Switzerland. In sharp contrast to the American government's restrictive policy, no such barriers were created by Japan. It permitted Swiss francs to be sent to Shanghai throughout the war by those willing to risk arrest in order to provide relief to their Jewish brethren. These included leaders such as Rabbi Abraham Kalmanowitz, a member of the presidium of the New York–based Vaad Hatzalah (the Orthodox rabbis' rescue committee). Ironically, by the end of 1943 Rabbi Kalmanowitz had convinced the U.S. State Department to allow money sent by all relief organizations to reach Jews in the ghetto in Shanghai or in occupied Europe.[78]

When Rabbi Kalmanowitz also drew up plans for the transfer of the rabbinical group in Shanghai to Sweden or Mexico, he not only obtained the approval of the United States and Japan but also was offered full cooperation by the Japanese. What eventually foiled these and other rescue plans was the Soviet Union's refusal to cooperate. Moreover, despite the creation of the ghetto, the Japanese authorities were still under the illusion that Jews marshaled inordinate power in the United States, as illustrated by the several (unsuccessful) attempts the Japanese made to send out peace feelers to the United States via unsuspecting Jews in Shanghai or Tientsin.[79]

In early January 1945 leaders of the Russian Jewish community of Tientsin were called to meet in Peking with Colonel Tomiaki Hidaka, head of a ten-man delegation from the Peking Military Mission. Hidaka discussed with the Jews the length of the war and the high number of casualties among the Americans, Jews, and Japanese. Getting to the heart of the matter, Hidaka revealed that everyone was aware of the powerful Jewish influence in the United States. He stressed the good treatment the Japanese had bestowed upon the Jews, especially the refugees. Hidaka then asked the Jews to appeal to their fellow Jews in the United States to persuade the government to halt the conflict. The embarrassed Jews managed a clever response. One of them said that although he would be glad to comply, such an appeal would make a negative impression on American Jews. They would assume that Japan was too weak to carry on, which would spur America to double its efforts to defeat her. This apparently satisfied the colonel.[80]

It was the Manchurian Faction's perception of the alleged Jewish Power that ultimately saved the Jews in China and Japan. Instead of adding to the tragedy of the Holocaust, the Japanese rescued close to eighteen thousand Jewish refugees from death at the hands of the Germans. And ironically, their actions were motivated by a unique form of anti-Semitism.

NOTES

1. A history of the Jews in Japan is still a desiderata; not a single scholarly article is devoted to this fascinating subject. At best there are Hyman Kublin's brief articles in the *Encyclopedia Judaica*, s.v. "Japan," "Kobe," and "Nagasaki." There is also a chapter (6) in Herman Dicker's undocumented volume *Wanderers and Settlers in the Far East* (New York, 1962), as well as a number of popular articles of varying accuracy by journalists and residents of Japan, some of which are cited below. (For a fairly

detailed listing, see David Kranzler, *Japanese, Nazis, and Jews: The Jewish Refugee Community of Shanghai, 1938–1945* [New York, 1976], 248 n. 2; see also a more complete bibliography on 583–97.) Therefore the statistics on Jews in Japan are at best good estimates. The sole accurate statistics, for Jewish refugees in Kobe during the period 1940–41, are found in ibid., chap. 11. For an estimate of the population statistics for the eight Jewish communities in Japan, Manchuria, and North China during the thirties, see ibid., 249.

2. Kublin, "Japan," *Encyclopedia Judaica*, vol. 9 (Jerusalem, 1972), 1280. See also Dicker, *Wanderers*, 162; Robert M. Lury, "Jews in Japan," *Jewish Center Yearbook* (Tokyo), 1956–57, 20; Abraham Black, "Jews in Japan," *Jewish Community Center Review* (Tokyo), 1957–58, 29; and Mary I. Swartz, "Jews in Japan," *Hadassah Magazine* (New York) 57 (1975), 10–11.

3. See n. 2. See also Stanley Jackson, *The Sassoons* (New York, 1968), 24, 41, 46.

4. Dicker, *Wanderers*, 162.

5. See esp. Jackson, *Sassoons*. See also Albert Parry, "Jews in East Asia," *Asia* 39 (September 1939), 513; and Kranzler, *Japanese, Nazis, and Jews*, chap. 2.

6. Joachim O. Ronall, "Jews in Japan," *Jewish Spectator*, February 1958, 20; Kublin, "Japan," 1281.

7. Kublin, "Kobe," *Encyclopedia Judaica*, vol. 10 (Jerusalem, 1972), 1118–19; Dicker, *Wanderers*, 163.

8. Kranzler, *Japanese, Nazis, and Jews*, 314–15.

9. Mark Wischnitzer, *To Dwell in Safety: The Story of Jewish Migration since 1800* (Philadelphia, 1948), 141–42; Dicker, *Wanderers*, 165–68. See also Kranzler, *Japanese, Nazis, and Jews*, 175–76; Swartz, "Jews," 50; and Black, "Jews," 29.

10. See esp. Kranzler, *Japanese, Nazis, and Jews*, chap. 11. Cf. Black, "Jews," 33–35; Dicker, *Wanderers*, 169–71; and Swartz, "Jews," 50.

11. Lury, "Jews," 2; see also Swartz, "Jews," 50.

12. Kublin, "Japan," 1280.

13. Parry, "Jews in East Asia," 515.

14. Dicker, *Wanderers*, 166, 172.

15. See esp. Kranzler, *Japanese, Nazis, and Jews*, chap. 7, which analyzes Japan's unique policy toward the Jews. For Schiff's role in creating the stereotype of the "influential international Jewish banker" who controlled the financial power of the United States and Britain and his influence on the Japanese, see esp. 175–76, 215 ff., and 240–41; and Dicker, *Wanderers*, 165–67. For the origin of these loans, see Cyrus Adler, *Jacob H. Schiff: His Life and Letters* (New York, 1928), esp. 213–30. See also Gary D. Best, "Financing a Foreign War," *American Jewish Historical Quarterly* 61 (December 1971), 371–82.

16. Adler, *Schiff,* chap. 7; Best, "Financing a Foreign War," 375–78; Parry, "Jews in East Asia," 514. For Schiff's public response to the Kishinev pogrom, see Kranzler, *Japanese, Nazis, and Jews*, 253 n. 16. On Schiff's relation to Takahashi, see Adler, *Schiff*, 237–39. See also Hideaki Kase, "Jews in Japan," *Chuo-Koron* 86 (May 1971), 234–47; Parry, "Jews in East Asia," 515–16. For Schiff's trip to Japan and the honors bestowed upon him, see Jacob H. Schiff, *Our Trip to Japan* (N.p., 1906); and Dicker, *Wanderers*, 164–65.

17. John Toland, *The Rising Sun* (New York, 1970), 61.

18. Kranzler, *Japanese, Nazis, and Jews*, 329–30.

19. Marius B. Jansen, "Einstein in Japan," *Princeton University Library Chronicle* 50, no. 2 (1989), 145–54; Tsutomu Kaneko, "Einstein's Impact on Japanese Intellectuals," in *The Comparative Reception of Relativity*, ed. Thomas F. Glick (New York, 1987), 351–79.

20. Based on a personal incident related by Professor Hyman Kublin, a world-renowned authority on Japan who resided there and taught for many years at Wasada University in Tokyo. See also Hyman Kublin, "Star of David and Rising Sun," *Jewish Frontier* 25 (April 1958), 15–22.

21. The first Japanese-language version of the *Merchant of Venice* was serialized in *Minkan zasshi*, nos. 98 and 99 (1877).

22. See esp. Kranzler, *Japanese, Nazis, and Jews*, 177–205. It is essential to realize two facets of Japanese society. First, it was the lower-echelon officers, such as captains and colonels, who "created" policy ideas, while the generals and government officials carried them out. Second, the relationship between classmates was closer even than blood relationships. This relationship existed between the two dozen or so members of the military and government that constituted the essential clique of Japanese anti-Semites who were responsible for the theory and implementation of the unique policy toward the Jews prior to and during the war in the Pacific.

23. Ibid., 176–78. For more information on the dissemination of the *Protocols*, see Norman Cohn, *Warrant for Genocide* (New York, 1967), esp. chaps. 5–7. See also Henri Rollin, *L'Apocalypse de notre temps: Les Dessous de la propaganda allemande d'après des documents inédits* (Paris, 1939). For the role of Admiral Kolchak and the influence of his anti-Semitism, see the excellent work by Zosa Szajkowski, *Kolchak, Jews, and the American Intervention in Northern Russia and Siberia, 1918–20* (New York, 1977), chaps. 7, 17.

24. Cohn, *Warrant*, 64.

25. For a summary of the *Protocols*, see ibid., 60–65. For the Jewish participation in the various Communist revolutions, see Jerry Z. Miller, "Communism, Anti-Semitism, and the Jews," *Commentary* 86 (August 1988), 28–39.

26. See, e.g., Kranzler, *Japanese, Nazis, and Jews,* 215–16.

27. Ibid., 170–71. The quotations from Yasue's works are taken from Rudolph Lowenthal, "Japanese and Chinese Materials Pertaining to the Jewish Catastrophe," an unpublished 293-page scholarly manuscript containing one- to two-page English-language summaries of Japanese anti-Semitic books and some articles (see esp. 265–74). The titles are given in Japanese, in transliteration as well as translation, as are the bibliographic details. This manuscript was originally prepared for the YIVO Institute for Jewish Research. A copy, with an added index, is in the author's possession, courtesy of Dr. Lowenthal.

28. For the problems resulting from modernization, see, e.g., two books by Edwin O. Reischauer: *Japan: Past and Present* (London, 1947) and *Japan: The Story of a Nation,* rev. ed. (New York, 1974). See also Ivan Morris, ed., *Japan, 1931–1945: Militarism, Fascism, Japanism?* (Boston, 1963); and Delmer Brown, *Nationalism in Japan* (Berkeley, 1955).

29. See Kranzler, *Japanese, Nazis, and Jews,* esp. 186–87, for the agrarian myth in both Japan and the United States.

30. Ibid., 178–82, 186–88.

31. *Yudaya-jin no inbo to heinichi mondai* (Osaka, 1924). The book is cited in Lowenthal, "Japanese and Chinese Materials," 73. See also Kranzler, *Japanese, Nazis, and Jews,* 205; and esp. Kase, "Jews," 234–37. For example, Setzuso Kotsuji wrote objective reports on the history and practices of Judaism. See copies of Kotsuji's papers in the Kogan Papers, Foreign Office, a collection of Japanese position papers relating to the Jews that were retrieved by Michael Kogan during the 1950s. They are a major source for my thesis on Japanese anti-Semitism. Most, but not all, of the Foreign Office documents have an identifying serial number. The originals and translations are in the possession of this author courtesy of Herman Dicker.

32. Kranzler, *Japanese, Nazis, and Jews,* 196–97.

33. During the 1920s the American industrialist Henry Ford published his viciously anti-Semitic book *The International Jew,* which was utilized by both Hitler and the Japanese for their own ends (see ibid., 196–97).

34. See n. 31.

35. Koreshige Inuzuka [Kiyo Utsunomiya, pseud.], "Shina jihan wa Yudaya mondai o bakurosu," *Kokusai Himitsu-Ryoku no Kenkyu* (Tokyo) 4 (1938), 28–47, cited in Lowenthal, "Japanese and Chinese Materials," 242–43 (*Kokusai Himitsu-Ryoku no Kenkyu* was an anti-Semitic journal). See also Kranzler, *Japanese, Nazis, and Jews,* 200–201, esp. n. 80.

36. Lowenthal, "Japanese and Chinese Materials," 73, 184.

37. Muto Taiti, *Angriff der Juden gegen Japan* (The Jewish attack on Japan) (Tokyo, 1939), 1–2; there is a three-page summary in German Foreign Office Inland 11, A/B Roll 120, microcopy no. 4667, *Juedisch-Japanische Beziehungen.* See also Lowenthal, "Japanese and Chinese Materials," 74, 115–16, 121, 189.

38. Kranzler, *Japanese, Nazis, and Jews,* 207–9, 216–17, 486.

39. Koreshige Inuzuka, "Report to the Naval General Staff, Jan. 18, 1939," cited in Kase, "Jews," 12.

40. Koreshige Inuzuka [Kiyo Utsunomiya, pseud.], *Yudaya mondai to Nihon* (Tokyo, 1939); Kranzler, *Japanese, Nazis, and Jews,* 200–201. For one of many examples of Inuzuka's help to the refugees, see 326–27.

41. For the Manchurian Faction and its relationship to the Japanese policy regarding the Jews, see ibid., 187–93. For a more detailed analysis of Ishiwara's ideology and its basis in Nichiren Buddhism, see Mark R. Peattie, *Ishiwara Kanji and Japan's Confrontation with the West* (Princeton, 1975). See also Toland, *Rising Sun,* esp. chaps. 4–5.

42. Kranzler, *Japanese, Nazis, and Jews,* 208–12.

43. Ibid.

44. For the experts' perception of American Jewry's power, see ibid., 219–31. For Stephen Wise's relationship to Roosevelt, see David Kranzler, "Stephen S. Wise and the Holocaust," in *Reverence, Righteousness, and Rahamanut: Essays in Memory of Rabbi Dr. Leo Jung,* ed. Jacob J. Schacter (New York, 1992), 169–75.

45. Kranzler, *Japanese, Nazis, and Jews,* 208–11.

46. For a brief background of the Birobidjan project, see Salo Baron, *The Russian Jew: Under Tsars and Soviets* (New York, 1964), 23–36. For the Japanese perception of "Jewish" Birobidjan, see Kranzler, *Japanese, Nazis, and Jews,* 224. For the plans for a Manchurian counterpart, with German refugees, see ibid., 237–38.

47. Kranzler, *Japanese, Nazis, and Jews,* 207 ff.

48. Ibid., 211–12.

49. Ibid., 212–13. See also Dicker, *Wanderers,* 35–55.

50. Kranzler, *Japanese, Nazis, and Jews,* 213.

51. Ibid., 213–18. In 1936 only Ayukawa's Five Year Plan was approved by the cabinet, while the "Jewish angle" was still evolving into what finally appeared full-blown on December 6, 1938.

52. Ibid., 213.

53. For an analysis of Yasue's speech, see ibid., 219–27; see also Dicker, *Wanderers*, 45 ff. For the text of the speech, see Kogan Papers, Foreign Office, January 13, 1938.

54. For Higuchi's speech, see Kogan Papers, FO S-9460-3-1640-1654, January 11, 1940. See also Kranzler, *Japanese, Nazis, and Jews*, 225–26.

55. Kogan Papers, FO-S-9460-3-1640-1654, January 11, 1940. See also Abraham Kaufman's report and version of this resolution, which he gave to the Russian Jews' representative, Lew Zikman, titled, "The Situation of the Jews in Japan and Manchukuo," 3–5. Zikman's correspondence with Herman Dicker is in the author's possession, courtesy of Dr. Dicker; see also Dicker, *Wanderers*, 46.

56. Kranzler, *Japanese, Nazis, and Jews*, 228–30, 264 n. 130.

57. Ibid., 228–29. Zikman's letter to Wise is in American Jewish Archives, Cincinnati, Ohio. See also the Zikman-Dicker correspondence.

58. Kogan Papers, Foreign Office, "Jewish Measures in View of the 1942 Situation," ca. January 1942. In addition to the factors mentioned in the text, the formalization of the slowly developing Japanese policy toward the Jews on December 8, 1938, was most likely the result of the confluence of a number of factors. One must take into consideration the timing, which drew Japan closer to the Axis and away from the West. For example, several weeks earlier, on November 2, the same day that it notified the League of Nations of its intention to withdraw, Japan had announced its New Order in East Asia. On November 19 Foreign Minister Hachiro Arita, a member of the Manchurian Faction, had announced that it would no longer permit an open-door economic policy in parts of China under Japanese influence. The availability of the German refugees at this crucial time in Japan's foreign policy was particularly important, since it fit neatly into the faction's view of helping Japan by being good to Jews.

59. Kranzler, *Japanese, Nazis, and Jews*, chap. 1, esp. 31.

60. Ibid., chap. 6. On the world's closing its doors to Jewish immigration, see Hans Habe, *The Mission* (New York, 1966); see also David S. Wyman, *Paper Walls: America and the Refugee Crisis, 1938–1941* (New York, 1968), esp. chaps. 2–3.

61. Kranzler, *Japanese, Nazis, and Jews*, 232–33, 236.

62. We have no details on Kotsuji's speech. Undoubtedly, his agenda was the same as that of the other Japanese authorities. It was his speaking in Hebrew that created the sensation (see ibid., 235, 322–23). In 1959 Kotsuji converted to Judaism and changed his first name to Abraham, the traditional Jewish name for converts. In his autobiography, *From Tokyo to Jerusalem* (New York, 1964), he only partially described his relations with the Jews under Japanese control in China and Japan, only hinting at his role as an adviser to the Japanese authorities on Jews (see, e.g., 143–44). He explained that people would not understand the times and the ideas. See also Kranzler, *Japanese, Nazis, and Jews*, 333–34; and Dicker, *Wanderers*, 183–86.

63. See *Japan Times*, March 1, 1939, 1; and Kranzler, *Japanese, Nazis, and Jews*, 233–35.

64. For Singer's dismissal, see Kranzler, *Japanese, Nazis, and Jews*, 217. If the response by the Japanese manager sounds strange, it is no more absurd than the Nazis' "Aryan" theory, which downgraded the study of psychology and psychiatry as "Jewish" sciences. One must also be aware that despite their alliance, the Japanese never overcame their mistrust of the Germans and their theory of the "Aryan" superiority over all other races, including the "yellow race" (see Raul Hilberg, *The Destruction of the European Jews* [Chicago, 1967], 45).

65. Kranzler, *Japanese, Nazis, and Jews*, 325–26. See also Rosenstock to Marvin Tokayer, April 15, 1974, Tokayer Papers, in the author's possession.

66. Although the Japanese public were vaguely aware of persistent government-sponsored anti-West propaganda, Tokyo's pro-Jewish policy was never explained to them. Even Arita's pronouncement of February 1939 had little impact on a populace that had only the slightest notion of who and what Jews were. See above, n. 20.

67. The speech is summarized in the *Shanghai Jewish Chronicle*, November 24, 1940, 7. For a summary of *Yudaya mondai to Nihon*, see Lowenthal, "Japanese and Chinese Materials," 245; see also ibid., 234–44. For the German reaction, see Kranzler, *Japanese, Nazis, and Jews*, 326–27.

68. This episode is detailed in Kranzler, *Japanese, Nazis, and Jews*, chap. 11; Sugihara's motivation had nothing to do with the official Japanese "Jewish" policy. In fact, there was no such thing as a Curaçao visa. Normally the governor's permission was required to settle in Curaçao. Zwartendijk stamped the refugees' passports with the statement, in French, "No Visa to Curaçao Necessary." With these in hand, the refugees went to Sugihara, who stamped the passports with brief

transit visas through Japan. He did this despite Tokyo's cabled instruction to halt this humanitarian practice.

69. Ibid., 318. See also Rabbi Joseph D. Epstein, interview by the author, Brooklyn, N.Y., October 15, 1968. Rabbi Epstein was the secretary of the Mirrer Yeshiva, and at times he served as the yeshiva's liaison with the Japanese authorities.

70. Kranzler, *Japanese, Nazis, and Jews,* 235, 322–23, 333–34. See also Kotsuji, *From Tokyo to Jerusalem,* chaps. 9–10.

71. Kranzler, *Japanese, Nazis, and Jews,* 322, 333–34.

72. Kogan Papers, Foreign Office, "Jewish Measures in View of the 1942 Situation."

73. See Kranzler, *Japanese, Nazis, and Jews,* chap. 16.

74. See ibid., chap. 17, for the establishment of the ghetto.

75. For life in the ghetto, see ibid., chaps. 17–18, esp. 454–55. The Russian Jews did suffer a few days of fear and jeopardy during the last days of the war, after the Soviet Union declared war on Japan on August 9, 1945, following the atomic bombing of Hiroshima and Nagasaki.

76. For portraits of Okura and Ghoya, see ibid., 496–500; their forenames are unknown.

77. Ronall, "Jews," 19–21.

78. See Kranzler, *Japanese, Nazis, and Jews,* 355–57, 432, 462, 558–62, 573 n. 57. See also David S. Wyman, *The Abandonment of the Jews: America and the Holocaust, 1941–1945* (New York, 1984), 248. In a 1968 taped interview with Dr. Joseph Schwartz, head of the JDC in Europe, I asked him why the State Department finally permitted the transfer of funds to Jews in enemy-occupied territory at the end of 1943, prior even to the establishment of the War Refugee Board on January 22, 1944. He responded, "There was a rabbi with a long white beard [i.e., Rabbi Abraham Kalmanowitz]. When he cried, even the State Department listened." For more detailed documentary evidence of this thesis as well as Vaad Hatzalah's influence on the State Department and the War Refugee Board, see David Kranzler, *Thy Brother's Blood: The Orthodox Jewish Response during the Holocaust* (New York, 1987), 38–41. See also the memo by William Riegelman, January 26, 1944, in State Department Papers, NA/SDDF 840.48 Refugees/5136, National Archives.

79. Kranzler, *Japanese, Nazis, and Jews,* 556–57, 562–63.

80. Ibid., 562–63.

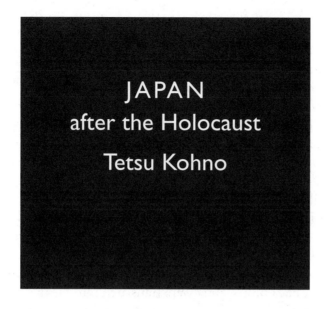

SEDIMENTS OF WARTIME ANTI-SEMITISM

Until the end of World War II, Japan's goal was to make "the divine land of Japan" the spiritual leader of the world, with the emperor enshrined as the messiah of all humanity. The Shintoist slogan "Hakkoh-Ichiu," literally, "all the world under one roof of his majesty's august virtue," was void of substance but managed, nevertheless, to inflate Japanese national pride.

Any form of treason against the emperor as the pillar of the national polity was unpardonable. This is why Japanese officers serving during the Siberian expedition (1918–22) could sympathize with their counterparts in the czarist army who were fighting the Bolshevik revolutionaries. Given the prominent role of some Jews in the Russian Revolution and the anti-Semitism so prevalent in Western countries, it is not surprising that even in Japan Bolshevism should have been equated with the so-called Jewish conspiracy, a conspiracy for global domination that allegedly caused all major wars, revolutions, assassinations, and a general moral degeneration.

After the Nazi accession to power and Japan's founding of its puppet state in Manchuria and its secession from the League of Nations, all in 1933, Japan fell under the domination of the military hierarchy and was being led toward fascism. Japan entered into the Anti-Comintern Pact with Germany in 1936 and joined Germany and Mussolini's Italy in the Triple Military Alliance in 1940. Once Japan became so closely linked with Germany, anti-Semitism became firmly institutionalized and the theory of a Jewish conspiracy was given fresh impetus by military leaders and ideologues whose main concern was to protect their nation and emperor against any impure, demonic foreign influences.

After Japan entered World War II in December 1941, anti-Semitic propaganda went unchallenged. Because of increased censorship of the press, the publication of expressions critical of Japan's militaristic national policies was prohibited. Unlike in liberal and antitotalitarian, democratic countries, there were very few opportunities for publicly ridiculing or denouncing the Jewish conspiracy theory in Japan. The United States, the United Kingdom, and all other hostile countries were alleged to be under Jewish influence. "The Greater East Asia War" (i.e., the Pacific War) was often called the war between Japan and the Jews. The feared "Jewish invasion" could seep into Japan like "frost on a chilly night" and then spread "like a fever."[1] Jews all over the world were labeled "profiteers taking advantage of wars" and typically were accused of amassing money and then controlling the mass media and entertainment industries, thus depriving all peoples of their national polity and vitality. Dozens of ideologues steadily produced such accusations against Jews. In the general election for the Japanese Diet in 1942, the virulently anti-Semitic Nobutaka Shioden (who had retired from the army with the rank of lieutenant general) received more votes than any other candidate.

Following *The Protocols of the Elders of Zion*, Hitler's *Mein Kampf* and numerous other books of Nazi propaganda were translated into Japanese. Fascinated with the Nazi spirit of national unity and the enormous military and industrial advancements made under the Führer, the eager reading public absorbed any new information provided by their model ally, including anti-Semitic materials. Even a work as specific as Othmar Krainz's *Juda Entdeckt Amerika* (Judah discovers America), a Nazi version of the history of Jews in America, was available in Japanese. This book led credulous readers to believe that Jews totally controlled major American political leaders and traditionally exploited every national emergency for speculative purposes. It asserted that Jews in Newport and Charleston initiated the slave trade and made enormous profits by using native African slave hunters, whom they paid with barrels of rum. This type of propaganda proved effective, for the Japanese were being taught that it was their role to help their one billion Asian "brothers" throw off the yoke of the Anglo-Saxon colonialists, who were under Jewish influence.

This widespread anti-Semitism did not disappear with the end of the war or even the democratization of the country. Though much diluted now, it still remains, like a sedimentary sludge that might be stirred to the surface whenever Japan needs a scapegoat to blame for a serious national crisis.

AUSCHWITZ RESONANT WITH NANJING AND HIROSHIMA

It is still a matter of conjecture whether the wartime Japanese government was aware of what was occurring in the Nazi concentration camps, particularly those built for exterminating Jews. In the first half of the 1930s, liberal Japanese intellectuals, such as journalists and academics living in Germany, were still allowed to publish articles critical of the Nazis' racial policies, and they did not fail to report on the outrageous persecutions of the Jews.[2] Like the Germans themselves, however, they underestimated Hitler, predicting that Jewish capitalists in Germany would never be oppressed and that the Nazi regime would eventually encounter significant opposition from antifascist forces in Germany.

Takayasu Senzoku, a student of philosophy and dramaturgy who went to live in

Berlin in 1932, claimed that he knew nothing about the Final Solution until the end of the war. But on November 9, 1938, he witnessed Kristallnacht. On his way to the university he saw a Jewish synagogue burning, storm troopers raiding Jewish stores, and Jews being evicted from their homes.[3] He remained in Berlin during the war as a part-time employee of the Japanese Embassy. Toward the end of the war, all embassy personnel were evacuated to Austria and eventually placed in the custody of the U.S. Army. It was only then, through a Salzburg newspaper, that Senzoku learned about the millions of Jews massacred by the Nazis. His profound shock was shared by all his colleagues.

Japanese anti-Semites should have been overjoyed to discover that the Final Solution had been implemented. But if they were, they kept their feelings to themselves. After August 1945 they disappeared from the public scene and were silent. There were no notable Jewish-related debates or publications in Japan until late 1952, when the Japanese translation of Anne Frank's *Diary of a Young Girl* was published. It was through the *Diary* that most Japanese learned about the Final Solution and the atrocities their former ally had perpetrated against the Jews and other "undesirable peoples."

The *Diary* became a best-seller immediately and went through one hundred printings (one million copies) by 1964. To commemorate the one-hundredth printing the publisher held a nationwide essay contest, gathering more than seven thousand contributions from high-school girls. Most of the writers expressed their hatred of war and the Nazis and sympathized with or praised the heroine, comparing her agony to that suffered by blacks or the Burakumin, a Japanese social minority traditionally considered outcast, perhaps because their ancestors included executioners, slaughterers, and leatherworkers. But one of the prizewinners wrote: "The fact that six million Jews had to be persecuted and massacred only because they were Jews made me think that it was not only because of the war but because something else had already existed."[4] This perceptive student managed to find a clue to what was really behind the Holocaust.

No public library in Japan lacks a copy or two of Anne Frank's *Diary*, and the book continues to sell briskly despite news from abroad suggesting that she might not have written it. Another Japanese translation of the *Diary*, based on the authenticated and unexpurgated Dutch edition, replaced the original version in 1986. As of January 1990 more than three million copies of the *Diary* have been printed since the first printing in 1952. The dramatized version of the *Diary* has been included in the repertoire of not a few high school and college theatrical clubs. The entry "Anne-no-nikki" (Anne's diary) appears (with the original Dutch title, *Het Achterhuis*) in such authoritative Japanese-language dictionaries as Iwanami's *Kojien* and Sanseido's *Daijirin*. Books and articles have been written by those who mourn Anne Frank's death. She has become a symbol for all persecuted Jewish adolescents and will be remembered for ages to come.

Some authors have visited the museum in Amsterdam that was once Anne's hiding place and felt obligated to extend their pilgrimage to Auschwitz. Machiyo Kurokawa, who made such a pilgrimage, described in her 1982 book *Anne-no Nikki-eno*

Tabi (A journey to Anne's diary) how she tried to put herself in Anne's place by drinking water from a faucet left running in one of the lavatories at Auschwitz. She later suffered terrible stomach cramps.[5] Others have flown directly to Poland. In December 1976 Shusaku Endo, a Catholic writer known for his *Chimmoku* (Silence), a novel about apostasy among the crypto-Christians in northwestern Kyushu under the late Tokugawa shogunate, made a three-hour tour of Auschwitz. Even after returning to Cracow he was unable to overcome his nausea and had difficulty breathing. He wrapped the shoes he had worn during the tour in newspapers and discarded them outside his hotel. "How could I put on the thing that trod on the ground soaked with rancor, curse, and grief?"[6]

Another author, the pacifist Katsumoto Saotome, recorded how he felt when he viewed the gas chamber and crematorium at the camp in *Aushuvittsu-to Watakushi* (Auschwitz and I): "My cheeks stiffened, my shoulder blades felt dislocated, and then my two legs seemed to grow leaden." He was continually obsessed by the thought "If it were I. . . ." Even a year after his return home he suffered from a recurring nightmare of being pushed into the gas chamber with his children "because of that specific medicine against forgetting he had gulped at Auschwitz": "With the iron door closed, the diesel motor starting to hum, and the lethal gas spreading like smoke, I hear a mother shrieking, 'Save this baby for God's sake!'"[7]

Both Kurokawa and Saotome are survivors of the ravages of war, Kurokawa of the atomic bombing of Hiroshima on August 6, 1945, and Saotome of the heaviest carpet bombing of downtown Tokyo, on March 10, 1945. As hard-core peace activists, both are aware not only of what it is to be a war victim but also of what it is to be on the side of the victimizers. In Holland, Kurokawa was told how cruelly Dutch prisoners had been persecuted in Japanese concentration camps in Indonesia and was asked why Emperor Hirohito had been reluctant to apologize for the atrocities committed by his soldiers. Kurokawa made a point of telling them how ashamed she was of what the Japanese armed forces had done in Asia before relating her own experience as an atomic-bomb survivor.

Saotome does not forget that the Japanese Empire was affiliated with the Nazis. He learned from Rudolf Höss's autobiography that the Japanese people's spirit of self-sacrifice for their country and for the emperor served as a glorious model for SS cadets. He also remembers that Hakushuh Kitahara, one of Japan's best contemporary poets, wrote a wartime song titled "Welcome, Hitler Jugend!" which began with the phrase "Brightly shining Hakenkreuz!" and ended with "Banzai Hitler Jugend! Banzai Nazis!"[8]

Following Anne Frank's *Diary*, Victor Frankl's *Ein Psycholog erlebt das Konzentrationslager* (first published in English as *From Death-Camp to Existentialism*, revised edition titled *Man's Search for Meaning*) and other books by concentration camp survivors were translated into Japanese. Frankl's book was published in Japan in 1956, and by January 1990 nearly half a million copies had been sold. It was released under the title *Yoru to Kiri* (Night and fog), perhaps to capitalize on the sensation created by Alain Resnais's documentary film *Nuit et Brouillard* in 1955. (This film, however, had been banned by the Japanese censors because of the excessive cruelties depicted in it. It was only in 1961 that it was shown publicly in Japan.) Frankl's book attempted to fathom the human psyche as it responded to the extreme circumstances of the camps. Japanese readers have been impressed by the fact that Frankl, a survivor of Auschwitz, could advocate such existential values as love, freedom, and responsibility, all of which were authenticated for him by the horrors he suffered.

So it was only in the early to mid-1950s that the grim revelations of Nazi atrocities were widely exposed in Japan. By then it was also widely known that the Japanese army, after occupying Nanjing in 1937, had committed countless brutalities, among them massacring approximately two hundred thousand noncombatant Chinese, exploding poison-gas shells in northern China, and practicing vivisection on Chinese prisoners (called "logs") in secret medical experiments at a facility near Harbin.

The similarities between Nanjing and Auschwitz were apparent. In both cases the oppressor's complete contempt for the oppressed was justified and intensified by crooked racial prejudices and notions of superiority. Only by committing barbarities did soldiers become heroes. What was worse, only by doing so could they stay alive in the army. Absolutely obedient to those in power, Japanese soldiers demanded absolute obedience from the powerless. Certainly the Japanese were not in a position to accuse the Germans of arrogance and cruelty. They were led to soberly reflect on the danger of being bound by ethnocentricity and prejudice.

Nevertheless, differences existed. Japanese brutalities had been committed against the Chinese as members of an enemy nation, and not merely because they were members of a specified racial group that had to be exterminated. (The Japanese army distributed "good-citizen certificates" to obedient Chinese in the occupied territories, while no Jews, however obedient, were ever regarded as "good citizens" by the Nazis.) This may have allowed the Japanese to feel that they were not so inhuman after all. At least the Japanese government held no equivalent of the Wannsee Conference to premeditate what was to occur in Nanjing.

After his visit to Auschwitz in 1961, novelist Ken Kaikoh, who reported on the Eichmann Trial and later on the Vietnam War, stated in a letter to a weekly book review that "fifteen years since, yet countless bits of human bones are scattered over the field like seashells on the beach. I vividly felt the excesses of the German spirit, and was left mute. Dante's imagination seems to be a child's ravings [in comparison]."[9] In another essay Kaikoh tried to explain the Germans' eerily enthusiastic devotion to the nationalism that caused them to disconnect themselves from their human nature more rigidly than any other people has done: "The Japanese brutalized in Nanjing, the Americans in Korea, and the French in Algeria, but these are cases of 'passion' gone berserk, rather like sexual frenzy, which could hardly be extended to the level of the Germans' sadism. Those non-Germans deftly thought twice before reaching a point at which their passion has its own way apart from the body. In certain cases, humanity hangs on something that the Nazis must have viewed as an impure and benighted animal sentimentality. Unfortunately, such a combination [of humanity with sentimentality] never occurred in the low-humidity zone of Auschwitz."[10]

The atomic bombs dropped on Hiroshima and Nagasaki reduced the Japanese to a vanquished people for the first time in their history. In Japan comparisons have been made between the atomic bombing and the Holocaust. This might be unacceptable to those who point to the absolute uniqueness of the Holocaust. If Japan had known better, it could be argued, the tragedy of Hiroshima might have been avoided, while the Holocaust could not have been avoided even if European Jews had known better. But Japan, like every nation, regards its own suffering as unique and claims that it can compare notes with any other whose ordeals seem to match its own.

After 159,000 mostly nonbelligerent people were killed by the atomic blast in Hiroshima followed by another 74,000 in Nagasaki three days later, the Japanese could not help suspecting that a racist motive lay behind this unparalleled nuclear devastation.[11] Many felt that the bombs would not have been dropped if the Japanese had had white rather than yellow skin. Allegedly the United States dropped the second bomb on Nagasaki to limit the Soviets' involvement in the war against Japan and to minimize their influence on postwar developments. The politics of power were more important than the lives of thousands of citizens. The Japanese also bitterly noted that Japanese Americans had been the only U.S. citizens of foreign ancestry forcibly confined in the so-called relocation camps during World War II. This treatment, as well as the nuclear holocaust, allowed the Japanese to understand what it was like for the Jews or any other people to be treated as pariahs. For the first time in their history the Japanese learned to put themselves in the shoes of the oppressed.

ARGUMENTS FOR AND AGAINST THE EICHMANN TRIAL

The 1961 trial of Adolf Otto Eichmann in Jerusalem attracted worldwide attention, and the Japanese media coverage was not behind that of other countries. Famous writers and veteran reporters were sent to attend the trial, and their reports home provided a forum for keen discussions of the Jewish Question, Nazism, and the state of Israel. There was a great deal of sympathy for the persecuted Jews, but the legality of the trial was questioned. For example, essayist Michiko Inukai censured Israel, stating: "The United Nations, however imperfect and weak, is still a supranational organization, actually the only one that could take a standpoint free from national rancor or retribution; therefore Israel should have entrusted the U.N. with final judgment over this case."[12] She upheld Martin Buber's opinion that if Israel wished to stand on a higher moral ground than the Nazis, no sentence should be passed on Eichmann. In its "Konnichi-no mondai" (Today's problem) column, the *Asahi Shimbun* agreed, deploring such eye-for-an-eye retribution: "It is more important to watch over the massive war machine that involved Eichmann himself and over the grim reality of nuclear weapons than to get rid of him as a key criminal."[13]

Ken Kaikoh labeled Eichmann's death sentence a form of terrorism disguised as justice: "Is this all there is to the wisdom of the Chosen Hebrews? . . . They just yielded to the common behavior any nation could exercise. . . . Eichmann should have been kept alive and set free to choose his own destiny. They should have banished him after branding a *Hakenkreuz* on his forehead."[14] Historian Masanori Miyazawa, author of *Yudayajin Ronkoh* (A study of Japanese debates on the Jew), claimed that the Japanese, who had been idle onlookers and even indirect supporters of Nazi inhumanities, were not entitled to ask Jews to act with saintly forgiveness: "We cannot be Bubers or Arendts."[15] Analyzing Kaikoh's statement that the Israelis "just yielded to the common behavior any nation could exercise," Miyazawa questioned whether such seemingly humanitarian opposition did not demand an unreasonably high level of ethical behavior from the Israelis alone. According to Miyazawa, suggestions that Israel should be a morally superior nation are certain to breed more prejudice against the Jews. This requires all the more attention because anti-Semitism is still so prevalent, especially in Germany itself, that the Jews themselves have been blamed for their own persecution. Miyazawa emphasized the importance of eliminating unrealistic expectations rather than worrying about the evil influences of retribution.

Critic Takeshi Muramatsu offered a clear-cut vindication of the trial. "It is an unprecedented, unheard-of event that one nation planned and implemented the extermination of another; where there is no precedent, there is no law, therefore procedures had to be primitive. A trial of a victimizer at the hands of the victims and their bereaved is similar in appearance to, but different in essence from, a trial of a defeated power at the hands of the victorious. Why not understand this point?" On the other hand, Muramatsu quoted Dr. Robert Servatius, counsel for the defense, who claimed that it was illogical for Israel to punish a person whose "crime against humanity" had not been committed against Israelis and had taken place before the birth of the Jewish state. Israel had also deceived the Argentine government with some plausible plan about the establishment of a new air route. However, Muramatsu reconsidered, if it is unacceptable to let a burglar retire with impunity, it is still more so to condone a key planner of the extermination of a people. He concluded that since both Germany and Argentina had refused to defend Eichmann, there was no country or international agency to decide the case; therefore, nobody was in a position to object to the judicial proceedings conducted by Israel, which represented the victimized Jews.[16]

While covering the Eichmann trial in Jerusalem, Muramatsu himself had to give interviews. He was often asked what he, as a member of the nation victimized by atomic bombs, thought of the trial. "That," his interviewers would say, "also was a genocide. What a pity that you could not put Truman on trial. But at least you fought against the Americans; the Jews were killed without even fighting against the Germans." He was at a loss what to answer because he was aware of a multitude of crimes that Japan had committed all over the Asian continent.[17]

The World Reacts to the Holocaust

DEBATES ON THE POPE'S SILENCE DURING THE HOLOCAUST

Though it had far less impact than the Eichmann trial, the year-long debate over Rolf Hochhuth's *Der Stellvertreter* (The deputy) between a secular academic—Michio Takeyama, a professor of German at the University of Tokyo as well as a much-publicized essayist and novelist[18]—and a Catholic ex-journalist—Shin Tatsuki (pen name of Nobuchika Ninomiya), formerly an editor of the *Yomiuri Shimbun*—mirrored the grave concern aroused among Japanese intellectuals about the Christian responsibility for acquiescing to the Nazi genocide of the Jews. Hochhuth's play bitterly indicted Pope Pius XII and the Roman Catholic Church for their silence during the Holocaust through the character of a young priest who, after his unsuccessful appeals to the papacy to use its influence for stopping the Nazi lunacy, dared to wear a yellow star like a Jew and go to Auschwitz to stand proxy for the pope. While Takeyama took Hochhuth's side, Tatsuki, an alumnus of the Jesuit-run Sophia University, tried to exonerate the pope of the dramatist's charge of negligence in the face of the Nazi atrocities.

Takeyama was one of the Japanese pioneers of Holocaust studies. In his research on the Nazi persecution of the Jews, he began to investigate how and why such horrors could have occurred among those professing Christianity. He was not satisfied by explanations attributing the Nazi phenomenon to the dehumanization and mechanization of modern civilization. After his visit to Dachau, he tentatively concluded that there must be some explanation in Christian theology. In his 1963 essay "Seisho-to Gasushitsu" (The Bible and the gas chamber), he established a connection between the Gospels and the Holocaust. On rereading the New Testament, he confirmed that it abounded in intolerant curses on heathens, particularly Jews. With a warning that this was not from Hitler's *Mein Kampf,* he quoted from the Gospel according to John, in which Jesus said to the Jews: "Your father is the devil and you choose to carry out your father's desires. He was a murderer from the beginning, and is not rooted in the truth; there is no truth in him" (8:31–44). He said that this biblical reference to Jews as children of the devil, conspirators, evildoers, and beasts in human form has been a sentiment fixed in the Christian "collective unconscious." To the Nazis and their rank and file, therefore, the beliefs of Hitler, Himmler, and other anti-Semites were self-evident and in keeping with what they had been taught. They had been prepared to endure all the costs incurred by the Final Solution, which was a heavy burden on the Nazi war effort and an utter folly in terms of lost labor. Takeyama noted, "Hitler betrayed the Christian teaching of love but invoked Christian curses faithfully."[19] Later he bolstered this conclusion with visits to Auschwitz and Terezin as well as with *Gottes Erste Liebe* (God's first love), a massive book by philosopher Friedrich Heer, who had thoroughly demonstrated that Hitler's words and deeds were a logical consequence of Christian teachings since the medieval period. Takeyama summarized the main part of Heer's tome in five installments in the magazine *Jiyu* (Liberty) in 1969.

Shin Tatsuki's rebuttal, "Roma Hohoh-ni Sekinin-wa Nakatta" (The pope was not responsible), was published ten months later in *Jiyu*. Tatsuki started by excoriating Hochhuth's "malicious distortions of facts." He said that Hochhuth's Protestant view of the pope was based on a biased protest against the Catholic Church or was the result of his inferiority complex regarding Catholicism. "Historical facts show that Pius XII was just the opposite of Hochhuth's description. . . . The pope resisted Nazism in word and deed."[20] He said that it was true that Pius XII had neither openly criticized the Nazi racism nor excommunicated Hitler from the Catholic Church. But what the pope had had to avoid at all costs was the exacerbation of the Nazi lunacy and the ensuing massacre of Catholics as well as Jews. He had had to desist from making openly critical statements in order to minimize further tragedies. While Hochhuth held the pope responsible for nonfeasance during the war, he made no mention of the Protestant collaboration with the Nazis. Through his criticism of Hochhuth, Tatsuki was also adumbrating his intention to reprove Takeyama for connecting the teachings of the Catholic Church with the Holocaust.

In a November 1964 essay in *Kokoro* magazine titled "Zaiseki—Roma Hohoh-to Tennoh-no Baai" (The liability for the wartime nonfeasance—the cases of the pope and the Japanese emperor) Takeyama echoed the cry of Hochhuth's protagonist, young Father Fontana, that the pope should have gone to Auschwitz with a yellow star sewn on his robe and emulated Peter, who, after asking "Quo vadis, Domine?" returned to Rome to be martyred. He said that Pius XII had paid more heed to the political conditions than to the Christian precept "For whosoever will save his life shall lose it: and whosoever will lose his life for my sake shall find it" (Matthew 16:25). Takeyama said that it was easy to give a sermon but difficult to practice what one preached, and he asked, "Didn't the pope sadden the Holy Spirit?" Takeyama then compared the pope and the Tenno (Emperor Hirohito). In contrast to the Tenno, whose authority as a living god was utilized by the autocratic military to sanctify expansionist purposes and eventually to terminate the war, the pope, as a proxy of God, was in the position to lead Christian souls all over the world. If, as Tatsuki said, the pope as such was not mighty enough to confront the Nazis, then, Takeyama wondered, who on earth was?[21]

Takeyama also challenged Tatsuki's assertion that charity begins at home, that it is not egocentric to save one's own child before another's. According to Tatsuki, if the pope had openly charged Hitler, Christians might have been victimized; therefore, it was natural for the pope to try to save Christians before Jews.[22] Takeyama, in response, pointed to Matthew 18:12–14: "Suppose a man has a hundred sheep. If one of them strays, does he not leave the other ninety-nine that never strayed. In the same way, it is not your heavenly Father's will that one of these little ones should be lost." Presumably, papal love should be different from such instinctive impulses as parental love.[23]

Tatsuki's rejoinder appeared in a February 1965 article in *Jiyu* titled "Yudayajin-no Shukumei" (The destiny of the Jews). He repeated that it had been an unequivocal imperative for Pius XII to maintain the Catholic Church and that given the central role played by the Jews as pernicious vermin undermining the German nation, the pope's admonitory bulls had had to avoid this sore point, addressing it obliquely in generic terms. In response to Takeyama's quotation from the parable of one stray sheep, Tatsuki referred to this stray sheep as a spiritually troubled one. It therefore followed, he said, that in equating the stray sheep to the persecuted Jews Takeyama had confused the case of troubled spirituality with that of political persecution. Tatsuki also objected to the connection Takeyama made between the infallibility of the pope and the inviolability of the Tenno. The pope had spiritual leadership only, while the Tenno was the very source of political and moral leadership during the war. Takeyama had been misguided in assuming that the pope bore the same kind of responsibility as the Tenno.[24] Tatsuki emphasized that the clergyman's primary duty lay in devotion to God's words.

Tatsuki admitted that there were anti-Jewish sentiments in the Gospels, especially in the fierce words in John 8:31–44, which had certainly stimulated religious and social anti-Semitism since the medieval period. These words, however, had been uttered to awaken the Jews, a provisional anti-Semitism, so to speak, and were entirely different from the Nazi anti-Semitism, which included the extermination of the Jews. Tatsuki concluded that it had been rash of Takeyama to connect the Gospels with the gas chambers.

Takeyama's countercharge came in the May 1965 issue of *Jiyu*. In "Kirisutokyou-to Yudayajin-no Mondai" (Christianity and the Jewish Question) Takeyama wrote that he could not abide Tatsuki's argument that the clergyman's role lay solely in his devotion to God's words and that therefore he should observe political neutrality and his actions should not go so far as to bring him into conflict with the forces of evil. Takeyama continued to blame the pope for his inaction during the war, saying that in view of his spiritual influence on Christendom as well as Hitler's reluctance to cause friction with the Catholic rank and file, the pope could have achieved significant results by resisting the Nazis. "Had Father Kolbe, a saint who starved to death in the place of a Jewish inmate at Auschwitz, or Cardinal Mindszenty, an opponent of Communism in Hungary who never compromised his principles, acted against the clergyman's code of behavior?" he asked.[25]

Nor could Takeyama accept Tatsuki's theory that anti-Semitism in the Gospels was a warning provisionally extended to unconverted Jews that unless they converted, they would remain the devil's children and targets of persecution. Tatsuki's pretext attested, therefore, to the undeniable historical fact of "conversion or persecution," which has been emulated even in modern political ideologies. Takeyama argued that theological anti-Semitism as manifested by Christianity was indissolubly linked with the political intolerances of fascism and Communism.

Here the argument ended, for Takeyama himself pointed to the futility of continuing to debate with a Catholic believer on a matter of faith. He admitted that from a Catholic point of view Pius XII might indeed have been a man of moral courage and of deep deliberation, as depicted by Tatsuki. It might not be wrong to say that the pope or the Catholics in general could be neutral to evil if they had to defend the Catholic Church. "If so," Takeyama remarked, "with all the beauty and splendor of its architecture, apparel, adornment, rituals, and lores, Christianity would pale into insignificance in my view."[26]

RESPONSES TO THE ARAB-ISRAELI CONFLICT

Through the early postwar period, from the founding of the nation of Israel to the Eichmann trial, the Japanese media were generally friendly to Jews and the new Jewish state. Japanese tourists visited Israel in increasing numbers. Not a few Japanese were fascinated with ancient Israel from a religious or historical standpoint. A group of Japanese archaeologists excavated ruins on a slope of Mount Carmel in 1961. The utopian kibbutz system was another attraction. One sociologist after another carried on fieldwork as temporary kibbutz members. In association with the Israeli Embassy in Tokyo, the Japan Kibbutz Institute was established in 1962; it has annually sponsored many young persons wishing to experience life on the Israeli kibbutzim.

Mikaru Ishihama, a college student who participated in this program, published a travelogue called *Sharomu Isuraeru* (Shalom Israel), in which she concluded that there seemed to be a stronger spirit of comradeship among Israelis than among Japanese.[27] While in her observations she was flexible enough to comprehend the complexities of the Arab-Israeli conflict, it should be pointed out that some Japanese kibbutz enthusiasts and pro-Israeli Christians with a strong messianic orientation tended to idealize Israel, calling themselves "Japanese Zionists," for example. Such attitudes would now be considered exceptional in Japan.

At the outbreak of the Six-Day War in 1967 there was a clash of opinions among Japanese intellectuals regarding the Arab-Israeli conflict. Some sided with Israel and criticized the simplistic dichotomy that not a few progressives had drawn between Jewish nationalism as an imperialist movement and Arab nationalism as an anticolonialist vanguard. They also asserted that Jews had consistently recognized the necessity of peaceful Arab-Israeli coexistence, as had been proven by the frequent Israeli peace appeals addressed to, but invariably rejected by, the Arabs since preindependence days.

Many more supported the Arab camp, attributing the Middle East turmoil to the establishment of the Zionist state in Palestine. In their view, Zionism was a degenerate ideology that aimed to develop a Jewish sector at Arab expense. It was vehemently insisted that Jews could not stand on a par with Arabs until they abandoned Zionism, severed their ties with Western imperialist powers, and became Palestinians. Of course the Jewish state was never to be tolerated in this Palestinian-centered perspective. The vitriolic diatribes of some pro-Arab disputants against Israel and Zionism as the root of all evil were reminiscent of those of the Jewish conspiracy theorists in the prewar days.

Such conflicting attitudes were clearly delineated in 1972, when three members of the Japanese Red Army shot passengers at Lod Airport. Pro-Arab Japanese students praised the attackers, two of whom died, as heroes and demanded the release of Kohzoh Okamoto, who had survived and been arrested. On Japanese campuses, donations were solicited for Okamoto's defense. On the other hand, the Japan-Israel

Friendship Association and other sympathizers with Israel immediately started collecting funds for the injured and the relatives of those who had been killed. A Christian group in Kyoto held a prayer meeting to mourn the innocent victims and repent before God and the Israeli people.

The Japanese government faced criticism at home when it dispatched an apologetic envoy offering *mimaikin* (literally, "sympathy money") to Israel. Katsuichi Honda, a journalist popular for his stories of downtrodden peoples everywhere, contended: "When Che Guevara conducted guerrilla operations in Cuba, did the Argentine government pay anything to the Batista regime in token of sympathy or compensation or whatever? Japan has not paid anything even to China, where millions of people were slaughtered by the Japanese forces. Our special envoy should rather have flown to Hanoi, where planes from U.S. carriers based in Japan are still indiscriminately bombing innocent people."[28]

Another example of Japan's generally pro-Arab stance was its reaction to the Arab massacre of eleven Israeli Olympic athletes in Munich in 1972. Only one Japanese official attended the memorial service at the main stadium, in sharp contrast to the whole Polish team, next-door neighbors in the Olympic village, standing in full dress. This conduct was deplored by at least one Japanese reporter, who accused the Japanese team of being "medal animals."[29]

After the onset of the Arab oil embargo in the final stages of the 1973 Yom Kippur War, Japan experienced severe inflation and recession. Various energy-saving measures were introduced. Car owners were asked not to drive, and gas stations did not open on Sundays. Air-conditioning units were operated for shorter periods of time with the thermostats set a few degrees higher. All over the country, panicked people anticipating shortages queued up at stores to buy more rolls of toilet paper and more boxes of detergent. Owing to continuous markups on construction materials, building expenses skyrocketed. Since then the general image of Israel as a troublemaker has lingered in Japan. Japanese intellectuals tend to express sympathy for the dispossessed Palestinians and to believe reports of Jewish injustices toward Arabs. There was even an abortive attempt to boycott a film about the Entebbe rescue.

In 1979 a large private university in Tokyo decided that ten of its teachers would hold a colloquium on the Middle East problem. However, eight of these professors were primarily interested in the Arab countries and did not know much about Israel. This ratio of eight to two was fairly representative of the pro-Arab inclinations then prevalent in Japan. There are some historical explanations for Israel's unpopularity. The Japanese have not forgotten the lessons drawn from their abject failure in expansionism, which started with the seizure of Manchukuo (Manchuria). It is no wonder that they were quick to associate the Israeli presence in Lebanon with the Japanese rule of old Manchuria. And Israel's disregard of the Palestine Liberation Organization (PLO) as a political entity reminded them of Japan's one-sided statement in 1937 that it would have nothing to do with Chiang Kai-shek's nationalist government.

The Israeli military occupation of the West Bank and Gaza reanimated Japan's sense of guilt as a former imperialist. The Japanese had repeatedly been reminded by the formerly colonized or invaded peoples that justice always stands on the side of the fighters for freedom and independence, while oppressors are destined to sink into moral degeneration. Israel's annexation of the Golan Heights in 1981 aroused suspicions about its territorial aspirations. The *Yomiuri Shimbun*, the newspaper with the largest circulation in Japan, remarked at the time: "With each move made by [Premier Menachem] Begin, the prospect for peace in the Middle East recedes."[30] There is no doubt that Israel's invasion of Lebanon in 1982 was far more emphatically condemned than its occupation of the West Bank. However, it was the media coverage of Israel's actions in the occupied territories, especially during the Intifada, that greatly damaged Israel's image in Japan.

Israel's policies were considered too reminiscent of the harshly oppressive colonial policies of the old Japanese Empire. In addition, since the end of World War II the Japanese have been unswervingly antimilitarist, conveniently ignoring the fact that their country is in effect under the protection of the American nuclear umbrella. The Israelis, in contrast, are known to allocate a very large proportion of their total resources to military defense and to be ever vigilant concerning the security of their beleaguered country. Israel's rallying cry is "Masada will never fall again," while Japan's is "No more Hiroshima." Japan's pacifist attitude has managed to prevent the repeal of the constitutional article on the eternal abandonment of armaments and has set a ceiling on the military budget of 1 percent of Japan's gross national product. It is therefore natural that there should be a lack of understanding between the two countries.

Finally, the Japanese view with profound distrust the religious arguments some Israeli leaders employ to justify their policies. They have dark memories of being taught to believe, according to the state religion, Shinto, that they were divinely chosen and divinely entitled to spread the empire. They cannot help, therefore, finding an analogy between the old Japanese expansionist policy and Israel's grip on the occupied territories. Japanese intellectuals are aware that the inconsistency between power and morality does not occur in Israel alone. Yet they insist on holding Israel to a different standard because of their belief that the Jews, who have such a long history of enduring and exposing unjustified persecutions, should be particularly sensitive about recognizing the harmful effects their own power politics have on other national groups.

These ingrained historical perceptions notwithstanding, Japan as a major economic power has been obliged to modify its foreign policy according to the ever-changing international situation. In view of Japan's dire need for Arab oil and the country's increasing trade with Arab countries, of course, it was not advisable to antagonize the Arab countries, nor was it beneficial to offend those Jewish American businessmen who dealt in some 40 percent of Japanese exports to the United States. As anticipated, the Conference of Presidents of Major American Jewish Organizations did not overlook Japan's compliance with the Arab pressure to boycott Israel. According to Daniel Elazar, the conference asked local Jewish communities to make their views known to the Japanese authorities, and "informal talk of a counterboycott (to any unfavorable Japanese actions) was encouraged or at least allowed to spread." There were indications that the presidents' conference had at least the tacit support of the U.S. government, which made its views on Japan's actions public.[31]

A brief survey of the relations between Japan and the United States prior to the Arab oil embargo is in order here. In 1971 President Richard Nixon suddenly and unilaterally erected barriers on the import of Japanese textiles, probably with an eye to satisfying those lobbies that would later help him through his reelection. The Japanese government was subjected to another "Nixon shock" when the United States did not even consult Japan about the historic U.S. rapprochement with Communist China; it was informed of Nixon's intended visit to Beijing only half an hour before his departure. Meanwhile, the war situation in Vietnam was getting so hopelessly out of control that the United States asked its allies to defend themselves with their own manpower (according to the so-called Nixon Doctrine). With the Japan-U.S. Security Treaty now in a slightly shakier state, Japan grew more concerned about its own strategic vulnerability and was driven to develop a more autonomous foreign policy. Then Japan faced the oil embargo of 1973, which naturally accelerated the Japanese consciousness of insecurity. This is why the Japanese response to the Yom Kippur War was uncharacteristically quick.

The Japanese government officially announced in the so-called Nikaido Communiqué in November 1973 that (1) no acquisition or occupation of territories by force was admissible; (2) all the Israeli forces should be withdrawn from those territories occupied during the 1967 war; (3) the territorial integrity and security of every nation in the Middle East should be respected; and (4) the legitimate rights of the Palestinians based on the United Nations Charter should be recognized and respected. This pro-Arab policy, which has been followed ever since, remains one of Japan's few foreign policies consistently supported by the media and the general public. It should be noted, however, that as pro-Arab as this communiqué might sound, the Japanese government was not rash enough to break off relations with Israel; nor did it specify any timetable or course of action.[32] Japan did not entirely sever economic ties. While actively trading with oil-rich Arab countries, Japan never failed to capitalize on its "Peaceful Constitution" (Article 9 of which stipulates relinquishing armaments forever) and claim its inability to supply any kind of weaponry or strategic materials to the Arabs. Obliged to avoid impairing its relationship with the United States and at the same time to avoid being targeted by the Arabs as a nonfriendly nation, Japan had to maintain an "equidistant Middle East diplomacy." In short, the Japanese policy toward Israel has been considered "more in a Japan-U.S. or Japan-Arab framework than as a relationship with Israel *per se*."[33]

Japan's attitude toward Israel during the 1970s and 1980s could be referred to as indifferent, if not hostile. Its official pro-Arab policy was supported by business circles, which had an enormous stake in the Middle East, as well as by intellectual circles, which tended to consider the Palestinian cause an integral part of modern Asian nationalism or rebellion against Eurocentric neocolonialism. Yet the "equidistant" diplomacy persisted. The PLO office in Tokyo, which opened in 1976, was never given formal diplomatic recognition, and Yassir Arafat, who visited Japan for the first time in 1981, was invited not by the government but by the Parliamentarians' League for Japan-Palestinian Friendship.

A marked change occurred in relations between Japan and Israel in 1986, when the volume of trade between the two nations suddenly increased by more than 50 percent. This increase in trade was accompanied by higher levels of exchange in the political and cultural fields. Japan's attitude toward Israel was tempered by such cataclysmic developments in Middle Eastern affairs as the Camp David accords, the Iran-Iraq War, and the war in Lebanon. The oil glut, and particularly the concomitant decline of the purchasing power once wielded by the oil-producing countries, made it necessary for Japan to reconsider its Middle East policy. Japan was no longer the largest exporter to the Gulf region. The Middle East became less important as a source of energy and as a potential market. The disharmonies among the Arab countries also allowed Japan to be less concerned about a possible backlash against a modified Middle Eastern policy. Israel had its own reasons to come into more positive contact with Japan. Besides its desire to make a political breakthrough, its business circles, hitherto oriented toward Europe and the United States, "now saw the outstanding potential market opportunities in Japan; they also saw Japan as a most fitting base for marketing in East Asia, particularly for the future penetration of China; thus the Israeli government explored seriously the possibility of inducing Japanese investment in the Israeli economy."[34]

In the fall of 1987 the two nations exchanged trade missions, and in the following summer Foreign Minister Sohsuke Uno (no relation to the anti-Semitic author Masami Uno) became the first cabinet member to pay an official visit to Israel. Diplomatic activity was further expanded after Israeli president Chaim Herzog attended the funeral of Emperor Showa (Hirohito) in February 1989. Later the same year, first Arafat and then Moshe Arens, Israel's prime minister, were officially invited by the Japanese foreign ministry as an expression of its eager concern over the conflict in the Middle East. During his stay in Tokyo, Arafat told his Japanese audience at a symposium that he was well aware of the rapprochements between Japan and Israel and reminded them of the widespread Palestinian influence in all of the Arab countries. Despite Arafat's reminder, there grew between Japan and Israel a more clearly bilateral economic relationship, which reached its climax when the Toyota Motor Company decided to cancel its trade embargo of Israel in mid-April 1991.

It should not be forgotten that Toyota's decision was announced immediately after the conference held in Los Angeles between Japanese premier Toshiki Kaifu and U.S. president George Bush. At the meeting Japan was pressured into seriously reconsidering its Middle East policy in connection with the Gulf crisis. Japan had acquired an unenviable international reputation because of its noncommittal attitude toward Iraq and its reluctant cooperation with the United States and its allies during the Gulf War. Even before facing this dilemma, Japanese leaders were comparing risks: which was more dangerous, complying with the Arab boycott, thus offending world Jewry, or trading with Israel, thus angering the Arabs? In view of Israel's utmost cooperation with the United States by not retaliating against Iraq's Scud missile attacks, and given the longtime concern of the powerful Jewish American lobbies with Japan's pro-Arab bias, the choice was obvious. If the Yom Kippur War facilitated Japan's compliance with the Arab boycott, the Gulf War provided the impetus for its rapprochement with Israel. Toyota's decision to start exporting its products to Israel was something more significant than a marketing move; it signaled a change in Japan's Middle East policy, proving at the same time the strong political pressures from across the Pacific. Japan's new stance toward Israel was vectored by Japanese-U.S. political dynamics.

Japanese business circles had for some time been worried that their pro-Arab bias might antagonize the Jewish lobbies in the United States, which could capitalize on Americans' already strong anti-Japanese feelings caused by trade frictions. Japanese industrialists and exporters feared that the Jewish lobbies might initiate an effective counterboycott at any time by joining forces with anti-Japanese politicians, whose enmity was evident in televised scenes of Japanese products being demolished with hammers. This phobia was amplified during the *endaka* (rising yen value) crisis and the concomitant economic downturn in the first half of the 1980s, thus creating an environment in which the old Jewish conspiracy theories were revived and a good number of Jewish-related books were published.

THE UNO PHENOMENON

In Japan in the 1920s all seditious or revolutionary ideas and movements, such as Bolshevism and democratic uprisings, were believed to have been engineered by the leaders of the Jewish conspiracy. In the 1930s and the early 1940s all foreign interventions against Japanese military expansion were immediately connected with the same conspirators. And even now, whenever a crisis arises from overwhelming external pressures, some Japanese continue to resurrect this theory. (Perhaps a parallel could be drawn with the Yellow Peril theory, which still persists in some Western countries.) As the trade frictions between the United States and Japan grew severe in the early 1980s, Japan faced much criticism of its "unfair" protectionist trade practices and then suffered from the unprecedented surge in the value of the yen against the dollar and its quick-freezing effect on exports. Such outside pressures caused a general malaise in Japan and drove people to seize with both hands any plausible explanation about the genesis of the problem. One explanation was the Jewish conspiracy.

In 1986 two paperbacks, *Yudaya-ga Wakaruto Sekai-ga Mietekuru* (If you know the Jews, you will understand the world) and *Yudaya-ga Wakaruto Nihon-ga Mietekuru* (If you know the Jews, you will understand Japan), were published, and by early 1987 more than a million copies had been sold.[35] Masami Uno, the author, claimed that the trade disputes between Japan and the United States and the "high yen" could be traced to the Jewish conspiracy. According to Uno, Japan's economic slowdown and industrial "hollowing out" had been engineered by the Jews, who surreptitiously controlled almost all major American corporations. But he cited no specific instances or documented individual cases to show that Jewish influence was in fact responsible for the alleged anti-Japanese economic activities, let alone prove that there was a Jewish conspiracy aimed at world dominion. Like the anti-Semitic theories that prevailed in the 1920s and 1930s, Uno's arguments were based on in-accurate data (he stated, for example, that Rockefeller, Morgan, du Pont, Mellon, Roosevelt, and Schultz were Jewish names) and hazy conjectures about an economic offensive being launched by international Jewish capital to take over one vulnerable Japanese enterprise after another.

On March 12, 1987, the *New York Times* ran Clyde Haberman's special report from Tokyo regarding Uno's two best-selling paperbacks. Entitled "Author Cites a 'Conspiracy of International Capital' and Sees Nation 'Bashed,'" this report prompted U.S. Senator Arlen Specter, a Republican from Pennsylvania, and Congressman Charles Schumer, a Democrat from New York, to send a joint letter to Premier Yasuhiro Nakasone, asking him to help prevent such extreme, prejudiced assertions. In April, in an article entitled "Johdan-janai! Yudaya Imbosetsu" (None of your Jew-ish conspiracy jokes!), published in the *Bungei Shunjuh,* one of Japan's most popu-lar monthlies, Professor Herbert Passin of Columbia University wrote a detailed exposé of Uno's attempts to pull all U.S. industrial and financial magnates and their combines under his immodestly reductionist umbrella of Jewish conspiracy. Passin was all the more emphatic because an executive of the Bank of Japan, the Japanese equivalent of the U.S. Federal Reserve Bank, had reportedly stated that "American high officials suddenly scrap the Japan-U.S. agreement meant for a more stable exchange rate. I found such tricks clearly explained in this book [of Uno's]."[36]

Stimulated by the foreign criticism, the Japanese media started analyzing the Uno phenomenon. Given the minuscule Jewish presence in Japan and the virtual lack among the Japanese of the anti-Semitic practices found in Western countries, it is evident that Jews themselves were not the direct cause of anti-Semitism in Japan. Just as inquisitions or witch hunts occurred in Western countries despite, or rather because of, nonexistent satans or witches, so anti-Semitism grew in places, including Japan, despite, or rather because of, nonexistent Jewish threats. In Japan one might feel free to say anything about Jews one has never met, but could one speak so freely about Koreans or Chinese, who live so near? In the absence of veri-fiable realities, one could hypothesize as audaciously as one pleased without any feeling of guilt. And the more audacious the hypothesis, the more intriguing. Thus, despite the absence of concrete proof, Jews were accused of being conspirators against national or global welfare, and anti-Semitic arguments tended to be abstract. Strangely, however, Uno had managed to sound less abstract and more realistic than past Japanese anti-Semites, probably because of the sense of imminent disaster then prevalent in the country.

In spite of Uno's stated desire to restore Japan's self-confidence and to promote a new form of nationalism, he actually encouraged the Japanese to impute their gen-eral malaise to some vague, hypothetical enemy whom they could freely hate and blame without the possibility of future retribution. It was certainly safer and easier to express national discontent and rancor against the Jews in general and against American Jewry in particular than against the United States. It is no exaggeration to say that what was referred to as Japanese anti-Semitism was a corollary of the latent antipathy among the Japanese to U.S. threats against Japanese trade and industry.

The delegates of the Jewish defense organizations who were sent to Japan after Uno and his ilk caused the so-called anti-Jewish furor could certainly collect a lot of anti-Jewish publications but could not find any anti-Jewish group or person.

Uno also knew how to row with the rising tide of neonationalism. Japan's successive achievements in industry and international trade in the past decades have inspired the Japanese to believe that their prosperity is due to their tradition of self-sacrifice and teamwork, which derives from the very homogeneity of the nation. There is a general conviction, expressed by former premier Nakasone himself, that such achievements could not be effected by a pluralistic society. Such ethnocentric pride easily leads to xenophobic paranoia when Japan considers itself to be threatened by foreign economic offensives. In such circumstances, Uno's prophecies about "another global depression being engineered by international Jewish capital" or "Japan's downfall through the reversion to the gold standard" can precipitate alarm among all social strata. Moreover, several incidents (exploited by Uno in his later publications) may have confirmed for some Japanese the suspicion that the powerful international Jewish leaders were capable of anything: the admission by an American Jew (who had made handsome donations to Jewish charities) that he had engaged in very profitable but illegal stock exchange deals; the conviction of another American Jew for spying for Israel; Israel's role in the secret supply of arms to Iran; the assertion by a disaffected Israeli operative who had worked in a top-security plant that Israel did possess nuclear bombs; and the revelation of the Israeli armament industry's links with South Africa and other countries.

Not all Japanese, of course, fell prey to Uno's theories. Critics and academics took Uno to task for his ignorance and arrogance. In May 1987 Masahiro Miyazaki, a journalist well versed in international politics and finances, published *Yudaya-ni Kodawaruto Sekai-ga Mienakunaru* (If you are sticky about Jews, you will not understand the world), in which he debunked Uno's ominous prophecies one after the other, revealing Uno's huge leaps in logic as well as his obvious lack of expertise. Miyazaki, who had covered the key world money markets, explained how major international banks and stock exchanges make deals in a matter of a few minutes to a few hours, constantly referring to a number of indexes. Miyazaki averred that "there can be no point of contact between these actual dealings and the so-called Jewish conspiracy." He asked, "If invincible whizzes at stock market arbitrage were all usurious (or Jewish) as Uno says, what are the House of Nomura and other big securities firms of Japan?" Miyazaki feared that "if an American equivalent of Uno changed the term 'Jews' into 'Japanese,' it would be easy for him to resurrect the Yellow Peril theory that has been latent among the whites for the past decades or centuries."[37]

Such responses clearly had a positive effect. For example, the Seibu Department Store, the flagship of the Seibu group, one of Japan's major conglomerates, and the Shohgakkan Press, one of Japan's largest and best publishers, canceled their jointly planned series of lectures to be given by Uno in early June 1987. Perhaps they had arranged the lectures to inform their clientele about Uno's theories on the national crisis. Flabbergasted at the overwhelming domestic and foreign rebuttals to Uno's books, both sponsors immediately notified all the lecture subscribers of the cancellation of the event with an apology. Uno countered public criticism with this message: "Jews always say, 'Scratch goyim, and there will appear anti-Semitism.' Their persecution mania is still deep-rooted. Their excessive reaction against my books serves as an example."[38] Then, Tokuma Shoten, the publisher of Uno's first two books, was dissuaded from following up with the third, which was issued by a minor press, Nihon Bungeisha, in 1988 under the title *Yudaya-ga Wakaruto Jidai-ga Mietekuru* (If you know the Jews, you will understand the times). Cut from the same cloth as the first two, this book purported again "to fully elucidate a shrewd plot to revert to the gold standard and to boldly present a way to escape this global panic."[39]

Uno published book after book, each with an intriguing title: *1992 nen-no Yudaya Keizai Senryaku* (Jewish economic strategy for 1992 [1989]), *Miezaru Teikoku* (The invisible empire: The Zionist Jews will dominate the world in 1993 [1989]), *Doitsu Daiyon Teikoku-no Bokkoh-to Yudaya Senryaku* (The rise of the German Fourth Reich and the Jewish strategy: The day the unified Germany will contain the Jews [1990]), *Hitorah-no Gyakushuh* (Hitler's counterattack: Japan's future is in the hands of the Germans and the Jews [1990]), *Busshu-no Nerai* (What Bush aims at: The conspiracy of the "original" Jews that will devour Japan [1991]),[40] *Yudaya-to Tatakatte Sekai-ga Wakatta* (Struggling with the Jews I understood the world: The collapse of white rule and "the two kinds of Jews" [1993]), *1994-nen Nihon-wa Chuhgoku-e Yuku* (Japan looks to China for partnership in 1994 [1993]), and others. It will suffice to list some of the theses he puts forth in these books:

1. The state of Israel was founded on the lie invented by the Ashkenazim, who do not derive from Palestine but rather from Khazaria. These Khazarians, who now dominate Israel with the Sephardim (the authentic Jews) as the underclass, ought to go back to Central Asia, which is really their homeland.[41]

2. The Holocaust is another lie spread by the Ashkenazic Jews. They have used it to legitimize the founding of the state of Israel, to secure free aid from the United States, and to demand compensation from Germany. The Jews have made a religion out of the Holocaust, and anyone who casts doubt on it is branded an anti-Semite. It is now a Zionist myth and the mightiest weapon of the Israeli propaganda machine. The myth is so strong that a Holocaust museum was built in the capital of the United States, to the annoyance of the American people. There is enough evidence to disprove the Holocaust: *(a)* That six million Jews were murdered by the Nazis is hyperbole: how could they cremate an average of five thousand people daily for three years? *(b)* Zyklon B is an insecticide and cannot kill men; moreover, no Zyklon B was detected in samples taken from the ceilings, walls, and floors of the so-called gas chambers. *(c)* The diary of Anne Frank, the most widely known book in Holocaust literature, was written by Meyer Levin at the request of Anne's father, Otto, for a fee of five thousand dollars.[42]

3. The Zionists made a secret deal with the Nazis. Former Israeli premier Yitzhak Shamir offered to yield such useless Jews as the aged, the diseased, and the very young into German hands in exchange for hard-core Zionists, who would devote themselves to the founding of a Jewish nation in Palestine. It is no wonder that the Zionists, who were ruthless even to their own kind, are more so to non-Jews. According

to the Talmud, only the Jews are human; non-Jews, *goyim,* are beasts. Zionists will go to any length to attain their objectives. The Anti-Defamation League (ADL), ostensibly an institute for advocating human rights, is in fact a criminal syndicate that inherited the underworld of Meyer Lansky, the most influential Jewish gangster of the twentieth century. The ADL actually controls the drug trade, and if anyone reveals this, he or she is immediately sued for anti-Semitic libel. Judicial authorities, major financial institutions, and even the police are under its influence. The ADL is the most powerful private secret police organization in the United States.[43]

In his 1993 book *Yudaya-to Tatakatte Sekai-ga Wakatta,* Uno declared that he was no longer pro-Jewish, but definitely anti-Zionist.[44] There is no doubt that he is heir to Nobutaka Shioden's mantle. Underlying Uno's anti-Semitism is a sort of Christian apocalyptic belief that there will be no peace until the Jews realize that the true messiah is Jesus and ask God's forgiveness for their wrongdoings. Uno demonstrates his etymological erudition by dividing the word "history" into "His" and "story," that is, God's story![45] He performs another verbal legerdemain when he asserts that the atomic bombing of Hiroshima and Nagasaki was virtually a Jewish plot. The *Enola Gay,* the plane that dropped the bomb over Hiroshima, Uno explains, was not the name of the pilot's mother but a Yiddish phrase meaning "Destroy the emperor!"[46] According to Willie Stern, a correspondent for *Maariv,* Israel's largest newspaper, Uno frankly admitted to foreign reporters that he was an imposter: he did not believe what he had written; he liked Jews, but nobody would buy his books if it turned out that he was pro-Jewish; and he intentionally wrote anti-Semitic tracts to draw attention to himself as a Japanese authority on the Jewish Question.[47] In *Yudaya-to Tatakatte Sekai-ga Wakatta* Uno affirmed that he had indeed been pro-Jewish when he met Stern in 1989. Only later did he discover that the reporter was an American Jew enthusiastic over the Zionist cause and had not understood him at all.[48]

One is at a loss how to explain why hundreds of thousands of Japanese readers have fallen prey to Uno's demagoguery. Some must have questioned his stories at first; but then they may have thought Uno's stories might not be entirely false. Even if his explanations are not cogent, something like the Jewish conspiracy might be encroaching upon Japan. One would hope that many more just sneer at his poorly made espionage tales, in which the code number of the hero is, of course, 001 *(cero cero uno).*

Herbert Passin concluded his aforementioned protest with the memorable line, "You would land up in trouble should this be the case: If You Know Uno, You Will Understand Japan."[49] David Goodman, a professor of Japanese literature at the University of Illinois, seems to have taken a cue from this statement when he analyzed the paranoid ethnocentrism of the Japanese. In an article titled "Han-yudayashugisha-toshiteno Momotaro" (Momotaro as an anti-Semite) he suggested that in the minds of Uno and his ilk, Jews are perhaps imagined as fiends *(oni)* who, with rancorous indignation, wish only to take revenge on the Japanese as former allies of the Nazis. The spirit of Momotaro (Peach Boy), a legendary hero in Japanese folklore who led the expedition (made up of a dog, a monkey, and a pheasant)

JAPAN AFTER THE HOLOCAUST

to suppress the evil Island of Fiends, was often invoked by the Japanese when they invaded neighboring territories. The Momotaro symbolism is now being revived, with the Jews as fiends, to promote a new type of aggressive nationalism that, Goodman asserted, is nothing less than a frontal attack against Japan's postwar democracy.[50]

The resurgence of the Jewish conspiracy theory was caused by the very real fear of an economic recession that would adversely affect the whole socioeconomic structure of Japan. This indeed is reminiscent of the conditions that led to Hitler's success after World War I. The Führer also told the German masses to beware of the nearby fiends, who, with rancorous indignation, were scheming to bring about the downfall of the Third Reich. Admittedly, present-day Japan, where there are only about a thousand Jews, is quite different from Germany in the 1920s and 1930s; but it is a historical fact that the demagogues of prewar Japan tried, as Hitler did, to blame national crises on Jews and on Marxism with considerable success. The resulting self-righteous foreign policy led Japan on the tragic road to ruin, as it did Germany.

It is therefore necessary to be aware of the possible consequences of the trade wars, which so often revive the old Jewish conspiracy theory, and to remember those spiritual guides in prewar Japan who, amidst the turmoil of anti-Semitic fever in an age of blind patriotism, could discern the true motives of the anti-Semites around them. For example, Sakuzo Yoshino, a former professor of political science at the University of Tokyo, proved his mettle as the theoretician of the democratic movement in the Taisho era (1912–26) when he pointed out that people were urged to fight the Jews in the cause of freedom and progress, while, in fact, freedom and progress were the very causes Japanese anti-Semites were doing their best to repudiate.[51] And in 1923 Tadao Yanaihara, an expert on colonial policies and later a president of the University of Tokyo, published a serious study of Zionism in which he declared, "Those who fear a Jewish conspiracy are those who suffer from nightmares of persecutions they themselves inflicted on Jews."[52]

NOTES

1. Hiroshi Izawa, *Yudaya Ronko* (Tokyo, 1944), 2, 251.

2. Ryokichi Minobe, "Daisan Teikoku-ni Taizaishite," *Kaizoh* (Tokyo), November 1934, as quoted in Masanori Miyazawa, *Yudayajin Ronkoh* (Tokyo, 1982), 88–89.

3. Yomiuri Shimbun, ed., *Showashi-no Tenno*, vol. 18 (Tokyo, 1972), 226.

4. Quoted in Tomiko Inui, "Teiko-to Shi-to Ai," *Asahi Journal* (Tokyo), July 24, 1966, 38.

5. Machiyo Kurokawa, *Anne-no Nikki-eno Tabi* (Tokyo, 1982), 157.

6. Shusaku Endo, "Aushuvittsu Shuyosho-wo Mite," *Shincho* (Tokyo), March 1977, 205.

7. Katsumoto Saotome, *Aushuvittsu-to Watakushi* (Tokyo, 1980), 38, 130.

8. Ibid., 96–97.

9. Ken Kaikoh, "Aushuvittsu-kara," *Nihon Dokusho Shimbun*, November 28, 1960.

10. Ken Kaikoh, "Soredemo Wakaranai," *Ah Kono Nijuhgonen* (Tokyo, 1983), 170.

11. *Heibonsha Dai Hyakka Jiten*, vol. 5 (Tokyo, 1984), 94. These figures for the number of A-bomb victims in Hiroshima and Nagasaki are given in the entry "Genshibakudansho."

12. Michiko Inukai, "Kokuren-ga Sabakubeki-datta," *Asahi Shimbun*, December 16, 1961.

13. "Konnichi-no mondai," ibid., evening edition.

14. Ken Kaikoh, *Koe-no Karyudo* (Tokyo, 1962), 67–70.

15. Miyazawa, *Yudayajin Ronkoh*, 160.

16. Takeshi Muramatsu, *Tairyosatsujin-no Shiso* (Tokyo, 1961), 92, 13, 91.

17. Ibid., 98.

18. Takeyama is best known for *Biruma-no Tategoto,* an antiwar novel about a Japanese army private who would not join his platoon at the POW camp for repatriation, but remained in Burma to pray for the repose of the Japanese soldiers who had fallen on the battlefields there. This novel was translated into English as *The Harp of Burma* by Howard Hibbett in 1966 and twice made into a film in Japan.

19. Michio Takeyama, "Seisho-to Gasushitsu," in *Ningen-ni Tsuite* (Tokyo, 1966), 21–23, 25.

20. Shin Tatsuki, "Roma Hohoh-ni Sekinin-wa Nakatta," *Jiyu* (Tokyo), May 1964, 114.

21. Michio Takeyama, "Zaiseki—Roma Hohoh-to Tennoh-no Baai," *Kokoro* (Tokyo), November 1964, 15–17.

22. Tatsuki, "Roma Hohoh-ni Sekinin-wa Nakatta," 118.

23. Takeyama, "Zaiseki," 17.

24. Shin Tatsuki, "Yudayajin-no Shukumei," *Jiyu,* February 1965, 119.

25. Takeyama, "Kirisutokyou-to Yudayajin Mondai," ibid., May 1965, 146.

26. Ibid., 147.

27. Mikaru Ishihama, *Sharomu Isuraeru* (Tokyo, 1965), 312.

28. Katsuichi Honda, "Musabetsu Gyakusatsu-to Nihonjin-no Sekinin," *Ushio,* August 1972, 100–101, 107.

29. Nobumasa Kawamoto, "Fujori-no Saiten," *Asahi Journal,* September 22, 1972, 102. Kawamoto's source was the *Mainichi Shimbun,* September 7, 1972.

30. "Golan Kogen-wa Dare-no Monoka," *Yomiuri Shimbun,* December 20, 1981.

31. Daniel Elazar, *Community and Polity* (Philadelphia, 1976), 363.

32. Susumu Nikaido was the cabinet secretary under premier Kakuei Tanaka.

33. Akifumi Ikeda, "Japan's Relations with Israel," in *Japan in the Contemporary Middle East,* edited by Kaoru Sugihara and J. A. Allan (London, 1993), 159.

34. Ibid., 162.

35. Both *Yudaya-ga Wakaruto Sekai-ga Mietekuru* and *Yudaya-ga Wakaruto Nihon-ga Mietekuru* were published by Tokuma Shoten, a major publisher in Tokyo.

36. Herbert Passin, "Johdan-janai! Yudaya Imbosetsu," *Bungei Shunjuh* (Tokyo), April 1987, 262.

37. Masahiro Miyazaki, *Yudaya-ni Kodawaruto Sekai-ga Mienakunaru* (Tokyo, 1987), 154, 25, 27.

38. Masami Uno, "Hanron!" *Bigman* (Tokyo), May 1987, 129.

39. Masami Uno, *Yudaya-ga Wakaruto Jidai-ga Mietekuru* (Tokyo, 1988), quotation on the book's jacket.

40. By "original" Jews Uno meant the authentic descendants of Abraham, Isaac, and Jacob, among whom he included the Rothschilds and the Warburgs, whose close business connections with the Rockefellers he hints at (see Masami Uno, *Busshu-no Nerai* [Tokyo, 1991], 189–90).

41. Ibid., 32.

42. Masami Uno, *Miezaru Teikoku* (Tokyo, 1989), 166–202. Uno closely follows what has been asserted by such deniers of the Holocaust as Robert Faurisson, Arthur Butz, and David Irving. As a corollary, he even denied the Nanjing Massacre of 1937, which he said was invented at the Tokyo Trial (see his *Doitsu Daiyon Teikoku-no Bokko-to Yudaya Senryaku* [Tokyo, 1990], 93).

Uno was followed by another denier of the Holocaust, Masanori Nishioka, a neurologist who published an article titled "Nachi Gasushitsu-wa Nakatta" (There was no Nazi gas chamber) in the February 1995 issue of *Marco Polo.* Nishioka summarized what had been put forth by Faurisson, Butz, and Irving. The Simon Wiesenthal Center in Los Angeles immediately reacted to this by asking Volkswagen, Microsoft, and other globally influential corporations to stop placing advertisements in the periodicals owned by the Bungei Shunjuh, publisher of *Marco Polo.* The strategy worked: the February issue was the magazine's last number, and the president of the company resigned his post. The Wiesenthal Center itself was surprised by this extreme response.

There were, however, repercussions from some Japanese journalists and academics. While they understood that the Bungei Shunjuh periodicals tended to overemphasize controversial topics and that the publication of Nishioka's problematic article was senseless and shameless, they questioned the Wiesenthal Center's method of protest. They believed that such financial pressure was too aggressive. According to journalist Hajime Takano, the center's strong-arm tactic could create a situation in which even reasonable debates on the subject would be taboo. Eventually, this might not be in the interest of the Jewish side. Takano felt that the Wiesenthal Center should have seized this occasion to expose the revisionist fallacies in *Marco Polo,* thereby enlightening the Japanese reading public on this important aspect of history. The

Bungei Shunjuh's sudden discontinuance of *Marco Polo* was nothing but an abdication of all responsibility in the affair, he said. The monthly's editorial staff should have featured the Holocaust in another issue, perhaps devoting the entire publication to the topic ("Media Should Not Amplify the 'Taboo,'" *SAPIO,* March 23, 1995, 20–22).

The *Asahi Shimbun*'s weekly *AERA* also criticized the Bungei Shunjuh for totally submitting to the protest without even a single argument ("Is the Nazi Holocaust a Taboo?" *AERA,* February 27, 1995, 21–23). It warned that such an attitude would only rouse anti-Jewish sentiments and emphasized that the Holocaust should not be rendered untouchable. To prove that the Jewish defense organizations were not always in the right, *AERA* cited a case involving free speech that was decided in U.S. federal court in favor of a revisionist who had sued the Wiesenthal Center and others for interfering with his contract for exhibit space for the Holocaust-denial activities of the Institute of Historical Review: *Simon Wiesenthal Center for Holocaust Studies, American Jewish Committee et al.* v. *McCalden.* *AERA*'s source was the *American Jewish Year Book, 1994* (New York, 1994), 131.

43. Masami Uno, *Yudaya-to Tatakatte Sekai-ga Wakatta* (Tokyo, 1993), 167–68, 40, 60, 35–38. Uno translated into Japanese *ADL,* a treatise jointly authored by Paul Goldstein and Jeffrey Steinberg (N.p., n.d.), which serves as the source for Uno's attacks on the ADL. Uno's translation, *Yudaya-no Kokuhaku,* was published in Tokyo in 1990.

44. Uno, *Yudaya-to Tatakatte Sekai-ga Wakatta,* 16.

45. Masami Uno, *Kyuyakuseisho-no Daiyogen* (Tokyo, 1982), 103, 184, 104.

46. Masami Uno, *1992 nen-no Yudaya Keizai Senryaku* (Tokyo, 1989), 148.

47. Willie Stern, "Makaritoru Yudaya Imboron-no Uso," *Asahi Journal,* August 25, 1989, 90.

48. Uno, *Yudaya-to Tatakatte Sekai-ga Wakatta,* 60–63.

49. Passin, "Johdan-janai! Yudaya Imbosetsu," 270.

50. David Goodman, "Han-yudayashugisha-toshiteno Momotaro," *Sekai,* January 1988, 337–39.

51. Sakuzo Yoshino, "Iwayuru Sekaiteki Himitsukessha-no Shotai," *Chuo Koron* (Tokyo), June 1921, 41, 24, 32.

52. Tadao Yanaihara, "Shion-Undo-ni Tsuite," *Yanaihara Tadao Zenshu,* vol. 1 (Tokyo, 1963), 543–44.

THE BRITISH SPHERE

GREAT BRITAIN
David Cesarani

BEFORE THE HOLOCAUST

The first small Jewish communities in England were established in the eleventh century, in the wake of the Norman Conquest. Jews were expelled from England in 1290, and no organized community existed until the resettlement of the Jews was approved by Oliver Cromwell in 1656. Under the Hanoverian monarchs, from 1714 to 1830, the number of Jews grew from a few hundred, mainly domiciled in London, to between 20,000 and 30,000. Two-thirds lived in the capital, and the remainder were scattered around ports on the south coast, market towns in the Home Counties, and northern cities. The Jewish population grew to around 80,000 by 1880, on the eve of the great immigration of Eastern European Jews. Between 1882 and 1914 some 120,000 Jews arrived, 100,000 of whom settled in London alone. The immigrants created large, new communities in the industrial cities of the north, northeast, and northwest of Britain as well as in towns in Wales, Scotland, and Ireland. In the 1920s the Jewish population stood at 300,000, and it grew by natural increase to around 335,000 by the mid-1930s. Jewish refugee immigration added approximately 60,000 Jews from Germany, Austria, and Czechoslovakia. The Jewish communities of the United Kingdom peaked at between 410,000 and 450,000 in the 1950s, and they have since declined steadily. In 1986 the Jewish population was estimated to be 330,000.[1]

The Protestant Reformation in England greatly modified the perception of Judaism and the Jews. During the period of religious toleration under Oliver Cromwell a favorable atmosphere developed for their readmission, although this did not proceed without opposition. Following the Restoration there were several attempts to expel them, curtail their rights, or prevent their further immigration. During the period between 1660 and 1701 the small, predominantly Sephardic Jewish community consolidated its institutions and expanded slowly with the immigration of Jews from Spain, Portugal, and the Netherlands. These Jews were "socially emancipated," but precisely because they were not enclosed in any kind of ghetto they were extremely conscious of their behavior. Unremitting scrutiny and intermittent attacks on the fledgling community took their toll, fostering a preoccupation with decorum and a determination to render the Jewish presence invisible.[2]

In the eighteenth century a small, acculturated elite of Sephardim and Ashkenazim achieved great wealth as financiers, merchants, and government factors. Below them was a stratum of traders, shopkeepers, and small manufacturers. The largest part of the Jewish population comprised peddlers, hawkers, and the poor. This section of Jewry was the source of unflattering images of the Jew as old-clothes man, criminal, and beggar. The Jewish religion was recognized by Parliament in 1698, but Jews were still treated as aliens. An attempt in 1753–54 to naturalize foreign-born Jews was vigorously resisted. Like Christian Nonconformists outside the Church of England, the Jews were barred from holding offices in state and local government. Whereas Catholics and most Protestant dissenters were relieved of this disability by 1830, Jews were still excluded.[3]

From 1829 to 1858 the leading families of London Jewry and their allies fought a campaign for civic equality that was as bitter as it was protracted. The emancipation debate gave wide currency to claims that the Jews were aliens who could not be loyal to their country of residence, were obsessed with financial gain, lacked culture, and were still guilty of deicide. It was not until 1858 that Jews won the provisional right to sit in the House of Commons, made permanent in 1866. The battle for emancipation shaped the institutions and identity of English Jews. To refute the charges made against the community, its leaders engaged in social engineering to modify the occupational profile, educational attainments, and cultural awareness of lower-middle-class and working-class Jews. The founders of the Reform congregation, which became the West London Synagogue of British Jews in 1842, were motivated by a desire to modify Jewish worship in accordance with the spirit of the times and the necessity of winning public approval for the Jews. Under Chief Rabbi Nathan Adler, elected in 1844, even the Orthodox ritual was gradually revised to meet the needs of the emancipation campaign.[4]

The mid-nineteenth century saw the crystallization of Anglo-Jewish identity. It was framed by a tacit "emancipation contract." Jews were emancipated on liberal universalistic grounds as individuals; Judaism was understood as another Nonconformist denomination, a private affair that did not detract from the rights and duties of citizenship. This did not imply recognition or acceptance of what it was that made Jews different: the classic liberal formulation did not readily comprehend the wider dimensions of Jewish existence or the associational ties between Jews. Indeed, although liberalism laid claim to universality, it actually assumed as norms the mores and beliefs of the Christian majority. Between 1858 and 1881 this assumption led to strain on the conditions implicit in the emancipation bargain. There was friction between Jews and Liberals over Sunday trading, marriage and divorce laws, military service, and state-funded education. The most serious controversy centered on the foreign agenda of British Jews. Most British Jews regarded Turkish rule as a better option for their coreligionists than the emerging Christian states of Romania and Bulgaria, backed as they were by Russia. When W. E. Gladstone led an outcry against the Turks over their treatment of Bulgarian Christians, Nonconformist Protestants in the ranks of the Liberal Party berated pro-Turkish British Jews for placing Jewish interests before those of the nation and, implicitly, Christians in need.[5]

By 1880 the Jews in Britain were well integrated into society and the economy. At their head was a network of rich families who controlled the central communal agencies. Members of this haute bourgeoisie sat in Parliament and mingled with the aristocracy. There was a large, prosperous Jewish middle class, engaged predominantly in retail and wholesale trading, small manufacturing, and commerce, with a foothold in the professions. Some 12,000 to 19,000 Jews who had emigrated from southern Germany and Eastern Europe in the mid-century already formed communities of artisans and workers in Manchester, Leeds, Liverpool, and the East End of London. The institutions of British Jewry were well established and highly centralized. In London the Board of Deputies (est. 1760), the Anglo-Jewish Association (est. 1871), the Board of Guardians (est. 1859), and the United Synagogue (est. 1870) handled, respectively, the domestic and foreign affairs of British Jews and philanthropic and religious matters. The charitable, educational, and religious structures of Jews in the major provincial centers closely resembled those of London Jewry.[6]

The immigrant Jews from Eastern Europe who arrived between 1882 and 1914 were concentrated in a narrow range of familiar occupations: tailoring, boot and shoe making, furniture making, and trade. They built their own synagogues, created a network of self-help organizations, and transplanted Yiddish culture to Great Britain along with ideologies from the Old Country, notably socialism and Zionism. Native Jews feared that their hard-won civic standing would be damaged by association with these newcomers. The Anglo-Jewish elite consequently used all the instruments at their disposal to remake the immigrants according to their values and in their image: Anglicized, middle-class, and patriotic. In addition, they did all they could to stem or limit the inflow. From the mid-1890s, Jewish relief organizations repatriated migrants who were not considered to be genuine "refugees" and those who seemed incapable of making their way in the new land. The policy of Anglicization and repatriation was driven by external pressure. From 1885 onwards, Jewish immigration became the subject of intense debate in the press, the labor movement, and Parliament. "Anti-alienism," as it was known, reached its climax between 1900 and 1905. Pressure inside and outside Parliament led to the appointment of a Royal Commission on Alien Immigration (1902–3), and a bill to restrict immigration was passed in 1905.[7]

In the years prior to World War I, the esteem accorded to Jews in British society diminished; there were currents of political anti-Semitism and outbursts of anti-Jewish violence. The political culture was still rooted in liberal ideology, but as we have seen, this was of equivocal significance for the Jews. Jewish behavior was further constrained by the contemporaneous construction of an English culture, with the emphasis on the monarchy, Parliament and the common law, the country house, and the pastoral mode in literature, music, and art. Englishness, while not always politically conservative, tended toward an Anglo-Saxon, white racism that was defined against, and excluded, Jews as well as other ethnic minorities in Britain.[8]

World War I fueled xenophobia and racism, particularly against German- and Russian-born Jews. From 1917, Jews were routinely associated with the revolution in Russia: reactionary elements claimed that Jews and Bolsheviks were all but identical. *The Protocols of the Elders of Zion* found its way to the United Kingdom during the British intervention in the civil war in Russia and attracted wide publicity. Domestic opposition to Britain's patronage of the Jewish National Home following the Balfour Declaration in 1917 was larded with anti-Jewish stereotypes, anti-Bolshevism, and anti-Semitism.[9]

Although anti-Bolshevism and anti-Zionism waned in the mid-1920s, immigrants remained the target of stringent anti-alien regulations, under which many were deported. Discrimination against non–British-born Jews was perpetuated in employment, housing, and education in the public sector and, less formally, in the economy, social life, and private schools. The essential legal position of British Jews remained unchanged, and the prosperity of the Jewish population advanced steadily. More and more Jews were able to move to new communities in the suburbs, but in the inner cities there remained large agglomerations of working-class Jews of immigrant origin, who bore the brunt of discrimination by the state and felt the lash of popular prejudice.[10]

When Hitler came to power, Ramsay MacDonald, a former Labour Party leader, was at the head of a national government dominated by Conservatives. Although the government was well informed about Hitler's worldview and objectives, it continued to regard the pursuit of disarmament and the doctrine of collective security as the most appropriate foreign policy. The press and certain public figures, such as Harold Nicolson, expressed concern about the random violence against Jews and the anti-Jewish policies of the German regime during 1933, but it was anticipated that this would blow over. Few understood the radical nature of Nazi anti-Semitism. Indeed, it was common for diplomats and reporters to blame anti-Semitism in Germany on the Jews themselves. The desire for cooperation with Germany prevailed over any misgivings about the handling of Jewish matters, even after the imposition of the Nuremberg Laws. Moreover, a significant part of British society evinced sympathy with Hitler's social policies and envied the recovery of the German economy. The persecution of Austrian Jews following the Anschluss and the events of Kristallnacht in Germany caused a strong reaction, but, as in 1933, public indignation quickly evaporated. A few champions of the refugees in Parliament, notably Eleanor Rathbone and Colonel Josiah Wedgwood, tried vainly to generate concern about the treatment of the Jews. However, Prime Minister Neville Chamberlain was fixed upon the appeasement of Germany, and the government tempered the expression of anti-German feeling.[11]

Official Jewish responses were formulated within these practical constraints as well as according to the long-established Anglo-Jewish ideology of the nineteenth century. Neville Laski, president of the Board of Deputies, and Leonard Montefiore, president of the Anglo-Jewish Association, followed Foreign Office promptings and advised Anglo-Jewry not to antagonize German opinion by engaging in public protests. This counsel did not reflect popular Jewish feeling. In March through July 1933 a spontaneous boycott of German goods and services took hold among Jews in the East End of London, and anti-Nazi demonstrations were organized. The communal leadership arranged an impressive indoor protest led by non-Jews in June 1933 and lobbied the Foreign Office to intervene on behalf of German Jews but rejected all calls to endorse and direct the boycott movement. As a result, a Jewish Representative Council was formed in September 1933, and for the next four years there was friction between activists and communal loyalists over the best means of registering Jewish ire against Germany.[12]

The German-Jewish refugee crisis proved no less divisive. Britain did not see itself as a country of immigration, and the government maintained the strict immigration controls put in place in 1919. These regulations required immigrants to have a work permit or means of support in order to be allowed to stay in Britain. To facilitate the entry of penniless and jobless refugees, the Jewish communal leadership offered financial guarantees to ensure that none would become a burden on the public purse. The corollary of this pledge was that Anglo-Jewry had to find large amounts of money and the number of refugee immigrants would be limited by the available funds. Only a few thousand refugees were anticipated, and from 1933 to 1938 the system worked reasonably well. In these years only around eleven thousand refugee immigrants arrived from Germany. Later on, during the stampede from Austria and Germany in 1938 and 1939, the refugee agencies ran out of funds, and the pledge proved to be a hostage to fortune. The communal leadership's fateful arrangement can be seen as a continuation of the behavior pattern based on the notion of an emancipation contract formed during the previous century. Loath to seek aid from the government as a community or to risk its administration of Jewish affairs, the Anglo-Jewish leadership preferred to finance and regulate refugee immigration itself.

In March 1938 this system broke down, and visas became required for those entering Britain from Germany. However, following Kristallnacht the government relaxed entry procedures by using the notion of temporary refuge prior to reemigration. Ministers were disturbed by the brutal treatment of the Jews and felt they had more latitude for sympathetic action due to concomitant public outrage. So in the period between Kristallnacht and the outbreak of war some forty thousand refugees from Central Europe, including nine thousand children, poured into the country.[13]

Anglo-Jewry quickly raised large sums to assist the Jews who fled Germany as well as those who remained. But Zionists and non-Zionists clashed over the disbursement of monies. To the influential Zionist donors, Palestine was the most logical, cost-effective, and long-term solution for the Jewish refugee problem. Non- and anti-Zionists in the communal leadership were happy to support Jewish institutions inside Germany, to assist Jews to go wherever they wished, and to investigate settlement options in any part of the world. To prevent competition between fundraising for Palestine and the succor of German Jewry, a compromise was negotiated. The Zionists suspended their most active fund in return for a fixed percentage of the money raised on behalf of German Jews. In return they had equal representation with anti- and non-Zionists on an allocations committee of the Central British Fund for German Jewry (CBF), which distributed funds on a merit basis. This did not stop strenuous argument within the CBF and some underhand behavior by both sides. The anti-Zionists, for example, ensured that loans to Palestinian enterprises were repaid to the CBF in London, although the amount of the loan was recorded as a permanent investment in Palestinian settlement projects. At one point Chaim Weizmann, who initially sat on the allocations committee, threatened to resign because of the antics of its anti-Zionist members.[14]

The response to the refugee crisis must be seen against the background of domestic fascism and anti-Semitism. In 1932 Sir Oswald Mosley, a charismatic former Labour Party minister, formed the British Union of Fascists (BUF). The BUF grew fast and attracted considerable support, claiming forty thousand members at its peak, with a wider penumbra of followers. However, the violence that accompanied BUF meetings and the repulsion that followed the Night of the Long Knives in Germany alienated most of its influential backers. Mosley kept the movement alive at the grass roots by taking up local grievances. During 1935 and 1936 BUF activists exploited discontent among the unemployed and the poor in the dockside and industrial districts of the East End. It was an area where old, established ethnic antagonisms were easily manipulated. At street-corner meetings that frequently resulted in violence, Jews were accused alternately of "sweating" (exploiting "British" workers) and of having Communist sympathies. The most serious confrontation occurred in October 1936, when police and antifascist protesters fought in the streets for a whole day. The Battle of Cable Street prompted the government to outlaw the wearing of uniforms and empowered the police to ban provocative marches. Nevertheless, the BUF continued to function, enabling government ministers dealing with Jewish refugee immigration to claim that too many immigrants would lead to a further upsurge of anti-Semitism. This line was strengthened by hostile comment on the refugees in sections of the mass-circulation press. On the eve of the World War II and throughout the Phony War (September 1939–April 1940), Mosley enjoyed a revival on the strength of his antiwar campaign. In his propaganda he accused the Jews of wanting war for their own interests and in defense of international finance.[15]

The Jewish response to domestic fascism was divided. The official leadership refused to engage in action that might be construed as political, such as allying the Jewish community with antifascist groups. They ascribed anti-Jewish feeling to ignorance or the perception of Jews as ostentatious, sharp in business, and insufficiently patriotic. Jews in East London objected to the idea that they were to blame for anti-Semitism and formed self-defense organizations. By mid-1936 the Board of Deputies was confronted by several rival bodies, the most significant being the Jewish People's Council. This forced the board to put greater resources into a visible, activist defense policy as well as behind-the-scenes meetings with police chiefs and political leaders. But a generation of young Jews came to see the Left as their savior, and many joined the ranks of the Labour Party, the Communists, or left-wing Zionist groups.[16]

In the course of these major prewar crises a pattern emerged. The Jewish leadership, fearing that Jewish behavior might have a negative impact on non-Jewish opinion, preferred a policy of temporization, quiet person-to-person lobbying in the corridors of government, and strict political neutrality. It shied away from reflexive protests, disliked public demonstrations by Jews as Jews, and deplored the evidence that large numbers of Jewish youth were turning to the Left. Whether Jewish behavior had any negative effect on the way Jews were perceived was debatable. However, this mentality, which was a legacy of the emancipation contract, ruled the policy of communal institutions and continued to hold good after 1939.

The reaction of the British government, civil service, and public opinion to specific Jewish demands suggests that such anxiety was not without foundation. Ministers and officials deplored the violence and intolerance in Nazi Germany, but many explained it as the result of allegedly provocative behavior by Jews or resentment of their supposed wealth and power. Foreign-policy imperatives and "appeasement" frequently overrode the feelings of those whose perceptions were not distorted by prejudice. A similar conjunction of bias and expediency underlay the government's decision to maintain a restrictive immigration policy. In this case, domestic anti-Semitism was summoned to justify their caution. Instead of meeting fascism head-on, the government made concessions to a movement that articulated certain of its own prejudices against the Jews.[17]

The struggle over Zionism, anti-Nazi policy, and fighting fascism left Anglo-Jewry weaker and more fractured than ever before. On the eve of World War II the Jews of Britain were divided geographically between the suburbs and the inner cities as well as by class, ideology, and generation.[18]

THE HOLOCAUST ERA

During the war, official governmental reactions to the fate of the Jews were determined by the pre-1939 agenda. Apprehensive about the level of domestic anti-Semitism, which could feed off antiwar and profascist sentiment, the government was keen to interdict anything that could give the impression that Britain was at war on behalf of the Jews. The ministry of information was ordered to play down any mention of Jewish suffering in official propaganda. The Foreign Office was already eager to avoid creating sympathy for the Jews, fearing that this might undermine enforcement of the 1939 White Paper on Palestine, which curtailed Jewish immigration.[19]

Nor was the climate of opinion conducive to the advancement of Jewish interests. At the outbreak of war, aliens were ordered to register with the police. Following the fall of France in May 1940 and the threat of invasion, press agitation and a security scare led the government to order the internment of twenty-seven thousand "enemy aliens," who were overwhelmingly Jewish refugees from Nazism. More than seven thousand were shipped to Canada and Australia. The internment and deportation process was halted only after several hundred people died when the SS *Arandora Star,* carrying internees to Canada, was torpedoed and sunk on July 2, 1940. Such was the fear of invasion and the clamor for security precautions that the entire press, including the *Jewish Chronicle,* supported mass internment until this tragedy stimulated a backlash that forced the government to reverse its policy.[20]

It is now generally accepted that the information about the Jews in Nazi Europe that reached Britain during the war was plentiful and accurate. However, as Walter Laqueur has pointed out, a chasm between knowing and believing characterized responses to the data. During 1939 and 1940 the *Jewish Chronicle* obtained precise data on the Jews in Warsaw and other Polish ghettos from Swedish newspapers, the Baltic States (until July 1941), and the Polish government-in-exile in London. It carried reports of the initial mass executions and the overcrowding, starvation, and epidemics in the ghettos from the winter of 1940–41 onwards. The possibilities for accurate coverage of developments in Poland and western Russia were reduced by the German invasion of the Soviet Union in June 1941. The Jewish press obtained little information about the *Einsatzgruppen,* or mobile SS killing units, and was consequently ill equipped to evaluate this critical stage in the evolution of the Nazis' genocidal policies.[21]

The nature of the Final Solution surfaced gradually and haphazardly. On November 7, 1941, the *Jewish Chronicle* documented the deportation of German Jews to Poland. On January 16, 1942, it carried a report from the Polish government-in-exile that eighty thousand Poles had died since 1939 and the Soviet disclosure that fifty-two thousand Jews had been killed in Kiev. At the start of February the paper publicized rumors that eighteen thousand Jews had died in Poltava and reported that fifteen thousand Jews had been killed at Borisov. And on April 10 a small article on the front page carried the news that twelve hundred Jews had been deported to the Mauthausen concentration camp, where they had been killed by "poison gas."

On June 19, 1942, the *Jewish Chronicle* announced in bold type on the front page: "News is filtering through of recent ghastly massacres of Jews in Nazi Europe. Some eighty-five thousand men, women, and children are mentioned in the reports to hand." Then on June 25 and 30 the *Daily Telegraph* printed a story provided by Shmuel Zygielbojm, a member of the Polish National Council in London, which said that seven hundred thousand Polish Jews had been killed. It was the first time that a British newspaper mentioned the routine use of gas in mass killings and named Chelmno as a killing site. Zygielbojm deliberately broke the story in the *Daily Telegraph* because there it would gain a wide readership and carry greater authority than if it appeared in the Jewish press. The news was also carried in the *Times,* the *Evening Standard,* the *News Chronicle,* the *Daily Mail,* the *Manchester Guardian,* and the *Scotsman.*[22]

On August 10, 1942, the government received a telegram from Dr. Gerhart Riegner, the representative of the World Jewish Congress in Geneva, to Sidney Silverman, M.P., in which for the first time a comprehensive plan to annihilate European Jewry was postulated. The response of civil servants in the Foreign Office ranged from incredulity to caution; for several weeks officials and ministers debated the matter internally as well as with the U.S. State Department. In early September the British prime minister, Winston Churchill, and the U.S. president, Franklin D. Roosevelt, issued a joint warning against the perpetration of war crimes, but they did not identify the Jews as the group most endangered by German policy. In October the essence of the Riegner telegram reached the press, whereupon World Jewish Congress leaders in London and Jewish members of Parliament lobbied the government to take more aggressive action. Again there was resistance, largely from within the Foreign Office and the Colonial Office. Certain officials dismissed the reports as "Jewish Agency 'sob stuff'" calculated to engender greater sympathy for Zionist efforts to get more refugee immigrants into Palestine. It was not until the beginning of December, after the *Times* printed a report on the Nazis' "Deliberate Policy for Extermination" and after protests by senior church leaders, that the government responded. On December 17, 1942, the foreign secretary, Anthony Eden, read to the House of Commons the Declaration of the Great Powers, which condemned Nazi war crimes and the extermination policy. Afterwards, M.P.'s stood in silence with bowed heads.[23]

Public opinion was deeply, if temporarily, stirred by the news reports and the Great Powers Declaration. A National Committee for Rescue from Nazi Terror was formed; included among its members were several members of Parliament and publicists, such as Victor Gollancz. The archbishop of Canterbury and other church figures added to the calls to aid the Jews. To appease this outcry, the British government reached an agreement with the U.S. administration to hold a conference on the plight of refugees. Held in Bermuda in April 1943, the conference was little more than a public-relations exercise. The two governments had agreed not to force each other to take any meaningful action. Indeed, since December the British authorities had done all they could to play down the news from Europe; only overseas listeners to the BBC European Service learned of Belzec, Sobibor, and Treblinka. By the spring of 1943 public concern had subsided, and the government could revert to a policy of inaction.[24]

The Anglo-Jewish organizations did not sustain a campaign for action much beyond December 1942 either. Their response needs to be set in the context of Jewish behavior during the war and the domestic pressures under which they were acting. Despite the news from Poland between 1939 and 1941, the *Jewish Chronicle* made few editorial comments. Nor did the communal leadership attempt to foster protests comparable to those in earlier periods when east European Jewry was persecuted. At the time, the future of Britain hung in the balance and everything was subordinated to national survival, as demonstrated by the earlier Jewish response to mass internment. During the blitz the entire British population was in peril and civilian suffering was intense. It was politic to avoid the impression that British Jews were unduly preoccupied with the fate of coreligionists at home or abroad.[25]

Confusion dogged the reports of *Einsatzgruppen* operations. The connection between the various appalling stories that did seep out to the West was not apparent to commentators; nor could it have been. Indeed, the framework for comprehension was drawn from the traditional experience of ghettoization and pogroms. Yet this only partially accounts for the erratic editorial comment in the Jewish press and the passivity of communal organizations: there was also a reluctance to express outrage on behalf of the Jews. The *Jewish Chronicle* reflected the official attitude that it was best not to assert a particularistic interest at a time of national struggle and thus subordinated its trepidation over the fate of the Jews under the banner of winning the war.[26]

The comments made by the *Jewish Chronicle* on the *Daily Telegraph* reports in late June 1942 exemplified the further problem of credulity. Sheer disbelief straitjacketed the formulation of an adequate response: "The hideous details now coming to hand . . . read like tales from the imagination of some drug-maddened creature seeking to portray a nightmare of hell. The average mind simply cannot believe the reality of such sickening revelations, or that men, even the vilest and most bestial, could be found to perpetrate such disgusting orgies of sadistic mania." As Richard Bolchover has demonstrated, Jewish leaders were not immune to incomprehension. Like the rest of the population, they were skeptical of "atrocity propaganda," and three years of warfare had desensitized them to reports of mass murder. Moreover, the news from Europe was without precedent and was impossible to grasp in the absence of an imaginative leap. Even then the truth created feelings of powerlessness that could lead to despair, resignation, and inner withdrawal.[27]

There were other reasons for the relative paucity of editorial comment in the Jewish press and the absence of a public Jewish response commensurate with the news it carried. Anglo-Jewry was preoccupied with the threat posed by domestic anti-Semitism and the question how best to fight it. Throughout the summer of 1942 more editorials in the Jewish press and speeches at communal meetings were devoted to domestic anti-Semitism than to the happenings in Europe. Greater attention was also paid to the progress of the Zionist movement and events in Palestine, which was regarded as the best hope for Jewish refugees.[28]

The *Jewish Chronicle*'s leading article on December 11, 1942, composed when it was possible for Jews to vent their feelings openly under the aegis of governmental concern, hints at the reasons for the paper's earlier reticence, like that of Anglo-Jewry. The initial quiescence may have been determined as much by what Jews would tolerate or believe as by anything else. "Week after week . . . this paper has striven to awaken the public mind to the facts of the Jewish-extermination being carried on by the Nazi masters in Europe. Again and again it has cried aloud that the oft-repeated Nazi threat of Jewish annihilation was seriously intended." But many Jews "complained that they could no longer read the *Jewish Chronicle* because the facts it recorded so harrowed the feelings."[29]

Over subsequent weeks expressions of indignation swept the Allied powers and Jewish communities in the free world. Yet in the course of 1943 the sense of urgency tailed off. This was not due to any interruption in the flow of information. To the contrary, Anglo-Jewry was able to follow the Warsaw Ghetto Uprising blow by blow. The Jewish press obtained accurate data on the decimation of the Jewish populations in Belgium, Holland, Vilna, and Salonika. Readers learned of Treblinka and Sobibor, and there were reports describing the gas chambers and the crematoria in the death camps. Yet throughout the first part of 1943 and even at the height of the Warsaw Ghetto Uprising the *Jewish Chronicle*'s leading articles dealt with domestic issues, notably the struggle between Zionists and non-Zionists for control of the Board of Deputies.[30]

For all but a few exceptional individuals, activity in connection with Europe's Jews was dissipated in discussion of Palestine and the creation of a Jewish army, neither of which could be of immediate practical help to Jews in occupied Europe. The Jewish response was distinguished by fragmentation, in-fighting between various bodies, and the absence of a coordinated strategy. It reflected both the anguish and bewilderment of Jews in Britain, who were powerless to intervene by themselves and fearful of pressing government agencies too hard. Indignation was sublimated into attacks on the poor response of the free world to requests for places of refuge, fury over the British government's Palestine policy, and demands for the creation of a Jewish army.[31]

The dilemmas of the Jewish situation were not of Jewry's own making. The German occupation of Hungary in March 1944 and the consequent deportation of Hungarian Jews to Auschwitz were known about in Britain virtually as they took place, but British governmental responses again displayed resistance to special measures in aid of Jews. The government responded coolly to an offer, transmitted by a Jewish intermediary, to ransom Jewish lives. Pleas by Jewish leaders, including the chief rabbi and Chaim Weizmann, president of the World Zionist Organization, to bomb the railway line to Auschwitz were rebuffed. Protest meetings were held, although Jewish communal organizations never attempted to embarrass the government by mounting major, public demonstrations. Yet it is an open question whether a more aggressive approach on the eve and in the midst of the Allied invasion of Europe would have had any effect; it might even have been counterproductive.[32]

In July 1944 the Red Army captured Majdanek, the death camp near Lublin. In the following month Western reporters were allowed to see the camp, and for the first time photographs and newsreels of crematoria appeared in British cinemas and newspapers. The *Jewish Chronicle* reflected bitterly that it was no longer possible to evade the reality of what had happened to Europe's Jews. The *Times,* however, questioned whether it was tasteful to display the horror of Majdanek. The *Illustrated London News* added to its photographs of the camp a commentary on the dangers of "atrocity propaganda"; Jews were not mentioned. The British journalist with the Red Army, Alexander Werth, was actually told by the BBC that his broadcast from Majdanek was considered "a propaganda stunt" and would not be used. The established pattern of disbelief, skepticism, and reluctance to give salience to the suffering of the Jews persisted up to the point of Liberation and the end of the war.[33]

THE POST-HOLOCAUST ERA

The way the war ended and the manner in which the last phase was characterized in British propaganda at the time had a lasting effect upon popular perceptions of why it had been fought and what it was about. British people were offered a distorted and partial account of the destruction of European Jewry. Over subsequent decades this version hardened into myth and became part of British identity, exercising a baneful influence on understandings of the Final Solution.

We have seen that the capture of Majdanek made little impact in Britain during the war; nor did listeners to the BBC or moviegoers learn much of the other killing centers in Poland. What information had been allowed to filter through was treated warily by broadcasters, journalists, and the public alike. Hence the shock when British soldiers and pressmen reached Bergen-Belsen was even greater than it would otherwise have been. The first witnesses repeatedly stated that it was only on beholding the corpses strewn around the camp that they began to believe what they had half heard during the previous years.[34]

The introduction to BBC war correspondents' dispatches, published in 1946, commented on the reports from Celle, Buchenwald, Bergen-Belsen, and Dachau that "of conditions in the concentration camps, and the behaviour of the Gestapo in occupied countries, we already knew a great deal. It was perhaps forgivable to have hoped that some part of this might be found to have been exaggerated, but the conditions laid bare by the advancing Allies confirmed—even exceeded—the worst accusations levelled at the Nazis' treatment of their victims." One serviceman, Squadron Leader F. J. Lyons, went to Belsen on June 18, 1945, two months after the entry of Allied troops, to see for himself whether the reports from Britain on the camps were "exaggerated propaganda." He wrote in a letter home, "I was anxious to take the opportunity of seeing it with my own eyes." Reassured, he concluded, "If in five years time I hear people saying that Belsen etc, were so much propaganda, I shall be in a position to argue with conviction."[35]

British press reports often revolved around the question of evidence and belief. The conservative weekly *Spectator* wrote: "As long as there was any conceivable loophole of doubt many in this country dared to hope that there was at least exaggeration about the hideousness and the scale of the atrocities committed in German concentration camps. Such doubts might well have been dispelled by the records of Lidice and Lublin, but if any still remained they must vanish forever in view of . . . Buchenwald."[36] In April 1945, C. E. M. Joad, the popular philosopher and commentator in the left-wing *New Statesman and Nation*, expressed impatience with those who refused to believe in the atrocities "even now." Yet he himself suspected that propaganda was at work behind the sudden wave of revelations. "The motive . . . is, I suspect, in part to whip up anger against the Germans and sharpen the demand for revenge." He recalled that when the liberal and left-wing press had denounced the Nazis before the war, their warnings had been dismissed because it had suited the ruling powers to downplay the atrocious record of the Germans. Joad implied that the public horror, though genuine, was being artificially stimulated and manipulated.[37]

Reporters and commentators failed to signify the enormity of what had befallen the Jews or their unique fate. The BBC dispatches by Chester Wilmot from Celle (April 14, 1945), Robert Reid from Buchenwald (April 17), Richard Dimbleby from Belsen (April 19), and Ian Wilson from Dachau (May 1) mentioned Jews only incidentally if at all. These broadcasts were brilliantly contrived and had enormous force when they were heard by home audiences, but the singular fate of the Jews was entirely omitted. The popular *Illustrated London News* carried a special four-page, detachable supplement on the camps in its issue on April 28, 1945. Jews were mentioned twice among the other "victims" of Nazi crimes in Nordhausen. Two later issues, which covered Belsen, did not cite Jews in any form. After this the *Illustrated London News* did not touch on the camps again.[38]

The editorial in the *Spectator* the week after its front-page leading article "Concentration Camp Hell" dealt with the budget. In the following month a leading article reflected on the visit by British Parliamentarians to Buchenwald. That camp and Belsen were rather sloppily described as "internment camps." Jews were mentioned twice among the now established list of inmates, which included political opponents of the Nazi regime, slave laborers, and prisoners of war.[39] Jews were identified only once in the second leader, "The Death Camps," in the *New Statesman and Nation* on April 28, 1945. This item was thirty-five lines long; it was followed by one of about thirty lines on rent control and another of similar length on an industrial plan for India. The writer of the article engaged in a relativization of the Nazis' conduct that revealed little understanding of their activities. He applauded the capacity for outrage among a British population that was weary and numbed by war but warned against hating the Germans as a people: the camps were, in fact, the emanation of an ideology. This ideology was shared by fascist Spain, Vichy France, and Italy, and it ill behooved those among the British who had been complicit with fascism before 1939 to become indignant.[40]

Reports and newsreels tended to focus exclusively on the concentration camps in the West, reinforcing the impression that this was the *locus classicus* of Nazi crimes. Tony Kushner has observed that this emphasis blurred the distinction between the purpose of the camps set up in the early years of the Nazi regime and the murderous accomplishments of the camps that operated between 1939 and 1945. Above all, it elided the intervening significance and specificity of the Final Solution, whose survivors had accidentally ended up in the concentration camps in western Germany following the death marches from camps located in the path of the Red Army.[41] In American and British propaganda, particularly in newsreels, the camps were used to vindicate the Allies' chief war aim of defeating fascism; but there was nothing in the commentaries about saving Jews or intercepting a genocidal system based on racism. Indeed, the Final Solution as carried out at the killing centers in the East had been over for several months by the time the British soldiers arrived at Belsen. The rescue of the Jews had never been a war aim, and the public was spared the agony of asking whether more should have been done earlier on. The myth of liberation circumvented this question and left it untouched for nearly thirty years.[42]

Photographs in the daily papers and in specially mounted exhibitions shocked the public. An exhibition sponsored by the *Daily Express* attracted large crowds, but not necessarily for the right reasons. The camps were projected in propaganda as symbols of Nazi brutality, often eroticized through the use of terms such as "sadism" and "bestiality," in contrast to the decency of the troops who liberated them. Subscribers to the *Illustrated London News* who had "young families" were warned that the special supplement on the camps, with photographs and sketches, was "intended for our adult readers only." It is unclear whether this was the result of prudishness or whether it was supposed to titillate and increase the appetite, but the textual emphasis on "sadism" and "brutality" did nothing to inform the public of the calculated and rational functioning of the *Konzentrationslager* system.[43]

The extermination of the Jews figured briefly in the press at the time of the Belsen trial and the Nuremberg trials. The fourth leader, on November 23, 1945, in the *Spectator,* praised these punctilious judicial proceedings as the best way of exposing the truth, "involving among other things the deliberate murder of 5,000,000 Jews." In May 1945 the *New Statesman and Nation* cautioned that the appetite for retribution would rapidly wane: "Let us have a quick end to it, that men's minds, released from the obsessions of war-cruelty and revenge, may turn the sooner to the task of rebuilding the ruins." In October of the following year, when the International Military Tribunal was still sitting, "Critic" pronounced: "The whole Nuremberg business has been a ghastly mess. At the end of the war I thought a drum-head court martial the best way of getting rid of Goering, Streicher etc."[44]

Although the Nuremberg trials had a substantial impact at the time, their effect should not be exaggerated. In fact, they were considered a bore by many people in Britain who were impatient to get on with peacetime affairs. In December 1945, when the *Reynolds News* polled 150 of its readers on their reactions to the trials, 72 replied that they were "not interested." Even the journal of the Association of Jewish Refugees in Britain regretted that the tribunal had "dragged on" for ten months. According to the historian John Wheeler-Bennett, who assisted with the prosecution of the German diplomats and generals in 1948, by this time "the British people were bored to death with war crimes trials."[45]

The attempted genocide of the Jews was only given prominence under the charge of crimes against humanity. Even then the element of incredulity prevented many from comprehending what had occurred. Peter Calvocoressi, the writer and journalist who contributed features on Nuremberg to the *Jewish Chronicle,* reported that in the course of the *Einsatzgruppen* trial, SS General Otto Ohlendorf admitted responsibility for the killing of ninety thousand people, but "there were many who found it impossible to grasp or believe this statement."[46]

Subsequent publications based on evidence given at the tribunal perpetuated the minimal attention awarded by the proceedings to the Jewish fate. In Calvocoressi's account of the trials, published in 1947, only one chapter dealt with war crimes and crimes against humanity, of which a small portion was devoted to the Final Solution. Lord Russell's *Scourge of the Swastika,* which appeared in 1954, focused on atrocities against Allied prisoners of war and civilian populations in the West. Auschwitz, discussed in the chapter on concentration camps, received the lion's share of attention, while Chelmno and Treblinka received under two pages of commentary; Belzec, Sobibor, and Majdanek were passed over in silence. There were twenty-five pages on the Final Solution, but Russell had clearly wearied of the material and expected the same response of his readers. He concluded: "This dreary catalogue of murders could be continued but it would be the same old story."[47]

Throughout the tribunal's sittings, newsprint rationing meant that reports from Germany were truncated or restricted to the high points, especially the sentencing. According to Calvocoressi,

It was a calamity that reports of the Nuremberg proceedings were restricted in England (as elsewhere) by the lack of newsprint. At the conclusion of the trial a spate of letters to the press showed that those who had taken an interest in the trial had been deprived of the opportunity of forming sensible views about it. Almost the whole of the evidence remained unrevealed to a very great proportion of the readers of newspapers. . . . As soon as the sentences and verdicts of the Tribunal had been announced voices were heard in England urging a reprieve for the condemned, among them being some of note and authority.

The enormity of the crimes, their geographical distance, and the time lag since they had been committed contributed to the erosion of public concern. In addition, the horrors of Belsen were eclipsed by those of Hiroshima and Nagasaki, which attracted far more coverage and comment during the latter part of 1945 and overshadowed the Nuremberg trials. The Allies were responsible for the use of the A-bomb, so the controversy over weapons of mass destruction touched domestic opinion directly. Calvocoressi observed that "developing a guilty conscience they began to feel that in the face of this wrong it had been unjust to punish the German leaders for their misdeeds." In a parliamentary speech made late in 1947, Richard Stokes, the right-wing, Catholic Labour member of Parliament for Norwich, said that "I find the greatest difficulty in deciding who is a war criminal. For example, is the man who lets off an atomic bomb a war criminal, or not? That may be a great crime against humanity."[48]

Gerd von Rundstedt, Erich von Manstein, and Adolf Strauss had served Hitler loyally to the end and were implicated in the commission of atrocities through the "commissar order," which gave official military sanction to the mass execution of Soviet state officials and Communist Party functionaries, who were assumed to be co-equivalent with male Jews. The order was issued on the eve of Operation Barbarossa. Yet it was commonly argued that these three men were, in the words of General Sir George Jeffreys, M.P., "elderly and distinguished officers who fought against us according to their lights as honourable opponents, and who we now know as an absolute fact were politically opposed to the regime in many ways and some suffered as a result." Winston Churchill contributed to the Manstein defense fund and, in the debate on the King's Speech in October 1948, asserted that with the exception of cases involving crimes against Allied prisoners, "the time has come to stop these denazification trials."[49]

According to the *Spectator* of September 3, 1948, "Public opinion would welcome the end of the whole business cordially." Responding to this feeling, the government edged toward a suspension of war crimes trials by the British authorities in Germany. Finally, the outcry over the Manstein case helped to force the government's hand. In October 1948 Herbert Morrison, the Lord President of the Council, announced that Britain would not conduct any more war crimes trials in Germany. The campaign to free Manstein did not end. In May 1949 the bishop of Chichester, Viscount Simon, and Lord Hankey pleaded in the House of Lords for his release. Members of the House of Commons argued that in the new context of the Cold War it was unwise to antagonize German opinion by persisting with the case.[50]

In 1945 Russia had been a valued friend. By 1948 she was perceived as Britain's main international adversary. The involvement of Russia in the Nuremberg trials was even held to have compromised, if not invalidated, their conduct. In an early example of revisionism, the writer Montgomery Belgion, in *Epitaph on Nuremberg* (1946), protested that journalists wrote nothing about the massacre at Katyn or the Soviet secret police (NKVD) camps. "The Nuremberg Trial was a gigantic 'put up show' . . . a gigantic piece of propaganda." Lord Hankey, an eminent former civil servant, was influenced by Belgion's tract. Bitterly opposed to war crimes trials in Europe or the Far East, he argued in *Politics Trials and Errors* (1950) that the trials were "victors' justice." Aside from the legalistic objections to war crimes trials, Hankey argued that Russia too was guilty of "waging a war of aggression" and committing atrocities. He maintained that the trials would do nothing to remove Nazi ideology from the minds of the German people; rather, an important ally against the Soviet Union was being unnecessarily alienated.[51]

Following the government's decision in 1949, war crimes trials were conducted in the British Zone of Germany by German courts. The sentences were frequently light, but only the Anglo-Jewish press voiced concern about this leniency and the policy of amnesties for those sentenced earlier. By now there was little general interest in war crimes cases. If Jewish people continued to observe German internal affairs with hostility, through the prism of the Final Solution, British public opinion toward Germany reflected the rehabilitation of the Federal Republic and the imperatives of the Cold War.[52]

Only the Jewish press protested that there was no statement of culpability for war crimes, mention of denazification, or restitution in the 1949 Basic Law of the Federal German Republic. The *Jewish Chronicle; AJR Information,* serving refugees from Central Europe who arrived before 1939; and the *Wiener Library Bulletin,* the journal of the library established in London in 1938 by anti-Nazi German-Jewish émigrés, were virtually alone in monitoring the progress of the Right in the first German postwar elections. They voiced the opposition of Jews to the rearming of West Germany and its admission into the European Defense Community. However, such was the climate in the Cold War that the *Jewish Chronicle,* which refused to accept advertisements for German goods or services, was forced to concede that German rearmament was a necessary corollary of Western European strategy to meet the Russian threat.[53]

Throughout the 1950s the Jewish population of Britain manifested a particular sensitivity to all matters related to Germany. Barnett Janner, a Jewish Labour M.P., was one of the few members of Parliament who took an interest in the appointment of former Waffen SS officers to the Bundeswehr. The attention paid to postwar politics in Austria was likewise distinctive to the Jewish press. *AJR Information* was one of the few publications in Britain in the 1950s to challenge the myth of Austria as "the first victim" of Nazi Germany.[54]

If outrage against the Nazis was tempered by time and circumstances, so was sympathy for the Jews. The British occupation forces in Europe were reluctant to recognize Jews as a distinct group with special needs for fear of appearing to accept the Zionist case that there was a Jewish nationality. Thus they treated Jews as members of the nationality to which they technically belonged. Latvian Jews who had survived the war thus found themselves in displaced person (DP) camps with Latvians, many of whom were former Nazi collaborators. German Jews were placed in refugee centers with Germans displaced from the East who were still fanatical Nazis. Moreover, they were denied DP status and rations, since this privilege was barred to Germans and *Volksdeutsche*. Dismayed by this treatment, thousands of Jews moved into the U.S. Zone, where the U.S. government had ordered that they be housed separately and treated as DPs.[55]

In January 1946, Lt. Gen. Sir Frederick Morgan, the British head of the United Nations Relief and Rehabilitation Administration (UNRRA) DP operations in Germany, caused an uproar when he accused the Zionist movement of manipulating the flight of Jews from Poland following a series of attacks on Jewish survivors who had returned to their homes. His reference to a Zionist conspiracy was particularly egregious, and there were calls for his resignation.[56] In fact, Morgan's statement reflected Foreign Office policy to keep Polish Jews out of the British Zone of Occupation and the British sector of Berlin for fear that they would become an embarrassment by then demanding the right to emigrate to Palestine. Although Morgan was "released" from his UNRRA post in August 1946, the Foreign Office continued its policy of excluding Jews from British-controlled territory. Strenuous efforts were made to deny any precedent for the movement of Jewish DPs to Britain, and the first line of defense became the border of the British Zone in Germany. The British occupation authorities were instructed not to provide rations or accommodation for Jews who were alleged to have entered the zone illegally.[57]

Immigration into Britain was still covered by the 1919 regulations, which were prohibitive when applied to Jewish DPs, who were mostly sick, poverty-stricken, or too young to work. Efforts were made by the Jewish communities in Britain to secure the admission of Jews from Europe, and in November 1945 the government responded with a scheme under which "distressed relatives" could be brought over. By January 1946 only 109 concentration camp survivors had been admitted, and Labour Home Secretary Chuter Ede was challenged in Parliament to explain why the number was so small. Although the total had risen to 790 by May, Ede was accused by Conservative M.P. Quintin Hogg of preserving an "illiberal" and "xenophobic" immigration policy. The under secretary at the Home Office explained that the paucity of results was due to "transport difficulties."[58]

By the end of 1949, 5,600 "distressed relatives" had been admitted to Britain, but the number of Jews among them was no more than about 2,000, including 740 orphans from the concentration camps. Nor were many Jews among the 1,000 Czechs and 6,000 aliens married to British citizens who were granted entry.[59] Over the same period, Britain also admitted more than 200,000 Eastern Europeans. First, 150,000 Polish servicemen and their dependents were settled in the United Kingdom as a consequence of Britain's wartime alliance with Poland and the employment of Poles in the British army. Then 93,000 European Voluntary Workers (EVWs), mainly Eastern Europeans recruited from DP camps, were imported into Britain via labor recruitment schemes intended to meet the critical shortage of manpower in certain sectors of British heavy industry that followed the economic crisis in the winter of 1946–47. In addition, 15,000 German and 8,000 Ukrainian POWs were later civilianized and worked under the same conditions as EVWs. The Ukrainians were brought to Britain from a POW camp near Rimini ostensibly because they were vulnerable to demands from Russia for their repatriation once Italy's postwar treaty with the Soviet Union went into effect and there was nowhere else for them to go.

This influx was not welcomed by some sections of British society, and the government exerted itself to placate the trades unions in particular. Nevertheless, the sense of obligation to the Poles, the need to find manpower for British industry, and political considerations were such that domestic opposition was either meliorated or disregarded.[60] The vast discrepancy between the numbers of Jews and non-Jews who were admitted to the country did not go unnoticed. When the EVW schemes were first announced early in 1947 there was praise in Jewish circles for the government's humanitarian and practical gesture and excited speculation about the roles Jewish DPs could fulfill. By the end of 1948 the excitement turned to disillusionment as it became evident that of the eighty-five thousand DPs that had entered Britain only an insignificant fraction were Jewish. Sidney Silverman, a Jewish Labour M.P., clashed with Ede over the differential, and Jewish organizations' suspicions were aroused when the Home Secretary spoke pejoratively about people of "alien blood."[61]

In fact, the EVW recruitment agencies were actively discriminating against Jews. The instructions for recruitment criteria sent from the Control Office in London to the British authorities in Vienna stated: "Ex-enemy nationals, Jews and Volksdeutsche are to be excluded from the field of recruitment but the possibility of considering some Volksdeutsche at a later date will be further examined."[62] Fear that Jewish DPs in the British Zone or in the United Kingdom would try to reach Palestine was one motive for this policy. Another reason was underscored in an account of the aims and operation of DP recruitment in Austria. In April 1947 Maj. Gen. T. J. Winterton, deputy commissioner in the Allied Commission for Austria—British Element, told Lord Pakenham, the chancellor of the Duchy of Lancaster, whose Whitehall office was responsible for the implementation of the schemes: "It seems to us . . . much more simple and more effective to recruit from the whole body of DPs without regard to nationality, except that we shall exclude Jews and Polish men because of the opposition from public opinion at home."[63]

The reference to domestic opinion was well founded. As early as May 1945 some Conservative members of Parliament were calling for the repatriation of Jewish refugees who had arrived in Britain before the war. In September 1945 the *Times* carried an article referring to claims that the refugees were responsible for the shortage of housing and suggested that it was time to return them whence they had come. In the London borough of Hampstead a petition was circulated to this effect. The British Medical Association also proposed that refugee doctors whose registration had elapsed should now be sent back to Central Europe. Despite pressure from the liberal press and from Labour members of Parliament, the government did nothing to relax the restrictions on alien immigration and referred to public unease to justify its policy. This was in contrast to the concerted efforts that were being made to win the public round to accepting Poles, Latvians, and Ukrainians for work in British factories and mines.[64]

The British government's reluctance to make special provision for the remnant of European Jewry rested on the high level of domestic anti-Semitism. In the autumn of 1945 anti-Semitism was becoming so serious that the Board of Deputies felt it necessary to demand a law on community libel. In March 1946 the *Jewish Chronicle* commented that "one of the most astonishing phenomena of the times is that the martyrdom of the Jewish people, instead of being followed by universal sympathy and reparation, has begotten only a new spate of anti-Jewish feeling." The storm of indignation that followed the exposure of the Western concentration camps in April and May 1945 was not focused on Jewish suffering and, in any case, had dissipated by early 1947. Thereafter, the authorities could rely on either indifference or outright hostility toward Jews to minimize popular pressure for a modification of its policies.[65]

The Palestine emergency of 1945–47 was the source of much of the animosity that welled up against Jews in Britain. Despite the clamor among the Jewish DPs who wanted to escape from Europe to Palestine, the British government stuck to its policy of blocking Jewish immigration. Angry Jewish organizations in the United States responded with anti-British propaganda. In Palestine the Haganah, the Jewish underground army, combined with the Irgun and Lehi, extreme nationalist Jewish underground groups, to mount a series of attacks on British targets. Terror and counterterror in Palestine escalated: in April 1946 Lehi killed six British paratroopers in cold blood, and a few weeks later the Irgun kidnapped five British officers from the officers' club in Tel Aviv. In July the Irgun blew up part of the King David Hotel, the British headquarters in Jerusalem, resulting in many lives being lost.[66]

The crisis had inexorable repercussions on the Jews in Britain. The *Spectator* accused the Zionist organizations of exploiting the plight of the Jewish DPs to embarrass the government. In a veiled threat it stated that "if such suspicions are justified—and if they are not it is within the means of influential Jewry in this country to put them at rest—then not only is irreparable harm being done to the cause of Zionism and countless hundreds and thousands of innocent Jews, but sympathy for that cause in this country will be dealt a heavy blow." It warned ominously that "clearly no right-minded individual has any wish to indict a Jew in this country for the actions of a co-religionist in Palestine unless there is evidence that these actions receive either his sympathy or his active support. Nobody would doubt the pressure of just and conflicting loyalties, but the responsibilities of British citizenship involve obligations to the state that cannot lightly be put aside." In January 1947 a *Sunday Times* editorial openly demanded that British Jews denounce terrorism in Palestine.[67]

Scare stories in the press that Jewish terrorists were about to launch a terror campaign in Britain heightened tension in the early weeks of 1947. The flogging of a British officer and three sergeants by the Irgun in Palestine was followed by acts of vandalism against two synagogues in London. Former Mosleyites who had revived the network of British fascists and taken to the streets again easily exploited anger over events in Palestine.[68]

The Palestine emergency reached its climax in July and August 1947, after two British sergeants were hung by the Irgun in revenge for the execution of one of its members. The murder of the sergeants was front-page news in the British press. The *Daily Express* illustrated the story with a photograph of the scene that could not fail to cause outrage. Over the August bank-holiday weekend, mobs of youths rampaged through the Jewish districts of Liverpool, Manchester, Salford, Glasgow, East London, and other towns. No one was seriously hurt, but Jewish-owned property was destroyed and looted, synagogues were attacked, and Jewish cemeteries were desecrated.[69]

Newspaper coverage of the killing of the sergeants was distinguished by hyperbole. According to the *Daily Express* on August 1, 1947, "Not in the black annals of Nazi wickedness is there any record of an outrage more vile than this." Even the *Manchester Guardian* opined that "in the whole record of political terrorism there has been no worse crime than the brutal and cold blooded murder of the two British sergeants." All the papers, including the Jewish press, agreed that, in the words of the *Times* leader writer, it was "difficult to estimate the damage that will be done to the Jewish cause." Harold Soref, editor of the Anglo-Jewish Association's *Jewish Monthly*, observed bitterly that because of the Zionist movement, "the victims of Hitler are being replaced in the popular imagination and sentiment by the victims of the Irgun Zvai Leumi."[70]

Yet the rioting also provoked shock and introspection. Fleet Street and politicians alike immediately condemned the weekend violence. The right-wing *Evening Standard* pronounced that "there is no excuse for terrorism here. . . . There is no place in Britain for the apostles of Hitler's satanic creed." The *Spectator* reminded readers that "chains of events of this kind have led in the past to mass-murder and the gas chambers. The brake must be applied at every point." Woodrow Wyatt, then a Labour member of Parliament, wrote pointedly in the *New Statesman and Nation* about the gathering strength of the fascists in East London and issued a clarion call to the Left to resist the temptation to rage against the Jews. Several members of Parliament approached the Home Secretary regarding the need to curtail fascist and anti-Semitic provocations, especially in the East End of London.[71]

Anti-Jewish feeling peaked in the winter of 1947–48, although it remained the subject for widespread public debate. Within Jewish communal organizations the fight against domestic fascism and anti-Semitism created tensions similar to those in the 1930s. It also sharpened the differences between Zionists and non-Zionists, since the latter blamed the former for the precipitous rise of Jew-hatred in Britain. Jewish energies were thus absorbed by defense issues and factionalism. It was an unpropitious atmosphere in which to meditate on the recent past or to seek public commemoration of those who had perished under the Nazis. Reviewing the previous year in September 1947, Harold Soref considered that "the sympathy aroused by the massacre of the six million Jewish martyrs and the concentration camp atrocities have been eclipsed by happenings in Palestine. Belsen, Auschwitz and Dachau have slipped from public memory."[72]

The evacuation of British forces from Palestine in April and May 1948 and the emergence of the state of Israel only partly defused the tension at home. Britain refused to extend even de facto recognition to the new state until January 29, 1949. Just a few days before that, Israeli fighter planes shot down five British fighters patrolling the border between Egypt and Israel, and for a moment it seemed as if the two countries might be at war.[73] However, once the United Nations took responsibility for Palestine and British forces were extricated, popular interest in the area waned.[74] Although the rioting of 1947 left local scars, by the close of the decade the cessation of the conflict, combined with easier domestic circumstances, contributed to the retreat of anti-Semitic feeling.

Nevertheless, diminished sympathy for the Jews and official reluctance to depart from liberal universalistic preconceptions and recognize Jews as a "special case" were evident in the handling of the restitution issue. The first regulations promulgated by the British zonal authorities in Germany were regarded as "highly unsatisfactory" by Jewish representative organizations because they only dealt with the return of property that still existed. A more comprehensive piece of legislation proceeded through Parliament at a snail's pace and was condemned by the refugee Council of Jews from Germany because its benefits were confined to residents in the British Zone. Even after the reparations arrangement with the West German government had been arrived at, the Treasury continued to prevent former German Jews living in England from enjoying it to the full. From 1951 to 1954 Jews paid taxes on their reparations payments in both West Germany and Britain. In 1954 a convention was reached between the two countries whereby double taxation was avoided, but it was not until 1961 that reparations payments were relieved of taxation entirely. It took another three years of lobbying before Britain and Germany signed a convention to allow for the payment of reparations to non-German nationals resident in the United Kingdom since 1945.[75]

In Britain during the 1950s, commemoration of the destruction of European Jewry was a small-scale and private affair. Refugee organizations, such as the Association of Jewish Refugees in Great Britain (est. 1941), the Association of Baltic Jews in Great Britain (est. 1944), the Federation of Czechoslovak Jews (est. 1939), and the Polish Jewish Ex-Servicemen's Association (est. 1945), marked dates of particular significance to their communities, notably the anniversaries of Kristallnacht and the Warsaw Ghetto Uprising. Commemoration of the latter, held in a communal venue, regularly attracted several hundred Polish and Eastern European Jews. There were memorial prayers and speeches in English and some in Yiddish, and the format was stark and introspective.[76]

In 1959 the *Jewish Chronicle* welcomed the Knesset decision to establish a Holocaust Memorial Day. It commented, significantly, that "the anniversary of the battle of the Warsaw Ghetto is an occasion which for many requires an effort to remember, while it rivets the attention and haunts the memories of a few." As the number of survivors dwindled and the events of the war grew more distant, there was a drive to institutionalize commemorative events and broaden their base.[77] From 1960 on, the anniversary of the revolt was marked on an increasingly grand scale and with greater sophistication. The Association of Jewish Refugees, composed predominantly of German and Austrian Jews, threw its weight behind the gathering and exhorted its members to attend. In 1971 *AJR Information* explained that it had "a twofold purpose: to keep alive the memory of our loved ones who perished, and to link the commemoration of the past with an assessment of the tasks incumbent on present-day Jewry." Commemoration of the uprising had thus been universalized and instrumentalized: it now represented all those who died in the Holocaust and had acquired an educational function.[78]

The universalization of the Warsaw Ghetto Uprising merged gradually into the Zionization and sanctification of the Holocaust. In the late 1970s, following the trend set in Israel, the pivotal month in the commemorative calendar became May, in close proximity to Israel's Independence Day. The title of the day of commemoration was changed first to the Anniversary of the Warsaw Ghetto and the Six Million Martyrs and then to Yom Hashoah.[79]

A parallel process saw the embodiment of the Holocaust in memorial objects. The practice of erecting memorials developed in the late 1960s. The first major communal discussion of a Holocaust memorial occurred at a meeting of the Board of Deputies in late 1960. An educational project was favored over a statue or sculpture, but nothing came of the debate. In the following decade it became increasingly common for individual synagogues to dedicate small-scale memorials. These took the form of plaques (St. John's Wood Synagogue), sculptures (Finchley Progressive Synagogue), or basins for the ritual washing of hands (Bushy Jewish Cemetery, Kenton District Synagogue).[80]

Public memorials in non-Jewish locations raised sensitive issues. In February 1971 the Association of Jewish Refugees unveiled a plaque at the site of Richborough camp, where many refugees had found sanctuary from 1938 to 1940. It marked a place of haven but also tragedy and trauma for German, Austrian, and Czech Jews. However, the wording chosen for the plaque was limited to a heartfelt expression of gratitude to the local population. When the Salisbury City Council discussed the erection in Salisbury Cemetery of a monument to the victims of the Holocaust, the proposal met strong objections from council members who thought it had no local relevance. By contrast, a universalistic memorial to prisoners of war and concentration camp inmates designed by the German-Jewish sculptor Fred Kormis was erected in Gladstone Park, in northwest London, in 1969. It was commissioned by the council of the London borough of Brent.[81]

Within Jewish circles debate over a national Holocaust memorial continued for more than five years. The first proposal, in 1979, was for a site opposite the Cenotaph in London, the monument to Britain's dead in two world wars. Since the 1920s the Cenotaph has been the focal point for the annual national day of remembrance, on the first Sunday in November, and it has become an emblem of British national identity. It is noteworthy that the project for a Holocaust memorial to be built in close proximity to this location never came to fruition. Eventually the British government presented to the Jewish community a small plot of land in The Dell, in Hyde Park, that had no evident meaning for Jews or non-Jews. A memorial designed by the architect Richard Seifert was placed there in 1983, and it became the Holocaust Memorial Garden. This is now the site for the annual commemorative gathering on Yom Hashoah.[82]

Visits or pilgrimages to Holocaust sites were also slow to develop. In an article published in August 1950, of a kind that was rare for the time, the German academic and writer Herbert Freeden recalled in *AJR Information* his visit to Dachau. Five years later *Daily Express* journalist Kenneth Macaulay went to see Auschwitz and capitalized on the originality of his trip to write a feature for the paper. In 1960 Barnett Janner, then president of the Board of Deputies, went to a memorial meeting at Auschwitz, beginning a ritual in the life of every president. The following year the Warsaw Ghetto Commemoration Committee organized what was intended to become an annual "pilgrimage" to Warsaw and Auschwitz. Since the early 1980s it has been de rigueur for Jewish youth groups to visit sites in Central and Eastern Europe. Educational tours have become commonplace, and official visits by Jewish communal figures have been institutionalized.[83]

The entry of the Holocaust into public space occurred in Britain in the 1970s and 1980s, once it had become established as a subject in scholarship and culture. Until then, members of the Jewish community complained with justice that their historical experience was marginalized. For example, in March 1958, on the twenty-fifth anniversary of Hitler's rise to power, the *Jewish Chronicle* noted that there was little to mark the occasion in the British press. In the same year the *Wiener Library Bulletin* remarked that during the important state visit to London by West German President Theodor Heuss, the Jews in Germany and the Holocaust were barely mentioned in the British press. In 1960 the *Bulletin* contrasted the ballyhoo over the twentieth anniversary of the Battle of Britain with the silence surrounding the twenty-fifth anniversary of the Nuremberg Laws, with which it coincided.[84]

The Final Solution had little immediate impact on historical scholarship, literature, and the arts. Few examples of memoir literature were published in Britain after the end of the war. Dr. Filip Friedman's testimony, *This Was Oswiecem,* appeared in 1946, but five years later Joseph Leftwich remarked in the *Jewish Chronicle* that most of the memoirs that were being printed were still being published in Yiddish.[85] The *Jewish Chronicle, AJR Information,* and the *Jewish Monthly* published accounts of relief work in Europe and some essays by survivors, but these were relatively few. In 1951 Michael Zylberberg, a Polish-born journalist, remarked that Bernard Goldstein's *The Stars Bear Witness* enjoyed critical acclaim because up to that time so few survivors' accounts had been published in Britain. Whereas a "catastrophe literature" had developed in several countries on the Continent, "an exception to this is England where, so far, we have almost nothing appertaining to this particular literary activity. Furthermore there is no echo in the Press of these foreign publications. The reader knows nothing of the interesting publications which have been written [by survivors]." After a slow start, the diary of Anne Frank, published in England in 1952 by Vallentine Mitchell, a subsidiary of Jewish Chronicle Newspapers, rapidly outstripped every other contemporary testimony in terms of both sales and readership. Its popularity may have been connected with its relatively anodyne content.[86]

Reminiscences by British servicemen who had been present at the liberation of the camps or had taken part in the trial of Nazi war criminals touched on the Final Solution, but usually only in a tangential fashion. For example, Derrick Sington's evocative *Belsen Uncovered* perforce reflected the limited perspective of those in the West who witnessed only the end of the final stage. While some of the journalistic accounts of Nuremberg, such as that by Calvocoressi, were solidly informative, others, like Victor Bernstein's *Final Judgement,* were sensational and misleading. Bernstein wrote twenty-five pages on the Jews under the Christocentric heading "Twentieth Century Calvary." This was followed by a chapter called "Six Million Slaves," which confused the numbers of Jewish dead with the millions of forced workers. The chapter titles "Ghoul's Gold" and "SScience" speak for themselves.[87]

The first comprehensive history of the Holocaust to appear in Britain was Gerald Reitlinger's *The Final Solution,* published by Vallentine Mitchell, in 1953. Reitlinger was a German-born, British-educated dilettante of independent means who customarily wrote on art history. His pioneering study was a work of considerable scholarship, but it attracted few reviews. Max Beloff, writing in the *Jewish Chronicle,* remarked that although there was now abundant proof that millions of Jews had been systematically destroyed, "public opinion outside Jewry nowhere really accepts this fact." The paucity of attention paid to Reitlinger's book was symptomatic of a wider malaise. In a similar vein, the *Manchester Guardian* critic said that "this book is needed as a record of what has already become blurred in many minds because of guilt-haunted attempts to minimise an unendurable horror."[88]

By contrast, Lord Russell's *The Scourge of the Swastika: A Short History of Nazi War Crimes,* published in 1954, went through four English editions in one year. Russell stated in his preface that his book was "intended to provide the ordinary reader with a truthful and accurate account of many of these German war crimes." He set out to demonstrate that unlike other war crimes in history, Nazi atrocities were central to their policy of conquest. However, the text was punctuated by tales of sadism and perversion. In the prurient mid-1950s it attracted readers as much for the pictures of naked women prisoners and shrunken heads as for the historical content, facts, and details. Reviewing the book in the *Observer,* the historian Edward Crankshaw objected that "the most serious problem of our age is exploited with a tastelessness and sensationalism normally associated with the worst kind of journalism." Russell's was a partial account, and what was worse, it veered toward the lurid and the bizarre.[89]

Mainstream British historical scholarship and the memoir literature of British statesmen, diplomats, and politicians revealed little awareness of the Final Solution. The first volume of Winston Churchill's wartime memoirs, *The Gathering Storm,* which covered the years up to 1939, failed to mention Kristallnacht. (The second volume did discuss Jewish attempts to reach Palestine from occupied Europe.) From the mid-1950s through the 1960s a series of reminiscences appeared that stoked the debate over appeasement, but again the Jewish dimension was notably absent.[90]

Collections of documents perpetuated the invisibility of the Jews by reflecting the lacunae in policy during the 1930s and 1940s. Only 12 out of 690 pages of *Documents on International Affairs, 1939–56,* volumes 1 and 2, edited for the Royal Institute for International Affairs by Arnold Toynbee and published in 1954, touched on the Jewish Question. *Documents on British Foreign Policy, 1919–1939* (1947–), edited by E. L. Woodward and Rohan Butler, was significant precisely because it did not contain anything about the plight of the Jews. British historians dealt with the Jews in a cursory manner, a predilection that later drew a scathing commentary from Lucy Dawidowicz in *The Holocaust and the Historians.* She was not the first to note this tendency, however. The *Jewish Monthly* criticized F. H. Hinsley for his failure to include material on Hilter's anti-Semitic outlook and the massacre of Jews in the Soviet Union in his book *Hitler's Strategy,* published in 1951. The *Wiener Library Bulletin* added to the plaudits for Alan Bullock's *Hitler: A Study in Tyranny* (1952) but chastised the author for not seeing anti-Semitism as a central and determining part of the Nazi *Weltanschauung.*[91]

A. J. P. Taylor's *Origins of the Second World War,* published in 1961, stimulated controversy because it challenged the demonization of Hitler and instead characterized him as an opportunistic statesman acting on the world stage no differently from his predecessors or his contemporaries. Taylor minimized the role of Nazi ideology and reduced the war to the accidental result of policies rather than the outcome of a deliberate drive for Lebensraum. But he was taken to task by a range of British historians, including F. H. Hinsley, Hugh Trevor-Roper, James Joll, and A. L. Rowse. The *Wiener Library Bulletin* expostulated that Taylor's book represented "history as she never was" and argued that it had met with "the hostile reception which it deserves," since it was calculated to cause "mischief and confusion."[92]

Serious attention to the history of anti-Semitism and the Final Solution was otherwise confined largely to Jewish émigré writers and Anglo-Jewish historians. In 1950 Eva Reichmann published *Hostages of Civilisation,* one of the first serious studies of the roots of Nazi anti-Semitism. Lionel Kochan's *Pogrom* (1957) was a rare example of a monograph on the unfolding of Nazi policy toward the Jews before the Final Solution. Roger Manvell and Heinrich Fraenkell published a biography of Goebbels in 1960. The Jewish-owned publishing houses Gollancz and Vallentine Mitchell were prominent in this field. *AJR Information* was almost alone in printing accounts of the internment and deportation of Jewish refugees between 1940 and 1944, while the *Jewish Quarterly,* founded by Czech-born Jacob Sonntag in 1953, published many important accounts of Jewish resistance in occupied Europe.[93]

The Wiener Library was a vital institutional base for scholarship in the United Kingdom. Its staff, under the direction of Dr. Alfred Wiener from 1938 to 1961, produced several seminal bibliographical volumes on the Nazi period. The *Wiener Library Bulletin* was a showcase for research abroad and in Britain. Many prominent British historians, including Alan Bullock, James Joll, A. J. P. Taylor, and J. W. Wheeler-Bennett, were also involved in the library's affairs. However, it was a telling comment on the library's marginality that from the early 1950s it experienced severe funding difficulties. In spite of its unique collection of documents on the Third Reich and the extermination of the European Jews, the library found it almost impossible to raise funds in Britain. It relied heavily on financial infusions from a few benefactors and the organizations disbursing restitution monies.[94]

There was not even much attention paid to the British dimension of the Jewish tragedy. Initiatives by Jewish-based organizations such as the Institute of Jewish Affairs or the Wiener Library were largely responsible for the progress that was made in this area. In the mid-1960s Andrew Sharf published the study *The British Press and Jews under Nazi Rule* (1964), and Ernest Hearst contributed two articles entitled "The British and the Slaughter of the Jews" to the *Wiener Library Bulletin.* Not until the 1970s did several major works bring Britain's role into prominence: A. J. Sherman's *Island Refuge: Britain and Refugees from the Third Reich, 1933–1939* (1973); Bernard Wasserstein's follow-up study, *Britain and the Jews of Europe, 1939–1945* (1979); Peter and Leni Gillman's study of internment, *Collar the Lot!* (1980); and Martin Gilbert's *Auschwitz and the Allies* (1981). The 1980s also saw the growth of studies concerning Jewish refugee immigration and settlement, again mostly thanks to the selfsame members of this community and British-born Jewish historians.[95]

Periodically, controversies that revolved around the history of the Final Solution broke through to a wider public. The Kasztner Affair and the question of Jewish collaboration with the Nazis were first discussed in the Jewish press in the mid-1950s, at the time of the Kasztner libel case in Israel. In 1958 Alex Weissberg published in English Joel Brand's account of the events in Hungary in 1944 and the thwarted rescue project in which Brand and Kasztner were involved. Because of Brand's sensational allegations that the Jewish Agency neglected the opportunity offered at that time, as well as his allegations about the involvement of British officials in Palestine and the Foreign Office, the subject caught the imagination of the British press. *Advocate for the Dead,* Brand's story, was serialized in the *Observer* and aroused a good deal of hostility from Jewish commentators. David Astor, editor of the *Observer,* was criticized by the *Jewish Observer and Middle East Review* for publishing what it viewed to be a partial as well as controversial narrative. He replied that on reflection it was one-sided, but "we consider [Brand's] story to be an important document and believe that its publication will help to increase public understanding in this country of the gigantic tragedy with which it is concerned, namely the attempted extermination of the Jewish communities of continental Europe by the Nazis. To attack this public ignorance and indifference is our motive." The BBC's flagship current-affairs program *Panorama* also devoted one broadcast to "The Joel Brand Story," and it was the subject of an Independent Television book program.[96]

A war of words was triggered by Arnold Toynbee's obiter dicta in volumes 7 and 8 of his monumental *Study of History* (1954–63). In the former he described Zionists as "the disciples of the Nazis." In the latter he elaborated on this proposition by arguing that in 1948 the Zionists in Palestine had chosen to "imitate some of the evil deeds that the Nazis had committed against the Jews" with regard to the way that they treated the Arabs. Toynbee was attacked by Jewish and non-Jewish critics alike for his poor understanding of Judaism, which was the root of his dislike of Zionism, and his loose historical metaphors.[97] The comparison of Zionists with Nazis was to recur later in pseudohistorical literature, anti-Zionist propaganda, and cultural works.

The capture of Adolf Eichmann in 1960 and his trial in Israel in 1961 attracted intense media attention. Although it was inevitably spasmodic, the extensive coverage provided new information about the Holocaust. The *Daily Herald* serialized Rudolf Vrba's important memoir of his experiences in Auschwitz and his escape. Newspapers sent prestigious correspondents to cover the trial: Hugh Trevor-Roper, for example, sent back reports for the *Sunday Times. The People* published a series of articles by Lord Russell, which it advertised in Yiddish for the presumed benefit of the Jewish reading public. On February 22, 1961, Associated Television broadcast a fifty-five-minute documentary on Eichmann that included interviews with a range of Holocaust survivors. Public interest was aroused: an "avalanche of letters" followed a discussion of the case on BBC radio's *Any Questions?* Even so, in April, when the trial was at its height, 29 percent of those interviewed for a Gallup poll thought it was a bad idea to remind the world about the concentration camps, while 25 percent either did not have an opinion about Eichmann or felt sorry for him.[98]

Some responses were ambivalent, sensationalist, or trivial. The *Solicitor's Journal* denounced Israel for arrogating the right to seize and try foreign nationals for alleged crimes against the Jews in any part of the world. Richard Crossman, writing in the *New Statesman,* condemned the trial process and, later, the death sentence passed on Eichmann. His qualms were widely reflected in the editorial columns of the press. The *Daily Express* echoed a prurient and silly strain in the public interest with its story headlined "Our Life by Mrs Eichmann."[99]

The testimony by Joel Brand briefly revived the controversy over British reactions to rescue opportunities in 1944 and the failure to bomb Auschwitz. More sustained attention was paid to the debate over the extent to which Jews had colluded with the Nazis in their own destruction. This heated exchange was triggered by the German-born New York Jewish intellectual Hannah Arendt and reached London when the *Observer* serialized her *New Yorker* articles on the trial. Arendt's views were influenced by Raul Hilberg, who had remarked in his monumental work *The Destruction of the European Jews* that Jewish responses to Nazi persecution were characterized by passivity and ill-judged attempts at cooperation. Indeed, even before the "Arendt debate" the Jewish press in Britain had been agitated by Hilberg's conclusions. Leading figures in the community of former German refugees, several of whom had been community leaders in Germany before 1939, took up arms. Herbert Reisser, Robert Weltsch, and Werner Rosenstock, writing in *AJR Information* in 1962, criticized Hilberg for failing to appreciate the "constructive resistance" of German Jews and blaming the victims. The World Jewish Congress organized a symposium in London on the "Arendt thesis." The following year, the Council of Jews from Germany formally passed a resolution condemning both Hilberg and Arendt. It was carried boldly on the front page of *AJR Information.*[100]

Publicity of a more lurid kind was generated by the 1964 court case in which Leon Uris, the author of *Exodus,* was sued for libel by Dr. Wladyslaw Dering, whom he had named in the novel as one of the doctors who performed experiments on inmates at Auschwitz. The London trial attracted a great deal of coverage, not least because of the sensational outcome. Uris was found to have been wrong in his precise facts, but Dering was awarded only one halfpenny in damages, a demonstration of the jury's abhorrence of the work Dering had carried out in the camp, regardless of the inexactitudes in *Exodus*.[101]

Gradually, the peripheral status of the Holocaust was modified. By 1982 it was possible for a British historian to protest that some Jewish colleagues were misguidedly treating the Final Solution as purely their own concern. This widening of interest beyond Jewish circles was not the result of a concerted attempt to foster Holocaust studies, as occurred in the United States. In the 1970s a remarkable body of British historians embarked on a reappraisal of modern German history that ineluctably touched on the origins of political anti-Semitism in Germany; the rise of the Nazis; the governance, policies, and ideology of the Third Reich; and the Final Solution. These British scholars contributed heavily to the debate between "intentionalist" and "functionalist" schools of analysis. The former, exemplified by Lucy Dawidowicz, held that Hitler had intended to exterminate the Jews from the outset of his career and bore the prime responsibility for instigating genocide. The latter, heavily represented by young British historians, argued that the Third Reich was a polycentric regime in which decisions emerged out of the struggles between center and periphery and between competing elites over which Hitler presided, often at a distance. Although this debate deepened academics' understanding of Hitler's Jewish policies, it was not matched by progress in university teaching about the Holocaust. The subject barely figured on British campuses, and few non-Jewish British historians attended the major international conference "Remembering for the Future," held at Oxford in 1988.[102]

As in the field of scholarship, in the arts and literature too the extermination of the Jews did not figure largely for decades after the event. Thanks to his immersion in Yiddish culture and his extensive prewar contacts with Yiddish authors in Europe, Joseph Leftwich was one of the few British-based authors who had access to the large and tragic store of *churban* (catastrophe) literature. In September 1948 he observed acutely that "the songs of the death-camps are the Jewish literature of our time." However, only a few in Britain shared his facility with the Yiddish language or his knowledge of contemporary Yiddish culture.[103]

The first novel about the Final Solution to make an impact in Britain was John Hersey's *The Wall*, published in 1950. Otherwise, a literary reckoning with the Holocaust was almost entirely confined to Jewish authors. Indeed, when Alexander Baron, a leading postwar Anglo-Jewish writer, was asked in an interview in 1957 what it was that made a Jewish writer's work distinctive, he replied: "In my opinion it is not the whole corpus of Jewish life, it is not the atmosphere in which we have grown up; it is one thing alone, the tragedy, the immense tragedy which consumed six million Jews. This has shocked us into facing up to the fact that we are Jewish. It has aroused in us this need to identify ourselves." The literary historian Efraim Sicher has argued that the Holocaust was central to the work of Anglo-Jewish novelists, dramatists, and poets.[104]

Few wrote explicit "Holocaust novels"; there has been an evident reluctance to do so. Even though he was one of the first to explore the issues raised by the Final Solution, in 1960 Frederic Raphael actually denounced Anglo-Jewry for being too Holocaust-centered. But this did not preclude Raphael and others from embarking on a subtle and penetrating analysis of the impact Nazi persecution had on survivors, refugees, and British-born Jews. Most Anglo-Jewish writers simply preferred to remain within a superficially parochial milieu that allowed them to write from experience: they explored the deeper resonances of the Holocaust in the society they knew best.[105]

Outside of Jewish circles the Holocaust registered only obliquely. When Arnold Toynbee asked the British writer Graham Greene in 1957 whether the extermination of the Jews had had any effect on literature, Greene replied: "Not direct, I should say, but certainly an indirect one. I rather think we were already living, before that, in a climate which made that kind of thing not only possible but probable." He added that many people believed Auschwitz to be just a propaganda creation. A year later, C. P. Snow, a central figure in Britain's literary establishment, reflected that the centenary of Darwin's *Origin of Species* was overshadowed by "the mass slaughter of the concentration camps." Yet this was hardly evident from the country's literary output. Thirty years later George Steiner commented bitterly that "leading [British] literary figures—Kingsley Amis, Philip Larkin—have written as though unaware that the Holocaust had ever taken place."[106]

The publication in English of Primo Levi's *If This Is a Man* (1958) and Elie Wiesel's *Night* (1960) created much interest, but these were foreign imports. Sylvia Plath's 1965 collection of poems, which exploited Holocaust imagery, was distinguished by its singularity. George Steiner was almost alone in connecting her poetry with the wider implications that Auschwitz had for literature.[107] The Holocaust only began to register in British novels, poetry, and drama in the 1980s. Steiner's *Portage to San Cristobal of A.H.* (1981), D. M. Thomas's *The White Hotel* (1982), and Thomas Keneally's *Schindler's Ark* (1983; published in the United States as *Schindler's List*) inaugurated a more sustained exploration of the Holocaust in novels and drama and an attendant critical interest. In 1991 Martin Amis's *Time's Arrow* was short-listed for the Booker Prize. Alan Massie's *The Sins of the Fathers,* a controversial novel that blurred the lines between Jews, Zionists, and Nazis, attracted attention when there were protests because it was *not* short-listed.

Theater, film, and television turned to the Holocaust as a subject somewhat later. Christopher Hampton's stage version of *Portage to San Cristobal of A.H.* (1982) caused particular disquiet among Jews because of the final peroration by the Hitler character, who declared, in terms reminiscent of Toynbee, that the Jews of Israel had learned from Nazi ideology and actions.[108] Peter Barnes's *Auschwitz* (1978) and Peter Flannery's *Singer* (1989), which looked at the impact of the Holocaust on the survivors and the quality of memory, were rare efforts by British playwrights. *Forbidden* (1986), directed by Anthony Page, and *Escape From Sobibor* (1987), by Jack Gold, were among the few British contributions to feature films in the genre. *The Evacuees* (1975), directed for television by Alan Parker from a Jack Rosenthal script, was the first dramatic depiction of the wartime experience of Jewish refugees in Britain. The Jewish Film Festival, which began in London in 1985, acted as a showcase for films on Holocaust subjects, and in its second year a large section of the festival was devoted to this theme. The entries have been almost entirely foreign-made, one prominent exception being Naomi Gryn's *Chasing Shadows* (1990).[109]

There was more activity by television producers in the fields of documentaries and current affairs. Productions of impressive quality included *The Warsaw Ghetto* (BBC, 1968); *Before Hindsight*, by Jonathan Lewis (BBC, 1978); and *The Gathering* (BBC, 1981) and *Auschwitz and the Allies* (BBC, 1983), both by Rex Bloomstein. *A Painful Reminder/Memory of the Camps*, the uncompleted and unscreened 1945 film by Sidney Bernstein, was finally shown by the BBC in 1985. BBC Television also showed Tom Bower's documentaries *Blind Eye to Murder* (1978) and *The Paperclip Conspiracy* (1987), which dealt with British complicity in the escape of Nazi war criminals. The independent television networks were responsible for the episode "Genocide," in the multipart series *World at War* (1975), directed by Michael Darlow for Thames Television, and *Kitty—Return to Auschwitz* (1979), directed by Peter Morley for Yorkshire TV. All the same, when Claude Lanzmann's *Shoah* was shown in two parts on television (Channel 4), it occasioned a mere fraction of the discussion that accompanied its transmission in the United States and Europe.[110]

The slow pace at which awareness of the Holocaust penetrated into academia and culture was not unrelated to its absence from secondary education. E. J. Passant's widely used student reader *A Short History of Germany, 1815–1945*, published in 1959, contained almost nothing on Jews or anti-Semitism. Until the 1960s, British school students learned little about European history after 1918. A survey conducted by the Wiener Library of four textbooks on modern European history showed that they contained no information on anti-Semitism or the Jews. These lacunae were called into question after the spate of swastika daubings and neo-Nazi activities in Britain in 1960 and 1961. A letter from the Wiener Library to the *Times Literary Supplement* calling for a good student reader on the period 1933–45 elicited correspondence from teachers expressing their agreement.[111]

Student responses to an exhibition on the Warsaw Ghetto at York University in 1965 confirmed, albeit on the basis of a narrow sample, that a large proportion of British youth simply did not know about the fate of the Jews in World War II. According to the professor of education responsible for the exhibition and the subsequent survey, "The average reaction was expressed by a student who declared: 'Since I didn't know about the Warsaw Ghetto uprising before, the printed sheet was interesting. The photos added a little to the story, but we have seen so many like them before, that they fail to make any great impact apart from the stock reaction of *Isn't it all sickening*.'" A *Daily Mail* survey in 1989 revealed that when a group of people aged eighteen to twenty-four were asked to give the meaning of Dachau and Auschwitz, 23 percent did not know or guessed incorrectly. Of the total, 57 percent answered correctly and 43 percent, incorrectly.[112]

In 1972 the Education and Youth Committee of the Board of Deputies organized a special, youth-oriented event in conjunction with the Warsaw Ghetto Uprising commemoration. However, such initiatives only reached Jewish youth. Ten years passed before the Board of Deputies arranged a seminar on teaching about the Holocaust aimed at Jewish and non-Jewish educators. Efforts were also made outside of the Jewish organizations to provide exhibitions and teaching materials. In 1981 the Polish "Auschwitz Exhibition" was brought to Britain and toured several cities to wide acclaim. An educational packet produced after the exhibition by the Inner London Education Authority was less well received. Entitled *Auschwitz: Yesterday's Racism,* it compromised the specificity of the Final Solution by trying to give it "relevance" for the 1980s and yoking it to the current antiracism campaign. In 1985 the "Anne Frank in the World" exhibition traveled around Britain and drew large crowds.[113]

The first major survey on teaching about the Holocaust was carried out in 1987 by John Fox under the auspices of the United Kingdom Yad Vashem Academic and Educational Sub-committee. It showed that in the great majority of sixth-form colleges, both public and independent, students were exposed to the history of the Third Reich, the Jewish Question, and the Final Solution. However, the Holocaust was almost always subsumed within a larger subject, and teachers reacted with suspicion to the notion that it should be taught separately. A similar profile was noted with respect to higher education. Only six universities and three polytechnics out of the forty and twenty-one, respectively, that responded to the survey offered a course on the Holocaust. This reflected not only the parlous state of Jewish studies in Britain at the tertiary level but also the unwillingness to tackle the Holocaust as a discrete subject and the perception that it "belonged" to one "faction."[114]

Between 1987 and 1990 the Conservative government instigated a fundamental reform of secondary education that included the introduction of a national history curriculum. The interim report of the working party on history syllabuses prepared for the Department of Education in 1989 initially excluded consideration of World War I, the rise of Hitler, and the Third Reich from the curriculum intended for fourteen- to sixteen-year-olds. It was only after considerable lobbying by Jewish teachers, ex-servicemen's associations, and members of Parliament that "the era of the Second World War, 1933–1948" was included in the final report. It recommended as a core subject "the causes of the war; Hitler; casualties of war. Genocide: the Holocaust."[115]

Fear that trivialization of the Holocaust and outright denial in Britain was gaining momentum lay behind much of the pressure to insert European history in the years 1933–45 into the national curriculum. Trivialization and Nazi kitsch had become familiar in Britain since the 1970s. In 1971, for instance, the marquess of Bath announced that he wanted to set up a "Hitler Room" in his stately home at Longleat; it was intended as an attraction to the public, who also visited the zoo on the grounds. In the mid-seventies skinheads regularly sported Nazi insignia, and T-shirts listing Hitler's "European Tour 1933–45" were sold in Carnaby Street. In 1991 the story of the forged "Hitler Diaries" was the subject for a major Thames Television comedy series.[116]

The ideologically driven denial of the Holocaust was a feature of the extreme

Right in Britain from the 1950s on. It expanded beyond these confines in 1974 with the publication of *Did Six Million Really Die?* by Richard Harwood (pen name of Richard Verrall). Verrall was then a prominent member of the extreme Right National Front, and the politics behind the publication were clear. In the wake of its wide distribution the Board of Deputies and several members of Parliament asked the government to take action against the pamphlet's author or publisher, but the attorney general declined.[117] In 1977 Arthur Butz's *Hoax of the Twentieth Century* was published in Britain by the Historical Review Press. Five years later a broadsheet entitled *Holocaust News,* which distilled the denial argument, was circulated to schools, universities, and parliamentarians. Despite renewed protests by Jewish organizations, no official steps were taken against the authors or publishers.[118]

These manifestations were clearly connected with the activities of the far Right, but a more complex and politically more evasive form of historical revisionism appeared in the 1970s. In *Hitler's War* (1977), David Irving suggested that Hitler had not known about the Final Solution and cited a document that he claimed proved that Hitler had actually intervened to prevent the deportation of Jews to the death camps. A. J. P. Taylor considered the book "too silly to be worth arguing about," and Hugh Trevor-Roper was likewise dismissive. But careful research by the historian Gerald Fleming later showed that the document on which Irving based his case had been utterly misconstrued. The reasons were doubtless those that caused Irving to call Anne Frank's diary a forgery in 1977. Throughout the 1980s Irving spoke regularly at meetings of neo-Nazi groups in West Germany. In 1989 his publishing company issued *The Leuchter Report,* which offered spurious "scientific" evidence to prove that no homicidal gas chambers had operated at Auschwitz. Irving wrote a laudatory introduction to it. This did not prevent the *Sunday Times* from hiring Irving to "transcribe" the Goebbels diaries ("discovered" in a Moscow archive) in June–July 1992, a step that suggested that sensitivity to Holocaust-related issues, as well as awareness of Holocaust denial, had failed to penetrate deeply into even sophisticated press circles.[119]

Holocaust denial was not confined to the far Right. After the 1975 U.N. resolution identifying Zionism as a form of racism, it became common for far Left anti-Zionist groups to couple the swastika with the Israeli flag and to assert that Zionism shared ideological features with Nazism. This claim originated in the Soviet Union, but it was spread in Britain by Trotskyite groups. In 1983 *The Beautiful Part of Myself,* a play by Tom Kempinski, a member of the Workers Revolutionary Party (WRP), was withdrawn from production after protests by Jews against the play's allegation that Zionists collaborated with the Nazis during the Holocaust. Four years later the play *Perdition* detonated another controversy, and it too was canceled following objections by Jewish groups. Jim Allen, the play's author, had once been a member of the WRP. His drama, based on the Kasztner Affair, combined the myth of a worldwide Jewish conspiracy with the myth of Zionism as a form of racism. Allen argued that Zionists found common ground with Nazi racial doctrine and deliberately withheld news about the destruction of Hungarian Jewry because Jewish suffering would foster support for their cause. These notions were widely peddled on university and polytechnic campuses around the United Kingdom and became a feature of student debate between 1977 and the late 1980s.[120]

One of the saddest aspects of this development was the effect it had on the survivors of the Holocaust. For the first two decades after their liberation they found themselves in a largely uncaring society. Many recall that even though they received assistance from the Jews in Britain, there was little understanding of their experiences and they were driven to seek companionship mainly among their own kind. Survivors emerged as a group only hesitantly. A dinner in 1963 that brought together the survivors of Bergen-Belsen with their liberators and war crimes prosecutors was an unusual event. In the same year, survivors of the concentration camps formed the '45 Aid Society, a self-help group with philanthropic and social objectives. By the seventies it was confident enough to organize major events. In 1978 its members donated four thousand pounds toward the establishment of a fellowship in Holocaust studies, the first such initiative in Britain.[121]

Major research into the complex of psychological phenomena known as survivors' syndrome, or post-traumatic stress syndrome, did not begin until 1977. The watershed was the conference on survivors' syndrome in October 1979, coorganized by the Raphael Clinic in northwest London. During the following decade more psychologists and psychoanalysts devoted themselves to understanding and ameliorating some of its effects. By this time the survivors and also child refugees had begun to define a distinctive profile for themselves. Several books were published on the *Kinderstransport,* culminating in 1989 and 1990 with publications as well as reunions and celebrations marking the fiftieth anniversary of their arrival in Britain.[122]

Survivors and former child refugees now had the time to dwell upon their histories or were freed from the distractions of work and family that formerly had shielded them from active memory. Poignant anniversaries, the prominence of the Holocaust in culture, and the swelling tide of Holocaust denial made continued evasion of the past more difficult in any case. All of these factors led to a dramatic increase in the numbers seeking counseling or companionship on the basis of shared traumas. In 1989, 75 percent of the patients attending the Raphael Clinic did so because of problems relating to the Holocaust, a twofold increase over the preceding year.[123]

The impact of the Holocaust on British society to date may be gauged by the war crimes issue that erupted in 1986 after the Simon Wiesenthal Center in Los Angeles submitted to the British government a dossier of material alleging that Eastern European war criminals were living in Great Britain. These men were immune to prosecution under English or Scottish law, since the crimes of which they were accused were committed in Eastern Europe when they were not British citizens. An All-Party Parliamentary War Crimes Group was subsequently formed by a dozen members of Parliament to campaign for measures against these alleged war criminals.

The lobby for war crimes trials argued that it was a universal issue, a matter of justice. This was to some extent a tactical line that reflected an acute consciousness of the liberal universalistic discourse that still prevailed over the more narrowly based, though no less valid, priorities of an ethnic group. It had little effect, in any case, since opponents of war crimes trials repeatedly attributed the campaign to a Jewish lobby. A powerful group of members of Parliament including former Prime Minister Edward Heath opposed the demands for an official inquiry into the allegations. However, the weight of evidence from the United States, the Soviet Union, and the War Crimes Group's own research helped sustain a public outcry that was too strong to ignore. A commission of inquiry was finally appointed by the Home Secretary in February 1988. Conducted by Sir Thomas Hetherington and William Chalmers, two former senior law officers, it showed that large numbers of Nazi collaborators had been able to enter the United Kingdom after the war and that several alleged war criminals were still alive. The authors recommended that a bill be introduced to deal with the anomaly that the suspects could not be tried in Britain.[124]

A bill was introduced by the government after the House of Commons indicated its support for such a measure, but a bloc of members of Parliament and a majority of peers in the House of Lords fought it step by step. Their arguments were heavily legal and constitutional, but important elements were also historical, moral, and religious. Some opponents of war crimes legislation argued that the campaign was a Jewish one, motivated by a spirit of revenge that was inherent to Judaism. Lord Hailsham, a former Lord Chancellor, and several churchmen appealed to the spirit of forgiveness that was identified exclusively with Christianity. Antagonists such as Conservative M.P. Ivor Stanbrook denied the specificity of the Holocaust and demanded to know why the bill did not comprehend crimes committed by the Japanese in the Far East or Stalin's secret police. Edward Heath called for bygones to be bygones and argued that in the new Europe it was time to stop raking up past quarrels that had once divided the Continent. Although the bill passed through the House of Commons with large majorities, it was twice rejected by the House of Lords. On the second occasion the government was obliged to invoke a rarely used constitutional procedure to override the upper chamber.[125]

While the opponents of war crimes legislation constantly adverted to Jewish suffering in the past, they were not able to understand its ramifications for the present. The existence of survivors, the desire for justice, and the importance of making a public statement that such crimes should never be passed over in silence seemed to elude them. Nor could they remain focused on the Holocaust: there was an almost irresistible urge to compare, relativize, and, ultimately, diminish the event. In one or two cases there was outright denial: Quentin Davies, M.P., for example, wanted to know "what crimes" were at issue, and Ivor Stanbrook spoke of "so-called offences."[126]

British Jews of all generations frequently complain with reference to the place of the Holocaust in British culture that their sensitivities are being ignored, and their experiences overlooked, by the wider society. Although a number of prominent churchmen in the United Kingdom have associated themselves with the reevaluation of Christian theology, interfaith dialogue about the Holocaust has been late, hesitant, and highly circumscribed. It has been driven forward by the Council of Christians and Jews, often at the initiative of its Jewish members. The silence that followed the television screening of Lanzmann's *Shoah* in 1987 and the lackluster response to the "Remembering for the Future" conference in 1988 indicate that British society is not very interested in the fate of the Jews under Nazism. The prevalence of Holocaust denial and the predisposition of speakers in the parliamentary debates to blur or belittle Nazi war crimes show that Jewish fears are not unfounded. By contrast, non-Jews object that they have the Holocaust "rammed down their throats" at every possible opportunity. These two perceptions are not unconnected. The notion that Jews are obsessed with the Holocaust is an outgrowth of the reluctance to accept the particularistic Jewish experience.[127]

It is true that Jewish responses can appear exaggerated. In the summer of 1958 the letter columns of the *Jewish Chronicle* were filled with arguments over whether Jews should employ German au pair girls. Clive Sinclair satirized this controversy in his 1988 novel *Blood Libels,* notwithstanding that his own fiction circles around anti-Semitism and is informed by images from the Final Solution. As the dedication of Holocaust memorials gathered pace and more energy was devoted to Holocaust education within Jewish circles, Chief Rabbi Lord Jakobovits warned against the tendency to use it as a crutch for Jewish identity. He wrote in the *Jewish Chronicle* in 1988 that "we must beware against nurturing and breeding a Holocaust mentality of morose despondency among our people, especially our youth."[128]

If Jakobovits is correct, the salience of the Holocaust is a relatively recent phenomenon. Studies of Anglo-Jewry such as *A Minority in Britain,* edited by Maurice Freedman (1955), and *Jewish Life in Modern Britain,* edited by Shaul Esh and Julius Gould (1964), barely registered any interest in the repercussions of the Final Solution on either the society or the psyche of British Jews. Chaim Bermant's *Troubled Eden: An Anatomy of British Jewry* (1969) was the first study to identify the influence of the Holocaust on Anglo-Jewry: "The Gentile has the Bomb hanging over his existence; the Jew has the Bomb and memories of the Holocaust. Auschwitz is hardly more than two decades away and there is hardly a Jewish family which did not have a close relative among its victims. And it is not only this which hurts. It is the very thought that a few years ago one could be hunted down and destroyed wholly and solely because one was Jewish." Bermant detected traces of this experience in the opulent and overblown celebration of family affairs and Jewish life-cycle events. He also located it in the deep feeling of insecurity that appeared to characterize British Jews, so markedly in contrast to their prosperity and integration into society.[129]

Each subsequent study of Anglo-Jewry has devoted an increasing amount of space to the seismic waves of the Holocaust. On the basis of many conversations with communal figures in 1988 and 1989, Stephen Brook divined that the losses suffered between 1939 and 1945 underlay the ferocity with which Orthodox groups in Britain defended their community and attacked progressive Jews. He was informed that Soviet Jewry activism was undergirded by the determination never to repeat the mistakes of the war years. Above all, his interlocutors testified that Anglo-Jewish identity was shot through with insecurities and was articulated largely around the Holocaust. Two years later Howard Cooper and Paul Morrison went still further. In their study of British Jewish identity they suggested that "at one level, the ache and the fear and the emptiness in British Jewry is a product of the Holocaust. . . . We can't understand contemporary Jewish families, our specific exile in Britain, Jewish politics, or Jewish spiritual wanderings without taking into account the Holocaust."130

According to George Steiner, "In Britain the Shoah has no reality, not even to the Jews. . . . Out of all the countries in the world with a sizeable Jewish population, Britain alone, out of the whole diaspora of remembrance is oblivious of the Shoah."131 The evidence suggests that the first part of his proposition is tenuous. Anglo-Jewry is deeply preoccupied by the Holocaust—to an unhealthy degree, some would say. The wider society is not, and there is a relationship between these two phenomena. It is precisely the absence of the Holocaust from British culture and society that niggles and worries Jews. This silence is a denial of something that they feel is now fundamental to their being and signifies a refusal to accept the reality of their experience.

As Judith Miller shows in her acute study of how Europe absorbed the significance of the Holocaust, the imperviousness of British culture and society is not unique.132 Moreover, there are clear reasons for its muted effect. The United Kingdom was spared occupation by the Nazis. Outside of the Channel Islands, a peculiar case, no British subjects were involved in either deportations or instances of collaboration. British troops were among the liberators of Europe and felt little cause for introspection. As we have seen, their entry into the concentration camps in the spring of 1945 actually acted as a barrier to comprehending the full scale and horror of the Final Solution. The unique configuration of events in 1945–48 certainly provides an explanation for why Britain failed to reckon with anti-Semitism and its legacy. News of the events in Palestine overwhelmed the revelations at Nuremberg and even caused an anti-Jewish backlash. This hardening of the heart was compounded by the parochialism that distinguished much of British postwar culture. As a victor nation, Britain felt that it had little to learn from prostrate Europe. Furthermore, it had its own preoccupations arising from the winding down of the empire.133

Yet this is to ignore ideology and the smothering embrace of liberal tolerance. It can be argued that the reluctance to engage with the Jewish tragedy in Europe signified a continuation of the discourse of liberalism about the Jews.134 Since 1945 it has still been the case that Jews are constructed in culture according to universalistic criteria that deny the specificities inherent to their existence. A discourse that hobbled British and Jewish responses to the Final Solution as it unfolded persists to this day. It continues to marginalize the historical experience of the Jews and inoculates the majority community against reckoning with its own complicity in events that occurred fifty years ago.

Throughout the years 1989–95, even the sustained run of anniversaries related to World War II, German reunification, the surge by the far Right in Europe, and the hugely successful film *Schindler's List*, which all drew attention to the wartime fate of Europe's Jews, only modified this cognitive framework. In January 1995 the mass media devoted unprecedented attention to the anniversary of the liberation of

Auschwitz, leaving popular consciousness of the Holocaust at a much higher level. And yet the anniversary of VE Day the following May was a singularly British event.[135] The Jewish and British experiences of the war were neatly bifurcated between the events marking the liberation of Auschwitz (and, to a lesser extent, Belsen), and the official celebrations marking the victory in Europe.

The tension between universalistic interpretations of the war and the specificity of the Holocaust was exemplified when, in December 1994, the Imperial War Museum (IWM) in London, the official repository of Britain's memory of the war, announced that it was considering the creation of several new galleries devoted to genocide in the twentieth century and the Holocaust in particular. This step marked a significant recognition of the Holocaust as a part of British history and demonstrated respect for the discrete experience of British Jews. However, early plans indicated that the new galleries would not be a Holocaust museum on the model of the U.S. Holocaust Memorial Museum. The fate of the Jews would be framed in a universal and comparative context. This initiative by a major national institution, though welcome, graphically exposed the ambivalence of British responses to the Holocaust.[136] But at least it is in the open, and the IWM has invited all interested parties to give their views of the proposed museum extension. Not before long, there will be a genuine national debate in which British Jews, survivors, former refugees, and their children will play a leading part.

NOTES

I would like to acknowledge the generous assistance of Dr. Tony Kushner, Parkes Lecturer, Department of History, Southampton University, in the preparation of this essay, which is on a subject about which he has already written widely and which forms part of his book *The Holocaust and the Liberal Imagination: A Social and Cultural History* (Oxford, 1994).

1. Cecil Roth, *History of the Jews in England* (Oxford, 1941); Stanley Waterman and Barry Kosmin, *British Jewry in the Eighties: A Statistical and Geographical Study* (London, 1986), 6–7. The total population of England, Wales, and Scotland in 1951 was 48.9 million; in 1961, 51.3 million; in 1971, 53.9 million; in 1981, 54.2 million; and in 1985, 55 million (Chris Cook and John Stevenson, *The Longman Handbook of Modern British History, 1714–1987* [London, 1989], 110–11).

2. David Katz, *Philo-Semitism and the Readmission of the Jews to England, 1603–1655* (Oxford, 1983); Roth, *History of the Jews in England,* 173–79.

3. Todd Endelman, *The Jews of Georgian England, 1714–1830* (Philadelphia, 1979).

4. M. C. N. Salbstein, *The Emancipation of the Jews in Britain* (New Brunswick, N.J., 1982); Vivian D. Lipman, *A History of the Jews in Britain since 1858* (Leicester, 1990), chap. 1.

5. Bill Williams, "The Anti-Semitism of Tolerance: Middle Class Manchester and the Jews, 1870–1900," in *City, Class, and Culture,* ed. A. J. Kidd and K. W. Roberts (Manchester, 1985), 74–102; Colin Holmes, *Anti-Semitism and British Society, 1879–1939* (London, 1979), 12–17.

6. Lipman, *History of the Jews in Britain,* chap. 2; I. Finestein, *Post-Emancipation Jewry: The Anglo-Jewish Experience* (Oxford, 1986).

7. Lloyd Gartner, *The Jewish Immigrant in England, 1870–1914* (London, 1960); Eugene Black, *The Social Politics of Anglo-Jewry, 1880–1920* (Oxford, 1989).

8. Holmes, *Anti-Semitism and British Society,* chap. 7; R. Colls and P. Dodds, eds., *Englishness, Politics, and Culture* (London, 1986); Hugh A. MacDougall, *Racial Myth in English History* (Hanover, 1982), 89–103; Billie Melman, "Claiming the Nation's Past: The Invention of an Anglo-Saxon Tradition," *Journal of Contemporary History* 26, nos. 3–4 (1991), 575–96; Raphael Samuels, ed., *Patriotism: The Making and Unmaking of British National Identity,* 3 vols. (London, 1989).

9. David Cesarani, "An Embattled Minority: The Jews in Britain during the First World War," in *The Politics of Marginality,* ed. Tony Kushner and Kenneth Lunn (London, 1990), 61–81; idem,

"Anti-Zionist Politics and Political Anti-Semitism in Britain, 1920–24," *Patterns of Prejudice* 23, no. 1 (1989), 28–45; Keith Wilson, "'The Protocols of Zion' and the 'Morning Post,' 1919–1920," ibid. 19, no. 3 (1985), 6–14; Sharman Kadish, "'Boche, Bolshie and the Jewish Bogey': The Russian Revolution and Press Antisemitism in Britain 1917–21," ibid. 22, no. 4 (1988), 24–39.

10. David Cesarani, "Anti-Alienism in Britain after the First World War," *Immigrants and Minorities* 6, no. 1 (1987), 14–29; idem, "Joynson-Hicks and the Radical Right in England after the First World War," in *Traditions of Intolerance,* ed. Tony Kushner and Kenneth Lunn (Manchester, 1989), 118–39.

11. Tony Kushner, "Beyond the Pale? British Reactions to Nazi Anti-Semitism, 1933–39," in Kushner and Lunn, *Politics of Marginality,* 143–60; John P. Fox, "Great Britain and the German Jews, 1933," *Wiener Library Bulletin* 26, nos. 1–2 (1976), 40–46. See also A. Sharf, *The British Press and the Jews under Nazi Rule* (Oxford, 1964); F. Gannon, *The British Press and Germany, 1936–1939* (Oxford, 1971); and Richard Griffiths, *Fellow Travellers of the Right: British Enthusiasts for Nazi Germany 1933–39* (Oxford, 1983).

12. Sharon Gewirtz, "Anglo-Jewish Responses to Nazi Germany, 1933–39: The Anti-Nazi Boycott and the Board of Deputies of British Jews," *Journal of Contemporary History* 26, no. 2 (1991), 255–76.

13. Louise London, "British Government Policy and Jewish Refugees, 1933–1945," *Patterns of Prejudice* 23, no. 4 (1989–90), 29–30; idem, "British Immigration Control Procedures and Jewish Refugees, 1933–1939," in *Second Chance: Two Centuries of German-Speaking Jews in the United Kingdom,* ed. Werner E. Mosse et al. (Tübingen, 1991), 485–518, esp. 505–13.

14. Louise London, "Jewish Refugees, Anglo-Jewry, and British Government Policy, 1930–1940," in *The Making of Modern Anglo-Jewry,* ed. David Cesarani (Oxford, 1990), 163–90; Vivian D. Lipman, "Anglo-Jewish Attitudes to the Refugees from Central Europe, 1933–1939," in Mosse et al., *Second Chance,* 519–31; David Cesarani, "Zionism in England, 1917–1939" (D.Phil. thesis, Oxford University, 1986), 355–69.

15. G. C. Webber, "Patterns of Membership and Support for the British Union of Fascists," *Journal of Contemporary History* 19, no. 4 (1984), 573–605; Robert Skidelsky, *Oswald Mosley* (London, 1975); Richard Thurlow, *Fascism in Britain: A History, 1918–1985* (Oxford, 1987).

16. Elaine Smith, "Jews and Politics in the East End of London, 1918–1939," in Cesarani, *Making of Modern Anglo-Jewry,* 141–62; idem, "Jewish Responses to Political Antisemitism and Fascism in the East End of London, 1920–1939," in Kushner and Lunn, *Traditions of Intolerance,* 53–71; David Cesarani, "The East End of Simon Blumenfeld's 'Jew Boy,'" *London Journal* 13, no. 1 (1987–88), 46–53.

17. Tony Kushner, "The Impact of British Anti-Semitism, 1918–1945," in Cesarani, *Making of Modern Anglo-Jewry,* 195–97; idem, "Beyond the Pale?" 143–60.

18. David Cesarani, "The Transformation of Jewish Communal Authority in Anglo-Jewry, 1914–1940," in Cesarani, *Making of Modern Anglo-Jewry,* 115–40.

19. Martin Gilbert, *Exile and Return: The Emergence of Jewish Statehood* (London, 1978), 236–51; Bernard Wasserstein, *Britain and the Jews of Europe, 1939–1945* (London, 1978), 163–65; Tony Kushner, *The Persistence of Prejudice: Antisemitism in British Society during the Second World War* (Manchester, 1989), 158–60; idem, "Different Worlds: British Perceptions of the Holocaust During the Second World War," in *The Final Solution: Origins and Implementation,* ed. David Cesarani (London, 1994), 249–51.

20. Peter Gillman and Leni Gillman, *Collar the Lot!* (London, 1980); Wasserstein, *Britain and the Jews of Europe,* 83–108; idem, "Patterns of Jewish Leadership in Great Britain during the Nazi Era," in *Jewish Leadership during the Nazi Era: Patterns of Behavior in the Free World,* ed. Randolph L. Braham (New York, 1985), 36–37; Kushner, *Persistence of Prejudice,* 142–52; David Cesarani and Tony Kushner, eds., *The Internment of Aliens in Twentieth Century Britain* (London, 1993).

21. Sharf, *British Press,* 113; Walter Laqueur, *The Terrible Secret* (London, 1980), 2–3. The *Jewish Chronicle,* edited by Ivan Greenberg, naturally strove to maintain the most exhaustive coverage. The stories it printed were also available to other newspapers via its own press service and the Jewish Telegraphic Agency (JTA). The Jewish press thus offers a good sense of what was known at the time and, in addition, gives an insight into Anglo-Jewish reactions. See David Cesarani, *The Jewish Chronicle and Anglo-Jewry, 1841–1991* (Cambridge, 1994), 165–83.

22. For summaries of the wider coverage, see *Jewish Chronicle,* July 3, 1942, 8.

23. John P. Fox, "The Jewish Factor in British War Crimes Policy in 1942," *English Historical Review* 92 (1977), 82–106; Wasserstein, *Britain and the Jews of Europe,* chap. 4; Laqueur, *Terrible Se-*

cret, 73–83; Martin Gilbert, *Auschwitz and the Allies* (London, 1981), 39–105; *JTA Bulletin,* October 28, 1942, 4, citing an editorial that appeared in the *Manchester Guardian* on October 27. For aspects of the general press response, see Sharf, *British Press,* 90–100. Eleanor Rathbone, an Independent M.P. who worked closely with the British Section of the World Jewish Congress (WJC), was feeding information from WJC sources in Europe to W. P. Crozier, editor of the *Manchester Guardian* (see Kushner, "Different Worlds," 254 and n. 38).

24. Cf. Wasserstein, *Britain and the Jews of Europe,* chap. 5. Kushner, "Different Worlds," 13–14, uses survey material from Mass-Observation, an independent research project that collected data on public attitudes from 1937 to 1945, to make important observations on the public response. See also idem, "The Rules of the Game: Britain, America, and the Holocaust in 1944," *Holocaust and Genocide Studies* 5, no. 4 (1990), 383–89. On Christian responses, see Marcus Braybrook, *Children of One God: A History of the Council of Christians and Jews* (London, 1991), 10–19.

25. For a full evaluation, see Richard Bolchover, *British Jewry and the Holocaust* (Cambridge, 1993); cf. Wasserstein, "Patterns of Jewish Leadership in Great Britain."

26. Bolchover, *British Jewry and the Holocaust,* 94–102, 103–20; cf. Wasserstein, "Patterns of Jewish Leadership," 38–43.

27. *Jewish Chronicle,* July 3, 1942, 8; Bolchover, *British Jewry and the Holocaust,* 13–18.

28. Kushner, *Persistence of Prejudice,* 167–84; Bolchover, *British Jewry and the Holocaust,* 31–53.

29. *Jewish Chronicle,* December 11, 1942, 8.

30. Ibid., May 7, 1943, 8, and subsequent issues. For the response of the general press and public, see Sharf, *British Press,* 111–13; and Bolchover, *British Jewry and the Holocaust,* 34–37. Auschwitz was mentioned in press reports during 1943, but its function was still unclear.

31. Bolchover, *British Jewry and the Holocaust,* 121–56.

32. Wasserstein, *Britain and the Jews of Europe,* 168–69, 249–70; Gilbert, *Auschwitz and the Allies,* 207–30; Kushner, "Rules of the Game," 389–93.

33. *Jewish Chronicle,* August 18, 1944, 7, 10; September 1, 1944, 10; September 22, 1944, 10. Alexander Werth, *Russia at War, 1941–45* (London, 1964), 888–90.

34. Laqueur, *Terrible Secret,* 1–3.

35. BBC, *War Report: A Record of Dispatches Broadcast by the BBC's War Correspondents with the Allied Expeditionary Force, 6 June 1944–5 May 1944* (London, 1946), 390; Paul Kemp, "The Liberation of Bergen-Belsen Concentration Camp in April 1945: The Testimony of Those Involved," *Imperial War Museum Review* 5 (1990), 28–41. See also Imperial War Museum, *The Relief of Belsen, April 1945: Eyewitness Accounts* (London, 1991).

36. Front-page leader comment, *Spectator,* April 20, 1945, 349–50.

37. *New Statesman and Nation,* April 28, 1945, 269.

38. BBC, *War Report,* 392–96, 401–4; *Illustrated London News,* April 28, May 5, June 2, 1945.

39. *Spectator,* April 27, 1945, front-page editorial; May 4, 1945, 402; May 25, 1945, 476–77.

40. *New Statesman and Nation,* April 28, 1945, 256–57. The same self-serving interpretation featured in "Critic"'s column, April 14, 1945, 237. The pro-Zionist Labour M.P. Richard Crossman chose to concentrate on the suffering of left-wing inmates when he reported from Buchenwald (June 23, 1945, 402–3).

41. "Critic," ibid., April 28, 1945, 269. Tony Kushner, "The Impact of the Holocaust on British Society and Culture," *Contemporary Record* 5, no. 2 (1991), 13.

42. Nicholas Pronay, "Defeated Germany in British Newsreels: 1944–45," in *Hitler's Fall: The Newsreel Witness,* ed. K. R. M. Short and Stephen Dolezel (London, 1990), 30–32, 40–45. See also Jon Bridgman, *The End of the Holocaust: The Liberation of the Camps* (London, 1990), 110–13, although his conclusions on the impact of the "liberation" and the decline of anti-Semitism have been criticized by Kushner in "Impact of the Holocaust," 357.

43. *Illustrated London News,* April 28, May 5, June 2, 1945. Cf. *Lest We Forget: The Horrors of the Nazi Concentration-Camps Revealed for All Times in the Most Terrible Photographs Ever Taken* (London, 1945), cited in Kushner, "Impact of the Holocaust," 11–13.

44. *Spectator,* November 23, 1945, 478; see also Harold Nicolson's comments, May 10, 1946, 478. *New Statesman and Nation,* May 5, 1945, 282; October 19, 1946, 277.

45. *Reynolds News,* December 16, 1945, cited in Ann Tusa and John Tusa, *The Nuremberg Trial* (London, 1983), 222; *AJR Information* 1 (September 1946), 46; Sir John Wheeler-Bennett, *Friends, Enemies, and Foreigners* (London, 1976), 114–15.

46. Peter Calvocoressi, *Nuremberg: The Facts, the Law, and the Consequences* (London, 1947), 24–25, 89–90.

47. Lord Russell of Liverpool, *The Scourge of the Swastika: A Short History of Nazi War Crimes* (London, 1954), 250.

48. Calvocoressi, *Nuremberg*, 120–23. For the impact of the A-bombs, for example, see *Spectator*, August 10, 1945, 117, and follow-up articles, which continued into 1946. *House of Commons Debates,* 5th ser., vol. 445, cols. 673–90.

49. 457 *H.C. Deb.* 5s., cols. 66, 256.

50. Ibid., cols. 256, 272. On the Manstein affair, see *House of Lords Debates,* vol. 162, cols. 389–91, and 465 *H.C. Deb.* 5s., col. 247. See also Wheeler-Bennett, *Friends, Enemies, and Foreigners,* 114–15.

51. Montgomery Belgion, *Epitaph on Nuremberg* (London, 1946), 25–35, 58–65, 89–90; Lord Hankey, *Politics Trials and Errors* (Oxford, 1950), 125–30. Hankey also contributed a postscript to Viscount Maugham's book, *U.N.O. and War Crimes* (London, 1951), which argued that there were no such things as "crimes against humanity."

52. *Jewish Chronicle,* April 15, 1949, 10; April 22, 1949, 10; December 23, 1949, 1; February 2, 1950, 12. *AJR Information* 3, no. 11 (1948), 1.

53. *Jewish Chronicle,* May 20, 1949, 12; August 19, 1949, 12; November 24, 1950, 12; May 30, 1952, 12. *AJR Information* 9, no. 11 (1954), 3; 10, no. 6 (1955), 1. The small British Communist Party was also vocally opposed to German rearmament.

54. *Jewish Chronicle,* September 19, 1947, 10; April 27, 1951, 10; October 14, 1949, 12. *AJR Information* 9, no. 2 (1954), 1; 10, no. 1 (1955), 1; 11, no. 12 (1956), 2. *Jewish Chronicle,* May 24, 1957, 16, protesting the appointment of Gen. Hans Speidel, chief of staff to Field Marshal Rommel in 1944, as commander of NATO land forces.

55. Gilbert, *Exile and Return,* 275–83.

56. Sir Frederick Morgan, *Peace and War: A Soldier's Life* (London, 1961), 235–38, 243–48, 253–68; Mark Wyman, *DP: Europe's Displaced Persons, 1945–1951* (Philadelphia, 1989), 134–37.

57. *Jewish Chronicle,* August 2, 1946, 8; August 16, 1946, 9; September 6, 1946, 9; January 24, 1947, 1. See PRO, FO 371/55979 and FO 945/754.

58. *Jewish Chronicle,* November 16, 1945, 5; February 8, 1946, 5; May 17, 1946, 5.

59. *AJR Information* 3, no. 7 (1946), 1, 2; 4, no. 4 (1949), 2; 4, no. 12 (1949), 2. *Jewish Chronicle,* August 16, 1946, 1; March 18, 1949, 5. See the report of statement by the under secretary of state at the Foreign Office, reported in *AJR Information* 4, no. 12 (1949), 2.

60. Elizabeth Stadulis, "The Resettlement of Displaced Persons in the United Kingdom," *Population Studies* 5 (1951–52), 207–37; Keith Sword, "The Absorption of Poles into Civilian Employment in Britain, 1945–1950," in *Refugees in the Age of Total War,* ed. Anna C. Bramwell (London, 1988), 233–52; Robert Miles and Diana Kay, "The

TUC [Trades Union Congress], Foreign Labour, and the Labour Government, 1945–1951," *Immigrants and Minorities* 9, no. 1 (1990), 85–108. See also Julius Isaac, *Post-War British Migration* (Cambridge, 1954), 162–92; and John Tannahill, *European Volunteer Workers in Britain* (Manchester, 1958).

61. *AJR Information* 1, no. 8 (1946), 59; 2, no. 6 (1947), 42, 43; 3, no. 7 (1948), 2. *Jewish Chronicle,* January 31, 1947, 1; March 7, 1947, 1, 9; June 6, 1947, 1, 10; July 29, 1949, 10; August 12, 1949, 12.

62. PRO, FO 371/66709; see also PRO, FO 945/470, on recruitment practice.

63. PRO, FO 371/66711.

64. *Jewish Chronicle,* May 25, 1945, 8; September 7, 1945, 12; October 19, 1945, 10; November 2, 1945, 5, 10. *AJR Information* 1, no. 7 (1946), 49–51; 1, no. 8 (1946), 59; 2, no. 2 (1947), 11, 27; 3, no. 12 (1948), 5; 6, no. 9 (1951), 2. *Jewish Chronicle,* August 10, 1951, 5.

65. *Jewish Chronicle,* September 7, 1945, 12; December 7, 1945, 10; December 21, 1945, 10; March 8, 1946, 10.

66. For the background, see Michael J. Cohen, *Palestine: Retreat from Mandate. The Making of British Policy, 1939–1945* (London, 1978); idem, *Palestine and the Great Powers, 1945–1948* (Princeton, 1982); and Nicholas Bethell, *The Palestine Triangle* (London, 1979).

67. *Spectator,* August 16, 1946, 156; *Jewish Chronicle,* January 3, 1947, 8, 12; January 17, 1947, 12.

68. *Jewish Chronicle,* November 15, 1946, 1; November 22, 1946, 1, 6, 9, 12; December 6, 1946, 12. *AJR Information* 1, no. 8 (1946), 57; 2, no. 5 (1947), 35. *Jewish Monthly,* April 1947, 36. On the revival of fascism, see Morris Beckman, *The 43 Group* (London, 1992); Colin Cross, *The Fascists in Britain* (London, 1964), 199–202; and Kushner, *Persistence of Prejudice,* 199–200.

69. *Jewish Chronicle,* July 25, 1947, 12; August 1, 1947, 1, 6, 12; August 8, 1947, 1, 2, 10; August 15, 1947, 1, 2; August 22, 1947, 10; August 29, 1947, 10; September 12, 1947, 1, 8, 12. David Leitch, "Explosion at the King David Hotel," in *The Age of Austerity,* ed. Michael Sissons and Phillip French (London, 1963), 59–72.

70. For British press responses, see *Jewish Monthly,* September 1947, 30–31, 33.

71. *Spectator,* August 8, 1947, 161; *New Statesman and Nation,* August 30, 1947, 161. For a survey of the reaction, see *Jewish Chronicle,* August 22, 1947, 10; *AJR Information* 2, no. 9 (1947), 67, and 2, no. 11 (November 1947), 85; and *Jewish Monthly,* September 1947, 30–31. For a judicious

assessment of the origins and impact of the riots, see Tony Kushner, "Anti-Semitism and Austerity: The August 1947 Riots in Britain," in *Racial Violence in Britain, 1840–1950,* ed. Panikos Panayi (Leicester, 1993), 149–68.

72. *AJR Information* 3, no. 1 (1948), 3; 3, no. 2 (1948), 3, 6; 3, no. 8 (1948), 6; 3, no. 10 (1948), 3. *Jewish Monthly,* October 1948, 407. *Jewish Chronicle,* March 19, 1948, 10. John Gross, "The Lynskey Tribunal," in Sissons and French, *Age of Austerity,* 255–75. *Jewish Monthly,* September 1947, 30.

73. Conor Cruise O'Brien, *The Siege* (London, 1986), 305–6.

74. In April 1948 only 1 percent of those questioned in a Gallup poll rated Palestine a chief problem of government, compared with 4 percent in January 1947. See George H. Gallup, ed., *The Gallup International Public Opinion Polls: Great Britain, 1937–1975,* vol. 1, *1937–1964* (New York, 1976), 148, 175.

75. *AJR Information* 4, no. 6 (1949), 1; 6, no. 12 (1951), 5; 7, no. 2 (1952), 1; 9, no. 5 (1954), 1–2; 9, no. 10 (1954), 3; 15, no. 7 (1960), 1; 16, no. 5 (1961), 1; 19, no. 10 (1964), 2.

76. See *The Jewish Year Book,* published in London annually since 1896. Refugee bodies are listed under "Foreign and Refugee Assistance Organisations" in the section on Anglo-Jewish Institutions. On Kristallnacht, see each November issue of *AJR Information.* The Ghetto Uprising memorial always received coverage in the Jewish press.

77. *Jewish Chronicle,* April 10, 1959, 34; April 17, 1959, 26.

78. *AJR Information* 15, no. 6 (1960), 12; 18, no. 5 (1963), 5; 19, no. 5 (1964), 15; 26, no. 4 (1971), 10.

79. Ibid. 33, no. 5 (1978), 4; 36, no. 4 (1981), 3.

80. *Jewish Chronicle,* December 18, 1959, 18. *AJR Information* 15, no. 1 (1960), 3; 32, no. 1 (1977), 3; 34, no. 7 (1979), 3; 35, no. 5 (1980), 3.

81. *AJR Information* 26, no. 2 (1971), 2; 16, no. 8 (1971), 3.

82. Ibid. 34, no. 12 (1979), 2; 37, no. 4 (1982), 3; 38, no. 8 (1983), 4; 38, no. 11 (1983), 4. The memorial also soon became the target for anti-Semitic and anti-Zionist graffiti.

83. Ibid. 5, no. 8 (1955), 3; 10, no. 9 (1955), 8; 15, no. 3 (1960), 30.

84. *Jewish Chronicle,* March 21, 1958, 22. *Wiener Library Bulletin* 12, nos. 5–6 (1958), 41–42; 14, no. 3 (1960), 41.

85. Filip Friedman, *This Was Oswiecem* (London, 1951); *Jewish Chronicle,* March 23, 1951, 12.

86. *Jewish Monthly,* April 1947, 19–23; August 1947, 29–32; February 1948, 20–21; December 1948, 524–31; January 1951, 662–63. For the slim bibliography of books in English, see *Wiener Library Bulletin* 3, no. 2 (1949), 11. Bernard Goldstein, *The Stars Bear Witness* (London, 1950). For the genesis of Anne Frank's diary in Britain, see Tony Kushner, "Anne Frank and the Liberal Imagination" (paper presented at a conference entitled "War and Memory in the Twentieth Century," Portsmouth University, March 25, 1994).

87. Derrick Sington, *Belsen Uncovered* (London, 1946); Victor Bernstein, *Final Judgement* (London, 1947).

88. *Jewish Chronicle,* May 1, 1953, 14. For a review of reviews, see *Wiener Library Bulletin* 7, nos. 3–4 (1953), 17.

89. *Observer,* August 22, 1954.

90. The *Wiener Library Bulletin* was a pitiless critic of these screeds. See *Wiener Library Bulletin* 13, nos. 5–6 (1959), 57; 15, no. 2 (1961), 27; 17, no. 3 (1963), 41.

91. Lucy Dawidowicz, *The Holocaust and the Historians* (Cambridge, Mass., 1981), 31–34; *Jewish Monthly,* August 1951, 611–12; *Wiener Library Bulletin* 6, nos. 5–6 (1952), 29.

92. A. J. P. Taylor, *Origins of the Second World War* (London, 1961); *Wiener Library Bulletin* 15, no. 3 (1961), 41–42. See also C. Robert Cole, "Critics of the Taylor View of History," ibid. 22, no. 3 (1968), 29–35.

93. Gollancz brought out Stefan Szende's *The Promise Hitler Kept* (1945), on the destruction of Polish Jewry; Jean-Jacques Bernard's *The Camp of Slow Death* (1946), on the Compiègne transit camp; and Eva Reichmann's *Hostages of Civilisation* (1950). Vallentine Mitchell was responsible for Reitlinger's seminal work and Anne Frank's diary. On the *Jewish Quarterly,* see Efraim Sicher, *Beyond Marginality: Anglo-Jewish Literature after the Holocaust* (New York, 1985), 19–23.

94. Reichmann, *Hostages of Civilisation;* Max Beloff, ed., *On the Track of Tyranny* (London, 1960). The *Bulletin,* which ran from 1946 to 1981, was edited by C. C. Aaronsfeld, 1965–66, Ernest Hearst, 1966–75, Hearst and Robert Wistrich, 1975–76, and Wistrich, 1976–81. For an appreciation of Dr. Wiener and the library, see *The Wiener Library Bulletin,* special issue (1982). On financial troubles see, e.g., plaint and warning by Alfred Wiener, "Does the Community Care?" *Jewish Monthly,* July 1951, 230–31; and on appeal for funds, *Wiener Library Bulletin* 11, nos. 1–2 (1957), 2–3.

95. See Kushner, "Rules of the Game," 382–83; on refugee studies, see Mosse et al., *Second Chance.*

96. *AJR Information* 9, no. 10 (1954), 5; *Wiener Library Bulletin* 9, nos. 3–4 (1955), 21. On the Joel Brand story, see *Observer,* April 20, 1958; critical

editorial comment in *Jewish Observer and Middle East Review,* March 21 and 28, 1958, for further comment and correspondence from David Astor, editor of the *Observer; Jewish Chronicle,* April 18, 1958, 18, 25.

97. Peter Kemp, "Toynbee and the Jews," *Wiener Library Bulletin* 21, no. 1 (1966–67), 21–28. See also Hugh Trevor-Roper, "Arnold Toynbee's Millennium," *Encounter* 8, no. 45 (1957), 71.

98. *Daily Herald,* February 27, 28, March 1, 2, 3, 1961; Hugh Trevor-Roper, *Sunday Times,* December 17, 1961; *The People,* October 16, 1960; on *Any Questions?,* see *Jewish Chronicle,* April 28, 1961, and poll, April 7, 1961.

99. *Solicitor's Journal,* quoted in *Daily Mail,* March 30, 1961; *New Statesman,* January 5, 1961; *Times,* December 16, 1961; *Daily Express,* December 12, 1961.

100. *Jewish Chronicle,* June 2, 1961. *AJR Information* 16, no. 8 (1961), 1, 17; 17, no. 6 (1962), 3; 18, no. 4 (1963), 3; 18, no. 10 (1963), 2; 18, no. 12 (1963), 2. *Anglo-Jewish Association Quarterly* 9, no. 2 (1964), 14–27. *Jewish Chronicle,* May 27, 1960, 1, 18, and subsequent issues. For a review of the impact of the trial, see ibid., July 28, 1961, 16; on press responses to the death sentence, ibid., December 22, 1961, 13; on the execution, ibid., June 8, 1962, 16. On Arendt, see ibid., May 17, 1963, 22; October 11, 1963, 27. On the question of Allied responses during the war, see ibid., June 9, 1961, 22.

101. For the story of the trial, see Mavis M. Hill and William L. Norman, *Auschwitz in England: A Record of a Libel Action* (London, 1965).

102. Geoff Eley, "Holocaust History," *London Review of Books,* March 3–17, 1982, 6–9. Between 1965 and 1990 major studies of fascism, Nazism, and the Third Reich were published by Robin Blackbourne, Jane Caplan, Geoff Eley, Richard Evans, John Farquharson, John Hiden, Ian Kershaw, Martin Kitchen, Tim Mason, Alan Milward, Anthony Nichols, Jeremy Noakes, Richard Overy, Geoffrey Pridham, Janet Stephenson, and Norman Stone. For a summary of the debate between the intentionalists and the functionalists with respect to the Holocaust, see Ian Kershaw, *The Nazi Dictatorship: Problems and Perspectives of Interpretation* (London, 1985), chap. 5.

103. *Jewish Monthly,* September 1948, 344–59.

104. See Leftwich's comments on *The Wall* in ibid., November 1950, 502–9. For the interview with Baron, see *Anglo-Jewish Association Quarterly* 3, no. 1 (1957), 8. See also Chaim Bermant, *Troubled Eden: An Anatomy of British Jewry* (London, 1969), 172–73; and Sicher, *Beyond Marginality,* 153–62.

105. *Jewish Chronicle,* September 23, 1960, 10; Stephen Brook, *The Club* (London, 1989), 329; Sicher, *Beyond Marginality,* 131–35. I am grateful to Dr. Bryan Cheyette for his assistance with the paragraphs on literary history.

106. *Observer,* September 15, 1957; July 13, 1958. Sicher, *Beyond Marginality,* 17–18. Ken Worpole, *Dockers and Detectives* (London, 1983), 49–53, 62–66. George Steiner, quoted in Brook, *The Club,* 421.

107. George Steiner, *Language and Silence: Essays on Language, Literature, and the Inhuman* (New York, 1967) and *In Bluebeard's Castle: Some Notes towards the Redefinition of Culture* (London, 1971).

108. *AJR Information* 37, no. 4 (1982), 3; C. C. Aaronsfeld, "Dr. Steiner's Fables," *Patterns of Prejudice* 16, no. 3 (1983), 35–40.

109. Jonathan Davis, ed., *Film History and the Jewish Experience: A Reader* (London, 1986).

110. For a full list of films and details, see Annette Insdorf, *Indelible Shadows: Film and the Holocaust,* 2d ed. (New York, 1989). For the response to *Shoah,* see Brook, *The Club,* 421–22.

111. *Anglo-Jewish Association Quarterly* 5, no. 2 (1959), 27. *Wiener Library Bulletin* 13, nos. 1–2 (1959), 11; 14, no. 1 (1960), 3–5; 14, no. 3 (1960), 42.

112. *Wiener Library Bulletin* 19, no. 4 (1965), 39–41; *Daily Mail,* August 26, 1989.

113. *AJR Information* 27, no. 3 (1972), 3; 37, no. 9 (1982), 3. On the exhibitions, see ibid., 36, no. 3 (1981), 3, and 38, no. 4 (1983), 2; and *Jewish Chronicle,* November 4, 1988, 26.

114. John P. Fox, *Teaching the Holocaust: The Report of a Survey in the United Kingdom (1987)* (Leicester, 1989); Sharman Kadish, *The Teaching of Jewish Civilization at British and Irish Universities and Other Institutions of Higher Learning* (Oxford, 1990).

115. *Holocaust Education Trust Bulletin* 1 (April–June 1990), 1.

116. *AJR Information* 27, no. 1 (1972), 3; 38, no. 6 (1983), 4, on the forged diaries.

117. Ibid., 29, no. 8 (1974), 3, and no. 9 (1974), 3. Gill Seidel, *The Holocaust Denial* (Leeds, 1986), 112–21; Roger Eatwell, "The Holocaust Denial: A Study in Propaganda Technique," in *Neo-Fascism in Europe,* ed. Luciano Cheles et al. (London, 1991), 120–23, 139–43.

118. *AJR Information* 32, no. 9 (1977), 3; 33, no. 4 (1978), 1–2; 37, no. 6 (1982), 3.

119. David Irving, *Hitler's War* (London, 1977); Gerald Fleming, *Hitler and the Final Solution* (London, 1985); *AJR Information* 32, no. 10 (1977), 1–2; Seidel, *Holocaust Denial,* 121–28; Eatwell, "Holo-

caust Denial," 141–42; David Cesarani, "Bad and Dangerous," *New Statesman and Society,* July 10, 1992.

120. Seidel, *Holocaust Denial,* 85–92; David Cesarani, "The *Perdition* Affair," in *Anti-Zionism and Antisemitism in the Contemporary World,* ed. Robert Wistrich (London, 1990), 53–60.

121. Anton Gill, *The Journey Back from Hell: Conversations with Concentration Camp Survivors* (London, 1988), esp. 137–87. Jewish Women in London Group, *Generations of Memory* (London, 1989), 120–21. *AJR Information* 20, no. 10 (1965), 3; 33, no. 8 (1978), 8.

122. *AJR Information* 32, no. 7 (1977), 3; 34, no. 11 (1979), 11. Gill, *Journey Back from Hell,* 57–70. Howard Cooper, ed., *Soul Searching: Studies in Judaism and Psychotherapy* (London, 1988), 91–101. Karen Gershon, *We Came as Children* (London, 1966), was one of the earliest of the "second generation" memoirs. See the *Kinderstransporte '38–'39 Commemoration, July 1989* brochure for one of the reunions.

123. For the effects of these anniversaries, see the entry on the Raphael Clinic in *Directory of Holocaust Education and Related Activity in the United Kingdom* (London, 1990).

124. Sir Thomas Hetherington and William Chalmers, *Report of the War Crimes Inquiry* (London, 1988).

125. David Cesarani, *Justice Delayed: How Britain Became a Refuge for Nazi War Criminals* (London, 1992), chaps. 9–10.

126. Ibid., 213–14, 229.

127. Braybrook, *Children of One God,* 52–53, 80–83, 95–96; *Jewish Chronicle,* August 8, 1958, 16, and subsequent issues; Clive Sinclair, *Blood Libels* (London, 1987); Brook, *The Club,* 421–22.

128. *Jewish Chronicle,* August 12, 1988, 25.

129. Bermant, *Troubled Eden,* 258–62.

130. Brook, *The Club,* 90, 158, 364, 418–25; Howard Cooper and Paul Morrison, *A Sense of Belonging: Dilemmas of British Jewish Identity* (London, 1991), 6, 88–94.

131. Brook, *The Club,* 421.

132. Judith Miller, *One, By One, By One: Facing the Holocaust* (New York, 1990).

133. Peter Hennessy, *Never Again: Britain 1945–1951* (London, 1992). Hennessy comprehensively sets out the trials and tribulations of postwar Britain, but apart from the highly publicized case of non-white immigrants, he overlooks the experience of minorities in British society. While this new, authoritative history accurately represents the preoccupations of 1945–51, it also replicates the myopia that prevented people from seeing beyond them to the wider issues.

134. Kushner, "Impact of the Holocaust," 350–51, 370.

135. The news stories and articles from the print media, and news items, current affairs programs, and special documentaries broadcast on the electronic media are too numerous to cite. The Wiener Library, London, collected a wide selection that is available for consultation.

136. See *Jewish Chronicle,* June 16, 1995. For a critique of an early plan for the proposed exhibition, see David Cesarani, "A Holocaust Museum for Britain?" *Aufbau,* June 9, 1995, 14–15.

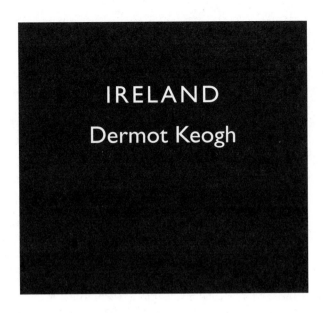

IRELAND
Dermot Keogh

BEFORE THE HOLOCAUST

The present Jewish community in Ireland can trace its existence to the early eighteenth century. There were earlier settlements, large enough to support the founding of synagogues and a cemetery at Ballybough, Dublin, but by 1820 there were only two Jewish families in the whole of Dublin. The reestablishment of the Jewish community was a slow process. In the period up to 1880 the Jews who immigrated to Ireland were, almost without exception, Ashkenazim, a marked change from the earlier period, in which Sephardim predominated. Although they originated mainly in Central and Eastern Europe, they came to Ireland from England, Holland, Poland, Germany, Russia, Lithuania, and Morocco. These immigrants were middle-class craftsmen: gold- and silversmiths, brassworkers, picture-frame carvers, watchmakers, jewelers, and grocers. In the beginning they lived and traded in the center of Dublin, but gradually, as they grew more prosperous, some moved to the suburbs.[1]

The community came together to found a synagogue, and Myer Nerwich, a scholar who had immigrated from Posen, Germany, served as its first spiritual leader. In 1829 the community moved to larger premises and set about trying to raise funds. Some help was received from Sir Moses Montefiore, who was a regular visitor to the synagogue, and other money was received from London. The extent of the contact between Jews in Ireland and those in the neighboring island is not clear. The community applied to affiliate itself to the Bevis Marks synagogue in London but was refused. Because the community was not yet large enough and had not been established long enough to produce spiritual leaders and teachers from within its own ranks, most of those who assumed such roles had gained broad experience elsewhere. One of the more notable of these leaders was Philip (Phineas) Bender, who made a name for himself by teaching students of all denominations.[2]

At this stage the Jewish community apparently had not distanced itself greatly from its neighbors. On arriving in Ireland the Jews may have found a common bond with the Catholic majority, since certain areas of public life were closed to both communities on religious grounds. The leaders of the two communities in England and Ireland shared ideas about how to further their respective emancipatory causes. In a letter to Isaac Goldsmid, the leader of the Jewish Emancipation Movement, Daniel O'Connell, the champion of Catholic emancipation in Ireland, wrote, "Ireland has claims on your ancient race, as it is the only that I know of unsullied by any one act of persecution against the Jews." At O'Connell's instigation, the obsolete law requiring Jews to wear special dress was repealed in 1846.[3]

The Jewish community in Ireland and elsewhere was quick to respond to the needs of those affected by the Great Famine of 1845–47. Baron Lionel Rothschild donated one thousand pounds, and the first appeal for aid in the United States was organized by Jewish banker August Belmont. It may be argued that the Jewish community did not simply coexist side by side with its Catholic and Protestant neighbors but took an active part in the public and commercial life of Ireland. In 1874 Lewis Harris became the first Jew to be elected to the Dublin Corporation (the city council); he died in 1876, just before he was to have been made lord mayor.[4]

In 1861 the national census recorded a total of 393 Jews living in Ireland. By the time of the census of 1871 this figure had dropped to 285. Of the 341 Jews living in 1861 in what is now the Republic of Ireland, 324 resided in the Dublin county borough. The register of births of the Jewish congregation in Dublin records that between November 25, 1838, and May 7, 1879, there were 308 births; and the register of deaths records 140 deaths between January 5, 1842, and February 8, 1879. The Jews of Dublin lived and traded in the inner city along the banks of the river Liffey. Perhaps the small size of the Jewish community helped facilitate their easy acceptance; anti-Semitism began to manifest itself after their numbers significantly increased following a wave of Jewish immigration from Eastern Europe in the 1880s.[5]

The promulgation of the May Laws in Russia in 1881 and the resulting pogroms prompted a mass exodus of Jews, many of whom went to Britain. A large number made their way to Ireland. While the number of Jews in Ireland increased by 71.3 percent between 1871 and 1881, the increase was more than 280 percent between 1881 and 1891, bringing the total Jewish population to 1,506. Another influx, in response to more official anti-Semitism in Eastern Europe, swelled the total to 3,006 by 1901, with 763 living in what is now Northern Ireland. The newcomers brought little wealth with them, and many could not speak English. Because of cultural and linguistic differences they were as isolated from their coreligionists as they were from the rest of the population.

Peddling was the primary occupation of the new immigrants. They sold blankets and other items, for which they were paid in installments. Over time these peddlers became more established as traders, and many went on to become wholesale merchants. Before such successes, however, the refugees' initial poverty had to be combated. To this end the Board of Guardians for the Relief of Jewish Poor of Dublin was established in 1889. While they still relied heavily on individual philanthropy, the Jews were moving toward a greater sense of community in all areas. It was at around this time that the first branches of Chovevei Zion were founded in Ireland (the Dublin branch was founded in 1890).[6] The Dublin community set up its own organization, the Brotherhood of Israel Association, to further the aim of resettlement in Palestine.

Members of the Jewish community also became prominent in Irish nationalist politics. The Judaeo-Irish Home Rule Association was founded in 1908. Among the individuals who made an impact in this movement were Jacob Elyan, who was asked by John Redmond, leader of the Irish Parliamentary Party, to run for the House of Commons as a member of that party, and Michael Noyk, a solicitor who became legal adviser to the Irish revolutionary leader Michael Collins.[7]

With this newly expanded population it became imperative to provide the community with suitable educational opportunities. The first schools were small and provided only religious education. A larger school was completed in 1892 that, with the help of the Irish Board of Education, provided both secular and religious instruction.[8]

The increase in the Jewish population produced major changes in the organization of the community and in the relationship between the Jews and the Irish people. In 1886 a Dublin poster campaign that was supported by letters to the newspapers protested against the arrival of the immigrants. The newspapers in question defended the Jews. The liberal nationalist daily *Freeman's Journal* wrote: "This sudden antipathy to the Jewish community in the city is either the work of some harebrain, or, what is more likely, the project of a set of ruffians having some ulterior object in view."[9] At least one radical nationalist politician, Arthur Griffith, allowed anti-Semitic articles and sentiments to appear in his newspaper, the *United Irishman*. The founder of Sinn Féin and the first leader of the future Irish state, Griffith was rabidly anti-Semitic and anti-Dreyfus. On August 5, 1899, he wrote: "While the Dublin Editors have fed the Irish public on the fables of the Jew Telegram Agencies, every diplomatist in Europe knows why Gallifet [the general chosen to review Dreyfus's guilty verdict] has been chosen to be the Tool of the Jews at the French War Office. He has been for many years their servile debtor, absolutely living on their loans, and only able to repay as interest his 'aristocratic service' in getting rich Jews into 'good society.'"[10] In other articles, Griffith stated that "two thirds of the Foreign journalists, who are not English or Yankee, are Jews"; and "I have in former years often declared that the Three Evil Influences of the century were the Pirate, the Freemason, and the Jew." Griffith continued his anti-Semitic writings into the 1900s.[11]

The most serious anti-Semitic outbreak in the history of the country took place in Limerick in 1904. Twenty Lithuanian Jewish families had settled there in the 1880s, and by 1896 their congregation had grown to 130. A synagogue had been opened, and in 1903 the Jewish community established a Board of Guardians and a Society for Relieving the Sick. The Jews engaged mainly in retail sales, and as they gained a greater fluency in English they began to mix more freely with the local people.

There were some displays of animosity toward the Jews in the early years, such as in 1884, when the house of a Jew was attacked by rioters throwing stones.[12] But in January 1904, during a time of celebration for the local Redemptorist Confraternity, a Fr. John Creagh preached an anti-Semitic sermon in which he said that "nowadays . . . [the Jews] dare not kidnap and slay Christian children but they will not hesitate to expose them to a longer and even more cruel martyrdom by taking the clothes off their back and the bit out of their mouths. . . . [T]hey came to our land to fasten themselves on us like leeches."[13] He also blamed the "Jews and the Free Masons" for being behind the expulsion of certain religious orders, including the Redemptorists, from France. His speech so inflamed the members of the confraternity that they carried out attacks on the street where many of Limerick's Jews lived. A group of youths also stoned the local rabbi. A boycott of Jewish businesses followed that lasted for more than three months, resulting in the dissolution of the Jewish community in the city.[14] Many of the Jews moved to Cork, which had an area known as Jewtown.

Jewtown was "a Lithuanian village inserted in the midst of a very parochial people." Most of the Jews who had settled in Cork were from Vilna and Kovno. They had founded a congregation in 1881 and leased a cemetery in 1885, buying it outright in 1887.[15] The earliest recorded marriage in the congregation took place in 1891. According to one prominent member of the community, Gerald Goldberg, who later became mayor of Cork, there was "no real co-ordination" among members in the early years of the community. At the turn of the century approximately four hundred Jews—about fifty-five families—lived in Jewtown. By 1939 only eleven families remained, most of the others having moved to other parts of the city.[16]

The Jewish immigrants were welcomed in Cork, and what few incidents of anti-Semitic behavior have been recorded seem to have been isolated. In 1888 two foreigners known by the name Katz threatened to import cheap labor and produce from abroad. The two were known popularly as Jews, although this has not been verified. The Cork Trades Union threatened the persecution of all Cork Jews. The mayor of Cork, John O'Brien, wrote a letter to the *Times* (London) disassociating the city's population from these threats. In 1894 some attacks on Jews occurred, and three of those responsible were imprisoned.[17] While there were occasional outbursts against the Jews in the city, they did not receive official support in any way.

Anti-Semitism was not widespread in Irish society between 1900 and 1922, but it did occur. The *Irish Worker*, a radical left-wing paper edited by the socialist revolutionary James Larkin, gave vent to anti-Semitism in parts of working-class Dublin. There were disturbing signs of its presence in nationalist, trade union, and church circles. Oliver St. John Gogarty, a doctor, novelist, and later a senator in the upper house of the Irish Free State, was of one mind with Griffith on the Jews. Writing in *Sinn Féin* on November 24, 1906, he said, "The Jews are upon us! . . . Meanwhile the struggle is approaching. Germany is healthy and must expand. Israel is rotten within and like a hollow elm holding her unwielding boughs together only by her bark. Her death is upon us. Devourer of the world, she must die from a surfeit undigested. Already her grave is open and the 'Chancerin' worm doth chide." And on December 1, 1906, he wrote, "I can smell a Jew, and in Ireland there's something rotten."[18]

A number of Catholic nationalist publications also published anti-Semitic articles. In 1916 the *Catholic Bulletin* featured an article titled "Ritual Murder among the Jews" by Fr. Thomas H. Burbage. The issue was advertised with publicity posters that proclaimed, "Murder by the Jews." The article began, "Does ritual murder exist among the Jews? This is one of those puzzling questions that is still awaiting a satisfactory answer. For centuries past and at frequent intervals Christians throughout the world have been shocked and alarmed by the discovery of murders that clearly belong to a special class. They show a startling similarity in their detail."[19]

Despite bitter complaints from the leaders of the Jewish community in Dublin and some public involvement, the *Catholic Bulletin* continued to publish articles by Burbage. The publication's editor, J. J. O'Kelly, went on in the 1920s to write about Jewish and Masonic plots.[20] As president of Sinn Féin in 1930, O'Kelly told its members: "In the signs of the Anti-Christ, England is today the prey of rival groups of unscrupulous Jews fighting for their lands." He told an audience in Cork City Hall in 1939 that "England's difficulty is Ireland's opportunity . . . it seems to me that England prefers to plant the Jews in Ireland, as she planted the Cromwellians, the Orangemen. . . . How many people in Ireland reflect that the Treaty of Versailles placed Germany . . . with the heel of the Jews on her neck . . . while Jewish usury emaciated and the Jewish White Slave Trade sought to corrupt the whole land?"[21] While O'Kelly was atypical of the majority of Irish people, his ideas represented a subcurrent that persisted throughout the 1920s and 1930s.

The Irish Free State (Saorstát Éireann) came into being in 1922 after a two-year war of independence. The outcome was dominion status for Irish nationalists, but the victory was tinged with bitterness. The island had been partitioned with the creation of the State of Northern Ireland in 1921. Then civil war erupted in 1922 in the Irish Free State between nationalists of differing views. The new border divided the Jews in the small Jewish community in Belfast and elsewhere in the north from their southern coreligionists. Politics also divided the Jewish community. This situation is brilliantly evoked by the writer David Marcus in his novel *A Land Not Theirs*.[22] The work focuses on the Jewish community in Cork and shows how it was drawn into the war of independence. Robert Briscoe, a founding member of the Fianna Fáil Party in 1926, was one of the most prominent members of the Jewish community to take the anti-Treatyite side and remain with Éamon de Valera, the future *taoiseach* (prime minister), in the 1920s. In his autobiography, *For the Life of Me,* he wrote: "Indeed, my race was a definite advantage in my extracurricular career—a Jewish member of the I.R.A. [Irish Republican Army] was almost as improbable as a Jewish Lord Mayor of Dublin."[23]

On an arms-buying trip to Germany during the war of independence Briscoe met the Sinn Féin envoy in Berlin, Charles Bewley. The descendant of an old Quaker family long associated with commercial life in Dublin, Bewley had been sent to Berlin to represent the interests of the newly emerging Irish state. The encounter between Briscoe and Bewley was not a happy one. In January 1922 Bewley arrived drunk at a Jewish-owned beer hall, where upon hearing Briscoe's name mentioned he "burst forth into a string of most abusive and filthy language. His chief point of argument as an excuse for this attitude was . . . [Briscoe's] faith."[24] Bewley was forcibly ejected from the premises, and Briscoe demanded that Bewley be removed from office. In his defense, Bewley reported to Dublin that he had been asked by a member of the bar staff if Briscoe was an Irish consul. "I said that he was not, and added that it was not likely that a Jew of this type would be appointed." He expressed regret for making the remark. Briscoe took his revenge by smashing up Bewley's office.[25]

Bewley remained an anti-Semite throughout his career. In 1933 he became Irish envoy extraordinary and minister plenipotentiary to Berlin. Bewley was atypical of most of the staff working in the government of the new state. Such overt prejudice as his was rarely displayed. Article 6 of the new Irish constitution protected all religious bodies in Ireland: "Freedom of conscience and the free profession and practice of religion are, subject to public order and morality, guaranteed to every citizen, and no law may be made either directly or indirectly to endow any religion." The new state, however, was strongly Gaelic, Catholic, and nationalist in ethos. It introduced very strict censorship laws regarding literature and films. It refused to introduce divorce and restricted the sale of contraceptive drugs, devices, and so on.[26] It did not interfere with denominational schooling, and the various churches and religious congregations generally were unimpeded by the state.

The good relations between the leaders of the Jewish community in Dublin and the rival political leaders, President William T. Cosgrave and de Valera of Fianna Fáil, owed much to the tact and diplomacy of Isaac Herzog, the chief rabbi of the Irish Free State. Herzog enjoyed an honored position in Jewish circles and in the larger society. According to Bernard Shillman, "The esteem and respect he enjoyed amongst Gentile circles in Ireland had the effect of raising the prestige of Irish Jewry in general."[27] When Herzog was appointed chief rabbi of Palestine in 1937, the *Irish Times* stated that "the appointment reflects high honour upon our nation."[28] Herzog also developed strong working relationships with the other religious leaders in the capital, which meant that any anti-Semitic utterances or writings were swiftly intercepted.

The Jewish community in Ireland did not increase appreciably during the 1920s and 1930s. The 1926 census recorded 3,686 Jews living in Ireland; in 1936 the figure was 3,749. Robert Briscoe was the only Jewish member of Dáil Éireann (Parliament) when de Valera won the general election in 1932. He was not senior enough in the party ranks to expect a ministry, but his presence in the Dáil ensured that the small Jewish community had an able spokesperson operating on its behalf. It also meant that the Jewish community had relatively easy access to the president of the executive council.

In this turbulent period Briscoe was very active. Anti-Semitism was introduced more directly into Irish politics with the founding of the fascist Blueshirts in 1933. The Blueshirts were a relatively ineffectual force and disappeared from public life within two years. They were xenophobic and accepted only Christians as members. An organization spokesman wrote in *The Blueshirt* on June 8, 1933, "I hope that when a Blueshirt Government is elected its first act will be to send all the foreign exploiters who have come in here during the past 12 or 13 years back to the land or lands of their birth."[29]

Throughout the 1930s, Catholic Ireland displayed considerable interest in the corporatist movement, which drew upon right-wing Continental Catholicism and the papal encyclicals of Pius XI for its intellectual inspiration. There was a risk that those espousing vocationalist views might also be influenced by the anti-Semitism that usually accompanied such ideas in France, Belgium, Holland, and Austria. The Jesuit Fr. Edward Cahill was one of the strongest supporters of radical Catholic Action, a movement dedicated to the establishment of a state based on papal encyclicals.[30] The author of a number of popular works, he viewed with great apprehension the power of international Freemasonry, Communism, and Jewry.[31] He was also a strong cultural nationalist and a friend of Éamon de Valera. De Valera did not espouse the priest's extreme political ideas, nor did Cahill ever succeed in developing a mass following.

The Holy Ghost Father Denis Fahey was among the more extreme of the anti-Semitic right-wing Catholic polemicists. He was ever conscious of world Jewish conspiracy; in his view, the influence of Freemasons, Jews, and Communists was ubiquitous. He was a prodigious writer, and his works, based on recycled French right-wing Catholic thought, enjoyed a certain vogue in the late 1930s.[32] Holding Jews responsible for the spread of Communism, he argued that the "real force behind Bolshevism in Russia are Jewish forces" and that Communism was "the most recent development in the age-long struggle waged by the Jewish Nation against the Supernatural Messiah, our Lord Jesus Christ." His works influenced Fr. Charles E. Coughlin in the United States.[33]

In the mid-1930s a series of explicitly anti-Semitic articles appeared in *The Cross* and other popular Catholic journals. One article involved the manner in which Jews butcher meat. "Why should privileges be given to foreigners in this country? It might be said that this was a religious matter, but if cannibals come to this country should they be allowed to eat the people because it was their religion?"[34] This and other such remarks were attempts by some people associated with the Blueshirts to foment anti-Semitic feelings in the country. They were probably aided and supported by elements in the German and Italian legations.[35] There was further evidence of anti-Semitism in the leadership of the Irish Christian Front, a group formed in the autumn of 1936 to support Francisco Franco during the Spanish Civil War.[36]

Thus, in the 1930s the Jewish community faced many difficulties in trying to protect itself from the prevailing European prejudices. It was fortunate that Chief Rabbi Herzog enjoyed the personal friendship of de Valera, who in 1937 made explicit reference in the new Irish constitution to the religious freedom of the Jews, together with other non-Catholic churches. Article 44 reads: "The State also recognises the Church of Ireland . . . as well as the Jewish Congregation."[37]

At about this time the activities of Charles Bewley began to cause new concern. In 1933 he assumed his diplomatic post in Berlin, where he was strongly influenced by the Nazis. In an interview in *Uhr Blatt,* a Berlin evening paper, Bewley was quoted as saying, "That your Reich and its leaders has many admirers among our youth is a well-known fact."[38] However, Bewley did have consular duties to perform in Berlin, and it is unlikely that he was sympathetic to Jews who wished to immigrate to Ireland. George Clare, author of *Last Waltz in Vienna,* moved to Ireland at the end of the 1930s with his mother to work in a factory in the midlands. He had to endure Kristallnacht in Berlin because Bewley had temporized over giving his mother a visa to enter the country.[39] If this was typical of Bewley's handling of consular work for Jews, then it is likely that many did not persevere and simply went elsewhere to find refuge. In mid-1939 Bewley left his post amid a welter of acrimony. His behavior, however, must be set against the background of a very restrictive Irish policy toward all refugees.

The law relating to the admission and regulation of aliens was governed by the Aliens Act (1935) and the orders made under that legislation. The most important order was the Aliens Order (1935), which provided that an alien coming from anywhere other than the United Kingdom could not land in Ireland unless the permission of an immigration officer had been obtained. Furthermore, an alien coming to Ireland had to possess a permit issued by the Department of Industry and Commerce addressed to his prospective employer. Such a permit was issued only when the department was satisfied that "no suitable Irish citizen is available" to fill the post. Aliens who did not possess an employment permit had to satisfy the immigration officer that they were in a position to support themselves and their dependents. Individual immigration officers had the authority to attach certain conditions to entry; for example, they could specify the duration of the stay or whether the immigrant would be allowed to work.

At the international Evian Conference in July 1938 Irish envoy Frank T. Cremins told the plenary session of the conference that his country was effectively closed to refugees:

> Ireland is a small country with jurisdiction over a population of something less than three million people. Notwithstanding the steady progress which has been made in recent years in regard to the creation of new industries, by far the greater part of our people still derive, and will continue to derive, their living from the land. I need not attempt to explain the land problems which have arisen in Ireland; it is sufficient to say that there is not enough land available to satisfy the needs of our own people.
>
> Although every effort is being made by the Government to expedite industrialisation in a country which has been greatly under-industrialised, the new industries are not yet capable of absorbing the regular increase in our population, so that each year numbers of young people are forced by circumstances to emigrate. While such emigration remains imposed upon our national economy, it is obvious that we can make no real contribution to the settlement of refugees.[40]

In 1938 and 1939 many continental Europeans wished to either study or work in Ireland. Most were refused entrance. In one such case in August 1938 the governing body of University College, Dublin, sought permission for twelve Austrian students to study at the college. The request had come from Catholic sources in Austria. The Department of Justice, citing the Evian arguments, refused permission. Only the direct intervention of the Department of the Taoiseach overturned the decision and allowed the students to study in the country.[41] In another case, even the intervention of Herzog and the Vatican could not convince the Irish authorities to allow Jewish doctors and dentists to immigrate.[42]

The German envoy Eduard Hempel, who had been posted to Dublin in 1937, reported to Berlin on December 7, 1938, that people were "beginning to be more lucid than before about the dangers of an increase in the Jewish population in Ireland and of the necessity of a fundamental solution of the Jewish question." He added: "The Irishman as such is generally not well disposed to Jews, in so far as he knows any." Hempel believed that the government feared anti-Semitic disturbances.[43]

There were new manifestations of anti-Semitism in the country. The *Irish Times* reported on February 23, 1939, that an unnamed organization was circulating a flyer that claimed that the group refused to "stand by and allow the Jewish hold on our economic life to develop. . . . [T]he whole question of racial aliens, their special moral code and values, is never widely appreciated until it is too late. When at last a remedy is applied to the evils engendered by leading Jewish propaganda the public is given no opportunity to judge for itself." In an editorial, the *Irish Times* took the organization in question to task for the "crudest form of anti-semitic propaganda. . . . We would treat this effusion with the contempt which it deserves but for the fact that attempts have been made of late to stir up anti-Jewish feeling in this country, which is famed justly for its tolerance. The statement that the English-speaking Press is in Jewish hands is merely laughable; but there are credulous people in Ireland, as in every other country, who will believe almost anything." The newspaper concluded: "Anti-Semitism in any country is foolish; in Ireland it is almost criminal."[44]

THE HOLOCAUST ERA

Ireland remained neutral during the war, a policy Taoiseach de Valera sought to implement very strictly.[45] From the outset, however, there was no doubt that Irish allegiance lay on the side of the Allies. Ireland was practically defenseless, and the British were its main source of military supplies. De Valera, despite his dependence on London, resolutely refused to allow the British to repossess the Irish ports they had only given up in 1938. The month of July 1940 was a time of great tension between Dublin and London, but differences were finally resolved as the British came to accept, albeit reluctantly, the intransigence of the Irish position. An accommodation was then worked out on a number of levels that proved satisfactory to the British. But the relationship was not without its difficult moments.[46]

From the beginning of the war the Irish government was aware that the Germans were engaged in a two-track policy toward Ireland. Diplomatic relations were conducted on a professional level, but the Abwehr had identified the IRA as a worthwhile collaborator. The IRA, having thrown its lot in with the Nazis, awaited with anticipation the "liberation" of the country. The chief of staff of the IRA, Seán Rus-

Buchenwald internment camp is one of incredulity . . . the people here find it difficult to believe that atrocities such as those alleged in radio broadcasts could possibly have happened." In the weeks following the lifting of censorship, letters to the
editor in Irish newspapers reflected the mental confusion and, in some cases, the disbelief. Some believed that the reports were the invention of British propaganda, the
result of a long period of conditioning in which it was considered prudent to treat
all British sources with skepticism. One author of a letter published in a Kilkenny
paper described the newsreels about Belsen as being "all propaganda" and alleged
that the British had used starving Indians to impersonate the prisoners housed
there.[58]

The Irish government, however, was not ignorant of what was happening to
Europe's Jews. It had contacts with the Catholic Church, which maintained an international network of clerics. Herzog and Jewish relief organizations regularly communicated with the Irish officials. The Irish government also received information
on the Holocaust from its missions abroad. The mission to the Holy See, in particular, was the most often used by de Valera to request information or to initiate
action on the genocide of the Jews. Therefore, the refugee policy of the Dublin government may not be explained on the basis of ignorance.

What was the government's policy regarding Jewish refugees? An explicit reference to the policy of excluding Jewish refugees from Ireland can be found in a Department of Justice memorandum written just after the war. The document discussed
the "admission of refugees from the continent," and in the section titled "Jews" it
stated that "the immigration of Jews is generally discouraged. The wealth and influence of the Jewish community in this country appear to have increased considerably
in recent years and there is some danger of exciting opposition and controversy if
this tendency continues. As Jews do not become assimilated with the native population, like other immigrants, any big increase in their number might create a social
problem."[59] Another Department of Justice document, written in February 1953 by
Peter Berry, who later became secretary of the department, stated:

> In the administration of the alien laws it has always been recognised in the Depart-
> ments of Justice, Industry and Commerce and External Affairs that the question of
> the admission of aliens of Jewish blood presents a special problem and the alien laws
> have been administered less liberally in their case. Although the Jewish community
> in Ireland is only 3,907, according to the 1946 census, there is a fairly strong anti-
> Semitic feeling throughout the country based, perhaps, on historical reasons, the fact
> that the Jews have remained a separate community within the community and have
> not permitted themselves to be assimilated, and that for their numbers they appear
> to have disproportionate wealth and influence.[60]

The general reluctance to allow aliens to enter the country was strongly supported by Colonel Daniel Bryan, the head of military intelligence. He wrote on January 6, 1945, "I see no reason to depart from the general principle adopted since the
start of the Emergency that aliens should not normally be allowed to come here.
When the emergency is over I shall have some very concrete recommendations to
make, based on the experience of the last six years, as to the future conditions under

which aliens should be allowed to take up permanent residence here." Turning to the question of Jewish refugees, he stated:

> Writing with full recognition that the Jewish problem is a very thorny and contentious one and that accusations of anti-Semitism are easily aroused, I wish to state that the extent to which Dublin has become what may be described as Jew conscious is frequently coming to the notice of this branch. It is a problem which has only a limited security aspect but I am quite satisfied that any relaxation of the control on aliens entering this country will lead to an influx of continental Jews here, in addition to those Jews who enter here as British subjects. The general problem needs serious investigation before any loosening of the control is effected.[61]

The government responded conscientiously, if often negatively, to the many individual requests for asylum it received during the war. For example, the Society of Swiss Writers sent an appeal to Dublin on October 31, 1941, requesting that the Irish government intercede on behalf of Paul Léon, James Joyce's close friend, who had been arrested by the Gestapo. A former Russian officer in exile since the revolution, Léon was of Jewish origins. He had remained in Paris after Joyce had gone to Switzerland in 1940. On November 5 the Irish government notified its envoy in Berlin, William Warnock: "In case there is danger that Léon be shot please intervene with Foreign Office on his behalf." Warnock replied on November 8 that "there is danger that intervention on behalf of L. might be regarded as interfering in internal German matters where no Irish citizen is involved and might even have some effect on our good relations." Dublin agreed that no action should be taken.[62] Léon was shot by the Nazis in 1942.

The files of the Department of Foreign Affairs reveal other instances similar to that of the Léon case. But there are many examples of intervention by the Irish government following a request from either the Agudat Israel World Organization or Herzog. De Valera, for instance, instructed Thomas J. Kiernan, Ireland's envoy to the Holy See, to intervene on behalf of Jews in Hungary and Slovakia, albeit unsuccessfully.[63]

Overall, the Irish government maintained excellent relations with the local Irish Jewish community throughout the war. The Jewish community felt that the government was responsive to its pleas for help. The U.S. diplomat Harry Clinton Reed, reporting from Dublin on May 17, 1949, noted that "during the Hitler regime Briscoe was instrumental in smuggling an undetermined number of Central European Jewish refugees into Ireland. When confronted by the Government authorities with proof that over 300 of these persons had illegally entered Ireland through his good offices, he staunchly denied it and has never admitted that he was engaged in this traffic."[64] Aware of what had been done clandestinely, the Jewish community ignored the rigidity of official Irish immigration policy.

THE POST-HOLOCAUST ERA

On May 3, 1945, the *Irish Press* reported that de Valera had "called on the German Minister to express his condolences on the death of Hitler."[65] Michael McDunphy, the secretary of President Douglas Hyde, had also visited the German minister.[66]

Both visits were monumental political gaffes and difficult to understand. In his defense, de Valera argued that he had been adhering strictly to what protocol dictated. There is no evidence that he harbored any admiration for Hitler. The government received only one letter in support of his actions. It read:

> The British Union of Fascists, which is still in existence, although it had to go underground for the time being, have instructed me to write to your Excellency, and to express their deep appreciation of the news that the secretary of the president of Eire has called on the German minister in Dublin to express condolences on behalf of the president on the death of Adolf Hitler. The British Union of Fascists begs of your Excellency to convey its gratitude to the government of Eire for thus honouring the memory of the greatest German in history.[67]

The international reaction was unrelentingly negative. There was a threat that the British and the American envoys would be recalled. Letters from private citizens, particularly from Irish Americans, expressed their outrage. There is no record of the Irish Jewish community's reaction. De Valera's clandestine support of the Allies throughout the war and the Irish Jewish community was eclipsed by his decision to visit the German minister.

Despite the controversy, the government continued to plan for the refugees it knew would apply to come to Ireland. The Department of Justice was prepared to grant visas to students provided it was satisfied that they would leave after completing their studies. Aliens married to Irish citizens and applying for permanent residence or asylum would "receive sympathetic consideration." Applications from aliens with special qualifications, such as scholars, would receive the same treatment provided they satisfied the Department of Industry and Commerce. Dependent relatives of aliens resident in Ireland were normally allowed in. The Department of Justice was not prepared to consider sympathetically "applications from refugees, who have no special qualifications, but who wish to come here for temporary or permanent refuge." In 1945 "an exception was made from this general rule, and approximately 150 'non-Aryan' refugees from Germany were admitted for temporary refuge." Approximately five hundred French children had been admitted, and other groups were expected. The plan was to place the children in boarding schools, and after their studies were completed they would be expected to return to France.[68]

Although the refugee policy was liberalized, the number of people admitted to the country in the postwar years never reached one hundred, the figure suggested by de Valera. However, the Irish Red Cross helped place or cared for a large number of children, including two hundred French schoolchildren and two hundred German schoolchildren in Glencree, County Wicklow; two hundred German schoolchildren to families to recuperate for periods from three months to three years; one hundred German children for the 1948 summer holidays; and one hundred Irish children from London for holidays. A number of the German children were ultimately allowed to stay permanently with Irish families.

The same treatment was not meted out generally to Jewish children. De Valera received a request in 1946 from the English chief rabbi's Religious Emergency Council that permission be granted for one hundred orphaned Jewish children to come to Ireland. The council had acquired Clonyn Castle and one hundred acres in Delvin in County Westmeath, where it hoped to accommodate the refugees, who were survivors of Bergen-Belsen. A Department of Justice document revealed that the council had stated "that they would undertake entire responsibility for the transport of the children and their maintenance in this country. They stated that they 'would be prepared to follow the advice of the Eire authorities' in regard to the ultimate settlement of the children, mentioning that the children might remain in this country or that, alternatively, the Council would undertake to make arrangements for their emigration after a specified period." The Department of Justice Minister Gerry Boland refused permission because of the fear that anti-Semitism would increase with their presence. In September 1946, however, Herzog visited de Valera in Dublin to intervene, whereupon the taoiseach "committed himself to granting the application."[69] In November 1946 the children were given permission to stay temporarily in County Westmeath.

On March, 26, 1948, the castle was broken into and gasoline was sprinkled on the floors of five rooms. An attempt was made to set a fire, but it did not catch, and the only damage done was a scorching of wood. The Department of Justice report on the incident noted that "while numbers of the local people do not like the proposal to house Jewish children in the castle, there is not, as far as the police are aware, any local organised agitation against the admission of the culture."[70]

The frigid attitude of senior officials in the Department of Justice toward the entry of Jewish refugees into Ireland stands in marked contrast to their willingness to offer refuge to right-wing European politicians. For example, in the postwar period the leader of the British Union of Fascists, Oswald Mosley, took up residence for a short time in Galway without any apparent difficulty being created by the Department of Justice. Perhaps the case that most reveals the stance of senior officials in this regard was the request for residency by Leon Degrelle, the leader of the Belgian fascist Rexist movement. Degrelle had been sentenced to death in absentia in Belgium after fleeing to Spain. The Department of Justice secretary, S. A. Roche, was strongly in favor of admitting him into Ireland, but Frederick Boland, secretary of the Department of External Affairs, was strongly opposed and blocked the application.[71] Between the end of the war and 1950 Ireland had admitted, according to the Department of Justice, about 925 aliens from the Continent. Of those, 355 were domestic servants, 170 were university students, and about 400 were children who were dependent relatives of people already living in the country or "aliens who have Irish relatives or some other connection with this country."[72]

De Valera, who had been taoiseach for sixteen years, lost power in February 1948 to a five-party coalition led by Fine Gael and a new nationalist party, Clann na Poblachta. John A. Costello was named taoiseach, and Seán MacBride was made minister for external affairs. Refugee policy did not change significantly in the three years of the interparty government. The cabinet met on September 26, 1950, to review the policy. It was decided that the Red Cross would be asked to help solve the special problems of transport, housing, and so forth, of refugees admitted for the purpose of employment and resettlement. Applications for an employment permit were to be considered on a case-by-case basis, provided the offers of employment were for a minimum of twelve months. As a result of this decision, 107 refugees were admitted to take up employment, and 50 for institutional care.

De Valera and Fianna Fáil returned to power in mid-1951. Robert Briscoe worked actively on behalf of Jewish refugees, but little changed. The government refused to accept refugees on a racial or religious basis.[73] The Department of Justice reaffirmed its stance in a February 28, 1953, memorandum, which also stated that about 2,700 aliens were registered as permanent residents in Ireland. That number did not include British subjects who were exempt from the application of the aliens laws, alien children under sixteen years of age, aliens who were wives or widows with Irish children, and aliens who had been in the country for less than three months. The corresponding figure for 1948 was 1,465. Approximately 620 of the 2,700 registered aliens were refugees or stateless persons. About 170 were students at universities who had guarantees of readmission to their own countries or elsewhere on completion of their studies. There were, in addition to the 2,700, about 800 (not counting approximately 300 of British origin) who had become Irish citizens by naturalization. Of these 800 naturalized Irish citizens more than 300 were former refugees or stateless persons. There are no records of the number of aliens, displaced persons, or naturalized Irish citizens who were of Jewish blood. According to the memorandum, "Official records are not kept on the basis of race or religion but observation from time to time seems to indicate that quite a number are Jews." About 1,000 refugee children, including 400 Germans, more than 200 Poles, and more than 200 Austrians, were admitted for temporary care in selected centers or in the homes of suitable people. This group also included 100 Jewish children. Almost all the children had left, but a small number had been informally adopted.[74]

The Jewish community had grown slightly during the war. By 1952 the total Jewish population in Ireland was 5,381, with 3,907 in the Republic of Ireland and 1,474 in Northern Ireland. By 1961 the total had dropped to 4,446: 3,255 in the Republic and 1,191 in the North. The figures for Northern Ireland dropped steadily to 959 in 1971 and to 517 in 1981. South of the border the population decrease was less dramatic, dropping to 2,633 in 1971 and 2,127 in 1981. By 1991 the population had dropped to 1,580, and by the mid-1990s the figure was little more than 1,200. The decline in the Jewish population was due mainly to heavy emigration, particularly by the younger members of the community, to Britain, Israel, and the United States. They left behind a community with a disproportionate number of old people. The annual rate of decline was 1.2 percent between 1946 and 1961, rising to 3 percent in the intercensal period 1981–91. Jewish fertility rates were lower than those in the Catholic community. The effect of intermarriage on the decline in the community's population appears to have been relatively small. Therefore, a recent study identifies immigration among the young Jews, sometimes to places like Manchester, England, to find marriage partners, as the major reason for the radical population decline of the community in Ireland.[75]

The demographic decline may be illustrated more clearly by focusing on the smaller towns. There were 252 Jews living in Cork city and county in 1946; that figure dropped to 120 in 1961, 75 in 1971, and 62 in 1981. In Waterford city and county the drop was from 23 in 1946 to 6 in 1961 and 4 in 1971. No Jews remained there in 1981. Limerick city and county were the exception: 13 Jews were living there in 1946, 3 in 1961, 10 in 1971, and 75 in 1981. Dublin, the capital of the Republic, remained the most important center of Jewish culture. The Jewish population there was 1,952 in 1981, having fallen dramatically from 3,511 in 1946 to 3,064 in 1961 and 2,451 in 1971.[76] That decline has continued into the 1990s.

The counselor of the U.S. Legation in Dublin, Vinton Chapin, wrote of the Jewish community in Ireland in 1949:

> Jews in Dublin are orthodox, maintain themselves aloof and inter-marriage with the Irish is uncommon. The bulk of the community lives in the South Circular district of the city which is serviced by a cathedral synagogue and a large national school partially built by the Irish Free state for Jewish children to receive instruction in Gaelic. The more well-to-do attend private schools and rely on four Zionist Centers for religious instruction. There are five other synagogues, a number of charitable organisations and a Talmud Torah. Jews attend the non-sectarian Trinity College and it is estimated that 20 per cent of the medical students there are Jewish. . . . [T]he majority of Jews in Dublin are small shop keepers and tradesmen but . . . they are also in the real estate and theatre business as well as the professions. As yet they are not engaged in the banking, stock exchange, journalism or newspaper business, but even so their influence is being increasingly felt in business and financial circles.[77]

The situation changed significantly between the 1950s and 1990s. In 1995 only one butcher's shop remained open in the old Jewish quarter of the city. There had been five such shops in that area twenty years earlier, before the dispersal of the community to Terenure and the suburbs. Only one Jewish bakery remained open in Dublin in 1995, and it was run by a non-Jewish family.[78]

The places of religious observance also suffered from the decline in the Jewish population. The main synagogue on South Circular Road closed in the 1970s. The Orthodox Hebrew Congregation Synagogue in Terenure opened in the 1950s. In 1995 the community was trying to decide whether to close the beautiful old synagogue on Adelaide Road, which is more than one hundred years old. There is a third tiny Orthodox synagogue in Harold's Cross, Dublin. The Dublin Jewish Progressive Congregation is situated on Rathgar Road. According to Andy Pollak, the religious-affairs correspondent of the *Irish Times,* this community interprets Jewish laws regarding the Sabbath and the preparation of food more liberally and grants membership to people not born of Jewish mothers.[79]

Two internal reports in 1986 recommended that the Jewish community's independent institutions—synagogues, school, sports club, and old people's home—be brought together under one unified governing body. The three Orthodox synagogues would be merged and situated on the Terenure site. The Adelaide Road community, in particular, was opposed. A succession of very talented chief rabbis have sought to unify the somewhat divided community. In 1993 Rabbi Simon Harris, seeking to push forward the consolidation, suggested that the Orthodox communities and the progressive congregation participate in joint prayer services. His efforts were not successful, and he returned to London in June 1994.[80] The struggle for restructuring continues.

One member of the Jewish community outlined the difficulty of maintaining the interest of the youth. This remains a struggle for them in the context of the dominant culture of the country. The Jewish Boy Scouts and Girl Guides, which have been in existence for more than fifty years, only provide part of the solution. Great efforts are made to run summer youth camps with leaders from abroad, but such efforts have had only a limited impact. It is not surprising that young Irish Jews wish to study and live in England, the United States, and Israel.

The Holocaust did not enter the discourse of postwar Irish politics significantly until the 1990s. Mary Robinson, elected president of Ireland in 1990, was among the first Irish public figures to attempt to raise Irish consciousness about the Holocaust. On a visit to Auschwitz-Birkenau on June 23, 1994, she laid a wreath at the Death Wall. Afterward, she wrote in the visitors' book: "On my own behalf and of the people of Ireland I have come to pay deep respect, to honour the victims, and to remember the terrible deeds in this place. We must always remember the inhumanity of man to men, to women and to children. Only if we remember will we remain eternally vigilant. Sadly, that vigilance is needed in our world today."[81] When asked by a Polish journalist at Birkenau whether she thought the concentration camps should be destroyed completely, she responded emphatically:

> I do not share that view. I believe that it is very important that not only the place would remain, but that it would remain as authentically as it remains at the moment. I know that it is difficult, and I know that for some families in particular it must be almost too painful to come. We must come here. We must take on board what happened here. We must do it because it must not be allowed to recur. And yet, we know in our hearts that the ingredients of racism, of anti-Semitism, of ethnic hatred are there, and none of us can be complacent or feel that we don't need places like this. Yet we do. It is most important that you keep and you value as I do the opportunity—that is, to see at first hand the capacity for inhumanity that is with us—so that it may bring out the capacity for compassion, for tolerance, for reaching out to each other and for being open to each other.

Robinson's visit was covered extensively in the Irish media and helped to focus Irish attention on the Holocaust.

Senior politicians endeavored to demonstrate Irish solidarity with the victims of the Holocaust in the anniversary year of 1995. Taoiseach John Bruton was very anxious to mark officially the liberation of Bergen-Belsen. His office felt it appropriate to choose the actual day of liberation, April 15. Invitations to a short ceremony at the War Memorial in Islandbridge were sent out. This was to be followed by a reception in the Royal Hospital in Kilmainham. When a journalist pointed out to the taoiseach's office that April 15 was the Jewish Sabbath and the first day of Passover, the date of the ceremony was changed immediately.[82]

Meanwhile, the Jewish community in Ireland had announced that it would officially commemorate the liberation of Bergen-Belsen on April 26 in the Terenure synagogue. This ceremony was a joint commemoration by the Jewish community and the Ireland-Israel Friendship League. Bruton attended, the first time such a ceremony had been attended by a taoiseach. Holocaust survivors resident in Ireland and children and grandchildren of survivors also participated. In all about four hundred people came, many representing churches, business and labor associations, and civic groups.[83]

In his speech, Bruton said: "We in Ireland have not been immune from the bigotry and the indifference which manifested themselves in Europe this century." He acknowledged that official Irish archives had revealed that Ireland's doors "were not freely open to those families and individuals fleeing from persecution and death." He said that some people "did find refuge and comfort in Ireland, but their numbers were not very great. We must acknowledge the consequences of this indifference. As a Society we have become more willing to accept our responsibility to respond to events beyond our shores." He continued, "Tonight, on behalf of the Irish government and people I honour the memory of those millions of European Jews who died in the Holocaust. I am also humble to be here when we have with us some of those who have borne witness personally to the horror and reality of the Holocaust."[84]

Bruton stated that fifty years after the liberation of the death camps, "the recognition of the colossal evil enacted in these places is branded deep in the moral conscience of modern man." The Holocaust was, he said, "first and foremost a crime against the Jewish people; more fundamentally it was a crime against all humanity. Its memory must always be kept alive. I would again quote Primo Levi when he said—'It happened, therefore it can happen again'. Too much in today's world tells us that we have yet to grasp the full significance of this fact."[85]

Bruton spoke about the Holocaust again two days later, at the rescheduled official commemoration ceremony at the Irish National War Memorial Park at Islandbridge, Dublin. He paid tribute to the Irish people who fought and died in the British forces in the war. He referred to the 150,000 Irish people, from North and South, who had volunteered to fight against "Nazi tyranny in Europe" and acknowledged the more than 100 who died while serving in British uniform. He remarked, "They fought to liberate Europe from the worst tyranny mankind has known, a tyranny that caused the death of 6 million Jews, simply because of their Jewish faith. Those who seek to understand the justice of the struggle against Nazi tyranny will find no better understanding than that contained in the recently published book, by Mary Rose Doorly, containing the personal recollections of survivors and witnesses to the holocaust now living in Ireland."[86]

Bruton's speeches were of significance in the Irish experience in two respects. First, he acknowledged the role played by Irish men and women in the British and American forces in the fight to defeat Nazism and fascism. In a more nationalistic era, the contribution of such a large number of Irish people during the war had been passed over in silence. Second, the taoiseach developed the themes introduced by President Robinson when she visited Auschwitz-Birkenau. Bruton, moreover, was the first member of the Irish government to acknowledge that Irish refugee policy had been lacking in the 1930s and 1940s and that Ireland had not offered refuge to those fleeing persecution and death.

The fiftieth anniversary of the end of World War II, therefore, may be viewed as a breakthrough in official Irish thinking concerning the Holocaust. Irish politicians from Éamon de Valera to Albert Reynolds had participated in various functions organized by the Jewish community, but on this occasion Bruton made a special effort to redress the official Irish silences regarding the Holocaust.

The Holocaust has never been given prominence in the history curricula of Irish primary and secondary schools. It is discussed only in very broad outline in Junior Certificate textbooks (studied by twelve- to fifteen-year-olds). Gerard Brockie and Raymond Walsh's text *The Modern World*, volume 3 of the Focus on the Past series, is among the best; the authors devote three pages to "Life in Nazi-Occupied Europe." This section comprises a small paragraph of text, an excerpt from Kitty Hart's eyewitness account of life in Auschwitz, and three photographs. The first photograph shows Jewish children being released from Dachau on May 12, 1945. The second is a graphic "scene of horror discovered by the Allies at Belsen concentration camp," and the third shows "leading Nazis on trial at Nuremberg in 1946." Brockie and Walsh write that "the war in Europe left a heavy toll of death and destruction in its wake. The full extent of the horrors of Nazi rule became clear as the Allies liberated German-occupied territory. In a plan known as 'the Final Solution' Hitler had exterminated some six million Jews in concentration camps throughout Europe such as Auschwitz, Dachau and Treblinka." The authors then explain that the Allies were "determined to bring the leading Nazi war criminals to justice." They note that twelve leading Nazis were sentenced to death, eleven were hanged, and Göring committed suicide while awaiting execution.[87]

Brockie and Walsh fail, however, in the second half of the book, which is devoted to Irish history, to make any reference to the government's reaction to the Holocaust or to the country's anti-Jewish refugee policy.[88] While this is defensible in the context of the Junior Certificate, writers of school texts for which are obliged to be hyperselective, the same defense cannot be offered for textbooks used at the senior level, for students preparing for the Leaving Certificate.[89] M. E. Collins's *History in the Making: Ireland, 1868–1966,* has not a single reference in the index to Jews, refugees, or the Holocaust. Her otherwise excellent thirteen-page treatment entitled "Neutral Ireland, 1939–1945," makes no reference to the government's wartime stance on the Holocaust, the censoring of information about the Holocaust, or the country's restrictive refugee policy.[90]

The opening in the early 1990s of government archives housing documents related to these issues may help explain why even the better school texts at the level of the Leaving Certificate do not set the Holocaust in the context of Irish society during the war years but rather treat it as part of the history of Europe, distant from Irish shores.[91] Perhaps the next generation of Irish history textbooks will incorporate contemporary scholarship on the question of the Holocaust and Ireland. There are also indications that the Holocaust will be given greater prominence in the curriculum, which is drawn up by the Department of Education.[92]

The Department of Education's failure to emphasize the importance of the Holocaust in history curricula and to integrate a challenge to popular prejudices against Jews into the general educational system may account in part for the continuation of those prejudices in some sectors of Irish society. Anti-Semitism remains a subcurrent in Irish society.

While relations between the major Christian churches and the Jewish community have always been very cordial, a small number of lay Catholic organizations have continued to foment anti-Semitism. In 1945 the anti-Semitic Fr. Denis Fahey founded the Maria Duce society, which, although it never attracted very many members, enjoyed good relations for a short time with the archbishop of Dublin, John Charles McQuaid. The group's literature represented in tone and content the continuation of interwar anti-Jewish Catholic propaganda. For example, society members picketed the American actor Danny Kaye when he performed in Dublin in the early 1950s.[93]

Elements from Maria Duce were responsible for the publication of an anti-Semitic sheet, *Saoirse* (Freedom), which appeared on September 9, 1950. The secretary of the Jewish Representative Council, Ernest Newman, and his father, Arthur Newman, asked Taoiseach John A. Costello and Department of Justice officials to take action against the publication. The Department of Justice was most anxious to avoid "any racial trouble in this country" and "could be expected to take any action within their power to prevent any encouragement of racial prejudice." An investigation revealed that *Saoirse* had a negligible circulation. Published at irregular intervals, it was distributed around the General Post Office in Dublin. The Department of Justice noted: "While it is anti-Jewish, it is mild in tone compared with a previous anti-Jewish publication called 'Penapa.'" Although one issue of *Saoirse* carried the headline "Communism is Jewism," its contents were deemed neither to be subversive nor to amount to criminal libel. The advice from the *gardaí* to the Jewish community was to "ignore the existence of this periodical." The *gardaí* discovered who was responsible for the sheet and where it was published. The IRA raided the premises on September 23, 1950, since which time no further issues have appeared.[94]

An opinion poll conducted in Dublin in 1977 concluded that there was "a moderate degree of anti-semitic prejudice" in the city. "The pattern of this prejudice is along classical lines, i.e., the negative monetary and religious myths are still believed by a significant percentage of Dublin adults." The most negative responses were to items that had commercial or financial implications. Almost 60 percent of those surveyed agreed that Jews played too large a role in the control of money matters; only 25 percent disagreed with that view. The poll noted that "it seems reasonable to conclude that this exceptionally high percentage of agreement with an unsubstantiated allegation against the Jews, may be attributed to Anti-Semitic prejudice and the acceptance by the vast majority of respondents of the common stereotypical view of the Jews as the controllers of money matters today."[95] This conclusion was confirmed by another question in the study. Of all those polled, 49.2 percent agreed that the Jews were behind the money-lending rackets in Dublin; only 28 percent disagreed with this view.

Micheál Mac Gréil, the author of the survey, thought that particular attention should be paid to the responses to the statement, "The Jews as a people are to blame for the crucifixion of Christ." This belief still lingered among one-sixth of those polled; only three-quarters of those polled denied it. Mac Gréil stated, "For a minority, therefore, to be convicted of deicide, or the 'killing of Christ,' is most serious in a society like Ireland. The evidence . . . concerning the ascription of blame to the Jews as a people for the crucifixion of Christ merits serious attention."[96] The survey included no questions about the Holocaust.

Given the findings of this poll, it is all the more surprising that the Department of Education did not undertake to ensure that prejudice and tolerance in European and Irish history would receive particular attention. An emphasis on the place of the Holocaust in the study of the twentieth century might also have served to counteract the continuation of anti-Jewish prejudices. But that problem, as Taoiseach John Bruton's speech in the Terenure synagogue indicated, was being treated with far greater sensitivity and seriousness in the 1990s than it had been in the early decades of the state's existence.

Bruton provided a number of reasons why Irish society was more willing to confront the full horror of the Holocaust in the 1990s. First, there was more willingness in Ireland to shoulder its international responsibilities. Second, there was a greater willingness to accept the inadequacies of the Irish government's policy in the past. Irish society had also become more cosmopolitan and diverse. The critical evaluation of concepts of identity had progressed since the 1960s, prompted in part by the problem of Northern Ireland. There was a new awareness of the diversity of Irish society and an acceptance of the role played by other religious groups in its development.

The place of the Jewish community was also more readily acknowledged. The community, which now numbered no more than twelve hundred in the Republic, had made a contribution "out of all proportion to its numbers" to the life of the nation, according to Fr. Michael O'Carroll, who had been engaged in Christian-Jewish dialogue for fifty years. He cited Jews' contributions to the world of learning, legal studies, the judiciary, the arts, medicine, business, and politics.[97]

There was, of course, Robert Briscoe, who represented de Valera's Fianna Fáil Party in the Dáil.[98] A veteran of the war of independence, he was first elected to the Dáil in 1927 and served as a deputy for a Dublin constituency until 1965. He was lord mayor of Dublin in 1956–57 and again in 1961–62.[99] His son Ben succeeded him in the Dáil in 1965 and became lord mayor of Dublin in 1988. Gerald Goldberg, a distinguished member of the diminishing Jewish community in Cork, was an independent member of that city's corporation for eight years before joining Fianna Fáil. In 1977 he became the first Jewish lord mayor of Cork in the eight hundred years of the mayoralty and, he commented sadly but probably accurately, "very likely its last."[100] There were three Jewish members in the twenty-seventh Dáil

(1992–94): Ben Briscoe; Mervyn Taylor, a lawyer and member of the Labour Party, who served as minister for equality and law reform; and Alan Shatter, a lawyer, who was a front-bench spokesperson for Fine Gael.

Jacob Weingreen and Erwin Schrödinger have contributed significantly to the world of higher learning. Herman Good, Hubert Wine, and Henry Barron have served in the judiciary. Good ran unsuccessfully for the Labour Party in 1944. Larry Elyan was a creative and innovative force in Irish theater. In the visual arts, Harry Kernoff is among Ireland's most prominent painters, along with Estella F. Solomons. Gerald Davis is a contemporary painter and gallery owner.

In the world of Irish literature, David Marcus stands out as the author of *A Land Not Theirs, A Land in Flames,* and a collection of short stories, *There Is No Such Thing As an Irish Jew.* As the literary editor of the *Irish Press* for many years, Marcus did much to encourage young writers. His work in this area dates back to the 1950s. His brother, Louie Marcus, is a distinguished filmmaker.

The Jewish community has also produced a number of very fine athletes. Bethel Solomons, later master of the Rotunda Hospital, played rugby ten times for Ireland in international competition. Louis Bookman played soccer for Ireland four times between 1914 and 1922, and Judge Hubert Wine played table tennis for Ireland.[101]

This list is indicative rather than exhaustive. But be it in the creative and visual arts, in the world of politics, or in the field of higher learning, the Irish Jewish community has made, and continues to make, a significant contribution. Yet it took until 1995 for Ireland to officially acknowledge that the Holocaust was above all a crime against the Jewish people.

In 1994 Mary Rose Doorly's book *Hidden Memories* was published in Dublin. This book, which contains the reminiscences of some members of Dublin's Jewish community who are Holocaust survivors, marked the end of a silence for the small number of Holocaust survivors living in Ireland. Together with the commemoration of the fiftieth anniversary of the Holocaust, it has had a significant impact on the growth of Irish consciousness about the genocide of the Jews during World War II. In *Hidden Memories* Doorly introduced the reminiscences of Joe Briscoe, the brother of the parliamentarian, Ben, when he recalled seeing newsreels of Belsen as a teenager in Dublin: "Like many Irish people, he regarded it as something that had happened in Europe and harboured a romantic notion that he would have taken to the hills with a rifle. The Nazis would never have taken him. Now, years later, knowing that 156 European members of his extended family perished in the Holocaust, he feels very different. He understands much more clearly the slow, methodical progression of Jewish extermination."[102] Briscoe and other members of the Irish Jewish community who lost family members in the Holocaust have begun to articulate their fears and memories. The exercise, which has only just started, is likely to encourage a wider review in Irish society of the country's role during World War II and its refusal to admit Jewish refugees.

A large number of articles on a range of topics were published for the fiftieth anniversary of the end of World War II. There was, however, an uncharacteristic concentration in the Irish media on the liberation of the death camps and upon the

Holocaust. The *Sunday Tribune* magazine section carried a four-page feature entitled: "After the Holocaust—50 Years On, Survivors in Ireland Recall the Horror." Dr. Johanna Collis, who lives in Ireland, was one of the first nurses, along with her late husband, Robert, to enter Belsen after Liberation. She said: "The fiftieth anniversary of the liberation of the camp is a milestone for me and for everyone. It seems a long time ago but when you see pictures and talk to other people about it, it does not seem so remote."[103]

As survivors of the Holocaust living in Ireland began to tell their stories in public—some were telling their stories for the first time—the media began to take an interest in Ireland's wartime record, particularly the country's policy on the admission of Jewish refugees. An article in the *Irish Times* entitled "Dublin Closed Doors on Jewish Refugees," which documented the attitude of the Department of Justice in particular, provoked considerable debate.[104] However, in the same issue the paper published a front-page piece whose title erroneously claimed that "Fewer than 10 Jews Were Given Shelter Here before the War." This gave rise to a series of letters to the editor. One writer stated that he was aware of many Jews who had been given refuge in Dublin during the war. Another recalled the "continuous stream of distinguished Jewish men from Germany, Czechoslovakia, and even Romania, staying in my parents' house in Mountjoy Square, sometimes for weeks, sometimes for months, on their way to the US. Although they were not medical doctors, they were all called 'Dr' which was very strange to us at the time." The trips, she believed, had been arranged by Michael Noyk, a Jewish solicitor who was very friendly with her father, having been in jail with him in Reading, Frongoch, and Wandsworth after 1916. She was sure that many other families had not shared the narrow views of the then minister of justice.[105]

Other letter writers took a very critical view of the government's wartime record. The most vigorous of such statements came from the Fine Gael member of the Dáil, Alan Shatter: "There has never been a State ceremony in Ireland to commemorate the 6 million Jews who were murdered in the Holocaust. There has never been any official expression of regret from any Irish government at the State's refusal to admit into Ireland the many Jews fleeing from Nazi terror."[106] Bruton's speech at the commemoration of the liberation of Bergen-Belsen came five days after this letter appeared. The Irish papers carried a large number of articles about the fiftieth anniversary of the end of the war and the legacy of the Holocaust.

Since the end of World War II a small number of ultra-right-wing groups have established themselves in Ireland. But they have been unrepresentative of the general population and politically inconsequential. The close proximity of England has meant that Dublin is sometimes viewed as a convenient outpost in which to locate printing operations. This was so in the 1970s in the case of the National Socialist Irish Workers' Party, an offshoot of a British neofascist organization. Operating out of a house in a poor area of Dublin, the party sought the "repatriation" of Jews, Asians, and blacks in order to preserve Ireland's distinctive culture.[107] The group attracted only a handful of followers in the capital. In the 1980s a neo-Nazi organization emerged in Cork, but it too was short-lived. These groups have recycled the literature containing the stereotypical beliefs of the far Right. Ireland has not proved to be a fertile recruiting ground for international neo-Nazi organizations.

There has been a popular tendency in Ireland and among some historians as well to use the term "holocaust" to refer to what happened to the Irish nation during the Great Famine in the mid-1840s, when an estimated one million died and another million emigrated. The distinguished historian Roy Foster wrote: "The figures for Famine deaths are equally stunning, and equally they raise problems. At least 775,000 died, mostly through disease, including cholera in the latter stages of the holocaust."[108] While the word here is being used to mean "catastrophe," it has been used by others far less cautiously to indict British policy in Ireland in the 1840s.

Anti-abortion groups in Ireland have frequently used the Holocaust in their rhetoric, for example, in the successful referendum campaign in 1983 to have abortion banned in the Irish constitution. When an Abortion Information Bill was published by the Irish government in March 1995, Justice Rory O'Hanlon criticized its content, saying that if he had remained silent, he would have been as guilty as a judge in Germany who had remained silent on the planning and execution of the Nazi Holocaust.[109] Fr. Brendan Purcell, a lecturer in philosophy at University College, Dublin, compared anti-abortion campaigners to a group of Berlin women whose protests saved their Jewish menfolk from the death camps.[110] Placards carried in anti-abortion street demonstrations often refer to abortion as a modern holocaust. There is also frequent use of such terms as "genocide," "mass murder," and the "slaughter of the innocents." This strident language is most evident in the demonstrations organized by youth groups associated with such campaigns.[111] The use of such inflated rhetoric was a defining characteristic of these referenda campaigns and displayed a great insensitivity on the part of those who freely used that vocabulary, pointing to the need in the 1990s for more extensive education on the Holocaust in Irish high schools and at the college level.

The manner in which the Holocaust was remembered in the country on the occasion of the fiftieth anniversary of the ending of World War II demonstrated that Irish political leaders were prepared to admit that they could learn from the parsimonious refugee policy of the war years. The visit by President Robinson to Auschwitz in 1994 helped raise Irish consciousness about the Holocaust. The admission by Taoiseach John Bruton that Ireland could have done more to provide a haven for Jewish refugees was significant. Then in 1995 survivors of the Holocaust living in Ireland spoke and wrote about their experiences, some doing so for the first time in public. After fifty years of silence, the Holocaust has finally become a topic of discussion in Irish public discourse.

NOTES

I would like to thank the Jewish Museum in Dublin and the staff of the National Archives, Dublin, who helped me in my research for this project. I would also like to thank Donal Ó Drisceoil, Finín O'Driscoll, Mervyn O'Driscoll, Kieran Madden, Áine Macneely, Aengus Nolan, Colette Cottor, and Ann Keogh.

1. P. L. S. Quinn, "The Re-entry of the Jew into England and Ireland and His Re-establishment There" (Ph.D. diss., National University of Ire-

land, 1966), 576; Louis Hyman, *The Jews of Ireland* (Shannon, 1972), 155–56. For the general history of the Jews in Ireland, see Hyman, *The Jews of Ireland;* and Bernard Shillman, *A Short History of the Jews in Ireland* (Dublin, 1945).

2. Quinn, "Re-Entry of the Jew," 578, 582; Hyman, *Jews of Ireland,* 124–32.

3. Quinn, "Re-Entry of the Jew," 580; Hyman, *Jews of Ireland,* 158.

4. Hyman, *Jews of Ireland,* 110.

5. Ibid., 156.

6. A. J. Leventhal, "What It Means to Be a Jew," *Bell* 10, no. 3 (1944), 209; this article appeared during World War II and was heavily censored by the government. See also Donal Ó Drisceoil, "Censorship in Ireland during the Second World War" (Ph.D. diss., National University of Ireland, 1994), 278; and Hyman, *Jews of Ireland,* 161, 193.

7. Hyman, *Jews of Ireland,* 200–201.

8. Hannah Berman and Melisande Zlotover, *Zlotover Story: A Dublin Story with a Difference* (Dublin, 1966), 59; Hyman, *Jews of Ireland,* 196–99.

9. *Freeman's Journal,* quoted in Hyman, *Jews of Ireland,* 161–62.

10. Arthur Griffith, in *United Irishman,* August 5, 1899.

11. Ibid., August 19, September 23, 1899. See also Manus O'Riordan, "The Sinn Féin Tradition," in *The Rise and Fall of Irish Anti-Semitism,* ed. Manus O'Riordan (Dublin, 1984), 18–36.

12. Hyman, *Jews of Ireland,* 210–13.

13. Fr. John Creagh, quoted in *Freeman's Journal,* January 18, 1904.

14. See Pat Feeley, "Rabbi Levin of Colooney Street," "Aspects of the 1904 Pogrom," and "Davitt and the Limerick Jews," all reprinted from the *Limerick Journal* in O'Riordan, *Irish Anti-Semitism,* 1–17. This book also includes the correspondence in the press following their publication.

15. Hyman, *Jews of Ireland,* 218.

16. John Crowley, "Narrative and Place—A Cultural History of the South Parish" (M.A. thesis, National University of Ireland, 1993), 80; Shillman, *Jews in Ireland,* 141; Hyman, *Jews of Ireland,* 218.

17. Hyman, *Jews of Ireland,* 218–21.

18. Both quotations are from O'Riordan, "Sinn Féin Tradition," 20–21.

19. Thomas H. Burbage, "Ritual Murder among the Jews," *Catholic Bulletin,* May–June 1916, 309–14, and July–August 1916, 433–44.

20. Thomas Burbage, "What Is Freemasonry?" (in three parts), ibid., May 1917, 309–16; June 1917, 376–84; July 1917, 429–36.

21. O'Riordan, "Sinn Féin Tradition," 21.

22. David Marcus, *A Land Not Theirs* (London, 1986).

23. Robert Briscoe, *For the Life of Me* (Boston, 1958), 77–210.

24. Mervyn Samuel O'Driscoll, "Irish German Relations, 1922–1939" (M.A. thesis, National University of Ireland, 1992), 4–25.

25. Briscoe, *For the Life of Me,* 259.

26. Dermot Keogh, *Twentieth Century Ireland* (Dublin, 1994), 1–63.

27. Shillman, *Jews in Ireland,* 124.

28. *Irish Times,* April 10, 1937.

29. K.C.C., "Ireland for the Irish," *The Blueshirt,* June 8, 1933.

30. See Finín O'Driscoll, "The Search for the Christian State: An Analysis of Irish Social Catholicism, 1913–1939" (M.A. thesis, National University of Ireland, 1994).

31. Cahill's works include the following: *Ireland's Peril* (Dublin, 1930); *The Framework of a Christian State* (Dublin, 1932); *The Irish Catholic Social Movement* (Dublin, 1932); and *An Alternative to Capitalism* (Dublin, 1936).

32. Among Fahey's works are *The Social Rights of Our Divine Lord Jesus Christ, the King* (Dublin, 1932); *The Mystical Body of Christ in the Modern World* (Dublin, 1935); *The Rulers of Russia* (Dublin, 1938); *Money, Manipulation, and Social Order* (Dublin, 1944); *The Mystical Body of Christ and the Reorganisation of Society* (Cork, 1944); *The Church and Farming* (Cork, 1953); and *The Kingship of Christ and the Conversion of the Jewish Nation* (Dublin, 1953). Fahey also contributed extensively to many popular Catholic journals.

33. Sr. Mary Christine Athans, "The Fahey-Coughlin Connection: Father Denis Fahey, C.S.Sp., Father Charles E. Coughlin, and Religious Anti-Semitism in the United States, 1938–1954" (Ann Arbor, Mich.: University Microfilms, 1982), 3–52. Athans's thesis was published as *The Coughlin-Fahey Connection: Father Denis Fahey, C.S.Sp., and Religious Anti-Semitism in the United States, 1938–1954* (New York, 1992).

34. "Cattle Slaughter Byelaws," *Irish Independent,* December 30, 1936.

35. The role of Axis diplomats in fomenting anti-Semitic ideas in Ireland has yet to be researched. But there is evidence that the Italian consul and later minister Lodi Fe harbored anti-Semitic feelings and expressed them in his reports, as did his successor, Vincenzo Berardis. The situation is less clear regarding the German legation. It is my view that at least one official there during

667

the war was responsible for encouraging the spread of anti-Semitism in Ireland.

36. Dermot Keogh, *Ireland and Europe,, 1919–1989* (Cork and Dublin, 1989), 61, 63–97.

37. See Dermot Keogh, "The Constitutional Revolution: An Analysis of the Making of the Constitution," *Administration* (Dublin) 35, no. 4 (1988), 4–85. When the constitution was amended in 1972, this section was deleted, along with the section stating that "the State recognises the special position of the Holy Catholic Apostolic and Roman Church as the guardian of the Faith professed by the great majority of the citizens."

38. Charles Bewley, quoted in *Irish Times,* April 6, 1937.

39. George Clare, *Last Waltz in Vienna: The Destruction of a Family* (London, 1980), 204–391.

40. Official Report of Plenary Session of the Evian Conference, July 1938, 36; Myron Taylor Papers, U.S. National Archives and Records Administration, Franklin D. Roosevelt Library, Hyde Park, New York.

41. Memorandum, November 14, 1938, Department of the Taoiseach, S11007A, National Archives, Dublin.

42. Herzog to de Valera, October 9, 1938, Department of Foreign Affairs, 131/143, National Archives, Dublin.

43. Eduard Hempel to the German Foreign Ministry, December 7, 1938, Records of the German Foreign Office received by the Department of State, microfilm, K834/K214845-849, National Archives, Washington D.C. I am grateful to Professor Matthew MacNamara for the translation of this document.

44. *Irish Times,* February 23, 1939.

45. Keogh, *Twentieth Century Ireland,* 108–56.

46. Keogh, *Ireland and Europe,* 121–64.

47. Keogh, *Twentieth Century Ireland,* 110–13. See also Robert Fisk, *In Time of War: Ireland, Ulster, and the Price of Neutrality, 1939–45* (London, 1983).

48. Carolle Carter, *The Shamrock and the Swastika: German Espionage in Ireland during World War II* (Palo Alto, 1977).

49. Fisk, *In Time of War,* 432–36.

50. Ó Drisceoil, "Censorship in Ireland," 279.

51. Oliver J. Flanagan to Denis Fahey, May 26, 1943, Denis Fahey Papers (Correspondence files), Holy Ghost Fathers' Archives, Provincial House, Dublin.

52. Dáil Debates, vol. 91, col. 569, July 9, 1943, quoted in Joseph T. Carroll, *Ireland in the War Years* (Newton Abbot, 1975), 137.

53. Dan Bryan, interview by author, Dublin,

1978. In July 1942 one of Breen's letters to the *Irish Press,* in which he complained that the paper was an instrument of British propaganda, was censored, and a copy was forwarded to Joe Walshe in the Department of External Affairs. Bryan was convinced that Breen was being influenced by Henning Thomsen, the second in command at the German legation. Breen was indiscriminately anti-British. As a backbencher, he was lionized by Axis diplomats in Dublin.

54. Controller of Censorship Thomas E. Coyne to chief press censor and staff, October 20, 1942, Office of the Controller of Censorship (OCC), 2/42, Military Archives, Dublin, quoted in Ó Drisceoil, "Censorship in Ireland," 188–89.

55. Ó Drisceoil, "Censorship in Ireland," 190–91.

56. Ibid., 192 ff.

57. Keogh, *Ireland and Europe,* 177–78.

58. Ó Drisceoil, "Censorship in Ireland," 195.

59. Department of Justice memorandum, September 24, 1945, S11007A, National Archives, Dublin.

60. Ibid., February 28, 1953, S11007B/2.

61. Dan Bryan, letter dated January 6, 1945, confidential source.

62. See Cian Ó hÉigeartaigh, "Léon's Last Letters," *Irish Times,* April 4, 1992.

63. Department of Foreign Affairs, Irish Legation to the Holy See, P4/2, Villa Spada, Rome.

64. Harry Clinton Reed to U.S. Department of State, May 17, 1949, G 84, Ireland, National Archives, Washington, D.C.

65. Secretary's files, P98, Department of Foreign Affairs, National Archives, Dublin.

66. Dermot Keogh, "Éamon de Valera and Hitler: An Analysis of International Reaction to the Visit to the German Minister, May 1945," *Irish Studies in International Affairs* 1, no. 1 (1989), 71.

67. Ibid., 88.

68. Maurice Moynihan minute, September 26, 1945, Department of the Taoiseach, S11007A, National Archives, Dublin.

69. Department of Justice memorandum, April 28, 1948, S11007B/1, ibid.

70. Ibid.

71. S. A. Roche to Frederick H. Boland, September 11, 1946, and draft of Boland to Roche, undated, Secretary's files, P253, Department of Foreign Affairs, National Archives, Dublin. There is no indication that Boland's letter was sent.

72. Department of Justice memorandum, February 28, 1953, Department of the Taoiseach, S11007B/2, National Archives, Dublin.

73. Peter Berry to Thomas E. Coyne, February 16, 1953, S11007B/2, ibid.

74. See Mary Rose Doorly, *Hidden Memories: The Personal Recollections of Survivors and Witnesses to the Holocaust Living in Ireland* (Dublin, 1994).

75. The population figures are from the Irish Jewish Museum, Dublin. See also Andy Pollak, "Dublin's Jewish Community Is Here for the Long Haul Despite Its Decline," *Irish Times,* March 7, 1995; and J. J. Sexton and Richard O'Leary, "Factors Affecting Population Decline in Minority Religious Communities in the Republic of Ireland," in *Building Trust in Ireland—Studies Commissioned by the Forum for Peace and Reconciliation* (Dublin, 1996), 255–332.

76. The population figures are from the Irish Jewish Museum, Dublin.

77. Vinton Chapin to State Department, May 17, 1949, G 84, State Department, Ireland (segregated security records), National Archives, Washington, D.C.

78. Irish Jewish Museum staff member, interview by author, Dublin, September 1995.

79. Ibid.; *Irish Times,* March 7, 1995.

80. *Irish Times,* March 7, 1995.

81. Ibid., June 24, 1994.

82. See Geraldine Kennedy, "Ceremony Changed after Passover Clash Revealed—Belsen to Be Commemorated," ibid., April 8, 1995.

83. See *Ireland-Israel Friendship League Newsletter* 1, no. 2 (1995).

84. Ibid.

85. Text of John Bruton's speech, April 26, 1995, kindly supplied by the Government Information Services.

86. Text of John Bruton's speech, April 28, 1995, kindly supplied by the Government Information Services.

87. Gerard Brockie and Raymond Walsh, *Focus on the Past,* vol. 3, *The Modern World* (Dublin, 1991), 73–75.

88. Ibid., 215–16.

89. Mark Tierney's *Ireland since 1870* (Dublin, 1988) is a Junior Certificate textbook. The index carries no reference to the Holocaust, and the chapter on the war years makes no reference to Ireland's foreign-policy position on the Holocaust.

90. M. E. Collins, *History in the Making: Ireland, 1868–1966* (Dublin, 1993), 370–84.

91. See Francis T. Holohan, *From Bismarck to DeGaulle: A History of Europe, 1870–1966* (Dublin, 1988), 201, 217, 224, 225, 310.

92. I am grateful to Professor Áine Hyland, Department of Education, University College, Cork, for her observations on this area.

93. See Maria Duce files, Fahey Papers.

94. See Department of Justice, S13/50/1, National Archives, Dublin.

95. Micheál Mac Gréil, *Prejudice and Tolerance in Ireland: Based on a Survey of Intergroup Attitudes of Dublin Adults and Other Sources* (Kildare, 1978), 333, 525.

96. Ibid., 333–35.

97. Michael O'Carroll, "Jews among Irish Catholics," *Christian Jewish Dialogue,* 1983, 51.

98. Ibid.

99. Ted Nealon, *Nealon's Guide to the 27th Dáil and Seanad: Election 1992* (Dublin, 1993).

100. Gerald Y. Goldberg, "The Freeman of Cork," *Cork Review,* special issue (1991), 58–59.

101. Information from the Jewish Museum, Dublin.

102. Doorly, *Hidden Memories,* 9–10.

103. *Sunday Tribune* (Dublin), January 22, 1995. Collis, her husband, Robert, and Hans Hogerzeil wrote about their experiences in *Straight On* (London, 1947).

104. Andy Pollak, "Dublin Closed Doors on Jewish Refugees," *Irish Times,* April 14, 15, 1995. Pollak wrote the article using a manuscript I had given to him.

105. A journalist for the newspaper, not Andy Pollak, had misinterpreted the remarks of Joe Briscoe quoted in the paper. Briscoe had said that his father, Robert, had been able to get fewer than ten—perhaps as few as two or three—Jewish refugees admitted to Ireland before the war (*Irish Times,* April 14, 15, 1995). That statement was wrongly attributed to my research, and the paper did not carry a correction (ibid., April 19, May 6, 1995).

106. Ibid., April 21, 1995; see also ibid., April 19, 26, 27, 1995.

107. "Irish Nazis: Why Dublin Is a Fascist Haven," *Dublin,* July 24, 1996, 24–27.

108. Roy Foster, *Modern Ireland, 1600–1972* (London, 1988), 324.

109. Frank McNally, "Review of the Week," *Irish Times,* March 4, 1995.

110. Brendan Purcell, "Courageous Protest by O'Hanlon Remains Valid," ibid., April 4, 1995. Purcell was referring to an episode in March 1943 in which "about 1,000 'Aryan' German women held a week-long round-the-clock protest outside a building near the centre of Berlin where their Jewish husbands and fiancees were being held prior to being shipped to death camps in the east. . . . Their protests were completely successful."

111. For general background, see Emily O'Reilly, *Masterminds of the Right* (Dublin, 1988).

SOUTH AFRICA
Milton Shain

Although Jews were among the early explorers who circumnavigated the Cape of Storms, they and other non-Protestants were denied the right to settle at the Cape during the rule of the Dutch East India Company (1652–1795). This practice was abrogated under the enlightened Batavian administration (1803–6), whose lead was followed by its administrative heirs, the British, in 1806.[1] A handful of Jews of mainly English and Dutch origin took advantage of the new circumstances. The majority settled in Cape Town, although a contingent of seventeen among the so-called 1820 Settlers located themselves in the eastern Cape.[2]

The first recorded manifestation of organized Jewish life was in 1841, when seventeen males attended a meeting and religious service in Cape Town on the eve of the Day of Atonement. One week later the Society of the Jewish Community of Cape Town, forerunner of the Cape Town Hebrew Congregation, was founded. New congregations were established in Grahamstown (1843), Port Elizabeth (1862), and Kimberley (1872); nonetheless, Jews made up a mere fraction of South Africa's white population. The majority resided in the Cape Colony, where in 1875 they constituted only 0.23 percent of the entire white population.[3] Most Jews were acculturated and well ensconced within the dominant English-speaking segment of white society. Religion was a private matter, and primary allegiance was accorded to the state.

Jews were perceived in much the same way as were their coreligionists in mid-Victorian England. While that image included some negative factors, it was on the whole benign. Certainly Jews in Cape Town, as well as an increasing number of German-Jewish traders in the hinterland, thrived in a society that separated church and state. An 1860 act empowering the government to appoint Jews as marriage officers and another act eight years later proscribing any differentiation or penalties based on religious belief were palpable indications of tolerance and goodwill. Within this atmosphere Jews were able to make important contributions to the colony. In particular, they were prominent in the mohair and merino fleece trade and, from the late 1860s, the diamond industry. Further afield, in Natal, Jews numbered among the early sugar pioneers.

The assassination of Czar Alexander II in 1881, followed by the discovery of gold on the Witwatersrand in 1886, generated the pull and push that were necessary for a new wave of Jewish immigration. The new arrivals, most of whom were part of a chain migration from Lithuania, spurred by stories of Jewish success, enlivened and boosted established urban and rural Jewish communities; but the vast majority were attracted to the Witwatersrand and its burgeoning economic opportunities. There they came under the rule of President Paul Kruger's South African Republic. Within a short period Jews constituted approximately 6 percent of Johannesburg's white community. Almost half were of "Russian" origin.[4]

Unlike the Cape Colony, the South African Republic bound church and state inextricably together, and Jews (together with other non-Protestants) were denied full civic and political equality. In effect, the constitution reflected a determined resolve on the part of the Dutch population, the Boers, all of whom were members of the Dutch Reformed Church, to maintain their hard-won independence from Britain and to keep control of the republic and its morals. In any event, at the time the constitution was drafted there were no Jews in the republic. The constitution, in other words, was not motivated by anti-Semitic intent, and Jews enjoyed complete economic and social freedom. The reluctance of Boer leaders to amend the constitution, despite substantial pressure from English immigrants, was motivated by fear that Boer power would be eroded and ultimately subsumed by new demographic realities. Pressures from the Uitlander (foreigner) community culminated eventually in the Anglo-Boer War (1899–1902), in which British forces ultimately tamed the Boers and established control over the South African Republic and the Orange Free State.

In the postwar years, Eastern European Jews continued to enter the country in large numbers. In 1910 the Transvaal, Natal, the Cape Colony, and the Orange Free State were amalgamated into the Union of South Africa, which was part of the British Empire. By then the total Jewish population stood at approximately forty-seven thousand, or 3.7 percent of the entire white population. Under the new union constitution Jews enjoyed full civic and political rights. Indeed, five Jews were elected to the first union parliament. But the burgeoning Jewish presence in South Africa did not go unnoticed. While many observers admired Jewish enterprise, loyalty, and sobriety, others cast aspersions on the Jews for alleged dishonesty and knavery. In particular, Jews were accused of illicit dealing on the diamond fields, and in the smaller towns Jewish traders and itinerant peddlers were often perceived as avaricious and exploitative. The coincidence of Jewish penetration into the rural economy and the disruption of traditional agrarian life explains to a large extent the crystallization of an anti-Jewish stereotype in the hinterland. Most farmers did not realize that social changes of a structural nature were undermining their former well-being and security. Disturbing feelings of alienation and displacement were instead simply projected onto the Jew, a readily available symbol of change.

The Jew became an even greater symbol of change and upheaval in the urban centers during the 1890s. In Johannesburg especially, Eastern European newcomers formed a conspicuous segment of the mining city's *lumpenproletariat* and a sector of the much-maligned Uitlander community. These hapless victims of czarist oppression and discrimination soon became the recipients of vicious class and race prejudice. It was not long before they acquired the pejorative label "Peruvian," a term of obscure origin.[5] The Peruvian rapidly became associated with the evils of Johannesburg, more specifically with the city's illicit liquor trade. The Peruvian was also associated with unsanitary living and the seamier side of Johannesburg's nightlife. Similarly negative depictions of the Jew were evident in Cape Town, where Peruvians were accused of undercutting the mercantile establishment and threatening the city's business morality.[6]

Emerging at the same time as the Peruvian stereotype, but far more sinister, was the image of the Jew as part of a network of international finance. This association had already taken root in Europe, and it found fertile ground in South Africa, where Jewish mining magnates were a prominent feature of society. Indeed, Jewish success was at least in part a product of access to international money markets. Their detractors, however, perceived that access as conspiratorial and subversive. Alleged Jewish machinations attracted widespread attention when John Atkinson Hobson, the *Manchester Guardian's* Johannesburg correspondent, popularized the notion that the Anglo-Boer War was fought in the interests of a "small group of international financiers, chiefly German in origin and Jewish in race."[7]

In the immediate postwar years, legislative attempts were made to curtail the influx of Eastern European Jews.[8] Although these efforts were unsuccessful, not least of all because of pressure from Jewish leaders, relations between Jew and gentile continued to be affected by negative stereotyping and harmful accusations. This was the period in which the cartoon caricature "Hoggenheimer" emerged. This quintessential parvenu, based on a character in the London stage musical *The Girl from Kays,* became a national symbol, personifying the power of mine magnates in South African society. By the 1930s he was specifically a symbol of Jewish exploitation.[9]

Although the Eastern European newcomers added a vitality to Jewish life, it was the Anglo-German Jewish establishment that shaped communal institutions. The South African Jewish Board of Deputies, founded in 1912, was thus modeled on the Board of Deputies for British Jews, and religious patterns followed the English example. In some cases, however, Eastern European Jews did establish their own congregations with their own liturgical traditions. Nonetheless, Anglo-Jews served as a reference group for the new arrivals. The years of large-scale immigration also witnessed the establishment of a South African Zionist Federation, in 1898, and a range of educational, charitable, and welfare associations. By the outbreak of World War I the Jewish community could boast of a corporate cohesion and unity of purpose envied by other Diaspora populations.

Jews were also prominent in public life and were able to contribute to the wider society. In particular they were conspicuous in local government and continued to play an important part in mining. In addition, Jews were successful in manufacturing industries, most notably furniture and textiles, where they took advantage of the Englishman's preference for foreign imports and the Afrikaner's attachment to the land. In other words, Jews were well placed, as one economic historian noted, to fulfill an entrepreneurial function.[10] Success generated more antagonism, however, and in 1913 further attempts were made to curtail Eastern European immigration. Although these efforts were once again thwarted, the sentiment against foreigners continued into the 1920s, when escalating unemployment among unskilled and recently urbanized "poor whites" ensured Jewish immigration an important place on the public agenda. In 1925, 1,353 Jewish immigrants entered South Africa, and by 1929 the number had more than doubled, to 2,738. Against the background of alleged Jewish or Bolshevik involvement in the 1922 Rand Rebellion, in which white workers violently clashed with the government-supported Chamber of Mines, nativist concerns were articulated by both English and Afrikaans speakers. The latter in particular saw the Jew as powerful and manipulative. To be sure, Jews were demonstrating a marked upward mobility. Besides entering the professions, many Jews, spurred by the shortage of goods and raw materials during World War I, made further inroads into secondary manufacturing, particularly of clothing and textiles. Their efforts were encouraged by legislation designed in the mid-1920s to stimulate local industry.[11] Success, however, provoked fear, even among those who admired Jewish enterprise and excellence. Herein lay a convergence between philo- and anti-Semitic sentiment.

In 1930 South African Jews were shocked by the introduction of the Immigration Quota Bill, which limited to a numerical quota immigrants of whatever race or creed born in quota, or "non-scheduled," countries. These included the countries of Southern and Eastern Europe and therefore directly affected Jewish immigration. Non-quota, or "scheduled," countries were free of restriction. These included countries of the British Commonwealth, Austria, Belgium, Denmark, France, Germany, Holland, Italy, Norway, Portugal, Spain, Sweden, Switzerland, and the United States. A remarkable consensus across language and party divides greeted the introduction of the bill, which was obviously aimed at keeping out the Eastern European Jew. "The Bill will commend itself to most citizens of the Union and has not been introduced a day too soon," noted an editorial in an eastern Cape newspaper, which captured prevailing public sentiment.[12]

Debate surrounding the Immigration Quota Bill demonstrated clearly the intensification of anti-Jewish sentiment and a movement away from simple cultural and literary stereotyping. In 1933 the South African Christian Nationalist Socialist Movement, whose followers were known as Greyshirts, was formed under the leadership of Louis T. Weichardt. The Greyshirts were patently inspired by Hitler's success and tactics, particularly brownshirt thuggery and Nazi propaganda. At its peak the movement had two thousand members, and its success inspired a number of similar organizations to mushroom across the country.[13]

Anti-Jewish hostility was further fueled by the entry of 3,614 German Jewish refugees in the three years following Hitler's ascent to power. The groundswell of anti-Jewish feeling, including demands from the opposition (mainly Afrikaans-speaking) National Party that action be taken against the Jewish community, prompted the ruling United Party to introduce in 1937 an Aliens Bill, which was designed to restrict Jewish immigration, particularly from Germany, although it did not mention the word "Jew." Immigrants were to be permitted entry by a selection board on the basis of good character and the likelihood of their assimilation into the European population.

The bill failed to satisfy the nationalists, who considered any Jewish immigration unacceptable. The bill, they argued, was in the interests of the Jewish community and the country. The most articulate exponent of this view was Dr. Hendrik Frensch Verwoerd, editor-in-chief of *Die Transvaler,* a nationalist mouthpiece of the far right. In one particularly lengthy editorial, "The Jewish Question from a Nationalist Point of View," Verwoerd summarized the whole corpus of South African anti-Semitic discourse: Jewish domination in business and the professions, the unassimilability of Jews, Jewish alienation from the Afrikaners, questionable Jewish commercial morality, and the use of money by Jews to influence government through the English-language press. Obviously the Jewish Question was no longer a concern solely of fringe fascist groups; by 1937 it was firmly entrenched within mainstream white politics.

This anti-Jewish hostility, of course, caused the South African Jewish Board of Deputies to engage in the defense of the Jewish community. Alliances were sought with non-Jewish liberals, and efforts were made to introduce antidefamation legislation. Whenever possible, litigation against anti-Jewish acts was encouraged. One of the board's most important successes in this respect was obtaining an injunction against the Greyshirts' using an adapted version of the notorious anti-Jewish forgery, *The Protocols of the Elders of Zion,* which the board alleged was stolen from a synagogue in Port Elizabeth.[14] The Board of Deputies also expended a great deal of effort monitoring anti-Jewish manifestations and refuting anti-Jewish literature. Nonetheless, Dr. Daniel Francois Malan's opposition National Party campaigned for the 1938 general election on an openly anti-Semitic ticket. Party propaganda was underpinned by an insistence on the prospect of Jewish domination. Afrikaner nationalists' fears were confirmed by the election results, which were illustrated in a cartoon in *Die Burger,* a nationalist newspaper. It depicted the United Party leader, James Barry Munnik Hertzog, and his deputy, Jan Christiaan Smuts, carrying Hoggenheimer to victory. In the election year there emerged yet another paramilitary, authoritarian movement, the Ossewabrandwag (Ox-Wagon Sentinel). Born out of the centenary celebrations of the Great Trek, a central episode in Afrikaner history in which thousands of Afrikaners moved into the interior in the 1830s to escape British control at the Cape Colony, the Ossewabrandwag attacked "British Jewish Masonic" imperialism and capitalism, British Jewish democracy, and Jewish money, power, and disloyalty. With its *fuhrer-prinzip,* its authoritarian philosophy, and its anti-Jewish stance, the movement was obviously a Nazi clone.

Anti-Semitism had become an integral part of "volkish" Afrikaner nationalism by the late 1930s. Many of the key theoreticians within the movement had studied in Germany, where they had become supporters of the corporate state, an idealist worldview, and an exclusivist nationalism. These ideas propelled a powerful republicanism rooted in notions of divine election, a leitmotif within the Afrikaners' civil religion. Like their European counterparts on the Right, Afrikaner nationalists were opposed to liberalism, Marxism, and laissez-faire capitalism. The latter, associated with British imperialism, was, of course, exemplified in Hoggenheimer, who, as one historian noted, was "English-speaking, imperialist and clearly Jewish."[15]

THE HOLOCAUST ERA

It is hardly surprising that Afrikaner nationalists empathized with the Third Reich. Even the Kristallnacht outrage was minimized, and details of rioting were ignored by nationalist newspapers. It was not for South Africa, argued *Die Burger,* to pronounce judgment upon Germany's treatment of some of her citizens.[16] Germany's expansionist policies were also minimized. Dr. Malan described them as "nothing else but an effort to get together in one country and under one Government what through race and language belongs together, and wants to be united."[17] It followed naturally that the Nationalists called for a policy of neutrality in the event of war. Of course, a German victory would have suited the aims of Malan's republicans, who wished to secede from the British Commonwealth. It should also be noted that the ruling United Party maintained cordial relations with the Third Reich during the thirties, despite a firm commitment to the British Commonwealth. State contracts were awarded to the German transport industry.[18]

When Britain and France declared war on Germany in 1939, Hertzog assumed that his case for neutrality would be supported. Indeed, he was convinced that white South Africans wished to avoid entanglement in yet another European conflagration, particularly one involving Germany, for whom many Afrikaners (who made up more than 50 percent of the white population) had substantial sympathy. However, the cabinet was divided, and the Parliament favored by 80 votes to 67 Smuts's argument to support the Commonwealth and resist Germany. Governor General Sir Patrick Duncan asked Smuts to form a government, and on September 6, 1939, South Africa proclaimed a state of war between itself and Germany.

South African Jewry fully supported Smuts and played a substantial role in the war effort. More than 10 percent of the entire Jewish population served in the Union Defence Force and other Allied forces. Of these, 357 were killed, 327 were wounded or injured, 143 were mentioned in dispatches, and 94 received various awards for distinguished service. On the home front, the Board of Deputies and the Zionist Federation established organizations to raise funds for refugees and the relief of European Jewry. The Jewish War Appeal in particular assisted Jewish victims of the war and South African Jewish soldiers and their dependents. This organization worked in conjunction with international agencies such as the American Joint Distribution Committee (JDC) and the South African Red Cross. In the later stages of the war, the Aliens and Refugees Committee raised funds to assist relief operations.[19]

In addition to fundraising and relief work, the Board of Deputies had to contend with a powerful antiwar and anti-Semitic movement orchestrated by the Osse-wabrandwag. By 1941 this organization claimed a membership of more than three hundred thousand, drawn mainly from the Afrikaner petite bourgeoisie. Their sentiments were shared by the avowedly pro-Nazi party, the New Order, founded by Oswald Pirow in 1940. A range of major National Party publications also demonstrated the formative influence of Mussolini and Hitler on the exclusivist nature of Afrikaner nationalism, in which the Jew had no place.[20] It is hardly surprising, therefore, that Nationalists and other extremists ignored stories of German atrocities, labeling them as unproven accusations or British propaganda. Even an alarming World Jewish Congress report on the appalling plight of European Jewry in June 1942 failed to generate concern. Indeed, attitudes remained unchanged in the wake of Anthony Eden's statement to the British House of Commons on December 17, 1942, that Hitler intended to exterminate the Jews. Such pronouncements did, however, galvanize supporters of the war effort, and a number of mass meetings addressed by non-Jewish leaders and Christian clergy denounced Nazi barbarism. As the minister of labor, Walter Madeley, put it, "The conscience of South Africa has been stirred."[21] South African troops certainly did acquit themselves well. Besides defending the Cape sea route and seizing Madagascar, which had backed Vichy France, two South African divisions fought the Germans and Italians in North Africa, and an armored division joined the American Fifth Army in Italy. All together, two hundred thousand South Africans took part in the war; almost nine thousand were killed.

The enormity of the catastrophe overtaking European Jewry was fully appreciated by the South African Jewish community. Jewish parliamentarian Morris Kentridge asserted in January 1943 that "two million Jews [had been] treacherously murdered in the slaughterhouse of Poland" and a further "five million more were in hourly peril of the same fate."[22] With such knowledge South African Jews could hardly divorce themselves from the European calamity. Many, of course, hailed from the regions most devastated by Hitler's war machine. Beginning in 1942, the Board of Deputies coordinated official days of mourning for South African Jewry. On each occasion Jewish businesses closed early and special synagogue services were held. The board also lobbied the government (unsuccessfully) to permit the entry of more Jewish refugees; Jewish immigration had virtually ceased with the advent of war. Sadly, Smuts feared that renewed Jewish immigration would lead to food shortages, pressure on Allied shipping, which was confined to war purposes, and further right-wing anti-Semitism. With regard to the latter, his fears were not unfounded. Even the uncovering of Buchenwald by the American Third Army in 1945 failed to evoke a reasonable response from opponents of the war. Of course, acknowledging such evidence would have discredited Germany and made the Allied cause acceptable. Hence the one-time diplomat Eric Hendrik Louw, who had supported Hertzog's policy of nonintervention, refused to take up the challenge of a private Jew to lead a parliamentary delegation (with the costs to be covered by private subscription) to German and Russian concentration camps. Louw instead argued that the money would be better spent on the republication of Emily Hobhouse's book *War without*

Glamour, on British concentration camps during the Anglo-Boer War. The South African government did, however, send officials attached to South Africa House in London to visit certain concentration camps in Germany. There they compiled a fully documented report, based both on their findings and on investigations then being undertaken by other governments.[23]

THE POST-HOLOCAUST ERA

Instead of acknowledging the horrors of Nazism, nationalists concentrated on the sufferings of the German people after the war, arguing that it was ironic that German war criminals were judged at Nuremberg by a country that had dropped the atom bomb.[24] But the Nuremberg trials were welcomed by progovernment newspapers, who gave them front-page coverage. As the *Cape Times* put it:

> The accused at Nuremberg are criminals on an international scale and the machinery of justice has been accordingly expanded. . . . Whatever the fate of the wretches who are being tried, Nuremberg will mark a stage in the development of the human race. The foundations are being laid for a wider and bolder conception of justice, a system of law under which evildoers will not easily escape retribution because murderers call themselves patriots and brutes and savages label themselves statesmen.[25]

Notwithstanding such sentiments and an obvious sympathy in government circles for the primary victims of Nazi aggression, Smuts remained opposed to large-scale Jewish immigration. The South African government considered Palestine to be the preferred solution for displaced Jewish persons. As a result, only 1,512 Jews entered South Africa between 1946 and 1948. Many of these newcomers were Jewish teachers, aged parents of South African citizens, or religious functionaries. The feeling was that such persons would not be a strain on the economy and would satisfy humane imperatives and the particular needs of the Jewish community.

For most South Africans the postwar period was a time to heal political rifts and tensions. More than that, it was a time to deal with South Africa's mounting racial problems. For the mainly Afrikaner National Party, the solution lay in the policy of *apartheid* (separate development), an alleged panacea that enabled the party to capture power in 1948. For the Jews, self-conscious and vulnerable since the early thirties, this election result was frightening. The new government, after all, included pro-Nazis and others avowedly hostile to the war effort. Nonetheless, Jewish leaders did manage to effect a rapprochement with the National Party, and South African Jews were soon able to enjoy the comfort and confidence they had experienced before the thirties. Of course, that comfort could not obliterate the memory and trauma of the war years. For the older generation, in particular, the destruction of European Jewry was intensely and understandably personalized; the vast majority had their roots in Lithuania, where 90 percent of Jews had been annihilated. The Board of Deputies had, in fact, convened a conference of *Landsmanshaften* of Lithuanian Jews in Johannesburg in 1945 to ensure a sense of responsibility on the part of all South African Jews for their surviving European brethren. Food and medical supplies were collected and sent to Europe via the well-established JDC. Help was also forthcoming from Cape Town, where the Vilna Society offered assistance.

In the ensuing months, long lists of survivors having relatives in South Africa were published. In the meantime, the Jewish War Appeal continued to send relief consignments of medicine, food, and clothing to Europe. Increasingly, the horrors of the European tragedy came to the fore as the Jewish press published survivors' accounts and stories. On May 29, 1946, a service was held in Johannesburg to commemorate the Warsaw Ghetto Uprising. Despite a disappointing attendance, the commemoration inspired the Board of Deputies to explore ways of further assisting Jewish survivors in Europe. It was decided that the Jewish War Appeal would collaborate with the World Jewish Congress in this endeavor. The Board of Deputies was also involved in assisting German Jewish refugees living in South Africa, and arrangements were made for restitution through the Control Office for Germany and Austria in London. In addition, the Federation of Lithuanian Jews, which was closely allied to the Jewish War Appeal, was established to assist surviving Lithuanian Jews in Europe. Their plight was vividly recounted in 1947 when Rabbi Ephraim Oshry, a Lithuanian survivor, visited South Africa and described the fate of five Lithuanian communities.[26]

Besides supporting aid-related activities, the Board of Deputies acknowledged its gratitude to governments that had aided Jewish refugees. In one instance a deputation was sent to the Danish consul general in Johannesburg to congratulate King Christian X of Denmark on his seventy-fifth birthday. The king had, of course, resolutely opposed Nazi attempts to impose restrictions on Danish Jews during the war.

By 1947 thirty-eight South African Jews, some in important positions, were engaged in relief activity in Europe as part of the JDC staff. And on the home front Jews tried, without success, to influence government immigration policy. In addition, an extraordinary national conference of the Jewish War Appeal met to raise further aid for European Jewish refugees. Although some apathy had begun to set in, interest in the death of six million Jews was not lost, and in 1948 the fifth anniversary of the Warsaw Ghetto Uprising was commemorated.

The Holocaust was thus firmly rooted in the South African Jewish consciousness. One of its most important short-term effects was to strengthen the already powerful South African Zionist movement. Certainly, in the immediate postwar years the fate of the survivors and the future of Jews in Palestine had been intimately connected. Intense lobbying and feverish political activity now characterized the Zionist movement. As the scholar Gideon Shimoni noted, "In the two years preceding the creation of the State of Israel, Zionism in South Africa reached the peak of its hegemony over the life of the Jewish community. Never before had the Jewish people been rallied on such a scale."[27] If anything, the Holocaust demonstrated the need for a Jewish homeland or sovereign state.

This connection between destruction and rebirth was further demonstrated in 1952 when the Board of Deputies issued an official date for commemorating the Holocaust and those who died in Israel's war of liberation. South African Jewry was to hold official services on April 22, 1952, and Jewish organizations were requested not to arrange any functions on that date so that there could be mass participation in the official functions throughout the country.[28] The board also decided on suitable material for the services and arranged for cards signifying financial pledges for the planting of trees in Israel's Martyr's Forest. Despite little publicity, the meetings were well attended, and the board's assessment that it had managed to keep the memory of this human tragedy alive was fully confirmed.

The imprint of the Holocaust was further strengthened by the formation of She'erith Hapletah, a survivors' group dedicated to keeping the memory of the Holocaust alive, to educating future generations about the enormity of the tragedy, and to promoting social and cultural ties among themselves. At its height She'erith Hapletah numbered more than two hundred members. Some of these survivors contributed to a worldwide memoir literature. One of the most prominent of these authors was Levi Shalit. Born in Kuybyshev, in Russia, Shalit had survived Dachau and founded *Unzer Weg* (Our Way), the first postwar Yiddish newspaper in Europe. In 1951 he had visited South Africa on a cultural mission as a guest of the Board of Deputies and had decided to stay. He acquired the magazine *Afrikaner Yiddishe Zeitung* and served as its managing editor for nearly thirty years. Shalit wrote widely, but he is perhaps best known for his reflective work on the Holocaust, *Beyond Dachau,* published in Johannesburg in 1980.[29]

A number of other memoirs have been published by survivors living in South Africa: Gabriella Rose, *Red Snow* (Cape Town, 1963); Clarissa Jacobi, *A Real Kavalsky and Other Stories* (Cape Town, 1972); Henia Brazg, *Passport to Life, Memories, and Dreams* (Johannesburg, 1981); and Gabriel Weiss, *And So He Survived* (Johannesburg, 1984). Another survivor, David Wolpe, editor of the literary monthly *Dorem Afrika,* embraced the Holocaust, with its themes of anguish and faith, in *A volk un a weg: Lider un poemes-oyfkleyb* (A cloud and a way: A collection of poems), published in Johannesburg in 1978. Numerous poems and essays relating to the Holocaust were also written by Yiddishist Louis Segal and, in Afrikaans, by Olga Kirsch, a Lithuanian-born South African now resident in Israel. But the most important contribution came from David Fram, a Lithuanian-born Jew, whose epic poem *Dos Letzte Kapitel* (The last chapter), published in London in 1947, is regarded as a classic. In this poem Fram recalls "an harmonious—and largely mythic—time when Jew and Christian lived peaceably in brotherhood" in Lithuania. But that dream was devastated.[30] In 1984 Harold Serebro published *The Devil and His Servant,* a novel about a chance encounter between an ex-Nazi and a medical doctor and the latter's search for the truth.[31]

In the immediate postwar period the anguish of the older generation was not shared by South Africa's Jewish youth. This disturbed the Jewish establishment, which believed that it was essential that young Jews "come to realise what these years meant to the Jewish destiny and what the Jewish people owe to the Jewish resistance."[32] Indifference on the part of the youth was considered the fault of the older generation, who were disinclined to let the life of the young be overshadowed by the horrors of Nazism. Efforts were then made for children to hear the story and learn the significance of the Holocaust. Consequently, South Africa's network of Jewish day schools—established in the postwar period—incorporated the study of the Holocaust in their curricula. In simple language and without too much emphasis on the horrible details of the Holocaust, children were told the truth about the Nazi plans for extermination, the execution of these plans, and Jewish resistance. The courage and heroism of the Jewish resistance were in turn linked to the establishment of the state of Israel. Once again, the connection between destruction and rebirth—a powerful dimension of contemporary Jewish awareness—was evident.

These educational initiatives appear to have been successful; it was not long before young Jews began to understand the grief of their parents and grandparents. By the mid-1950s youngsters were conspicuous at commemorative services, and in 1960 a special memorial service was arranged jointly by the Board of Deputies' youth department and the Zionist Youth Council in Johannesburg. A similar service held two years later could not contain the crowd. Clearly, young Jews had become fully conscious of the European tragedy by the early sixties. No doubt this was in part owing to the growth of the Jewish day school movement and the international focus on Jerusalem, where Hitler's lieutenant, Adolf Eichmann, was tried in 1961. This was also a period in which a number of memorials for the murdered six million were erected in South Africa.

This Jewish sensitivity was not shared by the wider South African population, black or white. Of course, all literate South Africans knew of the Jewish tragedy, but the subject was handled only indirectly. When it was touched upon, particularly by writers, it was usually in relation to South Africa's race policies.[33] The Jewish tragedy, in other words, was appropriated for local political purposes. This strategy had already been evident in 1945, when black leaders in the Non-European Unity Movement drew up a document informing the United Nations of the similarities between South African race laws and Nazism. Skin color substituted for the "Yellow patch," and like the Jews, the blacks in South Africa faced a whole host of discriminatory legislation. Of course, the authors of this document were well aware that South African racism did not imply genocide, but they nonetheless drew important analogies:

> But if there is no Buchenwald in South Africa, the sadistic fury with which the Herrenvolk policeman belabours the Non-European victim, guilty or not guilty is comparable only to the brutality of the SS Guards. Moreover, the treatment meted out to the Non-European in the Law Courts is comparable only to the fate of the Non-Aryan in the Nazi Law Courts. But the fundamental difference in law and morality is not only expressed in the different paragraphs of the Legal Statutes, it lies in the fundamentally different concept of the value of the life of a Non-European, as compared with the value placed on the life of a European. The life of a Non-European is very cheap in South Africa. As cheap as the life of a Jew in Nazi Germany.[34]

South African Jews may well have sympathized with the disenfranchised black majority, but they would not have drawn parallels between apartheid and Nazism. But such parallels were drawn by others, and indeed South African racism and Nazism was further elaborated in Brian Bunting's book *The Rise of the South African Reich,* published in 1964.[35] The writer, a one-time left-wing parliamentarian, systematically compared the Nuremberg Laws and South Africa's intricate apartheid legislation. Such comparisons, however problematic, were certainly necessary, given the worldwide apathy toward the suffering of millions of blacks. Of course, the majority of white South Africans supported "separate development" and failed to appreciate the immorality of racism in all its forms. And racism naturally did not stop with the blacks. Whites continued to stereotype local Jews, embellishing the earlier dimensions with accusations of liberalism and Communism, both of which were terms of abuse in the lexicon of white politics of the 1960s. A number of National Party members of Parliament even saw the Eichmann trial as an unnecessary display of revenge, which is hardly surprising given the pro-Nazi predilections of a fair number of Nationalists in prominent positions.

A particularly sinister development at this time was the introduction of anti-Semitic literature imported from abroad. Clearly pro-Hitler groups, albeit limited to the extreme fringe of the white political spectrum, continued to thrive in postwar South Africa, and it was not uncommon for anti-Jewish pamphlets, both local and foreign, to be distributed to Jewish-owned stores and for swastikas to be publicly displayed. Particularly galling was the celebration of Hitler's birthday in a popular Johannesburg beer hall in 1967. German songs were sung, "Sieg heil" was chanted, and a photograph of Hitler was allegedly displayed. Not surprisingly, the incident provoked clashes between indignant Jewish youths and German immigrants. The "Hillbrow Affair," named for the cosmopolitan suburb in which the events took place, was discussed by Chief Rabbi Bernard Casper in his Sabbath sermon. South Africa, he warned, "cannot be blind to some of the Nazi-oriented antisemitic literature that is coming into the country and being circulated, or the swastikas that are sent to various people in the mail, or the visits to this country of certain individuals with a pronounced Nazi antisemitic background." It was, he concluded, the task of the government to denounce neo-Nazi activities.[36]

Casper's admonitions notwithstanding, Hitler's birthday was celebrated regularly by neo-Nazi elements. Obviously such celebrations were limited to numerically few bigots, but the very fact that they took place concerned Jewish leaders. More disturbing, however, were the links between South African anti-Semites and neo-Nazis abroad. In 1975, for instance, one Dr. Manfred Roeder, a leader of West Germany's militant right-wing Deutsche Burger-Initiative (German Citizen Initiative), visited South Africa. In addition to praising Hitler for disciplining the German people, Roeder publicly denied that six million Jews had been murdered by the Nazis. Most significantly, he expressed pleasure at his reception in South Africa and noted that the German Reich had survived. According to the *Sunday Times* (Johannesburg), there were indeed secret Nazi cells in South Africa.[37]

In the 1970s, amidst fears that the government was becoming soft on race issues, the Afrikaner Weerstandsbeweging (Afrikaner Resistance Movement), or AWB, was formed. It patently modeled itself on the Nazi movement, with its leader, Eugene Terre'Blanche, employing volkish language and symbols in his demagoguery and its swastika-type emblem. The AWB made it clear that Jews would not have full rights in a Christian country under its leadership. Predictably, the AWB's propaganda claimed that Jews were making capital out of the Holocaust.[38]

The shared perspective of neo-Nazis in South Africa and abroad was most clearly evident in the reception accorded to Arthur R. Butz's book *The Hoax of the Twentieth Century* in the ultrarightist monthly *South African Observer*. This classic of Holocaust denial literature clearly suited the *South African Observer's* conspiratorial worldview, which had been molded by its editor, S. E. D. Brown. Brown applauded Butz's work, which, he argued, combined "the historian's mastery of documents with the technical knowledge of a scientist." This book, he maintained, "will remain the standard volume for many years to come." The review included a chapter-by-chapter summary and an invitation to readers to order the book through the *South African Observer*.[39] International neo-Nazi links were even more apparent in the publication of *Did Six Million Really Die?—The Truth at Last,* a booklet written by Richard Verrall under the pseudonym Richard Harwood, supposedly of the University of London, and disseminated widely in the United Kingdom.[40] Verrall's booklet denied the Holocaust. Not surprisingly, it was advertised and distributed for South African readers through Brown's *South African Observer*.

In June 1976 the Board of Deputies applied to the director of publications, under the terms of Section (10)(1)(a) of Publications Act No. 42 of 1944, for a decision whether *Did Six Million Really Die?* was "undesirable" and hence should be banned. This was certainly the view of Jewish leaders, who noted that the act provided, *inter alia,* that any publication shall be deemed to be "undesirable" if it, or any part of it, "brings any section of the inhabitants of the Republic into ridicule or contempt" or "is harmful to the relations between any section of the inhabitants of the Republic." The Publications Board declared the booklet to be undesirable, and further dissemination was prohibited.

In August 1976 the editor of the *South African Observer* and two private individuals lodged appeals against the Publications Board's decision. In preparation for an appeal, the board collected expert evidence and affidavits from individuals in Israel and England. When the case came before the Publications Appeal Board on September 7, 1977, the appellants withdrew their appeal, and the publication therefore remained undesirable. Having gathered such useful material, the Board of Deputies decided to publish it in a book titled *Six Million Did Die—The Truth Shall Prevail*.[41] Favorable responses to the publication revealed that most South Africans, including mainstream nationalists, were now prepared to acknowledge the truth about this period. Indeed, a reviewer in Johannesburg's *Sunday Times* recommended the book as "a very necessary document" in a world "where few school history books give more than a few paragraphs to the holocaust."[42]

But sensitivity still ran deep in certain quarters, as illustrated in the controversy surrounding the screening of the "Genocide" episode in the television series *The World at War*. But for substantial popular pressure, including representations made by the Board of Deputies, the state-controlled South African Broadcasting Corporation would have refrained from showing the episode on the grounds that it might disturb race relations and give offense to one of the population groups. However, good sense prevailed, and the "Genocide" episode was screened and indeed acclaimed in mainstream English and Afrikaans newspapers. *Die Beeld* even argued that anti-Semites especially should have watched the transmission.[43] Brian Barrow, a columnist in the prominent English daily newspaper *Cape Times*, was more forthright. He asked:

> Who would have been offended for instance by the harrowing concentration camp episodes? The Jews? The Germans? Our children? Or was there a fear that black men would see that white men could commit barbarities unheard of even in Darkest Africa? Every reason that comes to mind seems utterly childish compared to the far more important message of the death camp episode, namely that man's inhumanity to man is a universal condition and that what man has most to fear in this world are the dark subterranean areas of his own fundamental nature. It is an insult that most TV viewers in this country will not easily forget.[44]

Barrow's appropriation of this specifically Jewish tragedy for its universal message is significant, and it was echoed by other commentators. "No narrative of World War 2," noted the *Cape Argus*, "could be complete without the story of the extermination camps. It does not simply show what Hitler's Germany did, it shows what people can do to other people. It shows the inhumanity that can emerge in even the most advanced societies. It is a dreadful warning to us all."[45] Much the same line was taken by Dr. Louw Alberts, founder and member of the religious group Action Moral Standards: "I do not identify this horrible thing with either Germans or Jews. This was one of the low points in human history and I don't think this should be specifically assigned to the nations and people involved but rather to humanity as a whole which must recognize its guilt in allowing things to happen."[46] The universal message of the Holocaust, and indeed the tendency to relativize the tragedy, was taken even further by *Tempo*, an Afrikaans newspaper in Natal: "Even if it were only 6000 Jews that had died, it could not have been justified, but it should be remembered that there are many other nations who have also had to suffer the brutality of their fellow men."[47]

South Africans were thus able to draw on the Holocaust for its universal message. But Afrikaner nationalists avoided an examination of their own wartime behavior and actions. Ironically, the very people who opposed the war effort and even committed acts of sabotage against the government because of its opposition to Nazism were now cementing relations between South Africa and Israel. Veiled criticism of the Jews, so evident in the 1960s, had ended, and in 1976 South Africa's prime minister, Balthazar Johannes Vorster, visited Yad Vashem, Israel's Holocaust memorial. The irony of this visit by someone interned during the war for antigovernment and pro-Nazi activities was not lost on progressive South African Jews, who expressed consternation at the visit. But the overriding message survived: mainstream Afrikaners now accepted the reality of the Jewish tragedy.

This was not the case for members of the extreme Right, heirs to the fascist movements of the 1930s. For them, the decision to screen the controversial "Genocide" episode was a mockery of the South African Broadcasting Corporation's allegedly objective position. As *Die Afrikaner* noted, "The alleged slaughter of six million Jews is based on falsification and fraud and lies."[48] It was obviously people of this ilk who placed leaflets denying the Holocaust under the windshield wipers of cars parked outside a Johannesburg hotel where the producer of *The World at War,* Jeremy Isaacs, was giving a public lecture.

Predictably, the most vicious attack came from the *South African Observer,* which described the screening of "Genocide" as "the capitulation of the Vorster Government to the forces of world Zionism." The whole series, argued the newspaper, was "nothing more than history of the last war selected, compiled and purveyed, *not* by qualified historians, but by two Zionist Jews, Jeremy Isaacs and Charles Bloomberg." The "other side of the story," it was argued, "had been completely blacked out or smothered out." It was "nothing else than another instalment in the gross continuing libel against Germany and the German people as a whole at the hands of Zionists." Not surprisingly, the article cited "denial" literature, including Harwood's *Did Six Million Die?* and quoted the American historian Harry Elmer Barnes, a father of revisionist historiography, and the Frenchman Paul Rassinier, whose denial of the Holocaust won him notoriety in the late 1970s.[49] The *South African Observer* clearly was well connected to international neo-Nazi circles. Thus could the monthly conclude:

> For our part, if "The World at War" series—including the Genocide episode 20—has one lesson for the people of South Africa, it is the pressing need for the whole question of Zionism, Judaism and the Talmud, "anti-Semitism", the myth of the Six Million, and the whole matter of Jewish ethnocentricism to be opened up to free discussion and enquiry—in just the same way that Western man's customs, his traditions, his racism, his nationalism and his Christian faith, have since the end of the last war been subjected to the fierce and unremitting glare of public scrutiny by the Zionists themselves.[50]

The clamor of ultra-right-wing neo-Nazis notwithstanding, the "Genocide" episode appears to have made a substantial impact. Afrikaner educators even maintained that the episode was a necessity for South African viewers.[51] In practice, however, these suggestions have not been taken up, and the lessons of the Holocaust certainly have not filtered into the syllabuses of state schools. Thus high-school history courses that cover the period ignore or minimize the specific dimensions of the Jewish tragedy. Some textbooks do mention the denial of rights to Jews and acknowledge that they were persecuted but include them with other victims of the Nazis. Occasionally textbooks even treat Hitler as a successful social reformer, and at least one textbook has questioned the veracity of the figure six million.[52] *Mein Kampf* is generally described as a compilation of Hitler's political aims, and the implications of its anti-Jewish discourse are not developed. Perhaps in an apartheid society it is difficult to deal with the ultimate in racial discrimination.

The treatment of the Holocaust is very different in South Africa's well-established Jewish day schools. There major emphasis is placed upon "the war against the Jews" in both the general history and Jewish history syllabuses. In addition, these schools commemorate Yom Hashoah (Holocaust Day) with a memorial service and very often a photographic exhibition. There can be little doubt that graduates of these schools (more than 50 percent of all Jewish children) have a keen sense of this period, at least at the emotional level. Indeed, it could be argued that the ramifications of the Holocaust, together with Zionism, to a large extent constitute the essence of their Jewish identity. In 1981 a university group, the South African Union of Jewish Students, participated in the Gathering of Holocaust Survivors in Jerusalem. As a result, the so-called second generation made a pledge to educate all future generations about the Holocaust. Out of this conference came the Student Holocaust Interviewing Project (SHIP), which, as the organization explained, "enables students to get a first hand insight" into the Holocaust.[53] By the end of 1990 more than twenty interviews had been conducted with survivors in Johannesburg, Cape Town, and Durban.

By the 1980s black South Africans too were referring increasingly to the Holocaust. Once again they compared their plight to that of the Jews in Nazi Germany,[54] a viewpoint elaborated upon by Nobel Prize winner Archbishop Desmond Tutu when he was interviewed by Alan Fischer and Tzippi Hoffman as part of their study on perceptions of the Jew in South Africa:

> There is a kind of Jewish arrogance: one can only call it that. I do not know whether you've heard, but I sometimes say that apartheid is as evil as Nazism and there have been Jews who say I am insulting them. Jews seem to think that they have a corner on the market of suffering. In Germany, I was speaking to a German minister in the foreign office, and just mentioning the kind of things that were happening here, the forced removals, and so on, and he said: "It reminds one very much of the kind of things that they did to Jews in Germany". Maybe you would be able to explain to me how a Jew can claim to be insulted by a comparison of apartheid with Nazism, unless he's saying that, well, the South African government at least has not ordered six million to be liquidated. I am saying yes, we don't have gas chambers, but if you put people in a situation in resettlement camps where they will starve and children die every day, it's the same sort of thing . . . maybe less tidy. The Germans were more efficient: they put people in gas chambers.[55]

Tutu is not alone in this view. The late Percy Qobosa, one-time editor of the black Sunday newspaper *City Press,* similarly noted that the only horror that South African blacks had not experienced was Auschwitz. But, he added, "our people have also died in detention. Our people were stripped of their citizenship. The Jews couldn't fall in love with Germans and we're going to jail for falling in love with white people."[56]

Blacks have also argued that Jews ought, in the light of their own experience, to speak out more vociferously against the apartheid regime. A member of the African National Congress, Dr. Neo Mnumzama, put it as follows:

> Perhaps the most tragic experience in all of history befell the Jewish people under Hitlerite Nazism. One then wants to conclude that the Jewish people, having gone through that experience, would be in a better position to appreciate the similarities between Nazism and apartheid. We expect them to be in a better position to empathize with the South African people who have to daily endure the tragedy that apartheid visits upon them. It is perhaps the Jewish community of South Africa that one would have expected more than any other community to be most militantly involved in the struggle.[57]

Of course, this view had long been expounded by progressive Jewish youths who had invariably related to apartheid in terms of the Nazi paradigm. Indeed, that paradigm serves as an ultimate evil, one to which blacks can easily relate. It is even hinted that some future government may seek retribution against whites by appealing to the Jewish experience. A foretaste of this thinking emerged recently when Farid Esack, an anti-apartheid activist, defended a militant opponent of apartheid, Harry Gwala, for the latter's allegedly vengeful spirit. "What is it," asked Esack, "that allows Jews to comb the forests of Argentina—and the hamlets of the United Kingdom—for the Nazi criminals but is horrified at Gwala's 'tooth for a tooth.' The logic seems to be that the Jews belong to a 'civilized' world and their murderers to an 'uncivilized' one, whereas in South Africa the murderers belong to a 'civilized' world whilst the victims do not."[58]

The association of South Africa's apartheid policies and the Holocaust has ensured an important place for the Holocaust in the South African consciousness. But even without the apartheid dimension, the South African Jewish identity has been profoundly influenced by the Holocaust. Today, Holocaust memorial services are major features on the Jewish calendar. Intricate ceremonies have been devised that include poetry readings, song singing, and the delivery of keynote addresses, often by a prominent visitor. In addition, Holocaust memorials have been erected in South Africa and in major Jewish centers. Since the late 1980s South African Jews have joined the worldwide pilgrimages to Auschwitz, and in 1988 South African Jews joined world Jewry in commemorating the fiftieth anniversary of Kristallnacht, the Night of the Broken Glass. To mark the event, synagogues kept their lights burning throughout the night. For the occasion a panel of Holocaust survivors in Johannesburg recounted their experiences to an audience of more than four hundred, who listened in horrified fascination. Adult-education Holocaust study programs have been conducted in Johannesburg and Cape Town, in 1983 and 1990, respectively. The 1990 program, run by Dr. Ze'ev Mankowitz of the Hebrew University of Jerusalem, was organized by the Isaac and Jessie Kaplan Centre for Jewish Studies and Research at the University of Cape Town. The six weekly sessions were attended by 350 Jews and gentiles. Sadly, the penultimate lecture was clouded by ugly questions from a "denial" member of the audience.

Unfortunately, such beliefs still survive in South Africa. Indeed, a group of neo-Nazis commemorated the death of Rudolf Hess in 1987. Among those who gave a Nazi salute at the ceremony and sang "Der Gut Kameran" were members of the Afrikaner Weerstandsbeweging. Regrettably, as David Scher explains, "ignorance and gross insensitivity to the nature of the Holocaust has not been confined to the uneducated and benighted."[59] Scher was referring to a student dinner held at a residence of the University of Pretoria whose theme was "A Nazi Victory Feast." The hall was decorated with Nazi emblems, and waiters were dressed in Hitler Jugendbond outfits. "Sieg heil" and other Nazi salutes punctuated the evening. To make matters worse, a number of university officials were present. Very recently, ultra-right-wing individuals exasperated by President Frederik Willem de Klerk's political reforms have vilified Jews and expressed regret that the Final Solution did not succeed.[60]

In the main, South Africa is not experiencing the sort of neo-Nazism that is currently rearing its ugly head in Europe. The lessons of the Jewish tragedy have filtered down to a wide audience. Afrikaner poets such as Lina Spies and I. L. de Villiers have embraced Holocaust themes,[61] and a 1990 editorial in the *Cape Times* entitled "Lessons of the Holocaust" suggests that the lessons of the Jewish tragedy have indeed been absorbed:

> In the presence of survivors of Hitler's death camps, a monument was unveiled at Pinelands Cemetery on Sunday, as Cape Town honoured the memory of six million Jews who died in the Holocaust of 1939–1945. On the same day ceremonies of solemn remembrance were held in many places throughout the world.
>
> It is right and proper that what happened at Auschwitz, Bergen-Belsen, Treblinka, Dachau and other centres of Nazi infamy should never be allowed to fade from human memory. It is not a question of keeping alive a vengeful spirit. On the contrary. The Holocaust was so horrifying in its revelation of evil that there is a fatal inclination to avert the eyes and obliterate the horror.
>
> This kind of totalitarian nightmare can take hold of any society at any time if the conditions are propitious, and if the incipient evil is not recognized and resisted—as took place in Hitler's Germany in the 1930s when the victims were the Jews and many people looked the other way.
>
> In South Africa, as everywhere else, it is as well to be alert for the early warning signal—symptoms of militarism, pathological nationalism and racism—and to act swiftly to prevent the disease taking hold.[62]

NOTES

I wish to acknowledge the University of Cape Town for its financial assistance toward research for this study. I am also grateful to Margo Bastos for her assistance and to Marcia Leveson, Lilian Dubb, and Xavier Piat for their helpful suggestions.

1. For the early history of Jews in South Africa, see Louis Herrman, *A History of the Jews in South Africa from Earliest Times to 1895* (London, 1930), chaps. 1–6; and Israel Abrahams, *The Birth of a Community* (Cape Town, 1955), chap. 1.

2. 1820 Settlers was the name of a settlement scheme designed by the British government to provide a buffer of white settlers on the eastern frontier of the Cape Colony at little expense.

3. *Results of Census. Colony of the Cape of Good Hope, 1875,* G. 42-76 (Cape Town, 1877). A handful of Jews resided in the South African Republic (Transvaal), Natal, and the Orange Free State, future components of a united South Africa.

4. *Johannesburg Gezondheids Comite Sanitaire Departement, Census 15 July 1896* (Johannesburg, 1896).

5. The term "Peruvian" comes from "Peru," probably an acronym for the Polish and Russian Union, a Jewish club established in Kimberley in the 1870s. See Max Sonnenberg, *The Way I Saw It* (Cape Town, 1957), 52. According to Eric Partridge, "Peruvian" was a Transvaal colloquialism for Polish and Russian Jews (*A Dictionary of Slang and Unconventional English* [London, 1961], 620). There is also some evidence to suggest that the term refers to those immigrants who had sojourned in Argentina under Baron de Hirsch's settlement scheme before coming to South Africa. See the *Owl* (Cape Town), February 8, 1901; and *Johannesburg Times,* April 1, 1896.

6. Milton Shain, *Jewry and Cape Society: The Origins and Activities of the Jewish Board of Deputies for the Cape Colony* (Cape Town, 1983), chap. 3.

7. John Atkinson Hobson, *The War in South Africa: Its Causes and Effects* (London, 1900), 189.

8. See Shain, *Jewry and Cape Society,* chap. 2.

9. See Milton Shain, "Hoggenheimer—The Making of a Myth," *Jewish Affairs* 36 (September 1981), 112–16.

10. See Antony Arkin, "Economic Activities,"

in *South African Jewry: A Contemporary Survey,* ed. Marcus Arkin (Cape Town, 1984), 59.

11. For Jewish economic contributions, see Mendel Kaplan, *Jewish Roots in the South African Economy* (Cape Town, 1986).

12. *East London Daily Dispatch,* February 3, 1930.

13. For details, see Michael Cohen, "Anti-Jewish Manifestations in the Union of South Africa during the Nineteen-thirties" (B.A. thesis, University of Cape Town, 1968), 67–69.

14. See Gideon Shimoni, *Jews and Zionism: The South African Experience (1910–1967)* (Cape Town, 1980), 112.

15. T. Dunbar Moodie, *The Rise of Afrikanerdom: Power, Apartheid, and the Afrikaner Civil Religion* (Berkeley and Los Angeles, 1975), 15.

16. *Die Burger,* November 25, 1938, 6.

17. *House of Assembly Debates,* September 4, 1939, 50.

18. See Albrecht Hagemann, "Rassenpolitische Affinität und Machtpolitische Revalität. Das Dritte Reich und die Südafrikansche Union 1933–1945" (Ph.D. thesis, Bielefeld University, West Germany, 1987).

19. For details, see Michael A. Green, "South African Jewish Responses to the Holocaust, 1941–1948" (M.A. thesis, University of South Africa, 1987), chap. 4.

20. See William H. Vatcher, *White Laager: The Rise of Afrikaner Nationalism* (London, 1965), 68–75.

21. Walter Madeley, quoted in *South African Jewish Times,* January 1, 1943, 2.

22. Ibid.

23. For the report, see Arthur Suzman and Dennis Diamond, *Six Million Did Die—The Truth Shall Prevail* (Johannesburg, 1977), app. 4.

24. See Sharon L. Friedman, "Jews, Germans, and Afrikaners—Nationalist Press Reactions to the Final Solution" (B.A. thesis, University of Cape Town, 1982), chap. 4.

25. *Cape Times,* November 23, 1945, 6.

26. See Green, "South African Jewish Responses," 262.

27. Shimoni, *Jews and Zionism,* 197.

28. The date April 22 was appointed by the first Israeli Knesset in preference to April 19, the official date of the Warsaw Ghetto Uprising, so that the commemoration would never fall during the Passover period.

29. For further details, see Joseph Sherman, ed., *From a Land Far Off* (Cape Town, 1987), 182–87.

30. See Joseph Sherman, "'Singing with the Silence': The Poetry of David Fram," *Jewish Affairs* 44 (September–October 1988), 39–44.

31. Harold Serebro, *The Devil and His Servant* (London, 1984).

32. "Children's Lesson for Day of Mourning," *Jewish Affairs* 10 (March 1955), 55–57.

33. See, e.g., Peter Abrahams, *The Path of Thunder* (London, 1952), 88–89, and, most recently, Achmed Essop's short story "The Metamorphosis" in his collection *Noorjahan and Other Stories* (Johannesburg, 1990). Jewish writers such as Dan Jacobson have also dealt obliquely with the Holocaust. See Dan Jacobson, *The Beginners* (London, 1966).

34. Document 66, "A Declaration to the Nations of the World," statement of the Non-European Unity Movement, signed by the Rev. Z. R. Mahabane, Dr. G. H. Gool, and E. C. Roberts, July 1945, in *From Protest to Challenge: A Documentary History of African Politics in South Africa, 1882–1964,* ed. Thomas Karis and Gwendolen M. Carter, vol. 2, *Hope and Challenge, 1935–1952,* by Thomas Karis (Stanford, 1973), 357–61.

35. Brian Bunting, *The Rise of the South African Reich* (London, 1964).

36. Bernard Moses Casper, *A Decade with South African Jewry* (Cape Town, 1972), 20.

37. *Sunday Times* (Johannesburg), December 21, 1975, 9.

38. *Rand Daily Mail,* December 22, 1975, 3.

39. Arthur R. Butz, *The Hoax of the Twentieth Century* (Richmond, Surrey, 1975); S. E. D. Brown, review of *The Hoax of the Twentieth Century,* by Arthur R. Butz, *South African Observer,* September, 1976.

40. Richard Harwood [Richard Verrall], *Did Six Million Really Die?—The Truth at Last* (Richmond, Surrey, 1974). Interestingly, Verrall was the son of a British businessman with extensive South African interests.

41. Suzman and Diamond, *Six Million Did Die.* The book came out in a second edition in 1978.

42. *Sunday Times Magazine* (Johannesburg), May 28, 1978, 2.

43. *Die Beeld,* May 17, 1976, 6.

44. Brian Barrow, "Ban Strains TV Integrity," *Cape Times,* May 17, 1976, 3.

45. *Cape Argus,* May 17, 1976, 10.

46. Dr. Louw Alberts, quoted in the *Star,* May 19, 1976, 3.

47. *Tempo,* May 21, 1976, 6.

48. *Die Afrikaner,* May 21, 1976, 4.

49. *South African Observer,* June 1976, 3.

50. Ibid., 7.

51. *Die Vaderland,* May 19, 1976, 4.

52. E. H. W. Lategan and A. J. de Kock, *History*

in Perspective for Standard 10 (Johannesburg, 1978), 34.

53. Student Holocaust Interviewing Project (SHIP), pamphlet, ca. 1989.

54. See, e.g., Sipho Mzimela, *Apartheid: South African Nazism* (New York, 1983).

55. Archbishop Desmond Tutu, quoted in Tzippi Hoffman and Alan Fischer, *The Jews of South Africa: What Future?* (Johannesburg, 1988), 11.

56. Percy Qobosa, quoted in ibid., 85.

57. Dr. Neo Mnumzama, quoted in ibid., 75.

58. Farid Esack, quoted in *Cape Times,* August 21, 1990, 6.

59. David M. Scher, "Defaming the Holocaust," *Kleio* 21 (1989), 24.

60. *Sunday Star,* February 11, 1990, 16.

61. See Lina Spies, "Lied van die Kinders," and I. L. de Villiers, "Dietrich Bonhoeffer: Brief aan homself," in *Groot Verseboek,* ed. D. J. Opperman (Cape Town, 1980), 470, 483.

62. "Lessons of the Holocaust," editorial, *Cape Times,* April 24, 1990, 6.

NORTH AMERICA

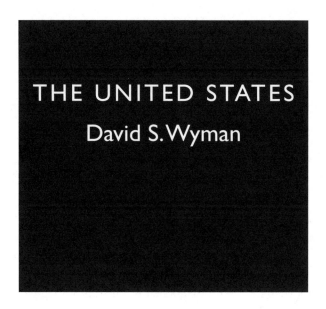

THE UNITED STATES
David S. Wyman

BEFORE THE HOLOCAUST

The first Jews to settle in what is now the United States arrived in New Amsterdam in September 1654. This group of twenty-three people had been part of a Dutch West India Company settlement in Recife, Brazil, which had been forced to leave when the Portuguese captured the area earlier that year. During the next decade the Jews of New Amsterdam never numbered more than fifty; nevertheless, the congregation they established remains in existence today. By 1664, when the English took over New Amsterdam (renaming it New York), the Jewish community there had nearly disappeared.[1]

During the century that followed, the economic opportunities and the religious toleration that prevailed in most of England's American colonies encouraged a small flow of Jewish immigration. By the time of the American Revolution about twenty-five hundred Jews lived in these English colonies, in settlements from New York to Newport, Philadelphia, Charleston, Savannah, and other locations. In a wider society whose economy revolved mainly around farming and the work of skilled artisans, a majority of the Jewish settlers were engaged in trade, some of it transatlantic. The Jews in colonial America were among the first Jews in the modern world to exist in an environment of toleration. Though generally excluded from voting and holding office until after the American Revolution, they interacted freely with the other colonists, carried on business with them, occasionally intermarried, and met with little anti-Semitism and almost no anti-Semitic violence.[2]

Between the American Revolution and the mid-1820s the American Jewish population grew to about six thousand. While substantial numbers were merchants, Jews began to turn also to banking and industrial undertakings as well as to law, medicine, and other professions. In these years Jews pressed for, and by 1826 obtained, full civil equality, including the right to vote and to hold office, in all but three states. Anti-Semitism remained at a very low level in the early United States, bearing out President George Washington's assertion of American tolerance in his letter to the Newport Jewish congregation in 1790: "The government of the United States . . . gives to bigotry no sanction, to persecution no assistance."[3]

What is generally termed the "second migration" of Jews to the United States lasted from roughly 1820 to 1880. In those years American Jewry increased from a small group to one of the major Jewish communities in the world, numbering close to 280,000. Until the 1820s, probably a majority of Jewish immigrants were of Sephardic (Spanish and Portuguese) background, though a great many were of Ashkenazic (German and Polish) origin. The largest part of the second migration came from German areas, though the influx also included many thousands of Jews from Eastern Europe, especially after 1870. The main reasons for the extensive migration, which peaked in the 1850s, were the political repression that followed the failed revolutions of 1848, an economic downturn in Europe in the 1850s, and particularly the open doors of a free and rapidly expanding United States. Much of the second migration flowed to New York City, Philadelphia, and Baltimore. By 1880 about one-quarter of American Jews lived in New York City, and another quarter lived elsewhere in the North Atlantic states. But a major part of the second migration settled in cities not located on the East Coast, cities such as Cleveland, Chicago, Detroit, Milwaukee, St. Louis, and even, with the Gold Rush, San Francisco.[4]

Many of the newcomers were craftsmen, such as tailors and carpenters, who continued to utilize their skills in the United States. Most American Jewish workers in this period, however, were involved in some form of commerce. A large proportion of them were peddlers, who filled an important economic need because of the scarcity of retail outlets everywhere except in the large cities. Many progressed from foot peddler to horse-and-wagon peddler to small shopkeeper. Some went on to become large merchandisers. Jews participated in the great economic boom that followed the Civil War, many as merchants, others as manufacturers and bankers.[5]

With the German Jews came the first ordained rabbis to serve American congregations. Most of the rabbis were adherents of Reform Judaism. Their efforts to harmonize Judaism with modern rationalism and with American life matched tendencies already under way in the Jewish community, tendencies aimed at simplifying religious observance and bringing it closer to Protestant forms. The result was a swift expansion of Reform Judaism in the United States in the 1860s and 1870s as the great majority of congregations adopted that form. This was also a time that saw a significant increase in synagogue construction.[6]

In the years from 1820 to 1880 American Jews continued to enjoy full rights and opportunities. There was not much anti-Semitism, and when bigotry did arise, Jews could fight it openly, sometimes with Christian help and always with the realization that it would receive no support from the government. One cloud did appear, however; it arose out of Jewish success: exclusion of Jews from elite hotels, resorts, social clubs, and other institutions of high society commenced in the 1870s.[7]

The German migration had virtually ended by 1880. It was immediately succeeded by the "third migration," a massive flow of Jews from Eastern Europe set off by worsening economic conditions along with a sequence of other disastrous events. In March 1881 Czar Alexander II was assassinated. The Russian government, as well as the general population, blamed the Jews. The responses were pogroms, which continued into the twentieth century, and laws aimed at removing Jews from economic and civil life in Russia. The numbers of Russian Jews coming to the United States increased rapidly in the last two decades of the nineteenth century and expanded again with the terrible Kishinev pogrom of 1903 and the pogroms that followed the Russian revolution of 1905. The influx was cut sharply by World War I. It began to reach high levels again soon after the war, only to be slowed nearly to a halt by the U.S. immigration restriction act of 1924. Between 1881 and 1930 more than 2.5 million Jews immigrated to the United States from Eastern Europe, giving the United States the largest Jewish population in the world. Even so, Jews constituted only about 10 percent of the total immigration during that period, a time that witnessed the historic movement of many millions of Europeans to the United States.[8]

In contrast to their German predecessors, most of the Jewish immigrants from Eastern Europe massed in slums in large cities, especially on New York's Lower East Side but also on Chicago's West Side, in South Philadelphia, in the North End of Boston, and in other densely populated areas. Large numbers of them made a meager living as laborers in the needle trades and other light manufacturing. Many of the rest earned a marginal subsistence from peddling and pushcart merchandising. Despite the poverty, these immigrants had very high aspirations. Most hoped eventually to own a business, however small. The children attended the public schools. Most worked hard in pursuit of Americanization and economic and social improvement. Many went to college. In just one generation a large proportion of the Eastern European Jews left the working class for white-collar and professional careers. By 1930 Jews played significant roles in several areas of the economy, including clothing manufacturing; the retailing of dry goods, furniture, and clothing; real estate; and the motion picture industry.[9]

The Eastern European Jews who had not become secularized were Orthodox. Their children, however, found traditional Orthodoxy foreign to their lives in the new land, and they found Reform Judaism irrelevant. They were leaving not only the synagogues but Judaism itself. In response, Orthodoxy's Jewish Theological Seminary was restructured in 1901 to adjust Orthodoxy to the American scene. It began to train Eastern European Jews to be English-speaking rabbis who combined modern training and approaches with many of the traditional rituals and practices. Though it was not its intention, this adaptation rapidly led to a separate movement in American Jewish life: Conservative Judaism. As one scholar summarized it, "The Conservative movement . . . captured the attention and loyalty of the largest portion of the children of the immigrants as they matured, acculturated, and moved up" because it offered them a Judaism that was "far more traditional than Reform, yet significantly more American and modern than the Orthodoxy of their parents." By 1935, it was estimated that 1,000,000 Jews identified themselves as Orthodox, 300,000 as Conservative, and 200,000 as Reform.[10]

In the years from 1880 to 1930, anti-Semitism was not a major problem, but it was definitely part of the American scene. During this period racial anti-Semitism became an important factor in the move to close America's doors to large-scale immigration. In the late nineteenth century, social scientists advanced supposedly objective theories concerning the differences between races and the determinant effects that race had on individual human beings. The theories that gained greatest currency in the United States maintained that southern and eastern Europeans, and Jews especially, belonged to races that were physically, mentally, and morally inferior to the Anglo-Saxon, Teutonic, and Nordic peoples of northern and western Europe who had settled America. Since the vast immigration that commenced in the 1880s consisted mostly of Catholics and Jews from southern and eastern Europe (Italy, Greece, Russia, Poland, etc.), numbers of Americans viewed the newcomers, with their high birthrates, as threatening to overwhelm the nation with masses of undesirable people. These views, which were especially strong among old-stock Protestant Americans, helped to fuel a growing anti-immigration movement in the early 1900s.[11]

Racism was not the only force involved, but it was of crucial importance in bringing about the enactment of the National Origins Immigration Act of 1924, which, when fully in force in 1929, set a maximum of 150,000 immigrants per year. By way of comparison, during the peak period of immigration (1905–14) an average of more than 1 million had entered each year. The new allotment of 150,000 per year was parceled out according to a quota system that assigned only 15 percent of the total to people from southern and eastern Europe (23,000 per year) and 85 percent to people from countries of northern and western Europe. Despite efforts by proponents of the legislation to disguise the fact, there is no question that anti-Catholicism and anti-Semitism were importantly involved in the decision to restrict immigration and in the final apportionment of the quotas.[12]

Along with the spread of racial anti-Semitism there were other manifestations of anti-Jewish attitudes in these years. The ugliest specific episode was the lynching of Leo Frank in Georgia in 1915. Far less vicious, but nevertheless increasingly pervasive and troubling, were several forms of discrimination. The earlier exclusion of Jews from clubs, hotels, and resorts continued. In the 1920s, several elite universities, among them Harvard, Yale, and Princeton, established quotas as a means of decreasing what had become fairly large Jewish enrollments. (Enrollment of Jews at Harvard, for example, fell from almost 22 percent in 1922 to 10 percent in 1928.) By the mid-1930s, quotas were prevalent throughout the nation's private colleges and medical schools. Jews were also excluded from some residential areas. They were discriminated against in much of the business world, from the secretarial and clerical levels to the top, as was openly displayed in employment advertisements in newspapers.[13]

To some degree, the growth of anti-Semitism was reflected by the Ku Klux Klan, which came to prominence in the 1920s. The Klan was anti-Catholic, anti-Jewish, and anti-immigrant, as well as anti-black, and it was strong in much of the North as well as in the South. Actually, however, the Klan paid only limited attention to the Jews. It had little support in the areas where Jews were most populous. Furthermore, it lost most of its influence by 1925.[14]

The most blatant anti-Semitism of the 1920s appeared in the *Dearborn (Mich.) Independent,* a newspaper owned by Henry Ford. The *Independent* published a long sequence of anti-Semitic articles as well as a serialization of *The Protocols of the Elders of Zion,* a faked document that supposedly proved the existence of a Jewish conspiracy to take control of the world. It required six years, three lawsuits, and a boycott of Ford products by both Jews and non-Jews to stop this dissemination of hatred and calumny. Finally, in 1927, Ford closed down the *Dearborn Independent* and issued a public statement retracting all his charges against Jews and apologizing to the Jewish people. By then, of course, Ford had spread a large amount of hate literature that helped lay the groundwork for the high level of anti-Semitism that developed in the United States in the 1930s and early 1940s.[15]

Although anti-Semitism increased in the United States in the years between 1880 and 1930, it is important not to overemphasize its extent. As one historian of the American Jewish experience observed, not one pogrom occurred, no political party of any importance supported anti-Semitism, the Catholic Church and mainline Protestantism condemned it, "and the pluralistic society produced and sustained a tolerance which would not permit excesses. Its chief expression remained in Jewish exclusion from significant aspects of American life."[16]

A crucial part of American Jewish life in the twentieth century has been the work of the several defense and overseas aid organizations. Some were formed to help Jews in other parts of the world by providing material aid, support for their rights under foreign rule, or assistance with migration. Others were established to counter anti-Semitism in the United States. A few were involved in multiple areas of action.

By 1902 three small organizations had merged to form the Hebrew Sheltering and Immigrant Aid Society (HIAS). This agency, established by American Jews of Eastern European origin, helped newly arrived immigrants comply with the immigration procedures, found lodging for them, and provided skills training, an employment agency, and other adjustment services. HIAS played a major part in the settlement of Jewish immigrants through the period of heaviest immigration and has continued its work up to the present.[17]

The earliest of the major defense organizations, and long the predominant one, was the American Jewish Committee. Founded in 1906 in response to the severe persecutions in Russia and the growing call for immigration restriction in the United States, its mission was to protect Jewish civil and religious rights throughout the world. Because it was dominated by a small, self-appointed group of very influential German Jews, it was frequently under attack from other, more broad-based Jewish organizations. It preferred a restrained, quiet approach and often worked through contacts with leading non-Jewish Americans and high officials of the government. It fought immigration restriction. It challenged American anti-Semitism, largely through education and dissemination of information about Jews. It sought to alleviate the Russian government's anti-Semitic policies by applying what influence it could on U.S. diplomatic policy.[18]

B'nai B'rith, a Jewish fraternal order that dated back to 1843, had, along with its mutual aid and social fellowship functions, involved itself from time to time in issues of Jewish rights. In 1913 the Anti-Defamation League was formed as part of B'nai B'rith. It rapidly became an important Jewish defense organization and a leader in the fight against anti-Semitism in the United States.[19]

World War I brought unprecedented disaster to heavily Jewish areas of Eastern Europe as the German and Russian armies moved back and forth, time and again, over the region. The American Jewish Committee succeeded in late 1914 in uniting the several American Jewish groups that had formed to collect funds to help the victims. The new organization, named the American Jewish Joint Distribution Committee (JDC), raised and distributed millions of dollars to aid Jews during the war. The urgent need for the JDC continued with the postwar chaos in Europe and then with the succession of emergencies that have confronted Jews around the world in the years since. Throughout that time the JDC has carried out its mission with the respect and financial backing of all sectors of American Jewry.[20]

During World War I, American Jewish leaders recognized the importance of sending a Jewish delegation to the peace conference to attempt to secure political and civil rights for the Jews of postwar Europe. At the same time, there was increasing support for formation of a more widely representative, more democratic organization to deal with this issue than the elitist American Jewish Committee. In 1916 representatives of a large number of Jewish organizations met to decide on the goals of what was by then called the American Jewish Congress. The American Jewish Committee, realizing that it could not stop the congress movement, agreed to support it on the condition that the congress would address itself only to the postwar peace conference and then dissolve. It was also agreed that the congress's delegation to the peace conference would press two issues: the protection of the Jews in the new states to be formed in Europe and the establishment of a Jewish national home to receive those Jews who wished to leave Europe. In mid-1917 American Jews elected nearly four hundred delegates to the American Jewish Congress. The congress officially convened in December 1918, elected officers, and chose a delegation to the Paris Peace Conference that reflected nearly all elements in American Jewry. At the peace conference the delegation succeeded in obtaining guarantees of civil rights for Jews (and other minorities as well) in the several newly formed European nations. Furthermore, the peace conference granted the mandate over Palestine to Great Britain, which had already pledged its support for a Jewish national home there. With its work completed, the delegation returned home and the American Jewish Congress disbanded.[21]

In 1922, however, the American Jewish Congress was revived and became a permanent Jewish defense organization, a mass-membership body made up largely of middle- and lower-middle-class Jews of Eastern European origin. It was Zionist in outlook and much more activist in approach than the American Jewish Committee. Another defense organization, the Jewish Labor Committee, came on the scene in

1934, to join in the struggle against Nazism. Representative of the American Jewish labor-union movement and some Jewish socialist groups, it had close ties with the American Federation of Labor. The Jewish Labor Committee was oriented toward democratic socialism and was for the most part anti-Zionist.[22]

Zionism, the movement for a Jewish state, emerged in Europe in the 1890s and took organized form at the first Zionist Congress, held in Basel in 1897. One year later the American Zionist organization was founded. But during the next several years it gained little following; by 1912 it had only 13,000 members. Many Jews, especially those of German origin, rejected Zionism as a compromise of their American citizenship and a possible indicator of dual loyalty. Between 1914 and 1919 the picture changed dramatically as American Zionism was transformed into a large, well-organized movement with 180,000 members. One vital reason for the growth was the leadership provided to the movement by Louis Brandeis from 1914 until 1916, when he was appointed to the U.S. Supreme Court. Brandeis brought efficiency to the Zionist movement's administration; but more importantly, his own stature and prestige brought respectability to the Zionist concept and effectively undercut the dual-loyalty issue. Also important for the expansion of the Zionist movement were the momentum and success of the American Jewish Congress, an undertaking in which Zionists played a pivotal role. A third significant factor was the British government's issuance in 1917 of the Balfour Declaration, which pledged British support for the establishment of a Jewish national home in Palestine. That commitment and the decision by the Paris Peace Conference to place Palestine under British control meant that the Zionist goal had become a real possibility.[23]

Yet only two years after the peace conference the Zionist movement split apart, its leadership bitterly divided over procedures, personalities, and ideology. By 1923 membership had dwindled to 15,000, and the movement remained weak into the 1930s. During the 1920s, American Zionism emphasized the physical and economic development of the Jewish settlements in Palestine and their importance as a place of refuge for Jews who were confronted again with severe anti-Semitism in Eastern Europe. Political Zionism (the drive for Jewish statehood) was to be held in abeyance indefinitely, pending the economic buildup. This emphasis made possible a degree of cooperation from "non-Zionists," people who opposed actual Jewish statehood but agreed that Palestine's Jewish settlements and economic capabilities should be expanded in order to provide an asylum for persecuted Jews in Europe and elsewhere. The Zionist movement made some gains in the 1930s as more and more American Jews recognized the importance of Palestine as a refuge for Jews fleeing Nazi persecution. By 1939 the Zionist Organization of America had increased to 44,000 members. But 1939 was also the year that the British government, breaking the pledge made in the Balfour Declaration, issued the White Paper that restricted Jewish immigration to Palestine to a maximum of 15,000 per year. This happened just as the need for Jews to leave Germany became extreme.[24]

The World Reacts to the Holocaust

The American response to the Holocaust fell far short of living up to the nation's underlying human and democratic values. In the pre-extermination years (1933–40) many hundreds of thousands of European Jews could have reached safe haven if the United States and other countries had been willing to open their doors. The United States could have set the example by a temporary widening of its immigration quotas. Instead, even the small quotas that were legally available were not allowed to be filled, except during a single two-year period. In the extermination years (1941–45) immigration was made even more difficult. And not until January 1944, fourteen months after it had incontrovertible evidence that genocide was occurring, did the U.S. government begin to take even limited steps toward rescue.[25]

The three main factors that lay behind America's failed response were the Great Depression, nativism, and anti-Semitism. In 1933, at the worst point in the Depression, unemployment in the United States reached 25 percent. By 1937 it was still at 15 percent. And in 1937–38 a recession occurred within the Depression, with the jobless rate rising to 18 percent. The decade of the 1930s was one of insecurity, fear, and anxiety. Many Americans worried that foreigners would come in and take their jobs. Even during World War II, when war production eliminated unemployment, there was widespread apprehension that the Depression would return with the end of hostilities. The argument that immigrants were consumers as well as workers and thus provided at least as many jobs as they took made little headway, though that is what had happened in the years of large-scale immigration.[26]

Nativist attitudes, which had run very high in the 1920s, remained prevalent in the 1930s. A great many Americans disliked foreigners of any kind and wanted to end or greatly cut the small flow of immigration that still existed. The issue was partly one of job competition, but many Americans also harbored fears about the cultural impact foreigners had on the United States. "America for the Americans" was their slogan.[27]

Anti-Semitism, already on the rise in the 1920s, increased significantly in the 1930s and reached its peak in American history in the late 1930s and early 1940s. The earlier types of discrimination continued, as did widely accepted views of the Jews as an undesirable race. Another very strong force in those years was a political anti-Semitism that drew on the fraudulent *Protocols of the Elders of Zion,* the emergence of the Soviet Union, and the growing strength of the international Communist movement since World War I. Anti-Semites now argued that there was a world Jewish conspiracy that secretly wielded vast international economic and political power. These "international Jews" supposedly manipulated the capitalist system through their stranglehold on international finance and simultaneously controlled the Soviet Union as well as the international Communist movement. Their alleged objective was to increase their power to the point where they could rule the world. While the theory as a whole was too extreme for very wide acceptance, parts of this mythology spread through American society: for instance, that the Jews were Communists and that they were at the same time capitalist manipulators intentionally imposing the Depression on the country.[28]

Although there can be no complete explanation for the increase in American anti-Semitism in this period, it is evident that the Great Depression was a central factor. Anxieties resulting from years of widespread unemployment led many to hunt for explanations, to ask who was to blame. The underlying negative image of Jews, deeply ingrained in Western society over the centuries, offered an answer to many Americans. The spread of the *Protocols* through the United States in the 1920s reinforced the tendency. The impulse was furthered by anti-Semitic propaganda that Nazi Germany circulated throughout the world.[29]

Anti-Semitic mass movements and demagogues spread fear and hatred throughout the United States. Over one hundred anti-Semitic organizations appeared, led by the Silver Shirts, the German-American Bund (American Nazis), and the Defenders of the Christian Faith. By far the most influential among the anti-Semitic demagogues was the Catholic priest Father Charles Coughlin, whose weekly radio broadcasts reached several million Americans. Opinion polls from 1938 through 1944 indicated that about 33 percent of the American public was anti-Semitic. Twelve percent of those polled were prepared to support an anti-Semitic campaign, and an additional 20 percent expressed sympathy for such a movement. During the war years the rhetoric of hate turned into violence in a few northeastern cities, where there were several episodes of teenage gangs beating Jewish schoolchildren.[30]

Troubling though the anti-Semitism of the thirties and forties was to American Jews, those who were hurt most by it were the Jews of Europe. The anti-Semitism of the 1920s had helped to close America's doors. The anti-Semitism of the thirties and forties was crucial in keeping them closed. However, despite the strength of the anti-Semites, their victory in the struggle concerning American refugee policy was not a foregone conclusion. The opinion polls also showed that if a campaign had been launched against Jews, almost one-third of Americans would have actively opposed it. Clearly, a reservoir of sympathy for endangered Jews existed in American society. But almost no leadership emerged to try to convert this concern into political pressure. The president and most of the rest of the political leadership made no effort to mobilize it. Very few Christian church leaders called for action to help the European Jews. Almost none of the mass media offered such leadership; in fact most of the media failed even to bring the Holocaust to the public's attention. Jewish leaders called on non-Jewish America for help, but few listened and even fewer acted.[31]

Almost as soon as Hitler and the Nazis took power in Germany in early 1933, they began their assault on the Jews. The first steps involved restriction of economic activity and educational opportunity, followed in 1935 by the Nuremberg Laws, which ended the right of Jews to vote or hold office. Some violent attacks also took place, though this was not yet a government policy. The aim of the persecution was to make life for Jews in Germany so difficult that they would emigrate. By the end of 1937, however, only 135,000—about 25 percent—had left. The doors of the outside world were not open to very many Jewish immigrants. Moreover, many German

Jews still did not believe that a modern, highly cultured society such as Germany would permit such persecution to continue indefinitely.[32]

Instead of any alleviation, 1938 brought a sharp increase in persecution. In March Germany absorbed Austria, and in September it took over part of Czechoslovakia. The German government's anti-Semitic policies of the previous five years were immediately imposed in these newly occupied areas, precipitating a rush of Jews attempting to flee. Growing persecution in Germany itself during 1938 came to a climax in November with the extreme violence of Kristallnacht, rapidly followed by drastic economic decrees. A huge fine was assessed on the Jews, and all remaining Jewish-owned businesses had to be transferred to non-Jewish hands. With almost no economic base remaining, and with large-scale violence now a constant possibility, Jews could no longer safely stay in Germany.[33]

The American response to the increasing persecution of the Jews was affected primarily by the immigration-quota law. The German quota was 25,957 per year. In 1930, with the onset of the Great Depression and rising unemployment, President Herbert Hoover ordered the use of all immigration quotas to be cut to 10 percent. Franklin D. Roosevelt succeeded Hoover in 1933. As the persecution worsened, Roosevelt gradually relaxed the restriction on the German quota, and by 1937 about 50 percent of the quota was available for use. In early 1938 the German annexation of Austria and the panicked rush of Jews to leave there, along with the increasing level of persecution in Germany, made it clear to the world that the refugee problem had turned into a major crisis. At that point Roosevelt opened the quotas for full use. They remained open for two years, a period that proved to be the high point of American generosity. It should not be concluded, however, that opening the quotas meant that any very great immigration would occur. The German, Austrian, and Czechoslovak quotas totaled 30,244 per year.[34]

At about the same time that he made the quotas fully available, President Roosevelt initiated a conference of thirty-two nations to address the refugee crisis. The American objective, as shown by State Department records, was "to get out in front" of expected pressures on the United States to take world leadership on the issue and to spread the responsibility as widely as possible. The conference took place in July 1938 at Evian, France. With the United States and Britain setting the example, nation after nation explained that it could accept few additional Jews. The main outcome at Evian was that the outside world made it clear that its doors were virtually closed.[35]

In November 1938, Kristallnacht occurred, and the pressure to leave Germany became intense. The world's leaders, with Roosevelt in the forefront, condemned the violent assault but did not open their doors. When President Roosevelt was asked whether he would recommend modification of the immigration laws to help the refugees, he replied, "That is not in contemplation; we have the quota system." He did take one very helpful step, however. He ordered that German refugees already in the United States on temporary visitor visas could remain indefinitely, thus providing safe haven to about 15,000 people.[36]

One result of Kristallnacht was a rising concern among some Americans, both

Jews and non-Jews, about the plight of the many thousands of Jewish children trapped in Germany. Because the quotas were completely filled, the Americans who wanted to help called for legislation permitting 20,000 German refugee children to enter the United States outside the quota. This was to be a one-time exception, not a permanent change in the immigration quotas. The plan was introduced in Congress in early 1939 as the Wagner-Rogers Children's Bill. The legislation received no support from the Roosevelt administration, and it failed even to reach the floor of Congress. Although seldom openly voiced, anti-Semitism was clearly the central factor in the defeat of the proposal. This was pointed out at the time by many observers, and it was proven one year later when Great Britain came under heavy bombardment by German aircraft. This time the American public urged action to bring British children across to safety, and Congress rushed through legislation enabling an unlimited number of British boys and girls to enter the United States. The difference was obvious: the German children were mostly Jewish, while the British children were virtually all Christian. Fewer than a thousand came, though, because the British government changed its original plan and decided to keep the children in Britain.[37]

While the Wagner-Rogers Children's Bill was struggling in Congress, the episode of the steamship *St. Louis* once more illustrated the closed doors. The *St. Louis* left Germany for Cuba in May 1939. When it reached Havana, more than 900 of the refugees on board were forbidden to land; the Cuban government had canceled their permits. The *St. Louis* sailed the coasts of Cuba and Florida for a week. Pleas were made to the Cuban government and to President Roosevelt. But the doors remained shut, and the *St. Louis* and its passengers returned to Europe.[38]

In the months of desperation that followed Kristallnacht the Wagner-Rogers Bill and the voyage of the *St. Louis* were not the only indicators of a world that had no room for the Jews. Also in the spring of 1939 Great Britain, which controlled Palestine under a League of Nations mandate, acceded to Arab pressures and severely reduced Jewish immigration to the area, limiting it to 15,000 per year. Actually, the British did not permit even that small quota to be fully met.[39]

One year later, in May and June 1940, Hitler's war machine swept across the Low Countries and France. Thousands of refugees, including Jews and political anti-Nazis, fled before the Germans and reached a precarious and temporary safety in the semi-autonomous Vichy sector of France. The political refugees faced immediate danger because the Vichy authorities were gradually rounding them up to turn them over to the Germans and likely death. Many of these refugees were intellectual and cultural leaders—writers, artists, labor leaders, clergy. Some were Jews, some non-Jews. Responding to urging by Eleanor Roosevelt, the American Federation of Labor, and some members of his administration, President Roosevelt agreed to a small program to save some of these people. Carefully selected political and intellectual refugees were issued temporary-visitor visas to the United States. Visitor visas were used because the regular quotas were still full and booked far ahead, while there were no numerical limits on visitor visas. Obviously, the regulations were stretched. These refugees were not really visitors; they would not be going home for a long time, if ever. About four thousand refugees were cleared for the special visas, but only two thousand actually received them and came to the United States. The other two thousand were blocked because just as the special visa program was getting under way, in June 1940, a stringent new policy on all immigration was emerging in the State Department.[40]

During the spring of 1940 a near hysteria swept the United States concerning the threat of Nazi spies' and saboteurs' infiltrating the country. It was fueled by rumors that the shockingly rapid defeat of France had been importantly abetted by such internal subversion. The American media burst with stories of "Trojan Horses," "enemies within our gates," and "Hitler's slave spies in America." The threat of subversion was, of course, a legitimate concern. Care had to be taken to keep Nazi agents and collaborators out. But instead of adding reasonable screening precautions to the immigration procedures, the State Department greatly exaggerated the problem and used it as a device to cut the use of the quotas in half. In view of the anti-immigration, anti-alien, and anti-Semitic attitudes current in the State Department, it is evident that the subversion issue was not the only factor behind the new policy.[41]

Since his appointment as assistant secretary of state in early 1940, Breckinridge Long had been in charge of refugee policy. Long was virulently anti-alien and, if not anti-Semitic, very close to it. He kept President Roosevelt posted on his policies, and the president approved or at least accepted the steps that Long took. In an internal State Department memorandum in June 1940 Long outlined the methods used in implementing the drastic reduction of immigration: "We can delay and effectively stop for a temporary period of indefinite length the number of immigrants into the United States. We could do this by simply advising our consuls to put every obstacle in the way and to require additional evidence and to resort to various administrative advices which would postpone and postpone and postpone the granting of the visas." The policy change was kept secret, but within weeks refugee aid organizations in the United States realized what had happened. They protested to President Roosevelt, to no avail.[42]

The 50 percent cut in immigration in mid-1940 was not the last of Long's changes. In the months that followed, he and the State Department concluded that there was increasing danger of foreign agents' entering the United States disguised as refugees. In July 1941 Long tightened visa procedures again and added a complicated, slow-moving review process through which all applications had to pass. Use of the quotas dropped to 25 percent. This time the State Department made the new procedures public. There were many protests. A small group of distinguished Americans met with President Roosevelt and requested changes, but the new policy remained in place.[43]

In the summer of 1941, as the new American visa policy took effect, the German policy of forced emigration of the Jews was about to change to one of physical extermination. With the German invasion of the Soviet Union in June 1941, special mobile killing units (*Einsatzgruppen*) operating directly behind the front lines began systematically to destroy the hundreds of thousands of Jews in the newly conquered areas. For the most part, the method was mass gunfire, carried out at the sides of ditches. By the end of 1942 the *Einsatzgruppen* had killed more than 1.3 million Jews in eastern Poland, the Baltic States, and the western Soviet Union. The decision to extend the genocide policy to all the European Jews was probably reached during the summer of 1941, certainly by October 1941. To kill the Jews outside the Eastern European regions where the *Einsatzgruppen* operated, six killing centers with large gas chambers were brought into operation by spring 1942. In the next three years about 3 million Jews from across Europe were deported, mostly via freight train, to the killing centers to be put to death in the gas chambers.[44]

For many months, only scattered information about the mass killings arrived in the West. But by August 1942 fairly conclusive evidence of systematic annihilation had reached the State Department. By late November 1942 the State Department had obtained enough additional information that it was willing to authorize Rabbi Stephen Wise, the foremost American Jewish leader of the time, to make the dreadful truth public. The news about the extermination, now amply documented and confirmed, received only minor attention in the American mass media. This pattern continued throughout the war, making it difficult for those who advocated governmental rescue action to build public support for it.[45]

On December 17, 1942, Great Britain, the United States, the Soviet Union, and eight other nations issued the Allied War Crimes Declaration. The declaration condemned Germany's policy of extermination of the Jews and pledged that the perpetrators would be brought to justice. But despite their condemnation, neither the British Foreign Office nor the American State Department was willing to attempt to rescue Jews. The British recognized that any significant flow of Jews out of Axis Europe would place great pressure on them to reverse their policy of tightly restricting Jewish immigration to Palestine, a policy they were adamantly unwilling to modify. The State Department also feared a large-scale exodus of Jews from Nazi Europe because that would put pressure on the United States to open its doors to some extent. For both governments, the real policy, though unannounced, was the avoidance of rescue.[46]

Despite limited coverage by the news media, information about the mass killing of the Jews circulated in the United States and Great Britain from November 1942 on. In Britain, Christian church leaders and many members of Parliament joined Jews in calling for rescue action. Some pressures for governmental rescue steps also arose in the United States. For a few months the effort for American government action was led by the Joint Emergency Committee on European Jewish Affairs (JEC), a council of several major Jewish organizations, including the American Jewish Committee, the American Jewish Congress, B'nai B'rith, the Jewish Labor Committee, the ultra-Orthodox Agudat Israel of America, and the Emergency Committee for Zionist Affairs. The JEC developed eleven specific rescue proposals and brought them to public attention through a series of forty mass meetings held in twenty states during the spring of 1943. The committee sought help from sympathetic members of Congress. It worked hard to persuade the State Department to give serious attention to the eleven-point rescue program, especially the parts concerning (1) acceptance of refugees into the United States, Palestine, and other Allied and neutral countries; (2) approaches to Germany and other Axis governments to release the Jews; and (3) organization of a system, working through neutral agencies such as the International Red Cross, to feed Jews who were unable to get out of Axis Europe.[47]

In a stratagem aimed at undermining the pressures for action, representatives of the British Foreign Office and the State Department met for twelve days at Bermuda in April 1943. The ostensible purpose of the conference was to look into ways to rescue the Jews who could still be saved. The findings of the Bermuda Conference were kept secret, but the diplomats announced that several recommendations for action had been sent on to the two governments. In reality, the Bermuda Conference recommended almost nothing in the way of rescue proposals. Nevertheless, its real objective had been accomplished: it had succeeded in dampening the pressures for action by giving the appearance of planning steps to rescue Jews. The Jewish leadership, however, was not deceived. The Joint Emergency Committee understood what had actually occurred at Bermuda and was devastated by the unmistakable demonstration of indifference by the two great democracies. The JEC, its hopes smashed, never recovered its former momentum.[48]

Despite the impact of the Bermuda Conference, the struggle for American governmental action persisted. By summer 1943 the main effort had shifted to a group of ten Palestinian Jews connected with the Irgun (a Jewish underground movement in Palestine) who had come to the United States in 1939 and 1940. Called the Bergson group, after their leader, Peter Bergson (Hillel Kook), these activists organized the Emergency Committee to Save the Jewish People of Europe. By means of full-page newspaper advertisements, pageants, and mass meetings, the Emergency Committee worked to publicize the Holocaust and to build support for a governmental rescue program. In October 1943 it organized a demonstration in Washington by four hundred Orthodox rabbis. Months of lobbying on Capitol Hill resulted in November in the introduction in Congress of a rescue resolution calling on President Roosevelt to establish a governmental rescue agency independent of the State Department. By the end of 1943, substantial support for the legislation was building in Congress.[49]

Meanwhile, in an unrelated set of developments, Treasury Department officials had learned that the State Department not only had done virtually nothing for rescue but had even impeded the rescue efforts American Jewish organizations were attempting on their own. Treasury officials also discovered that Breckinridge Long and the State Department had quietly cut the use of the immigration quotas to less than 10 percent, had taken steps in early 1943 to stop the transmission of Holocaust information from Europe, and had delivered altered documentation to the Treasury Department in an effort to cover up the information cutoff. The Treasury officials conveyed these and other findings to Secretary of the Treasury Henry Morgenthau, Jr., in a carefully documented report entitled "Acquiescence of This Government in the Murder of the Jews."[50]

Morgenthau carried the information to President Roosevelt in January 1944. Roosevelt, recognizing that a nasty scandal was imminent and realizing that the State Department's record would be debated within days when the rescue resolution reached the Senate floor, decided to head off the impending crisis. He accepted Morgenthau's recommendation that he establish a government rescue agency by executive order and charge it with doing all that was possible, consistent with the war effort, to save European Jews. The new agency was named the War Refugee Board.[51]

The War Refugee Board received little support from President Roosevelt and his administration. It became largely a Treasury Department operation in collaboration with private Jewish organizations. In planning its rescue programs, the board worked closely with American Jewish groups, and most of its overseas projects were implemented by Jewish organizations in Europe. In addition, government funding for the War Refugee Board was very small; consequently, more than 90 percent of the board's work was paid for by American Jewish organizations. By far the greatest part of the Jewish contributions were provided by the American Jewish Joint Distribution Committee, which supplied more aid to European Jews during World War II than all the world's governments combined. In its sixteen months of action, the War Refugee Board played a crucial role in saving the lives of about 200,000 Jews and at least 20,000 non-Jews. Nonetheless, as the board's director concluded years later: "What we did was little enough. . . . Late and little, I would say."[52]

THE POST-HOLOCAUST ERA

When World War II ended in Europe in May 1945, the Western Allies were confronted with the immense problem of more than 8 million displaced persons (DPs) in the sectors they occupied. The DPs included former slave laborers, concentration camp survivors, prisoners of war, Eastern Europeans who had fled the Russians, and others. In a highly effective operation, the Allied military succeeded in repatriating about 7 million by September 1945. More than 1 million, however, could not or would not return home. Among them were between 50,000 and 100,000 Jewish survivors of the Holocaust. Within a year that number grew to about 200,000. Most of the new arrivals were Polish Jews who had come out of hiding or had escaped to Russia during the war and had returned home. Finding little or nothing of their families in Poland and confronted with rampant anti-Semitism there, they fled to DP centers in Germany and Austria. (During 1945 and 1946 several hundred Jews were murdered in Poland, 42 of them in a single pogrom in Kielce in July 1946.)[53]

Care for the nonrepatriable DPs was to be handled jointly by the military forces and the United Nations Relief and Rehabilitation Administration (UNRRA). Because UNRRA proved unable to meet its responsibilities, the military had to fill the vacuum in this very difficult assignment, one for which it was not trained. The result was disastrous for the Jewish survivors. The U.S. Army, whose sector contained more than 90 percent of the Jewish DPs, had little understanding of or sympathy for the problems of these people, the ones most psychologically and physically damaged by the Nazis. Most Jews were held in inadequate camps (some of them former concentration camps) and provided with much the same rations they had received under the Nazis. One of the factors behind such treatment was anti-Semitism, which was quite widespread in the U.S. Army. A January 1946 opinion poll of American troops in Germany found that 22 percent agreed that "the Germans under Hitler had 'good reasons' for the persecution of the Jews." General George Patton, whose area of command included most of the DPs under American authority, described Jewish DPs as "lower than animals" and, "in the majority of cases, a sub-human species."[54]

In response to pressure from American Jewish leaders, President Harry S. Truman sent Earl G. Harrison, the former U.S. commissioner of immigration, to investigate the DP situation. Reporting to the president in August 1945, Harrison described the condition of the Jews as "far worse than that of other groups." He decried "the continuance of barbed-wire fences, armed guards, and prohibition against leaving the camp except by passes." In his strongest criticism, he asserted that "as matters now stand, we appear to be treating the Jews as the Nazis treated them except that we do not exterminate them." The War Department reacted to the Harrison report by instructing General Dwight Eisenhower, commander of Allied forces in Europe, to act quickly to improve the situation. Eisenhower issued several orders to that effect, and by late 1945 conditions had improved markedly, although some military officials showed little inclination to implement the new policy.[55]

In his report, Harrison pointed out that the only real solution to the problem of the Jewish DPs was to remove them from Europe as soon as possible. He recommended that 100,000 (which was most of them at that time) be admitted to Palestine and that "reasonable numbers" be allowed to enter the United States. Late in August 1945, shortly after receiving the Harrison report, President Truman urged the British government to permit 100,000 displaced Jews to go to Palestine. An official Anglo-American Committee of Inquiry was appointed to study the question. In April 1946, after months of investigation, and strongly influenced by its visit to the DP camps, the committee unanimously recommended the rapid evacuation of 100,000 of the Jewish survivors to Palestine. But the British government, until it departed from Palestine in 1948, adamantly refused to change its 1939 White Paper policy of tightly limiting Jewish immigration to Palestine.[56]

While awaiting the outcome of the Anglo-American Committee's investigations, President Truman, hoping to set an example for other nations, moved to expedite the admission of DPs to the United States. Just before Christmas 1945, in what was called the Truman Directive, the president reopened the American quotas for full use, with preference given to DPs. He also ordered the U.S. War Shipping Authority to arrange to transport them to the United States. Shortly afterward, high-ranking State Department and immigration officials traveled to the American zone of Germany to open visa offices. By June 1948, when this special program ended, 41,379 DPs had come to the United States. The Truman Directive had been issued to assist all DPs; there was no preference in it for Jews. But because Jewish relief organizations had gone into the camps earlier than others, they were better organized and more effective. As a result, although Jews then constituted about 20 percent of the DPs in Europe, two-thirds of those who immigrated under the Truman Directive were Jews.[57]

Meanwhile, in August 1946 President Truman concluded that special U.S. immigration legislation would be needed if the DP problem was ever to be solved. By then it was evident that the British were not going to permit anywhere near 100,000 Jews to enter Palestine. Moreover, tens of thousands of additional Jewish survivors were then fleeing from Poland to the DP camps in the wake of the Kielce pogrom. And it was clear that the Truman Directive, which was limited by the existing quota system, could make no more than a dent in the problem of resettling the million or so DPs still in Europe. Most of the DPs came from Eastern Europe, and the quotas for all the Eastern European countries combined totaled only 13,000 per year. Accordingly, Truman announced that he would seek congressional action.[58]

American Jews were divided by the president's decision. Zionists, who saw the plan for moving 100,000 Jewish DPs to Palestine as a critically important step toward a Jewish state, feared that Truman had given up on that proposal and intensified their work for a Jewish commonwealth. Non-Zionists, represented by the American Jewish Committee and the American Council for Judaism, formed a non-denominational Citizens Committee on Displaced Persons (CCDP) to concentrate on building public and congressional support for bringing 100,000 Jews to the United States. Even before the committee was fully formed, it widened its objective and called for admission over a four-year period of 400,000 DPs of all backgrounds. It was anticipated that 20–25 percent of that number would be Jews. Eventually, over one hundred labor, veterans, church, social work, and civic organizations endorsed the CCDP's program. Jews stayed in the background of the CCDP as much as possible; eminent non-Jews held most of the official posts. But it was Jewish work and Jewish funds that made the committee extremely effective as an educational and lobbying force.[59]

For eighteen months, the strong anti-immigration sentiment in Congress and in the nation withstood the gradually increasing public support for admission of DPs. Anti-Semitism, though it began to decline after the war, was still prevalent in American society, and it was a major factor in the resistance to DP legislation because members of Congress and Americans generally believed that most of the DPs were Jews. But as Congress became more aware of the DP situation in Europe, and as growing numbers of non-Jews became concerned about the issue, congressional resistance slowly decreased.[60]

In June 1948 the Displaced Persons Act was passed, permitting the immigration of 200,000 DPs over a two-year period. But the Jews in the CCDP, who had led the entire effort, were highly frustrated at the outcome. Anti-Semitic legislators, especially in the Senate, had framed the law in such a way that it indirectly but effectively discriminated heavily against Jews. The act reserved 30 percent of the visas for farmers, a provision made with clear knowledge that few Jewish DPs could qualify as farmers. The law also allotted 40 percent of the openings to DPs who had come from the Baltic area. Almost all of them were Christians fleeing Communism, and many of them had supported the Nazis during the war. And it restricted the program to people who had been in the DP camps by December 1945, thereby excluding the more than 100,000 Jewish survivors who had fled Poland during 1946.[61]

Despite its obvious discrimination against Jews, the DP Act of 1948 did provide important help for Jewish as well as non-Jewish DPs. This occurred because President Truman appointed pro-immigration people to the Displaced Persons Commission, the bureau set up by law to administer the act. The commission's goal was to move as many DPs as possible out of Europe as rapidly as it could, even though that meant disregarding the law's percentage requirements. As a historian of these events has stated, the commission "sought every loophole and stretched every ambiguity to help bring people to the United States." The commission's emphasis on fast action expedited the resettlement of DPs, but it also led to inadequate screening procedures in Europe. One consequence was surreptitious entry to the United States of an unknown but large number of Nazi collaborators and even war criminals, although the law explicitly excluded them.[62]

By 1949 the Displaced Persons Commission and the CCDP were advocating new legislation to permit additional numbers to enter and to eliminate the anti-Jewish aspects of the 1948 law. Public opinion and sentiment in Congress were moving in the same direction. Despite long-drawn-out opposition from Senator Pat McCarran, the powerful chairman of the Judiciary Committee, the Displaced Persons Act of 1950 was enacted in June of that year. It provided for the admission of more than 200,000 additional DPs, and it ended the discriminatory restrictions of the 1948 legislation. But McCarran and his backers did succeed in delaying enactment of the law for a year, and during that time many of the Jewish DPs still in Europe went to Israel, a choice that opened to them when the Jewish state came into existence in 1948.[63]

Under the two Displaced Persons Acts, the United States took in 405,616 DPs. Add to this the 41,379 who arrived earlier under the Truman Directive, and the total is 446,995. Of this number, approximately 96,000, or 21 percent, were Jewish survivors of the Holocaust. Though other countries took in scores of thousands of displaced persons, it was the American DP Acts that finally brought the mass exodus from the European camps. In 1951 the West German government took over the care of the few thousand remaining DPs, and in 1957 the last camp was closed.[64]

During the years they had to remain in the DP camps, waiting for the opportunity to relocate and to rebuild their shattered lives, the Jewish survivors found they had not been forgotten by America's Jews. From the time the U.S. Army arrived until most DPs had left Europe, they were helped by American Jewish Army chaplains and American Jewish soldiers. The Jews in the American military brought spiritual support, rebuilt morale and rekindled hope and confidence in the future, reconnected the survivors with the larger Jewish world, and drew American Jews' attention to their plight.[65]

Organized American Jewish aid, mostly through the American Jewish Joint Distribution Committee, did not begin until mid-June 1945, and then only on a limited scale. The JDC did not become fully operative in the DP areas until the end of 1945. The delays were caused by the military, which did not want the problem of dealing with private relief agencies. It was the impact of the Harrison report that forced the Army to let the JDC into the camps. The JDC's work there was critically important. It provided food, clothing, and other supplies to supplement the basic but marginal level of support furnished by the Army. Its staff protected the DPs'

rights and represented them before military and civil authorities. It offered education, health, personal counseling, and emigration services. Its representatives, like
the Jewish Army personnel, were able to help in the revival of morale, hope, and
confidence. And the JDC became a line of solidarity between American Jews, who
contributed the millions of dollars that it expended, and the surviving remnant of
European Jewry. The JDC also brought crucial help to the remaining Jewish communities in Hungary, Romania, Poland, Czechoslovakia, Yugoslavia, and Bulgaria
until 1949, when a large proportion of those Jews had gone to Israel and the Stalinist regimes of Eastern Europe expelled the JDC because of its supposed connection
with "American imperialism." In addition, in these years the JDC assisted in the
movement of many thousands of Jewish survivors from Europe to Palestine/Israel.[66]

Closely linked to the problem of the Jewish displaced persons was another important issue that came to the forefront at the end of World War II: the question of
Palestine. The American Zionist movement entered the 1930s as a weak minority on
the American Jewish scene. It increased its following to some extent during that
decade by focusing on refugee immigration into Palestine. The Zionists entered the
war period still emphasizing the expansion of the Jewish settlements in Palestine and
still holding the issue of actual statehood in abeyance. This enabled them to keep
the support of non-Zionists. Meanwhile, they projected that immigration would
move the Jewish population in Palestine toward majority status, which would presumably open the way for the emergence of a state sometime in the future. By 1941,
however, that strategy had lost viability as it had become clear that the British were
determined to keep the 1939 White Paper in force, limiting Jewish immigration to
Palestine to a trickle. In 1942 the world Zionist movement changed course and began
to advocate the establishment of a Jewish state in Palestine immediately after the war.
This would provide a home for the European Jews who survived (then expected to
number in the millions), and it would finally put an end to two thousand years of
Jewish homelessness, persecution, and disaster.[67]

The Zionists foresaw that their best opportunity for decades to come would
materialize at the end of the war, when there would be a fluidity in world affairs that
would very likely reopen the status of Palestine. They also realized that American
government support would be critically important in winning the Jewish state. The
first step toward their goal was to marshal all of American Jewry behind the Zionist
program. For that purpose, a widely representative American Jewish Conference was
convened in 1943. The five hundred delegates, who came from nearly all segments
of American Jewry, overwhelmingly ratified the Zionist statehood position. As a result, some non-Zionist organizations, including the very important American Jewish Committee, disassociated themselves from the conference. But the meeting had
demonstrated that the statehood position had acquired widespread, almost certainly
majority support among American Jews. In the months that followed, as more and
more information about the Holocaust came out of Europe, the Zionist viewpoint
gained additional backing. By September 1945 a Roper poll would show 80 percent
of American Jews firmly in favor of a Jewish state in Palestine.[68]

The Zionists' next step was to try to win the backing of the American people and their government. Starting in September 1943, the American Zionist Emergency Council, the political-action arm of the Zionist movement, organized more than four hundred local councils, situated in all the major American communities. These councils, building contacts with city governments, state legislatures, members of Congress, the local press, and thousands of non-Jewish groups and Jewish organizations, attained a level of effectiveness seldom surpassed on the American political scene. By the fall of 1944, three-quarters of the members of both the Senate and the House were on record in support of Jewish statehood. Twice during 1944, in March and in December, a resolution urging unlimited immigration of Jews into Palestine and the establishment there of "a free and democratic Jewish commonwealth" was on the verge of passing in both houses of Congress. But in each instance the State Department, with the backing of President Roosevelt, intervened and persuaded the congressional leadership to defer action. The argument was that passage would stir up the Arab world and risk violent upheavals in the Middle East. The real reason for the State Department's opposition, however, was its quiet but persistent anti-Zionist stance and its firm support of Britain's Palestine policy.[69]

As for President Roosevelt, he expressed support for a Jewish commonwealth in Palestine several times, and during the 1944 election campaign he specifically promised that "if reelected I shall help to bring about its realization." Yet a few days after the election, he asked the State Department to prevail upon the congressional leadership, for the second time, to postpone action on the Palestine statehood resolution. Furthermore, at least three times during 1944 and 1945 he confidentially assured Arab leaders that he would take no action on this issue without full consultation with them, which meant that the stalemate over Palestine would continue. Indeed, in the last of these instances (April 5, 1945) he reminded King Ibn Saud of Saudi Arabia that in their meeting in February "I assured you that I would take no action . . . which might prove hostile to the Arab people." Cordell Hull, Roosevelt's secretary of state, summed up Roosevelt's actions in his memoirs: "The President at times talked both ways to Zionists and Arabs, besieged as he was by each camp." The American chairman of the Anglo-American Committee of Inquiry was less diplomatic. Early in 1946, after reviewing State Department files on Palestine, he referred to Roosevelt as "a duplicitous son-of-a-bitch."[70]

The Palestine resolution, slightly weakened, finally came to a vote in Congress in December 1945. President Harry Truman, who had supported it as vice president, tried to have it delayed again, pending the completion of the Anglo-American Committee's investigation and his own negotiations with Britain for admission of 100,000 Jewish DPs into Palestine. This time the Zionists prevailed and the resolution was adopted overwhelmingly by both houses. The Palestine resolution did not require action by the president; it was a nonbinding congressional recommendation. What, then, was its value? The struggle for the Palestine resolution forced the question of Jewish statehood on Congress and brought it to the attention of the American public. The long debate over it solidified Jewish opinion behind the statehood policy and attracted considerable non-Jewish backing. The resolution, once adopted, became a constant reference point as Zionists worked to widen their support in the months that followed, support that became very important in 1947 and 1948, when the Jewish statehood issue built to a climax.[71]

Meanwhile, Jews in Palestine were growing increasingly restive. Expectations had been raised in August 1945 by President Truman's strong support of the Harrison report's call for admission to Palestine of 100,000 Jewish survivors. Formation in late 1945 of the Anglo-American Committee of Inquiry to study the issue at length was seen as a British delaying tactic. In the closing months of 1945, armed Jewish groups carried out several acts of violent sabotage in Palestine in protest against the continuing British limitation of Jewish immigration to 1,500 per month. Actions were also taken to assist with the landing of what the British termed "illegal" immigrants. These were Jewish survivors without immigration permits who, under the direction of emissaries from Palestine, made their way to European ports. There they crowded onto small, barely seaworthy boats for the voyage to Palestine and, they hoped, surreptitious entry into the country. Large numbers were captured by the British, who patrolled the Palestine coasts and much of the eastern Mediterranean with destroyers and airplanes. In Palestine, the British police and military worked to intercept those who reached land. The ones who were caught were placed in a detention camp near Haifa and, later, in camps in Cyprus. To assist the immigrants, Palestinian Jews hid the ones who got in, blew up British coast-guard stations, burned patrol aircraft, and attacked radar installations. The entire operation was costly for the British, not only in funds but especially in the worldwide negative publicity that it generated.[72]

The violence in Palestine escalated in 1946 after Great Britain refused to implement the Anglo-American Committee of Inquiry's unanimous recommendation for admission of 100,000 Jewish displaced persons. Jewish underground forces destroyed rail lines and bridges. The British searched Jewish settlements for arms and jailed more than 2,000 Jewish leaders. In July, members of a Jewish armed underground blew up the British military headquarters in Jerusalem, killing 91 people. The British answered with martial law, more arrests, and hangings. Throughout 1946 and into 1947 the violence went on, and the refugee boats kept coming. In February 1947 a frustrated British government, unable to devise an answer for Palestine and increasingly pressed financially, submitted the problem to the United Nations.[73]

The United Nations met on the issue in April 1947 and appointed a special eleven-nation committee to go to Palestine to investigate the situation. The committee's majority report recommended the partition of Palestine into an Arab state and a Jewish state. The minority report called for two semi-autonomous sectors under a federal government. The Arabs rejected both proposals. The Jews accepted the majority plan. In November 1947 the U.N. General Assembly, with both the United States and the Soviet Union voting in favor, approved the partition proposal. Behind the Soviet vote was probably the wish to weaken British influence in the Middle East. The decision of the U.S. government was made by President Truman, over State Department and Defense Department opposition. The reasons for Truman's decision (and for his decision the following May to recognize the newly established Jewish state) were complex and still cannot be clearly delineated. But without question the Zionists' years of work, propaganda, and building of public and political pressure had a significant impact on the outcome.[74]

Immediately after the U.N. decision, Arab governments in the Middle East started preparations to invade the Jewish state if it should actually be formed. At the same time, Arab guerrilla forces within Palestine launched attacks on Jewish targets, and war began. State and Defense Department officials, asserting that the hostilities proved that partition could not succeed, moved in March 1948 to urge the United Nations to back down on partition. But in Palestine, where the Jews were beginning to turn the tide of battle, Jewish leaders responded by announcing that they would establish a provisional government by May 15, the date Britain had set for its departure. The key issue then became whether the United States would recognize the new government. On May 14 Israel declared its independence. Eleven minutes later the White House announced American recognition. On May 17 the Soviet Union recognized the Jewish state. The surrounding Arab states invaded Israel, but by early 1949 the new nation had succeeded in driving them out.[75]

What part did the Holocaust have in building support for Jewish statehood? The most obvious connection involved the desperate plight of the Jewish survivors. The need to move them out of Europe became evident directly after the war, as did the lack of places to which they could go. The Harrison report's recommendation to send 100,000 of them to Palestine became a rallying point in the Zionist drive for a state. And the DPs became the central issue in the various diplomatic proceedings that led to the U.N. decision for partition in November 1947. Yet on a deeper level the six million Jews who died were the main force in bringing the Jewish state into existence. This concept, though difficult to document, is widely understood. It appeared, among other places, on the floor of Congress in late 1945. Senator Robert Taft of Ohio supported the plan for a Jewish commonwealth as "the best retribution we can give to the Jewish people who . . . have suffered the most intolerable tortures and the most frightful decimation." Or as seen by a Truman biographer writing three decades later about the complicated events that led up to the birth of Israel, "Above the maneuvers and strategies, above the pressures and irritations loomed the visage of Adolf Hitler."[76]

American support for Israel did not end with the formation of the Jewish state. Throughout the decades since 1948, despite ups and downs and sometimes sharp acrimony, the United States and Israel have shared a special relationship. Central to that relationship is a clear American commitment to the security and existence of Israel. As Secretary of State Henry Kissinger described it in 1975: "We have a historic commitment to the survival and the well-being of Israel. This is a basic national policy reaffirmed by every Administration." According to the opinion polls, the policy has also been consistently reaffirmed by the American people. The key question used across the years ("Are your sympathies more with Israel or more with the Arab nations?") has yielded percents generally in the mid-40s for Israel and in the single numbers to mid-teens for the Arab states. Although support for Israel dropped noticeably during the invasion of Lebanon in 1982 and the Palestinian uprising in the late 1980s, the declines were temporary. Since 1948, surveys of American Jews, asked whether they were pro-Israel or anti-Israel, have regularly found levels of support above 90 percent.[77]

Analysts point to several factors that have contributed to the special relationship that developed between the United States and Israel. Israel is a vital strategic asset for the United States, a reliable, stable, and militarily powerful partner in a pivotal sector of the world. The two nations have significant similarities, most importantly their firm commitment to a free and open democratic system. Many American Christians with close ties to the Bible and the Holy Land feel connected with the Jews of Israel. The American response to the Jewish state has also been affected by the strong identification of American Jews with Israel. Their high level of involvement in voting and political action and the very effective American Israel Public Affairs Committee (the outgrowth of the American Zionist Emergency Council of the 1940s) have had a continuing impact on Washington. But most significant of all—the original and most persistent impulse for American support—is the fact of the Holocaust. Help in bringing Israel into existence is perceived as a partial amends to the people who suffered the Holocaust. Support for Israel's continued existence is seen as helping to sustain a bulwark against another such tragedy's ever striking the Jewish people. "It's absolutely crucial," declared President Jimmy Carter in 1977, "that no one in our country or around the world ever doubt that our No. 1 commitment in the Middle East is to protect the right of Israel to exist, to exist permanently, and to exist in peace."[78]

A third important Holocaust-related development that unfolded in the aftermath of World War II was the endeavor to bring Nazi war criminals to justice. The Moscow Declaration, issued by the United States, Great Britain, and the Soviet Union in November 1943, had pledged that those responsible for German atrocities would be tried and punished. Shortly afterward the U.N. War Crimes Commission initiated steps to collect evidence and plan postwar punitive action. In the London Agreement of August 1945 the three Great Powers and France decided on the general structure and scope of the war crimes trials.[79]

Of the thousands of war crimes proceedings that took place over the next several years, the ones that received the most publicity and had the greatest worldwide impact were the Nuremberg trials of twenty-two major war criminals. The trials began in November 1945, and the final judgments were issued in October 1946. The London Agreement had established the International Military Tribunal (IMT) to conduct the trials. On it sat judges from the United States, Great Britain, the Soviet Union, and France. The trials dealt with four charges: (1) crimes against peace (planning or waging aggressive war), (2) war crimes (violations of the traditional laws of war, such as maltreatment of prisoners of war or killing and destruction with no military necessity), (3) crimes against humanity (murder, extermination, or enslavement of civilians, and political, racial, or religious persecution), and (4) a common plan or conspiracy to carry out the crimes included in the other three charges.[80]

The highest-ranking Nazis were not at the trial; Hitler, Himmler, and Goebbels had committed suicide. Of those tried by the IMT, twelve were condemned to death, including Göring, Ribbentrop, Streicher, Seyss-Inquart, and *(in absentia)* Bormann. Göring committed suicide after he was sentenced, and Bormann was not found. The other ten were hanged two weeks after the judgment was delivered. Three defendants were acquitted, three were given life in prison, and four received sentences ranging from ten to twenty years. The IMT also declared that the SS, the Gestapo, the SD, and the leadership corps of the Nazi Party were criminal organizations, but in any trial of members of these groups the individual's personal responsibility for crimes would have to be shown.[81]

Because it operated in uncharted areas of international law, the Nuremberg tribunal had to face some difficult problems. Were crimes against humanity and launching aggressive war legally punishable acts? Or was the IMT applying ex post facto law as a way to justify revenge? The judges recognized that "crimes against humanity" was a new legal concept, but they contended that it had evolved out of modern warfare. Furthermore, the Allies had repeatedly warned the Axis that policy formulators as well as the actual perpetrators would be punished for such crimes. The criminal designation of planning and waging aggressive war was more problematic, but the judges did not refrain from applying it. The conspiracy charge was questionable enough that the judges, behind the scenes, decided to use it only with reference to aggressive war. Throughout the proceedings the IMT ruled that following the orders of a superior was not an acceptable excuse for having carried out a crime.[82]

The prosecutors at Nuremberg followed a strategy that emphasized the aggressive-war charge and sought to demonstrate a conspiratorial plan to wage it. Accordingly, they made little room for testimony about atrocities. Yet crimes against Allied civilians and POWs, and especially the mass murder of the Jews, became central to the trial. When witnesses to the terrible atrocities did testify, the courtroom seemed to freeze in horror. The very nature of the testimony, along with the voluminous documentary evidence, forced the atrocities to the forefront. They made the strongest impression on the judges, and they drew their harshest judgments. The atrocities, particularly the extermination of the Jews, were the main message that the Nuremberg trials broadcast to the world. The newsreels and front-page photographs of the opening of the concentration camps in April 1945 had at last brought the horror of the Holocaust to the world's attention. But the news reports from Nuremberg, starting eight months later, cataloged the scope and enormity of the extermination and impressed them, along with the number six million, on the world's consciousness.[83]

In the United States, reactions to the Nuremberg trials varied but were mostly positive. Some Americans opposed the proceedings, maintaining that retroactive law was being imposed and that in any case the victors could not render impartial judgment. But 75 percent of the public approved of the IMT, the legal procedures used, and the results. The approval level in the press was only slightly less. President Truman praised the outcome as a deterrent to future international criminal acts. As for American Jews, they had no doubts about the legality of the trials, but there was widespread anger that three defendants had been acquitted and seven others had received only prison terms.[84]

Before the close of the Nuremberg trials of major war criminals, legal proceedings were under way for the less important war criminals. Thousands were extradited to where the crimes had occurred, to be tried in the courts of countries formerly occupied by Germany. Thousands more faced military courts that were established in each of the zones of occupation: U.S., British, Soviet, and French. Among the earliest of these actions was the Belsen trial, in which a British court tried 45 of the camp staff, sentencing the commandant and 10 others to hang and 19 more to prison terms. At about the same time, an American court convicted all 40 defendants in the Dachau trial, condemning 26 of them to death. A series of 12 trials held by U.S. military courts at Nuremberg (the Subsequent Nuremberg Proceedings) stretched from December 1946 to April 1949. The accused included 177 leaders of the Reich's ministries, army, industries, legal and medical establishments, and the SS and *Einsatzgruppen*. Twenty-five death sentences were handed down, along with several life sentences and many rather light penalties.[85]

The earlier trials brought the most severe sentencing. As time passed, anger tended to cool. By the end of 1947 interest in the whole undertaking had receded. The Germans for the most part resented the sentences as arbitrary and the whole trial process as victors' justice. German political and church leaders exerted increasing pressure against the trials and in favor of clemency for those already convicted. And in Washington by early 1948 the secretary of the Army was anxious to end the trials because they were impeding the goal of building a strong Germany in the face of the growing Soviet threat to Western Europe. In 1949 the trials in the American zone ended.[86]

In May 1949 John McCloy was appointed high commissioner of occupied Germany. NATO had just been formed to counter Soviet expansionism, and the Western Allies were about to establish the state of West Germany. McCloy's mission was to help build a democratic and economically viable state. In early 1950, under heavy pressure from German civic and church leaders, McCloy set up a clemency board of three Americans to review the cases of ninety war criminals convicted in the Subsequent Nuremberg Proceedings. In January 1951, after the board's and then his own study of the cases, McCloy announced his decisions, which undoubtedly had been influenced by the German leaders' continuing pressure on him. The pressure was magnified by the expansion of the Cold War in those same months as the Korean conflict began, requiring a military buildup in Western Europe against a possible Soviet thrust into West Germany. German cooperation was essential to that buildup.[87]

McCloy ruled that ten of the fifteen war criminals under sentence of death would instead serve prison terms. Four of the ten were *Einsatzgruppen* leaders. He also reduced the sentences of sixty-four of the remaining seventy-four convicts. Large decreases were made in the sentences of doctors convicted of experiments on concentration camp inmates. Most of those who had been judged guilty in the *Einsatzgruppen* case but not condemned to death had their sentences reduced. One-third of all the prisoners were eligible for immediate release. McCloy's leniency met with disbelief and outrage outside Germany. His critics included Winston Churchill and Eleanor Roosevelt. From inside Germany came anger at the decision to hang five of the criminals, though all five had participated directly in mass murders. There was a new barrage of pressure on McCloy, but the executions took place. One important result of McCloy's clemency was further to confirm the Germans in their belief that the war crimes trials had been arbitrary and unfair, thus helping them to continue to avoid facing the history of their nation's actions in World War II.[88]

In 1950, jurisdiction over as yet unprosecuted war crimes cases was turned over to the West German government. Very little investigation or prosecution took place in the next several years because politicians realized that most Germans opposed further confrontation with Nazi crimes. The Western Allies, for their part, had little interest in pressing the issue. They were mainly concerned about rearming Germany. The situation changed in the mid-1950s, when the extensive information collected in a case involving *Einsatzgruppen* killings in Lithuania indicated that some of the worst Nazi crimes had not yet been prosecuted. In late 1958 a German central office was formed to seek all available information about Nazi crimes and to initiate criminal proceedings. By 1986 nearly five thousand trials had been held, covering the full spectrum of Nazi crimes. But this effort came too late, and in the majority of cases convictions were not obtained. Evidence was often difficult to find, and witnesses could no longer remember details clearly. Even when convictions were made, the courts frequently handed down short sentences on the grounds that the defendants had been obeying the orders of superiors and thus had been only accessories to the crimes.[89]

In total, the three Western Allies convicted slightly more than 5,000 German war criminals. Of these, 806 received death sentences. Ultimately, 486 of them were executed. (The United States alone convicted 1,814 persons, including 462 who were sentenced to death, 283 of whom were executed.) No accurate figures are available for convictions by the Soviet Union, but the number is probably greater than the combined numbers of the Western Allies. One historian assessed the whole unprecedented undertaking in this way: "No one can say that justice was done. . . . Yet equally, no one can doubt the scale of the effort made to punish those who committed history's gravest crime."[90]

By 1952 the questions concerning the displaced persons, the status of Palestine, and the fate of the war criminals had been substantially dealt with. During the next two decades, Holocaust issues drew limited attention in the United States.

Before World War II ended, small gatherings began to be held in New York each April to commemorate the anniversary of the Warsaw Ghetto Uprising of 1943. In 1946 a national convention of Orthodox rabbis called for the establishment of a "universal memorial day" for all the Jewish victims of the Nazis, the date to be chosen in consultation with other groups. But nothing happened. Thirteen years later a similar plea went unanswered. The Warsaw Ghetto commemorations had continued, however, gradually assuming the role of memorializing all of the six million Jews who had perished.[91]

In Israel, meanwhile, an official Holocaust remembrance day was established in 1951 by the Knesset. It was called Yom Hashoah and the date was set for the twenty-seventh day of Nisan on the Hebrew lunar calendar. The date selected was a compromise. Holocaust remembrance in Israel, as in the United States, had begun in conjunction with the April 19 commemorations of the start of the Warsaw Ghetto Uprising. But Israelis insisted on placing the date on the Hebrew calendar. On the Hebrew calendar, April 19, 1943, was the fifteenth day of Nisan, the first night of Passover. Orthodox Israelis objected to combining the two events. The Holocaust commemoration would unacceptably impose on Passover. Furthermore, it would shadow that event of joy and liberation with one of destruction and mourning, effectively providing Hitler with a posthumous victory. After prolonged negotiations, a compromise was reached on a date that was after the Passover holiday but still close to the start of the ghetto revolt. That was the twenty-seventh of Nisan, four days following the end of Passover.[92]

Once it was officially established, Yom Hashoah was neglected in Israel for years. Only in 1959 did full commemoration begin. Two years later the *New York Times* reported that the New York observance of the eighteenth anniversary of the Warsaw Ghetto Uprising would be held on April 13, 1961, to coincide with the day of remembrance in Israel, Nisan 27. The *Times* also noted that the New York event commemorated both the ghetto revolt and all six million Jewish victims of the Nazis. The Israeli dating arrangement and the merger of the ghetto commemoration with the remembrance of the six million thus took permanent root in America. But the occasion would not be widely observed in the United States for nearly another two decades.[93]

During the 1950s most Americans who thought at all about the Holocaust probably did so because of the widely read diary of Anne Frank, which was published in the United States in 1952. Three years later it reached a larger audience as an extremely successful play, and in 1959 it appeared as an acclaimed Hollywood film. The book was mainly a personal account; it did not focus on Holocaust events, but brought the Holocaust to the reader only as background. In the play, and even more in the film, many of the Jewish aspects of Anne's book were removed or shaded in order to universalize the story and appeal to a larger audience. Some sections of the diary that dealt explicitly with the persecution of the Jews were omitted, though they could easily have been left in. Perhaps the greatest rearrangement was to change almost entirely an eloquent passage Anne wrote about Jewish suffering through the ages. It became: "We're not the only people that've had to suffer. There've always been people that've had to . . . Sometimes one race . . . Sometimes another." These alterations did not seem to disturb American Jewish leaders. The director of the Jewish Film Advisory Committee, which was funded by the National Jewish Community Relations Advisory Council, the American Jewish Committee, and the Anti-Defamation League, praised the film's universalization of suffering: "It could very easily have been an outdated Jewish tragedy by less creative or more emotional handling—even a Jewish 'Wailing Wall,' and hence regarded as mere propaganda." Apparently concern to keep a subdued Jewish profile still prevailed in some quarters, although American anti-Semitism had decreased significantly since 1944. Two other widely read books of the 1950s drew some attention to the Holocaust. They were John Hersey's *The Wall*, a novel about the Warsaw Ghetto, and Leon Uris's novel

Exodus, which told of the smuggling of Holocaust survivors into Palestine.[94]

In May 1960 the world was startled by headlines announcing that Israeli agents had captured Adolf Eichmann in Argentina and flown him to Israel to be tried for mass murders committed in World War II. Eichmann had headed the Gestapo office in charge of deporting Jews to the gas chambers. The Israeli government announced its intention to use the trial to expose the full story of the Holocaust, in all its horror, as a means of building world opinion to counter any repetition of such crimes. In fact, the trial did arouse great interest around the world. It focused attention more sharply on the Nazi extermination of the Jews than had the Nuremberg trials, where other crimes had also been under consideration.[95]

The Eichmann trial began in April 1961. The Israeli government paid for the accused's lawyer, a German who had acted as a defense attorney in the main Nuremberg proceedings. Eichmann pleaded not guilty to all charges. For two months the prosecution presented evidence of the Nazi crimes and Eichmann's role in them. More than one hundred witnesses testified, and some sixteen hundred documents, many bearing Eichmann's signature, were introduced, as a complete account of the Holocaust was laid out in its several stages and locations. Eichmann testified in late June and July. The defense did not really question the events portrayed or the accused's involvement in them. It argued instead that Eichmann was no more than an underling with no choice but to carry out the orders of his superiors, nothing but a small cog in the bureaucratic mechanism. The summations by both sides lasted until mid-August, at which time the trial was recessed. When the court reconvened in December 1961, it found the defendant guilty on all counts and sentenced him to hang. The court rejected the argument that he had only obeyed orders, pointing out that the evidence had proved that he had fully identified with the work and had pressed hard in the late stages of the war to complete the destruction of the Jews. In May 1962 Eichmann's appeal was rejected. He was hanged shortly afterward, and his ashes were scattered in the Mediterranean Sea.[96]

In the United States, the Eichmann trial received an exceptional amount of attention. It was headline news for more than a year and the subject of thousands of editorials. Coverage was also heavy on television and in mass-circulation news magazines. Until early 1961 the mass media focused on legal and jurisdictional matters: Israel's violation of Argentine sovereignty in kidnapping Eichmann, and whether Israel had jurisdiction over crimes that were committed outside its territory and before it existed. In the period just after Eichmann's capture, editorial opinion ran about 70 percent against Israel on these issues, but by the time the court proceedings began it had shifted to more than 75 percent in support of the trial. As the trial progressed, almost all the American mass media agreed that publicly documenting the Holocaust was important for educational reasons. Eyewitness testimonies were reported in detail. The press universally condemned Eichmann and for the most part presented him as a warning against totalitarianism and hatred.[97]

A Gallup poll taken during the trial found that 87 percent of the public had read or heard about it, an unusually large proportion for a public affairs event. Seventy-one percent agreed that the world ought to be reminded of the Nazi concentration camp horrors. But an in-depth survey in Oakland, California, raised serious questions about how deeply the highly publicized trial had penetrated into public consciousness. Conducted near the end of the trial, the study was based on hour-long interviews with a carefully weighted sample of 463 people. Eighty-four percent were aware that the trial was going on. Yet, when asked whether Eichmann was a Communist, a Nazi, or a Jew, only 50 percent of the total (59 percent of those aware of the trial) answered that he was a Nazi. And only 28 percent of the total (33 percent of those aware of the trial) were able to choose the correct figure of six million Jewish dead from a list of nine numbers ranging from ten thousand to ten million, even though the six-million figure had been prominently and repeatedly reported for many months. The authors of the study concluded that only a small part of the public had been "sufficiently interested or sophisticated to gain even the most elementary knowledge about the proceedings" and that the trial had thus "failed to reach and educate a substantial segment of the public."[98]

By chance, the day in December 1961 that Eichmann was sentenced was the day that the award-winning Hollywood film *Judgment at Nuremberg* premiered. Interest in the Eichmann trial undoubtedly contributed to the film's great commercial success, though surely less so than its all-star cast. The film broke new ground by incorporating documentary history (footage from the opening of the concentration camps in 1945) into a fictional presentation. And fiction it was. The extermination of the Jews was obscured as the Holocaust was universalized: the Jew emerged as a partner in suffering, one victim among many. As one film analyst emphasized, except for those in the documentary footage, there were no Jews in the film.[99]

From 1962 until 1978, Hollywood made almost no films directly related to the Holocaust. Several productions did graze its edges, films such as *Ship of Fools, Cabaret,* and *The Boys from Brazil. The Pawnbroker* provided a few background glimpses of the Jewish catastrophe while concentrating on a part of its legacy, a broken and brutalized survivor. *Voyage of the Damned,* released in 1976, was the first American film to focus on the Holocaust from a Jewish perspective. But even in that film the real hero was the German Christian who captained the ship *St. Louis* in its hopeless search for a haven for the hundreds of Jews on board. With the appearance of the TV miniseries *Holocaust* in 1978, the situation changed. Since then a stream of American films, fictional and documentary, have confronted Americans with many facets of the Holocaust.[100]

Several books dealing with the Holocaust came into print in the United States in the 1960s. *Night,* Elie Wiesel's autobiographical account of Auschwitz, appeared in English translation in 1960. During the following six years, Wiesel published *Dawn, The Accident, The Town beyond the Wall,* and *The Gates of the Forest,* while he barely made a living as a journalist. His books began to sell only in 1967.[101]

The first substantial American scholarship on the Holocaust, Raul Hilberg's monumental *The Destruction of the European Jews,* was published in 1961. This study, revised and expanded in 1985, has long been recognized as the most important work on the Holocaust in the world. The handling of Hilberg's book by the *New York Times Book Review* was an indicator of the limited attention then accorded the Holocaust in America, even after many months of very extensive publicity about the Eichmann trial. Hilberg's book, the second mentioned in a double review, received eight column inches beginning on page 22. The philosopher Hannah Arendt, who attended the Eichmann trial, did notice Hilberg's book, misread it, and combined her misperceptions with her interpretations of events at the trial. The result was a book that drew a great deal of attention and controversy, *Eichmann in Jerusalem*.[102]

In 1968 another *New York Times* reviewer, pondering two new books, Nora Levin's *The Holocaust* and Arthur Morse's *While Six Million Died*, asked: "But another book on 'the Final Solution'? Who—we ask each other with a smile, a shrug, understanding that surpasses embarrassment, apology in eyes—who needs it?" This was written when Holocaust scholarship was in its earliest stages, when knowledge of many aspects of the Holocaust was very limited, and when the first great outburst of Holocaust writing was still a decade away.[103]

The work that probably drew the greatest attention to the Holocaust in the United States in the 1960s was not American and not scholarship. It was *The Deputy*, written by Rolf Hochhuth, a German of Protestant origin. This extremely controversial play strongly criticized Pope Pius XII for his failure publicly to denounce the Nazi mass murder of the Jews. *The Deputy* was first performed in February 1963 in Berlin, where it immediately ignited an uproar that still echoes today. At the same time it was published as a book. When *The Deputy* opened on Broadway one year later, it attracted wide media attention, 150 pickets, and a capacity audience of 1,090. Its arrival also set off consultations between Catholic, Protestant, and Jewish leaders. The objective was to keep the controversial issues raised by *The Deputy* from harming the significant gains in interfaith relations that had been achieved in recent years. The religious leaders issued a statement calling for an open-minded approach to *The Deputy*. Several American Jewish groups avoided taking any position on the play.[104]

In fact, Christian-Jewish relations, and especially Catholic-Jewish relations, had taken a definite turn toward mutual understanding and respect in the years since the Holocaust. By the 1950s Christian and Jewish clergy, and to some extent laity, were holding conferences, institutes, and smaller gatherings for constructive discussion of their religious differences and to seek solutions to longstanding conflicts. The main impetus for this dialogue was the general recognition in Christian church circles that the anti-Semitism that had led to the Holocaust was the same anti-Semitism that the Christian church had carried and inculcated through the centuries. In 1961 the National Conference of Christians and Jews initiated a drive to eliminate anti-Semitic references from Protestant and Catholic texts and educational materials, and the World Council of Churches (Protestant) adopted a resolution condemning anti-Semitism as "a sin against God and man." Similar trends were under way in the Vatican; for example, in 1958 Pope John XXIII ordered removal of the phrase "perfidious Jew" from the Good Friday liturgy.[105]

When the Second Vatican Council (Vatican II) convened in Rome in 1962 to work toward a spiritual renewal of the Catholic Church, attitudes toward Jews and Judaism were part of the agenda. A draft statement, drawn up in consultation with

Jewish scholars and strongly supported by American Catholic leaders, was completed in 1964. It condemned anti-Semitism, past and present; called for the end of preaching or teaching anything that could give rise to hatred of or contempt for the Jews; and specifically rejected the charge that the Jewish people were guilty of deicide, the killing of Christ. Before the statement came to a vote, however, Arab Catholic leaders, anti-Semites in other sectors of the Church, and Arab political forces succeeded in revising it. The final version, as it appeared in *Nostra Aetate* in 1965, replaced "deplores, indeed condemns," anti-Semitism with "decries" anti-Semitism. It also deleted the word "deicide," though it did deny collective Jewish responsibility for Christ's death. The alterations weakened the document slightly and made it less decisive. But a historic change had nonetheless occurred. *Nostra Aetate* clearly required a new attitude toward Jews on the part of Catholics. In the United States the changes would become widely evident at the local parish level by the early 1980s.[106]

Less than two years after *Nostra Aetate* was proclaimed, Christian-Jewish relations in the United States suffered a setback. In the spring of 1967, with Arab armies massed on Israel's borders and Arab leaders threatening genocide, American Jews watched in dread as Jews once again appeared to face extermination. Jewish leaders expected their Christian colleagues to support their pleas to the U.S. government for help. Several important Protestant and Catholic religious leaders did speak out for Israel, but the official Christian church establishments were either silent or issued statements that were ambivalent. The largely Protestant National Council of Churches called for evenhanded neutrality on America's part. Shortly after hostilities broke out, the National Conference of Catholic Bishops released a general statement deploring the war and designating a day of prayer for peace. Jews and some Christian leaders decried the near silence and lack of support, the more so because it awakened memories of the Christian churches' virtual indifference during the Holocaust. The experience of the Six-Day War dampened Christian-Jewish dialogue, but only temporarily.[107]

The Yom Kippur War of 1973 generated a large groundswell of support for Israel from Catholic and Protestant leaders throughout the United States, especially those on the local and regional levels. In contrast, the National Council of Churches adopted a neutral resolution that omitted mention of the unanticipated Arab attack that had ignited the war. The National Council, which represented most of the mainline "liberal" Protestant churches, reflected the Arab connections that many of its member denominations had developed over more than a half-century of missionary activity in the Middle East. In addition, American Arab Christians exercised substantial influence in the council. Through the decades, the National Council of Churches has consistently taken a pro-Arab, anti-Israel stance. During the 1980s, however, some of its member denominations acted to eradicate the remaining elements of anti-Semitism from their theological doctrines. In 1987 the Presbyterian Church (U.S.A.) affirmed the full authenticity of the Jewish religion and called for an end to "the teaching of contempt for Jews," while the United Church of Christ declared that "Judaism has not been superseded by Christianity" and asked God's forgiveness for the Christian church's historic role in causing violence to the Jews.[108]

Christian-Jewish dialogue continued through the 1970s and 1980s. The growth of mutual understanding was especially strong on the Catholic side, despite tensions that arose from the pope's cordial reception of Austria's president, the ex-Nazi Kurt Waldheim, and the long-drawn-out dispute over the Carmelite convent at Auschwitz. Numerous convocations were held in the United States to reinforce and further implement Vatican II's declarations against anti-Semitism. As if to confirm the significant change in the Catholic Church's position since World War II, Joseph Cardinal Bernardin, the archbishop of Chicago, speaking at a memorial service on the fiftieth anniversary of Kristallnacht, pointed to the "moral blindness" of Christianity during the Holocaust and declared that "Christians, Catholics in particular, must accept their share of responsibility in what happened."[109]

The transformation in Christian-Jewish relations took place in a wider society where anti-Semitism was also undergoing a remarkable change. American anti-Semitism, which reached its historic high point during the 1930s and the war years, decreased strikingly between 1945 and 1960 and continued downward in the years that followed. The opinion poll question that had yielded frighteningly high levels of support for an anti-Semitic campaign from 1938 through March 1945 was discontinued in early 1946 because the numbers had fallen so low. Overt anti-Jewish agitation was limited mostly to isolated fringe groups that were themselves in decline. By the 1960s the American Jewish Committee reported that "few signs" of organized anti-Semitism remained. As for the general public's attitudes toward Jews, Charles Stember, a leading survey research analyst, after closely studying an extensive amount of polling data, concluded in 1966 that anti-Semitism had "dramatically fallen off" since World War II, that it had "in all its forms massively declined in the United States." A different set of polls conducted for the Anti-Defamation League reported similar findings.[110]

By the 1950s, restrictions against Jews were decreasing in employment, education, housing, and other areas. Whereas in 1945 the president of Dartmouth College had openly defended quotas limiting admissions of Jews, by 1965 quotas were described as "curiosities of the past," as Jews constituted 25 percent of the students at Ivy League colleges and universities. Exclusion from medical and engineering schools ended. Most employment discrimination was gone by the 1960s, except for executive posts in some areas such as insurance and banking—and gains were occurring there. Residential restrictions were falling, and only a few elite social clubs and resorts still kept Jews out. In many areas, court actions and fair-practice laws helped to obtain these results, as did organized action by Jews.[111]

As the barriers fell, a large proportion of American Jews shared fully in the postwar prosperity and were absorbed into the dominant suburban middle-class society. They attained educational success, economic affluence, and rising social status. By the 1950s they were mingling more with non-Jews, becoming less noticeably different from their Christian neighbors, and assimilating into the surrounding culture. The acceptance that came with the waning of anti-Semitism would in time lead to high levels of intermarriage, ironically posing, by the 1980s, a threat to the survival of Jewish culture. Surely neither Jewish immigration nor the Jewish birthrate offered an answer to that problem. At the end of World War II there were about 5 million Jews in the United States, making up 3.66 percent of the population (virtually the same percent as in 1927). The number in 1992 was estimated at 5.8 million, which by then was only 2.32 percent of the nation's population.[112]

The causes for the decline in anti-Semitism in post–World War II America cannot be clearly defined. But possible factors include the lowering of personal anxieties with the end of the war, the continuing good economic conditions, the realization that six million Jews had been killed in the Holocaust, the birth of Israel and the Jews' victory over the much more numerous Arabs, and the growing momentum of the civil-rights movement along with increasing social disapproval of openly expressed prejudice. The impact of the 1947 motion picture *Gentleman's Agreement* should not be overlooked. Based on the novel by Laura Z. Hobson, it became the best-known film on anti-Semitism ever to come out of Hollywood. Finally, the religious consensus that marked postwar American culture was both a result and an ongoing cause of decreasing anti-Semitism. The "new national creed," the Judeo-Christian faith, emphasized the common background and common central principles of both religions and affirmed that democracy was built on these foundations. President-elect Dwight Eisenhower summarized it in 1952: "Our form of government has no sense unless it is founded in a deeply felt religious faith. . . . With us of course it is the Judeo-Christian concept but it must be a religion that [says] all men are created equal."[113]

Since the 1960s, anti-Semitism has continued on a gradual downward course. A series of three opinion polls in 1964, 1981, and 1992 verified the trend. The *American Jewish Year Book,* in its annual sounding on the problem, found that "while anti-Semitism had by no means disappeared from the American scene in 1973, most Jews did not view it as a major problem affecting their daily lives." For 1979 and 1989, it reported that anti-Semitism remained at a low level, and in 1992, "by most major criteria, anti-Semitism continued to diminish." There was, however, one problem area. As a foremost scholar of American anti-Semitism wrote in 1987, by the 1970s anti-Jewish attitudes "seemed almost a thing of the past—except among blacks."[114]

Relations between blacks and Jews presented no special problems until 1966. That year, as the drive for black rights accelerated and was marked by violence, all black-white relations tended to worsen, and, as one report noted, "relations between Negroes and Jews grew noticeably acrimonious." By 1979 a Harris poll found that substantially higher percentages of blacks than whites held negative stereotypes about Jews. The anti-Jewish attitudes were most prevalent among younger and better-educated blacks and black leaders. Analysts believed that the most negative feelings revolved around the perception that "Jews have too much power in the United States," especially in the business world. Apparently, these views have frequently grown out of blacks' interactions with Jews who were landlords, store owners, and creditors. Other important points of conflict involved opposition by Jewish groups to affirmative-action quota systems and the anti-Israel attitudes of blacks who supported the PLO and the Arab cause generally. One very influential disseminator of anti-Jewish attitudes since 1975 has been Louis Farrakhan's Nation of Islam.[115]

The World Reacts to the Holocaust

During the 1950s and 1960s the Holocaust received only limited attention in the United States. In the early 1970s, however, a significant shift began to take place. What caused this change in the American reaction to the Holocaust? The Eichmann trial, though it may not have deeply affected the general American public, had a strong impact on American Jews, particularly Holocaust survivors. That a decade passed before that impact led to noticeably increased activity concerning the Holocaust should not cause surprise. In 1961 American Jews, most of whom had lost close relatives in the Nazi catastrophe, still held back from confronting the horrible tragedy. It remained too close and too raw. Facing the Holocaust would also have meant facing questions about what American Jews had done or not done to help, an issue so sensitive that a serious attempt to deal with it as late as 1983 splintered in acrimony. Nor were many Jews, well aware of their minority status, prepared yet to press two other inevitable questions, namely, the role of Christians in perpetrating the genocide and the role of the United States in the face of it.[116]

By the early 1970s the situation had changed. A generation separated the present from the catastrophe. It had become more bearable to look back. Also, by that time American Jews had found a new security in American society. They had been accepted. Anti-Semitism had greatly decreased. Jews felt freer than before to be publicly active on Jewish issues. The Holocaust could be openly addressed for what it was, a unique catastrophe that had struck the Jewish people, not part of a universalized partnership in suffering, a matter of one victim among many. Not that the tendency to universalize would entirely end, by any means. Or that most Jews would really feel secure in criticizing the Christian role in the mass murder and America's dreadfully failed response to the genocide. But important barriers to a more direct confrontation with the Holocaust had fallen.[117]

A key stimulus to the growth of Holocaust consciousness came from the Jewish survivors who had entered the United States as displaced persons soon after World War II. Most of them had arrived poor, physically and emotionally drained, and with little knowledge of English. In 1970 about eighty thousand were in the country. They had worked hard, raised families, and made the difficult adjustments to the new life. Their incomes, on average, were a little lower than those of other American Jews, but most had done very well and many were wealthy. A sizable number were willing to provide money and time for programs and activities to inform Americans about the Holocaust and to try to ensure that it would not be forgotten. They also realized that the time was approaching when they would be gone, and their witness with them.[118]

In earlier years the survivors had been virtually silenced by American Jews. Their accounts of the horror were usually discouraged or ignored. Soon after they arrived, they were typically told by their American relatives and friends to stop talking about their experiences. "Nobody's interested." The prevailing advice was to put it all behind them and get on with life. With the Eichmann trial, survivors began to speak about their past and finally to be heard to some extent. Then around 1970 the pressures to be silent ended. They were listened to, and their messages were increasingly sought. They were at last able to fulfill the pleas of their dying comrades, who had admonished them: "Don't forget us! Tell the world!" Through the years they had kept the commemoration services alive, and they had formed their own organizations to preserve the witness. Now, with the rising interest of the 1970s, they became a vital force for bringing knowledge of the Holocaust to the American people.[119]

The most important cause for increased *Jewish* consciousness of the Holocaust was the Six-Day War of 1967 and especially the anxious weeks that preceded it, when Arab forces stood at Israel's borders and Arab leaders threatened genocide. The terrifying possibility that the Holocaust was about to be repeated, that three million more Jews might be annihilated, that the world would stand by again, profoundly anguished American Jewry. The Holocaust was no longer only past experience; it was also a present danger. It became imperative to keep the Holocaust in the forefront of Jewish consciousness and to make the world, especially the United States, aware of what had happened before and what could occur again. The point was strongly reinforced by the Yom Kippur War of 1973. In the first days after the surprise attack, it appeared that Israel and much of its population might be destroyed by Arab might. The precariousness of Jewish existence was underscored once again. As one historian described it, "American Jews felt the Egyptian and Syrian armies threatening them, though they were six thousand miles away." In the aftermath of these wars, American Jews made determined efforts to extend knowledge of the Holocaust not only within the Jewish community but also to the wider society. These early efforts were supported to some degree by Christians, including those who had been involved over the years in Christian-Jewish dialogue.[120]

In the early and mid-1970s, several churches and increasing numbers of synagogues held annual services in remembrance of the six million Jewish victims. Courses on the Holocaust began to appear in colleges and some high schools. A few small memorials were dedicated, conferences on the Holocaust were held, and the first Holocaust educational centers opened. Films, novels, and scholarly works dealing with the Holocaust became more common. Each new Holocaust-related activity attracted additional attention and stimulated further action. By 1978 sufficient interest had built up across the United States to justify the risk of making the Holocaust the subject of a four-night prime-time TV feature film. It was broadcast during what had become the annual time of remembrance.[121]

The TV miniseries *Holocaust* aired in April 1978. It fastened the audience's attention on the Nazi destruction of the Jews by following the personal experiences of a fictional Jewish family as the Holocaust unfolded. Nearly half of the American population, 120 million people, watched one or more of the episodes. The book version sold one million copies in its first nine days. Press coverage was extremely heavy for one week and extensive for three more. The production was widely praised, not for its artistic merit but because it introduced many millions of otherwise unaware Americans to the fact of the Nazi genocide of the Jews. A Catholic leader further commended the film for teaching "that it is never too soon for Christians to come to the defense of Jews . . . threatened by any form of anti-Semitism." *Holocaust* was also harshly criticized by some as melodrama and trivialization of the subject. The counterargument was that even if this was the case, it was preferable to the absence of knowledge. One observer summarized the point when he described the film as a "sanitized presentation of genocide, love on the run and happy ending," which nevertheless succeeded in exposing "the essential *fact* of the Holocaust" to millions of people. Whatever its merits and demerits, *Holocaust* was spectacularly successful in bringing the Nazi genocide of the Jews to public attention. Beyond that, it was a key catalyst in loosing a torrent of Holocaust-related activity that continued at high levels for the next several years.[122]

Less than two weeks after the miniseries was broadcast, President Jimmy Carter announced his intention to appoint a commission to look into the establishment of a national Holocaust memorial. In this case, politics, not the T V film, was the reason for the decision. For about a year, Jews on Carter's staff had unsuccessfully encouraged such a step. By 1978, however, a significant rift had opened between Carter and the Jewish community over the president's endorsement of a Palestinian homeland, U.N. envoy Andrew Young's meeting with a PLO spokesman, and especially Carter's insistence on selling F-15 aircraft to Egypt and Saudi Arabia. In a move to recoup Jewish support, Carter formed the President's Commission on the Holocaust, with the well-known and respected survivor and author Elie Wiesel as chairman. The commission, composed largely of Jews, was charged with making recommendations for an appropriate memorial to the victims of the Holocaust and finding appropriate ways to implement annual national days of remembrance.[123]

The first national civic commemoration of the Holocaust took place in April 1979 in the rotunda of the Capitol, with President Carter, Vice President Walter Mondale, and Elie Wiesel as speakers. In September 1979, when the President's Commission on the Holocaust submitted its recommendations, they included a call for annual days of remembrance to be held in Washington and across the United States. The commission decided to follow the Israeli dating system for Yom Hashoah since it had already taken hold in the United States, although that meant that the observance day would shift each year. During the 1980s Holocaust commemorations spread to synagogues, churches, college and university campuses, and schools across the country. Before long, observances were held in all the state capitals and most major cities as well as in the national capital. Most of the ceremonies were initially coordinated by Jews, but increasingly non-Jews, including political and religious leaders, became involved.[124]

The main recommendation of the President's Commission on the Holocaust concerned the form the national Holocaust memorial should take. The commission proposed a museum with a strong educational outreach component rather than a monument. The museum was to be built on government land in Washington, D.C., but it was to be paid for with private contributions, obviously Jewish for the most part. Soon after the commission submitted its report, it dissolved, and President Carter established the United States Holocaust Memorial Council, with Wiesel as chairman, to plan the museum and raise the funds for its creation. A crucial problem confronting the council (and the commission before it) was President Carter's insistence, not revealed until a year after he first proposed the memorial, that the Holocaust consisted of the systematic extermination of eleven million victims, six million of them Jews. Concerned with ethnic political considerations, he had re-arranged historical reality by including in the Holocaust all civilians who had per-ished at the hands of Germany and its satellites. The council, after some resistance and much anguished discussion, accepted this politically imposed universalization of the Holocaust as a necessary cost of establishing an official national memorial. The struggle was sufficiently bitter that the Carter administration canceled the part of the 1980 Days of Remembrance ceremonies that had been scheduled for the White House.[125]

After several years of very slow progress in fundraising and museum planning, and after various shakeups in leadership, including Wiesel's withdrawal from active participation in 1986, the council opened the museum in April 1993. Located adja-cent to the National Mall and not far from the Washington Monument, the United States Holocaust Memorial Museum includes an educational center and a research center in addition to its vast exhibition areas. The council did incorporate many of the other victims of Nazi persecution into the museum, among them Gypsies, Poles, Soviet prisoners of war, and homosexuals, but it managed to keep the main empha-sis on the Holocaust. Visitors to the museum cannot miss the centrality there of the Jewish catastrophe. The potential for problems inherent in the museum's govern-mental connection has not ended, however. The completed museum was incorpo-rated into the U.S. Department of the Interior, which now operates and funds it. Appointments to the fifty-five-member U.S. Holocaust Memorial Council are made by the president and have for many years been used for political purposes. The mu-seum remains subject to the influences of American party politics and those who can wield political pressure.[126]

While the Washington museum was going through its planning stages, other museums were taking shape. Even earlier, in 1978, the Martyr's Memorial and Mu-seum of the Holocaust had been established in the office building of the Los Angeles Jewish Federation. The first freestanding museum, the Holocaust Memorial Center in suburban Detroit, opened its doors in 1984. A model of the medium-sized mu-seum, it presents the entire basic history: European Jewish life before the Holocaust, the rise of Nazism, and Germany's destruction of the Jews. It was followed by the Memorial Center for Holocaust Studies, located in the Dallas Jewish Community Center. In 1993, two months before the Washington museum went into operation, the Simon Wiesenthal Center inaugurated its Beit Hashoah—Museum of Tolerance in Los Angeles. The Los Angeles museum presents a multimedia experience in two settings, one focused on the Holocaust, the other dealing with the terrible costs of intolerance, historically and today. In the planning stages since 1983, but not yet built, is A Living Memorial to the Holocaust—Museum of Jewish Heritage. To be situated in New York City, on the tip of Manhattan Island opposite the Statue of Liberty, this institution will emphasize, along with the Holocaust, modern Jewish civilization before and since the Holocaust, giving special emphasis to the role of Jewish immigration in American history. All these museums offer library facilities and provide educational programs for schools and the wider community.[127]

Dozens of smaller Holocaust resource and education centers have come into existence all over the United States, most of them since the late 1970s and many associated with colleges or universities. They provide libraries, including audiovisual materials, assist with the development of school curricula on the Holocaust, offer teacher training, and sponsor adult-education programs. They organize lecture series and other community-oriented Holocaust-related activities, including Days of Remembrance observances. Many hold Holocaust conferences and seminars, publish newsletters, research bulletins, and bibliographies, and carry on oral history projects to preserve the testimonies of survivors.[128]

Since the late 1970s, Holocaust memorials and monuments have been placed throughout the United States. They range from plaques on synagogue walls to individual sculptures, memorial gardens, and very extensive monuments, such as the long wall and column in Tucson and the white sculptures of one survivor standing near the bodies of several victims in a San Francisco park. In Boston, survivors resisted a plan for a sculpture—similar to one in Liberty State Park, New Jersey—of an American soldier carrying an emaciated concentration camp survivor. They pointed out that the United States had done very little (and its military almost nothing) to rescue Jews during the Holocaust and that the proposed sculpture gave the false impression that American GIs had been sent with the purpose of liberating the camps. Consequently, an international competition was held that resulted in an impressive public art project, a row of six very high glass towers standing above and illuminated by glowing volcanic rocks in a black granite pit.[129]

Few events in history have brought forth so much published work in so short a time as the Holocaust has in the United States since the mid-1970s. A vast amount of energy has been devoted to the production of scholarship, memoirs, literature, poetry, and drama about the Jewish catastrophe. To observe the huge outflow one need only look through the Jewish Book Council's quarterly *Jewish Book World* or examine any Jewish book sales catalog. The flood of books and articles seems to have crested in the late 1980s, but the flow has continued at a high level. Interest and demand have been strong enough that commercial and university presses alike have printed large numbers of Holocaust-related books. The Holocaust Library, a publisher founded in 1978 by survivors, managed on very slim resources to produce more than thirty-five original and twenty reprint titles during its fifteen-year existence.[130]

Probably the greatest outpouring has come in the area of scholarship. Works in theology and religion, both Christian and Jewish, have become numerous. The output in history had become so large by 1987 that a bibliographical and historiographical essay on the field easily filled an entire volume. Several multivolume sets, containing thousands of pages of facsimiles of archival documents, have been published, opening some of the most important primary materials to scholars and students not having access to the originals. It would be futile within the context of this essay to attempt a discussion of any of the numerous categories of Holocaust scholarship or literature. The result would be no more than a list that would serve no purpose.[131]

Holocaust survivors have provided much of the initiative and the funding for the Holocaust museums, centers, memorials, and monuments that dot the country. Survivors have also made a vital contribution to knowledge about the Holocaust through the hundreds of memoirs and personal accounts they have written. As early as 1975 the amount of published survivor testimonies was voluminous, and it has expanded since then to the point where it is a significant category within the wider field of Holocaust literature.[132]

Despite the pain it often brings them, survivors have made themselves available on thousands of occasions as speakers at commemorative and other programs, as guests of the media, and most importantly as a precious resource in classrooms throughout the nation. They have also contributed many hours and much anguish to the audio and video recording of their experiences. Videotaped interviewing of survivors, which began by the early 1970s, exploded following the television showing of *Holocaust*. Dozens of Holocaust museums and centers began survivor oral history projects. A small, private initiative undertaken in 1979 in New Haven, Connecticut, joined forces three years later with Yale University to become the Yale Video Archive (later renamed the Fortunoff Video Archive at Yale). It soon expanded into the foremost collection in the country; in 1990 its holdings included 1,400 video interviews, indexed and available for research and educational use. By 1992 approximately 11,600 audio and video interviews were held by forty-three major collections and many smaller projects. The tapes provide experiences and feelings that documents could never record and are of course a powerful medium for preserving and transmitting the realities of the Holocaust. Survivors have held several large-scale convocations, beginning with a gathering of 5,000 in Jerusalem in 1981. Two years later, 20,000 survivors met in Washington for a three-day conference. Several other major conferences have taken place over the years, organized under the aegis of the American Gathering/Federation of Jewish Holocaust Survivors.[133]

The heightened interest in the Holocaust that marked the 1970s and 1980s spurred action on an issue that had long been quiescent, justice for war criminals. American immigration screening procedures, so severely applied when Jewish refugees needed to flee the Nazis, had been excessively relaxed during the early postwar years to facilitate the rapid entry of displaced persons. Thousands of war criminals, many of them Eastern European collaborators with the Nazis, succeeded in slipping in among the 350,000 non-Jewish DPs by falsifying their applications. In time they became citizens, lying on the naturalization forms about their past activities, and went on to enjoy the full opportunities offered in the United States. For decades there was virtually no interest in this matter, and no action was taken. Then in 1974 Congresswoman Elizabeth Holtzman of New York, joined by Congressman Joshua Eilberg of Pennsylvania, began to blast the Immigration and Naturalization Service for not investigating the issue. In 1979 Holtzman was able to prevail upon the Justice Department to establish an Office of Special Investigations (OSI) to initiate legal action against Nazi war criminals in the United States.[134]

Because the war crimes had not violated American law, the perpetrators could not be tried for them in the United States. What the OSI determined to do was to locate war criminals, have them denaturalized by proving that they had lied about their wartime activities on their citizenship applications, and then have them deported. It was possible, but not likely, that they would ultimately be tried where the crimes had been committed. The OSI faced obstacles, for, with few witnesses still available, it was difficult to prove guilt for criminal acts that had happened more than thirty years previously in a foreign country. But the office managed to gather substantial amounts of evidence, partly through cooperation from the Soviet Union, which provided documentation and permitted OSI officials to travel to the Soviet Union to take videotaped testimony from witnesses. By the end of 1992 the OSI had succeeded in having the citizenship of forty-three war criminals revoked. Thirty-two of them were deported, and three were extradited to other countries for trial. More than four hundred cases were still under investigation. The crimes were not minor; most of the war criminals had been directly involved in annihilating Jews.[135]

After 1992 the efforts of the OSI decreased. Reasons included the advanced age of the suspected war criminals and a decline in general interest in the program. But the main factor was the final outcome of the highly publicized case of Ukrainian-born John Demjanjuk. Using evidence that he was the man called "Ivan the Terrible" who had operated the gas chambers at Treblinka, the OSI obtained revocation of his American citizenship in 1981. After lengthy litigation he was extradited to Israel, tried for war crimes, and, in 1988, convicted and sentenced to death. Before the execution was carried out, however, new evidence was found in the former Soviet Union that pointed to the definite possibility that a different person was "Ivan the Terrible." The Israeli Supreme Court then acquitted him because reasonable doubt existed and returned him to the United States, having decided not to try him again even though strong additional evidence linked him to crimes at Sobibor. In the meantime, a U.S. appeals court had reopened Demjanjuk's 1985 extradition case. In late 1993 it overturned the extradition order and charged the OSI with professional misconduct for withholding evidence that would have helped Demjanjuk in the 1985 proceeding. Several months later the U.S. Supreme Court closed off any further action by ruling that Demjanjuk could not be deported.[136]

It had been known for decades that war criminals had passed through the loose screening procedures used for the displaced persons. It was not until the 1980s, however, that researchers discovered that in the early Cold War years U.S. government agencies had intentionally protected Nazi war criminals who they thought would be useful in the struggle against the Soviet Union. In 1983 it was learned that the U.S. Army Counter Intelligence Corps (CIC) had employed Klaus Barbie in Europe from 1947 to 1951 while aware that he had been a war criminal. When France wanted him for trial in 1950, the CIC lied, claiming that it did not know where he was. A year later the CIC engineered Barbie's escape to South America. Barbie was only one of a number of Nazi collaborators who escaped with CIC help.[137]

Beyond that, the CIC, the State Department, and the CIA were all involved in programs that knowingly, and for the most part illegally, brought significant numbers of war criminals and ex-Nazis to the United States for Cold War purposes. From 1947 to 1951 the CIC's project Paperclip recruited 765 German weapons scientists, engineers, and technicians and moved them to the United States. At least 50 percent of them had been Nazi Party members or SS men. The Army either faked or suppressed their wartime records in order to obtain visas for them. The State Department and the CIA also had programs that brought several thousand Europeans to the United States from 1945 to 1956 for use in intelligence work, propaganda and psychological warfare projects, laboratory research, and even for training as anti-Communist guerrilla troops. Most of these people were not war criminals, but many were. One specific instance was uncovered by an OSI investigator who found that more than 300 people, a sizable part of the wartime Nazi puppet government of Byelorussia and the SS brigade there, had been illegally brought to the United States. They were put to work in anti-Soviet propaganda projects, government research institutes, and as translators and consultants to military and academic organizations. Many of them were war criminals; the Byelorussian government and SS had cooperated extensively with the German *Einsatzgruppen*.[138]

Seven years had passed since the airing of *Holocaust*. Consciousness of the Nazi destruction of the Jews had spread throughout the nation during those years, and interest in the Holocaust was still at a high level. It was April 1985, one week before the annual Day of Remembrance. Three weeks earlier, President Ronald Reagan had explained that he would not be visiting a concentration camp during his coming trip to Germany because he did not want to reawaken painful memories. Into that context burst the White House's Bitburg announcement. The president, accompanied by West German Chancellor Helmut Kohl, would visit a German military cemetery at Bitburg. There he would lay a wreath in a spirit of reconciliation, marking the forty years of peace since the end of World War II. The announcement, soon followed by the discovery by the press that forty-nine of the two thousand dead soldiers at Bitburg had been members of the Waffen SS, set off weeks of protest.[139]

Jewish leaders and organizations strongly condemned the intended visit. They were joined in their criticism by the American Legion. Reagan's subsequent announcement that he had, after all, decided to lay a wreath at a concentration camp as well did not lessen the outcry. And when, on the Day of Remembrance, he told a meeting of editors and broadcasters that the young men in the cemetery were also victims of Nazism, "just as surely as the victims in the concentration camps," the uproar reached a high pitch. The U.S. Holocaust Memorial Council, after tabling a motion for mass resignation, telegraphed the president that it was shocked at his "distortion of what took place during the Holocaust." Among those who now criticized the Bitburg visit were Archbishop John O'Connor of New York; several Republicans, among them former U.N. ambassador Jeanne Kirkpatrick, Senator Robert Dole of Kansas, and Congressman Newt Gingrich of Georgia; and, in a *New York Times* advertisement, 143 Protestant and Catholic leaders. The controversy reached its climax the day after the president's comment about victims, at a long-planned White House ceremony in which Elie Wiesel received the Congressional Gold Medal of Achievement. In accepting the medal, Wiesel implored Reagan to cancel the visit to Bitburg: "That place, Mr. President, is not your place. Your place is with the victims of the SS." In the days that followed, both the Senate and the House overwhelmingly passed resolutions asking Reagan to reconsider the stop at

Bitburg. Despite the protests, the trip went forward essentially as planned. On May 5 Reagan laid a wreath at Bergen-Belsen and later stopped very briefly to place another at Bitburg. At Bergen-Belsen he delivered a sensitive and moving address. In a speech made minutes after he left the Bitburg cemetery, he directed this thought to Holocaust survivors: "Many of you are worried that reconciliation means forgetting. Well, I promise you, we will never forget."[140]

The Bitburg episode was a major blunder by the Reagan administration. The president had no intention of offending Jews. His record had been one of consistently warm relations with American Jewry and strong support of Israel. But many months before he had impulsively agreed to a request from Kohl to carry out the cemetery wreath-laying, a request apparently made to help Kohl buttress his own political position. According to Wiesel, Reagan tried in the midst of the crisis to persuade Kohl to agree to cancellation of the Bitburg part of the trip. But Kohl insisted that Reagan keep his word. Wiesel blamed Reagan's advisers, who gave him very poor guidance, for allowing the episode to get so out of hand. Reagan was poorly informed about the Holocaust and unaware of how critically important its remembrance is to Jews. The most discouraging aspect of the whole affair, however, was its revelation of the level of ignorance, or lack of interest, on the part of his circle of advisers. It indicated that despite all the attention given to the Holocaust—the TV miniseries, the publicity since then, the Days of Remembrance, and all the other efforts—there was no assurance that the facts were known, or their significance understood, even at the highest levels of government.[141]

In 1986, the year after he received the Congressional Gold Medal of Achievement, Elie Wiesel was awarded the Nobel Prize for Peace in recognition of his life's work on the Holocaust. In his Nobel lecture in Oslo, Wiesel passionately cried out against persecution, terrorism, hunger, and war. Bestowal of so high an honor on him was confirmation of the belief already held by millions of Americans, Jewish and non-Jewish, that Wiesel and his quiet greatness personified the deep significance of the Holocaust. The prize also validated, on the world level, the extreme importance of the Holocaust and its remembrance.[142]

Since the broadcast of *Holocaust* in 1978, a great many American films related to the Jewish catastrophe have appeared, so many that Holocaust films have come to constitute a separate category in cinematic studies. But it was not until *Schindler's List* arrived at theaters at the end of 1993 that a film struck its viewers with a force comparable to that of *Holocaust*. *Schindler's List,* lavishly praised by nearly all reviewers, won seven Academy Awards. Yet there was criticism of the anonymous, stereotypical nature of the Jewish characters in the film and the historical inaccuracies in it. Beyond that, some wondered why a major Holocaust-related film would concentrate on an exceptional Nazi. Or why it would tell the story of the survival of a few rather than center on death, which is what the Holocaust actually was. The answer, of course, was Hollywood, an answer which also explained the uplifting ending and the superfluous sex. *Schindler's List* attracted large crowds for several months and surely succeeded in impressing some basic information about the Holocaust on millions of Americans, many of them unborn or too young to have watched *Holo-*

caust in 1978. The extensive attention that *Schindler's List* drew did not, however, match the notice attracted by the TV miniseries fifteen years earlier.[143]

Before 1970 only a tiny number of high schools and colleges included the Holocaust in any of their offerings. Since then, paralleling several other sectors of American society, educational institutions have turned significant attention to the topic. On the college and university level, the tendency in the 1970s was to incorporate small segments on the German annihilation of the Jews into Jewish history survey courses or courses on World War II. In the 1980s full-semester courses devoted to the Holocaust became widespread. Offered mostly by history and religion departments, the courses attracted strong enrollments, providing thousands of undergraduates with a reasonably comprehensive overview of the Holocaust. In the same years, more specialized and advanced Holocaust courses, some of them on the graduate level, began to be available in such areas as religion, philosophy, literature, and specific aspects of history.[144]

Many high schools introduced the Holocaust into their curricula during the seventies and eighties. Although the topic has not yet become a standard part of a high-school education, by 1988 eight states, numerous large cities, and probably hundreds of suburban school districts had adopted curricula for teaching it. Usually the Holocaust is integrated into U.S. or world history, or studies of Nazism or World War II. Typically there are two goals: to impart basic information about the Holocaust and to teach such values as democracy, respect for differences, individual responsibility, and freedom from racial and religious prejudices. The Holocaust is presented as an extreme instance of what can happen if these values are persistently violated. Teachers generally use audiovisual material, readings, lectures, discussions, and role-playing sessions. By 1990 teaching aids were available in abundance—books and collected readings, model curricula, posters, computer software, films, videotapes, and filmstrips.[145]

One important source of assistance for middle- and high-school teachers has been the nonprofit organization Facing History and Ourselves, formed in 1976. It offers training conferences and disseminates curricula, videotapes, and texts that it has developed. By 1990, 30,000 teachers from forty-six states had participated in Facing History conferences and workshops. Each year more than 450,000 students have worked with Facing History materials. The American Gathering/Federation of Jewish Holocaust Survivors has provided another type of experience for high-school educators since 1984. It is a Holocaust summer study program carried out in Poland and Israel. By 1992 it had involved 340 teachers from forty states and had affected an estimated 100,000 students.[146]

An adequate selection of books and other reading materials has been available since the mid-1970s for courses or segments of courses specifically on the Holocaust. On the other hand, the coverage of the Holocaust in the textbooks used in the more general courses in history and the social sciences, while improved since the 1960s, has remained inadequate. A 1970 study of about twenty textbooks written for college and high-school survey courses in U.S., European, and world history found that most of them contained no mention, or virtually none, of the Holocaust. One book did provide excellent coverage, and two others had good though short treatments. The only other text that gave a noticeable amount of space to the Holocaust was marred by important errors. A more recent analysis of ninety-three high-school textbooks, published for the most part during the 1970s, pointed to some improvement, but not much. Fewer than half of these books had a paragraph or more on the Holocaust, and almost one-third of them provided two sentences or less. Many of the accounts contained inaccuracies. The same study analyzed fifty-five college textbooks (twenty-eight in history and twenty-seven in social sciences) and found their Holocaust coverage even weaker than that in the high-school texts. The author of the survey concluded that, of the high-school and college books consulted, the twelve with the most useful presentations of the Holocaust would teach a student more about that topic than all the other books combined. Despite the generally dismal picture, there are indications that textbook authors and publishers in the 1990s have started to devote more attention to the Holocaust.[147]

Along with America's expanded interest in the Holocaust since the early 1970s has come an increase in the activity of Holocaust deniers, those who insist that the Holocaust did not occur. The basic claim of the deniers is that the Holocaust is a myth devised by Jews to ruin Germany's reputation, extract monetary reparations from Germany, and win sympathy for their plan to establish Israel and for continued American assistance to the Jewish state. This fraudulent argument took hold in Europe as early as 1947 with assertions that all the evidence of the Holocaust, including photographs and eyewitness testimonies, was falsified. The main formative influence on Holocaust denial was Paul Rassinier, a French national, who maintained that the Jews invented the Holocaust as a means of controlling the world's finances and gaining support for Israel. The similarities to *The Protocols of the Elders of Zion* are evident. The mythical power of the Jews and their supposed conspiratorial deviousness are basic concepts in both.[148]

Although Holocaust denial reached the United States in the 1950s, for two decades it had little currency except in anti-Semitic publications and with extremist racist and anti-Semitic groups. During those earlier years the notion was taken up by Harry Elmer Barnes, a once prominent historian. By the 1960s he had accepted Rassinier's basic position, although he kept the anti-Semitism subdued. Barnes's main objective in denying the Holocaust was to rehabilitate the moral stature of Germany. Austin J. App, a son of German immigrants and a professor of medieval English literature, pursued the same goal of justifying Germany's actions in World War II in an effort to restore its standing in the world. A blatant anti-Semite, App in 1973 published a pamphlet, *The Six Million Swindle*, which set down the basic assertions used by Holocaust deniers to this day. App claimed, for instance, that the gas chambers never existed; that if Germany had intended to eliminate the Jews, there would not have been hundreds of thousands of survivors; that most Jews who died were actually underground fighters against Germany or else spies, saboteurs, or criminals; and that there was no evidence to prove that six million Jews died.[149]

The impact of Holocaust denial in the United States expanded noticeably with two developments during the 1970s. Both represented an attempt to tone down the anti-Semitic rhetoric and to assume the appearance of academic respectability and objectivity. One was the publication in 1976 of *The Hoax of the Twentieth Century*, a book by Arthur Butz, a professor of electrical engineering at Northwestern University. Butz applied a veneer of scholarship by including source notes, long quotations, references to reputable scholarly books, and a bibliography. He also gave an impression of objectivity by criticizing earlier denier writings, by conceding that up to one million Jews might have died under the Nazis, and by granting that Jews were persecuted and died in ghettos and camps because of the bad conditions there. Yet anti-Semitism, though somewhat subtle, remained central, and his conclusions were the usual ones: the European Jews had not been annihilated, all evidence of the Holocaust had been faked, the Holocaust was a hoax—a Jewish plot invented for Zionist purposes. Butz's book rapidly became, and still is, the main text of the denial movement. The other step to create an aura of academic respectability was the establishment of the Institute for Historical Review near Los Angeles in 1978. This organization, which has worked closely with racist and anti-Semitic groups, is a major distributor of Holocaust denial literature. In its attempts to draw publicity to the deniers' views, it holds supposedly academic conferences and publishes the *Journal of Historical Review*, a periodical containing Holocaust denial and other "revisionist" studies that is crafted to look like an authentic scholarly journal.[150]

The denial movement drew substantial publicity in the late 1980s because of Fred Leuchter, a self-proclaimed engineer and a specialist in designing and installing execution equipment. Leuchter spent four days at Auschwitz and Majdanek observing the gas chamber areas, then returned to the United States and published his findings as *The Leuchter Report*. He maintained that the design of the facilities and the analysis of materials he scraped from their walls proved that they were not and could not have been used as gas chambers. Leuchter's conclusions and Leuchter himself were rapidly discredited. It turned out that not only did he have no expertise in gas chambers but he was not even trained as an engineer: he had a bachelor's degree in history. Three years later, as he was about to be tried in Massachusetts for illegally practicing engineering, Leuchter signed a consent agreement to cease presenting himself as an engineer and to refrain from issuing reports involving engineering opinions. But *The Leuchter Report*, a proven fraud, took on its own life and has continued to be cited by deniers as proof that the gas chambers never existed. The propaganda of the deniers was not without its ridiculous irony, however. Butz, the engineer, pretended to be a historian, and Leuchter, with his history degree, claimed to be the engineer.[151]

In the early 1990s the deniers gained a lot of attention by attempting to place full-page advertisements arguing that the Holocaust was a hoax in dozens of university newspapers. The advertisements for the most part consisted of lies, distortions, and obfuscations. At least fifteen papers printed them, and twenty or more rejected them, but either way the deniers drew the publicity they wanted. The published ads created shock, anger, and a great deal of discussion. One result was that the deniers were perceived by many as proponents of a legitimate, though unpopular, interpretation that deserved serious consideration in the marketplace of ideas.

The rejected ads provided the deniers with the opportunity to cry censorship and violation of the right of free speech, specious arguments that had strongly influenced those editors and university administrators who had agreed to publish the advertisements. It is not true that a newspaper must publish whatever is submitted to it; in fact, the campus papers that did print the advertisements had preexisting policies that excluded racist, sexist, and religiously offensive advertising.[152]

Despite their efforts to appear academic and to obtain publicity, it seemed that the Holocaust deniers had made little impression by the early 1990s, either on high-school and college youth or on the adult population. The response to a question in a Roper poll of late 1992 appeared to contradict this observation when it indicated that 22 percent of Americans had doubts about the occurrence of the Holocaust and an additional 12 percent had no opinion. This result was so unexpected that skepticism was expressed about the wording of the question, which was indeed confusing: "Does it seem possible or does it seem impossible to you that the Nazi extermination of the Jews never happened?" For clarification, Roper repeated the survey in early 1994 using a more straightforward wording: "Does it seem possible to you that the Nazi extermination of the Jews never happened, or do you feel certain that it happened?" This time, 1 percent thought it possible that it had never happened, 8 percent did not know, and 91 percent were certain that it had occurred. A Gallup poll, also taken in early 1994, found that 79 percent thought that the Holocaust had definitely happened and 17 percent thought that it had probably happened, while 2 percent believed that it probably had not occurred, and fewer than one half of a percent answered that it definitely had not taken place.[153]

In search of information about the American public's overall attitudes about the Holocaust, a Yankelovich–Clancy Shulman survey in late 1990 found a high level of acceptance of the importance of the Holocaust and the need to continue education about it. Seventy-three percent regarded the Holocaust as a very significant historical event, second in the survey to American slavery (78 percent). Seventy-six percent thought it was essential (28 percent) or very important (48 percent) that all Americans know about and understand the Holocaust. Seventy-three percent thought it was essential (32 percent) or very important (41 percent) that the Holocaust be incorporated into American education. Seventy-six percent believed that the public schools were paying the right amount of attention (32 percent) or too little attention (44 percent) to the Holocaust (3 percent thought there was too much attention, and 21 percent did not know). And 85 percent agreed that it was important for Americans to continue to hear about the Holocaust so that it would not happen again. As to their own knowledge about the Holocaust, 27 percent of the respondents claimed to know a great deal and 36 percent a fair amount; the remaining 37 percent said they knew little or nothing. Analysts interpreting a 1994 Roper poll concluded that Americans' detailed knowledge of the Holocaust was still quite limited but comparable to their knowledge of other significant events of World War II.[154]

The shocking revelations that emerged with the opening of the German concentration camps in the spring of 1945 and the reports from Nuremberg a few months later forcefully drew the attention of the American people to the Holocaust. When the main war crimes trials faded from public view, however, so did the catastrophe of the European Jews. Other than the publicity that surrounded the Eichmann trial in the early 1960s, the Holocaust received little attention in the United States for a quarter of a century. Then, in the first years of the 1970s, an important change started to take place. Concern about the Holocaust increased substantially in the Jewish community and began to spread in non-Jewish America. In 1978 the subject was thrust to the national forefront by the TV miniseries *Holocaust*. While the intense interest generated by *Holocaust* could not, of course, be sustained, concern with the Jewish catastrophe remained at very high levels into 1986.[155]

The indications are that in 1986 attention to the Holocaust began to level off and to decline to some extent in the United States. New books, films, displays, courses, memorials, and works of art continued to appear but not with the frequency of the previous eight years. Despite the decline, the levels of Holocaust interest and activity have remained high, though not at the peaks attained during the period from 1978 to 1986. By the mid-1990s, recognition of the Holocaust as an issue of national importance had been embedded in American culture and institutionalized in many ways. It was by then a permanent and growing component of the nation's educational systems. Annual Days of Remembrance had become integral to the civic calendar in all parts of the country. The monuments and museums were fixtures on the American scene. The museums and the many Holocaust centers had established close connections with the educational community, including the public schools and the providers of adult programs. The Holocaust had been deeply impressed into literature, film, and scholarship and would continue to have a strong presence in those areas of work. It was also firmly integrated into theological studies and had become a core issue in Christian-Jewish relations.

Lastly, an American consensus had been reached on the importance of the remembrance of the Holocaust. And, at least verbally, agreement had emerged on the need for the United States to intervene to stop potential future genocides or, at the minimum, to act to alleviate the impacts of any such catastrophes. These commitments have been affirmed at America's highest levels of civic responsibility, by the Congress and by the presidency. One of the clearest instances is seen in the nation's capital, on the outside walls of the United States Holocaust Memorial Museum. Chiseled into the plain solidity of limestone drawn from the nation's heartland are the words of the three presidents who served during the years the museum was planned and constructed:

> Out of our memory of the Holocaust we must forge an unshakable oath with all civilized people that never again will the world stand silent, never again will the world fail to act in time to prevent this terrible crime of genocide.
>
> Jimmy Carter, September 1979

> We must make sure that from now until the end of days all humankind stares this evil in the face. And only then can we be sure that it will never arise again.
>
> Ronald Reagan, October 1988

Here we will learn that each of us bears responsibility for our actions and for our failure to act. Here we will learn that we must intervene when we see evil arise.

George Bush, February 1991

The commitment to remember has been acknowledged and recorded. The responsibility to act has been forcefully recognized. The commitment to remember has been strongly upheld; its continuing fulfillment appears assured. But the pledge to act remains thus far little more than words.[156]

NOTES

1. Eli Faber, *A Time for Planting: The First Migration, 1654–1820* (Baltimore, 1992), 4, 11–12; Abraham J. Karp, *Haven and Home: A History of the Jews in America* (New York, 1985), 6, 8; *Encyclopaedia Judaica*, 16 vols. (New York, 1971), 15:1586.

2. Faber, *A Time for Planting*, 1, 4, 14–17, 26, 28, 84–97, 142–43; Karp, *Haven and Home*, 22, 28; *Encyclopaedia Judaica*, 15:1586–90.

3. *Encyclopaedia Judaica*, 15:1595–96; Faber, *A Time for Planting*, 129, 134–40, 143; Hasia R. Diner, *A Time for Gathering: The Second Migration, 1820–1880* (Baltimore, 1992), 198; Howard M. Sachar, *A History of the Jews in America* (New York, 1992), 26.

4. *Encyclopaedia Judaica*, 15:1596; Lucy S. Dawidowicz, *On Equal Terms: Jews in America, 1881–1981* (New York, 1982), 25, 41; Karp, *Haven and Home*, 23, 27, 52, 63; Faber, *A Time for Planting*, 12–13, 24–26, 28; Diner, *A Time for Gathering*, 1, 4–5, 232.

5. Dawidowicz, *On Equal Terms*, 26–27; Karp, *Haven and Home*, 28; *Encyclopaedia Judaica*, 15: 1597, 1603.

6. Dawidowicz, *On Equal Terms*, 28–33; *Encyclopaedia Judaica*, 15:1599–1600, 1603–4; Sachar, *Jews in America*, 104–13; Karp, *Haven and Home*, 36, 84–86.

7. Karp, *Haven and Home*, 29; *Encyclopaedia Judaica*, 15:1597–98, 1607; Dawidowicz, *On Equal Terms*, 24; Diner, *A Time for Gathering*, 191, 197–200.

8. Karp, *Haven and Home*, 63, 111–13, 171; Dawidowicz, *On Equal Terms*, 41; Leonard Dinnerstein, *Uneasy at Home: Antisemitism and the American Jewish Experience* (New York, 1987), 16–18; Gerald Sorin, *A Time for Building: The Third Migration, 1880–1920* (Baltimore, 1992), 57; *Encyclopaedia Judaica*, 15:1608, 1611.

9. Dawidowicz, *On Equal Terms*, 46, 47, 51, 59, 95; Sorin, *A Time for Building*, 69–71, 136–52; Karp, *Haven and Home*, 121, 126, 190, 194–98.

10. Dawidowicz, *On Equal Terms*, 58; Sorin, *A Time for Building*, 181–90; Arthur Hertzberg, *The Jews in America: Four Centuries of an Uneasy Encounter: A History* (New York, 1989), 279. The quoted material is from Sorin, *A Time for Building*, 188, 190.

11. John Higham, *Strangers in the Land: Patterns of American Nativism, 1860–1925* (New York, 1963), esp. chaps. 6 and 11; Robert Singerman, "The Jew as Racial Alien: The Genetic Component of American Anti-Semitism," in *Anti-Semitism in American History*, ed. David A. Gerber (Urbana, 1987), 103–28; Karp, *Haven and Home*, 172; Sachar, *Jews in America*, 280–83.

12. Higham, *Strangers in the Land*, chap. 11; Sachar, *Jews in America*, 321–24; Sorin, *A Time for Building*, 58; U.S. Immigration and Naturalization Service, *Monthly Review*, June 1945, 158.

13. Sorin, *A Time for Building*, 167; Sachar, *Jews in America*, 300–306, 326–33; Dawidowicz, *On Equal Terms*, 91, 92; Karp, *Haven and Home*, 266, 271, 274.

14. David M. Chalmers, *Hooded Americanism: The History of the Ku Klux Klan* (Chicago, 1968), 71, 110, 197; Charles C. Alexander, *The Ku Klux Klan in the Southwest* (Lexington, Ky., 1966), 26; Sachar, *Jews in America*, 307.

15. Sachar, *Jews in America*, 310–19; Karp, *Haven and Home*, 269, 270; Dawidowicz, *On Equal Terms*, 90, 91.

16. Karp, *Haven and Home*, 274.

17. Ibid., 116; Sachar, *Jews in America*, 132–33; Sorin, *A Time for Building*, 49–50.

18. Karp, *Haven and Home*, 219–20; Dawidowicz, *On Equal Terms*, 66–67, 72–73, 75; Sachar, *Jews in America*, 228–29, 233.

19. Dawidowicz, *On Equal Terms*, 35; *Encyclopaedia Judaica*, 15:1601; Diner, *A Time for Gathering*, 112; Sachar, *Jews in America*, 307–8.

20. Sachar, *Jews in America*, 234–36; Dawidowicz, *On Equal Terms*, 78–79; Sorin, *A Time for Building*, 207–9; Karp, *Haven and Home*, 245–46.

21. Karp, *Haven and Home*, 228–32; Sorin, *A Time for Building*, 200, 211–14; Sachar, *Jews in*

America, 262–70; Dawidowicz, *On Equal Terms,* 83–85.

22. David S. Wyman, *The Abandonment of the Jews: America and the Holocaust, 1941–1945* (New York, 1984), 67–68; Karp, *Haven and Home,* 231–32.

23. Dawidowicz, *On Equal Terms,* 70, 71; Sorin, *A Time for Building,* 210–14, 219–27, 231; Karp, *Haven and Home,* 248–50; Sachar, *Jews in America,* 253.

24. Sachar, *Jews in America,* 504–8, 514; Sorin, *A Time for Building,* 232; Karp, *Haven and Home,* 251, 252; David S. Wyman, *Paper Walls: America and the Refugee Crisis, 1938–1941* (Amherst, 1968), 37.

25. Wyman, *Paper Walls,* vii, 155–205, 209; idem, *Abandonment of the Jews,* preface and chaps. 7, 10, and 11.

26. Wyman, *Paper Walls,* 3–9; idem, *Abandonment of the Jews,* 6–9.

27. Wyman, *Paper Walls,* 10–14.

28. Ibid., 14, 16–17, 20–23; Wyman, *Abandonment of the Jews,* 9.

29. Lloyd P. Gartner, "The Two Continuities of Antisemitism in the United States," in *Antisemitism through the Ages,* ed. Shmuel Almog (Oxford, 1988), 317–18; Wyman, *Paper Walls,* 35.

30. Wyman, *Paper Walls,* 14–22; idem, *Abandonment of the Jews,* 9–11, 14–15.

31. Wyman, *Paper Walls,* chap. 1; Charles H. Stember et al., *Jews in the Mind of America* (New York, 1966), 130–33; Wyman, *Abandonment of the Jews,* preface and chap. 16.

32. Wyman, *Paper Walls,* 27–29, 35–36, 39.

33. Ibid., 29–30, 37, 71–72.

34. Ibid., 4–5, 29–30, 43, 168–72, 221; U.S. Immigration and Naturalization Service, *Monthly Review,* June 1945, 158.

35. Wyman, *Paper Walls,* 43, 44, 48–51.

36. Ibid., 71–73.

37. Ibid., 75–76, 85–86, 91–92, 95–97, 117–28, 132.

38. Ibid., 38; Richard Breitman and Alan M. Kraut, *American Refugee Policy and European Jewry, 1933–1945* (Bloomington, 1987), 70–73, 232.

39. Wyman, *Paper Walls,* 37; idem, *Abandonment of the Jews,* 157–58.

40. Wyman, *Paper Walls,* 116, 137–41, 148–50.

41. Ibid., 172–78, 182–91; Wyman, *Abandonment of the Jews,* 124–25, 130–32.

42. Wyman, *Paper Walls,* 143–47, 177–78, 200–201; idem, *Abandonment of the Jews,* 108–9, 190–91. The quotation is from Wyman, *Paper Walls,* 173.

43. Wyman, *Paper Walls,* 191–201; idem, *Abandonment of the Jews,* 125.

44. Wyman, *Abandonment of the Jews,* 3–5.

45. Ibid., 19–55, 61–62, 321–22; Deborah E. Lipstadt, *Beyond Belief: The American Press and the Coming of the Holocaust, 1933–1945* (New York, 1986), 180–88.

46. Wyman, *Abandonment of the Jews,* 73–76, 97–100.

47. Ibid., 63–73, 87–89, 93–100, 104–5, 107.

48. Ibid., 105–8, 112–22, 168–69.

49. Ibid., 84–87, 90–92, 143–50, 152–56, 193–94, 201, 203–4.

50. Ibid., chap. 10.

51. Ibid., 187, 203–5, 209.

52. Ibid., 209–15, 285, 287, 330.

53. Leonard Dinnerstein, *America and the Survivors of the Holocaust* (New York, 1982), 9, 18, 24, 101, 107–12; Dawidowicz, *On Equal Terms,* 126–27; Yehuda Bauer, *Out of the Ashes: The Impact of American Jews on Post-Holocaust European Jewry* (Oxford, 1989), 71–82, 131–32; Dora Drutman, "The Displaced Jews in the American Zone of Germany," *Jewish Journal of Sociology* 3 (1961), 262; *American Jewish Year Book, 1947–48* (Philadelphia, 1947), 520–21.

54. Dinnerstein, *America and the Survivors,* 10–13, 16–17, 24, 28, 33–34, 40–41, 47, 301; *American Jewish Year Book, 1948–49* (Philadelphia, 1949), 457; Wyman, *Abandonment of the Jews,* 13–14, 324–25; *New York Times,* January 25, 1946, 5.

55. Dinnerstein, *America and the Survivors,* 34, 36, 42–51, 291, 295, 300–302.

56. Ibid., 42–43, 73, 79–80, 86–88, 92–95, 296, 298–300.

57. Ibid., 112–13, 181, 201–5, 251; *American Jewish Year Book, 1946–47* (Philadelphia, 1946), 219; *New York Times,* December 23, 1945, 1, December 29, 1945, 1; Bauer, *Out of the Ashes,* 87.

58. Dinnerstein, *America and the Survivors,* 101, 113–15, 117, 119; *American Jewish Year Book, 1947–48,* 561.

59. Dinnerstein, *America and the Survivors,* 117, 121–27, 130–31, 146–51, 158–61, 315–19; *American Jewish Year Book, 1947–48,* 220.

60. *American Jewish Year Book, 1946–47,* 172–87, *1950* (New York and Philadelphia, 1950), 110; Dinnerstein, *America and the Survivors,* 5–6, 127–34, 146–67, 267.

61. Dinnerstein, *America and the Survivors,* 166–81, 267–70.

62. Ibid., 183–84, 191–98, 215, 260; Allan A. Ryan, Jr., *Quiet Neighbors: Prosecuting Nazi War Criminals in America* (San Diego, 1984), 5–6, 8, 13–28, 31, 264, 325–31, 344; John Loftus, *The Belarus Secret* (New York, 1982), 86–101, 104–5.

63. Dinnerstein, *America and the Survivors,* 214–53.

64. Ibid., 251–52, 255–56. Jews made up about two-thirds of the DPs who came under the Truman Directive but only 16 percent of those who entered under the DP Acts (Dinnerstein, *America and the Survivors,* 287). Other countries took in the following approximate numbers of DPs: Australia, 176,000; Israel, 136,000; Canada, 113,000; the United Kingdom, 104,000; France, 42,000; Belgium, 36,000; Argentina, 33,000; Brazil, 29,000; and Venezuela, 19,000 (ibid., 284). Both of the DP Acts were emergency legislation; thus neither changed the National Origins Immigration Act of 1924, with anti-Catholic and anti-Jewish bias built into its quota structure. The Immigration Act of 1965 finally eliminated the quota system, replacing it with an arrangement allotting major preference (74 percent of visas) to those with relatives in the United States and substantial preference (20 percent) to people with special skills. A small proportion (6 percent) was reserved for refugees (*American Jewish Year Book, 1966* [New York and Philadelphia, 1966], 164–75).

65. Bauer, *Out of the Ashes,* 39–41, 56, 69, 296, 298.

66. Ibid., xxv, 41–42, 51, 69–70, 76–80, 92–94, 133–80, 185–86, 203, 208, 256–59.

67. Aaron Berman, *Nazism, the Jews, and American Zionism, 1933–1948* (Detroit, 1990), 33, 80–89, 106–7, 155; Wyman, *Abandonment of the Jews,* 160.

68. Wyman, *Abandonment of the Jews,* 160–66, 174–75; *New York Times,* November 17, 1945, 8; *American Jewish Year Book, 1946–47,* 244.

69. Wyman, *Abandonment of the Jews,* 159, 170–73; Zvi Ganin, *Truman, American Jewry, and Israel, 1945–1948* (New York, 1979), 13, 44; Sachar, *Jews in America,* 567.

70. Wyman, *Abandonment of the Jews,* 173; Selig Adler, "Franklin D. Roosevelt and Zionism—The Wartime Record," *Judaism* 21 (1972), 265–69, 271, 275–76; Sachar, *Jews in America,* 573–79; Herbert Parzen, "The Roosevelt Palestine Policy, 1933–1945," *American Jewish Archives* 26 (1974), 63; Emanuel Neumann, *In The Arena: An Autobiographical Memoir* (New York, 1976), 199–201. The Roosevelt quotations are from U.S. Department of State, *Foreign Relations of the United States, 1944,* vol. 5, *The Near East, South Asia, Africa, the Far East* (Washington, D.C., 1965), 616, and *1945,* vol. 8, *The Near East and Africa* (Washington, D.C., 1969), 698. The Hull quotation is from Cordell Hull, *The Memoirs of Cordell Hull,* 2 vols. (New York, 1948), 2:1536. The quotation by the American chairman of the Anglo-American Committee, Joseph Hutcheson, is from Dinnerstein, *America and the Survivors,* 74.

71. Ganin, *Truman, American Jewry, and Israel,* 44–47; *New York Times,* November 30, 1945, 10, December 18, 1945, 1, December 20, 1945, 12; *Congressional Record,* 79th Cong., 1st sess., 91:12138; Wyman, *Abandonment of the Jews,* 174; John Snetsinger, *Truman, the Jewish Vote, and the Creation of Israel* (Stanford, 1974), 24–25.

72. Dinnerstein, *America and the Survivors,* 80, 107; Snetsinger, *Truman, the Jewish Vote, and the Creation of Israel,* 22, 51–52; *American Jewish Year Book, 1946–47,* 235, 381–84; *New York Times,* November 14, 1945, 1; Berman, *Nazism, the Jews, and American Zionism,* 170; Sachar, *Jews in America,* 615.

73. Dinnerstein, *America and the Survivors,* 106–7; Sachar, *Jews in America,* 587, 596–97; Berman, *Nazism, the Jews, and American Zionism,* 170, 177; *American Jewish Year Book, 1947–48,* 106, 251, 252, 256.

74. Berman, *Nazism, the Jews, and American Zionism,* 177–79, 182–83; Sachar, *Jews in America,* 596–600; Dawidowicz, *On Equal Terms,* 128; Robert J. Donovan, *Conflict and Crisis: The Presidency of Harry S Truman, 1945–1948* (New York, 1977), 319–31, 377–78, 381, 386–87; Nadav Safran, *Israel: The Embattled Ally* (Cambridge, Mass., 1978), 38–40; Snetsinger, *Truman, the Jewish Vote, and the Creation of Israel,* xi; Ganin, *Truman, American Jewry, and Israel,* xiii–xvi, 47, 64, 104–5, 108–9, 145–46, 188; Michael J. Cohen, *Truman and Israel* (Berkeley, 1990), 59–60, 259, 279. An October 1947 Gallup poll indicated that 65 percent of the American public supported partition, 10 percent opposed it, and 25 percent did not have an opinion (Eytan Gilboa, *American Public Opinion toward Israel and the Arab-Israeli Conflict* [Lexington, Mass., 1987], 18, 21). The history of the developments that led to the formation of Israel is highly complicated, and the course followed by President Truman was often vacillating and inconsistent. The reasons behind Truman's various actions continue to be debated. The books by Donovan, Snetsinger, Ganin, and Cohen mentioned above offer a good introduction to the literature.

75. Donovan, *Conflict and Crisis,* 369–87; Sachar, *Jews in America,* 602–12; Safran, *Israel,* 38, 43–44, 60; Ganin, *Truman, American Jewry, and Israel,* 147–52, 178–89; Cohen, *Truman and Israel,* 175–98, 208–22; Snetsinger, *Truman, the Jewish Vote, and the Creation of Israel,* 110–11, 139; *American Jewish Year Book, 1950,* 394. Surplus World War II arms, paid for by American Jews and in part smuggled out of the United States, contributed to the Jewish military victory. In an entirely unrelated effort during the

early post–World War II years, American Jewry, acting mainly through the United Jewish Appeal, gave hundreds of millions of dollars for the development of Palestine/Israel. This assistance to Israel has continued into the present (Sachar, *Jews in America,* 613–19, 713–14, 880–81).

76. *American Jewish Year Book, 1948–49,* 473; Berman, *Nazism, the Jews, and American Zionism,* 156–60; David Rosenthal, "She'erit ha-Pleytah," *Midstream* 36 (August 1990), 25; Donovan, *Conflict and Crisis,* 331, 378; Dawidowicz, *On Equal Terms,* 128; Safran, *Israel,* 41–42, 572; Gilboa, *American Public Opinion toward Israel,* 15. The Taft quotation is from *Congressional Record,* 79th Cong., 1st sess., 91: 12141. The final quotation is from Donovan, *Conflict and Crisis,* 387.

77. Donovan, *Conflict and Crisis,* 386; Gilboa, *American Public Opinion toward Israel,* 1, 33–35, 47–48, 75, 90–91, 127–28, 163, 241–42, 306, 321; Bat-Ami Zucker, "The Genesis of the Special Relationship between the United States and Israel, 1948–1973," *American Jewish Archives* 44 (1992), 565–66; David Schoenbaum, *The United States and the State of Israel* (New York, 1993), 3–4; Safran, *Israel,* 571; *American Jewish Year Book, 1985* (New York and Philadelphia, 1984), 110, *1990* (New York and Philadelphia, 1990), 212–13; Alvin Richman, "The Polls—A Report," *Public Opinion Quarterly* 53 (1989), 417. The Kissinger quotation is from *U.S. News and World Report,* June 23, 1975, 23.

78. Zucker, "The Genesis of the Special Relationship," 565, 569–75; Schoenbaum, *The United States and the State of Israel,* 5, 6, 320; Cohen, *Truman and Israel,* 274, 280–81, 567–68; Safran, *Israel,* 572–73; Gilboa, *American Public Opinion toward Israel,* 1. The Carter quotation is from *New York Times,* May 13, 1977, 12.

79. Henry Friedlander and Earlean M. McCarrick, "Nazi Criminals in the United States: The Fedorenko Case," *Simon Wiesenthal Center Annual* 2 (1985), 63; Israel Gutman, ed., *Encyclopedia of the Holocaust,* 4 vols. (New York, 1990), 4:1496; William J. Bosch, *Judgment on Nuremberg: American Attitudes toward the Major German War-Crime Trials* (Chapel Hill, 1970), 11, 21–27; Wyman, *Abandonment of the Jews,* 257, 260.

80. Bosch, *Judgment on Nuremberg,* 11–13, 27; Gutman, *Encyclopedia of the Holocaust,* 4:1488, 1491; Bradley F. Smith, *Reaching Judgment at Nuremberg* (New York, 1977), 13–15; *American Jewish Year Book, 1947–48,* 583.

81. Smith, *Reaching Judgment at Nuremberg,* xiii, 8, 164, 299–300, 307; *American Jewish Year Book, 1947–48,* 588; Bosch, *Judgment on Nuremberg,* 13.

82. Smith, *Reaching Judgment at Nuremberg,* xiv,

xviii, 14–15, 89, 135–36; *American Jewish Year Book, 1947–48,* 589; Gutman, *Encyclopedia of the Holocaust,* 4:1493.

83. Smith, *Reaching Judgment at Nuremberg,* 88–89; Friedlander and McCarrick, "Nazi Criminals in the United States," 64; Wyman, *Abandonment of the Jews,* 325–26; *New York Times,* e.g., December 13, 1945, 12, December 15, 1945, 8, January 4, 1946, 6, January 8, 1946, 10.

84. *American Jewish Year Book, 1947–48,* 588; Bosch, *Judgment on Nuremberg,* 28, 109, 118–19.

85. *American Jewish Year Book, 1948–49,* 494–99, *1952* (New York and Philadelphia, 1952), 445; Gutman, *Encyclopedia of the Holocaust,* 4:1489, 1501–4; Henry Friedlander, "The Judiciary and Nazi Crimes in Postwar Germany," *Simon Wiesenthal Center Annual* 1 (1984), 30; Tom Bower, *The Pledge Betrayed: America and Britain and the Denazification of Postwar Germany* (Garden City, N.Y., 1982), 178–84; *New York Times,* December 14, 1945, 11, December 15, 1945, 1.

86. Smith, *Reaching Judgment at Nuremberg,* 303–4; *American Jewish Year Book, 1948–49,* 500, *1952,* 446; Gutman, *Encyclopedia of the Holocaust,* 4:1504; Bower, *The Pledge Betrayed,* chap. 12.

87. Kai Bird, *The Chairman: John J. McCloy: The Making of the American Establishment* (New York, 1992), 310–11, 330–31, 333, 335, 338–39, 362–64, 368, 371.

88. Ibid., 364, 369–73; Thomas A. Schwartz, "John J. McCloy and the Landsberg Cases," in *American Policy and the Reconstruction of West Germany, 1945–1955,* edited by Jeffry M. Diefendorf et al. (Cambridge, 1993), 433–54.

89. Gutman, *Encyclopedia of the Holocaust,* 4:1505–8; *American Jewish Year Book, 1952,* 447.

90. Bower, *The Pledge Betrayed,* 361; Friedlander, "The Judiciary and Nazi Crimes," 30; *American Jewish Year Book, 1952,* 446. The quotation is from Paul Johnson, *A History of the Jews* (New York, 1987), 514.

91. Wyman, *Abandonment of the Jews,* 337; *New York Times,* April 20, 1946, 6, July 11, 1946, 7, May 3, 1954, 10, April 22, 1957, 2, April 21, 1958, 22, May 24, 1959, 58.

92. Irving Greenberg, "The Struggle over a Date for Yom haShoah," *Moment* 14 (June 1989), 34; more fully in idem, *The Jewish Way: Living the Holidays* (New York, 1988), 326–43.

93. Greenberg, *The Jewish Way,* 333; *New York Times,* April 13, 1961, 2, April 14, 1961, 8.

94. Judith E. Doneson, *The Holocaust in American Film* (Philadelphia, 1987), 60–62, 66–76, 82, 218; Anne Frank, *Anne Frank: The Diary of a Young Girl* (New York, 1959), 184; John Hersey, *The Wall*

(New York, 1950); Leon Uris, *Exodus* (Garden City, N.Y., 1958). *Exodus* appeared as a film in 1960; *The Wall,* not until 1982 (Annette Insdorf, *Indelible Shadows: Film and the Holocaust,* 2d ed. [Cambridge, 1989], 10, 22). The two quotations are from Doneson, *The Holocaust in American Film,* 69–70 and 72.

95. *New York Times,* May 24, 1960, 1; Charles Y. Glock, Gertrude J. Selznick, and Joe L. Spaeth, *The Apathetic Majority: A Study Based on Public Responses to the Eichmann Trial* (New York, 1966), xi, 1, 11–12; Stember et al., *Jews in the Mind of America,* 193; Gutman, *Encyclopedia of the Holocaust,* 2:429; Irving Crespi, "Public Reaction to the Eichmann Trial," *Public Opinion Quarterly* 28 (1964), 91.

96. Glock, Selznick, and Spaeth, *The Apathetic Majority,* 12–14; Gutman, *Encyclopedia of the Holocaust,* 2:430–32; *American Jewish Year Book, 1962* (New York and Philadelphia, 1962), 85, *1963* (New York and Philadelphia, 1963), 247.

97. *American Jewish Year Book, 1962,* 85–89, 93–96; Crespi, "Public Reaction to the Eichmann Trial," 91; Glock, Selznick, and Spaeth, *The Apathetic Majority,* 3, 18–19, 129; *New York Times Index,* 1961, 538–42.

98. *American Jewish Year Book, 1962,* 101–2; Glock, Selznick, and Spaeth, *The Apathetic Majority,* 6–7, 18–19, 24–29, 50–51, 141 (quotations on 50–51).

99. Doneson, *The Holocaust in American Film,* 94, 97–103, 106.

100. Insdorf, *Indelible Shadows,* 3, 10–12, 15, 29–34, 50–52; Doneson, *The Holocaust in American Film,* 110–18, 121–27, 130–31. Other films made between 1962 and 1978 that barely touched on the Holocaust were *The Condemned of Altona, The Man in the Glass Booth, Julia,* and *The Serpent's Egg* (Insdorf, *Indelible Shadows,* 45–49, 99–102, 180–82; Doneson, *The Holocaust in American Film,* 132–38). Insdorf names twenty-three American feature films and thirty-four documentaries on the Holocaust made from 1980 to 1989 and cautions that her list is "by no means complete" (267–76).

101. Elie Wiesel, *Night* (New York, 1960), *Dawn* (New York, 1961), *The Accident* (New York, 1962), *The Town beyond the Wall* (New York, 1964), *The Gates of the Forest* (New York, 1966). On Wiesel, see Yosef I. Abramowitz, "Is Elie Wiesel Happy?" *Moment* 19 (February 1994), 34.

102. Raul Hilberg, *The Destruction of the European Jews,* 3 vols., rev. ed. (New York, 1985); *New York Times Book Review,* November 19, 1961; Hannah Arendt, *Eichmann in Jerusalem* (New York, 1964). For a discussion of *Eichmann in Jerusalem,*

see Walter Laqueur, "Hannah Arendt in Jerusalem: The Controversy Revisited," in *Western Society after the Holocaust,* ed. Lyman H. Legters (Boulder, 1983), 107–29.

103. *New York Times,* February 12, 1968, 37; Nora Levin, *The Holocaust: The Destruction of European Jewry, 1933–1945* (New York, 1968); Arthur D. Morse, *While Six Million Died: A Chronicle of American Apathy* (New York, 1968).

104. Rolf Hochhuth, *The Deputy* (New York, 1964), 4; *New York Times,* February 20, 1964, 59, February 23, 1964, sec. 2, p. 1, February 25, 1964, 23, February 27, 1964, 26, February 28, 1964, 18, 28, March 8, 1964, sec. 4, p. 4.

105. *Holocaust and Genocide Studies* 5 (1990), 351–52; *American Jewish Year Book, 1966,* 72–73; Sachar, *Jews in America,* 844; *New York Times,* May 19, 1961, 10, October 20, 1961, 17, December 4, 1961, 13, January 25, 1965, 87, January 28, 1965, 7.

106. *American Jewish Year Book, 1966,* 45–48, 51–52, 57–68, 74–77; Eugene Fisher, "Anti-Semitism: A Contemporary Christian Perspective," *Judaism* 30 (1981), 276–77.

107. *American Jewish Year Book, 1968* (New York and Philadelphia, 1968), 204, 218–24, 233, *1974–75* (New York and Philadelphia, 1974), 196; Sachar, *Jews in America,* 735–36; Malcolm L. Diamond, "Christian Silence on Israel: An End to Dialogue?" *Judaism* 16 (1967), 411–17.

108. *American Jewish Year Book, 1968,* 220, *1974–75,* 194–96, *1989* (New York and Philadelphia, 1989), 171–72, *1992* (New York and Philadelphia, 1992), 196, *1994* (New York, 1994), 135; Judith H. Banki, *Anti-Israel Influence in American Churches: A Background Report* (New York, 1979), 1–15; Franklin H. Littell, "The Voice of Christian Conscience," *Judaism* 20 (1971), 122–23; idem, "The Future of Anti-Semitism," ibid. 40 (1991), 518. The quotations are from *American Jewish Year Book, 1989,* 171–72.

109. *Interreligious Currents* (Union of American Hebrew Congregations), fall 1994–winter 1995; *American Jewish Year Book, 1977* (New York and Philadelphia, 1976), 54, *1987* (New York and Philadelphia, 1987), 132–33, *1988* (New York and Philadelphia, 1988), 158, *1989, 165–69, 1990,* 220, *1992, 191–94, 1994,* 137. The quotation is from the *Chicago Tribune,* November 11, 1988, sec. 2, p. 9.

110. Dinnerstein, *Uneasy at Home,* 193; Stember et al., *Jews in the Mind of America,* 7, 67, 131–33, 208; *American Jewish Year Book, 1947–48,* 188, 191, *1950,* 110, *1952,* 135–39, *1967* (New York and Philadelphia, 1967), 63; *New York Times,* October 20, 1951, 17. The quoted comments of Charles Stem-

ber are from Stember et al., *Jews in the Mind of America,* 67 and 208.

111. Dinnerstein, *Uneasy at Home,* 192–93; Edward S. Shapiro, *A Time for Healing: American Jewry since World War II* (Baltimore, 1992), 39, 50–51; *Encyclopaedia Judaica,* 15:1656; *American Jewish Year Book, 1967,* 64.

112. *Encyclopaedia Judaica,* 15:1656; Shapiro, *A Time for Healing,* 50–51; Doneson, *The Holocaust in American Film,* 65; Hertzberg, *The Jews in America,* 383; *American Jewish Year Book, 1946–47,* 599, 603, *1994,* 206; Dawidowicz, *On Equal Terms,* 167.

113. Dinnerstein, *Uneasy at Home,* 188, 193; Gartner, "The Two Continuities of Antisemitism in the United States," 318; Stember et al., *Jews in the Mind of America,* 290–94; Doneson, *The Holocaust in American Film,* 51–56; Mark Silk, *Spiritual Politics: Religion and America since World War II* (New York, 1988), chap. 2. The quotation is from *New York Times,* December 23, 1952, 16.

114. Project for the Study of Anti-Semitism, Tel Aviv University, *Anti-Semitism Worldwide, 1994* (Tel Aviv, 1995), 188–89; *American Jewish Year Book, 1974–75,* 106, *1981* (New York and Philadelphia, 1980), 130, *1983* (New York and Philadelphia, 1982), 67–68, *1991* (New York and Philadelphia, 1991), 121, *1994,* 127; Tom W. Smith, "The Polls—A Review," *Public Opinion Quarterly* 57 (1993), 389. The quotations from *American Jewish Year Book* are from *1974–75,* 106, and *1994,* 127. The final quotation in the paragraph is from Dinnerstein, *Uneasy at Home,* 193.

115. *American Jewish Year Book, 1967,* 63, *1981,* 121; Harold E. Quinley and Charles Y. Glock, *Anti-Semitism in America* (New Brunswick, N.J., 1983), xx–xxiii; Project for the Study of Anti-Semitism, *Anti-Semitism Worldwide, 1994,* 190–91. The quotation is from *American Jewish Year Book, 1967,* 63.

116. Leon A. Jick, "The Holocaust: Its Use and Abuse within the American Public," *Yad Vashem Studies* 14 (1981), 310; Greenberg, *The Jewish Way,* 334; *New York Times,* January 4, 1983, 1, January 14, 1983, 26, January 20, 1983, 1, February 9, 1983, sec. 2, p. 11, February 10, 1983, 18, March 21, 1984, 1; Leonard Dinnerstein, "What Should American Jews Have Done to Rescue Their European Brethren?" *Simon Wiesenthal Center Annual* 3 (1986), 277–87.

117. Judith Miller, *One, by One, by One: Facing the Holocaust* (New York, 1990), 224; Jick, "The Holocaust," 311.

118. William B. Helmreich, "The Impact of Holocaust Survivors on American Society: A Socio-Cultural Portrait," *Judaism* 39 (1990), 14–15,

19–20; Abraham J. Peck, "Special Lives: Survivors of the Holocaust and the American Dream," in *Remembering for the Future: Working Papers and Addenda,* ed. Yehuda Bauer, 3 vols. (Oxford, 1989), 1:1151–52; Doneson, *The Holocaust in American Film,* 200; Jick, "The Holocaust," 311; William B. Helmreich, "The Impact of Holocaust Survivors on American Society: A Socio-Cultural Portrait," in Bauer, *Remembering for the Future,* 1:372; Miller, *One, by One, by One,* 224.

119. William B. Helmreich, *Against All Odds: Holocaust Survivors and the Successful Lives They Made in America* (New York, 1992), 38; Miller, *One, by One, by One,* 221–22; Peck, "Special Lives," 1151–52; Alvin H. Rosenfeld, "The Americanization of the Holocaust," *Commentary* 99 (June 1995), 38; Helmreich, "The Impact of Holocaust Survivors," *Judaism* 39 (1990), 23.

120. Robert Alter, "Deformations of the Holocaust," *Commentary* 71 (February 1981), 48; Jick, "The Holocaust," 312–14; Greenberg, *The Jewish Way,* 334–36; Diamond, "Christian Silence on Israel," 415; *American Jewish Year Book, 1968,* 204; Shapiro, *A Time for Healing,* 27, 207–8; Michael Berenbaum, "The Nativization of the Holocaust," *Judaism* 35 (1986), 448. The quotation is from Karp, *Haven and Home,* 330.

121. Philadelphia Center on the Holocaust, Genocide, and Human Rights, *Newsletter* [January 1993]; *New York Times,* February 27, 1972, sec. 4, p. 9, May 15, 1977, 53, September 18, 1977, 23, October 7, 1977, 21, October 31, 1977, 34; Doneson, *The Holocaust in American Film,* 149; Yaffa Eliach, "Documenting the Landscape of Death: The Politics of Commemoration and Holocaust Studies," in Bauer, *Remembering for the Future,* 3:2862.

122. Doneson, *The Holocaust in American Film,* 157, 189–90; *New York Times,* May 7, 1978, sec. 7, p. 50, June 11, 1989, sec. 2, p. 1; *American Jewish Year Book, 1980* (New York and Philadelphia, 1979), 85–86; Judith E. Doneson, "American Films on the Holocaust: An Aid to Memory or Trivialization?" in Bauer, *Remembering for the Future,* 2:1673, 1676–77; Richard Libowitz, "Holocaust Studies," *Modern Judaism* 10 (1990), 272–73. The first quotation, by Msgr. George Higgins, is from *American Jewish Year Book, 1980,* 85. The second quotation is from Libowitz, "Holocaust Studies," 272–73.

123. Edward T. Linenthal, *Preserving Memory: The Struggle to Create America's Holocaust Museum* (New York, 1995), 17–19, 23; Jick, "The Holocaust," 316; Miller, *One, by One, by One,* 256–57.

124. Greenberg, *The Jewish Way,* 335, 342; Linen-

thal, *Preserving Memory*, 26–27, 38, 271; Berenbaum, "The Nativization of the Holocaust," 448; Philadelphia Center on the Holocaust, *Newsletter* [January 1993]; Libowitz, "Holocaust Studies," 271; Miller, *One, by One, by One*, 300–301. In the United States in the late 1980s, the term *Yom Hashoah* seems to have taken on general usage, being employed interchangeably with the phrase "Days of Remembrance" (*New York Times*, April 27, 1987, sec. 2, p. 3).

125. Miller, *One, by One, by One*, 227; Linenthal, *Preserving Memory*, 19–20, 27, 35–55; Judith Miller, "Holocaust Museum: A Troubled Start," *New York Times Magazine*, April 22, 1990, 42; Rosenfeld, "The Americanization of the Holocaust," 35; Deborah E. Lipstadt, "Invoking the Holocaust," *Judaism* 30 (1981), 341; Henryk Grynberg, "Appropriating the Holocaust," *Commentary* 74 (November 1982), 56–57; Berenbaum, "The Nativization of the Holocaust," 448, 452–53.

126. Gutman, *Encyclopedia of the Holocaust*, 3:1019; Linenthal, *Preserving Memory*, 133, 257–60, 319; Monroe H. Freedman, "Michael Berenbaum's 'Distortions of the Holocaust,'" *Midstream* 37 (May 1991), 47; *American Jewish Year Book, 1987*, 118.

127. Yitzchak Mais, "Institutionalizing the Holocaust: Issues Related to the Establishment of Holocaust Memorial Centers," in Bauer, *Remembering for the Future*, 2:1788; James E. Young, *The Texture of Memory: Holocaust Memorials and Meaning* (New Haven, 1993), 296–97, 302–4; Holocaust Memorial Center (West Bloomfield, Mich.), *Our 10th Anniversary* (program), October 9, 1994; *New York Times*, February 10, 1993, 16; Daniel Landes, "Wake Them Up," *Forum* 5 (summer 1993), 24–26; Edward Norden, "Yes and No to the Holocaust Museums," *Commentary* 96 (August 1993), 23–24; David Altshuler, "Work in Progress," *Forum* 5 (summer 1993), 26–27; Gutman, *Encyclopedia of the Holocaust*, 3:1012–13.

128. United States Holocaust Memorial Council, *Directory of Holocaust Resource Centers, Institutions, and Organizations in North America* [Washington, D.C., 1985]; David M. Szonyi, ed., *The Holocaust: An Annotated Bibliography and Resource Guide* (New York, 1985), 260–72; Judith H. Muffs and Dennis B. Klein, eds., *The Holocaust in Books and Films: A Selected, Annotated List*, 3d ed. (New York, 1986), 135–42; Libowitz, "Holocaust Studies," 271.

129. Szonyi, *The Holocaust*, 278–305; Young, *Texture of Memory*, 294, 298–300, 309–19, 323–26, 332–33; Eliezer Trepman, "Subtle Revisionism,"

O[ne] G[eneration] A[fter] Newsletter (Boston) 10 (November 1988), 18.

130. Jick, "The Holocaust," 315; Libowitz, "Holocaust Studies," 273; Holocaust Publications, Holocaust Library catalog for 1989. What remained of the Holocaust Library was absorbed by the U.S. Holocaust Memorial Museum in 1993 (minutes of Academic Committee, U.S. Holocaust Memorial Museum, April 9, 1993).

131. The historiographical essay is Michael R. Marrus, *The Holocaust in History* (Hanover, N.H., 1987). Two useful bibliographical essays appeared in *Modern Judaism* 10 (1990), 271–96: Richard Libowitz, "Holocaust Studies," and Deborah E. Lipstadt, "America and the Holocaust." Studies on literature include Alvin H. Rosenfeld, *A Double Dying: Reflections on Holocaust Literature* (Bloomington, 1980); and Lawrence L. Langer, *The Holocaust and the Literary Imagination* (New Haven, 1975). See also Robert Skloot, *The Darkness We Carry: The Drama of the Holocaust* (Madison, 1988). General bibliographies on the Holocaust include Szonyi, *The Holocaust;* Muffs and Klein, *The Holocaust in Books and Films;* and Harry J. Cargas, *The Holocaust: An Annotated Bibliography*, 2d ed. (Chicago, 1985).

132. Rosenfeld, "The Americanization of the Holocaust," 38; Terrence Des Pres, *The Survivor: An Anatomy of Life in the Death Camps* (Oxford, 1976), 211.

133. Rosenfeld, "The Americanization of the Holocaust," 38; Libowitz, "Holocaust Studies," 271; Helmreich, "The Impact of Holocaust Survivors," *Judaism* 39 (1990), 26; Geoffrey H. Hartman, "Learning from Survivors: Notes on the Video Archive at Yale," in Bauer, *Remembering for the Future*, 2:1716; Eliach, "Documenting the Landscape of Death," 2862; *New York Times Book Review*, April 21, 1991, 7; Muffs and Klein, *The Holocaust in Books and Films*, 140; *Martyrdom and Resistance* 19 (March–April 1993), 3; Miller, *One, by One, by One*, 268; Joan Ringelheim, *A Catalog of Audio and Video Collections of Holocaust Testimony*, 2d ed. (Westport, Conn., 1992); Berenbaum, "The Nativization of the Holocaust," 451. In late 1994 filmmaker Steven Spielberg announced his inauguration of a major oral history project (*New York Times*, November 10, 1994, C22).

134. Ryan, *Quiet Neighbors*, 5–6, 31–45, 53–62, 264, 324–26, 332–34, 344; Friedlander and McCarrick, "Nazi Criminals in the United States," 65–66; Dinnerstein, *America and the Survivors*, 197–98; Gutman, *Encyclopedia of the Holocaust*, 3:1083.

135. Friedlander and McCarrick, "Nazi Criminals in the United States," 66–68; Ryan, *Quiet Neighbors,* 65–93, 261; *American Jewish Year Book, 1994,* 148; Gutman, *Encyclopedia of the Holocaust,* 3:1083.

136. Gutman, *Encyclopedia of the Holocaust,* 1:357–59; Ryan, *Quiet Neighbors,* 94–141, 354; *American Jewish Year Book, 1994,* 149–50, *1995* (New York, 1995), 124; *New York Times,* December 31, 1993, 13, February 25, 1994, 16, October 4, 1994, 18.

137. Christopher Simpson, *Blowback: America's Recruitment of Nazis and Its Effects on the Cold War* (New York, 1988), 192–93; Ryan, *Quiet Neighbors,* 287–321; Earlean M. McCarrick, "American Anti-Nazism: A Cold War Casualty," *Simon Wiesenthal Center Annual* 6 (1989), 225.

138. Simpson, *Blowback,* xi–xv, 6–11, 27–51, 66–73, 138–42, 199–216; Tom Bower, *The Paperclip Conspiracy: The Hunt for Nazi Scientists* (Boston, 1987), 4, 7, 96, 110, 122–26, 131, 157–87, 195–213, 234–39; Loftus, *The Belarus Secret,* 4–7, 11, 18–33, 86–89, 105, 108, 119.

139. Geoffrey H. Hartman, ed., *Bitburg in Moral and Political Perspective* (Bloomington, 1986), xiii–xiv; *American Jewish Year Book, 1987,* 117.

140. Deborah E. Lipstadt, "The Bitburg Controversy," *American Jewish Year Book, 1987,* 21, 24–25, 27, 32; Doneson, *The Holocaust in American Film,* 202; *American Jewish Year Book, 1987,* 118; Hartman, *Bitburg,* xiv–xvi. The quotations are from ibid., 240, xiv, 243, 258.

141. Lipstadt, "The Bitburg Controversy," 21–22, 28, 37; *American Jewish Year Book, 1987,* 118, *1991,* 140; Miller, *One, by One, by One,* 228; Charles E. Silberman, *A Certain People: American Jews and Their Lives Today* (New York, 1985), 363–64; Elie Wiesel, "A Time to Speak," *Bostonia,* summer 1995, 16; Hartman, *Bitburg,* 8. Polls taken in the midst of the Bitburg controversy showed that 44 percent of Americans approved of the Bitburg visit, while 52 percent thought it should be canceled (Lipstadt, "The Bitburg Controversy," 31).

142. *New York Times,* December 11, 1986, 1, December 12, 1986, 12.

143. Libowitz, "Holocaust Studies," 273; *New York Times,* December 20, 1993, C16, January 2, 1994, sec. 4, p. 9, January 23, 1994, sec. 2, p. 13, March 22, 1994, 1, C15; Philip Gourevitch, "A Dissent on 'Schindler's List,'" *Commentary* 97 (February 1994), 49–52; Rosenfeld, "The Americanization of the Holocaust," 39; Molly M. Hoagland, "What *Schindler* Missed," *Midstream* 40 (April 1994), 34; *New York Times Index,* 1978, 1993, 1994.

144. Libowitz, "Holocaust Studies," 278–80; Joel J. Epstein, "Holocaust Education in the United States: The Church Related Institution," in Bauer, *Remembering for the Future,* 2:1168–69. Some public-school Holocaust teaching began as early as 1953. A Tucson teacher recalled his principal's attempting to dissuade him from it: "Stop teaching that Jewish stuff, Ray. It's not in the textbooks" (*NEA Retired* 2 [May 1995], 15; Ray Davies, interview by author, Washington, D.C., February 19, 1996). A few college courses on the Holocaust existed by 1959 (Libowitz, "Holocaust Studies," 278).

145. Samuel Totten, "Review: Facing History and Ourselves," *Holocaust and Genocide Studies* 5 (1990), 463; *New York Times,* September 18, 1977, 23, October 7, 1977, 21, December 12, 1982, sec. 11, p. 3; *American Jewish Year Book, 1990,* 222; Lucy S. Dawidowicz, "How They Teach the Holocaust," *Commentary* 90 (December 1990), 25–26; Michael E. Siegel, "The Importance of the Holocaust in History and Social Studies Courses," *Peabody Journal of Education* 57 (October 1979), 40–43; Berenbaum, "The Nativization of the Holocaust," 453–54; Social Studies School Service, *Teaching the Holocaust: Resources and Materials,* sales catalog (Culver City, Calif., 1992).

146. Totten, "Review," 463–64; American Gathering/Federation of Jewish Holocaust Survivors, form letter, September 1992.

147. Gerd Korman, "Silence in the American Textbooks," *Yad Vashem Studies* 8 (1970), 183–202; Glenn S. Pate, "The United States of America," in *The Treatment of the Holocaust in Textbooks,* ed. Randolph L. Braham (New York, 1987), 243–45, 255–57, 265–66, 288–304, 309; Alan Brinkley et al., *American History: A Survey,* 8th ed. (New York, 1991), chap. 27.

148. Deborah E. Lipstadt, *Denying the Holocaust: The Growing Assault on Truth and Memory* (New York, 1993), 1, 17, 22–24, 50–65.

149. Ibid., 65, 74–87, 99–102.

150. Ibid., 102, 123–26, 136–37; Randolph L. Braham, "Historical Revisionism and the New Right," in Bauer, *Remembering for the Future,* 2:2095–96; Arthur R. Butz, *The Hoax of the Twentieth Century* (Richmond, Surrey, 1976); Project for the Study of Anti-Semitism, *Anti-Semitism Worldwide, 1994,* 195.

151. Lipstadt, *Denying the Holocaust,* 162–67, 172–73; *Washington Post,* June 18, 1991, 6.

152. Lipstadt, *Denying the Holocaust,* 17, 26, 183–84, 190–201, 208, 265.

153. Ibid., 3; Miller, *One, by One, by One,* 280; Tom W. Smith, "The Polls—A Review: The Holo-

caust Denial Controversy," *Public Opinion Quarterly* 59 (1995), 269–71, 282–84; *New York Times,* May 20, 1994, 12, July 8, 1994, 10.

154. *Dimensions: A Journal of Holocaust Studies,* 6, no. 2 (1991), 2–6; Yankelovich–Clancy Shulman, "American Public Awareness of and Attitudes toward the Holocaust, Part I: A Case for Further Education," unpublished, January 1991, 8, 38, 42; *New York Times,* July 8, 1994, 10; Smith, "The Polls—A Review," 272–75.

155. The periodization of developments from about 1970 to 1994 that is presented in this and the following paragraph is based on the research that underlies this essay, on personal observation of Holocaust-related activities, and on close examination of the *New York Times Index,* 1970–94.

156. The inscriptions of the three presidents' words are on the Raoul Wallenberg Place side of the museum. President Bill Clinton, in ceremonies dedicating the museum in April 1993, spoke these words: "For those of us here today representing the nations of the West, we must live forever with this knowledge—even as our fragmentary awareness of crimes grew into indisputable facts, far too little was done. Before the war even started, doors to liberty were shut, and even after the United States and the Allies attacked Germany, rail lines to the camps within miles of militarily significant targets were left undisturbed" (National Public Radio, *All Things Considered,* April 22, 1993).

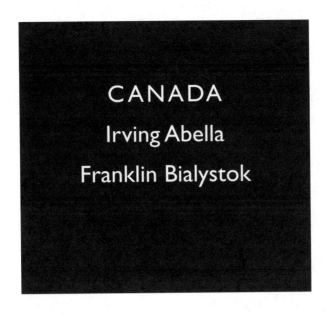

CANADA

Irving Abella

Franklin Bialystok

BEFORE THE HOLOCAUST

In June 1934 occurred one of the most bizarre strikes in Canadian history, and for the Jewish community the most telling. Samuel Rabinovich, a young medical student who had graduated first in his class at the University of Montreal, was offered an internship at Notre Dame Hospital. On the day he was to begin work all fourteen of his fellow interns walked out, refusing, as they put it, to work with a Jew. They picketed the hospital and refused to accept even emergency cases, their newly sworn Hippocratic oath notwithstanding. They were soon joined by fellow interns from five surrounding Catholic hospitals, as well as by the clergy of neighboring parishes.

It was a sensational story, and the French-language press gave it front-page coverage. The interns were all interviewed and their story told sympathetically. None wished to spend a full year working with a Jew—who could blame them, asked Quebec's leading French-language newspaper, *Le Devoir*—and all were concerned that Catholic patients would find it "repugnant" to be treated, or even touched, by a Jewish physician. To the support of the indignant interns came such organizations as the Jean Baptiste Society, the Association of Young Catholics, various county councils and cooperatives, as well as prominent members of the Catholic clergy. Within a few days Rabinovich submitted his resignation, and the hospital promised never to hire any Jewish doctors. Jews, a Quebec paper gloated, have now learned their place, and "it is not in Quebec."[1]

The *grève des internes* was one of the literally hundreds of anti-Semitic incidents that marked Canadian society in the years between the wars. In Toronto in August 1933, for example, the Christie Pits riots broke out. Large numbers of youths, members and supporters of a local anti-Semitic club, terrorized a Jewish baseball team in a battle that poured out onto surrounding streets and lasted most of the night, as reinforcements for both sides arrived.[2] There was also violence in the streets of Winnipeg and Vancouver as anti-Jewish gangs and Jews confronted one another.

These were, of course, isolated incidents. Canada was not Eastern Europe. Although there was some harassment and certainly some vandalism against synagogues and Jewish schools and businesses, there were few violent outbursts. Yet it is evident that the Canada of the 1920s and 1930s was a country permeated with anti-Semitism. A committee of the Canadian Jewish Congress (CJC) reported in 1937:

> During the past few years we have witnessed an amazing growth of anti-semitism. Manifestations of an intensified anti-Jewish sentiment have been springing up everywhere. . . . Jews have been barred from hotels, beaches, golf courses and parks. . . . [There are] many sign posters in front of parks and beaches to the effect that Gentiles only are admitted. . . . [There has been] a startling increase in the number of individuals and companies who refuse to rent living quarters to Jews. . . . [There is] a spreading policy of not employing Jews; the boycott of all Jewish firms; the sporadic attempts by various organizations to involve Jews in disturbances and violence.[3]

In 1938 the CJC commissioned a study on the status of the Jew in English Canada.[4] What was discovered was so profoundly unsettling—though hardly surprising to Canadian Jewry—that the report was never released. For Canadian Jews, it reported, quotas and restrictions had become a way of life. According to the study, few of the country's teachers and none of its principals were Jewish. The banks, insurance companies, and the large industrial and commercial interests, it charged, also excluded Jews from employment. Department stores did not hire Jews as salespeople; Jewish doctors could not get hospital appointments. There were no Jewish judges, and Jewish lawyers were excluded from most firms. Not only did universities and professional schools devise quotas against Jewish students but they did not hire Jewish faculty. The academic staffs of Canadian universities were totally *judenrein*. Few civil servants were Jews, and those few were rarely promoted. The report added that it was almost impossible for Jewish nurses, architects, and engineers to find jobs in their fields. And some succeeded only when they adopted Christian surnames—until they were unmasked.

If Jews found it difficult to find a job or obtain an education, it was perhaps even more difficult for them to find a suitable place to live or to vacation. Increasingly, restrictive covenants were put on various properties preventing them from being sold to Jews. Signs sprang up at beaches and resorts throughout the nation informing the Jew that he was not welcome. A Toronto beach warned: "No Jews or Dogs allowed." A tourist camp in Gimli, Manitoba, posted signs warning Jews to keep away. Throughout the Laurentians in Quebec and the Muskoka area in Ontario warnings were posted by various hotels informing Jews that they were not welcome. The growth of nativist groups such as Social Credit in Alberta, the Ku Klux Klan in Saskatchewan, and various fascist groups in British Columbia and particularly Manitoba spawned so much anti-Jewish activity and propaganda that the Manitoba legislature passed an anti-hate bill to control these groups.[5]

Indeed so threatening did the situation appear that a Jewish member of the Ontario legislature warned his coreligionists: "Unless something is done quickly the Jewish people may well meet the same fate in Canada that the Jews are meeting in Germany. . . . No fire is so easily kindled as anti-semitism. The fire is dormant in Canada, it has not yet blazed up, but the spark is there. Germany is not the only place with prejudice. Look at Quebec."[6] And indeed it was in Quebec that Jews were most threatened. In Quebec both the Roman Catholic Church and its lay allies in the French Canadian nationalist movement were aggressively anti-Jewish. As a leading Toronto rabbi put it: "In Quebec anti-semitism is a way of life. In the rest of Canada it is more an afterthought. Here it is much more subtle. There it is widespread and demonic."[7]

To the French Canadian nationalist of this period the Jews—indeed all foreigners—were a threat. Surrounded by the pervasive, all-encompassing American way of life and in their own country dominated by an apparently narrow-minded English-speaking majority, French Canadians have always felt threatened; their way of life, traditions, language, culture, and religion have been, at least in their eyes, constantly under attack, and never more so than in the 1920s and 1930s. And anything that tended to undermine the influence and role of the church was anathema. Most dangerous of course were modernism, materialism, and their purveyor, the Jew. It was he who personified the danger; he was, in the words of one church leader and scholar, the worldwide carrier of the bacillus of secularism, materialism, Communism, and internationalism. He was perceived to be the propagator of the American way of life and the major source of social disruption and moral decay.[8]

In the writings and speeches of many leading church and nationalist figures in Quebec the Jew was commonly depicted as a parasite, a germ spreading an insidious disease that was undermining the national health. The remedy for all diseases was quarantine and eradication. Therefore the elite of Quebec society worked strenuously to bar all Jews from entering Canada and to ostracize those already there. They led anti-immigration crusades, lobbied strenuously, and worked indefatigably to keep Jews out of Canada. As for those living in Quebec, the call went out for a total boycott. "If we do not buy from them," thundered *Action Catholique,* an official church journal, "they will leave." From this sprung up the Achat Chez Nous movement, sponsored by leading church officials, urging French Canadians to buy from their coreligionists and to stay away from Jewish storekeepers, who, in the words of *Le Devoir,* "have cheating and corruption in the bloodstream." Though it originally began as a nationalistic tool for the economic advancement of French Canadians, as a form of self-defense, it soon turned into a campaign to boycott all Jews. As one senior clergyman told his fellow priests, "It is to free us from Jews and usurers."[9]

The movement had the total support of the Catholic Church, most of the press, and, of course, local merchants. As the Restaurant Association's journal, *Le Restaurateur,* warned, "Do you want to be poisoned? Buy your food from Jews." Actively pushing the boycott as well was the massive ultranationalist Jean Baptiste Society, whose rallies on behalf of the movement throughout the province ended with the parting vow repeated by all those present: "I promise that under no circumstances shall I ever buy from a Jew."[10]

It would be misleading to maintain that anti-Semitism existed primarily in Quebec. Such nationwide organizations as the Social Credit Party, the Native Sons of Canada, and the Orange Order were rife with anti-Semitic feeling. Throughout the 1930s anti-Jewish outbursts on the editorial pages of some of the nation's newspapers, as well as from Protestant pulpits, became more frequent. Worst of all, at least from the point of view of those Jews desperate to flee Nazi-dominated Europe, anti-Semitism had permeated the upper levels of the Canadian government. Few capital cities anywhere, said Joe Garner, a senior British official and later high commissioner to Canada, were more subtly anti-Jewish than Ottawa. As an atheist, he worried on his arrival whether he could eat, sleep, or drink in a city in which so many hotels, clubs, and restaurants were restricted to Christians, but he was reassured that the restriction applied only to Jews.[11]

Why was Canada so anti-Semitic? The widespread anti-Semitic propaganda of the Nazis had a certain impact. Some were taken in by it and by such American hatemongers as Henry Ford, Father Coughlin, Gerald L. K. Smith, and dozens of others. They formed such anti-Jewish groupings as the Canadian Union of Fascists and the Swastika Club. It was also a time of economic depression, and the search for scapegoats invariably ended at a Jewish doorstep. Jews were also publicly seen and denounced as troublemakers. The prominence of Jewish names in the left-wing movement seduced many Canadians into believing that most Jews were Communists. In addition, many Canadians were reacting to three decades of almost unlimited immigration. The rapid rise of nativism in the 1920s grew out of a concern for the type of Canada these millions of uneducated, illiterate aliens would produce. For many, the Jew, since he tended to live in cities and therefore was the most visible of immigrants, symbolized this "mongrelization." Anti-Semitism to many, therefore, was simply an extreme form of Canadian nationalism. Also, many non-Jewish immigrants, particularly from Eastern Europe, had brought with them their traditional anti-Semitic phobias. An anti-Jewish tradition of many generations could not be dissolved overnight. Obviously, many hated Jews for religious reasons. Much of the anti-Semitism in Quebec and in fundamentalist areas of western Canada originated from religious teachings. Jews had killed Christ, had refused to repent or convert to Christianity, and therefore were damned.

All of these factors contributed to the anti-Semitism that permeated Canada in these years. One factor, however, stands out: a feeling among Canadians, especially the opinion-makers—the politicians, academics, writers, businessmen, and journalists who set the tone for a society—that the Jew simply did not fit into their concept of Canada. Theirs was a country of homesteaders and farmers; and despite the fact that the Jews in Palestine at the time were turning a desert green, few Canadians thought that Jews could be successful agriculturalists. Those immigrants who did not farm were expected to go into the woods, mines, smelters, canneries, or textile mills or to join the construction gangs needed to build and fuel the great Canadian boom of the first thirty years of this century. Most Canadians thought that Jews did not fit this pattern. The Jews were city people in a country attempting to build up its rural base; they were peddlers and shopkeepers in a country that wanted loggers and miners. They were seen as a people with brains in a country that preferred brawn, as a people with strong minds in a country that wanted strong backs.[12]

What is most astonishing about this anti-Semitism is how few and powerless Canadian Jews were at this time. Constituting just over 1 percent of the population and with little political or economic clout, they could be seen as a threat only by the paranoid. Equally surprising was the silence of the churches in the face of this frightful and oppressive anti-Jewish feeling and of course the acquiescence of both the media and the government. But Canadian Jews were not surprised. They expected nothing different. There were only about 156,000 Jews in Canada in the 1930s, most of them recent arrivals or children of immigrants.[13] They felt marginal and frightened. But this had not always been the case.

Jewish settlement in Canada began in the 1750s with a tiny influx of some ten families from the New England colonies to Halifax, Nova Scotia. But it was the 1759 defeat of the French in Quebec by the British general James Wolfe that finally opened up Canada to Jewish immigrants. And for the next one hundred years the English Jews who settled in Canada, mostly in Montreal, were largely successful and prosperous. It was only with the beginning of the mass migration from Eastern Europe in the 1880s and 1890s that a stifling curtain of anti-Semitism descended on Canada.[14]

The mass migration between the 1880s and 1914 drastically changed the makeup of Jewish Canada. The community became a significant minority in the country rather than a negligible one, increasing from around twenty-five hundred in 1882 to well over one hundred thousand by the 1920s. In that decade Jews constituted more than 6 percent of the population in the country's three largest cities—Toronto, Montreal, and Winnipeg—and constituted the largest immigrant community in each. Meanwhile, Ottawa's Jewish population burgeoned from twenty people to three thousand, while Vancouver's grew from a few dozen to more than one thousand. Other cities and towns experienced similar growth.[15]

More significant than the growth in numbers, however, was the change in composition. By the 1920s the acculturated Anglo-Jewish community had all but disappeared. Gone was their serene, comfortable, stable world. In its place emerged the new world of Canadian Jewry, the crowded, chaotic, noisy Yiddish world of the Eastern European newcomers. Leadership still remained in the hands of the old guard; their wealth, influence, contacts, and ability to speak English assured that. But they were losing their control over the Jewish community.[16]

Times were difficult for the Jews. It was a period of dreadful living and working conditions, of poverty and want. Yet the Jewish community exuded vitality, experimentation, passion, and creativity. The Yiddish-speaking immigrants were tearing off the fetters of the old world and adapting to the new. Their community was in constant ideological turmoil as Orthodox fought secularist and Zionist fought Bundist. The many varieties of socialists clashed with each other, as territorialists, cultur-alists, revisionists, separatists, and integrationists all pressed their views, their conflicting agendas for their survival as Jews.

Theirs was the world of the Jewish farmer, small-town storekeeper, and factory worker. In every town, village, and hamlet, at every railroad crossing, there was a Jewish presence—a store, a family, a farm, a peddler, a Yiddish word. There were even stations along the Canadian Pacific Railway main line named for Jews. Passengers could get off at Levine, Unger, or Ginsberg. Towns and villages also had Jewish names: Hirsch, Sonnenfeldt, Lipton, Edenbridge (Yidden Bridge).

But theirs also was the world of quotas, restrictions, and boycotts. For many Canadians the Jew represented a foreign culture that would undermine their beliefs and way of life. Every public-opinion poll taken in the years before 1945 showed that the Jews and Asians were the immigrants least wanted by the Canadian people, but in the 1930s and 1940s Jews were also the immigrants most in need of a place to go. The attitude of the Canadian people ensured that Canada was not to be that place.[17]

What Canadian history books until recently did not mention, and what few Canadians talk about, is that of all the receiving countries in the world, Canada had the worst record in providing sanctuary to European Jewry at the time of its greatest need. Canada could find no room for more than a handful of the European Jews who were searching desperately and in vain for a haven. Of the more than eight hundred thousand Jews seeking refuge from the Third Reich in the years 1933–39 Canada admitted approximately four thousand. Even in a world that was decidedly inhospitable to refugees, Canada's stinginess was striking. Even penurious Mexico and Colombia had each accepted far more Jews than Canada. Canadian immigration policy has always been as ethnically selective as it was economically self-serving. When economic necessity dictated the admission of non-British and non-American immigrants, it was always in descending order of ethnic preference. Following British and American immigrants, northern Europeans and then central Europeans were given preference. At the bottom were Jews, Asians, and blacks. Those "non-preferred immigrants" were acceptable as long as they were out of sight—in the mines and smelters of the West and North, in lumber camps deep in the forest, or farming the more marginal areas of the western wheat frontier. Those immigrants who chose to compete for jobs with native or British-born artisans in Canada's urban centers were less acceptable. And to immigration officials the worst culprits were the Jews.

The person entrusted with the task of ensuring that there was no breach in this scheme was Frederick Charles Blair. As director of the Immigration Branch during these years, Blair made almost all of the decisions, no matter how small, concerning who was allowed to enter Canada. And from the point of view of European Jewry this was most unfortunate. Just when they most needed a friend at the gate, they had an enemy; instead of a humanitarian, they got a narrow-minded bureaucrat. Perhaps Blair stayed in his job for so long because his inflexibility, his fetish for regulations, and his unchallenged control over immigration matters were a convenience to an administration that had no intention of allowing Jewish refugees into the country but wished to avoid being vilified for not doing so.

To Blair, "refugee" was a code word for "Jew." Unless "safeguards" were adopted, he warned, Canada was in danger of being "flooded with Jewish people." His task, as he saw it, was to make sure that the safeguards did not fail. Indeed, he was inordinately proud of his success in keeping out Jews. "Pressure on the part of Jewish people to get into Canada has never been greater than it is now," he said, "and I am glad to be able to add, after 35 years experience here, that it was never so well controlled." Blair expressed a strong personal distaste for Jews and especially for "certain of their habits." He saw them as unassimilable, as people apart, "who can organize [their] affairs better than other people" and therefore accomplish more. He complained that Jews were "utterly selfish in their attempts to force through a permit for the admission of relatives or friends." "They do not believe," he added, "that 'No' means more than 'Perhaps.'" Furthermore, he lamented, Jews "make any kind of promise to get the door open but . . . never cease their agitation until they get in the whole lot." Behind these Jewish attempts to get their coreligionists into the country Blair saw a conspiracy "to bring immigration regulations into disrepute and create an atmosphere favourable to those who cannot comply with the law." As he commiserated to the traffic manager of the Canadian Pacific Railway, "If there is any surer way to close the door in their own face, I do not know of it."

Only a short time after the outbreak of hostilities in Europe in 1939 Blair confided to his immigration commissioner in London: "Someone has facetiously said that numbers of our Jewish refugees lustfully sing 'Onward *Christian* Soldiers' but are very content to stay here and grab up all opportunities." And in a letter to a strong opponent of Jewish immigration Blair wrote:

> I suggested recently to three Jewish gentlemen with whom I am well acquainted, that it might be a very good thing if they would call a conference and have a day of humiliation and prayer which might profitably be extended for a week or more where they would honestly try to answer the question of why they are so unpopular almost everywhere. . . . I often think that instead of persecution it would be far better if we more often told them frankly why many of them are unpopular. If they would divest themselves of certain of their habits I am sure they could be just as popular in Canada as our Scandinavians. . . . Just because Jewish people would not understand the frank kind of statements I have made in this letter to you, I have marked it confidential.[18]

Although it was Blair who gave the final interpretation of governmental regulations and who acted as the de facto judge and jury on individual requests for admission, to blame him alone for Canada's response to the refugee crisis would be both overly simplistic and incorrect. After all, he was only a civil servant, albeit a powerful one. As a functionary he simply reflected the wishes of his superiors; it was they who were ultimately responsible for governmental policy. Not to accept refugees was a political decision, not a bureaucratic one. It was the prime minister and his cabinet who, in the final analysis, must shoulder the responsibility.

The prime minister of Canada, William Lyon Mackenzie King, was obsessed with Jews. He dreamt of them constantly and filled his diary with his thoughts on the Jewish people. While he saw the Jews as the "people of the Book" and as somewhat mystical, he was also capable of repeating—and believing—the most bilious anti-Semitic slanders. He believed that allowing in Jewish refugees "of even the best type" would destroy Canada. He confided to his diary: "We must seek to keep Canada free from unrest and too great an intermixture of foreign strains of blood." Jews, he feared, would not only "pollute" the Canadian bloodstream but also cause riots and worsen relations between the federal government and the provinces. Accepting Jewish refugees, he told his cabinet, could undermine Canadian unity, alienate many Canadians, strengthen the forces of Quebec separatism, and bring about bloodshed in the streets.[19]

King's policy is best symbolized by the instructions he gave Hume Wrong, the Canadian delegate to the Evian Conference in 1938. He told Wrong that his job was simply "to listen, make notes and say as little as possible" and under no circumstances make any promises. Canada, King said, was at Evian simply to gain information, actually only for cosmetic purposes. Should any other delegate make any concrete suggestions to solve the refugee problem, Wrong was to oppose them "without seeming to be obstructionist." Canada would do everything it could to find these refugees a haven, King said, "in some other country."[20]

THE HOLOCAUST ERA

King meant precisely what he said. In June 1939, when the *St. Louis,* a boat carrying nine hundred Jews forced out of Germany by the Nazis, attempted to land in Canada the Canadian government held firm. This was not a "Canadian problem," said the prime minister, and he did not wish to make it one by admitting these refugees. There would be no exceptions. Turned away by Cuba, the United States, and Canada, the so-called Voyage of the Damned headed back to Europe, where many of the ship's passengers would die in the gas chambers of the Third Reich.[21]

In the face of this hostility the Jewish community could do little. Aside from the occasional positive editorial and the encouragement of a few sympathetic church leaders and the committed but ineffective League of Nations Society, there was little public support for accepting any Jewish refugees. Officials of the CJC, the representative voice of Canadian Jewry, thought that their only tactic was quiet persuasion.

Regularly, and with no publicity, Jewish leaders traveled to Ottawa to lobby governmental authorities. They were made promises that were never kept. Indeed, some prominent Jews were rewarded with special immigration permits to be distributed to a fortunate few in the community. It was a cynical activity, but it worked. For the most part, Canadian Jewry, though restive, remained quiescent and supportive of the government. After all, on immigration matters the opposition parties were even more obdurate.

Even the onset of the war made little impact on Canada. In contrast to the hundreds of thousands of Jews who escaped to France, Holland, Spain, Portugal, Japan, and Shanghai, between 1939 and 1945, except for about one thousand interned refugees from Britain, Canada allowed in only a few hundred, even though many of those applying had skills Canada was short of or could bring with them thousands of needed dollars. When the opportunity arose in 1941 to rescue several thousand

Jewish orphans in Vichy France whose parents had been sent east by the Nazis, the Canadian government delayed. Officials worried that the children might not be orphans and that if admitted to Canada they might after the war sponsor their parents as immigrants, thus embarrassing the government. Others were concerned that since it was a longstanding policy not to break up families, if the children—all under ten years of age—wished to come they must bring their parents as well. By the time officials came to a decision it was too late: the Nazis had already shipped the children to Auschwitz, where none of them survived.[22]

By late 1942 Canadian officials largely knew what was happening to the Jews of Europe. Through the Polish underground, Jewish sources, and the other Allied governments, Canadian officials received graphic details of the plight of the Jews in occupied Europe. In fact, at the CJC plenary session in January 1942, Nahum Goldmann, president of the World Jewish Congress, gravely announced that "European Jewry is, for all intents and purposes, no longer existent." Yet even this information did not sway the cabinet. They were determined to keep Jewish refugees away from Canada, a position that seems to have been widely supported by the Canadian people. Poll after poll indicated that the vast majority of Canadians favored a restrictive policy. What is more telling, as the war continued and the suffering of Europe's Jews became more apparent, Canadian attitudes hardened. For example, a Gallup poll taken in January 1944 revealed that the number favoring a closed-door policy had increased almost exponentially—about 50 percent—in just one year.[23] Analyzing public opinion on the refugee issue, officials of Canada's War Information Board reported to the cabinet that it was abundantly clear that Canadians wanted "no Jews."[24]

It was not surprising, therefore, that Canadian politicians regularly turned aside all requests to help European Jewry. Indeed, in February 1943, when Great Britain and the United States jointly suggested that Ottawa would be an ideal location for a conference to discuss the refugee problem, the Canadian government demurred for fear that the meeting would focus world attention on Canada's dismal record in accepting Jewish refugees. The conference was eventually held in Bermuda; Canada, predictably, refused to attend.[25]

Similarly, when the two great powers approached Canada in the summer of 1944 to be prepared to accept some refugees should a deal be struck with the Nazis to barter Hungarian Jews, Canadian authorities were opposed. Indeed, Canada's most senior diplomat, Vincent Massey, remarked that the scheme to save Hungarian Jews was simply an election-year ploy by Roosevelt to win Jewish support. Massey joked: "The Democrats apparently want the Jewish vote without taking in more Jews, because if they allow more Jews they would lose the Roman Catholic vote."[26] The plan came to nought, as did the heroic efforts of Canadian Jewish leaders to force a change of policy in Ottawa. Despite strenuous lobbying by officials of the CJC, the Canadian government remained obdurate. It was obvious that no change was possible for politicians who believed not only that they were doing the right thing but also that they had the fulsome support of the Canadian people. And so to the very end of the war Canada turned her back on Jewish refugees.

THE POST-HOLOCAUST ERA

The revelations of the Nazi atrocities following the war came as no surprise to most Canadians. Since the early months of 1943, Canadian newspapers had carried eye-witness accounts of the slaughter of European Jewry. In fact, in November 1943 *Liberty,* the country's most popular magazine, published a horrifying, firsthand description of the massacre of thousands of Jews at Babi Yar in Kiev. In later issues *Liberty,* as well as most of the country's major newspapers, reported in detail on the liberation of the Nazi death camps by an advancing Soviet army. Names such as Treblinka, Majdenek, Belzec, and Sobibor now entered the lexicon and became synonymous with previously unimagined brutality. *Liberty* editorialized: "Close your eyes and ears and hearts against the horror and the cruelty of the Judenrein. Call the Jew an alien race. Wash your hands of responsibility as Pilate did. But a Gentile race that does not call for justice for the Jew will be forever accused."[27]

Predictably, the Canadian government did not rise to the challenge. The country's doors would remain closed. Not even the heartrending stories of the survivors of Auschwitz, which were extensively covered by the Canadian press following the camp's capture by the Red Army, stirred the Canadian government. As a memorandum from the Immigration Branch reassured the prime minister, "though the number of Jewish people who have been done away with must be enormous," survivors were not Canada's problem.[28]

Thus, even after the war, even after the world became fully aware of the extent of the Nazi atrocities, Canada adamantly refused to accept any Jewish refugees. And in keeping the gates closed the government likely had the support of most Canadians. In a very revealing poll taken in 1946, respondents were asked to list nationalities that the country ought not accept as immigrants. Topping the list were the Japanese. Right behind them were Jews; almost 50 percent wanted to keep Jews out of Canada. Well down the list were Germans; only a third of those polled thought Germans should be barred from Canada. Thus, despite the revelations of Nazi barbarity, Canadians preferred almost anyone—including Germans—to Jews.[29]

For almost three years after the end of the hostilities and the discovery of the death camps, immigration officials blocked the admission of Jewish survivors. Various schemes were devised to bring in displaced persons with special skills, such as woodworkers, farmers, nurses, domestics, and miners, but each one stipulated that no Jews be accepted. Finally, under pressure from Jews across the country, the government acceded to an arrangement to bring in several thousand Jewish garment workers from the camps. At the last moment, however, just as teams were moving into the camps to recruit, the Canadian cabinet ordered that only half those accepted could be Jewish. In other words, for every Jewish tailor accepted, a non-Jewish one also had to be found. It is no wonder that a stupefied Canadian relief official complained to her superiors that "it is easier to come to Canada if you are a Nazi than a Jew."[30]

Nevertheless, World War II was a watershed for Canada despite its attitude toward Jews and its refugee policy. It was clear that millions of Europeans would never return to their homes. It was also clear that the world would expect Canada to become part of the solution of this postwar refugee crisis. Canada willingly joined the International Refugee Organization; less willingly, however, did she open her doors to refugees. Aside from special groups, such as Polish soldiers, some Jewish orphans, and contract laborers from the displaced persons camps, few refugees were allowed into Canada in the first two years after the war.

By 1948, however, Canada seemed prepared to do her duty. The expected postwar recession never materialized. Rather, the country was booming as it strove to feed, clothe, defend, and rebuild a ravaged Europe. Canada was also coming under irresistible pressure from her U.N. allies as well as from domestic ethnic communities to accept large numbers of displaced persons. Of more importance, however, was a generous, farsighted view that had taken hold of both government and immigration officials as a new administration took over in Ottawa. If Canada was to retain her leading role in the postwar world, she needed more people; at least that was the attitude of key Ottawa officials. Thus, by the end of the decade boatloads of Baltic, German, Eastern European, and even Jewish refugees were arriving in Canada. In the ten years following the war more than 1.25 million immigrants, more than one hundred thousand of whom were displaced persons, entered the country. Naturally, the discriminatory aspect of Canadian policy did not change. In a famous speech outlining the future principles of the country's immigration policy in May 1947, Mackenzie King reassured his fellow citizens that only those people considered "desirable" and "adaptable" would be acceptable. Pointedly he added that this did not mean "Orientals and others."[31]

Canada is an enormous country, the second largest in the world, but one of the least populated. And Jewish life, like that of all Canadians, is influenced by the vastness of the land. If Jews suffer from an excess of history, then Canadians suffer from an excess of geography, and Canadian Jews suffer from both. Canada has been called the world's largest small nation. That sense of smallness and the immensity of the country may well have contributed to the sense of insecurity and marginality that has dominated the Canadian Jewish community for so much of its history in this century.

The proportion of Jews in Canada's population has remained relatively static at 1.5 percent since the 1920s. In 1951 there were 204,836 Jews (1.5 percent). According to the 1991 census, that figure grew to 356,315, although the proportion dropped slightly, to 1.3 percent of the total.[32] The Jewish population is more concentrated in the largest urban centers than the population as a whole. In 1991 there were 162,000 Jews in Greater Toronto, 101,000 in Montreal, 19,000 in Vancouver, 15,000 in Winnipeg, and 11,000 in Ottawa. Eighty-seven percent of Canadian Jews live in these five metropolitan areas.[33]

The number of Holocaust survivors and their descendants in Canada is difficult to ascertain. Of the 98,000 refugees admitted between 1947 and 1951 approximately 11,000 were Jews who emigrated directly from displaced persons camps. After Poles and Ukrainians, Jews were the third-largest group of displaced persons admitted to Canada.[34] From the end of the war to March 1951, 24,393 Jewish immigrants entered

Canada, representing 5.1 percent of all immigrants to Canada in that period. Further, the net immigration during that time was 19,873 Jews, indicating that nearly 5,000 Jewish immigrants had left Canada. This information does not convey the exact number of Holocaust survivors admitted, although one can assume that all of the displaced persons were survivors and that most of the remaining immigrants were also survivors. Thus, by 1951 there were probably 15,000 to 18,000 survivors, representing 7–9 percent of the total number of Jews in Canada.

From 1951 to 1956 another 21,660 Jewish immigrants arrived, of whom 20,193 remained. Again, we do not know how many were Holocaust survivors, although we can assume that a smaller proportion of the immigrants in this period were survivors than in the first six years following the war. We can establish that one estimate of 36,500 survivors resident in Canada by 1953 is too high, since it postulates that all the immigrants to that time were survivors. We can also determine that one estimate that 12–15 percent of Canadian Jews were survivors by 1951 is also too high.[35] By adding the figures from 1951–56 to those for 1945–51 we may conclude that 30,000 to 35,000 survivors and their descendants immigrated to and remained in Canada, representing 13–15 percent of Canadian Jews by 1956. Also, there was a natural increase of 27,286 Jews between 1945 and 1956, about 4,000 of whom were children born to survivors.[36] In 1957 another 6,000 Hungarian Jews immigrated, most of whom were survivors.[37] In absolute terms, the influx of survivors to Canada was small in comparison with the estimated 250,000 who immigrated to Israel and the overall figure of 137,500 Jews (survivors and nonsurvivors) who immigrated to the United States before 1952.[38] In relative terms, however, the influx of survivors was extremely high. They represented 3 percent of the total immigrants to Canada in the decade following the war, and more significantly, their proportion of the total Jewish population (13–15 percent) was far greater than the proportion of survivors who made up American Jewry in the same period (approximately 4 percent). Consequently, the impact of the survivors and their children on the political and social dynamic of the Canadian Jewish community became increasingly dramatic in the decades following the war. It is estimated that in Montreal in 1978, 20 percent of Jewish households were headed by survivors and there were thirty-one active organizations of Holocaust survivors.[39]

The central question with regard to the immediate postwar response to the Holocaust in the countries of the Western Hemisphere is why more than 250,000 Jewish refugees were languishing in displaced persons camps three years after Liberation.[40] In Canada the prohibitions against Jewish refugees were not modified until 1947. They were increasingly relaxed in subsequent years, allowing for the entry of some 40,000 Jewish immigrants. Changes in the immigration policy, however, almost wholly reflected political and economic developments. Compassion for the plight of the survivors played a marginal role.

King was the grand old man of Canadian politics in 1947. No Canadian leader has served longer than King's twenty-one years as prime minister and twenty-eight years as Liberal Party leader. No Canadian leader has been as astute in assessing the public mood and designing social and economic policies that reflected it. Thus, when King rose in the House of Commons on May 1, 1947, to outline his government's long-term program, which would determine immigration policy for the next fifteen years, he was responding to the country's needs and its international situation. King's speech articulated six major themes: enlarging the population, enlarging the domestic market, selective immigration, immigration related to absorptive capacity, control of immigration as a national prerogative, and continued restriction of Asiatic immigration so as not to "distort the present character of the Canadian population." King's speech mirrored information given to the Senate's Committee on Immigration and Labour, appointed the previous year. The committee's proceedings revealed that public opinion on immigration was mixed (Germans were more desirable than Jews, Chinese and Japanese were less desirable) and that there was a strong demand for labor.[41] The demand for labor was the most significant factor affecting immigration policy since King's architect for postwar reconstruction, C. D. Howe, had become the de facto head of immigration. Howe's economic policies, including the need for an increased labor force that would buy Canadian-made products, were unquestioned.[42]

King's announcement led to an easing of restrictions against European refugees in the next year. Following his speech, the quota of displaced persons to be admitted was set at 5,000, but it was increased to 30,000 in April 1948 and 40,000 by September. In all, 65,000 immigrants arrived by March 1948, of whom 8,000 were Jewish. The first large groups of Jewish immigrants were admitted as the result of an easing of the "first degree relative" policy (children, parents, and siblings). In addition, under pressure from Jewish organizations and the Canadian Labour Congress, the number of needleworkers, furriers, and orphans was increased.[43]

Canada's belated response to the plight of postwar Jewish refugees should not be interpreted as representing the government's recognition of the survivors' suffering. In the first two years following Liberation there was little appreciation, and even less sympathy, for Jewish refugees. Several examples attest to this attitude among Canadian diplomats, bureaucrats, politicians, and officers. In a national radio address on May 2, 1945, General Georges Vanier, Canada's ambassador to France, spoke at length about the horrors of Buchenwald without once mentioning the Jewish victims.[44] A memorandum from Minister of National Health Brooke Claxton to King on April 20, 1946, describing the horrible conditions in the camps and asking for permission to allow the entry of foster children, went unheeded for a year.[45] A directive to the Immigration Branch on February 6, 1946, stated that there were no concrete proposals for refugee resettlement but that when there were, they would be based on national status (since Jews were not a "nation," they were without status). A memo in August stated that the cabinet "commits nothing" on the state of displaced persons.[46] An internal memo of the Canadian armed forces in Germany dated November 18, 1946, placed Jews at the bottom of the list of preferential groups for admission since "they demonstrate less charity to others not members of their own group than do the remaining nationals."[47] In the House of Commons, a member of Parliament stated on July 9, 1946, that "the government is breeding a monster which sooner or later will devour it. Let it beware of the hammer and sickle. The Jewish-

Masonic gang can effect the worst interventions in Canada."[48] Even after King's speech and the relaxation of restrictions, J. B. Salsberg, a member of the Ontario legislature, wrote on December 12, 1947, following an investigation of immigration proceedings in Europe, that there was widespread anti-Jewish discrimination and incompetence on the part of Canadian officials.[49]

By the time the new wave of Jewish immigrants began arriving the pervasive anti-Semitism had begun to recede. The horrors of the Holocaust had shocked many Canadians, and others became caught up in the dramatic struggle for the creation of Israel. Although officially Canada supported the British attempts to prevent Jewish refugees from entering Palestine, large numbers of Canadians sympathized with the plucky, beleaguered Jews there.

It was at this moment that the Jewish leadership in Canada decided to launch an all-out offensive against discrimination. Their efforts were fueled by anger at the treatment of Jewish soldiers who returned from overseas to find the old restrictions barring their full entrance into society. In one much-publicized incident a veteran was fired from his sales job in Toronto when it was discovered that he was Jewish. Others were refused admission to skating rinks, swimming pools, golf clubs, and hotels, despite their sacrifices for the country.[50] With the help of sympathetic politicians, journalists, and jurists, Jewish leaders successfully lobbied for the introduction of antidiscrimination, fair-employment, and open-housing legislation.

With surprising rapidity, the barriers were torn down, opening Canadian society to all immigrant and ethnic groups. Universities dropped their quotas; hospitals accepted Jewish doctors; banks appointed Jewish directors. There was not a sector of society in which Jews were not able to play a role. Indeed, by the 1970s Canada had its first Jewish provincial premier and its first Jewish federal chief justice, as well as Jewish ambassadors, deputy ministers, and university presidents. All barriers, except perhaps the psychological ones, were gone.

And yet, in spite of these achievements and their status, there is still a general sense of unease in the Canadian Jewish community in the 1990s. A nervous cynic might ask, If everything is so good, why is everything so bad? The question illustrates the strange balance between hope and despair, between good news and bad news, that seems fundamental to the Jewish condition. The good news is that institutional discrimination against Jews has all but disappeared. The bad news is that much of the prejudice still remains.

Public-opinion polls seem to indicate that all is well, that anti-Semitism is not a problem in Canada now and has not been for years. Jews have become "white"; real prejudice is now focused on visible minorities: blacks, aboriginals, Hispanics, and Asians. And the pollsters are right. Never in Canadian history have Jews enjoyed such security, comfort, success, and acceptance as they do now.[51]

Yet pollsters have uncovered serious areas of concern. In 1984 a Goldfarb Poll indicated that 6 percent of Canadians considered themselves anti-Semites.[52] Although that percentage is low, it means that more than a million and a half Canadians hate Jews. Furthermore, according to the same poll, another 20–25 percent—approximately five million Canadians—admit to some prejudice against Jews. Thus, if this poll is accurate, nearly seven million Canadians dislike something about Jews. They may dislike other groups more, but significant anti-Jewish feeling has not disappeared.

Soundings taken in 1985 by the Gallup organization after the first trial of Holocaust denier Ernst Zundel concluded that the trial had a positive impact on Canadians.[53] Of those who followed the trial 25 percent were more sympathetic to Jews than they had been beforehand. One finding of the Gallup survey was troubling, however. When asked what they thought their neighbors felt about the Holocaust after the revelations of the Zundel trial, a substantial number of people stated that they believed their neighbors had real doubts about the extent of the Holocaust and were more suspicious of Jews than they had been before. Some analysts of this poll concluded that many of those respondents were saying about their neighbors what they themselves felt but were too polite or embarrassed to tell the pollsters. In saying that friends and neighbors—people with whom they spent a good deal of time and whose ideals and values they likely share—had become less sympathetic toward Jews, they may really have been saying that they themselves had become less sympathetic.

More encouraging were the results of the 1984 Canadian National Election Study, which indicated that only 14 percent of Canadians held negative feelings toward Jews, although in Quebec the percentage of people with hostile attitudes was much higher.[54] Supporting this conclusion was a much more comprehensive study conducted in 1986 by the Institute for Social Research at York University, which found levels of anti-Semitism in French Canada to be almost double those in English Canada.[55] This study also found anti-Jewish feeling in Canada to be about 25 percent higher than in the United States. Large numbers of Canadians still held negative Jewish stereotypes, although far fewer than in the 1950s.[56]

Anti-Semitism persists despite the determined efforts of Jewish organizations, increased interfaith activity, enhanced civil- and human-rights legislation, creative educational programs, and, above all, awareness of the Holocaust. Indeed, since the latter part of the 1980s there has been an increase in anti-Semitic activity, such as synagogue and cemetery desecration and verbal harassment. Of greater concern is the growing bravado of white-supremacist organizations, whose once aging ranks have been swelled by skinheads and unemployed youths. Although these organizations' recruiting rallies and rock concerts have not proved very successful, they do have ominous resonances.[57]

Perhaps the greatest present cause for concern relates to the changing nature of anti-Semitism in Canada. In the past, Canadian anti-Semitism was essentially a social disease, a prejudice that found its expression in predictable forms—not wanting to work for a Jew, live near one, hire one, or golf with one. But now, according to many observers, the number of people with these feelings is relatively small. Anti-Jewish attitudes have instead become more insidious. The charges are that Jews now have too much power and that they are more loyal to Israel than to their own countries. There seems to be a growing sense in Canada that Jews are getting more than their fair share, that they are far too influential for their small numbers. Many are saying that Jews are too visible—that they are too wealthy, too well educated, too integrated; that there are too many of them in high political, judicial, cultural, medical, and educational positions; that they control too many industries, are too prominent in the media, and dominate the entertainment and other businesses. In essence, according to anti-Semites, they play far too important a role in Canadian society given their insignificant number.

Though still relatively small in number, a variety of hate groups in Canada actively propagate Holocaust denial. Jews, they claim, were not the victims but the victimizers, who managed to pull off the greatest hoax in history. In the process they not only destroyed the good name of Germany but managed to steal billions of dollars in reparations.

Canada has become a haven for some of the world's leading hatemongers. Chief among them is Ernst Zundel, a German immigrant who throughout the 1970s and early 1980s was the principal source of Holocaust denial and neo-Nazi material shipped to Germany and Latin America. His imprint, Samisdat Press, is one of the world's major publishers of hate material.[58] In 1985 in Toronto Zundel was charged with disseminating false information deemed likely to cause injury or mischief to the public interest after he called the Holocaust a hoax in several of his publications. After a lengthy trial Zundel was convicted by a jury and sentenced to jail. On appeal the decision was reversed on a legal technicality. In 1988 Zundel was again tried and convicted. Then in 1993 the Supreme Court of Canada ruled that the law under which he had been convicted was vague and therefore unconstitutional. Zundel is a free man despite Canada's hate-law provisions.

Another Holocaust denier was brought to trial in 1984 in Red Deer, Alberta, for willfully promoting hatred against the Jewish people. Jim Keegstra, a high-school teacher in a small Alberta town in which he was also the mayor, had taught in his social-studies course that the Jews were the allies of the devil in the cosmic struggle between good and evil and that the Holocaust was a fraud. Although Keegstra was found guilty, his conviction was overturned on appeal.[59] In 1992 Keegstra was again tried and again convicted of disseminating hate. This time the Supreme Court of Canada upheld the constitutionality of the act under which Keegstra was charged, and his conviction stood. He was fined five thousand dollars.

Canadian courts have been busy dealing with Holocaust deniers. A New Brunswick teacher was barred from the classroom by a human-rights tribunal, a decision overturned on appeal, but ultimately upheld by a unanimous decision of the Supreme Court of Canada in April 1996. The Canadian government has also deported several well-known deniers, including David Irving, for entering the country illegally and for spewing hatred.[60]

Another issue that has caused great friction between Canada's Jewish community and its government has been the presence of Nazi war criminals in Canada. For many years there was incontrovertible evidence from a variety of sources that since the end of the war a number of Nazi war criminals had made their way to Canada. The exact number is not known, but a recent government commission found evidence that in 1985 there were several hundred potential war criminals worthy of further investigation.[61] Only the Jewish community seemed concerned, and the Canadian government did nothing. In 1982 the West German government demanded the extradition of Canadian citizen Helmut Rauca on the charge that he had been complicit in the murder of thousands of Lithuanian Jews. Only then did the Canadian government respond to the clamor of the Jewish community to rid the country of its unwelcome guest. Rauca was deported to Germany, where he died in jail awaiting trial.[62]

Finally in 1985 the Conservative government began a judicial inquiry into the presence of Nazi war criminals in Canada, headed by Justice Jules Deschênes of Quebec. A year later Deschênes recommended that the government bring immediate action against some twenty potential war criminals in Canada and that it investigate a number of others. The inquiry also recommended that the government amend the criminal code to allow prosecution in Canada.[63] This the government did. However, its performance in prosecuting alleged Nazis in Canada has bitterly disappointed the Jewish community. Since 1986 only one war criminal, a Dutch collaborator, has been deported from Canada. No one else has been convicted, and few have been charged. It is clear that successive Canadian governments, fearing political repercussions from various Eastern European ethnic groups, have been loath to make the prosecution of war criminals a priority. And the more hesitant the government has become, the more impatient Holocaust survivors have become to bring these alleged Nazis to justice.[64]

□

At a general assembly of the CJC in November 1993 ten resolutions out of fifty were related to the Holocaust. Seven dealt with the issue of Nazi war criminals resident in Canada, two with the dissemination of hate propaganda and Holocaust denial, and one with Holocaust remembrance. In contrast, no resolutions connected to the Holocaust were made at congress assemblies in the period from 1945 to 1950, and only two were made in the fifties.

The Holocaust Remembrance Committee of the Jewish Federation of Greater Toronto sponsors a Holocaust Education Week for the community each year. In 1993 this program offered fifty-three lectures, films, and discussions in synagogues, churches, libraries, and community centers by scholars, survivors, students, media representatives, and clergy.[65] Until the late seventies, in contrast, aside from commemorations, there had been no public education programs regarding the Holocaust in any Canadian city.

In short, the reaction to the Holocaust within the Canadian Jewish community was delayed for a generation. Aside from commemorations held on the anniversary of the Warsaw Ghetto Uprising, the Jewish community concentrated on freeing the surviving remnant from refugee camps and then helping them integrate into a new society. The established Jewish community, that is, those who had not experienced the Holocaust, did not regard the Holocaust as a defining point of its ethnic identity. The delayed response to the Holocaust within the Jewish community can be understood by examining how the established Jewish community and the survivor community were affected by certain events. The development of the response to the Holocaust falls into three clearly delineated time periods: the late 1940s to 1960; 1960 to 1973; and 1973 to 1985. The year 1985 proved to be a watershed in this process because of three important events, namely, the trials of Keegstra and Zundel, the establishment of the Deschênes Commission, and the first gathering of Canadian Holocaust survivors and their children. Since that time the Holocaust has become part of the fabric of Jewish self-definition in Canada. A brief examination of the Jewish community during these periods indicates that its response to the destruction of European Jewry was delayed for approximately twenty-five years.

From the late 1940s to 1960 the community was concerned with relief, restitution, and the absorption of the Holocaust survivors and their families. It had little interest in commemorating the Holocaust and even less in understanding the survivor experience or educating its members about the event. From 1960 until 1973 a struggle between the associations of survivors and the established communal organizations led to the determination to commemorate the Holocaust, to sponsor Holocaust education programs, and to muster political opposition, via legislation, to hate propaganda. Since 1973 Canadian Jews, through commemoration, education, and legislation, have made the Holocaust one of the central pillars of their self-definition as a unique ethnic community within the national mosaic. This phenomenon gained momentum after the events of 1985.

In the immediate postwar era the Canadian Jewish community was led by the children and grandchildren of settlers who had moved to Canada during the great wave of immigration that began in the 1880s and ended in 1914. The leaders' most immediate goal was to integrate Canadian Jewry into the Canadian polity. Stung by the federal government's reluctance to open the gates to Jews trapped in Nazi-occupied Europe and appalled by the venomous displays of anti-Semitism in the interwar period, communal leaders were conscious of the divisions within the Jewish community and their lack of clout in the body politic. These leaders, notably Samuel Bronfman, president of the CJC, were most concerned with transforming a diverse community into a unified body. At the national level, a unified voice representative of Canadian Jews was necessary to deal with federal politicians and bureaucrats on issues most pertinent to the community: the establishment of a Jewish state in Palestine and the easing of immigration restrictions for Jewish refugees in Europe. To a large measure this effort proved fruitful, more as a result of domestic needs and international developments than as a result of communal pressure.[66]

At the local level, the Jewish communities were in a state of transition. The established Jews in the largest cities, those Jews who had lived there since before World War II, were preoccupied with advancing from the fringes into the mainstream of Canadian society. They moved from the prewar Jewish neighborhoods, located in the inner-city cores, to the suburbs, a reflection of changes that had occurred within the community. The most significant transformation was the emergence of an upwardly mobile professional and business class. Its members distanced themselves from the working-class origins of previous generations, both psychologically and geographically. They considered themselves to be Canadians, and they were increasingly accepted as such. Communal structures were expanded and moved to new locations in the suburbs. Thus, during the decade and a half following the war the Jewish community succeeded in articulating a national voice and gaining acceptance as "ordinary" Canadians.[67]

During this period of transition the concentration on creating a unified voice and gaining recognition from English and French Canadians left little opportunity for established Jewry to comprehend the experiences of the refugees who inundated the community. The established community was most preoccupied with the immediate needs of the survivors. The community's efforts were underscored by several notable initiatives. Joint committees of the Jewish Immigrant Aid Service, the Canadian Jewish Congress, and the Jewish Labour Committee persuaded the government under the Group Movement Plan to admit 1,110 war orphans, at a cost of $1,880,000 to the community. Approximately 1,500 tailors and furriers gained entry under the Skilled Workers Project. These programs began in 1947, before the changes in the Immigration Act of the following year allowed more refugees to enter. Aside from resettlement, the CJC was active in sending supplies to refugee camps. In March and April 1948, for example, $195,000 worth of food was dispatched to Europe. Other organizations, such as the National Council of Jewish Women and the Jewish Vocational Service, played key roles in relief and restitution efforts.[68]

While a major wave of Jewish immigrants came between 1948 and 1954, the acceptance of established Jews into the mainstream of Canadian society bespoke the decline in systemic anti-Semitism among the Canadian polity and the increasing importance they placed on civil liberties and individual rights. The established Jews felt secure in a tolerant and prosperous postwar nation. They did not feel that the Holocaust was part of their world. Major community organizations were ill disposed to pressure the government about the entry of Nazi war criminals or sympathizers or to campaign against hate propaganda. The relative quietude of anti-Judaism in Canada, together with the corresponding relative tranquility of anti-Semitism abroad, reinforced their sense of security.[69]

As a result, a breach developed between the established Jewish community and the survivors. The established community viewed the survivors as immigrants, not essentially different from those Jewish refugees who had fled czarist restrictions and pogroms before World War I or from those who had escaped from the massacres in Ukraine and the anti-Semitic outbursts elsewhere after World War I. Furthermore, the survivors came from a Europe that the established community thought of as pre-industrial and Yiddish-speaking, a collection of *shtetlakh*. In reality, in the 1930s most European Jews lived in urban, somewhat acculturated surroundings as citizens of modern nation-states and were fluent in the national language.

The surviving fragment had already begun establishing new lives in the refugee camps and cities. Many had married or remarried, borne children, resumed their education or learned new occupations, and prepared themselves for integration into North American culture and society before they set sail. Upon their arrival in Canada the great majority of survivors were consumed with finding accommodations and employment and establishing communal networks with other survivors. For the most part, they were not concerned with sharing their experiences with the established Jews, especially since their memories were so fresh and painful. For the survivors who did speak to established Jews about their experiences, the response ranged from shock to incomprehension to derision. Ultimately, this experience created a schism between the established community, which represented about 85 percent of Canada's Jews by 1951, and the survivors. This break was evident in the separation of neighborhoods, in communal organizations, and, most importantly, in the articulation of ethnic identification. It must be pointed out, however, that in smaller Jewish communities this gulf was much narrower than in Montreal and Toronto.[70]

The community's contentment with its position became increasingly undermined from 1960 to 1973. Domestic events and international developments showed Canadian Jews that they and fellow Jews were vulnerable to anti-Jewish elements at home and abroad. By the early 1970s a rapprochement was occurring between the two groups. This was most apparent in the campaign to legislate against hate propaganda and in the increase of commemorative events.

Five sets of events occurring in close proximity to one another during the 1960s and early 1970s swung the mood of the Jewish community from its comfortable perch within the Canadian social fabric to a fear that a reemergence of anti-Jewish forces was primed to restrict its gains. The first development was a sudden rise of anti-Jewish activity in the winter of 1959–60, when a widespread, spontaneous outburst of swastika daubings occurred in Jewish communities worldwide. No clear cause was established. In Canada scores of daubings, including some in smaller towns with few Jews, outraged Canadians. Joan Seager, writing in the small-town *Burlington Gazette,* remarked that "I occasionally received chain letters and other garbage from anonymous sources which 'proved' that the Jews were responsible for—among other things—all the wars in history, the weather, strikes, Edward the Eighth's abdication, sexy movies and cancer. . . . I could feel the hate dripping off the paper. I could hear the sick mind vomiting its filth."[71]

These desecrations were soon followed by the widespread dissemination of hate propaganda, which was largely anti-Jewish but also aimed at Afro-Canadians, indigenous peoples, and Catholics. The event most responsible for changing the mood of Toronto Jews was a neo-Nazi demonstration that led to a riot instigated by anti-Nazi protesters on May 30, 1965. Among the rioters were prominent Holocaust survivors. Established community organizations, notably the CJC, responded by denouncing the rioters. This broadened the gulf between Jewish communal leaders, who tended to support the status quo, and the Holocaust survivors, who, emboldened by their success in establishing a foothold in their adopted country, advocated a more dynamic response to threats to Jews in Canada and abroad.[72] While the neo-Nazi party was ultimately proven to be minute, the CJC was spurred to create an anti-Nazi committee, which soothed some of the survivors' frustration about the lack of communal response.[73]

The third development was the rise of American Nazi organizations, such as the American Nazi Party, led by George Lincoln Rockwell. Interviews with Rockwell were aired by the publicly funded Canadian Broadcasting Corporation, which infuriated the community. The reemergence of Nazis in West Germany in the mid-sixties was also a source of concern. The initial success of the German National Democratic Party, the exposure given to its leader, Eric Von Thadden, and the legislative debates to invoke a statute of limitations on war crimes alerted Canadian Jews to the anti-Jewish climate still alive in Germany. A protest rally in Toronto on January 29, 1967, which drew three thousand Jews, helped to bridge the gulf between the established Jews and the survivors.[74]

Echoes of the Holocaust resonated in Canada during the capture, trial, and execution of Adolf Eichmann by Israel from 1960 to 1962. Canadian Jewry was not unique in responding to this fourth development. The Eichmann episode was perhaps the single most important event in the world reaction to the Holocaust. In Canada the trial, with its months of testimony and the picture of the average-looking man in the glass booth transmitted on television screens, did more to inform and alarm Jews and other Canadians than any other event. This was especially true in smaller Canadian cities, such as Vancouver, which were not as plagued as Toronto and Montreal with anti-Semitic outbursts.[75]

The fifth development was the Israeli wars in 1967 and 1973. These conflicts also rattled Canadian and world Jewry. Israel's swift victory in June 1967 only underlined the threat Israel faced from its immediate neighbors and the Islamic countries. The rise of the Palestine Liberation Organization, the anti-Israeli resolutions in the United Nations, the war of attrition, the consolidated attack by Syria and Egypt in October 1973, and the subsequent oil embargo alerted Canadian Jews to the possibility that Israel's existence was precarious. This realization helped solidify the Canadian Jewish community and must be seen as a precursor to the community's decision to appropriate the Holocaust as a source of ethnic identity.[76]

The Jewish community's response to all these developments was manifested in two ways. First, communal organizations pressured the federal government to enact legislation to ban hate propaganda. Spurred by the accusations by associations of Holocaust survivors that the established community was not responding sufficiently to these developments, the CJC resolved in 1962 "to bring about amendments to the Criminal Code which will make it a criminal offence to practice genocide and race hatred." A bill in the Canadian Senate led to the establishment of a committee, headed by Professor Maxwell Cohen, which included the future prime minister Pierre Trudeau. The committee's report in 1966 led to the passage in June 1970 of a law prohibiting the espousal of racial hatred. While pressing for this anti-hate legislation, the community also investigated the entry of Nazi war criminals into Canada in the immediate postwar era and discussed the possibility of enacting legislation to prosecute them.[77]

The second response of the Jewish community was to develop a concerted program of commemoration and education about the Holocaust within the community. At its plenary session in November 1971 the CJC resolved to "establish a permanent national memorial to the Holocaust" and to "intensify its efforts to motivate the interest to learn about the Holocaust and develop appropriate programs." This led to the creation of the National Holocaust Committee in 1973.[78]

With the formation of this committee, which was renamed the Holocaust Remembrance Committee later that year, the appropriation of the Holocaust as a defining point of ethnic identity by Canadian Jewry was under way. Holocaust commemoration and education thus became part of the matrix of communal identification. From the 1970s a new generation of leaders from both communities was instrumental in advancing this process, which culminated in 1985 with three seminal events: legislation to prosecute Nazi war criminals resident in Canada; the trials of Ernst Zundel for publishing anti-Semitic materials, specifically Holocaust-denial literature, and James Keegstra for teaching the same; and the gathering of Holocaust survivors and their children in Ottawa on the fortieth anniversary of the liberation of the camps.

Five factors accounted for these developments. Most significant was the evolution of the survivors as a force within the Jewish community.[79] One measure of their impact was the erection of Holocaust memorials within the Jewish community centers in Montreal and Toronto in the 1980s and in Vancouver in the early 1990s.[80] Another is that survivors and their children have been elected to prominent positions as lay leaders in the mainstream organizations. They have been instrumental in campaigning for legislation against hate propaganda and for the prosecution of Nazi war criminals. Finally, survivors have taken the front line in educating the Jewish and non-Jewish community as speakers and writers about the Holocaust and its contemporary implications.

The second factor was the perception by Canadian Jewry that anti-Semitism was increasing both at home and abroad. In 1990 a survey indicated that 79 percent of Canadian Jews felt that there was a "great deal" of anti-Semitism in Canada, even though 86 percent of the Canadian population was either favorably disposed or neutral in its attitude toward Jews.[81] Nevertheless, studies of the right wing in Canada consistently indicate that anti-Semitism is the "fundamental causal force" in the ideology of white-supremacist groups.[82] One bulwark against the spread of anti-Semitism, it was felt, was knowledge about the Holocaust through education of the public irrespective of age.[83] Consequently, programs such as Holocaust Education Week, sponsored by the Toronto Jewish Congress under the auspices of the CJC beginning in 1981, and Yom Hashoah commemoratives proliferated. By the late 1980s Jewish youths were being encouraged to participate in these ceremonies, to enter essay competitions about the significance of the Holocaust, and to join the March of the Living trips to Poland and Israel, the ultimate act of remembrance.

Third, disclosures about the lackadaisical immigration procedures in the immediate postwar period regarding the admission of possible Nazi collaborators fueled an already growing campaign by Canadian Jews for the federal government to investigate and prosecute suspected war criminals. The community's pressure on federal authorities to remedy the situation was another indication of the growing impact of the Holocaust.

Fourth, in 1970 the federal government adopted multiculturalism as official policy. The first decade after its adoption was essentially a recognition and celebration of the diversity of Canadians. Since the early 1980s, however, multiculturalism has come to mean that discrimination on the basis of creed, race, or ethnicity is not only illegal but contrary to the spirit and definition of what it means to be Canadian.[84] Multiculturalism was the final step in the official acceptance of Jews into the Canadian social fabric. Teaching the lessons of the Holocaust came to be viewed as one way to deal with racism and intolerance. This became most evident in public education.

Finally, since the mid-1970s the Holocaust has become a topic of widespread research and discussion in scholarly works, popular literature, and the visual media. The outpouring of materials has been most apparent in the United States, Europe, and Israel and certainly resonated with Canadian Jews. Canadians also discovered that there was a uniquely national aspect to the Holocaust, namely, Canada's shameful immigration policies during the Third Reich and the anti-Semitism of its governments and nativist groups in the interwar years and during World War II.[85] Learning about Canada's role in the Holocaust, although it is relatively insignificant in the wider and more horrible picture, has been both shocking and instructive to Canadians. Research on this topic has engendered seminars, discussions, and courses on university campuses and in synagogues and church basements.

For the first twenty years following the influx of survivors into Canada the observance of and discussion about the Holocaust were largely confined to the *landsmanschaften.* Since the mid-seventies the impact of the Holocaust on the wider Jewish community has created a competition among national organizations concerning the form Holocaust commemoration and education should take and how concern about anti-Semitism should be expressed. In Toronto alone, aside from the *landsmanschaften,* five organizations purport to represent the correct approach to Holocaust commemoration and education—the Holocaust Remembrance Committee of the Jewish Federation of Greater Toronto (under the umbrella of the CJC); the League for Human Rights of B'nai B'rith; the Holocaust Remembrance Association; the Canadian Friends of Yad Vashem; and the Simon Wiesenthal Center. While their different paths may indicate conflicting ideologies and a struggle for power and respect within the community, their efforts also bespeak the centrality of the Holocaust in the consciousness of Canadian Jews.

□

The curricula of the public schools in the first three decades following World War II provided very little information about the Holocaust. Crucial historical events, such as decolonization, Hiroshima, the struggle for civil rights, and the Holocaust, were absent or glossed over. One study found that of seventy-two history textbooks dealing with the modern world that were in use in Canada half had nothing, or less than one paragraph, on the Holocaust. Only three books did a "good" job on the topic. Further, of 208 high-school students attending a seminar on the Holocaust in 1981 only 28 percent had a "good" knowledge of the subject according to their self-evaluation after the seminar.[86]

A specific example of the lack of Holocaust education in public schools can be found in *The Modern Age,* a high-school history textbook printed in 1963. It was the sole text for the compulsory senior course on Western civilization in Ontario schools and was widely used in other provinces. Its author, an outstanding professor of education who trained a generation of teachers, made only the slightest reference to the Holocaust. He limited his comments to a few statements: that Hitler "blamed the Jews for many of Germany's troubles" and that in Germany "most of them [the Jews] were slaughtered. They numbered about half a million but they had incurred the hatred of many peoples for their success in business and the professions, and the Nazis delighted in destroying them." In 1987 *The Modern Age: Ideas in Western Civilization* was published and became one of the approved texts for the optional course on Western civilization. The book contains sixteen pages of selected readings from *Anne Frank: The Diary of a Young Girl,* Elie Wiesel's *Night,* Yevgeny Yevtushenko's *Babi Yar,* Paul Tillich's *The Courage to Be,* and Dietrich Bonhoeffer's *Letters and Papers from Prison.*[87]

The evolution from *The Modern Age* of the 1960s to the similarly titled work some twenty-four years later is indicative of the delayed response to the Holocaust in public education in Canada. Whereas the former text provided little and erroneous information, the latter used carefully chosen primary materials. That all senior students in Ontario in the first case learned little about the Holocaust and that some students who elect to study modern history today may learn a fair amount indicates how the Holocaust has entered into the public discourse in the last decade. That entry has been due to three interrelated factors: the broadening of educational perspectives, Canada's official adoption of multiculturalism, and the efforts of the Jewish community.

In May 1984 the Association of Large School Boards in Ontario (ALSBO) debated a resolution that the "Provincial and Territorial Ministers of Education incorporate studies of the Holocaust in the History, English and Social Studies curriculum" in order to "foster greater understanding of cultural relations in our schools," "to combat racism," and to stem the "seeming growth of intolerance towards immigrant and ethnic groups."[88] Shortly thereafter, the Ontario ministry of education stated that students "should develop an understanding of the background to and scope of the Holocaust" in the course on twentieth-century world history. The ministry stated that in the course on modern Western civilization a "sample teaching strategy" on democracy should employ "the background, the progress, and the horrors of the Holocaust."[89]

Similar initiatives to incorporate the Holocaust into curricula in other provinces have occurred in the late eighties and early nineties. In all cases, however, the unit on the Holocaust is only a recommended unit of study, usually in optional courses. The only province to mandate the teaching of the Holocaust is New Brunswick.[90] As the ALSBO report indicates, a primary reason for Holocaust education has been the adoption of multiculturalism as official policy in Canada. Concurrently, a new generation of teachers has been instrumental in developing new methodologies and exploring new areas of research. One indication of the impact of this thrust was the summer 1986 issue of the *History and Social Science Teacher,* the most widely read professional journal in Canadian education. Most of the issue was devoted to methodologies on teaching the Holocaust. In the summer of 1995 the journal, now named *Canadian Social Studies,* devoted another special issue to the Holocaust.[91]

Another indication of public education's interest in the Holocaust has been the development of specific curricula. In North York, a city in metropolitan Toronto, the board of education developed a curriculum for ninth-grade students in English literature, while the Toronto Board of Education decided that an interdisciplinary curriculum for high-school students best suited its needs.[92] This interdisciplinary curriculum contained units for teaching the Holocaust in twelfth-grade history, ninth- and twelfth-grade English, twelfth-grade economics, thirteenth-grade science, and senior-level (grades eleven to thirteen) art. This curriculum was adopted by teachers both in Toronto and in other cities across the country according to their specific requirements. The commitment of money and resources by local school boards and the inclusion of Holocaust studies by provincial ministries of education in the 1980s signify the advent of the Holocaust in the national public discourse. One example of this phenomenon was the schools in Waterloo County, seventy miles west of Toronto. Almost half of the county's population is of German descent, yet the study showed that all thirteen secondary schools taught the Holocaust in a compulsory course on contemporary Canada. Moreover, six hundred students from the county attend an annual one-day seminar on the Holocaust.[93] The oldest ongoing seminars for secondary-school students are the two one-day symposia held annually at the University of British Columbia since 1976.[94]

School boards, ministries, and teachers' associations have also sponsored professional-development programs for teachers. In New Brunswick, eight teachers have participated in tours to Germany, Poland, and Israel sponsored by the League for Human Rights of B'nai B'rith between 1986 and 1992, with partial funding by the New Brunswick Teachers' Association. New Brunswick teachers have worked with scholars and survivors in ongoing education programs. The 1993 annual New Brunswick Teachers' Association's meeting was devoted to the Holocaust and antiracist education.[95] The Toronto Board of Education has a standing committee on the Holocaust, which has sponsored professional-development programs since 1986, and the Waterloo County board adopted a similar agenda in 1989.[96]

Another reason for the growing interest in Holocaust studies in the public-education system has been the increased support of the Jewish community. Holocaust-education committees affiliated with the CJC have provided resources and survivor speakers to local school boards across the country. They have been the driving force in the creation of student seminars and professional-development programs for teachers. The Toronto committee has held workshops for survivors on the art of speaking to students and maintains the Holocaust Memorial, which some fifteen thousand children visit annually. A similar number of students attend programs at the Montreal memorial, while the edifice built in Vancouver in 1994 meets the needs of students and children there. In Saint John, New Brunswick, the tiny Jewish community has created a historical museum containing display and resource materials that are used by educators throughout the province.[97]

The explosion of Holocaust-related themes in the media since the late 1970s has also propelled the teaching of the subject. Most significant was the television miniseries *Holocaust,* aired in April 1978 in the United States and shown simultaneously in Canada. In anticipation of its showing the National Holocaust Remembrance Committee distributed a "Viewer's Guide to the Holocaust," prepared by the National Education Association, to its local committees. The committee in Toronto sent educational materials to the heads of history departments in all the Ontario secondary schools.[98] Other developments, such as the publication of *None Is Too Many* in 1982 and the showing of the documentary *Shoah* in 1985, created some interest among educators. Neither of these, however, had the impact for teachers and students that came with the release of the movie *Schindler's List* in 1993. Seminars on the movie and the book have been held, and some survivors have become active in speaking to students about the movie in particular and the issue of rescue in general.

Another arena in which the interest in the Holocaust has been evident in Canada in the last twenty years is the arts. Here the Holocaust has become inscribed into the experience of Canadian Jews. It has been difficult for many commentators, writers, and artists to disengage their Jewishness from the impact that the Holocaust has had on their lives. George Woodcock, a noted analyst of Canadian culture, has characterized literature written by Canadian Jews in the following way: "Jewish writers have revealed with a peculiar force and sensitivity the tensions that are characteristic of Canadian life. . . . It might be a metaphorical exaggeration to describe Canada as a land of invisible ghettos, but certainly it is, both historically and geographically, a country of minorities that have never achieved assimilation."[99]

Jewish Canadian writers, filmmakers, and artists find themselves in a no-man's-land, dispossessed from Europe and uncomfortable in Canada. They are immigrants and descendants of immigrants trapped between continuity and assimilation. As Michael Greenstein has written, "This 'being elsewhere,' this *difference,* constitute[s] the unresolved ambivalence of otherness in a ubiquitous diaspora from Europe to North America. Jewish-Canadian literature, in particular, turns back to a lost European tradition to help forge a new identity in its relatively unsettled Canadian homeland of vestigial ghettos."[100] Woodcock's and Greenstein's visions are even more relevant to the representation of the Holocaust in the arts. Survivors and their children, marked by their experiences, have been doubly disengaged, first from the mainstream and second from the established Jews in Canada. Nevertheless, the Holocaust has played an integral role in the artistic output both of established Jews and of the survivors and their children.

Modern Jewish Canadian literature rests on the shoulders of a colossus. Abraham Moses Klein was born in Lithuania and raised in Montreal. By profession he was a lawyer, by avocation a novelist, poet, and short-story writer. The Holocaust was the subject of several of his works. *The Hitleriad* (1943) is an eight-hundred-line poem exposing Hitler as a charlatan. It begins:

> See him, at last, the culprit twelve man damn.
> Is this the face that launched the master-race

And burned the topless towers of Rotterdam?
Why, it's a face like any other face
Among a sea of faces in a mob

And it continues:

Judge not the man for his face
Out of Neanderthal!
'Tis true 'tis commonplace
Mediocral,
But the evil of the race
Informs that skull! . . .
His strength is as the strength
Of ten, and ten times ten;
For through him, magnified
Smallness comes to our ken—
The total bigness of
All little men.[101]

After the war, Klein mourned the extinguishing of European Jewish civilization in his poem *Elegy* (1947). Then in 1951 he published his outstanding novel *The Second Scroll,* whose five chapters parallel the five books of the Torah; the novel posits the establishment of Israel as the vindication of Jewish suffering in the Holocaust.[102] Klein's work marks a watershed in Jewish Canadian literature by bridging the gap between the European background and the Canadian experience and by making the transition from Yiddish to English as the language of artistic expression.[103]

Canada's most prolific poet is Irving Layton, a friend of Klein's and a fellow Montrealer who regards Klein as a mentor. Layton has invoked the Holocaust both as a source of Jewish strength and as a way of identifying the marginalization of Jews, especially the survivors, in Canadian society. In *Ex-Nazi,* two neighbors, one a Jew and one a German, meet. The poem begins:

She tells me she was a Nazi; her father also.
Her brother lies buried under the defeat
and rubble of Stalingrad.
She tells me this, her mortal enemy, a Jew.[104]

A generation later, another Montrealer, Leonard Cohen, a poet, novelist, songwriter, and musician, invoked the Holocaust in his work. One collection of poems, *Flowers for Hitler* (1964), included the poem "All There Is to Know about Adolf Eichmann." The poem mirrors Klein's *Hitleriad* in showing that iniquity can corrupt otherwise ordinary people:

EYES . . . . Medium
HAIR . . . . Medium
WEIGHT . . . . Medium
DISTINGUISHING FEATURES . . . . None
NUMBER OF FINGERS . . . . Ten
NUMBER OF TOES . . . . Ten
INTELLIGENCE . . . . Medium

What did you expect?
Talons?
Oversize incisors?
Green saliva?
Madness?[105]

Among the writings of Jews who arrived in Canada as a result of the Nazi seizure of power, the most trenchant are the novels of Henry Kreisel, who escaped from Austria and settled in Canada in 1938 and died in 1993. His novels *The Rich Man* and *The Betrayal* employ the motif of the double man, dispossessed from his European roots and trying to integrate himself into the new culture while carrying the wounds of his experience.[106] J. J. Steinfeld is a younger writer whose dark, humorous stories about survivors and their children deal with guilt and adjustment.[107] Other notable novels by survivors include Andre Stein's *Broken Silence* and Jack Kuper's *Child of the Holocaust*.[108] Donia Clenman, a Toronto poet, has published several volumes. Many of her works, including the title poem of *I Dream in Good English Too,* tell of the difficult adjustments that survivors have been forced to make since the war.[109]

In recent years many survivors have published their memoirs, and many more are in the process of doing so. They include works of resistance fighters such as Amnon Aizenstadt, who escaped the Warsaw ghetto in a Wehrmacht uniform; Helene Mosckiewicz, who worked in the Belgian underground; the Smuschkowitz brothers, David and Peter, and Peter Silverman, who were Jewish partisan fighters in Lithuania; and Faye Shulman, a partisan fighter in Russia.[110] Memoirs of ghetto and camp conditions have been written by Joachim Schoenfeld, who combined scholarly research with an account of his experiences, and Eva Brewster and Eta Fuchs Berk, both of whom wrote about Auschwitz. Other notable memoirs include Michael Hanusiak's recollection of ghettos in Poland and Ukraine, Anita Mayer's account of her experience as a Dutch girl who was deported with Anne Frank, and Maria Jacobs's memoir of how her family hid Jews in Holland.[111]

Representations of the Holocaust in the visual arts have been important, especially as educational resources. Five documentary films in the last decade stand out. David Harel's *Buried Alive: Raoul Wallenberg* (1983) is an early review of rescue, a phenomenon that has been widely explored in recent years. Irene Angelico's *Dark Lullabies* (1985), a full-length movie, deals with a survivor's return to Europe. Two other documentaries explore this theme as well. Saul Rubinek, a native of Toronto and a Hollywood star, filmed his parents' return to Poland to meet the family that saved them in *So Many Miracles* (1988). Rubinek also wrote a book about the experience. *Return to the Warsaw Ghetto* (1993), a film Steve Paiken made for TV Ontario, chronicles the Canadian survivors and their children in Poland during the commemoration of the fiftieth anniversary of the Warsaw Ghetto Uprising. *Voices of Survival* (1989), a film made by Alan Handel for the CJC, combines oral history and documentary footage as seven survivors living in Canada tell their story in the context of the war. This documentary is accompanied by an educational guide that is widely used in Canadian classrooms.[112] *Art Out of Agony,* a series of radio documentaries on art and the Holocaust narrated by Stephen Lewis, Canada's ambassador to the United Nations at the time, aired in 1984. The series has also been produced in print.[113]

Representations of the Holocaust in paintings, sculpture, and architecture abound. Works in Holocaust museums and memorials (there are five just in Toronto) as well as in public galleries and private collections attest to the outpouring in these fields. As George Woodcock and Michael Greenstein have noted, the creation of mental ghettos has been a hallmark of the Canadian Jewish cultural experience. This phenomenon is not unique to Canadian Jews but is widespread in the artistic expressions of other minorities in Canada. For Holocaust survivors and their children this separation from the mainstream has been doubly difficult, yet the plethora of books, films, and art, especially in the last decade, are an indication that they are finally adjusting to their status as Canadians rather than transplanted, dispossessed Europeans. Unfortunately, this process has taken half a century.

□

Despite the persistence of some racism and anti-Semitism, the new multicultural Canada of the 1980s and 1990s is very different from the benighted, parochial, xenophobic country it was a generation or two ago, when Jews were excluded from every sector of Canadian society and were even excluded from the country itself by a government and a people who felt there were already far too many. Today the Canadian mosaic is the country's national cliché; pluralism is its most important national characteristic. Protected against discrimination by legislation, encouraged to maintain their culture and heritage by government largesse, Canada's minorities are finally playing their proper role in society. Prejudice and hostility are giving way to tolerance and respect; the new Canada is a nation that tries to celebrate differences and to accommodate as much diversity as possible.

And in bringing these changes about few communities have been as instrumental as Canada's Jews. Inspired by the arrival of large numbers of Holocaust survivors who brought with them a commitment to succeed and a self-assertiveness and a passion that had been largely lacking from the staid expression of Jewish life in the past, members of the Jewish community either as individuals or through their organizations, such as the CJC, have been in the forefront of fighting racism, attacking inequality, and lobbying for more liberal immigration policies. And they have succeeded beyond their wildest expectations.

What better symbol of their success and of the legacy of the Holocaust in Canada than that nearly fifty years after Canada turned its back on European Jews and abandoned to certain death the passengers of the ill-fated *St. Louis,* Canada was awarded the Nansen Medal by the United Nations for its "outstanding" record of assisting the world's refugees throughout the 1980s. It was present-day Canada's eloquent snub in the face of its own history, of its Mackenzie Kings and Frederick Blairs. Above all it was international recognition that a new, different, and better Canada had come into being.

NOTES

1. See the file on the *grève des internes* in the Canadian Jewish Congress (CJC) National Archives, Montreal; and *Le Devoir*, June 10–24, 1934.

2. Cyrill Levitt and William Shaffir, *The Riot at Christie Pits* (Toronto, 1987).

3. Report on Anti-Semitic Activities, 1937, 4–6, CJC National Archives.

4. Report on Anti-Semitic Activities, 1938, ibid.

5. Irving Abella, "Anti-Semitism in Canada in the Interwar Years," in *The Jews of North America*, edited by Moses Rischin (Detroit, 1987), 235–47. See also Rose Betcherman, *The Swastika and the Maple Leaf* (Toronto, 1984).

6. *Toronto Star*, April 24, 1933.

7. Rabbi Maurice Eisendrath, "Statement on Anti-Semitism," June 1938, CJC National Archives.

8. Abbe Grondin, quoted in Robert Rumilly, *Histoire de la province de Quebec,* vol. 16 (Montreal, 1955), 172.

9. See Esther Delisle, *The Traitor and the Jew: Anti-Semitism and the Delirium of Extremist Right-Wing Nationalism in French Canada from 1929 to 1939* (Montreal, 1993).

10. *Le Restaurateur,* September 1933; *L'Action nationale,* December 1934.

11. Irving Abella and Harold Troper, *None Is Too Many: Canada and the Jews of Europe, 1933–1948* (Toronto, 1982), 282.

12. Irving Abella, *A Coat of Many Colours: Two Centuries of Jewish Life in Canada* (Toronto, 1990).

13. Louis Rosenberg, *Canada's Jews: A Social and Economic Study of the Jews in Canada* (Montreal, 1939).

14. See Gerald Tulchinsky, *Taking Root: The Origins of the Canadian Jewish Community* (Toronto, 1993).

15. Rosenberg, *Canada's Jews,* 130–310.

16. Abella, *Coat of Many Colours,* 147–79.

17. Abella and Troper, *None Is Too Many.* The information in the next several paragraphs comes from pp. 1–38 of this source.

18. Ibid., 9.

19. Ibid., 17–18.

20. William Lyon Mackenzie King to Hume Wrong, June 30, 1938, King Papers, National Archives of Canada, Ottawa (NAC).

21. King Diary, June 8, 1939, ibid.

22. Abella and Troper, *None Is Too Many,* 101–25.

23. Ibid., 161.

24. War Information Board Survey, F.S. 12, 1944, *Privy Council Office,* vol. 49, NAC.

25. Abella and Troper, *None Is Too Many,* 126–48.

26. Ibid., 177–78.

27. *Liberty,* November 1943.

28. Memorandum, Immigration Branch to the prime minister, February 2, 1945, Immigration Records, file 673931, NAC.

29. Nancy Tienhora, "Canadian Viewpoints on Immigration and Population: An Analysis of Post-War Gallup Polls," in *A Report of the Canadian Immigration and Population Study* (Ottawa, 1974), 59.

30. Abella and Troper, *None Is Too Many,* 226–27.

31. Irving Abella, "Canadian Refugee Policy to 1980: An Overview," in *The International Refugee Crisis: British and Canadian Response,* edited by Vaughn Robinson (Oxford, 1993), 89.

32. Joseph Kage, *With Faith and Thanksgiving: The Story of Two Hundred Years of Jewish Immigration and Immigrant Aid Effort in Canada (1760–1960)* (Montreal, 1962), 263; J. Torczyner and G. Goldmann, "Demographic Challenges Facing Canadian Jewry," *Canadian Jewish News,* December 12, 1993, 1–2, 11. Torczyner and Goldmann used a liberal definition of Jews that encompassed all those who identified themselves in the 1991 census as "Jewish by religion and\or ethnicity." They excluded those who identified themselves as of "Jewish ethnicity and\or religion and a religion other than Judaism."

33. Torczyner and Goldmann, "Demographic Challenges."

34. Kage, *With Faith and Thanksgiving,* 129.

35. Ibid., 129, 261, 262.

36. William Helmreich, in "The Impact of Holocaust Survivors on American Society: A Sociocultural Portrait," in *Remembering for the Future: Jews and Christians during and after the Holocaust* (Oxford, 1988), 363, equates "immigrants" with "survivors" in using Kage's estimate of 36,500 by 1953. John J. Sigal and Morton Weinfeld, in *Trauma and Rebirth: Intergenerational Effects of the Holocaust* (New York, 1989), 6, employ Kage's figures in their 1951 estimate.

37. Kage, *With Faith and Thanksgiving,* 261–62.

38. The figure 250,000 is cited by Abraham J. Peck in "Special Lives: Survivors of the Holocaust and the American Dream," in *Remembering for the Future,* 1151. The figure 137,500 is cited by Helmreich in "Impact of Holocaust Survivors," 381, where he equates the number of Jewish immigrants with the number of survivors.

39. From 1946 to 1955, 1,222,319 persons immigrated to Canada (see Reginald Whitaker, *Canadian Immigration Policy since Confederation,* Canadian

Historical Association Booklet No. 15 [Ottawa, 1991], 2). During the same time there were 46,053 Jewish immigrants (3.8 percent of the total), of whom 40,066 remained, as cited in Kage, *With Faith and Thanksgiving,* 261–62. See also Sigal and Weinfeld, *Trauma and Rebirth,* 6–7.

40. Michael R. Marrus, *The Unwanted: European Refugees in the Twentieth Century* (Toronto, 1985), 331–39.

41. Freda Hawkins, *Canada and Immigration: Public Policy and Public Concern* (Montreal, 1972), 80–109.

42. Abella and Troper, *None Is Too Many,* chap. 8. Howe was referred to as "minister of everything." See also R. Bothwell, I. Drummond, and J. English, *Canada since 1945: Power, Politics, and Provincialism* (Toronto, 1982), 75–77, 98; and Reginald Whitaker, *The Government Party: Organizing and Financing the Liberal Party of Canada, 1930–1958* (Toronto, 1977), 168, 180–81.

43. Abella and Troper, *None Is Too Many,* chap. 8.

44. Speech by Georges Vanier, NAC, reprinted in Paula Draper and Harold Troper, *Archives of the Holocaust,* vol. 15, *National Archives of Canada, Ottawa and Canadian Jewish Congress Archives, Montreal* (New York, 1991), 340–45.

45. Brooke Claxton to Prime Minister (King), NAC, in ibid., 351–55.

46. Norman Robertson, Director of External Affairs, to Director of Immigration, NAC, in ibid., 358–62; Hume Wrong, Department of External Affairs, to Minister of Mines and Immigration, NAC, in ibid., 366–69.

47. Wing Commander J. W. P. Thompson to Colonel Seamen Morley Scott, NAC, in ibid., 387–88.

48. Louis Rosenberg, CJC, to Saul Hayes, CJC, memorandum on a speech by Liguori Lacombe, member for Laval–Two Mountains, NAC, in ibid., 386.

49. J. B. Salsberg to Hayes, NAC, in ibid., 393–96.

50. Abella, *Coat of Many Colours,* 209–30.

51. Robert Brym, William Shaffir, and Morton Weinfeld, eds., *The Jews in Canada* (Toronto, 1993).

52. Goldfarb Consultants, "Perception of Jews in Canada," May 1984.

53. Gabriel Weimann and Conrad Winn, *Hate on Trial: The Zundel Affair, the Media, and Public Opinion in Canada* (Oakville, Ont., 1986).

54. R. Brym and R. Lenton, "The Distribution of Anti-Semitism in Canada in 1984," in Brym, Shaffir, and Weinfeld, *Jews in Canada,* 116–19.

55. Paul Sniderman et al., *The Charter of Rights Study* (Toronto, 1988).

56. Irving Abella and Paul Sniderman, "Stubborn Stereotypes," *Toronto Globe and Mail,* April 9, 1988.

57. Reports of Community Relations Committee, 1990–95, CJC National Archives. See also Irving Abella, "The New Anti-Semitism," *Viewpoints,* March 1990.

58. Manuel Prutschi, "The Zundel Affair," in *Anti-Semitism in Canada,* edited by Alan Davies (Waterloo, Ont., 1992), 249–78.

59. Alan Davies, "The Keegstra Affair," in ibid., 227–48.

60. Reports of Community Relations Committee, 1992–96, CJC National Archives.

61. *Report of the Commission of Inquiry on War Criminals in Canada* (Ottawa, 1987).

62. Sol Littman, *War Criminals on Trial: The Rauca Case* (Toronto, 1983).

63. David Matas and Susan Charendoff, *Justice Delayed: Nazi War Criminals in Canada* (Toronto, 1987).

64. Reports of the Committee on Nazi War Criminals, 1992–96, CJC National Archives.

65. Plenary Sessions, CJC National Archives; "Holocaust Education Week," supplement to the *Canadian Jewish News,* October 28, 1993.

66. Abella and Troper, *None Is Too Many,* chap. 8; Michael R. Marrus, *Mr. Sam: The Life and Times of Samuel Bronfman* (Toronto, 1992), 288–92, 329–33, 420–24; Samuel Bronfman, "Presidential Address," CJC Plenary, 1947, Plenary Sessions, CJC National Archives; David J. Bercuson, "The Zionist Lobby and Canada's Palestine Policy 1941–1948," in *The Domestic Battleground: Canada and the Arab-Israeli Conflict,* edited by D. Goldberg and D. Taras (Montreal, 1989); David J. Bercuson, *Canada and the Birth of Israel: A Study in Canadian Foreign Policy* (Toronto, 1985).

67. Abella, *Coat of Many Colours,* chap. 9.

68. Kage, *With Faith and Thanksgiving;* Ben Lappin, *The Redeemed Children: The Story of the Rescue of War Orphans by the Jewish Community of Canada* (Toronto, 1963); Inter-Office Information, April 29, 1948, CJC National Archives; Abella, *Coat of Many Colours,* 230–31; Joseph Kage, interview by author, November 17, 1993, Montreal.

69. Hawkins, *Canada and Immigration,* chap. 4; Reginald Whitaker, *Double Standard: The Secret History of Canadian Immigration* (Toronto, 1987), 63–69.

70. Leslie Anne Hulse, "The Holocaust Survivor and the Canadian Jewish Community"

(M.A. thesis, Carleton University, 1979), published under the same title in *Viewpoints,* fall 1980, 34–42; Jean Miriam Gerber, "Immigration and Integration in Post-War Canada: A Case Study of Holocaust Survivors in Vancouver 1947–1970" (M.A. thesis, University of British Columbia, 1989); Myra Giberovitch, "The Contributions of Montreal Holocaust Survivor Organizations to Canadian Jewish Communal Life" (M.A. thesis, McGill University, 1988); Association of Survivors of Nazi Oppression, ZC1, ZC2, ZF Publication File, CJC National Archives.

71. Joan Seager, "The Fatal Disease of Anti-Semitism," *Burlington Gazette,* reprinted in *Toronto Telegram,* January 23, 1960; Joint Community Relations Committee, box 12, file 32, Ontario Jewish Archives (OJA), Ontario.

72. Minutes of the Executive of the Central Region of CJC, June 24, July 8, 1965, OJA; Association of Former Concentration Camp Inmates Survivors of Nazi Oppression, Open Letter, June 6, 1965, Jewish Public Library (JPL) Archives, Montreal.

73. Minutes of the Community Anti-Nazi Committee, January 3, March 13, 1966, OJA.

74. Minutes of the Joint Community Relations Committee, January 13, 1967, March 23, 1969, ibid.

75. Joint Community Relations Committee, 1961, file 13A, ibid.

76. Interviews by author with Sam Rothstein, November 28, 1993, Vancouver; Professor Moe Steinberg, November 29, 1993, Vancouver, who stated that "Israel and Holocaust awareness are inseparable"; and Professor Sid Olyan, director of the Jewish Federation of Vancouver in the 1960s, October 12, 1993, Toronto, on the impact of the 1967 war.

77. Plenary Sessions 1962, 1965, 1968, 1971, CJC National Archives; Harold Troper and Morton Weinfeld, *Old Wounds: Jews, Ukrainians, and the Hunt for Nazi War Criminals in Canada* (Toronto, 1989); Whitaker, *Double Standard,* 102–19.

78. Plenary Sessions 1971, 1974, CJC National Archives; CJC Holocaust Memorial Committee File, Minutes of Meetings, Canadiana Collection, JPL Archives.

79. CJC presidents since 1980 were born or raised in the postwar era: Les Scheininger, a child of survivors, was first president of the Ontario Region and then national president; Gerda Frieberg, a Holocaust survivor, was Ontario Region president from 1992 to 1995; and Ralph Snow, another survivor, was president of B'nai B'rith Canada in 1988–89.

80. Interviews by author with Dr. Robert Krell, November 28, 1993, Vancouver, and Nathan Leipciger, November 10, 1995, Toronto.

81. J. Brodbar-Nemzer et al., "An Overview of the Canadian Jewish Community," in Brym, Shaffir, and Weinfeld, *Jews in Canada,* 56.

82. Stanley Barrett, "White Supremacists and Neo-Fascists: Laboratories for the Analysis of Racism in Wider Society," in *Racism in Canada,* edited by O. McKague (Saskatoon, 1991), 90–94. See also Stanley Barrett, *Is God a Racist? The Right Wing in Canada* (Toronto, 1987), 339, 347–51.

83. Yaacov Glickman, "Anti-Semitism and Jewish Social Cohesion in Canada," in McKague, *Racism in Canada,* 55–57.

84. Karl Peter, "The Myth of Multiculturalism and Other Political Factors," in *Ethnicity, Power, and Politics in Canada,* edited by J. Dahlie and T. Fernando (Toronto, 1981); Harold Troper, "As Canadian as Multiculturalism: An Historian's Perspective on Multicultural Policy" (plenary address, Canadian Ethnic Studies Association, Vancouver, 1993).

85. For a sample of these studies, see Abella and Troper, *None Is Too Many;* Betcherman, *The Swastika and the Maple Leaf;* Eric Koch, *Deemed Suspect: A Wartime Blunder* (Toronto, 1985); Levitt and Shaffir, *Riot at Christie Pits;* and Delisle, *The Traitor and the Jew.*

86. Yaacov Glickman and Alan Bardikoff, *The Treatment of the Holocaust in Canadian History and Social Science Textbooks* (Toronto, 1982), 12–13 and app. C.

87. J. E. Cruickshank, *The Modern Age* (Toronto, 1963), 468, 470; Arthur Haberman, *The Modern Age: Ideas in Western Civilization, Selected Readings* (Toronto, 1987), 417–21, 431–39, 487–88.

88. Report of the Task Force on Holocaust Studies to the ALSBO Curriculum Committee, September 14, 1985, Toronto Board of Education, Equity Studies Centre.

89. Ontario Ministry of Education, *Curriculum Guideline, History and Contemporary Studies, Senior Division* (Toronto, 1987), 49; idem, *Curriculum Guideline, History and Contemporary Studies, Ontario Academic Courses* (Toronto, 1987), 26.

90. New Brunswick Department of Education, Program Development and Implementation Branch, *The Holocaust: A Topic of Study in History 111–112–113* (Fredericton, N.B., September 1988). This course, while optional, is taken by 90 percent of eleventh-grade students. According to ministry officials interviewed by the author in 1991, all students taking this course will study the mandatory unit on the Holocaust.

91. Alan Bardikoff, guest ed., *History and Social Science Teacher* 21 (summer 1986); Michael Charles, theme ed., *Canadian Social Studies* 29 (summer 1995).

92. See Jane Griesdorf and Alan Bardikoff, *The Holocaust* (North York, 1982); Frank Bialystok and Barbara Walther, *The Holocaust and Its Contemporary Implications*, 3 vols. (Toronto, 1985).

93. W. D. McClelland, Superintendent of Curriculum and Program Development, to Barry Preston, History Consultant, Waterloo County Board of Education, May 11, 1989, regarding Holocaust Studies, in the files of the Waterloo County Holocaust Education Committee, Kitchener, Ontario.

94. Holocaust Memorial Committee Minutes, box 31, Archives of the Jewish Historical Society of British Columbia, Vancouver.

95. *Focus: The Publication of the Social Studies Council of the New Brunswick Teachers' Association* 21, no. 2 (1991), and 23, nos. 1 (1992) and 2 (1993). Plenary session addresses at the 1993 annual meeting were given by Frank Bialystok ("The Antiracist Agenda for the 90s"), Herman Newman ("Reflections of a Holocaust Survivor"), and Rev. Jim Leland ("Jewish-Christian Relations and Holocaust Denial").

96. For a comprehensive account on the state of Holocaust education, see Frank Bialystok, "The Holocaust: Pedagogical Considerations," *Canadian Social Studies* 29 (summer 1995), 137–39.

97. Minutes of the Holocaust Remembrance Committee of the Jewish Federation of Greater Toronto, OJA. For Montreal, see the Archives of the Holocaust Memorial Centre; for Vancouver, the Archives of the Jewish Historial Society of British Columbia, Files on the Standing Committee on the Holocaust and the Holocaust Memorial Committee; and for Saint John, the Archives of the St. John Jewish Historical Museum.

98. Holocaust Remembrance Committee of Toronto Jewish Congress, 1978 files, OJA.

99. George Woodcock, quoted in Michael Greenstein, *Third Solitudes: Tradition and Discontinuity in Jewish-Canadian Literature* (Montreal, 1989), 15.

100. Greenstein, *Third Solitudes*, 15.

101. Abraham Moses Klein, *The Hitleriad*, quoted in Usher Caplan, *Like One That Dreamed: A Portrait of A. M. Klein* (Toronto, 1982), 111–17.

102. Rachel Felday Brenner, "Klein, Abraham Moses," in *The Blackwell Companion to Jewish Culture*, edited by Glenda Abrahamson (Oxford, 1988), 415–16; A. M. Klein, *Elegy* (Montreal, 1947); idem, *The Second Scroll* (Toronto, 1951).

103. Greenstein, *Third Solitudes*, 18–34.

104. Ibid., 38; Brenner, "Klein," 447; Irving Layton, *The Collected Poems of Irving Layton* (Toronto, 1971).

105. Leonard Cohen, *Selected Poems, 1956–1968* (Toronto, 1968), 122. For an assessment of Cohen's contribution, see Greenstein, *Third Solitudes,* 41–47, 119–41.

106. Henry Kreisel, *The Rich Man* (Toronto, 1948); idem, *The Betrayal* (Toronto, 1962); Greenstein, *Third Solitudes,* 54–67.

107. J. J. Steinfeld, *Forms of Captivity and Escape* (Saskatoon, 1988); idem, *Dancing at the Club Holocaust* (Charlottetown, Prince Edward Island, 1993).

108. Andre Stein, *Broken Silence: Dialogues from the Edge* (Toronto, 1984); Jack Kuper, *Child of the Holocaust* (Markham, Ont., 1984).

109. Donia Blumenfeld Clenman, *I Dream in Good English Too* (North York, Ont., 1988).

110. Amnon Aizenstadt, *Endurance: Chronicles of Jewish Resistance* (Oakville, Ont., 1987); Helen Mosckiewicz, *Inside the Gestapo: A Jewish Woman's Secret War* (Agincourt, Ont., 1985); David Smuschkowitz, Peter Silverman, and Peter Smuschkowitz, *From Victims to Victors* (Toronto, n.d.); Faye Schulman, *A Partisan's Memoir: Woman of the Holocaust* (Toronto, 1995).

111. Joachim Schoenfeld, *Holocaust Memoirs: Jews in the Lwow Ghetto, the Janowski Concentration Camp and as Deportees in Siberia,* foreword by Simon Wiesenthal (Hoboken, N.J., 1985); Eva Brewster, *Vanished in Darkness: An Auschwitz Memoir* (Edmonton, 1986); Eta Fuchs Berk, *Chosen: A Holocaust Memoir* (Fredericton, New Brunswick, 1992); Michael Hanusiak, *Lest We Forget,* 3d ed. (Toronto, 1976); Anita Mayer, *One Who Came Back* (Ottawa, 1981); Maria Jacobs, *Precautions against Death* (Oakville, Ont., 1983).

112. Frank Bialystok and Sharon Weintraub, *Voices of Survival: Education Guide* (Montreal, 1990).

113. Stephen Lewis, ed., *Art Out of Agony: The Holocaust Theme in Literature, Sculpture, and Film* (Toronto, 1984).

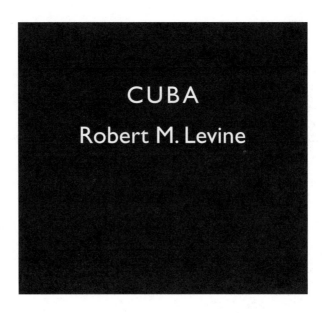

CUBA
Robert M. Levine

BEFORE THE HOLOCAUST

Cuba gained sovereignty from Spain only after three costly wars of independence (1868–98), U.S. intervention, and the proclamation of a republic on May 20, 1902, eight decades after the rest of Latin America achieved independence from European colonialism. Jewish arrivals to the island after 1902, as beleaguered refugees from Old World nations in turmoil, encountered a situation unique in the Western Hemisphere. There had been very few Jews in Cuba before 1900. The Spanish crown had excluded Jews from Cuba. Until 1898 Jews in Cuba could pray at home but not in synagogues.[1] Yet there was no modern tradition of institutional prejudice against Jews, and cultural and economic links to the nearby United States were great, with the result that Cuba's post-1920 Jewish population was able to maintain close contact with Jewish groups in the United States and Canada. Vicious anti-Semitism, from its eruption after the nationalistic revolution of 1933 until it was suppressed by President Fulgencio Batista during World War II, was principally an imported phenomenon, brought to Cuba by Falangist Spaniards as well as by agents of Mussolini and Hitler in the form of crude racist tracts. Since most Cubans supported the Spanish Republic, their sympathies remained with their Jewish compatriots, especially after information about the Holocaust reached Cuba. This was true even in elite circles, where the affinity for Franco and the Axis powers provided fertile soil for anti-Semitism and right-wing nationalism.[2] Jews were not permitted to become citizens until the 1930s, and then they were subjected to hardships that encouraged many to attempt to leave. Of the twenty-five thousand Jews who entered Cuba between 1918 and 1947, more than half emigrated, most to the United States, in spite of great difficulties posed by U.S. legislation.[3] The Jewish colony numbered no more than thirteen thousand at its height, between 1940 and 1942; even then it was clearly divided into subgroups based on language, customs, and levels of affluence.

782

Historical accounts of the Jewish colony's evolution have tended to emphasize early Jewish "connections with Cuba" by including as Jews *conversos* (those who converted to Catholicism) as well as *marranos* (covert Jews who nominally converted) and men and women of possible *marrano* descent.[4] Thus, even if Columbus is not claimed as a Jew, Luís de Torres, the expedition's interpreter (and, as a *converso,* an observant Catholic), is, based on the fact that he knew Hebrew, Aramaic, and Arabic, as well as several European languages. The Holy Inquisition, which was established in Havana in 1520, frequently accused *conversos* of being crypto-Jews, although it did not issue its first sentence until nearly a century later, in 1613. During the next decades many suspected Jews were arrested and fined, and some were burned at the stake, although Cuba also served briefly as a refuge for Jews and Calvinists fleeing Dutch Brazil after the Portuguese victory there in 1654. We also know that some Jews were forcibly baptized in Europe before being shipped to the New World, including some Jewish women who "accompanied the armed forces that Spain sent to the island" in the early sixteenth century.[5]

Things changed rapidly during the late nineteenth century. Following decades of conflict against the metropolis, culminating in the Ten Years' War (1868–1878), Spain's Cuban colony emerged broken. Times became especially hard during the 1880s, when unemployment reached desperate proportions. By the early 1890s some thirty-five thousand cigar makers were without work, and another group of roughly the same number were reduced to part-time employment. During the time of the Spanish-American War, in 1898, five or six Jewish families, including the Brandons, the Marchenas, the Machados, and the Dovelles, who had come from Panama, Curaçao, and Surinam, lived in Cuba; they were wealthy and kept to themselves. Most married outside their faith, and their children were raised as Catholics. Spain's prohibition of any religious practice except Roman Catholicism remained in effect until the termination of the Spanish-American War.[6]

José Martí, who became Cuba's hero of independence, enjoyed good relations with Jews in New York and attracted many to his cause. During and after the conflict with Spain, as early as 1892, some helped Martí raise funds; others, mostly Jewish immigrants from Europe, joined the patriots' Army of Liberation. Also participating were a handful of individual European Jews, including Louis Schlesinger, a Hungarian who had fought in the 1848 revolution and ended up in the United States, and Akiva Rolland (Rolloff), a "Ukrainian Jewish adventurer," who became a general in the Cuban army and the first finance minister of the nominally independent republic.[7]

The Spanish-American War and the occupation that followed brought hundreds of American Jews to the island. Jewish military casualties were buried in a Jewish cemetery at Guanabacoa, on the outskirts of Havana, at the request of American Jewish leaders. In 1904 the first Reform synagogue, the United Hebrew Congregation, was established for American Jews who settled in Cuba to do business. This congregation, affluent from the start and surviving into the 1960s, conducted services in English. Although it was always known as American, some of its members were Romanian Jews who had emigrated to the United States, learned the language, and been naturalized. Taken together, the American Jews in Cuba came to number about three hundred families by 1900. By 1910 this colony was prospering, establishing dry goods stores, factories, and department stores.[8]

Cuba's "American" Jews stood aloof from the impoverished (and Orthodox) Ladino-speaking Sephardic immigrants from European Turkey and North Africa, who began to arrive after 1900. Because of their language, which derived from medieval Spanish written in Hebrew script, the Sephardim adapted fairly easily, becoming occupied in commerce and striving to maintain their tightly knit extended-family and community structure on the North African–Levantine pattern.

The Sephardic colony increased after 1907, reaching fifty-seven hundred persons by 1914. Some of the Sephardim had been forced to leave their countries because they had participated in revolts against the Ottoman sultan, who was finally overthrown in 1908. In 1910 several hundred Jews arrived. Most were Sephardic, although many of the arrivals were Yiddish-speaking Ashkenazic Jews from Eastern Europe.

Most of the Jewish newcomers were destitute, seeking work as peddlers and domestics. Havana's American Jewish colony provided some aid but never truly welcomed the immigrants. The Orthodox Congregation Unión Hebrea Chevet Ajim was founded by Sephardic Jews in November 1914, and the Ashkenazic Centro Israelita was founded a few years later.[9] Almost all the Jewish immigrants brought nothing with them and were generally unskilled. Most settled in Havana, although some Sephardic families took up residence in provincial capitals. Ashkenazim tended to cluster in rented rooms and garrets in Havana's old commercial district in Old Havana, rarely venturing far from the congested Yiddish-speaking sections of that quarter.

A period of relative stability within the Jewish colony followed. Immigration from North Africa and the Mediterranean slowed, and both Sephardic and American Jews enjoyed the brief postwar prosperity, which reached its height in 1920 because of high sugar export profits. But the prosperity was short-lived. Prices fell in 1921, and high unemployment persisted until 1924–25. A study conducted by the United States National Council of Jewish Women found 90 percent of the Eastern European Jews in Cuba in May 1924 to be without work. Yet more than seven thousand Ashkenazic Jewish immigrants landed between 1921 and 1924, because Cuba—called Akhsanie Kuba (Hotel Cuba) by waiting immigrants—still offered the hope of access to the United States.

The arrival of so many Ashkenazic Jews created logistical difficulties, although politicians did not seem to mind. A more negative climate, aggravated by the postwar Red scare, arose in the United States, where beginning in early 1921 Congress voted to limit severely immigration from Eastern Europe. But the new American regulations preserved a loophole whereby immigrants denied entrance to the United States could use Cuba as a stopover on the way to subsequent legal entry. Steamship companies, faced with the loss of revenue for steerage-class passage to the United States, began to publicize in the European Yiddish-language press Cuba's lack of immigration laws and the fact that Cuban officials permitted anyone disembarking in

Havana harbor to remain. Since U.S. immigration laws did not restrict immigration from Latin America, persons remaining in transit in Cuba could reemigrate to the United States after a year's stay. Large numbers of Eastern European Jews began to arrive in Havana after March 1921, seeking to work for a year to make ends meet and then leave for New York or other American cities. Ninety percent entered through Havana, the rest at smaller ports, becoming the first Jewish residents of such towns and cities as Matanzas, Camagüey, Guantánamo, and Santiago de Cuba.[10]

Faced with large numbers of Jewish indigents, the Hebrew Immigrant Aid Society (HIAS) in New York, with supplemental funding from the Joint Distribution Committee (JDC), stepped in and provided relief. HIAS, in turn, asked that the local American Jews, through their United Hebrew Congregation (UHC), pledge more aid. This resulted in a campaign that raised several thousand dollars in the short term but fell off sharply by the end of 1921. Further negotiations caused the UHC to divide organizationally. Temple Beth Israel was created to provide religious services, and the Centro Macabeo was created to assume communal functions and to continue to provide indigent relief. But as Jeffrey A. Kahn points out, the mutual disdain between the established community and the newcomers would govern their interactions for the duration of Cuban Jewish history.[11] The Sephardic Jews, self-segregated and not particularly affluent, provided virtually no assistance to the Ashkenazim.

The Centro Macabeo provided legal-aid services, Spanish and English classes, and a canteen offering inexpensive or free meals to immigrants. Half of the Centro's funds came from the JDC in New York, half from Cuba's English-speaking Jews. But when the JDC's assistance ended after two years, the local colony curtailed the Centro's activities and provided neither food nor shelter to the needy. By late 1923 all relief efforts of the center ceased. The plight of the refugees soon worsened, however, when the U.S. Congress enacted the Johnson Act of 1924, which permitted only Cuban nationals to enter the United States, thus stemming the flow of emigrants using Cuba as a way station. Four thousand transient Jews from Eastern Europe had entered the United States this way, but now a thousand were barred, and more immigrants continued to arrive in Cuba each day. The island's proximity to the United States lent a sense of irony: the immigrants were so near, yet so far. The mainland was within broadcasting distance, and those who owned large radios could listen to concerts and news reports without difficulty.[12]

By the early 1930s, slow improvements in living standards among the immigrants were threatened by the impact of the Depression and worsening political instability across Cuba. The dictator, General Geraldo Machado, turned openly xenophobic and for the first time demonstrated antipathy against Jews. This took two specific forms. First, he encouraged Dr. José Ignacio Rivero, the editor of Havana's pro-Falangist newspapers, *Alerta* and *Avance,* as well as the conservative *Diário de la Marina,* Cuba's first newspaper, founded one hundred years earlier, to publish translations of the Nazi Julius Streicher's anti-Semitic diatribes. Second, in May 1932 Machado outlawed all Jewish cultural, social, and religious activities. Panic resulted. Some Sephardic and Ashkenazic leaders went into hiding or fled to the United

States. But three months later Machado was ousted, his departure prompted by the presence of U.S. Navy ships in Havana harbor and by diplomatic pressure applied by the U.S. envoy Sumner Welles.[13]

Control of the government was taken by army sergeant Fulgencio Batista y Zalvidar. In September 1933 Batista installed Ramón Grau San Martín, an aristocrat linked to *Alerta* and to the Spanish Falange, as president. The United States revoked the Platt Amendment, in force since 1903, which legitimated American intervention in Cuba, and Cuba was therefore elevated, for the first time, to the status of a diplomatic equal under the Good Neighbor Policy. Grau signed the Law of the 50 Percent, requiring that at least half of all employees in a business enterprise be Cuban-born nationals, thus extending xenophobic legislation to all of Cuba. The law drove thousands out of work, leading them to enter the much more poorly paid underground economy of home sweatshops or to bribe officials who were willing to overlook the new law. The law was not directed only against Jews; in fact, lower-class Spanish immigrants were the primary target. Jews were now permitted to apply for citizenship, which had not been possible under Machado, but high fees and other barriers made it difficult for large numbers of immigrants to earn a living legally.[14]

Hostility toward the Eastern European Jewish immigrants continued unabated. When *Alerta* published an editorial on Yom Kippur Eve (September 29), 1933, accusing Jewish strikers of firing on soldiers from rooftops during an antigovernment demonstration that had turned into a street battle and claiming further that Jews would close their businesses in a show of opposition to the army, military police descended upon Ashkenazic homes and businesses on Yom Kippur morning, arresting several dozen businessmen and forcing others to open their shops.[15] Jewish community leaders also worried about the impact of the Escuela Alemana, which opened in the Vedado suburb, flying the swastika from its gate and, after hours, providing facilities for the paramilitary exercises of the teenage auxiliary of the Asociación Nazista de Cuba.

In some cases, however, the nationalistic pressures actually benefited peddlers and other shopkeepers by forcing them to streamline their business practices or to become manufacturers. In spite of the difficult economic climate, moreover, many of the immigrants found their lot improving. But good fortune for individual Cuban Jews and the visibility it attracted brought new anti-Semitic propaganda, which now could be directed at evidence of Jewish monopolistic power and economic penetration. Despite this, efforts to organize a Cuban Jewish committee among representatives from the three major components of the colony failed. Most hoped that the anti-Semitic ugliness, previously foreign to Cuban life, would go away. In 1934 a report issued by the United States Foreign Policy Association concluded that "so far, no racial feeling of any marked extent has arisen between the Jewish colony and the Cubans."[16]

During the years of Batista's domination, relations between the Jewish colony and officialdom followed the rather personalistic formula required by the fact that Batista was de facto the head of state. When anti-Semitic broadcasts on one radio station increased in bellicosity in 1935, representatives from the UHC paid a visit to Batista during which they pledged ten thousand dollars toward the campaign to build a new national library; and they used the opportunity to ask that something be done about the broadcasts. Batista denied that he had any power to influence things but reminded the congregation's Rabbi Meier Lasker that a visit to Cuba's president (who lived upstairs in the same Havana apartment building) might help. Pleasantries were exchanged, and the visit ended. Within a few days unknown vandals smashed the radio station, and the offensive broadcasts were stilled.[17]

The respite did not last long. In 1936 the Nazi Embassy in Havana took the offensive. The attack, which was mounted in Dr. José Ignacio Rivero's newspapers and on the radio, focused on stopping Jewish immigration, calling Jews fleeing the Axis powers "human garbage." The attack grew in intensity daily, finding a sympathetic audience among the thousands of pro-Falange Spaniards living in Cuba. Anti-Semitism, which had been virtually absent from Cuban life, now became a prominent part of it. Rivero charged the biweekly Yiddish- and Spanish-language newspaper *Havaner Lebn—Vida Habanera* with disseminating leftist and anti-Cuban views; as a result, the editor, Sender M. Kaplan, was arrested in late March 1936 and detained for four weeks.[18] The UHC sent a delegation to meet privately with Fulgencio Batista, still the most powerful figure in Cuba, and he promised to help stamp out anti-Semitism. Nonetheless, the attacks continued, and institutional efforts to join the American and Eastern European Jews in common cause failed.

Then an incident took place that epitomized the patronizing attitude of the United States and further fueled the anti-Semitic storm. Without consulting any Cuban Jewish group, a U.S. Congressman, Dr. William I. Sirovich, met with Cuban authorities and proposed that at least one hundred thousand German Jews be resettled in Cuba, with Louis B. Mayer, chairman of Metro-Goldwyn-Mayer Studios, heading the project. Although Cuba lacked restrictive immigration laws, many Cubans reacted with hostility, and the plan was angrily rejected. With the rising crisis in Europe and the need for desperate actions to rescue refugees, further efforts to involve Cuba in resettlement plans were taken up by major U.S. Jewish organizations, principally the JDC, which opened a Havana office in early 1937 under the name Jewish Relief Committee. Cuban Jewish groups, with their history of internal divisiveness, remained uninvolved.

Cuba's initial response was very cooperative. By mid-1938 three thousand mostly German-speaking refugees had landed in Havana. Eighteen months later that figure had doubled. Hundreds of newly arrived refugees pressed into the Jewish Relief Committee's tiny office seeking money to live on and help for relatives still stranded in Europe. The committee also endeavored to combat the continuing wave of anti-Semitic propaganda. The government's legalization of the Cuban Nazi Party and the National Fascist Party on October 20, 1938, accompanied by a call from both groups to boycott Jewish firms and to "rise up against the Jewish menace," escalated the atmosphere of crisis. Still, the Relief Committee's advisory board, made up mostly of UHC members, declined to extend the committee's activities beyond charitable work among the German refugees. The board also insisted that all funds come from outside Cuba. Meanwhile, Cuban anti-Semitism reached a crescendo, and immigrants continued to pour in.[19]

Nazi and Falange sympathies reached their peak in mid-1938, when the fascists held a series of outdoor masses in the plaza of the Havana Cathedral and a host of fascist front organizations were organized. Germany had entered the picture as soon as Hitler came to power. The chief of the Abwehr, the German intelligence service, Admiral Wilhelm Canaris, recruited a cadre of Cuban agents, headed by Enrique Augusto Lunin, a businessman, and gave them the task of providing reports about merchant marine activity in Cuban waters.[20]

Cuban sympathy for the Falangist side in the Spanish Civil War grew, and on May 19, 1939, the Cuban government bestowed its Order of Merit on Nazi ministers Joachim von Ribbentrop and Vico von Bulow Schwant.[21] The *New York Herald Tribune* in 1939 estimated the number of Cuban Nazis and Nazi sympathizers at five thousand.[22] The Cuban Falange Party, legalized since July 1936, worked closely with Nazi agents and with Spanish consular officials in Havana and in the provinces. A considerable amount of Spanish-language anti-Semitic material was imported and distributed through these channels. The Falange Party was primarily influential in three sectors—commercial associations (especially the Lonja del Comercio), traditional secondary schools (especially the Colegio del Belén), and the newspapers, the *Diário de la Marina, Alerta, Avance, La Discusíon,* and *Sí*.[23]

THE HOLOCAUST ERA

Pro-Nazi Cubans became increasingly bold in their public behavior. Newspapers printed photographs of handsomely dressed men and women giving the straight-armed fascist salute. Opposition to further German Jewish immigration mounted. The opposition was centered in labor and business groups who were fearful that the newcomers would displace native workers and that they would place a burden on the still depressed economy, in spite of the fact that the Law of the 50 Percent would have protected most workers. On January 13, 1939, President Laredo Brú, who had been appointed and was largely controlled by Batista, responded to the rising tide of anti-immigrant arguments and decreed for the first time a distinction between immigrants and tourists.[24] Henceforth all foreigners would be required to have a visa jointly approved by the secretaries of the State and Labor departments and by the director general of the Immigration Department in order to enter. All foreigners wishing to immigrate would also have to post a five-hundred-dollar bond as guarantee.

The head of the Immigration Department, Manuel Benítez González, a comrade of Batista's during the 1933 coup, who had been appointed to the post when it was meaningless, opened what amounted to a private immigration bureau in the Hotel Plaza in January 1939. Landing permits, typed on Immigration Department stationery and personally signed by Benítez, with the written proviso that the holder would stay in Cuba only "for such time as necessary to obtain a visa for the United

States," were sold for $150.[25] More than four thousand permits were issued in this manner between January and May 1939. Travel agents bought lots containing dozens of permits at $150 each and resold them in Europe for much higher prices, generally from $500 to $600 each. One former member of the Cuban government later stated that some Jews paid as much as $50,000 or $100,000 for legal entry visas.[26] The Hamburg-Amerika Steamship Line offered package deals to passengers able to pay for the ship passage as well as landing papers that presumably were valid.

The Gestapo, which had quickly and efficiently cleared Vienna and Prague of Jews, now began picking up Jews on the street in Germany at random and telling them that they would have to emigrate immediately or face deportation to a concentration camp. The Gestapo also encouraged the purchase of visas and landing permits from Latin American consulates even if the papers were illegal.[27] It is not known whether Manuel Benítez knew that authorities would refuse to honor his permits, but he had sold them wholesale to the Hamburg-Amerika company without checking. His racket earned him a personal fortune estimated at more than half a million prewar dollars. According to Gordon Thomas and Max Morgan Witts, when other Cuban officials, including President Brú, demanded a share, they were refused, and the "bureau" was closed.[28]

On May 4, 1939, Cuban newspapers printed a report distributed by the German Embassy that a ship, the S.S. *St. Louis,* was transporting nearly a thousand Jewish refugees from Hamburg to Havana. President Brú then asked the Congress "to [prohibit] repeated immigrations of Hebrews who have been inundating the Republic and prohibit . . . permits that are being issued for the entrance of such Jews to Cuba."[29] The next day, the Congress issued Decree 937, abolishing landing permits and invalidating ones issued previously. Neither the local Jewish colony nor the JDC in New York tried to block enforcement of the decree. The London-based Intergovernmental Committee on Political Refugees, established after the 1938 Evian Conference, had warned the Hamburg-Amerika Steamship Line that the passengers probably would not be permitted to disembark, but Reich officials ordered the firm to sail nonetheless. On May 26, 1939, armed guards barred Immigration Director General Benítez's office and prevented any further permits from being issued.

Other ships from Europe carrying Jewish refugees, although not as many as on the *St. Louis,* also arrived in mid- and late May 1939. Passengers on these ships, the British liners *Orduña* and *Quanza* and the French ship *Flanders,* were authorized to land only if they held regular Cuban visas. As a result, 204 Jews holding Benítez's permits were denied permission to disembark. Newspaper reports, however, overlooked these ships and concentrated on the *St. Louis,* the target of the barrage of antirefugee propaganda. A sign of the ship's special status was that unlike the other ships, when the *St. Louis* approached Havana, the Cuban secretary of state telegraphed instructions for it to anchor in Havana's harbor, not at its pier.[30]

Berlin's ministry of propaganda dispatched press notices that the *St. Louis* passengers were "fleeing with stolen hoards of money, and much else."[31] Dr. José Rivero's newspapers carried these stories. Rivero wrote: "We must react with the same energy as have other peoples of the globe. Otherwise we will be absorbed and the day will come when the blood of our martyrs and heroes shall have served solely to enable the Jews to enjoy a country conquered by our ancestors."[32]

Statements issued by the Cuban Nazi Party alleging that the refugees were Communists were reprinted in virtually every Cuban newspaper. Daily reports of the location of the approaching ship fanned the crisis and led to the largest anti-Semitic demonstration in Cuba's history. Deposed President Grau San Martín, now leader of the opposition National Fascist Party and a senator, called for a "Rally against the Jews" on May 8. Forty thousand attended; tens of thousands more listened over national radio. A spokesman for Grau, Primitivo Rodríguez Medina, called for the people to "fight the Jews until the last one is driven out of the country."[33]

The various Cuban Jewish groups met once again to organize cooperatively, establishing on May 9 the Fareinigten Komitet Zum Bakemfn dem Antisemitism in Kuba (United Committee to Combat Anti-Semitism in Cuba), but it was too late. The ship arrived on May 15 and was ordered to remain in the harbor. Only twenty-two passengers with regularly issued visas were allowed ashore. No one from the island was permitted to board the vessel, although Rabbi Lasker was taken by launch to the ship's mooring place to receive the bodies of a Jewish old man and child who had died aboard the *St. Louis* and required burial.[34]

The JDC flew Lawrence Berenson, formerly the president of the Cuban Chamber of Commerce in the United States and a personal confidant of Fulgencio Batista, to Havana to negotiate. In February 1939 Batista had personally intervened to rescue seven Jewish refugees who had arrived without visas and had won the lasting gratitude of Cuban Jews. But he did not help in the case of the *St. Louis*. When Berenson pledged $250,000 to free the passengers, the local Jewish Relief Committee advisory board voted unanimously to forbid Berenson and his party from representing them to the Cuban government. President Brú demanded a bond of $453,000, and after lengthy talks Berenson withdrew his offer, pleading lack of time to obtain more funds. The *St. Louis* sailed out of Cuban waters for a week while Berenson continued to talk with government officials. Historical accounts claim that the ship sailed around the Caribbean for seven days.[35] The ship returned to Cuba in the hope that some agreement could be reached. But nothing else worked. On June 6, 1939, twenty-two days after arriving in Cuba, the *St. Louis* was ordered out, and it began its journey back across the Atlantic. Its passengers were disembarked in four groups, in England, Belgium, Holland, and France. Only the ones who landed in England all survived the war; most of the others ultimately perished in concentration camps when their host countries were overrun by the Nazis.

The sordid *St. Louis* incident was all the more tragic because the ship came so close to the U.S. and Cuban shores that deck passengers could see the lights of Miami Beach and Havana and in some cases spoke with officials and even relatives who were given permission to board the ship briefly before it was forced to return to Europe. Relatives in Havana sent pineapples and bananas aboard as gifts. While the *St. Louis* sat at anchor at the far end of Havana harbor the anti-Semitic fusillade continued, even in the Cuban Congress, where rival political factions speculated on how families of the hapless refugees could be made to pay millions of dollars for their relatives to be allowed to land.[36]

After the ship's departure, the *Miami Herald*'s correspondent in Havana during the episode, Stephen Trumbull, filed his report. He noted that twenty-two of the "heartsick and bewildered" Jewish refugees had been permitted to disembark in Havana when officials found their papers to be in "legal order."[37] One other passenger, an attorney named Loeb, who in desperation had stabbed and flung himself into Havana harbor trying to commit suicide but was rescued by sailors and taken to a Havana hospital, managed to stay. His wife and fifteen-year-old daughter were left on board. Before finding passage on the ship, Loeb had been arrested during Kristallnacht and sent to Dachau at a time when prisoners were sometimes released and had managed to gain his freedom. Trumbull also mentioned the valiant efforts of the ship's captain, Gustav Schroeder, and Jewish organizations in the United States.[38] The youngest passengers were infants; the oldest was a man of ninety-three.[39]

The *St. Louis,* as we have seen, was not the only "errant vessel" (as ships carrying refugees seeking safe harbors at which to land were called) to ply the coasts of the nations of the Caribbean and Latin America. Cuban authorities quietly relaxed their exclusionary policy beginning in early 1940. Slightly fewer than two thousand Jewish refugees arrived during 1940 on sixty-seven different ships, some from other Latin American countries where they had failed to gain permanent status.[40] The Italian ship *Conte Grande* and two Hamburg-Amerika passenger ships carried refugees to Uruguay, but they were refused landing rights; local Jewish refugee-aid societies ultimately gained entrance for these and other ship passengers to Chile and in Paraguay. The ordeal of the errant vessels involved bribery, swindles, and clandestine landings.[41] Three thousand Jews who had been sold counterfeit documents in Europe promising visas to Bolivia were turned away, although a compromise was worked out through which most were admitted.

The *St. Louis* affair must be seen in perspective. The ship's tragic fate proved an ominous turning point in a number of ways. It in effect shut the last open door for refugees fleeing from Europe to the Americas. For Jews around the world it dashed hopes for further rescues. This traumatic episode, popularized in a 1974 book titled *Voyage of the Damned,*[42] signaled the triumph of neoisolationism in the Western Hemisphere and, ironically, gave a major propaganda victory to the Nazis, who gleefully used the incident to affirm that no country wanted Jews. Before June 1939 the quasi-legal practice of obtaining landing permits from third-party nations, not only Cuba but Haiti, Panama, the Dominican Republic, and other Latin American countries, was the best that Jewish organizations could do to aid refugees to escape from Europe. The JDC helped arrange for the permits and paid for the costs of sheltering the refugees in Lisbon, Seville, and other ports while emigration transport was arranged. Cuba was caught in the middle, exposed to pressures far too great for it to handle. The Roosevelt administration, which probably could have applied sufficient coercion on Havana to permit the passengers to disembark, also could have responded to Captain Schroeder's appeals to allow the *St. Louis* to disembark passengers at Miami. The failure to find willing nations to accept refugees signaled a new and frightening escalation in the pressure put on European Jewry: now individuals and families could not afford to worry about shipping their household goods or assets; the best thing they could hope for was to simply save themselves. On September 19, 1941, the Nazis forced Jews in Germany to wear the yellow Jewish star in public. The decision to carry out the Final Solution had been made.[43]

U.S. State Department planners claimed later that they had hoped that individual Latin American nations would step forward to accept refugees, repeating the nineteenth-century policies of Domingo F. Sarmiento and other Latin American statesmen seeking to populate the region with Europeans. But the Evian Conference in mid-1938 produced only a pledge by the Dominican Republic to accept "agricultural" refugees to a farm colony at Sosua.[44] Nor did the Lima Conference in February 1939 help, despite oblique lobbying by Secretary of State Cordell Hull, who at the behest of the Roosevelt administration attached a rider favoring more liberal immigration policies to a Cuban resolution condemning persecution of minorities. In that same month, representatives from Argentina, Uruguay, and Paraguay meeting to discuss trade signed a convention placing greater restrictions than before on refugees and promised to cooperate among themselves to keep out undesirables.

Several Latin American nations justified their refusal to open their doors to Jewish refugees with the argument that admitting refugees would pose security risks. The U.S. State Department and the Federal Bureau of Investigation (FBI) did not help dissuade foreign states from making these arguments; in fact, both agencies were sympathetic to the security-risk excuse. In all likelihood, few spies succeeded in infiltrating by posing as refugees, although two Abwehr agents were exposed in Rabbi Lasker's own UHC, identified by other refugees.[45]

The anti-Semitic barrage reached its peak before Cuba entered the war on the Allied side. A massive public rally was called by the Cuban Young Fascists (Juventude Fascista de Cuba) for the Paseo del Prado in December 1939. Bands played and speakers attacked "fifth columnist Jews," "Yanqui imperialists," and "communist fellow travelers."[46] The German-American Bund (Amerikadeutscher Volksbund), headquartered in New York, sent representatives to participate.

The new Cuban constitution, written during 1939–40, contained provisions introduced during the stormy controversy over Jewish immigration, including a prohibition against immigrants' practicing law or medicine and regulations forbidding entry to political or religious refugees. Congressman Tirso Domínguez Fumero introduced a bill on July 3, 1940, calling for a census of all Jews who had entered Cuba after January 1, 1937, as a prelude to expelling them. The Labor Department recommended legislation barring immigrants from starting businesses that would compete with Cuban-owned firms. The Polish consul general in Havana issued a statement pointing out that the *polacos* (Eastern European Jews) were not "genuine" Poles, but Jews for which he had no concern.[47]

When the new constitution went into effect on September 15, 1940, Fulgencio Batista became president of the Republic of Cuba. Batista, although a personal friend of individual Jews, never interceded to stop any anti-Semitic propaganda, but as president he prohibited members of his government from enforcing the anti-Semitic articles of the constitution. In late 1939, bowing to American pressure, he had out-lawed the Cuban Nazi and Fascist parties. Some fringe front groups that were not formally linked to either one were permitted to continue to function but were kept under surveillance. An extensive Nazi spy network operated, its existence providing a pretext for the Latin American Division of the U.S. State Department in June 1940 to discourage Caribbean and Central American nations from accepting German Jew-ish expatriates on the grounds that spies had infiltrated the refugee stream.[48]

These fears owed as much to anti-Semitism within the U.S. State Department as to reality, but wartime anxiety was running high and Nazi infiltration of the Caribbean was significant. This was especially true in Cuba and in the Dominican Republic, where Dr. Adolf Meyer, an acquaintance of General Rafael Trujillo, con-trolled a network of agents in contact with German submarines, aircraft, and tele-graph installations. Gestapo agents carried out murders of turncoat Nazis, includ-ing Joaquin Wirkenstaedt, the manager of a German chemical plant in Cuba, Quimicas Schering S.A.[49] New right-wing front organizations funded by the Axis were formed, such as the Legión Nacional Revolucionaria Sindicalista (National Revolutionary Sindicalist Legion).[50]

With the German Jewish refugees who did manage to land in Cuba came oth-ers, including non-Jewish Europeans. Many were Social Democrats or Communists and therefore political refugees. There were German citizens as well as Poles, Ukraini-ans, and Ruthenians—about a thousand in all. Ironically, because the restrictions against working that applied to the new Jewish refugees also applied to these poor immigrants, many became dependent on their Jewish *landsmen* and many learned Yiddish, which was easier for them to learn than Spanish. Most of these refugees were single men, and their social life revolved around the Jewish colony rather than around the larger Cuban society.[51]

In Cuba the restrictive labor legislation still made earning a living during war-time very difficult, and as a result most refugees had to be supported entirely by pri-vate philanthropy, much of it from HIAS and the JDC in the United States. The major Jewish world organizations turned their efforts to helping the most recent refugees. For the first time, ORT established a Havana branch, headed by Hugo Semler and devoted to vocational training through trade schools, farm colonies, and nonprofit industrial workshops.[52] In November 1942 all Jewish refugees were in-vited to register and sign up for classes.

German Jewish refugees in Cuba kept in close touch with refugees who had gained admittance to the United States through the New York–based newspaper *Aufbau* and its network of community groups. In 1942 funds were raised to pub-lish a newsletter in Havana, *Unterwegs,* which appeared with articles in three lan-guages—German, Spanish, and (occasionally) English. *Unterwegs* combined news about the war effort with advertisements by German-speaking Cuban businessmen and establishments where German was spoken (hairdressers, health clinics, Spanish- and English-language academies, opticians, lawyers, cafés, nightclubs, and cinemas showing American movies). Another feature was a weekly series of English phrases for those learning English to memorize.

Unable to work, members of the refugee colony devoted considerable time and effort to showing their support for the war effort. An umbrella group, Loyalty Action, was organized to link the myriad refugee groups, which arrayed themselves along national lines: ORT's Asociación Democratica de Refugiados Hebreos (ADRH), the Asociación Italo-Cubana Antifascista, the Free Poles, the Free Yugoslavs, the Free Hungarians, the Free French, and so on.[53] Some of the members of the Ashkenazic community attempted to work with the refugees, although there were hard feelings over the perception that the German Jews would be more successful in gaining entry to the United States than would the Eastern European Cuban Jews, who would have to remain on the island and who were, for the most part, still finding economic conditions in Cuba very hard. ORT, through the ADRH, was the major vehicle linking the German and Eastern European Jews. That group's newsletter, V..., published occasional appeals for solidarity within the Jewish colony.[54] V... also provided detailed war news, including articles describing the plight of the surviving Jews in Europe. Because of the weekly's close ties with Jewish organizations in the United States and because Cuban print journalism was closely linked to the North American press and wire services, newspaper audiences in Cuba learned about events in Europe at the same time as readers in the United States and Canada.[55]

The "Free Peoples" groups in Cuba were antifascist associations organized to complement the antifascist Freies Deutschland (Free Germany) movement, which was a Communist front with member groups throughout the Western Hemisphere, notably Mexico. The Cuban branch of Free Germany, the Comité Alemán Antifascista de Cuba (CAAC), was created in late 1942 and early 1943. Its members were both Jewish and non-Jewish. The CAAC broadcast half-hour radio programs over the Havana station COK on a regular schedule, starting on July 24, 1943. The programs provided anti-Hitler material, including information about the concentration camps established in Germany and in German-occupied territory and news about the resistance movement in occupied lands.[56]

Cubans were overwhelmingly sympathetic when they heard about the atrocities. Leizer Ran, an ORT teacher who broadcast a series of radio appeals in Yiddish for funds to aid refugees, recalls that on the day after one of his radio broadcasts a man came to tell him that his mother, a seamstress, had sold her sewing machine to be able to donate something. The broadcast had been about the Warsaw Ghetto.[57]

Throughout the second half of the war detailed summaries of the numbers of Jews murdered in Europe were regularly reported through the JDC and by representatives of other agencies, and articles written for the American press were regularly translated and reprinted in Cuban newspapers and magazines.[58] Note was taken of the fact that of the one million Jewish children in Europe prior to Hitler, only 150,000 survived the war. This fact was emphasized in appeals for money to Sephardic (and larger Cuban) audiences, who were known for their strong traditional sense of family.[59] The JDC spent more than a million dollars in Cuba in the last eight months of the war alone, about 2 percent of its entire relief budget.[60]

After the United States, Cuba was the most generous recipient of German Jewish refugees in the Western Hemisphere. Although the exact number is not known, from twelve thousand to twenty thousand Jewish immigrants entered Cuba between 1933 and 1944. Most had tourist or transit visas, and many were able to use them to wait in Cuba for permanent visas to the United States or Mexico. The U.S. State Department closed its consulates in Germany, Italy, and Nazi-occupied Europe five months before Pearl Harbor, but Cuban consulates in those places remained open for another year. In April 1942 the Cuban government announced that it would no longer accept immigrants born in Axis countries.[61] Only the Dominican Republic and Ecuador continued to accept Jews beyond 1942, but in extremely limited numbers.

For a few months after the April 1942 announcement, though, Cuba issued new visas to refugees, although by this time it was very difficult for Jews to escape Axis-occupied countries. Exceptions included diamond cutters from Antwerp, who eventually started the Cuban diamond industry.[62] Belgian Grand Rabbi Srul Sapira was allowed to enter in 1942 to join the UHC when Rabbi Lasker departed for the United States. Also permitted were a number of German-born professors who obtained university positions and several Jewish writers and artists.[63]

Things changed quickly in Cuba as the war drew to its close. The remaining permanent colonies of Eastern European, Sephardic, and American Jews stabilized. Some of the antagonisms among the subgroups had become muted, although the groups still rarely intermingled. Many of the World War II–era refugees gained entry to the United States after V-J Day. In 1944 Batista's candidate lost the presidential election to former president Ramón Grau San Martín, his chief rival. Grau was considered to be anti-Semitic by many, but his position was actually ambiguous. Grau's Auténticos, the Cuban Revolutionary Party, promised economic and political independence and pledged to remove corruption from the government.

THE POST-HOLOCAUST ERA

Although some feared an increase in anti-Semitic activities, the first two years of Grau San Martín's second presidency (1944–48) proved quiet. The Cuban Jewish press reported only a few isolated hostile incidents, including efforts to bar Jewish tourists from registering in hotels on Varadero Beach. Grau maintained good relations with Washington and did not provoke the Cuban Jewish colony.[64] Anti-Semitic activity surfaced again in 1946–47 with the debate in the new United Nations over the partition of Palestine. Politicians split over the issue. Cuban Zionists in 1944 had organized the Comité Cubano Pro Palestina Hebrea (Cuban Committee for Jewish Palestine) with the support of liberal and leftist Cubans as well as Fulgencio Batista and the secretary-general of the Cuban Communist Party, Juan Marinello.[65] Some dissident Grau supporters also pledged their support. The most active member of the committee was its secretary, Ofelia Domínguez y Navarro, a lawyer and human-rights worker who considered the formation of a Jewish state to be a humanitarian matter.[66] The Cuban Senate endorsed unanimously a resolution reaffirming the Senate's 1919 vote supporting the Balfour Declaration. President Grau and the presidents of the Senate and Congress received a delegation of Jewish leaders in late 1946 and publicly pledged support for the Jewish drive to establish a nation in Palestine.[67]

It was thus very surprising when Guillermo Belt y Ramírez, ambassador to the United States and head of the delegation to the United Nations in 1947, cast Cuba's vote in 1947 against the creation of the state of Israel, the only negative vote from a Western Hemisphere nation. Despite this, most members of Cuba's delegation to the United Nations were pro-Israel. This incident and the allegation that Belt was driven by personal ambition have been cited to identify his motives as anti-Semitic.[68] Margalit Bejarano, an Israeli scholar who has studied this matter carefully, finds that there is no basis for saying that he was anti-Semitic. As Havana's mayor in 1935 Belt was considered to be sympathetic to Jews. The U.N. vote was actually cast by Belt's deputy, Ernesto Dihigo, who Bejarano suspects acted on instructions from Grau himself. One possible reason for this was Grau's relationship with Raul Roa, whose wife was a member of the Khouri family, which backed Grau's candidate, Carlos Prío Socarrás, considered to be pro-Arab.[69] Yet Prío Socarrás's election brought about recognition of the state of Israel in early 1949 and a positive vote in the U.N. Security Council for Israel's admission to the United Nations.[70]

During 1947 two new organizations—the Liga Nacional de Trabajadores Anti-Comunistas (National League of Anti-Communist Workers) and Defensa Revolucionaria (Revolutionary Defense)—launched a wave of hostile propaganda, accusing Cuban Jews of illegal acts, including clandestine immigration, and claiming that Jews in league with Communists had taken control of the island's commerce and industry.[71] Individual members of Cuba's Lebanese community who were not connected to these two groups, including Dr. Antonio Faber and Dr. Pedro Khouri, established the Comité Pan Arabe de Cuba (Cuban Pan-Arab Committee), which opposed the Jewish state. Some members of all of these groups had supported Nazi and Falange causes during the war, but most, especially members of the Lebanese group, had worked for the Allied side. Some of the Pan-Arab Committee literature, though, included anti-Jewish propaganda, including excerpts from the notorious *Protocols of the Elders of Zion,* the anti-Semitic forgery written by the czar's secret police before World War I. Another widely circulated book, by Enrique Trinchet (1947), cited Jews as "national tumors" and called the Cuban-Jewish *polacos* a "foreign plague."[72]

There was a brief wave of anti-Semitic pamphleteering by the Liga Nacional in late 1948 and early 1949 in Havana, and an anti-Semitic radio program produced by Eladio Cortina and Enrique Trinchet was broadcast daily. Complaints led police to stop the broadcasts and the pamphlets. This was one of the last times the large-scale, overt anti-Semitic acts occurred in public. During the rest of the 1950s they were limited to a series of snide articles in the daily *Tiempo* accusing individual Jews of Communist sympathies and of abusing workers, avoiding payment of taxes, and smuggling. Ironically, one of the authors of the series was "Cabi," Rodolfo Can-Birenholz, a Jewish refugee from Belgium.[73]

Batista's return to power in a bloodless military coup on March 10, 1952, terminated the democratic system and ushered in an era of martial law. University of Havana students ceremoniously buried a copy of the democratic constitution of 1940. But Batista was popular in the business community. He was personally charming and was seen as a man of the people, not representing special interests. Cuban Jews viewed him as sympathetic to Jewish humanitarian causes. His prime minister, Jorge García Montes, had worked as a lawyer for the Jewish Relief Committee during the war and had helped defend the cause of refugees. The Cuban government began to support Jewish causes, and even the old anti-Semitic newspaper *Alerta* modified its approach. The paper's editor, Roman Vasconsellos, who had taken part in its anti-Semitic campaign between 1934 and 1946, praised the planting of a forest in Israel named for Cuba's liberator, José Martí.[74]

An effort to consolidate and centralize Cuban Jewish community activities began in 1950, when *Havaner Lebn* initiated a campaign for a community center in suburban Vedado. The Jewish community had emerged from the war in safety and showing evidence, in some quarters, of significant prosperity, showcased by the luxurious Patronato de la Casa de la Comunidad Hebrea de Cuba, the Hebrew community center, built at a cost of more than three-quarters of a million dollars. The Ashkenazic Centro Israelita and the Orthodox kehillah had opposed the construction at the new site, but their influence was now restricted to the older and less affluent members of the Eastern European colony, still located downtown in the Old City commercial district. President Batista, his prime minister, and several high Cuban officials personally attended the laying of the cornerstone of the Patronato on October 27, 1953. It was dedicated in October 1955. The handsome Patronato building was designed by one of Cuba's leading architects, Achilles Capablanca.[75] It contained a synagogue, large clubrooms, a library, offices, even a cafeteria. The first Patronato board of directors was headed by three men, one with a German name, one with an Eastern European name, and one with a Sephardic name.[76]

The Patronato functioned as a community social and cultural center, pointedly apolitical. Overwhelmingly, Cuban Jews refrained from participating in national politics, not because they were barred, but because they brought with them no tradition of political involvement from Europe. Jewish youths who were politically concerned tended to join secret organizations (in order to hide their activities from their parents).[77] A few Jewish students participated in the rebellious Twenty-Sixth of July movement, but most did not. Looking back, community members explain this as a result of the still early stage of assimilation for the community in the 1950s.

Cuban Jews encountered slights of different kinds during the fifties. Ashkenazim continued to be called *polacos,* or, as small children, *polaquitos.* The word was used casually and not necessarily in a mean way. Sephardic Jews also called the Eastern Europeans *polacos* and were in turn called *turcos* (Turks), a term that was applied without distinction by both non-Jewish Cubans and Ashkenazim to Sephardic Jews as well as to Syrian and Lebanese Arabs. *Polaco* and *turco* were not necessarily used pejoratively, but both names were rooted in the acknowledgment that the Jews were different, foreigners in a society that did not value cultural pluralism. Everything depended on whether the names were uttered neutrally or with disdain.[78]

Although Cuban Jews now enjoyed a very good life compared with the difficult conditions of the prewar period, their lifestyle could not approach the luxurious lifestyle of the upper-class Cubans and Spaniards, whose lives revolved around the "Big Five" social clubs. Although these clubs were not formally closed to Jews, Jews almost never frequented them.[79] Nor did Jews join most of the second-tier social clubs, even though their incomes equaled those of the Cubans who frequented them. When they did join clubs, notably in towns and cities in the provinces, they found themselves associating with Cubans of a lower economic status than their own.[80]

Cuban Jews built their own clubs, which became the main social institutions of their communities, and beginning in the early 1940s, they built their own clinics and hospitals. Jewish merchants and businessmen also made financial contributions to government clinics for the poor.[81] The main Jewish health-related organization was the Anti-Tuberculosis Society, maintained by annual subscriptions.[82] A new monthly magazine, *Israelia*, founded in 1949, presented a potpourri of articles on cultural, literary, and domestic ("For Women," "For Children") themes and boasted a column devoted exclusively to the social life of "Hebrew-Cuban physicians." Students with Ashkenazic names studying at the medical faculty of the University of Havana were frequently mentioned, evidence of how far the Eastern European Jews had come in little more than two decades.[83]

During the 1950s Cuba mixed prosperity for the rich with poverty for the poor under Batista's dictatorship. Thousands of foreign businessmen settled or worked in Cuba, as did American gangsters, who obtained control of a good portion of the lavish tourist industry. Beneath the surface festered unrest, which exploded in armed insurrection in July 1953 under the leadership of Fidel Castro, a disenchanted law graduate, and his comrades of the Twenty-Sixth of July movement. Castro triumphantly entered Havana on January 1, 1959, after two years of guerrilla fighting in the mountains and countryside. Cuba underwent a temporary period of euphoria about the prospects of erasing the legacy of deep-seated corruption and special privilege that had characterized the military dictatorship. Under Batista (and his predecessors), governmental action was not expedited without a *padrino,* someone watching out for one's interests.[84] Collectively, the Jewish community had fared well because individual merchants and businessmen had learned the rules of the game, regularly visiting the presidential residence, where officials and even Batista's own relatives had accepted bribes in exchange for preferred treatment and exemption from restrictive regulations.[85]

Jews were not persecuted as Jews in any manner by the new revolutionary government. They were not harmed by the political trials held in the first months of the new regime or by the purges of Batista regime officials, since few Jews had entered government.[86] Castro and his comrades spoke out passionately in favor of human rights and social equality and attacked discrimination against minorities, especially blacks. Pent-up anger over institutionalized corruption at least partially explains the wave of relief that greeted Castro's seizure of power in 1959, which was accompanied by mobs' sacking the gambling casinos and other symbols of the toppled regime's glitter. Reaction to the pre-1959 atmosphere may also explain the Castro regime's puritanism. The Cuban Catholic Church in the 1950s as well as after the revolution backed moral stringency; priests spoke out against the moral degeneracy of "free enterprise" governments and backed Castro's stern measures to eliminate vice. Churchmen even adopted the new language: a Cuban priest remarked in 1964 that "in moral terms, Cuba before Castro seemed the creature of its 'decadent capitalist bourgeoisie.'"[87]

Affluent Cubans, including the immigrants and their children who had made their homes in Cuba and had accommodated to it, had accepted the unsavory aspects of life on the island during the Batista regime as a fact of life, and good for business. So had the resident colony of sixty-five hundred Americans in Havana, most of whom lived remarkably privileged lives and loyally supported the Batista regime.[88] But when the revolution came, other Jews were revealed as having played instrumental roles. Dr. Carlos Mizrachi, a Jewish surgeon living in Santa Clara, was the first physician to serve with Castro.[89] Enrique Oltuski Osachki, of a Polish Jewish immigrant family, had joined Castro in 1955 and served in the Las Vilas province with Castro's forces; at twenty-seven years of age he was made minister of communications, the only Jew ever to hold a cabinet-level position in Cuba. He left the government in 1960.[90] Some of the Polish Jewish immigrants had been Communists for years. A few of them, such as Manuel (Stolik) Novigrad and Fabio Grobart (Abraham Simchowitz), attempted to assert themselves as spokesmen for the Jewish community, but their efforts were rejected.[91] According to the *American Jewish Year Book* for 1962, the Castro regime employed thirty veteran Jewish Communists and about one hundred Jews who had worked for the revolution or who had stepped forth to serve it.[92] Most Cuban Jews, however, were anything but Marxist-Leninist sympathizers and found themselves embarrassed by their compatriots who had stubbornly clung to the socialism of the twenties and thirties.

Castro proceeded to reorganize Cuban society and to institutionalize the revolution. Labor unions were revitalized, but they lost their independence. Factories, agricultural land, and private businesses were turned over to the government in the name of their workers; foreign enterprises were nationalized. Moderates were purged from Cuban labor unions in January 1960, and Cuba moved closer to the Soviet orbit. President Dwight D. Eisenhower imposed an embargo on all U.S. exports to Cuba in October 1960, and diplomatic relations were severed three months later. The failed Bay of Pigs invasion took place in April 1961.

The nationalization of businesses and the socialization of the economy, and not discrimination or any threat of mistreatment, were the main reasons why most members of the Jewish community left Cuba. Three thousand Cuban Jews emigrated between July 1959 and the 1960 High Holy Days, including most of the leaders of Jewish communal organizations. By the early 1960s the UHC had virtually ceased functioning, and the Patronato's membership had dropped by half. Most of the Jews who resisted leaving were older residents of the Orthodox community located in the Old City or Jews who had intermarried or had otherwise ceased Jewish observance. *Havaner Lebn* suspended publication on December 31, 1960, and its editors left for the United States. By the end of 1961 an additional thirty-eight hundred Jews had left Cuba and another thousand were prepared to do so. (Altogether, thirty thousand Cubans had left the island by this date.)[93] On January 1, 1962, the third anniversary of the revolution, a group of veteran Jewish Communists and a hundred pro-Castro Jewish students seized the Patronato and "took control of the Jewish colony."[94]

Those who desired to emigrate to Israel were assisted by the Jewish Agency, an Israeli organization that helps Jews settle in Israel. Some Jewish businessmen whose companies were absorbed under the program of nationalization were compensated, but others were not. An Israeli diplomat estimated that 45 percent of the Jews who remained in Cuba through the mid-1960s were unemployed, living off the gradual sale of their possessions. Some homes and businesses were invaded by militiamen. In some cases, servants turned employers in to the police. But the Jews' treatment was entirely consistent with the treatment of other persons considered unfriendly to the regime; they were not treated differently because they were Jews.[95] Conditions deteriorated rapidly. Tourism suffered, and unemployment rose. The hard-line face of the regime solidified; personal freedoms vanished. President Carlos Manuel Urrutia Lleo, who had opposed Batista but who was an anti-Communist, was forced from office. The Communist Party, named the Popular Socialist Party, gained sole recognition for the right to carry out political activity, and Jews were permitted to join, unlike in Romania and Hungary.

Even as his regime tightened its grip on Cuban life, Castro bent over backwards not to appear to be persecuting Jews. Havana's five synagogues (three Ashkenazic, two Sephardic) continued to function, although most of their members had flocked into exile; no communal property was taken; and Jewish institutional buildings as well as cemeteries were maintained by the state.[96] Jewish parochial schools were exempted from the nationalization decree, although the Centro Israelita's school became a public school, named after Albert Einstein. It offered classes in Hebrew, Yiddish, and Jewish history, which were open to any students at the school who elected to take them. The government subsidized two buses to transport Jewish children to the school from distant locations. But all of these special arrangements were canceled in 1975, ostensibly for lack of interest and because there was a shortage of teachers able to teach Jewish subjects.[97]

Castro's relations with Israel were less sanguine, although initially the government maintained Batista's policy of total support. The revolutionary government accepted resident Israeli ministers in Havana, first Dr. Jonathan Prato (1961–63), then Haim Yaari (1963–65). Yaari later remarked that Castro's friendliness was extraordinary.[98] Castro, after all, had grown up in Cuban cultural and intellectual circles that were sympathetic to the victims of Nazism. The Cubans identified with the Israeli struggle for independence, and the Castroites initially saw Israel as a model socialist nation. Although Batista had been equally friendly, there had been no exchange of ambassadors between 1951 and 1960. Sender Kaplan of the *Havaner Lebn* had served as Israel's honorary consul for several years during this period. The Israeli consulate opened in Havana in 1952, and diplomatic relations were established in

1954, when the Israeli minister to Mexico, Joseph Kessari, presented his credentials in Cuba.[99]

Consistent with its emergence as a member of the Cold War Communist bloc, Cuba taught the Holocaust period in its schools as part of a required tenth-grade syllabus on the history of world Communism and movements of national liberation, explicitly ignoring the fact that millions of Holocaust victims were Jews. In the entire textbook treatment of the 1930s and 1940s, which included sections on World War II resistance movements, German military aggression, the war in Asia, repercussions of the war in Latin America, the end of the war, Potsdam, and the Nuremberg trials, the words "Jew," "Jewish," "genocide," and "refugee" did not appear once in any Cuban schoolbook. There was no mention of concentration or death camps and no reference to the word "Holocaust," although the texts referred to Nazi "cruelty and sadism," the death of "fifty-four million people," and the "crimes" of Hitler, Goebbels, Himmler, and Göring.[100] Throughout the Castro period, public references to the Holocaust have been rare. For the average Cuban, the term "Holocaust" conjures up images of the dropping of the atomic bomb on Japan by the United States, not of Nazi persecution of Jews. Castro-era historians typically have followed the Soviet line on World War II, either ignoring the murder of Jews or submerging it in the story of fascist atrocities, referring to Nazi victims as "antifascists" without mentioning their ethnic identity.[101] Cuban historical journals and other publications have devoted virtually no space to the Holocaust during Castro's regime.

In foreign affairs, Cuba asserted its self-defined role as a champion of Third World revolution and, as part of this orientation, a close supporter of the Arab bloc. A turning point came at the First Tri-Continental Conference of Solidarity with the Peoples of Asia, Africa, and Latin America, held in Havana in early January 1966. At the conference a resolution condemning Zionism and the state of Israel was passed with the support of most Latin American countries. Reportedly, some governments later questioned the actions of their representatives, who were for the most part left-wing nationals invited to the conference, but the resolution was only repealed by the U.N. General Assembly in 1991, after the collapse of the Soviet Union and the Soviet bloc and after the conclusion of the Gulf War.[102] Cuba severed diplomatic relations with Israel in 1973, maintaining no formal contacts until late 1989, when commercial and technical personnel exchanged visits.[103]

By the mid-seventies Cuban relations with the Palestinian Liberation Organization (PLO) had become so close that Cuba was accused of cooperating with Palestinian radicals in arms trafficking and of using Palestinian channels to import arms for guerrilla groups in El Salvador, Guatemala, and Chile. A veteran Cuban diplomat, Hector Aguililla Saladrigas, claimed after his defection to the United States that the Cuban Embassy in Damascus routinely provided shipments of arms and ammunition to pro-Marxist groups in the Bekka Valley.[104] Cuba became one of the most strident supporters of the radical Palestinian cause and, therefore, an implacable political opponent of the state of Israel, the "Jewish lobby," and Zionism in the international arena.[105]

By the end of 1965, Cuba's permanent Jewish colony was reduced to an aging, dwindling remnant. Only nineteen hundred acknowledged Jews still lived in Havana, and another four hundred lived in the provinces. Most stayed because their spouses were not Jewish, because they had families they did not want to leave behind, because they had sons of military age (and therefore could not leave), or because their husbands or wives had died and they did not want to abandon their graves. The average age of Cuban Jewish males rose from thirty-eight to between sixty and sixty-five.[106] Eight remaining families continued to worship at the UHC. All Jewish organizations except for the Patronato ceased to exist, and the communal functions of the Patronato passed to the Cuban government. From 1960 to 1961 the Patronato incurred a deficit of $90,989, which its remaining officers asked the JDC in New York to pay in the form of a loan.[107]

Havana's last rabbi died in 1975 at the age of eighty-two. Eighty-five percent of the nearly ten thousand Jews who left Cuba went to South Florida; the rest went to Israel, Canada, and other Latin American countries. About half of the arrivals in Florida stayed; most of the rest went on to the New York City area. The newcomers in New York settled in Brooklyn in a neighborhood dubbed Santos Tzoris, a pun on the affluent Havana suburb Santos Suárez, where many had lived.[108] Some managed to get money and possessions out of Cuba; some left with nothing but their suitcases. Those who had purchased Israel bonds in Cuba were able to redeem them in the United States. Fewer than a thousand resettled Cuban Jewish refugees needed relief assistance in the United States. The Ashkenazic and Sephardic communities remained separated in exile, just as in Cuba.

Four hundred Jews numbered among the tens of thousands of refugees permitted to leave by the Castro regime in the Mariel boatlift in early 1980. After that, exactly 807 observant Jews, nearly all elderly, were counted in Cuba, nearly all of them living in Havana's crumbling Old City.[109] Thousands of others, of course, who were descended from the original Jewish immigrants but had given up public identification with the Jewish community, who had converted, or who simply had cast off any religious identification still remained. Relations between the Jewish community and the Cuban Communist Party were formally cordial; as the 1980s passed, these relations focused on providing assistance for the remaining observant Jews, the majority of whom were more than seventy years of age.[110]

By the early 1980s the PLO maintained what amounted to full diplomatic relations with Cuba and sent representatives to meetings of the Cuban-Arabic-PLO Friendship Association, a group explicitly identified with the PLO, not simply with Cuban-Arab culture. University research centers in Cuba followed the standard Third World anti-Zionist line, equating Zionism with racism. "Zionism," declared the director of Havana's Center for African and Middle Eastern Studies in December 1985, "is intimately related to capitalist imperialism and would not be possible without the backing of powerful circles in the international financial oligarchy."[111] Still, the government claimed an openhanded policy, awarding visas to Israelis who sought to attend international conferences in Cuba. But anti-Israel articles appeared almost daily in the Cuban press. A visiting Orthodox Venezuelan rabbi stated in November 1987, after flying to Havana with Bishop Alfredo Rodriguez of Caracas to meet with Fidel Castro to appeal for the right of five Jews previously refused exit visas to emigrate, that in Cuba "heroism is required in order to approach the synagogue."[112]

The Jewish community, which had coalesced only during the 1950s, was moribund in the late 1980s. From time to time, representatives from foreign Jewish associations, especially the Canadian Jewish Congress and the Central Jewish Committee of Mexico, traveled to Cuba to offer assistance. Always the Cuban government formally pledged cooperation, which was dutifully acknowledged by the foreign bureaus. But not all efforts worked smoothly. A shipment of 16,500 pounds of Passover food was delayed for more than three weeks in 1986 by "bad weather" and was never unloaded, although Jewish leaders dutifully said that it had been distributed. Occasionally foreign rabbis came to officiate at services, as did a Lubovitch Hasidic rabbi from Brazil in 1986. The Jewish colony as a whole neared extinction, not as the result of any hostility from Cuba's government or from its people, but from attrition and its inability to regenerate itself.

Circumstances changed suddenly during the mid-1990s when Cuban Jewish youths in Havana—almost all products of mixed marriages—responded to the government's new air of religious toleration by participating in a revival of Jewish expression. The community became less isolated, now receiving regular visits from Jews in the United States as well as from Canada and Latin America.[113] But it remained a shadow of its former self, a fading remnant.

NOTES

A grant from the Lucius N. Littauer Foundation of New York City to support research costs is gratefully acknowledged. I would like to thank the following persons for their participation during various stages of the research project carried out at the University of Miami: Dr. Robert Kirsner, Omar Cuan, Shlomit Oz, and, in Philadelphia, Rabbi Meier Lasker. Dr. Hannah Wartenberg's assistance in New York and in Miami was especially valuable. She, more than any other volunteer working with the project, devoted time to search for materials in archives; she conducted interviews, located useful books, and helped translate German-language materials.

1. See Jerry W. Knudson, "Anti-Semitism in Latin America: Barometer of Social Change," *Patterns of Prejudice* (London) 6, no. 5 (1972), 9; and Arnold Roller, "The Jews of Cuba," *Menorah Journal* 17, no. 3 (1929), 258.

2. Margalit Bejarano, "The Problem of Anti-Semitism in Cuba, 1944–1963," manuscript, courtesy of author. See also idem, "Deproletarization of Cuban Jews," in *Judaica Latinoamericana* (Jerusalem, 1988); and Salvador Díaz Versón, *El nazismo en Cuba* (Havana, 1944).

3. Judith Laikin Elkin, *Jews of the Latin American Republics* (Chapel Hill, N.C., 1980), 87.

4. See, e.g., Max J. Kohler, "Los Judíos en Cuba," *Revista Bimestra Cubana* 10 (1920), 125–29; and Leizer Ran, ed., *Comunidad hebrea en tierra cubana: Almanaque commemorativo del 25° aniversario del Centro Israelita de Cuba: 1925–1950* (Havana, 1951).

5. Jeffrey A. Kahn, "The History of the Jewish Colony in Cuba" (thesis submitted in partial fulfillment for ordination, Hebrew Union College—Jewish Institute of Religion, 1981), 7–8; Elkin, *Jews,* 8–9.

6. Kohler, "Los Judíos," 128; Seymour Liebman, "Cuban Jewish Community in South Florida," *American Jewish Year Book* 70 (Philadelphia, 1969), 239–49.

7. Joseph Steinberg, who raised money for Martí, was appointed by Tomás Estrada Palma as captain of the Army of Liberation; other volunteers and filibusterers included a Captain Kaminsky, formerly a peddler in Florida, and Horace (Horácio) Rubens, a Jewish attorney from New York. See Elkin, *Jews,* 69; Kahn, "History," 15–16; and Eduardo Weinfeld, "Cuba," in *Enciclopedia Judaica Castellana,* 252–69.

8. Elkin, *Jews,* 69; George Weinberger, "The Jews in Cuba," *American Hebrew and Jewish Messenger,* February 8, 1918, 1.

9. Boris Sapir, *The Jewish Community of Cuba* (New York, 1948), 14–15.

10. See Kohler, "Los Judios," 7.

11. Kahn, "History," 27.

12. See *El Estudiante Hebreo* (Havana), October 15, 1929.

13. For a cynical view of the transition, see George Black, *The Good Neighbor: How the United States Wrote the History of Central America and the Caribbean* (New York, 1988), 58–60.

14. The Law of the 50 Percent was not uniformly enforced, but where it was, it put large numbers of foreigners out of work. A visiting commission of the Foreign Policy Association from New York estimated in 1935 that from twenty-five thousand to thirty thousand foreign workers had lost their jobs because of the law. The law also caused problems for manufacturers, who faced complaints from labor unions that some of their members—mostly Spanish immigrants—had been adversely affected. See *Diário de la Marina,* August 23, 1934, 1.

15. American and Sephardic Jews were left alone; the Americans even received police permission for their congregants to break the evening curfew to attend services (Rabbi Meier Lasker, interview by author, November 14, 1989, Elkins Park, Pa.).

16. Raymond Buell et al., *Problems of New Cuba* (New York, 1935), 27.

17. Lasker, interview, November 14, 1989.

18. Kahn, "History," 57. *Havaner Lebn* appeared in November 1932, succeeding the Centro Israelita's *Oifgang* (1927–30).

19. Kahn, "History," 61.

20. Juan Chongo Leiva, *El fracaso de Hitler en Cuba* (Havana, 1989), 14. Leiva cites the names of other German agents, including a Cuban colonel, Andrés Pedro Golowchenco. Lunin later was apprehended by the Cuban counterespionage agency, Servicio de Inteligencia de Actividades Enemigas (SIAE), and confessed to having worked as a German spy.

21. Leiva, *Fracaso,* 16.

22. Jack O'Brien, *Herald Tribune* Havana correspondent, article translated as "Las actividades del fascismo en Cuba," *Mediodia,* April 18, 1939, 1.

23. On Cuban volunteer participation in the Spanish Civil War, see Pablo de la Torriente Brau, *Peleando con los milicionanos,* 2d ed. (Havana, 1987); and Ramón Nicolau González et al., *Cuba y la defensa de la republica Española (1936–1939)* (Havana, 1981).

24. Kahn, "History," 61. This was Decree 55, of January 13, 1939. During the 1930s Batista remained behind the scenes but dominated the Cuban government, personally selecting a succession of shadow presidents (Grau San Martín, Carlos Mendieta, José A. Barnet, Miguel Mariano Gómez, Federico Laredo Brú) through 1940. See Louis A. Pérez, Jr., *Cuba between Reform and Revolution* (New York, 1988), 277.

25. The typed permits certified that the bearers were in good health and would not participate in any kind of employment while in Cuba. See, e.g., a copy of the permit signed by Manuel Benítez Gonzales for Oscar and Regina Schwartz, refugees from Germany on the S.S. *St. Louis,* April 5, 1939, JDC Archive, New York.

26. Carlos and Uva Marques Sterling, interview by Mark D. Szuchman and Robert M. Levine, March 26, 1984, Tape 14VA, Otto G. Richter Library, University of Miami, Coral Gables.

27. See Henry L. Feingold, *The Politics of Rescue: The Roosevelt Administration and the Holocaust, 1938–1945* (New Brunswick, N.J., 1970), 64–65.

28. Gordon Thomas and Max Morgan Witts, *Voyage of the Damned* (New York, 1974), 88.

29. Irwin F. Gellman, "The St. Louis Tragedy," *American Jewish Historical Quarterly* 61 (December 1971), 147.

30. Kahn, "History," 64–67.

31. Ibid., 66.

32. Thomas and Witts, *Voyage,* 106. Rivero died in 1944. In 1954, when the *Diário de la Marina* published its special issue commemorating the 125th anniversary of the newspaper, it included an apologetic biographical statement about Rivero, saying that his support of fascism had been based on the fact that he considered it the only realistic defense against the Communist menace.

33. "Review of the Year 5699," *American Jewish Year Book (1939–40)* (Philadelphia, 1940), 355–56; Kahn, "History," 64.

34. Lasker, interview, November 14, 1989.

35. In interviews on November 14, 1989, January 23, 1990, and April 17, 1992, Rabbi Meier Lasker maintained that the ship actually headed to Panama, where officials permitted some forty or fifty refugees to land quietly after having been paid bribes arranged through Panamanian relatives of the Cuban Maduro family. This is a highly perplexing assertion. Rabbi Lasker, who participated at the center of the negotiations in Havana and who was one of the few persons to be allowed to board the *St. Louis,* adamantly claimed the story to be accurate. He explained that a brother-in-law of one of the passengers, a man from New Jersey, acted in behalf of the Cuban Jewish Maduro family and hastily flew to Panama to make the arrangements, aided

by members of the Panamanian branch of the Maduros. But Rabbi Lasker had no notion of how the passengers were actually disembarked, how they were selected, or what happened to them after they supposedly entered Panama. No other survivor from the ship with whom I have had contact can vouch for this story; nor does Captain Schroeder's book, which emphasizes everything he did to aid the passengers, mention such an effort. Unless further evidence comes to light, the story will have to be considered unproven.

36. See *Diário de la Marina,* June 4, 6, 8, 1939. The *Diário* articles were written in a fairly neutral tone and did not cast racist aspersions. Opposition to admitting the refugees was explained on the basis of Cuba's poverty and inability to absorb newcomers (courtesy of Carolina Amram).

37. *Miami Herald,* June 8, 1939 (courtesy of Richard Bard).

38. For Captain Gustav Schroeder's detailed recollections of the voyage, see his memoir, *Heimatlos auf Hoher See* (Berlin, 1949). The standard accounts of the *St. Louis* episode relate that only one passenger, Mr. Loeb, was able to land. This discrepancy has not been explained.

39. Diary of Albert Eskenazy (courtesy of Dr. Martin Lackner, Los Angeles).

40. Jacques Rieur, "The Jewish Colony of Cuba," report to the American Jewish Committee, New York, 1954, YIVO Archive.

41. Elkin, *Jews,* 85.

42. The book *Voyage of the Damned* appeared in 1974 (see above, n. 28), the motion picture in 1977. For documentation on behind-the-scenes efforts in the United States to rescue more refugees, including copies of appeals for assistance to Professor Hans Morgenthau of the University of Chicago, who was believed to be close to Roosevelt, see the JDC Archive in New York City. Dutch author and playwright Jan de Hartog also popularized the story of the *St. Louis* in his *Schipper naast God* (Baarn, Netherlands, 1944).

43. See Yehuda Bauer, *American Jewry and the Holocaust: The American Jewish Joint Distribution Committee, 1939–1945* (Detroit, 1981), 45–64.

44. Ibid., 200–201. Dictator Rafael L. Trujillo publicly said that he would take one hundred thousand colonists, but few believed that he meant it. More likely he made this statement to attract attention and to raise funds to finance his plans for agricultural development. The JDC invested $1,423,000 in the project, hoping that Sosua would succeed and therefore encourage other countries to permit Jews to enter as farmers. A second project, the Sociedad Colonizadora, was initiated in

Bolivia in 1941; 142 refugees were admitted to the country to participate, but most drifted away from the agricultural project.

45. The American Embassy also asked Rabbi Lasker regularly to examine dossiers of Jews seeking entrance to Cuba under special circumstances in order to weed out spies (Lasker, interview, November 14, 1989).

46. Díaz Versón, *El Nazismo,* 14–15.

47. Kahn, "History," 69; Rieur, "Jewish Colony," 16. Polish scholarship on immigration to Cuba virtually ignores the fact that more than 90 percent of Poles entering Cuba were Jews. Polish writers either concentrate on the tiny percentage of Roman Catholic Poles who went to Cuba, most of them miners who ended up in the Matahambre mine in Pinar del Rio, or further minimize the Jewish presence by lumping together non-Catholic emigrants as "Jews and Ukrainians." Polish writers also tend to avoid commenting on why the Jews left except to say that they sought to "make better money." They express anger at the fact that Jews were called *polacos* and that the term was used to mean someone "dirty, miserable, and lazy." See Marcin Kula, "La emigración polaca en Cuba en el período entre guerras," *Revista de la Biblioteca Nacional José Martí* 22 (1980), 131–49.

48. Judith Laikin Elkin, "The Reception of the Muses in the Circum-Caribbean," in *The Muses Flee Hitler: Cultural Transfer and Adaptation, 1930–1945,* ed. Jarrell C. Jackman and Carla M. Borden (Washington, D.C., 1983), 297–98.

49. Díaz Versón, *El Nazismo,* 53.

50. J. Pando González, chief of the Press and Publicity Bureau, statement to press, May 13, 1941, Havana.

51. Rieur, "Jewish Colony," 17.

52. See Philip Block, Executive Director, American ORT Federation, to Hugo Semler, October 19, 1942, YIVO Archive. ORT worked through the existing Jewish Relief Committee.

53. *Unterwegs,* June 19, 1942, 7. See also fund-raising letter, Amadeo Pacifico, President, Asociación Italo-Cubana Antifascista, September 1944, Havana, YIVO Archive.

54. See, e.g., S[ender] M. Kaplan, "Dos corrientes immigratorias Hebreas—Un destino," *V...* (Havana), no. 41 (June 26, 1944), 1–5.

55. See, e.g., "The Situation of Surviving Jews in Europe," ibid., no. 47 (March 19, 1945), 4–5; and "10 Jahre Aufbauarbeit in Suedamerika," ibid., no. 50 (August 22, 1945), 1.

56. See Patrik von zur Muehlen, *Fluchtziel Lateinamerika: Die deutsche Emigration 1933–1945:*

Politische Aktivitäten und soziokulturelle Integration (Bonn, 1988), 264–67.

57. Leizer Ran, interview by author, November 25, 1989, Jackson Heights, N.Y.

58. See, e.g., open letter from Alberto Hartman, General Chairman, Joint (JDC) Committee in Cuba, October 10, 1945.

59. See open letter from Joint (JDC) Comité de Campaña en Cuba, September 1945, Havana. The committee was headed by David H. Brandon, one of the leaders of the UHC, and its board included representatives from both Sephardic and Ashkenazic groups, including Isidoro Abravanel, Isaac Behar, David Chajmovich (president of ORT), David Utianski, and Juan Habib.

60. Alberto Hartman, President, Cuban Joint Campaign, to David Chajmovich, President, ORT de Cuba, October 15, 1945, Havana, YIVO Archive.

61. See Elkin, "Reception of the Muses," 296–97.

62. Kahn, "History," 70.

63. Elkin, "Reception of the Muses," 89. The professors included Boris Goldenberg in sociology, Heinrich Friedlander in economics, and Desiderio Weiss in languages.

64. See *Havaner Lebn,* November 30, December 25, 1946; and *Kubaner Yiddishe Wort,* January 11, April 5, 1946, all cited in Bejarano, "Problem," 2. See also Hubert Herring, *A History of Latin America,* 3d ed. (New York, 1968), 406. At one point it was claimed that Cuban hotel owners were not acting on their own, but in response to the wishes of guests from the United States who did not wish to stay in hotels where Jews were also staying. This same argument was also used to exclude blacks and was commonly offered as a rationalization for barring minorities in tourist locations throughout the hemisphere, including Canada. See Adrian Spies, "Made in the U.S.A.," *Commentary* 1, no. 6 (1946), 88–89.

65. Pro-Zionist community organizations in Cuba date back to the 1920s. See, e.g., *El Estudiante Hebreo,* a monthly publication started in 1929 under the direction of Fiodor Valbe.

66. Bejarano, "Problem," 3, citing Ofelia Domínguez y Navarro, *50 años de una vida* (Havana, 1971), 453–73. Domínguez y Navarro spent a good deal of time speaking to the Sephardic colony, attempting to garner support and raise awareness about the Palestinian question. See, e.g., flier circulated by the Circulo Universitario Hebreo de Cuba (July 15, 1947) announcing a pro-Israel cultural program at the Unión Hebrea Chevet-Ahim featuring Ofelia Domínguez y Navarro as speaker;

and "Manifesto al pueblo cubana por un Comité Pro Palestina," *El Avance Criollo,* April 14, 1944.

67. Bejarano, "Problem," 3.

68. See Moshe A. Tov, *El murmullo de Israel* (Jerusalem, 1983), 152–53; and *Havaner Lebn,* May 4, 1948, cited in Bejarano, "Problem," 5.

69. See "A la colonia arabe de Cuba," *El Mundo,* May 18, 1948, cited in Bejarano, "Problem," 6.

70. Cuba's formal recognition of the state of Israel came on January 14, 1949. The decree was signed by Minister Carlos Hevia y Reyes Gavilan in the presence of Israel's representative, Dr. Solomon Rosenthal. See *Redención* (Havana), March 1949, 74.

71. Bejarano, "Problem," 3.

72. Enrique Trinchet, *Jirones cubanos (Conozca la politica, cierta prensa, el comercio judio y español y la didactica como son: tumores nacionales)* (Havana, 1947).

73. *Tiempo,* June 10, 13–15, 17, 22, 1952, Leizer Ran Collection, YIVO Archive.

74. Bejarano, "Problem," 8.

75. The architect, not Jewish, visited several Jewish centers in the United States before finishing his plans. In the late 1950s the Orthodox (Ashkenazic) synagogue in Old Havana, Adath Israel, was rebuilt at a cost of a quarter of a million dollars. See Report, Joseph Kage, National Executive Director, Canadian Jewish Congress (CJC), to Saul Hayes, Executive Vice-President, CJC, March 14, 1961, JDC Archive.

76. The three were Herman Heisler, Isaac Gurwitz, and Julio Carity. See Patronato, *Boletin #25,* June 30, 1953.

77. Max Lesnick, interview by Margalit Bejarano, June 1984, Miami.

78. See Nahman Solowiejczyk, "Ashkenazim y Sefaradim," translated from the Yiddish, in *Der Gruntshteyn* (n.p., n.d.), 43–44, YIVO Archive.

79. Bejarano, "Problem," 11, citing Alfred Padula, "The Fall of the Bourgeoisie, Cuba, 1959–1961" (Ph.D. diss., University of New Mexico, 1974), 8–25. Adolfo Kates, for example, one of the leaders of the UHC and a founder of the Patronato de la Casa de la Comunidad Hebrea de Cuba, was a thirty-third-degree Mason, a member of the Unión and Habana yacht clubs, ex-commodore of the Almendares Yacht Club, founder of the Miramar Yacht Club, a member of the American Chamber of Commerce and the Cuban Chamber of Commerce, a member and ex-director of the Cuban Rotary Club, and the president of honor of the Pro-Israel Committee in Cuba.

80. Bejarano, "Problem," 11.

81. Dionisio Castiel, "Algunos apuntes sobre la

contribución de los Hebreos al desarrollo de Cuba," *La Voz de Mariano,* 1949–50, 60.

82. Foreign Policy Association, *Problems of the New Cuba: Report of the Commission on Cuban Affairs* (New York, 1935), 38–39; Rieur, "Jewish Colony," 40. In the 1950s the Anti-Tuberculosis Society expanded its work to include the mentally ill.

83. José Achuili Levy, "Noticiario médico Hebreo-Cubano," *Israelia* 3, no. 9 (1952), 25. The magazine also reprinted caricatures of "Jewish personalities interpreted by Cuban artists," not as a protest, but in appreciation. The issue cited reproduces Massaguer's caricature of Vladimir Horowitz, "the most eminent 'virtuoso' of our times" (suppl. C).

84. Alfredo Rodríguez, interview by author, September 16, 1983, Domino Park, Little Havana, Miami.

85. One of the keys to success in business was being able to get around customs duties. Most businessmen needed to pay off customs agents, who then charged duty on less expensive items. The system is described in detail in interviews with Moisés Pitchón and Osher (Jaime) Schuchinsky, deposited in the Otto G. Richter Library of the University of Miami. See, e.g., tapes Pitchón 2B and Schuchinsky 4A–B. See also E. Vignier G. Alonso, *La corrupción política administrativa en Cuba, 1944–1952* (Havana, 1973), not so much an indictment of the system of corruption as a condemnation of government failures to provide for the poor and to administer in good faith.

86. Bejarano, "Problem," 12.

87. Oscar Tisyera, *Cuba marxista vista por un católico* (Buenos Aires, 1964), 167; Frederick C. Turner, *Catholicism and Political Development in Latin America* (Chapel Hill, N.C., 1971), 110.

88. See the photographs of Constantino Arias, the house photographer of the Hotel Nacional, documenting the lavish as well as the mundane aspects of the good life with, as George Black writes, a sense of irony that very likely escaped his subjects (Black, *Good Neighbor,* 96). Arias was interviewed in 1984 by Marucha and Sandra Levinson; excerpts from the videotape sound track were published in Center for Cuban Studies, *Cuba: A View from Inside, Forty Years of Cuban Life in the Work and Words of Twenty Photographers* (New York, 1985), 25.

89. Kahn, "History," 83.

90. See Bejarano, "Problem," 11; and Maurice Halperin, *The Taming of Fidel Castro* (Berkeley and Los Angeles, 1981), 90–92.

91. Grobart, who worked as a tailor on first arriving in Cuba from Poland in 1927, was a member of the editorial board of *Cuba Socialista,* the monthly theoretical journal of the Cuban Marxist-Leninist movement. Many of the left-wing activists never attempted to fit into Cuban life: at early Cuban Communist Party meetings, they spoke in Yiddish and needed Spanish translators. See Hugh Thomas, *Cuba or the Pursuit of Freedom* (New York, 1970), 576, 597, 697; and Tad Szulc, "Two Reds behind Scenes," *New York Times,* March 10, 1962, American Jewish Committee (AJC) Clipping File, AJC Archive, New York.

92. Bejarano, "Problem," 13. See Jorge García Montes and Antonio Alonso Avila, *Historia del Partido Comunista de Cuba* (Miami, 1970); and Abraham Dubelman, "Cuba," *American Jewish Year Book, 1962* (Philadelphia, 1962), 481–85.

93. Memorandum, Seymour Samet, Miami, to David Danzig, AJC, New York, December 16, 1961, AJC Archive.

94. Kahn, "History," 88. They soon lost interest, however, and returned the building to the remaining skeletal Patronato board.

95. Bejarano, "Problem," 14, 15.

96. See memorandum, Dr. Simon Segal to Dr. Hannah Desser, AJC, Mexico City, October 10, 1966, AJC Archive.

97. Bejarano, "Problem," 17.

98. Haim Yaari, interview by Margalit Bejarano, 1981, cited in ibid.

99. "Cuba-Israel," Consejo Plenario Sionista (Plenary Zionist Council), Havana, 1954, in Utiansky Collection, Institute of Contemporary Jewry, Jerusalem, cited in Bejarano, "Problem," 17.

100. Roberto Lagar Quintero, Teresita Bacallao Reyes, Bárbara Rafael Vázquez, Raquel Guevara Pérez, and Gladys Avila Molina, *Historia del Movimiento Comunista, Obrero y de Liberación Nacional y er II Cubano (1917–1945), 10 grado* (Havana, 1987).

101. See Zvi Gitelman, "History, Memory, and Politics: The Holocaust in the Soviet Union," *Holocaust and Genocide Studies* 5, no. 1 (1990), 23–37, esp. 23.

102. On the original resolution, see memorandum, Buenos Aires Office, AJC, to Dr. Hannah Desser, New York, May 4, 1966, AJC Archive.

103. Jarkow Institute for Latin America of the Anti-Defamation League of B'nai B'rith, *Latin American Report* 7, no. 3 (1989), 9.

104. Weapons of U.S., Israeli, or Italian manufacture were said to be favored because they would help disguise "socialist involvement" in the trafficking. Cuban military advisers also allegedly trained Palestinians as frogmen and in weapons' use and techniques of falsifying passports and engaging in clandestine correspondence. See "Cuban

Diplomat Defects," *Washington Post,* January 26, 1989.

105. See, e.g., transcript of the Eighteenth United Nations Seminar on the Question of Palestine, Palacio de las Convenciones, Havana, December 15–17, 1987. The meeting was convened under the auspices of the United Nations Division for Palestinian Rights and was mostly hostile to Israel, but among the participants was retired Israeli General Mattityahu Peled of the Peace Now movement.

106. Kahn, "History," 89.

107. Memorandum No. 816, Boris Sapir to Moses A. Leavitt, JDC, New York, February 1, 1961, 1, JDC Archive. A similar appeal was made to the JDC to cover the deficit of the Colegio Hebreo del Centro Israelita de Cuba.

108. Miramar was the most affluent and desirable suburban neighborhood where Jews lived in Havana. Between 1961 and 1977 some 140,000 Cubans flew to Spain, with 10 percent remaining. It is not known whether any Jews formed part of this group. See Michael R. Marrus, *The Unwanted: European Refugees in the Twentieth Century* (New York, 1985), 369–70.

109. Josh Friedman, "A Dwindling Community," *Miami Herald,* December 26, 1983. The figure 807 is so precise because it represents the total number of Jews who registered at the Patronato to receive packages of matzo and kosher meat from Canada, a service organized by the Canadian Jewish Congress, which became the major intermediary between Cuban Jews and the outside Jewish world because of the difficulties posed by hostilities between the United States and Cuba.

110. On March 18, 1985, Dr. José Felipe Carneado, the director of the Division of Religious Affairs of the Central Committee of the Cuban Communist Party, met with Patronato officials and pledged to continue to maintain Jewish cemeteries and any other institution still functioning (comment by Adela Dworin of the Patronato, cited in *Latin American Report* 3, no. 2 [1985], 7).

111. Armando Entralgo, director of CEAMO, Symposium, "Zionism and the International Community," December 1985, cited in ibid. 4, no. 2 (1986), 8.

112. Rabbi Pynchas Brener of Union Israelita, Caracas, president of the Committee of Relations between Synagogues and Churches in Venezuela. See ibid. 3, no. 4 (1987), 6. See also Tzvi Medin, *Cuba: The Shaping of Revolutionary Consciousness* (New York, 1990).

113. See Robert M. Levine, *Tropical Diaspora: The Jewish Experience in Cuba* (Gainesville, Fla., 1993), and the documentary film "Havana Nagila," produced by Laura Paull (Modesto, Calif., 1995).

BEYOND
THE CONFLICT

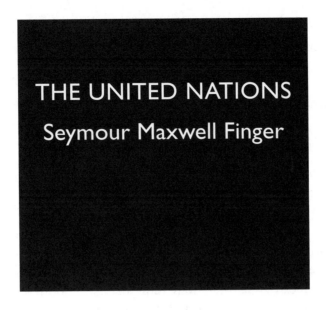

THE UNITED NATIONS
Seymour Maxwell Finger

The Holocaust had a significant impact on the work of the United Nations during its early years, particularly in the area of human rights and humanitarian issues. The most direct result was the adoption of the International Convention on the Prevention and Punishment of the Crime of Genocide in 1948. The crime targeted, genocide, was exactly that of the Holocaust, and the driving force behind the drafting and adoption of the convention was a Polish Jew, Raphael Lemkin, who had lost seventy-two of the seventy-four members of his family in that catastrophe.

A number of other important U.N. instruments related to the Holocaust were adopted during the period from 1946 to 1968: the statutes of the International Refugee Organization (1946), which defined refugees as, *inter alia,* "victims of the nazi or fascist regimes"; the Declaration of Death of Missing Persons (1949); the Convention Relating to the Status of Refugees (1951); the Convention Relating to the Status of Stateless Persons (1954); the Convention on the Reduction of Statelessness (1961); the Convention on the Elimination of All Forms of Racial Discrimination (1965); and the Convention on the Non-Applicability of Statutory Limitations on War Crimes and Crimes against Humanity (1968).

In the pages that follow we trace the relationship between the Holocaust and this formidable array of human-rights instruments. We then describe the reversal that took place after 1968, when the Soviet bloc and the Afro-Asian group, prodded by the twenty-one Arab states, provided a General Assembly majority that was hostile to Israel. The clearest example of this hostility was Resolution 3379 (1975), which equated Zionism with racism and served as a convenient pretext for anti-Semitic measures around the world. So the organization that had started out working against the kinds of crimes committed during the Holocaust was at this stage being used against the Jewish people, the victims of the Holocaust. Finally, we discuss the improvement in Israel's position at the United Nations in the 1990s, as evidenced by the General Assembly's decision in 1991 to rescind Resolution 3379.

THE INTERNATIONAL REFUGEE ORGANIZATION

At its very beginning the United Nations was confronted with a serious consequence of the Holocaust, the presence of hundreds of thousands of survivors in displaced-person (DP) camps or living precariously elsewhere in Europe. These were the remnants of the more than seven million Jews who were living in Europe when Hitler came to power. For most of them a return to their former homeland was either dangerous or impossible, and emigration was a slow process.

On August 5, 1946, a group of Jewish organizations submitted a memorandum on the subject to the Fifth Session of the council of the United Nations Relief and Rehabilitation Administration (UNRRA). The memorandum, submitted by the World Jewish Congress, the American Jewish Congress, and the Board of Deputies of British Jews, indicated that there were more than 500,000 Jewish displaced persons in Romania, Hungary, Bulgaria, and Italy and more than 100,000 in Germany and Austria, the great majority of whom were nonrepatriable. Other estimates put the number of Jewish refugees and displaced persons at 281,000 out of a total of 1,279,000.[1]

The United Nations responded by establishing the International Refugee Organization (IRO) in 1946. The five U.N. members from the Soviet bloc cast the only votes against its creation. They contended that the solution for the refugees and displaced persons was repatriation. Italy, a former Axis power and thus not yet a member of the United Nations, applied for membership in the IRO and had the support of the Jewish Agency for Palestine "in consideration [of the] generous attitude [of the] Italian people and government."[2]

As stated in Annex 1 of the founding resolution, 205 (III), the "object of the Organization will be to bring about a rapid and positive solution of the problem of *bona fide* refugees and displaced persons, which shall be just and equitable to all concerned." The annex also stipulates that "no international assistance shall be given to traitors, quislings and war criminals." Most important was the definition of bona fide refugees as persons who were "victims of the nazi or fascist regimes or regimes which took part on their side in the second world war . . . whether enjoying international status as refugees or not," as well as victims of the Falangist regime in Spain and other prewar refugees. Also defined as refugees are "persons who, having resided in Germany or Austria, and being of Jewish origin or foreigners or stateless persons, were victims of nazi persecution and were detained in, or were obliged to flee from, and were subsequently returned to, one of those countries as a result of enemy action, or of war circumstances, and have not yet been firmly resettled therein and unaccompanied children, 16 years of age or under, who were war orphans or whose parents had disappeared."

Section B of the annex defines a displaced person as one who, as a result of actions by the Axis regimes and their allies, "has been deported from, or has been obliged to leave, his country of nationality or of former habitual residence, such as persons who were compelled to undertake forced labor or who were deported for racial, religious or political reasons."

While the word "Holocaust" does not appear, it is clear that a substantial number of the people whom the IRO was established to help were victims of the Nazis and that the need for such help gave impetus to its establishment. The refugees and displaced persons, as defined in the founding resolution, became the concern of the IRO and received significant help from that organization, both in facilitating emigration and in ameliorating living conditions pending such emigration. By the end of 1951, when the IRO's operational activities ceased, more than a million people had been resettled.[3] Nevertheless, large numbers of people, including survivors of the Holocaust, remained refugees, and many were stateless, having lost their original nationality. To ameliorate their situation, the United Nations developed three significant international instruments: the Convention Relating to the Status of Refugees (1951); the Convention Relating to the Status of Stateless Persons (1954); and the Convention on the Reduction of Statelessness (1961).

THE UNITED NATIONS EDUCATIONAL, SCIENTIFIC, AND CULTURAL ORGANIZATION

At its inception the United Nations Educational, Scientific, and Cultural Organization (UNESCO) defined as its most important goal "the struggle against racism, prejudice and stereotyping and the defence of human rights and peace hoping to prevent any return of the hideous ideology of which the Jewish people had been the victim."[4] Over the years UNESCO conferences have, in fact, devoted considerable attention to these goals; however, there has been relatively little attention directed to the Holocaust and its victims. At the first UNESCO conference, in 1946, there was a brief discussion of UNRRA. The U.S. representative emphasized that UNESCO should not become a relief agency, receiving and distributing funds, because this was a task for which UNRRA already had responsibility.[5] At its second conference UNESCO ratified an agreement with the IRO, the successor to UNRRA.[6] Thereafter, numerous references to refugees and appeals for aid were concerned with Greek, Asian, and, repeatedly, Palestinian refugees but not with Jewish refugees. Virtually every conference adopted resolutions on racism, but these did not deal specifically with the Holocaust or anti-Semitism.

It is perhaps significant that in a book on UNESCO coauthored by the man who was its deputy director general from 1947 to 1950 there are no references in the index to the Holocaust, genocide, displaced persons, Jews, or the IRO.[7] UNESCO's emphasis has been on the overall struggle against racism and the defense of human rights rather than on the specific issues of the Holocaust, Jewish refugees, or Jewish displaced persons.

THE HOLOCAUST AND PALESTINE

British restrictions on Jewish immigration to the mandated territory of Palestine, imposed in response to pressure from the Arabs, closed one of the escape routes of Jews fleeing Nazi persecution. Britain's White Paper of May 17, 1939, restricted the number of Jews who could enter Palestine to fifteen thousand per year for five years and promised to end such immigration entirely thereafter. In fact, the British used various means to reduce Jewish immigration even further and did not even allow the quota of fifteen thousand per year to be met.[8]

With the end of the war and the pressure of hundreds of thousands of Jewish refugees or displaced persons, Zionist organizations mounted an intensive campaign to achieve the Jewish homeland promised in the Balfour Declaration of 1917 and incorporated in the Palestine mandate accorded to the British government by the League of Nations in 1922. Alfred James Lord Balfour, Britain's foreign secretary, had stated: "His Majesty's Government view with favor the establishment of a national home for the Jewish people and will use their best endeavors to facilitate this object, it being clearly understood that nothing shall be done which may prejudice the civil and religious rights of existing non-Jewish communities in Palestine, or the rights and political status enjoyed by Jews in any other country."[9] The Arabs continued to resist Jewish immigration to Palestine. The British government, caught between the pressures of Arabs and Jews, decided to turn the issue over to the United Nations, which considered the question in the First Special Session of the General Assembly, which convened April 28, 1947. The British asked the General Assembly to make recommendations concerning the future government of Palestine in accordance with Article 10 of the U.N. Charter.

Egypt, Iraq, Syria, Lebanon, and Saudi Arabia, insisting that the question of self-determination and the problem of Jewish homelessness in Europe were separate and unrelated issues, requested that an additional item be put on the agenda: "The termination of the Mandate over Palestine and the declaration of its independence." The General (Steering) Committee of the General Assembly decided by a vote of 8 to 1, with 3 abstentions, not to recommend inclusion of the item. The General Assembly not only accepted that recommendation but also decided to grant a hearing to the Jewish Agency for Palestine. The Arab Higher Committee was granted a hearing before the Assembly's First Committee. All other requests for hearings were denied.[10]

The ideological struggle between Arabs and Jews was further joined over the terms of reference for the U.N. Special Committee on Palestine (UNSCOP), established by Resolution 106 (S-1) of May 15, 1947. Specifically, it was contested whether the Special Committee should confine its investigation and inquiry to Palestine itself or also make inquiries and investigations in the areas where the refugees and displaced persons were located. Speaking for the Jewish Agency, Moshe Shertok (subsequently Sharett) argued that Jewish resettlement was a necessary corollary of the national rights of Jews as recognized by the international community. He stated: "If it is granted that the Jewish people are in Palestine as of right, then all implications and corollaries of that premise must be accepted. The foremost is that the Jews must be allowed to resettle in Palestine in unlimited numbers, provided only they do not displace or worsen the lot of existing inhabitants who are also there as of right."[11] Thus, from the Zionist viewpoint, the Jewish problem in Europe was inextricably linked to the Palestine problem that was before the United Nations. The

Zionists believed that Jews the world over had a national right to settle in Palestine and to determine their own future in accordance with the principle of national self-determination.

In the end the Zionist viewpoint prevailed. Resolution 106 did not refer specifically to the refugees in Europe, but UNSCOP's mandate was not restricted to visiting Palestine. The committee was authorized to conduct investigations anywhere it considered them necessary. And, in fact, after visiting Palestine and Transjordan, UNSCOP moved to Geneva, whence it sent a subcommittee to visit DP camps in Germany and Austria prior to preparing its report. The resolution provided, in paragraph 2, that "the Special Committee shall have the widest powers to ascertain and record facts, and to investigate all questions and issues relevant to the problem of Palestine." Paragraph 4 authorized it "to conduct investigations in Palestine and wherever it may deem useful, receive and examine written or oral testimony . . . from the mandatory Power, from representatives of the population of Palestine, from Governments and from such organizations and individuals as it may deem necessary."

The UNSCOP members were divided in their viewpoints and recommendations to the General Assembly, with a majority favoring the partition of Palestine into Jewish and Arab states. The majority report, supported by Canada, Czechoslovakia, Guatemala, the Netherlands, Peru, Sweden, and Uruguay, stated: "Jewish immigration is the central issue in Palestine today, and is the one factor above all, that rules out the necessary cooperation between the Arab and Jewish communities in a single State. The creation of a Jewish state under a partition scheme is the only hope of removing this issue from the arena of conflict."[12] The three UNSCOP members who opposed partition—India, Iran, and Yugoslavia—favored a federal state. The eleventh member, Australia, abstained.

Uruguay was particularly emphatic in making the link between the survivors of the Holocaust and the need to establish a Jewish state. It declared: "It is obvious that if the Palestine problem is directly linked with the problem of immigration, this latter problem has in turn been connected with, and is stimulated by, two well-known facts: first the nazi persecution which cost the Jewish people of Europe the lives of six million persons, who were systematically exterminated in the gas chambers and crematories of the nazi regime; and second, anti-semitism, which has continued to exist and may result in fresh outbursts of persecution and violence." UNSCOP's final resolution called for the creation of independent Jewish and Arab states in Palestine, a system of economic cooperation between the two states, and a "special system of administration for the City of Jerusalem and other Holy Places in Palestine." It incorporated the fundamental points proposed by Uruguay and supported by the Jewish Agency.[13]

These points formed the basis of Resolution 181 (II)A, adopted on November 29, 1947, calling for partition with economic union and the termination of the British mandate no later than August 1, 1948. Part II of the resolution defines the boundaries of the Arab and Jewish states, and part III the boundaries of the city of Jerusalem, to be administered by the United Nations. The resolution was adopted by a vote of

33 to 13, with 10 abstentions. Almost all of the affirmative votes came from European and Western Hemisphere countries, together with Liberia, the Philippines, Australia, and New Zealand; Cuba provided the lone negative vote from Latin America. The other negative votes came from African and Asian countries, then in a minority in the United Nations, and Greece.[14] The resolution on partition, opposed by the Arabs and their allies, was clearly a victory for the Zionists and was significantly influenced by concern for the survivors of the Holocaust.

Predictably, the partition resolution was accepted by the Jewish Agency, despite its misgivings about the small amount of territory accorded to the Jewish state, and rejected by the Arab states. On May 14, 1948, the establishment of the state of Israel was proclaimed. Immediately thereafter armed forces from Syria, Lebanon, Transjordan, and Egypt attacked the new state. Israel survived because of the successful defense provided by its own armed forces and, in the process, enlarged the area specified in the partition resolution. Nevertheless, the General Assembly's partition resolution gave legitimacy to the new state, and Israel's admission into the United Nations in 1949 served to enhance that legitimacy.

THE ADMISSION OF ISRAEL TO U.N. MEMBERSHIP

The debate over the admission of Israel to the United Nations also indicated that many countries were moved by recollections of the Holocaust, which made them sympathetic to the idea of a Jewish state. The proposal for admission was cosponsored by the United States and Guatemala. The Polish representative, speaking in support of Israel's admission, stated that Poland had actively assisted the Jews in achieving their aspirations not only for a national home but also for full statehood. The Poles and the Jews had suffered together, and many Jews had suffered from racial hatred encouraged by "the reactionary elements predominant in Poland's prewar government circles."

France, expressing support for Israel's admission, observed that "the thoughts of many were turned to those who had suffered persecution throughout the long years under the yoke of the totalitarian regimes." But, hedging its bets, France also referred to its "strong attachment to the countries of the Middle East."

Uruguay's representative, Rodriguez Fabregat, made an impassioned argument for admission, pointing out that "six million Jews had died at the hands of the Nazis merely because they were Jews." He asserted that all the old problems of persecution, pogroms, ghettos, stateless persons, religious segregation, and racial discrimination would disappear with the advent of the Jewish state.

The Arabs, of course, opposed Israel's admission and tried to block the vote. In the Ad Hoc Political Committee, Lebanon introduced a motion to defer the question of Israel's admission until the next session of the General Assembly. The motion was defeated, 25 votes to 19, with 12 abstentions. Iraq argued that the Security Council's recommendation of Israel's admission was of questionable legality, since one permanent member (the United Kingdom) had abstained; it proposed referring the question to the International Court of Justice, obviously a delaying tactic. The Iraqi representative pointed out that under Article 27 of the U.N. Charter, substantive decisions of the Security Council required "the concurring votes of the Permanent Members." He argued that an abstention was not a concurring vote. While this is technically correct, the practice of the U.N. Security Council since 1946 had been not to regard the abstention of a permanent member as constituting a veto. The president of the General Assembly ruled that the manner in which the recommendation of the Security Council had been adopted was the concern of the internal government and procedure of the Council and that it must be accepted by the General Assembly.

The General Assembly then proceeded to a vote on the proposal to admit Israel as a member, which was adopted by a vote of 33 to 12, with 12 abstentions. The pattern of voting was very similar to the vote on Resolution 181. Almost all the affirmative votes came from the European and Western Hemisphere states (in this instance Cuba also voted in favor), plus Australia, New Zealand, Liberia, and the Philippines. The twelve negative votes came from the African and Asian members, who were mostly Islamic. Thanking the U.N. members for their vote to admit Israel, Foreign Minister Moshe Sharett spoke of "mankind's revulsion against the European tragedy."[15]

THE GENOCIDE CONVENTION

The most direct U.N. reaction to the Holocaust was the International Convention on the Prevention and Punishment of the Crime of Genocide, adopted unanimously by the General Assembly in Paris on December 9, 1948. The driving force behind the drafting and adoption of the convention was Raphael Lemkin, who is now largely forgotten. Lemkin was born in Bezwodene, Poland, on June 23, 1900, and earned a law degree from the University of Lvov. He served as secretary of the Court of Appeals in Warsaw from 1926 to 1929 and as public prosecutor from 1929 to 1934. He engaged in private law practice in Warsaw until 1939, when the Germans invaded Poland. Lemkin escaped and worked as a lecturer at the University of Stockholm from 1939 to 1941 and then at Duke University from 1941 to 1942. In 1942 he became chief consultant to the Board of Economic Warfare, serving until 1944. In 1945 Lemkin became an adviser on foreign affairs to the U.S. War Department, and in this capacity he served on the U.S. Army prosecution staff at the Nuremberg trials as chief prosecutor on Axis criminality. In 1948 he moved to Yale University, where he was a professor of law until his death in 1959.[16] Lemkin published his monumental work *Axis Rule in Occupied Europe* in 1944. In it he coined the word "genocide" and laid much of the groundwork for the Nuremberg trials and the Genocide Convention.[17]

Lemkin initially focused his efforts to prevent genocide on the U.S. government. He prodded its representatives to take a leading role in prompting the United Nations to prepare a convention and to see to its adoption. Many nongovernmental organizations, especially those concerned with human rights, also provided a strong lead in that direction. These included the World Jewish Congress, B'nai B'rith, and the American Jewish Committee.

Lemkin started his campaign when the U.N. General Assembly met in London in its first session in January 1946. From that time on, he buttonholed representatives in the corridors and meeting rooms of the United Nations and groomed Senator Warren Austin, the U.S. permanent representative to the United Nations, and Ricardo Alfaro of Panama. His lobbying bore fruit. Panama, Cuba, and India introduced a resolution calling on the United Nations "to study the problem of genocide and to prepare a report on the possibilities of declaring genocide an international crime."[18] At its meeting in Paris on December 11, 1946, the General Assembly unanimously adopted Resolution 96 (I) (which Lemkin was credited with drafting), which established a committee to prepare a convention.

The Ad Hoc Committee on Genocide met at Lake Success, New York, from April 5 to May 10, 1948, under the chairmanship of the U.S. member, John Maktos. The Soviet representative, Platon Morozov, proposed that the convention "declare that the crime of genocide is organically bound up with fascism-nazism and other similar race 'theories' which preach racism and national hatred, the domination of the so-called races and the extermination of the so-called lower races." This proposal was rejected by a vote of 5 to 2 (the Soviet Union and Poland cast the two affirmative votes), its opponents arguing that there were other causes of genocide. Also rejected, by a vote of 6 to 1, was a proposal by the French representative, Pierre Ordonneau, to define genocide as a crime against humanity. On the draft convention as a whole, the vote was 5 (China, France, Lebanon, the United States, Venezuela) to 1 (the Soviet Union), with 1 abstention (Poland).[19] The definition finally adopted appears as Article II of the convention, which is quoted in full below. Much of the adopted text had been drafted by Lemkin, who was obsessed with the project; he worked on it night and day, passing his drafts to the U.S. representative.[20]

The draft convention came up for consideration when the U.N. General Assembly met in Paris in the autumn. It was adopted unanimously as the International Convention on the Prevention and Punishment of the Crime of Genocide, GA Resolution 260 (III), on December 9, 1948. The Soviets introduced an amendment similar to their proposal that had been rejected in the Ad Hoc Committee, but it was rejected by a vote of 36 to 7. In opposing the amendment, Ernest Gross, the U.S. representative, argued that it would have a limiting effect. Gross noted that the convention was organically linked to the genocide committed by the Nazis and their collaborators in World War II, as recognized by the Nuremberg tribunal. The vote on the convention "reflected the determination to insure that the barbarous crimes which had shocked the conscience of mankind in the preceding years would never again be repeated." The convention, Gross declared, "would constitute a milestone in the progress of international law."[21] Ricardo Alfaro of Panama, chairman of the Sixth (Legal) Committee, to which the draft convention was assigned for consideration, described genocide as "a crime which had been perpetrated throughout history but had never reached the depths of premeditated cruelty to which it had sunk recently."[22]

Article 1 of the convention states that "the Contracting Parties confirm that genocide, whether committed in time of peace or in time of war, is a crime under international law which they undertake to prevent and to punish." Article 2 defines genocide:

> In the present Convention, genocide means any of the following committed with intent to destroy, in whole or in part, a national, ethnical, racial or religious group, as such:
> (a) Killing members of the group;
> (b) Causing serious bodily or mental harm to members of the group;
> (c) Deliberately inflicting on the group conditions of life calculated to bring about its physical destruction in whole or in part;
> (d) Imposing measures intended to prevent births within the group;
> (e) Forcibly transferring children of the group to another group.

Article 6 provides that persons charged with genocide "shall be tried by a competent tribunal of the State in the territory of which the act was committed, or by such international tribunal as may have jurisdiction." The idea of an international criminal court like the Nuremberg tribunal has not been realized, though it continues to be evoked. At the Forty-fifth Session of the U.N. General Assembly in 1990, it was endorsed by the prime minister of Trinidad and Tobago, Arthur Robinson, speaking in the general debate. At the same session, the Sixth (Legal) Committee also considered the question, but its discussion revealed a wide range of views on the advisability of establishing such a court at that time. The committee also discussed inconclusively a draft code of Crimes against the Peace and Security of Mankind, which some representatives considered a necessary prerequisite to the establishment of an international criminal court.

By October 14, 1950, there were enough ratifications (twenty) to bring the convention into force, and by 1973 seventy-six countries had ratified or acceded to the convention. The United States, which took a leading role in the drafting and adoption of the convention, was one of the last to ratify it. The Senate gave its advice and consent in 1988, forty years after the convention was adopted unanimously by the General Assembly. This long delay was particularly surprising in light of President Harry Truman's support for the convention. In his message to the Senate on June 16, 1949, Truman declared: "By the leading part the United States has taken in the United Nations in producing an effective international legal instrument outlawing the world-shocking crime of genocide, we have established before the world our firm and clear policy toward that crime."[23]

But Truman's support was not strong enough to overcome a belief among many senators that international conventions dealing with human rights might interfere in matters that they thought should be subject only to domestic jurisdiction. Early in 1950 public hearings were held by a subcommittee of the Senate Committee on Foreign Relations. On May 23, 1950, the subcommittee reported on the convention to the full committee with four specific understandings and one declaration designed to clarify its meaning. Since misgivings continued, the understandings were redrafted as reservations by the full committee. The committee, however, did not recommend the convention to the Senate, and no further action was taken for more than thirty years. Those senators opposing ratification, although they generally condemned genocide, argued that the convention "raises important questions and does not resolve them in a manner consistent with our form of government." They maintained that genocide had never occurred in the United States and so action of any kind was unnecessary. Moreover, the convention might provide a vehicle whereby nations could intervene in one another's domestic affairs. Concern was also expressed that a treaty whose implementation required the passing of domestic laws might provide a basis for enhancing federal powers at the expense of powers traditionally exercised by the states.[24]

These misgivings were concretized in a proposed amendment to the U.S. Constitution in 1953. The amendment would prevent the United States from signing such treaties. While it was not pursued, the amendment did inhibit the executive branch from seeking ratification of the convention from Congress. There followed a period of many years during which the United States took a negative stance toward all conventions and covenants in the area of human rights, and successive administrations did not press the Senate to act on the Genocide Convention.[25]

During the 1960s and 1970s, repeated efforts were made, particularly by B'nai B'rith and other Jewish organizations, to spur the Senate into action on the convention. In March 1971 Justice Arthur J. Goldberg, speaking on behalf of the Ad Hoc Committee on the Human Rights and Genocide Treaties, said to a Senate subcommittee: "It is inconceivable that we should hesitate any longer in making an international commitment against mass murder." Earlier, in December 1968, Chief Justice Earl Warren had told an American audience that "we as a nation should have been the first to ratify the genocide convention. . . . Instead, we may well be near the last," a prediction that came true.[26] President Jimmy Carter urged the Senate to act at least three times, to no avail.[27] Finally, in November 1988, the eighth year of the Reagan administration, the Senate gave its advice and consent to the Genocide Convention.

Four years later the United States was in the forefront of countries expressing outrage at the "ethnic cleansing" taking place in Bosnia. No one has yet been tried for a violation of the Genocide Convention, despite mass killings of ethnic groups in Cambodia, Iraq, the former Yugoslavia, Rwanda, and elsewhere. Still, Raphael Lemkin's prodigious labors to bring the Genocide Convention into being have not been in vain. The convention does offer a legal basis for the trial and punishment of offenders and a standard of reference for the international community. And trials may yet take place.

THE CONVENTION ON DECLARATION OF DEATH OF MISSING PERSONS

The massive scale of killing during the Holocaust and the methods employed made it virtually impossible to identify the individual victims, let alone find death certificates. The importance and complexity of the issue was pointed out by the World Jewish Congress in a memorandum to the U.N. Conference on Declaration of Death of Missing Persons. It noted that in many instances the missing person was not a national or even permanent resident of the country from which he or she was deported. This was true in the case of victims of Nazi persecution on racial or religious grounds who were forced to leave their home country (e.g., Germany, Austria, or Czechoslovakia) before the war and who found temporary asylum in lands that subsequently were overrun by the Germans (France, Belgium, Holland) or came under German domination or control (e.g., Italy). Moreover, the victims of racial and religious persecution were annihilated en masse, so that very frequently almost an entire minority group disappeared. In many communities, 90 percent of the total Jewish population were destroyed as a result of mass slaughter.

The establishment of the death of close and distant relatives was of the greatest importance in determining the legal rights of those who succeeded somehow in surviving the Holocaust. Some of the missing persons possessed commercial interests, bank deposits, or other property outside their home country or usual place of residence. Others were entitled to such property as the closest heirs of persons who died intestate abroad or because they were beneficiaries in the wills of such persons. The problem involved not only matters concerning property rights but, more importantly, those related to the personal status of widows and orphans and the adoption of orphans. No widow could remarry or orphan be adopted until the death of the spouse or the parents had been definitely established.[28]

The U.N. Conference on Declaration of Death of Missing Persons took place from March 15 through April 6, 1950. It had before it the report of an ad hoc committee established by Resolution 209 (VIII), March 2, 1949, of the U.N. Economic and Social Council, including a draft convention prepared by the committee and memorandums submitted by the Consultative Council of Jewish Organizations and the World Jewish Congress.

At its conclusion on April 6, 1950, the conference established and opened for accession by states the Convention on Declaration of Death of Missing Persons. The procedure for obtaining a declaration of death is set forth in Article 3. It provides that "any competent tribunal in each contracting State shall, at the instance of any natural or juridical person having a legal interest in the matter or of an authority charged with the protection of the public interest, or acting on its own motion, issue a declaration of death of a missing person" provided that certain requirements are met. Among these requirements are that the person disappeared in the years 1939–45 under circumstances that afford reasonable ground to infer that the person died in consequence of events of war or of racial, religious, political, or national persecution; that at least five years have passed since the person was last known to be alive; and that during the proceedings public notice has been given to afford the person assumed dead an opportunity to make it known that he is alive.

Article 8 provides for the establishment within the framework of the United Nations of an International Bureau for Declarations of Death, including a central registry. The bureau was also empowered to receive from governments or individuals authenticated copies of declarations of death of missing persons issued before the adoption of the convention. Article 12 exempts people initiating proceedings under the convention from all costs and charges and provides for free legal aid in all cases in which, under national law, such exemption or aid is granted to nationals of the country where a proceeding is pending.

It was not necessary for the General Assembly to discuss the convention at its Fifth Session (1950), since that had been done by the conference. However, it did take up the question of establishing the international bureau in a draft resolution submitted by Belgium, Denmark, Sweden, and Uruguay.[29] The introduction of this resolution permitted the Soviet representative, Platon Morozov, to criticize the convention as "inexpedient." He pointed out that the conference had been attended by only twenty-five delegations, less than half the membership of the United Nations. Moreover, he argued, the bureau was unnecessary, and its establishment would involve considerable expense. Despite these objections, the draft resolution (A/1510) was adopted by 38 votes to 6 (the Soviet Union, Byelorussia, Ukraine, Poland, Czechoslovakia, and Yugoslavia), with 13 abstentions. It provided that "the expenses of the organization should be assessed upon such non-member States as may become parties to the convention, in accordance with the principle adopted in this respect in connection with the expenses of the International Court of Justice."

Unquestionably, the convention was of substantial importance to survivors of the Holocaust and the families of its victims. For many of them, the ability to establish their relatives' deaths and thus to validate their claims as heirs, to recover confiscated possessions, or to claim damages under restitution law was a matter of dire necessity. Moreover, the declarations of death were very important for those planning adoptions and marriages.

THE EICHMANN AFFAIR

In May 1960 officers of the Israel Security Services apprehended Adolf Eichmann, a major Nazi war criminal who was living in Argentina under an assumed name. They then took him to Israel; according to the Israeli government, he went voluntarily. The Argentine government protested to the government of Israel that this act was a violation of Argentine sovereignty. In a note dated June 3, 1960, Israel apologized, stating:

> If the volunteer group violated Argentine law or interfered with matters within the sovereignty of Argentina, the Government of Israel wishes to express its regret. The Government of Israel requests that the special significance of bringing to trial the man responsible for the murder of millions of persons belonging to the Jewish people be taken into account, and asks that due weight be given to the fact that the volunteers, who were themselves survivors of that massacre, placed this historic mission above all other considerations.[30]

Despite this apology and a meeting between the foreign ministers of the two countries, Argentina was not satisfied and decided to bring the issue to the U.N. Security Council. When the council met on June 22, Argentina argued that it was not so much objecting to an isolated, specific incident as it was defending an important principle: the rule of law over arbitrariness. Argentina introduced a draft resolution asserting that acts of this type, "which affect the sovereignty of a Member State and therefore cause international friction, may, if repeated, endanger international peace and security." This contention brought the matter under Chapter VI of the U.N. Charter, thus making it appropriate for Security Council consideration. The resolution also called upon Israel to make "appropriate reparation," which, in Argentina's view, would include the return of Eichmann to Argentina and the punishment of those Israelis responsible for taking him to Israel.[31]

Under ordinary circumstances the Argentine resolution might have been accepted by the Security Council without change. But these circumstances were far from ordinary, as Israeli Foreign Minister Golda Meir pointed out. Noting that the act in question had been carried out by certain Israeli nationals and not by her government, she observed: "But my Government sincerely believes that this isolated violation of Argentine law must be seen in light of the exceptional and unique character of the crimes attributed to Eichmann, on the one hand, and the motives of those that acted in this unusual manner, on the other hand. These men belong, as do I, to a people whose tragedy in the Second World War is unmatched in history. No people in modern times has ever mourned the loss of one third of its population."[32]

In the same vein, U.S. Ambassador Henry Cabot Lodge maintained that the whole matter could not be considered apart from the monstrous acts with which Eichmann was charged, "the systematic slaughter of some six million people." He then submitted two amendments to Argentina's draft resolution. One would add the following preambular phrase: "Mindful of the universal condemnation of the persecution of the Jews under the Nazis and of the concern of people in all countries that Eichmann should be brought to appropriate justice for the crimes of which he is accused." The second would add the operative sentence, "[The Security Council] expresses the hope that the traditionally friendly relations between Argentina and Israel will be advanced."[33]

Before the vote the question of the meaning of the "appropriate reparation" Israel would be requested to make under paragraph 2 of the draft resolution, in which the Security Council "requests the Government of Israel to make appropriate reparation in accordance with the Charter of the United Nations and the rules of international law," was raised. Lodge said that reparation would consist of the adoption of the resolution, together with a statement of apology by the Israeli foreign minister on behalf of the government of Israel.[34] This interpretation was supported by the United Kingdom and was not challenged by any other member. Argentina accepted the U.S. amendments, stated that it would not interpret the phrase "appropriate reparation," and declared that, as a party to the dispute, it would not participate in the vote. (By not challenging the U.S. interpretation of reparation, Argentina was in effect abandoning its original position that "adequate reparation" would mean the return of Eichmann to Argentina and the punishment of those responsible for taking him to Israel.) Obviously, there had been considerable negotiation behind the scenes and substantial agreement among all members except Poland and the Soviet Union. The resolution was adopted by a vote of 8 to 0, with Poland and the Soviet Union abstaining and Argentina not participating.

Poland explained that it had abstained because the question of Eichmann's fate was left unanswered. The Soviets doubted whether the matter should have been an issue for the Security Council at all, asking how it endangered peace and security. In any case, they declared, paragraph 2 could not be considered the basis for returning Eichmann to Argentina. With obvious satisfaction, Golda Meir stated that she was "deeply moved by the unanimous expression of horror and revulsion by Council members."[35] The Security Council's discussion clearly revealed that its decision had been significantly influenced by the Holocaust. Eichmann was kept in Israel, tried for his war crimes, condemned, and executed.

THE INTERNATIONAL CONVENTION ON THE ELIMINATION OF ALL FORMS OF RACIAL DISCRIMINATION

In 1959 and 1960 the attention of the United Nations was drawn to an outbreak of anti-Semitic incidents in Europe and other parts of the world. The Sub-Commission on Prevention of Discrimination and Protection of Minorities responded in January 1960 with a resolution.[36] Two months later the Commission on Human Rights also condemned these incidents, and on December 12 the General Assembly adopted Resolution 1510 (XV) denouncing all manifestations and practices of racial, religious, and national hatred as violations of the U.N. Charter.

In July 1961 the Economic and Social Council recommended to the General Assembly the adoption of a draft resolution entitled "Manifestations of Racial Prejudice and National and Religious Intolerance."[37] The General Assembly adopted this resolution in 1962 with a few minor amendments. Referring to the "continued existence and manifestations of racial prejudice and religious intolerance in various parts of the world," the resolution invited governments to make efforts to educate their people in order to eradicate such manifestations; to rescind discriminatory laws; to adopt legislation, if necessary, for prohibiting discrimination; and generally to take measures to combat prejudices and intolerance.[38]

After the adoption of that resolution, the Third Committee considered a draft resolution submitted by six African delegations proposing the preparation of an international convention on the elimination of all forms of racial discrimination. The discussion revealed a significant difference between those countries that wanted to maintain the emphasis on anti-Semitism and those that did not, notably the Arab and Communist states. The Arabs wanted to remove the question of anti-Semitism, and the Communists did not consider religious discrimination an important matter. As a compromise, the Third Committee and the General Assembly adopted two resolutions: 1780 (XVII) called for a draft declaration and a draft convention on the elimination of all forms of racial discrimination; and 1781 (XVII) called for the same with respect to all forms of religious intolerance.[39] This discussion and its outcome reflected the increasing influence of the new member states, formerly colonies, and the fact that the Holocaust had ended seventeen years earlier.

The U.N. Declaration on the Elimination of All Forms of Racial Discrimination, GA Resolution 1904 (XVII), was adopted a year later. The General Assembly adopted another resolution, 1906 (XVII), requesting that the Economic and Social

Council ask the Commission on Human Rights to give absolute priority to the preparation of a draft international convention on racial discrimination. The commission and its Subcommission on Prevention of Discrimination and Protection of Minorities did indeed give the draft convention absolute priority, completing its work by March 1964, only three months after the General Assembly's request. In July the substantive articles of the draft convention were considered by the Economic and Social Council, which in turn transmitted them to the General Assembly, along with an amendment by the United States dealing with anti-Semitism and a subamendment thereto submitted by the Soviet Union.

The U.S. amendment stated: "States Parties condemn anti-Semitism and will take action as appropriate for its speedy eradication in the territories subject to their jurisdiction." The Soviet subamendment read: "States Parties condemn anti-Semitism, Zionism, nazism, neo-nazism and all other forms of the policy and ideology of colonialism, national and race hatred and exclusiveness."[40] The Soviet proposal was noteworthy as the first official attempt to equate Zionism with racism in a U.N. body and as a ploy to defeat the American effort to specify anti-Semitism as a form of racism.

During the debate on these amendments, Greece and Hungary introduced a draft resolution to cut off all consideration of the U.S. amendment, the Soviet subamendment, and other related amendments. Thus, the Assembly's Third Committee did not include in the draft convention any reference to specific forms of racial discrimination. This decision did not affect the already adopted article on apartheid, a matter of obvious concern and importance to the numerous African delegations.

The Israeli representative, Michael Comay, opposed the Greek-Hungarian move, insisting that anti-Semitism should be expressly mentioned in the convention. He pointed out that the convention owed its origins to the manifestations of anti-Semitism in a number of countries in 1959 and 1960. He considered the Soviet amendment bracketing Zionism with anti-Semitism, Nazism, and neo-Nazism "an affront to Israel and to the Jewish people everywhere."[41] Even so, the resolution was adopted by a vote of 82 to 12, with 10 abstentions.

Regarding the shift in the Soviet stance, Natan Lerner, in his book on the convention, observed that it

> may be explained in many ways. The developments around the position of the Jewish minority in Russia, as well as the increasing Soviet involvement in the Middle East conflict, obviously played a major role. While this seems to be beyond doubt, it is however regrettable that one of the most persistent manifestations of racial discrimination and prejudice in the history of mankind, and precisely the one that most directly put into motion the United Nations effort that led to the Convention, should not have been mentioned, at least in the Preamble. This exclusion is still more striking since it was agreed to mention apartheid in the Preamble, in addition to a special article on it.[42]

The Convention on the Elimination of All Forms of Racial Discrimination was adopted unanimously, 106 to 0, on December 21, 1965. Mexico registered the sole abstention but later announced that it was voting in favor of the convention. Despite the regrettable fact that the convention makes no specific reference to anti-Semitism, it is clearly one of the transgressions that the convention condemns, declares punishable, and attempts to eliminate.[43]

Certain countries, and particularly the United States, had problems with Article 4, under which the States Parties would "declare an offence punishable by law all ideas based on racial superiority or hatred" and "shall declare illegal and prohibit organizations . . . which promote and incite racial discrimination." This language is clearly in conflict with the rights of freedom of speech and assembly guaranteed in the First Amendment to the U.S. Constitution. These problems were somewhat mitigated by the addition of the phrase "with due regard to the principles embodied in the Universal Declaration and the rights expressly set forth in Article 5 of the Convention." (Article 5 includes the right to freedom of opinion and expression and freedom of peaceful assembly and association.) This phrase was introduced on the initiative of the U.S. delegation. In signing the convention, the United States declared: "The Constitution of the United States contains provisions for the protection of individual rights, such as the right of free speech, and nothing in this Convention shall be deemed to require or to authorize legislation or other action by the United States of America incompatible with the Constitution of the United States of America."[44] To date the United States has not become a party to the convention, its rationale being the same one that kept it from ratifying the Genocide Convention for forty years.

THE CONVENTION ON THE NON-APPLICABILITY OF STATUTORY LIMITATIONS TO WAR CRIMES AND CRIMES AGAINST HUMANITY

In many respects the Convention on the Non-Applicability of Statutory Limitations to War Crimes and Crimes against Humanity, in 1968, marked a watershed. It was the last U.N. convention to deal expressly with the Holocaust and war crimes and crimes against humanity. Moreover, the Soviet bloc countries and Israel supported the convention, whereas in subsequent years the bloc turned strongly against Israel. And most Western European and Latin American countries, as well as Canada, New Zealand, and the United States, which had stood together with Israel on most important issues before the United Nations, did not support the convention. Israel found itself voting with a group of African and Asian nations and the Soviet bloc, by and large the very countries that were to make the U.N. General Assembly an uncomfortable place for Israel during the next two decades. This voting lineup resulted in part from the inclusion of "inhuman acts resulting from the policy of apartheid" along with war crimes. The convention was approved in the Third Committee by a vote of 58 to 6, with 32 abstentions.

Article 1, the source of the most problems for Western and Latin American delegations, reads as follows:

> No statutory limitation shall apply to the following crimes, irrespective of the date of their commission:

826

(a) War crimes as they are defined in the Charter of the International Military Tribunal, Nürnberg, of 8 August 1945 and confirmed by resolutions 3 (1) of 13 February 1946 and 95 (1) of 11 December 1946 of the General Assembly of the United Nations, particularly the "grave breaches" enumerated in the Geneva Conventions of 12 August 1949 for the protection of war victims;

(b) Crimes against humanity whether committed in time of war or in time of peace as they are defined in the Charter of the International Military Tribunal, Nürnberg, of 8 August 1945 and confirmed by resolutions 3 (1) of 11 December 1946 of the General Assembly of the United Nations, eviction by armed attack or occupation and inhuman acts resulting from the policy of apartheid, and the crime of genocide as defined in the 1948 Convention on the Prevention and Punishment of the Crime of Genocide, even if such acts do not constitute violations of the domestic law of the country in which they were committed.[45]

Jean Picker, the U.S. representative in the General Assembly's Third Committee, explaining her negative vote, expressed regret that the convention as adopted would not receive the broadest possible respect among governments, scholars, lawyers, and the public in general. Article 1 (a), in her view, should have made clear that the convention related only to war crimes of a grave nature. She also felt that Article 1 (b) had been very poorly drafted and lacked the clarity and precision required in a legal document.[46] France also objected to Article 1, "which created new and dangerously vague offenses termed 'crimes against humanity' and confused the drafting of a legal instrument which would have serious consequences in the political field with the enunciation of a political doctrine." Similar objections were raised by the representatives of Argentina, the United Kingdom, Belgium, the Netherlands, Canada, Austria, Italy, Finland, Mexico, and Brazil.[47] It is noteworthy that a number of these countries had been the victims of Nazi war crimes.

While Israel may have had some misgivings about the inadequacies, it nevertheless voted in favor of the convention. Given the enormity of the crimes committed against the Jews, Israel would have found it difficult not to support a convention that removed statutory limitations on those crimes. In doing so, it found itself in the strange company of the Arabs and the Soviet bloc. But as Israeli delegate Shabtai Rosenne stated, his country felt that the convention answered a real need, since a large number of Nazi criminals had evaded punishment.

THE UPSURGE OF ANTI-ZIONISM

Thus, in its first twenty-three years the United Nations adopted a series of declarations and conventions condemning racism, which had reached its climax in the Holocaust. Moreover, the support for the establishment of a Jewish state was, for many governments, linked to their sympathy for the survivors of the Holocaust. Two major factors led to a change in the attitudes of the majority. The first was the entry into the United Nations of more than a hundred new countries. Most of these were African and Asian former European colonies. The Holocaust was not part of their experience. They were much more concerned with anticolonialism and making demands on the West for economic assistance. They formed a nonaligned movement of some 120 countries that dominated the agenda and the resolutions of the General

Assembly. With 21 Arab countries among them, they were usually inclined to go along with the Arabs on anti-Israel moves in usually tacit exchange for Arab support on anticolonial and antiapartheid resolutions.

The other major change was in the position of the Soviet Union. The Soviets had given full support to General Assembly Resolution 181 (II)A, November 29, 1947, calling for the partition of Palestine, the establishment of Jewish and Arab states, and the termination of the British mandate for Palestine. By 1961, however, the Soviet attitude toward Zionism at the United Nations had changed profoundly.

In the Soviet Union itself there had been virulent anti-Semitism during Stalin's last years, manifestations of which led to the anticosmopolitan campaign and the Doctors' Plot. In the late 1950s Nikita Khrushchev embarked on a general antireligious campaign that became vicious when it was applied to Judaism. When Jewish nongovernmental organizations such as the Consultative Council of Jewish Organizations, Agudat Israel, and the Women's International Zionist Organization submitted documents on these matters to the Commission on Human Rights and its Subcommission on the Prevention of Discrimination and the Protection of Minorities, Soviet representatives at the United Nations attacked them. They termed the documents "slanderous," rudely interrupted statements being made by the representatives of these organizations, and attempted to have their consultative status with the United Nations taken away.[48]

In their campaign of vilification Soviet representatives regularly equated Israel with the Nazis. This was particularly so in the period following the Six-Day War, when the Soviets were embittered by the quick, decisive defeat of Egypt and Syria, both of which had been armed with Soviet weapons. Ambassador Nikolai Fedorenko, speaking in the Security Council on June 9, 1967, denounced Israel's move into Syria as following in "the bloody footsteps of Hitler's executioners."[49] Ten days later Prime Minister Aleksei Kosygin, speaking at the opening of the Fifth Emergency Special Session of the General Assembly, stated: "In the same way as Hitler's Germany used to appoint gauleiters in the occupied regions, the Israeli government is establishing an occupation administration in the territories it has seized and is appointing military governors there."[50]

Similarly, the prime minister of Ukraine denounced "the Israeli invaders, whose actions and arguments remind us so much of the black days of Hitler's aggression." As that special session was drawing to a close on July 4, 1967, Soviet Foreign Minister Andrei Gromyko charged that "the propagandists from Tel Aviv . . . sing . . . Old Goebbels songs," and his Ukrainian counterpart stated that the "perfidy" of Israel's rulers was "comparable to [that of] rulers of Hitler's Germany."[51] This distorted comparison was quickly picked up by the Arab and other Moslem countries. After the Six-Day War, Jordan's representative declared that the Israelis "are using the same tactics as those used by the Nazis," and similar language was employed by the representatives of Egypt, Syria, Mauritania, Mali, and Guinea.[52]

The Soviet equivalence of Zionism with fascism (Nazism) was reiterated starkly and graphically by Ambassador Yakov Malik in 1971. Addressing the Security Council on September 25, he said: "Mr. Tekoah [the Israeli ambassador to the United Nations] was indignant at our parallel between Zionism and fascism. But why not? . . . Both are racist ideologies. . . . The chosen people: is that not racism? What is the difference between Zionism and fascism, if the essence of the ideology is racism, hatred toward other peoples?"[53]

Developments in the early 1970s strengthened the Arab position at the United Nations. The nonaligned countries came to dominate the international organization's agenda and the resolutions of the General Assembly. The Arab countries, with twenty-one votes, were frequently able to manipulate the group to support anti-Israel resolutions. Their speeches and arguments began also to equate Israel and its treatment of the Palestinian Arabs with South Africa and its apartheid policies. It followed naturally that they supported African resolutions against apartheid and denounced the South African government.

Following the Yom Kippur War of 1973 almost all African countries broke relations with Israel. By the end of 1973 only three out of forty-two African states still maintained relations with the Jewish state. When the Organization of Petroleum Exporting Countries (OPEC) successfully quadrupled the price of oil in 1974, many of the poorer, developing countries saw this act as a successful defiance of the West and viewed the newly enriched Arab oil producers as a potential source of substantial aid.[54]

In the summer of 1975 the linkage of Zionism with racism (and apartheid) was vigorously pressed in various international forums by a coalition of Soviet and Arab countries. In July the World Conference of the International Women's Year in Mexico City called for the elimination of various racist evils, including Zionism. Soon afterward the Organization of African Unity (OAU), meeting in Uganda, labeled Zionism "a danger to world peace" and called for a campaign against "the racist, aggressive nature of the Zionist entity." A similar resolution was adopted in August by a conference of nonaligned nations in Lima, Peru.[55]

Thus the groundwork was laid for action at the General Assembly's Thirtieth Session. An item on the launching of a Decade for Action to Combat Racism and Racial Discrimination was referred to the Third Committee. Under this item more than twenty nonaligned delegations sponsored a draft resolution citing condemnations of Zionism voiced in Mexico, Uganda, and Peru and confirming "that Zionism is a form of racism and racial discrimination." Not all of the members of the OAU and the nonaligned movement were prepared to support the draft resolution. Most of the Latin American countries and some African countries opposed the draft because they considered it anti-Semitic and thought that it would likely hinder peace efforts in the Middle East and certainly disturb the consensus reached on the program for the Decade for Action to Combat Racism and Racial Discrimination. In fact, the resolution did just that: the United States and a number of other important Western countries withheld their support for the program. U.N. Secretary-General Kurt Waldheim, concerned about the damage the resolution would do to the standing of the United Nations in the United States and Western Europe, tried unofficially to get Iran to exert its influence to thwart it.[56]

The U.S. permanent representative, Daniel Patrick Moynihan, made a number of eloquent, impassioned speeches against the resolution in an effort to defeat it. This strategy may have backfired. Certain African delegates thought that the resolution might have been deferred or sidetracked had he not highlighted the issue.[57] In any event, on November 19, 1975, the General Assembly adopted Resolution 3379 by a vote of 72 to 35, with 32 abstentions. Among those voting in favor were the Arab and other Islamic countries, the Soviet bloc, China, Brazil, Cuba, India, and Yugoslavia. Among those voting against were Canada, Australia, New Zealand, the United States, the Central African Republic, the Ivory Coast, Malawi, Swaziland, and most European and Latin American countries.

There can be little doubt that adoption of this resolution was a major reason for the decline in U.S. support of the United Nations. In the Soviet Union it was used to provide a cloak of legitimacy to a major campaign of vicious anti-Semitism.[58] Many of the African and other nonaligned countries realized that they had been led astray by the Soviets and Arabs.[59] Thus, in the fall of 1984, when the General Assembly's Third Committee was considering the program for a second U.N. Decade for Action to Combat Racism and Racial Discrimination, a Soviet attempt to include a reference to "Zionism equals racism" was defeated by the Western and moderate Third World countries.[60]

The public perception of a decline in the United Nations' integrity and fairness was accentuated by the scandal surrounding Kurt Waldheim, who was secretary-general from 1971 to 1981. During Waldheim's campaign to become president of Austria in 1986 it was revealed that he had served as an intelligence officer with German army units involved in war crimes in Yugoslavia and Greece. These crimes included the murder of Yugoslav civilians, the execution of captured British commandos, and the deportation of Jews to concentration camps. In his memoirs, *In the Eye of the Storm,* Waldheim carefully avoided any mention of his wartime service in the Balkans and repeatedly lied about it to his closest associates in the U.N. Secretariat.[61] There is no evidence that Waldheim ordered, incited, or personally committed a war crime. But whatever qualms he might have had about the Nazi crimes in the Balkans, he did nothing to stop or impede them. Indeed, as a bureaucratic accessory, he was part of the deadly machine. The intelligence reports he processed included information used by Nazi military authorities in identifying targets for destruction.[62]

Waldheim appears to have been more an opportunist than a Jew-hater. Indeed, he appeared to go out of his way to cultivate American Jews in New York. Each of his last three books was written with the help of a Jew. His lawyer and doctor in New York were both Jewish, as is Lord Weidenfeld, a former classmate in Vienna and the publisher of several of his books. And he showed no evidence of anti-Semitism during his ten years as secretary-general.[63] It should be noted that the United States, Britain, France, and the Soviet Union all supported him for a third five-year term in 1981. Waldheim's reelection was blocked only by China, which vetoed it not as a criticism of the Austrian but because the country believed it was time for a secretary-general from the Third World. Even Israel raised no question about Waldheim's wartime record during his campaigns for secretary-general in 1971, 1976, and 1981.[64]

As time passes, the interest of governments in Nazi activities is waning. This change is illustrated by their attitudes toward opening the files of the U.N. War Crimes Commission (UNWCC). When the UNWCC, a body independent of the United Nations, was dissolved in 1948, those materials in the archives that were not returned to the governments that had provided them were placed in the custody of the United Nations. At that time rules for access were drawn up by the U.N. Secretariat in consultation with the legal adviser and the former chairman of the commission. Under these rules a large part of the material was made available for "serious research." However, the individual charge files were subject to restrictions "in order to preserve their confidentiality as they contain information which, for the most part, has not been communicated to the individuals concerned and not subject to judicial evaluation."[65] This restriction also applied to the lists of war criminals, suspects, and witnesses; related indexes; and the formal charges and related papers. These restricted records could be inspected and used only for official U.N. purposes, meaning the prosecution of war crimes. Access was granted only to governments for that purpose upon written request and with the understanding that the records were strictly confidential and were to be handled on the same basis of confidentiality as any other material being used in a criminal investigation would be.[66]

These rules for access remained unchallenged by any government for thirty-seven years. Then in May 1986 Ambassador Benjamin Netanyahu of Israel addressed a letter to Secretary-General Xavier Perez de Cuellar requesting that he "take the immediate steps necessary to ensure free access to the general public to all the material stored in the archives of the United Nations War Crimes Commission."

Netanyahu's move was made on his own initiative. Following the public revelations of Waldheim's wartime activities, Netanyahu informed the government of Israel that he intended to examine the files of the UNWCC for information on Waldheim. He took along members of his staff who could read the various languages involved in the documents and made photostatic copies of relevant materials. In the process he noticed the thousands of files stored in the building and decided to request free access to all of them. Again the Israeli government did not object to his proposed action.[67]

Perez de Cuellar decided that any changes in the rules should be made only after consultation with the seventeen governments that had been members of the UNWCC. (The Soviets had been invited but refused to join.) The first consultation revealed that most of the governments were reluctant to change the rule to provide wider access to the files. Initially, only Australia gave its agreement, followed by the Netherlands and Yugoslavia. Then the Israelis, with a nod from the secretary-general, went public. For a year and a half they lobbied the other governments and fed related stories to the press, especially the *New York Times.* The United States then changed its stance, and after that most of the other governments fell into line. Most reluctant were Poland and France, the latter contending that the files should remain closed until one hundred years after the death of the individuals concerned. Perhaps the French were aware that the files contained charges against many of their nationals, including some who were currently involved in French politics. This might explain their reluctance to see a Pandora's box opened, particularly since some of the charges that had not been investigated might have been false and malicious. Meanwhile, the secretary-general had been beleaguered by those who wanted the files opened. Finally he indicated that unless the rules were changed, he would hand all the files back to the governments concerned. In due course, having ascertained that no government would protest vehemently, he went ahead with liberalizing access.[68]

RECENT CHANGES IN THE POLITICAL CLIMATE

Changes in the world political situation have resulted in a marked improvement in Israel's standing at the United Nations. After the dramatic political upheavals in Eastern Europe in 1988–89 most of the new regimes restored diplomatic relations with Israel. Russia has restored relations with Israel and has permitted Jews to leave for Israel in numbers that vastly exceed the small trickle of exodus it had allowed in the 1980s. Of course, the new openness has also permitted anti-Semitism to surface in deeply disturbing ways. However, the official positions of the governments as manifested at the United Nations have become more favorably disposed toward Israel. Also, many other countries, notably in Africa, have restored or initiated diplomatic relations with Israel, which in the 1990s has diplomatic ties with twice as many countries (over 110) as it did in the 1980s. These changes are also reflected at the United Nations.

The clearest evidence of Israel's improved position was the General Assembly's decision on December 16, 1991, to revoke its Resolution 3379 of 1975 equating Zionism with racism. The vote was 111 to 25, with 13 abstentions.[69] The 111 affirmative votes are particularly impressive; they constitute more than three times the number of countries that stood with Israel in voting against Resolution 3379 in 1975. The majority included virtually all the members of the Soviet bloc, plus an overwhelming majority of African, Asian, Latin American, and European countries. The 25 negative votes came from Islamic countries and three radical Communist regimes, in Vietnam, Cuba, and North Korea. Even among Islamic countries, Turkey abstained, while Bahrain, Egypt, Kuwait, Morocco, Niger, Oman, Senegal, and Tunisia were absent. China was also absent.

Another indication of the altered political climate is the decline in support for a proposal that would reject the credentials of the delegation of Israel and thus deny it participation in the General Assembly. Such action has been taken against only one other member state, South Africa in 1974, which was not able to participate in the General Assembly until the government of Nelson Mandela took power. Attempts to apply the same tactic of exclusion against Israel began in 1982. U.S. Secretary of State George Shultz met this attempt head-on. Speaking to the General Assembly, Shultz stated bluntly that such action would be a clear violation of the U.N. Charter, would create further conflict and division, and would do grave damage to the entire U.N. system. He warned that if the action were taken, the United States would withdraw from participation in the General Assembly and withhold its assessed contribution. His warning, made more credible by the withdrawal of the U.S. delegation to the Conference of the International Atomic Energy Agency following the rejection of Israeli credentials there, had a strong impact on U.N. delegations. Moreover, Secretary-General Perez de Cuellar forcefully lobbied against the attempt to expel Israel, arguing that it would spell disaster for the organization.[70]

The majority of Arab nations then backed away from such action, whereupon Iran attempted to bring the issue to a vote. That attempt was easily blocked through a procedural move by Finland that won overwhelming support.[71] Attempts to exclude Israel continued, but support for them declined as Israel's political position improved.

Another indication of the changing political environment was witnessed in March 1994. The U.N. Commission on Human Rights adopted a resolution, L 14 Rev. 1, which, for the first time in thirty-four years, specifically includes anti-Semitism among the forms of "racism, racial discrimination, xenophobia and related intolerance" that persist and are even growing in magnitude.[72] While the move to include anti-Semitism was led by the United States, it is indicative of the change in the international political climate that Russia, Hungary, Poland, and Romania joined the sponsoring group.

Despite this marked improvement in Israel's political position, the General Assembly, dominated as it is by the nonaligned countries, has continued year after year to adopt resolutions biased against Israel.[73] It is disheartening that this bias has superseded the wave of sympathy that was extended to the Jewish people and their new state, Israel, in the years following the Holocaust. It should be noted, however, that General Assembly resolutions, while some of them may have a damaging propaganda impact, are not binding on governments. Only the Security Council can make such binding decisions, and there Israel has received fairer treatment. While the nonaligned countries can put together a blocking majority in the Security Council, they cannot by themselves force the council to take action. The United States can veto any resolution it considers unfair or ill-advised. In numerous instances it has done so. In others it has used the threat of a veto to negotiate a more balanced text.

The Security Council has also taken a number of actions that have been useful to Israel, notably the positioning of a U.N. peacekeeping force between the Egyptian and Israeli forces in 1973, which forestalled a Soviet-U.S. confrontation on the Suez Canal and eventually helped to bring peace between Egypt and Israel. Shortly thereafter the Security Council placed a force in the Golan Heights, which has helped to keep that border peaceful for two decades.[74] The Security Council also produced Resolution 242 of November 22, 1967, which has been accepted by both Israel and its Arab neighbors as a basis for negotiation. The resolution calls for a just and lasting peace in the Middle East to include the application of both the following principles: "(i) Withdrawal of Israeli armed forces from territories occupied in the recent conflict" and "(ii) Termination of all claims or states of belligerency and respect for the acknowledgment of the sovereignty, territorial integrity and political independence of every state in the area and their right to live in peace within secure and recognized boundaries free from threats or acts of force."[75] These provisions are noteworthy in that they make Israel's withdrawal contingent on peace with its neighbors and do not call for withdrawal to the boundary lines existing on June 5,

1967, when the Six-Day War started. The resolution further provides that the settlements be negotiated by the parties themselves, as was done in the peace agreements between Israel and Egypt and Israel and Jordan, not dictated from outside. On a few occasions over the past fifty years the United States has not vetoed a Security Council resolution opposed by Israel, but these instances have been rare and none has done damage to Israel. Thus, where it can be seriously hurt, Israel has been protected against blatant unfairness.

NOTES

1. United Nations, *Yearbook of the United Nations, 1946–47* (New York, 1947).

2. Nachum Goldman to the Jewish Agency, New York, September 11, 1946, cable reporting the decision by the Jewish Agency Executive, Zionist Archives, Jerusalem.

3. *Worldmark Encyclopedia of the Nations,* 4th ed. (New York, 1971), 108.

4. Address by Frederico Mayor, director general of UNESCO, Granada, Spain, December 8, 1993; the occasion of the address was an international symposium convened by UNESCO following the agreement negotiated in Washington, D.C., by Israel and the PLO.

5. Walter Laves and Charles A. Thompson, *UNESCO: Purpose, Progress, Prospects* (Bloomington, Ind., 1957), 27.

6. UNESCO, 2 c/Res IX Annex VII (12).

7. Laves and Thompson, *UNESCO.* Laves was the deputy director general.

8. David S. Wyman, *The Abandonment of the Jews: America and the Holocaust, 1941–1945* (New York, 1984), 157–58.

9. Edward J. Osmanczyk, *Encyclopedia of the United Nations and International Agreements* (Philadelphia, 1985), 66.

10. U.N. General Assembly Official Records (GAOR), Second Session, Supplement 11, 1947.

11. Jacob Robinson, *Palestine and the United Nations: Prelude to Solution* (Washington, D.C., 1947), 204.

12. GAOR, Second Session, Supplement 11, 1947.

13. Ibid., 48.

14. United Nations, *Yearbook of the United Nations, 1947–48* (New York, 1949), 227–56.

15. All quotations in this section are from GA Doc. A/P.V.207, May 12, 1949. The roll-call vote was as follows: Voting in favor of the proposal were the Union of Soviet Socialist Republics, the United States of America, Uruguay, Venezuela, Yugoslavia, Argentina, Australia, Bolivia, the Byelorussian Soviet Socialist Republic, Canada, Chile, China, Colombia, Costa Rica, Cuba, Czechoslovakia, the Dominican Republic, Ecuador, France, Guatemala, Haiti, Honduras, Iceland, Liberia, Luxembourg, Mexico, the Netherlands, New Zealand, Nicaragua, Norway, Panama, Peru, the Philippines, Poland, the Ukrainian Soviet Socialist Republic, and the Union of South Africa. Voting against were Yemen, Afghanistan, Burma, Egypt, Ethiopia, India, Iran, Iraq, Lebanon, Pakistan, Saudi Arabia, and Syria. And abstaining were the United Kingdom, Belgium, Brazil, Denmark, Salvador, Greece, Siam, Sweden, and Turkey.

16. *Who Was Who in America,* vol. 3 (Chicago, 1966).

17. Raphael Lemkin, *Axis Rule in Occupied Europe: Laws of Occupation, Analysis of Government, Proposals for Redress* (Washington, D.C., 1944).

18. Raphael Lemkin to the editor of the *New York Times,* November 8, 1949, editorial page.

19. *Report of the Ad Hoc Committee on Genocide,* U.N. Doc. E 1794, May 10, 1948.

20. Hannah Loewy (unpaid assistant to Lemkin during the drafting of the Genocide Convention), interview by author, June 28, 1990, New York.

21. GAOR, Third Session, 178th meeting, December 9, 1948.

22. Ibid.

23. Truman, quoted in William Korey, "The Embarrassed American," *Saturday Review,* October 31, 1964, 24.

24. U.S. Congress, Senate, Subcommittee on the United Nations Charter, *Human Rights, Domestic Jurisdiction and the United Nations Charter,* 84th Cong., 1st sess. (Washington, D.C., 1955), 11–12, 17–20.

25. Korey, "The Embarrassed American," 25.

26. William Korey, "On Banning Genocide: 'We Should Have Been the First,'" *World Magazine,* September 1972, 28–32.

27. William Korey, "Time to Adopt the First Human Rights Treaty," *Wall Street Journal,* March 15, 1979.

28. GAOR, Doc. A/Conf. 1/6, March 15, 1950, 1–3.

29. GAOR, Fifth Session, Plenary Meetings, November 16, 1950, 388–90.

30. U.N. Security Council (UNSC) Doc. S/4342, sec. 1, June 3, 1960.

31. U.N. Security Council Official Records (UNSCOR), 865th meeting, June 22, 1960.

32. Ibid., 866th meeting, June 24, 1960.

33. Ibid.

34. Ibid., 867th meeting, June 24, 1960.

35. Ibid.

36. Resolution of the U.N. Sub-Commission on Prevention of Discrimination and Protection of Minorities, January 1960, in U.N. Economic and Social Council (ECOSOC) Doc. E/CN 4/800, par. 163.

37. ECOSOC Res. 826 B (XXXII), July 27, 1961.

38. GA Res. 1780 (XII), December 7, 1962.

39. Natan Lerner, *The U.N. Convention on the Elimination of All Forms of Racial Discrimination* (Rockville, Md., 1980), 2–3.

40. Ibid., 70–71.

41. Ibid., 71.

42. Ibid., 72–73.

43. Ibid., 72.

44. GA Doc. A/C/SR 1373, November 1965.

45. Convention on the Non-Applicability of Statutory Limitations to War Crimes and Crimes against Humanity, November 26, 1968.

46. Ibid., par. 11.

47. Ibid., pars. 11–24.

48. William Korey, "Soviet Anti-semitism at the UN," in *Anti-semitism: Threat to Western Civilization,* ed. M. Z. Rosensaft and Yehuda Bauer (Jerusalem, 1988), 52–82.

49. UNSCOR, 22d year, S/PV 1352, June 9, 1967, 6.

50. Aleksei Kosygin, quoted in Korey, "Soviet Anti-semitism," 72.

51. Ibid., 73–74.

52. Ibid., 74–75.

53. Ibid., 84.

54. S. M. Finger and Z. Flamhaft, "The Issue of Zionism and Racism in the United Nations," *Middle East Review* 18, no. 3 (1986), 49–52.

55. Korey, "Soviet Anti-semitism," 87.

56. S. M. Finger and A. A. Saltzman, *Bending with the Winds: Kurt Waldheim and the United Nations* (New York, 1990), 50.

57. S. M. Finger, *American Ambassadors at the U.N.* (New York, 1988), 240–41.

58. Korey, "Soviet Anti-semitism," 87–102.

59. Dr. James Jonah (a national of Sierra Leone and under-secretary-general at the United Nations with widespread contacts with African delegations), interview by author, October 1992, New York.

60. Korey, "Soviet Anti-semitism," 87.

61. Kurt Waldheim, *In the Eye of the Storm* (Bethesda, Md., 1986); Finger and Saltzman, *Bending with the Winds,* 1.

62. Finger and Saltzman, *Bending with the Winds,* 9–10. See also Robert Edwin Herzstein, *Waldheim: The Missing Years* (New York, 1988); and World Jewish Congress, *Waldheim's Nazi Past* (New York, 1988).

63. Finger and Saltzman, *Bending with the Winds,* 75.

64. Ibid., 36.

65. GA Doc. A/41/1343, May 16, 1986.

66. U.N. Press Release SG/SM 3864, May 2, 1986.

67. Benjamin Netanyahu (deputy foreign minister of Israel), interview by author, August 8, 1986, Jerusalem.

68. Finger and Saltzman, *Bending with the Winds,* 36–38.

69. GA Res. 46/86, December 16, 1991. For the text and the recorded vote, see U.N. Press Release GA/8307, January 21, 1992, 58.

70. Finger, *American Ambassadors,* 304–5.

71. Ibid., 305.

72. *Report of the U.N. Commission on Human Rights on its 50th Session,* Doc. E/1994/24, June 5, 1994, 185–86.

73. For a detailed account of the General Assembly's anti-Israel, pro-PLO bias, see Harris Schoenberg, *A Mandate for Terror: The United Nations and the PLO* (New York, 1989); and Yehuda Blum, *Eroding the United Nations Charter* (Boston, 1993).

74. Brian Urquhart, *A Life in Peace and War* (New York, 1987), 239–43, 249–53.

75. S. M. Finger, *A New World Balance and Peace in the Middle East: Reality or Mirage?* (Cranbury, N.J., 1975), 258–61.

ISRAEL
Dalia Ofer

In the Israel of the 1990s there are opposing perspectives concerning what some would call the meaning, and others the demeaning, of the Holocaust. The ongoing dialogue regarding the Holocaust is an effort to fathom its significance. Thus the visual arts, films, theater, music, and folk songs, together with historical and social science research, reflect the genuine interest Israelis from different walks of life have in Holocaust images, conceptions, and reconstructed reality.

In this essay I analyze the impact of the Holocaust on the life of Israel, as a Jewish and Zionist state, in the context of a social, political, and cultural reality that contains many other elements. The awareness, and in some respects the fear, that the experience of the Holocaust might determine the very nature of Jewish social and intellectual life loomed over the state of Israel during its first decade. At the same time, there was a concern that the memory of the Holocaust might fade away and that the memory of Jewish life in Europe, which had been destroyed, would disappear, thus fulfilling Hitler's aim of obliterating the Jews.

The Holocaust was often mentioned in the country's political discourse in relation to both internal and external issues, including, for example, Israel's place among the family of nations; the uniqueness of Jewish history, which had prevented the Jews from becoming a "normal people"; and the intents of the Palestinian Liberation Organization (PLO) and the Arab states to destroy Israel. Concurrently, the collective memory of Israeli society was being shaped and conditioned to contemplate the relationship between present and past. The memory of the Holocaust is dynamic, and many individual recollections and testimonies have entered the "collective knowledge." As Saul Friedländer put it: "The representation of the *Shoah,* although more widespread than ever, is not crystallizing in the historical consciousness of the victims, as well as in general public discourse, into some monumental and mythical narrative; we are in fact dealing with a *non-structured public memory.*"[1]

To describe the role of the Holocaust in shaping Israelis' opinions on the political, social, and cultural affairs of their state is a very complicated task.[2] It is always difficult to isolate one factor from the many others that influence a society, and still more difficult to qualitatively measure it. Generally, clusters of factors, events, emotions, thoughts, and memories mold the self-understanding and the self-image of a society. A study of the transitions and the historical developments of Israel and the Yishuv, the Jewish community in Palestine that preceded the Jewish state, will provide an understanding of the role of the Holocaust in shaping Israeli society and politics.

In the first decade after Israel gained its independence, the patterns of commemoration of the Holocaust were established by the Israeli Knesset. Through these patterns, the symbolism that would furnish the collective memory was standardized.[3] In the 1950s and 1960s the people involved in the work of commemorative institutions largely reflected the views of Holocaust survivors, who had received most of their education before the war. Their views and ideologies contributed to the understanding of the Holocaust and its aftermath. However, the Israeli public represented a multifaceted and multivoiced discourse on the Holocaust; furthermore, a number of generations were involved. Among them we find people from different social backgrounds and different experiences, some coming from Europe and the Islamic countries, others born in Israel. The discourse, which began during the Holocaust and has continued in the dialogue between the present and the past, has been colored by various ideologies and dramatic political events that shaped the collective memory.

The reaction of Israel to the Holocaust was moved by many currents and undercurrents. Some of these were anticipated by intellectuals and politicians, while others came as a complete surprise. Throughout the years, reality produced an ongoing dialogue between the interpretation of the Holocaust and the understanding of Jewish history and Jewish destiny.

From its outset Zionism, one of the main Jewish national movements and ultimately the victorious one, was involved in political efforts to obtain for Jews the right to immigrate ("return" in its discourse) to Palestine and establish a Jewish state there. Since the late 1800s the Zionist movement had also been involved in the development of Jewish settlements in Palestine. When in 1917, toward the end of World War I, Great Britain conquered Palestine, which had been under Ottoman rule, the Zionists' hopes of accomplishing their political goals increased. In November 1917 the British foreign minister, Lord Balfour, announced in a letter to Lord Rothschild Britain's intention of establishing a Jewish national home in Palestine. The letter, known as the Balfour Declaration, was added to the Mandate charter when the League of Nations placed Palestine under British mandate for a twenty-five-year period in 1920. Hence, part of the British responsibility in Palestine was to prepare the country to become a Jewish national home.[4]

During the Mandate period, the Jews of Palestine (the Yishuv) were organized in a system of quasi self-rule containing institutions whose personnel were elected by all Jewish adults. The Va'ad Leumi (National Committee) was responsible for education, culture, health, and welfare. In 1929 the Jewish Agency (JA) was established; its tasks, as defined by the Zionist movement and the Mandate charter, were to represent the Yishuv in its relations with the Mandate government and to encourage the economic development of the Jewish sector.[5] The JA was composed of representatives of the political parties of the Zionist movement according to their proportion at the Zionist Congresses, whose electorate comprised all Jews who had paid a symbolic fee to become members of the Zionist movement. The JA also included members of non-Zionist organizations who were interested in the development of the Jewish national home.

The economic development of Jewish Palestine was aimed primarily at increasing the capacity of the country to absorb Jews, and as a result the largest share of the movement's economic resources was allocated to acquiring land and establishing agricultural settlements. One of the major causes of friction between the Jews of Palestine and the British Mandatory authorities was the application of the principle of economic absorption, which determined the number of immigrants to be allowed into the country. The authorities permitted only as many Jews to immigrate to the country as could, by their calculations, be economically absorbed. These quotas were decided following a survey, carried out by the JA, of the demand for labor in the Jewish sector. Only Jews who had capital (1,000 or 500 pounds sterling, depending on their occupation) could immigrate without restrictions.

The JA could not impose taxes, this right being reserved for the Mandatory authorities, but it could appeal for voluntary contributions. The resources for the development of Palestine came from Jewish contributions to Zionist funds, and as a result the Zionist budget was dependent on economic and political conditions outside Palestine. For the internal needs of the Yishuv, such as education, welfare, and health, very limited public funds were made available, partly by the government of Palestine and partly by institutions such as the Histadrut, the labor federation.[6]

The Yishuv was a highly politicized community, divided on the left into a variety of socialist Zionist parties. In 1930 these parties combined to form one majority labor party, Mapai, headed by David Ben-Gurion. The unity of Mapai was very fragile, as a deep rift developed between the middle-of-the-road socialists and a large Marxist minority. The two major leaders of the Marxist Left were Yitzhak Tabenkin of the Kibbutz Me'uhad (United Kibbutz), the largest kibbutz movement, and Meir Ya'ari (who was not affiliated with Mapai) of Hashomer Hatza'ir (the Young Guard), an elitist youth movement that had established a number of kibbutzim in Palestine. All the segments of Mapai had affiliated youth movements in Palestine and abroad in the Diaspora. The central goal of these youth movements was to promote immigration to Palestine and life on a kibbutz.

To the right of the political spectrum was the radical nationalist conservative Revisionist Party, with its Betar youth movement in the Diaspora and Palestine, headed by Ze'ev Jabotinsky. In 1935 the Revisionists seceded from the Zionist movement and established the New Zionist Organization (Hatzah). Thus the Revisionists did not participate in the JA. The main political conflicts in the Yishuv were between

Labor and the Revisionists and extended to all topics, such as social economic policy and the policy to be adopted toward the British rulers.[7] The largest party in the center was the Tziyonim Klaliyim (General Zionists), which also had a number of affiliated youth movements. Two major religious parties represented the religious community: the Mizrahi (Religious Zionists), whose youth affiliated in Palestine and the Diaspora with Bnei Akiva (Sons of Akiva), and Agudat Israel (Union of Israel), an anti-Zionist movement.[8]

The Yishuv (except for the minority of non-Zionists such as Agudat Israel and Neturei Karta [City Guardians], another extreme religious group) saw itself as an elite vanguard preparing the ground for Jewish autonomy and later independence in Palestine. It was the Zionists' plan that the Jewish masses would eventually join their enterprise in Palestine, following a thorough transformation. The Jewish people would go from being a people living in the Diaspora, which did not allow for regular economic and social activities, to being a people who could live on their own land and conduct their own enterprises. This view reflected the Zionists' hopes that the Jewish people would thus be normalized and return to history as a nation among nations and thus contribute their ingenuity to humanity. It reflected a strong existential negation of Diaspora life, where Jews as a minority were perceived as unable to live in freedom and as impaired socially, politically, and culturally.[9] It was in this context that the Zionist idea regarding the commitment of Diaspora Jewry to the well-being of the Yishuv was formulated. The Zionists needed all possible support to lay the foundations for the accomplishment of their mission. This challenged Zionism with a great educational goal and demanded that Diaspora Jews provide substantial human and economic support for the development of Palestine.

At the beginning of the 1930s the Yishuv numbered some 170,000 people, almost three times as many as in 1920. However, it was still smaller than the average medium-sized Jewish community in Poland. Cities such as Warsaw and Lodz each had more Jews than there were in all of Palestine, and the number of Jews in Germany was almost three times as large as the number in Palestine. The Yishuv was slowly recovering from an economic depression that had brought immigration almost to a halt and caused increased emigration from the country. This recovery was enhanced by the first wave of German Jews to arrive in Palestine after the initial shock of the Nazi rise to power. This wave consisted mostly of Zionists, who were able to bring some of their belongings with them.

Six years later, by the time World War II broke out, the Yishuv's population had almost tripled, to slightly more than half a million Jews. In spite of this demographic growth, the Jews remained a minority in the country, which had some three-quarters of a million Arab inhabitants. This relative weakness was reflected in the development of the Palestinian Arab national movement in the mid-1930s, which demanded the establishment of an Arab state in Palestine. A major threat to the Palestinian Arabs was the growing immigration of Jews to the country, and as a precondition to any talks with the British the Arabs demanded an end to Jewish immigration.[10]

The World Reacts to the Holocaust

The First Stage of the War, 1933–1941

Nazism confronted Zionist ideology with a frightening perspective, confirming the most dire predictions concerning the fate of the Jews in the Diaspora. The violence of Nazi anti-Semitism, the indifference of most Germans toward the assaults against the Jews, and the participation of non-Nazis in depriving German Jews of their basic human and civil rights could all be understood as the awful realization of what Theodor Herzl, the founder of the Zionist movement, had predicted. Herzl believed that violence was unavoidable for Jews who could not or would not assimilate in their non-Jewish societies and would not separate themselves from the European societies. Anti-Semitism was a central element in the relationship between Jews and non-Jews in history, and Zionist analysis pointed to the increasing difficulty for Jews of leading a normal Jewish life in modern times in the countries where they resided. Herzl cited the widespread anti-Semitism generated by the Dreyfus Affair (1894) in Paris. He understood it as the social, political, and cultural reaction of national groups that resented the attempt of another minority—the Jews—to integrate in their midst. Herzl thought that anti-Semitism might disappear if the Jews separated themselves from the European societies and established their own independent Jewish state. This, he conjectured, would happen with the help of the European countries.[11]

Historical developments did not conform to Herzl's theory. At the Versailles peace talks the Zionists favored a British mandate (which would include the Balfour Declaration, a document somewhat similar to the charter Herzl had in mind). At the same time, the European Jews made major progress in their own emancipation and in their involvement in their own societies. Thus, the Zionist enterprise in Palestine and the building of the Yishuv proceeded while many new horizons dawned for Jewish hopes in the Diaspora. Both the building of Palestine and the achievements of the Jews in the Diaspora, especially in Eastern Europe, involved many difficulties and disappointments, but also successes.

As a result of these successes, the crisis of German Jewry in the early 1930s was not only shocking from the human and Jewish perspectives; in the context of the ideological debate between the Zionists and the non- or anti-Zionists it also attained the status of a Judgment Day. On the one hand, it could be viewed as demonstrating how little the Jews had succeeded in integrating in the different societies: if German Jewry could suffer such a blow, there must be wider support for the Palestine option. On the other hand, it could be viewed as evidence of a danger that transcended the immediate risk to German Jewry and proved that the solution to the Jewish Problem was not to be found in immigration to Palestine, but in large-scale immigration to other territories. Thus, the implications of what was happening in Germany could be interpreted as either favoring or opposing Zionism.

The Zionist movement had to consider whether it should participate in the fight against Nazi anti-Semitism even if, as Zionist ideology had it, the chances of overcoming it were negligible. Jews in Poland and in the United States initiated a boycott of German goods after Hitler's rise to power. A demonstration of Jewish concern and solidarity, the effort gained large-scale public support in Palestine, especially among the Revisionists.[12]

In general, the Yishuv's Zionist leaders examined Zionist ideological tenets in relation to two major issues: the timespan required for the implementation of Zionist goals and the selection of immigrants. The events of the first months after Hitler's rise to power moved major leaders of the labor movement, such as Chaim Arlosoroff (who was murdered in June 1933), Ben-Gurion (who was elected chairman of the JA at the Zionist Congress of 1933), and others, to express the belief that Nazism had forced the Yishuv to adopt a more rapid pace for building Palestine.[13] Arthur Ruppin, one of the major personalities who shaped the policy of agricultural settlement and the economy of Palestine, talked at the 1933 Zionist Congress in Prague of the immigration of 100,000 people per year for ten years. He thought the young would come to Palestine, while the others would immigrate to other countries. He urged the formulation of a policy that would use Jewish wealth from Germany, contributions from world Jewry, and the assistance of other countries to absorb German Jews and Jews from other European countries in Palestine.[14] These efforts would make the immigration of a million Jews from all over Europe feasible. At his suggestion, the Zionist Congress agreed to establish a special body to aid the immigration of German Jews, which was headed by Chaim Weizmann.[15]

In 1936 Jabotinsky proposed the emigration of a million Jews from Poland to Palestine over a ten-year period. He too thought that increasing the speed and the volume of immigration to Palestine was crucial for saving the Jews under the new anti-Semitic regime in Poland, as well as for implementing Zionism and expanding and developing the Yishuv.[16] But changing the pace of implementing the Zionist dream raised another issue: would it be carried out by *halutzim* (young pioneers), who underwent agricultural training in preparation for their move to Palestine, or by regular immigrants, particularly by the refugees whose numbers increased dramatically after 1938? This was a central issue in particular among the Labor Zionists, who shared a vision of creating in Palestine a just and socialist society. Ben-Gurion offered a flexible concept: he thought that under the new circumstances the movement should broaden its definition of the pioneer to include all young Jewish people of middle-class background who were prepared to invest, live, and work in Palestine.[17] This proposition presented a major threat to the social vision of the Left, as the regular immigrants were not pioneers and the cities and towns were growing faster than the communal settlements (kibbutzim and moshavim). Palestine was experiencing large-scale immigration for the second time (the first time had been during the years 1924–26), and the immigrants mirrored the Jewish population in Germany, Austria, Poland, and other Eastern European countries.

The policies the Yishuv adopted during the 1930s were understandably influenced greatly by the events in Europe and by the Great Arab Revolt (1936–39), caused primarily by the growing number of Jews. From the first days of the rise of Nazism the Yishuv displayed a pragmatic response that reflected both its disbelief in the possibility of defeating Hitler on the Jewish issue and the need to promote the Jewish national home. The Yishuv demonstrated its belief in the centrality of Palestine and its unique role in assuring the future of the Jewish people through three major efforts: the Transfer Agreement, Youth Aliyah, and Illegal Immigration. In each case its response reflected a facet of the Yishuv's self-understanding and its potential to be the leader of the Jewish people.

The Transfer Agreement. During the first three years of Nazi rule the Yishuv offered a haven for some 33,000 German Jews; it was a refuge for the largest number of these Jews. (Until 1936 only some 20,000 Jews immigrated to the Americas.)[18] The Yishuv was interested in ensuring that German Jews immigrated to Palestine with their property. This infusion of capital would strengthen the Palestinian economy and enable the immigration of more young Jews, people without capital, from Poland and Germany.

Jews who were ready to leave Germany faced two problems: the ban on taking out foreign exchange and the low prices they got for their property in Germany. Since the unregulated sale of Jewish assets would have caused a further decline in prices, both the Nazis and the Jews who wanted to emigrate desired an arrangement that would encourage and regulate Jewish emigration. Talks between Jewish individuals and the German authorities on this subject had already started in the spring of 1933.

The basic agreement they reached involved the transfer of the assets of German Jews to Palestine in the form of German industrial goods. A trusteeship was established to receive deposits from German Jews in local currency. Upon arrival in Palestine, the German Jews would receive their funds, partly in cash and partly in industrial bonds. At first German goods were imported to Palestine by the Yishuv's industries; later they were imported according to the planned economic policy of the Bureau for the Settlement of German Jewry, established in 1933.

It was in the Germans' interest to minimize the impact of the economic boycott against them. They hoped that in addition to encouraging Jewish immigration, the agreement would result in a market for their goods, spare parts, and industrial knowledge. This would provide them with hard currency and a future market for their products. During the first years of the Transfer Agreement, those Jews who immigrated and others who planned their immigration were able to recover a considerable percentage of their assets.

The Transfer Agreement was criticized harshly by many Jews in Palestine, by the Revisionist Party, and by many of the religious non-Zionists. In spite of its pragmatic nature, it was seen as an accommodation of Nazism. The opposition within and outside the Zionist camps claimed that the Transfer Agreement was a brutal violation of Jewish solidarity and that the Nazis' interest in it demonstrated their desperate position. Indeed, it was claimed, the Nazis' primary goal was to create friction among the Jews and undermine the development of a united Jewish front that would lead the boycott. Therefore, the opposition continued, the Yishuv leadership had adopted a deceptive and selfish policy, one that only took into account the short-term benefits to the Jews in Palestine and a relatively small number of future immigrants, thus proving its disloyalty to the general Jewish cause and values.

The Transfer Agreement helped some 19,000 German Jews to recover part of their capital and facilitated the importation into Palestine of about 8 million pounds sterling, which represented approximately 14 percent of the total Jewish capital inflow of some 55.486 million pounds sterling in the years 1933–39.[19] In 1938, after the annexation of Austria, the JA tried to reach a similar agreement for Austrian Jewry, but the Nazis immediately turned it down. The Nazis were already conducting a massive Aryanization of Jewish property and were moving toward a policy of forced emigration and expulsion.

Youth Aliyah. Although the idea of bringing young people to Palestine to be educated in the spirit of Zionism had been discussed and practiced before the rise of Nazism, after 1933 it became a major project of the Yishuv and the Zionist movement. It was ultimately headed by the prominent American Zionist Henrietta Szold.[20] In organizing Youth Aliyah (YA), the JA demonstrated its partnership with Diaspora Jewry. It aimed to benefit all the parties concerned: German Jewry, by rescuing some of its youth from the humiliation and dangers of Nazism; the free and rich Jewish communities of the West, by mobilizing their aid for a constructive program; and the Yishuv, by having it lead the project and increase the number of young people dedicated to the Zionist cause.

The project also met with British approval, and the Mandatory authorities established special immigration quotas for children between the ages of twelve and sixteen. In spite of its daring character, YA functioned very cautiously as an institution. The young people were selected according to strict guidelines related to their health, social adaptability, and family background. Children of single-parent families were refused, and cooperation with parents was considered vital. Jewish middle-class parents wanted to ensure for their children a good vocational education in Palestine.

In spite of parents' apprehensions about agricultural training and the concerns of some people in YA that they might not offer the most appropriate social and educational setting, the kibbutzim became the principal hosts of YA groups. This came about as the result of both economic considerations and an identification among the heads of YA and the JA with the values represented by the kibbutzim. Thus, YA eventually became identified with the kibbutz movement, and its success was measured by how many of its graduates joined that movement. (About 85 percent of the YA graduates between 1933 and 1939 joined established kibbutzim or established new ones.)

YA brought some 6,000 youths to Palestine between 1933 and 1939. After the war broke out, its directors had to make the rules governing the selection of candidates more flexible. Orphans and the children of refugees had to be rescued and brought to Palestine under the YA quotas. During the war years approximately 3,000 youths and children were saved in this way. Furthermore, between 1945 and the establishment of the state of Israel about 15,000 youths were brought to Palestine through YA and absorbed into kibbutzim and special youth villages and institutions. It was difficult to educate those young people who had lost their families or experienced expulsion, cruelty, or indifference to their fate about the importance of communal life and shared responsibilities. The JA assumed full responsibility for YA after Kristallnacht in November 1938. During 1939 many parents pleaded for younger children to be permitted to enroll in YA. The organization responded positively, and in later years even children as young as eight were accepted. The Mandatory government did not allocate enough entry visas to accommodate the increased demand, so the YA began to send the youngsters to other countries in Europe with the intention of arranging for their immigration to Palestine at a later time. During the summer and fall of 1939 approximately 30,000 children from Germany were sent by YA (in cooperation with other organizations) to Great Britain, Belgium, Luxembourg, the Netherlands, and the Scandinavian countries.[21] The resources of YA came from special funds, mostly from the Zionist Women (Hadassah) in the United States. The heads of the JA nevertheless viewed the YA project as a Yishuv enterprise, integrating the Yishuv's own goals with its response to Nazism.

Illegal Immigration. The phrases "illegal immigration" and "irregular immigration" were used by the British to describe the clandestine entrance of Jews into Palestine without the formal certificates required by the authorities. The Jews referred to this immigration as Aliyah Bet ("Aliyah B") or *ha'apalah.* The first term is a more neutral one, indicating the type of immigration: "A" denoted immigration with the required official certificate, "B" immigration without such a certificate. *Ha'apalah,* however, implies a strenuous climb to reach the top.[22] Although there had been illegal immigration even before the 1930s, only in the late 1930s did it become a massive movement involving thousands of Jews. At this stage, "illegal immigration" both revealed the desperate need of Jews to find safe havens and constituted a protest against the British immigration restrictions. The leadership of the JA was ambivalent about Aliyah Bet, as it challenged its authority in the selection of immigrants and threatened to impair the JA's relationship with the British, which was vital to the development of the Yishuv. Another misgiving about Aliyah Bet was that it used the means of an underground movement, which were not suitable for the Zionist movement, now recognized by the international community as a formal political entity.

In the summer of 1938 the circumstances changed, and with them the Yishuv leadership's attitude toward Aliyah Bet. The problem of Jewish refugees mounted as the Nazi policy reached the stage of forced emigration.[23] On the other hand, the British policy in Palestine was now opposed to the Jewish national home. Following the Great Arab Revolt, the British, in conjunction with the neighboring Arab states, had formulated a new policy for Palestine. The White Paper published by the British government in May 1939 announced a plan that provided for the creation of an independent Palestinian state. Jewish immigration would be limited to 75,000 people (including 25,000 refugees) during the following five years, after which the further immigration of Jews would be dependent upon Arab consent. The purchase of land by Jews would be restricted to certain areas, and a legislative council would be elected by both Arabs and Jews.[24]

The leaders of the JA debated their response to the White Paper, seeking ways to reverse its policies. Illegal immigration seemed to provide a response that linked both the needs of the Yishuv and those of the persecuted Jews in Europe. This response did not involve force but actively opposed British immigration policy on moral grounds, as denying Jewish refugees a safe haven. The British responded by detaining refugees who reached Palestine, returning them to their countries of origin or sending them to detention camps in various British colonies. These steps embarrassed the British. Although both Labor and the Revisionists agreed on the need to foster illegal immigration, the political rivalry between them resulted in non-cooperation and conflicts.[25]

From the fall of 1938 through the end of 1939, 17,240 "illegal" immigrants, or 43 percent of the total of 40,147 immigrants, reached Palestine. Ben-Gurion hoped that the embarrassment illegal immigration caused the British in the international arena and in public opinion at home would force it to reverse the policy expressed in its White Paper. At that stage his hopes proved wrong.[26]

The beginning of the war challenged the Yishuv to reconsider its political agenda. Information on the ruthless Nazi actions against Polish Jewry had reached Palestine immediately. The accounts of refugees who had fled to Romania, Hungary, and Yugoslavia were reported in the Hebrew press, which carried detailed reports on the events in Poland and reflected the fears and anxieties of the people of the Yishuv. Words such as "destruction," "annihilation," and "catastrophe" were quite common in the press and in general discourse. However, these words were used for events that, serious as they were, gave little hint of what was to happen later. The Yishuv's emissaries to Hehalutz (an umbrella organization uniting the pioneer youth groups) had left Poland shortly after the beginning of the war and reached Palestine between November 1939 and January 1940. A number of Polish Zionist leaders who had fled to the Soviet Union also arrived in Palestine during the first year of the war. All told of the terrible fate of the Jews and predicted the decimation of the Jewish population.[27]

An analysis of these reports and discussions with the Polish Zionist leaders indicates that the information concerning the events in Poland was perceived as part of the general chaos in which the civilian population was involved because of the war and the first steps of occupation, with the cruelty of the Nazis aimed at the Poles in general and the Jews in particular. The fate of the Jews in occupied Europe was seen as being tied to the developments in the war. The Committee to Aid Polish Jewry, established in September 1939, planned to help Polish Jewish refugees who had fled to the Balkan countries. It sent aid and immigration certificates to Jews in Poland and also devoted time to deliberating on the rights of Jews in postwar Poland, expressing in this way its belief that the war would end shortly.[28]

The distressing information was somewhat eased by accounts of the continuation of community life in Poland and the reconstruction of the Zionist youth movement. This information reached Palestine via Geneva, whence representatives of the Yishuv, such as the activists of illegal immigration, Hehalutz representatives, and others, kept in contact with Poland and watched the developments there. They corresponded with a number of individuals and groups affiliated with the Zionist movement. The extreme expressions of the dire fate of the Jews arriving with reports on restructuring the activities of the youth movements and the renewal of social life aroused a great deal of confusion in Palestine and among the emissaries. Some reporters suspected that the situation had been exaggerated and wrote that the chaos of the early days would no doubt be replaced by a safer situation.[29]

Once the war began, the three responses to Nazism mentioned above became almost invalid. The Transfer Agreement had already lost its importance in 1938–39, when the Jews were banned from taking out all but a fraction of their property. YA arrangements had been based on free contacts between Germany and Palestine and on the permission of the British. The war changed both. The British refused to allow enemy aliens, including Jews under Nazi rule, into their territories. Although the British continued to allow immigration from the unoccupied countries, all regular immigration from Nazi territories came to a halt. In this context, illegal immigration became even more important. The number of people who were ready to undertake the difficult passage increased, and a larger scale of operation was needed. In practice, however, this did not take place. The availability of boats decreased because of strict regulations by all governments regarding the sale or charter of ships during wartime. The recruitment of seamen was more expensive and more difficult. Above all, however, illegal immigration was no longer a preferred Zionist policy, as it conflicted with other political goals of the Yishuv.

The Yishuv saw itself as part of the anti-Nazi front, and the JA leadership explored ways to implement its position in cooperation with Great Britain. For a number of reasons this was a complicated task: The various political leaders, such as Ben-Gurion, Weizmann, and Shertok, differed about the goals of such cooperation. Some stressed the defense interests of the Yishuv, while others felt that the Yishuv's moral obligation, both as Jews and as liberals, to fight Hitler was central. Furthermore, it was very difficult for the Yishuv leadership to cooperate with Great Britain, given the tense relationship between the Mandatory government and the Yishuv and the militant attitude adopted by the Yishuv toward the British, as evinced by numerous public declarations and actions since May 1939, when the White Paper was issued. The confrontations between Britain and the Zionists over the White Paper climaxed in the summer and fall of 1939, mostly through the illegal immigration organized separately by the Revisionists and Labor. The British, for their part, seized whatever illegal boats they could, interned the passengers, and then subtracted their numbers from the regular immigration quota. Furthermore, beginning in the second half of 1939, the immigration quota was no longer released. British immigration policy became even more radical during the first two years of the war, and in December 1940 illegal immigrants who reached Palestine were deported to the British colony of Mauritius.[30] This policy, together with the Land Regulations issued in January 1940 preventing Jews from buying land in most of Palestine, reinforced the opposition to the Mandatory authorities, in particular among the left wing of the Labor Party.

In September 1939 Ben-Gurion offered his party a formula that would separate the Yishuv's attitudes and actions toward Great Britain into two components: "We shall fight against the British on the White Paper policy as if the war did not exist, and fight with Great Britain against Hitler as if the White Paper did not exist," he offered in a speech to his party.[31] Ben-Gurion, Weizmann, and Shertok were the architects of the new policy that expressed both the Yishuv's moral commitment to fight the Nazis and its political goal to reverse the British White Paper. World War I had brought the Balfour Declaration, said Ben-Gurion, and this war should bring the Jewish state.[32]

The JA offered to establish a Jewish army supervised by the British and to participate in intelligence missions in the occupied European countries. The Jews of Palestine comprised immigrants from almost all the European countries, and their knowledge of the languages, geography, cultures, and politics of these countries could be used for intelligence operations. Behind these proposals lay the additional goal of strengthening the defense capability of the Yishuv during the war years. Ben-Gurion, Weizmann, and Shertok hoped that once the Yishuv was counted among the nations that had fought against Hitler, it would gain its political share in the future peace settlement and in the international arrangements that would follow the war.[33]

To accomplish its strategy, the JA thought that it was imperative to draft a concrete political plan for the situation after the war. In April 1942 the Biltmore Resolution was accepted by the Zionist Convention in the United States (the superior body of American Zionism), and in October 1942 it was ratified by the Small Zionist Action Committee in Jerusalem, the body authorized by the Zionist Congress to formulate and decide on policy. The resolution called for the establishment of a Jewish commonwealth in all of Palestine and for the transfer from Europe to Palestine of two million Jews by the war's end.[34]

The British were aware of the Zionist political agenda, and the large majority in the British Cabinet who supported the White Paper were radically opposed to accepting the Zionist offer of cooperation. Thus, the grand design of Zionist leadership was hindered in the British Cabinet. However, the JA did not give up. While it stressed its central role in organizing the recruitment drive among the Yishuv for the British army and encouraging young people to enlist, it continued to negotiate with the British on less pretentious schemes. It was only in June 1944, though, that the Jewish Brigade was finally established; it participated in the last battle on the Italian front in 1945.

Throughout the war the policy goal of encouraging Yishuv members to volunteer for the British army had to be constantly reconsidered and redefined. Besides the political, ideological, and moral considerations voiced by the politicians and expressed in the press, three other factors influenced the rate of enlistment: the economic situation and the rate of unemployment; the progress of the Nazis in North Africa, which posed a direct threat to Palestine; and the fate of European Jewry. The military experience of the enlisted was, on the whole, rather poor. Many of the Jewish volunteers were not sent to the front lines, and they had to spend long months guarding military installations in Palestine and Egypt. However, the soldiers in general expressed a sense of mission that became stronger as the war progressed and the unique and tragic fate of the Jews became evident. Until the end of 1942, cooperation with the British was perceived by all segments of the Yishuv as the appropriate response to the fate of European Jewry. This was true as long as the Jewish fate in occupied Europe was comprehended as being similar to, though more acute than, that of the general population.[35]

The Second Stage of the War, 1942–1945

Historians view November 1942 as a turning point in the understanding both by the Yishuv and the Allied leadership of the true fate of European Jewry. The watershed event was an agreement with Germany that permitted the return to Palestine of Jewish men, women, and children from the ghettos and labor camps in Eastern Europe in exchange for the return of German citizens from Palestine to Germany. The exchanged Jews, who had lived in Palestine before 1939, had been caught in the war while visiting in Europe and had been unable to return to the country. Three exchange groups totaling some one hundred people ultimately arrived in Palestine.[36]

These people had lived through the initial stages of Nazi policy—persecution, starvation, and humiliation—and since early 1942 they had experienced the terrifying days of deportations to the killing centers and the eradication of the Jewish community. Their testimony, given upon their arrival, shocked all. Although a great deal of information on Jewish suffering, of the murder of Jews and even of mass killings, had been published in the Palestinian Jewish press and the leadership had been privy to even more information, meeting these people and listening to their stories led to a new understanding of the situation.

This was the final layer, built on the foundation laid by the information accumulated from a number of sources, both Jewish and non-Jewish, relating to the persecution and mass killing of the Jews in Europe. In the fall of 1942 this new information was linked to information that had been transmitted in August 1942 from Geneva by the World Jewish Congress (WJC) delegate Gerhart Riegner and Richard Lichtheim of the JA about the decision taken at Hitler's headquarters to exterminate three to four million European Jews in special installations in the East.[37] Thus, the testimony of these people helped to integrate a number of elements that, taken together, established an understanding about the decision made by the Nazis to implement a systematic process for killing all Jews. At that point the Yishuv began to truly grasp the meaning of the terminology and propaganda of Nazi anti-Semitism, as embodied in the Final Solution. The mounting numbers of murdered Jews during the first three years of the Occupation were finally understood to be part of the plan to deliberately destroy the Jewish people, and not merely the inevitable suffering caused by a world war. The Jewish fate was thus in a category of its own, apart from the killing of millions of soldiers and civilians in occupied Europe. The unparalleled meaning of this information for the future of the Jewish people and Zionism was slowly perceived and confronted.

The response of the public and the leadership to the knowledge of the systematic and deliberate killing of European Jewry developed over a period of time. Throughout 1943 and even after the news of the Warsaw Ghetto Uprising had reached the Yishuv, many of the people who were exposed to the major sources of information in Palestine still hoped that the annihilation of the Jews would not really be total and that there were still camps such as Auschwitz and Birkenau (!), where the young and healthy worked and thus were not murdered.[38] Others sank into despair, thinking that there was no hope of any rescue. As Dina Porat stated in her comprehensive research on the Yishuv's policy in response to the Final Solution, the Jews of Palestine did not react radically. They did not break the rules and norms of their private or public lives. The routine of life in Palestine continued. Individuals and the leadership conformed to the new reality and responded to the information on the destruction of European Jewry with restraint or silent shock. This reaction was criticized by some groups in the Yishuv, such as Al Domi, a group of intellectuals who protested against the self-control exercised by the members of the Yishuv. Indeed, this stoicism, which was so evident during the war years, caused bewilderment among Israelis in later years, as I shall note later.[39]

The Yishuv's reaction to the news from Europe took three forms: proposals of action; ideological and philosophical reflections; and actual actions embarked upon. In the first category, people expressed their feelings of bewilderment, anger, and revenge. In letters to the JA, some offered to organize groups of volunteers that would infiltrate European countries, join the Jews in the ghettos, and organize them for resistance and rescue. Others offered to join the Jews and die with them. Yet others sought ties with underground movements in Europe, with the Vatican, and with the Allies to press them into launching rescue operations and finding ways to deter the Nazis from carrying out the killings. Other ideas included bombing German cities and dropping leaflets informing the German population that the bombings were in retaliation for the killing of the Jews; punishing German citizens residing in the West; and killing Nazi prisoners of war.[40]

In the second category, ideological and philosophical reflections, people shared their bitter thoughts about the relationship between the Jews and non-Jews in the wake of modern history and the emancipation of the Jews. They raised questions about the missed opportunities for establishing stronger relations between the Yishuv and Diaspora Jewry, as well as the implications of the Zionist immigration policy in the 1920s and early 1930s. These thoughts indicated self-criticism and soul-searching, particularly in regard to the concept of the negation of the Diaspora, which may have led to feelings of estrangement toward the Jews in the Diaspora. Thus, faced with the imminent destruction of European Jewry, some observers focused on the Yishuv's responsibility to assure the future of the Jewish people. The Yishuv had to move from being the favored—one might almost say pampered—son of the Jewish people to being the one with the responsibility of shouldering all their duties and concerns.[41]

Among the leaders of the Zionist movement, people such as Richard Lichtheim, the JA delegate to the League of Nations, who resided in Geneva, thought that the outcome of Hitler's policy would be the end of the Zionist movement and the hopes of the Yishuv.[42] Zionism, Lichtheim claimed in a letter to Nahum Goldmann, a leader of the WJC who had stayed in the United States, was doomed. The small number of Jews who would survive the war would be mostly from Western Europe.

After the war they would return to their countries of origin. American Jews did not think that immigration to Palestine was intended for them, and the remaining Jewish people, after the above groups were discounted, were the relatively small number of Jews in Islamic countries, in particular in North Africa. However, these Jews had never been at the core of the Zionist movement, and it was not worth going through all the pain of building Palestine just for this fraction of the Jewish people since the plan could no longer succeed.

On the other end of the spectrum were figures such as Yizhak Gruenbaum and Yitzhak Tabenkin, who thought that the destruction in Europe had made the Yishuv even more important. The Yishuv was the only true heir of the dead communities, and it was now its duty to reconstruct a meaningful Jewish life and create a new future for the Jewish people. The Yishuv should therefore dedicate all its resources to creating a future haven for the European survivors and for the rest of the Jews.[43] A contrary view was expressed by the labor-union leaders Golda Meyerson and David Remez, who felt that Zionism's only duty now was to rescue Jews by any means possible, such as sending aid, bribing officials in occupied Europe and the Balkans, and buying ships for illegal immigration. The conflict between those who favored marshaling all the Yishuv's efforts and resources for rescue and those who thought those resources should be devoted to the continued development of Palestine was expressed in speeches and demonstrated in the decisions of the various leaders.[44]

Between these two extreme positions stood the main leaders of the Yishuv—Ben-Gurion, Shertok, and Weizmann—who adopted a pragmatic approach. They realized that Lichtheim's ominous prediction might be accurate but thought that the Jewish people would transcend even this tragedy. During the winter of 1943 two emotions dominated the Yishuv: despair over the loss of family, friends, and communities and a resolve that came from the realization that there would be survivors, remnants of the communities, who needed all the help that could be extended to them. The various political parties and social groups reached the consensus that after the catastrophe it was the role of the Yishuv to rebuild the Jewish people. The remnant of European Jewry needed the Zionist movement, and the Zionist movement needed the remnant.[45] And Ben-Gurion expanded the definition of the remnant to include not only those who had directly survived Nazi persecution but all living Jews in the East, the West, the Islamic countries, the Americas, and Palestine.[46]

The destruction of European Jewry emphasized even more the need to break the political impasse. Although the Biltmore Program had become obsolete in its call for the immigration of two million European Jews at the war's end, the essence of the resolution, that is, the need for an independent Jewish entity in Palestine, was even more relevant. The Jews could not afford to lose Palestine, and Ben-Gurion, Weizmann, and Shertok remained faithful to their basic conceptions of the Zionist policy in spite of their failure with the British and the changes in the situation.

The fear that the anti-Zionist Jewish forces would try to weaken Zionism even further continued to loom. How to shift the support of the rich Jewish community in the United States from reconstructing the European communities to concentrating all the remnants in Palestine was of great concern. Thus, Zionist leaders still felt that they had to defend their political goals against the non- or anti-Zionist organizations.

In planning any substantial rescue operation or other aid to the Jews in Europe, the Yishuv realized its dependency on the Great Powers, in particular Great Britain. A number of large-scale rescue schemes were not feasible without the extensive cooperation of the Allies. The neutral countries whose collaboration was mandatory for the success of any migration plan would not consider cooperating unless requested to do so by the Allies. Thus, the alternatives were limited, and avenues had to be found within this framework.[47]

The political leadership in general and Ben-Gurion and Shertok in particular were looking for a direct Jewish presence in the Allied military that would facilitate direct contacts with European Jews. Such contacts were important for all rescue and relief operations. They would help in providing a better network of ties with the Jewish communities and, through them, with the remnants of Jews in the forests and camps. In March 1943 a rescue committee representing all segments of the Yishuv, including the religious anti-Zionist Agudat Israel and the Revisionists, neither of whom was part of the JA, was established. The fund-raising for mobilization was expanded to include rescue, and the rescue committee supported and expanded the delegations of the Yishuv in Istanbul and Geneva. These two centers became the basis for rescue and relief projects carried out by the Yishuv's emissaries. They received information from occupied Europe and transmitted it to other parts of Europe, the United States, and Palestine. They also sent money and information from Palestine to refugees in Europe. They maintained contacts with Red Cross delegates in the neutral countries and the Balkans. Their analysis of the situation helped Jews in the free world to plan aid and rescue efforts and to push their governments to support such projects. They also assisted Jewish leaders in occupied Europe in assessing different rescue possibilities.[48]

An issue of great concern to the political leadership was the future attitude of the Jewish survivors toward their Jewish identity in general and their Zionist affiliation in particular. Therefore, the contacts and the aid and rescue efforts transcended national and religious boundaries and were linked to various political considerations. It was of the utmost importance for the Zionists that the survivors immigrate to Palestine and that this immigration be known in the international arena.[49]

Thus two courses were taken. The first centered on persuading the Allies, and especially the British, to support aid and rescue efforts aimed at the European Jews by establishing a Jewish Brigade within the British army; supporting the mission of sending parachutists from the Yishuv to Europe; negotiating with the Nazis to save the Jews of Bulgaria and the remaining Jews of Slovakia and other countries from deportation; and, from the spring of 1944, seeking to alleviate the plight of Hungarian Jews. The second course was labeled "minor projects." It included relief work and illegal immigration, carried out by the Yishuv's delegations and financed by the Yishuv and Jewish organizations, in particular the Joint Distribution Committee (JDC), the great American Jewish relief organization established in 1914.[50] The first course never materialized, and so the "minor projects" became the central manifestation of the Yishuv's rescue efforts. Some sixty-five hundred illegal immigrants succeeded in leaving the Balkan countries between 1943 and 1945; thousands of food parcels were sent to refugees in the Soviet Union and occupied Europe; and money was transferred to Zionist movements in support of aid programs and border crossings.

The people who devoted all their time to rescue efforts were the thirty Yishuv delegates in Geneva and Istanbul. They complained that the central leadership was not interested in rescue work. They constantly demanded that a prominent person, such as Shertok or Kaplan, join them for an extended period of time, but both visited Istanbul for only a few weeks. These delegates criticized the rescue committee in Jerusalem for its directives concerning the selection of immigrants and for how it viewed its relationship with the Jews in Europe. They also thought that the share of the special Mobilization and Rescue Fund established in 1943 that was allocated to rescue was too small. They believed that the distance between Turkey and Palestine created an unbridgeable psychological gap in the Yishuv that made it difficult to establish the correct priorities.

Nevertheless, in 1943, 25 percent of the JA's budget was dedicated to rescue, and most of it was spent on aid to Jews in occupied Europe. (Illegal immigration had a separate budget.) This was the single largest item in the JA budget (320,000 pounds sterling out of a total budget of 1.15 million pounds) and represented a 34 percent share of the MRF (218,000 pounds sterling out of a total of 702,000). From February 1943 to June 1945 the Yishuv spent 1.325 million pounds sterling on rescue (equivalent to approximately $40 million in 1994) out of a budget of 4.5 million pounds sterling. Of the total product of the Jewish economy for the years 1943–45, however, it amounted to only 0.5 percent.[51]

AFTER THE HOLOCAUST

The period between the end of the war in Europe in May 1945 and the establishment of the state of Israel in May 1948 was one of sharp transition for the Yishuv. In this short time the Yishuv moved from concentrating on the destruction of the Jews of Europe to ensuring the rebirth of the Jewish nation. In the spring and summer of 1945 the Yishuv and its leadership stood at one of the most difficult crossroads in recent history. Despite economic growth, the creation of a defense organization, and an experienced corps of soldiers in the British army, the Zionist war policy had failed in its central goal of changing British policy toward Palestine. The foundation of the Arab League in March 1944 pointed to a stronger British alliance with the Arab states, and the new Labour government in Britain, elected in the summer of 1945, proved extremely uncooperative on the Palestine issue.

The political conflicts and disunity in the Yishuv did not shrink in the face of the European tragedy, and the means for achieving Zionist goals were debated vehemently. The rift within Labor, the ruling party, swelled, and in the summer of 1944 a new leftist political movement, Hatnu'ah Leahdut Ha'avodah (the United Labor Movement), was established by former Mapai members. The quarrels between the

Left and the Revisionists became more acute and almost led to a civil war, causing tremendous frustration. Despite opposition and disagreements within Mapai and the other parties, Ben-Gurion was unyielding on the Biltmore political agenda for large-scale immigration and the establishment of a Jewish state. He viewed it as a twofold policy. On the one hand, it challenged the Yishuv to assume the responsibility of building the Jewish future. Ben-Gurion proclaimed to his party members, "Nothing Jewish is alien to us."[52] On the other hand, the policy relied on the remnants, She'erit Hapletah, to immigrate to Palestine. This "old" policy was a genuine postwar response to the destruction of the Jews in Europe; it offered a practical solution (even if it was not yet feasible) that expressed both the wishes of the Yishuv and the deep feelings of displacement and desire for rehabilitation of the survivors.

Immediately after the war the survivors established their own social, cultural, and educational institutions in the displaced persons (DP) camps in Austria, Germany, Italy, and other European countries. Their devotion to Zionism and their willingness to act on its behalf were displayed in numerous resolutions and newspaper articles. "They sensed," wrote Zeev Mankowitz, "that they were situated at a fateful crossroads that could well determine the future of their people. They were persuaded that the Exodus from Egypt and the Exodus from Europe were fully analogous."[53] For example, the *Landsberger lager Cajtung,* the Yiddish weekly of the Landsberg DP camp, published the following statement on November 22, 1945: "Only the setting up of a Jewish state in Eretz Israel will make it possible to change the whole situation and lay a formal political foundation from which we shall be able to move forward as a political force, keeping our own political accounts and thereby able to interact with the corresponding interests of other peoples."[54] It conformed completely with the political program set by the leadership of the Yishuv.

An analysis of the various joint efforts by the Yishuv's emissaries and the survivors to achieve Zionist goals is beyond the scope of this essay. Suffice it to mention that a central pillar of Zionist policy was illegal immigration to Palestine. Unlike during the prewar and war years, when a limited number managed to arrive, in the immediate postwar period illegal immigration became a mass movement. Without the preparation and organization of all Yishuv emissaries and the strong will of the survivors to support this Zionist goal, the movement of seventy thousand illegal immigrants to Palestine could not have occurred. Two-thirds of these immigrants were intercepted on their way to Palestine and deported by the British to Cyprus, where they were detained in special camps. Most of them reached Palestine only after the establishment of the state of Israel.[55]

Five major groups of emissaries comprising some 500 persons were dispatched to Europe to work with survivors. The largest group, numbering about 250 envoys, was the relief team adjunct to the United Nations Relief and Rehabilitation Administration, headed by Haim (Hoffmann) Yahil. Others included an educational team of about 100 teachers and 115 representatives of YA. A special group was sent to Eastern Europe to help organize clandestine border crossings between the DP camps in Germany and the Mediterranean ports of France and Italy. This group worked closely with the illegal immigration activists among the survivors and the emissaries of the various youth movements. In 1947 a mission of the Jewish Palestine underground defense forces began providing paramilitary training to the young in the DP camps. All these Zionist activities provided an important moral boost and helped the survivors overcome the difficulties of daily life and a prolonged stay in the camps. They encouraged the survivors not to abandon the hope that they would eventually immigrate to Palestine. The emissaries felt that they were preparing the survivors for their future life in Palestine.[56]

The DP problem and the illegal immigration to Palestine positively influenced the U.S. government as well as European public opinion toward Zionism. Despite the hardships and the often dangerous journeys, illegal immigration inspired the survivors and reinforced their confidence in the Yishuv during the long period of idleness and homelessness. Many survivors joined the underground defense forces of Palestine and immigrated to Palestine/Israel even during the difficult months of the War of Independence, from November 1947 to January 1949. By January 1949 survivors constituted approximately 20 percent of the Israel Defense Force.[57]

The Trail of Commemoration

It is difficult to obtain direct information about the spontaneous commemoration of the Nazis' victims by individuals or groups. It is evident, however, that people who knew that their relatives or friends had died remembered their loved ones in the traditional Jewish ways: reciting the yearly *Kaddish* prayers on the anniversary of the death, kindling a *Yizkor* (memorial) candle on that day, and giving the names of deceased relatives to newborns. Some hung pictures of their dead family members in their homes. Nevertheless, for most people it was still too early to commemorate their loved ones, as they were not sure what had happened to them. During the war, no credible information was available about individuals. Sometimes specific information was obtained about the fate of one's relatives or friends from refugees who had arrived in Palestine during the war. This information was, however, very limited. Years after the war had ended, many were still searching for relatives and reliable information about their fate in the hope that they were still alive. Well into the 1950s a special office of the JA broadcast daily on the radio the names of people about whom relatives were seeking information.

The lack of a burial site and precise date of death hindered the survivors' ability to follow the traditional rituals. It became apparent that there was a need for a formal memorial day to remember those who had been killed. Two dates were observed in the Yishuv: April 19, the beginning of the Warsaw Ghetto Uprising, and the tenth day of the Hebrew month of Tevet, the traditional date of the general *Kaddish,* designated by the chief rabbinate and endorsed by the religious sector of the Yishuv.

Another way to remember and reflect on the fate of the Jews was to write testimonies and memoirs. In 1942 Berl Katznelson founded the series Min Hamoked (From the Fire), which was published by Am Oved, the major publishing house of the Histadrut, until 1949. The books in the series told the stories of refugees who had managed to reach Palestine during the war and revealed the conditions in the ghettos and labor camps. The series also printed letters sent to Palestine about the efforts to survive and about the death and suffering in Europe. Anthologies were compiled about Jewish heroism and suffering, along with historical accounts such as Moshe Prager's *On the Jewish Tragedy and the Conscience of the World*, a documentary on the destruction of Jewish life.[58] Intentionally or unintentionally, these books served as memorials to friends, community leaders, and rabbis who had been murdered by the Nazis.

More than a decade passed between the first proposal in September 1942 and the time when the Knesset passed the Yad Vashem Law in August 1953.[59] The internal debate concerning the character and framework of the commemoration was influenced both by political and social events and by an understanding of the nature and scope of the destruction. The Jews of Palestine and the Israeli society were faced with an extensive chain of commemorative places and times, which represented not only the development of an understanding of the reality of the Shoah but also the particular manner in which Israel wanted to remember this era and to connect it to the establishment of an independent Jewish state.

In September 1942, at the height of the murder in Europe and before the news about the Final Solution reached the Yishuv, the first plan to commemorate the victims of Nazism was introduced to the Jewish National Fund (JNF), the body responsible for obtaining and developing land in Palestine. Mordechai Shenhabi, a member of the Mishmar Ha'emek kibbutz and an emissary to Germany in the 1930s, proposed planting "a Garden of the Nation" that would become a multipurpose center commemorating the tragedy of the European Jews in World War II and the achievement of building Palestine. The complex would include a hall in which the names of Jewish soldiers who had fallen in the war against Hitler and the names of the Jews murdered by the Nazis would be listed. There would be a symbolic cemetery, a youth village for the war orphans who would come to Palestine, and lodging for Jewish visitors from abroad who would come to mourn in the "Garden of the Nation."

The concept of the memorial was based on cooperation between the JNF and the Diaspora Jewish communities, which would be ready to accept the leadership of Palestine. Shenhabi reasoned that the Jewish communities that had lost so many of their members would wish to build a memorial center in Palestine and would allocate money and human resources for this purpose. From the Yishuv's perspective, it would be of the utmost importance to create, after the devastating war, another focus of interest connecting Diaspora Jews, both Zionist and non-Zionist, with Palestine. Shenhabi entitled his first proposal "Mif'al 'Am" (Nation's Project).[60]

Then in 1945 a national committee responsible for commemoration was established. It was under the authority of the Va'ad Leumi and included representatives of other institutions of the Yishuv among its members. At first, committee membership was not stable, but the JA, the JNF, and a number of cultural institutions, including the Hebrew University, participated. The committee was named Yad Vashem, an expression taken from Isaiah 56:5: "Even unto them will I give in My house and within My walls *a monument and a memorial*, better than sons and daughters." The verse expressed the idea of God's eternal remembrance of those converts who join the Jewish people and follow the Lord's laws, even if they themselves are unable to bear children. In addition to this public effort, various private bodies were founded, including, for example, the *landsmannschaften*, who were anxious to express their sorrow publicly.[61]

In May 1945 Shenhabi submitted to the JNF and the National Committee a more comprehensive proposal, which was entitled "Yad Lagolah Haneherevet" (A Memorial to the Diaspora Which Was Destroyed). It was also published in a number of newspapers and received a positive public response.[62] The plan reflected the realization that a civilization, a culture, and almost an entire people had perished. Aimed at linking old Jewish commemorative traditions with modern ones to frame a collective memory of the Holocaust, the plan included a memorial and a place of ritual observance for individuals and for large groups. The site was to be located in a forest to be planted in memory of the dead Jews. In the tradition of the Zionists and the Yishuv, planting trees symbolized the new life in the land of Israel. It was also an old Jewish custom to plant trees on the fifteenth day of the Jewish month of Shevat, at the beginning of spring.[63] Thus, Shenhabi's proposal combined sorrow and mourning for the past with hope for the future.

Shenhabi also suggested activities to preserve a living memory of the murdered Jews. Lists of the names of victims from each community were to be collected, along with descriptions of their struggles for survival, their heroism, and their resistance. Jewish participation in the war against Hitler was to be part of the history of the Holocaust; therefore, the names of all the fallen Jewish soldiers in all the Allied armies were also to be recorded at the commemoration site. To be remembered as well were the efforts by Jews to leave Europe, particularly on the illegal boats organized with the help of the Yishuv. The proposal incorporated a special monument to the Righteous Gentiles who helped rescue Jews during the Nazi era. These ideas eventually became the commemoration patterns followed in Israel today. Both of Shenhabi's proposals reflected the Yishuv's view that it was responsible for the commemoration of the Jewish victims, just as other countries commemorated their fallen soldiers or civilian victims of war. The Yishuv leadership viewed the Jews of Europe as potential members of the Jewish community in Palestine. Most were, of course, citizens of other countries.

In August 1945 the executive committee of the Zionist movement assembled in London. It was their first meeting after the end of the war, and a meeting of representatives who had been cut off from one another during the war years. Holocaust survivors were among the delegates, and one of the issues on the agenda was the official ratification of the Yad Vashem national committee. Initially, Yad Vashem was meant to represent Jewish welfare organizations such as the WJC, established in 1934 to aid German Jews and involved in rescue efforts of European Jews since that time, and cultural institutions such as Yidisher Visenshaftlicher Institut, or YIVO, the Institute for Jewish Research, which since 1940 had centered its activities in New York. After the Yad Vashem committee was formally established, most of the private bodies that had been founded in Palestine to commemorate the dead disbanded, transferring their allegiance, plans, and financial support to Yad Vashem.[64]

In many respects the years 1946–49 were the formative years for ideas of commemoration. These ideas were influenced heavily by the political struggle for a Jewish state and the direct encounter with Holocaust survivors. When Palestinian Jews met with survivors in DP camps and elsewhere in Europe, and when they saw the sites of destruction, their reactions were extremely complex. Listening to the actual survivors' accounts of what the Jewish people and the survivors had gone through brought a totally new dimension to the Palestinian Jews' understanding of the plight of the European Jews, which they could never have obtained from reading the published accounts.

For some survivors, remembering was a compulsive act, and they thought that their lives had to be dedicated to telling the story of the destruction. Furthermore, some survivors maintained that the public memorial ceremonies, the collection of testimonies, and other acts of remembrance were very important for their rehabilitation.[65] Others, however, tried to forget and return to some form of normalcy. Many were somewhere between these positions. Attitudes in the Yishuv were similar, and some emissaries warned that if the survivors immersed themselves in the past, their rehabilitation would be hindered. Abba Kovner, the leader of the resistance in the Vilna ghetto, a poet, and a major figure in shaping the commemoration patterns in Israel, said in one of his Memorial Day talks: "To remember everything is madness, but to forget is a betrayal."[66] Indeed, what to remember, how much to remember, and how to commemorate were central issues for the survivors from the very first days of Liberation.

The first acts of collecting testimony and documents on the Jews during the Holocaust had been initiated and conducted by the Jews themselves under the Occupation. The historian Emanuel Ringelblum founded the Oneg Shabbath Archive in Warsaw, and there were less comprehensive attempts in other ghettos, such as Vilna and Lodz. From 1944 on (1943 in the case of France), the survivors in the liberated countries continued this tradition even while they were still underground or in hiding. They set up historical committees, which then established networks of workers to cover the European countries and the large number of survivors.[67]

In Bergen Belsen the Central Jewish Committee established a special archival department. On November 1, 1945, the archivists put out a call for sources dating from the war years. The committee was interested in all kinds of documents, such as diaries, newspapers, advertisements by the *Judenräte*, and Nazi orders. Explaining the importance of such an archive, its members emphasized the need to remember the past and to facilitate research in the future. They assembled the materials, which were then sent to Palestine, with copies to YIVO in New York.[68]

Although public commemoration had already begun among the survivors in the DP camps and in other locations in Europe, the patterns of commemoration had not yet been established, and the search for a proper model veered between the traditional and the new. The *Yizkor* prayer, for example, opened the ceremonies, but the content of the prayer was secularized and addressed not the Almighty but the Jewish people.[69] In a number of places, people connected with the Zionist movement took the lead in organizing these ceremonies. The relationship that developed between the Yishuv emissaries and the survivors provided a channel through which patterns of commemoration were passed from one group to the other. Thus the emissaries became a bridge between the two communities.

The members of the committee charged with establishing the commemoration authority, also named Yad Vashem, represented four main groups: (1) members of the JA and other Yishuv institutions who had been active in rescue and aid efforts during the war; (2) members of the WJC, such as Aryeh Leon Kubovy (Kubowitzki) and Arieh Tartakower, who had maintained contact with Jews in occupied Europe and had endeavored to push the U.S. government and various organizations into taking part in rescue operations; (3) intellectuals from the Hebrew University, such as Professors Benzion Dinur (Dinaburg) and Gershom Scholem, and teachers in the Bezalel Art Academy (some of whom, such as Dinur, had lobbied the JA and the Histadrut to participate more actively in rescue efforts); and (4) members of the JNF and the rescue fund. Both ideologically and religiously this was a diverse group. Its discussions reflected the challenges the participants faced and the sense of responsibility they shared. In 1946 the Yishuv leadership was not involved in the issue of commemoration.[70]

From the end of 1945, the committee's various subcommittees convened more frequently, and the scope of their activities extended into different areas. Along with some private people, they proposed a number of plans to the committee. All the plans included a number of similar elements. They stressed a firm commitment to assuring the future of Jewish life and the conviction that the land of Israel was the place to erect a commemorative site. All suggested building a physical monument of some type that would reflect the dimensions of the tragedy. Some proposed creating new settlements named after the destroyed communities, with each such settlement housing a memorial structure of some kind. Others suggested establishing a "city of the dead" (*'Ir hametim*) that would include museums in memory of the victims of the Holocaust and a center for the study of the social history, culture, and politics of the destroyed Jewish world. Thus the study of Jewish life would become part of the project. Such a commemorative site in the land of Israel would eventually become a center for Jews from all over the world, who would come to honor the dead.[71]

Some of the religious members of the Yad Vashem committee felt that monuments and gravestones were not in keeping with the Jewish way of commemorating the victims. Aaron Barth, a member of the JNF and of Mizrahi, the religious segment of the Zionist organization, complained that the commemoration plans, by giving the monument such an important place, made the commemoration resemble a ritual of the dead, which was alien to Jewish tradition. Barth proposed that centers of higher Jewish learning—yeshivot—be established instead. The nonreligious members of the committee agreed that learning and research were central to any commemorative project, but they had in mind historical and sociological research projects that would further aim at understanding the circumstances that had led to the Holocaust and explore the mechanism of destruction and the responses of the Jewish leadership and ordinary Jews in the ghettos and camps. Shenhabi and those who thought that a physical monument was necessary were influenced by the patterns of commemoration in Western Europe, but what they sought was a memorial that was imposing but not megalomaniacal.

Another controversy among the committee members concerned fund-raising. This was a delicate issue, as the fundraisers believed that raising funds for the commemorative site would compromise the regular Zionist fund-raising efforts. Some thought that funds for the commemoration project should come from the JNF and other organizations, such as the WJC and the JA, that would administer Yad Vashem.[72] On September 16, 1946, a subcommittee was appointed to offer concrete plans for commemoration, taking into account the different perspectives that had been raised in the previous discussions. This subcommittee was given a budget of 100,000 pounds sterling.[73] The Hebrew University was requested to be involved in order to ensure a proper academic level for the historical work and documentation that would be involved.

The ideology of the Zionists and many others nevertheless held that the ultimate commemoration of the destruction must be a sovereign Jewish society in the land of Israel. Therefore, all commemoration plans were dependent on other urgent needs of the Zionist movement, such as illegal immigration and building the defense forces and settlements. As early as June 1945, in one of the first discussions concerning the commemoration of the Holocaust, Eliyahu Dobkin, a central figure in the immigration department of the JA, who had spent long months visiting survivors of the Holocaust, said that the best memorial to the victims of the destruction would be a Jewish state.[74]

The link between the Holocaust and the establishment of the state of Israel—the concept of *Shoah Utekumah* (Holocaust and rebirth)—dominated the minds of people in the Yishuv and, later, in Israel and was supported by many Jews in the Diaspora. It became a central part of the legacy of Israeli society, the essence of a commemorative view that evolved and was molded by the experience of a generation active in the rehabilitation and absorption of survivors and in the foundation of the state.[75]

On June 1, 1947, Dr. Chaim Weizmann was invited to be the president of Yad Vashem, and David Remez, a leading member of the Mapai labor party and the head of the Va'ad Leumi, was appointed chairman. Two committees, for finance and program, were elected. The latter was made up of historians from the Hebrew University and representatives of various archives, the Bezalel Art Academy, and the Institute for Jewish Folklore (Yed'a 'Am).[76]

On July 31, 1947, an international conference linked to the first Congress for Jewish Studies convened in Jerusalem to discuss the politics and programs of research and commemoration of the Holocaust. It also formalized the mission of Yad Vashem. The goals of the conference were to establish the centrality of Yad Vashem in all commemorative and research activities; to work with the existing historical committees and institutions that were involved in documenting and commemorating the Holocaust; and to establish the formal structure of Yad Vashem and its international committees and delegates.[77] Cooperation with the other organizations was deemed crucial from a political perspective. If Yad Vashem was to become the central commemorative institution in the Jewish world, an agreement with various prestigious research and learning institutions, such as YIVO, was essential. From both the moral and material perspectives, it was important to obtain the formal endorsement of major Jewish organizations. The first international conference on research of the Holocaust and heroism, sponsored by the Hebrew University and Yad Vashem, defined the goals of Yad Vashem: *(a)* to commemorate the Holocaust; *(b)* to spearhead research on the Holocaust and to publish documents and testimonies; and *(c)* to establish Jerusalem as the center of Jewish commemoration of the Holocaust.[78] Thus, before the state of Israel was established, the responsibility of the Yishuv to preserve the memory of the Holocaust was acknowledged as part of its commitment to provide a haven and a home for the survivors of the Holocaust.

This initial progress stalled when a number of crises consumed the Yishuv: the War of Independence; the declaration of the state of Israel; and the immigration of huge numbers of people to the new nation. The Yad Vashem committee, feeling that the government and the public had lost interest in implementing its Holocaust commemoration plans, resigned in March 1949, protesting that it was unable to act because of a lack of funding.[79]

During the first years of statehood the commemoration of those killed in the Holocaust had to compete with the remembrance of the soldiers who died in the War of Independence. No less than 1 percent of the total population of Israel died in the War of Independence. Individuals, institutions, communities, and the state searched for a way to honor the war dead. Various ideas were proposed and practiced until March 1953, when the Knesset decided on a national day of remembrance. Interestingly, the first call in the Knesset for the Yad Vashem Law was heard one month after the ratification of the law to honor the fallen soldiers.[80]

The Hok Yom Hazikharon Lashoah Ulemered Hagetaot (Memorial Day for the Holocaust and the Ghetto Rebellion Law) became law on April 12, 1951. Commonly called the Yom Hashoah Law, it set aside the twenty-seventh day of the Hebrew month Nisan as the formal memorial day. The debate concerning selection of that particular date demonstrates how legislators had dealt with the spontaneous commemoration practices previously. The two days of commemoration, one secular, April 19, the other religious, the tenth day of the Hebrew month Tevet, reflected different ideologies and ways of life. The first stressed the centrality of Jewish heroism and armed resistance during the war and sought to view Jewish fate through that prism. The second followed Jewish tradition and suggested that this continuity embodied the authentic Jewish reaction to the Holocaust. The commemorations on both days, however, were not regular, and in some years they were neglected altogether. Sometimes April 19 would occur during Passover. Therefore, the need to establish one day that would reflect a unified, national approach seemed important.

In order to make the remembrance of the Holocaust a national observance, the lawmakers endeavored to choose a date that would unite all segments of Israeli society. In settling on the twenty-seventh day of Nisan, the legislators followed the Jewish tradition and selected a date according to the Hebrew calendar. April 19, the non-Jewish date of the start of the Warsaw Ghetto Uprising, was not acceptable. The Hebrew date of the beginning of the uprising—the fourteenth day of Nisan—was not appropriate for commemoration because it was the day before the festival of Passover. However, the month of Nisan itself was most suitable. The uprising had lasted more than six weeks, and according to Jewish tradition the seven weeks from the first day of Passover until the holiday of Shavu'ot (Pentecost) contain a stretch of thirty-three days of mourning commemorating the persecution of the Jewish sages and their pupils in the second century. Over the years, other memorial days were added during this period to commemorate all the Jews who had died in pogroms during the Crusades and during the Chmielnicki massacres in Poland in the seventeenth century. Thus, the selection of the twenty-seventh of Nisan answered the needs of both the religious and the nonreligious. The Knesset accepted this date unanimously. Since seven days—the traditional period of mourning, or *Shiv'ah,* for Jews—separate the twenty-seventh of Nisan from Israel's Independence Day, the fifth day of Iyyar, the date chosen complemented the conceptual framework of *Shoah Utekumah.*[81]

The Yad Vashem Law, 1953

Two years after passage of the Yom Hashoah Law the Knesset debated the Yad Vashem (Remembrance of the Holocaust and Heroism) Law. The legislators relied heavily on the experiences gained by the committees that had discussed the issue of commemoration since 1945 and passed a law that could be interpreted in different ways. The law not only provided the framework of commemoration but also defined its content and goals. A council and an executive committee nominated by the government were to direct the work of Yad Vashem; the ministry of education was responsible for its funding and also for ensuring that the spirit of the law be kept and that activities be organized.

The preamble to the law conveyed the three basic concepts of the Holocaust: Shoah, Gevurah (heroism), and 'Oz ruah (the courage of the spirit). *Shoah* is an all-encompassing term that refers both to the acts of the Nazi perpetrators, which culminated in the mass murder, and to the humiliation and helplessness of their Jewish victims. The term also indicates a period of time that included the Gevurah, the armed resistance of the ghetto fighters and the partisans in the forests, which served as a beacon of light and a source of inspiration to the Jews during the Holocaust and later. 'Oz ruah was the daily struggle of most Jews to survive the difficulties of the war years and to preserve their dignity and human spirit. These concepts had to be integrated into a comprehensive image that would nourish the collective memory and the historic conscience of the Jews.[82]

Yad Vashem would initiate activities, public ceremonies, and other cultural projects to transmit information about the Holocaust and foster patterns of commemoration. The law described in detail the people and institutions to be remembered and commemorated: the Jewish families involved; the Jewish communities, including their synagogues, organizations, and cultural, educational, and religious institutions; all the Jews who had struggled to preserve their humanity and had died in the ghettos and camps; the ghetto fighters; the partisans; all the Jewish soldiers in all the different armies, including the Allied forces, and underground military units; the people who attempted to reach Palestine illegally and perished in the process; the emissaries of the Yishuv who had died in their missions, such as the parachutists, to save Jews; and the righteous among the nations who had helped to save Jews.

Yad Vashem's scholarly responsibility was to collect and publish the testimonies of survivors and to promote historical and social research about the Holocaust. Its Israeli and Jewish viewpoint obliged Yad Vashem to convey the heroism and spiritual courage of the Jews to future generations and to teach the lessons of the Holocaust, although there were no definitions of what those lessons might be. It had to formulate the patterns of remembrance for Yom Hashoah, which would then pass from Israel to the Jewish communities in the Diaspora. Yad Vashem was also ordered to grant all the Jewish victims of the Holocaust "Israeli memorial citizenship," a status created to connect the victims to the state of Israel. This was a very unusual assignment, laden with emotional and ideological meaning.[83] Yad Vashem was also charged with taking the lead in cooperating with other Jewish (and perhaps non-Jewish) institutions that commemorated the victims of the Holocaust and representing Israel on the different international commemoration projects that might arise.[84]

The minister of education, Professor Benzion Dinur, presented the law to the Knesset and thus opened the Knesset debate. Those who took part in the deliberations emphasized certain principles in accordance with their own political inclinations. The presentation of the Holocaust and the establishment of the state of Israel—*Shoah Utekumah*—in the context of cause and effect illuminated the main agreements and differences between the speakers of the various parties.

The final wording of the law clearly reflected the wish to minimize the political rifts among the various parties. The phrasing emphasized the themes on which all agreed, including the commemoration of individuals and the need to take into account the spontaneous commemorations that had developed since the 1940s. The recognition of Israel as the manifestation of Jewish life and culture was expressed in the general debate about the law and by Haim Ben Asher of Mapai as follows: "The existence of the people and the existence of the State (of Israel) are one."[85] The law's emphasis was on study and research rather than on a monument (a major element in the proposals of the 1940s). The character of the memorial day, however, was to be determined by the leadership of Yad Vashem and by the traditions that would develop.

Following the ratification of the Yad Vashem Law, the government set aside a site for the Yad Vashem complex. It was located on the western side of the Mount of Remembrance (Har Hazikaron, later renamed Mount Herzl), on which Herzl's tomb had been built in 1950. On the eastern side a cemetery for the soldiers who fell in Israel's wars was established. For seven days each year, from the end of Holocaust Day to the beginning of the Day of Independence, Mount Herzl hosts the Jewish state's major ceremonies, both those for mourning and those for rejoicing. Thus, the temporal flow of the Jewish calendar, along with the institutions built on this mountain, created a historical focal point for the new nation that embraced the meaning of *Shoah Utekumah.*[86]

The Memorial Day for the Holocaust and the Heroism Law, 1959

On June 18, 1958, eight years after the dedication of the twenty-seventh of Nisan as the memorial day for the Holocaust, Mordechai Nurock, a Mizrahi representative, asked the Knesset to define in detail how that day was to be nationally observed. Nurock expressed his disappointment at the lack of attention given to the memorial day. Theaters, movie houses, and coffee shops all maintained their regular schedules. No consistent commemoration programs existed in the school system, on the radio, or within various official bodies. His discontent was shared by many survivors, *landsmannschaften,* and Jewish institutions abroad. Nurock found it alarming that the memory of the Holocaust was fading only thirteen years after the end of World War II and that in another generation, when the survivors were no longer alive, the Holocaust might be totally forgotten. Although Minister of the Interior Israel Bar-Yehudah questioned both Nurock's criticism about the attitude of the people and the patterns of observance of the memorial day, the idea of passing such a law was accepted. On April 8, 1959, the law was approved by the Knesset.[87]

It was decided that the Yom Hashoah commemoration would incorporate symbols of national mourning: lowering flags to half-staff; breaking the normal daily routine with two minutes of silence, during which all activity throughout the country would cease; discontinuing regular public entertainment between the evening of the twenty-sixth of Nisan and the evening of the twenty-seventh; and dedicating the content of all cultural programs to the Holocaust and its meaning. The law also mandated the broadcasting of special radio programs and, in 1967, when television came to Israel, special television programs.

By the provisions of this law and the Yad Vashem Law, a national ceremony was to be held on the eve of Holocaust Day during which the president would open the formal commemoration. The commemoration incorporated the traditional elements of the *Yizkor* prayer and the lighting of six torches (in memory of the six million who had perished), along with modern Zionist observances, such as musical presentations and speeches. This ceremony was broadcast on the radio and later on television.

Ceremonies were also held at various sites and museums, including the Ghetto Fighters Museum and the museum at Kibbutz Yad Mordehkai, which was named after Mordechai Anielewicz, the leader of the Warsaw Ghetto Uprising. Many of the original members of the kibbutz were Holocaust survivors. The ceremony at the kibbutz reflected the attitudes of the fighters and their political connection with Labor Zionism. During the 1960s and 1970s the number of people who participated in these ceremonies grew considerably. Discussions, documentaries, and literary and theatrical works about the Holocaust and survivors' testimonies dominated the radio and television programs on Holocaust Day. The attempt to make the public commemoration more meaningful was evident in a project entitled "Every Man Has a Name," started during the 1980s, which gave individuals the opportunity to announce and list the names of relatives who had been murdered in the Holocaust. This idea had been suggested in the 1940s and was included in the Yad Vashem Law, but the response of the general public had been very limited until the 1980s. The relatively recent success of public ceremonies of "listing names" is a clear demonstration of the change in the patterns of observation of Holocaust Day as public and private commemorations have merged.

The Eichmann Trial, a Turning Point

Israel in the 1950s. During the 1950s, Israel's population increased to almost 2 million Jews and almost 250,000 Arabs and other minorities. More than 60 percent of the Jews had immigrated after the declaration of the state in 1948. More than half of the Israeli Jews were of European origin, and the remaining 48 percent were from Islamic countries. Some 350,000 of the immigrants were Holocaust survivors.[88] Many of the Israelis of European origin had personally experienced the loss of family and friends. Altogether, more than half of the Jews in Israel were connected directly or indirectly to the Holocaust.

Economic conditions were very difficult, although they improved toward the early 1960s. Inflation and unemployment hindered the economic growth of the country, which was burdened with both a high level of immigration and national security expenses. Immigrants had to work hard to provide for their families without resorting to welfare. However, Holocaust survivors fared considerably better than immigrants from non-European countries. A number of factors account for their higher economic level: *(a)* better social networks, relatives, friends, and acquaintances from the Old Country; *(b)* the knowledge of Yiddish, which many of the earlier immigrants spoke; *(c)* money received from the reparations agreement with West Germany; and *(d)* their not being hindered by the prejudice against Jews from Islamic countries. While the Holocaust survivors differed from the earlier settlers in many ways, the differences between the two groups were still far fewer than those between the earlier settlers and the Jews from Islamic countries.[89] There was also a more objective factor: a large number of Holocaust survivors had come to the country in the early stages of the mass immigration that followed the declaration of the state, and their absorption process was thus easier. For example, toward the end of the War of Independence, Holocaust survivors made up 20 percent of the Israeli Defense Force. They lived in the central parts of the country, many in deserted Arab towns such as Jaffa, Lydda, Ramle, and Haifa. In the early 1960s most of these immigrants were employed, owned their own homes, and were able to educate their children, equipping them with the means to become successful members of Israeli society. In the sixties Holocaust survivors were among the leading artists, writers, actors, university professors, and scholars in the country, and a few had been elected to the Knesset. However, many Holocaust survivors preferred not to publicly identify themselves as such, and most of their commemorative activities were centered in their own intimate social circles.

The general atmosphere in the country did not encourage discussion about the past, for it was considered a hindrance to the survivors' rehabilitation. The future was what counted, with new assignments and hopes and a strong denial of bonds with the Diaspora.[90] In YA, for example, the formal policy for counselors was specifically not to provide a time or place for a discussion of the past. As far as they were concerned, the beginning of the survivors' new lives was the date of their immigration. A popular topic for school essays was "Aliyati la'aretz" (My Immigration), as if the student's biography had only begun then. Children and youths with foreign names were asked to change them to Hebrew ones.[91] A public announcement requested that families with foreign-sounding last names replace them with Hebrew names. For many survivors, though, their names were the only remembrance they might have of their lost families.

While the survivors and their children might have long and painful discussions in which they recalled again and again their days in the ghettos and camps and their final rescue, they were usually held with friends who were also survivors or on the occasion of a *yohrzeit,* the anniversary of the death of a loved one. Associations of ghetto fighters, war veterans and partisans, and concentration camp survivors were established, indicating the need for formal identification.

Survivors initiated the erection of the first commemorative sites, shipped the ashes of Jews murdered in Poland and buried them in cemeteries in Israel, and published *Yizkor* books (memorial volumes) for different communities. The survivors wrote their memoirs in their native languages, and some were translated into Hebrew and published. Thus they developed a channel through which people were able to relate to the Holocaust and its reality from the perspective of the individual.[92]

Nevertheless, the large majority of survivors were not involved in formulating any specific way for the Holocaust to become an important subject for reflection and thought. The public discourse on the Holocaust was linked to the political rhetoric of death and rebirth, with the fighting in the forests and ghettos linked to the fighting of Israeli soldiers in the War of Independence and later battles. The call to remember was accompanied by a description of what exactly to remember. Speakers at Holocaust commemorations coupled the shame of those "going like sheep to the slaughter" with the valor of those who chose to die in battle. This contrast stressed the breach between the common people and the few heroes. Most of the survivors asked to speak at such ceremonies were drawn from the "fighters," such as Kovner, Yizhak Zukerman of the Warsaw ghetto, and Reizl Korchak of Bialystok. The other survivors participated in the ceremonies as part of the audience. The press reported that thousands attended these ceremonies. In those organized by municipalities, *landsmannschaften* activists were among the speakers, and they used the same rhetoric. The common people, everyday life under the Nazis, and the dilemmas of leadership under the incredibly difficult circumstances of Nazi rule were hardly ever mentioned.[93]

This soon changed. Two events occurred that moved large numbers of survivors to publicly voice their thoughts on the Holocaust and Israel. One was the reparations agreement with Germany in 1952, and the other was the Kasztner Affair in 1954. In both cases the survivors articulated what the public in general felt.

The Reparations Agreement. On March 13, 1951, the foreign minister of Israel, Moshe Sharett (Shertok), stated in the Knesset that Israel had submitted to the four Allied governments a request for compensation to the state of Israel of $1.5 billion from West Germany.[94] The sum was based on the approximate cost of the state's absorption and rehabilitation of half a million Holocaust survivors, calculated at a cost of $3,000 per capita. The Allied governments refused to handle the claim. A few months later, German Prime Minister Konrad Adenauer declared that West Germany was ready to compensate the Jews for material losses, and he invited representatives of Diaspora Jewish organizations and Israel to negotiate a plan. In January 1952 the Knesset approved the launching of the negotiations, and in September 1952 an agreement was signed. Germany agreed to pay Israel $845 million in goods in annual installments over a period of fourteen years.

In the Knesset the opposition to a reparations agreement with West Germany crossed political lines. The debates were highly emotional; protesters filled the streets, hurling insults at the government, calling for new elections, and resorting to violence. The street demonstrations were organized by both the Right and the Left—by Herut, headed by Menachem Begin, and by Mapam and the Communists. Every protest succeeded in drawing great numbers of people.[95]

The largest and most violent demonstration took place on January 7 and 8, 1952, when the Knesset was debating whether to empower the government to start negotiations with Germany. Highest on the agenda were the moral issues concerning the meaning of the agreement. Would it serve as a pardon to Germany, forsaking the remembrance of the Nazi crimes and the memory of Jewish suffering? These issues were raised in the context of Israel's role to protect Jewish honor, along with its responsibility to fashion the collective memory and to educate the young.[96] In this context, the establishment of any kind of relationship with Germany, even for the advancement of a just cause such as the absorption of the immigrants, was bitterly argued. Other major issues related to world order and politics: To what extent would the agreement contribute to Germany's return into the "family of nations"? How would the agreement reflect on the conflicting political goals of East and West?[97]

The government suggested a rational argument, using the same political grounds for reparations as those used by the Allies in their demands of Germany. Israel requested only a fraction of the public Jewish wealth that still remained in Germany for the rehabilitation of the survivors. Israel's success and growth were the only meaningful response to the Nazi crimes, and thus the "ingathering of the exiles," the phrase used in Zionist rhetoric to describe the mass immigration, was the primary goal that justified the negotiations with Germany. The agreement was not a pardon of Germany or a legitimization of a new Germany.

The reparations debate was important not only because it mobilized large numbers of survivors but also because it made the Holocaust an open topic of political bickering in the Knesset and in election campaigns. Herut accused the government of pursuing a policy that was indifferent toward the fate of the Jews. Mapam presented the reparations agreement as a betrayal of the "progressive and peace-loving nations," that is, the Soviet bloc, and it competed with the Communists in the use of politically correct rhetoric. These criticisms became major weapons against the government during the Kasztner Affair, which erupted in 1953.

The Kasztner Affair. Rudolf (Rezso) Israel Kasztner, a Zionist activist from Cluj, Transylvania, worked with a Zionist rescue committee in Budapest beginning in 1942. After the Nazi occupation of Hungary, the Germans made an offer to Joel Brand, the head of the Zionist rescue committee, to exchange Jews for goods that Germany needed for its war effort on the eastern front. Brand negotiated with Adolf Eichmann for the rescue of Hungarian Jews, whom the Germans planned to deport to Auschwitz. In May 1944 Brand was sent to Istanbul to convey Eichmann's offer to the Western powers. Meanwhile, the deportation of Hungarian Jews to Auschwitz went forward. In June 1944 Brand was arrested by the British and sent to Cairo.[98]

Kasztner, along with Brand's wife, Hanzi, took over the negotiations with the Nazis. He managed to rescue 1,685 Jews, who were sent by special train to Germany and eventually to Switzerland. During the last months of the war, Kasztner visited the concentration camps in Germany where Hungarian Jews had been deported and, with the help of Kurt Becher, a member of the economic division of the SS who was responsible for the confiscation of the wealth of Hungarian Jewry, helped to provide these camp inmates with food and clothing. These activities helped save the lives of many Jews in the winter of 1945. In 1947 Kasztner immigrated to Israel. He became active in the Mapai Party, held a government job, and was a potential candidate for the Knesset.[99]

In 1953 Malkiel Gruenwald, a Hungarian Jew, accused Kasztner in a mimeographed leaflet of being a Nazi collaborator and assisting in the deportation of the Hungarian Jews. Gruenwald claimed that in return for the rescue of the 1,685 Jews, a group that included members of Kasztner's family and friends, he had concealed from the general Jewish public information about the true destination of their deportation—Auschwitz. As Kasztner was a government official, the attorney general of Israel, Haim Cohen, who had helped structure the country's legal system, insisted that Kasztner or the state should sue Gruenwald for libel.

In January 1954 the trial began in Jerusalem. Gruenwald was defended by a young and talented lawyer, Shmuel Tamir, the Israeli-born son of a very prominent Revisionist family, the Katzenelsons, who had been an activist in the Irgun (the underground movement of the Revisionist Party during the Mandate period) and involved in the new Herut Party. Tamir left the party after failing to form a strong opposition to Menachem Begin. Kasztner's case was presented by Cohen, a German Jew who had immigrated to Palestine in the early 1930s. On June 22, 1955, Judge Binyamin Halevy, also a German Jew who had come to Palestine after the rise of Hitler, cleared Gruenwald. He accepted Gruenwald's three allegations against Kasztner: that he had collaborated with the Nazis; assisted in the preparations leading to the murder of Hungarian Jewry; and testified at the Nuremberg trials on behalf of a Nazi war criminal, Kurt Becher, who was acquitted. The court also blamed Kasztner for the tragic fate of Jewish parachutists from Palestine who had been dropped into Hungary in July 1944 by the British. He was accused of failing to act in the case of one of these parachutists, Hannah Senesh, who had been captured when she crossed the border from Yugoslavia to Hungary and then languished in prison for several months before being tried and sentenced to death by a Hungarian court. The judge ruled that Kasztner had ignored the plea of Hannah Senesh's mother to find a jurist to defend her daughter in court. The most striking sentence in the verdict was that "Kasztner sold his soul to Satan." This became the headline in all the papers and a theme that echoed for many years in the minds of Israelis. During the trial, in which Kasztner was ostensibly the plaintiff, he in fact became the accused and had to defend himself against the allegations made by Tamir. Halevy's verdict endorsed Tamir's claims, and soon there were calls to have Kasztner tried under the Law for the Punishment of Nazis and Nazi Collaborators.

The government appealed the verdict to the High Court, and in January 1958 the court reversed Halevy's decision, finding Gruenwald guilty on all charges and clearing Kasztner of all charges except that of testifying on behalf of Kurt Becher. However, the judges disagreed with Halevy's assessment that Kasztner's testimony had been decisive in Becher's release. The decision of the High Court was, however, too late for Kasztner, who was assassinated on March 4, 1957, by three right-wing extremists.

Kasztner's trial, the appeal, his murder, and the debates that followed reflected Israelis' understanding of and stereotypes regarding the Holocaust. The Kasztner Affair started a process of listening that made an open dialogue about the Holocaust possible in Israel. The trial raised four major issues, all of which were important in the political and social context of Israel and its ideological conventions: *(a)* the response of the Jews to the Final Solution; *(b)* the behavior of the Jewish leadership under Nazi occupation; *(c)* the reaction and policies of the Yishuv to the fate of European Jewry; and *(d)* the conflicting images and perceptions of the free, proud, active Israeli and the passive, submissive, and weak Diaspora Jew.

The last of these issues became the leitmotif of the trial. The compliance of the Jewish masses with the deportation orders was contrasted by Tamir with the possibility of engaging in armed resistance. The passivity of the Jews was condemned, and images of Jews who willingly concentrated in the ghettos and climbed into the deportation trains were widely conjured. The Hungarian Jews were portrayed as having been able to choose between resisting an uprising such as the one that occurred in the Warsaw ghetto and collaborating with the *Judenräte*. Although the ultimate outcome of either choice was death, one at least represented an honorable way to die. Tamir built his case using crude stereotypes to characterize the *Judenräte* and to attack Kasztner, even though Kasztner had never been a member of a *Judenrat* and the situation of Hungary had been very different from that of Poland.

Tamir did not invent the simplified portraits of Jewish leadership, the radical young Zionist *halutz* and fighter and the intimidated middle-class *galut* (Diaspora) Jew, exemplified by the *Judenrat* member, the negotiator and collaborator with the Nazis. These stereotypes had been sustained by the ghetto fighters and partisans, who after the war had continued their debates with the *Judenräte* in their own circles and in public presentations. They were also supported by the *Zeitgeist* of the years following the War of Independence. The need for heroes in Israel in the fifties was expressed in numerous books about fallen soldiers, such as *Haverim mesaprim 'al Gimi* (Friends speaking about Gimi), and in anthologies, such as *Sefer Haparti-zanim* (Partisan book), *Sefer Lohamei Hagetaot* (Ghetto fighter book), *Sefer Hama-'apilim* (The illegal immigration book), and *Sefer Hapalmah* (The Palmah book).[100] Tamir used these stereotypes to the hilt and completely ignored the implications of a more complex approach to the *Judenräte*.

Because of Tamir's viewpoint (which was totally opposite Kasztner's), rescue (as employed by Kasztner) was not presented as a viable alternative, nor was it justified in the courtroom. The images of the partisan heroes Anielewicz, Zukerman, and Mordechai Teneneboim-Tamaroff of Bialystok loomed over the court proceedings, and their actions and deaths became models of proper behavior. Accordingly, Hungarian Jewry was considered to have been a strong and large community in 1944 that nevertheless was unable to respond with honor to the Nazi threat, even during the last stages of the war. As portrayed by Tamir, the Hungarian Jewish leadership lacked heroes, and when the Yishuv sent its heroes, the parachutists Senesh, Goldstein, and Palgi, to Hungary, the Jewish leadership was unable to appreciate their potential contribution to the Jewish resistance, and the parachutists were extradited to the Nazis.

This portrait of Hungary was presented with all the benefits of hindsight and colored by the political conflicts in Israel. From Tamir's examination, one would assume that the Hungarian Jews had been free to decide how to organize and what sort of institutions to establish. Tamir maintained that the Jews of Hungary should have learned a lesson from the fate of their brethren in Poland. The Hungarian Jewish leadership, he claimed, could have arranged for a border crossing into Romania if only it had told the people what the Nazi policy held in store for them. Kasztner, Tamir suggested, should have urged the Jews to disobey the orders of the Nazis and the Hungarian police; in this way, said Tamir, he could have saved many. Tamir provided a simple explanation for all of Kasztner's alleged faults. The process of negotiation had inevitably corrupted Kasztner, leading him to the wrong decisions and into direct cooperation with the Nazis. He had concealed the truth from the Jews, frustrated their resistance, and assisted in their submissiveness. This was the culpability of the *Judenräte*.

The main thrust of Tamir's attack, however, was aimed at the Yishuv's leadership. Kasztner was one example of corrupted leadership, but his teachers were not in Poland, Lithuania, or other parts of occupied Europe but in Palestine. Since the early thirties the architects of cooperation, including Weizmann, Ben-Gurion, and Sharett (prime minister during the year of the trial), who had been responsible for the policy of cooperation with the British, had poisoned Jewish politics. They had deserted German Jewry in return for the Transfer Agreement, and they had mocked the evacuation plan Jabotinsky had offered for rescuing Polish Jewry because they were too blind to read the writing on the wall. They had continued to forsake European Jewry during the war years, suppressing the information they had available on the Final Solution. Finally, when Hungarian Jewry came under the Nazi yoke, they were ready to neglect the rescue mission of Joel Brand because of British opposition. The peak of their treachery was demonstrated in Palestine, when they handed over to the British the true freedom fighters of Israel, the members of the Irgun and of Lehi, a more extreme group that had split off from the Irgun.[101]

Tamir drew a straight line between the cooperation of the Yishuv's leadership with the British and collaboration under the Nazi occupation. The *Judenräte* embodied the Diaspora mentality, and the Yishuv leaders had planted this Diaspora mentality in Israel. Thus, stated Tamir, the roots of Kasztner's cooperation with the Nazis rested in Palestine. Moving to the issue of Jewish honor, Tamir stated that the defamation of the Jews had originated in Palestine and in the Zionist movement, which he and his political friends had abandoned to create a new Zionist movement. The trial revealed that the "king was naked," Tamir claimed, and that the government had rushed to support Kasztner to protect itself. For how long would this leadership be allowed to mislead the people? asked Tamir. In fact, Tamir and his supporters coined the term "kasztnerism" to describe authority used in a corrupt and unfaithful way; this, according to Tamir, was the heritage the Diaspora mentality left to the Mapai government and independent Israel.

The atmosphere in the courtroom was extremely emotional. Survivors of Hungarian Jewry, many of them the sole remnants of their families, attended. Some of them had been after Kasztner for several years, blaming him for the deaths of their loved ones. Kasztner was astounded that in the process of the trial he had become the accused. He had to defend his actions and credibility and vindicate himself as a person who had dedicated long and dangerous years to rescuing his fellow Jews. His friends and family, all the people in the rescue train, and those who had been active with him in his rescue efforts were tarred by the trial. The air in the courtroom was thick with disillusionment, fear, and anxiety.

As long as the trial continued, the press, according to Israeli law, could only report on what was occurring in the courtroom. After the verdict had been rendered, detailed analysis of the trial began. The political credos that had played a major role throughout in the trial continued to influence the interpretation of the trial. The verdict was handed down a few weeks before the elections of July 1955, and naturally the issue of the Yishuv leadership and its successor, the Mapai government, became central in the campaigns of both Right and Left. The left-wing Mapam party had split, and a new party, Ahdut Ha'avodah, formed in 1954, attracted disillusioned members of the Mapai and Mapam parties. In their rivalry, Mapam and Ahdut Ha'avodah both presented their followers as the leaders of the resistance during the Holocaust and as the elite underground unit Palmah during the War of Independence. The two parties of the Left competed in "collecting" heroes, and to some extent Mapai tried to follow the same course. The Communists were extreme in their loyalty to the Soviet bloc, which was in the midst of a major anti-Zionist and anti-Semitic campaign. They attacked the government for its "capitalist-neo-fascist" alliance with the West and were ready to endorse Tamir's interpretation of the pro-British approach of the Yishuv leadership.

All the parties except Mapai stressed the differences between a "proud, true

Israeli Zionist response" and that of the Jewish leaders in Europe during the Holocaust. Any attempt to offer a more moderate interpretation, one that accounted for the differences between countries and the periods of the war involved or one that avoided the simplistic stereotypes of the *Judenräte* and the resistance, was criticized as apologetic. The election in the summer of 1955 reflected great changes in Israel's political makeup. It would be wrong to refer to the Kasztner Affair and the verdict as the dominant factors in these changes. However, the emergence of Herut, the party Tamir belonged to, as the second strongest party, with 15 seats in the Knesset, can largely be attributed to the atmosphere created by the trial and the verdict. Mapai lost 5 seats but still remained the strongest party, with 40 seats in the Knesset (of a total of 120 members).

In general, the public and most of the parties respected the verdict, and even Mapai found itself in a difficult situation, as it was reluctant to undermine the status of the court. Yet more thoughtful and reserved responses were not totally absent. Articles by Moshe Keren, Natan Alterman, and Alex Barzel offered alternative viewpoints.[102] A major concern was whether the courtroom was an appropriate place for analyzing the methods Jewish leaders had employed in their rescue efforts. Keren compared the court's effort to reach a clear conclusion about Kasztner's activities and motivations to trying to clear fog with a sharp knife. It was a hopeless task. Keren believed that an investigative committee would reach a more accurate interpretation because it could study the whole period in depth.[103]

But the primary criticism of the trial and the verdict was that they forced a clear dichotomy between two Jewish responses under the Nazis: that of resistance and the *Judenräte.* Alterman declared forcefully that this easy division was a major error. The main tactic of the Jews under the Nazis was to work within the *Judenräte.* Indeed, even the different youth movements had cooperated with the *Judenräte* until the Nazi policy reached the very last stage of the Final Solution. The resistance realized that they could not demand an armed revolt as long as the slightest chance of survival remained. During the ghetto years, resistance members did not separate themselves from the rest of the community or from the Jewish leadership. They argued with the *Judenräte,* claiming that it was wrong to believe that negotiations, bribes, or the profits that the industry of the ghetto provided for the military or the SS might save the Jews. However, they were not ready to risk the entire ghetto unless there was no doubt that the end was at hand, with the deportation to extermination sites. They were bound by family bonds to the ghetto, and they shared the mutual responsibility of the entire community, which was threatened with collective capital punishment even for any minor insult. Even in the very last stages many of the young fighters debated whether to leave for the forests and hope for ultimate rescue or to stay and fight in the ghetto and surely die.[104]

Barzel related this point to the specific situation in Hungary. Any activity by Hungarian Jewry on Jewish matters was carried out through negotiations with the authorities. Bribes were common at the local and national levels and proved beneficial to the Jews. Barzel pointed to the social conditions of Hungarian Jewry, including the tension with the local population and the rampant anti-Semitism in the country. Many acts of terror were perpetrated against Jews in the annexed territories of Hungary, Transylvania, and Novisad. The forced recruitment of all male Jews between the ages of eighteen and forty-five into labor brigades had resulted in a Jewish population that consisted mostly of the elderly, women, and children.

The ghettos in Hungary, unlike those in Poland, merely served as assembly points prior to deportation, without the potential of self-organization. The deportations happened so quickly that in a few months some 600,000 people had been deported. At the time, the Russians were near the borders and Allied planes were bombing Budapest. How long can the war go on? Jews asked. Ironically, said Barzel, in the spring of 1944 Jews were more optimistic that the war was finally coming to an end. "Could anyone think of a revolt in that situation?" he asked. The natural response was to negotiate, bribe, gain time, and try to save as many as possible in various ways.[105]

Both Keren and Alterman believed that Tamir's assumption about the issue of Jewish knowledge and resistance was wrong. Even if the Almighty himself had come down to tell the Jews about Auschwitz, Alterman stated, they would not have been able to comprehend this information or react as the courtroom in Jerusalem thought they would have. The Nazis deceived the Jews in sophisticated ways, and their lies were easier to believe than any information about total annihilation. The sad reality was that the chances of the majority for being rescued on their own initiative or being smuggled over the borders were very small.[106]

Keren stated bluntly that if Kasztner was guilty, all the Jewish leaders and all the members of the rescue committee were collaborators. This was inconceivable; thus, he continued, the question to be raised was what had gone wrong in the courtroom. Alterman's most forceful outcry was against the perspective used in judging Kasztner. The Israeli set of values about fighting and heroism was inappropriate for the evaluation of the Jews in Nazi Europe. Israelis, including the resistance fighters themselves, had become captives of their own rhetoric, reflecting in it their own needs and the political rivalry among the different parties. This hindered their ability to think clearly. Heroes of a certain mold were admired, and Israeli public discourse froze them into stereotypes. "Our heroes," proclaimed Alterman, "were different, and we were unable to appreciate and admire them."[107]

The assassination of Kasztner in 1957 and the January 1958 decision of the High Court overturning, in a thorough and detailed analysis, the conclusions and assumptions of Judge Halevy could not be ignored.[108] The calls for constraint and for recognition of certain limits in dealing with such cases became more acceptable. This view was expressed in the press, often by the same people who had denounced Kasztner in 1955.[109]

However, the fierce debates did not extend beyond a small intellectual and semi-intellectual elite that read the literary supplements. Most people only heard the election propaganda of the political parties and read the clichés the reporters continued to use. For the public in general, the affair was a political one that only concerned Hungarian Jewry. For survivors, the assaults on the behavior of the Jewish leadership and the Jews in general under the Nazis proved once more that it was wise to keep a low profile about the Holocaust unless one had been a ghetto fighter or a partisan. This may explain why those who were rescued by Kasztner were silent in public.

The Eichmann Trial. On May 23, 1960, Prime Minister David Ben-Gurion announced in the Knesset that Adolf Eichmann, the chief architect of the Final Solution, had been captured in Argentina and brought to Israel to be tried under the 1950 Law for the Punishment of Nazis and Nazi Collaborators.[110] On April 11, 1961, Eichmann's trial began in Jerusalem, and on May 31, 1962, he was executed. The Eichmann trial was a turning point in the Israelis' attitude toward the Holocaust. During the two years between Eichmann's arrival in Israel and his execution Israelis began to confront the past with some humility and with greater sincerity than ever before. Moreover, in the wake of the trial, Israelis reflected on their self-image, their Zionist tenets, and their bonds with Diaspora Jewry. "No one would leave this court hall the same person as he was when he entered," wrote Haim Gouri, a well-known poet who reported on the trial.[111]

In a special Independence Day address in 1961, Israel's Bar Mitzvah year (the thirteenth year, which in the Jewish tradition marks the entrance to adulthood), Prime Minister Ben-Gurion called the Eichmann trial, which had just begun, one of most significant events in Jewish history and in the history of the state of Israel. This trial transcended the confines of common legal process since it was about "historical justice." The state of Israel was connected to the Holocaust in a tragic bond, and the murder of European Jewry had almost prevented the establishment of a Jewish state. Eichmann was not the only defendant in the court; the Nazi system as a whole and the entire phenomenon of Jew hatred, which had prepared the ground for the Holocaust, were also on trial. Ben-Gurion was convinced that Israel was the appropriate venue for this trial, for the Jewish state would not only do justice in the legal sense but also represent historical justice.[112] Ben-Gurion placed the Eichmann trial in the general ideological context of the role of Zionism in Jewish history, demonstrating once more the purpose of the Jewish state.

The Eichmann trial achieved numerous political, social, and educational goals. The motivations for holding this rather complex trial were many. The punishment of Nazi criminals was a basic desire of many survivors, some of whom had dedicated their lives to the achievement of this goal.[113] The Nuremberg trials had proven extremely disappointing to Holocaust survivors, for they barely touched upon the Holocaust, and the Jewish aspects of the history of World War II had remained a marginal topic. In order for a Nazi criminal to stand trial in Israel, force was required, such as in the abduction of Eichmann. Ben-Gurion's decision to try Eichmann must have been inspired by a very strong commitment, for only thus could he have justified such irregular action on behalf of the state of Israel. The motivations behind Ben-Gurion's actions rested on his understanding of the Holocaust and its meaning to the future of the Jews and on his strong belief that, by judging Eichmann, Israel would render a major service to itself and the world.

Ben-Gurion himself disclosed part of his reasoning. He stated that the lack of knowledge about the Holocaust on the part of young Israelis and new immigrants from Islamic countries was a barrier to their full understanding of Israel's objectives and everyday reality. A survey of Israeli schools disclosed that about half of them did not commemorate Holocaust Day and that the Holocaust was not even included in the school curriculum of the ministry of education. A short survey taken by an Israeli radio station on May 23, 1960, indicated that many Israelis were not familiar with the name Eichmann.[114] Ben-Gurion evidently thought that the time was ripe to confront the Holocaust and to come to terms with its history.

The atmosphere in Israel following the news of Eichmann's abduction was described as national hysteria. Government officials, in particular Minister of Justice Pinhas Rosen, and reporters tried to calm the situation so that a proper trial could be conducted. Others warned that people would expect from the trial what it could not render: the victims would not come back to life, and no punishment would be sufficient for the crimes Eichmann had committed.[115] The Israeli people and the Israeli government found it difficult to understand the reaction of Argentina, which protested to the U.N. Security Council that Israel had violated its sovereignty by kidnapping Eichmann. The unfavorable debate in the United Nations and international criticism forced the government to consider the implications of the trial, to define its goals more precisely, and to face its political and judicial ramifications.

The Eichmann trial presented the Israeli judiciary system with great challenges. Two primary principles of justice, an unprejudiced court and justice fairly dispensed, could easily be jeopardized. The basic assumption that the accused is innocent until proven guilty was difficult to maintain in the case of Eichmann. Public opinion and the accumulated knowledge about Eichmann left little room for assuming his innocence. Judge Halevy, who was supposed to preside over the court, had already referred to Eichmann as "Satan" in the Kasztner trial. Another issue that concerned critics was Eichmann's defense. Could an Israeli lawyer defend Eichmann adequately? Would the law allow for a foreign attorney to fulfill the task? Israel was criticized by a number of prominent international court authorities, who claimed that its desire to try Eichmann was a primitive quest for revenge and that it was unable to carry out a fair trial. They therefore maintained that Eichmann be tried either in an international court or in Germany. Because of all this criticism, it was important that the government and the legal authorities ensure that all the formal and necessary procedures of justice were performed to perfection.[116]

The most important decision the ministry of justice had to make had to do with the scope of the trial. One option was to restrict the trial to Eichmann's direct actions. Another option was to present Eichmann's crimes within the larger context of the origins of the Final Solution and its execution, providing a political, social, and cultural background of Europe between the two world wars and during World War II. The latter was chosen because the knowledge provided by the trial would enrich the understanding of the Holocaust in Israel and in the world.[117]

Government officials declared that both absolute justice and historical justice compelled Israel to try Eichmann, and they received overwhelming support from the Israeli public. For Israelis, who already believed that the establishment of the state was connected to the tragic fate of European Jewry, the trial added another dimension to the meaning of the Israeli Jewish reality. It was a mission fulfilled and homage paid to the victims (potential Israeli citizens) and a confirmation of the vitality of the state and its people.[118] It was Israel's duty, as derived from the ancient (and modern) perception of the Jews' universal mission to expose the Jewish and universal meanings of the Holocaust. No less important was the need to demonstrate that crimes against Jews were now accountable and that Israel was the true guardian of the Jewish people.[119]

Before the trial opened, the press was filled with articles from all political perspectives that revealed Israelis' limited understanding of the Jewish condition during the Holocaust. Israel's isolation in the world community, as demonstrated in the U.N. Security Council debate and criticism of the forthcoming trial, was compared by Israelis, for example, to the desertion of the Jews in occupied Europe. An analogy was drawn between the Allies' indifference to the plight of the Jews and the world's ignorance regarding Israel's right to try Eichmann. Some took this even further, claiming that those who opposed Israel's right to judge Eichmann were aiming at the destruction of Israel.[120] These sentiments revealed not only an attachment to the memory of the Holocaust but also a willingness to use it for common purposes. Thus most Israelis expressed pride at being the heirs of the Jewish victims without, however, really penetrating deeply into the meaning of the trial.

The positive feelings the forthcoming trial raised in Israel were accompanied by suspicion and reservations. Some feared the revelation of "concealed dark incidents," such as Jews' collaboration with the Nazis or their passivity. Others remembered the Kasztner trial and the way it had been manipulated in internal Israeli politics. This issue was particularly sensitive because the Knesset passed a special law to allow a High Court judge to preside over the trial, a position that was to be filled by Halevy. As the trial approached, the doubts increased. The feeling that a soul-searching process was fast approaching was deeply disturbing. How would it end? Where would Israel be when it was over?[121] Much anxiety was also demonstrated in the attitude toward Dr. Robert Servatius, Eichmann's German attorney. A special law was passed permitting a foreign lawyer to defend Eichmann. Servatius was watched constantly, and he was often criticized by the press. Many agreed that if he was ready to defend Eichmann, and he had already defended other Nazi criminals at Nuremberg, Servatius must be a Nazi.[122]

On April 17 and 18, in an eight-hour opening address, Gideon Hausner, the attorney general of Israel, who served as the prosecutor, presented a general picture of the Holocaust from its beginnings in Germany in 1933 through the end of the war. His first sentences electrified the spectators and the entire Israeli public: "As I stand before you, Judges of Israel, to lead the prosecution of Adolf Eichmann, I do not stand alone. With me, in this place and at this hour, stand six million accusers. But they cannot rise to their feet and point an accusing finger toward the man who sits in the glass dock and cry: 'I accuse.'" Hausner accused Eichmann of four categories of crimes: *(a)* crimes against the Jewish people, *(b)* crimes against humanity, *(c)* war crimes, and *(d)* participation in hostile organizations. He stated that Eichmann's role as an initiator, planner, organizer, and executer of the Final Solution would be proven through documents and testimony. Some of the witnesses had actually met Eichmann when the crimes were committed, and others had heard about his direct involvement.[123]

Since Hausner wanted to place the Holocaust in its historical context, Professor Salo Baron began the testimony by providing a historical account. He described Jewish life in Europe, along with its institutional and normative background. He established that anti-Semitism was the central motivation in Nazi Jewish policy and that Nazi anti-Semitism was a continuation of the Jew hatred of the past but maintained a singular racial dimension.[124] Then began the survivors' accounts.

Forty-six witnesses carefully selected by Hausner took the stand. The survivors, mostly Israelis from all walks of life, represented all the Jewish communities. Their testimonies reflected their deep pain and loss and told the stories of average people who had endured ghetto life, labor camps, mass murder, or hiding with Christians. Partisans, ghetto fighters, and the leaders of various communities also testified. Other witnesses provided a different perspective of the past. The testimonies of Christians who had saved Jews while risking their own lives proved that humanism had not disappeared totally. The testimonies of all the witnesses had an unforgettable impact on the audience, the reporters, and the court. On most days the hall was packed with people, not only survivors but also Israelis of all ages and ethnic backgrounds. Entrance tickets had to be ordered days ahead.[125]

Hausner kept to a certain pattern in examining the survivors. Each witness gave his personal story, and in some cases Hausner asked, "Why didn't you resist?" Thus he required many to deal with the issue of resistance. In most cases the answers were self-evident. Resistance was simply impossible in the situation of terror, starvation, humiliation, and isolation. Still, the answers revealed people's differing perspectives, the differing situations in different countries and localities in Europe, and the changes in each community as the war progressed. Thus, the testimony portrayed young and old, parents with children, and singles who were the sole providers for their parents and siblings. They demonstrated how complex the Jewish condition was and how sensitive and open-minded one had to be to understand it.

The Nazi system of punishing the whole Jewish community for the actions of an individual Jew was presented. The historical value of mutual responsibility among Jews had prevented many individuals from engaging in acts that might have been blamed on the whole population and caused more death and misery.[126] The hope of enduring and surviving was illustrated repeatedly, and various strategies of survival were mentioned. Some told how they kept thinking and rethinking their chances to live in the context of the political events, the progress of the war, and so on. Others noted that they simply kept from thinking about anything except the next minute, the next hour, or the next day in order to continue to have some hope.[127] In the context of the detailed accounts about Nazi policy regarding everyday life in the ghettos and camps, these strategies no longer seemed passive. A number of the witnesses told of their escapes from forced-labor camps or mass-murder sites and of jumping from trains on their way to the killing centers. Although told in an undertone and with reluctance, these were acts of extraordinary courage. When examined with the proper historical background, the survivors' hopes for a swift Russian offensive sounded quite logical. This became especially true after information about partisan warfare, the German defeat in North Africa, and the Allies' progress on the western front after June 1944 had infiltrated into the ghettos and camps. All of these together were suddenly regarded as reasons to hope.[128]

Hausner wanted the testimony to have such a compelling impact on the audience and the public that they would be able to identify with and understand the Jews' impossible situation under the Nazis. During the trial, the major themes of Holocaust discourse in Israel in the fifties were reexamined. The notions that the Jews went as sheep to the slaughter and that the only resistance is armed resistance came under renewed scrutiny. The attitudes of veteran Israelis toward the survivors began to change. The trial of Eichmann also personalized the murderer, which made the evil even more terrible and difficult to understand.[129]

The image of the Jews going as sheep to the slaughter was weakened by the personal descriptions of the circumstances. These accounts created great turmoil, as the combination of shame and pain was difficult to comprehend. Gouri wrote, "I don't want to listen to the long and painful account of this small and broken man . . . 'We were bitten, hungry, wet' . . . I don't want to see him. . . . However, I felt as if he were gripping my throat with unimaginable power and commanding me: 'Sit down and listen. . . . These are also part of your own people. You will not escape from this court.'"[130]

Only after hearing many different witnesses give many different answers to the repeated question, "Why didn't you resist?" were the public and the press able to understand their own inability to comprehend what had happened. They stopped grading the answers given by the witnesses. "We should all lower our heads in admiration after hearing these answers," wrote Moshe Tavor, a reporter of the trial.[131]

Following this realization, the press expressed its clear admiration for the survivors. The revelation of one of the witnesses, a survivor of mass killings and a forced-labor and death camp, that he was able to endure all the suffering and losses by keeping a diary to record all the events and the names of people whom he saw murdered left many breathless. It was the victims' wish that their story be told to the world, he said, and that Jews and other people never forget what happened.[132] The *Jerusalem Post* gave a moving account of the average people who went to their deaths without fighting back: "They were human beings. They had families and homes and dreams and had been kind to people and other people had been kind to them, and they had cooked their meals and washed the children and laughed over a good story. And now they were being asked to believe that human beings like themselves intended not only to starve them, to throw them out of their homes, to load them into trucks and carry them off and make them work like slaves; not only that but also to tear their babies apart, like tearing a cloth and to . . . it is no use. It really is unbelievable."[133] However, coupled with this wonder at the tenacity of the survivors were the seeds for distancing oneself from the Holocaust. The Holocaust was so unimaginable, unbelievable, and non-understandable that one could give up any effort to comprehend.

A new definition of resistance was formulated after the survivors gave their accounts. "There was resistance everywhere. The Jewish woman who spat in the face of a Nazi in the streets of Lwow was a resistance fighter. So were the prisoners of the ghettos and camps who, in the face of prohibitions backed by immediate death penalties in case of discovery, were clandestinely celebrating the Sabbath, lighting candles on Hanukkah, gathering for prayers on holidays, organizing schools and activities, even holding debates on national issues. All these were national resistance heroes."[134]

While there was now a deeper understanding of the Jewish condition, the uneasiness about the stereotypes had not yet dissipated, and the witnesses' testimony about the armed resistance was awaited eagerly. *Hazofeh,* the daily of the Religious Zionists, shed light on the prevailing Israeli attitude. Jewish resistance, *Hazofeh* believed, was based on two pillars: spiritual resistance and armed resistance. During the trial, *Hazofeh*'s reports stressed the Jews' courage in keeping the religious laws and the importance of the various self-help organizations that had sprung up in the ghettos, marking the continuation of the traditional community organization (the kehillah).[135] In reaction to Hausner's question, "Why didn't you resist?" following one survivor's testimony, *Hazofeh*'s reporter asked, "How come anybody resisted?"[136] However, when the paper described the Warsaw Ghetto Uprising, it elevated the revolt to the highest symbol of Jewish pride: "We are proud of the ghetto fighters, our sisters and brothers who saved the honor of Israel, who performed wonders in heroic acts and proved to the murderers, to Amalek [the symbol of evil and the traditional enemy of the Jews], that the people of Israel were not led as sheep to the slaughter, and that they were able to die with bravery. All generations should cherish and appreciate the memory of their sacrifice."[137]

This reaction demonstrates an interesting outcome of the deliberations and reflections on Jewish responses during the Holocaust. Following the testimony of witnesses, a greater understanding and empathy had developed for the "average Jew," "the men and women in the ghetto and the camp," and the behavior of the Jewish masses in general. As a result, armed resistance was even further glorified. While the dichotomy between the passive and active responses had been blurred, armed resistance now stood in even greater contrast to the logical options available to the Jews. The tangible description of the Jews' fear and their inability to oppose the Nazis actively, along with sympathy for the starving Jews and their suffering, created amazement at their endurance and their continued struggle for survival.

In this context, the testimony of the resistance leaders, with their careful descriptions of the painful process of understanding that the mass annihilation of the Jews was a planned policy of the Nazis, created even greater admiration for them. Hearing how difficult it was to get organized before the mass deportations of the summer of 1942 and how the isolation of the ghetto had made the acquisition of arms and other supplies impossible, the audience was compelled to acknowledge how unique the uprising was.[138]

The armed revolts and partisan warfare had been presented as unique acts of human courage and heroism ever since information about them had reached the Yishuv in 1943. Since then they had been revered in the public discourse, literature, and politics of Israel. During the forties and fifties these heroic acts assisted Israelis in identifying with the Holocaust, and in this respect they also demonstrated a need of the Israelis. The Eichmann trial signified a change in this perspective. Those acts that had already been internalized in the minds of Israelis were enhanced, and the first steps were taken to include them as part of the Holocaust sequence. Armed resistance was no longer regarded as a complete deviation from the general fate of the Jews but as a phenomenon that could somehow be placed in a chain of historical events and as part of the reactions of the Jews. The singularity of Jewish armed resistance was demonstrated in the context of the hopeless Jewish situation and by comparison with the various non-Jewish resistance movements.

The argument that only those who were there could really understand the reality and judge its protagonists was voiced and reenforced by the testimony of the writer K. Zetnik. The author described the "other planet Auschwitz": "Time does not run there as it does here on earth. Every fraction of a second there passes on a different scale of time. The inhabitants of this planet had no names; they had no parents; they were not born there and they did not beget children. They breathed according to different laws of nature. They did not live nor did they die according to the laws of this world."[139] The telling of the events, the detailed accounts by living people who had recovered their lives, studied, and were now serving as judges, doctors, carpenters, mechanics, and so on, transported the Holocaust even more than before to another planet. It was the only satisfying way to view something so difficult to grasp. Unlike in the forties and fifties, in the sixties this other planet occupied a prominent place in the Israeli consciousness. From the 1960s on, both the mystification and the historicization of the Holocaust were evident in the minds and scholarly works of many Israelis.

After the trial all the Zukermans, Roses, and Rechts who had testified went on living in the midst of Israeli society. The attitude toward the survivors had undergone an important transformation. During the first months after the capture of Eichmann, and in particular while the international debate raged, the survivors were the subject of pride. They were "entitled" to vengeance in its direct, instinctive sense. There was widespread sympathy for their feelings, and their various suggestions for punishing Eichmann were heard with understanding. But during the trial the survivors emerged as heroes who were not interested in an "instinctive primitive revenge." They embodied in their rehabilitation the meaning of Jewish rebirth.[140] By the end of the trial they had become "living memorials." In a society where the formation of the collective memory was of such importance, this was a central role. The survivors as a group became an essential part of the dialogue and negotiation with the Holocaust. Many felt impelled to employ their personal testimony for the education of future generations. They were asked to tell their stories to both students and soldiers. Education became a central component in the heritage of the Holocaust.

As a result of the Eichmann trial, the survivors would no longer be an anonymous group. They became individuals with names and biographies. The press expressed feelings of guilt about both the past and the present. The past was seen as a period of unawareness, with lectures, social life, and ideological debates going on as usual while the Jews in Europe were suffering so terribly. In the present this unawareness had continued. The Israelis had not appreciated the Greenspans and the Beiskies they worked with, sat next to in theaters, and passed on the streets.[141] The solidarity that grew from this realization called for deeper contemplation of the Holocaust and its meaning. Israelis felt they needed to make a stronger effort to empathize with the survivors and the memories that impinged on their daily lives. They expressed greater appreciation for the survivors' personal achievements. The artist Yehuda Bacon, the writer K. Zetnik, and the poet Abba Kovner were looked upon as spiritual giants who were to construct and preserve Israel's memory.[142]

Many survivors who before the trial had been hesitant to share their experiences with nonsurvivors came to feel, in the course of the trial and later, a responsibility to do so. The legitimization resulting from the opportunity to tell their stories publicly and the willingness of people to listen had just begun. Almost another decade would pass, however, before the nascent affirmation would completely erase their former silence.

Five Years and Six Days: A Memory and an Experience Intersect

After the Eichmann trial, public discussions of the Holocaust were more frequent. Many Israelis had learned of Yad Vashem's activities during the trial, and more young people visited the site as part of their high-school education. A comparison of articles on the Holocaust written in the 1950s with those written in the 1960s shows that during the earlier decade the daily papers limited themselves primarily to reporting about the commemoration ceremonies and major addresses given on the topic. In the 1960s, however, the press started to publish more scholarly articles on the Holocaust, along with interviews with survivors. This more thoughtful coverage provided new information, cast light on unknown events, and offered fresh interpretations of various incidents that occurred during the Holocaust.[143]

Despite the new sensitivity that developed during the Eichmann trial, the central themes in Holocaust discourse remained armed resistance, the passivity of European Jewry, the need to remember the lessons of the Holocaust, and the vow "Never Again." The tone of many articles had changed but not the subjects. Quite frequently articles reflected ambivalence about the issue of resistance. An interesting example is an article entitled "Why Didn't They Escape? Why Didn't They Resist?" After the author explained all the reasons why armed resistance and escape were so difficult, he concluded, "If millions would have broken the ghettos' gates when the occupation was in its first stages, . . . it could have been more difficult for the Germans to concentrate them in the ghettos and camps and implement the Final Solution. Had it not been for such shortcomings, hundreds and thousands of Jews could yet have lived with us."[144] The judgmental approach had not yet dissipated, and many were still unable emotionally to accept the logical explanations of what had occurred. Treating the Holocaust as "another planet" enabled Israelis to avoid historical explanations; it was easier to relate to the individual stories of the survivors. The desire existed to learn and understand what had actually happened, but in the minds of many Israelis the events of the Holocaust were still unstructured and unconnected pieces of information about what had happened "over there."[145]

Five years after Eichmann was put to death, Israel experienced the trauma of "death and rebirth" in a very concrete way. During May and June 1967 the expression "death and rebirth," which had been employed regularly in Holocaust Day addresses and discussed in the aftermath of the Eichmann trial, moved from mere academic discourse to becoming part of the life experience of every adult Israeli Jew, regardless of age or origin. On June 6, 1967, the Six-Day War broke out. In a week of fierce battles Israel fought its three Arab neighbors—Egypt, Syria, and Jordan—and managed to conquer the Sinai Desert, the Golan Heights, the West Bank, and East Jerusalem, including the Old City.

The three weeks before the war started were fraught with anxiety. The Arabs' threats to destroy Israel and the political and military steps taken by Egypt and then by Syria and Jordan compelled Israel to prepare for war. Internationally, Israel felt deserted by the United States and Europe; France announced its neutrality; and the Soviet bloc was vociferously anti-Israel. The U.S. position seemed inconsistent, with the State Department and President Lyndon B. Johnson speaking at cross-purposes. This caused embarrassment and uncertainty in Israel. The situation seemed very dangerous, and many military experts abroad warned that Israel would suffer considerable losses if it had to confront a military coalition of Egypt, Syria, and Jordan.[146]

The fear mounted in Israel. The whole country was mobilized; most men aged eighteen to forty-five were in the army for long weeks, and the atmosphere was very tense. The Arabs' rhetoric consisted of extreme propaganda, including threats to destroy Israel, wipe it from the face of the earth, and push it into the sea. These sentiments were regularly voiced in large gatherings in Arab capitals, followed by long and inflammatory speeches.

Regardless of the true intentions of Nasser and other Arab rulers, this constant incitement was taken at face value by many Israelis. The Holocaust had taught them to fear such threats. "Never consider such rhetoric as merely that" was the message of many news articles. Jews had suffered in the past for not believing the rhetoric they heard; they had made the mistake of thinking that propaganda was meant to appeal to the emotions of the masses but was not to be taken seriously.[147] Partisan and survivor organizations cabled various governments and associations of war veterans in Europe and the United States asking them to press the Arabs to stop their belligerence and to denounce their call to destroy Israel. These appeals referred to the Holocaust and the Nazis' policy of annihilation and to the high toll the world and the Jews had paid for not being aware in time of the Nazis' real intentions.[148]

Two comparisons from the Holocaust period frequently appeared in the press: Egypt's ruler Gamal Abdel Nasser was likened to Hitler, and Czechoslovakia before the Munich agreement of September 1938 was compared with Israel. The first comparison was adopted by many and elaborated through textual comparisons of Hitler's and Nasser's rhetoric. In the latter comparison, however, the differences were stressed. Unlike the Czechs, the Israelis, who had learned the lesson of the Holocaust, were ready to fight for their independence. Jews had experienced abandonment during the Holocaust and had learned that they could rely only on themselves.[149]

The Holocaust was also mentioned by Prime Minister Levi Eshkol in a letter to Soviet Prime Minister Aleksei Kosygin on June 7, 1967. Eshkol referred to Nasser's scheme to "destroy the State of Israel, which embodies the memories of victims and the hopes of an old nation. In the last generation, the Jews lost millions of people, who were murdered by the Nazis in the most cruel way."[150] By connecting the Jewish experience during the Holocaust and the Arabs' belligerence with Israel as the embodiment of the visions and hopes of the victims of the Holocaust, Eshkol demonstrated to Kosygin the complex nature of Israel's reaction to any incitement to use force against it. As prime minister, Eshkol of course expressed the basic responsibility of the government for the safety of its citizens. However, he also revealed a deeper awareness of Israel's broader responsibility to ensure the future of the Jewish people, which was conditional on Jewish independence, as proven by the Holocaust experience. After the war had ended, a young Israeli-born soldier expressed it another way: "The Jewish aspect of the war applies to each one of us. Something in our education has made us very conscious of the Jewish tragedy. The war was a link in a chain of actions that derive from this tragic feeling. Our opponents, the Arabs, are really equal partners in this tragic conflict. But, unlike us, they're quite unprepared to fill the role. In this instance their role was to be defeated. The Jews, as they appear in this conflict, have undertaken to struggle for survival."[151]

In his book *The Israelis: Fathers and Sons* Amos Elon described the transformation of Israelis after the 1967 war:

> In the Six Day War of 1967, the Israeli people came of age. . . . The 1948 war of independence had been harder to win; but it had taken place before the arrival of mass immigration. The 1948 war had been a unique moment of grace; during their first war with the Arabs the Israelis had been able to rely upon the support of the USA and the Soviet Union. . . . This time they stood alone. When most was at stake, they could stand up and shape their own future. They proved it to others, but above all to themselves. . . . The psychological effect was even greater. For Israelis it marked the transition from adolescence to maturity.[152]

What did this coming of age mean in the context of the Holocaust? Not all Israelis had the same experience. Even in the same ethnic or social group, different generations experienced the war differently. Since the social history of Israel remains to be written, I will examine the experience of only one social group, Israelis of European origin. Whether born to native Israeli parents or to parents who had been educated in the country since early adolescence, they can help us understand what the experience of the Six-Day War meant in the context of the Holocaust.[153] The Six-Day War demonstrated this generation's ties and commitment to their country and the meaning of their contribution to it. Since they had been brought up with a legacy of heroes—the founding fathers of Israel—but also with the images of the dishonored Jewish condition in the pre-Israel Diaspora, their self-image included both shame and pride.

Everyday life in Israel in the sixties before the war was difficult economically, as a depression engulfed the country from 1964 to 1966. The political structure was shattered by a political crisis that followed Ben-Gurion's withdrawal from the Labor Party and his establishment of a new political party, Rafi, in June 1965. The feuds among the veteran leadership, on the one hand, and the control by the ruling party, Mapai, of the power centers, on the other, caused many young Israelis to despise politics. The options offered to young people for "heroic fulfillment" in the service of their country were few. Whereas some Israelis made the army the focus of their identification, for many personal fulfillment and a professional career became central. In this context, the generation aged twenty-five to thirty-five in the late 1960s searched for their identity and their particular role in the social and political life of Israel.[154]

After the War of Independence, in which 1 percent of the population (6,000 of the 600,000 people of the Yishuv) had been killed, bereavement had dampened the excitement of the great moment. In comparison, the human toll of the Six-Day War, while painful, was much smaller than had been anticipated, with 777 killed and 2,586 injured out of a population of approximately 2.5 million. Both the great anxiety before the war and the swift victory, with relatively few casualties, made jubilation possible. People realized how fine a line divided death and life, and thus the expression "from death to rebirth," which had been utilized so frequently, was now filled with significance. For twenty years this expression had been but a conception, but now it had become a reality.[155]

Soldiers who were members of kibbutzim (and who belonged to the same demographic group mentioned above) were interviewed shortly after the 1967 war about its goals, its meaning, and its outcome. The Holocaust was referred to directly and indirectly in these interviews. The image these soldiers had of the Holocaust demonstrated part of the collective memory. They talked about their impressions of their visits to Yad Vashem, the commemoration ceremonies in school, and personal associations with survivors. The soldiers often expressed great confusion about how they had confronted the Holocaust prior to the war.[156]

One soldier reflected on the fact that he had been sitting idly on the northern front and absorbing heavy shelling from the Syrians on the Golan Heights. His family had remained in a kibbutz on the Syrian border that had suffered a lot of the shelling. The order to start the operation to conquer the Golan Heights was not given until the fourth day of the war. This enforced idleness at a time when his family and home were in danger and throughout the rest of the country the Israelis were moving forward victoriously led to certain associations with the Jews during the Holocaust. "We discussed this question. We said a thing like that couldn't happen.

The Jewish people would never forgive a thing like that—letting them in to wipe out a whole settlement. Perhaps that is our link with the Jews of Europe. . . . It's a subject one doesn't think about consciously. But for all that, it does have a role to play. In fact, . . . we can't permit a similar thing to recur. The memory and the lesson of the gas chambers are part of our national honor, part of our lives here."[157]

One way Israelis interpreted the meaning of the Holocaust before and during the war was as a command to survive. The fear of being occupied by the enemy, a natural fear for any country that fights a war on its own soil, was magnified because of the memory of the Holocaust, and the idleness on the northern front was taken out of its natural context as part of a military strategy. The idleness was seen as shameful behavior because it was reminiscent of the passivity of European Jewry during the Holocaust. Another soldier, Menahem Shelah, the son of a survivor, connected the Holocaust to his war experience in a totally different way: "I felt uneasy about being part of a victorious army, a strong army. If I had any clear awareness of the World War years and the fate of European Jewry it was once when I was going up the Jericho road and the refugees were going down it. I identified directly with them. When I saw parents dragging their children along by the hand, I actually almost saw myself being dragged along by my own father."[158]

The Holocaust acted as a two-edged sword. Together with Jewish history and Zionist ideology, it served both as a source of justification for ruling the belligerent Arabs and as a source of criticism for the occupation system and the military rule imposed on the West Bank and Gaza. The justification stemmed from the political situation before the war and from the state of siege that had caused such fear and anxiety on Israel's part. The conviction that Israel was morally right since it had been forced to fight was strengthened by the reactions of the West before and during the war. Following the Six-Day War, the issues concerning the Holocaust in Israeli public discourse changed.

During the 1970s and 1980s four major events greatly influenced the way the Holocaust was viewed and examined in Israel. In October 1973 the difficult and costly Yom Kippur War with Egypt and Syria surprised Israel and prompted Israelis to question much of the self-confidence they felt about their military power. In 1978 Israel and Egypt signed the Camp David Accords. In July 1983 Israel started a war in Lebanon because of the military buildup of the PLO and was dragged into a complicated venture in dominating another Arab population. Finally, in 1987 the Intifada, an uprising of the Palestinians in Gaza and the West Bank against the Israeli occupation, began.

A growing and painful internal political and social rift split Israel. The predominant issues concerned Israel's conflict with the Arabs and Palestinians and the future of the occupied territories. The expansion of Jewish settlements in the territories and the political and paramilitary development of the PLO added to the hostility of the conflict. The struggle of the two nations over the same piece of land was concretized in Israel's rule over two million Palestinians and the daily encounters with a civilian population that grew more desperate and aggressive.

These issues dominated defense and security concerns as well as the destiny of

Israel as a Jewish, democratic state. They were also inevitably linked to discussions about Jewish history, Judaism, and the Holocaust. The traditional political division in Israel between Left and Right changed during these years, as the debates cut across traditional party lines. Left and Right were defined according to each party's willingness or unwillingness to compromise on a new partition of the land between the two nations. The Holocaust was invoked in the arguments of all the political factions, and its moral implications were cited often, with diametrically opposed interpretations being given to its significance. The Holocaust became even more a political tool of both the Right and the Left.

Research on the Holocaust advanced rapidly. In 1961 the first chair of Holocaust studies was created at Bar Ilan University. The Institute of Contemporary Jewry was established at the Hebrew University of Jerusalem in 1962, and a chair for Holocaust studies was founded. Other universities followed, and master's theses and doctoral dissertations were written on a variety of aspects of the life of the Jews during the Holocaust. Yad Vashem's research programs were also expanded, and a research committee composed of historians was established. Primary documents, such as the papers of the *Judenräte* of Bialystok and Lublin, were published, and important monographs were written on Warsaw, Vilna, Slovakia, Romania, and the death camps. *Yad Vashem Studies,* a scholarly publication sponsored by Yad Vashem, became an important outlet for the new research, and other periodicals dedicated to the Holocaust, such as *Yalkut Moreshet,* were developed. Beginning in 1968 Yad Vashem has hosted international academic conferences every four years in which specific topics of the Holocaust have been explored in the context of Jewish history, Nazism, and World War II. The first such conference dealt with Jewish resistance, and armed resistance was presented as only one of its manifestations. Other conferences examined rescue during the Holocaust, Jewish leadership in occupied Europe, the death camps, and more.

The uniqueness of the Holocaust is one aspect that has been examined by Israeli historians and intellectuals. The view that the Holocaust is a singular event in history is generally accepted in the scholarly community and among the public. The combination of Nazi racial anti-Semitism, which had been built on the foundations of late-nineteenth-century anti-Semitism, together with the deliberate and systematic plan to murder all the Jews, confers particularity upon the Holocaust. However, the Holocaust cannot be separated from the more general phenomenon of genocide, which is defined as the attempts by the Nazis and other governments before and after World War II to destroy entire populations.[159]

The impact of academic research on public discourse was not always evident, but more commemoration addresses and articles in the press began to raise major questions that had been taken up by researchers, and these scholars' findings were used by speakers and writers to buttress their views. A dialogue between the collective memory of the Holocaust and the new conclusions arrived at through research influenced Israelis' understanding of the Holocaust.[160] Thus, the issues addressed below demonstrate not only the strong impact of social and political reality but also the stage of the intellectual scholarly debate in Israel.

The World Reacts to the Holocaust

The major issues in the public discourse concerned the relationship between the free world and the Holocaust; the relationship between the Holocaust and the Arab/Palestinian–Israeli conflict; and the universal and moral implications of the Holocaust.

The Free World and the Holocaust. As mentioned earlier, in the three weeks preceding the Six-Day War the Israelis were extremely disappointed by the lack of support provided by Europe and, to a lesser extent, the United States. Expressions such as "The world is against us" and "We stand alone as did the Jews during the Holocaust" appeared in the press. However, the anxiety was so strong, and the situation seemed so grave, that sympathy and support were sought everywhere, and the anger about abandonment was mitigated somewhat in the press by reports of supportive public opinion among certain political groups in Europe, the positive attitude of the American president, and the tremendous support of the Jewish world. In the wake of victory, Israel's confidence increased, but the world's reaction became more crucial. It was manifested in the commemoration addresses of Israeli officials and in articles that examined the political situation.

In a commemoration address in Tel Aviv, Deputy Prime Minister and Minister of Education Yigal Allon talked about the lessons of the Holocaust after the Six-Day War.[161] He listed three lessons learned from the war, which were actually traditional Zionist tenets that had been proclaimed on numerous occasions since 1948. The first was that Israel was here to stay and no justifications for its existence were needed. Israel lived because its people wanted it, and it had proved its viability and its ability to defend itself. The second lesson was that the Jewish people were no longer a pawn of history; they had entered world history actively and now determined their own destiny. The third lesson was that nobody was entitled to teach Israel its moral obligations. Israel had proved this when it faced the ultimate moral demand of self-defense, despite the abandonment of the West—the same West that had fought against Hitler and yet had not cared to rescue the Jews. Israel was therefore free to set the conditions of its security and political arrangements with its Arab neighbors. Prime Minister Levi Eshkol gave a speech in Jerusalem at Yad Vashem that was reported in the press under the headline, "The Prime Minister to the Nations of the World: You Did Not Help Us in Our War—Don't Help after the Victory."[162] In later years this response to criticism grew stronger.

The Holocaust and the Conflict between the Israelis and the Arabs and Palestinians. The media depicted the Arabs as the successors of the Nazis, and Nasser and his successor in Egypt, Anwar Sadat, as following in the footsteps of Hitler. The fact that young Sadat had supported Nazi Germany during the early 1940s in the hope of gaining Egypt's independence was often cited to confirm his anti-Jewish feelings. The swastika appeared in newspaper cartoons about Sadat or Nasser. The PLO and its leader, Yassir Arafat, supposedly inspired by Hitler's ideology, were described as planning a new "Final Solution."[163]

The issue of anti-Semitism came up more frequently in the press and public discussions during the 1970s and 1980s. The increase in the number of neo-Nazi groups in Europe and the anti-Israeli and anti-Semitic rhetoric of the radical Right and Left in the West and in the Communist bloc alarmed Israelis and led to associations with the Holocaust.[164] On the occasion of the commemoration of the thirtieth anniversary of the Warsaw Ghetto Uprising in April 1973, the speakers in a special session of the Knesset drew parallels between past and present events and condemned anti-Semitism and stressed its dangers. The report of these Knesset speeches in the newspaper *Haaretz* was entitled "Even Today the Movement of Jew Hatred Has Not Ceased: This Was the Background That Made the Holocaust Possible."[165]

On November 9, 1975, Israel was humiliated and appalled by a U.N. resolution that defined Zionism as "a form of racism and racial discrimination." Seventy-five delegates voted for the resolution, twenty-two opposed it, and twenty-five abstained. It was initiated by the PLO with the support of the Arab states, the Soviet bloc, and most African and Asian countries. The resolution reflected the influence on the Third World of the Soviets and the Arabs, who together made up a substantial majority in the U.N. General Assembly. Israelis were outraged; in their minds, the resolution embodied the convergence of anti-Israeli politics, anti-Semitism, and the influence of Nazism. The Holocaust was frequently mentioned in the public discussions that followed, in such statements as "Israel will not be a second Czechoslovakia" or "The memory of the six million was dishonored."[166] The fact that the U.N. vote took place on the thirty-seventh anniversary of Kristallnacht made the connection with the Holocaust even more significant. The press and the Knesset reminded Israelis of their responsibility to remember. "Slander Preceded Destruction," warned an article published in *Haaretz*. Thus, the PLO, Arab enmity, and Nazism were directly related. The press, however, also described the opposition of most Western European countries and the United States to the resolution.[167]

The Universal and Moral Implications of the Holocaust. The universal and moral implications of the Holocaust were frequently raised in public discussions and in intellectuals' deliberations after the Six-Day War, and the repercussions of ruling almost two million Palestinians in the occupied territories became more apparent. The Holocaust was mentioned in the context of examining the meaning of Zionism in the new political and social context of a more secure Israel. The Holocaust was by no means the center of the debate, nor was it always examined in a deep and sincere way. Since different groups used the Holocaust to gain support for their political position—the expansion of Israeli settlements, the establishment of a Palestinian state in the West Bank and Gaza, and many other concrete sociopolitical problems—it emerged frequently in public discussions. That the Holocaust was used in such different contexts exemplified how central it had become in the collective memory of Israel. The radical Left claimed that the Right abused the Holocaust by stressing only its national Jewish character and neglecting completely its meaning for all humankind. The Right, they added, reinforced the manipulation of the memory of the Holocaust to fan hostility against the Palestinians, so that the interpretation of the Holocaust as a unique historical event unparalleled in human history had come to serve an ideology of Jewish isolation among the nations and the singularity of the Jewish fate and history. The Left maintained that the Right encouraged a mythic, noncomparative, ahistorical perspective of the Holocaust and that politically it had established a "Holocaust complex" in Israel.[168] The Left also attacked the research at Yad Vashem, claiming that the unclear division within the organization between commemoration and scholarship had led its researchers to present the history of the Holocaust within a narrow Jewish perspective and that their scholarship was loaded with ideology.[169] A 1986 issue of *Politika,* a quarterly published by the Ratz Party, that was dedicated to the Holocaust demonstrated this position. The opening article, by Adi Ofir, attacked the practice of viewing the Holocaust as unique and asked Israelis to abandon all national conclusions drawn from the history of the Holocaust and to see the Holocaust as a manifestation of universal evil.[170]

Yehuda Elkana harshly criticized the "nationalization" and "internalization" of the Holocaust in an article entitled "The Need to Forget."[171] Responding to the public outrage at the army's violent response during the first months of the Intifada, Elkana proposed that the way the Holocaust was remembered in Israel caused Israelis to view themselves as permanent victims. As a result, they not only ignored their victimization of others but also overreacted when their soldiers aggressively confronted rioting masses of civilians.

Despite twenty years of domination over the West Bank and Gaza, Israel was unprepared for the active resistance of a civilian population in which women and young children often led the attacks. Storms of stones and other forms of homemade ammunition rained upon Israeli soldiers in the narrow alleys of Arab towns and villages. The first reaction of the army authorities was very forceful, and the aggressiveness of the response came as a surprise to Israeli soldiers and the general public. Shots of Israeli soldiers beating captive Palestinians or running to catch teenagers and smaller children were shocking. All the political parties were embarrassed. The Left, which opposed the occupation altogether, protested against the army's policy, which it claimed did not respect the basic principles of human rights or the accepted code of behavior during wartime. The Left also criticized the educational system and accused the army of the corruption that inevitably arises during a long occupation. The Right felt that the criticism of the army was unjustified. The Palestinians chose to attack the army with mobs of children and women, and the soldiers simply had to defend themselves. If, however, the army exerted more force than was necessary, this was because of the pressure and anxiety it was experiencing.

Elkana's article on this controversy provides an interesting perspective. Elkana was a boy of ten when the Red Army liberated him from Auschwitz. Afterward he spent a few months in Soviet "liberation camps." He wrote that his personal experiences had taught him that anybody could conduct acts of extreme cruelty and that "what happened in Germany could happen anywhere, and to any people, also to my own."[172] He claimed he was immune from confusion and overreaction when he was confronted with what people would call "anomalous incidents," such as soldiers' beating young captive Palestinians.

Elkana realized that the extreme reactions of the public to the brutalities of Israeli soldiers were rooted in nonrational thinking. He surmised that both the reaction of the army and the protests of the public came from "a profound existential *Angst,* fed by a particular interpretation of the lessons of the Holocaust and the readiness to believe that the whole world is against us, and that we are the eternal victim." Israel's future as a democratic state was at stake because of these fears that led Israelis to nonrational conclusions. "Had the Holocaust not penetrated so deeply into the national consciousness, I doubt whether the conflict between Israelis and Palestinians would have led to so many anomalies," wrote Elkana. The command to remember the Holocaust distorted the self-understanding of Israelis. Elkana concluded that instead of remembering, "we must learn to forget. . . . We must uproot the domination of that historical 'remember!' over our lives."[173]

While Elkana did not offer a substantial explanation of the behavior of Israeli soldiers in the Intifada or articulate the existential fear in the history of Israel, his attempt to understand the use of excessive force at this stage of the Israeli-Palestinian conflict through reference to the Holocaust demonstrated the importance given to the dialogue between Israel and the Holocaust. However, the nationalistic interpretation of the dichotomy between the universal and particular meanings of the Holocaust did not result in a rich historical debate, nor did it enrich the public discourse on the Holocaust; it merely reflected the radicalization in the political expression of the dialogue during the 1970s and 1980s.[174] These issues crystallized in the discussion about the Holocaust and education in Israel.

The Holocaust and Education

Every educational system is situated at the crossroads between the past and future. Its primary responsibility is to prepare the young to live in the world of the future while safeguarding the continuity of the society from the past through the present to the future. An education must provide the knowledge and emotional experiences to foster the solidarity of the society and strengthen the identification of the individual with the heritage and culture of that society. The role of education was of utmost importance in the Zionist revolution. Zionism faced conflicts between religious and nonreligious Zionists, on the one hand, and between the negation of the Diaspora and the affirmation of its cultural heritage, on the other. Thus, from its outset Hebrew education in Palestine confronted special difficulties concerning its content, educational goals, and the traditional values of most parents and the majority of teachers. Many parents and intellectuals of the Zionist movement, for example, were unable to agree to an educational system that would not contain the study of the traditional Jewish literature. Thus, the revolutionary messages of Zionist ideas, together with the influence of new educational thinking, created tension that burdened the educational system.[175]

In this context, a complicated task in curriculum planning was to select those events from Diaspora history that would enhance Zionism without breaking altogether with past traditions. It was important to construct a heroic past based on all of Jewish history without alienating the youth from Diaspora Jewry, for it was hoped that its members would eventually immigrate and join the Yishuv in Palestine and, later, Israel. It may be appropriate to quote in this context the French writer André Malraux: "The Israelis are not simply a continuation of the Jew, they represent his transformation." Yet it would appear that this transformation was too great a challenge.[176]

The success of the Yishuv and Israel in achieving both the continuation of Jewish tradition and the transformation of the Jewish self-image was limited. In practice, Israeli youth felt superior to Diaspora Jews and very far removed from their cultural heritage. In spite of their activities in helping survivors to reorganize their lives in the DP camps and their work in illegal immigration, the young Israeli was detached from the Diaspora Jew.

"The Zionist Period," 1948–1977. It is therefore natural that issues concerning the younger generation's knowledge of the Holocaust and its meaning have come to the fore since the late 1940s. The incomprehensibility of the Holocaust and the possibility that the memory of the Holocaust would fade away and the knowledge about European Jewry and its social and spiritual world would disappear were of great concern to the Israeli political elite of the 1950s. This, they feared, would fulfill Hitler's wish to obliterate the Jews.[177]

A sense of unease was expressed in discussions about the teaching of the Holocaust and the ability to transmit an understanding of it to later generations. This concern derived not only from the innate incomprehensibility of the Holocaust but from anxiety that the terrible stories of the Holocaust might cause emotional damage to the youngsters and from the denigration with which Israeli youth treated Jewish history in the Diaspora in general and the Holocaust in particular. Many young Israeli students had negative stereotypes of Diaspora Jewry that were supported by the Hebrew literature they studied. Much of the modern Hebrew literature stressed the poverty and humiliation of the Jews of Eastern Europe and contained many anti-Semitic stereotypes.

Jewish history after the destruction of the Second Temple was perceived mostly as a series of persecutions and pogroms and a period of the rule of outdated religious and rabbinic law. Many of the nonreligious youngsters, picking up on the direct and indirect messages of their parents, felt detached from that reality. On the other hand, they felt admiration for the free, proud, brave, straightforward native-born Sabras, who displayed a remarkable sense of solidarity with their peer group and dedication to national causes.[178]

Very little was actually taught about the Holocaust in Israeli schools until the late 1970s. In 1979 the Holocaust was introduced as an independent unit in the high-school curriculum, and in 1981 it was introduced as a unit of the matriculation exams, thereby sanctioning its being taught to graduating classes. This did not occur earlier because of the great ambivalence toward the Holocaust in Israel during its first two decades.

Until the early 1970s most of the information students gained on the Holocaust was through various commemoration ceremonies, but even these did not become a mandatory part of the school curriculum until 1958. Thus, the knowledge students acquired was neither systematic nor coherent and was completely divorced from any historical context. Furthermore, it was laden with phrases suitable for commemoration ceremonies, aimed mostly at eliciting an emotional response. Students' difficulty in relating to the events of the Holocaust was intensified by the lack of information and any real intellectual challenge. Young people often cited the passivity of the Jews or their going as sheep to the slaughter to explain the large number of Jews murdered in Europe.

In the early 1960s two new high-school history textbooks incorporated substantial units on the Holocaust. However, an analysis of these books reveals a strong emotional and ideological bias.[179] In 1963 the ministry of education offered a course entitled "The Ghetto during the Holocaust" as an elective in the matriculation examinations. However, because there were few satisfactory course materials and teachers' knowledge of the subject was limited, very few students chose the course.

Sociological research on the attitudes of Israeli high-school students conducted after the Eichmann trial reflected a change. The students displayed a more positive attitude toward Diaspora Jewry and made an effort to understand its hopeless situation. Indeed, some 88 percent of the young people—the vast majority—now felt proud of the behavior of European Jewry during the Holocaust. The nonreligious youth related mostly to Jewish resistance, while the religious youth expressed their admiration for the efforts of Jews in the Holocaust to keep the religious laws and their willingness to sanctify God. The students now viewed the Holocaust as a meaningful event in Israel's life.[180] A study conducted a few years after the trial using a group of Israeli soldiers who had been in high school at the time of the trial confirmed these findings and indicated that students' level of interest in the history of the Holocaust was higher after the trial than before.[181] In general the studies demonstrated that students had a more positive attitude toward the Holocaust than their teachers had thought.

It is interesting that many high-school students who endured a prolonged teachers' strike in the spring of 1961 used the opportunity to visit the hall where the Eichmann trial was taking place. Some of the second generation of Holocaust researchers attribute their acute interest in the subject to their experience as spectators at the trial. Only a minority of the students could visit the trial, however, and because of the strike the teachers were unable to use the months of the trial to deepen their knowledge of the Holocaust.

Given all this, curricula did not change considerably during the Eichmann trial. Teachers realized that they lacked the appropriate materials for the classroom. The ministry of education initiated some teachers' seminars in cooperation with the Ghetto Fighters Museum, but these were insufficient. Many teachers complained that they lacked a basic knowledge of the Holocaust and were unable to confront the issues raised during the trial.[182]

Even after the Eichmann trial and throughout the 1960s the ministry did not initiate any methodical program for the study of the Holocaust. It was suggested that a few lessons be dedicated to the subject in conjunction with the Remembrance Day ceremonies and that the Holocaust be studied in each subject of the humanities, particularly history and literature. A few collections of documents, abstracts, and segments of articles published by Yad Vashem were offered to the teachers, and exhibitions, mostly of photographs along with some documentation, were assembled and displayed in school lobbies and libraries during the week of Remembrance Day.[183]

The Humanistic Approach, 1978 to the 1990s. During the 1970s the educational system's interest in teaching the Holocaust increased markedly. This was the outcome of various political and social developments after the wars of 1967 and 1973. The two experiences had caused deep anxiety and fear, and their frequent comparison to the Holocaust made educators and historians realize how inadequate their knowledge about the Holocaust was. Faced with increasing criticism of its curriculum planning, the ministry of education could no longer avoid creating a structured Holocaust curriculum.

The ongoing expansion of scholarship on the Holocaust provided more suitable books for teachers and made more knowledge available. The university graduates who had studied the Holocaust in an academic framework became a new generation of teachers who were able to introduce changes into the teaching of the Holocaust. Many of these teachers had been high-school students during the Eichmann trial and soldiers in the 1967 and 1973 wars. They shared the criticisms voiced by a number of historians and educators about the substandard teaching of the Holocaust.

One article that played an important part in influencing the ministry of education to reconsider its programs was "Trends in the Understanding of the Holocaust in Israeli Society," by the historian and educator Haim Schatzker.[184] Schatzker criticized the teaching of the Holocaust in Israel on a number of levels: it lacked a conceptual foundation; it emphasized the emotional rather than the intellectual; it lacked historical context; and it provided no understanding of the universal meaning of the Holocaust. Schatzker regretted that the schools failed to employ serious historical methodology in their teaching of the Holocaust. Most study activities were aimed at the emotional level and centered around memorial ceremonies. Since students were provided with no conceptual framework in which to understand the Holocaust and its causes, they had many fears, and their natural reactions were to separate the memory of the Holocaust from their daily life experiences. As a result, they demonized the perpetrators and were unable to empathize with the victims. Thus, they relied on irrational statements regarding the Jews, the Germans, and the other nations of the world to explain the horrible events.

Schatzker stated that without a sincere effort to study the Holocaust in the broad historical context of Jewish and European history and from a comparative rather than a particularistic perspective, the Holocaust would be mythologized. If a particularistic approach were adopted, the Holocaust would be understood as an event that had happened outside of the normal course of history, as some kind of accident, and people would not learn from it. Schatzker called upon Israelis to rid their minds of the commemoration framework and to set regular goals for the study of the Holocaust, applying to it the same standards they would employ in the study of any other subject. Knowledge and historical analysis were basic elements that all teachers should demand. Schatzker also noted that the Holocaust was presented in Israel's educational framework as a uniquely Jewish event but that its universal context and meanings were just as important. The annihilation of the Jews extended the limits of Jewish history, and its meaning could be understood only if it was looked at in both the Jewish and the universal context.[185]

In the early 1970s a new trend in curriculum planning downplayed the significance of any specific content as long as the general subject matter was studied. High school was to provide the students with an understanding of the general subject matter and methodology. Therefore, in any field of knowledge teachers could decide which topics to cover. This trend encouraged clearly defining the goals to be achieved in teaching the Holocaust.

Three major approaches emerged. The first emphasized the need to strengthen Zionist identity through the Holocaust. This was particularly evident in history textbooks published until the late 1970s and used throughout the 1980s (and in some schools in the 1990s). In these books, "the authors of the 'Zionist' period (1948–1977) tried to explain these phenomena [i.e., the events of the Holocaust] by using historical methods combined with personal emotions. These emotions are expressed in an extreme, heavily emotionally charged terminology. Their technical tools are stereotypic, deprecatory terms, and persuasive definitions."[186] The message transmitted through this approach was that the Jews had not seen the "writing on the wall" because of their false hopes concerning Jewish emancipation. The events of the Holocaust destroyed these illusions forever, and thus the return to Israel embodied the "lesson" learned from the Holocaust. The establishment of the state of Israel was the miraculous manifestation of both the Holocaust and Zionism.[187]

The second approach, promoted by Arie Carmon, viewed the main goal of teaching the Holocaust as "Education toward Values." Its purpose was "to focus on the student in his search for meaning and the importance of his life as a human being, as a Jew and as an Israeli. . . . The principles, aims, content, and methods are all meant to derive from and serve the intellectual needs of the student as an individual who is both searching for his identity and reflecting on his role and function in society."[188] Carmon proposed that the Holocaust be studied through an analysis of dilemmas. The teacher was to present students with a set of problems confronted by the Jewish leadership, youth movements, and parents and children during the Holocaust and then examine the possible alternatives. This method was also to be applied in the study unit on the Germans. Carmon stated that the Israeli youngsters could identify with the young Germans more readily than with their Jewish counterparts. Therefore, the socialization of German youth into Nazi society and its effect on the thinking of young Germans was a very important topic. The relationships of German adolescents with their parents, German attitudes toward the Jews, and the influence of anti-Semitism would all be examined.[189]

The third approach regarded gaining the knowledge itself as the primary purpose for studying the Holocaust. Beginning in the late 1970s Schatzker, Yisrael Gutman, and other historians have promoted this approach. They stated that in spite of the new trends in curriculum planning, the Holocaust should not be treated as just another subject. The Holocaust, as "an epoch-making event," had to be studied in depth. It was inconceivable that young Israelis might not know the events of the Holocaust. The goal was knowledge for its own sake, and the methodology to be used was systematic historical analysis that would raise the major issues through the readings of primary documents and a comprehensive comparative study. Schatzker and Gutman's textbook *The Holocaust and Its Meaning,* which followed these guidelines, became the most popular textbook on the Holocaust. However, despite the authors' claim that the dissemination of knowledge about the Holocaust was their primary goal, the textbook emphasized the meaning of the Holocaust from a broad Jewish and human perspective. The Zionist message was clearly presented as one of the options open to Jews, but the universal human message was also clearly stated.[190]

Because of these and other developments, the genuine participation of Israeli youth in the dialogue about the Holocaust has become more meaningful in the last two decades. The opportunities for young Israelis to engage in the shaping of this dialogue also increased as the Holocaust became a more frequent topic of reflection in Israeli cultural life and because of political changes in Europe. The ministry of education initiated a program for high-school students that includes a visit to Poland and the camps. The program has become common in the last few years, and a number of studies have demonstrated the strong impact these visits have had on students' understanding of themselves and their Jewish identity. Since 1989 more than half a million Jews have immigrated to Israel from the former Soviet Union. Families have been reunited, and descriptions of Jewish life in those countries have challenged Israelis to review the meaning and the long-term influences of the Holocaust. The ability to travel to Eastern Europe motivated many Israelis to visit their birthplaces, often with their children and grandchildren.

The year 1995 marked the fiftieth anniversary of the end of World War II, along with the liberation of Auschwitz and the concentration and labor camps in Germany. This milestone inspired new studies and renewed reflections on the Holocaust. The Israeli educational system has already come a long way in terms of its ability to meaningfully confront the Holocaust period.

Hebrew Literature: The Holocaust and Israeli Society

Hebrew literature reflects Israeli society's encounter with the Holocaust. The large number of survivors in Israel made literary works on the Holocaust relevant to large segments of Israeli society as well as more painful. Those who had not experienced the destruction personally searched in the literature for its significance. The survivors felt that existing languages were unable to express their experiences and that a new language had to be invented. They felt that the traditional Jewish way of responding to calamity in literature could not reflect the human condition during the Holocaust.[191]

Abba Kovner, a poet and a survivor who had been a leader of the resistance in the Vilna ghetto, stated that after the Holocaust some metaphors were unusable in the Hebrew language. He recalled his "literary shock" shortly after his arrival in Palestine in 1947. The famous poet Abraham Shlonsky had given him his newly published book 'Al Milet (On abundance). Very excited, Kovner read the poems until he reached the expression *shad tahuah* (literally, "crumbling-earth bosom"), describing the relationship between a hill and the farmer who had cultivated it. He was unable to continue reading. How could a Hebrew poet use such a metaphor while in the fields of Europe human bodies fertilized the soil and the farmers who did their plowing found human flesh and bones?[192]

Kovner also wrestled with the broader issue of the "human language that had turned into the language of murder. How would it become human again? Just by the scrawling of a pencil?"[193] Aharon Appelfeld, a survivor of Transnistria and one of the most prominent Hebrew writers on the Holocaust, stated this theme in another way:

> By its nature, when it comes to describing reality, art always demands a certain intensification. . . . However, that is not the case with the Holocaust. Everything in it already seems so thoroughly unreal, as if it no longer belongs to the experience of our generation, but to mythology. Hence the need to bring it down to the human realm. This is not a mechanical problem, but an essential one. When I say "to bring it down," I do not mean to simplify, to attenuate, or to sweeten the horror, but to attempt to make the events speak through the individual and in his language, to rescue the suffering from huge numbers, from dreadful anonymity, and to restore the person's given and family name, to give the tortured person back his human form, which was snatched away from him.[194]

Writing on the Holocaust began during the war, reflecting the need to describe and elaborate on the historical situation and the human condition. Poetry was written in the ghettos and camps by such people as Izhak Katzenelson, who wrote poems on the Jewish people while in Warsaw and Vittel; David Fogel, who wrote a poem in Vittel; Moshe Bosack (Meir Busak), who wrote poetry in Plaszow; and Abba Kovner, who wrote in the ghetto of Vilna and in the forests.[195] After the war many memoirs and stories were published in Palestine and then in Israel. Although not written in Hebrew, they were soon translated and thus became a channel through which the people of the Yishuv and Israel could relate to the Holocaust as experienced by individuals. Among many such works were the very popular memoir by Reizl (Ruz'ka) Korchak, *Lehavot Baefer* (Flames in the ash), which had a documentary appendix and was reprinted a number of times, and Haika Grossman's *Anshei Hamahtereth* (People of the underground).[196]

Hebrew Writers with a Diaspora Background. During the war, when information about the Jewish suffering reached Palestine and when the full extent of the tragedy was revealed, Hebrew writers and poets were accused of being mute, which in a sense hinted at their being deaf, about the catastrophe. Hebrew literature was expected to express the "national grief,"[197] and it was not doing so. In Zionism, as in many other national movements, poets and writers played a major role in shaping feelings and attitudes. Hebrew literature held a special place in the Zionist movement, for the revival of the Hebrew language, its transformation into a living and growing language, was one of Zionism's primary goals. The Zionists expected writers to transcend the feelings of the individual and mobilize the Jewish public into a nation concerned about national causes. During World War II, writers and poets addressed the ongoing political issues in regular columns in the press, the most famous being Natan Alterman's "Hatur Hashvi'i" (The seventh column), and at specially convened authors' conventions.

It is interesting to note that in the 1990s the accusation about the silence of Hebrew literature has been voiced again, but in a different context. The literary critic Avi Catzman complained that between the 1940s and the 1960s the Yishuv and then Israel turned away from the Holocaust and did not confront its reality or its impact on Israel.[198] In this context, the article "Hamilhamah veshoat Yisrael beshiratenu" (The war and the Holocaust in our poetry), by literary critic B. Y. Mikhaeli, warrants mention.[199] In Mikhaeli's view, the public was too impatient for artistic expressions of the Holocaust. He explained that a poetic reaction to the destruction was not yet possible. The events were too immediate and too difficult to comprehend. A poet's response develops from within and not from external demands. Although most of the poets in the Yishuv had lost family members and friends, they had not experienced the suffering and horrors firsthand. He asserted that even if poets and writers felt compelled to keep silent, their silence was an authentic expression of their pain.

Mikhaeli also offered a literary rationalization. He thought that Haim Nachman Bialik's monumental poem *Be'ir haharegah* (In the city of slaughter), a reaction to the pogroms against Jews in Russia between 1903 and 1906, had become a paradigm of a modern literary reaction to slaughter. In many respects Bialik had continued the traditions of *kinoth* (lamentations) and *piyutim* (holy poetry that entered the prayer book), which had been produced after great catastrophes throughout Jewish history.[200] Having this poem as a model, he thought, paralyzed many individuals, as the events in 1903 were utterly different from the annihilation of the Jews during World War II. He took the argument one step further, saying somewhat hesitantly that the capability of literature to express the reality of the Shoah was limited.[201]

Hebrew literature indeed responded to the events, beginning with the early days of Nazi rule. Poems, stories, and articles were published in periodicals, mostly by a generation of Hebrew writers who had immigrated to Palestine in the 1920s and 1930s. Their work could be understood as a general reaction to the persecution of German Jews and the spread of Nazi policy and hatred to other countries. However, some saw prophetic qualities in these writings.[202] Despite the shock that the unforeseen developments in Germany and Austria had caused, they initially conformed with what had occurred during the first two decades of the 1900s, namely, the pogroms in Russia between 1903 and 1906 and in Ukraine between 1920 and 1922. An example of an early poetic reaction to the fate of German Jews is the poem "Harugei

Tirmonia" (The murdered of Tirmonia), by Saul Tchernichowsky, which alludes to medieval persecutions as an analogy to present events. S. Y. Agnon's novel *A Guest for the Night*, written in 1939, describes the feelings of the narrator as he visits his hometown in Galicia and senses its demolition. A poem by Yizhak Lamdan, "Masada," expressing despair after the Ukraine massacres, was perceived by many in 1940 to be a response to the Shoah, and it became a primary text for Jewish youth movements and resistance activists in Poland.[203] The poem was reprinted nearly every year during the 1930s and early 1940s. In spite of the poet's conviction that life in the Diaspora was doomed and his great doubts about the safe future of the Yishuv, the public remembered the poem's central message, "Masada will never fall again."

Writers' responses to the Holocaust were inevitably personal. They grappled with the destruction by examining their own feelings about family, friends, and childhood experiences.[204] Poetry preceded prose as a literary reaction to the Holocaust. The common threads in this poetry included expressions of anger, calls for vengeance, curses on all Germans, pleas to God to reappear and prove his covenant with Israel, and statements of bewilderment that nature was unaffected by the horror and continued to move along at its normal pace. Another frequently voiced theme was the indictment of the free nations, which had remained indifferent to the fate of the Jews and had thereby been accessories to murder.[205] The poet Abraham Shlonsky wanted the Germans to be hated forever and feared that the hatred and the memory of the Holocaust would fade. He sought a vocabulary that would express this hate.[206] Avigdor Hameiri voiced anger and hate and the fear of becoming like "them." "It is so easy to become a dog," he said. "It may happen overnight."[207]

At the same time, poets longed for the world that was now lost. They remembered the beauty of their former lands, the closely knit communities, and the warm and kind homes. Shmuel Bass, who considered himself a defeated and shameful person and grieved that he was alive, found refuge for his lonely soul in poetry.[208] Guilt, expressed in many forms, constituted a central theme in the poetry of the first generation of writers who dealt with the Holocaust.[209] A son mourning his father was described by Alterman in his poem "On the Boy Avram" and by Amir Gilbo'a in "Isaac." The sacrifice of Isaac is a frequent motif in modern Hebrew literature. In Gilbo'a's poem, as Abraham and his son walk to Mount Moriah with the fire and the knife, Isaac calls out:

> Father, Father hurry and save me
> And no one will be missing at lunchtime.

To which Abraham replies:

> It is I who am being slaughtered, my son,
> And my blood is already on the leaves.

Isaac then reflects:

> And Father's voice was stifled.
> And his face pale.

> And I wanted to cry out, writhing not to believe
> And tearing open the eyes.
> And I woke up.
> And bloodless was the right hand.[210]

The poetry of this generation often involved the very painful confession by new immigrants to Palestine that they had failed in their efforts to disassociate themselves from the Diaspora. They suffered an agonizing longing for their former homes and guilt about leaving all they had loved. Avraham Rosenzweig expressed these feelings in his poem "Tov lishon baleilot, vetov li shenishart" (Good to sleep at night, good that you remained).[211] Shimson Meltzer described similar feelings in a dedication to a poem of lamentation. Written in the style of Hebrew tombstone epitaphs, it reads:

> To the memory of the righteous and innocent of my town, at one with God and with themselves, who in my childhood loved me, spoiled me, and sought to guide me in the right path. But I turned away from them to the path of the free-thinker, together with all the youth, and so caused them much pain. The Lord who knows men's hearts knows how much I have grieved over this. For it was not from them that I sought to separate myself, but from their lives, the life of the Exile. Let their souls be bound up in the bond of life.[212]

These poets also examined the meaning of the Zionist experience after the Holocaust. The Zionist vision of a new Jewish life had been crushed. This was due not only to the destruction but also to the attitude of the Yishuv. During that terrible time the Yishuv had continued to live normally. The endless internal political confrontations and manipulations taking place in the Yishuv while Europe was going up in flames had voided its claim to responsibility for leading Jewish life in the future.[213] In his long poem "Keter Kinah le-Khol Beit Yisrael" (Crown of lamentation for the whole house of Israel), Uri Zvi Greenberg, the foremost poet of the Holocaust, described in detail how the Jews were deported to their deaths and also related it to the Yishuv:

> If only our sainted ones could have drawn back our curtains
> And peeked with the blood of their eyes through our windows
> And seen how we lived our lives:
> An inferno engulfed them while Paradise surrounded us.[214]

Some poets used biblical forms to express anger and lamentation; others were lyrical and sentimental and depicted their love of the people and the communities that had vanished. The bald reality of atrocities and death was hinted at in words like "the railroad," "the trains," and "walls," which became the code words of Holocaust literature. Irony was another way of avoiding direct references to the horrors.[215]

The Hebrew press also published in translation poetry and prose that reached Palestine from occupied Europe. In June 1944 poems by Zvi Nesher were translated from German and published. One series, entitled "Poems from the City of Death," included a poem about the Cyanide Boy:

Many in the ghetto commit suicide.
In the street of the ghetto
A young boy peddles cyanide.

Cyanide, people, you ought to buy
A practical item for everyone to try.
Better painlessly your foe defy
Than from torture to die.

O you human mortals
Buy your cyanide potions.
Compassionately will it by you abide,
On the day of genocide.[216]

A poem written by Abba Kovner was published in September 1944. Songs that were sung by Jews in the ghettos were also translated and published when they reached Palestine.[217] These are but a few examples of the works that introduced the reader to the literary expression of the Holocaust as viewed from the inside.

The first monumental poetic response to the Holocaust in the Hebrew language was Uri Zvi Greenberg's *Rehovot Hanahar: Sefer Hailiyot Vehakoah* (Streets of the river: The book of dirges and power).[218] A controversial figure in the history of the Zionist movement and the Yishuv, Greenberg immigrated to Palestine in 1924. Initially he supported Labor Zionism, sharing its visions of the new man and a just society in the land of Israel. In the late 1920s, however, he moved away from socialist Zionism and became very active in the Zionist Right. He became a militant writer and political prophet of Revisionist Zionism, and in the five years preceding World War II he reported for the Revisionist Yiddish press in Warsaw.[219] Two weeks after the beginning of the war Greenberg escaped to Palestine, leaving his family behind in Poland.[220] Greenberg believed that poetry played a central role in shaping and directing the Zionist revolution. According to Yaacov Shavit, he was "a poet with a sense of mission that was profound, lofty, sweeping, and powerfully self-confident; one who did not remain secluded in a poetic ivory tower but 'descended to the street' and took part in the various public and political debates which were agitating the *Yishuv* and Zionism at the time."[221]

During the long years of the war Greenberg did not publish any poetry. Instead he wrote his great poetic work *Rehovot Hanahar.* The external framework of the book is a lamentation for his murdered family, their destroyed community, and their entire cultural and spiritual world. The book contains 140 poems written in an expressionistic style that create a kind of a narrative. Continuity is maintained from one poem to the next through the repetition of verses and themes. In the work Greenberg's family members move from being real personalities to mythological images, and his conversations with them move from the realistic to the mystical and mythic. Thus Greenberg is able to encompass the collective and the personal by freely traversing these two realms. Throughout the book, the story of the destruction in all its horrific forms is described directly and indirectly through a conversation with the murdered. The dead reveal their reality, which is contrasted with the poet's life, creating an awareness of the past. The reader thus experiences the ordeal of destruction as described from within, not by an outsider who was a witness or who, having been saved from destruction, lived a "normal" life. In a slow but inescapable process the totality of the destruction and the unimaginable loss are revealed.[222] "To listen to the inner voice of *Streets of the River*," wrote Alan Mintz,

> means to be exposed to a series of troubling questions about the responsibility and experience of the bystander to catastrophe, the bystander who is kinsman and brother to the victims (both the individual and the collective, the poet and the Yishuv); about the possibilities and means of purification from the ordeal of loss and guilt; about the function of myths of apocalyptic damnation and deliverance in the response to catastrophe and about the problems of their authentic realization; and about the pressures of the catastrophic event upon the boundaries of the identity of the individual ego.[223]

Greenberg centers his rage on the gentile murderers and on the indifferent. He recounts the bloody relationship between gentiles and Jews from ancient times to modern pogroms and the destruction in Europe. Unlike Bialik in his "In the City of Slaughter," Greenberg does not believe that self-defense can change the fate of the Jews, and he does not feel shame about Jewish "passivity." The gentiles thought of the Jews as sheep to be slaughtered, and Greenberg uses the phrase "sheep of God" (*'edrei Elohim*). The gentiles, he says, were responsible for the murder of the Jews.[224] He depicts the partisans, however, as the thirty-six righteous individuals who, according to Jewish legend, preserved the world.[225]

Greenberg portrays the loss as irreparable. However, the subtext of the poems endeavors to demonstrate a way to continue with life and conveys the message that there must be a future. The role of the poet is similar to that of the prophet, and the power of poetry opens new avenues. Greenberg does not idealize the past or the surviving remnant of European Jewry. He strongly believes that the Zionist movement faces a social and human situation unlike anything it expected before the Holocaust.[226] The Jews are depicted as a bride without beauty or charm who is preparing for her wedding. All of her loved ones have died, but she will nevertheless bear children. This sad image, on the edge of despair, stresses the loss, but it also stresses the obligation to go on living. In the poem "Iliat benayim" (Between dirges) Greenberg writes that one is permitted to weep and mourn but that the crying and mourning will be in vain if the people of Israel do not turn into an iron rim.[227] A sense of redemption is gained by the lyrical association of Greenberg's dead parents with the patriarchs of Israel:

> At the Rim of the Heavens
> Like Abraham and Sarah by the terebinths of
> Mamre before the precious tidings, and like
> David and Bathsheba, in the king's palace,
> in the tenderness of their first night—
> my martyred father and mother rise in the
> West over the sea with all the aureoles
> of God upon them. Weighed down by their
> beauty they sink, slowly. Above their heads

flows the mighty ocean, beneath it is their
deep home.[228]

A New Generation of Hebrew Writers. Between the end of the war and the establishment of the state of Israel a new generation of writers and poets confronted the reality of the Holocaust. Made up mostly of young artists who had been born or educated in the Yishuv before and during World War II, this group was named Dor Baaretz (A generation in the land). Some of its members had taken part in missions in Europe and had met with survivors in the DP camps, along the trails of the Brichah (an underground escape organization), or on the illegal boats. Most of them were in their twenties, and Mintz described them as having "no personal experience, nor memories of [the Diaspora's] Jewish life; most had little contact with grandparents, who had stayed behind. Raised in Hebrew, their speech registered the development of a living community. This was reflected in the range of cultural allusion in their written style. Their secular gymnasium education, though it included Bible and Jewish history, left them alien to the world of Talmudic erudition."[229] Mintz concluded that this generation's response to the Holocaust was to avoid it and that "it was shame and not the shock of loss and grieving over the destruction that caused the conspicuous avoidance of the Holocaust in the literature of the period."[230]

Gershon Shaked claimed that these writers were not able to describe the Diaspora Jews from within but only from an outside perspective. They were bound to the superstructure of the Zionist story and history. However, said Shaked, they did express major issues of self-identity following the Holocaust. Dor Baaretz looked for new ways to reconcile their self-image with the Jewish tradition of the past and with the world that had been destroyed in the Holocaust.[231]

Dan Laor reached a different conclusion. His examination of Dor Baaretz led him to believe that the Holocaust was a central theme in their works. He divided the writers into four subgroups, based on the frequency with which they related to the Holocaust. The first group was made up of writers who avoided the Holocaust altogether, such as S. Izhar. At the other end of the spectrum, the fourth subgroup comprised writers who made the Holocaust a central theme in their work, such as Haim Gouri, Hanoch Bartov, Aharon Meged, and Amir Gilbo'a.[232] In the second group were writers who related to the Holocaust rarely, such as Nathan Yonatan and Avner Trainin. The third subgroup was made up of those who did not make the Holocaust a major theme in their work but dedicated at least one major work to the subject. This was the largest group, and it included such major writers as Yehudit Handel, Yehudah Amihai, Dan Ben Amotz, Benyamin Tammuz, Yoram Kenuik, and others.[233] The main themes in the works of the authors in the third and fourth categories are the survivors and their fate, their efforts to rebuild their lives, and the fate of their communities. The memory of the Holocaust and their fears beset the survivors as they seek to reconstruct their lives, placing a heavy burden on their relationships with other survivors—the new immigrants—and the immigrants already living in Israel. Some of the works depict the survivors' lives in Europe after the war (Gouri, Bartov) and their encounters with Israeli society after immigration. Yehudit

Handel criticized the Israeli society, which was unable to open its mind and heart to the "other" and to appreciate other ways of life. Meged illustrated the gap between the generations in his story of a child of a survivor who is unable to give his own child the name of his grandfather, Mendel.

The works of most of these writers describe the feelings, inner struggles, and misunderstandings of the Holocaust survivors and the Israeli-born and those between the generations. They question the positive images the Israelis have of themselves and criticize the smug self-satisfaction of the "new Jew," brought up in freedom. The writings of Meged, Gouri, Handel, and others nevertheless refer to the Zionist "superstory" as demonstrated in the great events of the years between 1940 and 1950—the mass murder and subsequent rebirth of the Jewish people, the great transition from World War II and the Holocaust to the War of Independence, the establishment of the Jewish state, and the massive ingathering of exiles between 1948 and 1951.[234] These writers therefore identify with the heroism manifested in the partisans' war against the Nazis and in the ghetto uprisings. Yizhak Zukerman, a leader of the underground in Warsaw, is a paradigm for many characterizations, such as Yonat and Alexander Sened's *Bein Hahaim Vehametim* (Between the living and the dead). Within the overall Zionist framework, Yonat and Alexander Sened depart from the regular stereotypes of the Jews as passive victims. Laor believes that some of these works have strong literary qualities, demonstrating these writers' ability to penetrate and identify with the situation of the Jews in general and the survivors in particular.[235]

Survivor Writers

A new group of writers emerged during the 1960s. These writers, such as Abba Kovner, Aharon Appelfeld, Shamai Golan, Dan Pagis, and Uri Orlev, were survivors. During the Holocaust they literally lived for the day when they could tell their stories. After Liberation, though, they turned silent. Appelfeld wrote that "the desire to keep silent and the desire to speak both became deeper; and only the artistic expression which came years later could attempt to bridge those two difficult imperatives. Artistic expression did not arise quickly. It called for a human form that would hint at the available possibilities."[236] Kovner expressed this idea in a slightly different manner: "A whole generation had to pass, a new life experience, until our language could assimilate the powerful drama, until it could express it without pathos, without a cry, with indifference, quietly, that it was so."[237]

These writers began to publish after they had been in Israel for a decade or so and after the Eichmann trial had taken place. One exception was Yehiel Dinur, whose pen name was K. Zetnik, a survivor who published in the late forties and early fifties and whose works appealed to readers of all ages. Dinur described the struggle of everyday life for the inmates of the death and concentration camps.[238]

Most survivor writers dealt with their wartime experiences, their existential dilemmas as survivors, and how, still possessed by the past, they were struggling to return to "normalcy."[239] They added a personal dimension to the literary expression of the Holocaust. In works that departed from the realistic and expressionistic styles and were heavy with symbolism, they demonstrated that the survivors carried the Holocaust within themselves forever (Appelfeld's *Bertha* is an example). Unlike Dor Baaretz, these writers did not espouse the Zionist metaplot. In their works the survivor is depicted as an outsider (Appelfeld) endeavoring to join the inner circle of Israeli society (Golan).[240] This literature presented a new image of Israelis: the self-restrained young survivor with doubts and fears who conducts an ongoing examination of the Zionist dream. The "native" Israeli seems dull and self-centered and certainly less cultured in comparison with the Israeli survivor.

These survivor writers influenced the work of writers whose lives were linked to the Holocaust through lost childhoods in Europe and the memory of family and friends who had been left to die. The Eichmann trial had granted the survivors the legitimacy to deal with a wide variety of Holocaust experiences and personal recollections.

The Literature of the 1970s, 1980s, and 1990s. In the late sixties two new trends began to appear in Holocaust literature. The first is represented by authors such as Yehudah Amihai (*Lo Me'akhshav Lo Mikan* [Not now, not here]), Benyamin Tammuz (*Eliakum, Sefer Hahazaiot* [Eliakum, book of prophesies]), Yoram Kenuik (*Adam Ben Kelev* [Adam the son of a dog] and *Avi* [My father]), and Nathan Shaham (*Rosendorff Quartet).* Some of their major works were on the Holocaust and reflected a change in the approach toward Jewish life in the past and toward the reality of life in Israel. The second trend is represented by a younger generation of Israeli writers educated in Israel, such as Amos Oz (*Michael Sheli,* published in English as *My Michael),* A. B. Yehoshu'a (*Molkho),* and David Grossman (*'Ayen Erech Ahavah,* published in English as *See Under: Love).* They explored the relationship between Israeli society and the Holocaust.[241]

The writers in the first group confronted the Holocaust after two decades of independence. They examined their past, their roots, and their own Israeli and Jewish identities. Amihai, born in Germany and educated in Palestine from early adolescence, described, in his autobiographical novel *Lo Me'akhshav Lo Mikan,* the return of a young adult to his birthplace in Germany. In his search for his lost childhood, Yoel, the protagonist, finds an old and dying Jewish community in which people live on their memories and wait for the return of their beloved lost relatives. This experience throws Yoel into turmoil about his identity as a Jew and an Israeli, but it also proves to him that any other identity is inconceivable. It is interesting that Yoel, who grew up in the Yishuv, speaks Hebrew, and fought in the War of Independence, feels like an outsider in his hometown and in Israel, just as the survivors do.[242]

Yoram Kenuik, in his very painful autobiographical novel *Avi,* described with sympathy and longing his father's admiration for and rejection of Germany. His father had left Germany in the early 1930s, fully aware of the dangers of Nazism, yet he never felt at home in Palestine. Both father and son are fundamentally alienated. Shaham sympathetically examined the integration into the Yishuv of the refugee-immigrant German Jews in the 1930s in his *Rosendorff Quartet.* His heroes question the Zionist dream with some irony and doubt that they will ever be able to establish a new identity.[243]

The younger generation of writers, represented by Oz and Yehoshu'a, generally dealt with the Holocaust only through their descriptions of the Israeli environment or of the past. Their protagonists relate to the Holocaust through the memories or experiences of relatives or friends or in noting how the Holocaust is treated in Israel. Although he was a member of this group of writers, David Grossman eschewed this removed vantage and attempted to confront the Holocaust directly. His effort, *See Under: Love,* was a breakthrough in Holocaust literature and deserves closer examination.

Shaked stated that *See Under: Love* was the first work not written by a survivor to touch the Holocaust from within.[244] The first part of the book introduces the child Momik, who desires to understand his parents through a mysterious expression they utter in their most intimate conversations: "the Nazi beast." The imaginative nine-year-old lives in the shadow of his parents' unspoken memories and through his old grandfather Wassermann, also a survivor. Momik tries to breed the "Nazi beast" by collecting all kinds of stray animals and giving them special treatment. He keeps in mind what he once heard from his relative and neighbor Bella, that "the 'Nazi beast' could come out of any kind of animal if it got the right care and nourishment."[245] Finding the Nazi beast, assumes Momik, will provide him with a better understanding of the hidden pain of his parents and relieve his grandfather's nightmares. Then he will be able to rescue them from their pain and save the land "Over There," which they lost and miss so much. The reader learns of the concerns of a number of survivors and of the inescapable memories that torment them. Kiryat Yovel, the part of Jerusalem inhabited by new immigrants from all over the world, is filled with silent and painful memories, which the children, living "normal lives," sense.[246]

The other parts of the book, in which Momik has grown up and is a father, take the reader from Israel to Poland. In Poland Momik experiences the suicide of an artist, the Polish Jewish writer Bruno Schultz. Grossman describes Bruno's death in a complex, allegorical way. Grossman also explores the reality of a death camp through the relationship between Momik's grandfather, who will not die (the eternal Jew?), and the commander of the camp, Neigel. Wassermann, a writer of children's stories, nightly spins tales for Neigel about the "Children of the Heart" from books Wassermann had written before the war, in freedom, and which Neigel had read and adored as a child. As Wassermann tells the story, he and the Nazi commandant live under its spell. The last part of the book is an encyclopedia of the life of Kaszick, the Jewish protagonist of Wassermann's story and a symbol of all the victims of the Holocaust, a man who lives a full life in twenty-two hours. This section contains many of the subplots of the book.

This monumental novel is an attempt to understand, through the reality of the Holocaust, the problems of survival and life. Grossman's interest is life and the ability to live it with meaning. The survivors are portrayed as living "dead lives." They are constantly on guard, protecting themselves from the dangers they confronted earlier and which are now sealed in their memories. Thus, they are unable to appreciate the meaning of life. The gray and difficult everyday existence of the survivor parents is examined by the child with remorse, but he rejects their way of life when he becomes an adult.

As a child Momik manifests the dilemma of the perpetrator and the victim. He is the victim of his parents' lives, and when he tries to rescue them by breeding the Nazi beast he becomes a perpetrator. In the death camp, the connection between the victims and perpetrators is the focus of the relationship between Wassermann and Neigel. Momik reveals that Neigel is a part of himself, just as Wassermann and Kaszick are. He is also prevented by an unending process of self-protection from becoming both a victim and a perpetrator.

Although in the first part of the book the reader realizes with Momik that imagination does not make it possible to reenact the reality of the Holocaust, in the third part of the book Grossman dares to do just that. Is he able to confront his questions on the "other planet" of the death camps? Grossman leaves the reader with no answers, which he confirms in the last part of the book. In the encyclopedia of Kaszick's life, "love" and "life" are left unexplained: "love: see sex" and "life: the meaning of."[247] A partial answer is implied, Shaked suggested, in the literary imagination and innocence of the children who exist only in the imagination of the author. Both have prevented the deaths of Wassermann and Schultz and can even influence the Nazi commandant.[248]

The publication of *See Under: Love* caused a stormy public debate. Critics argued that the book was an insult to the survivors, that it revealed a misconception of the Holocaust, and that it attempted to touch untouchable themes, such as the feelings of the victims in the gas chambers. They claimed that it demonstrated a distorted historical perception of the Holocaust, that its author was someone born in Israel who had been pondering the current political issue of the victimization of Palestinians.[249]

Grossman's attempt to write about the Holocaust can be seen as a response to claims by Kovner and Appelfeld that literature could not describe the horrors of the Holocaust. However, *See Under: Love* can also be viewed as an attempt to understand the contradictions between life and survival and the link between the victim and the perpetrator. In this interpretation, the reality of the Holocaust is not central, though it is the stage on which the story takes place.

The Holocaust and Political Messages. Another major novel on the Holocaust is Izhak Laor's *Am Maachal Melachim* (The people, food fit for a king), published in 1993.[250] It is the story of a military supply base in the Negev on the eve of the Six-Day War, in the spring of 1967. Corruption, low morale, and social animosity prevail. All the characters are dull and mediocre people strangled by national conventions and petit bourgeois material values. In this respect it is a novel of antiheroes. The memory of the Holocaust is portrayed with skepticism and almost brutality, which, claimed Laor, is a reflection of the political and social manipulation of the Holocaust by politicians, intellectuals, and the educational system. The officers in the army molest their soldiers and justify their behavior by their own experiences as Holocaust victims. The contempt for "the other"—the Arab, the refugee, or the new immigrant— is rationalized by exploiting the Jewish memory of persecution.

As Sidra Ezrahi has pointed out, some authors perceive the Holocaust "as a historical event to be engaged on the level of social and political reality, and as a mythic force inducing terror and capitulation."[251] Laor questions the basic conventions of the Jewish state and uses irony and even grotesquery to illustrate what he sees as the demeaning of the Holocaust. His book departs completely from the Zionist meta-plot and demonstrates that Israelis manipulate the memory of the Holocaust without the pain and compassion.

Ezrahi noted that the Holocaust imagery in the official political rhetoric "appeals to history only to affirm the pathos of the eternal status of the Jew as victim and to grant the Israeli collective a sense of moral impunity." She demonstrated how the poetry written after the war in Lebanon in 1982–83 echoed ironic martyrological literature. She quoted a poem by Tzvi 'Atzmon, *Yizkor* (Remembrance): "Exiled . . . persecuted . . . murdered . . . stoned . . . poisoned . . . burned . . . slaughtered . . . buried alive . . . one gets up one morning, sees / children shot while the sun was shining . . . Arab children. And there is no consolation."[252]

Ten years later, Laor showed how far Hebrew literature had been able to depart from the images of the strong and fearless young Israelis, the visions of the just society, and the dedication to the Zionist dream.

The Holocaust in Drama

No discussion about the Holocaust in Israeli society can be complete without citing the developments in drama and theater. Ben Ami Feingold pointed out in *Hashoah Badramah Ha'ivrit* (The theme of the Holocaust in Hebrew drama) that until the 1980s the theater displayed little interest in the Holocaust. The few dramas that were staged in the early 1960s included Lea Goldberg's *Ba'alat Haarmon* (Mistress of the Palace), about the dilemmas concerning the rescue of children hidden by Christians; and Aharon Meged's *Haonah Habo'eret* (The High Season), which leveled criticism at the Jews who returned to Germany or continued to live in countries where the hatred toward Jews had not disappeared. Other than in these and a few other plays the subject was marginal in Israeli theater.

In the early 1980s this began to change. Playwrights, theater groups, and theater houses became interested in producing dramas dealing with the Holocaust. As in Israeli literature, this turnabout reflected Israeli literature, a genuine interest in the life of the Jews during the Holocaust and the Diaspora in general. It also reflected a search for self-identity and a criticism of Israeli society and Zionist visions. A few types of plays can be identified. One type describes the search for lost childhood and the wish to transfer memories to the third generation, the grandchildren. This category includes Nola Chelton's *Hamesh* (Five [1983]), on the fate of five women survivors, and Alizah Ulmert's *Duet Lepsanter* (Duet for a Piano [1994]), about a woman who returns to her hometown in Poland to find her piano.[253]

Another type includes dramas dedicated to the Holocaust, such as Yehoshua Sobol's *Ghetto* (1989) and Hanokh Levin's *The Patriot and Queen of the Bathroom* (1989). Both Sobol and Levin are leading Israeli playwrights whose works have been performed by major theaters. *Ghetto* is one of the most important plays about the Holocaust. Sobol, a native Israeli active in the political Left, describes in the drama the dilemmas of the Jews and the Jewish leadership in the ghetto. The plot of the play revolves around the creation of a theater in Vilna just after the mass deportation to Ponary. Sobol uses a theater within a theater to portray ghetto life and to move with ease to the imaginary world on the theater stage.

While Sobol's characters are not polarized between "good" and "bad," his criticism of Gens, the head of the Jewish police, and of the *Judenrat* encompasses the ghetto leadership. Gens, a Zionist and a member of the Revisionist movement, is devoted to Hebrew culture. Through this character, Sobol is able to criticize the Zionist ethos. His nationalistic views prompt Gens to devise a strategy in which a few Jews—the young, the strong, and the brave, who will be the seed for the future Jewish nation—are to be rescued at the expense of the others. Gens does not act for personal gain and believes that through his understanding of the situation—the interests of the Germans, the progress of the war, and how the Jews can benefit the Germans who rule the ghetto—he will be able to arrange for the rescue of large numbers of Jews. Gens confronts moral dilemmas, but he must act, and his decisions cannot always be right or moral. Sobol also alludes to the fact that without the Zionist ideology, which justified his strategy, Gens would not have reached these conclusions.

Sobol portrays Gens as the manifestation of the Nazi inside the Jew and prompts the viewer to ask whether Gens personifies any Jew, every Jew, or only a Zionist Jew. Gens obeys the Nazis to the point of cooperating in the deportations to Ponary. Constrained by Nazi orders, he takes it upon himself to decide who will die and who will live, thus traversing moral limits. Gens's decision then pushes him to use force against the Jews, which he does without reservations. The three Nazis who rule the ghetto, seal its fate, and personally murder many of its inhabitants also are not totally evil. These Nazis show an interest in art through the theater of the ghetto, love music, and display knowledge about Judaica. They demonstrate the Jew inside the Nazi, not only in their love of art and books but also in their killing of the theater group in the final act of the play.

Thus, Sobol introduced into the Hebrew theater two controversial elements: the criticism of Zionist chauvinism and its outcome and the interpretation of the Holocaust as a universal evil. He does not present the Holocaust as a unique historical event that resulted from centuries of anti-Semitism and enmity between Jews and non-Jews, but rather as a tragic event that sprang out of the evil of ordinary people. The Holocaust therefore endangers every society and every human being. Any nation or person can become a perpetrator and a victim. Sobol aims this message at Israeli society and the evils he perceives: the occupation of the West Bank and the Lebanon war.[254] Thus Sobol, like Laor and Grossman, departed from the generally accepted metaplot of the Holocaust and Zionism.

The same process occurred in films and in television movies. Television has played a major role in provoking debates and representing a wide spectrum of subjects and interpretations of the Holocaust. On numerous occasions Israeli television has presented programs on the Holocaust, and television's role on Remembrance Day is central.

CONCLUSION

When we remember the past, we imagine it and when we imagine the future, we remember it.

Yehoshua Sobol[255]

The commemoration in Jerusalem during the week of January 22–27, 1995, of the fiftieth anniversary of the liberation of Auschwitz illuminated the living dialogue that is taking place in Israel about the Holocaust. In the opening event at Yad Vashem on January 22 the solemnity and vitality of a few thousand Jewish survivors from Israel and abroad was evident. The survivors expressed their feelings about Auschwitz in different ways: some wore striped pajamas like those they had worn at Auschwitz, others carried their Auschwitz numbers on their chests, a few came with their children and grandchildren, but most just came. They smiled, hugged, and kissed friends and acquaintances and seemed anxious to listen and to compare memories and experiences. The great majority of these people had never been active in planning a public commemoration, nor had they been involved in the politics of remembrance. They assembled to remember because a half-century had passed. Even after fifty years they wanted to listen and share again their long years of suffering at Auschwitz, but discussing their lives after the war was just as important to them. The large number of participants in this gathering and at other conventions of survivors in the late 1980s and early 1990s is an indication of the new readiness of survivors to be seen publicly. This is also manifested in the large number of memoirs that have been published in recent years. Survivors ask to be interviewed, and in institutions such as Yad Vashem videotaping oral history interviews has became a major project.

Many survivors share the concern voiced at this gathering that there is a widespread tendency in many quarters to portray Auschwitz as a symbol of universal evil and to downplay the fact that most victims of the Auschwitz-Birkenau killing center were Jews. Survivors feel that their personal and concrete Jewish experience in Auschwitz has been subsumed under an all-embracing general concept or has been regarded as a universal metaphor for evil. These interpretations, they say, are unfaithful to the past as it really was. Survivors and others in Israel are committed to stressing the Jewish perspective of the Holocaust, while various factions in the world try to reduce it. In Poland Auschwitz was regarded as the killing center of the Poles, and an attempt to establish a Carmelite convent on the site aroused ill feelings among many Jews. In the countries of the former Communist bloc the Jewish identity of the victims was concealed, and the commemoration plaques posted at the killing centers and other memorial sites avoided any indication that the victims were Jewish. Although the Poles have made changes since the late 1980s, the misgivings of

Jewish organizations and many survivors in Israel have not dissipated. Their apprehensions are exacerbated by anti-Semites and neo-Nazi groups who purposely deny the Holocaust, claiming that it would have been impossible to kill so many people in Auschwitz; they present the Jewish remembrance of Auschwitz as a manipulation of the Jewish conspiracy.

In Israel this concern is shared by many, including Holocaust survivors, researchers, and politicians. In the preparations for the Auschwitz commemoration in Poland this issue became a central obstacle to the planned cooperation between Poland, Israel, and other Jewish organizations. The debate revolving around the "nationalization" of the Holocaust in a narrow Israeli or Jewish sense placed this issue on the Israeli political agenda.

On January 23, 1995, the Knesset held a special session to commemorate the liberation of Auschwitz. The discussion was overshadowed by the funerals of twenty victims of a terrorist raid that had occurred in the center of Israel the previous day. The gloom that gripped the country was palpable in the hall and echoed in the Holocaust rhetoric commonly heard on such occasions. Shevah Weiss, the speaker of the House and a Holocaust survivor, opened the discussion with personal remarks about the symbolism of his presiding over the commemoration. Among the several parties' speakers were many members of the Knesset whose families came from Islamic countries and who thus had no personal ties to the Holocaust. The speakers stressed Auschwitz's significance for Israel, for the Jews, and for humanity as a whole. The connection between the present political situation and the ongoing terrorist attacks was mentioned by many, who talked about the past and expressed grief over the newly dead. This occasion, like many others, demonstrated how the memory of the Holocaust and current events intersected in political rhetoric.

As much as the dialogue with the Holocaust is interwoven with political reality, however, and in spite of its vulgarization, it would be wrong to view it only through the political prism. Since the early 1940s the responses to what we today define as the Holocaust have been an integral part of the thinking of the Yishuv. Those who had immigrated to Palestine and experienced the destruction of their homes and communities from a distance tried to keep the images of the past in their minds and hearts. This was demonstrated in the poetry of the 1940s. The images of their villages, families, and friends remained frozen in time. In spite of their feelings of guilt for not being there on doomsday, the decision they had made to leave the Diaspora and immigrate seemed to have been the correct one.

Their memories of the world that was destroyed were the origins of the dialogue that would slowly develop with the Holocaust, and their feelings of guilt, regret, and mourning were transformed into an authentic solidarity with the Jewish people and the Jewish state. The Holocaust was perceived by many Jews and non-Jews as a major factor that motivated Jews and others to support the establishment of the Jewish state. The Holocaust proved the necessity of the state and became an important factor in unifying Israelis and Jews all over the world. The Hebrew phrase *Shoah Utekumah* grew to reflect an active modern Zionist transformation of the traditional Jewish response to catastrophes.

The World Reacts to the Holocaust

During the years 1945–49 the dialogue regarding the Holocaust progressed in a minor tone. The ideological perception that the Yishuv had a responsibility to redeem the Jewish people became more evident. As contacts between the Yishuv's emissaries and the survivors in the DP camps and other European countries increased, Yishuv members came to admire the survivors' vitality, although they disapproved of their materialism and other unappealing characteristics. The Yishuv tended to patronize the Holocaust survivors and immigrants in general. This complex emotional relationship was expressed in a deep ambivalence. Thus, Yishuv veterans and survivors were close but distant, unwilling to listen but eager to speak. Their relationship was described by Yablonka as one between "Foreign Brothers."[256]

Zionism allowed many survivors to sublimate their desire for revenge against the Germans, the hostile population of Europe that had cooperated with the Nazis, and the bystanders who had been indifferent to the Jews' fate. Survivors channeled their energies into the reconstruction of their lives by participating in the struggle for a Jewish state and the renewal of Jewish life as a whole. Israel, as a new state and a society of immigrants, enabled the survivors to associate their personal rehabilitation with the collective goals of the state. This became an important source of identification that united the different segments of the Israeli Jewish society. In many respects the expression "death and rebirth" was a reflection of the genuine feelings of Israel's citizens and of reality. Thus, the Holocaust became an authentic part of the national legacy of Israel and was transmitted and shared within the society at large.

During the 1950s and early 1960s, interaction with the Holocaust occurred on many levels. The dialogue and negotiation with the memories of the Holocaust did not progress along a straight path. The minor tone was replaced by a rhetoric of pathos. The concept of "death and rebirth" now had to account for the deaths of those killed in the War of Independence. This synthesis elicited a painful comparison between those who had died in vain, as had the Jews during the Holocaust, and those who had died for a cause, as had the Israeli soldiers, among them Holocaust survivors. Many memorial books were written about the fallen soldiers of the War of Independence, but those survivors who slowly developed the kehillah books (reference books for Jewish community organizations) and wrote a few memoirs, in particular about the resistance, concealed their longing for what had disappeared as well as their pain. The reaction seemed an appropriate one, and it almost became the strategy of Israeli society. This suppressed pain, however, undermined the feelings of identification and solidarity created during the struggle for independence. These conflicting emotions dwelled side by side for many years without any overt confrontation.

Thus, during the first fifteen years after the establishment of Israel, dialogue regarding the Holocaust was impaired. The reciprocity necessary for a meaningful discussion was missing. Israel was talking rather than listening. Nevertheless, during this period and until the Eichmann trial the hidden past erupted at frequent intervals. These eruptions included the legislation regarding commemoration, the German reparations agreement, the Kasztner Affair, and the arms sale to Germany. All of these events provided opportunities for examining the past that would have enabled Israelis to listen. However, this did not happen. Israeli society, which was charged with the need to unite, to dedicate tremendous efforts to solving the social and economic problems of mass immigration, and to establish a stable political system, was unable to listen, nor did it view the survivors as conveying a particular message. The political and ideological divisions made the social and cultural situation more vulnerable.

After the Six-Day War, and in particular after 1973, the dialogue carried a new complexity that incorporated the impact of the Eichmann trial. Thus, a new two-way road was paved for a discussion that would move onto a more mature and meaningful plane. The second generation of Israelis, many of them the sons and daughters of the immigrants of the 1950s, who had been born or educated in the Jewish state, strived to make the unstructured interpretations of the past more coherent and started to listen. The innocence of Israel's first two decades was challenged by a new and more difficult political and moral reality, and the Zionist narrative began to be transformed. The clear credos of the late 1940s and the early 1950s were thrown into doubt and emphasized many unanswered questions that had been raised.

A strong Israel that had experienced anxiety, failure, and victory opened the political and social stage to new actors. The traditional leaders, the successors of the founding fathers, with their European origins and left-wing orientation, lost their hegemony. The political opponents to Labor, particularly the Israelis of eastern origins, took the lead in the new era, and they had their own social and political agendas. Thus, a new concern about the Holocaust emerged, nourished by a willingness to adopt a new Zionist narrative and new stereotypes but also by a more critical attitude. The heroic past had to be brought into line with tragic interpretations of the past and the present, and in particular with the recognition of various difficult dilemmas. This negotiation with the Holocaust progressed and produced different definitions of heroism, cooperation, and collaboration. Old and new concepts and interpretations were provided by research, and the new political factions argued about how and what to remember of the Holocaust, while the vulgarization of Holocaust rhetoric increased. What will be the direction of the dialogue in the future? Will the political manipulation of the Holocaust impair the meaningful dialogue that is occurring today? These questions and many others will be left to the historian of future years.

NOTES

I would like to thank my research assistant, Yael Orvieto, for her assistance and dedication in the preparation of this essay.

1. Saul Friedländer, "The *Shoah* between Memory and History," *Jerusalem Quarterly*, no. 53 (winter 1990), 116.

2. For a very radical approach, see Yehuda Elkana, "Bizkhut Ha'shikhekhah," *Haaretz*, March

2, 1988, 13. That the Holocaust is manipulated for political purposes is one of the claims advanced by Tom Segev, *The Seventh Million: The Israelis and the Holocaust* (New York, 1993).

3. Pierre Nora, "Between Memory and History: Les Lieux de Memoire," *Representations* 26, no. 9 (1985), cited in Yael Zerubavel, *Recovered Roots:*

Collective Memory and the Making of Israeli National Tradition (Chicago, 1994).

4. On the Balfour Declaration, see Leonard Stein, *The Balfour Declaration* (London, 1961). On the beginnings of British rule in Palestine and the Mandate, see ESCO Foundation, *Palestine: A Study of Jewish, Arab, and British Policies,* 2 vols. (New Haven, 1947).

5. On the establishment of the Jewish institutions and bodies of self-government in the Mandate period, see Don Horowitz and Moshe Lissak, *The Origins of Israeli Polity: The Mandate Period* (Chicago, 1978), 37–104. For a historical account of the establishment of the Jewish Agency, see Yigal Elam, *Hasokhnut hayehudit* (Jerusalem, 1990), esp. 1–146.

6. Only in 1940, because of the war, was an effort made to collect contributions from all the people of the Yishuv, through a fund known as Kofer Ha'yishuv, which, however, never managed to obtain contributions from all the members of the Jewish population.

7. On the Revisionist movement, see Joseph Schechtman, *The Life and Time of Vladimir Jabotinsky,* 2 vols. (New York, 1961); and Raphaela Bilski Ben-Hur, *Every Individual a King* (Washington, D.C., 1993).

8. On the political and social structure of the Yishuv and its development during the Mandate years, see Horowitz and Lissak, *Origins of Israeli Policy,* 105–19. Agudat Israel did not participate in the JA but was represented in the other Yishuv political institutions, such as Va'ad Leumi.

9. The concept of the "negation of the Diaspora" is complex. The founding fathers of Zionism were very skeptical about the prospects for a viable life for Jews in the Diaspora, both in countries where Jews had been emancipated and in countries, such as Russia, where they had not. Part of the skepticism about Diaspora life reflected opposition to the prevailing Jewish social structure, to the strategies Jews had developed as a minority, and to the dominant role of religious values in the social and cultural life of the Jewish people. At one extreme, Zionist thinkers reflected the view of those who negated all aspects of Diaspora life, including the cultural creativity of that life. Those at the other extreme viewed the problems of living in the Diaspora as part of the modern transformation of the Jews and the societies in which they were living but did not deny the spiritual importance of Jewish creativity in the past. The majority of Yishuv leaders tended to favor abandoning all past traditions, although there was much support for incorporating the cultural achievements of the past into Zionist life. In the educational framework of the time, criticism of the Diaspora was evident in the literature taught and in the effort to strengthen the students' ties to the land and its environment. Thus young Jews in Palestine felt removed from the difficulties of the Diaspora and identified with the criticism of the Diaspora.

10. For further elaboration on Palestinian nationalism, see Yehoshua Porat, *The Emergence of the Palestinian National Movement: 1919–1929* (London, 1974); and idem, *The Palestinian Arab National Movement from Riots to Rebellion: 1929–1939* (London, 1977).

11. Theodore Herzl, *The Jewish State* (London, 1934), 22–33.

12. On the boycott movement, see M. Gottlieb, "The Anti-Nazi Boycott Movement in the United States—An Ideological and Sociological Appreciation," *Jewish Social Studies* 34 (1973), 198–227; E. W. Braatz, "German Commercial Interests in Palestine, Zionism, and the Boycott of German Goods, 1933–1934," *European Studies Review* 9 (1979), 481–513; and Yoav Gelber, *Moledeth Hadashah* (Jerusalem, 1990), 1–7.

13. Anita Shapira, "Time Perception as a Factor in the Partition Plans, 1937–1947," in *Iyunim Betokhniot Halukah,* ed. Meir Avizohar and Isia Friedman (Beersheba, 1984).

14. Arthur Ruppin, "The Settlement of German Jewry," in *Three Decades of Palestine: Speeches and Papers on the Upbuilding of the Jewish National Home* (Jerusalem, 1936).

15. On the establishment of the Office for German Jewry, see Gelber, *Moledeth Hadashah,* 40–51; and Chaim Weizmann to Oliver D'Avigdor-Goldsmith, August 14, 1933, in *The Letters and Papers of Chaim Weizmann, Series A: Letters Vol. XVI, June 1933–August 1935,* ed. Gabriel Sheffer (Jerusalem, 1978), 25–28.

16. Ze'ev Jabotinsky, "On the Evacuation, a Speech at the Doctors and Engineers Club, Warsaw, October 1936," in *Cetavim* (Jerusalem, 1948). On the evacuation, see Bilski Ben-Hur, *Every Individual a King,* 164–75.

17. Dalia Ofer, "Ha'aliya, hayishuv vehagola: Ben-Gurion Bitkufat hashoah," *Cathedra,* no. 43 (1987), 69–90.

18. On the Transfer Agreement, see Werner Feilchenfeld et al., *Haavara—Transfer nach Palastina und Einwanderung deutscher Juden: 1933–1939* (Tubingen, 1972); and Gelber, *Moledeth Hadashah,* 7–51. On the public Jewish reaction to the agreement, see Central Zionist Archive, Jerusalem (CZA), L9/101. On the reaction in Palestine, see *Haaretz,* August 25, 27, 28, 1933, and *Davar,* August 24, 1933 (the

latter is the daily of the Histadrut). For criticism at the seventeenth Zionist Congress, in Geneva, see the discussions of the Political Committee, August 29, 1933, CZA, Z4/232/4; see also the newspapers in Palestine throughout the spring of 1933 on the boycott. For a very anti-Zionist and critical analysis of the Transfer Agreement in relation to the boycott, see Edwine Black, *The Transfer Agreement: The Untold Story of the Secret Agreement between the Third Reich and Jewish Palestine* (New York, 1984); and Gelber, *Moledeth Hadashah,* 60.

19. For sources for the number of German immigrants and the transfer money involved, see Gelber, *Moledeth Hadashah,* 60 (table 4). For sources for the Jewish capital inflow figures, see Nadav Halevi, "The Political Economy of Absorptive Capacity: Growth and Cycles in Jewish Palestine under the British Mandate," *Middle Eastern Studies* 19, no. 4 (1983), 460 (table 2).

20. For an extensive account of Youth Aliyah, see Raphael Gat, "Aliyat Hano'ar," *Cathedra,* no. 37 (1985), 149–76; Gelber, *Moledeth Hadashah,* 186–221; Sarah Kadosh, "Youth Aliyah and the Rescue and Absorption of Youth during the Holocaust, 1935–1945" (Ph.D. diss., Columbia University, 1994); and the many memoirs of YA workers.

21. Gelber, *Moledeth Hadashah,* 214–21.

22. See Dalia Ofer, *Escaping the Holocaust: Illegal Immigration to the Land of Israel, 1939–1944* (New York, 1990), 1. On the origins of the *ha'apalah,* see David Shapira, *La'alot Bekhol Hadrakhim* (Tel Aviv, 1994), 1–29.

23. For the development of the Nazi Jewish policy in the Reich, see Karl Schleunes, *The Twisted Road to Auschwitz, 1933–1945: Nazi Policy towards German Jews* (Urbana, Ill., 1970). On its implications for illegal immigration, see Ofer, *Escaping the Holocaust,* 98–103.

24. See Porat, *Palestinian Arab National Movement,* 274–94; and Michael J. Cohen, *Palestine: Retreat from the Mandate, the Making of British Policy, 1936–45* (London, 1978), 66–87.

25. On Ben-Gurion and illegal immigration, see Shabbetai Tevet, *Hakark'a Habo'ereth,* vol. 3 (Tel Aviv, 1987), 326–29; Yitzhak Avneri, "Mered Haaliyah," *Cathedra,* no. 44 (1987), 126–57; and Meir Avi Zohar, *Zikhronoth Ben Gurion,* vol. 5 (Tel Aviv, 1989), 17–60. On the illegal immigration of the Revisionists and their relationship with Labor, see Ofer, *Escaping the Holocaust,* 69–88.

26. For a more detailed discussion of the movement during these years, see Ofer, *Escaping the Holocaust,* 17–21, 23–30. It is important to note that the Zionists outside of Palestine, in particular the General Zionists in the United States, opposed illegal immigration. They did not approve of the unlawful actions of a legitimate, recognized political movement; they thought that all actions taken by the movement should be in line with legal international behavior.

27. For a fuller description of the information available during the first months of the war, see Hava Eshkoli (Wagman), *Elem: Mapai lenokhah hashoah, 1939–1942* (Jerusalem, 1994), 57–85.

28. Ibid., 61–64.

29. *Davar,* October 3, 1939 (commentary by Berl Katznelson), December 11, 1939; Raya Choen, "A Test of Jewish Solidarity: The Activities of the Geneva Liaison Offices in Switzerland, 1939–1942" (Ph.D. diss., University of Tel Aviv, 1991), 68–76, 125–58.

30. For a more detailed description, see Ofer, *Escaping the Holocaust,* 31–39, 98–127.

31. Mapai Archive, Beit Berl, meeting of the Central Committee, September 12, 1939. On the establishment of a number of new settlements during the summer of 1939 and the confrontation with the British on the arrival of the illegal boats *Tiger Hill* and *Naomi Julia,* both in September 1939, see ibid.

32. David Ben-Gurion, *Bama'arakhah,* vol. 3 (Tel Aviv, 1949), 14.

33. This political concept was based on the Treaty of Versailles, after World War I, which had demonstrated the advantage accruing to those who had fought with the victorious nations when the political map was redrawn. For a wide-ranging analysis of this issue, see Joseph Heller, *Bema'avak Lemedinah* (Jerusalem, 1985), 34–45; and Yoav Gelber, *Toldoth Hahitnadvut,* vol. 1 (Jerusalem, 1979), 61–84.

34. Heller, *Bema'avak Lemedinah,* 45–50, 332–45. It is important to note that the left wing of the Labor Party strongly opposed the Biltmore Resolution. The Left was doubtful about both the strategy of cooperation with the British and the establishment of a Jewish commonwealth. Tabenkin and Ya'ari feared that the active resentment toward the British would decline with the Yishuv's cooperation with them. Their opposition rested on their view of Great Britain as an imperialist state, of its treachery toward Zionism, and of the limits it wanted to place on the operations of a Jewish army. Both opposed sending soldiers of the Yishuv to serve outside Palestine.

35. "Convention of Hebrew Writers," *Mozna'im,* no. 14 (1942), 370–96.

36. Dina Porat, *The Blue and Yellow Star of David* (Cambridge, Mass., 1990), 33–40.

37. In May 1942 the Bund Report, the first comprehensive report on the mass killing in Poland, which had begun with the invasion of the Soviet Union in June 1941, reached the West. It was sent to the Polish government-in-exile in London by the Bund, the General Jewish Workers Party in Poland, an anti-Zionist Jewish socialist party. The report was partly broadcast on the BBC on June 2, 1942. Information about an order by Hitler to annihilate all European Jewry was sent to London and Washington in August 1942 by Gerhard Riegner. The Jewish leaders in the West and Palestine also received letters from Lichtheim, sent on August 15, 1942, stressing that the sources of information were very reliable. The reaction of the leaders, including people such as Yizhak Gruenbaum, who had been involved with aid to Poland from the beginning of the war, was one of disbelief. Gruenbaum, for example, sent a cable to Rabbi Ehrenpreis in Stockholm in an effort to verify the information. Participants in the JA meeting of October 25, 1942, still referred to the information as a rumor.

38. Yechiam Weitz, *Mudauth vehoser onim: Mapai Lenockah ah Hashoa, 1943–1945* (Jerusalem, 1994), 42; see also 38–49, 100–101.

39. Porat, *Blue and Yellow Star,* 49–53; Ofer, *Escaping the Holocaust,* 205. On the Al Domi group, see Dina Porat, "*Al Domi:* Palestinian Intellectuals and the Holocaust, 1943–45," *Studies in Zionism* 5, no. 1 (1984), 97–124.

40. Small Zionist Committee, January 18, 1943, CZA, S25/259.

41. Ofer, *Escaping the Holocaust,* 199–201; Porat, *Blue and Yellow Star,* 41–47; Eshkoli, *Elem,* 322–28.

42. Ofer, *Escaping the Holocaust,* 199–202.

43. Ibid., 199–210; *Davar,* March 23, 1943.

44. See Weitz, *Mudauth vehoser onim,* 95–98.

45. Ibid., 87–100; Ofer, *Escaping the Holocaust,* 206–10.

46. For Ben-Gurion's view of the remnant (She'erit Hapletah), see Dalia Ofer, "From Survivors to New Immigrants: *She'erit Hapletah* and *Aliyah,*" in *She'erit Hapletah, 1944–1948: Rehabilitation and Political Struggle,* Proceedings of the Sixth Yad Vashem International Historical Conference, ed. Yisrael Gutman and Avital Saf (Jerusalem, 1990), 304–37. On Ben-Gurion's understanding concerning the role of the remnants, see Tuvia Friling, "Changing Roles: The Relationship between Ben Gurion, the *Yishuv,* and She'erit Hapletah: 1942–1945," ibid., 450–80.

47. After November 1942 the anger toward Great Britain stood in contrast to the increased desire to fight against Hitler. Enlistment in the British army expressed even more a response to the Jewish plight in Europe. After the defeat of the Germans at El Alamein in October 1942, the danger of a Nazi invasion of Palestine disappeared. Young people, however, continued to join the military in considerable numbers. During the years 1943–45, 7,226 out of a total pool of 27,028 (26.7 percent) enlisted, even though unemployment had decreased considerably (see Yoav Gelber, *Toldoth Hahitnadvut,* vol. 4 [Jerusalem, 1984], 282–88, 300–301).

48. Ofer, *Escaping the Holocaust,* 211–14; Dalia Ofer, "The Activities of the Jewish Agency Delegation in Istanbul, 1943," in *Rescue Attempts during the Holocaust,* ed. Yisrael Gutman and Ephraim Zuroff (Jerusalem, 1977), 435–51; Porat, *Blue and Yellow Star,* 120–26.

49. See the discussions of the Political Committee of Mapai, December 12, 1943, to January 26, 1944, in particular the talk of Ze'ev Shind, a central figure in the Illegal Immigration Organization and an emissary in Istanbul from 1942 on, and Eliyahu Dobkin, assistant head of the Immigration Department of the JA and a central member of Mapai, September 24, 1944, in Mapai Archive, 26/43, 26/44. See also Ofer, *Escaping the Holocaust,* 206–10, 286–90; and Weitz, *Mudauth vehoser onim,* 100–128.

50. A three-volume examination of the work of the JDC was written by Yehuda Bauer: *My Brother's Keeper: A History of the American Jewish Joint Distribution Committee, 1929–1939* (Philadelphia, 1974); *American Jewry and the Holocaust: The American Jewish Joint Distribution Committee, 1939–1945* (Detroit, 1981); and *Out of the Ashes: The Impact of American Jews on Post-Holocaust European Jewry* (Oxford, 1989).

51. See Porat, *Blue and Yellow Star,* 91–92; and Yaakov Mezer and Oded Kaplan, *Meshek Yehudi Umeshek 'Aravi Beeretz Yisrael: Ta'asukah Uzmihah Bitkufat Hamandat* (Jerusalem, 1990), 145 (table 8/1).

52. Ben-Gurion Diary, August 17, 1945, Ben Gurion Archive, Sdeh Boker, quoted in Friling, "Changing Roles," 477.

53. Zeev Mankowitz, "Zionism and She'erit Hapletah," in Gutman and Saf, *She'erit Hapletah,* 224.

54. Quoted in ibid., 222.

55. On the Cyprus detention camps, see Nahum Bogner, *Ei Hagerush* (Tel Aviv, 1991).

56. For elaborate discussions on the emissaries of the Yishuv, see Irit Keynan, "The Meeting of the Eretz-Israel Envoys with the She'erith-Hapletah in the Displaced Persons Camps in Germany,

1945–1948" (Ph.D. diss., University of Tel Aviv, 1994); Haim (Hoffmann) Yahil, "Hamishlahat haaretz Yisraelit Lesherit Hapletah," *Yalkut Moreshet,* nos. 30 (November 1980), 7–40, and 31 (April 1981), 133–76; and Shlomo Bargil, "Youth Aliyah: Rescue and Rehabilitation of Holocaust Survivors Policy and Activities, 1945–1955" (Ph.D. diss., Hebrew University, Jerusalem, 1996). The numbers of emissaries given are the total in 1947.

57. Hanah Yablonka, *Ahim Vezarim* (Jerusalem, 1994), 79–154.

58. Eighteen books were published in the series, as well as a number of booklets. Most of the books were written in Hebrew by writers from Palestine who interviewed the survivors; some were written by the survivors themselves. A book by the Soviet author Vasilli Grosmann was also included in the series. The purpose of the series is explained on the back cover of one of the books, *Shneim-'asar pelitim,* ed. Brachah Habas (Tel Aviv, 1942): "To strengthen our awareness and our war efforts. . . . The books describe the life of Nazi victims in the ghettos and in the torture camps, stories of refugees, and the adventures of the documents which were rescued and which pertain to the underground struggle." See also Y. Shragai to the Executive of the Va'ad Leumi, CZA, J1/6442, October 6 and 10, 1944.

59. *Divrei Haknesset,* vol. 4 (Jerusalem, [1950?]), 1949 ff., 1409.

60. Moreshet Archive (Archive of the Shomer Hatza'ir, Givat Havivah), personal archive of Mordechai Shenhabi, September 9, 1942. See also Segev, *Seventh Million,* 427–29. In an interview in 1953, after the Yad Vashem Law had passed, Shenhabi told a reporter that he had thought of commemorating Jewish life in Germany while still an emissary of the Hashomer Hatza'ir youth movement in Nazi Germany. As there was no future for Jewish life there, he thought it should be remembered by future Jewish generations through a commemorative site such as a forest. The idea was that German Jews who left Germany would establish such a site. He had expressed this idea to Weizmann in London and received his support.

61. Committee to Commemorate European Jewry (Yad Leyahadut Eiropa) to the National Committee, September 6, 1945, CZA, J1/3610I.

62. Shenhabi, "A Memorial to the Diaspora Which Was Destroyed," May 2, 1945, CZA, S26/1326. See also *Davar,* May 25, 1945, 3–4; *Hamishmar,* May 25, 1945, 3; *Hatzofeh,* May 25, 1945, 5.

63. In later years a number of articles in the Israeli press referred to the traditional meaning of planting trees. Many articles were published in the

spring of 1952, when the Ya'ar Hakedoshim, the Martyrs' Forest, was planted (see the dailies *Hador, Haaretz, Hatzofeh,* all of April 21, 1952; see also James E. Young, *The Texture of Memory: Holocaust Memorials and Meaning* [New Haven, Conn., 1993], 219–20).

64. Yad Vashem, meeting following the resolution adopted at the World Zionist Conference, August 7, 1945, CZA, J1/3601a.

65. Yosef Rosensaft, Jewish Committee in Bergen Belsen, to the Yad Lagolah Committee, December 6, 1945, and reply, January 17, 1946, CZA, J1/3610I.

66. Abba Kovner, speaking at a meeting dedicated to the establishment of Yad Vashem during the last day of the First Congress for Jewish Studies, July 13–14, 1947, CZA, JI/6449. Kovner's talk, "The Hill of Warning," is cited in its entirety in *Hamishmar,* July 25, 1947.

67. Samuel Krakowski, "Memorial Projects and Memorial Institutions Initiated by She'erit Hapletah," in Gutman and Saf, *She'erit Hapletah,* 388–98.

68. CZA, J1/3610a. In June 1950 Gruenbaum reported that the historical committees had sent forty-three boxes of documents to Israel to be housed in the archive of Yad Vashem (*Davar,* June 4, 1950).

69. See Moshe Beham's letter in *Davar,* May 16, 1945; and Emmanuel Sivan, *Dor Tashah: Mitos, deyokan, vezikaron* (Tel Aviv, 1991), 172–82. On the first *Yizkor* book published in the Yishuv and the debate over it, see John Frankel, "Sefer Yizkor Mishnat 1911—He'arah 'al Mitosim Bitkufat Ha-'aliyah Hashniyah," *Yahadut Zemaneinu* 4 (1988), 67–97.

70. *Hatzofeh,* June 11, 1945, applauded the Va'ad Leumi's decision to take responsibility for Yad Vashem.

71. An early and important discussion on the subject was held on June 4, 1945, in the Va'ad Leumi. Its goal was to prepare a proposal for the first postwar meeting of the Zionist executive meeting in London. During this meeting, a number of proposals were raised and discussed (the proposals are collected in CZA, JI/1360a).

72. Meeting of the JNF directorate (Keren Hayesod), September 16, 1946, CZA, S53/1671. See also a statement by David Remez on the obligation to avoid vulgarity in fund-raising for this purpose (July 13, 1947, CZA, J1/6449; as well as the criticism of Dr. Dov Soloveichik, of the Religious Zionists, on May 6, 1946, at a special meeting of the Va'ad Leumi).

73. On the budget, see the meeting regarding

the establishment of the Yad Vashem center on June 1, 1947, CZA, S46/306; and meetings of June 8 and June 10, 1947, of the committee responsible for the establishment of Yad Vashem, CZA, S53/1671.

74. Ibid.

75. On February 19, 1946, at a meeting of the executive committee of Yad Vashem, the name offered for the institute was Yad Vashem Lagolah Haneherevet Ulmilhemet Hashihrur (Yad Vashem [i.e., a Memorial] for the Destroyed Diaspora and for the War of Independence). This name demonstrates that the political struggle for Jewish independence and the Holocaust were two aspects of the same event (CZA, J1/6442). For a more elaborate discussion on the conceptual development of *Shoah Utekumah,* see Dalia Ofer, "The Holocaust in the Public Discourse of Palestine and Israel: 1942–1953," *Journal of Contemporary History,* July 1996.

76. CZA, S46/306. See also the letter of the directorate of the JNF to Remez of June 6, 1947, about fund-raising and publicity in the press.

77. Minutes of the meeting of the preparatory committee, June 29, 1947, CZA, S26/1326.

78. July 13–14, 1947, CZA, S26/1326.

79. *Haboker* (daily of the Central Zionists), March 11, 12, 1951. The debate over the obligation of the state to go on with the commemoration plans of Yad Vashem continued in the press. See, e.g., *Davar,* June 26, September 30, 1951; and *Al Hamishmar* (daily of the left Zionist Mapam party), September 30, 1951. See also Joseph Klausner, memorandum on Yad Vashem, July 5, 1951, Israel State Archive (ISA), GL/1087.

80. *Divrei Haknesset,* vol. 14 (Jerusalem, 1954), 1051–70.

81. Ibid., vol. 9 (Jerusalem, 1952), 1655–57, 1708. For an interesting interpretation of the "temporal flow" between Passover, Yom Hashoah, Yom Hazikaron, and the Day of Independence, see Don Handelman, *Models and Mirrors: Towards an Anthropology of Public Events* (Cambridge, 1990), 194–201.

82. For the law and the Knesset debate, see *Divrei Haknesset,* 14:1310–14, 1331–54, 2402–10. For a detailed elaboration of the development of the concepts of Shoah, Gevurah, and 'Oz ruah and their relation to the public discourse and understanding of the meaning of the events of the war and the Jewish fate, see Ofer, "Holocaust in Public Discourse."

83. The issue of memorial citizenship *(Ezrahut Zikaron)* for the victims of the Holocaust raised a debate on the use of citizenship, a legal concept denoting a concrete status that grants the person holding that status certain rights and obligations. After all, those who had been killed had all been citizens of other countries (see the opinion of the deputy attorney general to the minister of education, May 26, 1952, ISA, 1087/907-3).

84. The people of Yad Vashem and the government were alarmed by the plans of the Centre de Documentation Juive Contemporaine in Paris, established by Isaac Schneersohn in France in 1943 as an underground research center to collect information on the fate of the French Jews. After the war the center had extended its activities and received the support of prominent Jewish and non-Jewish leaders in France and of Jewish institutions elsewhere, such as YIVO in New York. It initiated a project to erect a Tomb of the Unknown Jewish Martyr, and it established an international committee of prominent people in France and throughout the Jewish world to develop the plans. The plans were completed in 1951, and in December 1952 the opening ceremony was held (see Justin Godart [honorary president of the Documentation Center] to Ben-Gurion, June 18, 1951, and December 17, 1952; and Benzion Dinur [minister of education] to Ben-Gurion, April 3, 1953, ISA, G/5564/40/9).

85. *Divrei Haknesset,* 14:1347.

86. Handelman, *Models and Mirrors,* 194–201.

87. *Divrei Haknesset,* vol. 24a (Jerusalem, 1958), 2118–19; vol. 26 (Jerusalem, 1959), 1992–93.

88. The sources for the numbers are *Statistical Abstract of Israel, 1989,* vol. 40 (Jerusalem, 1990), 83 (table B/24); and, for the number of immigrant survivors, *Israel Census, 1961* (Jerusalem, 1962), booklet 42, 13 (table 3). I subtracted from the total number of 406,140 immigrants from European countries the 52,435 children aged 14 and younger, who were born abroad after the end of the war. These children and those who were born to survivors in Israel were considered the second generation of Holocaust survivors.

89. Moshe Lissak, "Dimuei Olim—Stereotipim vetiug bitkufat ha'aliyah hagdolah bishnot hahamishim," *Cathedra,* no. 43 (1987), 125–44; Dalia Ofer, "Holocaust Survivors as Immigrants: The Case of Israel and the Cyprus Detainees," *Modern Judaism,* February 1996, 1–23.

90. For a broader discussion of the attitudes toward the survivors and their experiences, see Yablonka, *Ahim Vezarim,* 71–78, 139–54, 234–38; and Segev, *Seventh Million.*

91. On YA, see Yablonka, *Ahim Vezarim,* 196–215; and Bargil, "Youth Aliya."

92. One of the most widely read prose writers

in Israel in the late 1940s and early 1950s was a survivor, Yehiel Dinur, who used the pen name K. Zetnik; he described the daily struggle of inmates of the death and concentration camps. See his *Salamandra* (Tel Aviv, 1946); *Karu lo Pipel* (Tel Aviv, 1961); and *Beit Habubot* (Tel Aviv, 1972). See also Reizl (Ruz'ka) Korczak, *Lehavot Baefer* (Merhavia, 1946). Korczak's memoir, with its documentary appendix, had a great impact on young people and adults and was reprinted a number of times.

93. *Al Hamishmar,* April 26, 1955; *Yediot Aharonot,* April 15, 1955.

94. For a thorough discussion of the reparations agreement, see Nana Sagi, *German Reparations: A History of the Negotiations* (Jerusalem, 1980).

95. David Ben-Gurion, *Medinat Israel Hamehudeshet,* vol. 1 (Tel Aviv, 1969), 421–23. See *Divrei Haknesset,* vol. 8 (Jerusalem, 1952), 1547–61, for the debate on April 2, 1951, and vol. 10 (Jerusalem, 1953), 895–964, for the stormy debates on January 7–8, 1952.

96. For a detailed account of the relations between Israel and Germany after the Holocaust, see Ne'imah Barzel, "Yisrael Vegermania, 1945–1956: Hitpathut yahas hamedinah vehahevrah beyisrael legermania aharei hashoah" (Ph.D. diss., University of Haifa, 1990).

97. One aspect of the normalization in the relationship between West Germany and Israel was the renewal of Jewish life in Germany. On this issue, see Frank Stern, *Whitewashing the Yellow Badge* (London, 1991); and Ne'imah Barzel, "Kium Haim Yehudiim Begermania, 1945–1953," *Yahadut Zemaneinu* 8 (1993), 99–134.

98. Bauer, *American Jewry and the Holocaust,* 380–99.

99. This section is based on the following sources: Dov Dinur, *Kasztner, Leader or Villain?* (Haifa, 1987), 15–99; Yehiam Weitz, *Hayav, mishpato umoto shel Israel Kasztner* (Jerusalem, 1995); idem, "The Herut Movement and the Kasztner Trial," *Holocaust and Genocide Studies* 8, no. 3 (1994), 349–71; Shalom Rosenfeld, *Tik plili 124: mishpat Gruenwald Kasztner* (Tel Aviv, 1955); Pninah Lahav, *Israeli Justice: An Intellectual Biography of Chief Justice Simon Agranat* (forthcoming); Roni Shetauber, "Havikuah hapoliti al mishpat Kasztner al pi ha'itonut hamiflagtit," *Measef Ha-zionut* 13 (1988), 219–46.

100. *Haverim mesaprim 'al Gimi* (Tel Aviv, 1952); Moshe Gefen et al., eds., *Sefer Hapartizanim* (Tel Aviv, 1959); Yizhak Zukerman et al., eds., *Sefer Lohamie Hagetaot* (Tel Aviv, 1954); Moshe Basok, ed., *Sefer Hama'apilim* (Jerusalem, 1947); Zerubavel

Gilad, ed., *Sefer Hapalmah* (Tel Aviv, 1952).

101. On the Irgun, see David Niv, *Hairgun Hazvai Haleumi,* 4 vols. (Tel Aviv, 1967–75); on Lehi, see Joseph Heller, *Lehi Ideologiah upolitikah: 1940–1949,* 2 vols. (Jerusalem, 1989).

102. See Moshe Keren's articles in *Haaretz,* July 8–15, 1955; they were later collected in *Be'ayot holofot ube'ayot shel kev'a* (Jerusalem, 1978), 187–238. For Alterman's poems and commentaries, see *Davar,* April 30, May 28, 1954; July 1, 22, 29, August 12, 1955; and April 12, 1957. Some were published in his *Hatur Hashvi'i: Cetavim,* vol. 3 (Tel Aviv, 1962), 407–40; Dan Laor, ed., *'Al Shetei Hadrakhim: Dapim min hapinkas* (Tel Aviv, 1989), contains the drafts Alterman prepared before writing his poems in 1954–57. And see Alex Barzel, "Following the Kasztner Trial," *Igeret Lahaverim,* no. 186, July 7, 1955; no. 187, July 14, 1955; no. 188, July 21, 1955; no. 189, July 28, 1955.

103. Keren, *Be'ayot holofot,* 187–92; Laor, *'Al Shetei Hadrakhim,* 124.

104. Alterman, *Hatur Hashvi'i,* 407, 413–20, 422–23; Laor, *'Al Shetei Hadrakhim,* 97–103, 110–11.

105. Barzel, *Igeret Lahaverim,* nos. 186, 187.

106. Alterman, *Hatur Hashvi'i,* 434–40; Keren, *Be'ayot holofot,* 197–204.

107. Alterman, *Hatur Hashvi'i,* 434–40; Laor, *'Al Shetei Hadrakhim,* 18–25, 119–21.

108. Pninah Lahav, "The Kasztner Affair," in *Israeli Justice.*

109. Yehiam Weitz, "Hashinui bedimuyo shel Israel Kasztner," *Cathedra,* no. 69 (1993), 134–51.

110. For Ben-Gurion's declaration, see *Divrei Haknesset,* vol. 29 (Jerusalem, 1960), 1286; for the Law for the Punishment of Nazis and Nazi Collaborators, see ibid., vol. 6 (Jerusalem, 1950), August 10, 2397. The discussions on the first reading were on March 27 (ibid., vol. 5 (Jerusalem, 1950), 1142–62).

111. Haim Gouri, *Mul Ta Hazkhukhit: Mishpat Yerushalayim* (Tel Aviv, 1963), 73.

112. David Ben-Gurion, *Medinat Israel Hamehudeshet,* vol. 2 (Tel Aviv, 1969), 672.

113. Simon Wiesenthal, *Ich jagte Eichmann* (Guetersloh, 1961); Tuvia Friedman, *Nazi Hunter* (Haifa, 1961). The idea of vengeance was voiced by a number of the survivors, including such well-known personalities as Kovner (see Segev, *Seventh Million,* 149–52).

114. Nili Keren, "Hashpaot me'azvei da'at hakahal umehkar hashoah 'al hadiun hakhinukhi beyisrael, 1948–1981" (Ph.D. diss., Hebrew University, Jerusalem, 1985), 50. See also Ben-Gurion to Yisrael Galili, in *Davar,* May 27, 1960.

115. P. B., "After the Capture of Eichmann," *Haboker,* May 26, 1960, 2; Y. Shifman, "Would Ben-Gurion's Government Withdraw from the Issue of Eichmann?" *Herut,* May 27, 1960; Ahron Dolev, "Eichmann Is Not a Human Being," *Ma'ariv,* June 3, 1960, 4.

116. Pninah Lahav, "The Eichmann Trial: Between Universalism and Particularism," in *Israeli Justice; Haboker,* May 27, 1960, which discusses Eichmann's actions and the report of the last testaments of Jews calling for revenge by killing all murderers; Eliezer Livneh, "Thoughts around Eichmann," *Yediot Aharonot,* June 3, 1960, 3. See also the debate in the Knesset on the budget of the ministry of justice when the issue of the trial arose, in particular what Haim Zadok said about restraining the press (*Divrei Haknesset,* 29:2106–8).

117. Gideon Hausner, *Justice in Jerusalem,* vol. 2 (New York, 1968), 292–307; Abraham Axelrod, "On a Show Trial to Eichmann," *Herut,* June 17, 1960; Aryeh L. Kubovy, "The Portent of the Capture of Adolf Eichman: The Second Meeting of the Yad Vashem Council," in *Im Eshkahekh Shoah* (Jerusalem, 1967), 60–63; Nehemiah Robinson, "Eichmann: His Past and Future; His Prospective Punishment," *Gesher* 2 (December 1960), 70–90; "The Best Confession of Eichmann," *Sulam,* December 1960; Moshe Prager, "On the Payment of 20,000 Dollars for the Defence of Eichmann," *Davar,* January 6, 1961, 2, 4.

118. See *Davar, Haboker, Al Hamishmar,* and *Haaretz* of June 3, 1960, for reactions to the suggestion of Nahum Goldmann, the head of the Zionist movement, that Eichmann not be tried in Israel. See also Sara Nishmit, "Our Right and Responsibility to Try Eichmann," *Lamerhav,* June 8, 1960, 2; Jacob Shabbetai, "A Letter to General Frondizi from a Survivor," *Davar,* June 17, 1960, 2; Robinson, "Eichmann"; and reports in all the papers on December 19, 1960, of a press conference by Ben-Gurion, who stated that the punishment of Eichmann was not as important as holding the trial in Jerusalem ("The Israeli Dispatch," *Haaretz,* June 8, 1960, 2; "The Insult to Argentina," *Davar,* June 10, 1960, 2; "The Trial in Jerusalem," *Hazofeh,* April 11, 1961, 1; "The Lesson," ibid., May 27, 1960, 2. See also Ben-Gurion, remarks in a press conference on June 18, 1960, "Only Israel Had the Right to Judge Eichmann," *Davar,* June 19, 1960, 2). For an interesting article on the universality of Nazi crimes against the Jews and thus on the contribution of the trial to humanity, see Moshe Prager, "Why Not an International Court," ibid., January 27, 1961, 5.

119. Y. D., "Their Sleep Will Be Disturbed," *Herut,* May 26, 1960, 1; "Jewish War against Nazism," *Lamerhav,* June 19, 1960, 5.

120. *Haaretz* and *Lamerhav,* June 8, 1960. See also Yizhak Rubin, "Eichmann in the UN," *Haboker,* June 29, 1960, 2: "This was the great day of hatred not only toward Israel but to all Jews, that came after the general disregard of Jewish tragedy. . . . It was a day of paradox in the history of the UN. Instead of guarding morals it became a legalistic mill that crushed the most terrible tragedies of our nation."

121. "The Witness Is Not Here," *Haolam Hazeh,* September 9, 1960, 8–9, 35 (the article asks what Kasztner could have told about Eichmann had he been alive, as well as what Eichmann could have revealed about his activities); "What Has Life Magazine Revealed about Eichmann?" ibid., December 12, 1960; Hagai Lahav, "In the Month of March," *Lamerhav,* December 1, 1960, 2; S. Rosenfeld, "Let Him Go," *Ma'ariv,* January 27, 1961, 3; M. Brai, "Eichmann Trial, the Nuremberg Trials," *Hazofeh,* April 6, 1961, 5. On the political issues, see David Lior, "Servatius Dictates His Terms to Rosen," *Ya'ad,* January 2 1961; P. B., "Eichmann Law," *Haboker,* January 18, 1961, 2. Most papers criticized the legislation.

122. "Eichmann's Attorney," *Davar,* September 30, 1960, 3 (about the fact that the public would have to get used to the idea that Eichmann had an attorney); Y. Ezer, "Eichmann's Attorney Is Recommended," *Hazofeh,* December 25, 1960, 2; M. H., "The Servatius Affair," *Al Hamishmar,* January 27, 1961, 1; S. Rosenfeld, "Let Him Go," 3; "The Servatius Affair," *Haboker,* January 29, 1961, 2; "Eichmann Trial a Trap to Israel," *Panim El Panim,* October 19, 1960.

123. *6,000,000 Accusers: Israel's Case against Eichmann—The Opening Speech and Legal Argument of Mr. Gideon Hausner, Attorney-General* (Jerusalem, 1961). The proceedings of the trial were published by the government in four volumes in Hebrew, which included the opening and closing addresses of Hausner and all testimonies and cross-examinations: *Hayoetz Hamishpati Lamemshalah Neged Adolf Eichmann: Neum Hapetihah,* 4 vols. (Jerusalem, 1961); the opening address was published in volume 1; see 1:7, 129–30. Gouri, *Mul Ta Hazkhukhit,* 12–16. Reports on Hausner's address were carried in all the papers the following day, April 18, 1961. The evaluation of his general performance in the trial was mixed (see Nahum Pundak, "The Man with the Black Robe," *Dvar Hashavu'a,* July 7, 1961; Moshe Tavor, "Trial Diary," *Davar,* April 19, 1961, 10; "Eichmann's Victims Became His Judge," ibid., 12; "Trial Diary,"

ibid., 3; Uri Avneri, "The Great Failure," *Ha'olam Hazeh*, July 12, 1961, 5; Ephraim Kishon, "Had Gadia," *Ma'ariv*, July 21, 1961, 4; and Simeon Avidan, "Notes from the Trial," *Hapo'el Hatza'ir*, April 25, 1961, 15–16).

124. *Hayoetz Hamishpati*, 1:5–41.

125. On the selection of witnesses, see Rahel Auerbach, "Edim Veeduiot Bamishpat," *Yediot Yad Vashem* 28 (1961), 35–41; and Gouri, *Mul Ta Hazkhukhit*, 72.

126. See, e.g., the testimony of Zivia Lubetkin, *Hayoetz Hamishpati*, 1:243.

127. *Hayoetz Hamishpati*, 1:158–64, 176–225.

128. Tavor, "Trial Diary," *Davar*, May 2, 1961, 5; May 3, 1961, 4. D. R. Elston, "Resistance Has Many Faces," *Jerusalem Post*, May 5, 1961, 4.

129. The press reflected this painful process of reevaluation. See, e.g., Abraham Axelrod, "A Heretic on the Trial," *Herut*, June 17, 1960, 2; A. S., "Echoes, Not Revenge," *Davar*, September 8, 1960, 2; M. H., "With the Presentation of the Indictment," *Al Hamishmar*, February 2, 1961, 1; Eli Eyal, "Eichmann Trial and the Young Generation," *Haaretz*, January 1, 1961, 5; Fay Doron, "But for the Grace of God," *Jerusalem Post*, May 14, 1961, 4; and Rivkah Gruber, "Lamentation," *Devar Hapo'elet*, July 8, 1961, 222–23.

130. Gouri, *Mul Ta Hazkhukhit*, 33.

131. Tavor, "Trial Diary," *Davar*, May 2, 1961, 5.

132. Ibid., May 3, 1961. Testimony of Dr. Leon Weliczker Wells, *Hayoetz Hamishpati*, 1:195–216.

133. Elston, "Resistance," 4.

134. K. Shabbetai, *As Sheep to the Slaughter* (Beit Dagan, 1962), 5–6. See also K. Zetnik, "I Was in Another Universe," *Davar*, June 8, 1961, 3; and D. R. Elston, "The Heroes of Sosnowiec," *Jerusalem Post*, May 5, 1961, 4.

135. Areh L. Kubovy, "A Turning Point," *Hazofeh*, April 13, 1961, 2; M. Nurock, "Sabbath Candles," ibid., May 5, 1961, 2.

136. Ya'akov Even Hen, "Trial Diary," ibid., May 5, 1961, 1.

137. N. Aminah, "Shem'a Yisrael," ibid., April 11, 1961, 1; see also his article in ibid., May 11, 1961, 2.

138. *Hayoetz Hamishpati*, 1:242–96, 301–20, 335–66.

139. Ibid., 1:1122–23.

140. L. Magi, "Eichmann Was Captured," *Hazofeh*, May 25, 1960, 2; Yehudah Levy, "A Just Trial for Eichmann," ibid., May 26, 1960, 2.; H. D., "Changing Jobs," *Davar*, May 26, 1960, 2.

141. Tavor, "Trial Diary," *Davar*, May 2, 1961, 2. Fay Doron wrote that "this shock treatment . . . should make the rest of us more grateful for our blessings, more understanding of our neighbors who survived the death camps" (Doron, "But for the Grace of God," 4).

142. Tavor, "Trial Diary," *Davar*, May 3, 1961, 5; K. Zetnik, "I Was in Another Universe," 3; Even Hen, "Trial Diary," *Hazofeh*, May 2, 1961, 1, June 4, 1961, 1, 3; Pundak, "Man with the Black Robe."

143. See, e.g., Naftali Lavi, "This Holocaust Is Unforgettable," *Haaretz*, April 13, 1961, 5; Yehuda Ariel, "The Prayer Book That Was Written in the Bunker," ibid.; idem, "They Started to Write Since the Memory Is Fading," ibid., April 9, 1964, 9; Moshe Kahanowitz, "Why Didn't They Escape? Why Didn't They Resist?" ibid., April 17, 1966, 9; idem, "Jewish Women—Heroines in the Soviet Partisan Movement," ibid., May 7, 1967, 8; and Eliyahu 'Amikam, "The Two Flags That Were Not Burned," *Yediot Aharonot*, May 7, 1967, 3.

144. Kahanowitz, "Why Didn't They Escape?" 9.

145. See the articles listed in n. 143; in addition, see the editorial in *Haaretz*, April 9, 1964, 4.

146. On the Six-Day War, see Moshe A. Gilbo'a, *Shesh Shanim Shisha Yamim* (Tel Aviv, 1969). The feelings and impressions of the public before and during the war are derived from the press, Knesset proceedings, and published materials.

147. Letters to the editor, *Haaretz*, May 30, 31, June 5, 1967, 4; *Davar*, May 28, 1967, 3, June 4, 1967, 3.

148. "Partisans' Organizations Call Upon World Public Opinion to Protect Israel," *Davar*, May 28, 1967, 3. On the survivors' greater awareness of the danger, see "Our Readers Write," ibid., June 4, 1967, 3; "Against Concessions," Letters to the editor, ibid.; Amnon Rubinstein, "A Popular Army," *Haaretz*, May 29, 1967, 4; Letters to the editor, ibid., May 31, 1967, 6, June 4, 1967, 6.

149. Eliezer Livneh, "The Danger of Hitler," *Haaretz*, May 31, 1967, 2; "Between Hitler and Nasser," ibid., June 5, 1967, 2. See also the comment of one government official in a meeting on the situation, "All the time I live with the memories of Munich, when the world let Hitler take Czechoslovakia" (Gilbo'a, *Shesh Shanim*, 16; see also Shabbatai Tevet, *The Tanks of Tammuz* [London, 1969], 275).

150. Levi Eshkol, quoted in "A Challenge to the Soviet Prime Minister," *Davar*, June 6, 1967, 2.

151. Henry Near, ed., *The Seventh Day: Soldiers' Talk about the Six-Day War* (Tel Aviv, 1970), 164.

152. Amos Elon, *The Israelis: Founders and Sons* (Tel Aviv, 1981), 28–29.

153. For an interesting account of Israeli-born generations, see ibid., 189–256.

154. Ibid., 251–55.

155. Eliezer Schweid, "Yemei Shivah," *Ptahim*, October 1, fall 1967, 9–37. See also the response of Amos Oz to Schweid's article and Schweid's answer to Oz, in ibid., December 2, 1967, 49–51; and the reaction of Pinhas Rosenbleit to Schweid's article, in ibid., March 3, 1968, 32–35.

156. Near, *Seventh Day*, 151–52, 167–75.

157. Ibid., 153.

158. Ibid., 163.

159. On the uniqueness of the Holocaust, see Michael R. Marrus, *The Holocaust in History* (Hanover, N.H., 1987), 18–30; Yehuda Bauer, *The Holocaust in Historical Perspective* (Seattle, 1978); and *Divrei Haknesset*, vol. 55 (Jerusalem, 1968), 3492–95, concerning the genocide in Biafra, where the Ibo tribe was murdered by the Nigerian government in a civil war that lasted from 1966 to 1969.

160. Keren, *Hashpaot*, 191–201.

161. "Allon: We Have Decided Not to Be Apologetic about Our Existence," *Haaretz*, April 15, 1969, 2.

162. Ibid., 1–2. In the following years this topic appeared frequently in the speeches of the major politicians at commemoration ceremonies (see *Haaretz*, April 22, 1971; "Golda Meir, We Know That We Have No One to Rely Upon," ibid., April 12, 1972, 3; Golda Meir, "European Nations That Did Not Assist during the Holocaust Are Not Entitled to Preach to Us," a speech at Kibbutz Yad Mordekhai, ibid., April 30, 1973, 3; and "Christian Europe, Which 30 Years Ago Betrayed the Jews Who Lived in Its Midst and Abandoned Them to be Massacred and Annihilated by the Nazis Was Ready to Abandon Us in 1973," speech by Minister of Tourism Moshe Kol in a commemoration ceremony at Tel Yizhak, ibid., April 18, 1974, 5).

163. "Allon," 2; Yehoshu'a Tirah, "Even Today the Movement of Jew Hatred Has Not Ceased: This Was the Background That Made the Holocaust Possible," *Haaretz*, April 30, 1973, 3; Moshe Zeliger, "A World Protest against the Decision of Zionism as Racism," *Davar*, September 6, 1975, 6. For cartoons, see, e.g., *Haaretz*, October 19, 1975, 9; and *Hazofeh*, October 31, 1975, 2.

164. For an elaborate discussion of anti-Semitism and anti-Zionism, see Robert S. Wistrich, ed., *Anti-Zionism and Antisemitism in the Contemporary World* (New York, 1990).

165. See Tirah, "Even Today," 3.

166. Letters to the editor, *Haaretz*, November 12, 1975.

167. *Haaretz*, October 19, 1975, 9, written before the resolution was adopted; *Divrei Knesset*, vol. 75 (Jerusalem, 1976), 299–330. See also Yonah Cohen, "The *Knesset* Identifies with Zionism," *Hazofeh*, November 14, 1975, 6; and "The Knesset Call," *Davar*, November 21, 1975, 1.

168. Yehoshu'a Tirah, "Holocaust Complex," *Haaretz*, April 30, 1973, 3; Yehuda Elkana, "The Need to Forget," ibid., March 2, 1988, 4.

169. Haim Schatzker, "Trends in the Understanding of the Holocaust in the Israeli Society," ibid., May 1, 1970, 22.

170. Adi Ofir, "On the Renewal of the Name," *Politika* 8 (June–July 1986), 2–7.

171. Elkana, "Need to Forget," 13.

172. Ibid.

173. Ibid.

174. An interesting example of an attempt to find a middle way between the two extreme perspectives was demonstrated in a symposium entitled "The Meaning of the Holocaust in Our Times," *Mibifnim* 45, nos. 1–4 (1983), 235–67.

175. Rachel Elboim-Dror, *Hahinukh Ha'ivri Be'eretz Israel*, vol. 1 (Jerusalem, 1986), 1–9, 396–403.

176. André Malraux, quoted in Haim Gouri, "Facing the Glass Booth," *Holocaust Remembrance: The Shape of a Memory*, ed. Geoffrey H. Hartman (Oxford, 1994), 155.

177. Keren, *Hashpaot*, 24–30, 71–85; *Divrei Haknesset*, 14:1346–52; Jacob Shelhav, "Hashoah Betoda'at Dorenu," *Yediot Yad Vashem* 15–16 (April 1958), 2–3; B. Ofir, "'Al Limud Hashoah Beveit Hasefer Beyisrael," ibid. 19–20 (May 1959), 18–19.

178. Amnon Rubinstein, *Liheyot 'Am Hofshi* (Tel Aviv, 1977), 101–11; Anita Shapira, "Dor Ba'aretz," *Alpayim* 2 (1990), 178–203. On the teaching of Jewish history in the schools, see *The First Conventions of High School Students to Discuss the Projects of Commemoration in the Years 1964–1965*, Yad Vashem Archive (YVA), File of the Committee to Commemorate Jewish Communities by Schools in Israel and the Diaspora.

179. Samuel Ettinger and Michael Ziv, *Divrei Hayamim*, vol. 4/2 (Jerusalem, 1960); Ephraim Shmueli, *Toldot Amenu*, vol. 7 (Tel Aviv, 1961).

180. Simon N. Herman, Yohanan Peres, and Ephraim Yuchtman, "Reaction to the Eichmann Trial in Israel, A Study of Involvement," *Scripta Hierosolymitana* 14 (1965), 98–118.

181. Akiva W. Deutsch, *The Eichmann Trial in the Eyes of Israel Youngsters* (Ramat Gan, 1974), 36. See also Hillel Klein and Uriel Last, "Cognitive and Emotional Aspects of the Attitudes of American and Israeli Jewish Youth towards the Victims of the Holocaust," *Israeli Annals of Psychiatry and Related Disciplines* 12, no. 2 (1974), 110–23.

182. Keren, *Hashpaot,* 116–34; *Hozer Mankal,* 22/11, November 1960 (Jerusalem, 1960).

183. *Hashoah vehagvurah* (Jerusalem, 1966). Of the thirty-two photographs in the exhibition, two-thirds depicted ghetto fighters, partisans, and other underground movements (*Shoah Umeri: Yalkut leveit Hasefer* [Jerusalem, 1967]). This exhibition was intended for students in the seventh and eighth grades.

184. Haim Schatzker, "Trends in the Understanding of the Holocaust in Israeli Society," *Haaretz,* May 1, 1970, 22.

185. Haim Schatzker, "Ba'ayot Didaktiyot Behoraat Hashoah," *Masuah* 1 (1973), 18–26. See also Arie Simon, "He'arot leba'ayat hashoah behinukhenu," in *Da'at Uma'as Behinukh Sefer Arnon,* ed. Yohanan Tverski (Tel Aviv, 1963), 360–65.

186. Ruth Firer, "The Holocaust in Textbooks in Israel," in *The Treatment of the Holocaust in Textbooks,* ed. Randolph L. Braham (New York, 1987), 178.

187. Ibid., 188.

188. Arie Carmon, "Teaching the Holocaust in Israel," in *Methodology in the Academic Teaching of the Holocaust,* ed. Zev Garber (Lanham, Md., 1988), 75–91. See also Arie Carmon, "Teaching the Holocaust as a Means of Fostering Values," *Curriculum Inquiry* 9, no. 3 (1979), 209–28.

189. Arie Carmon, *Hashoah,* 2 vols. (Jerusalem, 1980).

190. Yisrael Gutman and Haim Schatzker, *The Holocaust and Its Meaning* (Jerusalem, 1990).

191. For a detailed discussion of the traditional literary reaction to catastrophe in Jewish history, see Alan Mintz, *Hurban: Responses to Catastrophe in Hebrew Literature* (New York, 1984); and David G. Roskies, *Against the Apocalypse: Responses to the Catastrophe in Modern Jewish Culture* (Cambridge, 1984).

192. Abba Kovner, *'Al Hagesher Hatzar* (Tel Aviv, 1981), 145–46.

193. Ibid., 144.

194. Aharon Appelfeld, "After the Holocaust," in *Writing and the Holocaust,* ed. Berl Lang (New York, 1988), 83–92.

195. Izhak Katzenelson was an important poet who wrote in Yiddish and Hebrew. He was in the Warsaw ghetto until 1943, when he was sent to France as part of an exchange agreement (he had a Honduran visa). In 1944 he was deported from Vittel to Auschwitz, where he perished. Some of his writings survived and were published in the 1950s. His writings include a famous poem on the murdered Jewish people and a diary of Vittel (see *Ktavim Aharonim* [Tel Aviv, 1956]). David Fogel was a famous young Hebrew poet when he was interned in France in 1941 and then deported to Poland with his family. Only one of his poems, *Sha'atat Zevaot,* survives from the war years (see David Fogel, *Kol Hashirim,* ed. Dan Pagis [Tel Aviv, 1966]). Meir Busak, a Hebrew poet, was interned in Plaszow, where he wrote the poem *Mima'amakim,* which was published in *Davar* in 1947. He immigrated to Israel in 1949 and wrote extensively on the Holocaust.

196. Reizl (Ruz'ka) Korchak, *Lehavot Baefer* (Sifriyat Hapo'alim, 1946); Haika Grossman, *Anshei Hamahtereth* (Tel Aviv, 1947); Manfred Riefer, *Mas'a Hamavet* (Tel Aviv, 1947).

197. B. Y. Mikhaeli, "Hamilhamah veshoat yisrael beshiratenu," in *Divrei Sofrim: Measef Sofrei Eretz-Yisrael,* ed. Asher Barash and Yizhak Lamdan (Tel Aviv, 1944), 323–29.

198. Avi Catzman, "Mul hadan hashotek," *Efes* 2, no. 2 (1993), 97–119.

199. Mikhaeli, "Hamilhamah."

200. On Bialik's mission to Russia to report on the pogroms, see Israel Halprin, ed., *Sefer Hagevura,* 3 vols. (Tel Aviv, 1941–50), 3:ix–xvii, 1–230; Bialik's written report is on pp. 4–16. For commentary on Bialik's poem, see Mintz, *Hurban,* 129–54; and Roskies, *Against the Apocalypse,* 79–108.

201. Mikhaeli, "Hamilhamah," 321. Mikhaeli did not conclude, as did Theodor W. Adorno, that no poetry could be written after Auschwitz. Adorno is quoted in *The Holocaust and the Literary Imagination,* by Lawrence L. Langer (New Haven, Conn., 1975), 2. Langer challenges this assumption by coining the expression "art of atrocity" (30).

202. Sidra DeKoven Ezrahi, *By Words Alone: The Holocaust in Literature* (Chicago, 1980), 103–4.

203. Saul Tchernichowsky, *Kol Hashirim* (Tel Aviv, 1950), 615–20; Yizhak Lamdan, *Masada* (Tel Aviv, 1927). For further elaboration on the Masada symbol, see Barry Schwartz, Yael Zrubavel, and Bernice M. Barnett, "The Recovery of Masada: A Study in Collective Memory," *Sociological Quarterly* 27, no. 2 (1987), 147–64; and Anita Shapira, *Land and Power* (New York, 1992), 314–18.

204. In *Mibifnim,* the major journal of the kibbutz movement in Palestine, a great number of stories and poems published between the years 1943 and 1944 related to the Holocaust. There were also many articles about Jewish heroism and Jewish responses to the Nazis. See, for example, *Mibifnim* 9, no. 1 (1943), much of which is devoted to the Holocaust and the Diaspora.

205. Ya'akov Cohen, "Reu et harash'a" and

"Minivkhe zarotenu sheol," both quoted in Barash and Lamdan, *Divrei Sofrim,* 322; Ya'akov Fikhman, "Shem hanevalim," ibid.; Yehudah Karni, "Kamatz alef aa," ibid., 323.

206. Abraham Shlonsky, "Hamilim sheshunu meod," ibid., 325. Shlonsky expressed the same idea in the poem "Neder," which he wrote after the war (see Hannah Yaoz, *Shlosha Dorot Bashirah Ha'ivrit Benose Hashoah* [Tel Aviv, 1990], 13).

207. Avigdor Hameiri, "Behevel pi hamiflezet," in Barash and Lamdan, *Divrei Sofrim,* 323.

208. Shmuel Bass, "Shir-'anavim lenefesh bodedah," ibid., 325.

209. Yizhak Lamdan, "Marot laylah"; Yocheved Bat Miriam, "Beshulei hayamim"; and Binyamin Teneboim, "Shaharit," in ibid., 325, 325, and 328, respectively.

210. Ezrahi, *By Words Alone,* 105.

211. Avraham Rosenzweig, "Tov lishon baleilot, vetov li shenishart," in Barash and Lamdan, *Divrei Sofrim,* 324.

212. Shimson Meltzer, quoted in Mintz, *Hurban,* 162.

213. Mordekhai Temkin, "Mileti dami ve'imum halom; limshorerei hazman," in Barash and Lamdan, *Divrei Sofrim,* 324; Avigdor Hameiri, "Berega zeh," in Yaoz, *Shlosha Dorot,* 12.

214. Uri Zvi Greenberg, "Keter Kinah le-Khol Beit Yisrael," in Greenberg, *Rehovot Hanahar: Sefer Hailiyot Vehaoah* (Tel Aviv, 1950), 55. Translation from Ezrahi, *By Words Alone,* 104.

215. A beautiful example of the lyrical and sentimental poems is *Zviyah* by Zrubavel, dedicated to Zivia Lubetkin, a young member of the hehalutz in Warsaw, which appeared in *Mibifnim* 9, no. 2 (1943), 243.

216. Zvi Nesher, in ibid. 10, no. 2 (1944), 135–37, translated from the German by Moshe Basok. The English translation is quoted from Murry J. Kohn, *The Voice of My Blood Cries Out: The Holocaust as Reflected in Hebrew Poetry* (New York, 1979), 41–42.

217. *Mibifnim* 10, no. 2 (1944), 137. Kovner's poem was published in *Haaretz,* September 1, 1944.

218. See above, n. 214.

219. Yaacov Shavit, "Uri Zvi Greenberg: Conservative Revolutionarism and National Messianism," *Jerusalem Quarterly,* no. 48 (fall 1988), 63–72; idem, *Hamitologia Shel Hayamin* (Tel Aviv, 1986), 180–200.

220. Mintz, *Hurban,* 171. This interpretation of Greenberg's poetry is based on the excellent chapter on him in Mintz's book (165–202).

221. Shavit, "Uri Zvi Greenberg," 64.

222. One of the poems that portrays these elements clearly, with a very strong sense of self-criticism, is "Keter kinah le-Khol beit Yisrael" (Greenberg, *Rehovot Hanahar,* 47–62). In the middle of the poem, between descriptions of a mass killing and deportation in a sealed train car, eighteen lines describe how people in the Yishuv continue to live normally (55–56).

223. Mintz, *Hurban,* 173–74.

224. The metaphor of sheep is used in a variety of expressions in Hebrew, and generally its sense is not negative (Greenberg, *Rehovot Hanahar,* 58).

225. Ibid., 76–79, "Lishivah shel matah."

226. Ibid., 203, "'Enei hanefesh be'enei habasar."

227. Ibid., 207.

228. English translation quoted from Mintz, *Hurban,* 195–96.

229. Ibid., 159–60. See also Gershon Shaked, *Behevlei Hazman,* vol. 4 of *Hasiporet Ha'ivrit 1880–1980* (Jerusalem, 1993), 26–27.

230. Mintz, *Hurban,* 162.

231. Gershon Shaked, *Ein Makom Aher* (Tel Aviv, 1988), 106–13; idem, *Ein Makom Aher, Gal Hadash Basiporet Ha'ivrit* (Tel Aviv, 1971), 71–86.

232. Dan Laor, "Dor Baaretz Bisvach Hashoah" (paper presented at the Yad Vashem International Conference, Jerusalem, 1993).

233. Among their works are Hanoch Bartov's *Brigade* (Tel Aviv, 1969) and *Shesh Knafaim Le'ehad* (Tel Aviv, 1988); Haim Gouri's *'Iskat hashokolad* (Tel Aviv, 1965); Yehudit Handel's *Bahazer shel Momo* (Tel Aviv, 1969); Aharon Meged's *Yad Vashem* (Tel Aviv, 1968); and Yehudah Amihai, *Pa'amonim verakavot* (Tel Aviv, 1968).

234. On the relationship between the great historical events and the Hebrew writers and the acceptance of the Zionist superstory, see Shaked, *Behevlei Hazman,* 14–36.

235. Laor, "Dor Baaretz."

236. Appelfeld, "Beyond the Tragedy," *Yedioth Aharonot,* August 4, 1978, quoted by Ben Shalom Lurie, "Abba Kovner the Man and His Mission," in Kovner, *'Al Hagesher Hatzar,* 237 and n. 30. See also Appelfeld, "After the Holocaust," 89.

237. Kovner, *'Al Hagesher Hatzar,* 147. Kovner compares Bialik's protest in *Be'ir haharegah* to the protest of the post-Holocaust generation (185).

238. See above, n. 92. An interesting article on K. Zetnik and his place in the Israeli educational framework is Dan Meron's "Bein sefer leefer," *Al-payim* 10 (1994), 196–224.

239. Yaoz, *Shlosha Dorot,* 3–5; Hanna Yaoz, *Hashoah beshirat dor hamedinah* (Tel Aviv, 1984), 5–12.

240. Aharon Appelfeld, *'Ashan* (Tel Aviv, 1962);

Shamai Golan, *Baashmoret Aharonah* (Tel Aviv, 1963).

241. Amos Oz, *Michael Sheli* (Tel Aviv, 1968); A. B. Yehoshu'a, *Molkho* (Jerusalem, 1987); David Grossman, *'Ayen Erech Ahavah* (Tel Aviv, 1986); Yehudah Amihai, *Lo Me'akhshav Lo Mikan* (Jerusalem, 1963); Benyamin Tammuz, *Eliakum, Sefer Hahazaiot* (Tel Aviv, 1969); Yoram Kenuik, *Adam Ben Kelev* (Tel Aviv, 1969); idem, *Avi* (Tel Aviv, 1992); Nathan Shaham, *Rosendorff Quartet: A Novel* (New York, 1991).

242. Amihai's radio drama, "Pa'amonim Vrakavot," is also autobiographical (Shaked, *Gal Hadash,* 76–77).

243. Shaked, *Behevlei Hazman,* 17.

244. Ibid., 358 n. 26.

245. Quoted from the English translation, *See Under: Love* (New York, 1991), 13.

246. For my interpretation of this novel I have relied extensively on Gavriel Zuran, "Mibeit Mazmil Leeretz Sham," *Siman Kriah* 20 (May 1990), 245–50. See also Menahem Peri, "Misaviv Lanekudah," *Siman Kriah* 18 (May 1986), 7–9.

247. Grossman, *See Under: Love,* 305, 351.

248. Gershon Shaked, *Sifrut: Az Kan Ve'akhshav* (Tel Aviv, 1993), 115–19.

249. Irena Liebermann, "Od 'al Grosman," *'Iton 77,* no. 78–79 (1986), 5. Liebermann wrote a very emotional letter from the perspective of a survivor. Amela Einat, "Rohav halashon veaminut hameser," ibid., no. 76 (1986), 7. Einat, a writer and reporter, questioned Grossman's motivation and his ability to portray a credible picture of the Holocaust. See also Eli Shealtiel, "Haroman hehadash shel Grosman, ha'im yesh lanu eru'a," *Koteret Rashit,* no. 165 (June 1986), 47.

250. Izhak Laor, *Am Maachal Melachim* (Tel Aviv, 1993).

251. Sidra DeKoven Ezrahi, "Revisioning the Past: The Changing Legacy of the Holocaust in Hebrew Literature," *Salmagundi: The Literary Imagination and the Sense of the Past,* no. 68–69 (fall 1985–winter 1986), 265.

252. Ibid., 267. 'Atzman's poem is *Ein tikhlah lakeravot velahereg: shira politit bemilhemet Levanon,* ed. Hanan Hever and Moshe Ron (Tel Aviv, 1984).

253. Ben Ami Feingold, *Hashoah Badramah Ha'ivrit* (Tel Aviv, 1989), 13. Both Chelton's *Hamesh* and Ulmert's *Duet Lepsanter* were performed on stage in Israel in September 1994.

254. See Feingold, *Hashoah,* 93–113; and Yael Feldman, "'Identification with the Aggressor'—or the 'Victim Complex'? Holocaust and Ideology in Israeli Theater: *Ghetto* by Joshua Sobol," *Modern Judaism* 9, no. 2 (1989), 165–77.

255. The quotation of Sobol is taken from the program of the play *Tony Hayafeh,* staged at the Khan Theater in Jerusalem in 1995.

256. Yablonka, *Ahim Vezarim.*

INDEX

Page references to tables are followed by an italic *t*.

Abakumova, Raisa, 311
Abortion Information Bill (Ireland), 666
Abs, Hermann Josef, 409
Abwehr, 364, 650, 651, 788, 792
academia, Holocaust in (England), 628–30
Academy of Sciences (East Germany), Central Institute for History, 464
Accident, The (Wiesel), 721
acculturation: of Jews in Austria, 479; in Hungary, 210, 213; in Russia/Soviet Union, 300; in South Africa, 670
Achat Chez Nous movement, 751
"Acquiescence of This Government in the Murder of the Jews" (report), 706
Action against Anti-Semitism, 503–4
Action Catholique (journal), 751
Action française, 8
Action Moral Standards, 683
Action Party (Italy), 528
Adam, Uwe Dietrich, 420
Adam Ben Kelev (Adam the son of a dog) (Kenuik), 903
Adam and the Train (Böll), 415
Adenauer, Konrad, 402, 403, 406–9, 411, 416, 454, 456, 496, 866
Adevarul (newspaper), 246, 248
Adler, Cyrus, 563
Adler, Jacques, 14, 31
Adler, Nathan, 600
Advocate for the Dead (Brand), 624
Africa, relations of, with Israel, 832
African countries, U.N. votes/actions, 816, 817, 824, 825, 826, 827–28, 829, 830, 832, 887
Afrikaner, Die, 683–84
Afrikaner National Party, 677
Afrikaner Weerstandsbeweging (Afrikaner Resistance Movement) (AWB), 681–82, 686
Afrikaner Yiddishe Zeitung (magazine), 679
Afrikaners, 674–75
Afro-Canadians, 768
aggressive-war charge (Nuremberg), 715, 716
Agnon, S. Y., 897
Agrarian Union (Bulgaria), 267, 268, 271
agricultural settlement campaigns (Russia), 299, 301
Agudat Israel (Union of Israel), 92; of America, 705; in Israel, 828, 839, 851; in Latvia, 360, 361; World Organization, 654
Aguililla Saladrigas, Hector, 801
Ahdut Ha'avodah, 870

Aichinger, Ilse, 414–15, 416
aid to Jews, xx-xxi, 856; from American Jews, 110, 116, 247, 726, 760; in Austria, 492, 503; in Bulgaria, 270, 278, 279–81, 282, 283, 285; in Canada, 767; in Cuba, 785; in Czechoslovakia, 168, 171, 172, 188; in England, 603–4, 607, 609, 631; in France, 13; in Hungary, 205, 207, 218, 867; in Ireland, 660, 665; in Italy, 514, 524, 530, 532, 543, 545; in Lithuania, 334–35, 342, 345; Palestine and, 851, 858; in Poland, 106, 107, 119, 124, 138; in South Africa, 677–78; by Soviets in Latvia, 369; U.S. and, 707, 710–11; by Zionists, 852
aid organizations, U.S., 697
Aizenstadt, Amon, 776
Aizsargi (Land Guard) (Latvia), 381
Aizsilnieks, Arnolds, 378
AJR Information, 614, 620, 621, 623, 625
Akhromeyer, Sergei, 318
Akhsanie Kuba (Hotel Cuba), 784
Aktion(s), 376; in Hungary, 205; in Italy, 526; in Lithuania, 334; in Soviet Union, 310
Aktion Gitter (Operation Bars), 167
Al Domi, 849
'Al Milet (On abundance) (Shlonsky), 895
Alberts, Louw, 683
Alecsandri, Vasile, 226, 227, 228
Aleichem, Shalom, 297
Alerta (newspaper), 785, 786, 788, 797
Alexander of Battenberg (prince), 258, 259
Alexander II (czar), 296, 671, 695
Alexandru, Radu F., 247
Alexianu, Gheorghe, 231, 235
Alfaro, Ricardo, 818
Algemeen Handelsblad (General Business Journal), 63
Algeria, 21, 32; war in, 22, 29
aliens, Jews as: in England, 600, 605; in Hungary, 200, 205, 214; in Italy, 521; in Netherlands, 50; in Romania, 226
Aliens Bill (South Africa), 674
Aliens and Refugees Committee (South Africa), 675
Aliyah Bet ("Aliyah B; *ha'apolah*), 844. *See also* immigration
"All Because They Were Jews" (exhibition), 464
All-Party Parliamentary War Crimes Group (England), 631, 632
"All There Is to Know about Adolf Eichmann" (Cohen), 775–76
Allen, Jim, 630
Alliance israélite universelle (AIU), 6, 227, 228, 260, 261

Index

Index

Index

Index

Index

Index

Index

Index

Index

Index

Index

Index

Index

Index

Index

Index

Index

Index

Index

Index

Index

Index

Index

Index

Index

Index

Smith, Gerald L. K., 752

Smrt Krásných Srnců (Death of the Beautiful Roebucks) (film), 186

Smuschkowitz, David, 776

Smuschkowitz, Peter, 776

Smuts, Jan Christiaan, 674, 675, 676, 677

Snow, C. P., 627

So Many Miracles (film), 776

So oder So? (Either this or that) (Harand), 482

Sobibor (camp), 81, 144, 491, 607, 608, 612, 732, 758

Sobol, Yehoshua, 907

Social, Cultural, and Educational Organization of the Jews of the People's Republic of Bulgaria, 274, 281, 284, 285, 287

Social Credit Party, 750, 752

Social Darwinism, 89

Social-Democratic Labor Party (Russia), 298

Social Democratic Party, 268, 271; in Austria, 478, 480, 493, 496; in Germany (SPD), 398, 416, 425, 427, 429, 430, 432, 436; in Italy, 529; in Latvia, 357, 378; in Netherlands, 65

Social Democratic Workers' Party (SDAP), 478

Social Revolutionary movement (Lithuania), 335

socialism, 47; in England, 601; in Italy, 528; in Japan, 558; Jewish, 88, 271, 297; in Poland, 115–16, 118–19, 121–22; in Russia/Soviet Union, 298, 301

Socialist International, 499

Socialist Party: in Bulgaria, 286–87; SPÖ, in Austria, 494

Socialist Unity Party (SED), 448, 453, 462; Central Committee, 455, 456

Socialist Work Party (Romania), 251–52

Society of Children of the Holocaust, 144

Society of the Jewish Community of Cape Town, 670

Society for Relieving the Sick (Limerick), 644

Society of Survivors from the Riga Ghetto, 375

Society of Swiss Writers, 654

socioeconomic conditions, and anti-Semitism, 157, 214. *See also* economic conditions and anti-Semitism; economy

Soetendorp, Jacob, 59

Sofia, 257, 258, 260, 261, 263, 266, 273, 276; Allied bombing of, 267; Jewish ghetto in, 279; synagogue in, 274, 285; University, 279

Sofia Press Agency, 285

Solicitor's Journal, The, 625

Solidarity (Poland), 121, 130–32, 133, 134, 135–36, 141, 144; split in, 142

Solidarity movement (France), 14

Solomon, Norman, 464

Solomons, Bethel, 664

Solomons, Estella F., 664

Sonino, Giuseppe, 517

Sonntag, Jacob, 623

Soref, Harold, 618–19

Sorescu, Constantin, 239

Šormová, Eva, 180

South Africa, 336, 590, 670–89, 829, 832; Jews in society, 670–71; immigration policy in, 673, 674, 678; political equality in, 671; racial problems in, 677

South Africa House (London), 677

South African Broadcasting Corporation, 682, 683

South African Jewish Board of Deputies, 672, 674

South African Jews: before the Holocaust, 670–75; Holocaust-era, 675–77; number of, 670, 672; post-Holocaust era, 677–87

South African Observer (periodical), 682, 684

South African Red Cross, 675

South African Union of Jewish Students, 685

South African Zionist Federation, 672

South Manchurian Railroad, 566

Soviet bloc, 801; anti-Zionist/anti-Semitic campaign, 870; disintegration of, 200–201, 213, 218; and Six-Day War, 881; U.N. votes/actions, 811, 812, 818, 822, 823, 825, 826, 827, 828–29, 830, 831, 832, 887

Soviet Communist Party, 276

Soviet-German nonaggression pact, 264, 302. *See also* Nazi-Soviet Non-Aggression Pact; Ribbentrop-Molotov Agreement

Soviet Jews: activism of, 633; before the Holocaust, 295–302; Holocaust-era, 302–6; number of, 295, 303; post-Holocaust era, 306–21; war against, 305–6; in West Germany, 437–38

Soviet Occupied Zone, 447–48, 450, 451, 457, 717

Soviet Union, xiii, xxi, 26, 91, 107, 171, 204, 229, 231, 232, 270, 295–324, 498, 616, 630, 700, 705; anti-British foreign policy of, 271; anti-Semitic campaign, 210; anti-Zionist campaign, 175, 209–10; Bulgaria and, 264, 267, 274; and Cold War, xiv, 405; collapse of, 246, 320–21, 343, 801; Cuba and, 799; East Germany's liberation by, 448; German invasion of, 265, 268, 606, 704; historiography, 176; information on Holocaust in, 377; invasion of, 233; invasion of Poland by, 96, 99; and Israel, 110–11; and Italy, 527; Japan's relations with, 560, 565, 567, 568; Jewish emigration and protest movement in, 342; Jews fled to, 172; Jews from, in Israel, 894; Jewish hatred in, 300–301; liberating role of, 186, 189; and liberation of Budapest, 207; and occupation of Czechoslovakia, 238; and occupation of Poland, 102–4, 114–15, 119, 122; politicization of Holocaust by, 319–21; purges in, 301, 302, 303; reaction to Holocaust in Latvia, 371–72; recognition of Israel by, 714; relations of, with West, 278; role of, in defeating Germany, 179; in Romania, 242; U.N. votes/actions, 713; and war crimes trials, 718; and war criminals, 732

Soviet Writers Union, 313

Sovietish haimland (journal), 312, 314

Sovietization, 127, 208, 303, 369; of Lithuania, 330, 331, 332, 339, 340, 342, 346

Sozialistische Kampf (newspaper), 486

Spain, 46, 47, 440, 611, 756, 782, 783; and Cuba, 782; expulsion of Jews from, 515, 522; German-Italian collaboration in, 520

Spanish-American War, 783

Spanish Civil War, 8, 648, 788

Spanish Falange, 782, 786

Spanish Riding School, 488

Spann, Gustav, 502

specificity of Holocaust, 29, 36, 635; blurred in Soviet historiography, 307, 308–9, 310; generalized, 36, 339,

Index

Index

Index

Index

Library of Congress Cataloging-in-Publication Data

The world reacts to the Holocaust / David S. Wyman, editor ; Charles H.
Rosenzveig, project director.

    p.   cm.

   Includes index.

   ISBN 0-8018-4969-1

   1. Holocaust, Jewish (1939–1945)—Public opinion.   2. Holocaust, Jewish
(1939–1945)—Influence.   I. Wyman, David S.   II. Rosenzveig, Charles H.

D804.44.W67   1996

940.53′18—dc20   96-15395